CASSELL'S COMPACT

Latin–English
English–Latin
Dictionary

Compiled by
D. P. SIMPSON, M.A.
Assistant Master and formerly Head of
Classical Department at Eton College

Published by
Dell Publishing Co., Inc.
1 Dag Hammarskjold Plaza
New York, New York 10017

Laurel ® TM 674623, Dell Publishing Co., Inc.

ISBN: 0-440-31101-2

Reprinted by arrangement with
Macmillan Publishing Co., Inc.

Printed in the United States of America
One Previous Laurel Edition
New Laurel Edition
First printing—September 1981
Fifth printing—November 1984

PREFACE

THE first Latin Dictionary published by Cassell appeared in 1854. It was the work of two Unitarian divines, J. R. Beard and his son Charles Beard, and consisted of two sections of equal length, Latin-English and English-Latin. The first of these sections was "revised, enlarged, and in part rewritten" for publication in 1886, by J. R. V. Marchant, who was for a short time a master at St. Paul's School, but later was called to the Bar, and became a County Court Judge. By 1892 the second section, English-Latin, had also been revised, and considerably shortened, by J. F. Charles, probably with help from Marchant. Charles had been a pupil, with Marchant, at the City of London School, and after graduating at London and Oxford he returned there as a master. The combined work of Marchant and Charles was reprinted at short intervals for the next sixty years. In 1927 a shortened version of it appeared, under the name of "Cassell's Compact Latin-English English-Latin Dictionary." This was prepared by Miss Millicent Thomas, M.A. (London), sometime Classics and Senior Mistress of Tottenham High School, and an assistant examiner in Classics for the University of London. She dispensed with most of the prolegomena printed by Marchant and Charles, and in her main text reduced both the length and the number of articles, leaving the rarer words out of account and removing the illustrative quotations from Latin authors. In her book, as in that of Marchant and Charles, the English-Latin section was little more than half as long as the Latin-English.

In 1959 Cassell published their "New Latin Dictionary." which was a complete revision by the present author of both sections of Marchant and Charles. The new "compact" dictionary follows as an abbreviation of this, the result of much the same process of selection and simplification as Miss Thomas applied to its predecessor.

This book resembles every other Latin dictionary so far produced by Cassell, in concerning itself with "classical" Latin, as used from about 200 B.C. to A.D. 100. It also conforms to the principle maintained since the time of Marchant and Charles, that the English-Latin section should be kept relatively short, in the hope that the user will refer from it to the Latin-English for fuller information. Both English and Latin words are treated in alphabetical order, except that adverbs appear under the adjectives from which they are derived, participles under verbs, and so on; certain synonyms, also, are grouped together within a single article. The spelling of Latin words is intended to correspond to what will be found in the more recent editions of Latin authors; I, i replaces J, j throughout, but V, v is retained. In the Latin-English section most vowels in Latin words are marked short (˘) or long (¯); in the English-Latin this has been done more sparingly, for the special purpose of distinguishing between words of similar form, or of indicating declension or conjugation.

D.P.S.

LIST OF SPECIAL TERMS

abbrev. abbreviated, abbreviation.
abl. ablative.
absol. absolute.
abstr. abstract.
acc. accusative.
act. active.
adj. adjective.
adv. adverb.
adversat. adversative.
architect. architectural.
c. common (both m. and f.).
class. classical.
coll. collective.
colloq. colloquial.
commerc. commercial.
compar. comparative.
concr. concrete.
conj. conjunction.
dat. dative.
dep. deponent.
dim. diminutive.
distrib. distributive.
e.g. exempli gratia (for example).
esp. especially.
etc. et cetera.
exclam. exclamatory.
f. feminine.
fig. figure, figurative.
foll. followed.
fut. future.
gen. general, generally.
genit. genitive.
gram., grammat. grammatical.
i.e. id est (that is).
imperf. imperfect.
impers. impersonal.
indecl. indeclinable.
indef. indefinite.
indic. indicative.
infin. infinitive.
interj. interjection.
interrog. interrogative.
intransit. intransitive.
logic. logical.

m. masculine.
medic. medical.
meton. by metonymy.
milit. military.
myth. mythological.
n. neuter.
naut. nautical.
neg. negative.
nom. nominative.
num. numeral.
obs. obsolete.
occ. occasionally.
opp. opposite (to).
partic. participle.
pass. passive.
perf. perfect.
pers. person.
personif. personified.
philosoph. philosophy, philosophical.
phr. phrase.
pl., plur. plural.
poet. poetical.
polit. political.
posit. positive.
prep. preposition.
pres. present.
pron. pronoun.
q.v. quod vide, quae vide (i.e. see article concerned).
reflex. reflexive.
relat. relative.
relig. religious.
rhet. rhetoric, rhetorical.
sc. scilicet (that is to say).
sing. singular.
subj. subjunctive.
subst. substantive.
superl. superlative.
t.t. technical term.
transf. transferred (i.e. used in altered sense).
transit. transitive.
voc. vocative.

CASSELL'S LATIN-ENGLISH DICTIONARY

A

A, a, the first letter of the Latin Alphabet.

a, ah, interj. *Ah!*

a, ab, abs, prep. with abl. (1) of motion or measurement in space, *from, away from*. (2) of time, *from, after*. (3) of separation, difference, change, *from*; so of position or number, *counting from*; and of the relation of part to whole, *out of, of*. (4) or origin and agency; especially with passive verbs, *by, at the hands of, because of*. (5) *viewed from, on the side of*: a tergo, *in the rear*; hence *in connexion with, as regards*.

ăbăcus -i, m. *a square board*; hence *sideboard, counting-board, gaming-board, ceiling panel*.

ăbălĭēnātĭo -ōnis, f. *transfer of property.*

ăbălĭēno -are, *to make alien, separate, estrange.*

ăbăvus -i, m. *great-great-grandfather.*

Abdēra -ōrum, n. pl.; also -ae, f., *a town in Thrace, noted for the stupidity of its inhabitants.*

abdĭcātĭo -ōnis, f. *disowning, renunciation.*

¹abdīco -are, *to renounce, reject*; esp. of magistracies, *to abdicate*, often with reflex. and ablative of office.

²abdīco -dīcĕre -dixi -dictum, in augury, *to disapprove of.*

abdo -dĕre -dĭdi -dĭtum, *to put away, withdraw, remove*; esp. *to secrete, hide.*

  Hence partic. **abdĭtus** -a -um, *concealed, secret.* Adv. **abdĭtē.**

abdōmen -ĭnis, n. *belly*; hence *gluttony.*

abdūco -dūcĕre -duxi -ductum, *to lead or take away, detach, withdraw.*

ăbĕo -ire -ĭi -ĭtum, *to go away*; abi, *be off with you*; abi in malam rem, *go to the devil.* Transf., *to retire from office; to depart from life, die; in discussion, to digress*; in form, *to change*; of things, *to pass away, disappear, vanish; to pass over from owner to owner.*

ăbĕquĭto -are, *to ride off.*

ăberrātĭo -ōnis, f. *escape, relief.*

ăberro -are, *to wander, deviate, escape.*

abhinc (1) *hereafter.* (2) *ago*: abhinc annos tres, or annis tribus *three years ago.*

ăbhorreo -ēre, *to shrink back from*; hence *to be inconsistent with* or *opposed to; a fide, to be incredible.* Pres. part., as adj., *unseasonable, inappropriate.*

ăbĭcĭo -icĕre -ĭēci -iectum, *to throw down or away.* Transf., *to pronounce carelessly, break off abruptly; to get rid of, give up; to dash to the ground, weaken, dishearten.*

  Hence partic. **ăbiectus** -a -um; of position, *low, common*; of character, *cowardly, mean*; of style, *without force, prosaic.* Adv. **ăbiectē,** *without spirit, meanly.*

ăbĭectĭo -ōnis, f. *throwing away*; animi, *despondency, despair.*

ăbĭegnus -a -um, *of fir wood or deal.*

ăbĭēs ĕtis, f. *the silver fir*; meton., *anything made of deal, such as a ship or spear.*

ăbĭgo -ĕre -ēgi -actum, *to drive away*; of cattle, *to remove, steal.* Transf., *to banish, be rid of* : uxorem, *to divorce.*

ăbĭtĭo -ōnis, f. and **ăbĭtus** -ūs, m., *going away, departure; place of egress.*

abĭūdĭco -are, *to take away by a judgment.*

abĭungo -iungĕre -iunxi -iunctum, *to unharness*; hence *to estrange, detach.*

abĭuro -are, *to abjure, deny on oath.*

ablātīvus -a -um, *ablative.*

ablēgātĭo -ōnis, f. *sending away, banishment.*

ablēgo -are, *to send away, remove to a distance.*

ablĭgūrĭo -ire, *to lick away*; hence *to squander.*

ablūdo -ĕre, *to be out of tune.*

ablŭo -lŭĕre -lŭi -lūtum. *to wash clean; to wash away.*

abnĕgo -are, *to deny, refuse.*

abnĕpōs -ōtis, m. *great-great-grandson.*

abneptis -is, f. *great-great-granddaughter.*

abnocto -are, *to stay out all night.*

abnormis -e, *irregular, unconventional.*

abnŭo -nŭĕre -nŭi, fut. partic. -nūitūrus, *to refuse by a gesture, to deny.*

ăbŏleo -ēre -ēvi -itum, *to destroy, do away with.*

ăbŏlesco -ĕre -ēvi, *to perish.*

ăbŏlĭtĭo -ōnis, f. *removing, annulling, abolition.*

ăbolla -ae, f. *a cloak of thick woollen cloth.*

ăbōmĭno -are, and **ăbōmĭnor** -ari, dep. (1) *to deprecate*: quod abominor, *God forbid.* (2) *to hate, detest.*

ăbŏrĭor -ōriri -ortus, dep.: of heavenly bodies, *to set*; poet., of the voice, *to fail.*

ăbŏriscor -i = aborior: q.v.

ăbortĭo -ōnis, f. *untimely birth, miscarriage.*

ăbortīvus -a -um, *prematurely born.*

ăbortus -ūs, m. *miscarriage.*

abrādo -radĕre -rāsi -rāsum, *to scrape off, shave.* Transf., *to squeeze out, to extort.*

abrĭpĭo -rĭpĕre -rĭpŭi -reptum *to, snatch away, drag off, remove, detach.*

abrōdo -rōdĕre -rōsi -rōsum, *to gnaw off.*

abrŏgātĭo -ōnis, f. *annulling, repealing.*

abrŏgo -are. *to repeal, annul, remove, take away.*

abrŏtŏnum -i, n. and abrŏtŏnus -i, m. *southern-wood.*

abrumpo -rumpĕre -rūpi -ruptum, *to break off, sever; to remove, dissociate; to break off prematurely, destroy.* Hence partic. abruptus -a -um, *steep, precipitous, abrupt, rough.* N. as subst., *a steep place.* Adv. abruptē.

abruptio -ōnis, f. *tearing away;* hence *divorce.*

abscēdo -cēdĕre -cessi -cessum, *to go away, depart, retire, desert.*

abscessio -ōnis, f. *going away, separation.*

abscessus -ūs, m. *going away, withdrawal.*

abscīdo -cīdĕre -cīdi -cīsum, *to cut off; to separate or take away.* Hence partic. abscīsus -a -um, *precipitous, abrupt, short.*

abscindo -scindĕre -scīdi -scissum, *to tear off, wrench away;* venas, *to cut open the veins;* poet., abscissa comas, *with her hair torn.* Transf., *to divide or separate.*

abscondo -ōnis, -condĕre -condi (-condidi) -condĭtum (-consum), *to conceal; to lose sight of;* pass., of stars, *to set.* Adv. from partic., absconditē, *obscurely.*

absens -entis, *absent;* see also absum.

absentia -ae, f. *absence.*

absĭlio -ire, -ĭi or -ŭi, *to spring forth or away.*

absĭmilis -e, *unlike.*

absinthĭum -i, n. *wormwood.*

absisto -sistĕre -stĭti, *to go away from a place or person; to desist from an action.*

absŏlūtio -ōnis, f. (1) *acquittal.* (2) *perfection.*

absŏlūtōrius -a -um, *relating to acquittal.*

absolvo -solvĕre -solvi -sŏlūtum, *to loosen, to free;* of an accused person, *to acquit;* of a subject, *to dispose of, relate in full;* in gen. *to complete.* Hence partic. absŏlūtus -a -um, *perfect, complete; unfettered, unconditional.* Adv. absŏlūtē, *perfectly, completely.*

absŏnus -a -um, *inharmonious, discordant, disagreeing.*

absorbĕo -ēre -ŭi, *to swallow, gulp down;* hence *to carry away, engross.*

absque, prep. with abl. *without.*

abstēmius -a -um, *temperate, abstemious.*

abstergĕo -tergĕre -tersi -tersum, *to wipe off, clean away.*

absterrĕo -ēre, *to frighten away.*

abstĭnentia -ae, f. *self-denial, temperance;* sometimes *fasting.*

abstĭnĕo -tĭnēre -tĭnŭi -tentum: transit., *to hold back;* intransit., *to abstain from.* Hence present partic. abstĭnens -entis, *temperate.* Adv. abstĭnenter.

absto -are, *to stand aloof.*

abstrăho -trăhĕre -traxi -tractum *to drag away;* hence *to remove, exclude, restrain.*

abstrūdo -trūdĕre -trūsi -trūsum, *to push away, hide.* Hence partic. abstrūsus -a -um, *concealed, secret, abstruse;* of character, *reserved.*

absum, ăbesse, āfŭi. (1) *to be away, be absent or missing;* hence *to take no part in a thing, fail to help.* (2) *to be far away, be distant;* hence *to be far from doing a thing, to be free from a fault.*

absūmo -sūmĕre -sumpsi -sumptum, *to reduce, consume, waste, destroy.*

absurdus -a -um, *unmelodious, harsh.* Transf., *foolish, unreasonable, out of place;* of persons, *incapable.* Hence adv. absurdē, *harshly, discordantly; foolishly.*

ăbundantia -ae, f. *abundance, plenty; riches, wealth.*

ăbundē, *copiously, abundantly;* with est and genit., *there is plenty of a thing.*

ăbundo -are, *to overflow; to grow in abundance; to abound, be rich in,* esp. with abl. Hence partic. ăbundans -antis, *overflowing; abundant, numerous; abounding in;* adv. ăbundanter, *abundantly, copiously.*

ăbusquĕ, prep. with abl., *from.*

ăbūsus -ūs, m. *using up, wasting.*

ăbūtor -ūti -ūsus, dep., with abl. (1) *to make full use of.* (2) *to abuse, waste;* esp. *to use a word wrongly.*

ac; see atque.

Ăcădēmīa -ae, f., *the Academy,* a grove near Athens where Plato taught; meton., *the Academic school of philosophy.* Hence adj. Ăcădēmĭcus -a -um; n. pl. Ăcădēmĭca, *Cicero's treatise on the Academic philosophy.*

ăcălanthis and ăcanthis -ĭdis, f., *a small bird, perhaps siskin.*

ăcanthus -i, m. (1) *bear's foot,* a plant. (2) *a thorny evergreen tree.*

Acarnānĭa -ae, *Acarnania,* a country in western Greece.

Acca Lārentĭa, *a Roman goddess;* Lārentālĭa or Accālĭa -ĭum, n. pl. *her festival at Rome in December.*

accēdo -cēdĕre -cessi -cessum, *to approach, come near;* of persons, *to enter upon a course;* ad rem publicam, *to begin public life;* of things, *to be added;* huc accedit ut, *it is also true that, moreover.*

accĕlĕro -are: transit., *to quicken, accelerate;* intransit., *to hasten.*

accendo -cendĕre -cendi -censum, *to kindle, set alight, set on fire.* Transf., *to fire, inflame, excite.*

accensĕo -censēre -censum, *to reckon in addition.* Hence partic. accensus -a -um, *reckoned with;* m. as subst., *an attendant;* in plural, accensi, *reserve troops, supernumeraries.*

acceptio -ōnis, f. *reception, acceptance.*

accepto -are, *to receive.*

acceptus -a -um, partic. from accipio; q.v.

accerso = arcesso; q.v.

accessĭo -ōnis, f. *a going or coming to; increase; a thing added, appendage.*

accessus -ūs, m. *approach, access; means of approach, entrance.*

¹**accīdo** -cīdĕre -cīdi -cīsum, *to hew or hack at; hence to weaken, ruin.*

²**accĭdo** -cīdĕre -cīdi, *to fall down;* ad pedes, *to fall at a person's feet.* Transf., *to happen, fall out.*

accĭĕo -ēre, obs. form of accio; q.v.

accingo -cingĕre -cinxi -cinctum, *to gird on a weapon; to equip, arm a person;* with reflex., or in pass., *to arm oneself,* hence *to make oneself ready.*

accĭo -īre -īvi (-ĭi) -ītum, *to call, summon.*

accĭpĭo -cĭpĕre -cēpi -ceptum, *to take, receive, accept.* Esp. with the senses, *to hear, feel, etc.;* with the understanding, *to grasp, to learn;* also *to take, interpret in a certain sense;* of persons, *to receive hospitably,* or *to treat in any particular manner;* in business, acceptum referre, *to enter on the credit side of an account book,* hence *to consider oneself indebted to someone for a thing.* Hence partic. **acceptus** -a -um, *welcome, pleasant, agreeable.*

accĭpĭter -tris, m. *a hawk.*

accītus -ūs, m. *a summons.*

Accĭus -a -um, *name of a Roman gens;* esp. of L. Accius, tragic poet (170-c. 85 B.C.).

acclāmātĭo -ōnis, f. *a loud cry.*

acclāmo -are, *to cry out* (in approval or otherwise); with acc. of person, *to name by acclamation.*

acclāro -are, *to make clear, reveal.*

acclīnis -e, *leaning towards, inclined to.*

acclīno -are, *to lean towards, incline to.*

acclīvis -e, *inclined upwards.*

acclīvĭtās -ātis, f. *upward slope.*

acclīvus -a -um, = acclivis; q.v.

accŏla -ae, m. or f. *neighbour;* as adj. *living near, neighbouring.*

accŏlo -cŏlĕre -cŏlŭi -cultum, *to live near.*

accommŏdātĭo -ōnis, f. (1) *proportion or adjusting.* (2) *courteousness, complaisance.*

accommŏdātus -a -um, partic. from accommodo; q.v.

accommŏdo -are, *to fit, put on equipment, etc.; to make suitable, adjust, adapt.* Hence partic. **accommŏdātus** -a -um, *adapted, suitable;* adv. **accommŏdātē,** *agreeably.*

accommŏdus -a -um, *fit, adapted.*

accrēdo -crēdĕre -crēdĭdi -crēdĭtum, *to believe* (with dat.).

accresco -crescĕre -crēvi -crētum, *to grow, increase;* with dat., *to be joined to a thing.*

accŭbĭtĭo -ōnis, f. and **accŭbĭtus** -ūs, m. *the act of reclining at table.*

accŭbo -are, *to lie, or recline beside,* esp. at table; apud hominem, *to dine at a man's house.*

accumbo -cumbĕre -cŭbŭi -cŭbĭtum, *to lie down or recline,* esp. at table.

accŭmŭlātor -ōris, m. *one who heaps together.*

accŭmŭlo -are, *to heap up, accumulate; to heap things on a person, give in abundance; to ply, overwhelm a person with things; to increase.* Adv. from partic. **accŭmŭlātē,** *abundantly, copiously.*

accūrātĭo -ōnis, f. *accuracy, carefulness.*

accūro -are, *to take care of, prepare with care.* Hence partic. **accūrātus** -a -um, *done with care, careful, exact, accurate.* Adv. **accūrātē.**

accurro -currĕre -curri (-cŭcurri) -cursum, *to run to;* of ideas, *to occur.*

accursus -ūs, m. *running, concourse.*

accūsābĭlis -e, *blameworthy.*

accūsātĭo -ōnis, f. *an accusation, indictment.*

accūsātor -ōris, m. *an accuser;* hence *an informer.*

accūsātōrĭus -a -um, *of or like an accuser;* adv. **accūsātōrĭē.**

accūsātrix -icis, f. *a female accuser.*

accūso -are, *to accuse;* in gen., *to blame, find fault with.*

¹**ācer** -ĕris, n. *the maple tree or maple wood.*

²**ācer** -cris -cre, *sharp, cutting, keen.* Hence, to taste, *biting;* to touch, *sharp;* of sounds, *shrill;* of smells, *penetrating;* of sight, *keen;* of emotions, *painful;* of understanding or character, *quick, vigorous, energetic.* Adv. **ācrĭter,** *sharply, keenly.*

ācerbĭtās -ātis, f. *bitterness, harshness, painfulness;* in plur., *calamities.*

ācerbo -are, *to make bitter, to aggravate.*

ācerbus -a -um, *bitter.* Hence, of sounds, *harsh;* of looks, *dark, gloomy;* of speech or writing, *bitter;* of events, etc., *painful, severe;* of persons, *morose;* from the notion of unripeness, *premature.* Adv. **ācerbē,** *bitterly, harshly.*

ācernus -a -um, *made of maple wood.*

ācerra -ae, f. *a casket for incense.*

ăcervātim, *by accumulation;* dicere, *to sum up.*

ăcervo -are, *to heap up.*

ăcervus -i, m. *a heap, mass;* in logic, *argument by accumulation.*

ăcesco ăcescĕre ăcŭi, *to grow sour.*

ăcētum -i, n. *vinegar.*

Ăchāĭa or **Ăchāĭa** -ae, f., *the Greek country of Achaia, in the Peloponnese,* or in gen. *Greece;* after 146 B.C., *the Roman province of Achaea.* Hence adj. and subst. **Ăchaeus** and **Ăchīvus,** *Achaean, an Achaean* (or *Greek*).

Ăchātes -ae, m. *friend of Aeneas.*

Ăchĕron -ontis, m. (older form **Ăchĕruns** -untis) *mythol. river in the lower world; the lower world itself.*

Ăchillēs s, and **Ăchillēus** -ei, m. *a Greek hero, son of Peleus and Thetis.* Adj. **Ăchillēus** -a -um.

Ăchīvus -a -um; see **Ăchāĭa.**

ăcĭdus -a -um, *sharp, sour.*

ăciēs -ei, f. *keenness, edge*; *of the mind, penetration, insight*; *of the eye, a piercing look or keen vision*; *sometimes the pupil of the eye, or the eye itself.* Milit., *battle-line*; hence *battle, battlefield.*

ăcīnăcēs -is, m. *a Persian sabre.*

ăcinus -i, m. and **ăcinum** -i, n. *a berry; the seed of a berry.*

ăcipenser -eris, also **ăcipensis** -is, m. *the sturgeon.*

ăclys -ўdis, f. *a small javelin.*

ăcŏnītum -i, n. *monk's hood, aconite*; in gen., *strong poison.*

acq- = adq-; q.v.

ăcrātŏphŏrum -i, n. *a vessel for unmixed wine.*

ăcrēdŭla -ae, f. *a bird, perhaps thrush, owl, or nightingale.*

ăcrĭcŭlus -a -um, *somewhat sharp in temper.*

ăcrĭmōnĭa -ae, f. *sharpness, keenness.*

ăcrĭter, adv. from acer; q.v.

ăcrŏāma -ătis, n. *an entertainment, esp. musical*; *an entertainer, i.e. reader, actor, or singer.*

ăcrŏāsis -is, f. *reading aloud, recitation.*

Ăcrŏcĕraunia -orum, n. pl. *part of the Ceraunian mountains*; hence *any dangerous place.*

¹acta -ae, f. *sea-shore, beach*; meton., *life at the seaside.*

²acta -orum, from partic. of ago; q.v.

Actaeon -ōnis, m. *a hunter turned into a stag by Diana, and killed by his hounds.*

actĭo -ōnis, f. *action, doing*; gratiarum, *giving of thanks.* Esp. *the action of a magistrate, a proposal*; *in the theatre, a plot*; *at law, an action or the bringing of it or right to bring it*; also *a legal formula or speech on an indictment.*

actĭto -are, *to be busy, in law-court or theatre.*

Actĭum -i, n. *a promontory in Acarnania, near which Augustus conquered Antony and Cleopatra (31 B.C.).* Adj. **Actĭacus** and **Actĭus** -a -um.

actor -ōris, m. (1) *a driver.* (2) *a doer*; esp. *a dramatic actor, player*; *a public speaker*; *the plaintiff in an action*; *a manager of property.*

actŭārĭŏlum -i, n. *a small skiff.*

actŭārĭus -a -um *swift*; actuaria (navis), *a fast-sailing vessel.*

actŭōsus -a -um, *active*; adv. **actŭōsē.**

actus -ūs, m. (1) *driving, movement*; esp. *of cattle*; hence *right of way for driving cattle, etc.* (2) *doing, action, esp. on the stage*; hence *the presentation of a piece on the stage*; also *a division of a piece, an act.*

actŭtum, adv. *immediately, directly.*

ăcŭlĕātus -a -um, *provided with prickles or stings*; hence *pointed, stinging*; *hair-splitting, subtle.*

ăcŭlĕus -i, m. *sting, point*; fig., esp. in plur., *painful thoughts, cutting remarks.*

ăcūmen -ĭnis, n. *sharp point*; hence *the point of remarks, etc.*; *sharpness of intellect*; *cunning, trickery.*

ăcŭo -ŭĕre -ŭi -ūtum, *to sharpen, whet*; *to quicken, make expert*; *to inflame, encourage, incite.*

Hence partic. **ăcūtus** -a °um, *sharpened, pointed, acute*; *to the hearing, shrill*; *to touch, piercing*; *of events, etc., sharp, painful*; *of minds, sharp, keen, intelligent*; *of orators, effective.* Adv. **acūte**, *keenly, sharply.*

ăcus -ūs, f. *a needle, bodkin*; acu pingere, *to embroider*; acu rem tangere, *to hit the nail on the head.*

ăcūtŭlus -a -um *rather subtle.*

ăcūtus; see acuo.

ad, prep. with acc. (1) *of motion, towards, to a person or place*; ad Dianae (sc. aedem) *to Diana's temple*; ad me, *to my house*; often strengthened by usque. (2) *of rest, at or near.* (3) *of time*: either *to, until, or at, about.* (4) *of other relations*: *towards, for a purpose*; *concerning, bearing on*; *compared with, in addition to*; *in conformity with*; *approximating to, about*; *in consequence of an event*; *as far as, up to a certain degree*; ad summam, *on the whole*; ad verbum, *literally.*

ădactĭo -ōnis, f. *driving, compulsion.*

ădactus -ūs, m. *bringing to, application.*

ădaeque, *in like manner.*

ădaequo -are: transit., *to make equal*; hence *to compare*; intransit., *to match, come near to.*

ădămantēus -a -um, *hard as steel.*

ădămantĭnus -a -um, *made of steel.*

ădămas -antis, m. *the hardest steel, adamant*; poet., *anything firm, unyielding, durable.*

ădambŭlo -are, *to walk by or near.*

ădămo -are, *to fall in love with, find pleasure in.*

ădăpĕrĭo -ăpĕrīre -ăpĕrui -ăpertum, *to open fully.*

ădauctus -ūs, m. *increase.*

ădaugĕo -ēre -auxi -auctum, *to increase, augment.*

ădaugesco, -ĕre, *to begin to increase.*

adbĭbo -bĭbĕre -bĭbi -bĭbitum, *to drink in.*

addenseo -ēre, and **addenso** -are, *to make thick or compact.*

addīco -dīcĕre -dixi -dictum, *to assent to*; *in augury, to promise well*; *of a judge (especially the praetor), to award*; *of an auctioneer, to knock down a lot*; *of an owner, to put up for sale.* Hence in gen., *to give up or over, doom, dedicate, surrender*; partic. **addictus**, *bound, pledged.*

addictĭo -ōnis, f. *a judge's award.*

addisco -discĕre -didici, *to learn in addition.*

addĭtāmentum -i, n. *an addition.*

addo addĕre addidi addĭtum. (1) *to give, bring, place*; *of feelings, to inspire, cause.* (2) *to add, join*; esp. *in speech or writing*; adde, or adde huc, or eo, *add to this, take also into consideration.*

addŏcĕo -ēre, *to teach in addition.*

addŭbĭto -are, *to begin to doubt.*

addūco -dūcĕre -duxi -ductum. (1) *to bring or lead to a person, place, or* condition; of persons, *to bring to a certain state of mind, to influence, induce.* (2) *to draw to oneself, pull in;* hence *to contract;* partic. **adductus** -a -um, *contracted, taut;* of persons, *strict.* Compar. adv. in gen., *union.* **adductius.**

ădĕdo -esse -ēdi -ēsum, *to nibble, gnaw; to consume, waste away.*

ădemptio -ōnis, f. *taking away.*

ădĕo, adv., *to that point, so far;* often strengthened by usque; of space, *so far;* of time, *so long;* of degree, *so much, so, to such an extent;* sometimes, *even, what is more;* enclitically, with pron. or conjunction, *just.*

ădĕo -īre -ii -ĭtum, *to go or come to, approach, visit;* in ius, *to go to law;* of business, etc., *to undertake, undergo, incur;* adire hereditatem, *to enter on an inheritance.*

ădeps -ipis, c. *soft fat.*

ădeptio -ōnis, f. *attainment, obtaining.*

ădequito -are, *to ride to.*

ădesdum, or **ades dum,** *come hither.*

adfābilis -e, *easy to speak to, affable.*

adfābilitās -ātis, f. *affability.*

adfabrē, *in a workmanlike way.*

adfātim, *sufficiently, enough.*

adfātus -ūs, m. *address, speech.*

adfectātio -ōnis, f. *striving, eagerness.*

adfectātor -ōris, m. *a striver.*

adfectio -ōnis, f. *manner of being affected;* hence *relation* to a thing or person, or *change,* or *state, condition;* sometimes *favourable state of mind, good-will.*

adfecto -are, *to strive after, grasp at, aim at, aspire to;* polit. *to try to win over;* in literary style, *to affect;* partic. **adfectātus** -a -um, *studied.*

adfectus -ūs, m. *condition, disposition;* esp. of the mind, *a feeling;* often *friendly feeling, good-will.*

adfectus -a -um, partic. from adficio; q.v.

adfero adferre attŭli adlātum, *to carry to, bring to;* esp. of messages, and news; absol., *to bring news, report.* Transf., *to apply, bring to bear;* vim, *to offer violence; to cause, bring about; to bring forward* by way of excuse or reason; *to bring by way of help, contribute.*

adficio -ficĕre -fēci -fectum, *to influence, work upon;* with adverbs, *to affect;* with abl. of nouns, *to treat with, present with;* nominem sepultura, *to bury;* poena, *to punish,* beneficio adfici, *to be benefited;* absol., of the body, *to affect adversely, weaken.* Hence partic. **adfectus** -a -um, *affected, influenced;* with abl. *furnished with, treated with;* absol., of the body, *weakened, sick;* of undertakings, *worked upon,* and so *nearly finished.*

adfigo -figĕre -fixi -fixum, *to fasten to, affix;* litteram ad caput, *to brand;* adfigi animis, *to be imprinted.*

adfingo -fingĕre -finxi -fictum, *to form or invent in addition.*

adfinis -e *neighbouring;* hence *connected with, privy to;* also *related by marriage;* as subst., *a relative.*

adfinitās -ātis, f., *relationship by marriage;* meton., *relations by marriage;* in gen., *union.*

adfirmatio -ōnis, f. *positive assertion.*

adfirmo -are *to strengthen; to support a statement, to prove; to assert as true.* Adv. from partic., **adfirmatē,** *positively.*

adflatus -ūs, m. *blowing or breathing on, breath;* maris, *sea breeze.* Transf. *inspiration.*

adflĕo -flēre -flēvi -flētum, *to weep at.*

adflictātio -ōnis, f. *pain, torture.*

adflicto -are, *to agitate, knock about, harass, distress.*

adflictor -ōris, m., *a subverter.*

adfligo -flīgĕre -flixi -flictum, *to dash, knock down, knock about; to weaken, discourage, injure;* causam susceptam, *to drop.* Hence partic. **adflictus** -a -um, *damaged, shattered;* of spirits, *broken down, desponding;* of character, *vile, contemptible.*

adflo -are, *to blow on or breathe on.*

adflŭentia -ae, f. *overflow, abundance.*

adflŭo -flŭĕre -fluxi -fluxum, *to flow to, flow near;* of men, *to stream, to flock together.* Transf., *to flow freely, to be abundant,* with abl., *to abound in.* Hence partic. **adflŭens** -entis, *rich, abounding.* Compar. adv. **adflŭentius.**

adfor -ari, dep. *to accost, address;* esp. *to say farewell* to the dead, and *to pray to gods.*

adfulgĕo -fulgĕre -fulsi, *to shine, glitter; to shine upon, favour,* with dat.

adfundo -fundĕre -fūdi -fusum, *to pour upon;* colonia amne adfusa, *washed by a river;* adfundere se, or adfundi, *to prostrate oneself.* Transf., *to throw in, add.*

adgĕmo -ĕre, *to groan at,* with dat.

adgĕro -gĕrĕre -gessi -gestum, *to carry to, bring up.*

adgestus -ūs, m. *carrying to, accumulation.*

adglŏmĕro -are, *to wind on a ball;* hence *to add.*

adglūtino -are, *to glue to, fasten to.*

adgrăvesco -ĕre, *to grow worse* (of sickness).

adgrăvo -are, *to make heavier;* hence, *to make worse.*

adgrĕdĭor -grĕdi -gressus, dep. *to go to, approach;* with words, *to address;* of enemies, *to attack;* of business, etc., *to begin, undertake, attempt.*

adgrĕgo -are, *to add to the flock;* so *to attach, associate.*

adgressio -ōnis, f. *the introduction to a speech.*

ădhaerĕo -haerēre -haesi -haesum, *to hang to, stick to, adhere;* of places, *to border on, be near;* fig., *to depend on, cling to.*

adhaeresco -haerescĕre -haesi -haesum, *to hang on to, adhere.* Transf., *to* cling to, hang on, attach oneself; in speaking, to stick fast, stop.

adhaesio -ōnis, f. and **adhaesus** -ūs, m. adhering, clinging.

ădhĭbĕo -ēre -ŭi -ĭtum, to bring up to, apply, bring to bear; of persons, to invite, call in, employ for a purpose; with adv., to treat.

ădhinnĭo -ire, to neigh after, neigh at.

ădhortātĭo -ōnis, f. exhortation.

ădhortātor -ōris, m. one who exhorts.

ădhortor -ari, dep. to exhort, encourage (esp. of soldiers).

ădhūc, of time, hitherto, till now, till then; still, even now; in gen., besides, also; with comparatives, even, still.

ădiăcĕo -ēre, to lie by the side of, be adjacent. N. pl. of partic. as subst. **adiăcentia**, the neighbourhood.

adĭcĭo -icĕre -iēci -iectum, to throw to; hence to cast, direct, apply; also to add; at an auction, to outbid.

adiectĭo -ōnis, f. addition, advance.

adiectus -ūs, m. addition.

ădĭgo -igĕre -ēgi -actum, to drive, force, compel; hominem ad iusiurandum, or iureiurando, to put a man on his oath.

ădĭmo -ĭmĕre -ēmi -emptum, to take away.
Hence partic. **ădemptus** -a -um, poet., dead.

ădĭpatus -a -um, fatty, greasy; n. pl. as subst., pastry. Transf., o style, bombastic.

ădĭpiscor -ĭpisci -eptus, dep. to come up to, overtake; hence to obtain. Perf. partic. adeptus, used passively, = obtained.

ădĭtĭo -ōnis, f. approach.

ădĭtus -ūs, m. approach, access; hence also right or possibility of entrance; homo rari aditus, difficult of access; concr., an entrance to a place, approach. Transf., opportunity of obtaining.

adiŭdĭco -are, to award as a judge, assign, grant.

adiŭmentum -i, n. help, assistance.

adiunctĭo -ōnis, f. joining, addition, union; rhet. a limitation, or repetition.

adiunctor -ōris, m., one who joins.

adiungo -iungĕre -iunxi -iunctum, to join, connect; adiunctus fundus, neighbouring; of immaterial things, to associate, impart; of persons, to attach, esp. as partner, friend, etc.
Hence partic. **adiunctus** -a -um, bound to, belonging to; n. pl. as subst. collateral circumstances.

adiūro, -are, to swear in addition; to swear to a thing, promise on oath.

adiŭto -are, to be serviceable, help.

adiŭtor -ōris, m., a helper, assistant, deputy.

adiŭtrix -:cis, f., of females and f. nouns, an assistant, aid; used of reserve legions under the empire.

adiŭvo -iŭvāre -iūvi -iūtum, to help, assist, support.

adlābor -lābi -lapsus, dep. to glide to, flow to, with dat or acc.

adlābŏro -are, to labour at; also to add to by labour.

adlacrĭmo -are, to weep at.

adlapsus -ūs, m., a gliding approach.

adlatro -are, to bark at, rail at.

adlaudābilis -e, praiseworthy.

adlecto -are, to entice.

adlēgātĭo -ōnis, f. the sending of a person on a mission.

adlēgo -are., to send on private business, to commission; adlegati, deputies. Transf., to instigate, suborn; to adduce or allege in excuse.

adlēgo -lēgĕre -lēgi -lectum, to choose, elect.

adlĕvāmentum -i, n., a means of alleviation.

adlĕvātĭo -ōnis, f., a lifting up; hence alleviation.

adlĕvo -are, to lift up, erect; hence to lighten, alleviate; pass., adlevari, to be cheered.

adlĭcĭo -licĕre -lexi -lectum, to allure, entice.

adlīdo -līdĕre -lisi -līsum, to strike against, dash against; pass., adlidi, to suffer damage.

adlĭgo -are, to tie to, bind to; of wounds, to bind up. Transf., in gen., to fetter, bind, confine; esp. to bind by friendship, obligations, promise, etc.; pass., to become an accomplice in, make oneself responsible for; perf. partic. adligatus, implicated, involved.

adlĭno -linĕre -lēvi -litum, to smear on, bedaub.

adlŏcūtĭo -ōnis, f. an address; esp. a word of comfort.

adlŏquĭum -i, n., exhortation, encouragement, consolation.

adlŏquor -lŏqui -lŏcūtus, dep. to address; esp. to encourage, appeal to.

adlūcĕo -lūcēre -luxi, to shine at, or upon.

adlūdo -lūdĕre -lūsi -lūsum, to jest at, sport with; of waves, to play or dash upon.

adlŭo -lūĕre -lŭi, to wash, of the sea.

adlŭvĭēs -ēi, f., a pool caused by flooding.

adlŭvĭo -ōnis, f., alluvial land.

admātūro -are, to hasten.

admētĭor mētiri -mensus, dep. to measure out to.

Admētus -i, m. husband of Alcestis.

admĭnĭcŭlor -ari, dep. to support, prop.

admĭnĭcŭlum -i, n. prop, support; in gen., aid, help.

admĭnister -stri, m. attendant, assistant.

admĭnistra -ae, f. a (female) helper.

admĭnistrātĭo -ōnis, f. the giving of help; direction, government.

admĭnistrātor -ōris, m. administrator, manager.

admĭnistro -are. to help, assist; to manage, direct, administer; navem, to steer.

admīrābĭlis -e. admirable; astonishing, strange. Adv., **admīrābĭliter**.

admīrābĭlĭtās -ātis, f. admirableness; admiration.

admīrātĭo -ōnis, f. admiration; plur. outbursts of admiration; wonder, astonishment.

admīror -ari, dep. *to admire; to be astonished, to wonder.* Hence gerundive admīrandus -a -um, *admirable.*

admiscēo -miscēre -miscŭi -mixtum (-mistum), *to mix with, to join;* admisceri novis sermonibus *to become familiar with.*

admissārĭus -i, m. *stallion.*

admissĭo -onis, f. *audience,* esp. with kings, etc.

admitto -mittĕre -mīsi -missum, *to send to, admit;* esp. of horses, *to let go, put to a gallop.* Transf., *to allow; to admit a crime to one's record, so to commit;* hence n. of partic. as subst. admissum -i, *a crime.*

admixtĭo -ōnis, f. *an admixture.*

admŏdĕrātē, *appropriately.*

admŏdum, *up to the measure, up to the mark;* hence, *completely.* With adjectives and other parts of speech, *wholly, quite;* puer admodum, *a mere boy;* with numbers, *just about;* in affirmative answers, *certainly.*

admŏnĕo -ēre -ŭi -itum, *to admonish, remind,* of a fact or duty. N, of partic. as subst. admŏnĭtum -i, *an admonition.*

admŏnĭtĭo -ōnis, f. *a reminding;* esp. *a friendly admonition.*

admŏnĭtor -ōris, m. *one who reminds.*

admŏnĭtū, abl. sing. m., *by reminding, by warning.*

admordēo -mordēre -morsum, *to bite at, gnaw;* fig. *to fleece.*

admōtĭo -ōnis, f. *moving to, application.*

admŏvĕo -mŏvēre -mōvi -mōtum, *to move to, bring up, apply;* manum operi, *to engage in a work;* manus nocentibus, *to lay hands on the guilty;* milit. *to bring up* war-machines or soldiers.

admŭgĭo -ire, *to bellow after.*

admurmŭrātĭo -ōnis, f. *murmuring.*

admurmŭro -are, *to murmur at.*

adnāto -are, *to swim to or beside.*

adnecto -nectĕre -nexŭi -nexum, *to bind to, connect with.*

adnexus -ūs, m. *binding, connexion.*

adnītor -niti -nisus or -nixus, dep. *to press against, lean upon.* Transf., *to strive after.*

adno -are, *to swim to, or near, or beside.*

adnŏto -are, *to note, remark on.*

adnŭmĕro -are, *to count out, pay; to reckon in with,* with acc. and dat.

adnŭo -nŭĕre -nŭi -nūtum, *to nod to; to indicate by nodding; to nod assent to;* in gen., *to agree; also to agree to give or do a thing.*

¹adŏlĕo -ēre -ŭi, *to worship, offer sacrifice, burn a sacrifice; to sacrifice* on an altar; in gen., *to burn.*

²adŏlĕo -ēre, *to smell.*

adŏlescens = adulescens; q.v.

adŏlesco -ŏlescĕre -ŏlēvi, (1) *to grow up, come to maturity.* (2) *to be heaped up,* or perhaps *to burn* (cf. adoleo). Hence partic. adultus -a -um, *grown up, adult, mature.*

Ădōnis -is or -idis, *a beautiful young man, beloved of Venus.*

ădŏpĕrĭo -ŏpĕrire -ŏpĕrŭi -ŏpertum, *to cover or close.*

ădŏpĭnor -ari, dep. *to guess.*

ădoptātĭo -ōnis, f. *adopting.*

ădoptĭo -ōnis, f. *the adoption of a child.*

ădoptīvus -a -um, *adopted, connected with adoption;* of plants, *grafted.*

ădopto -are, *to choose for oneself;* esp. *to adopt,* as child or grandchild; of plants, *to graft.*

ădŏr -oris, n. *a species of grain, spelt.*

ădōrātĭo -ōnis, f. *praying to, adoration.*

ădōrĕus -a -um, *of spelt;* f. as subst. *a reward for valour* (originally a gift of corn).

ădŏrĭor -ŏriri -ortus, dep. *to rise up at;* hence *to attack, set about, attempt, undertake.*

ădorno -are, *to prepare, furnish, provide; to adorn.*

ădŏro -are, *to speak to;* esp. *to address a deity,* in worship or entreaty; sometimes *to ask a deity for a thing.*

adp-; see under app-.

adquiesco -quiescĕre -quiēvi quiētum, *to rest, repose, be undisturbed, find comfort.*

adquiro -quirĕre -quisivi -quisitum, *to acquire, get,* esp. in addition to previous possessions.

adrādo -rādĕre -rāsi -rāsum, *to scrape, shave.*

adrectus -a -um, partic. from adrigo; q.v.

adrēpo -rēpĕre -repsi -reptum, *to creep up, glide gently to.*

Adria = Hadria; q.v.

adrīdĕo -ridēre -risi -risum, *to laugh to, to smile upon.* Transf., *to be favourable to; to please.*

adrĭgo rĭgēre -rexi -rectum, *to erect, lift up;* hence *to excite, arouse.*

adrĭpĭo -rĭpĕre -rĭpŭi -reptum, *to seize, snatch, appropriate;* poet., terram velis, *to sail quickly to;* mentally, *to grasp, comprehend quickly;* legal, *to arrest, bring to court, accuse;* hence perhaps *to satirize.*

adrīsor -ōris, m. *a flatterer.*

adrōdo -rōdĕre -rōsi -rōsum, *to gnaw at.*

adrŏgans, partic. from adrogo; q.v.

adrŏgantĭa -ae, f. *assumption,* hence *pride, haughtiness.*

adrŏgo -are, polit., *to associate in office;* in gen., either *to take to oneself* (sibi), *to claim, assume,* or *to adjudge, grant to another* (dat.). Hence partic. adrŏgans -antis, *assuming, arrogant, haughty;* adv. adrŏganter.

adsc-; see under asc-.

adsectātĭo -ōnis, f. *respectful attendance.*

adsectātor -ōris, m. *a companion, follower.*

adsector -ari, dep. *to follow, attend respectfully.*

adsĕcŭla (adsecla) -ae, m. *follower, servant, sycophant.*

adsensĭo -ōnis, *assent, agreement, applause;* philosoph. *belief in the reality of sensible appearances.*

adsensor -ōris, m. *one who assents or agrees.*

adsensus -ūs, m. *assent, agreement;* philosoph. *belief in the reality of sensible appearances;* poet., *echo.*

adsentātio -ōnis, f. *flattering assent or applause, flattery.*

adsentātiuncŭla -ae, f. *trivial flattery.*

adsentātor -ōris, m. *a flatterer.*

adsentātōriē, *flatteringly.*

adsentio -sentīre -sensi -sensum, and **adsentior** -sentīri, -sensus, dep. *to assent to, agree with.*

adsentor -ari, dep. *to assent constantly;* hence *to flatter.*

adsĕquor -sĕqui -secūtus, dep. *to follow after: to reach by following, to come up to, attain;* mentally, *to grasp.*

¹**adsĕro** -sĕrēre -sēvi -sĭtum, *to plant at or near.*

²**adsĕro** -sĕrēre -sērŭi -sertum, *to lay hold of a slave, and thereby either claim him* or *declare him free;* in gen. *to set free, protect,* or *to claim.*

adsertor -ōris, m. *one who asserts the freedom of another person or claims him as his own.*

adservio -ire, *to assist, help.*

adservo -are, *to preserve, watch.*

adsessio -ōnis, f. *a sitting by the side of one* (to console).

adsessor -ōris, m. *one who sits by, or assists.*

adsĕvĕrātio -ōnis, f. *earnestness, vehemence;* esp. *vehement assertion, asseveration.*

adsĕvĕro -are, *to be earnest;* esp. *to assert confidently or strongly.* Adv. from partic. **adsĕvĕranter,** *earnestly.*

adsĭdĕo -sidēre -sēdi -sessum, *to sit near, sit beside,* esp. *beside a person, to give comfort, advice, etc.;* usually with dat. Hence, *to devote oneself to; to approximate to;* milit., *to besiege, blockade.*

adsīdo -sidĕre -sēdi -sessum, *to sit down.*

adsĭdŭĭtās -atis, f. *continual presence, regular attention.* Hence *constancy; constant repetition;* epistularum, *regular correspondence.*

¹**adsĭdŭus** -a -um, *continuously in one place,* or *one occupation,* in gen. *constant, persistent.* Adv. **adsĭdŭē** and **adsĭdŭō,** *continuously, without remission.*

²**adsĭdŭus** -i, m. *a taxpaying citizen.*

adsignātio -ōnis, f. *assignment, allotment.*

adsigno -are. (1) *to assign, allot;* hence *to impute, ascribe.* (2) *to seal;* hence *to impress upon.*

adsĭlio -silire -silŭi, *to leap to, or on.*

adsĭmilis -e, *like, similar.*

adsĭmŭlo -are, *to make like; to compare.*

Hence partic. **adsĭmŭlatus** -a -um, *similar, pretended, simulated.*

adsisto adsistĕre adstĭti or astĭti, *to place oneself at, to stand by;* at law, *to defend.*

adsŏlĕo -ēre, *to be accustomed;* ut adsolet, *as is usual.*

adsŏno -are, *to answer with a sound.*

adsp-; see under asp-.

adsterno -ĕre, *to strew or spread upon.*

adstĭpŭlātor -ōris, m. *a supporter.*

adstĭpŭlor -ari, dep. *to agree with.*

adsto -stare -stĭti, *to stand up, stand by* esp. *to stand by to help, to assist.*

adstrĕpo -ĕre, *to make a noise at;* esp. *to applaud.*

adstringo -stringĕre -strinxi -strictum, *to tighten, draw together, contract, make fast;* in writing or speech, *to compress;* of persons, *to bind, oblige;* with reflex., se adstringere, *to commit oneself to, become guilty of.*

Hence partic. **adstrictus** -a -um, *tight, compressed, drawn together; close-fisted, avaricious;* of oratory, *concise;* adv. **adstrictē.**

adstrŭo -strŭĕre -struxi -structum, *to build to or near;* hence *to add to.*

adstŭpĕo -ēre, *to be astonished at,* with dat.

adsŭĕfācĭo -fācĕre -fēci -factum, *to accustom* a person *to* a thing.

adsuesco -suescĕre -suēvi -suētum: intransit., *to grow accustomed:* adsuevi, *I am accustomed;* transit., *to accustom;* poet., of things, *to make familiar.*

Hence partic. **adsuētus** -a -um, *customary, usual; accustomed to.*

adsuētūdo -ĭnis, f. *custom, use.*

adsuētus -a -um, partic. from adsuesco; q.v.

adsulto -are, *to leap violently upon; to attack, assault.*

adsultus -u, m. *leaping up, assault.*

adsum adesse adfŭi, *to be present, to be at or near;* esp. *to be present and ready, to stand by;* hence, *to support, be favourable to;* sometimes *to be present for a special purpose,* esp. political or legal; of the mind, adesse animo or animis, *to attend;* of things, *to be near, at hand.*

adsūmo -sūmĕre -sumpsi -sumptum, *to take to oneself,* or *take in addition* a person or thing; hence *to claim, appropriate, call in;* in logic, *to state the minor premises of a syllogism.*

adsumptio -ōnis, f. *choice, adoption;* in logic, *the minor premise of a syllogism.*

adsumptīvus -a -um, *deriving its defence from a extraneous cause.*

adsŭo -ĕre, *to sew on.*

adsurgo -surgĕre -surrexi -surrectum, *to rise up, stand up;* with dat., *to rise in the presence of a person, as a sign of respect:* of feelings, *to rise, be aroused;* of style, *to become elevated;* of material things, *to rise up.*

adt-; see under att-.

ădūlātĭo -ōnis, f. *fawning, cringing, flattery.*

ădūlātor -ōris, m. *flatterer.*

ădūlescens (ădŏlescens) -entis: as adj., *young, growing;* as subst., *a young man or young woman.*

ădūlescentia -ae, f. *youth.*

ădūlescentŭlus -i, m. *a young man.*

ădūlo -are, *to fawn* (*upon*).

ădūlor -ari, dep. *to fawn;* with acc. or dat., *to flatter, cringe before.*

ădulter -eri, m., **ădultĕra** -ae, f. *an adulterer, adulteress.*

ădulter -era -erum, adj. *adulterous.*

ădultĕrīnus -a -um, *adulterous; not genuine, forged.*

ădultĕrĭum -i, n. *adultery.*

ădultĕro -are, *to commit adultery, to defile.* Transf. *to falsify, defile, corrupt.*

ădultus -a -um, partic. from adolesco; q.v.

ădumbrātim, *in outline.*

ădumbrātĭo -ōnis, f. *a sketch.*

ădumbro -are, *to shade in, to sketch,* esp. in words. Partic. **ădumbrātus** -a -um, *sketched;* hence *imperfect, shadowy, unreal.*

ăduncĭtās -ātis, f. *a bending, curvature.*

ăduncus -a -um, *bent in, crooked.*

ădurgĕo -ēre, *to press against;* poet., *to pursue closely.*

ădūro -ūrēre -ussi -ustum, *to set fire to, kindle, singe;* of frost or wind, *to nip.* Hence partic. **ădustus** -a -um, *burnt:* hominum color, *sunburnt.*

ădusquĕ: prep. with acc., *as far as;* adv. *thoroughly, entirely.*

advectīcĭus -a -um, *brought from a distance, foreign.*

advecto -are, *to convey often.*

advectus -us, m. *conveying, carrying.*

advĕho -vĕhĕre -vexi -vectum, *to carry, bring, convey to a place;* pass., *to ride up, sail to,* etc.

advēlo -are, *to veil.*

advĕna -ae, c. *a stranger, foreigner.*

advĕnĭo -vĕnire -vēni -ventum, *to come to, arrive.* Transf., of time, *to come;* of events, *to happen, come near, break out;* of property, *to come to an owner.*

adventīcĭus -a -um, *coming from without;* esp. *coming from abroad, foreign.*

advento -are, *to approach, come near.*

adventor -ōris, m. *a visitor, guest.*

adventus -ūs, m. *an arrival.*

adversārĭus -a -um. (1) *turned towards;* n. pl. as subst. *a day-book, journal, memorandum.* (2) *turned against, opposed, contrary;* as subst., m. and f. *an antagonist, rival;* n. pl., *the assertions of an opponent.*

adversor -ari, dep. *to oppose, resist.*

adversus -a -um, partic. from adverto; q.v.

adversus, adversum. Adv., *against, opposite;* adversum ire *or* venire, *go to meet.* Prep. with acc.: of place, *towards, opposite;* of action, etc., *against, in answer to;* of behaviour, *towards;* of comparison, *compared with.*

adverto (advorto) -vertĕre -verti -versum, *to turn towards;* of the senses, etc. *to direct towards an object;* esp. of the mind, animum (or mentem) advertere, *to direct one's attention to, to perceive,* and of offences, *to punish;* of the object of attention, *to attract.*

Hence partic. **adversus** -a -um, *turned towards, fronting, opposite;* solem adversum intueri, *to look straight at the sun;* adverso flumine, *against the stream;* venti adversi, *contrary winds;* hence, in gen., of persons and things, *opposed, unfavourable;* adversa valetudo, *ill health;* proelium, *unsuccessful;* n. as subst. *misfortune.*

advespĕrascit -avit, *evening approaches.*

advĭgĭlo -are, *to watch by, guard, be vigilant.*

advŏcātĭo -ōnis, f. *a calling to one's aid;* hence *legal assistance;* concr., *the bar.*

advŏco -are, *to summon, call;* esp. *to call to one's aid:* as legal t. t., *to call in as adviser, to consult an advocate.* M. of partic. as subst. **advŏcātus** -i, m. *one called in to help,* esp. in court *as witness or advocate.*

advŏlo -are, *to fly to;* hence *to hasten or rush to.*

advolvo -volvĕre -volvi -vŏlūtum, *to roll to;* of suppliants, advolvi, *or* se advolvere, *to throw oneself down before a person.*

advors- advort- = advers-, advert-; q.v.

ădȳtum -i, n. *shrine;* poet., ex adyto cordis, *from the bottom of the heart.*

Aeăcus -i, m. *king of Aegina, grandfather of Achilles; after death a judge in the infernal regions.* Hence subst. **Aeăcĭdes** -ae, m. *a male descendant of Aeacus.*

aedēs (aedis) -is, f. *a building;* in sing., usually *a temple;* plur., *rooms,* or *a house;* of bees, *cells.*

aedĭcŭla -ae, f. *a small building,* esp. *a small temple or shrine;* in plur., *a little house.*

aedĭfĭcātĭo -ōnis. f.: abstr., *the act of building;* concr., *a building, structure.*

aedĭfĭcātor -ōris, m. *a builder, architect.*

aedĭfĭcĭum -i, n. *a building.*

aedĭfĭco -are, *to build, erect, establish; to create, frame.*

aedīlĭcĭus -a -um, *relating to the aediles;* m. as subst. *an ex-aedile.*

aedīlis -is, m. *an aedile, a public officer at Rome, in charge of streets, markets and public games.*

aedīlĭtās -ātis, f. *aedileship.*

aedĭtĭmus -i, and **aedĭtŭens** -entis, and **aedĭtŭus** -i, m. *keeper of a temple, sacristan.*

Aeēta and **Aeētēs** -ae, m., *king of Colchis, father of Medea.* Hence f. subst. **Aeētĭas** -ădis, and **Aeētĭne** -es, = *Medea.*

Aegaeus -a -um, *Aegean;* n. as subst. **Aegaeum** -i, *the Aegean Sea.*

Aegātes -um, f. pl. *three islands off the west coast of Sicily.*

aeger -gra -grum, *sick, ill,* physically or mentally; aeger consilii, *infirm of purpose;* aegris oculis, *with envious eyes;* politically *unsound, mutinous.* M. as subst. *an invalid.* Adv. **aegrĕ** *with pain, regret or difficulty;* hence *hardly, scarcely* (cf. vix).

Aegeus -ĕi, m., *king of Athens, father of Theseus.*

Aegīna -ae, f. *an island near Athens.*

aegis -ĭdis, f. *an aegis, or shield,* esp. *that of Jupiter or Minerva.* Transf., *a protection, bulwark.*

Aegisthus -i, m. *murderer of Agamemnon, afterwards husband of Clytemnestra.*

aegrē, adv. from aeger; q.v.

aegreo -ēre, *to be sick.*

aegresco -ēre, *to fall ill;* mentally, *to become troubled;* of bad things, *to become worse.*

aegrĭmōnĭa -ae, f., *grief, trouble of mind.*

aegrĭtūdo -ĭnis, f. *sickness,* esp. *of the mind.*

aegrōtātĭo -ōnis, f. *sickness,* of body or mind.

aegrōto -are *to be sick or ill,* in body or mind.

aegrōtus -a -um, *sick, ill,* in body or mind.

Aegyptus -i. (1) m., *a king of Egypt, brother of Danaus.* (2) f. *Egypt;* adj. **Aegyptĭus** and **Aegyptĭācus** -a -um, *Egyptian.*

aelinos -i, m. *a dirge.*

Aemĭlĭus -a -um, *name of an old patrician family at Rome.* Hence adj. **Aemĭlĭānus** -a -um, *relating to the gens Aemilia; a surname of Scipio Africanus minor.*

Aemōnĭa = Haemonia; q.v.

aemŭlātĭo -ōnis, f., *a striving after, emulation;* in bad sense, *jealousy, rivalry.*

aemŭlātor -ōris, m., *a rival, imitator.*

aemŭlor -ari, dep. *to rival, emulate;* with dat., *to envy.*

aemŭlus -a -um, *emulous, rivalling;* in bad sense, *jealous.* M. or f. as subst., *a rival,* esp. in love.

Aemus = Haemus; q.v.

Aenēās -ae, m., *son of Venus and Anchises, hero of Vergil's Aeneid.* Hence subst. **Aenĕădēs** -ae, m., *a male descendant of Aeneas;* **Aenēĭs** -ĭdos, f. *Vergil's Aeneid.*

āēnĕus and **ăhēnĕus** -a -um, *made of copper or bronze; hard as bronze, brazen.*

aenigma -ătis, n., *a riddle, mystery.*

āēnĭpēs -pĕdis, *brazen-footed.*

āēnus (**ăhēnus**) -a -um, *made of copper or bronze;* poet., *hard as bronze.* N. as subst., *a brazen vessel.*

Aeŏles -um, m. *the Aeolians, Greeks living in Greece and Asia Minor.* Hence adj. **Aeŏlĭcus** and **Aeŏlĭus** -a -um, *Aeolic.*

Aeŏlĭa -ae, f. *north part of the coast of Asia Minor.*

Aeŏlus -i, m. *ruler of the Aeolian islands and of the winds.*

aequābĭlis -e, *like, similar, equal.* Transf., *equal to itself, uniform, consistent; fair, impartial.* Hence adv. **aequābĭlĭter**, *equably, uniformly, fairly.*

aequābĭlĭtās -ātis, f., *uniformity, equability;* hence *evenness* in style, *impartiality* in law.

aequaevus -a -um, *of equal age.*

aequālis -e, *even;* of places, *level.* Transf., *equal;* esp. *of time, of the same age, contemporary, coexistent.* M. or f. as subst., *a comrade, person of the same age.* Adv. **aequālĭter**, *evenly, equally.*

aequālĭtās -ātis, f., *evenness;* of places, *smoothness.* Transf., *equality,* esp. *equality of age.*

aequănĭmĭtās -ātis, f. *impartiality.*

aequātĭo -ōnis, f. *making equal;* bonorum, *communism.*

Aequi -orum, m. *a people of central Italy.*

aequĭlībrĭtās -ātis, f. *equal distribution of natural forces.*

aequĭnoctĭālis -e, *equinoctial.*

aequĭnoctĭum -i, n., *the equinox.*

aequĭpăro (**aequĭpĕro**) -are, *to compare; to equal.*

aequĭtās -ātis, f., *uniformity, evenness.* Transf., *equanimity;* also *impartiality, fairness, justice.*

aequo -are. (1) *to make level* or *equal.* (2) *to compare.* (3) *to equal, come up to.*

aequor -ōris, n., *a flat level surface;* esp. of a *plain,* or of the *sea;* rarely of a *river.*

aequŏrĕus -a -um, *belonging to the sea.*

aequus -a -um, adj. *equal.* (1) *equal in itself, even, level;* ex aequo loco loqui, *to speak in the senate;* milit., aequa frons, *a straight line.* (2) *equal to something else:* ex aequo, in aequo, *on even terms.* Transf., of places or times, *favourable, advantageous;* of battles, *even,* and so *indecisive;* of temper, *even, contented, easy;* aequo animo, *patiently, with resignation;* of behaviour, etc., *equal, impartial;* of persons, *fair;* aequum est, *it is just.* N. as subst. aequum -i, *level ground; fairness, equity.* Adv. **aequē**, *in like manner, equally; fairly, justly.*

āēr āĕris, m., *the lower air, the atmosphere.*

aerārĭus -a -um, *of or belonging to bronze or copper;* hence *belonging to (copper) money;* tribuni, *paymasters.* M. as subst. *a copper-smith;* in plur., aerarii, *the citizens of the lowest class in Rome.* N. as subst. *a treasury,* esp. *the public treasury at Rome.*

aerātus -a -um, *made of or fitted with copper or bronze;* hence *provided with money, rich.*

aerĕus -a -um, *made of or fitted with copper or bronze.*

aerĭfer -fĕra -fĕrum, *bearing brazen cymbals.*

aerĭpēs -pĕdis, *brazen-footed.*

āērĭus (**āĕrĕus**) -a -um, *belonging to the air, airy;* hence *high in the air, lofty.*

aerūgo -ĭnis, f., *the rust of copper, verdigris; rusty money.* Transf., *envy* or *avarice.*

aerumna -ae, f. *labour, toil, hardship.*

aerumnōsus -a -um, adj., *full of hardship.*

aes, aeris, n. *copper ore,* and *the alloy of copper, bronze.* Transf., *anything made of bronze; a vessel, statue,* *trumpet, kettle*; aera aere repulsa, cymbals; aes publicum, *public inscriptions.* Esp. *copper* or *bronze money*; aes grave, *the* as; aes signatum, *coined money*; also *money generally, pay*; aes alienum, *debt.*

Aeschўlus -i, m. *an Athenian tragic poet.*

Aescŭlāpĭus -i, m. *the god of medicine.* Hence subst. **Aescŭlāpĭum** -i, n. *a temple of Aesculapius.*

aescŭlētum -i, n., *an oak forest.*

aescŭlĕus -a -um, *relating to the (winter) oak.*

aescŭlus -i, f. *the winter or Italian oak.*

Aesōn -ōnis, m., *a Thessalian prince, father of Jason.* Hence subst. **Aesōnĭdēs** -ae, m. *a male descendant of Aeson,* = *Jason*; adj. **Aesōnĭus** -a -um.

Aesōpus -i, m. *a Greek fabulist of Phrygia.*

aestās -ātis, f. *summer*; hence *summer weather, summer heat.*

aestĭfer -fĕra -fĕrum, *heatbringing.*

aestĭmābĭlis -e, *valuable.*

aestĭmātĭo -ōnis, f. *an appraising in terms of money*; litis, *assessment of damages.* Transf., in gen., *valuation, worth, value.*

aestĭmātor -ōris, m. *one who estimates, an appraiser.*

aestĭmo (aestŭmo) -are, *to appraise, rate, estimate the value of*; litem, *to assess the damages in a law-suit*; in a wider sense, *to value* a thing or person; hence, in gen., *to judge.*

aestīvus -a -um, *relating to summer.* N. pl. as subst. **aestīva** -orum, *a summer camp*, and hence, *a campaign*; *summer pastures for cattle.*

aestŭārĭum -i, n., *low ground covered by the sea at high water*; *a firth, creek.*

aestŭo -are, *to be agitated or hot*; of liquids, *to boil, seethe*; fig., of emotional excitement, *to burn*; of perplexity, *to waver.*

aestŭōsus -a -um, *hot, agitated*; adv. **aestŭōsē.**

aestus -ūs, m., *agitation, heat*; of liquids, esp. of the sea, *seething, raging*; also of the sea's *tide*, and *spray*; fig., of persons, *dizziness*; also *emotional excitement, heat, fury,* and *perplexity, anxiety.*

aetās -ātis, f., *age*: of human life, either *a lifetime* or *a time of life, age*; id aetatis, *of that age*; bona (or iniens) aetas, flos aetatis, *youth*; aetas ingravescens, or provecta, *old age.* Meton., *the persons of a particular age*: aetas puerilis, *boys.* In gen., *time, age, a period of time, epoch.*

aetātŭla -ae, f., *youth.*

aeternĭtas -ātis, f., *eternity, immortality.*

aeterno -are, *to make eternal, immortalize.*

aeternus -a -um, *eternal, everlasting*: aeternum, or in aeternum, *for ever.*

aether -ĕris, acc. -ĕra, m., *the upper air*; poet., *heaven*, or *the upper world.*

aethĕrĭus -a -um, *of the air* or *upper air*; aqua, *rain*; poet., *heavenly*, or *belonging to the upper world.*

Aethĭōpĭa -ae, f., *Ethiopia*; adj. **Aethĭōpĭcus** -a -um. and **Aethĭops** -ōpis, *Ethiopian, Negro.*

aethra -ae, f., *the upper air, clear sky.*

Aetna -ae and **Aetnē** -ēs, f. *Etna, a volcano in Sicily*; adj. **Aetnaeus** -a -um.

Aetōlĭa -ae, f., *Aetolia, a country in the west of Greece*; adj. **Aetōlus, Aetōlĭcus, Aetōlĭus** -a -um.

aevĭtās -ātis, f. = aetas; q.v.

aevum -in, n., also **aevus** -i, m., *eternity.* Transf., *time, lifetime*, or *time of life*; flos aevi, *youth*; in gen., *a period of time.*

Āfer -fra -frum, adj. and subst., *African, from Africa*; esp. *from Carthage.* Hence subst. **Āfrĭca** -ae, f. *the continent of Africa*; esp. either *the country round Carthage* or *the Roman province of Africa.* Adj. **Āfrĭcānus** -a -um, *African, belonging to Africa*; esp. as a surname, conferred upon two of the Scipios. Also adj. **Āfrĭcus** -a -um; ventus Africus, *or simply* Africus, *the S.W. wind* (bringing *rain and storms*).

aff-; see under **adf-**.

Ăgămemnon -ōnis, m. *leader of the Greek expedition to Troy.*

Ăgănippē -ēs, f. *a fountain in Boeotia, sacred to the Muses*; adj. **Ăgănippēus** -a -um, *sacred to the Muses.*

ăgāso -ōnis, m. *a groom, lackey.*

ăgellus -i, m. *a little field.*

ăgēma -ātis, n. *a corps in the Macedonian army.*

Ăgēnor -ōris, m. *father of Cadmus and Europa*; hence adj. **Ăgēnŏrĕus** -a -um, and subst. **Ăgēnŏrĭdēs** -ae, m. *a male descendant of Agenor.*

ăger, agri, m. *land, territory*; as cultivated, *a field*; *open country* (opp. towns); *land,* (opp. sea).

agg- (except agger and aggero); see **adg-**.

agger -ĕris, m. *heap, mound*; milit., *rampart*; poet., *any high place.*

aggĕro -are, *to form a mound, heap up, increase.*

ăgĭlis -e, *easily moved, light, nimble, active.*

ăgĭlĭtās -ātis, f. *quickness, agility.*

ăgĭtābĭlis -e, *easily moved, light.*

ăgĭtātĭo -ōnis, f., *movement, agitation, activity*; rerum magnarum, *management.*

ăgĭtātor -ōris, m. *driver*; esp. *charioteer.*

ăgĭto -are, *to put in motion, drive about* (cf. ago); of animals, *to drive or hunt*; of water, *to toss.* Transf. (1) *to vex, harry, trouble* persons, etc. (2) *to deal with, be engaged upon, argue, discuss, consider* a subject; *to maintain* a state of affairs; *to conduct* a business; *to keep* a holiday; *to spend* time; so, absol., *to live.*

Ăglăĭa -ae or **Ăglăĭē** -ēs, f. *one of the Graces.*

agmĕn -ĭnis, n. *a driving movement or a mass in (orderly)movement, a stream, band, train*; esp. milit., *an army on the march.*

agna -ae, f. *a ewe lamb.*

agnascor -nasci, -nātus, dep., of children, *to be born after their father's will.* M. of partic. as subst. **agnātus** -i, *a relation descended from a common ancestor in the male line; a child born into a family where a regular heir already exists.*

agnātĭo -ōnis, f. *relationship reckoned through males only.*

agnellus -i, m. *a little lamb.*

agnīnus -a -um, *of a lamb*; f. as subst., *lamb's flesh.*

agnĭtĭo -ōnis, f. *recognition*; in gen., *knowledge.*

agnōmen -ĭnis, n., *surname.*

agnosco -noscĕre -nōvi -nĭtum, *to know again, recognise; to know by inference or report, understand; to express knowledge, admit, acknowledge.*

agnus -i, m. *lamb.*

ăgo ăgĕre ēgi actum, *to set in motion, drive*; of animals, *to drive or hunt*; se agere, *to go*; animam, *to give up the ghost*; radices, *to strike root.* Transf., *to incite to action; to deal with, be engaged upon; to treat of a subject;* hoc agere, *to attend to the matter in hand*; pass., *to be concerned, be at stake*; actum est de, *it is settled about, so it is all over with*; bene agere cum homine, *to treat a person well*; grates, gratias, *to express thanks*; pacem, *to keep the peace*; of time, *to spend*; so absol., *to spend time, live*; on the stage, *to act, play*; primas partes, *to play the leading part*; legal and polit., *to take a matter up publicly*; agere (iure, or lege), *to go to law*; agere causam, *to plead a cause.* Pres. partic. **ăgens** -entis, as adj. *effective.*

ăgōn -ōnis, m. *a contest in the public games.*

ăgōnālĭa -ĭum and -orum, n. *a festival of Janus.*

agrārĭus -a -um, *relating to land*; m. pl. as subst., *the agrarian party,* aiming at a general distribution of public land.

agrestis -e, *belonging to the field or country; wild, rustic*; hence, *countrified, boorish, clownish.* M. as subst. **agrestis** -is, *a countryman.*

¹agrĭcŏla -ae, m. *farmer.*

²Agrĭcŏla -ae, m. Gnaeus Julius, *governor of Britain, and father-in-law of Tacitus.*

agricult-; see under **cult-**.

Agrĭgentum -i, n.; also **Acrăgās** -antis, m.; *a Doric town in S.W. Sicily.*

agrĭpēta -ae, m. *a land-grabber, squatter.*

Agrippa -ae, m. *a Roman family name.*

Agrippīna -ae, f. *the name of several Roman women, esp. Nero's mother.* Hence **Colonia Agrippinensis** (now Cologne).

ah or **a**, *ah! oh!*

Āhāla -ae, m., C. Servilius, *master of the horse under the dictator Cincinnatus,* 439 B.C.

ai, *ah!*, interjection of grief.

Āiax -ācis, m. *name of two Homeric heroes, sons of Telamon and of Oileus.*

āio, defective verb. *to say yes, to affirm, assert, state*; ain tu? *you don't say?* Hence pres. partic. **aiens** -entis, *affirmative.*

āla -ae, f. *a wing*; poet., of the *sails or oars* of a ship; of a man, *the armpit*; milit., *a wing, squadron.*

ălăbaster -stri, m., with pl. **ălăbastra,** *a perfume casket.*

ălăcer -cris -cre, and **ălacris** -e, *quick, lively, animated.*

ălacrĭtās -ātis, f. *quickness, eagerness, animation.*

ălăpa -ae, f. *a box on the ear,* given by a master to his slave when freeing him.

ālārĭus -a -um, and **ālāris** -e, *belonging to the wings of an army*; m. pl. as subst., *allied troops.*

ālātus -a -um, *winged.*

ălauda -ae, f. *a lark*; also *the name of a legion formed by Caesar in Gaul*; in pl. **Alaudae** -arum, *the soldiers of this legion.*

Alba -ae, *Alba Longa,* the oldest Latin town; hence adj. **Albānus** -a -um.

albātus -a -um, *clothed in white.*

albĕo -ēre, *to be white.*

albesco -ĕre, *to become white.*

albĭco -are, *to be white.*

albĭdus -a -um, *whitish.*

Albĭon -ōnis, f. *old name of Great Britain.*

Albis -is, m. *the Elbe.*

albŭlus -a -um, *whitish*; f. as subst. **Albŭla** -ae (sc. aqua), *old name of the Tiber.*

album -i; *see* albus.

albus -a -um, *white, dead white*; hence *pale* or *bright*; sometimes *making bright*; fig., *fortunate.* N. as subst. **album** -i, *white colour; a white writing-tablet, a list.*

Alcaeus -i, m. *a Greek lyric poet* (about 600 B.C.).

alcēdo -inis and **alcyōn** -onis, f. *the kingfisher.* Hence n. pl. **alcēdōnĭa** -orum, *the kingfisher's time, quietness, calm.*

alces -is, f. *the elk.*

Alcestis -is, and **Alcestē** -ēs, f. *wife of Admetus, who saved her husband by dying for him.*

Alcēūs -ēi and -ĕos, m. *grandfather of Hercules.* Hence subst. **Alcīdes** -ae, m. esp. of Hercules.

Alcĭbĭădēs -is, m. *an Athenian general, pupil of Socrates.*

Alcĭnoūs -i, m. *king of the Phaeacians, host of Odysseus.*

Alcmēna -ae, also **Alcmēnē** -ēs, f. *mother of Hercules.*

alcyōn = alcedo; q.v.

ālĕa -ae, f. *a game of dice, game of hazard*; hence *chance, risk, uncertainty.*

aiĕātor -ōris, m. *dicer, gambler.*

alĕātōrĭus -um, *of a gambler.*

ālec = allec; q.v.

āles ălĭtis, *winged;* hence *swift;* as subst., *a bird,* esp. *a large bird or bird of omen;* poet., *an omen, sign.*

ālesco -ĕre, *to grow up.*

Ālexander -dri, m. (1) = *Paris, son of Priam, king of Troy.* (2) *Alexander the Great* (356-323 B.C.), *king of Macedonia.* Hence **Alexandrīa** or **ēa** -ae, f. *a city founded by Alexander,* esp. *Alexandria in Egypt;* adj. **Alexandrīnus** -a -um, *of Alexandria.*

alga -ae, f. *sea-weed.*

algĕo algēre alsi, *to be cold;* partic. **algens** -entis, *cold.*

algesco algescĕre alsi, *to catch cold.*

¹algĭdus -a -um, *cold.*

²Algĭdus -i, m. *a mountain in Latium;* adj. **Algĭdus** -a -um, *of Algidus.*

algor -ōris, m. *cold.*

algus -ūs, = algor; q.v.

ālĭas, see under alius.

ălĭbī. (1) *elsewhere, at another place;* alibi . . . alibi, *here . . . there.* (2) *otherwise, in other respects.*

ālĭca -ae, f. *spelt, or a drink prepared from spelt.*

ălĭcŭbi, *anywhere, somewhere.*

ălĭcundĕ, *from anywhere, from somewhere.*

ălĭēnātĭo -ōnis, f. *a transference, alienation;* mentis, *aberration of mind.*

ălĭēnĭgĕna -ae, m. *strange, foreign;* as subst., *a foreigner.*

ălĭēnĭgĕnus -a -um, *of different elements, heterogeneous.*

ălĭēno -are, *to make something another's, let go, transfer; to estrange* one person from another; *to put a thing out of one's mind, forget;* with mentem, etc., *to cause a person to lose his reason;* pass., alienari, *to go out of one's mind.*

ălĭēnus -a -um, *belonging to another;* aes, *another's money, and so debt;* in gen., *strange, foreign, unrelated;* esp. of persons, *not at home, unfamiliar, or estranged, unfriendly;* of things, *unfavourable.* M. as subst., alienus, *a stranger;* n. as subst. alienum, *another person's property.*

ālĭger -gĕra -gĕrum, *winged.*

ălĭmentārĭus -a -um, *relating to food.*

ălĭmentum -i, n. (1) *food.* (2) *maintenance.*

ălĭmōnĭum -i, n. *nourishment.*

ālĭo; see under alius.

ălĭōquī and ălĭōquīn. (1) *otherwise, in other respects.* (2) *in general, in most respects.* (3) *else, in other conditions.*

ălĭorsum and ălĭorsus. (1) *in another direction, elsewhere.* (2) *in another manner.*

ālĭpēs -pĕdis, *having wings on the feet;* hence *swift;* m. pl. as subst., *horses.*

ălĭpta and ālĭptēs -ae, m. *the anointer in the wrestling-school or the baths.*

aliqua, aliquamdiu, aliquammultus; see under aliquis.

ălĭquandō, *at any time, once; sometimes, occasionally; at last.*

ălĭquantŭlus -a -um, *little, small;* n. as adv. *a little.*

ălĭquantus -a -um, *of some size, moderate.* N. as subst. **ălĭquantum** -i, *a good deal;* acc. aliquantum, and (with compar.) abl. aliquanto, *somewhat, considerably.*

ălĭquātĕnus, *to a certain degree.*

ălĭqui, aliquae, or aliqua, aliquod, adj. *some.*

ălĭquis aliquid, pron. *someone, something; anyone, anything.* N. aliquid often with partitive genit., *a certain amount or number of;* as adv., *in any respect.* Transf., *somebody or something great* or *significant.* Hence adv. **ălĭquō,** *some whither, in some direction;* adv. **ālĭquā,** *by some road, in some way;* adv. **ălĭquamdiu,** *for some time;* adj. **ălĭquammultus,** *considerable* in number or quantity.

ălĭquot, indecl., *some, several.*

ălĭquŏtiē(n)s, *several times.*

ālis, alid, old form of alius, aliud; q.v.

ălĭter; see under alius.

ālĭum or allĭum -i, *garlic.*

ălĭundĕ, *from some other direction;* alii aliunde, *from various directions.*

ālĭus -a -ud, adj. and pronoun, *another, other, different.* Distributively, *one, another:* alii . . . alii, *some . . . others;* alii alia censent, *some think one thing, some another.* In comparison, *other than,* followed by atque, quam, etc. Rarely, in plur., *all other, the rest;* in sing. = alter, *one of two.* Hence adv. **ālĭās.** (1) *at another time;* alius alias, *one person at one time, another at another.* (2) *otherwise.* Adv. **ālĭō,** *to another place;* alius alio *in various directions.* Transf., *to another person or object; for another end.* Adv. **ālĭtĕr.** (1) *otherwise, in another way;* alius aliter, *in different ways.* (2) *else, in other conditions.*

ālĭusmŏdi, *of another kind.*

all-, v. also under adl-.

allec or ālec -ēcis, n. *fish-pickle.*

Allecto or Alecto, *one of the three Furies.*

Allĭa (Alĭa) -ae, f. *river in Latium;* adj. **Allĭensis** -e.

Allobrox -ōgis, and pl. **Allobrŏges** -um, m. *the Allobroges, a Gallic people.*

almus -a -um, *nourishing, kind.*

alnus -i, f. *the alder;* meton, *a ship of alderwood.*

ălo ălĕre ălŭi altum (or ălĭtum), *to nourish, support, rear, feed;* hence in gen., *to strengthen, increase, promote, advance.*

Hence partic. **altus** -a -um, *grown, great.* As seen from below, *high,* hence, of the voice, *shrill;* of character, dignity, rank, *lofty, noble.* As seen from above, *deep;* hence of quiet, *deep;* of thoughts, *secret, deep-seated;* of time, *reaching far back, ancient.* N. as subst. **altum** -i, either *height* or *depth*. Adv. **alte**, *highly* or *deeply*.

ălŏē -ēs, f., *the aloe; bitterness.*

Alpēs -ium, f. *the Alps;* adj. **Alpīnus** and **Alpicus** -a -um, *Alpine.*

Alphēus or **Alphēos** -i, m. *the chief river of the Peloponnese.*

alsĭus -a -um, *frosty, cold.*

altāria -ium, n. pl. *an erection upon an altar;* hence *high altars,* or *a high altar.*

alter -těra -těrum, *one of two, the one, the other;* as a numeral, *second;* unus et alter, *one or two;* in pl., of a second set. Hence of quality, *second, next best;* of similarity, *another, a second;* alter idem, *a second self;* of difference, *other, changed.*

altercātio -ōnis, f., *dispute, wrangling; legal, cross-examination.*

altercor -ari, dep. *to dispute, contend, quarrel; legal, to cross-examine, cross-question.*

alterno -are, *to do first one thing, then another;* transit, *to interchange;* intransit., *to alternate, waver.*

alternus -a -um, *one after the other, by turns, alternate, interchanging;* sermones, *dialogue;* of metre, *elegiac* (with hexameter and pentameter alternating).

altěrŭter -utra -utrum, *one of two.*

altĭlis -e, *fattened, fed;* f. as subst. (sc. avis), *a fowl.*

altĭsŏnus -a -um, *sounding from on high; high-sounding, sublime.*

altĭtūdo -inis, f. (1) *height;* hence *sublimity.* (2) *depth;* animi, *secrecy, reserve.*

altor -ōris, m, *nourisher, foster-father.*

altrix -īcis, f. *nurse, foster-mother.*

altus -a -um, **alte**, etc.; see under alo.

ălūcĭnor -ari, dep. *to wander in mind, dream, talk idly.*

ălumnus -a -um, adj. used as noun, *nursling, foster-child;* hence *pupil.*

ălūta -ae, f. *soft leather; a shoe, purse* or *patch.*

alvĕārĭum -i, n. *beehive.*

alvĕŏlus -i, m. *tray, trough, bucket; gaming-board.*

alvĕus -i, m. *a hollow, cavity, trough;* hence *boat;* also *the hold of a ship; bath-tub; bed of a stream; beehive; gaming-table.*

alvus -i, f. *belly, womb, stomach; hold of a ship, beehive.*

ămābĭlis -e, *amiable, lovely;* adv. **ămābĭlĭter.**

Ămalthēa -ae, f. either *a nymph, the nurse of Jupiter in Crete* or *the goat on the milk of which Jupiter was reared.*

ămandātĭo -ōnis, f. *a sending away.*

ămando -are, *to send away.*

ămans = partic. of amo; q.v.

ămānŭensis -is, m. *secretary, clerk.*

ămārācĭnus -a -um, *made of marjoram;* n. as subst. *marjoram ointment.*

ămārăcus -i, c. and **ămărăcum** -i, n. *marjoram.*

ămărantus -i, m., *the amaranth.*

ămărĭtiēs -ēi, f., *bitterness.*

ămārĭtūdo -inis, f. *bitterness;* vocis, *harshness of voice.*

ămāror -ōris, m., *bitterness.*

ămārus -a -um, *bitter, pungent.* Hence, of things, *disagreeable, unpleasant;* of persons, *irritable;* of speech, *biting, acrimonious.* Adv. **ămārē**, *bitterly.*

ămātor -ōris, m. *a lover, friend, admirer;* esp. *the lover of a woman.*

ămātōrĭus -a -um, *loving, amorous;* n. as subst. *a love philtre.* Adv. **ămātōrĭē.**

ămātrix -īcis, f. *mistress, sweet-heart.*

Ămāzon -ŏnis, f.; gen. in plur. **Ămāzŏnes** -um, myth., *nation of female warriors.* Hence subst. **Ămāzŏnis** -ĭdis, f. = Amazon; adj. **Ămāzŏnĭcus, Ămāzŏnĭus** -a -um.

ambactus -i, m. *vassal.*

ambāges, abl. -e, -f. (of sing. only abl. found) *a roundabout way, winding.* Hence, in speech, etc., either *circumlocution* or *obscurity, ambiguity.*

ambēdo -esse -ēdi -ēsum, *to eat round, consume.*

ambĭgo -ěre, *to go about or round.* Transf., (1) *to doubt, hesitate;* ambigitur, impers., *it is in doubt;* (2) *to dispute, contend.*

ambĭgŭĭtās -ātis, f. *ambiguity.*

ambĭgŭus -a -um, *moving from side to side, doubtful, uncertain, insecure, unreliable;* of speech, *ambiguous, obscure;* n. as subst. *uncertainty, doubt, ambiguity.* Adv. **ambĭgŭē**, *ambiguously, indecisively.*

ambĭo -ire -īvi -or -ii -itum *to go round.* Hence (1) *to surround.* (2) *to go round from person to person, to approach, entreat, canvass* (for votes, help, etc.).

Ambĭŏrix -rigis, m. *chief of the Eburones in Gallia Belgica.*

ambĭtĭo -ōnis, f. *canvassing for office* (in a lawful manner); in gen., *desire for office, popularity* or *fame.*

ambĭtĭōsus -a -um, *going round;* esp. *active in seeking office, popularity* or *fame; ambitious, ostentatious.* Adv. **ambĭtĭōsē**, *ambitiously, ostentatiously.*

ambĭtus -ūs, m. *a going round, circuit, revolution.* Hence, of things, *border, edge* or *extent;* in speech, *circumlocution;* in relation to persons, *illegal canvassing for office, bribery, striving after popularity* or *effect.*

ambō -ae -ŏ, *both, two together.*

ambrŏsĭa -ae, f. *ambrosia, the food or unguent of the gods.*

ambrŏsĭus -a -um, *divine, immortal, ambrosial.*

ambūbāia -ae, f., *a Syrian flute-girl.*

ambŭlātĭo -ōnis, f. *a walk or place for walking.*

ambŭlātĭuncŭla -ae, f. *a little walk or place for walking, promenade.*

ambŭlo -are, *to walk, go for a walk, travel, march:* bene ambula, "*bon voyage*"; with acc., *to traverse.*

ambūro -ūrěre -ussi -ustum, *to burn*

round, scorch; of cold, *to nip, numb*; in gen., *to injure.*

ămellus -i, m. *the purple Italian starwort.*

ămens -entis, *mad, insane, senseless.*

ămentia -ae, f. *madness, senselessness.*

ămento -are, *to furnish with a strap.*

ămentum -i, n. *a strap, thong.*

ămes -ĭtis, m. *a forked pole.*

ămĕthystĭnus -a -um, *amethyst-coloured*; n. pl. as subst., *dresses of amethyst colour.*

ămĕthystus -i, f. *an amethyst.*

amfractus = anfractus; q.v.

ămīcĭo -īcīre -īcŭi or -ixi -ictum, *to clothe, wrap round, wrap up, cover, conceal.*

ămīcĭtĭa -ae, f. *friendship*; in plur., concrete, = *friends.*

ămīcĭtĭēs -ēi, f. = amicitia; q.v.

ămictus -ūs, m., *the putting on of a garment, esp. the toga.* Transf., *a garment, covering.*

ămīcŭla -ae, f. *a little mistress.*

ămīcŭlum -i, n. *a mantle, cloak.*

ămīcŭlus -i, m. *a dear friend.*

ămīcus -a -um, *friendly, well-wishing, favourable.* M. as subst., **ămīcus** -i, *a friend*; in plur., *retinue*; f. as subst., **ămīca** -ae, *a friend or mistress.* Adv. **ămīcē** and **ămīcĭter**, *in a friendly manner.*

ămissĭo -ōnis, f. *loss.*

ămissus -ūs, m. = amissio; q.v.

ămīta -ae, f. *a father's sister, aunt.*

ămitto -mittĕre -mĭsi -missum, *to send away, let go, let slip*; hence, in gen., *to lose.*

Ammōn (Hammōn) (ōnis, m. *a Libyan deity, worshipped at Rome under the name of Jupiter Ammon.*

amnĭcŏla -ae, c. *dwelling by the river-side.*

amnĭcŭlus -i, m. *a little river.*

amnis -is, m. *a stream, river, torrent*; poet., *current, river water.*

ămo -are, *to love (passionately), be fond of*; amare se, *to be selfish or pleased with oneself*; amabo te, or amabo, *please, be so good*; with infin., *to like to do a thing, also to be wont, be accustomed.*

Hence partic. **ămans** -antis, *loving, fond*; as subst., *a lover.* Adv. **ămanter**, *lovingly.*

ămoenĭtās -ātis, f. *pleasantness, esp. of places.*

ămoenus -a -um, *pleasant, delightful, esp. of places.*

ămōlĭor -iri, dep. *to remove by an effort, set aside, get rid of*; amoliri se, *to take oneself off.*

ămōmum -i, n. *a shrub.*

ămor -ōris, m. *love, passion, fondness, desire*; meton., *an object of love, darling*; personified, *Love, Cupid.*

ămōtĭo -ōnis, f. *removal.*

ămŏvĕo -mŏvēre -mōvi -mōtum, *to move away, withdraw*; se amovere, *to depart*; in insulam, *to banish to an island*; of ideas or feelings, *to put aside.*

amphĭbŏlĭa -ae, f. *ambiguity, double meaning.*

Amphictўōnes -aum, m. plur., *the Amphictyons, religious representatives of the Greek states.*

Amphīōn -ōnis, m. *king of Thebes, husband of Niobe.*

amphĭthĕātrum -i, n. *amphitheatre.*

Amphitrītē -ēs, f. *wife of Neptune, goddess of the sea.*

amphŏra -ae, f. (1) *a two-handled jar.* (2) *a measure*: liquid, = about 7 gallons; of shipping, = about 1/40 of our ton.

amplector -plecti -plexus, dep., *to embrace, twine round, enclose, surround.* Transf., *to welcome, love, esteem*; in thought or speech, *to take in, consider, deal with*; *to include, comprise.*

amplexor -ari, dep. *to embrace*; *to welcome, love.*

amplexus -ūs, m. *encircling, embrace.*

amplĭfĭcātĭo -ōnis, f. *enlarging, heightening, amplification.*

amplĭfĭcātor -ōris, m. *one who enlarges.*

amplĭfĭco -are, *to enlarge, heighten, increase, magnify.*

amplĭo -are, *to enlarge, increase, magnify*; legal, *to adjourn a case.*

amplĭtūdo -ĭnis, f. *breadth, size; greatness, dignity, grandeur.*

amplus -a -um, *large, spacious, ample.* Transf., *great, important, honourable; eminent, distinguished*; amplissimi viri, *men of the highest position*; rhet., *grand, full.* Adv. **amplē** and **amplĭter**, *fully, grandly.* Compar. adv. and n. subst., **amplius**, *more, further, besides*; with numerals, often = *more than.*

ampulla -ae, f. *flask, bottle.* Transf., *bombast.*

ampullor -ari, dep. *to speak bombastically.*

ampŭtātĭo -ōnis, f. *cutting off, pruning.*

ampŭto -are, *to cut off, esp. of trees, to lop, prune*; of limbs, *to amputate*; hence, in gen., *to remove, diminish*; amputata loqui, *to speak disconnectedly.*

Āmūlĭus -i, m. *king of Alba Longa, brother of Numitor.*

ămurca -ae, f. *oil-lees.*

ămygdălum -i, n., *almond.*

Āmyntas -ae, m., *name of several Macedonian kings.*

ămystis -ĭdis, f., *the emptying of a goblet at a draught.*

ăn, conj.: in direct questions, *or*; in indirect questions, *or whether.*

ănăbathrum -i, n. *a raised seat.*

ănădēma -ătis, n. *a head ornament, fillet.*

ănagnostēs -ae, m. *reader.*

ănălecta -ae, m. *a dining-room slave.*

ănălŏgĭa -ae, f. *proportion, comparison, analogy.*

ănăpaestus -a -um: pes, *a metrical foot, anapaest*; n. as subst. *a poem in anapaestic verse.*

ănăphŏra -ae, f. in rhetoric, *the repetition of a word at the beginning of several sentences.*

ănas ănătis, f. *duck.*

ănătícŭla -ae, f. *little duck.*

ănătōcismus -i, m. *compound interest.*

Ănaxagoras -ae, m. *a Greek philosopher of the fifth century B.C.*

anceps -cĭpĭtis, *two-headed; hence with two peaks or edges.* Transf., *coming on or from both sides; of two natures; ambiguous, uncertain, undecided;* hence *dangerous;* n. as subst., *danger.*

Anchīsēs -ae, m. *father of Aeneas.* Hence subst. **Anchīsíădēs** -ae, m. *a male descendant of Anchises, Aeneas.*

ancīle -is, n., *a sacred shield, supposed to have fallen from heaven.*

ancilla -ae, f. *maid-servant, female slave.*

ancillāris -e *of a maid-servant.*

ancillor -ari, dep. *to serve (as a maid).*

ancillŭla -ae, f. *a little maid-servant.*

ancīsus -a -um, *cut round.*

Ancōn -onis, and **Ancōna** -ae, f. *a town on the Adriatic coast of Italy.*

ancŏra -ae, f. *an anchor;* ancoram tollere, *to weigh anchor.*

ancŏrāle -is, n. *a cable.*

ancŏrārĭus -a -um, *belonging to an anchor.*

Ancus (Marcius) -i, *fourth king of Rome.*

Ancӯra -ae, f. *capital of Galatia, in Asia Minor.*

andrŏgӯnus -i, m. or **andrŏgӯne** -es, f. *hermaphrodite.*

Andrŏmáchē -ēs and **-cha** -ae, f. *wife of Hector.*

Andrŏmĕdē -ēs, f. and **-da** -ae, f. *wife of Perseus.*

andrōn -ōnis, m., *corridor.*

Andrŏnīcus -i, m. L. Livius, *Roman dramatic and epic poet of the third century B.C.*

ānellus -i, m. *a little ring.*

ānēthum -i, n. *dill, anise.*

anfractus -ūs, m. *a turning, a bend;* solis, *revolution;* vallis, *winding.* Transf., *legal intricacies, circumlocution, digression.*

angellus -i, m. *a little corner.*

angĭportum -i, n. and **angiportus** -ūs, m. *a narrow street.*

ango -ĕre, *to press tightly;* of the throat, *to strangle, throttle;* in gen., *to hurt, distress;* of the mind, *to torment, make anxious.*

angor -ōris, m. *compression of the throat, suffocation;* of the mind, *distress, anguish, trouble.*

anguĭcŏmus -a -um, *having snaky hair.*

anguĭfer -fĕra -fĕrum, *snake-bearing.*

anguĭgĕna -ae, m. *snake-born.*

anguilla -ae, f. *an eel.*

anguĭmānus -a -um, *snake-handed.*

anguĭnĕus -a -um, *of a snake, snaky.*

anguīnus -a -um, *snaky.*

anguĭpēs -pĕdis, *snake-footed.*

anguis -is, c. *a snake;* in astronomy, *the constellation Draco,* or *Hydra,* or *the Serpent.*

Anguĭtĕnens -entis, m., *the Snake-holder,* i.e. *the constellation Ophiuchus.*

angŭlātus -a -um, *angular, cornered.*

angŭlus -i, m. *a corner, angle;* esp.

either *a quiet corner, retired spot,* or, fig., *an awkward corner, strait.*

angustiae -arum, f. pl. *narrowness;* hence, of space, *a strait, narrow place;* spiritūs, *shortness of breath;* of time, *shortness;* of supplies, *shortness, poverty;* of circumstances, *difficulty, distress;* of disposition, *narrow-mindedness;* of reasoning, *subtlety.*

angustus -a -um, *narrow, confined;* habenae, *tightly-drawn reins;* spiritus angustior, *constricted breath;* of time, *short;* of supplies, *short, scarce;* of circumstances, *precarious, critical;* of mind or speech, *narrow, petty, limited;* of style, *brief, simple.* N. as subst. **angustum** -i, a narrow space. Adv. **angustē,** *narrowly, sparingly, in a narrow, confined manner;* of speech, *briefly.*

ănhēlĭtus -ūs, m. *puffing, panting.* Transf., in gen., *breath; exhalaticn, vapour.*

ănhēlo -are, *to puff, pant;* transit., *to pant out words;* also *to pant for a thing, desire eagerly.*

ănhēlus -a -um, *puffing, panting;* febris, *causing to pant.*

ănĭcŭla -ae, f. *a little old woman.*

ănīlis -e *belonging to* or *like an old woman.* Adv. **ănīlĭter.**

ănīlĭtās -ātis, f. *old age (of women).*

ănĭma -ae, f. *breath, wind, air.* Transf., *the breath of life, vital principle, soul;* animam edere, *to give up the ghost;* poet., *life-blood;* meton., *a living being;* sometimes = animus, *rational soul.*

ănĭmadversĭo -ōnis, f. *perception, observation, notice;* esp. *unfavourable notice; censure, blame, punishment.*

ănĭmadversor -ōris, m. *an observer.*

ănĭmadverto (ănĭmadvorto) -vertĕre -verti -versum *to turn or give the mind to.* Hence *to take notice of, attend to; to perceive, observe.* Esp. *to take notice of a fault, blame, censure, punish.*

ănĭmăl -ālis, n. *a living being, animal.*

ănĭmālis -e. (1) *consisting of air, airy.* (2) *living.*

ănĭmans -antis, *living;* as subst., *a living being, animal.*

ănĭmātĭo -ōnis, f. *animating;* hence, *a living being.*

ănĭmo -are. (1) (anima), *to animate, give life to.* (2) (animus), *to endow with a particular disposition.* Hence partic. **ănĭmātus** -a -um. (1) *having life, alive.* (2) *having a disposition, inclined, disposed;* esp. *having courage, spirited.*

ănĭmōsus -a -um. (1) (anima), *full of breath, airy.* (2) (animus), *full of spirit* or *courage.* Adv. **ănĭmōsē,** *courageously.*

ănĭmŭla -ae, f. *a little soul, little life.*

ănĭmus -i, m. *the spiritual* or *rational principle of life in man.* More specifically: (1) *the seat of feeling, the heart;* animi causa, *for pleasure;* loc. (or genit.) animi, *at heart.* (2)

character, disposition; as a trait of character (esp. in plur.) *courage, spirit, vivacity*; also *pride, arrogance*. (3) *the seat of the will, intention*: habeo in animo, *I am resolved*. (4) *the seat of thought, intellect, mind, memory, consciousness*.

Ănio -ēnis, and poet. **Ăniēnus** -i, m. *the Anio, a tributary of the Tiber*.

Anna -ae, f., *sister of Dido*; Anna Perenna, *an Italian goddess*.

annālis -e *lasting a year, or relating to a year*. M. as subst., usually plur. **annālēs** -ium, *yearly records, annals*.

anniversārius -a -um, *recurring every year*.

annōna -ae, f. *yearly produce, crop*, esp. of grain; *the price of provisions* (esp. corn), *the cost of living*.

annōsus -a -um, *full of years, long-lived*.

annōtinus -a -um, *a year old, belonging to last year*.

annus -i, m. *a circuit of the sun, year*; exeunte anno, *at the end of the year*; annos LXX natus, *seventy years old*; habere annos viginti, *to be twenty*; esp. *year of office, or of eligibility for office*; poet., *time of year, season*.

annŭus -a -um, *lasting for a year; returning every year, annual*. N. plur. as subst. *a salary, pension*.

anquiro -quirĕre -quisivi -quisitum, *to seek carefully, inquire after, investigate*; legal, *to set an inquiry on foot*.

ansa -ae, f. *a handle*; hence, *occasion, opportunity*.

ansātus -a -um, *with a handle*; homo, *a man with arms akimbo*.

anser -ĕris, m. *goose*.

Antaeus -i, m. *a giant killed by Hercules*.

ante. Adv., *before*, of place or time. Prep., *before*, of place or time; ante urbem conditam, *before the founding of the city*; of preference, *sooner than, above*.

anteā, *before, formerly*.

anteămbŭlo -ōnis, m. *a footman to clear the way ahead*.

antĕcăpio -căpĕre -cēpi -ceptum, *to seize beforehand*; hence *to anticipate, not to wait for*; philosoph., antecepta informatio, *an innate idea*.

antĕcēdo -cēdĕre -cessi -cessum, *to go before, precede*, in space or time; *to excel* (with dat. or acc.). Hence partic. **antĕcēdens** -entis, *preceding, antecedent*.

antĕcello -ĕre, *to be outstanding, excel* (with dat. or acc.).

antĕcessio -ōnis, f. *a preceding or going before*; philosoph., *the antecedent cause*.

antĕcursor -ōris, m. *a forerunner*; in pl., *pioneers*.

anteĕo -ire -ii *to go before*, in space or time; hence *to excel* (with dat. or acc.).

antĕfĕro -ferre -tŭli -lātum, *to carry before*. Transf., *to prefer*; *to anticipate, consider before*.

antĕfixus -a -um, *astened in front*; n. as subst. *ornaments fixed on roofs*.

antĕgrĕdior -grĕdi -gressus, dep. *to*

go before; philosoph., *of antecedent causes*.

antehăbĕo -ēre, *to prefer*.

antĕhāc, *before this time, formerly*.

antĕlūcānus -a -um, *happening before daybreak*.

antĕmĕrīdiānus -a -um, *before noon*.

antemitto -mittĕre -mīsi -missum, *to send before*.

antemna or **antenna** -ae, f. *a sail-yard*.

anteoccŭpātio -ōnis, f. *an exception*.

antēpēs -pĕdis, m. *the forefoot*.

antĕpilāni -orum, m. *front line soldiers* (i.e. *the* hastati *and* principes).

antĕpōno -pōnĕre -pŏsŭi -pŏsitum, *to place before, to prefer*.

antĕquam, conjunction, *before*.

antēs -ium, m. pl. *rows or ranks*.

antesignanus -i, m. usually plur., *soldiers chosen for a place in front of the standards*; hence, sing., *a leader*.

antesto (**antisto**) -stare -stĕti, *to stand before*; *to excel, surpass*.

antestor -ari, dep. legal, *to call as a witness*.

antĕvĕnio -vĕnire -vēni -ventum. *to come before, get the start of*. Transf., *to anticipate, prevent*; *to excel*.

antĕverto (-**vorto**) -vertĕre -verti -versum, *to come or go before, precede*. Transf., *to anticipate, prevent*; *to prefer*.

anticĭpātio -ōnis, f. *a preconception, innate idea*.

anticĭpo -are *to receive before, anticipate*; viam, *to travel over before*.

antīcus -a -um, *forward, in front*.

antidea, antideo, antidhac; see antea, anteeo, antehac, of which they are old forms.

Antigŏnē -ēs, f. and **Antigŏna** -ae, f. *daughter of Oedipus, put to death for burying her brother*.

Antigŏnus -i, m., *name of several of the successors of Alexander the Great*.

Antiŏchīa or **Antiŏchēa** -ae, f. *Antioch, name of several Asiatic towns*.

Antipăter -tri, m. *name of several kings of Macedonia*.

antiquārius -a -um *belonging to antiquity*; m. or f. as subst. *an antiquary*.

antiquĭtās -ātis, f. *antiquity, ancient times*; *the history of ancient times*; in plur., *the ancients*.

antiquĭtus v. antiquus.

antiquo -are, *to leave in its former state*; legem, *to reject a bill*.

antiquus -a -um, *coming before; previous, earlier*; absol., *old, ancient, primitive*. In compar. and superl., *preferred, more important*. M. pl. as subst. antiqui -orum, *the people of old time*, esp. *ancient authors*. Hence adv. antiquē, *in the ancient manner*; also **antiquitus**, *from of old or long ago*.

antistēs -stĭtis, c. *a presiding priest* or *priestess*.

antistĭta -ae, f., *a presiding priestess*.

antisto, v. antesto.

antĭthĕton -i, n. *antithesis; opposition*.

Antĭum -i, n. *an old town of Latium on the sea-coast.*

antlĭa -ae, f., *a pump.*

Antōnīnus -i, m. *name of several Roman emperors.*

Antōnĭus -a -um, *the name of a Roman gens.*

antrum -i, n. *a cave, hollow.*

Ănūbis -bis or -bĭdis, m. *an Egyptian god.*

ānŭlārĭus -a -um, *of a ring:* m. as subst. *a ring-maker.*

ānŭlus -i, m. *a ring;* anulus equestris, *the badge of knighthood at Rome.*

¹ānus -i, m. *the fundament.*

²ānus -ūs, f. *an old woman;* also used like adj., *old.*

anxĭĕtās -ātis, f., *anxiety, grief, anguish.*

anxĭfer -fĕra -fĕrum, *causing anxiety.*

anxĭtūdo -ĭnis, f. *anxiousness.*

anxĭus -a -um, *anxious, uneasy.* Transf., *causing anxiety.* Adv. **anxĭē.**

Anxŭr -ūris, n. *an old town of the Volsci.*

Ăōnes -um, *the Boeotians;* **Ăōnĭa** -ae, f. *part of Boeotia, resort of the Muses;* hence **Ăōnĭdĕs** -um, f. *the Muses;* adj. **Ăōnĭus** -a -um.

Ăornos -i, m., *the lake of Avernus.*

ăpăgĕ, interj. *away! be off!*

Ăpellēs -is, m., *a Greek painter, friend of Alexander the Great.* Adj. **Ăpellēus** -a -um.

ăper apri, m. *a wild boar.*

ăpĕrĭo ăpĕrīre ăpĕrŭi ăpertum. (1) *to uncover, lay bare;* hence in gen. *to reveal.* (2) *to open what was shut, open up;* ludum, *to open a school;* annum, *to begin the year.*
Hence partic. **ăpertus** -a -um. (1) *uncovered, clear, unconcealed, manifest;* of speech, *clear, intelligible, frank;* of character, *frank, straight-forward, open.* (2) *unclosed, accessible, exposed.* N. as subst., *an open space.* Adv. **ăpertē**, *openly, frankly.*

ăpex -ĭcis, m. *the top;* esp. *the top of the conical cap of the Roman flamines, or the cap itself;* hence *any crown, tiara, helmet;* fig., *highest honour, crown;* gram., *the long mark over a vowel.*

aphractus -i, f. *a long undecked boat.*

ăpĭcātus -a -um, *wearing the priest's cap.*

ăpīnae -arum, f. pl. *trifles.*

ăpis or **ăpes** -is, f. *a bee.*

Ăpis -is, m., *Apis, the ox-god of the Egyptians.*

ăpiscor apisci aptus, dep., *to attain, come to, come by.*

ăpĭum -i, n. *parsley or celery.*

aplustrĕ -is, n. generally plur. aplustria -ium, and aplustra -orum, *the carved stern of a ship.*

ăpŏdўtērĭum -i, n. *the undressing-room in a bath.*

Ăpollo -ĭnis, m. *Apollo, god of the sun, born at Delos;* ad Apollinis (sc. aedem), *to the temple of Apollo.* Adj. **Ăpollĭnāris** -e, and **Ăpollĭnēus** -a -um.

ăpŏlŏgus -i, m. *a narrative, fable.*

ăpŏphŏrēta -orum, n. *presents given to guests.*

ăpŏthēca -ae, f. *store-room.*

appărātē, adv. from apparo; q.v.

appărātĭo -ōnis, f. *preparation.*

appărātus -ūs, m.: abstr., *preparation, preparing;* concr., *provision, equipment, apparatus,* esp. on a pretentious scale; hence *splendour, magnificence, pomp, parade.*

appārĕo -ēre -ŭi -ĭtum, *to become visible, appear, be manifest;* apparet, *it is clear;* sometimes *to appear as a servant, to serve* (with dat.).

appārĭo -ēre, *to get, obtain.*

appārĭtĭo -ōnis, f. *waiting upon, serving;* meton., plur. *servants.*

appārĭtor -ōris, m. *a servant;* esp. *a public servant,* e.g. lictor.

appăro -are, *to prepare, get ready, provide.*
Hence partic. **appărātus** -a -um, *prepared, well supplied* or *sumptuous.* Adv. **appărātē**, *sumptuously.*

appellātĭo -ōnis, f. *addressing, speech; legal, an appeal; a naming, name, title; pronunciation.*

appellātor -ōris, m. *an appellant.*

appellĭto -are, *to be accustomed to name.*

¹appello -are. (1) *to address, accost, speak to;* esp. *of asking favours, to approach, entreat, sue;* legal, *to appeal to.* (2) *to name, entitle;* hence, *to mention by name, make known.* (3) *to pronounce.*

²appello -pellĕre -pŭli -pulsum, *to drive to, bring to, apply;* nautical, *to bring to land;* huc appelle, *put in here.*

appendix -ĭcis, f. *appendage, addition.*

appendo -pendĕre -pendi -pensum, *to weigh to, deal out by weight.*

Appennīnus -i, m. *the chain of the Appennines.*

appĕtentĭa -ae, f. and **appĕtĭtĭo** -ōnis, f. *desire, longing.*

appĕtītus -ūs, m. *longing, appetite;* plur., *the passions.*

appĕto -ĕre -ivi or -ii -ītum, *to make for, grasp at, seek;* of places, *to make for* or *go to;* in hostile sense, *to attack:* intransit., of time, *to draw near.*
Hence partic. **appĕtens** -entis, *eager, desirous, avaricious.* Adv. **appĕtenter**, *greedily.*

appingo -pingĕre -pinxi -pictum, *to paint to,* or *upon; to write in addition.*

Appĭus -i, m., **Appĭa** -ae, f. *a Roman praenomen common in the gens Claudia;* as adj. **Appĭus** -a -um, *Appian:* via, *the Appian Way, a road from Rome to Capua, afterwards extended to Brundisium;* also adj. **Appĭanus** -a -um, *belonging to an Appius, Appian.*

applaudo -plaudĕre -plausi -plausum. *to strike upon, clap.*

applĭcātĭo -ōnis, f. *attachment, application.*

applĭco -are -avi -atum, and -ŭi -ĭtum, *to apply to, place to* or *near;* corpora corporibus, *to close up the ranks;* naut., *to lay a ship to* or *beside;*

absol., *to land.* Transf. in gen., *to attach, connect*; with reflex. *to attach oneself, devote oneself.* Perf. partic. pass. **applĭcātus** -a -um, *situated near, built near.*

applōro -are, *to lament, deplore.*

appōno -pōnĕre -pŏsŭi -pŏsĭtum, *to place near, put to*; esp. *to serve, put on table*; *to appoint a person, to add* a thing; appone lucro, *reckon as gain.* Hence partic. **appŏsĭtus** -a -um, *placed near, lying near; approaching, near to; fit appropriate, apposite*; adv. **appŏsĭtē,** *appropriately.*

apporrectus -a -um, *extended near.*

apporto -are, *to carry, bring to.*

apposco -ĕre, *to ask in addition.*

apprecor -ari, dep. *to worship, pray to.*

apprĕhendo -prehendĕre -prĕhendi -prehensum, and poet. **apprendo,** *to seize, lay hold of.*

apprimē, *above all, exceedingly.*

apprimo -primĕre -pressi -pressum, *to press to.*

approbātio -ōnis, f. *approval, assent*; in philosophy, *proof.*

approbātor -ōris, m. *one who approves or assents.*

approbo -are, *to approve of, assent to; to prove, establish; to make acceptable to another.*

apprōmitto -mittĕre -misi -missum, *to promise in addition.*

apprŏpĕro -are, *to hasten, hasten on.*

apprŏpinquātio -ōnis, f. *approach.*

apprŏpinquo -are, *to approach, draw near.*

appugno -are, *to assault, fight against.*

Appulia v. Apulia.

appulsus -ūs, m. *a driving towards*; hence *approach, influence*; naut. *landing.*

aprīcātio -ōnis, f. *sun-bathing.*

apricor -ari, dep. *to sun oneself.*

apricus -a -um, adj. *open to the sun, sunny; loving the sun.*

Aprilis -e *of April*; m. as subst. *the month of April.*

apto -are, *to fit, adapt, adjust; to make ready or fit.*

aptus -a -um. (1) as partic. *fitted, fastened, connected.* Transf., *depending on*; also *prepared, fitted out; fitted up with, equipped with,* with abl. (2) as adj. *suitable, appropriate, fitting.* Adv. **aptē.**

ăpŭd, prep. with acc. *at, near, by, with*; apud me, *at my house.* Of other relations; apud se, *in one's senses*; apud me valet, *it weighs with me*; apud patres *in our fathers' time*; apud Ciceronem, *in the works of Cicero.*

Āpŭlia or **Appūlia** -ae, f. *Apulia,* a region in S. Italy. Adj. **Āpūlicus** and **Āpūlus** -a -um.

ăqua -ae, f. *water*; aqua et ignis, *the necessaries of life*; aqua et igni interdicere homini, *to banish a person*; aquam terramque poscere, *to demand submission.* Esp. *the water of the sea, a lake, a river,* or *rain*; in

plur. (*medicinal) springs*; often *water in the water-clock.*

aquaeductus -ūs, m. *an aqueduct; the right of conveying water.*

ăquārius -a -um, *belonging to water*; m. as subst. *a water-carrier* or *an inspector of conduits.*

ăquātĭcus -a -um, *living in water,* or *full of water, watery.*

ăquātĭlis -e, *living in water.*

ăquātio -ōnis, f. *a fetching of water*; meton., *a watering-place.*

ăquātor -ōris, m. *a water-carrier.*

ăquila -ae, f. *an eagle*; milit., *an eagle as the standard of a Roman legion*; architect, *gable* or *pediment.*

ăquĭlĭfer -fĕri m. *an eagle-* or *standard-bearer.*

ăquilo -ōnis, m. *the north wind; the north.*

ăquĭlōnius -a -um, *northern.*

ăquilus -a -um, *dark-coloured, blackish.*

Ăquitānia -ae, f. *Aquitania, the south-west part of Gaul.* Adj. **Ăquitānus** -a -um.

ăquor -ari, dep. *to fetch water.*

ăquōsus -a -um, *full of water, watery.*

ăquŭla -ae, f. *a little water, small stream.*

āra -ae, f. *altar*; hence *refuge, protection*; arae, plur., *name of certain rocks at sea.*

Ărăbĭa -ae, f. *Arabia.* Adj. **Ărăbĭus** and **Ărăbĭcus** -a -um, *Arabian*; adj. and subst. **Ărabs** -ăbis and **Ărăbus** -a -um *Arabian, an Arabian.*

Ărachnē -ēs, f. *a Lydian maiden turned into a spider by Minerva.*

ărănĕa -ae, f. *a spider*; menton., *the spider's web.*

ărănĕŏla -ae, f. and **ărănĕŏlus** -i, m. *a little spider.*

ărănĕōsus -a -um, *full of cobwebs.*

¹ărănĕus -i, m. *a spider.*

²ărănĕus -a -um, *of a spider*; n. as subst. *a cobweb.*

ărātio -ōnis, f. *ploughing, agriculture*; meton., *a ploughed field.*

ărātor -ōris, m. *ploughman, husband-man.*

ărātrum -i, n. *plough.*

arbĭter -tri, m. *a witness, spectator, legal, an umpire, arbitrator*; hence *any judge, ruler, master.*

arbitra -ae, f. *a female witness.*

arbitrārius -a -um, *arbitrary, uncertain.*

arbitrātus, -ūs, m. *will, choice, decision.*

arbitrĭum -i, n. (1) *the presence of witnesses.* (2) *the decision of an umpire*; hence *any decision, judgment, authority*; arbitrio suo, *under his own control.*

arbĭtro, are, and **arbĭtror** -ari, dep. (1) *to witness; to bear witness.* (2) *to arbitrate, judge, decide.*

arbŏr (**arbōs**) -ōris, f. *a tree*; also any wooden object, such as an *oar, mast, ship*; arbor infelix, *the gallows.*

arbŏrĕus -a -um, *relating to trees; treelike.*

arbustus -a -um, *planted with trees.*

N. as subst. **arbustum** -i, *a planta-tion, vineyard planted with trees.*

arbŭtĕus -a -um, *of the arbutus.*

arbŭtum -i, n. *the fruit, leaves, etc., of the wild strawberry or arbutus tree.*

arbŭtus -i, f. *the wild strawberry or arbutus tree.*

arca -ae, f. *a chest, box; esp. a money-box or coffin; also a cell.*

Arcădia -ae, f. *part of the Peloponnesus.* adj. **Arcădĭus** and **Arcădĭcus** -a -um.

arcānus -a -um, *shut, closed; hence silent, secret.* N. as subst. *a secret.* Adv. **arcāno,** *secretly.*

Arcăs -ădis, m. adj. and subst., *Arcadian, an Arcadian.*

arcĕo -ēre -ŭi. (1) *to shut in.* (2) *to keep at a distance, hinder, prevent, keep away.*

accessĭtor -ōris, m. *a summoner.*

accessĭtū abl. sing. m. *at the summons* (of a person).

accesso (**accerso**) -ĕre -īvi -ītum, *to fetch, call, summon; legal, to summon, bring before a court of justice; in gen., to fetch, derive, obtain.*
Hence partic. **accessītus,** *strained, far-fetched.*

archĕtypus -a -um *original.*

Archĭās -ae, m., Aulus Licinius, *a Greek poet defended by Cicero.*

archĭmăgīrus -i, m. *head cook.*

Archĭmēdes -is, m. *a mathematician and inventor, killed at the capture of Syracuse* (212 B.C.).

archĭpīrāta -ae, m. *chief pirate.*

architectōn -ŏnis, m. *master-builder.*

architĕctor -ari, dep. *to build, devise.*

architectūra -ae, f. *architecture.*

architectus -i, m. *an architect, master-builder, inventor, maker.*

archōn -ontis, m. *an archon, an Athenian magistrate.*

arcĭtĕnens -entis, *holding the bow.*

Arctŏs -i, f. *the Great and Little Bear;* hence *the north.*

arctōus -a -um, *belonging to the Bear;* hence, *northern.*

Arctūrus -i, m. *the brightest star of Bootes.*

arcŭla -ae, f. *a casket.* Transf., *rhetorical ornament.*

arcŭo -are, *to bend or shape like a bow.*

arcus -ūs, m. *a bow, arch, arc; esp. the rainbow.*

ardĕa -ae, f. *a heron.*

ardēlĭo -ŏnis, m. *a busybody.*

ardĕo ardēre arsi, *to burn, glow, be on fire;* of bright objects, *to gleam;* of feeling (esp. of love), *to burn, smart;* of political disorder, *to be ablaze.*
Hence partic. **ardens** -entis, *hot, glowing, burning, fiery, eager;* adv. **ardenter.**

ardesco -ĕre *to take fire;* of bright objects, *to glitter;* of passions, *to become inflamed;* of strife, *to blaze up.*

ardor -ōris, m. *flame, burning, heat;* of bright objects, *gleam;* of feelings (esp. of love), *heat, eagerness;* meton., *an object of love, loved one.*

ardŭus -a -um, *steep, towering, lofty.*

Transf., *difficult to undertake or reach;* n. as subst., *difficulty.*

ārĕa -ae, f. *a level or open space, site, court-yard, threshing floor; esp. a playground;* hence, in gen., *play, scope.*

ārĕfăcĭo -făcĕre -fēci -factum, *to make dry.*

ārĕna = harena; q.v.

ārĕo -ēre, *to be dry;* partic. **ārens** -entis, *dry, thirsty.*

Ārĕŏpăgus -i, m. *Mars' hill at Athens, where a court sat.* Hence **Ārĕŏpăgītes** -ae, m. *a member of the court.*

Ārĕs -is, m. *the Greek god of war,* Latin *Mars.*

āresco -ĕre *to become dry.*

ārĕtălŏgus -i, m. *a babbler about virtue.*

Ărĕthūsa -ae, f. *a fountain at Syracuse;* myth. *a nymph chased by the river Alpheus under the sea to Sicily.*

argentārĭus -a -um *relating to silver or money; taberna, a banker's stall.* M. as subst. *a money-changer, banker;* f. as subst., *the office or trade of a banker; also a silver mine.*

argentātus -a -um *ornamented with silver.*

argentĕus -a -um, *of silver.* Transf., *ornamented with silver; of the colour of silver; belonging to the Silver Age.*

argentum -i, n. *silver; esp. silver plate or silver coin;* hence, in gen., *money.*

Argīlētum -i, n. *the booksellers' district in Rome.*

argilla -ae, f. *white clay, potter's clay.*

Argō, Argūs, f. *the ship Argo.*

Argŏnautae -arum, m. pl. *the Argonauts, the heroes who sailed in the Argo.*

Argŏs, n. and **Argi** -orum, m. pl. *Argos, capital of Argolis in the Peloponnese.* Adj. **Argēus** and **Argīvus** -a -um : plur. subst. **Argīvi,** m. *the Argives or Greeks.* Hence f. subst. **Argŏlis** -idis, *the district Argolis;* adj. **Argŏlĭcus** -a -um.

argūmentātĭo -ōnis, f. *the bringing forward of a proof.*

argūmentor -ari, dep. *to bring forward a proof, allege as a proof.*

argūmentum -i, n. *argument, proof; subject, contents, matter.*

argŭo -ŭĕre -ŭi -ūtum, *to put in clear light; to declare, prove; to accuse, blame, expose, convict.*
Hence partic. **argūtus** -a -um: to the eye, *expressive, lively;* to the ear, *piercing, shrill, noisy;* of omens, *clear, significant;* of persons, *sagacious, cunning.* Adv. **argūtē,** *sagaciously.*

Argus -i, m. *the hundred-eyed guardian of Io.*

argūtiae -arum, f. pl. *liveliness, animation;* of the mind, *cleverness, sagacity, cunning.*

argūtŭlus -a -um, *somewhat acute.*

Ărĭadna -ae and **Ărĭadnē** -ēs, f. *daughter of Minos of Crete.*

ārĭdŭlus -a -um *somewhat dry.*

ārĭdus -a -um, adj. *dry, arid, thirsty;*

febris, *parching*; crura, *shrivelled*; of living conditions, *meagre*; intellectually *dry, jejune*; of character, *avaricious.* N. as subst., *dry ground.*

ārĭēs -ĭĕtis, m. *a ram; a battering ram; a prop, beam.*

ărĭēto -are, *to butt like a ram.*

Ărĭōn -ŏnis, m. *a cithara player, saved from drowning by a dolphin.*

Ărĭovistus -i, m. *a Germanic prince.*

ărista -ae, f. *the beard of an ear of grain; hence the ear itself; also a harvest.*

Ărĭstŏphănēs -is, m., *the Athenian comic dramatist.* Adj. **Ărĭstŏphănēus** -a -um.

Ărĭstŏtĕlēs -is and -i, m. *the Greek philosopher, pupil of Plato, founder of the Peripatetic school.* Adj. **Ărĭstŏtēlēus** and **Ărĭstŏtēlĭus** -a -um.

ărithmētĭca -ae and **-e** -ēs, f.; also **ărithmētĭca** -orum, n. pl.; *arithmetic.*

arma -orum, n. pl. *defensive arms, armour, weapons of war*; hence *war; soldiers, military power; protection, defence*; in gen., *tools, equipment.*

armāmenta -orum, n. pl. *implements, tackle*, esp. of a ship.

armāmentārĭum -i, n. *an armoury.*

armārĭum -i, n. *a cupboard, chest.*

armātŭ, abl. sing. m. *with armour*; gravi armatu, *with heavy-armed troops.*

armātūra -ae, f. *equipment, armour*; meton., *armed soldiers.*

armentālis -e, *belonging to a herd.*

armentārĭus -i, m. *herdsman.*

armentum -i, n. *cattle for ploughing*; coll., *a herd.*

armĭfer -fĕra -fĕrum *bearing arms, warlike.*

armĭger -gĕra -gĕrum *bearing arms*; as subst., m. or f., *an armour-bearer.*

armilla -ae, f. *bracelet.*

armillātus -a -um *adorned with a bracelet.*

armĭpŏtens -entis *mighty in arms, warlike.*

armĭsŏnus -a -um *resounding with arms.*

armo -are, *to provide with arms, arm, equip, fit out.*

armus -i, m. *shoulder or shoulder-blade*; also, of an animal, *the side.*

Arnus -i, m. *chief river of Etruria* (now *Arno*).

ăro -are, *to plough, farm, cultivate.* Transf., *to furrow, wrinkle*; of ships, *to plough the sea.*

Arpīnum -i, n. *a Volscian hill-town, birthplace of Cicero*; adj. and subst. **Arpīnas** -atis; adj. **Arpīnus** -a -um.

arquātus -a -um, *relating to jaundice*; m. as subst., *a sufferer from jaundice.*

arr -; see also adr-.

arrha -ae, f. and **arrhābo** -ōnis, m. *earnest money.*

ars -tis, f. (1) *skill, method, technique*; ex arte, *according to the rules of art.* (2) *an occupation, profession.* (3) *concrete*, in pl., *works of art.* (4) *con-*

duct, character, method of acting; bonae artes, *good qualities.*

Artaxerxēs -is, m. *name of several Persian kings.*

artēria -ae, f. *the wind-pipe; an artery.*

arthrĭtĭcus -a -um *gouty.*

artĭcŭlāris -e *of the joints*; morbus, *gout.*

artĭcŭlātim, *piecemeal, joint by joint, distinctly.*

artĭcŭlo -are, *to articulate, speak distinctly.*

artĭcŭlus -i, m.: in the body, *a small joint*; in plants, *a knob, knot*; of time, *a moment, crisis*; in gen., *a part, division, point.*

artĭfex -fĭcis, m. As adj.: act., *skilled, clever*; pass., *skilfully made.* As subst., *worker, craftsman, maker, creator, expert.*

artĭfĭcĭōsus -a -um. *skilful, accomplished; skilfully made*; hence *artificial.* Adv. **artĭfĭcĭōsē**, *skilfully.*

artĭfĭcĭum -i, n. *occupation, craft, art*; also *the theory, system of an art*; concr., *work of art*; in gen., *cleverness, skill, cunning.*

arto -are *to press together, reduce, abridge.*

artŏlăgănus -i, m. *a cake made of meal, wine, milk*, etc.

artŏpta -ae, m. *a baker; a bread pan.*

¹artus (arctus) -a -um, *narrow, tight, close*; somnus, *fast, sound*; of supplies, *small, meagre*; of circumstances, *difficult, distressing.* N. as subst. *a narrow space*; in gen., *difficulty, constraint.* Adv. **artē**, *narrowly, tightly, closely*; dormire, *soundly, fast*: artius appellare. *to cut a name short.*

²artus -ūs, m. normally plur., *the joints*; dolor artuum, *gout*: poet., *limbs.*

ārŭla -ae, f. *a little altar.*

ărund-; see harund-.

Aruns, *an Etruscan name for a younger son.*

arvīna -ae, f. *fat, lard.*

arvus -a -um, *ploughed.* N. as subst. **arvum** -i, *ploughed land, a field*; in gen., *a region.*

arx -cis, f. *fortress, citadel, stronghold, height*; fig., *bulwark, protection, headquarters.*

as, assis, m. *a whole, a unit*, divided into 12 parts (unciae); heres ex asse, *sole heir*; as a small coin, *the as*; as a weight, *a pound.*

Ascănĭus -i, m. *son of Aeneas.*

ascendo -scendĕre -scendi -scensum *to mount, ascend, rise.*

ascensĭo -ōnis, f. *ascent*; oratorum *lofty flight.*

ascensus -ūs, m. *a going up, ascent*; meton., *a way up.*

ascĭa -ae, f. *a carpenter's axe; a mason's trowel.*

ascĭo -scire, *to take to oneself, adopt as one's own.*

ascisco asciscĕre ascivi ascitum, *to receive, admit*; of persons, *to adopt*; of things, *to take up, to approve.*

Hence partic. **ascītus** -a -um, *foreign, acquired.*

Ascra -ae, f. *town in Boeotia, home of Hesiod*; adj. **Ascraeus** -a -um.

ascrībo -scrībĕre -scripsi -scriptum: of things, *to write in, add in writing*; hence *to attribute, impute*; of persons, *to enrol, include, put on a list.*

ascriptīcius -a -um, *enrolled as member of a community.*

ascriptĭo -ōnis, f. *addition in writing.*

ascriptor -ōris, m. *one who approves.*

ăsella -ae, f. *she-ass.*

ăsellus -i, m. *ass.*

Ăsia -ae, f. (1) *a town and district in Lydia.* (2) *the continent of Asia.* (3) *the peninsula of Asia Minor.* (4) *the Roman province of Asia, formed in* 133 B.C. Hence adj. **Asiānus**, **Asiăticus** and **Asius** -a -um; subst. **Asis** -ĭdis, f., poet., *Asia.*

ăsilus -i, m. *gad-fly.*

ăsĭna -ae, f. *she-ass.*

ăsĭnus -i, m. *ass.*

ăsŏtus -i, m. *sensualist, libertine.*

aspărăgus -i, m. *asparagus.*

aspargo, v. aspergo.

aspectăbĭlis -e, *visible.*

aspecto -are, *to look at earnestly, look towards, observe, attend to.*

aspectus -ūs, m.: act., *looking, sight, range* or *power of vision*; pass., *sight, power of being seen, look, aspect, appearance.*

aspello -ĕre, *to drive away.*

asper -ĕra -ĕrum, *rough, uneven*; to the taste, *pungent, sour*; to the hearing, *harsh, grating*; of weather *rough, stormy*; of character or circumstances, *rough, wild, harsh, difficult, severe.* N. as subst. *roughness, a rough place.* Adv. **aspĕrē**, *roughly.*

¹**aspergo (aspargo)** -spergĕre -spersi -spersum, *to sprinkle upon* or *besprinkle with.*

²**aspergo (aspargo)** -inis, f. *sprinkling, spray.*

aspĕrĭtās -ātis, f. *roughness, unevenness*; to the taste, *sourness*; to the ear, *harshness*; of character or circumstances, *harshness, fierceness, severity, difficulty.*

aspernātĭo -ōnis, f. *contempt.*

aspernor -ari, dep. *to despise, reject, spurn.*

aspĕro -are, *to make rough* or *sharp; to excite, arouse.*

aspersĭo -ōnis, f. *sprinkling.*

aspĭcĭo -spĭcĕre -spexi -spectum, *to look at, behold, survey, inspect, confront.* Transf., mentally, *to investigate, consider*; of places, *to look towards, face.*

aspīrātĭo -ōnis, f. *breathing, exhalation*; in speech, *pronunciation of the letter H, aspiration.*

aspīro -are: intransit., *to breathe, blow, exhale*; fig. *to be favourable, assist*; also *to climb up, reach towards a thing*; transit., *to blow air*; fig. *to infuse spirit,* etc.

aspis -ĭdis, f. *an adder, asp.*

asportātĭo -ōnis, f. *a taking away carrying off.*

asporto -are, *to carry off, take away.*

asprēta -orum, n. pl. *rough, uneven places.*

asser -ĕris, m. *a stake, pole.*

assŭla -ae, f. *a shaving, chip.*

assus -a -um *dried, roasted*; n. pl. as subst. *a sweating bath.*

ast = at; q. v.

ast -; see also adst -.

astrŏlŏgĭa -ae, f. *astronomy.*

astrŏlŏgus -i, m. *an astronomer* or *astrologer.*

astrum -i, n. *a star,* or *constellation.* Transf., esp. plur., *the heights, glory, immortality.*

astu, n. *a city,* esp. *Athens.*

astus -ūs, m. *cleverness, cunning.*

astūtĭa -ae, f. *adroitness, craft*; in pl. *tricks.*

astūtus -a -um, *adroit, clever, crafty*; adv. **astūtē.**

āsylum -i, n. *a sanctuary, place of refuge.*

ăsymbŏlus -a -um, *contributing nothing to the cost of an entertainment.*

at (ast), *but, yet, moreover*; sometimes introducing an imaginary objection, *but, you may say.*

ătăt, attat, attatae, attattatae, etc. interj. *oh! ah! alas!*

ătăvus -i, m. *a great-great-great-grandfather*; in gen., *an ancestor.*

Ātella -ae, f. *a city in Campania*; adj. **Ātellānus** -a -um; f. as subst. (sc. *fabella*) *a kind of popular farce*; m. as subst., *a player in these farces*; adj. **Ātellānius** or **Ātellānicus** -a -um, *of Atellane farces.*

āter atra atrum, *dead black, dark*; poet. *clothed in black.* Transf., *dark, gloomy, sad*; *malicious, poisonous.*

Ăthēnae -arum, f. pl. *Athens*; meton., *leaning.* Adj. **Ăthēnaeus** -a -um, *Athenian*; adj. and subst. **Ăthēniensis** -e, *Athenian, an Athenian.*

ătheos and **ătheus** -i, m. *an atheist.*

athlēta -ae, m. *wrestler, athlete.*

athlēticus -a -um, *relating to an athlete*; adv. **athlēticē,** *athletically.*

Atlās -antis, m. (1) *a mountain in Mauretania.* (2) *a mythical king and giant, changed into Mount Atlas.* Hence **Atlantĭădes** -ae, m. *a male descendant of Atlas*; **Atlantis** -ĭdis, f. *a female descendant of Atlas*; adj. **Atlanticus, Atlantēus** -a -um.

ătŏmus -i, f. *an atom.*

atque and **ac**, *and, and also, and indeed* In comparisons: of similarity, with such words as aequus or idem, *as*; of difference, with such words as alius or secus, *than, from.*

atquī, *nevertheless, but in fact*; sometimes confirmatory, *indeed, certainly.*

ātrāmentum -i, n. *black fluid, such as ink* or *shoemaker's black.*

ātrātus -a -um, *clothed in black in mourning.*

Atreus -ei, m. *son of Pelops, father of*

Agamemnon and Menelaus. Hence **Atrīdēs** or **Atrīda** -ae, m. *a son of Atreus.*

ātriensis -is, m. *head slave, steward.*

ātriŏlum -i, n. *a little* atrium, *an ante-chamber.*

ātrĭum -i, n. *the hall* or *entrance room in a Roman house temple* or *public building.*

atrōcĭtās -ātis, f. *frightfulness, cruelty, harshness, barbarity.*

Atrŏpŏs -i, f. *one of the three Parcae* or *Fates.*

atrox -ōcis, *terrible cruel, horrible;* of human character, *harsh, fierce, severe.* Adv. **atrōcĭtĕr.**

attactū abl. sing. m., *by touch, by contact.*

attăgēn -ēnis, m. and **attăgēna** -ae, f. *the black partridge.*

Attălus -i, m. *name of several kings of Pergamum:* adj. **Attălĭcus** -a -um.

attāmen or **at tāmen,** *but yet.*

attempĕro -are *to fit, adjust to;* adv. from partic., **attempĕrātē,** *appropriately.*

attendo -tendĕre -tendi -tentum, *to stretch to;* usually with animum (animos) or absol., *to direct the attention towards, attend to.* Hence partic. **attentus,** *attentive, careful:* adv. **attentē.**

attentĭo -ōnis, f. *attentiveness, attention.*

attento or **attempto** -are, *to try, test, essay; to tamper with, try to corrupt,* or *to attack.*

attĕnŭo -are, *to make thin, reduce, weaken.* Hence partic. **attĕnŭātus,** *made weak;* of style, *abbreviated, over-refined,* or *unadorned;* adv. **attĕnŭātē,** *simply, without ornament.*

attĕro -tĕrĕre -trīvi (-tĕrŭi) -trītum, *to rub against, rub away;* in gen., *to weaken, ruin.* Hence partic. **attrītus** -a -um, *rubbed away, worn out;* fig., frons, *shameless.*

attestor -ari, dep. *to attest, bear witness to.*

attexo -texĕre -texŭi -textum, *to weave* or *plait on* or *to;* hence, in gen., *to add.*

Atthis -ĭdis, f. adj., *Attic, Athenian.*

Attĭca -ae, f. *Attica, the district of Greece containing Athens.*

¹**Attĭcus** -a -um, *belonging to Attica* or *Athens, Attic, Athenian;* adv. **Attĭcē,** *in the Attic* or *Athenian manner.*

²**Attĭcus,** T. Pomponius, *the friend of Cicero.*

attĭnĕo -tĭnēre -tĭnŭi -tentum: transit., *to hold, keep, detain;* intransit., *to pertain to,* or *concern,* only in third person: quod ad me attinet, *as far as I am concerned;* nihil attinet, *it is pointless.*

attingo -tingĕre -tĭgi -tactum, *to touch, to reach;* of places, *to border upon;* of enemies, *to attack,* or *strike.* Transf., *to handle, manage, be concerned* or *connected with;* of feelings,

to affect a person; in writing or speech, *to touch upon, to mention.*

attollo -tollĕre, *to raise, lift up.* Transf., *to elevate, excite, exalt.*

attondĕo -tondēre -tondi -tonsum, *to cut, clip, prune;* in gen., *to diminish.*

attōno -tōnare -tōnŭi -tŏnĭtum, *to strike with thunder, stun.* Hence partic. **attŏnĭtus** -a -um, *struck by thunder; stunned, senseless; inspired, frantic.*

attorquĕo -ēre, *to whirl, swing upward.*

attrăho -trăhĕre -traxi -tractum, *to draw, drag, attract.*

attrecto -are, *to touch, handle, lay hands on.*

attrĭbŭo -ŭĕre -ŭi -ūtum, *to allot, assign, hand over.* Transf., in gen., *to give, ascribe, add;* of taxes, *to impose.* N. of partic. as subst. **attrĭbūtum** -i, *a predicate, attribute.*

attrĭbūtĭo -ōnis, f. *the assignment of a debt;* rhet. *an attribute.*

attrītus -a -um, partic. from attero; q.v.

au, interj., *oh!*

auceps -cūpis, m. *a fowler, bird-catcher; a spy, eavesdropper,* or *caviller.*

auctĭfĭcus -a -um, *increasing.*

auctĭo -ōnis, f. *an increasing;* hence, from the bidding, *an auction.*

auctĭōnārĭus -a -um, *relating to an auction.*

auctĭōnor -ari, dep. *to hold an auction.*

auctĭto -are and **aucto** -are, *to increase very much.*

auctŏr -ōris, m. *one that gives increase.* Hence (1) *an originator, causer, doer; founder* of a family; *architect* of a building; *author* of a book; *originator* of or *leader in* an enterprise; *source of* or *warrant for* a piece of information. (2) *a backer, supporter, approver, surety.*

auctōrāmentum -i, n. *a contract; wages.*

auctōrĭtās -ātis, f. (1) *support, backing, lead, warrant ;* polit., *sanction* (esp. of the senate). (2) *power conferred, rights, command; legal title.* (3) in gen., *influence, authority, prestige;* meton., *an influential person.*

auctōro -are, *to bind* or *hire for money.*

auctumnus = autumnus; q.v.

auctus -ūs m. *increase, enlargement, growth.*

aucŭpātĭo -ōnis, f. *fowling, bird-catching.*

aucŭpĭum -i, n. *bird-catching, fowling;* hence, in gen., *hunting, watching, eavesdropping;* aucupia verborum, *cavilling, quibbling.*

aucŭpor -ari, dep. *to catch birds;* in gen., *to watch out for, lie in wait for.*

audācĭa -ae, f. *courage, daring;* in bad sense, *audacity, impudence, temerity;* in plur., *audacious deeds.*

audax -ācis, *bold* (in good or bad sense); adv. **audactĕr** or **audācĭtĕr.**

audentĭa -ae, f. *boldness, courage.*

audĕo audēre ausus sum, *to be daring to dare, venture, bring oneself to.*

Hence partic. **audens** -entis, *daring, bold*; compar. adv. **audentius.**

audientia -ae, f. *hearing, attention.*

audio -ire, *to hear, listen; to learn a thing by hearing;* sometimes *to listen to and believe* (or *obey*); rarely *to be called;* bene audire, *to be well spoken of.* Hence partic. **audiens** -entis, as adj., *obedient;* as subst., *a hearer.*

auditio -ōnis, f. *hearing, listening;* concr., *hearsay report.*

auditor -ōris, m. *a hearer, auditor, scholar.*

auditōrium -i, n. *a place of audience. lecture-room, court of justice,* etc.

auditus -ūs, m. *hearing, sense of hearing;* concr., *a report.*

aufĕro auferre abstŭli ablātum, *to carry away, remove:* in bad sense, *to make away with, carry off, steal.*

Aufidus -i, m. *a river in Apulia.*

aufŭgio fūgĕre -fūgi, *to flee, escape.*

augĕo augēre auxi auctum, *to enlarge, increase;* of rivers, in pass., *to be swollen;* in speech, *to extol, set forth;* with abl., *to enrich with, furnish with;* in transit. (rare), *to grow.* Hence partic. **auctus** -a -um, *increased, enriched.*

augesco -ĕre, *to increase, begin to grow.*

augmĕn -Inis, n. *increase, growth.*

augur -ŭris, c. *augur, soothsayer, seer.*

augŭrālis -e, *relating to an augur or augury;* n. as subst. **augŭrāle** -is, *part of the Roman camp, where auspices were taken.*

augŭrātio -ōnis, f. *divining, soothsaying.*

augŭrātus -ūs, m. *the office of augur.*

augŭrium -i, n., *the office and work of an augur, observation and interpretation of omens, augury;* in gen., *an omen, prophecy, presentiment.*

augŭrius -a -um, *relating to an augur.*

augŭro -are, *to act as an augur, take auguries;* locus auguratur, *the place is consecrated by auguries;* in gen., *to have a foreboding* or *presentiment.*

augŭror -ari, dep. *to act as an augur, foretell by auguries;* hence, in gen., *to foretell* or *to guess.*

Augusta -ae, f. *a name for any female elative of the Roman emperor,* or *town named after him.*

Augustālis -e, *belonging to* or *in honour of the Emperor Augustus.*

¹augustus -a -um, *consecrated, holy; majestic, dignified.* Adv. **augustē,** *reverently.*

²Augustus -i, m. *a name assumed by all Roman emperors.*

³Augustus -a -um, *relating to Augustus;* mensis, *August.*

aula -ae, f. *fore-court, court-yard;* poet = atrium, *an inner court.* Transf., *a palace, royal court;* meton., *courtiers.*

aula = olla; q.v.

aulaeum -i, n. usually plur., *embroidered work, tapestry curtains* (esp. of a theatre).

aulicus -a -um, *of the court, princely.*

auloedus -i, m. *one who sings to the flute.*

aura -ae, *air, esp. air breathed* or *blowing, breath, wind;* poet., esp. plur., *upper air, heaven;* superas ad auras. *to the light of day;* ferre sub auras. *to make known;* poet. (rarely), *smell, glitter* or *echo.*

aurārius -a -um, *golden, of gold;* f. as subst., *a gold-mine.*

aurātus -a -um, *golden* or *adorned with gold.*

Aurēlius -a -um, *name of a Roman plebeian gens.*

aurĕolus -a -um, *golden, glittering. splendid.*

aurĕus -a -um, *golden, made of gold* or *adorned with gold;* poet., *of the colour of gold;* and, in gen., *excellent, beautiful.*

aurichalchum = orichalchum; q.v.

auricŏmus -a -um, *with golden hair* or *leaves.*

auricŭla -ae, f. *the lobe of the ear;* in gen., *the ear.*

aurifer -fĕra -fĕrum, *gold-bearing. gold-producing.*

aurifex -ficis, m. *a goldsmith.*

auriga -ae, c. *charioteer, driver;* of a ship, *helmsman;* as a constellation *the Waggoner.*

auriger -gĕra -gĕrum, *gold-bearing.*

aurigo -are, *to drive a chariot.*

auris -is, f. *the ear;* hence *hearing;* of a plough, *the earth-* or *mould-board.*

aurītus -a -um, *long-eared;* hence *attentive.*

aurōra -ae, f. *dawn, break of day;* personified, *Aurora, goddess of morning;* mcton., *the east.*

aurum -i, n. *gold; anything made of gold, gold plate, coin, a cup, ring,* etc.; *the golden age.*

Aurunca -ae, f. *a town in Campania.*

auscultātor -ōris, m. *a listener.*

ausculto -are, *to hear attentively, listen to;* sometimes also *to obey;* of servants, *to attend, wait.*

ausim, as subjunctive of audeo; q.v.

Ausŏnia -ae, f. *Ausonia, Lower Italy,* and in gen., *Italy;* adj. **Ausŏnius** -a -um.

auspex -ĭcis, c. *one who watches birds and divines from them;* esp. *an official witness of marriage contracts;* poet., in gen., *a leader.*

auspicium -i, n. *divination by means of birds, the taking of* or *right to take auspices.* Transf., *any omen* or *sign;* poet. *leadership, guidance.*

auspĭco -are, *to take the auspices.* Hence partic. **auspĭcātus** -a -um, *consecrated by auguries;* as adj., *favourable, auspicious.* Abl. abs. **auspĭcāto,** *after taking auspices;* hence *in a fortunate hour.*

auspĭcor -ari, dep., *to take the auspices;* hence *to begin favourably.*

auster -stri, m. *the south wind;* meton. *the south.*

austĕritās -ātis, f., *harshness, strictness, severity.*

austērus -a -um, *sour, harsh, strict, severe, gloomy.* Adv. **austērē.**

austrālis -e, *southern.*

austrīnus -a -um, *southern.*

ausum -i, n. *a daring deed, undertaking.*

aut, *or, or else*; repeated, aut . . . aut . . ., *either . . . or . . .*

autem, *but, on the other hand, however, moreover, now.*

authepsa -ae, f. *a cooking-stove.*

Autŏmĕdōn -ontis, m. *charioteer of Achilles.*

autumnālis -e, *autumnal.*

¹**autumnus** -i, m. *autumn.*

²**autumnus** -a -um, adj., *autumnal.*

autŭmo -are, *to say, assert.*

auxiliāris -e, *giving help, assisting:* m. pl. as subst., *auxiliary* or *allied troops.*

auxiliārius -a -um, *helping*; milites, *auxiliary troops.*

auxiliātŏr -ōris, m. *a helper.*

auxiliātus -ūs, m. *help, assistance.*

auxilior -ari, dep., *to help, assist, support.*

auxilium -i, n. *help, aid, assistance*; milit., often plur., *auxiliary troops,* or in gen., *military power.*

ăvāritia -ae and **ăvārĭtiēs** -ēi f. *avarice, covetousness.*

ăvārus -a -um, *covetous, greedy*; adv. **ăvārē** and **ăvārĭtĕr.**

ăvĕho -vĕhĕre -vexi -vectum, *to carry off, bear away*; pass., *to ride* or *sail off.*

ăvello -vellĕre -velli and -vulsi (-volsi) -vulsum (-volsum), *to tear away, pluck away* (esp. with violence).

ăvēna -ae, f. *oats* or *wild oats*; hence *oaten pipe, shepherd's pipe*; in gen., *any stalk, straw.*

Ăventīnus -i, n. and **Ăventīnus** -i, m. *the Aventine, one of the seven hills of Rome.*

¹**ăvĕo** -ēre, *to long for, desire.*

²**ăvĕo** (**hăvĕo**) -ēre, *to be well*; found only in imperat. and infin.; ave, *hail!* or *farewell!*

Ăvernus -i, m. *a lake near Puteoli, said to be an entrance to the infernal regions*; meton., *the infernal regions*; adj **Ăvernus** -a -um, **Ăvernālis** -e.

ăverrunco -are, *to turn away, avert.*

ăversābilis, *from which one must turn away, horrible.*

¹**āversor** -ari, dep. *to turn away* (in shame, disgust, etc.); with acc., *to turn away from, avoid, shun.*

²**aversŏr** -ōris, m. *an embezzler.*

averto (avorto) -vertĕre -verti (-vorti) -versum (-vorsum), *to turn away, remove*; flumina, *to divert*; of feelings, *to estrange*; of property, *to carry off, appropriate embezzle*; poet., intransit., *to retire.*

Hence partic. **āversus** -a -um, *turned away, backward, behind*; of feeling, *disinclined, unfavourable, hostile.*

ăvia -ae. f. *a grandmother.*

ăviārium -i, *an aviary*; also *the haunts of wild birds.*

ăvĭdĭtās -ātis, f. *desire, longing*; esp. *desire for money, avarice.*

ăvĭdus -a -um, *desiring, longing for*; esp. *greedy for money, avaricious*; adv. **ăvĭdē.**

ăvis -is, f. *a bird*; often *a bird of omen,* and in gen., *an omen.*

ăvītus -a -um, *of a grandfather, ancestral.*

ăvĭus -a -um: of places, *out of the way, untrodden*; of persons, *wandering, astray, lost.*

ăvŏcātĭo -ōnis, f. *a calling away, diversion.*

ăvŏco -are, *to call away,* or *off, to withdraw, remove, divert.*

ăvŏlo -are, *to fly away, hasten away.*

ăvuncŭlus -i, m. *a mother's brother, uncle.*

ăvus -i, m. *a grandfather*; poet., in gen., *an ancestor.*

axis (or **assis**) -is, m. *an axle.* Hence (1) *a wheel*; meton., *a chariot, waggon.* (2) *the axis of the earth*; meton. *the north pole* or *the heavens*; sub axe, *in the open air.* (3) *a board, plank.*

B

B, b, the second letter of the Latin Alphabet.

băbae or **păpae**, interj. *wonderful!*

Băbўlōn -ōnis, f. *a city on the Euphrates*; **Băbўlōnia** -ae, f. *Babylonia, between the Euphrates and the Tigris*; adj. **Băbўlōnicus** and **Băbўlōnius** -a -um.

bāca (**bacca**) -ae, f. *a berry, fruit*; *a pearl.*

bācātus -a -um, *set with pearls.*

baccar (**bacchar**) -āris, n. and **baccaris** -is, f. *a plant, perhaps sowbread.*

Baccha -ae, f. *a Bacchante, female worshipper of Bacchus.*

Bacchānal -is. n. *the place where Bacchus was worshipped*; plur. **Bacchānālia** -ium, *the (Greek) festival of Dionysus* or *Bacchus.*

bacchātĭo -ōnis, f. *revelling in Bacchanalian fashion.*

bacchor -ari, dep. *to celebrate the festival of Bacchus*: as passive, of places, *to be made the scene of Bacchic revels*; in gen., *to rage, rave like a Bacchante.* Partic. **bacchantes** = Bacchae; see Baccha.

Bacchus -i, m. *the god of wine*: meton., *the vine,* or *wine,* or *the Bacchic cry* (Io Bacche). Adj. **Bacchēus, Bacchĭcus,** and **Bacchĭus** -a -um.

bacifer -fĕra -fĕrum, *bearing berries.*

băcillum -i, n. *a little staff*; esp. *the lictor's staff.*

băcŭlum -i, n. and **băcŭlus** -i, m. *a staff, walking-stick.*

Baetis -is, m. *a river in Spain*; adj. **Baeticus** -a -um, *relating to the Baetis*; f. subst. **Baetĭca** -ae, f. *the*

Bai

26

bĕn

Roman province of Baetica on the Baetis.

Baiae -arum, f. pl. *a holiday-resort on the coast of Campania*; adj. **Baiānus** -a -um.

băiŭlo -are, *to carry a burden.*

băiŭlus -i, m. *a porter.*

bālaena -ae, f. *a whale.*

bălănus -i, f. rarely m. *an acorn, bennut, chestnut or date.*

bălatro -ōnis, m. *buffoon, jester.*

bālātus -ūs, m. *the bleating of sheep or goats.*

balbus -a -um, *stammering*; adv. **balbē.**

balbūtio -ire, *to stammer, stutter*; hence in gen., *to speak obscurely.*

Bāliāres (**Bălĕāres**) -ium, f. pl. *the Balearic Islands*; adj. **Bāliāris** -e, **Bāliāricus** -a -um.

bălĭnĕum or **balnĕum** -i, n. esp. in pl.; also heteroclite pl. **bălĭnĕae** or **balnĕae** -arum; *a bath, bathing place.*

ballista -ae, f. *a military engine for throwing large stones.*

balnĕae, v. balineum.

balnĕārius -a -um, *belonging to the bath*; n. pl. as subst. *baths, bathing-rooms.*

balnĕātor -ōris, m. *the keeper of a bath.*

balnĕŏlum -i, n. *a little bathroom.*

balnĕum, v. balineum.

bālo -are, *to bleat.*

balsămum -i, n. *the balsam-tree, or its gum.*

baltĕus -i, m. and **baltĕum** -i, n. *a girdle.*

bărathrum -i, n. *a pit, abyss*; esp. *of the lower world.*

barba -ae, f. *beard*; promittere barbam, *to let the beard grow.*

barbăria -ae and **barbărĭēs,** f. *a foreign country,* as opposed to Greece and Rome; *want of culture, rudeness, savagery.*

barbărĭcus -a -um, *foreign,* i.e., not Greek or Roman.

barbărus -a -um, *foreign, strange; uncultivated, rough, savage*; as subst., *a foreigner.* Adv. **barbărē,** *like a foreigner; roughly, barbarously.*

barbātŭlus -a -um, *with a slight beard.*

barbātus -a -um, *bearded.*

barbĭger -gĕra -gĕrum, *wearing a beard.*

barbĭtos, m. and f. *a lyre.*

barbŭla -ae, f. *a little beard.*

bardŏcŭcullus -i, m. *a Gallic overcoat.*

bardus -a -um, *stupid, slow, dull.*

băris -ĭdos, f. *an Egyptian barge.*

barītus (**barrītus**) -ūs, m. *a German war-cry.*

bāro -ōnis, m. *a blockhead, simpleton.*

barrus -i, m. *elephant.*

bascauda -ae, f. *a basket.*

bāsĭātĭo -ōnis, f. *kissing, a kiss.*

bāsĭātor -ōris, m. *a kisser.*

bāsĭlĭcus -a -um, *royal, kingly, princely.* M. as subst., *the best cast of the dice*; n. as subst., *a royal robe*; f. as subst., **băsĭlĭca** -ae, *a basilica, a building with double colonnades, where merchants met and courts were held.* Adv. **băsĭlĭcē,** *royally.*

bāsĭo -are, *to kiss.*

băsis -is and ĕos, f. *a pedestal, base; villae, foundation-wall*; trianguli, *base.*

bāsĭum -i, n. *a kiss.*

Bassārĕus -ei, m. *a name of Bacchus.*

bătillum (or **vătillum**) -i, n. *a chafing-dish or shovel.*

battŭo (**bātŭo**) -ĕre, *to beat, knock.*

baubor -ari, dep., *to bark gently.*

bĕātĭtās -ātis, f. and **bĕātĭtūdo** -ĭnis, f. *happiness, blessedness.*

bĕātus -a -um, partic. from beo; q.v.

Belgae -arum, m. *the Belgae, a warlike people in the north of Gaul.*

bellāria -orum, n. pl. *dessert.*

bellātor -ōris, m. and **bellatrix** -ĭcis, f., *a warrior*; as adj. *warlike, courageous.*

bellātōrius -a -um, *warlike.*

bellicōsus -a -um, *warlike.*

bellĭcus -a -um, *of war, warlike.* N. as subst. **bellĭcum** -i, *the signal for march or attack.*

bellĭger -gĕra -gĕrum, *waging war, warlike.*

bellĭgĕro -are, *to wage war.*

bellĭpŏtens -entis, *mighty in war.*

bello -are and **bellor** -ari, dep. *to wage war, fight.*

Bellōna -ae, f. *the goddess of war.*

bellŭa, v. belua.

bellŭlus -a -um, *pretty, elegant.*

bellum -i, n. (old form, **duellum**), *war, fighting*; in bello, or loc., belli, *in time of war.*

bellus -a -um, colloq., *pretty, handsome*; adv. **bellē.**

bēlŭa -ae, f. *a beast, large animal*; as a term of reproach, *monster, brute, beast.*

bēlŭōsus -a -um, *full of monsters.*

Bēlus -j, m. *a king, founder of Babylon.* Hence f. pl. subst., **Bēlĭdes** -um, *the granddaughters of Belus, the Danaides.*

bĕnĕ, adv.; comp. **mĕlĭus**; superl. **optĭmē**; *well, rightly, properly*; bene rem gerere, *to succeed*; with adj. or adv., *thoroughly, very*; as an exclamation, *good, excellent*; bene facis, *I am obliged to you*; bene facta (or benefacta), *good deeds, benefits.*

bĕnĕfĭcentia -ae, f. *kindness.*

bĕnĕfĭcĭārius -a -um, *of a favour*; m. pl. as subst., *privileged soldiers.*

bĕnĕfĭcĭum -i, n. *a kindness, favour, service*; in political life, *favour, distinction, promotion,* also *privilege, exemption.*

bĕnĕfĭcus -a -um, comp. -entior, superl. -entissimus, *kind, generous, obliging.*

Bĕnĕventum -i, n. *a town in Samnium.*

bĕnĕvŏlens -entis, *well-wishing, obliging.*

bĕnĕvŏlentĭa -ae, f. *good-will, kindness.*

bĕnĕvŏlus -a -um, *kind, obliging, well disposed*; adv. **bĕnĕvŏlē.**

bĕnignĭtās -ātis, f. *kindness, generosity.*

bĕnignus -a -um, *kind, friendly, generous*; of things, *abundant, fruitful.* Adv. **bĕnignē,** *kindly, generously*; colloq., benigne dicis, or benigne, *much obliged* (accepting or refusing an offer).

bĕo -are, *to bless, enrich, make happy.*
Hence partic. **bĕātus** -a -um,
happy, blessed, prosperous; well off;
n. as subst. *happiness.* Adv. **bĕātē,**
happily.

bĕryllus -i, c. *a beryl.*

bēs bessis, m. *two-thirds.*

bestia -ae, f. *an animal without reason,
a brute, beast.*

bestiārius -a -um, *belonging to animals;*
m. as subst., *one who fought with wild
beasts at the public shows.*

bestiŏla -ae, f. *a small animal.*

¹bēta -ae, f. *a vegetable, beet.*

²bēta, n. indecl. *beta, the second letter in
the Greek alphabet.*

bibliŏpōla -ae, m. *a book-seller.*

bibliŏthēca -ae, f. and **bibliŏthēcē** -es,
f. *a collection of books, library.*

bibo bibĕre bibi bibitum, *to drink, drink
in.*

Bibracte -is, n. *a town in Gaul.*

bibŭlus -a -um, *fond of drinking,
thirsty;* charta, *blotting paper.*

biceps -cĭpitis, *two-headed.*

bicŏlor -ōris, *of two colours.*

bicorniger -gĕri, m. *two-horned.*

bicornis -e, *two-horned, two-pronged;*
luna, *the new moon;* Rhenus, *with
two mouths.*

bicorpor -ōris, *having two bodies.*

bidens -entis, *having two teeth.* As
subst.: m., *a hoe with two crooked
teeth;* f., *a sheep.*

bidental -ālis, n. *a sacred enclosure.*

bidŭum -i, n. *a space of two days;*
abl., biduo, *in the course of two days.*

biennium -i, n. *a space of two years.*

bifāriam, *in two parts.*

bifer -fĕra -fĕrum, *of a tree, bearing
fruit twice a year.*

bifidus -a -um, *split into two parts.*

biforis -e, *having two doors or openings.*

biformātus -a -um and **biformis** -e, *of
double form.*

bifrons -frontis, *with double forehead or
countenance.*

bifurcus -a -um, *having two prongs or
forks.*

bigae -arum, f. pl. (and sing. **biga**
-ae) *a pair of horses, or a chariot
drawn by a pair.*

bigātus -a -um, *stamped with the
effigy of a pair of horses;* m. as subst.,
a silver coin so marked.

biiugis -e and **biiugus** -a -um,
yoked two together; m. pl. as subst.,
*a pair of horses or a chariot drawn by
a pair.*

bilibra -ae, f. *two pounds weight.*

bilibris -e, *weighing or containing two
pounds.*

bilinguis -e, *having two tongues, or
speaking two languages;* hence *double-
tongued, treacherous.*

bilis -is, f. *gall, bile, anger, displeasure;*
atra (or nigra) bilis, *black bile,* i.e.
melancholy, madness.

bilix -Icis, *having a double thread.*

bilustris -e, *lasting ten years.*

bimāris -e, *lying on two seas.*

bimārĭtus, m. *the husband of two wives.*

bimātris -e, *having two mothers.*

bimembris -e, *having two kinds of
limbs;* m. pl. as subst., *Centaurs.*

bimestris -e, *lasting two months:* porcus,
a pig two months old.

bimŭlus -a -um, *two years old.*

bimus -a -um, *two years old or lasting
two years.*

bini -ae, -a, *twofold.* Hence *two
apiece,* sometimes simply *two;* of
things that match, *a pair;* findi in
bina, *to be cleft in twain;* bis bina,
twice two.

binoctium -i, n. *a space of two nights.*

binōminis -e, *having two names.*

bipalmis -e, *two palms or spans long
or broad.*

bipartitus or **bipertitus** -a -um,
divided in two; abl. as adv., bipartito
or bipertito, *in two parts, in two
ways.*

bipatens -entis, *doubly open, open in
two directions.*

bipĕdālis -e, *two feet long, broad,
thick or high.*

bipennifer -fĕra -fĕrum, *armed with a
two-edged axe.*

bipennis -e, *having two wings or edges;*
f. as subst., *a double-edged axe.*

bipēs -ēdis, *having two feet;* as subst.
biped.

birēmis -e, *two-oared;* f. as subst., *a
boat with two oars or a ship with two
banks of oars.*

bis, *twice.*

Bistōnes -um, m. *a Thracian people;*
adj. **Bistōnius** -a -um, *Bistonian or
Thracian.*

bisulcus -a -um, *split into two parts,
forked.*

Bithȳnia -ae, f. *a country in north-west
Asia.Minor.*

bito -ĕre, *to go.*

bitūmen -Inis, n. *asphalt, bitumen.*

bitūmĭnĕus -a -um, *bituminous.*

bivius -a -um, *having two ways or
passages;* n. as subst. **bivium,** *a
place where two roads meet.*

blaesus -a -um, *lisping, indistinct.*

blandimentum -i, n. *flattery, allurement.*

blandior -iri, dep. *to flatter, caress,
coax,* with dat.
Hence partic. **blandītus** -a -um,
charming.

blanditia -ae, f. *flattery, allurement,
attraction, charm.*

blandus -a -um, adj. *flattering, caressing,
alluring, tempting.* Adv. **blandē** and
blandĭtĕr, *flatteringly.*

blătĕro -are, *to chatter, babble.*

blatta -ae, f. *a cockroach.*

bŏārius and **bŏvārius** -a -um, *relating
to cattle.*

Boeōti -orum or -um, and **Boeōtii,** m.
*the inhabitants of Boeotia, a district in
Greece to the west of Attica.*

Bōii -orum, m. pl. *a Celtic people of
north Italy, Germany and Gaul.*

bōlētus -i, m. *a mushroom.*

bŏlus -i, m. *a throw;* hence *the haul
or catch of a fishing net.*

bombus -i, m. *a boom, deep hollow noise.*

bombȳcinus -a -um, *silken.*

bombyx -ȳcis, m. and f. *the silkworm,* or *silk.*

bŏnĭtās -ātis, f. *goodness, excellence;* esp. *moral goodness, kindness, integrity.*

bŏnus -a -um; compar. **mĕlior** -ius; superl. **optĭmus** -a -um; *good:* in gen., *good of its kind;* nummi boni, *genuine coin;* bona aetas, *youth;* bona verba, *words of good omen;* bona pars, *a good* (i.e. *considerable) proportion;* in a particular respect of tools, workmen, etc. *useful, efficient;* morally *good, virtuous, honest, kind;* polit., *patriotic, loyal.* N. as subst. **bŏnum** -i, *good;* in gen., *profit, advantage;* bonum publicum, *the common weal;* cui bono fuisset, *for whose advantage;* materially, usually pl., *goods, property;* morally, *the good:* summum bonum, *the supreme good.*

bŏo -are, *to shout, roar, echo.*

Bŏōtēs -ae, m. *a constellation in the northern hemisphere.*

Bŏrĕās -ae, m. *the north wind;* meton., *the north.* Adj. **Bŏrĕus** -a -um, *northern.*

bōs, bŏvis, c. (1) *ox, bullock, cow;* bos Lucas, *elephant.* (2) *a kind of flat fish.*

Bospŏrus (Bosphŏrus) -i, m. *name of various straits;* esp. *those between Thrace and Asia Minor.*

bŏtŭlus -i, m. *a sausage.*

bŏvile = bubile; q.v.

Bŏvillae -ārum, f. pl. *a town in Latium.*

bŏvillus -a -um, *relating to oxen.*

brăbeuta -ae, m. *a judge, umpire.*

brācae (braccae) -ārum, f. pl. *breeches, trousers.*

brācātus (braccātus) -a -um, *wearing breeches;* Gallia Bracata, *Gaul on the north side of the Alps.*

brācchium -i, n. *the forearm, arm from elbow to wrist; any limb of a living creature; any other thing like an arm,* e.g. *branch, spur, yard, outwork of a fortification, mole.*

bractĕa (brattĕa) -ae, f. *a thin plate of metal; gold leaf.*

brassĭca -ae, f. *cabbage.*

brĕvĭārium -i, n. *a summary, epitome.*

brĕvĭlŏquens -entis, *brief in speech.*

brĕvĭlŏquentia -ae f. *brevity of speech.*

brĕvis -e, *short,* in space or time; of water, *shallow;* of living things, conditions, etc., *short-lived;* of style, *concise;* n. abl. **brĕvī,** *shortly, soon, briefly;* n. pl. as subst. **brĕvĭa** -ium, *shallows, shoals.* Adv. **brĕvĭtĕr,** *shortly, briefly.*

brĕvĭtās ātis, f. *shortness,* in space or time; of style, *brevity, conciseness.*

Briărēus -ei, m. *a giant with a hundred arms.*

Brĭtanni -orum, m. pl. *the Britons;* **Brĭtannĭa** -ae, f. *Britain;* adj. **Brĭtannĭcus** -a -um, *British;* m. sing. as a *title commemorating successes in Britain.*

Brŏmĭus -i, m. *a surname of Bacchus.*

brūma -ae, f. *the winter solstice;* in gen., *winter, wintry cold.*

brūmālis -e, *relating to the shortest day;* in gen., *wintry.*

Brundĭsĭum -i, n. *a seaport in Calabria;* adj. **Brundĭsĭnus** -a -um.

Bruttii (Brūtĭi, Brittĭi) -orum, m. *the inhabitants of the southern extremity of Italy.*

¹brūtus -a -um, *heavy, immoveable; dull, without feeling or reason.*

²Brūtus -i, m. *a cognomen of the Roman Gens Iunia.*

bŭbile -is, n. *an ox-stall.*

bŭbo -ōnis, m., *the owl.*

bŭbulcus -i m. *one who ploughs with oxen.*

bŭbŭlus -a -um, *relating to cows or oxen;* f. as subst. (sc. caro), *beef.*

bucca -ae, f. *the cheek,* esp. when puffed out. Transf., *a declaimer, bawler; a parasite; a mouthful.*

buccĭna, buccĭnātor, etc.; v. bucina, etc.

buccŭla -ae, f. *a small cheek;* of a helmet, *beaver, visor.*

bŭcĕrus and **bŭcĕrius** -a -um, *having ox's horns.*

būcĭna -ae, f. *a crooked trumpet or horn.*

būcĭnātor -ōris, m. *a trumpeter.*

būcōlica -orum, n. pl. *pastoral poems.*

būcŭla -ae, f. *a heifer.*

būfo -ōnis, m. *a toad.*

bulbus -i, m. *an onion.*

būleutērion -i, n. *the place of meeting of a Greek council.*

bulla -ae, f. *a round swelling;* in water, *a bubble;* on furniture or equipment, *a boss, stud;* bulla aurea, *a golden ornament, an amulet.*

bullātus -a -um. (1) *inflated, bombastic,* or perhaps *transitory.* (2) *wearing the bulla* (q.v.).

būmastus -i, f. *a kind of vine.*

būris -is, m. *the crooked hinder part of the plough.*

bustŭārius -a -um, *belonging to the place where corpses were burned.*

bustum -i, n. *the place where corpses were burned and buried;* hence *grave, sepulchre.*

buxĭfer -fĕra -fĕrum, *producing the box-tree.*

buxus -i, f. and **buxum** -i, n. *the evergreen box-tree; box-wood;* an *article made of box-wood.*

Byzantĭum -i, n. *Byzantium, a Greek city on the Bosphorus.*

C

C, c, the third letter of the Latin Alphabet.

căballus -i, m. *pack-horse, nag, hack.*

căchinnātĭo -ōnis, f. *violent laughter.*

¹căchinno -are, *to laugh aloud.*

²căchinno -ōnis, m. *jester, scoffer.*

căchinnus -i m. *loud laughter.*

căcŏēthēs -is, n. *an obstinate disease.*

căcŭmen -ĭnis, n. *the extreme point, top, tip, zenith.*

căcŭmino -are, *to point, make pointed.*

cădāver -ĕris, n. *dead body, carcass.*

cădāvĕrōsus -a -um, *corpse-like.*

Cadmus -i, m. *the founder of Thebes;* adj. **Cadmēus** -a -um, *Theban.*

cădo cădĕre cĕcĭdi, *to fall, sink, drop;* vela cadunt, *are furled;* iuxta solem cadentem, *in the west;* of living beings, often *to fall in death, die;* hence *to be destroyed, to subside, sink, flag, fail;* cadere animis, *to lose heart;* with in or sub, *to come under, be subject to;* with in, *to agree with, be consistent with;* of events, *to fall out, happen;* of payments, *to fall due.*

cădūcĕātor -ōris, m. *herald.*

cădūcĕus -i, m. and **cădūcĕum** -i, n. *a herald's staff.*

cădūcĭfer -fĕra -fĕrum, *bearing the caduceus* (of Mercury).

cădūcus -a -um. (1) *fallen or falling.* (2) *inclined or ready to fall;* esp. *destined to die, devoted to death;* in gen., *frail, perishable, transitory.*

cădus -i, m. *jar or urn.*

caecĭgĕnus -a -um, *born blind.*

Caecilius -a -um, *name of a plebeian gens.*

caecĭtās -ātis, f. *blindness.*

caeco -are, *to make blind or dark.*

Caecŭbum -i, n. and **Caecŭbus ager**, *a marshy district in Latium, famous for its wine;* (vinum) Caecubum, *Caecuban wine.*

caecus -a -um: act., *blind, not seeing; intellectually or morally blind; uncertain, objectless;* pass., *unseen, hidden, obscure, dark.*

caedēs -is, f. *cutting down, killing, slaughter.* Transf., *persons slain; blood shed in slaughter.*

caedo caedĕre cĕcĭdi caesum. (1) *to cut.* (2) *to beat, knock about.* (3) *to kill, slay.*

caelāmen -ĭnis, n. *bas-relief.*

caelātor -ōris, m. *chaser, graver, carver.*

caelātūra -ae, f. *the art of engraving or chasing; an engraving.*

caelebs -lĭbis, *unmarried, single* (of men); of trees, *to which no vine is trained.*

caelēs -ītis, *heavenly;* as subst., *a dweller in heaven, god.*

caelestis -e, *belonging to heaven, coming from heaven;* n. pl. as subst. *things in heaven, heavenly bodies.* Transf., *belonging to the gods, celestial, divine, superhuman;* as subst., esp. plur., *the gods.*

caelĭcŏla -ae, *dwelling in heaven;* as subst. *a god.*

caelĭfer -fĕra -fĕrum, *bearing the heavens.*

Caelius -a -um. *name of a Roman plebeian gens;* Caelius Mons, *a hill in Rome.*

caelo -are, *to engrave or chase, to carve in bas-relief, to fashion.*

¹caelum -i, n. *the burin or engraving tool.*

²caelum -i, n. *the heavens, sky, air, climate.* Esp. *heaven* as the home of the gods; fig., *heaven* as the height of joy, renown, etc.

caementum -i, n. *rough stone from the quarry.*

caenōsus -a -um, *muddy.*

caenum -i, n. *mud, dirt, filth.*

caepa (**cēpa**) -ae, f. and **caepe** (**cēpe**) -is, n. *onion.*

Caerē, n. *a very old city of Etruria;* adj. **Caerēs** -ītis and -ētis.

caerĭmōnia -ae, f. *holiness, sanctity; holy awe, reverence; religious usage, sacred ceremony.*

caerŭlĕus (poet. also **caerŭlus**) -a -um, *blue, dark blue* (esp. of the sea or sky).

Caesar -ăris, m. *a Roman family name of the gens Iulia;* esp. of C. Iulius Caesar, *the general and dictator, and later of all the emperors.*

caesărĭēs -ēi, f. *hair, a head of hair.*

caesim, *with cutting;* fig. of style, *in short sentences.*

caesius -a -um, *bluish grey* (esp. of eyes).

caespĕs (**cespĕs**) -ĭtis, m. *a turf, sod.* Transf., *a hut or altar of turf.*

caestus -ūs, m. *gauntlet for boxers.*

caetra (**cetra**) -ae, f. *short Spanish shield.*

caetrātus -a -um, *armed with the caetra.*

Caius = Gaius; q.v.

Călabria -ae, f. *the peninsula at the south-east extremity of Italy;* adj. and subst. **Călăber** -bra -brum, *Calabrian, a Calabrian.*

călămister -tri, m. and **călămistrum** -tri, n. *a curling-iron for the hair.* Transf., *excessive ornament or flourish in style.*

călămistrātus -a -um, *curled with the curling-iron.*

călămĭtās -ātis, f. *loss, failure, misfortune, damage, a reverse.*

călămĭtōsus -a -um: act., *causing loss, destructive;* pass., *suffering loss, miserable.* Adv. **călămĭtōsē**, *disastrously.*

călămus -i, m. *reed;* hence *anything made of reed,* e.g. *a pen, a reed pipe, an arrow,*

călăthiscus -i, m. *a small wicker basket.*

călăthus -i, m. *a wicker basket;* and of other containers, e.g. *a milk-pail, wine-bowl.*

călātor -ōris, m. *attendant.*

calcar -āris, n. *spur.*

calcĕāmentum -i, n. *covering for the foot.*

calcĕo -are, *to shoe, provide with shoes.*

calcĕus -i, m. *shoe.*

calcitro -are, *to kick; to resist obstinately.*

calco -are, *to tread, trample on.*

calcŭlus -i, m. *a little stone, pebble.* Esp. *a piece used in the Roman game of draughts; a voting pebble; a counter for reckoning;* hence *a calculation.*

caldus = calidus; q.v.

Călēdŏnia -ae, f. *the highlands of Scotland;* adj. **Călēdŏnĭus** -a -um.

călĕfăcio (**calfăcio**) -făcĕre -fēci -factum, pass. călĕfīo, etc., *to make warm, heat; to disturb, excite.*

călĕfacto -are, *to make warm, heat.*

Călendae = Kalendae; q.v.

călĕo -ēre -ŭi, to be warm, to glow; of feeling, etc. to be inflamed, aroused, excited.

călesco -ĕre, to become warm, grow hot.

călidus (caldus) -a -um, warm, hot; fiery, passionate. F. sing. as subst., **călida (calda)** -ae, warm water; n. sing. **călĭdum** -i, warm wine and water.

căliendrum -i, n. a lady's wig.

căliga -ae, f. a stout shoe or boot (esp. a soldier's).

călĭgātus -a -um, wearing heavy boots; m. as subst., a private soldier.

călĭgĭnōsus -a -um, foggy, misty, dark.

¹călīgo -ĭnis, f. fog, mist, darkness. Transf., mental darkness, dullness; calamity, affliction, gloom.

²călīgo -are: transit., to spread a dark mist around, to make dizzy; intransit., to be dark, misty.

Călĭgŭla -ae, m. a little soldier's shoe; nickname given by the soldiers to the emperor Gaius.

călix -ĭcis, m. a drinking or cooking vessel.

callĕo -ēre, to be thick-skinned. Transf.: intransit., to be practised, experienced; transit., to know by experience, understand.

callĭdĭtās -ātis, f. expertness, cleverness; in bad sense, cunning, craft, artifice.

callidus -a -um, experienced, clever, dexterous, skilful; in bad sense, cunning, subtle, sly. Adv. **callĭdē**.

Callĭŏpē -ēs and **Callĭŏpēa** -ae, f. Calliope, the Muse of epic poetry.

callis -is, m. or f. narrow track, footpath, cattle track.

callōsus -a -um, hard-skinned, solid.

callum -i, n. hard skin or flesh; toughness, insensibility.

¹călo (kălo) -are, to call, summon.

²călo -ōnis, m. a soldier's servant; in gen., a drudge.

călor -ōris, m. warmth, heat, glow; passion, excitement.

Calpurnius -a -um, name of a Roman plebeian gens.

caltha -ae, f. a plant, prob. marigold.

călumnia -ae, f. trick, artifice, chicanery, craft; at law, a false accusation, or an action for false accusation.

călumnĭātor -ōris, m. a false accuser, pettifogger.

călumnĭor -ari, dep. to accuse falsely, misrepresent; in gen., to practise trickery.

calva -ae, f. the bald scalp of the head.

calvĭtĭēs -ēi, f. and **calvĭtĭum** -i, n. baldness.

calvus -a -um, bald, without hair.

¹calx -cis, f. the heel.

²calx -cis, f. rarely m. a stone, pebble; collectively, lime, chalk; meton., a goal (marked with chalk), an end.

Călypsō -ūs, a nymph who entertained Ulysses.

cămella -ae, f. a goblet.

cămēlus -i, m. and f. a camel or dromedary.

Cămēna -ae, f. usually pl., Latin goddesses of poetry, identified with the Greek Muses.

cămĕra (cămăra) -ae, f. a vaulted chamber, vault; a flat covered boat.

Cămillus -i, m. cognomen of several members of the gens Furia.

cămīnus -i, m. a forge, fire-place, fire.

cammărus -i, m. a crustacean, perhaps crayfish.

Campānia -ae, f. a district of Central Italy.

campester -tris -tre: in gen., on level ground, flat; esp. relating to the Campus Martius and its exercises and elections. N. sing. as subst., a loin-cloth worn by wrestlers; n. pl. as subst., a plain.

campus -i, m. a level space, plain, field; esp. of the Campus Martius at Rome, as a place for various exercises, and for meetings of the comitia. Transf., any free space, field, or theatre of action; any level surface; poet., the sea.

Camulōdūnum -i n. a town in Britain (now Colchester).

cămŭr -a -um, hooked, curved.

cănālis -is, m. waterpipe, channel canal.

cancelli -orum, m. pl. lattice, railing, grating. Transf., bounds, limits.

cancer -cri, m. crab; a sign of the Zodiac; meton., the south, or summer heat; the disease cancer.

candēla -ae, f. a wax or tallow candle, taper; a cord coated with wax.

candēlābrum -i, n. a candle-stick.

candĕo -ēre -ŭi, to shine, white, glitter or glow with heat.

candesco -ēre -ŭi, to begin to shine or glow.

candĭdātōrius -a -um, relating to a candidate.

candĭdātus -a -um, clothed in white; as subst. a candidate for office.

candĭdŭlus -a -um, shining, dazzling.

candĭdus -a -um, shining white; of persons, with the suggestion of beauty, fair. Transf., of time or fortune, happy; of writing, clear, lucid; of character, honest, straight-forward; of dress, clothed in white; sententia candida, a vote for acquittal. N. as subst. **candĭdum** -i, white colour. Adv. **candĭdē**, in white; clearly candidly.

candor -ōris, m. shining whiteness, lustre; of character, sincerity, candour; of writing, clarity, simplicity.

cănĕo -ēre -ŭi, to be white, or hoary.

cănesco -ēre, to become white or hoary; hence to become old.

cănĭcŭla -ae, f. little bitch; sometimes a term of abuse. Transf., Dog-star, Sirius; the worst throw at dice.

cănīnus -a -um, of a dog, canine. Transf., snarling, spiteful; littera, the letter R.

cănis -is, c. dog, hound; of persons, as a term of abuse; in dice, the worst throw.

cănistra -orum, n. pl. baskets.

cănĭtĭēs, acc. -em. *whitish-grey colour*; esp. of the hair; meton., *grey hair*, *old age*.

canna -ae, f. *reed*. Transf., *a reed-pipe*; *a small boat*.

cannăbis -is, and **cannăbum** -i, n. *hemp*.

Cannae -arum, f. pl. *town in Apulia*, *where Hannibal defeated the Romans* (216 B.C.). Adj. **Cannensis** -e.

căno cănĕre cĕcĭni cantum, *to sing* or *play*. Intransit. *to sing*; of cocks, *to crow*; of frogs, *to croak*; also (with -abl.), *to play on an instrument*; canere receptui, *to sound the signal for retreat*; of instruments, *to sound*. Transit.: (1) *to sing with the voice*. (2) *to sing of*, *celebrate in song*. (3) *to sound* or *play an instrument*. (4) *to prophesy*.

cănor -ōris, m. *melody, song, sound*.

cănōrus -a -um, *melodious, harmonious, sweet-sounding*; n. as subst., *harmonious sound*.

Cantăbrĭa -ae, f. *a region in north-west Spain*.

cantāmen -ĭnis, n. *incantation*.

canthăris -ĭdis, f. *a beetle*: esp. *the Spanish fly*.

canthărus -i, m. *a tankard; a sea-fish, the black bream*.

canthērĭus -i, m. *a gelding, nag*.

canthus -i, m. *the tire of a wheel*.

cantĭcum -i, n. *a scene in Roman comedy, accompanied by music and dancing; a song; sing-song delivery in an orator*.

cantĭlēna -ae, f. *an old song, twaddle, chatter*.

cantĭo -ōnis, f. *a song; an incantation, enchantment*.

cantĭto -are, *to sing* or *play often*.

Cantĭum -i, n. *a district in Britain* (now Kent).

cantĭuncŭla -ae, f. *a flattering song*.

canto -are -avi -atum, *to sing* or *play*. Intransit., of persons, *to sing*; of cocks, *to crow*; also *to play on an instrument*; of instruments, *to sound*. Transit. (1) *to sing*. (2) *to sing of, celebrate, continually mention*. (3) *to predict*.

cantor -ōris, m. *a singer, poet, musician; an actor*.

cantus -ūs, m. *song, melody music, poetry; prophecy; incantation*.

cănus -a -um, *whitish-grey*; hence *aged*; m. pl. as subst., *grey hair*.

căpācĭtās -ātis, f. *breadth, capacity*.

căpax -ācis, *able to hold, broad, wide, roomy*. Transf., *receptive, able to grasp, capable, fit for*.

căpēdo -ĭnis, f. *a bowl used in sacrifices*.

căpella -ae, f. *a she-goat; a star in the constellation Auriga*.

Căpēna -ae, f. *a town in Etruria*; adj. **Căpēnus** -a -um; porta Capena, *a gate in Rome at the beginning of the Via Appia*.

căper -ri, m. *he-goat*.

căpesso -ĕre -īvi and -ĭi -ītum, *to seize, grasp eagerly*; of places, *to strive to reach, to make for*; of

business, etc., *to take up, undertake*; rempublicam *to enter public life*.

căpillātus -a -um, *hairy, having hair*.

căpillus -i, m. *a hair*; usually pl., or collect. sing., *the hair of the head or beard*.

căpĭo căpĕre cēpi captum, *to take*. (1) in gen. *to take, seize*; of places, *to choose, reach*, or *take possession of*; of business, opportunities, etc. *to take up, take in hand, adopt*; of persons, *to choose*. (2) *to catch, take in a violent or hostile manner*; hence, *to attack, injure*; pass. capi, *to be injured or diseased*; oculis et auribus captus, *blind and deaf*; also *to charm, captivate, take in*; at law, *to convict*. (3) *to receive*, esp. of money; in gen., *to suffer, undergo, take on*. (4) *to take in, hold, contain, keep in*; mentally, *to grasp, comprehend*.

căpis -ĭdis, f. *a one-handled vessel*.

căpistro -are, *to fasten with a halter*.

căpistrum -i, n. *a halter*.

căpĭtālis -e, *relating to the head*, or *to life*. Transf., *deadly, mortal; first, chief, distinguished*. N. as subst. **căpĭtal** and **căpĭtălĕ**, *a capital crime*.

căpĭto -onis, m. *a man with a large head*.

Căpĭtōlĭum -i, n. *the temple of Jupiter at Rome, the Capitol*; adj. **Căpĭtōlĭnus** -a -um; m. pl. as subst., *superintendents of games in honour of Jupiter Capitolinus*.

căpĭtŭlum -i, n. *a little head*.

Cappădŏcĭa -ae, f. *a district in Asia Minor*.

capra -ae, f. *a she-goat*; also *a star in the constellation Auriga*.

caprĕa -ae, f. *a roe*.

Caprĕae -arum, f. *small island off the Campanian coast* (now Capri).

caprĕŏlus -i, m. *a roebuck*; in plur., *props, supports*.

Capricornus -i, m. *Capricorn, a sign of the Zodiac*.

caprĭfĭcus -i, f. *the wild fig-tree*, and *its fruit*.

caprĭgĕnus -a -um, *born of goats*.

caprĭmulgus -i, m. *goat-milker*—i.e. *a countryman*.

caprīnus -a -um, *relating to a goat*.

caprĭpēs -pĕdis, *goat-footed*.

capsa -ae, f. *a box* or *case*, esp. *for books*.

capsārĭus -i, m. *a slave who carried his young master's satchel*.

capsŭla -ae, f. *a little chest*.

captātĭo -ōnis, f. *an eager seizing*; verborum, *quibbling*.

captātor -ōris, m. *one who eagerly seizes*; esp. *a legacy-hunter*.

captĭo -ōnis, f. (1) *a cheat, deception*. (2) *harm, loss*. (3) *a fallacy, sophism*.

captĭōsus -a -um, *deceitful; captious*; n. pl. as subst. *sophistries*. Adv. **captĭōsē**.

captĭuncŭla -ae, f. *fallacy, quibble*.

captīvĭtās -ātis, f. *captivity, capture*; collectively, *a number of captives*.

captīvus -a -um, *captured, taken*, esp. *in war*. Transf., *of a prisoner*.

M. and f. as subst., *a prisoner, captive.*

capto -are, *to seize, catch at*; in gen., *to strive after, desire, seek.*

captus -ūs, m. *catching, taking*; hence *power* or *manner of comprehension, idea.*

Capŭa -ae, f. *chief town of Campania.*

căpŭlus -i, m. (1) *a coffin.* (2) *a handle*; esp. *the hilt of a sword.*

căput -itis, n. *the head*; meton., *a living individual, esp. of human beings, a person*; also of *a person's life, existence, esp.,* in Rome, *a man's political and social rights.* Transf., of lifeless things, *the top, summit, extremity*; of rivers, etc., *the source*; of persons and things, *the head, leader, chief, headquarters, chief point*; of places, *the capital.*

carbăsĕus -a -um, *made of canvas.*

carbăsus -i, f.; heteroclite pl. **carbăsa** -orum, n.; *flax*; meton., *anything made of flax, e.g. garments, curtains, sails.*

carbo -ōnis, m. *burning or burnt wood.*

carbōnārĭus -i, m. *a charcoal burner.*

carcer -ĕris, m. *prison, cell*; in plur., **carceres,** *the starting-place of a race-course.*

carchēsĭum -i, n. *a goblet with handles.* Transf., *the top of a mast, scuttle.*

cardĭăcus -a -um, *pertaining to the stomach*; m. as subst., *one who suffers from a disease of the stomach.*

cardo -inis, m. *a hinge; any pole or pivot*: cardo duplex, *the ends of the earth's axis; a cardinal point, main consideration.*

cardŭus -i, m. *thistle.*

cārectum -i, n. *a sedgy spot.*

cārĕo -ēre -ŭi, *to be without* (with abl); of a place, *to absent oneself from.*

cārex -icis, f. *rush, sedge.*

cărĭēs, acc. -em. abl. -e, f. *rottenness, decay.*

cărīna -ae, f. *the keel of a ship*; meton., *a ship, vessel.*

cărĭōsus -a -um, *rotten, decayed.*

cāris -Idis, f. *a kind of crab.*

cārĭtās -atis, f. *dearness, high price*; esp. *high cost of living.* Transf., *affection, love, esteem.*

carmen -inis, n. *a song, tune, vocal or instrumental; a poem, poetry, verse; a prediction; an incantation; a religious or legal formula.*

Carmentis -is, and **Carmenta** -ae, f. *a prophetess, mother of Evander*; adj. **Carmentālis** -e.

carnĭfex -fĭcis, m. *an executioner, hangman.*

carnĭfĭcīna -ae, f. *the work of a hang-man; execution, torture.*

carnĭfĭco -are, *to behead, or mangle.*

¹cāro -ĕre, *to card.*

²cāro carnis, f. *flesh.*

carpentum -i, n. *a two-wheeled carriage.*

carpo carpĕre carpsi carptum, *to pluck, pull off, select, choose out*; and so *to enjoy*; of animals, *to graze.* Transf., *to proceed on a journey; to pass over a place; to carp at, slander a person*;

to weaken, annoy, harass an enemy; *to break up, separate, divide* forces.

carptim, *in pieces, in small parts; in different places; at different times.*

carptor -ōris, m. *one who carves food.*

carrūca -ae, f. *a four-wheeled carriage.*

carrus -i, m. *a four-wheeled baggage-waggon.*

Carthāgo (Karthāgo) -inis, f. (1) *the city of Carthage in N. Africa.* (2) Carthago (Nova), *a colony of the Carthaginians in Spain* (now *Cartagena*). Adj. **Carthāgĭnĭensis** -e.

cărunчŭla -ae, f. *a small piece of flesh.*

cārus -a -um, adj. *high-priced, dear, costly.* Transf., *dear, beloved.*

căsa -ae, f. *hut, cottage, cabin.*

cāsĕolus -i, m. *a little cheese.*

cāsĕus -i, m. *cheese.*

căsia -ae, f. (1) *a tree with an aromatic bark, like cinnamon.* (2) *the sweet-smelling mezereon.*

Cassandra -ae, f. *a prophetess, daughter of Priam.*

cassēs -ĭum, m. pl. *a net; a trap* ;*nare*; also *a spider's web.*

cassĭda -ae, f. = cassis; q.v.

Cassĭŏpē -ēs, f. *mother of Andromeda.*

cassis -ĭdis and **cassĭda** -ae, f. *a metal helmet.*

Cassĭus -a -um, *name of a Roman gens*; adj. **Cassĭānus** -a -um.

cassus -a -um, *empty, hollow*; with abl., *devoid of.* Transf., *worthless, useless, vain*; in **cassum** or **in-cassum** as adv., *in vain.*

Castālĭa -ae, f. *a spring on Mount Parnassus, sacred to Apollo and the Muses.*

castănĕa -ae f. *a chestnut* or *chestnut-tree.*

castellānus -a -um, *relating to a fort-ress*; m. pl. as subst., *the garrison of a fortress.*

castellātim, *in single fortresses.*

castellum -i, n. *a castle, fortress, fort; a shelter, refuge.*

castĭgātĭo -ōnis, f. *punishment, reproof.*

castĭgātor -ōris, m. *one who reproves or corrects.*

castĭgo -are, *to reprove, chasten, punish; to check, restrain.*
Hence partic. **castĭgātus** -a -um, *restrained, orderly, neat.*

castĭmōnĭa -ae, f. *purity.*

castĭtās -ātis, f. *chastity.*

¹castor -ōris, m. *the beaver.*

²Castor -ōris, m. *twin-brother of Pollux.* Hence **ecastor** and **mecastor,** *By Castor!*

castŏrĕum -i, n. *an aromatic secretion obtained from the beaver.*

castrensis -e, *pertaining to a camp.*

castro -are, *to castrate, enervate, weaken.*

castrum -i, n.: sing., *a castle, fort, fortress*; plur. **castra** -orum, *a camp, encampment*; aestiva, *summer quarters*; hiberna, *winter quarters.* Transf.: *a day's march; martial service; a party, faction.*

castus -a -um, *clean, pure, chaste*; with reference to religion, *pious,* *religious, holy.* Adv. **castē,** *purely piously, religiously.*

căsŭla -ae, f. *a little hut, cottage.*

căsus -ūs, m. *a falling, fall.* Transf.: (1) *what befalls, an accident, event, occurrence.* (2) *occasion, opportunity.* (3) *destruction, downfall, collapse*; and, in gen., *end.* (4) in grammar, *a case.*

cătaphractēs -ae, m. *a breastplate of iron scales.*

cătaphractus -a -um, *mail-clad.*

cătaplūs -i, m. *the arrival of a ship; a ship that is arriving.*

cătăpulta -ae, f. *an engine of war, a catapult.*

cătăracta (cătarracta) -ae, f. and **cătăractēs** -ae, m. *a waterfall; a sluice or flood-gate; a portcullis.*

cătasta -ae, f. *a stage upon which slaves were exposed in the market.*

cătēia -ae, f. *a kind of spear.*

¹**cătellus** -i, m. and **cătella** -ae, f. *a little dog, puppy.*

²**cătellus** -i, m. and **cătella** -ae f. *a little chain.*

cătēna -ae, f. *a chain, fetter.* Transf., (1) *restraint.* (2) *a series.*

cătēnātus -a -um, *chained, bound, linked together*; labores, *continuous.*

căterva -ae, f. *crowd, troop, flock.*

cătervātim, *in troops, in masses.*

căthedra -ae, *a chair; esp. a soft one for ladies, or one occupied by a professor.*

Cătilīna -ae, m. L. Sergius, *a Roman noble, killed at the head of a conspiracy in 62 B.C.* Hence adj. **Cătilīnārĭus** -a -um.

cătillus -i, m. *a small dish or plate.*

cătinus -i, m. *a deep dish or bowl.*

Căto -ōnis, m. *a cognomen belonging to members of the gens Porcia*; adj. **Cătōnĭānus** -a -um; subst. **Cătōnīni** -orum, m. *the party of M. Porcius Cato Uticensis, the younger Cato.*

Cătōnĭum -i, n. *the lower world* (with a play on the word Cato).

Cătullus -i, m. C. Valerius (c. 85-55 B.C.) *the Roman lyric and epigrammatic poet.*

cătŭlus -i, m. *a young animal,* esp. *a whelp, puppy.*

cătus -a -um, *sharp, cunning*; adv. **cătē.**

cauda (cōda) -ae, f. *the tail of an animal.*

caudex = codex ; q.v.

Caudium -i, n. *an old city in Samnium, near the pass of the Caudine Forks.* Adj. **Caudīnus** -a -um.

caulae -arum, f. pl. *a hole, opening; a sheep-fold.*

caulis -is, m. *the stalk of a plant*; esp. of a cabbage.

caupo -ōnis, m. *a small shopkeeper* or *inn-keeper.*

caupōna -ae, f. *a tavern, inn.*

caupōnor -ari, dep. *to trade.*

caupōnŭla -ae, f. *a little inn.*

Caurus (Cōrus) -i, m. *the north-west wind.*

causa (caussa) -ae, f. *a cause,* in all senses of the English word. (1) *a*

reason, motive, pretext. (2) *interest*; abl., causā, *on account of, for the sake of.* with genit., meā, etc. (3) *a case at law, law-suit, claim, contention*; causam dicere, *to plead.* (4) *situation, condition, case.*

causārius -a -um, *sickly, diseased*; m. pl., milit., *men invalided out of the army.*

causidicus -i, m. *an advocate, barrister* (often used contemptuously).

causor -ari, dep. *to give as a reason,* or *pretext; to plead, pretend.*

causŭla -ae, f. *a little cause or case.*

cautēs -is, f. *a rough sharp rock.*

cautio -ōnis, f. *caution, care, fore-sight, precaution*; legal, *security, bail, bond.*

cautor -ōris, m. *one who is on his guard,* or *who gives bail for another.*

cautus -a -um, partic. from caveo; q.v.

căvaedĭum -i, n. *an inner quadrangle.*

căvĕa -ae, f. *a hollow place, cavity.* Esp. *an enclosure, den, cage,* the seats in a theatre.

căvĕo căvēre căvi cautum, *to be on one's guard*; with acc. *to be on one's guard against*: cave ignoscas, *take care not to forgive*; with ut and the subj., *to take care that*; with dat. of person, *to take care for, provide for.* Commercial and legal, *to give security* or *to get security*; also *to provide, order,* in a will, treaty or law. Hence partic. **cautus** -a -um: of persons, etc., *cautious, wary, careful*; of property, *made safe, secured.* Adv. **cautē, cautim,** *cautiously* or *with security.*

căverna -ae, f. *a hollow place, cavern*: navis, *the hold*; caeli, *the vault of heaven.*

căvillātĭo -ōnis, f. *raillery, jesting, irony.* Transf., *sophistry.*

căvillātor -ōris, m. *a jester* joker. Transf., *a quibbler.*

căvillor -ari, dep. *to jest, joke, satirize.* Transf., *to quibble.*

căvo -are, *to hollow out, excavate, pierce.*

căvum -i, n. and **căvus** -i, m. *a hollow, hole, cavity.*

căvus -a -um, *hollow, concave.*

-cĕ, a demonstrative particle joined on to pronouns and adverbs—e.g. hisce.

Cecrops -ōpis, m. *the mythical first king of Athens*; adj. **Cecrōpĭus** -a -um, *Cecropian, Athenian.*

¹**cēdo** cēdĕre cessi cessum, *to go, proceed*: of things, *to turn out, happen; to fall to the lot of* a person; *to change into something else; to go away, withdraw, retire*; with dat., *to give ground to, submit to,* hence *to be inferior to*; transit., *to grant, yield.*

²**cēdŏ** and plur. **cettĕ,** colloquial imperat., *give, hand over, out with it!*

cedrus -i, f. *the cedar*; meton. *cedar-wood* or *cedar oil.*

cēlātor -ōris, m. *a concealer.*

cĕlĕber -bris -bre, *filled, crowded*; of places, *frequented*; of occasions, *well attended*; of sayings, *often repeated*;

of persons and things, *celebrated, famous, renowned.*

cĕlĕbrātĭo -ōnis, f. *a numerous assembly or attendance.*

cĕlĕbrātŏr -ōris, m. *one who praises.*

cĕlĕbrĭtās -ātis, f. *a crowd, multitude, numerous attendance;* of a festival, *celebration;* in gen., *fame, renown.*

cĕlĕbro -are, *to visit frequently, or in large numbers; to fill; to celebrate, solemnize; to publish, make known; to sing the praises of, to honour; to practise often, repeat, exercise.*
    Hence partic. **cĕlĕbrātus** -a -um: of places, *much frequented:* of festivals, *kept solemn, festive;* in gen., *famous, celebrated.*

cĕler -ĕris -ĕre, *swift, quick, rapid;* in a bad sense, *hasty, rash.* Adv. **cĕlĕrē** and **cĕlĕrĭtĕr.**

Cĕlĕres -um, m. *early name for Roman nobles,* esp. *the body-guard of the kings.*

cĕlĕrĭpēs -pĕdis, *swift-footed.*

cĕlĕrĭtās -ātis, f. *quickness, swiftness.*

cĕlĕro -are: transit., *to make quick, accelerate;* intransit., *to hasten.*

cella -ae, f. *a room:* esp. *a store-room or a garret, mean apartment;* in a temple, *the shrine of the god's image.*

cellārĭus -a -um, *of a store-room;* as subst. *a cellarer.*

cēlo -are, *to hide, conceal, keep secret.*

cĕlōx -ōcis, *swift, quick;* f. as subst. *a swift vessel, yacht.*

celsus -a -um, *upraised, high, lofty, elevated;* in bad sense, *proud, haughty.*

Celtae -arum, m. pl. *the Celts,* esp. those of Central Gaul. Adj. **Celtĭcus** -a -um.

Celtĭbēri -orum, m. *the Celtiberians, a people in the middle of Spain.*

cēna -ae, f. *dinner, the main Roman meal;* meton., *a dish or course at a dinner.*

cēnācŭlum -i, n. *a garret, attic.*

cēnātĭo -ōnis, f. *a dining-hall.*

cēnātōrĭus -a -um, *relating to dinner;* n. pl. as subst. *clothes to dine in.*

cēnĭto -are, *to dine often.*

cēno -are: intransit., *to dine, sup;* transit, *to dine on, to eat.* Perf. partic., with middle meaning, **cēnātus,** *having dined, after dinner.*

censĕo censēre censŭi censum, *to estimate, to form or express an opinion or valuation of a person or thing;* esp. of the censor at Rome, *to take an account of the names and property of Roman citizens.* In gen., *to express an opinion, be of opinion, vote, advise, recommend;* of the senate, *to resolve.*

censor -ōris, m. *the censor, a Roman magistrate.* Transf., *a severe judge, rigid moralist.*

censōrĭus -a -um, *relating to the censor;* homo, *an ex-censor;* tabulae, *the censor's lists.* Transf., *rigid, severe.*

censūra -ae, f. *the censor's office, censorship.* Transf., *judgment.*

census -ūs, m. *the census, an enrolment of names and assessment of property.* Transf., *the censor's list; the amount of property necessary for enrolment in a certain rank;* in gen., *property, wealth.*

centaurēum and **centaurīum** -i, n. *the plant centaury.*

Centaurus -i, m. *a centaur,* i.e. *a monster of Thessaly, half man and half horse.*

centēni -ae -a (poet. also sing.), *a hundred together, a hundred each.*

centēsĭmus -a -um, *the hundredth.* F. sing. as subst. *the hundredth part;* hence *a tax of one per cent,* or as interest on money, *one per cent,* (reckoned at Rome by the month, therefore = 12 per cent. per annum).

centĭceps -cĭpĭtis, *hundred-headed.*

centĭens or **centĭēs,** *a hundred times.*

centĭmānus -a -um, *hundred-handed.*

cento -ōnis, m. *patchwork;* in war, *coverings to ward off missiles or extinguish fires.*

centum, *a hundred;* also *any indefinitely large number.*

centumgĕmĭnus -a -um, *hundred-fold.*

centumvĭrālis -e, *relating to the centumviri.*

centum vĭri or **centumvĭri** -orum, *a bench of judges dealing with civil suits.*

centuncŭlus -i, m. *a little piece of patchwork or a saddle-cloth.*

centuplex -ĭcis, *a hundred-fold.*

centŭrĭa -ae, f. *a division of 100; a company of soldiers; a century, a part of the Roman people, as divided by Servius Tullius.*

centŭrĭātim, *by centuries or companies.*

centŭrĭātus -ūs, m. *a division into companies or centuries; the centurion's office.*

¹centŭrĭo -are, *to divide into centuries;* comitia centuriata, *the assembly in which the whole Roman people voted in their centuries.*

²centŭrĭo -ōnis, m. *commander of a century, centurion.*

centŭrĭōnātus -ūs, m. *an election of centurions.*

cēnŭla -ae, f. *a little meal.*

cenum, see caenum.

cēra -ae, f. *wax; a waxen writing-tablet, wax seal, or waxen image.*

cērārĭum -i, n. *a fee for sealing a document.*

cērastēs -ae, m. *the horned snake.*

cĕrāsus -i, f. *a cherry-tree or a cherry.*

Cerbĕrus -i, m. *the dog guarding Hades.*

cercōpĭthēcus -i, m. *a kind of ape.*

cercūrus -i, m. *a species of vessel peculiar to Cyprus; a sea-fish.*

cerdo -ōnis, m. *a workman, artisan.*

cĕrebrōsus -a -um, *hot-tempered.*

cĕrebrum -i, n. *the brain; the understanding; hot temper.*

Cĕrēs -ĕris, f. *the Roman goddess of agriculture.* Transf., *bread, grain, corn.* Adj. **Cĕrĕālis** -e; n. pl. as subst. *the festival of Ceres on April 10.*

cĕrĕus -a -um, *waxen, or resembling wax;* m. as subst., *a wax taper.*

cērintha -ae, f. *the wax flower.*

cĕrīnus -a -um, *wax-coloured*: n. pl. as subst. *wax-coloured garments.*

cerno cernĕre crēvi crētum, *to separate, sift.* Transf., *to distinguish,* with the senses or with the mind; *to decide, resolve, determine.*

cernŭus -a -um, *falling headlong.*

cēro -are, *to smear or cover with wax.*

cērōma -ătis, n. *an ointment of oil and wax used by wrestlers.*

cērōmăticus -a -um, *anointed with the ceroma.*

cerrītus -a -um, *frantic, mad.*

certāmen -ĭnis, n. *contest, struggle.*

certātim, adv. *emulously, eagerly.*

certātĭo -ōnis, f. *contest, rivalry.*

certē and certō, adv. from certus; q.v.

certo -are, *to settle by contest;* hence *to contend, struggle, dispute.*

certus -a -um, adj. *settled, resolved, decided,* of projects and persons; *definite, certain, fixed; sure, to be depended on;* of things as known, *undoubted, sure;* certum scio, *I know for certain;* pro certo habeo, *I feel sure;* of persons *knowing, sure, certain;* certiorem facere, *to inform.* Adv. certē and certō, *certainly, assuredly.*

cērŭla -ae, f. *a little piece of wax.*

cērussa -ae, f. *white lead.*

cērussātus -a -um, *painted with white lead.*

cerva -ae, f. *hind;* poet., *deer.*

cervīcal -ālis, n. *cushion, pillow.*

cervīcŭla -ae, f. *a little neck.*

cervīnus -a -um, *relating to a stag.*

cervix -īcis, f. *the nape of the neck, the neck;* dare cervices, *to submit to the executioner.*

cervus -i, m. *stag, deer;* pl., milit., *stakes stuck in the ground as a palisade.*

cespes; see caespes.

cessātĭo -ōnis, f. *delaying, inactivity, laziness.*

cessātor -ōris, m. *one who loiters.*

cessĭo -ōnis, f. *a giving up, a cession.*

cesso -are, *to leave off, cease work, be idle, rest;* of things, *to be left alone, do nothing;* so of land, *to lie fallow.*

cestrosphendŏnē -ēs, f. *engine for hurling stones.*

¹cestus and cestos -i, m. *a girdle.*

²cēstus -us, m; see caestus.

cētārĭum -i, n. *a fish-pond.*

cētārĭus -i, m. *a fishmonger.*

cētĕrōqui or cētĕrōquin, *otherwise, else.*

cētĕrus -a -um, *the other, the rest;* usually plur., cētĕri -ae, -a; et cetera, *and so on.* Acc. n. sing. as adv. cētĕrum, *otherwise, moreover, but.*

Cĕthēgus -i, m. C. Cornelius, *a conspirator with Catiline, put to death by Cicero in 63 B.C.*

cētra; see caetra.

cette; see cedo.

cētus -i, m. and cētos n.; plur. cete; *any large sea-creature,* such as *whale, seal, dolphin.*

ceu, adv., *as, like as;* sometimes *as if.*

Chalcis -ĭdis or -ĭdos, f. *the chief city of Euboea.*

Chaldaei -orum, m. pl. *the Chaldaeans, famous as astrologers.*

chălўbēius -a -um, *of steel.*

chălybs -ўbis, m. *steel;* an article made of steel, such as *a sword, a horse's bit, the tip of an arrow.*

chănē or channē -ēs, f. *the sea perch.*

Chăos, acc. Chaos, abl. Chao, n. *boundless empty space.* Hence *the lower world;* personified, *Chaos, the father of Night and Erebus; the shapeless mass out of which the universe was made.*

chara -ae, f. *an edible root.*

Chărĭtes -um, f. pl. *the Graces,* i.e. *Aglaia, Euphrosyne, and Thalia.*

Chărōn -ontis, m. *Charon, who ferried souls over the Styx.*

charta -ae, f. *a leaf of Egyptian papyrus, paper; anything written on paper,* a *letter, poem,* etc.

chartŭla -ae, f. *a little paper, small piece of writing.*

Chărybdis -is, f. *a whirlpool opposite the rock Scylla.*

Chatti (Catti) -orum, m. *a Germanic people.*

Chauci -orum, m. *a Germanic people on the coast of the North Sea.*

chēlўdrus -i, m. *an amphibious snake.*

chĕlys, acc. -yn, f. *the tortoise;* hence, *the lyre made of its shell.*

chĕragra and chiragra -ae, f. *the gout in the hands.*

Cherrŏnēsus and Chersŏnēsus -i, f. *a peninsula;* esp. *of Gallipoli or the Crimea.*

chĭlĭarchēs -ae, and chĭlĭarchus -i, m. *a commander of 1,000 soldiers;* among Persians, *chancellor,* or *prime minister.*

Chĭmaera -ae, f. *a monster killed by Bellerophon.*

chĭmaerĭfer -fĕra -fĕrum, *producing the Chimaera.*

Chĭos or Chĭus -i, f. *an island in the Aegean Sea, famous for wine and marble.*

chīrŏgrăphum -i, n. *an autograph, a person's own handwriting.*

chīrŏnŏmos -i, and chīrŏnŏmōn -ontis, m. *a gesticulator, a mime.*

chīrurgĭa -ae, f. *surgery.*

chlămўdātus -a -um, *dressed in a chlamys.*

chlămys -ўdis, f. *a large upper garment of wool.*

chŏrăgĭum -i, n. *the training and production of a chorus.*

chŏrăgus -i, m. *he who pays for a chorus.*

chŏraulēs -ae, m. *a flute-player, accompanying the chorus.*

chorda -ae, f. *cat-gut;* usually as the *string of a musical instrument.*

chŏrĕa -ae, f. *a dance in a ring.*

chŏrēus and chŏrĭus -i, m. *the metrical foot afterwards called a trochee.*

chŏrus -i, m. *dance in a circle, choral dance.* Transf., *the persons singing and dancing, the chorus;* hence *a crowd, troop.*

Christus -i, m. *Christ;* **Christiānus** -i, m. *a Christian.*

chrōmis -is, c. *a sea-fish.*

chrȳsanthus -i, m. *a flower,* perhaps *marigold.*

chrȳsŏlithos -i, m. and f. *chrysolite,* or *topaz.*

chrȳsophrys, acc. -yn. f. *a sea-fish.*

cibārius -a -um, *relating to food;* n. pl. as subst., *food, rations.* Transf. (*from the food of slaves*), *ordinary, common.*

cibātus -ūs, m. *food, nourishment.*

cibŏrium -i, n. *a large drinking-vessel.*

cibus -i, m. *food, fodder, nourishment, sustenance.*

cicāda -ae, f. *a cicada,* or *tree cricket.*

cicatrix -icis, f. *a scar;* on plants, *a mark of incision;* also *a patch on an old shoe.*

cicer -eris, n. *a chick-pea.*

Cicěro -onis, M. Tullius, *Roman Statesman, orator, and writer* (106-43 B.C.); adj. **Cicěrōniānus** -a -um.

cichŏrēum -i, n. *succory* or *endive.*

cicōnia -ae, f. *a stork.*

cicur -ūris, *tame.*

cicūta -ae, f. *hemlock; poison extracted from the hemlock; a shepherd's pipe, made of hemlock stalk.*

ciěo ciēre civi citum, *to move, stir, agitate.* Transf., *to give rise to, excite, arouse; to summon; to call by name.*
 Hence partic. **citus** -a -um, *quick, speedy.* Adv. **citŏ,** *quickly;* citius quam, *sooner than, rather than.*

Cilicia -ae, f. *a region in Asia Minor.*

Cimber -bri, m.; usually pl. **Cimbri,** *the Cimbrians, a German tribe;* adj. **Cimbricus** -a -um.

cimex -icis, m. *a bug.*

Cimměrii -orum, m. pl. (1) *a Thracian people, living on the Dnieper.* (2) *a mythical people, living in eternal darkness.*

cinaedus -i, m. *a wanton* or *shameless person.*

¹**cincinnatus** -a -um, *having curled hair.*

²**Cincinnatus** -i, m. *a cognomen in the gens Quinctia.*

cincinnus -i, m. *curled hair, a lock of hair.* Transf., *artificial rhetorical ornament.*

Cincius -a -um, *name of a Roman gens.*

cinctūra -ae, f. *a girdle.*

cinctus -ūs, m. *a girding, a way of wearing the toga.* Transf., *a girdle.*

cinctūtus -a -um, *girded.*

cinĕfactus -a -um, *turned to ashes.*

cingo cingĕre cinxi cinctum, *to surround* or *equip the head* or *body;* pass., cingi, *to gird oneself;* in gen., *to surround;* esp. *to surround* with hostile intent, or for protection; of persons, *to escort, accompany.*

cingŭla -ae, f. *a girdle.*

cingŭlum -i, n. *a girdle, sword-belt.*

cingŭlus -i, m. *a girdle of the earth, zone.*

cīniflo -onis, m. = cinerarius.

cinis -ěris, m. rarely f. *ashes.*

Cinna -ae, m. *a Roman cognomen,* esp. of L. Cornelius Cinna, *supporter of Marius, noted for his cruelty.* Adj. **Cinnānus** -a -um.

cinnămōmum or **cinnămum** -i, n. *cinnamon.*

cippus -i, m. *a pale, stake;* esp. *a tombstone;* plur., milit., *palisades.*

circā. Adv., *around, round about.* Prep. with acc.: of space, *around, near;* of persons, *around* or *with;* of time or number, *about.*

circāmoerium -i, n. = pomerium; q.v.

Circē -ēs and -ae, f. *an enchantress, daughter of the Sun;* adj. **Circaeus** -a -um.

Circēii -orum, m. pl. *a town in Latium.*

circensis -e, *belonging to the circus;* m. pl. as subst. (sc. ludi), *the circus games.*

circino -are, *to form into a circle* hence *to fly round.*

circinus -i, m. *a pair of compasses.*

circiter, adv., and prep. with acc., *about.*

circlus = circulus; q.v.

circŭeo; see circumeo.

circŭitio and **circŭmitio** -ōnis, f. *a going round, patrol.* Transf., *a roundabout way of speaking.*

circŭitus -ūs, m. *a going round in a circle, circuit.* Hence *a roundabout way, circuitous course;* also *compass, circumference, extent;* rhet., *a period.*

circŭlor -ari, dep. *to gather in groups,* or *collect a group around oneself.*

circŭlus (circlus) -i, m. *a circle, circular figure, circuit; any circular body; a circle* or *group for conversation.*

circum. Adv. *roundabout, around.* Prep. with acc. *round, around, round about, near.*

circŭmăgo -ăgĕre -ēgi -actum. (1) *to turn round;* esp. in the ceremonial manumission of a slave; of time, circumagi or circumagere se, *to pass away, be spent;* of the feelings, *to influence, bring round.* (2) *to drive about from one place to another; to distract.*

circumăro -are, *to plough round.*

circumcaesūra -ae, f. *the external outline of a body.*

circumcīdo -cidĕre cidi -cisum, *to cut round, to cut, trim.* Transf., *to make less, by cutting, diminish.*
 Hence partic. **circumcīsus** -a -um, of places, *abrupt, steep, inaccessible;* of style, *abridged, brief.*

circumcircā, *all round about.*

circumclūdo -clūdĕre -clūsi -clūsum, *to shut in, enclose, surround.*

circumcŏlo -ere, *to dwell around, dwell near.*

circumcurso -are, *to run round.*

circumdo -dăre -dĕdi -dătum, *surround.* (1) *to put something round,* with acc. of the thing placed, and dat. of that round which it is placed. (2)

to surround with something, with acc. and abl. (rarely double acc.).

circumdŭco -dūcĕre -duxi -ductum, *to lead round, move or drive round.* Transf., *to cheat; to extend, amplify.*

circŭmĕo (**circŭĕo**) -ire, -ii or -ivi, circŭĭtum, *to go round*; milit., *to surround; to go the rounds of; to visit*; hence *to canvass or solicit.* Transf., *to cheat, circumvent.*

circŭmĕquĭto -are, *to ride round.*

circumfĕro -ferre -tŭli -lātum, *to carry round, take round*; esp. of the eyes, *to turn all round*; in religion, *to lustrate, purify*, by carrying round consecrated objects. Transf., *to spread*, esp. *to spread news.*

circumflecto -flectĕre -flexi -flexum, *to bend round, turn about.*

circumflo -are, *to blow round.*

circumflŭo -flŭĕre -fluxi -fluxum, *to flow round.* Transf., *to overflow, abound*; with abl., *to abound in.*

circumflŭus -a -um: act., *flowing round, circumfluent*; pass., *flowed round, surrounded by water.*

circumfŏrānĕus -a -um. (1) *round the forum*: aes, *money borrowed from bankers.* (2) *attending at markets.*

circumfundo -fundĕre -fūdi -fūsum. (1) *to pour around*; in pass., or with reflexive, *to be poured round = to surround.* (2) act., *to surround, encompass*, and pass., *to be surrounded*; usually with instrumental abl.

circumgĕmo -ĕre, *to growl round.*

circumgesto -are, *to carry round.*

circumgrĕdĭor -grĕdi -gressus, dep., *to go round, travel round.*

circumiăcĕo -ĕre, *to lie round about, adjoin.*

circumicio -icĕre -iēci -iectum. (1) *to throw round, put round.* (2) *to surround* one thing with another.

Hence partic. **circumiectus** -a -um, *thrown round, so surrounding, adjacent.*

circumiectus -ūs, m. *a surrounding, enclosing.*

circumĭtĭo = circuitio; q.v.

circumlĭgo -are. (1) *to bind round, bind to.* (2) *to bind round with* something.

circumlĭno -lĭnĕre -lĭtum. (1) *to smear one thing over another.* (2) *to besmear with, bedaub*; hence poet., *to cover.*

circumlŭo -lŭĕre, *to wash round, flow round.*

circumlŭvĭo -ōnis, f. *alluvial land.*

circummitto -mittĕre -mīsi -missum, *to send round.*

circummūnĭo -ire, *to wall round, to shut in by lines of circumvallation.*

circummūnĭtĭo -ōnis, f. *circumvallation.*

circumpădānus -a -um, *near the river Po.*

circumplector -plecti -plexus, dep. *to embrace, enclose, surround.*

circumplĭco -are, *to fold round, wind round.*

circumpono -pōnĕre -pŏsŭi -pŏsĭtum, *to place or put round.*

circumrētĭo -ire, *to enclose in a net, ensnare.*

circumrōdo -rōdĕre -rōsi, *to gnaw round.* Transf., *to slander.*

circumsaepĭo -saepire -saeptum, *to hedge round, enclose.*

circumscindo -ĕre, *to tear off, round, to strip.*

circumscrībo -scrībĕre -scripsi -scriptum, *to describe a circle round, to enclose in a circular line.* Transf., (1) *to confine, define, limit, restrict.* (2) *to set aside, exclude.* (3) *to take in, ensnare, defraud*; vectigalia, *to embezzle.*

Hence partic. **circumscriptus** -a -um, as rhet. t. t. *rounded, periodic*; also *concise.* Adv. **circumscriptē.** *in rhetorical periods, fully.*

circumscriptĭo -ōnis, f. *an encircling*; hence *circumference.* Transf., (1) *outline, boundary, limit*; in rhetoric, *a period.* (2) *swindling, defrauding.*

circumscriptor -ōris; m. *a cheat, swindler.*

circumsĕco -sĕcare -sectum *to cut round.*

circumsĕdĕo -sĕdēre -sēdi -sessum, *to sit round*; esp. *to besiege, beleaguer.*

circumsessĭo -ōnis, f. *encircling, beleaguering.*

circumsido -ĕre, *to besiege.*

circumsĭlĭo -ire, *to leap or jump round.*

circumsisto -sistĕre -stĕti or -stĭti, *to stand round, surround.*

circumsŏno -sonare -sonui: transit., *to sound all around* or *to make to resound*; intransit., *to resound, to echo.*

circumsŏnus -a -um, *sounding all around.*

circumspectĭo -ōnis, f. *looking about, circumspection, caution.*

circumspecto -are: intransit., *to look round repeatedly*; transit., *to look round at* or *for.*

[1]**circumspectus** -a -um; see circumspicio.

[2]**circumspectus** -ūs, m. *looking round at*; hence *attention to; prospect, view all round.*

circumspĭcĭo -spĭcĕre -spexi -spectum: intransit., *to look round*, esp. *anxiously*; hence *to consider*; transit., *to look round at, survey*; hence *to consider carefully*; also *to look about for, seek* for.

Hence partic. **circumspectus** -a -um: pass., of things, *deliberate, well considered*; act., of persons, *circumspect, cautious.*

circumsto -stare -stĕti: intransit., *to stand round* or *in a circle*; partic. as subst., circumstantes, *the bystanders*; transit., *to surround, beleaguer.*

circumstrĕpo -ĕre, *to make a loud noise around.*

circumsurgens -entis, *rising round.*

circumtĕro -tĕrĕre, *to rub against on all sides.*

circumtextus -a -um, *woven all round.*

circumtŏno -tŏnare -tŏnŭi, *to thunder round.*

circumtonsus -a -um, *shorn all round; of discourse, artificial.*

circumvădo -vādĕre -vāsi, *to attack from every side, to surround.*

circumvăgus -a -um, *wandering round, flowing round.*

circumvallo -are, *to blockade, beleaguer.*

circumvectĭo -ōnis, f. *a carrying round of merchandise:* portorium circumvectionis, *transit dues;* in gen., *circuit, revolution.*

circumvector -ari, *to ride or sail round;* poet., *to go through, describe.*

circumvĕhor -vĕhi -vectus, *to ride or sail round;* poet., *to describe.*

circumvēlo -are, *to veil round, envelop.*

circumvĕnĭo -vĕnire -vēni -ventum, *to come round, surround, encircle.* Transf., *to beset, assail; to cheat, defraud.*

circumvertor (**-vortor**) -verti, *to turn oneself round.*

circumvestĭo -ire, *to clothe all round.*

circumvŏlĭto -are, *to fly round, rove about.*

circumvŏlo -are, *to fly round.*

circumvolvo -volvĕre -volvi -vŏlūtum, *to roll round;* usually pass., *to revolve.*

circus -i, m. *a ring, circle, orbit:* candens, *the milky way;* also *an oval course for races.*

ciris -is, f. *a bird, into which Scylla was transformed.*

cirrātus -a -um, *curly-haired.*

Cirrha -ae, f. *a city near Delphi, sacred to Apollo;* adj. **Cirrhaeus** -a -um.

cirrus -i, m. *a lock, or ringlet of hair; the fringe of a garment.*

cis, prep., with acc., *on this side of, within.*

Cisalpīnus -a -um, *on this (the Roman) side of the Alps.*

cisium -i, n. *a light two-wheeled vehicle.*

Cisrhenānus -a -um, *on this (the Roman) side of the Rhine.*

cista -ae, f. *a chest, box.*

cistella -ae, f. *a little chest or box.*

cisterna -ae, f. *reservoir, cistern.*

cistŏphŏrus -i, m. *an Asiatic coin.*

cistŭla -ae, f. *a little chest or box.*

citātus -a -um, partic. from ²cito; q.v.

citĕr -tra -trum, *on this side;* usually compar., **citĕrior** -us, genit. -oris, *on this side, nearer;* superl. **citĭmus** -a -um, *nearest.*

cithăra -ae, f. *a stringed instrument, lyre, lute.*

cithărista -ae, m. *a player on the cithara.*

cithăristria -ae, f. *a female player on the cithara.*

cithărizo -are, *to play the cithara.*

cithăroedus -i, m. *one who plays the cithara with voice accompanying.*

¹**cĭto**, adv. from cieo; q.v.

²**cĭto** -are (1) *to put in motion, excite, start up.* (2) *to summon, call forward;* esp. *for legal, political or military purposes;* hence *to appeal to, point to authorities, etc.*

Hence partic. **cĭtātus** -a -um,

quick, speedy: citato equo, *at full gallop.* Adv. **cĭtātim.**

citrā (abl. f. from citer). Adv. *on this side, nearer.* Prep. with acc., *on this side of, nearer than;* of time, *since;* hence, in gen., *short of, without.*

citrĕus -a -um, *belonging to the citrus-tree or citron-tree.*

citrō, adv. found only with ultro: ultro (et) citro, *up and down, hither and thither.*

citrus -i, m. (1) *the citrus, a kind of African cypress.* (2) *the citron-tree.*

citus -a -um, partic. from cieo; q.v.

cīvĭcus -a -um, *relating to a citizen, civic;* civica (corona), *the civic crown, awarded to one who had saved the life of a Roman in war.*

cīvīlis -e, *relating to a citizen, civic, civil;* esp. ius civile, *the Roman civil law or civil rights; befitting a citizen;* hence, *popular, affable, courteous; relating to public life or the state.* Adv. **cīvīliter,** *like a citizen; politely.*

cīvīlitās -ātis, f. (1) *the science of politics.* (2) *politeness, civility.*

cīvis -is, c. *citizen;* also *a fellow citizen:* under a king, *a subject.*

cīvĭtās -ātis, f.: abstr., *citizenship;* concr., *a union of citizens, state, commonwealth; the inhabitants of a city, townsfolk;* (rarely) *a city, town.*

clādēs -is, f. *destruction;* in gen., *disaster, injury, defeat.*

clam. Adv., *secretly, in secret:* esse, *to remain unknown.* Prep. with acc. or abl., *unknown to, without the knowledge of.*

clāmātor -ōris, m. *a shouter, noisy speaker.*

clāmĭto -are, *to cry aloud, shout violently.*

clāmo -are, *to call, shout, cry aloud;* with object, *to call to or upon a person, to shout something;* sometimes *to proclaim, declare.*

clāmor -ōris, m. *a loud shouting, cry;* poet., *of lifeless things, echo, reverberation.*

clāmōsus -a -um: act., *noisy, clamorous* pass., *filled with noise.*

clanculum. Adv. *secretly, in secret.* Prep. with acc., *unknown to.*

clandestīnus -a -um, *secret, clandestine;* Adv. **clandestīnō.**

clangor -ōris, m. *sound, clang, noise.*

clārĕo -ēre, *to be bright, to shine.* Transf., *to be evident; to be distinguished.*

clāresco clārescĕre clārŭi, *to become clear to the senses.* Transf., *to become evident; to become illustrious.*

clārĭgo -are, *to demand satisfaction,* used of the Fetials.

clārĭsŏnus -a -um, *clearly sounding.*

clārĭtās -ātis, f. *clearness, brightness.* Transf., *clearness to the mind, plainness; fame, celebrity.*

clārĭtūdo -īnis, f. *clearness, brilliancy.* Transf., *fame, celebrity.*

clāro -are, *to make bright or clear.* Transf., *to make plain to the mind; to make illustrious.*

clārus -a -um, *bright, clear, distinct*; poet., of the wind, *making clear, bringing fair weather.* Transf., to the understanding, *clear, evident, plain*; of reputation, *illustrious, distinguished*; in bad sense, *notorious.* Hence adj. **clārē,** *clearly, brightly, distinctly; illustriously.*

classiārius -a -um, *of the fleet*; m. pl. as subst., *marines.*

classĭcus -a -um. (1) *relating to the different classes of Roman citizens.* (2) *relating to the armed forces,* esp. to the fleet: m. pl. as subst., *marines*: n. sing. as subst., *the signal for battle or the trumpet giving this.*

classis -is, f. *a group as summoned, a division, class.* (1) *one of the classes into which Servius Tullius divided the Roman people.* (2) *the armed forces,* esp. *the fleet.* (3) in gen., *a class, group.*

clatri -orum, m. pl., *trellis, grating.*

claudĕo -ēre and **claudo** -ēre, *to limp, halt, be lame.*

claudicātĭo -ōnis, f. *a limping.*

claudĭco -are, *to limp, be lame.* Transf., *to incline, be deflected; to halt, waver.*

Claudĭus (**Clōdĭus**) -a -um, *the name of two Roman gentes*; esp. *of the emperor Claudius* (10 B.C.-A.D. 54). Adj. **Claudĭānus** -a -um, **Claudĭālis** -e.

¹**claudo** claudĕre clausi clausum (and **clūdo**) *to close, shut up, make inaccessible*; of military positions, *to blockade, invest*; of prisoners, etc., *to shut in, confine.* Transf., *to conclude*; agmen, *to bring up the rear.* Hence partic. **clausus** -a -um, of character, *close, reserved*; n. as subst., *an enclosed place.*

²**claudo** = claudeo; q.v.

claudus -a -um, *limping, lame.* Transf., *crippled, defective*; poet. carmina alterno versu, *elegiac verse.*

claustrum -i, n., gen. plur., *a means of closing or shutting in: a bolt, bar; an enclosure, prison, den; a barricade, dam, fortress*; milit., *the key to a position.*

clausŭla -ae, f. *end, conclusion:* in rhetoric, *the close of a period.*

clāva -ae, f. *staff or cudgel.*

clāvārĭum -i, n. *an allowance to soldiers for buying shoe-nails.*

clāvĭcŭla -ae, f. *the tendril by which the vine clings to its prop.*

¹**clāvĭger** -gĕri, m. *the club-bearer,* of Hercules.

²**clāvĭger** -gĕri, m. *the key-bearer,* of Janus.

clāvis -is, f. *a key*: claves adimere uxori, *to separate from one's wife.* Transf., *a stick for trundling a hoop.*

clāvus -i, m. (1) *a nail, spike.* (2) *a tiller, helm, rudder.* (3) *a stripe of purple on the tunic, worn broad by senators, narrow by knights.*

clēmens -entis, *mild, kind, merciful*; adv. **clēmenter,** *gently.*

clēmentĭa -ae, f. *mildness, gentleness, mercy.*

Clĕŏpatra -ae, f. *the queen of Egypt and mistress of Antony, defeated with him at Actium.*

clĕpo clĕpere clepsi cleptum, *to steal*; se, *to conceal oneself.*

clepsydra -ae, f. *a water clock,* esp. as used to measure the time allotted to orators.

clĭens -entis, m. *a client, dependent on a patronus* (q.v.); in gen., *a vassal or ally.*

clĭenta -ae, f. *a female client.*

clĭentēla -ae, f. *clientship, the relation between client and patron*; hence, in gen., *dependence.* Transf. (gen. plur.) *clients.*

clīnāmen -inis, n. *inclination, swerving aside.*

clīnātus -a -um, *inclined, leaning.*

Clĭō -ūs, f. *the Muse of history.*

clĭpĕātus -a -um, *armed with a shield*; m. pl. as subst., *soldiers with shields.*

clĭpĕus -i, m. and **clĭpĕum** -i, n. *a (round) shield.* Transf., *the disk of the sun; a medallion portrait.*

clĭtellae -arum, f. pl. *a pack-saddle, pair of panniers.*

clīvōsus -a -um, *hilly, steep.*

clīvus -i, m. *a slope, rise, gradient.*

clŏāca -ae, f. *a sewer, drain.*

Clŏācīna -ae, f. *the cleanser, surname of Venus.*

Clōdĭus = Claudius; q.v.

Clōthō, f. *the spinner, one of the Parcae.*

clŭĕo -ēre, *I hear myself called, am named.*

clūnis -is, m. and f. *the buttocks.*

Clūsĭum -i, n. *a town of Etruria*; adj. **Clūsīnus** -a -um.

Clҫtaemnestra -ae, f. *wife of Agamemnon who killed her husband, and was killed by her son Orestes.*

Cnĭdus (-os), or **Gnĭdus** (-os), -i, f. *a town in Caria, famous for the worship of Venus*; adj. **Cnĭdĭus** -a -um.

Cnossus = Gnossus; q.v.

cŏăcervātĭo -ōnis, f. *a heaping up.*

cŏăcervo -are, *to heap up, accumulate.*

cŏăcesco -ăcescĕre -ăcŭi, *to become sour.*

cŏacto -are, *to compel.*

cŏactor -ōris, m. *a collector of money*; coactores agminis, *the rear-guard.*

cŏactū, abl. sing. m. *by force, under compulsion.*

cŏactum -i, n. subst. from cogo; q.v

cŏaedĭfĭco -are, *to build on.*

cŏaequo -are, *to level, make even.*

cŏagmentātĭo -ōnis, *a connexion, binding together.*

cŏagmento -are, *to join together*; pacem, *to conclude.*

cŏagmentum -i, n. *a joining joint.*

cŏagŭlum -i, n. *rennet or curds.*

cŏalesco -ălescĕre -ălŭi -ălĭtum, *to grow together; to take root, grow*; hence *to become established or firm.*

cŏangusto -are, *to limit, confine.*

cŏarcto, etc. = coarto, etc.; q.v.

cŏargŭo -ŭĕre -ŭi, *to show clearly.*

demonstrate fully; esp. to prove wrong or guilty.

cŏartātĭo -ōnis, f. a confining in a small space.

cŏarto -are, to confine, draw together; of discourse, to compress; of time, to shorten.

coccĭnātus -a -um, clad in scarlet.

coccĭnus -a -um, scarlet-coloured; n. pl. as subst., scarlet clothes.

coccum -i, n. the berry of the scarlet oak; hence scarlet dye; sometimes scarlet cloth or garments.

coclĕa (cochlĕa) -ae, f. a snail or snail-shell.

coclĕāre (cochlĕāre) -is, n. and coclĕārĭum -i, n. a spoon.

Cocles, Roman cognomen, esp. of Horatius Cocles, the Roman who defended the bridge over the Tiber against Porsenna.

coctĭlis -a, baked; muri, made of burnt brick.

Cōcȳtŏs and -us, -i. m. a river of the lower world.

cōda = cauda; q.v.

cōdex (older caudex) -dĭcis, m. the trunk of a tree; as a term of abuse, dolt, blockhead. Transf., a book (made up of wooden tablets, covered with wax); esp. an account-book, ledger.

cōdĭcārĭus (caudĭcārĭus) -a -um, made of tree trunks.

cōdĭcillī -orum, m. little trunks, logs. Transf., small tablets for memoranda; hence a letter, petition, codicil, rescript.

coel-; see cael-.

cŏēmo -ēmĕre -ēmi -emptum, to buy up.

cŏemptĭo -ōnis, f. a form of marriage; a fictitious sale of an estate.

coen-; see caen-.

cŏĕo -ire -ĭi -ĭvi -ĭtum, to go or come together, assemble; of enemies, to engage; of friends, etc., to unite, combine; transit., societatem coire, to form an alliance; of things, to unite, come together; of blood, to curdle; of water, to freeze.

cŏepio cŏepĕre, coepi coeptum (only the perfect-stem tenses are class.; see incipio), to begin, commence. N. of partic. as subst. coeptum -i, a thing begun or undertaken.

cŏepto -are, to begin or undertake (eagerly).

cŏeptus -ūs, m. (only in plur.), a beginning.

cŏerceo -cēre -cŭi -cĭtum, to enclose, shut in, confine, restrain; vitem, to prune.

cŏercĭtĭo -ōnis, f. confining, restraint; hence punishment.

coerŭlĕus = caeruleus; q.v.

coetus (cŏĭtus) -ūs, m. meeting together, union, assemblage.

cōgĭtātĭo -ōnis, f. thinking, conception, reflection, reasoning; sometimes a particular thought, idea or intention.

cōgĭto -are, to turn over in the mind, to think, reflect; sometimes to intend, plan.

Hence partic. cōgĭtātus -a -um, considered, deliberate: n. pl. as subst. thoughts, reflections, ideas. Adv. cōgĭtātē, thoughtfully.

cognātĭo -ōnis, f. relationship, connexion by blood; meton., persons related, kindred, family: in gen., connexion, agreement, resemblance.

cognātus -a -um, related, connected by blood; m. and f. as subst. a relation either on the father's or mother's side. Transf., akin, similar.

cognĭtĭo -ōnis, f. getting to know, study, knowledge, acquaintance; recognition; legal inquiry, investigation; in plur., ideas, conceptions.

cognĭtor -ōris, m. a knower; legal, a witness or an attorney; in gen., a supporter.

cognōmĕn -ĭnis, n. a surname, family name.

cognōmentum -i, n. a surname, a name.

cognōmĭnātus -a -um, of the same meaning; verba, synonyms.

cognōmĭnis -e, having the same name.

cognosco -gnoscĕre -gnōvi -gnĭtum, to become acquainted with, get to know, learn; in perf. tenses, to know; to know again, recognize; of judges, to examine, hear, decide.

Hence partic. cognĭtus -a -um, known, proved.

cōgo cōgĕre cōēgi cŏactum, to bring, drive, or draw to one point, to collect; to bring close together, compress: of liquids, etc. to thicken, curdle; milit., agmen cogere, to bring up the rear. Transf., to restrict, confine; to compel.

Hence partic., cŏactus, constrained: n. as subst., thick cloth, felt.

cŏhaerentĭa -ae, f. coherence.

cŏhaerĕo -haerēre -haesi -haesum: of a whole, to cohere, hold together; of one thing (or person), to cling, adhere, be connected to another.

cŏhaeresco -haerescĕre -haesi, to hang together.

cŏhērēs -ēdis, m. a coheir.

cŏhĭbĕo -ēre -ŭi -ĭtum, to hold in, hold together: hence to confine, restrain, hold back, repress.

cŏhŏnesto -are, to do honour to.

cŏhorresco -horrescĕre -horrŭi, to shudder or shiver.

cŏhors -tis, f. an enclosure, yard. Transf., a troop, company, throng; milit., a cohort, the tenth part of a legion; praetoria cohors, the retinue of the governor of a province.

cŏhortātĭo -ōnis, f. exhortation, encouragement.

cŏhortor -ari, dep. to encourage, incite, exhort.

cŏĭtĭo -ōnis, f. a coming together, meeting; a faction, coalition, conspiracy.

cŏĭtus -us, see coetus.

cōlăphus -i, m. a cuff, box on the ear.

Colchis -ĭdis, f. Colchis, a country on the Black Sea; adj. Colchĭcus and

Colchus -a -um; f. adj. **Colchis** -Idis.

cōlĕus -i; see culeus.

cōlĭphĭa (**cōlȳphĭa**) -orum, n. *a food used by athletes.*

cōlis = caulis; q.v.

coll-; see also conl-.

Collātia -ae, f. *a town in Latium*; adj. **Collātinus** -a -um.

collīnus -a -um, *hilly, relating to a hill*: porta Collina, *a gate of Rome near the Quirinal Hill.*

collis -is, m. *hill, high ground.*

collum -i, n. (**collus** -i, m.) *neck.*

collȳbus -i, m. *exchange of money, or rate of exchange.*

collȳrium -i, n. *eye-salve.*

cōlo cōlĕre cōlŭi cultum, *to cultivate, till, tend; to dwell in, inhabit a place;* in gen., *to take care of, attend to; foster, honour, worship, court.* Hence partic. **cultus** -a -um, *cultivated, tilled, planted*; n. pl. as subst., *cultivated land.* Transf., physically, *tidy, well-dressed, smart;* mentally, *refined.* Adv. **cultē,** *elegantly.*

cōlŏcāsĭa -orum, n. pl. *the Egyptian bean.*

cōlōna -ae, f. *a country-woman.*

cōlōnĭa -ae, f. *a farm, estate; a colony*; meton., *colonists.*

cōlōnĭcus -a -um, *relating to agriculture or to a colony.*

cōlōnus -i, m. *a farmer, sometimes a tenant farmer; a colonist, inhabitant of a colony.*

cŏlor (**cŏlōs**) -ōris, m. *colour, tint, hue*; esp. *complexion;* sometimes *beautiful complexion, beauty.* Transf., *outward show, external appearance; cast, character, tone; an artful excuse.*

cŏlōro -are, *to colour*; partic. **cŏlōrātus** -a -um, *coloured*: of complexion, *tanned, dark.*

cŏlossĕus and **cŏlossĭcus** -a -um, *colossal, gigantic.*

cŏlossus -i, m. *a colossus, statue larger than life;* esp. *that of Apollo at Rhodes.*

cŏlŭber -bri, m. *serpent, snake.*

cŏlubra -ae, f. *female serpent.*

cŏlubrĭfer -fĕra -fĕrum, *snake-bearing, snaky-haired* (of Medusa).

cōlum -i, n. *colander, sieve, strainer.*

cŏlumba -ae, f. *a pigeon, dove.*

cŏlumbīnus -a -um, *belonging to a pigeon.*

cŏlumbus -i, m. *a male dove or pigeon.*

cŏlŭmella -ae, f. *a little column.*

cŏlŭmen -ĭnis, n. *a height, summit, ridge;* of buildings, *roof, gable.* Transf., *chief, summit, crown; support, pillar.*

cŏlumna -ae, f. *a pillar, column;* columnae, *pillars as signs of book-sellers' shops in Rome;* columnae Herculis, *the pillars of Hercules.* Transf., *a support, pillar of the state; a water-spout.*

cŏlumnārium -i, n. *a tax on pillars.*

cŏlumnārĭus, *a rascal, thief.*

cŏlurnus -a -um, *of hazel-wood.*

cŏlus -i and -ūs, f. or m., *a distaff.*

cŏma -ae, f. *the hair of the head.* Transf., *leaves; rays of light.*

cŏmans -antis, *hairy*: galea, *crested*; stella, *a comet.*

cŏmātus -a -um, *hairy;* Gallia Comata, *a name for Transalpine Gaul*: comata silva, *in full leaf.*

[1]**combĭbo** -bĭbĕre -bĭbi, *to drink in, suck up.*

[2]**combĭbo** -ōnis, m. *a comrade in drinking.*

combūro -ūrĕre -ussi -ustum, *to burn up;* hence *to ruin or consume.*

cŏmĕdo -esse -ēdi -ēsum or -estum, *to eat up, consume;* of property, *to waste, squander.*

cŏmĕs -ĭtis, c. *a fellow-traveller;* hence *a companion, comrade;* sometimes *attendant;* in plur., comites, *retinue.*

cŏmētēs -ae, m. *a comet.*

cŏmĭcus -a -um, *of comedy, comic;* esp. *represented in comedy.* M. as subst. *an actor in comedy or writer of comedy.* Adv. **cŏmĭcē,** *in the manner of comedy.*

cominus = comminus; q.v.

cōmis -e, *courteous, kind, friendly, obliging;* adv. **cōmĭter.**

cōmissābundus -a -um, *revelling, rioting.*

cōmissātĭo -ōnis, f. *a revel, riotous procession.*

cōmissātor -ōris, m. *a reveller.*

cōmissor -ari, dep. *to revel.*

cōmĭtās -ātis, f. *courtesy, friendliness, civility.*

cŏmĭtātus -ūs, m. *train, retinue, following.*

cōmĭter, adv. from comis; q.v.

cŏmĭtĭa; see comitium.

cŏmĭtĭālis -e, *relating to the comitia.*

cŏmĭtĭātus -ūs, m. *the assembly of the people in the comitia.*

cŏmĭtĭum -i, n. *a place of assembly,* esp. *one in the forum at Rome;* plur. **cŏmĭtĭa,** *the assembly of the Roman people for the election of magistrates,* etc.; hence *elections.*

cŏmĭto -are, *to accompany:* esp. as partic. **cŏmĭtātus** -a -um, *accompanied.*

cŏmĭtor -ari, dep. *to attend, accompany, follow.*

commācŭlo -are, *to pollute.*

commānĭpŭlāris -is, m. *a soldier belonging to the same company.*

commĕātus -ūs, m., *free passage, going and coming;* milit., *leave of absence, furlough;* also (often plur.) *supply of provisions, food, forage.*

commĕdĭtor -ari, dep. *to practise, represent.*

commĕmĭni -isse, *to remember fully.*

commĕmŏrābĭlis -e, *worthy of mention, memorable.*

commĕmŏrātĭo -ōnis, f. *reminding, mention.*

commĕmŏro -are, *to call to mind, recollect; to remind another, so to mention, relate, recount.*

commendābĭlis -e, *commendable, praiseworthy.*

commendātīcius -a -um, *giving recommendation.*

commendātio -ōnis, f. *recommendation; that which recommends, excellence.*

commendātor -ōris, m. and **commendātrix** -īcis, f., *one that commends.*

commendo -are, *to commit to the care or protection of anyone.* Hence, in gen., *to commit; to recommend; to set off, render agreeable.*

commensus partic. of commetior; q.v.

commentāriolum -i, n. *a short treatise.*

commentārius -i, m. and **commentārium** -i, n. *a memorandum, note-book;* as the title of a book, *a memoir* (usually plur.); legal, *a brief.*

commentātio -ōnis, f. *reflection, careful consideration; practice.*

commentīcius -a -um, *invented, fictitious.*

1commentor -ari, dep. *to consider thoroughly; to practise, prepare; to invent, compose, write.*

2commentor -ōris, m. *an inventor.*

commeo -are, *to go up and down, come and go.*

commercium -i, n. *trade, commerce;* meton. *the right to trade,* or *an article of traffic, merchandise,* or *a place of trade, depot.* Hence in gen., *intercourse, communication.*

commercor -ari, dep. *to buy up.*

commereo -ēre (also **commereor,** dep.) *to deserve fully; to commit a fault.*

commētior -mētiri -mensus, dep. *to measure;* sometimes *to measure one thing against another, compare.*

commēto -are, *to go frequently.*

commigro -are, *to move in a body, migrate.*

commīlitium -i, n. *companionship in war* or *military service;* in gen., *fellowship.*

commīlito -ōnis, m. *a fellow-soldier.*

comminātio -ōnis, f. *threatening, threat.*

commingo -mingēre -minxi -mictum, *to make water on, defile.*

comminiscor -minisci -mentus, dep. *to think out, contrive, invent.* Perf. partic. in passive sense, **commentus** -a -um, *feigned, invented;* n. as subst. **commentum** -i, n. *a fiction, invention, contrivance.*

comminor -ari, dep. *to threaten.*

comminuo -ŭēre -ŭi -ūtum, *to make small, break up, diminish, weaken.*

comminus, *hand to hand,* esp. *in close combat;* in gen., *close up, close at hand.*

commisceo -miscēre -miscŭi -mixtum, *to mix together, mix up.*

commisĕrātio -ōnis, f. *pity;* rhet. *the exciting of pity.*

commisĕresco -ēre, *to pity.*

commisĕror -ari, dep. *to pity, bewail;* of a speaker, *to excite pity.*

commissio -ōnis, f. *a setting together:* hence *the start of games, contests,* etc.

commissūra -ae, f. *a joining together, connexion, joint*

committo -mittēre -misi -um.miss (1) *to unite, connect, combine;* esp. *to bring together in a contest, to match:* hence *to compare.* (2) *to begin, set on foot, initiate:* with ut and the subj., *to bring it about that;* esp. of crimes, etc., *to commit, perpetrate,* and of penalties *to incur.* (3) *to entrust, commit,* esp. with reflex. N. of partic. as subst. **commissum** -i. *an undertaking; a crime, fault; a trust, secret.*

commŏditās -ātis, f. *proportion, fitness;* hence *a fit occasion,* also *convenience, advantage;* of persons, *kindness.*

commŏdo -are, *to make fit, adapt;* hence *to adapt oneself to a person, to please, oblige, serve;* with acc. *to furnish, lend, give.*

commŏdus -a -um, *to measure, in full, complete;* hence *proper, fit, appropriate;* of persons, *character,* etc., *friendly, obliging, pleasant.* N. as subst. **commodum** -i, *suitable time, opportunity, convenience; use, advantage, interest; remuneration, loan.* N. acc. as adv. **commodum,** *at the right time, opportunely; just then.* Adv. **commode,** *rightly, properly, fitly; pleasantly, comfortably, kindly*

commōlior -iri, dep. *to set in motion.*

commŏnĕfăcio -făcĕre -fēci -factum, *to remind, warn* a person, or *to call to mind* a thing.

commŏnĕo -ēre, *to remind, warn* a person, or *to call to mind* a thing.

commonstro -are, *to show fully.*

commŏrātio -ōnis, f. *delaying, lingering.*

commŏror -ari, dep. *to linger, stay;* transit., *to delay.*

commōtio -ōnis. *violent movement excitement.*

commŏvĕo -mŏvēre -mōvi -mōtum, *to move violently, shake, disturb, carry about* or *away;* nummum, *to employ in commerce;* esp. of the mind or passions, *to excite, influence, upset;* of abstract things, *to start up, produce cause.*

Hence partic. **commōtus** -a -um, *insecure, unsteady; excited, upset.*

commūnĭcātio -ōnis, f. *communicating, imparting.*

commūnĭco -are (1) *to share out, give a share in;* hence *to communicate, impart a matter;* without object, or *to take counsel, confer with* a person. (2) *to join, unite.* (3) *to take a share participate.*

1commūnio -ire, *to fortify thoroughly.*

2commūnio -ōnis, f. *sharing, mutual participation.*

commūnis -e, *shared, common, universal, public;* loca, *public places;* loci, *commonplaces;* of persons, *approachable, affable.* N. as subst. **commūne,** *common property,* esp. in plur.; *state, commonwealth;* in **commūne,** *for the public good,* also *in general.* Adv. **commūnĭter,** *jointly, generally.*

commūnĭtās -ātis, f. *community, fellowship; sense of fellowship, affability.*

commurmŭror -ari, dep. *to mutter, murmur.*

commūtābĭlis -e, *changeable.*

commūtātus -ūs, m. *change, alteration.*

commūto -are, *to change, alter; to exchange, barter, interchange.*

cōmo cōmēre compsi comptum, *to put together, make tidy, arrange, adorn;* esp. of the hair.
Hence partic. **comptus** -a -um, *formed, framed; adorned, neat.*

cōmoedĭa -ae, f. *comedy.*

cōmoedus, *comic;* m. as subst., *a comic actor.*

cōmōsus -a -um, *hairy;* of plants, *leafy.*

compactĭo -ōnis, f. *joining together.*

compactum or **compectum** -i, n. *an agreement.*

compāgēs -is, f. *a joining together, connexion:* hence either *something that joins, a joint, seam,* or *something joined together, a structure.*

compāgo -inis, f. *a joining together.*

compār -păris: as subst., *an equal, companion. mate;* as adj. *like, similar.*

compărābĭlis -e, *capable of comparison, comparable.*

¹**compărātĭo** -onis, f. *preparing, providing.*

²**compărātĭo** -onis, f. *a putting together;* hence, *comparison.*

compărātivus -a -um, *relating to comparison, comparative.*

comparco (**comperco**) -parcĕre -parsi or -persi, *to scrape together, save up.*

compārĕo -pārēre -pāruī *to appear, be visible; to be present, be in existence.*

¹**compăro** -are, *to prepare, get ready, provide;* hence *to arrange, settle.*

²**compăro** -are, *to couple together,* esp. for a contest, *to match.* Transf., *to liken, compare.*

compasco -pascĕre -pastum, *to feed* (cattle) *together.*

compascŭus -a -um, *of common pasturage.*

compellātĭo -ōnis, f. *accosting, rebuking.*

¹**compello** -pellĕre -pŭli -pulsum, *to drive together, collect; to force, compel.*

²**compello** -are, *to address, accost;* esp. *to reproach, rebuke;* legal, *to accuse before a court.*

compendĭārĭus -a -um *short;* f. and n. as subst., *a short cut.*

compendĭum -i, n. *saving, profit, advantage; shortening, abbreviation;* compendi facere, *to make short;* in plur. *short ways, short cuts.*

compensātĭo -ōnis, f. *balancing, compensation.*

compenso -are, *to weight together, balance.*

comperco = comparco; q.v.

compĕrendĭnātĭo -ōnis, f. and **compĕrendĭnātus** -ūs, m. *a putting off to the next day but one.*

compĕrendĭno -are, *to remand to the next day but one.*

complector -plecti -plexus, dep. *to embrace, surround, encompass.* Transf., *to hold fast, master; to attach oneself to, esteem;* of the mind, *to embrace,*

grasp, comprehend; *to unite in oneself. to include.*

complementum -i, n. *a complement.*

compleo -plēre -plēvi -plētum, *to fill up;* milit., *to man,* or *to bring up to strength;* of a sum, *to make up;* of fate, etc., *to fulfil;* of a task, *to finish.*
Hence partic. **complētus** -a -um, *perfect, complete.*

complexĭo -ōnis, f. *connexion, combination;* in rhetoric, *a summary* or *a period;* in logic, *the statement of a syllogism* or *a dilemma.*

complexus -ūs, m. of persons, *embrace, grasp,* either *in love* or *in combat;* of things, *compass* or *connexion.*

complĭco -are *to fold together;* complicata notio, *confused, intricate.*

complōrātĭo -ōnis, f. and **complōrātus** -ūs, m. *lamentation.*

complōro -are, *to bewail, lament.*

complūres, -ĭum, *several.*

complūvĭum -i, n. *roofless space in the centre of a Roman house.*

compōno -pōnĕre -pŏsŭi -pŏsĭtum. (1) *to put together;* esp. of unlike persons or things, either *to match as opponents,* or *to compare.* (2) *to make up a whole, compose.* (3) *to put in place, arrange, settle;* of enemies, *to reconcile.*
Hence partic. **compŏsĭtus** -a -um. *constructed, put together; arranged in order, settled;* hence *adapted* to a purpose. Adv. **compŏsĭtē,** *in an orderly way.*

comporto -are, *to bring together, collect.*

compōs -pŏtis, *having control of, possessed of, sharing in.*

compŏsĭtĭo -ōnis, f. *putting together;* of opponents, *matching; composing, compounding; orderly arrangement, settlement.*

compŏsĭtor -ōris, m. *an arranger, adjuster.*

compŏsĭtūra -ae, f. *connexion, joining.*

compŏsĭtus -a -um, partic. from compono; q.v.

compōtātĭo -ōnis, f. *drinking party.*

compōtor -ōris, m. and **compōtrix** -ĭcis, f. *a drinking-companion.*

compransor -ōris, m. *a dinner companion.*

comprĕcātĭo -ōnis, f. (*common*) *supplication.*

comprĕcor -ari, dep. *to pray to* or *for, supplicate.*

comprĕhendo -prĕhendere -prĕhendi -prĕhensum and **comprendo** -prendĕre -prendi -prensum, *to grasp; to take together, unite;* hence *to embrace, include; to take firmly, seize;* ignem, *to catch fire;* often of persons, *to capture, arrest;* of criminals, *to catch red-handed.* Transf., *to comprehend, perceive.*

comprĕhensĭbĭlis -e, *comprehensible.*

comprĕhensĭo -ōnis, f. (1) *a taking together, uniting;* rhet., *a period.* (2) *seizing, arrest.* Transf., *comprehending, comprehension.*

comprendo = comprehendo; q.v.

compressĭo -ōnis, f. *an embrace; compression of style, conciseness.*

compressū, abl. sing. m. *by pressing together; by embracing.*

comprĭmo -prĭmĕre -pressi -pressum, *to press together; to press tightly; hence to embrace; to check, restrain, suppress.* Hence compar. adv. **compressius**, *more (or rather) concisely.*

comprŏbātĭo -ōnis, f. *approval.*

comprŏbātor -ōris, m. *one who approves.*

comprŏbo -are (1) *to approve fully.* (2) *to confirm, prove, establish.*

comprōmissum -i, n. *reference to arbitrator.*

comprōmitto -mittĕre -misi -missum, *to agree to refer a cause to arbitration.*

¹comptus -a -um, partic. from como; q.v.

²comptus -ūs, m. *a head-dress; a band, tie.*

compungo -pungĕre -punxi -punctum, *to prick, puncture; hence to tattoo.*

compŭto -are, *to reckon together, calculate, compute.*

compŭtresco -ĕre, *to rot, putrefy.*

Cōmum -i, n. *a lake-side town in Cisalpine Gaul (now Como).*

cōnāmen -mĭnis, n. *effort, endeavour; concr., a support.*

cōnātus -i, n. *an undertaking.*

cōnātus -ūs, m. *an exertion, effort; sometimes impulse, inclination; an undertaking.*

concaedēs -ium, f. pl. *a barricade of trees.*

concălĕfăcĭo -făcĕre -fēci -factum (pass. **concălĕfīo**) *to warm thoroughly.*

concălesco -călescĕre -călŭi, *to become thoroughly warm.*

concallesco -callescĕre -callŭi, *to become thoroughly hard; hence to become practised* or *callous.*

concăvo -are, *to hollow out, make concave.*

concăvus -a -um, *hollow, vaulted, arched, concave; aqua, swelling.*

concēdo -cēdĕre -cessi -cessum: intransit., *to retire, withdraw;* concedere vita, *to die;* hence *to yield, submit, give way to,* with dat.; concedere naturae, *to die a natural death;* transit., *to yield, grant, give up;* of faults, *to pardon, overlook;* of actions, *to permit, allow.*

concĕlĕbro -are. *to visit often,* or *in large companies; to pursue an occupation eagerly; to celebrate a festivity; also to praise, extol a person* or *thing.*

concēnātĭo -ōnis, f. *supping together.*

concentĭo -ōnis, f. *singing together, harmony.*

concentus -ūs, m. *singing together, harmony; hence agreement, unity, concord.*

conceptĭo -ōnis, f. *conception, becoming pregnant; drawing up of legal formulae.*

conceptus -ūs, m. *conceiving, pregnancy; collecting,* or *a collection.*

concerpo -cerpĕre -cerpsi -cerptum, *to tear in pieces.* Transf., *to abuse.*

concertātĭo -ōnis, f. *contest, strife, dispute.*

concertātor -ōris, m. *a rival.*

concertātōrĭus -a -um, *relating to a contest.*

concerto -are, *to strive eagerly.*

concessĭo -ōnis, f. *yielding, granting.*

concessū, abl. sing. m. *by permission, with leave.*

concha -ae, f. *a sea-shell;* hence *a shell-fish,* esp. *mussel* or *pearl-oyster* or *the fish yielding purple dye;* poet., *a pearl* or *purple dye.* Transf., *a vessel like a shell,* e.g. *a salt-cellar* or *trumpet.*

conchȳlĭātus -a -um, *dyed with purple* or *dressed in purple.*

conchȳlĭum -i, n. *a shell-fish* esp. *a mussel* or *oyster,* or *the shell-fish which yielded the purple dye;* meton., *purple dye* or *a purple garment.*

¹concĭdo -cĭdĕre -cĭdi, *to fall down.* Transf., *to sink, perish;* of winds, *to subside;* of persons, *to be ruined, to fail,* esp. at law.

²concīdo -cidĕre -cidi, -cisum, *to cut up, cut down, destroy.* Transf., *to ruin, strike down.*
    Hence partic. **concīsus** -a -um, *cut up small, brief, concise.* Adv. **concīsē.**

concĭĕo -cĭēre -cĭvi -cĭtum and **concĭo** -ire. (1) *to collect, bring together.* (2) *to move violently, excite, arouse, stir up.*

concĭlĭābŭlum -i, n. *a place of assembly.*

concĭlĭātĭo -ōnis, f. *a bringing together, uniting, conciliating, causing of good-will; sometimes inclination.*

concĭlĭātor -ōris, m. *one who brings about a result.*

concĭlĭātrix -īcis, f. *she who unites; hence a match-maker.*

concĭlĭātū, abl. sing. m., *by union, by connexion.*

concĭlĭo -are, *to bring together, unite, reconcile, win over;* hence of results, *to bring about, cause.*
    Hence partic. **concĭlĭātus** -a -um, *won over, inclined, favourable.*

concĭlĭum -i, n. *bringing together, connexion, assembling, union;* esp. *an assembly for deliberation, a council.*

concinnĭtās -ātis, and **concinnĭtūdo** -ĭnis, f. *elegance, harmony,* esp. of style.

concinno -are, *to put together carefully, to arrange;* hence *to produce, cause.*

concinnus -a -um, *well put together;* hence *pleasing, elegant, neat,* esp. of style. Adv. **concinnē,** *elegantly.*

concĭno -cĭnĕre -cĭnŭi: intransit., *to sing in chorus, play together;* hence *to agree in saying* and in gen. *to agree;* transit., of songs, *to sing together;* of festivals, *to celebrate;* of the future, *to prophesy.*

¹concĭo = concieo; q.v.

²concĭo -ōnis = contio; q.v.

concĭpĭo -cĭpĕre -cēpi -ceptum. (1) *to take together, contain, hold;* of ideas, *to express in a certain form of*

words. (2) *to take completely in,*
absorb; of fluids, *to suck in*; of fire,
to catch; of air, *to draw in*; often
also *to conceive.* Transf., *to take in,*
grasp by senses or intellect; *to conceive,*
imagine; of passions, *to begin to feel*;
of action, *to devise,* esp. in bad sense.

concisio -ōnis, f. *the breaking up of a*
clause into divisions.

concisus -a -um, partic. from ²concido;
q.v.

concitātio -ōnis, f. *violent movement.*
Hence *tumult, sedition*; also *dis-*
turbance of mind, passion.

concitātor -ōris, m. *one who stirs up.*

concito -are, *to move violently, stir up,*
excite; equum calcaribus, *to spur to a*
gallop; aciem, *to move forward the*
army. Hence in gen., *to stir up,*
incite; of results, *to cause, produce.*
Hence partic. **concitātus** -a -um,
quick, rapid; *excited, violent, passion-*
ate. Adv. **concitātē,** *excitedly.*

concitor -ōris, m. *one who stirs up.*

conclāmātio -ōnis, f. *loud or combined*
shouting.

conclāmo -are. (1) *to shout together*
or *loudly*; with ut, *to demand loudly*
that; with acc. of a dead person, *to*
bewail. (2) *to call together.*

conclāve -is, n. *a room, chamber.*

conclūdo -clūdĕre -clūsi -clūsum *to*
shut up, enclose, confine. Hence *to*
include, comprise; *to bring to an end*;
in logic, *to argue, infer.* Adv. from
partic., **conclūsē,** *with well-turned*
periods.

conclūsio -ōnis, f. *a shutting, closing*;
milit, *a blockade.* Transf., *a close,*
conclusion; rhet., *the conclusion of a*
speech, peroration, or *a period*; in
logic, *a conclusion, consequence.*

conclūsiuncŭla -ae, f. *a foolish*
inference.

concŏlor -ōris, *similar in colour.*

concŏquo -cŏquĕre -coxi -coctum.
to boil or *cook thoroughly*; hence *to*
digest. Transf., *to bear, endure,*
stomach; *to consider well, deliberate*
upon.

concordia -ae, f. *agreement, union,*
harmony.

concorditer, adv. from concors; q.v.

concordo -are, *to agree, be in harmony.*

concors -dis, *of one mind* or *opinion,*
agreeing, harmonious. Adv. **con-**
corditer.

concrēbresco -brescĕre -brŭi *to*
increase.

concrēdo -crēdĕre -crēdidi -crēditum,
to entrust, commit.

concrĕmo -are, *to burn down, burn*
entirely.

concrĕpo -are -ŭi -ĭtum: intransit.,
to rattle, creak, clash; digitis concrepare, *to snap the fingers*; transit.,
to rattle, strike upon.

concresco -crescĕre -crēvi -crētum.
to grow, collect, be formed; *to become*
stiff, congeal, harden.
Hence perf. partic. **concrētus** -a
-um, *compounded*; *congealed, stiff.*

concrētio -ōnis, f. *a growing together,*
congealing; *matter.*

concrūcio -are, *to torture violently.*

concŭbina -ae, f. *a concubine.*

concŭbinus -i. m. *a man living with*
a concubine.

concŭbitus -ūs. m. *lying* or *reclining*
together; hence *copulation.*

concŭbius -a -um, in the phrase
concubia nocte, *at the time of first*
sleep, at dead of night.

conculco -are, *to tread down, trample*
under foot.

concumbo -cumbĕre -cūbŭi -cūbitum,
to lie or *recline together* (at table);
to lie with, have intercourse with.

concŭpisco -piscere -pīvi or -pĭi
-pītum, *to desire eagerly, covet, aim*
at.

concurro -currĕre -curri (or -cŭcurri)
-cursum, *to assemble hurriedly, flock*
to one spot; *to rush together, clash,*
esp. *to meet in conflict, engage.*

concursātio -ōnis, f. *running together,*
concourse; hence *coincidence*; in
gen., *running about*; milit. *skirmishing.*

concursātor -ōris, m. *a skirmisher.*

concursio -ōnis, f. *running together,*
concourse; rhet., *frequent repetition*
of a word.

concurso -are, *to run about, rush to*
and fro; milit., *to skirmish.*

concursus -ūs, m. *running together,*
concourse, union; *a rushing together,*
clashing; *a hostile encounter.*

concussū, abl. sing. m. *by shaking, by*
concussion.

concŭtio -cŭtĕre -cussi -cussum *to*
shake together, agitate, disturb. Hence,
physically, *to shatter, impair*; of
persons, *to shake the clothes of,* and
so *to examine*; mentally, *to alarm,*
trouble, excite.

condĕcŏro -are, *to adorn carefully.*

condemnātor -ōris, m. *one who causes*
condemnation, an accuser.

condemno -are, *to condemn*; of an
accuser, *to urge* or *effect the condemna-*
tion of a person; in gen.. *to blame,*
disapprove.

condenso -are and **condensĕo** -ēre,
to make thick, press close together.

condensus -a -um, *dense, thick.*

condicio -ōnis, f. *an arrangement,*
agreement. Hence (1) *a condition,*
stipulation, provision; esp. *conditions*
of marriage, marriage contract. (2)
state, condition, place, circumstances.

condico -dicĕre -dixi -dictum, *to*
make arrangement, agree, fix, settle;
esp. *to agree to dine with a person.*

condignus -a -um, *very worthy*; adv.
condignē.

condimentum -i, n. *spice. seasoning,*
sauce, condiment.

condio -ire; of fruits, etc., *to pickle,*
preserve; of corpses, *to embalm*; in
gen., *to season, temper.*
Hence partic. **conditus** -a -um,
seasoned, savoury.

condiscĭpŭlus -i, m. and **condiscĭpŭla**
-ae, f. *a schoolfellow.*

condisco -discĕre -dĭdĭci, *to learn thoroughly.*

¹condĭtĭo = conidicio; q.v.

²condĭtĭo -ōnis, f. *pickling* or *seasoning.*

condĭtor -ōris, m. *a founder*; hence, in gen., *contriver, composer, author.*

condĭtōrĭum -i, n. *the place in which a corpse or its ashes are preserved.*

condo -dĕre -dĭdi -dĭtum. (1) *to build, found; form, establish;* of literary work, *to compose, write* a poem, etc., and also *to write of* a subject. (2) *to put up, put away safely, store, to hide, withdraw;* of corpses, *to bury;* of time, *to pass, dispose of.*

condŏcĕfăcĭo -făcĕre -fēci -factum, *to train, instruct, teach.*

condŏlesco -dŏlescĕre -dŏlŭi, *to suffer severely, feel much pain.*

condōnātĭo -ōnis, f. *a giving away.*

condōno -are, *to give away, present, give up, sacrifice;* of debts, *to excuse;* of faults, *to overlook, forgive;* sometimes *to forgive an injury for the sake of a third party* (dat.).

condūco -dūcĕre -duxi -ductum: transit., *to bring* or *lead together: collect, unite, connect;* as commercial term, *to hire,* also *to contract for, farm;* intransit. (3rd person only), *to be of use, to profit, serve,* with dat.

conductĭcĭus -a -um, *hired.*

conductĭo -ōnis, f. *a bringing together, uniting;* commerc., *hiring, farming.*

conductor -ōris, m. *one who hires: a contractor.*

condŭplĭco -are, *to double.*

condūro -are, *to harden.*

cŏnecto -nectĕre -nexŭi -nexum, *to fasten, tie together, connect, join, unite.* Hence partic. **cŏnexus** -a -um, *joined, connected;* n. as subst. *logical connexion.*

cŏnexĭo -ōnis, f. *binding together; logical sequence.*

cŏnexus -ūs, m. *connexion, union.*

confābŭlor -ari, dep. *to talk, converse.*

confarrĕātĭo -ōnis, f. *a Roman form of marriage.*

confarrĕo -are, *to marry by the ceremony of* confarreatio.

confātālis -e, *determined by the same fate.*

confectĭo -ōnis, f. (1) *production, completion;* tributi, *complete exaction.* (2) *consumption.*

confector -ōris, m. *one who produces or completes; a destroyer, consumer.*

confercĭo -fercire -fertum, *to press close together, compress, cram together;* usually in perf. partic. **confertus** -a -um, *compressed, dense;* of troops, *in close formation;* with abl., *stuffed with, full of;* adv. **confertim**, *compactly.*

confĕro -ferre -tŭli -lātum. (1) *to bring* or *put together, collect, concentrate;* of money, etc. *to contribute;* milit., *to bring into contact* or *collision;* pedem (cum pede), *to fight foot to foot;* signa conferre, *to engage;* of speech and ideas, *to interchange,*

discuss; of diverse things, *to compare* (2) *to bring to a particular place, sphere, task, etc.;* se conferre, *to betake oneself,* or *to devote oneself;* in time, *to put off, postpone;* of responsibility, *to impute, attribute.*

confertus; see confercio.

confervĕfăcĭo -făcĕre, *to make very hot, melt.*

confervesco -fervescĕre -ferbŭi, *to begin to boil* or *glow.*

confessĭo -ōnis, f., *a confession, acknowledgment.*

confessus -a -um, partic. from confiteor; q.v.

confestim, *immediately, without delay.*

confĭcĭo -fĭcĕre -fēci -fectum. (1) *to finish, make ready, bring about, accomplish;* of arrangements, *to conclude, settle;* of time or space, *to complete, pass through;* of results, *to produce, cause.* (2) *to get together, obtain, win over.* (3) *to use up, exhaust, consume:* of food, *to chew, eat* and also *to digest;* of property, *to waste;* of living creatures, *to destroy kill;* in gen., *to weaken, wear out,* esp. of persons.
    Hence partic. **confĭcĭens** -entis *productive, efficient.*

confictĭo -ōnis, f. *a fabrication, invention.*

confĭdens, confĭdenter; see confido.

confĭdentĭa -ae, f. *confidence;* in bad sense, *impudence, boldness.*

confīdo -fīdĕre -fīsus sum, *to have complete trust in, be assured.*
    Hence partic. **confīdens** -entis, *confident, self-reliant;* in bad sense *bold, self-assured;* adv. **confĭdenter.**

confīgo -fīgĕre -fixi -fixum, *to fasten together;* *to pierce through, transfix, pin down.*

confingo -fingĕre -finxi -fictum, *construct, fashion, fabricate.*

confīnis -e. *having the same boundary, adjacent;* m. as subst. *a neighbour.* Transf., *closely allied, similar.*

confīnĭum -i, n. *a confine, boundary border.*

confirmātĭo -ōnis, f. *a thorough strengthening;* of an institution, *a securing, making firm;* of a person, *consolation, encouragement, support;* of a fact or statement, *confirmation, verification.*

confirmātor -ōris, m. *one who confirms.*

confirmo -are, *to make firm, strengthen, support;* se confirmare, *to recover strength;* polit. *to ratify;* of persons, *to strengthen in mind, encourage;* of assertions, either *to corroborate, establish* or *to affirm, state positively.*
    Hence partic. **confirmātus** -a -um *encouraged, emboldened;* of things. *certain.*

confisco -are, *to lay up, preserve in a chest; to appropriate to the imperial treasury, to confiscate.*

confisĭo -ōnis, f. *confidence, assurance.*

confĭtĕor -fĭtēri -fessus sum, dep. *to confess, admit, acknowledge; to reveal, make known.*

Hence partic. **confessus** -a -um:
in act. sense, *having confessed*; pass.,
undoubted, acknowledged, certain.

conflagro -are, *to blaze up, be well
alight.*

conflictio -ōnis, f. *collision, conflict.*

conflicto -are, pass. or intransit., *to
collide, contend*; transit., *to harass*;
pass. *to be harassed or tormented.*

conflictū, abl. sing. m. *by striking
together.*

confligo -flīgĕre -flixi, flictum: transit.,
*to strike or throw together; to bring
together in order to compare*; intransit.,
to collide, clash, come into conflict.

conflo -are, *to blow up; blow into flame*;
of metals, *to melt or forge*; of money
to coin. Transf., *to excite; to forge,
fabricate, put together.*

confluo -fluĕre -fluxi, *to flow, stream or
flock together.* Partic. **confluens**
-entis, *flowing together*; m. sing. or
pl. as subst. *the confluence of two
rivers*; as a place-name **Confluentes**,
f. pl. *Coblenz.*

confŏdio -fŏdĕre -fōdi -fossum, *to dig
thoroughly; to stab, pierce through.*

conformātio -ōnis, f. *form, shape*;
vocis, *expression*; verborum, *arrangement*; philosoph., *an idea*; rhet., *a
figure of speech.*

conformo -are, *to form, to put together,
to adapt one thing to another.*

confrăgōsus -a -um, *rugged, uneven*;
n. pl. as subst., *uneven places.*

confrăgus -a -um = confragosus; q.v.

confrĕmo -frĕmĕre -frĕmŭi, *to murmur,
make a noise.*

confrico -fricare -frĭcŭi -fricatum, *to
rub hard.*

confringo -fringĕre -frēgi -fractum, *to
break in pieces; to destroy.*

confŭgio -fŭgĕre -fūgi, *to fly, take
refuge; to have recourse to.*

confŭgium -i, n. *a place of refuge.*

confulcio -fulcire -fultus, *to prop up.*

confundo -fundĕre -fūdi -fūsum, *to
pour; to pour together, mingle, mix,
join*; hence *to confuse, throw into
disorder, trouble, disturb, upset.*
Hence partic. **confūsus** -a -um,
disorderly, confused; mentally, *embarrassed, troubled.* Adv. **confūsē.**

confūsio -ōnis, f. *blending, union;
confusion, disorder.*

confūto -are, *to check, repress*; by
speech, *to put down, silence.*

congĕlo -are: transit., *to freeze, harden,
thicken*; intransit., *to freeze up,
become inert.*

congĕmino -are, *to redouble.*

congĕmo -gĕmĕre -gĕmŭi: intransit.,
to sigh or groan loudly; transit., *to
bewail, lament.*

conger -gri, m. *a sea or conger eel.*

congĕriēs -ēi, f. *a heap, mass, esp. of
wood*; rhet., *accumulation.*

congĕro -gĕrĕre -gessi -gestum, *to
bring together, collect, pile up, accumulate; esp. to build up*; in discourse,
to bring together, comprise; of benefits,
abuse, etc., to heap upon a person.

congestīcius -a -um, *heaped up.*

congestus -ūs, m. *a heaping together*;
of birds, *the building of nests.* Transf.,
a heap, mass.

congiārium -i, n. *a donation* (originally
of wine, oil, etc.).

congius -i, m. *a Roman liquid measure*
(= *six sextarii*).

conglăcio -are; intransit., *to freeze,
be inert*; transit. *to turn to ice.*

conglŏbātio -ōnis, f. *a heaping or
crowding together.*

conglŏbo -are, *to form into a ball,
press tightly together.*

conglŏmĕro -are, *to roll, twist,
entangle.*

conglūtinātio -ōnis, f. *cementing together, connexion.*

conglūtino -are, *to cement together,
connect, bind closely.*

congrātŭlor -ari, dep. *to wish joy to,
congratulate.*

congrĕdior -grĕdi -gressus, dep. *to
meet, esp. in conflict; in words, to
dispute, argue.*

congrĕgābilis -e, *sociable, inclined to
collect.*

congrĕgātio -ōnis, f. *an assembling,
society, union.*

congrĕgo -are, *to collect into a flock or
swarm*; of men, *to gather together*;
with reflex., or in pass., *to swarm,
assemble.*

congressio -ōnis, f. *meeting, intercourse, association.*

congressus -ūs, m. *a meeting*; either *a
friendly meeting, social intercourse, or a
hostile encounter, combat.*

congrŭentia -ae, f. *agreement, symmetry,
proportion.*

congrŭo -ŭĕre, -ŭi, *to run together,
come together, meet*; in time, *to
coincide*; in gen., *to be suited to,
correspond with, agree.*
Hence partic. **congruens** -entis,
agreeing, fit, appropriate, suitable;
concentus, *harmonious, uniform*;
clamor, *unanimous.* Adv. **congruen-
tĕr**, *agreeably, suitably.*

congrŭus -a -um, *agreeing, fit, suitable.*

conicio -icĕre -iēci -ectum, *to throw
together; to cast lots*; mentally, *to
put two and two together, conjecture,
guess; to interpret dreams, etc.*; in
gen., *to throw, hurl*; se conicere, *to
betake oneself, flee*; of abstract things,
to bring up, bring in; of money, *to
throw away.*

coniectio -ōnis, f. *hurling, throwing;
conjectural interpretation.*

coniecto -are, *to throw together*; hence
*to put two and two together; conclude,
infer, guess.*

coniector -ōris, m. *an interpreter.*

coniectūra -ae, f. *a guess, conjecture,
inference; interpretation of dreams and
omens, divination.*

coniectūrālis -e, *conjectural.*

coniectus -ūs, m. *a throwing or throwing
together.*

cōnĭfĕr -fĕra -fĕrum and **cōnĭgĕr**,
cone-bearing.

cōnītor -nīti -nisus or -nixus, dep.
to lean or press hard; to make a great

effort, *physical* or *mental*; transit., of offspring, *to bring forth with difficulty*.

coniŭgālis -e, *of marriage, conjugal*.

coniŭgātio -ōnis, f. *etymological connexion of words*.

coniŭgātor -ōris, m., *one who connects*.

coniŭgiālis -e, *of marriage, conjugal*.

coniŭgium -i, n., *a close connexion, union*; esp. *marriage, wedlock*; meton. *a husband or wife*.

coniŭgo -are, *to bind together, connect*.

coniunctio -ōnis, f. *uniting, joining together, connexion*; grammat., *a connecting particle, conjunction*; of persons, *union, association, connexion* (esp. by blood or marriage).

coniungo -iungĕre -iunxi -iunctum, *to join together, connect, unite*; amicitias, *to form*; esp. *to unite* persons *by marriage, friendship, alliance*, etc. Hence partic. **coniunctus** -a -um, *connected, joined, agreeing, allied*; of place, with dat. *bordering on, near*; of time, *contemporary*; of persons, *connected* by blood or marriage or friendship. N. as subst., *an inherent property or quality*; rhet., *connexion*. Adv. **coniunctē**, *conjointly, in connexion*; *intimately, on friendly terms*; **coniunctim**, *conjointly, in common*.

coniunx (**coniux**) -iŭgis, c. *a husband or wife*; poet. *a betrothed virgin, bride*.

coniūrātio -ōnis, f. *a union confirmed by an oath*; in bad sense, *conspiracy, plot*; meton., *conspirators*.

coniūro -are, *to take an oath together*; in bad sense, *to plot, conspire*; perf. partic. (in act. sense) **coniūrātus** -a -um, *sworn, united by oath*; m. pl. as subst. *conspirators*.

coniux = coniunx; q.v.

cōnīvĕo -nīvēre -nīvi or -nixi, *to close the eyes, wink, blink*. Transf. *to wink at, let pass*.

conlăbĕfacto -are, *to cause to totter, to soften up*.

conlăbĕfio -fiēri -factus, *to be made to totter, to be softened or broken*.

conlābor -lābi -lapsus, dep. *to fall or sink down, collapse*; *to fall down in a swoon or death*.

conlăcĕrātus -a -um, *much lacerated or torn*.

conlacrĭmātio -ōnis, f. *a weeping together*.

conlacrĭmo -are, *to weep together or weep much*; transit., *to weep for*.

conlactĕus -i, m., and -a -ae, f., *a foster-brother or sister*.

conlātio -ōnis, f. *a bringing together*; signorum, *a battle*; of money, *a contribution, collection*. Transf., *a comparison, simile, analogy*.

conlātus -a -um, partic. from confero; q.v.

conlaudātio -ōnis, f. *strong praise*.

conlaudo -are, *to praise very much*.

conlaxo -are, *to widen, extend*.

conlecta -ae, f. *a contribution in money*.

conlectīcius -a -um, *gathered together*; exercitus, *quickly levied*.

conlectio -ōnis, f. *a gathering together, collection*; rhet. *a brief recapitulation*; in logic, *a conclusion, inference*.

conlēga -ae, m. *a colleague, partner in office*; in gen., *an associate*.

conlēgium -i, n.; abstr., *colleagueship*; concr., *persons united as colleagues, a body, guild, corporation, college*.

conlībertus -i, m. *a fellow-freedman*.

conlĭbet or **conlŭbet** -bēre -bŭit or -bĭtum est, impers., *it pleases, is agreeable*.

conlīdo līdĕre -līsi -līsum, *to strike or dash together, to bring into hostile collision*.

conlīgātio -ōnis, f. *a binding together connexion*.

¹conlĭgo -ligĕre -lēgi -lectum, *to gather or bring together, collect*; poet., *to gather into a smaller space, contract*; conligere se, or animum, or mentem, *to compose oneself, gain courage*; in the mind, *to put together*, hence *to infer, conclude*.

²conlĭgo -are, *to bind, tie, fasten together, connect*; sometimes *to detain, hinder, tie down*.

conlīnĕo are, *to direct in a straight line*.

conlĭno -linĕre -lēvi -litum, *to besmear, daub*.

conliquĕfactus -a -um, *liquefied melted*.

conlŏcātio -ōnis, f. *a placing, arrangment*; esp. *a giving in marriage*.

conlŏco -are, *to place, lay, set, arrange*; of time, money, etc. *to lay out, employ, spend*; of persons, *to settle, place*; of troops, *to billet, quarter*; of women, *to settle in marriage*.

conlŏcuplēto -are, *to enrich*.

conlŏcūtio -ōnis, f. *conversation*.

conlŏquium, -i, n., *talk, conversation, conference*.

conlŏquor -lŏqui -lŏcūtus, dep. *to speak to, converse with, to treat or negotiate with*.

conlūcĕo -ēre, *to shine on all sides, be completely illuminated*.

conlūdo -lūdĕre -lūsi -lūsum, *to play with*; *to have a secret understanding with, to act in collusion*.

conlŭo -luĕre -lŭi -lūtum, *to wash thoroughly, rinse*.

conlūsio -ōnis, f. *secret understanding*.

conlūsor -ōris, m. *a play-fellow*; *a fellow-gambler*.

conlustro -are, *to illuminate on all sides*; *to survey, look at on all sides*.

conlŭvĭo -ōnis and **conlŭvĭēs** -ēi *collection of impurities, filth*; of people, *scum, rabble*.

conm-; see comm-.

conn-; see con-.

cōnōpēum or **cōnōpĭum** -i, n. *a mosquito net*.

cōnor -ari, dep. *to undertake, try, strive*.

conp-; see comp-.

conquassātio -ōnis, f., *a violent shaking*.

conquasso -are, *to shake thoroughly, shatter*.

conquĕror -quĕri -questus, dep. *to complain loudly (of)*.

conquestio -ōnis, f. *a loud complaint*.

conquestū, abl. sing. m. *by loud complaint.*

conquiesco -quiescĕre -quiēvi -quiētum, *to take rest, repose, be still, stop.*

conquiro -quirĕre -quisivi -quisitum, *to seek out, get together.* Hence partic. **conquisitus** -a -um, *carefully sought out, chosen, costly.*

conquisitio -ōnis, f. *search, collection;* of soldiers, *levying conscription.*

conquisitor -ōris, m., *a recruiting officer.*

conr-: see **corr-.**

consaepio -saepire -saepsi -saeptum, *to fence round, hedge in;* n. of partic. as subst. **consaeptum** -i, *an enclosure.*

consălūtātio -ōnis, f., *mutual salutation.*

consălūto -are, *to greet (mutually), hail, salute.*

consănesco -sănescĕre -sānŭi, *to become healthy, get well.*

consanguĭnĕus -a -um, *related by blood, brotherly, sisterly;* m. as subst., *brother;* f., *sister;* m. plur., *relations.*

consanguĭnĭtās -ătis, f., *relationship by blood, consanguinity.*

conscĕlĕro -are, *to defile with crime;* partic. **conscĕlĕrātus** -a -um, *villainous, depraved.*

conscendo -scendĕre -scendi -scensum, *to ascend, mount, go up;* equum, *to mount on horseback;* naut. (with or without navem, etc.), *to go on board ship, embark.*

conscensio -ōnis, f. *embarkation.*

conscientia -ae, f., *knowledge shared with others, "being in the know";* *joint knowledge; knowledge shared with oneself,* i.e. *consciousness,* esp. *of right or wrong, a good or a bad conscience.*

conscindo -scindĕre -scĭdi -scissum, *to tear in pieces.*

conscio -ire, *to be conscious of guilt.*

conscisco -sciscĕre -scivi and -scii -scitum, *to agree on, resolve, decree; to inflict upon oneself (with or without sibi).*

conscĭus -a -um. *sharing knowledge with others, privy to a thing, cognizant of;* m. or f. as subst., *an accomplice, fellow-conspirator; sharing knowledge with oneself,* i.e. *conscious,* esp. *of right or wrong.*

conscrībo -scribĕre -scripsi -scriptum, *to enter on a list, enroll;* of troops, *to levy;* patres conscripti (patres et conscripti), *senators; to write, compose;* of physicians, *to prescribe; to write all over an object.*

conscriptio -ōnis, f. *writing, composition.*

consĕco -sĕcare -sĕcŭi -sectum, *to cut up, dismember.*

consecrātio -ōnis, f. *dedication, consecration;* of dead emperors, *apotheosis.*

consecro -are, *to consecrate;* sometimes *to dedicate to the gods below, to curse;* of persons, *to deify;* in gen., *to make holy or immortal.*

consectārĭus -a -um, *following logically,* consequent; n. pl. as subst., *logical conclusions, inferences.*

consectātio -ōnis, f. *eager pursuit, striving after.*

consectātrix -icis, f., *an eager pursuer, devoted friend.*

consectio -ōnis, f., *cutting to pieces.*

consector -ari, dep. *to follow, pursue eagerly; to make for, try to join, imitate, attain;* in hostile sense, *to chase, hunt.*

consĕcūtio -ōnis, f.: philosoph., *an effect, consequence;* rhet., *order, connexion, arrangement.*

consĕnesco -sĕnescĕre -sĕnŭi, *to become old, lose one's strength, decay.*

consensio -ōnis, f., *agreement, harmony, consent;* in bad sense, *plot, conspiracy.*

consensus -ūs m. *agreement, concord;* abl. consensu, *unanimously;* in bad sense, *secret agreement, conspiracy.*

consentānĕus -a -um, *agreeing, fit, suitable;* consentaneum est, *it is reasonable* or *suitable.*

consentio -sentire -sensi -sensum; of physical sensation, *to feel together;* of thought or sentiment, *to agree, assent, resolve unanimously;* with acc., bellum, *to resolve upon war:* in bad sense, *to plot, conspire;* of things, *to agree, harmonize.* Hence partic. **consentiens** -entis, *harmonious.*

consēpio = consaepio; q.v.

consĕquentia -ae, f., *a consequence, succession.*

consĕquia -ae, f. = consequentia; q.v.

consĕquor -sĕqui -sĕcūtus, dep. (1) *to follow, go after;* in hostile sense, *to pursue; to follow in time, follow logically, result.* (2) *to follow right up, reach, obtain, catch, get;* of states and events, *to befall, happen to a person;* in speech or thought, *to understand, grasp.* Hence partic. **consĕquens** -entis, *appropriate, consequent;* n. as subst. *a logical consequence.*

¹consĕro -sĕrĕre -sēvi -situm, *to sow, plant.* Transf., *to cover.*

²consĕro -sĕrĕre -sĕrŭi -sertum, *to connect, join, twine together;* milit., *to join in conflict,* esp. manum (or manus) conserere, *to engage.* Hence, from partic., adv. **consertē,** *connectedly.*

conserva -ae, f. *fellow slave.*

conservātio -ōnis, f. *preservation, keeping, laying up.*

conservātor -ōris, m., *preserver.*

conservo -are, *to keep, preserve, maintain.* Pres. partic. as adj. **conservans** antis, *preserving.*

conservus -i, m. *fellow slave.*

consessor ōris, m., *one who sits near, a neighbour;* in court, *an assessor.*

consessus -ūs, m. *assembly.*

considĕrātio -ōnis, f., *consideration, contemplation.*

considĕro -are, *to look at, regard carefully, contemplate;* mentally, *to consider, reflect upon.*

Hence partic. **consīdĕrātus** -a -um; pass., *well weighed, deliberate*; act., of persons, *cautious, circumspect.* Adv. **consīdĕrātē,** *thoughtfully, carefully.*

consīdo -sīdĕre -sēdi -sessum, *to sit down, to settle*; esp. *to sit down in an assembly or court*; milit., *to take up one's position or encamp.* Transf.: of things, *to settle, sink, subside*; *to be overcome or neglected*; of ideas, *to sink in*; of feelings, *to subside.*

consigno -are, *to seal; to vouch for, authenticate; to record.*

consiliārius -a -um, *deliberating*; m. as subst. *an adviser, assessor, interpreter.*

consiliātor -ōris, m., *counsellor, adviser.*

consilior -ari, dep. *to consult, take counsel; to give counsel, advise.*

consilium -i, n. (1) *deliberation, consultation*; meton., *persons in consultation, an assembly, council*; as a quality, *judgment, understanding.* (2) *a resolution, plan*; abl., *consilio, intentionally, designedly.* (3) *advice, suggestion.*

consimilis -e, *exactly similar.*

consīpio -sĭpēre, *to be in one's right mind.*

consisto -sistĕre -stĭti -stĭtum, *to take one's stand, place oneself; to stand still, stop; to be posted or to halt.* Transf., of things, *to fall to, come upon, rest on; to stop, stay; to stand firm*; with abl. etc., *to consist, be formed of.*

consĭtio -ōnis, and **consĭtūra** -ae f., *sowing, planting.*

consĭtor -ōris, m., *sower, planter.*

consōbrīnus -i, m. and **consōbrīna** -ae, f., *cousin (on the mother's side).*

consŏciātio -ōnis, f., *union, connexion.*

consŏcio -are, *to unite, connect, share, make common.*

Hence partic. **consŏciātus** -a -um, *united, harmonious.*

consōlābilis -e, *consolable.*

consōlātio -ōnis, f., *consolation, encouragement, alleviation; consoling words.*

consōlātor -ōris, m., *consoler.*

consōlātōrius -a -um, *consolatory.*

consōlor -ari, dep.: of persons, *to console, comfort, encourage*; of things, *to alleviate, lighten.*

consŏno -sŏnare -sŏnŭi. (1) *to sound together*; hence *to harmonize, agree.* (2) *to resound, echo.*

consŏnus -a -um, *sounding together, harmonious, accordant, suitable.*

consōpio -ire, *to lull to sleep, stupefy.*

consors -sortis: act., *sharing in, partaking of*; as subst., *brother or sister*; as adj., *brotherly, sisterly*; pass., *shared.*

consortio -ōnis, f., *companionship, partnership.*

consortium -i, n., *partnership, participation.*

¹**conspectus** -a -um, partic. from conspicio; q.v.

²**conspectus** -ūs m.: act., *seeing, look,* *sight, view*; hence *mental view, survey*; pass., *appearance.*

conspergo -spergĕre -spersi -spersum, *to sprinkle or moisten by sprinkling.*

conspĭcio -spĭcĕre -spexi -spectum, *to catch sight of, behold, perceive; to look at with attention, watch*; pass., conspici, *to attract notice, be gazed at.* Transf., *to see mentally, understand.*

Hence partic. **conspectus** -a -um, *visible; striking, remarkable, conspicuous.* Gerundive **conspĭcĭendus** -a -um, *worth looking at, notable.*

conspĭcor -ari, dep. *to catch sight of perceive.*

conspĭcŭus -a -um, *visible; remarkable, striking, conspicuous.*

conspīrātio -ōnis, f., *blowing or breathing together; harmony, agreement, union*; in bad sense, *conspiracy, plot.*

conspīro -are, *to blow or breathe together*; of instruments, *to blow together, sound together.* Transf., *to agree, harmonize in opinion and feeling*; in bad sense, *to conspire.*

Hence partic. **conspīrātus** -a -um, *sworn together, united by oath*; m. as subst., *a conspirator.*

consponsor -ōris, m. *a joint surety.*

conspŭo -spŭĕre, *to spit upon.*

conspurco -are, *to cover with dirt, defile.*

conspūto -are, *to spit upon.*

constans -antis, partic. from consto; q.v.

constantĭa -ae, f., *steadiness, firmness.*

consternātio -ōnis, f., *fear, alarm, dismay, confusion; mutiny, tumult.*

¹**consterno** -sternĕre -strāvi -strātum, *to strew, scatter, cover by strewing.*

Hence partic. **constrātus** -a -um; esp. constrata navis, *a decked ship*; n. as subst., *flooring, deck.*

²**consterno** -are, *to throw into confusion, alarm, frighten; to stampede.*

constipo -are, *to press, crowd together.*

constĭtŭo -stĭtŭĕre -stĭtŭi -stĭtūtum, *to cause to stand, set up, place, establish, settle*; milit., *to post, station, arrange, bring to a halt; to settle people in homes or quarters; to found, set up buildings, et:.* Transf., *to appoint a person to an office; to settle, fix upon an amount, time, etc.; to decide about a fact, decide that; to decide on a course of action, decide to.*

Hence partic. **constĭtūtus** -a -um, *arranged, settled*; n. as subst., *anything arranged, settled or agreed upon.*

constĭtūtio -ōnis, f., *the act of settling; settled condition, disposition; a regulation, order, ordinance*; rhet., *the issue, point in dispute.*

consto -stare -stĭti -stātum. (1) *to stand together*; hence *to be composed, consist; to depend upon, rest upon; to correspond, be consistent* (with dat.); with abl., *to cost.* (2) *to stand firm, stand still; to remain the same, be unaltered*; of resolves, *to be fixed, firm*; of evidence, facts, etc., *to be*

established, sure, well-known; impers.
constat, *it is agreed*; in gen., *to exist.*
Hence partic. **constans** -antis,
*steady, firm, unchanging, constant,
consistent, resolute*; adv. **constantĕr,**
steadily, firmly.

constringo -stringĕre -strinxi -strictum,
*to bind together, bind fast, confine,
restrain*; in speech, *to compress,
abbreviate.*

constructĭo -ōnis, f., *putting together,
building, construction.*

constrŭo -strŭĕre -struxi -structum, *to
heap up together; to construct, build
up; to arrange.*

constuprātor -ōris, m. *ravisher, de-
baucher.*

constupro -are *to debauch, ravish,
corrupt.*

consuāsor -ōris, m. *an adviser.*

consuĕfācĭo -făcĕre -fēci -factum, *to
accustom, habituate.*

consuesco -suescĕre -suēvi -suētum:
transit., *to accustom, habituate*; intransit., *to accustom oneself*; in perf.,
consuevi, *I am accustomed*; cum
homine, *to cohabit with a person.*
Hence partic. **consuetus** -a -um:
of persons, *accustomed to*; of things,
accustomed, usual.

consuētūdo -inis, f., *custom, usage,
habit*; of relations with persons,
intimacy, familiar acquaintance; of
lovers, *intrigue.*

consuētus -a -um, partic. from consuesco; q.v.

consul -sŭlis, m., *a consul*; plur.,
consules, the consuls, *the two chief
magistrates at Rome under the Republic*; consul designatus, *consul
elect*; pro consule, *an officer in the
place of the consul, a proconsul, e.g. a
governor of a province.*

consŭlāris -e. (1) *relating to a consul,
consular.* (2) *having been a consul*;
m. as subst., *an ex-consul,* or *provincial governor of consular rank.*
Adv. **consŭlārĭtĕr**, *in a manner
worthy of a consul.*

consŭlātus -ūs, m. *the office of consul,
consulship.*

consŭlo -sŭlĕre -sŭlŭi -sultum. (1) *to
reflect, consult, consider*; with dat.,
to look to the interests of; as a result of
deliberation, *to come to a conclusion,
to take measures*; boni (or optimi)
consulere, *to take in good part.* (2) *to
ask the advice of, consult.*
Hence partic. **consultus** -a -um:
of things, *well considered, deliberated
upon*; of persons, *experienced* (with
genit). N. as subst. **consultum** -i:
the act of deliberation, *reflection,
consideration*; the result of deliberation, *a resolution, plan, decision*; esp.
a decree of the senate at Rome.
Abl. as adv. **consulto**, *deliberately,
designedly.* Adv. **consultē**, *advisedly,
after consideration.*

consultātĭo -ōnis, f.. *a full consideration, deliberation; an asking for
advice, inquiry.*

consulto -are. (1) *to consider maturely,*

weigh, ponder; with dat., *to look to
the interests of.* (2) *to consult, ask
advice of.*

consultor -ōris, m. (1) *an adviser.*
(2) *one who asks advice, esp. legal
advice; a client.*

consummātĭo -ōnis, f. *a summing up,
adding up; a finishing, completion.*

consummo -are, *to add together, sum
up; to form a whole, complete,
perfect.*
Hence partic. **consummātus** -a
-um, *complete, perfect.*

consūmo -sūmĕre -sumpsi -sumptum,
to spend, employ on a purpose; in
gen., *to use up, finish, waste away,
destroy.*

consŭo -sŭĕre -sŭi -sūtum, *to stitch* or
put together; to form.

consurgo -surgĕre -surrexi -surrectum,
to rise up, stand up, esp. *to speak,* or
as a mark of respect. Transf.: of
persons, *to be roused to action*; of
things, *to arise, break out.*

consurrectĭo -ōnis, f., *a general
standing up.*

contābesco -tābescĕre -tābŭi, *to waste
away gradually.*

contăbŭlātĭo -ōnis, f., *planking, floor,
storey.*

contăbŭlo -are, *to cover with boards,
equip with floors* or *storeys.*

contactus -ūs, m., *contact, touching;
contagion.*

contāgēs -is, f., *touch, contact.*

contāgĭo -ōnis, f., and **contāgĭum** -i,
n., *touching, contact*; hence *contagion,
infection.*

contāmĭno -are, *to pollute, infect*; of
authors, *to blend (and so spoil)* Greek
plays.

contĕgo -tĕgĕre -texi -tectum, *to
cover, shield.*

contemno -temnĕre -tempsi -temptum,
to think meanly of, despise, contemn.
Hence partic. **contemptus** -a -um,
despised; despicable, contemptible.

contemplātĭo -ōnis, f., *surveying,
contemplation.*

contemplor -ari, dep., *to mark out*;
hence *to look at attentively, survey,
regard; to consider carefully.*

contemptim, *contemptuously.*

contemptĭo -ōnis, f., *contempt, scorn,
disdain.*

contemptor -ōris, m., **contemptrix**
-ricis, f., adj. and subst., *a despiser,
contemptuous.*

¹**contemptus** -a -um, partic. from
contemno; q.v.

²**contemptus** -ūs, m., *contempt, disdain.*

contendo -tendĕre -tendi -tentum, *to
strain, stretch, exert*; of missiles, *to
shoot, cast*; intransit., *to strive,
strain, exert oneself, hasten*; of statements, *to assert with confidence,
maintain.* In relation to another:
transit., *to compare, contrast*; intransit., *to compete.*
Hence partic. **contentus** -a -um,
*strained, stretched, tense; eager,
zealous.* Adv. **contentē**, *eagerly,
earnestly.*

¹**contentē**, adv. from contendo; q.v.
²**contentē**, adv. from contineo; q.v.
contentio -ōnis, f., *exertion, effort, straining, striving.* In relation to another, *contrast, comparison*; or *combat, contest, strife.*
¹**contentus** -a -um, partic. from contendo; q.v.
²**contentus** -a -um, *contented*, partic. from contineo; q.v.
conterminus -a -um, *bordering upon, adjacent, near.*
contĕro -tĕrĕre -trīvi -trītum, *to rub away, grind, pound*; in gen., *to wear away, destroy, obliterate*; of time, *to consume, spend.*
conterrĕo -ēre, *to terrify, frighten much.*
contestor -ari, dep. *to call to witness*; litem, *to start an action by calling witnesses*; partic. **contestātus** -a -um, in pass. sense, *witnessed to, approved.*
contexo -texĕre -texŭi -textum, *to weave* or *twine together, connect, unite, construct, form.*
    Hence partic. **contextus** -a -um, *interwoven, connected, united.* adv. **contextē**, *in close connexion.*
¹**contextus** -a -um, partic. from contexo; q.v.
²**contextus** -ūs, m., *uniting, connexion.*
conticesco (**contĭcisco**) -ticescĕre -ticŭi, *to become silent, be stilled, abate.*
contignātio -ōnis, f., *floor of planks.*
contigno -are, *to floor with planks.*
contiguus -a -um, *touching, contiguous, near*; with dat., *within reach of.*
continens -entis, partic. from contineo; q.v.
continentia -ae, f., *self-control, moderation, temperance.*
continĕo -tinēre -tinŭi -tentum. (1) *to hold together, keep together*; to connect, join. (2) *to keep in, surround, contain, confine*; hence *to include, comprise.* (3) *to hold back, restrain.* Hence pres. partic. **continens** -entis. (1) *lying near, adjacent.* (2) *hanging together, unbroken, continuous*; f. as subst., *a continent*; n. as subst., rhet., *a main point.* (3) *self-controlled, temperate, continent.* Adv. **continenter**, *without break, continuously*; *continently, temperately.* Partic. **contentus** -a -um, *contented, satisfied* (with abl.).
contingo -tingĕre -tĭgi -tactum: transit., *to touch, reach, grasp*; *to touch with* something, *smear* or *sprinkle* with; hence *to affect, infect* (esp. in perf. partic.); geograph. *to border on*; intransit., *to happen, befall*, usually of good luck (with dat.).
continŭātio -ōnis, f., *unbroken continuance* or *succession*; rhet., *a period.*
continŭĭtās -ātis, f., *continuity, unbroken succession.*
¹**continŭō**, adv. from continuus; q.v.
²**continŭo** -are, *to connect up, unite, make continuous, form into a series*; verba, *to make into a sentence*; magistratum, *to prolong.*

continŭus -a -um, *connected up, hanging together, continuous, uninterrupted.* N. abl. as adv. **continŭō**, *immediately, at once*; in argument, *necessarily, as an immediate consequence.*
contio -ōnis, f., *an assembly, public meeting.* Transf. *a speech made in such an assembly*, or *the speaker's platform.*
contiōnābundus -a -um, *haranguing, speaking in public.*
contiōnālis -e and **contiōnārius** -a -um, *relating to a public assembly.*
contiōnātor -ōris, m., *a popular orator, demagogue.*
contiōnor -ari, dep., *to attend an assembly*; esp. *to speak in public before an assembly.*
contiuncŭla -ae, f., *a short harangue.*
contorquĕo -torquēre -torsi -tortum *to twist, whirl, turn violently, contort*; *to whirl* a spear, etc., in throwing, and so *to hurl.*
    Hence partic. **contortus** -a -um. (1) *intricate, confused, complicated.* (2) *whirling*; so *powerful, vigorous.* Adv. **contortē**, *intricately.*
contortio -ōnis, f., *whirling, twisting, intricacy.*
contra. Adv., *opposite, over against, on the opposite side*; of equivalence, *in return back*; of difference, *otherwise*; of opposition, *against.* Prep., with acc., *opposite to, over against*; *against, in opposition to.*
contractio -ōnis, f., *drawing together, contraction*; orationis, *abbreviation*; animi, *anxiety, depression.*
contractus -a -um, partic. from contraho; q.v.
contrādico -dicĕre -dixi -dictum, *to gainsay, contradict.*
contrādictio -ōnis, f., *a speaking against, contradiction.*
contrāho -trahĕre -traxi -tractum. (1) *to draw together, collect, unite*; *to conclude* or *complete* any arrangement; in gen., *to cause, bring on, bring about*; aes alienum, *to contract debt.* (2) *to shorten, narrow, contract, reduce*; frontem, *to frown*; vela, *to furl one's sails*; of the spirits, *to depress.*
    Hence partic. **contractus** -a -um, *contracted, narrow, straitened*; of persons, *retired, quiet.*
contrārius -a -um, *opposite, opposed, contrary*; vulnera, *wounds in front*; with genit. or dat., *opposed to*; in gen., *hostile, injurious.* N. as subst. **contrārium** -i, *the opposite*; ex contrario, *on the other side.* Adv. **contrāriē**, *in an opposite direction* or *manner.*
contrectātio -ōnis, f., *touching, handling.*
contrecto -are, *to touch, feel, handle*; of familiar handling, *to violate*; mentally, *to consider.*
contrĕmisco -trĕmiscĕre -trĕmŭi: intransit., *to tremble, quake*; transit, *to tremble before, be afraid of.*

contrĕmo -ĕre, *to tremble, quake.*

contrĭbŭo -trĭbŭĕre -trĭbŭi -trĭbūtum, *to brigade with, incorporate, unite;* of contributions, *to bring in.*

contristo -are, *to make sad or gloomy.*

contrītus -a -um, partic. from contero; q.v.

contrŏversĭa -ae, f., *a dispute* (esp. at law); sine controversia, *indisputably.*

contrŏversĭōsus -a -um, *strongly disputed.*

contrŏversus -a -um, *disputed, controverted.*

contrūcīdo -are, *to cut in pieces, hew down, slay.*

contrūdo -trūdĕre -trūsi -trūsum, *to thrust, push together.*

contrunco -are, *to cut in pieces.*

contŭbernālis -is, c. (1) *a messmate comrade.* (2) *a young staff-officer.*

contŭbernĭum -i, n. Concrete, *a soldiers' tent; the common dwelling of a male and female slave.* Abstract, *comradeship, companionship, intimacy; concubinage; junior staff duties.*

contŭĕor -tŭēri -tŭĭtus, dep. *to see, survey, look at attentively;* mentally, *to consider, reflect upon.*

contŭĭtū (contūtū), abl. sing. m., *by surveying.*

contŭmācĭa -ae, f., *firmness, stubbornness, obstinacy.*

contŭmax -ācis, *firm, stubborn, obstinate;* adv. contŭmācĭtĕr.

contŭmēlĭa -ae, f. *outrage, physical violence;* of speech, *insult, affront.*

contŭmēlĭōsus -a -um, adj. *outrageous, insulting, abusive;* adv. contŭmēlĭōsē.

contŭmŭlo -are, *to bury, inter.*

contundo -tundĕre -tūdi -tūsum, *to bruise, crush, pound, beat up, break up, demolish.*

contŭor -i = contueor; q.v.

conturbātĭo -ōnis f., *disorder, confusion.*

conturbo -are, *to throw into disorder, disturb, distress; to ruin, make bankrupt.*

contus -i, m. *a pole used in boating; a long spear or pike.*

cōnus -i, m., *a cone; the apex of a helmet.*

convălesco -vălescĕre -vălŭi, *to become strong, establish oneself;* esp. *to recover from a disease, get well.*

convallis -is, f., *an enclosed valley.*

convāso -are, *to pack up baggage.*

convecto -are, *to bring together, collect.*

convector -ōris, m. *a fellow-traveller.*

convĕho -vĕhĕre -vexi -vectum, *to bring together, carry into one place.*

convello -vellĕre -velli -vulsum, *to pluck up, pull away, wrench off;* milit., convellere signa, *to decamp;* in gen., *to weaken, overthrow, destroy.*

convĕna -ae, c.: adj. *coming together;* as subst., in plur., *a concourse, assembled multitude.*

convĕnĭentĭa -ae, f., *agreement, harmony, conformity.*

convĕnĭo -vĕnīre -vēni -ventum. (1) *to meet;* intransit., *to come to-* gether, assemble; legal, convenire in manum, of the wife, *to come into the power of her husband;* transit., *to visit, meet, call upon.* (2) *to fit, be suitable, be congenial;* impers. convenit, *it is fitting.* (3) *to agree;* usually in pass. sense, *to be agreed upon;* impers., convenit, *it is agreed.* Hence partic. convĕnĭens -entis *agreeing, unanimous, concordant; fit, appropriate, suitable;* adv. convĕnĭentĕr, *agreeably, suitably.* N. of perf. partic. as subst., conventum -i, *an agreement, compact.*

conventĭcŭlum -i, n., *a coming together, assembly, association; a place of meeting.*

conventĭo -ōnis, f. *assembly; agreement, compact.*

conventum; see convenio.

conventus -ūs, m. *coming together, assembly, union, congress;* conventus agere, *to hold assizes;* in gen., *agreement.*

converro -verrĕre -verri -versum, *to sweep together, brush up; to beat thoroughly; to scrape together.*

conversātĭo -ōnis, f., *frequent use;* esp. *frequent sojourn in a place,* or *regular dealings with persons.*

conversĭo -ōnis, f. *a turning round, alteration,* or *periodical return;* rhet. *rounding off of a period,* or *repetition of word at the end of a clause.*

converso -are, *to turn round often;* pass. in middle sense, *to live, consort, have dealings.*

converto -vertĕre -verti -versum. (1) *to turn round, whirl round;* se convertere, *to revolve, to turn back;* milit., signa convertere, *to wheel round;* terga, or se, convertĕre, *to flee.* Transf., *to change, alter;* of books, *to translate.* (2) *to turn in any direction, direct;* conversus ad, *facing.* Transf., *to direct, devote* (esp. with reflex.); rarely intransit.); pecuniam publicam domum, *to embezzle.*

convestĭo -ire, *to clothe; to cover, surround.*

convexus -a -um. (1) *vaulted, arched, convex;* n. as subst., arch. (2) *sloping downwards.*

convīcĭātor -ōris, m., *a railer, reviler.*

convīcĭor -ari, dep., *to rail, revile.*

convīcĭum -i, n. *a loud cry, shout, clamour;* esp. *abuse, reproach, insult;* hence, in gen., *censure, reproof*

convictĭo -ōnis, f. *intercourse, familiarity;* meton., *familiar friends.*

convictor -ōris, m., *a constant associate.*

convictus -ūs, m. *living together, intercourse; entertainment, feast.*

convinco -vincĕre -vici -victum, *to convict of a crime; to prove mistaken;* of things, esp. *crimes or mistakes, to prove conclusively, demonstrate.*

convīso -ere, *to examine carefully;* poet. *to beam upon.*

convīva -ae, m. *guest.*

convīvālis -e, *of a feast.*

convīvātor -ōris, m. *a host.*

convīvĭum -i, n. *a feast, entertainment, banquet*; meton., *the company assembled, guests.*

convīvo -vīvĕre -vixi -victum, *to live with, to feast with.*

convīvor -ari, dep. *to feast* (as a guest).

convŏcātĭo -ōnis, f. *calling together.*

convŏco -are, *to call together, assemble, convoke.*

convŏlo -are, *to fly together, run together.*

convolvo -volvĕre -volvi -vōlūtum, *to roll together* or *roll round; to intertwine.*

convŏmo -ere, *to vomit all over.*

convulsus -a -um, partic. of convello; q.v.

cŏŏpĕrĭo -ŏpĕrīre -ŏpĕrŭi -ŏpertum, *to cover up, envelop, overwhelm;* lapidibus *to stone to death.*

cŏoptātĭo -ōnis, f., *election of a colleague, co-optation;* censoria, *filling up of the senate by the censors.*

cŏopto -are, *to choose, elect, co-opt.*

cŏŏrĭor -ŏrīri -ortus, dep., *to arise, come forth together;* of things, *to appear, to break out;* of people, *to rise for insurrection or fight.*

cŏortus -ūs, m., *arising, breaking forth.*

Cŏos (Cŏus) = Cos; q.v.

cōphĭnus -i, m , *basket, hamper.*

cōpĭa -ae, f., *plenty, abundance* (of persons or things); milit., *supplies, provisions;* also *troops, forces* (esp. plur.). Transf., *means, opportunity;* with genit. of person, *access to.*

cōpĭōsus -a -um, *richly provided, wealthy; plentiful, abundant;* of speech, *copious, eloquent.* Adv. **cōpĭōsē**, *abundantly, plentifully, copiously.*

cōpo, cōpōna = caupo, caupona; q.v.

cōpŭla -ae, f., *a link, bond, tie, connexion; a rope, a leash;* plur. grapnels.

cōpŭlātĭo -ōnis, f., *union, connexion.*

cōpŭlo -are, *to join together, connect, unite.*
Hence partic. **cōpŭlātus** -a -um, *connected, united, coupled.*

cŏquo cŏquĕre coxi coctum, *to cook, prepare food; to burn, ripen; to digest;* mentally: *to think of, meditate, contrive a thing; to harass a person.*

cŏquus (cŏcus) -i m. and **cŏqua** -ae, f., *a cook.*

cŏr, cordis, n., *the heart;* often as seat of emotions or thought, *heart, mind, judgment;* meton., *a person.*

cŏram. Adv., *personally, openly, face to face.* Prep., with abl. *in presence of.*

corbis -is, m. and f. *a wicker basket.*

corbīta -ae, f., *a slow-sailing merchant vessel.*

corcŭlum -i, n., *little heart.*

Corcȳra -ae, f., *Corcyra, an island in the Ionian Sea.*

cordātus -a -um, *prudent, wise;* adv. **cordātē.**

Cordŭba -ae, f. *a town in Hispania Baetica* (now *Cordova*).

Cŏrinthus -i, f. *Corinth, a city of Greece.*

Cŏrĭŏli -orum, m. pl. *a town of the Volsci in Latium;* adj. **Cŏrĭŏlānus** -a -um.

cŏrĭum -i, n. *hide, skin, leather; a leathern thong, strap.*

Cornēlĭus -a -um, *name of a Roman gens, including the Scipios.* Adj. **Cornēlĭānus** -a -um.

cornĕŏlus -a -um, *horny.*

¹cornĕus -a -um, *horny, made of horn; like horn, hard.*

²cornĕus -a -um, *of cornel-tree;* or *cornel-wood.*

cornĭcĕn -cĭnis, m., *a horn-blower.*

cornĭcŭlum -i, n. *a little horn; a horn-shaped decoration for soldiers.*

cornĭger -gĕra -gĕrum, *horned.*

cornĭpēs -pĕdis, *horn-footed, hoofed.*

cornix -īcis, f. *crow.*

cornū -ūs, n. *a horn;* fig., *strength, courage; anything made of horn,* esp. *a bow, trumpet, lantern; anything resembling a horn,* esp. *a hoof, beak, tip of a helmet, end of a stick* or *spar, end of a promontory, wing of an army.*

Cornūcōpĭa -ae, *the horn of Amalthea, symbol of plenty.*

cornum -i, n. *the cornel-cherry;* meton. *a spear of cornel-wood.*

cornus -i (and -ūs), f. *the cornel-tree;* hence *the wood of the cornel-tree, a spear of cornel-wood.*

cornūtus -a -um, *horned.*

cŏrolla -ae, f., *a little crown.*

cŏrollārĭum -i, n. *a garland of flowers; a present, gratuity.*

cŏrōna -ae, f. *garland, chaplet, crown;* sub corona vendere, *to sell into slavery prisoners of war (wearing chaplets).* Transf., *anything resembling a crown; a constellation; a circle of people, audience;* milit. *besiegers* (or *defenders*) *of a city.*

cŏrōnārĭus -a -um, *of a garland.*

cŏrōno -are, *to wreath, crown with a garland; to surround, enclose in a circle.*

corpŏrĕus -a -um, *of the body, bodily; of flesh.*

corpŭlentus -a -um, *fat, stout.*

corpus -pŏris, n. *body, substance, matter;* esp. *the body* of men and animals; *flesh, the trunk;* sometimes *a corpse.* Transf., *a person, "a body";* the "*body politic*"; in gen., *the main mass* of a thing.

corpuscŭlum -i, n. *a little particle, atom; a small body.*

corrādo -rādĕre -rāsi -rāsum, *to scrape* or *rake together.*

correctĭo -ōnis, f., *straightening out, improvement, amendment.*

corrector -ōris, m. *improver, amender, corrector.*

correpo -rēpere -repsi -reptum, *to creep, slink, crawl.*

correptĭus, compar. adv. from corripio; q.v.

corrĭgĭa -ae, f. *a shoe-string, boot-lace.*

corrĭgo -rĭgĕre -rexi -rectum, *to put straight, set right, reform, amend.*

corrĭpĭo -rĭpĕre -rĭpŭi -reptum, *to seize, snatch up; pecuniam, to steal;*

viam, *to hasten on a journey*; se, *to hurry off.* Transf., of disease, etc., *to attack*; of the passions, *to over-come*; of persons, *to blame, rebuke, accuse, bring to trial*; in time, *to shorten*; hence, from partic., compar. adv. **correptius**, *more shortly.*

corrŏbŏro -are, *to strengthen, invigorate.*

corrōdo -rōdere -rōsi, -rōsum, *to gnaw away.*

corrŏgo -are, *to get together, collect by begging.*

corrūgo -are, *to wrinkle up.*

corrumpo -rumpĕre -rūpi -ruptum. (1) *to break up, destroy, annihilate.* (2) *to spoil, make worse, weaken*; of documents, *to falsify*; of characters, *to corrupt*; corrumpere pecuniā, *to bribe.*
     Hence partic. **corruptus** -a -um, *spoilt, damaged, corrupt*; adv. **cor-ruptē**, *corruptly, incorrectly.*

corrŭo -rŭere -rŭi: intransit. *to fall to the ground, sink down, be ruined*; transit., *to throw down, overthrow.*

corruptēla -ae, f., *corruption, bribery, seduction*; meton., *a corrupter.*

corruptĭo -ōnis, f. *corrupting; a corrupt state.*

corruptor -ōris, m. *corrupter, seducer, briber.*

corruptus -a -um, partic. from corrumpo; q.v.

cors = cohors; q.v.

Corsĭca -ae, f. *the island of Corsica*; adj. **Corsus** and **Corsĭcus** -a -um.

cortex -tĭcis, m. and f. *bark, rind, shell*; esp. *the bark of the cork tree, cork.*

cortīna -ae, f. *a round kettle or cauldron*; esp. *the cauldron-shaped Delphic tripod*: cortina Phoebi, *the oracle of Apollo.*

cŏrŭlus = corylus; q.v.

cŏrus = caurus; q.v.

cŏrusco -are: transit., *to move quickly, swing, shake*; intransit., *to tremble, flutter*; of light, *to twinkle, flash.*

cŏruscus -a -um, *shaking, trembling*: of light, *twinkling, flashing.*

corvus -i, m. *a raven*; perhaps also *a rook.*

Cŏrȳbantes -ium, m. pl. *the priests of Cybele.*

cŏrȳcus -i, m. *a sand-bag, a punch-ball.*

cŏrȳlētum -i, n. *a hazel copse.*

cŏrȳlus -i, f. *a hazel tree.*

cŏrymbus -i, m. *a bunch of flowers or fruit*, esp. *a cluster of ivy berries.*

cŏryphaeus -i, m. *a leader, chief.*

cŏrȳtus or **cŏrȳtos** -i, m. *a quiver.*

¹**cōs** cōtis, f. *any hard, flinty stone*; esp. *a whetstone, grindstone.*

²**Cōs** or **Cŏus (Cŏos)** Coi, f. *a small island in the Aegean Sea*; adj. **Cŏus** -a -um; n. sing. as subst., *Coan wine*; n. plur., *Coan garments.*

cosmēta -ae, m. *a woman's valet.*

cosmĭcos -a -um, *of the world*; m. as subst. *a citizen of the world.*

costa -ae, f. *a rib or side.*

costum -i, n. *an eastern aromatic plant.*

cŏthurnātus -a -um, *in buskins*; hence *tragic, elevated.*

cŏthurnus -i, m. *a large hunting boot; a boot or buskin worn by tragic actors*; hence *tragedy, elevated style.*

cotid. = cottid.; q.v.

cottăna (cotŏna, coctŏna, coctăna) -orum, n. *a kind of small fig.*

cŏturnix -īcis, f. *a quail.*

cŏvinnārĭus -i, m. *a soldier in a war chariot.*

cŏvinnus -i, m. *a war-chariot; a travelling-chariot.*

coxa -ae, f. *the hip-bone.*

coxendix -īcis, f. *the hip.*

crabro -ōnis, m. *a hornet.*

crambē -ēs, f. *cabbage.*

crāpŭla -ae, f. *drunkenness*; its *after-effects*, "*hangover*"

crās, *tomorrow.*

crassĭtūdo -ĭnis, f. *thickness, density.*

¹**crassus** -a -um, *thick, dense, solid*; aer, *misty, heavy*; of intellect, *dull or uneducated.* Adv. **crassē**, *roughly, rudely.*

²**Crassus** -i, m. *name of a family in the gens Licinia*; q.v.

crastĭnus -a -um, *of tomorrow*; n. as subst. *the morrow.*

crātēra -ae, f. and **crātēr** -ēris, m. *a bowl, esp. for mixing wine with water*; *the crater of a volcano*; *a constellation, the Bowl.*

crātis -is, *a wicker frame, hurdle, a harrow*; milit. *fascines*; favorum, *honeycomb*; spinae, *the joints of the backbone.*

creātio -ōnis, f., *choice, election.*

creātor -ōris, m. and **creātrix** -īcis, f. *maker, founder; parent.*

creber -bra -brum; of space, *thick, crowded together, close, numerous*; with abl., *crowded with, full of*; of time, *repeated, numerous, frequent*; of persons, to signify *repeated* action, e.g. creber pulsat, *he beats repeatedly.* Adv. **crēbrō**, *repeatedly, often.*

crēbresco (crēbesco) -escĕre -ŭi, *to become frequent, increase, gather strength.*

crēbrītās -ātis, f. *frequency.*

crēbrō, adv. from creber; q.v.

crēdĭbilis -e, *credible, worthy of belief*; adv. **crēdĭbĭliter**, *credibly.*

crēdĭtor -ōris, m., *a creditor.*

crēdo -dĕre -dĭdi -dĭtum, *to trust*: with acc. and dat., *to entrust, commit*, esp. of secrets and money; n. of perf. partic. as subst., creditum, *a loan*; with dat., *to trust in, rely upon*; also with dat., *to believe, give credence to*; with acc., *to believe as a fact, to accept as true*; in gen., *to believe, think, be of opinion.*

crēdŭlĭtās -ātis, f., *credulity.*

crēdŭlus -a -um, *believing easily, credulous, confiding.*

crĕmo -are, *to burn, consume with fire.*

crĕmor -ōris, m. *juice, pulp, cream.*

crĕo -are, *to make, create, produce; to elect* to an office; of parents, *to beget, bear.*

crĕpīda -ae, f. *sandal.*

crĕpīdātus -a -um, *wearing sandals.*

crěpīdo -ĭnis, f., *a base, foundation, pedestal; a quay, pier, dam.*

crěpĭtācŭlum and **crěpĭtācillum** -i, n. *a rattle.*

crěpĭto -are, *to rattle, creak, crackle, rustle.*

crěpĭtus -ūs, m. *rattling, creaking, rustling, clattering:* digitorum, *snapping of the fingers.*

crěpo -are -ŭi -ĭtum: intransit., *to creak, rattle, rustle, crackle;* digiti crepantis signa, *a snapping of the fingers;* transit., *to make resound; to chatter about.*

crěpundĭa -orum, n. pl. *a child's plaything; a rattle or amulet.*

crěpuscŭlum -i, n. *twilight.*

cresco crescěre crēvi crētum. (1) *to come into existence, spring forth, arise;* past partic. crētus, *sprung (from).* (2) *of what exists, to grow, grow up, increase in size, height,* etc.; luna crescens, *waxing;* fig., *to increase in fame, power,* etc.

¹Crēta -ae, f. and **Crētē** -ēs, f. *Crete.* Hence m. adj. and subst. **Crēs** -ētis; f. adj. and subst. **Cressa** -ae; adj. **Crētensis** -e, and **Crēticus** -a -um, *Cretan.*

²crēta -ae, f. *chalk,* or *fuller's earth.*

crētātus -a -um, *chalked;* hence *in white.*

crētĭo -ōnis, f. *a declaration by an heir accepting an inheritance.*

crētōsus -a -um, *abounding in chalk.*

crētŭla -ae, f. *white clay for sealing.*

Crěūsa -ae, f. *wife of Aeneas.*

cribrum -i, n. *a sieve.*

crimen -ĭnis, n. (1) *an accusation, charge:* esse in crimine, *to be accused;* meton., *an object of reproach.* (2) *fault, guilt, crime;* meton., *cause of crime.*

crimĭnātĭo -ōnis, f. *accusation, calumny, charge.*

crimĭnātor -ōris, m. *accuser, calumniator.*

crimĭnor -ari, dep: with acc. of person, *to accuse, charge;* esp. *to calumniate;* with acc. of offence, *to complain of, bring up.*

crimĭnōsus -a -um, *reproachful, calumnious, slanderous;* adv. **crimĭnōsē,** *by way of accusation, reproachfully.*

crīnālis -e, *of* or *for the hair;* n. as subst. *a hair-band.*

crīnis -is, m. *hair;* esp. in pl.; of a comet, *the tail.*

crīnītus -a -um, *hairy, with long hair;* stella crinita, *a comet;* galea, *crested.*

crispĭsulcans -antis, *forked, wavy.*

crispo -are, *to curl; to move rapidly, brandish;* intransit. partic. **crispans** -antis, *curled, wavy.*

crispŭlus -a -um, *curly-haired, curly.*

crispus -a -um, *curly, curly-headed; trembling, quivering.*

crista -ae, f., *the crest, plume;* of a cock, *the comb.*

cristātus -a -um, *with a crest, plume* or *comb.*

crŏcěus -a -um, *of saffron; saffron-coloured, golden, yellow.*

crŏcĭnus -a -um, *of saffron, saffron-*

coloured, yellow; n. as subst. *saffron oil.*

crŏcŏdīlus -i, m. *crocodile.*

crŏcŏtŭla -ae, f., *a saffron-coloured robe.*

crŏcus -i, m. and **crŏcum** -i n. *the crocus; saffron,* prepared from crocus; hence *the colour of saffron, yellow.*

Croesus -i, m., *a king of Lydia, famous for his wealth.*

crŏtālĭa -orum, n. *ear-rings.*

crŏtālistrĭa -ae, f. *a castanet-dancer*

crŏtălum -i, n. *a castanet.*

Crŏtōn -ōnis, c. *a Greek town near the " toe " of Italy.*

crŭcĭāmentum -i, n. *torture.*

crŭcĭātus -ūs, m., *torture, torment.*

crŭcĭo -are, *to torture, torment.*

crūdēlis -e, adj. *unfeeling, cruel;* adv. **crūdēlĭter.**

crūdēlĭtās -ātis, f., *cruelty, inhumanity.*

crūdesco -escěre -ŭi, *to become hard* or *violent.*

crūdĭtās -ātis, f., *overloading of the stomach, indigestion.*

crūdus -a -um, adj. (1) *bleeding.* (2) *uncooked, raw;* of material, *fresh, not prepared;* of fruit *unripe,* in gen. *green, fresh, immature, untimely;* of food, *undigested;* of persons, *stuffed, dyspeptic;* of feeling, etc., *hard, cruel;* of the voice, *harsh.*

crŭento -are, *to make bloody, stain with blood.*

crŭentus -a -um, *bloody, bloodthirsty; blood-red.*

crŭmēna -ae, f. *a pouch, purse; store of money, funds.*

crŭor -ōris, m. *blood shed, gore; murder, slaughter.*

crūs crūris, n. *the shin, shin-bone, leg;* of a bridge, *pier, support.*

crusta -ae, f. (1) *crust, rind, shell, bark.* (2) *inlaid work, bas-relief, embossing.*

crustŭlum -i, n. *a little cake.*

crustum -i, n. *bread, cake.*

crux crŭcis, f. *a cross;* hence *torment, trouble;* as a term of abuse, *gallows bird.*

crypta -ae, f. *covered gallery, vault, grotto.*

crystallĭnus -a -um, *of crystal;* pl. as subst., *crystal vases.*

crystallus -i, f. and **crystallum** -i, n. *crystal; a crystal drinking vessel; a precious stone looking like crystal.*

cŭbĭcŭlāris -e, *of a bedchamber.*

cŭbĭcŭlārĭus -a -um, *of a bedchamber;* m. as subst. *a chamber-servant.*

cŭbĭcŭlum -i, n. *bedroom.*

cŭbīle -is, n. *bed;* esp. *marriage-bed;* of animals, *lair, den, nest;* of bees, *hives;* in. gen., *seat, resting-place.*

cŭbĭtal -tālis, n., *an elbow cushion.*

cŭbĭtālis -e, *one cubit long.*

cŭbĭto -are, *to lie down often.*

cŭbĭtum -i, n. *the elbow; a cubit.*

cŭbĭtus -ūs, m. *lying down.*

cŭbo -are -ŭi -ĭtum, *to lie down, recline;* esp. *at table or in bed; to be ill in bed;* cubitum ire, *to go to bed;* of things, *to lie;* partic. cubans, *sloping.*

cŭcullus -i, m. *a hood, cowl.*

cŭcŭlus -i, m. *cuckoo.*

cŭcŭmis -měris, m. *cucumber.*

cŭcurbĭta -ae, f. *a gourd; a cupping-glass.*

cŭdo -ĕre, *to beat, pound, thresh;* of metals, *to forge, stamp, coin.*

cŭiās -ātis, *of what country?*

cuicuimŏdi *of whatever kind.*

cŭius (quoius) -a -um: interrog., *whose?;* relat., *whose;* quoia causa, *wherefore.*

cŭiuscěmŏdi, *of whatever kind.*

cŭiusdammŏdi, *of a certain kind.*

cŭiusmŏdi, *of what kind?*

cŭiusquěmŏdi, *of every kind.*

culcĭta -ae, f. *bolster, pillow.*

cŭlěus = culleus; q.v.

cŭlex -ĭcis, m. *gnat, midge.*

cŭlina -ae, f. *kitchen;* meton., *food, fare.*

cullěus (cūlěus) -i, m. *a leather sack.*

culmen -ĭnis, n. *top, summit; the ridge of a roof; a stalk.*

culmus -i, m. *stalk, haulm, thatch.*

culpa -ae, f. *fault, blame;* esp. *the fault of unchastity;* meton., *a cause of error or sin.*

culpo -are, *to blame, find fault with, disapprove.*

cultellus -i, m. *a little knife.*

culter -tri, m. *a knife; a ploughshare, coulter.*

cultĭo -ōnis, f. *cultivation, agriculture.*

cultor -ōris, m., *a cultivator, planter, husbandman;* with genit., *an inhabitant, occupier of a place; a friend, supporter of a person; a worshipper of gods.*

cultrix -ĭcis f. *she who tends* or *takes care; an inhabitant.*

cultūra -ae, f. *tilling, culture, cultivation, husbandry;* animi, *mental culture, cultivation;* potentis amici, *courting of.*

¹cultus -a -um, partic. from colo; q.v.

²cultus -ūs, m. *tilling, cultivation, tending;* in gen., *care, careful treatment;* deorum, *reverence,* animi, *training, education;* hence *refinement, culture, civilization.*

cŭlullus -i, m. *a drinking-vessel.*

¹cum (older form quom) conj., *when; whenever; since; although;* cum . . . tum . . ., *both . . . and. . . .*

²cum, prep., with abl., *with, together with; at the same time as;* cum eo quod, ut, or ne, *on condition that.*

Cŭmae -arum, f. *a city of Campania;* adj. Cūmānus and Cūmaeus -a -um.

cumba (cymba) -ae, f. *small boat, skiff.*

cŭměra -ae, f. *a corn-bin.*

cŭmĭnum -i, n. *a herb, cummin.*

cumprimis, see primus.

cumque (cunque, quomque) adverb, usually found added to a relative, with the force of *-ever, -soever.*

cŭmŭlo -are, *to heap up, pile up, increase, heighten; to fill up, overload;* cumulatus laude, *loaded with praise;* also *to crown, bring to perfection.*

Hence partic. cŭmŭlātus -a -um: *heaped up, increased, enlarged; crowned, perfected.* Adv. cŭmŭlātē, *abundantly, fully.*

cŭmŭlus -i, m. *heap, pile, mass; addition, increase, finishing touch.*

cūnābŭla -orum, n. pl. *cradle.*

cūnae -arum, f. pl., *cradle,* of young birds, *nest.*

cunctābundus -a -um, *loitering, dilatory.*

cunctātĭo -ōnis, f. *delay, lingering hesitation.*

cunctātor -ōris, m. *one who delays.*

cunctor -ari, dep. *to delay, linger, hesitate;* of things, *to move slowly.*

Hence partic. cunctans -antis, *lingering, slow;* adv. cunctanter.

cunctus -a -um, *all, all collectively, the whole.*

cūněātim, *in wedge formation.*

cūněo -are, *to secure with wedges; to shape like a wedge.*

Hence partic. cūněātŭs -a -um, *pointed like a wedge.*

cūněus -i, m. *a wedge; troops in wedge formation; any triangular figure;* often *of the wedge-shaped compartments into which the seats of a theatre were divided.*

cŭnĭcŭlōsus -a -um, *full of rabbits (or of caverns).*

cŭnĭcŭlus -i, m. (1) *a rabbit, cony.* (2) *an underground passage;* milit. *a mine.*

cūpa -ae, f. *cask, butt.*

cŭpĭdĭtās -ātis, f. *eager desire, passionate longing.* Esp. *ambition; avarice, factiousness, party spirit.*

cŭpīdo -ĭnis, f. and poet. m., *longing, desire.* Esp. *desire for power, ambition; avarice; physical desire, love.* Personified, Cŭpīdo -ĭnis, m. *Cupid,* god of love; plur. Cŭpīdĭnes, *Cupids;* adj. Cŭpīdĭněus -a -um.

cŭpĭdus -a -um, *desirous, eager, keen.* Esp. *eager for power, ambitious; avaricious;* physically, *desirous, passionate;* towards persons, *attached, partial.* Adv. cŭpĭdē, *eagerly, passionately.*

cŭpĭo cŭpĕre cŭpīvi or -ii -ĭtum, *to desire, long for, wish for.*

Hence partic. cŭpĭens -entis *longing, eager;* as adj., with genit.; adv. cŭpĭenter.

cŭpĭtor -ōris, m. *one who desires.*

¹cuppēdĭa -ae, f. *taste for delicacies.*

²cuppēdĭa -orum, n. pl. *delicacies, tit-bits.*

cuppēdĭnārĭus -i, m. *a confectioner.*

cuppēdo = cupido; q.v.

cupressētum -i, n. *a cypress wood.*

cupressěus -a -um, *made of cypress wood.*

cupressĭfer -fěra -fěrum, *cypress-bearing.*

cupressus -i (-ūs), f. *the cypress; a casket of cypress wood.*

cūr (quor) *why? wherefore?*

cūra -ae, f. *care:* (1) *care taken, carefulness, pains, attention, minding of* things *or* persons; of *business, management, administration;* meton., *an object of care,* or *a guardian, care-*

taker, (2) *care felt, anxiety, worry, disquiet.*

cūrālium -i, n. *coral, esp. red coral.*

cūrātio -ōnis, f. *care, attention;* esp. *medical attention, healing, curing;* of business *management, administration;* frumenti, *commission to buy corn;* agraria, *commission to divide land.*

cūrātor -ōris, m. *guardian, overseer.*

cūrātus, partic. from curo; q.v.

curcūlio -ōnis, m. *a weevil, corn-worm.*

Cūrēs -ium, f. *a town of the Sabines;* adj. **Cūrensis** -e.

Cūrētes -ûm, m. *ancient inhabitants of Crete;* adj. **Cūrētis** -idis = *Cretan.*

cūria -ae, f. (1) *a curia, a division of the Roman patricians;* meton., *the meeting-place of a curia.* (2) *the meeting-place of the senate, senate-house;* at Athens, *the Areopagus.*

cūriālis -e, *belonging to the same curia.*

cūriātim, *by curiae.*

cūriātus -a -um, *relating to* curiae; comitia curiata, *the original assembly of the Roman people.*

cūrio -ōnis, m. *the priest of a curia; a herald, crier.*

cūriōsitās -atis, *inquisitiveness.*

cūriōsus -a -um. (1) *careful, attentive.* (2) *inquisitive.* (3) *wasted by cares.* Adv. **cūriōsē,** *carefully; inquisitively.*

cūris or **quīris,** f. *a spear.*

cūro -are, *to care for, pay attention to, trouble about;* with gerundive *to see to a thing being done;* of business, *to manage, administer;* physically, *to minister to, cure, rest;* in business *to provide or procure money;* curare Romae, *to be in charge at Rome.* Hence partic. **cūrātus** -a -um, *cared for; showing care.* Compar. adv. **cūrātius,** *more carefully.*

curriculum -i, n. *running; a contest in running, race; raceground, course, lap; a racing chariot.*

curro currēre cŭcurri cursum, *to run, hasten;* esp. *to run in a race;* at sea, *to sail;* of time, *to pass.*

currus -ūs, m. *a chariot, car;* esp. one used in racing, or war, or at a triumph; meton., *a triumph.* Transf., *a plough with wheels; a ship.*

cursim, *hastily, quickly.*

cursito -are, *to run up and down.*

curso -are, *to run hither and thither.*

cursor -ōris, m. *a runner; a courier, messenger; a running footman.*

cursus -ūs, m. *running, rapid motion; course, direction, movement, journey.*

curto -are, *to shorten, abbreviate.*

curtus -a -um, *shortened, mutilated, defective;* esp. *gelded.*

cūrūlis -e, *relating to a chariot;* equi, *horses provided for the Circus;* (sella) curulis, *the curule chair,* official seat of consuls, praetors, and curule aediles.

curvāmen -ĭnis, n. and **curvātūra** -ae, f. *curving, arching.*

curvo -are, *to bend, arch, curve; to influence.*

curvus -a -um, *bent, bowed, arched, curved, winding;* morally, *crooked.*

cuspis -īdis, f. *point, esp. of a spear;* hence *a spear, lance; a trident; a spit.*

custōdia -ae, f. *watching, guarding, custody, care;* milit. *keeping guard, watch;* of prisoners, *custody, safe-keeping;* custodia libera, *house-arrest.* Transf., *persons guarding, guards, sentinels; the station of the guard, post, prison; persons guarded, prisoners.*

custōdio -ire, *to guard, watch, keep, take care of; to keep in sight, observe; to keep in prison, hold captive.*

custōs -ōdis, c. *guardian, watchman, keeper, attendant; a gaoler, sentinel guard, spy.*

cutīcula -ae, f. *skin, cuticle.*

cutis -is, f. *skin, hide, leather.*

cyāthus -i, m. *a ladle for filling goblets with wine;* as *measure of capacity* = one-twelfth of a sextarius.

cybaea -ae, f. (with or without navis), *a merchantman.*

Cybēlē or **Cybēbē** -ēs f. *a Phrygian goddess, worshipped at Rome.*

²**cyclas** -ādis, f., *a female robe of state.*

¹**Cyclas** -ādis, f., gen. plur., **Cyclādes.** *a group of islands in the Aegean Sea.*

cyclicus -a -um, *cyclic.*

Cyclops -clōpis, m. *a Cyclops,* gen. plur., **Cyclōpes,** *the Cyclopes, a gigantic one-eyed race;* adj. **Cyclōpius** -a -um.

cycnēus or **cygnēus** -a -um, *belonging to the swan.*

cycnus or **cygnus** -i, m. *the swan.*

cylindrus -dri, m. *a cylinder; a roller.*

Cyllēnē -ēs and -ae, f. *a mountain in Arcadia, where Mercury was born.* Adj. **Cyllēnēus** and **Cyllēnius** -a -um.

cymba -ae, f. = cumba; q.v.

cymbălum -i, n. *a cymbal.*

cymbium -i, n., *a small drinking-vessel.*

Cynicus -a -um *Cynic, of the Cynic school.*

cynŏcéphălus -i m. *the dog-faced baboon.*

Cynŏsūra -ae, f., *the constellation Ursa Minor.*

Cynthus -i, m. *a mountain in Delos, birth-place of Apollo and Diana;* hence adj. as subst., m. **Cynthius** -i, *Apollo,* f. **Cynthia** -ae, *Diana.*

Cypārissus, f = cupressus; q.v.

Cyprus or **Cypros** -i, f., *the island of Cyprus;* adj. **Cyprius** -a -um, *Cyprian;* f. as subst. *Venus.*

Cyrēne -es and **Cyrēnae** -arum, f. *a city of north-eastern Africa;* adj. **Cyrēnaeus** and **Cyrēnāïcus** -a -um, *Cyrenaic;* m. pl. as subst., *the Cyrenaic philosophers.*

Cythēra -orum, n., *the island Cythera, sacred to Venus;* adj. **Cythērēus** and **Cythērēïus** -a -um, *Cytherean;* f. as subst. = *Venus.*

cytisus -i, c. *clover or lucerne.*

D

D, d the fourth letter of the Latin alphabet.

Dăci -orum, m. *the Dacians, a warlike people on the Lower Danube.* **Dācia** -ae, f. *their country.*

dactўlicus -a -um, *dactylic.*

dactўliŏthēca -ae, f. *a casket for rings.*

dactўlŭs -i, m. *a metrical foot, a dactyl* (— ⌣ ⌣).

daedălus -a -um : act., *skilful;* (natura) daedala rerum, *quaint artificer;* pass., *curiously wrought, variegated.*

²Daedălus -i, m., *mythical Athenian, builder of the Cretan labyrinth;* adj. **Daedălĕus** and **Daedălius** -a -um.

Dalmătae (Delmătae) -arum, m. pl., *the Dalmatians, inhabitants of Dalmatia.*

Dămascus -i, f. *Damascus, capital of Syria;* adj. **Dămascēnus** -a -um. *Damascene;* pruna, *damsons.*

damma (older **dāma**) -ae, f. or m. *a fallow-deer, chamois, antelope:* as meat *venison.*

damnātio -ōnis, f. *condemnation.*

damnātōrius -a -um, *condemnatory.*

damno -are, *to cause loss or injury to;* at law, *to condemn, sentence, punish* (offence usually genit., punishment genit. or abl.); damnari inter sicarios, *to be condemned as an assassin;* in gen., *to condemn, disapprove of;* of deities, damnare voti or voto, *to grant a person's wish, and compel him to discharge his vow;* also *to assign, devote, make over.*

damnŏsus -a -um: act.. *causing loss or damage, detrimental;* pass., *damaged, injured;* middle sense, *self-injuring.* Adv. **damnōsē,** *ruinously.*

damnum -i, n. *loss, damage, injury;* at law, *a fine.*

Dănäē -ēs, f. *mother of Perseus.*

Dănäus -i, m. *son of Belus, who left Egypt for Argos;* adj. **Dănäus** -a -um, *Argive, Greek;* m. pl. **Dănăi** -orum, *the Greeks;* **Dănăïdes** -um, f. *the fifty daughters of Danaus.*

dănista -ae, m. *money-lender.*

dăno = old form of do; q.v.

Dănūvius -i, m. *the Danube.*

Daphnē -ēs, f. *daughter of Peneus, changed into a laurel-tree.*

daphnōn -ōnis, m. *a grove of laurels.*

daps, dăpis, f. *a sacrificial feast, religious banquet;* in gen., *meal, feast, banquet.*

dapsilis -e, *sumptuous, plentiful.*

Dardăni -orum, m. pl. *a warlike Illyrian people.*

Dardănus -i, m. *son of Jupiter, mythical ancestor of the royal family of Troy;* adj. **Dardănus** and **Dardănius** -a -um, *Trojan;* subst. **Dardănia** -ae, f. = *Troy;* **Dardănides** -ae, m. *a male descendant of Dardanus;* **Dardănis** -ĭdis, *a Trojan woman.*

Dărēus -i, m. *name of several Persian kings.*

dătio -ōnis, f. *a giving;* legal, *right of alienation.*

dătīvus -a -um, *to do with giving;* (casus) dativus, *the dative case.*

dăto -are, *to give away.*

dător -ōris, m. *giver.*

Daunus -i, m. *a mythical king of Apulia, ancestor of Turnus;* adj. **Daunïus** -a -um, *Daunian;* f. subst., **Daunïas** -ădis, *Apulia.*

dē, prep., with abl. (1) in space, *down from, away from.* Transf., *coming from* an origin; *taken from* a class or stock, *made from* a material, *changed from* a previous state; of information, *from* a source. (2) in time; *following from, after; in the course of, during.* (3) *about* a subject; *on account of* a cause; *according to* a standard.

dĕa -ae, f. *goddess.*

dĕalbo -are, *to whitewash, plaster.*

dĕambŭlo -are, *to take a walk.*

dĕarmo -are, *to disarm.*

dĕbacchor -ari, dep. *to rave, revel furiously.*

dēbellātor -ōris, m., *a conqueror.*

dēbello -are: intransit.. *to fight to the end, finish a war;* transit. *to fight out a fight; to conquer an enemy.*

dēbĕo -ēre -ūi -itum, *to owe.* Lit. of money, etc.; n. of perf. partic. pass. as subst., debitum -i, *a debt.* Transf., *to be indebted to* somebody *for anything;* with infin., *to be due to do a thing, be morally bound to* or *be bound by* logic or *necessity or law to; to have to pay* because of fate, *to be destined to give.*

dēbilis -e, *feeble, weak.*

dēbilitās -ātis, f. *weakness, feebleness.*

dēbilitātio -ōnis, f. *weakening, disabling.*

dēbilito -are, *to weaken, enfeeble, disable; to enervate, break down.*

dēbĭtio -ōnis, f. *owing, debt.*

dēbĭtor -ōris, m. *one who owes, a debtor.*

dēbĭtum -i, subst. from debeo; q.v.

dēcanto -are: transit., *to sing* or *say repeatedly;* intransit., *to leave off singing.*

dēcēdo -cēdĕre -cessi -cessum. (1) *to move away, withdraw, retire;* milit. *to march away.* Transf., *to retire, give up;* with dat., *to yield to, retire in favour of,* esp. *to depart from life, to die.* (2) of things, *to retire, abate, cease;* sol decedens, *setting.* (3) *to go astray, deviate.*

dĕcem, indecl. *ten.*

Dĕcember -bris, adj. *of December* (originally the tenth Roman month); December (mensis), *December.*

dĕcempĕda -ae, f. *a ten-foot rule.*

dĕcempĕdātor -ōris, m. *a land-surveyor.*

dĕcemprimi -orum, m. pl. *the ten chief men in the senate of a municipium* or *colonia.*

dĕcemvir -i, m.; usually plur., *a board of ten commissioners at Rome for various purposes.*

dĕcemvirālis -e *relating to the decemvirs.*

dĕcemvirātus -ūs, m. *the office of decemvir.*

děcennis -e, *of ten years.*

děcens -entis, partic. from decet; q.v.

děcentia -ae, f., *propriety, comeliness*

děcerno -cernĕre -crēvi -crētum, *to decide, determine; to settle that a thing is so; and of action, to decide to do or to give a thing; of a body, to decide, decree;* as a member of a body, *to move, propose;* of combatants, *to settle by fighting.*
Hence partic. **děcrētus -a -um**; n. as subst. **děcrētum -i**, *a resolve, decree;* philosoph. *doctrine, principle.*

děcerpo -cerpĕre -cerpsi -cerptum, *to pluck off, pluck away.* Transf., *to gather; to derive; to take away.*

děcertātio -onis, f. *contest.*

děcerto -are, *to contend, fight to a finish.*

děcessio -ōnis, f., *a withdrawing, departure;* esp. *of a governor retiring from his province.* Transf., *deduction, diminution.*

děcessor -ōris, m., *one who retires from an office, a predecessor.*

děcessus -ūs, m. *withdrawal, departure.* Esp. *the retirement of an official; death;* of water, *ebb.*

děcet -ēre -ūit, *it is proper, it is fitting* (physically or morally).
Hence partic. **děcens -entis**, *proper, fit;* adv. **děcenter.**

¹děcido -cidĕre -cidi, *to fall down, to fall dead, die;* in gen., *to sink, fall.*

²děcido -cidĕre -cidi -cisum, *to cut down, cut off; to cut short, to settle, to arrange.*

děciens and děciēs, *ten times.*

decim-; see also decum-.

děcimus (older **děcŭmus**) **-a -um**, *tenth;* decimum, *for the tenth time.*

děcipio -cipĕre -cēpi -ceptum, *to catch;* hence *to cheat, deceive, beguile* (esp. of time).

děcisio -onis, f. *a settlement, decision.*

Děcius -a -um, *name of a Roman gens;* adj. **Děciānus -a -um.**

děclāmātio -ōnis, f., *loud, violent speaking, declamation; practice in oratory, or a theme for such practice.*

děclāmātor -ōris, m. *a declaimer.*

děclāmātōrius -a -um, *of declamation, rhetorical.*

děclāmito -are, *to speak loudly, declaim;* esp. *to practise public speaking;* causas, *to plead for practice.*

děclāmo -are, *to speak loudly;* esp. *to practise speaking in public;* with object, *to declaim.*

děclārātio -ōnis, f. *making clear, open expression.*

děclāro -are, *to make clear, explain, reveal, declare;* of appointments, *to proclaim* a person as chosen.

děclīnātio -ōnis, f. *bending away, turning aside.* Transf., *an avoiding, declining;* rhet. *a digression;* grammat. *inflexion, declension.*

děclino -are: transit., *to bend aside, turn away, deflect.* Transf., *to avoid, to shun;* intransit., *to deviate, swerve, digress.*

děclīvis -e, *inclined downwards, sloping;*

n. as subst. **děclīvě -is**, *a slope declivity.*

děclīvītās -ātis, f., *a declivity.*

děcocta -ae, f. subst. from decoquo; q.v.

děcoctor -ōris, m., *spendthrift, bankrupt.*

děcollo -are, *to behead.*

děcōlo -are, *to trickle away.*

děcŏlor -ōris, *off-colour, pale.*

děcŏlōrātio -ōnis, f. *discolouring.*

děcŏlōro -are, *to discolour.*

děcŏquo -cŏquĕre -coxi -coctum, *to boil thoroughly; to boil down, boil away;* of metals, *to melt away;* of property, *to waste;* commerc., *to ruin oneself, become bankrupt.*
Hence partic. **děcoctus -a -um**, *boiled down;* of style, *insipid;* f. as subst. *a cold drink.*

děcor -ōris, m. *grace, comeliness beauty.*

děcŏro -are, *to embellish, beautify, adorn.*

děcŏrus -a -um, physically, *graceful, beautiful comely;* morally, *proper, fit, becoming.* N. as subst. **děcōrum -i**, *propriety, grace.* Adv. **děcōrē**, *fitly, becomingly.*

děcrēpitus -a -um, *infirm, decrepit.*

děcresco -crescĕre -crēvi -crētum, *to grow down, become smaller, decrease.*

děcrētum -i, subst. from decerno; q.v.

děcŭma (děcĭma) -ae, f. *a tenth part tithe* (as an offering, tax or largess).

děcŭmānus (děcĭmānus) -a -um, *of the tenth.* (1) *relating to the provincial tax of a tenth;* m. as subst. *the farmer of such a tax.* (2) *belonging to the tenth legion;* m. pl. as subst. *its members.* (3) *belonging to the tenth cohort.*

děcŭmātes -ium, pl. adj. *relating to tithes.*

děcumbo -cumbĕre -cŭbŭi, *to lie down, fall, fall down.*

děcŭmo (děcĭmo) -are, *to take a tithe;* milit. *to decimate troops.*

děcŭria -ae, f. *a body of ten men; a class, division,* esp. of jurors; *a party, club.*

děcŭriātio -ōnis, f. and **děcŭriātus -ūs**, m., *a dividing into decuriae.*

¹děcŭrio -are, *to divide into bodies of ten, or into classes in gen.*

²děcŭrio -ōnis, m., *head of a body of ten;* milit. *company-commander in the cavalry;* polit., *a senator of a municipium or colonia.*

děcurro -currĕre -cŭcurri or -curri -cursum., *to run down, hasten down;* milit. *to move down or to manoeuvre.* Transf., *to run in a race;* transit. to *run through, traverse a set course; to have recourse to, take refuge in;* of ships *to sail downstream or to land;* of water, *to run down.*

děcursio -ōnis, f., milit., *a manoeuvre or charge.*

děcursus -ūs, m. *a running down;* milit. *a manoeuvre, a charge, attack.* Transf., *the completion of a course;* rhet., *rhythmical movement.*

dēcurtatus -a -um., *mutilated* (of style).

dĕcŭs -ŏris, n. *distinction, honour, glory, grace*; moral *dignity, virtue*; of persons, *pride, glory*; plur., decora, *distinguished acts.*

dĕcŭtio -cŭtĕre -cussi -cussum, *to shake down, shake off, knock off.*

dēdĕcet -dĕcēre -dĕcŭit, *it is un-becoming, unsuitable, unfitting.*

dēdĕcŏro -are, *to dishonour, bring shame upon.*

dēdĕcŏrus -a -um, *shameful, dis-honourable.*

dēdĕcus -ŏris, n. *shame, dishonour, disgrace; a dishonourable action, crime, vice.*

dēdicātio -ōnis, f., *consecration.*

dēdico -are, *to dedicate, consecrate; to specify, indicate.*

dēdignor -ari, dep. *to think unworthy, scorn, reject.*

dēdisco -discĕre -didici, *to unlearn, forget.*

dēdĭticius -a -um, *relating to sur-render*; m. plur., dediticii, *subjects of Rome without rights.*

dēditio -ōnis, *unconditional surrender, capitulation.*

dēdo dēdĕre -didi -ditum, *to give up, surrender*; esp. of the conquered, *to give up, surrender.* Transf., *to give up to, dedicate, devote.* Hence partic. **dēditus** -a -um *devoted to, addicted to*; deditā operā, *intentionally.*

dēdŏceo -ēre, *to cause to unlearn, to unteach; teach not to.*

dēdŏleo -dŏlēre -dŏlŭi, *to make an end of grieving.*

dēdūco -dūcĕre -duxi -ductum, *to lead or bring down*; in time, from the past, *to trace downwards to the present*; in amount, *to reduce*, or, from an amount, *to subtract*; in gen., *to lead or draw away; to lead forth colonists, to found a colony; to escort a person to a place*; of persons and things, *to bring out of one state, opinion, etc. into another*; in weaving, *to draw threads*; hence, *to draw out, spin out* in speech or writing.

dēductio -ōnis, f. *a leading down; a reduction; a leading away* of colonists, etc.

deerro -are, *to wander from the right path, go astray.*

dēfătigātio -ōnis, f. *exhaustion, fatigue.*

dēfătigo -are, *to weary, fatigue.*

dēfătiscor = defetiscor; q.v.

dēfectio -ōnis, f. *failure.* Hence *defection, rebellion; weakening, failing, vanishing.* Partic. **dēfectus** -a -um, *failing, deficient.*

dēfector -ōris, m. *rebel, deserter.*

[1]**dēfectus** -a -um, partic. of deficio; q.v.

[2]**dēfectus** -ūs, m., *a failing, disappear-ing*; esp. *a failing of light, eclipse.*

dēfendo -fendĕre -fendi -fensum. (1) *to repel, repulse, ward off, drive away.* (2) *to defend, protect*; esp. *to defend in court*; in argument, *to maintain a proposition or statement; to sustain a part.*

dēfensio -ōnis, f. (1) *a warding off.* (2) *defence.*

dēfensito -are, *to defend frequently.*

dēfenso -are, *to defend vigorously.*

dēfensor -ōris, m. (1) *one who wards off or averts.* (2) *a defender, protector*, esp. in court.

dēfero -ferre -tŭli -lātum, *to bring down, carry down*; in gen., *to bring or carry away*, esp. *to a particular place*; deferre rationes, *to hand in accounts*; fig., *to offer, hand over, refer*; of news, *to communicate, report*, esp. *to authority; legal,* deferre nomen *to inform against* a person, *indict*; deferre crimen, *to bring a charge.*

dēfervesco -fervescĕre -fervi or ferbŭi, *to cease boiling*; of passion, *to cease to rage.*

dēfetiscor (**dēfătiscor**) -fētisci -fessus, dep. *to become tired, grow weary*: esp. in perf. partic. **dēfessus** -a -um, *weary, tired.*

dēficio -ficĕre -fēci -fectum: intransit. *to do less than one might, to fail*; hence, *to desert, rebel, revolt*; of things, *to fail, run short*; of sun or moon, *to become eclipsed*; of fire, *to go out*; of water, *to ebb*; of strength, etc., *to fail, become weak*; animo deficere, *to lose heart*; transit., *to abandon, leave, fail*; rarely pass. defici, *to be failed.* Hence partic. **dēfectus** -a -um, *feeble*, esp. because of age.

dēfigo -fīgĕre -fixi -fixum, *to fasten down, fix in*; in gen., *to secure, plant firmly*; of sight or thought, *to concentrate, fix upon*; of persons, *to fix, make motionless, with astonish-ment*, etc.; partic. defixus, *astounded*; of enchantment, *to bind by a spell.*

dēfingo -fingĕre -finxi, *to form, mould.*

dēfinio -ire, *to limit, bound, mark out; to set limits to a thing, confine; to set as a limit, appoint, assign; to interpret* ideas or words in terms of each other, *to understand one thing by another*; in logic, *to define.* Hence partic. **dēfinĭtus** -a -um, *definite, distinct*; adv. **dēfinītē.**

dēfinītio -ōnis, f., *limiting, prescribing*; in logic, *a definition.*

dēfinītivus -a -um, *definitive ex-planatory.*

dēfit (as from defio), *fails.*

dēflagrātio -ōnis, f. *burning, destruc-tion by fire.*

dēflagro -are, *to be burnt down, des-troyed by fire*; in gen., *to be destroyed*; of passions, *to cease burning, abate, cool.* Partic. in pass. sense, **dēfla-grātus** -a -um, *burnt down, destroyed.*

dēflecto -flectĕre -flexi -flexum: transit., *to bend down or aside*: intransit., *to turn aside, turn away*; in speech, *to digress.*

dēflěo -flēre -flēvi -flētum, *to bewail, weep for.*

dēfloccatus -a -um, *bald.*

dēflōresco -flōrescĕre -flōrŭi, *to shed blossom, fade, wither.*

dēflŭo -flŭĕre -fluxi. (1) *to flow down, slip down, descend;* abstr., *to come down,* esp. of the gifts of heaven. (2) *to flow away, disappear, be lost.*

dēfōdĭo -fŏdĕre fōdi -fossum, *to dig down into; to form by digging, excavate; to dig in, cover, bury, conceal.*

dēfōrmātĭo -ōnis, f. *deforming, disfiguring; degradation.*

dēfōrmis -e. (1) *deformed, misshapen, ugly, disgusting.* Transf., *foul, shameful.* (2) *formless, shapeless.* Adv. **dēfōrmĭter,** *in an ugly fashion.*

dēfōrmĭtās -ātis, f. *deformity, ugliness; disgrace, dishonour.*

dēfōrmo -are. (1) *to form, fashion; to delineate.* (2) *to put out of shape, disfigure; to disgrace, dishonour.*

dēfraudo (**dēfrudo**) -are, *to deceive, cheat;* genium suum, *to deprive oneself of pleasure.*

dēfrēnātus -a -um, *unbridled, unrestrained.*

dēfrĭco -fricare -frĭcŭi -frictum, *to rub down;* fig. *to satirize, lash.*

dēfringo -fringĕre -frēgi -fractum, *to break down, break off.*

dēfrŭtum -i, n. *new wine boiled down.*

dēfŭgĭo -fŭgĕre -fūgi: intransit., *to flee away;* transit., *to fly from, avoid.*

dēfundo -fundĕre -fūdi -fūsum, *to pour down, pour out.*

dēfungor -fungi -functus, dep. *to perform, discharge, have done with;* (vita) defungi, *to die.*

dēgĕner -ĕris, *fallen away from one's origin, unworthy of one's race, degenerate, unworthy, ignoble.*

dēgĕnĕro -are: intransit., *to become unlike one's kind, to fall off, degenerate;* transit., *to cause to degenerate, or disgrace by degeneracy.*

dēgĕro -ĕre, *to carry off.*

dēgo dēgĕre dēgi, *to pass time;* absol., *to live.*

dēgrandĭnat, impers., *it hails violently,* or (perhaps) *it ceases to hail.*

dēgrăvo -are, *to weigh down, bring down, lower.*

dēgrĕdĭor -grĕdi -gressus, dep., *to step down, march down.*

dēgusto -are, *to take a taste from, taste;* of fire, *to lick;* of a weapon, *to graze;* in gen., *to try, make a trial of, sound.*

dēhinc, *from here, hence; from this time, henceforth, immediately after that time, thereupon.*

dēhisco -ĕre, *to gape, open, split down.*

dēhŏnestāmentum -i, n. *blemish, deformity disgrace.*

dēhŏnesto -are, *to dishonour, disgrace.*

dēhortor -ari, dep. *to discourage, dissuade.*

dēĭcĭo -icĕre -iēci -iectum, *to throw, cast, hurl down;* with reflex., *to rush down;* of upright things, *to throw to the ground, fell;* of persons, *to kill, bring down.* In gen., *to fling away or*

aside; naut., deici, *to be thrown off course;* milit. *to dislodge; to eject, dispossess; to shift a person from an opinion, attitude; to disappoint.*

Hence partic. **dēiectus** -a -um *low-lying; dispirited, dejected.*

dēĭectĭo -ōnis, f. *throwing down; eviction from property.*

¹**dēĭectus** -a -um, partic. from deicio; q.v.

²**dēĭectus** -ūs, m. *a throwing down; a declivity, steep slope.*

dēĭero -are, *to swear.*

dein; see deinde.

dēinceps, *one after another, successively.*

dēinde, and abbrev. **dēin:** of space, *from that place;* of time, *thereafter, thereupon, then, afterwards;* in enumerations, *next, and then.*

Dēiŏtărus -i, m. *a king of Galatia, defended by Cicero.*

dēiungo -ĕre, *to disconnect.*

dēlābor -labi -lapsus, dep. *to glide down, fall down, sink;* of liquids, *to flow down.* Transf., *to sink to, come down to circumstances, etc.; to proceed from, be derived from an origin; to fall unawares among people.*

dēlăcĕro -are, *to tear to pieces.*

dēlāmentor -ari, dep. *to bewail, lament.*

dēlasso -are, *to weary, tire out.*

dēlātĭo -ōnis, f. *reporting, giving information against, denunciation.*

dēlātor -ōris, m., *an informer, denouncer.*

dēlectābĭlis -c, *delightful, pleasant.*

dēlectāmentum -i, n. *delight, amusement.*

dēlectātĭo -ōnis, f. *delight, pleasure.*

dēlecto -are, *to divert, attract, delight;* in pass., with abl. *to take delight in:* in pass. with infin., *to delight to.*

dēlectus -ūs, m. *choosing, choice.*

dēlēgātĭo -ōnis, f. *assignment of a debt.*

dēlēgo -are, *to transfer, commit, assign; to impute, attribute, ascribe.*

dēlēnimentum -i, n. *what soothes or charms.*

dēlēnĭo (**dēlĭnĭo**) -ire, *to soften down; to soothe or charm.*

dēlēnītor -ōris, m. *one who soothes or cajoles.*

dēlĕo -lēre -lēvi -lētum, *to blot out, efface;* in gen., *to destroy, annihilate.*

dēlībĕrābundus -a -um, *carefully considering, deliberating.*

dēlībĕrātĭo -ōnis, f. *consideration, consultation.*

dēlībĕrātīvus -a -um, *relating to deliberation.*

dēlībĕrātor -ōris, m., *one who deliberates.*

dēlībĕro -are, *to weigh carefully, consider, consult about; to ask advice,* esp. *of an oracle; as a result of deliberation, to resolve.*

Hence partic. **dēlībĕrātus** -a -um. *resolved, determined.*

dēlībo -are, *to take a little from, to taste;* in gen., *to extract, derive; to take from so as to enjoy; to take from so as to lessen or spoil.*

dēlibro -are, *to peel the bark off.*

dēlibūtus -a -um, *steeped.*

dēlĭcātus -a -um, *soft, tender*; in bad sense, *luxurious* of things, *spoilt, effeminate* of persons; of tastes, *fastidious, dainty, nice.* Adv. **dēlĭcātē,** *luxuriously.*

dēliciae -arum, f. pl. *allurements, charms, delights, fancies*; esse in deliciis, *to be a favourite*; concr., *darling, sweetheart.*

dēlĭcĭŏlae -arum, f. p . *a darling.*

dēlictum -i, n. *a fault crime.*

¹**dēlĭgo** -lĭgĕre -lēgi -lectum *to pick, pluck; to choose, select.*

²**dēlĭgo** -are, *to fasten, bind up.*

dēlingo -ere, *to lick off, lick up.*

dēlinquo -linquĕre -liqui -lictum, *to fail, be wanting,* esp. *to fail in duty, commit a crime.*

dēlĭquesco -liquescĕre -lĭcŭi, *to melt, dissolve; to vanish, disappear.*

dēliquo and **dēlico** -are, *to clarify; to explain.*

dēlīrātĭo -ōnis. f. *folly. silliness, dotage.*

dēlīro -are, *" to go off the rails " act crazily, rave.*

dēlīrus -a -um, *silly, crazy doting.*

dēlitesco -litescĕre -litŭi, *to conceal oneself, lie hid, take refuge.*

dēlĭtigo -are, *to scold furiously.*

Dēlos -i, f., *a small island in the Aegean Sea, birth-place of Apollo and Diana*; adj. **Dēlĭăcus** and **Dēlĭus** -a -um, *of Delos*; as subst. **Dēlĭus** -i, m. = *Apollo*; **Dēlĭa** -ae, f. = *Diana.*

Delphi -orum, m. *a town in Phocis, famous for its oracle of Apollo*; adj. **Delphĭcus** -a -um.

delphīnus -i and **delphīn** -īnis, m. *dolphin.*

dēlūbrum -i, n. *a shrine. temple.*

dēluctor -ari, dep. and **dēlucto** -are, *to wrestle.*

dēlūdo -lūdĕre -lūsi -lūsum, *to mock, cheat.*

dēlumbo -are, *to lame, enervate, weaken.*

dēmădesco -mădescĕre -mădŭi, *to become wet through.*

dēmando -are, *to entrust, commit.*

dēmens -mentis, *out of one's mind, insane, senseless*; adv. **dēmenter.**

dēmentĭa -ae, f., *senselessness, insanity*; in plur., *mad actions.*

dēmentĭo -ire, *to be mad, rave.*

dēmĕrĕo -ēre and **dēmĕrĕor** -ēri, dep. *to earn thoroughly; to deserve well of a person, to oblige.*

dēmergo -mergĕre -mersi -mersum, *to sink, plunge into, dip under*; aere alieno demersus, *over head and ears in debt.*

dēmētĭor -mētiri -mensus, dep. *to measure out*; partic. **dēmensus** -a -um, in pass. sense, with n. as subst., *an allowance.*

dēmĕto -mētĕre -messŭi -messum, *to mow, reap, cut down* or *off.*

dēmigro -are, *to emigrate. depart.* Transf., *to die.*

dēmĭnŭo -mĭnŭĕre -mīnŭi -mĭnūtum, *to take away from, diminish, lessen*; capite se deminuere, *to suffer a loss of civil rights.*

dēmĭnūtĭo -ōnis, f. *lessening, diminution*; sui, *loss of prestige*; capitis, *loss of civil rights; right of alienation.*

dēmiror -ari, dep. *to wonder* (at).

dēmissio -ōnis, f., *sinking, lowering*; animi, *dejection.*

dēmītĭgo -ari, *to make mild, soften.*

dēmitto -mittĕre -mīsi -missum, *to send down, lower, put down*; tunica demissa, *hanging loosely*; demissi capilli, *growing long*; milit., *to lead down*; naut., *to lower gear* or *bring a vessel downstream* or *to land.* Transf., *to sink, bury, plunge*; of spirits, *to lower.*
    Hence partic. **dēmissus** -a -um, *hanging down*; of dress and hair, *long, loose*; of places, *low-lying.* Transf., *feeble, weak; unassuming, modest; down-cast, dispirited.* Adv. **dēmissē,** *low, near the ground.* Transf., *modestly, humbly meanly.*

dēmo dēmĕre dempsi demptum, *to take away, subtract.*

Dēmocrĭtus -i, m. *a philosopher of Abdera* (c. 460-370 B.C.). Hence adj. **Dēmocrĭticus** -a -um

dēmōlĭor -iri, dep. *to throw down. demolish.*

dēmōlĭtĭo -ōnis, f. *throwing down, demolition.*

dēmonstrātĭo -ōnis, f. *pointing out, indication, explanation, description*; rhet., *oratory concerned with praise and censure.*

dēmonstrātīvus -a -um, *demonstrative*; rhet., *of oratory, concerned with praise and censure.*

dēmonstrātor -ōris, m., *one who points out* or *indicates.*

dēmonstro -are *to indicate, explain, describe.*

dēmōrior -mŏri -mortŭus, dep. *to die, die off*; with acc. of person, *to die for love of.*

dēmŏror -ari dep.: intransit., *to delay, loiter*; transit., *to stop, delay, retard.*

Dēmosthĕnēs -is (also -i), *the Athenian orator* (384-322 B.C.).

dēmŏvĕo -mŏvēre -mŏvi -mōtum, *to move away, remove*; hominem de sententia, *to make a person change his opinion.*

dēmūgītus -a -um, *filled with the noise of lowing.*

dēmulcĕo -mulcēre -mulsi, *to stroke down, caress by stroking.*

dēmum, of time, *at length, at last*; in enumerations, *finally, in short*; id demum, *that and that alone.*

dēmurmŭro -are, *to murmur* or *mutter over.*

dēmūtātĭo -ōnis, f., *change, alteration,* esp. *for the worse.*

dēmūto -are: transit., *to change, alter a thing,* esp. *for the worse*; intransit. *to change one's mind* or *become different.*

dēnārĭus -a -um, *containing ten;* denarius nummus, or denarius alone, *a Roman silver coin.*

dēnarro -are, *to narrate, tell, relate.*

dēnăto -are, *to swim down.*

dēnĕgo -are, *to deny, say no; to deny, refuse, reject a request.*

dēni -ae, -a, *ten by ten, ten at a time, by tens.*

dēnĭcālis -e, *releasing from death;* feriae, *a funeral ceremony.*

dēnĭquĕ: in time, *at last, finally;* in enumerations, *again, further or finally;* in short, in fine.

dēnōmĭno -are, *to name.*

dēnormo -are, *to make crooked.*

dēnŏto -are, *to mark out for another, designate precisely; to take note of.*

dens dentis, m. *a tooth.* Transf., of things resembling a tooth, e.g., *a mattock or sickle;* abstr., of anything sharp, biting, destructive.

denso -are, and **densĕo** -ēre, *to make thick, condense, press together.*

densus -a -um, *thick close, dense;* in time, *frequent;* in degree, *intense, vehement;* in style, of work or author, *condensed.* Adv. **densē,** *densely;* of time, *frequently.*

dentālĭa -ium, n. pl. *the share-beam of a plough.*

dentātus -a -um, *provided with teeth, toothed; polished by teeth.*

dentĭo -ire, *to cut teeth;* of teeth, *to grow.*

dēnūbo -nūbĕre -nupsi -nuptum, *to be married off, to marry (of the woman),* esp. *beneath her.*

dēnūdo -are, *to lay bare, uncover, reveal.* Transf., *to rob, plunder.*

dēnuntĭātĭo -ōnis, f. *announcement, declaration, threat.*

dēnuntĭo -are, *to announce, give notice, declare, threaten;* bellum denuntiare, *to declare war;* legal, *to give notice, serve a summons.*

dēnŭo, *anew; again; a second time.*

deōnĕro -are, *to unload, disburden.*

dēorsum or **dĕorsus,** *downwards;* sursum deorsum, *up and down, backwards and forwards.*

dēpāciscor = depeciscor; q.v.

dēpactus -a -um, *fastened down, firmly fixed.*

dēpasco -pascĕre -pāvi -pastum and **dēpascor** -pasci, dep. *to feed off;* in gen., *to eat up, consume, reduce.*

dēpĕciscor -pĕcisci -pectus, dep. *to make a bargain for or about; to settle for, accept a condition.*

dēpecto -pectĕre -pexum, *to comb down;* in comedy, *to beat soundly.*

dēpĕcŭlātor -ōris, m. *plunderer embezzler.*

dēpĕcŭlor -ari, dep. *to rob, plunder.*

dēpello -pellĕre -pŭli -pulsum, *to drive down, or away, expel, remove;* milit., *to dislodge;* naut., *to drive off course;* in gen., *to drive away, avert;* of persons, *to dissuade.*

dēpendĕo -ēre, *to hang down; to depend upon; to be derived from.*

dēpendo -pendĕre -pendi -pensum, *to weigh out and pay over.*

dēperdo -perdĕre -perdidi -perditum, *to lose, waste, destroy;* esp. of the effects of love.

dēpĕrĕo -pĕrire -pĕrii, *to perish or be ruined utterly; to be desperately in love.*

dēpĭlo -are, *to strip of hair or feathers.*

dēpingo -pingĕre -pinxi -pictum, *to paint, depict, portray.*

dēplango -plangĕre -planxi, *to bewail, lament.*

dēplexus -a -um, *clasping.*

dēplōro -are: intransit., *to weep bitterly, lament;* transit., *to lament, bewail; to regard as lost, give up.*

dēplŭit -plŭĕre, *rains down.*

dēpōno -pōnĕre -pŏsŭi -pŏsĭtum. (1) *to lay down, put down;* esp. *to lay as wager or prize.* (2) for safekeeping, *to put down, deposit; to commit, entrust.* (3) *to lay aside, have done with.*
     Hence partic. **dēpŏsĭtus** -a -um, (1) *laid out; dying, despaired of, dead.* (2) *entrusted;* n. as subst. *a deposit.*

dēpŏpŭlātĭo -ōnis, f., *laying waste ravaging.*

dēpŏpŭlātor -ōris, m. *a ravager.*

dēpŏpŭlor -ari, dep.; also **dēpŏpŭlo** -are, *to lay waste, ravage, destroy.*

dēporto -are, *to carry down, carry off, take away; to bring home; to banish for life* (with loss of rights and property).

dēposco -poscĕre -pŏposci, *to demand,* usually for a purpose, esp. for punishment.

dēprāvātĭo -ōnis, f. *perverting, distorting;* animi *depravity.*

dēprāvo -are, *to make crooked, pervert, disfigure;* verbally, *to distort, misrepresent;* morally, *to spoil, corrupt.* Adv. from partic., **dēprāvātē,** *perversely.*

dēprĕcābundus -a -um, *earnestly entreating.*

dēprĕcātĭo -ōnis, f. (1) *an attempt to avert by entreaty, deprecating.* (2) *an entreaty against a person,* for his punishment.

dēprĕcātor -ōris, m. (1) *one that begs off, an intercessor.* (2) *one that pleads for.*

dēprĕcor -ari, dep. (1) *to try to avert by entreaty, to deprecate; to allege in excuse* (so as to avoid punishment). (2) *to entreat against a person, to curse.* (3) *to entreat for, beg for, intercede.*

dēprĕhendo and **dēprendo** -endĕre -endi -ensum, *to seize upon, catch hold of;* esp. *to surprise, catch, detect a person in a crime or fault; to discover, detect, observe a thing.*

dēprĕhensĭo -ōnis, f. *detection.*

dēprimo -primĕre -pressi -pressum, *to press down, depress;* esp. *to plant deep in the ground, dig deep;* of ships, *to sink.*
     Hence partic. **depressus** -a -um, *low-lying.*

dēproelians -antis, *struggling violently.*

dēprōmo -prōmĕre -prompsi -promptum, *to take down produce, fetch out.*

dēprōpĕro: intransit., *to hasten;* transit., *to hasten over, produce in haste.*

dēpŭdet -pŭdēre -pŭdŭit, *ceases to be ashamed, loses all sense of shame.*

dēpugno -are, *to fight hard, fight it out.*

dēpulsio -ōnis, f. *driving away;* rhet. *defence.*

dēpulsor -ōris, m. *an averter.*

dēpŭto -are. (1) *to prune, cut off.* (2) *to count, estimate.*

deque; *see* susque deque.

dērēlinquo -linquĕre -liqui -lictum. *to forsake, desert, abandon.*

dērēpentē, *suddenly.*

dērēpo -rēpĕre -repsi, *to creep, crawl down.*

dērīdĕo -rīdēre -rīsi -rīsum, *to laugh at, mock, deride.*

dērīdĭcŭlus -a -um, *very laughable;* n. as subst. *ridicule;* esse deridiculo, *to be an object of ridicule.*

dērigo -rĭgĕre -rexi -rectum, *to set straight, direct;* of placing (also in form dirigo), *to order, dispose;* milit. *to draw up.* Transf., *to direct, aim, guide* abstr. things.

dērigŭi, perf., *grew quite stiff.*

dērĭpio -rĭpĕre -rĭpŭi -reptum, *to tear down, snatch away.*

dērīsor -ōris, m. *a mocker.*

dērīsus -ūs, m. *mockery, derision.*

dērīvātio -ōnis, f. *turning away or diversion of water.*

dērīvo -are, *to turn into another channel, to divert.*

dērŏgo -are, *to modify a law;* in gen., *to diminish, detract from.*

dērōsus -a -um, *gnawed away.*

dēruncino -are, *to cheat, fleece.*

dērŭo -rŭēre -rŭi -rŭtum, *to cast down, make to fall.*

dēruptus -a -um, *broken off;* hence *precipitous, steep;* n. pl. as subst., *precipices.*

dēsaevio -ire -ĭi -ĭtum, *to rage violently.*

dēscendo -scendĕre -scendi -scensum, *to climb down, come down, descend;* milit., *to march down;* of things, *to sink, pierce, penetrate;* of mountains, *to slope down;* of the voice, *to sink.* Transf., of persons, *to lower oneself, stoop;* of things, *to sink in, penetrate.*

dēscensio -ōnis, f. *going down, descent;* Tiberina, *voyage down the Tiber.*

dēscensus -ūs, m. *going down, descent; way down.*

dēscisco -sciscĕre -scivi or -scii -scitum, *to break away, revolt, withdraw, diverge.*

dēscribo -scrībĕre -scripsi -scriptum. (1) *to transcribe, copy.* (2) *to describe, delineate, represent, portray.*

dēscriptio -ōnis, f. (1) *a copy.* (2) *a representation, figure, description.*

dēsĕco -sĕcare -sĕcŭi -sectum, *to hew off, cut off.*

dēsĕro -sĕrĕre -sĕrŭi -sertum, *to forsake, abandon, leave; to neglect, disregard.*

Hence partic. dēsertus -a -um, *forsaken, abandoned;* n. pl. as subst., *deserts, wildernesses.*

dēsertor -ōris, m. *one who forsakes,* milit., *deserter.*

dēservio -ire, *to serve zealously, be a slave to.*

dēsēs -sĭdis, m. (nom. sing. not found), *idle, lazy, inactive.*

dēsĭdĕo -sĭdēre -sēdi -sessum, *to sit idle, be slothful.*

dēsīdĕrābĭlis -e, *desirable.*

dēsīdĕrātio -ōnis, f. *desire longing.*

dēsīdĕrium -i, n. *desire or longing, grief for the absence or loss of a person or thing;* in gen., *a desire or request.*

dēsīdĕro -are, *to long for what is absent or lost, to wish for; to miss, find a lack of;* milit., *to lose.*

dēsĭdia -ae, f. *idleness, inactivity, apathy.*

dēsĭdĭōsus -a -um, *slothful, idle, lazy;* adv. dēsĭdĭōsē.

dēsīdo -sīdĕre -sēdi, *to sink down, subside, settle.* Transf., *to deteriorate.*

dēsignātio -ōnis, f. *marking out, designation: appointment to an office.*

dēsignātor -ōris, m. = dissignator; q.v.

dēsignātor -ōris, m. = dissignator; q.v.

dēsigno -are, *to mark out, trace, plan;* in gen., *to point out, indicate, signify; to portray, delineate;* polit., *to nominate, elect;* partic. dēsignātus, *elected, designate.*

dēsĭlio -sĭlire -sĭlŭi -sultum, *to leap down;* ad pedes, *dismount.*

dēsĭno -sĭnĕre -sii -sĭtum: transit., *to cease, desist from;* intransit., *to cease, stop, end;* with in and acc., *to end in.*

dēsĭpientia -ae, f. *foolishness.*

dēsĭpio -sĭpĕre, *to be foolish, act foolishly.*

dēsisto -sistĕre -stĭti -stĭtum, *to stand away:* from a person, *to withdraw;* from action, etc., *to desist, leave off, cease.*

dēsōlo -are, *to leave solitary, forsake.*

dēspecto -are, *to regard from above, look down upon; to despise.*

1dēspectus -a -um, partic. from despicio; q.v.

2dēspectus -ūs, m. *a looking down, downward view; an object of contempt.*

dēspērātio -ōnis, f. *hopelessness, despair.*

dēspēro -are: intransit., *to be without hope, despair;* transit., *to despair of, give up.* Adv. from pres. partic., dēspēranter, *despairingly, hopelessly.* Perf. partic. dēspērātus -a -um; in pass. sense, *despaired of;* in middle sense, *desperate.*

dēspĭcātio -ōnis, f. and dēspĭcātus -ūs, m. *contempt.*

dēspĭcientia -ae, f., *looking down upon; contempt.*

dēspĭcio -spĭcĕre -spexi -spectum, *to look down, regard from above; to look down upon, despise.* Pres. partic. act. dēspĭciens, *contemptuous.* Perf. partic. pass. dēspectus -a -um, *despised, contemptible.*

dēspīcor -ari, *to look down upon, despise.* Perf. partic. in pass. sense **despicātus** -a -um, *despised, contemptible.*

dēspŏlio -are, *to plunder, despoil.*

dēspondĕo -spondēre -spondi -sponsum, *to pledge, to promise,* esp. *to promise in marriage, betroth*; in gen., *to pledge, devote*; with animum or animos, *to lose heart, despair.*

dēspūmo -are. (1) *to skim off.* Transf., *to digest.* (2) *to drop foam.*

dēspŭo -spŭĕre, *to spit down, spit on the ground.* Transf., *to reject.*

dēsquāmo -are, *to take off the scales, to scale.*

dēsterto -stertĕre -stertŭi, *to finish snoring or dreaming.*

dēstillo -are, *to drip down, distil.*

dēstinātio -ōnis, f. *fixing, determining, appointment.*

dēstino -are, *to make fast, fix down; to fix, determine, settle, appoint*; with infin., *to resolve to do*; of persons, *to appoint to an office*; of things *to fix upon, intend to buy.*
  Hence partic. **dēstinātus** -a -um, *fixed, determined*; n. as subst., *an objective or intention*; (ex) destinato, *intentionally.*

dēstĭtŭo -stĭtŭēre -stĭtŭi -stĭtūtum, *to set down, place*; esp. *to leave in the lurch, forsake, desert.*

dēstĭtūtio -ōnis, f. *forsaking, abandoning.*

dēstringo -stringĕre -strinxi -strictum. (1) *to strip*; esp. *to draw or bare a sword.* Transf., *to satirize, censure.* (2) *to touch lightly, graze.*
  Hence partic. **dēstrictus** -a -um, *severe.*

dēstrŭo -strŭĕre -struxi -structum, *to pull down, dismantle, destroy, ruin.*

dēsŭbĭto (or **dē sŭbĭto**), *suddenly.*

dēsŭdo -are, *to sweat violently, exert oneself hard.*

dēsuēfio -fĭĕri -factus sum, pass., *to be made unaccustomed.*

dēsuesco -suescĕre -suēvi -suētum, *to become unaccustomed*; esp. partic. **dēsuētus** -a -um: in pass. sense, *disused*; in middle sense, *unaccustomed, unused to.*

dēsuētūdo -ĭnis, f. *disuse.*

dēsultor -ōris, m. *a leaper, acrobat.* Transf., *an inconstant person.*

dēsultōrius -a -um, *relating to a desultor.*

dēsum -esse -fŭi, *to be down, fall short, fail, be missing or remiss.*

dēsūmo -sūmĕre -sumpsi -sumptum, *to take out, choose, select.*

dēsŭpĕr, *from above.*

dēsurgo -surgĕre -surrexi -surrectum, *to rise and go down or out.*

dētĕgo -tĕgĕre -texi -tectum, *to uncover, lay bare, disclose.*

dētendo -tendĕre -tensum, *to unstretch*; tabernacula, *to strike tents.*

dētergĕo -tergēre -tersi -tersum. (1) *to wipe off, clear away, brush off.* (2) *to cleanse by wiping.*

dētĕrior -ius, genit. -ōris, compar. (superl. deterrimus), *lower, inferior, poorer, worse.* Adv. **dētĕrius**, *worse.*

dētermĭnātio -ōnis, f., *boundary, end.*

dētermĭno -are, *to bound, fix the limits of, determine.*

dētĕro -tĕrĕre trivi -tritum, *to rub away, wear out; to detract from, weaken.*

dētĕrrĕo -terrēre -terrŭi -territum, *to frighten away, deter, discourage.*

dētestābĭlis -e, *abominable, horrible.*

dētestātio -ōnis, f. (1) *a cursing, execration.* (2) *a warding off, averting.*

dētestor -ari, dep. (1) *to pray against: to pray for deliverance from a person or thing, or to curse, execrate.* (2) of the gods' action, *to avert, remove.*

dētexo -texĕre -texŭi -textum, *to make by plaiting; to finish, complete.*

dētĭnĕo -tĭnēre -tĭnŭi -tentum, *to hold back, detain; to prevent; to engage, occupy exclusively.*

dētondĕo -tondēre -tŏtondi and -tondi -tonsum, *to shear, clip.*

dētŏno -tŏnāre -tŏnŭi *to cease to thunder or rage.*

dētorquĕo -torquēre -torsi -tortum. (1) *to turn away, bend aside.* (2) *to twist out of shape, distort.*

dētractio -ōnis, f. *drawing off, withdrawal, taking away*; rhet., *ellipsis.*

dētracto = detrecto; q.v.

dētractor -ōris, m., *detractor, disparager.*

dētrăho -trăhĕre -traxi -tractum. (1) *to draw down, drag down; to lower, humiliate.* (2) *to draw off, drag away, remove*; numerically, *to subtract*; in speech, *to detract from a person, disparage, slander.*

dētrectātio -ōnis, f. *refusal.*

dētrectātor -ōris, m. *disparager, detractor.*

dētrecto -are. (1) *to decline, refuse, shirk.* (2) *to disparage, detract from, depreciate.*

dētrīmentōsus -a -um, *detrimental, hurtful.*

dētrīmentum -i, n. *loss, damage, injury*; milit., *loss, defeat.*

dētrītus -a -um, partic. from detero; q.v.

dētrūdo -trūdĕre -trūsi -trūsum, *to push down, thrust down*; milit., *to dislodge*; legal, *to dispossess, eject.* Transf., of persons, *to force, compel*; of functions, *to put off, postpone.*

dētrunco -are, *to lop or cut off; to mutilate.*

dēturbo -are, *to force away, dash down*; milit., *to dislodge*; legal, *to eject dispossess.*

Deucălĭōn -ōnis, m. *son of Prometheus, saved in an ark from a great flood, with his wife Pyrrha.*

deunx -uncis, m. *eleven-twelfths of a unit.*

deūro -ūrĕre -ussi -ustum, *to burn down*; of cold, *to destroy, nip.*

dĕus -i, m. *a god, a deity*; di meliora (ferant), *God forbid.*

dēvasto -are, *to lay waste, devastate.*

dĕvĕho -vĕhĕre -vexi -vectum, *to carry away* or *down*; pass. devehi (sc. navi), *to sail.*

dēvello -vellere -velli -vulsum, *to pluck, tear away.*

dēvēlo -are, *to unveil, uncover.*

dēvĕnĕror -ari, dep. (1) *to worship, revere.* (2) *to avert by prayers.*

dēvĕnĭo -vĕnire -vēni -ventum, *to come to, arrive at, reach.*

dēverbĕro -are, *to thrash soundly.*

¹dēversor -ari, dep., *to lodge as a guest.*

²dēversor -ōris, m., *a guest.*

dēversōrĭŏlum -i, n. *a small lodging.*

dēversōrĭus -a -um, *fit to lodge in*; n. as subst. *an inn, lodging, refuge .*

dēvertĭcŭlum (dēvort-) -i, n. (1) *a by-way, by-path*; hence *digression.* (2) *an inn, lodging, refuge, resort.*

dēverto (dēvorto) -vertĕre -verti -versum; *to turn aside*; esp. *to turn aside to a lodging, to put up at, stay with.* Transf., *to digress.*

dēvexus -a -um, *moving downwards, descending, sinking*; of position, *sloping down, shelving, steep*; of tendency, *inclining to.*

dēvincio -vincire -vinxi -vinctum, *to bind, tie fast, attach, connect.* Hence partic. **dēvinctus** -a -um, *attached, devoted.*

dēvinco -vincĕre -vīci -victum, *to conquer thoroughly, subjugate, overcome.*

dēvītātĭo -ōnis, f. *avoiding.*

dēvīto -are, *to avoid.*

dēvĭus -a -um, *off the beaten track, out of the way, solitary, retired*; in mind, *erroneous, unreasonable.*

dēvŏco -are, *to call down* or *away*; devocare in dubium, *to bring into danger.*

dēvŏlo -are, *to fly down, hasten down.*

dēvolvo -volvĕre -volvi -vŏlūtum, *to roll down*; pass., *to roll down, fall headlong, sink back.*

dēvŏro -are, *to swallow, devour, seize upon*; of words, *to articulate badly, mispronounce*; of property, *to consume, waste*; of disagreeable things, *to swallow, accept, put up with.*

dēvorticŭlum; see deverticulum.

dēvortĭum -i, n., *a by-way, by-path.*

dēvōtĭo -ōnis, f. (1) *consecrating, devoting.* (2) *cursing.* (3) *enchantment, incantation.*

dēvŏto -are, *to consecrate* or *devote to death.*

dēvŏvĕo -vŏvĕre -vŏvi -vŏtum, *to consecrate, devote,* esp. *to a god, or to death; to curse, execrate; to bewitch, enchant*; in gen., *to devote, give up.* Hence partic. **dēvōtus** -a -um, *devoted; accursed; attached* to a person; m. pl. as subst. *faithful followers.*

dextella -ae, f., *a little right hand.*

dexter -tĕra -tĕrum, or -tra -trum; compar. **dextĕrĭor** -ius, superl. **deximus** -a -um; *right, on the right hand, on the right side.* Transf., *dexterous, skilful; propitious, favourable, opportune.* F. as subst., **dextĕra** or **dextra** -ae, *the right hand*; (a) dextra, *on the right*; esp. *the right hand* as pledge of faith; sometimes, in gen. *the hand.* Adv. **dextĕrē** or **dextrē**; compar. **dextĕrĭus**; *dexterously, skilfully.*

dextĕrĭtās -ātis, f., *skilfulness, readiness.*

dextrorsum and **dextrorsus**, *on the right, towards the right.*

Dīa -ae, f. *mother of Mercury.*

dĭădēma -ātis, n., *a royal headband, diadem.*

dĭaeta -ae, f. (1) *a way of living prescribed by a physician, regimen, diet.* (2) *a living-room.*

dĭălecticus -a -um, *of discussion, dialectical*; m. as subst., **dĭālectĭcus** -i, *a dialectician, logician*; f. **dĭālectĭca** -ae, and **dĭālectĭcē** -es, *the art of dialectic, logic*; n. pl. **dĭālectĭca** -orum, *dialectical discussion*; adv. **dĭālectĭcē**, *dialectically.*

dĭālis -e, *relating to Jupiter*; (flamen) dialis, *the priest of Jupiter.*

dĭălŏgus -i, m., *a philosophical conversation.*

Dĭāna (older **Dĭāna**) -ae, f. *the virgin goddess of the moon and of hunting*; adj. **Dĭānĭus** -a -um, *belonging to Diana.*

dĭārĭa -orum, n. pl. *a day's allowance of food* or *pay.*

dĭbăphus (-a) -um, *double-dyed*; as f. subst. **dĭbăphus** -i, *the purple-striped robe of the higher magistrates in Rome.*

dĭca -ae, f., *law-suit, action* in a Greek court.

dĭcācĭtās -ātis, f. *wit, satire, raillery.*

dĭcātĭo -ōnis, f. *settling as a citizen.*

dĭcax -ācis, *ready of speech; witty, satirical, sarcastic.*

dĭchŏrēus -i, m. *a double trochee.*

dĭcĭō -ōnis, f. *power, sovereignty, authority.*

dĭcis (genit.); dicis causa, dicis gratia, *for form's sake, for the sake of appearances.*

¹dĭco -are, *to consecrate, dedicate, devote to the gods; to deify, place among the gods; to inaugurate.* Transf., *to devote, give up, set apart*; se civitati, or in civitatem, *to become a citizen.*

²dĭco -dicĕre dixi dictum, *to indicate; to appoint;* most commonly, *to say, speak, tell, mention*; in pass. with infin., *to be said to*; impersonally, dicitur, *it is said that*; of values, *to express, put into words*; ius, *to administer law, give rulings*; of persons or things, *to mention, speak of, tell of, relate; to name, call; to mean, refer to.* N. of partic. as subst. **dictum** -i, *a word, saying, speech; a witty saying, a bon-mot; a prediction; an order, command.*

dĭcrŏtum -i, n. *a vessel with two banks of oars.*

dictamnus -i, f. *dittany, a plant.*

dictātor -ōris, m. *a dictator*; in Rome, *an extraordinary magistrate, elected* *in emergency and granted absolute power*; elsewhere, *a chief magistrate*,

dictātōrius -a -um, *belonging to a dictator, dictatorial.*

dictātūra -ae, f., *the office of dictator, dictatorship.*

dictio -ōnis, f. *saying, speaking, talk, oratory.*

dictito -are, *to say often, reiterate, assert repeatedly*; dictitare causas, *to plead frequently.*

dicto -are, *to say often; to say over, dictate a thing to be written; hence to get written down.*

dictum -i, n. subst. from =dico; q.v.

¹Dīdō -ūs, f., *the founder of Carthage, also called Elisa or Elissa.*

²dīdo didēre didīdi diditum, *to divide, distribute, spread round.*

dīdūco -dūcēre -duxi -ductum, *to draw apart, separate*; milit., *to divide, distribute*, also *to scatter, disperse.*

diēcŭla -ae, f. *a little day, a short time.*

diērectus -a -um, *an abusive expression, like go and be hanged!*

diēs -ēi, m. or f., *daytime, day; a day, period of twenty-four hours; diem ex die, from day to day*; in dies, *daily, esp. of a continuing process of change*; in diem vivere, *to live for the day*; meton., *the business or events of the day*; in gen., *time.* Esp. *a particular day, fixed date; a historic day; day of death; anniversary, esp. birthday.*

Diespiter -tris, m. *a name for Jupiter.*

diffāmo -are, *to spread evil reports about, to defame.*

differentia -ae, f., *difference, distinction.*

differĭtās -ātis, f. *difference.*

diffēro differre distŭli dīlātum. Transit., *to carry in different directions, spread abroad, scatter; to spread news; to harass, disturb, discredit a person; in time, to delay, postpone business, to put off persons.* Intransit., *to differ, be different*; nihil differt, *there is no difference.*

differtus -a -um, *stuffed full, crammed.*

difficilis -e, *difficult*; of character, *hard to deal with, morose, obstinate.* Adv. **difficilĭtěr** and **difficultěr**, *with difficulty.*

difficultās -ātis, f., *difficulty, need, trouble, distress*; of character, *obstinacy, moroseness.*

diffīdentia -ae, f., *want of confidence, distrust, despair.*

diffīdo -fīděre -fīsus sum, *to have no confidence, mistrust, despair*; partic. **diffīdens** -entis, *distrustful, diffident*; adv. **diffīdentěr.**

diffindo -finděre -fĭdi -fissum, *to split, cleave, open*; legal, diem, *to postpone business.*

diffingo -ěre, *to form again, forge anew; fig., to change.*

diffitěor -ěri, dep. *to deny, disavow.*

difflo -are, *to blow apart.*

diffluo -fluěre -fluxi -fluxum, *to flow in different directions, to dissolve, melt away.*

diffringo -fringěre -fractum, *to shatter.*

diffŭgio -fŭgěre -fūgi -fŭgitum, *to fly in different directions, to disperse.*

diffŭgium -i, n. *dispersion.*

diffundīto -are, *to scatter.*

diffundo -funděre -fūdi -fūsum, *to pour in different directions, to spread out, diffuse, extend*; esp. *to make relax, brighten up, gladden.* Hence partic. **diffūsus** -a -um, *spread out, extensive, wide*; adv. **diffūsē,** *copiously, diffusely.*

diffūsilis -e, *capable of spreading, elastic.*

dīgěro -gerěre -gessi -gestum, *to carry in different directions, to separate, spread*; esp. *in orderly fashion, to arrange.*

dīgestio -ōnis, f. *arrangement, distribution.*

dīgestus -a -um, partic. from digero; q.v.

dīgitŭlus -i, m. *a little finger; the touch of a finger.*

dīgitus -i, m. (1) *a finger*; digitus pollex, *the thumb*; index, *the forefinger*; as a measure, *a finger's breadth, an inch.* (2) *a toe.*

dīglădior -ari, dep. *to flourish the sword; to fight, struggle fiercely*; in words, *to dispute.*

dignātio -ōnis, f. *esteem; dignity, reputation, honour.*

dignĭtās -ātis, f. *worth, worthiness, merit.* Transf., *dignified appearance or style; dignified position, esteem, honour*; esp. *official rank*; plur. dignitates, *persons of rank.*

digno -are, and **dignor** -ari, dep. *to consider worthy*; with infin., *to deign to.*

dignosco (dinosco) -noscěre -nōvi, *to recognize as different, to distinguish.*

dignus -a -um. (1) *worthy, deserving*; esp. of persons, usually with abl. or genit. (2) *of things, worth having, deserved, suitable, fittings*; dignum est, foll. by infin., *it is proper.* Adv. **dignē.**

dīgrēdior -grědi -gressus, dep. *to go apart, depart, deviate*; in speech, *to digress.*

dīgressio -ōnis, f. and **dīgressus** -ūs, m. *separation, departure*; in speech, *digression.*

dīiūdicātio -ōnis, f. *judging, decision.*

dīiūdico -are. (1) *to judge between parties, to decide, determine.* (2) *to distinguish, find a difference between.*

dīiun-; see disiun-.

dīlābor -lābi -lapsus, dep., *to glide apart*: of solids, *to fall to pieces, fall down, melt, dissolve*; of liquids, gases, etc., *to flow apart, run away*; of persons in groups, *to break up, slip away*; in gen., *to break up, vanish* of time, *to go by.*

dīlācěro -are, *to tear in pieces.*

dīlāmino -are, *to split in two.*

dīlānio -are, *to tear in pieces.*

dīlāpĭdo -are, *to demolish.*

dīlargior -īri, dep. *to hand round, give liberally.*

dīlātio -ōnis, f. *putting off, postponing.*

dīlāto -are, *to spread out, extend;* litteras, *to pronounce broadly.*

dīlātor -ōris, m., *a dilatory person, loiterer.*

dīlātus, partic. from differo; q.v.

dīlaudo -are, *to praise highly.*

¹dīlectus -a -um, partic. from diligo; q.v.

²dīlectus -ūs, m.: in gen., *choosing, choice, selection;* milit., *a levy, recruiting of troops, conscription;* meton., *troops so raised.*

dīligens -entis partic. from diligo; q.v.

dīligentia -ae, f., *carefulness, attentiveness, accuracy;* esp. *care in management, economy.*

dīligo -līgēre -lexi -lectum, *to choose out; to prize, love, esteem highly.* Hence pres. partic. dīligens -entis, *attentive, careful;* esp. *careful in housekeeping, economical, saving;* adv. dīligentēr, *attentively, carefully.*

dīlōrico -are, *to tear open.*

dīlūcĕo -ēre, *to be clear, evident.*

dīlūcesco -lūcescēre -luxi, *to grow light, become day; to become clear.*

dīlūcidus -a -um, *clear, lucid, plain;* adv. dīlūcidē.

dīlūcŭlum -i, n., *the break of day, dawn.*

dīlūdium -i, n., *an interval, breathing-space.*

dīlŭo -lŭēre -lŭi -lūtum. (1) *to wash apart, separate, dissolve;* of troubles, *to remove, resolve;* of puzzles, *to clear up.* (2) *to dilute, temper; to weaken, lessen, impair.*

dīlŭvĭēs -ēi, f. *washing away, inundation.*

dīlŭvio -are, *to flood, inundate.*

dīlŭvium -i, n. *flood, deluge, inundation.*

dīmāno -are, *to flow in different directions, spread abroad.*

dīmensio -ōnis, f. *measuring.*

dīmētĭor -mētīri -mensus, dep. *to measure out.*

dīmēto -are and dep. dīmētor -ari, *to measure out.*

dīmĭcātĭo -ōnis, f., *a fight, struggle, battle.*

dīmĭco -are, -avi, *to brandish weapons;* hence *to fight, contend, struggle.*

dīmĭdĭātus -a -um, *halved, divided, half.*

dīmĭdius -a -um, *halved, divided in half;* dimidia pars, *half.* N. as subst. dīmĭdium -i, *half:* dimidio minus, *less by half.*

dīmĭnūtĭo; see deminutio.

dīmissĭo -ōnis, f. (1) *a sending out.* (2) *a dismissing, discharging.*

dīmitto -mittēre -misi -missum. (1) *to send forth, send in different directions; without object, to send (word) round.* (2) *to send away, let go, let fall;* milit. *to disband or to detach;* of a gathering, *to break up, dismiss;* of places, *to*

give up, leave; of abstr. things, *to give up, renounce, abandon.*

dimmĭnŭo -ēre, *to dash to pieces.*

dīmŏvĕo -mŏvēre -mōvi -mōtum. (1) *to move asunder, part, divide.* (2) *to separate, remove, take away.*

dīnosco = dignosco; q.v.

dīnŭmĕrātĭo -ōnis, f. *enumeration.*

dīnŭmĕro -are, *to count,* esp. *to count money, to pay.*

dĭoecēsis -ĕos and -is, f., *a district under a governor.*

dĭoecētēs -ae, m., *a revenue official or treasurer.*

Dĭōmēdēs -is, m. (1) *a hero of the Trojan War, son of Tydeus.* (2) *king of the Bistones in Thrace.*

Dĭōnē -ēs, f. and Dĭōna -ae, f. (1) *the mother of Venus.* (2) *Venus.* Adj. Dĭōnaeus -a -um.

Dĭōnÿsus (-os) -i, m., *the Greek name of Bacchus.* Hence Dĭōnÿsĭa -orum, n. pl. *the feast of Dionysus.*

dīōta -ae, f. *a two-handled wine-jar.*

dĭplōma -ătis, n. (1) *a letter of introduction given to travellers.* (2) *a government document conferring privileges.*

dīremptus -ūs, m. *a separation.*

dīreptĭo -ōnis, f. *plundering, pillaging.*

dīreptor -ōris, m., *plunderer, pillager.*

dīrĭbĕo -ēre -ĭtum, *to sort tablets when taken out of the ballot-box.*

dīrĭbĭtĭo -ōnis, f. *sorting of voting tablets.*

dīrĭbĭtor -ōris, m., *the officer who sorted voting tablets.*

dīrĭgo -rĭgēre -rexi -rectum, *to arrange, direct.* Hence partic. dīrectus -a -um, *straight, direct; straightforward, plain, simple.* Abl. as adv. dīrectō and adv. dīrectē, *straight, directly.* See also derigo.

dīrĭmo -imēre -ēmi -emptum, *to part, separate, divide.* Transf., *to break off, interrupt, stop temporarily or permanently.*

dīrĭpĭo -rĭpēre -rĭpŭi -reptum, *to snatch apart, tear to pieces;* of spoil, *to divide, hence,* milit., *to pillage, lay waste; to tear away.*

dīrĭtās -ātis, f. *misfortune, disaster; cruelty, fierceness.*

dīrumpo -rumpēre -rūpi -ruptum, *to break apart or to pieces, shatter;* of friendship, etc., *to sever, break up;* in pass., dirumpi, *to burst with envy, grief, anger.*

dīrŭo -rŭēre -ŭi -ūtum, *to pull apart, demolish, destroy, break up;* financially, *to ruin.*

dīrus -a -um, *fearful, horrible, frightful, cruel.* N. pl. dīra -orum, and f. pl. dīrae -arum, as subst., *unlucky omens, curses;* Dīrae -arum, as name for the Furies.

¹Dīs, Ditis, m. *a name of Pluto, god of the Lower World.*

²dīs, dītis (contracted from dives), *rich; having or containing or bringing wealth.*

discēdo -cēdēre -cessi -cessum. (1) *to*

go asunder, part, separate. (2) to
depart, go away; milit., to march
away; discedere ab signis, to break
the ranks; ab armis, to lay down
arms; to come out of a contest, to come
off; in gen., to depart, pass away;
to deviate, swerve, digress; polit., of
the senate, in sententiam discedere,
to support a resolution.

disceptātiō -ōnis, f. debate, discussion,
controversy.

disceptātor -ōris, m. and disceptātrix
-tricis, f. an arbitrator.

discepto -are. (1) to decide, settle,
determine. (2) to dispute, debate,
discuss.

discerno -cernĕre -crēvi -crētum, to
sever, separate, set apart. Transf.,
to distinguish, discern.

discerpo -cerpĕre -cerpsi -cerptum,
to pluck to pieces, dismember.

discessiō -ōnis, f. (1) going separate
ways, separation; polit., voting, a
division in the senate. (2) a going
away, departure.

discessus -ūs, m. (1) parting, separation. (2) departure, going away;
milit., marching off; banishment.

discidium -i, n. tearing apart; separation, division; separation in feelings,
disagreement.

discido -ĕre, to cut in pieces.

discindo -ĕre -scĭdi -scissum, to cleave
asunder, split.

discingo -cingĕre -cinxi -cinctum, to
take off the girdle, ungird. Partic.
discinctus -a -um, ungirt; at ease,
careless, dissolute.

disciplīna -ae, f., instruction, teaching;
training, education; esp. military
training. Transf., results of training,
discipline, ordered way of life; that
which is taught, learning, body of
knowledge, science; a rhetorical or
philosophical school or system.

discipŭla -ae, f., a female pupil.

discipŭlus -i, m, a pupil, apprentice.

disclūdo -clūdĕre -clūsi -clūsum to
shut away, separate, divide.

disco discĕre didici, to learn, get to
know; discere fidibus, to learn to
play on the lyre; in gen., to receive
information, find out; to become
acquainted with, learn to recognize.

discŏlor -ōris, of different colours; in
gen., different.

disconvĕnio -ire, to disagree, not to
harmonize.

discordābilis -e. disagreeing.

discordĭa -ae, f. dissension, disagreement; milit., mutiny, sedition.

discordĭōsus -a -um, full of discord,
mutinous.

discordo -are, to be at discord, disagree,
be opposed; milit., to be mutinous.

discors -cordis, disagreeing, inharmonious, opposed, different.

discrĕpantĭa -ae, f. disagreement,
difference.

discrĕpātĭo -ōnis, f, disagreement,
disunion.

discrĕpĭto -are, to be quite unlike.

discrĕpo -are -ŭi, to differ in sound, be

discordant; to disagree, be different.
Res discrepat, or impers., discrepat,
people are not agreed; with acc. and
infin., it is inconsistent that.

discrībo -scrībĕre -scripsi -scriptum,
to mark out, arrange, classify, define;
to allot, fix, appoint.
Hence partic. discriptus -a -um,
classified, arranged; adv. discripte.

discrīmen -ĭnis, n. (1) dividing line,
distinction, difference, interval.
(2) turning-point, critical moment;
crisis, hazard, danger.

discrīmino -are, to separate, sunder,
divide.

discriptĭo -ōnis, f. an arrangement
definition, distribution.

discrŭcĭo -are, to torture, torment,
esp. mentally.

discumbo -cumbĕre -cŭbŭi -cŭbĭtum.
(1) to recline at table. (2) to go to bed.

discŭpĭo -cŭpĕre (colloq.), to long.

discurro -currĕre -cŭcurri and -curri
-cursum, to run about, run to and fro.

discursus -ūs, m. a running about,
running to and fro.

discus -i, m., a quoit.

discŭtĭo -cŭtĕre -cussi -cussum, to
shatter. Transf., to disperse, scatter,
break up.

disertus -a -um, eloquent, expressive;
adv. diserte and disertim.

disĭcĭo disĭcĕre disĭĕci disiectum, to
throw in different directions, cast
asunder; of buildings, etc., to throw
down; of military formations, to
break up, disperse; of abstr. things,
to break up, frustrate.

disĭecto -are, to toss about.

¹disĭectus -a -um, partic. from disicio.
q.v.

²disĭectus -us, m., scattering, dispersing.

disiunctĭo -ōnis, f. separation, estrangement; in logic, a disjunctive proposition.

disiungo (diiungo) -iungĕre -iunxi
-iunctum, to unbind, loosen, separate,
remove, distinguish.
Hence partic. disiunctus -a -um,
separated, apart, distant, remote; of
speech, disconnected; in logic, disjunctive. Compar. adv. disiunctius,
rather in disjunctive fashion.

dispando -pandĕre -pandi -pansum, or
-pessum, to expand, stretch out.

dispār -păris, unlike, dissimilar, unequal.

dispărilis -e, unlike, dissimilar, unequal.

dispăro -are, to separate, part, divide;
n. of partic. as subst. dispărātum -i.
rhet., the contradictory proposition.

dispartio = dispertio; q.v.

dispello -pellĕre -pŭli -pulsum, to
drive in different directions, to scatter.

dispendĭum -i, n. expenditure, expense
loss.

dispenno = dispando; q.v.

dispensātĭo -ōnis, f., weighing out;
management, administration; the office
of a treasurer.

dispensātor -ōris, m. steward, bailiff
treasurer.

dispenso -are, to weigh out or pay out;
in gen., to distribute, to arrange.

disperdo -děre -dīdi -dītum, *to squander, ruin, spoil.*

dispěrěo -ire -ii, *to perish utterly, be squandered, ruined.*

dispergo -spergěre -spersi -spersum, *to scatter, disperse.* Adv. from perf. partic. **dispersē,** *dispersedly, here and there.*

dispertio -ire, and dep. **dispertior** -iri, *to separate, divide, distribute.*

dispīcio -spicěre -spexi -spectum, *to see clearly,* esp. by an effort; *to make out, discern, perceive; to reflect upon, consider.*

displicěo -ēre, *to displease;* displicere sibi, *to be dissatisfied with oneself, be out of spirits.*

displōdo -plōděre -plōsi -plōsum, *to burst noisily.*

dispōno -pōněre -pōsǔi -pōsĭtum, *to put in different places, to distribute, put in order;* milit., *to station at intervals.*

Hence partic. **dispōsĭtus** -a -um, *arranged, orderly;* adv. **dispōsĭtē,** *in order, methodically.*

dispōsĭtio -ōnis, f. *regular arrangement or order in a speech.*

dispōsĭtū abl. sing. m., *in or by arranging.*

dispōsĭtūra -ae, f., *arrangement, order.*

dispǔdet -ēre -ǔit, *it is a great shame.*

dispǔtātio -ōnis, f. *arguing, debate.*

dispǔtātor -ōris, m. *debater, disputant.*

dispǔto -are, *to reckon up; to debate, discuss, argue.*

disquīro -ěre, *to inquire into, investigate.*

disquīsĭtio -ōnis, f. *inquiry, investigation.*

dissaepio -saepire -saepsi -saeptum, *to hedge off, separate, divide;* n. of perf. partic. as subst. **dissaeptum** -i, *barrier, partition.*

dissěco -sěcare -sěcǔi -sectum, *to cut up.*

dissēmĭno -are, *to spread abroad, disseminate.*

dissensio -ōnis, f. *difference in feeling or opinion; disagreement, variance, conflict, opposition.*

dissensus -ūs, m. *disunion, disagreement.*

dissentāněus -a -um, *disagreeing, different.*

dissentio -sentire -sensi -sensum, *to be of different feeling or opinion, to be opposed, not to agree.*

dissěrēnat -are, impers., *it is clearing up all round,* of the weather.

¹dissěro -sěrěre -sěvi -sĭtum, *to scatter seed, sow; to spread about.*

²dissěro -sěrěre -sěrǔi -sertum, *to set in order;* hence *to examine, treat of, discuss.*

disserpo -ere, *to creep about, spread.*

dissertio -ōnis, f. *a severance.*

disserto -are, *to treat of, discuss, argue.*

dissĭděo -sīděre -sēdi -sessum, *to sit apart, be distant, disagree, be opposed;* of clothes, *to sit unevenly.*

dissīdo -sīděre -sēdi, *to fall apart, disagree.*

dissignātio -ōnis, f. *arrangement.*

dissignātor -ōris, m. *one that arranges, a supervisor.*

dissigno -are, *to arrange, regulate, manage.*

dissĭlio -silire -silǔi, *to eap apart, break asunder.*

dissĭmĭlis -e, *unlike, dissimilar;* adv. **dissĭmĭlĭtěr,** *differently.*

dissĭmĭlĭtūdo -ĭnis, f. *unlikeness, difference.*

dissĭmŭlātio -ōnis, f. *a concealing, dissembling,* esp. *of irony.*

dissĭmŭlātor -ōris, m. *dissembler, concealer.*

dissĭmŭlo -are. (1) *to dissemble, disguise, keep secret;* pass. with middle force, dissimulata deam, *concealing her divinity.* (2) *to ignore, leave unnoticed.* Adv. from pres. partic. **dissĭmŭlantěr,** *in a dissembling manner.*

dissĭpābĭlis -e, *that can be scattered.*

dissĭpātio -ōnis, f. *scattering.*

dissĭpo or **dissŭpo** -are, *to scatter, disperse;* milit. *to break up, rout; to break up, destroy, squander.*

Hence partic. **dissĭpātus** -a -um, *disconnected.*

dissĭtus, partic. from dissero; q.v.

dissŏcĭābĭlis -e: act., *separating;* pass. *unable to be united.*

dissŏcĭātio -ōnis, f. *separation, parting.*

dissŏcĭo -are, *to separate, sever, divide;* in feeling, *to estrange.*

dissŏlūbĭlis -e, *dissoluble, separable.*

dissŏlūtio -ōnis, f. *breaking up, dissolution, destruction;* naturae, *death;* navigii, *shipwreck;* criminum, *refutation;* rhet., *want of connexion.*

dissolvo -solvěre -solvi -sōlūtum, *to loosen, break up, undo, destroy;* glaciem, *to melt;* animam, *to die;* criminationem, *to refute;* of debts, *to pay, discharge; to release a person from difficulties, to unravel, explain a difficulty.*

Hence partic. **dissŏlūtus** -a -um, *loose;* navigium, *leaky;* of style, *disconnected;* of character, *wanting in energy, lax; profligate, dissolute.* Adv. **dissŏlūtē,** *disconnectedly, loosely; carelessly, negligently, without energy.*

dissŏnus -a -um, *discordant, different, disagreeing.*

dissors -sortis, *having a different lot or fate.*

dissuāděo suāděre -suāsi -suāsum, *to advise against, oppose by argument.*

dissuāsio -ōnis, f. *advising to the contrary, speaking against.*

dissuāsor -ōris, m. *one who advises to the contrary, one who speaks against.*

dissulto -are, *to leap apart, burst asunder.*

dissǔo -sǔěre -sǔi -sūtum, *to unstitch, undo.*

distaedet -ēre, *causes boredom or disgust.*

distantia -ae, f. *distance, difference, diversity.*

distendo (distenno) -tenděre -tendi -tentum, *to stretch apart, expand,* esp.

to *fill full*, distend. Transf., *to distract, perplex.*

Hence partic. **distentus** -a -um, *distended, full.*

distermino -are, *to separate by a boundary, divide.*

distichon distichi, n., *a poem of two lines, distich.*

distinctio -ōnis, f. *a distinction, difference; the finding of a difference, the act of distinguishing, discriminating;* rhet., *a division in a speech; a pause, stop.*

¹**distinctus** -a -um, partic. from distinguo; q.v.

²**distinctus** -ūs, m. *difference, distinction.*

distiněo -tiněre -tinŭi -tentum, *to hold asunder, keep apart, separate.* Transf., *to divide in feeling; to distract; to keep away, prevent a thing from happening.*

Hence partic. **distentus** -a -um, *distracted, occupied.*

distinguo -stinguěre -stinxi -stinctum, *to mark off, distinguish, divide.* Transf., *to separate, distinguish;* gram., *to punctuate; to set off, decorate, adorn.*

Hence partic. **distinctus** -a -um, *separate, distinct; set off, diversified, adorned.* Adv. **distinctē**, *clearly, distinctly.*

disto -are, *to be apart, be distant; to differ, be distinct;* impers., distat, *there is a difference.*

distorquěo torquēre -torsi -tortum, *to twist apart, distort; to torture.*

Hence partic. **distortus** -a -um, *distorted, deformed;* of speech, *perverse.*

distortio -ōnis, f. *distortion.*

distractio -ōnis, f. *pulling apart, separation, disunion.*

distrăho -trăhěre -traxi -tractum, *to pull apart or pull to pieces;* of associations, *to break up, dissolve;* of persons, *to draw away, estrange,* also *to distract;* of property, *to sell up;* gram., *to leave a hiatus in a verse.*

distribŭo -ŭěre -ŭi -ŭtum, *to distribute, divide.* Adv. from partic. **distribūtē**, *methodically, with logical arrangement.*

distribūtio -ōnis, f. *division, distribution.*

distringo -stringěre -strinxi -strictum, *to draw apart, stretch out, to engage at different points, divert, occupy.*

Hence partic. **districtus** -a -um, *busy, occupied, engaged.*

disturbātio -ōnis, f. *destruction.*

disturbo -are, *to drive apart in confusion; to destroy, raze to the ground; to bring to naught, frustrate, ruin.*

ditesco -ere, *to become rich.*

dithўrambicus -a -um, *dithyrambic.*

dithўrambus -i, m. *a dithyrambic poem* (originally in honour of Bacchus).

ditio, better dicio; q.v.

ditior, ditissimus; see dis.

dito -are, *to enrich, make wealthy.*

diū, adv. (1) *by day.* (2) *for a long time.* (3) *a long time ago.* Compar. **diūtius,** *longer; too long.* Superl. **diūtissimē.**

dĭurnus -a -um, *belonging to a day or lasting for a day;* n. as subst. *a journal, account-book* or *a daily allowance.*

dĭus -a -um, *divine, god-like;* hence *fine, noble;* also (apparently) *out of doors, in the open air.*

diūtinus -a -um, *lasting a long time long;* adv. **diūtinē.**

diūtius, diūtissimē; see diu.

diūturnĭtās -ātis, f. *long duration.*

diūturnus -a -um, adj., *lasting a long time, of long duration.*

dīvārĭco -are, *to stretch apart, spread out.*

dīvello -vellěre -velli -vulsum (-volsum), *to pluck apart, tear asunder, break up, destroy, interrupt; to distract, pull away, remove, separate.*

dīvendo -venděre -venditum, *to sell in separate lots.*

dīverběro -are, *to strike apart, cleave, divide.*

dīverbium -i, n. *dialogue on the stage.*

dīversĭtās -ātis, f. *contrariety, contradiction; difference, diversity.*

dīversōrĭum; see deversorium.

dīverto (dīvorto) -vertěre -verti -versum, *to turn different ways;* hence *to differ.*

Hence partic. **dīversus** -a -um, *turned away, turned in different directions;* of places, *out of the way, remote;* of character, *fluctuating, irresolute;* in gen., *different, unlike, opposed, hostile.* Adv. **dīversē,** *differently, diversely.*

dīves -vĭtis, *rich, wealthy;* with abl. or genit., *rich in.*

dīvexo -are, *to tear asunder;* hence *to destroy, plunder, to distract.*

dīvidia -ae, f. *division, trouble.*

dīvido -viděre -vīsi -vīsum. (1) *to divide up, separate into parts;* esp. *to divide among persons, distribute, allot;* polit., sententiam, *to divide a resolution into parts so that each part can be voted on;* in music, *to accompany.* (2) *to separate from one another; to distinguish; to set off, to adorn.*

Hence partic. **dīvīsus** -a -um, *separate.*

dīvidŭus -a -um, *divisible; divided, parted;* fig., *distracted.*

dīvīnātĭo -ōnis, f. *the gift of prophecy, divination;* legal, *the selection of a prosecutor.*

dīvīnĭtās -ātis, f. *divine nature, divinity; the power of prophecy or divination; excellence, surpassing merit.*

dīvīnĭtŭs, *divinely, by divine influence; by inspiration, by means of divination; admirably, nobly.*

dīvīno -are, *to foretell, prophesy, forebode.*

dīvīnus -a -um. (1) *belonging or relating to a deity, divine;* res divina, *the service of the gods;* n. as subst. *a sacrifice,* in plur. *divine things or attributes.* (2) *divinely inspired, prophetic;* vates, *a poet;* m. as subst., *a seer.* (3) *noble, admirable.* Adv. **dīvīnē,** *divinely, by divine* *power; by divine inspiration, prophetically; admirably, excellently.*

divisio -ōnis, f. *division, distribution.*

divisor -ōris, m. *a divider; a distributor,* esp. *of lands; a hired bribery agent.*

divisŭī, dat. sing. m., *for division.*

divitiae -arum, f. pl. *riches, wealth; ornaments, rich offerings;* of soil, *richness.*

divortium -i, n. *divergence, separation;* of things, *a boundary, parting of the ways;* of persons, *separation, divorce.*

divorto; see diverto.

divulgo -are, *to make common, publish, spread abroad.*

    Hence partic. **divulgātus** -a -um, *spread abroad, made common.*

divus -a -um: as adj., *divine* or *deified;* as subst., m. *a god* and f. *a goddess* (often as epithet of dead and deified emperors); **sub divo** (neuter), *in the open air.*

do dăre dĕdi dătum. (1) *to offer, give, grant, lend, bestow; to hand over, commit, devote;* of letters, *to give for dispatch;* vela dare ventis, *to sail;* poenas, *to pay a penalty;* verba, *to give words only,* i.e., *to cheat;* of news, *to tell, communicate.* (2) *to cause, bring about, put.*

dŏcĕo dŏcēre dŏcŭi doctum, *to teach, instruct* (with acc. of person and/or of thing); *with clause, to inform that* or *how;* docere fabulam *to teach a play to the actors, to bring out, exhibit.*

    Hence partic. **doctus** -a -um, *taught; learned, instructed, well-informed; experienced, clever, shrewd.* Adv. **doctē,** *learnedly, skilfully; cleverly, shrewdly.*

dochmius -i, m. *a metrical foot, the dochmiac.*

dŏcĭlis -e, *teachable, docile.*

dŏcĭlĭtās -ātis, f. *teachableness, docility.*

doctor -ōris, m. *a teacher.*

doctrina -ae, f. *teaching, instruction; knowledge, learning.*

doctus -a -um, partic. from doceo; q.v.

dŏcŭmen -inis, n. and **dŏcŭmentum** -i, n., *example, pattern, warning, proof.*

dodrans -antis, m. *three fourths;* as a measure of length, *nine inches.*

dogma -ătis, n. *a philosophical doctrine.*

Dŏlăbella -ae, m. *a Roman family name in the gens Cornelia.*

dŏlabra -ae, f. *a pick-axe.*

dŏlĕo dŏlēre dŏlŭi, *to suffer pain,* physical or mental, *to be pained, to grieve;* of things, *to cause pain.*

    Hence partic. **dŏlens,** *painful;* adv. **dŏlentĕr,** *painfully, sorrowfully.*

dŏlium -i, n. *a wine-jar, cask.*

¹**dŏlo** -are, *to hew with an axe, to work roughly;* caput fuste, *to cudgel.*

²**dŏlo** or **dŏlōn** -ōnis, m. (1) *a pike, sword-stick.* (2) *a small foresail.*

dŏlor -ōris, m., *pain,* physical or mental; esp. *disappointment, resentment.* Transf., *cause of sorrow;* rhet., *pathos.*

dŏlōsus -a -um, *crafty, deceitful, cunning;* adv. **dŏlōse.**

dŏlus -i, m. *a device, artifice; fraud, deceit, guile; a trap.*

dōmābĭlis -e, *tameable.*

dōmesticus -a -um. (1) *belonging to house* or *family, domestic;* m. as subst., esp. plur., *members of one's family.* (2) *native;* crudelitas, *towards citizens;* bellum, *civil war.*

dŏmicĭlium -i, n. *place of residence, dwelling.*

dŏmĭna -ae, f. *mistress of a household; wife, mistress, lady;* of abstr. things, *ruler, controller.*

dŏmĭnātio -ōnis, f. *mastery, control, irresponsible power, despotism.*

dŏmĭnātor -ōris, m. *ruler, governor.*

dŏmĭnātrix -icis, f. *a female ruler, mistress.*

dŏmĭnātus -ūs, m. *mastery, absolute power.*

dŏmĭnium -i, n. (1) *rule, power, ownership.* (2) *a feast, banquet.*

dŏmĭnor -ari, dep., *to rule, be supreme, domineer.*

dŏminus -i, m. *master of a house, lord, master.* Transf. *husband* or *lover; a master, owner, possessor; employer; ruler, lord, controller.*

dŏmĭporta -ae, f. *one with her house on her back, the snail.*

Dŏmĭtiānus -i, m. *son of Vespasian, brother of Titus; Emperor from 81 to 96 A.D.*

Dŏmĭtius -a -um, *name of a plebeian gens in Rome.*

dŏmito -are, *to tame, subdue, break in.*

dŏmĭtor -ōris, m, *tamer, conqueror, victor.*

dŏmitrix -icis, f. *she who tames.*

dŏmĭtus -ūs, m. *taming.*

dŏmo dŏmare dŏmŭi dŏmĭtum, *to tame, break in, conquer, subdue.*

dŏmus -ūs, f. *a house, home;* locative domi, *at home, in the house;* domi habere, *to have at home, to possess;* domum, *home, homewards;* domo, *from home.* Transf., *dwelling, abode; native country; household; philosophical school* or *sect.*

dōnārium -i, n. (1) *a temple, shrine, altar.* (2) *a votive offering.*

dōnātio -ōnis, f. *giving, donation.*

dōnātivum -i, n. *an imperial largess.*

dōnĕc (older **donicum**). (1) *up to the time when, until.* (2) *so long as, while.*

dōno -are. (1) *rem homini, to give as a present, to present, grant, bestow, give up;* esp. *to remit a debt* or *obligation; to forgive, pardon.* (2) hominem re, *to present with.*

dōnum -i, n. *a gift, present;* dono dare, *to give as a present;* esp. *a votive offering.*

dorcas -ādis, f. *gazelle, antelope.*

Dōres -um, m., *the Dorians, one of the Hellenic tribes;* adj. **Dōricus** and **Dōrius** -a -um, *Dorian, Greek.* F. **Dōris** -idis: as adj., *Dorian;* as subst., *the country of the Dorians; the wife of Nereus;* meton., *the sea.*

dormio -ire, *to sleep; to rest, be inactive.*

dormito -are, *to be sleepy, begin to sleep, nod; to dream, be lazy; of a lamp, iam dormitante lucerna, iust going out.*

dormitōrius -a -um, *for sleeping.*

dorsum -i, n. *the back, of men, animals or things; immane dorsum mari summo, a reef; a mountain ridge, 'hog's back'.*

dōs dōtis, f., *a dowry, marriage portion; a gift, quality, endowment.*

dōtālis -e, *belonging to or forming a dowry.*

dōto -are, *to provide with a dowry, endow;* partic. **dōtātus** -a -um, *richly endowed.*

drachma (drachŭma) -ae, f., *a drachma, a small Greek coin.*

drăco -ōnis, m., *a kind of snake, dragon.*

drăcōnigĕna -ae, c. *dragon-born.*

drăpēta -ae, m. *a runaway slave.*

Drĕpănum -i, n. and **Drĕpăna** -orum, plur., *a town on the west coast of Sicily.*

drŏmas -ādis, m. *a dromedary.*

Drŭentia -ae, f. *a river in Gaul (now Durance).*

Drŭïdēs -um and **Drŭïdae** -arum, m. *the Druids.*

Drŭsus -i, m. *a cognomen of the gens Livia; hence adj.* **Drŭsiănus** and **Drŭsinus** -a -um, *of Drusus:* subst. **Drŭsilla** -ae, f. *name of several females of the gens Livia.*

Drўăs -ādis, f. *a wood nymph, Dryad.*

dŭbĭtābĭlis -e, *doubtful, uncertain.*

dŭbĭtātĭo -ōnis, f., *doubt, uncertainty; hesitation, irresolution.*

dŭbĭto -are, (1) *to doubt, waver in opinion, be uncertain.* (2) *to waver as to action, be irresolute, hesitate.* Adv. from partic., **dŭbĭtantĕr**, *doubtingly, hesitatingly.*

dŭbius -a -um, *doubtful.* (1) act., *wavering:* in opinion, *doubting; uncertain;* as to action, *hesitating, irresolute.* (2) pass., *uncertain, doubted, doubtful;* n. as subst.; in dubium vocare, *to call in question;* procul dubio, *without doubt.* (3) fig., *doubtful, dangerous, critical.* Adv. **dŭbiē**, *doubtfully;* haud dubie, *certainly.*

dŭcēni -ae, -a, *a group of two hundred, or two hundred each.*

dŭcentēsĭma -ae, f. *the two hundredth part, one-half per cent.*

dŭcenti -ae, -a, *two hundred.*

dŭcentie(n)s, *two hundred times.*

dŭco dūcĕre duxi ductum. (1) *to draw; to draw along or away;* hence *to shape anything long, to construct; carmina, to make verses;* of time, *either to spend or to delay, protract.* Transf., *to charm, influence, mislead; to derive.* (2) *to draw in;* aera spiritu, *to inhale;* pocula, *to quaff.* (3) *to lead;* in marriage, *to marry a wife;* milit., *either to lead on the march,* or *to command.* (4) *to calculate, count, reckon; to esteem, consider.*

ductim, *by drawing; in a stream.*

ductĭto and **ducto** -are, *to lead, esp.*

to lead home a wife. Transf., *to cheat.*

ductor -ōris, m. *a leader, commander; a guide.*

ductus -ūs, m. (1) *drawing, drawing off.* (2) *shaping, shape;* oris, *the lineaments of the face;* muri, *line of a wall.* (3) *leading, command, leadership.*

dŭdum, *some time ago; a little while ago, not long since; a long while ago or for a long time.*

dŭellum, dŭellicus, dŭellātor = bellum, bellicus, bellator; q.v.

Dŭilius -a -um, *name of a Roman gens.*

dulcēdo -inis, f., *sweetness, pleasantness, charm.*

dulcesco -ĕre, *to become sweet.*

dulcĭcŭlus -a -um, *somewhat sweet.*

dulcis -e, *sweet;* unda, *fresh water;* in gen., *pleasant, delightful, agreeable;* of persons, *friendly, dear.* N. acc. **dulcĕ** and adv. **dulcĭter,** *sweetly.*

dulcĭtūdo -inis, f. *sweetness.*

dum. (1) adv., joined as an enclitic with other words; nondum, *not yet;* vixdum, *scarcely yet;* nedum, *not to say;* age dum, *come now.* (2) conj.: *while, during the time that; while, throughout the time that; so long as, provided that; until.*

dūmētum -i, n. *a thorn brake, thicket.*

dummŏdo, *provided that, so long as.*

dūmōsus -a -um, *covered with thorn bushes, bushy.*

dumtaxat. (1) *at least, not less than.* (2) *at most, not more than.*

dūmus -i, m. *a thorn bush, bramble.*

dŭŏ -ae, -ŏ, *two.*

dŭŏdĕcĭe(n)s, *twelve times.*

dŭŏdĕcim, *twelve.*

dŭŏdĕcĭmus -a -um, *twelfth.*

dŭŏdēni -ae, -a, *twelve at a time* or *twelve each.*

dŭŏdĕquādrāgēsĭmus, *thirty-eighth.*

dŭŏdĕquādrāgĭnta, *thirty-eight.*

dŭŏdĕquinquāgēsĭmus -a -um, *forty-eighth.*

dŭŏdētrĭcĭe(n)s, *twenty-eight times.*

dŭŏdētrĭgĭnta, *twenty-eight.*

dŭŏdēvīcēni -ae -a, *eighteen each.*

dŭŏdēvīgĭnti, *eighteen.*

dŭŏetvīcēsĭmāni -orum, m. *soldiers of the 22nd legion.*

dŭŏetvīcēsĭmus -a -um, *twenty-second.*

duplex -plicis, *double, doubled, twofold.* Transf. (1) plur., *both.* (2) *two-faced, deceitful, equivocal.* Adv. **duplĭcĭtĕr,** *doubly.*

duplĭcārius -a -um: miles, *a soldier who gets double pay.*

duplĭco -are, *to double;* of words, *to repeat;* also *to form compound words.* Transf., *to bend double;* in gen., *to lengthen, increase.*

duplus -a -um, *twice as much, double;* n. as subst. *double, esp. a double penalty.*

dŭpondius -i, m., *a coin of two asses.*

dūrābĭlis -e, *lasting, durable.*

dūrāmen -inis, n. *hardness.*

dūrātĕus -a -um, *wooden.*

duresco dūrescĕre dūrŭi, *to grow hard;* of water, *to freeze.*

dūrĭtās -ātis, f., *harshness, unfriendliness.*

dūrĭtĭa -ae, and **dūrĭtĭēs** -ēi, f., *hardness;* fig., *austerity, harshness, severity.*

dūro -are: transit., *to make hard or hardy, to inure;* intransit., *to become hard or dry; to be hard or callous; to endure, hold out; to last, remain, continue.*

dūrus -a -um, *hard, harsh; tough, strong, enduring;* in demeanour or tastes, *rough, rude, uncouth;* in character, *hard, austere,* sometimes *brazen, shameless;* of things, *hard, awkward, difficult, adverse.* Adv. **dūrē** and **dūrĭtĕr**, *hardly, hardily; roughly, rudely; harshly, unpleasantly, severely.*

dŭumvir and **dŭŏvir** -vĭri, m. usually pl., *a pair of magistrates, a commission of two.*

dux dŭcis, c. (1) *a guide, conductor.* (2) *a leader, ruler, commander.*

dўnastēs -is, m. *ruler, prince.*

Dyrrhăchĭum -i, n. *a port in Illyria.*

E

E, e, the fifth letter of the Latin alphabet.

e, prep. = ex; q.v.

ēă, adv. = abl. of is; q.v.

ĕādem, *by the same way, likewise.*

ĕātĕnus, *so far.*

ĕbēnus -i, m. = hebenus; q.v.

ēbĭbo -bĭbĕre -bĭbi, bĭbum, *to drink up.*

ēblandĭor -iri, dep. *to obtain by flattery.*

ēbrĭĕtās -atis, f. *drunkenness.*

ēbrĭŏlus -a -um, *tipsy.*

ēbrĭōsĭtās -ātis, f. *love of drink, drunkenness.*

ēbrĭōsus -a -um, *drink-loving.*

ēbrĭus -a -um, *drunk, intoxicated.*

ēbullĭo -ire, *to boil up; to boast of.*

ēbŭlum -i, n. (or **-us** -i, m.), *the dwarf elder.*

ēbur -ŏris, n. *ivory.* Transf. (1) of things made of ivory. (2) *the elephant.*

ēburnĕŏlus -a -um, *made of ivory.*

ēburnĕus or **ēburnus** -a -um, *made of ivory, white as ivory.*

ēcastor; see Castor.

ecce, *behold! lo! see!*

eccĕrĕ, *there you are!*

ecclēsĭa -ae, f., *an assembly of the (Greek) people.*

ecdĭcus -i, m. *a solicitor for a community.*

Ēcĕtra -ae, f. *capital of the Volsci.*

ecf-; see eff-.

ĕchĕnĕĭs -ĭdis, f., *a sucking fish, the remora.*

ĕchīnus -i, m. (1) *an edible sea-urchin.* (2) *a copper dish.*

ĕchō -ūs, f. *an echo;* personif., *Echo, a wood-nymph.*

eclŏgārĭi -orum, m. pl. *select passages or extracts.*

ecquando, adv., *ever? at any time?*

ecqui, ecquae or ecqua, ecquod, in-

---

terrog. adj., *is there any . . . that? does any . . .?*

ecquis, ecquid, interrog. pron., *is there any that? does anyone?* Hence **ecquid** or **ecqui,** *at all?* or *whether?* **ecquō,** *whither?*

ĕcŭlĕus i, m. *a little horse, colt; a rack, instrument of torture.*

ĕdācĭtās -ātis, f. *greediness, gluttony.*

ĕdax -ācis, f. *greedy, gluttonous; destructive, consuming.*

ēdĕpol; see Pollux.

ēdīco -dīcĕre -dixi -dictum, *to announce, declare;* esp. of a magistrate, *to decree, ordain by proclamation.* Hence n. of partic. as subst. **ēdictum** -i, *a decree, edict.*

ēdictĭo -ōnis, f. *an edict.*

ēdicto -are, *to proclaim.*

ēdisco -discĕre -dĭdici, *to learn thoroughly.*

ēdissĕro -sĕrĕre -sĕrŭi -sertum, *to explain, set forth, relate fully.*

ēdisserto -are, *to explain exactly.*

ēdĭtīcĭus -a -um, *announced, proposed:* iudices, *jurors chosen by a plaintiff.*

ēdĭtĭo -ōnis, f. *the publishing of a book; a statement;* editio tribuum, *a proposal by a plaintiff for the choice of a jury.*

¹ĕdo ĕdĕre or esse ēdi ēsum, *to eat, devour, consume, waste.*

²ēdo -dĕre -dĭdi -dĭtum, *to put forth, give out;* animam, *to breathe one's last, die;* clamorem, *to utter.* Esp. (1) *to bring into the world, to bring forth, give birth to;* of things, *to produce.* (2) *to make known:* of writings, *to publish;* of ideas and information, *to divulge, spread;* officially, *to proclaim;* as legal t. t., *to fix, determine, nominate.* (3) *to bring about, cause, produce;* of magistrates, *to provide games for the people.*
    Hence partic. **ēditus** -a -um, *raised, high, lofty;* n. as subst. *a high place, eminence.*

ēdŏcĕo -dŏcēre -dŏcŭi -doctum, *to instruct thoroughly, inform fully.*

ēdŏmo -dŏmāre -dŏmŭi -dŏmĭtum, *to tame thoroughly, entirely subdue.*

Ēdōni -orum, *a Thracian people, famed for the worship of Bacchus;* adj **Ēdōnus** -a -um, and **Ēdōnis** -nĭdis, f. *Thracian.*

ēdormĭo -ire, *to have one's sleep out;* transit., *to sleep off.*

ēdormisco -ĕre, *to sleep off.*

ēdŭcātĭo -ōnis, f. *bringing up, training, education.*

ēdŭcātor -ōris, m. *one who brings up; a foster-father* or *a tutor.*

ēdŭcātrix -icis, f. *a foster-mother, nurse.*

¹ēdŭco -are, *to bring up, raise, rear, educate.*

²ēdūco -dūcĕre -duxi -ductum. (1) *to draw out, lead out;* of time, *to spend;* milit., *to march troops out;* legal, *to bring before a court of law;* naut., *to take a ship out of port.* (2) *to raise up* (of persons and buildings); in astra, *to praise sky-high.* (3) *to bring up, rear.*

ĕdūlis -e, *eatable.*

ēdūro -are, *to last, endure.*

ēdūrus -a -um, *very hard.*

effarcio = effercio; q.v.

effātum -i, n. from partic. of effor; q.v.

effectĭo -ōnis, f. *practising.* Transf., *an efficient cause.*

effector -ōris, m. *one who produces, causes, originates.*

effectrix -tricis, f. *she that causes or produces.*

¹effectus -a -um, partic. of efficio; q.v.

²effectus -ūs, m. *doing, execution, performance; effect, result.*

effēmĭno -are, *to make into a woman; in character, to make effeminate.*
Hence partic. **effēmĭnātus** -a -um, *effeminate, womanish;* adv. **effēmĭnātē.**

effercio or **effarcio** -fercire, -fertum, *to stuff full;* partic. **effertus,** *stuffed.*

effĕrĭtās -ātis, f., *wildness, savagery.*

¹effĕro -are, *to make wild, make savage;* partic. **effĕrātus** -a -um, *wild, savage.*

²effĕro (ecfero) efferre extūli ēlātum. (1) *to carry out, bring out;* efferre signa, *to march out.* Esp. *to carry to the grave, bury;* pass., efferri, *to be borne out, buried;* of the earth, *to bring forth, bear; to utter, express, publish words or ideas.* (2) *to carry off or away;* pass., efferri *to be carried away by feelings.* (3) *to raise up, lift up; to praise, extol;* efferri or se efferre, *to pride oneself, be puffed up.* (4) *to endure to the end.*
Hence partic. **ēlātus** -a -um, *elevated, exalted;* adv. **ēlātē,** *loftily.*

effertus -a -um, partic. from effercio; q.v.

effĕrus -a -um, *wild, savage.*

effervesco -fervescĕre -fervi, *to boil up, effervesce;* of an orator, *to be passionate.*

effervo -ĕre, *to boil up or over; to swarm forth.*

effētus -a -um, *weakened* (by giving birth); *effete.*

efficācĭtās -ātis, f. *efficacy.*

efficax -ācis, *effective, efficient, efficacious;* adv. **efficācĭter.**

efficĭens -entis, partic. from efficio; q.v.

efficientĭa -ae, f. *efficiency.*

efficio -ficĕre -fēci -fectum, *to do, produce, effect, make;* of results, *to bring about, cause* (esp. with ut and subj.); of numbers, *to make up, amount to;* philosoph. *to prove, show;* of appointments and changes, *to make.*
Hence partic. **efficĭens** -entis, *effective:* causa, *efficient cause;* adv. **efficientĕr,** *efficiently, powerfully.*

effigĭēs -ēi, or **effigĭa** -ae, f. *an image, likeness, effigy; a shade, ghost; an ideal.*

effingo -fingĕre -finxi -fictum. (1) *to wipe.* (2) *to mould, form, fashion;* esp. *to form one thing like another, and so*

to copy, represent, express in words, *conceive* in thought.

effĭo (ecf-) -fĭĕri, old pass. of efficio; q.v.

efflāgĭtātĭo -ōnis, f., *an urgent demand.*

efflāgĭtātū abl. sing. m., at *an urgent request.*

efflāgĭto -are, *to ask earnestly, demand, entreat.*

effligo -ĕre -flixi -flictum, *to destroy.*

efflo -are, *to blow out, breathe out:* animam, *to die.*

efflōresco -flōrescĕre -flōrŭi, *to blossom, break into bloom.*

efflŭo (ecflŭo) -flŭĕre -fluxi, *to flow out.* Transf. (1) *to vanish, drop off.* (2) *to pass out of mind, be forgotten.* (3) *to come to light, become known.*

efflŭvĭum -i, n., *flowing out, outlet.*

effŏdĭo -fŏdĕre -fōdi -fossum. (1) *to dig out, gouge out.* (2) *to make by digging, to excavate.* (3) *to gut, to rummage.*

effor (ecfor) -fari -fatus, dep. *to speak out, express, speak:* in logic, *to state a proposition;* in religion, *formally to dedicate a place.*
Hence partic. (in pass. sense) **effātus** -a -um, *pronounced; dedicated.*

effrēnātĭo -ōnis, f. *unbridled impetuosity.*

effrēno -are, *to unbridle, let loose;* partic. **effrēnātus** -a -um, *unbridled, unrestrained, violent;* adv. **effrēnātē.**

effrēnus -a -um, *unbridled, unrestrained.*

effringo -fringĕre -frēgi -fractum, *to break open.*

effŭgĭo -fŭgĕre -fūgi -fūgĭtum: in-transit. *to flee, fly away, escape, get off;* transit., *to escape from, avoid, shun.*

effŭgĭum -i, n. *a flying away, flight; means or opportunity of flight.*

effulgĕo -fulgēre -fulsi, *to shine out, glitter; to be distinguished, conspicuous.*

effultus -a -um, *resting upon, supported by.*

effundo (ecf-) -fundĕre -fūdi -fūsum, *to pour out, pour forth, shed;* of solids, *to fling out, empty out;* with violence, *to throw off, fling down;* esp. of horses, *to throw their riders;* of weapons, *to discharge;* spiritum extremum, *to die;* se effundere, and effundi, *to stream forth, pour forth,* also *to give oneself up to, indulge in:* of sounds, *to utter;* with ideas of generosity, *waste, etc. to pour out freely, squander;* habenas, *to slacken.*
Hence partic. **effūsus** -a -um, *poured out;* hence *widespread, extensive; extravagant, wasteful; unrestrained;* adv. **effūsē.**

effūsĭo -ōnis, f. *a pouring forth; violent movement; extravagance, prodigality; exuberance of spirits.*

effūsus, partic. from effundo; q.v.

effūtĭo -ire, *to blab out, chatter.*

ēgĕlĭdus -a -um, *with the chill off; lukewarm, tepid.*

ĕgens -entis, partic. from egeo; q.v.

ĕgēnus -a -um, *needy, destitute*; with genit. or abl., *in need of.*

ĕgĕo -ēre -ŭi, *to want, be in need*; with genit. or abl. *to be in want of, to be without, not to have*; also *to desire, wish for, want.*
Hence partic. **ĕgens** -entis, *needy, destitute*; with genit., *in need of.*

Ėgĕrĭa -ae, f. *a nymph, instructress of Numa Pompilius.*

ĕgĕro -gĕrĕre -gessi -gestum, *carry out or off.*

ĕgestās -ātis, f. *poverty, indigence, need*; with genit., *want of.*

ĕgestĭo -ōnis, f. *wasting.*

ĕgŏ, I; plur. nos. *we* (often used for sing.); alter ego, *my second self*; ad me, *to my house*; apud me, *at my house*, also *in my senses.*

ĕgrĕdĭor -grĕdi -gressus, dep.: in-transit., *to go out, pass out*; milit., *to march out*; naut., egredi (ex) navi, *to disembark*; in speech, *to digress*; sometimes *to go up, ascend*; transit., *to go out of, pass beyond, overstep, pass.*

ĕgrĕgĭus -a -um, *not of the common herd; excellent, extraordinary, distinguished*; adv. **ĕgrĕgĭē**.

ĕgressus -ūs, m. *going out, departure*; esp. *landing from a ship, disembarkation.* Transf., *a passage out; the mouth of a river*; in speech, *digression.*

ehem, *oho!*

ĕheu, *alas! woe!*

ĕhŏ, *hi!*

ei (hei), *ah! woe!*

eiă and **heiă**: expressing joy or surprise, *well!*; in exhortation, *come on!*

ĕiăcŭlor -ari, dep. *to throw out, hurl out.*

ĕicĭo -icĕre -iēci -iectum, *to throw out, cast out, eject*; vocem, *to utter*; armum, *to dislocate*; se eicere, *to rush out*; naut., *to bring to shore*; pass., *to be cast ashore, stranded*; eiectus, *a shipwrecked person.* Transf., *to drive out, expel, dispossess*; domo, *to divorce*; ex patria, *to banish*; of feelings *to cast out, put aside.*

ĕiectāmentum -i, n. *that which is thrown up.*

ĕiectĭo -ōnis, f. *banishment, exile.*

ĕiecto -are, *to hurl out, eject.*

ĕiectus -ūs, m. *casting out.*

ĕiŭlātĭo -ōnis, f., and **ĕiŭlātus** -ūs, m. *wailing, lamenting.*

ĕiŭlo are, *to wail, lament.*

ĕiūro and **ĕiĕro** -are, *to refuse* or *deny on oath*; bonam copiam, *to swear that one is insolvent*; forum sibi iniquum, *to declare that a court is partial*; magistratum, imperium, *to resign, abdicate*; in gen., *to give up, disown.*

ĕiusdemmŏdi, *of the same kind.*

ĕiusmŏdi, *of this kind, such, so.*

ēlābor -lābi -lapsus, dep. *to glide out, slip away, escape, disappear.*

ēlăbōro -are; intransit., *to labour hard, strive, take pains*; transit., *to labour on, work out, elaborate*, esp. in partic.

ēlăbōrātus, -a -um, *elaborate, artificial.*

ēlămentābĭlis -e, *very lamentable.*

ēlanguesco -guescĕre -gŭi, *to become weak, be relaxed.*

ēlātĭo -onis, f. *a lifting up*; fig., *exaltation.*

ēlātro -are, *to bark out, cry out.*

ēlātus -a -um, partic. from effero; q.v.

Ėlĕa or **Vĕlĭa** -ae, f. *town in Lucania, birth-place of Parmenides and Zeno, the founders of the Eleatic school of philosophy*; subst. **Ėlĕātes** -ae, m. Zeno; adj. **Ėlĕātĭcus** -a -um, *Eleatic.*

ēlectĭo -ōnis, f. *choice, selection.*

ēlectrum -i, n. *amber*; plur. *amber balls; an alloy of gold and silver, resembling amber.*

¹ēlectus -a -um, partic. from eligo; q.v.

²ēlectus -ūs, m. *choosing, choice.*

ēlĕgans -antis, *choice, fine, neat, tasteful*; in bad sense, *fastidious, fussy*; adv. **ēlĕgantēr**.

ēlĕgantĭa -ae, f. *taste, refinement, grace*; in bad sense, *fastidiousness.*

ēlĕgi -orum, m. pl. *elegiac verses.*

ēlĕgīa and **ēlĕgēa** -ae, f. *an elegy.*

ēlēmentum -i, n. *an element, first principle*; in plur., *physical elements; letters of the alphabet, beginnings, the elements of any science or art.*

ēlenchus -i, m. *a pearl pendant worn as an ear-ring.*

ēlĕphantus -i, c. *an elephant; ivory.*

ēlĕphās (-ans) -phantis, m. *an elephant; the disease elephantiasis.*

ēlĕvo -are, *to lift up, raise, elevate; to weaken, impair, disparage; to alleviate, lighten.*

ēlĭcĭo -licĕre -lĭcŭi -licitum, *to lure out, entice, call forth*; inferorum animas, *to conjure up.*

ēlīdo -līdĕre -līsi -līsum, (1) *to strike, knock, thrust out, expel.* (2) *to dash to pieces, shatter.*

ēlĭgo -ligĕre -lēgi -lectum, *to pick out, choose, select*; fig., *to root out.*
Hence partic. **ēlectus** -a -um, *chosen, select*; adv., **ēlectē**, *choicely.*

ēlīmĭno -are, *to carry out of doors*; dicta, *to blab.*

ēlīmo -are, *to file off, polish, elaborate, perfect.*

ēlinguis -e, *speechless* or *without eloquence.*

Ėlissa (Ėlīsa) -ae, f. *another name of Dido.*

ēlixus -a -um, *boiled, sodden.*

ellĕbŏrus (hell-) -i, m. and **ellĕbŏrum (hell-)** -i, n. *hellebore*, a plant considered a remedy for madness.

ēlŏco -are, *to let, hire out.*

ēlŏcūtĭo -ōnis, f. *oratorical delivery, elocution.*

ēlŏgĭum -i, n. *a short saying, maxim; an inscription*; esp. *on a gravestone, epitaph; a clause in a will, codicil; a record of a case.*

ēlŏquentĭa -ae, f. and **ēlŏquĭum** -i, n. *eloquence.*

ēlŏquor -lŏqui -lŏcūtus, dep. *to speak out, express*; esp. *to speak eloquently*; partic. **ēlŏquens** -entis, *eloquent*; adv. **ēlŏquentēr**.

ēlūcĕo -lūcēre -luxi, *to beam forth, shine out, glitter*.

ēluctor -ari, dep: intransit., *to struggle out*; transit., *to struggle out of, surmount a difficulty*.

ēlūcubro -are, and **ēlūcubror** -ari, dep. *to compose by lamplight*.

ēlūdo -lūdĕre -lūsi -lūsum: intransit., *to finish playing*, esp. of the waves of the sea; transit., *to parry a blow; to ward off, evade; to beat an opponent in play; to delude, mock*.

ēlūgĕo -lūgēre -luxi, *to mourn for the prescribed period*.

ēlumbis -e, *weak, feeble*.

ēlŭo -lŭĕre -lŭi -lūtum, *to wash out, wash clean, rinse, cleanse*. Transf., *to squander; to wash away, efface, remove*.
Hence partic. **ēlūtus** -a -um, *washed out, watery, insipid*.

ēlŭviēs -ēi, f. *a flowing out, discharge; a flowing over, flood*.

ēlŭvĭo -ōnis, f., *an inundation*.

Ēlȳsĭum -i, n., *Elysium, the abode of the blessed*; adj. **Ēlȳsĭus** -a -um; m. plur. as subst. *the Elysian fields*.

¹em = hem; q.v.

²em, interj. *here! hi!*

ēmācĭtās -ātis, f. *fondness for buying*.

ēmancĭpātĭo -ōnis, f. *emancipation or transfer*.

ēmancĭpo (-cŭpo) -are, *to release or emancipate a son from the patria potestas; to transfer or make over property; to give up persons*.

ēmāno -are, *to flow out; to arise, spring, emanate, spread abroad*.

Ēmăthĭa -ae, f. *a district of Macedonia*; adj. **Ēmăthĭus** -a -um, and f. **Ēmăthis** -ĭdis, *Macedonian*; Ema- thides, *the Muses*.

ēmātūresco -tūrescĕre -tūrŭi, *to become mature, to ripen; to become mild, be softened*.

ēmax -ācis, *fond of buying*.

emblēma -ātis, n. *inlaid or mosaic work*.

embŏlĭum -i, n. *a dramatic interlude*.

ēmendābĭlis -e, *that may be amended*.

ēmendātĭo -ōnis, f. *improvement, emendation, amendment*.

ēmendātor -ōris, m. and **ēmendātrix** -īcis, f. *amender, corrector*.

ēmendo -are, *to free from errors, correct, improve*; partic. **ēmen- dātus** -a -um, *free from mistakes, correct, faultless*; adv. **ēmendātē**.

ēmentĭor -iri -itus, dep. *to devise falsely, feign, counterfeit*; absol., *to make false statements*.

ēmercor -ari, dep. *to buy up*.

ēmĕrĕo -ēre -ŭi -itum and **ēmĕrĕor** -ēri -ĭtus, dep. *to obtain by service, earn completely; to deserve well of a person*; milit., *to earn pay, to serve, finish one's time*.
Hence partic. **ēmĕrĭtus** -a -um:

m. as subst., *a soldier that has served his time, a veteran*; as adj. *worn out, finished with*.

ēmergo -mergĕre -mersi -mersum: transit., *to cause to rise up*; emergere se or emergi, *to rise up, emerge, free oneself*; intransit., *to come forth, come up, emerge, free oneself, get clear*; also *to rise, come to the top; to come to light, appear*.

ēmērĭtus -a -um, partic. from emereo; q.v.

ēmētĭor -iri -mensus, dep., *to measure out*. Transf., *to pass over, traverse a distance*; partic. emensus -a -um in pass. sense, *traversed; to pass through, live through a period of time*.

ēmēto -ere, *to reap away*.

ēmĭco -mĭcare -mĭcŭi -mĭcatum. (1) *to spring out, leap forth*. (2) *to gleam, shine forth, be conspicuous*.

ēmĭgro -are, *to move from a place, migrate*; e vita, *to die*.

ēmĭnentĭa -ae, f. *standing out, pro- minence; the lights of a picture*.

ēmĭnĕo -minēre -minŭi, *to project, stand out, be conspicuous, be remark- able*.
Hence partic. **ēmĭnens** -entis, *outstanding, projecting; distinguished, eminent*.

ēmĭnor -ari, *to threaten*.

ēmĭnus, *at a distance, from a distance*.

ēmīror -ari, dep. *to wonder exceedingly, be astonished at*.

ēmissārĭum -i, n. *an outlet for water*.

ēmissārĭus -i, m. *an emissary, spy*.

ēmissĭo -ōnis, f. *sending forth, letting loose*.

ēmissus -ūs, m. *sending forth*.

ēmitto -mittĕre -mīsi -missum, *to send forth, send out*. Hence (1) *to dispatch, send on a chosen course*; of books, *to publish*. (2) *to let go, let loose, free, let slip*.

ēmo ēmĕre ēmi emptum, *to buy, purchase*; male or magno, *dear*; bene or parvo *cheap*. Transf., *to bribe, buy*.

ēmŏdĕror -ari, dep., *to moderate*.

ēmŏdŭlor -ari, dep., *to put to music*.

ēmŏlĭor -iri, dep., *to achieve by effort*.

ēmollĭo -ire -īvi -itum, *to soften, make mild or effeminate*.

ēmŏlo -ĕre, *to grind away*.

ēmŏlŭmentum -i, n. *result of effort; gain, advantage*.

ēmŏnĕo -ēre, *to warn, admonish*.

ēmŏrĭor -mŏri -mortuus, dep. *to die off, perish*.

ēmŏvĕo -mŏvēre -mōvi -mōtum, *to move out or away, remove*.

Empĕdŏcles -is, m. *a poet and philoso- pher of Agrigentum, of the fifth century* B.C.; adj. **Empĕdŏclēus** -a -um; n. pl. as subst. *the doctrines of Empedocles*.

empīrĭcus -i, m. *an unscientific physician, empiric*.

empŏrĭum -i, n. *a place of trade, market*.

emptĭo -ōnis, f. *buying, purchasing; a purchase*.

emptīto -are, *to buy up.*

emptor -ōris, m. *buyer, purchaser.*

ēmūgio -ire, *to bellow.*

ēmulgĕo -mulgēre -mulsum, *to drain out, exhaust.*

ēmungo -mungēre -munxi -munctum, *to clean a nose;* with reflex. or in pass., *to wipe one's nose.* Transf. *to cheat a person.*
Hence partic. **ēmunctus** -a -um: emunctae naris, *with a clean nose,* i.e. *shrewd, discerning.*

ēmūnio -ire, *to fortify, make safe; to build up;* paludes, *to clear up.*

ēn (sometimes **ĕm**) *lo! behold! see!* Interrog., *look, say;* with imperat., *come!*

ēnarrābilis -e. *that can be narrated or told.*

ēnarrātio -onis, f. *exposition; scansion.*

ēnarro -are, *to narrate or explain.*

ēnascor -nasci -nātus, dep. *to grow out, spring forth, arise.*

ēnăto -are, *to swim away, escape by swimming, to extricate oneself.*

ēnāvigo -are, *to sail away;* undam, *over the waves.*

endo; archaic = in.

endrŏmis -idis, f. *a rough cloak worn after exercise.*

Endymiōn -ōnis, m. *a beautiful young man, loved by the Moon.*

ēnĕco (**ēnico**) -nĕcare -nĕcŭi -nectum, *to kill off; to wear out, exhaust, torture.*

ēnervis -e, *powerless, weak.*

ēnervo -are, *to remove the sinews from; to weaken.*
Hence partic. **ēnervātus** -a -um, *weakened, powerless.*

ēnico = eneco; q.v.

ĕnim, conj. *for; namely, for instance; indeed, truly, certainly;* at enim, *but you may object . . . ;* sed enim, *but indeed.*

ĕnimvēro, *to be sure, certainly.*

ēnĭtĕo -ēre -ŭi, *to shine out, shine forth, be conspicuous.*

ēnĭtesco -ĕre, *to gleam, shine forth.*

ēnĭtor -nīti -nīsus or -nixus, dep. *to work one's way up, struggle up, ascend;* with acc., *to climb;* in gen., *to strive, struggle, make an effort;* also transit., *to bring forth, bear.*
Hence partic. **ēnixus** -a -um, *strenuous, eager;* adv. **ēnixē.**

Enna = Henna; q.v.

Ennius -i, m., Q. (239-169 B.C.), *the 'father of Roman poetry'.*

ēno -are, *to swim out, escape by swimming, flee.*

ēnōdātio -ōnis, f. *untying;* hence *explanation.*

ēnōdis -e, *without knots; clear, plain.*

ēnōdo -are, *to free from knots; to make clear, explain;* adv. from partic., **ēnōdātē,** *clearly, plainly.*

ēnormis -e, *irregular, unusual; very large, immense, enormous.*

ēnormĭtās -ātis, *irregular shape.*

ēnōtesco -nōtescĕre -nōtŭi, *to become known, be made public.*

ensĭfĕr -fĕra -fĕrum and **ensĭgĕr** -gĕra -gĕrum, *sword-bearing.*

ensis -is, m. *sword.*

enthȳmēma -ătis, n., *a thought, line of thought, argument;* esp. *a kind of syllogism.*

ēnūbo -nūbĕre -nupsi -nuptum, of a woman, *to marry out of her rank.*

ēnuclĕo -are, *to take out the kernel;* hence *to explain in detail;* partic. **ēnuclĕātus** -a -um, *straightforward, simple, clear;* adv. **ēnuclĕātē.**

ēnŭmĕrātio -ōnis, f. *counting up, enumeration; recapitulation.*

ēnŭmĕro -are, *to reckon, count up, enumerate;* esp. *to pay out;* also *to recount, recapitulate.*

ēnuntiātio -ōnis, f. *an enunciation, proposition.*

ēnuntio -are, *to tell, divulge, announce, express in words;* in logic, *to state a proposition;* also *to pronounce clearly.* N. of partic. as subst., **ēnuntiātum** -i, *a proposition.*

ēnuptio -ōnis, f.: gentis, *a woman's marrying out of her gens.*

ēnūtrio -ire, *to nourish, rear, bring up.*

'ĕo ire ivi and ii Itum, *to go;* cubitum ire, *to go to bed;* milit., ire ad arma, *to fly to arms;* polit. (pedibus) ire in sententiam, *to support a motion.* Transf., *to pass, proceed;* in exclamations, i, go to; melius ire, *to go better;* ire in, with acc., *to be changed to.*

²ĕō. (1) old dat., *thither, to that point;* of degree, so far, *to such a pitch.* (2) locative, *there;* esp. with loci (partitive genit.). (3) abl., *for that, on that account.*

ĕōdem. (1) old dat., *to the same place; to the same point or person.* (2) locative, *in the same place; in the same condition.*

Ēos, f. *dawn;* adj. **Ēoüs** and **Ēous** -a -um, *belonging to the morning, or eastern.*

ēpastus -a -um, *eaten up.*

ĕphēbus -i, m. *a young man between eighteen and twenty.*

ĕphēmĕris -idis, f. *a journal, diary.*

ĕphippiātus -a -um, *provided with a saddle.*

ĕphippium -i, n., *a horse-cloth, saddle.*

ĕphŏrus -i, m., *an ephor, a Spartan magistrate.*

ĕpicōpus -a -um, *provided with oars.*

ĕpicrōcus -a -um, *transparent, fine.*

Ĕpicūrus -i, m. *an Athenian philosopher, founder of the Epicurean school* (342-270 B.C.): adj. and subst. **Ĕpicūrēus** -a -um, *Epicurean, an Epicurean.*

ĕpicus -a -um, *epic.*

ĕpidīcticus -a -um, *for display.*

ĕpidīpnis -idis, f., *dessert.*

ĕpigramma -ătis, n. *an inscription; an epigram.*

ĕpilŏgus -i, m. *a conclusion, peroration, epilogue.*

ĕpimĕnia -orum, n. pl. *a month's rations.*

ĕpirēdium -i, n., *the strap by which a horse was fastened to a vehicle; a trace.*

Ēpīrus -i, f., *a region in north-west Greece*; adj. **Ēpīrensis** -e, *of Epirus*; subst. **Ēpīrōtes** -ae, m., *an Epirote*.

ĕpistŏlĭum -i, n. *a little letter, note*.

ĕpistŭla (or **ĕpistŏla**) -ae, f., *a written communication, letter, epistle*; ab epistulis, *to do with correspondence*, of secretaries. Transf., *sending of letters, post*.

ĕpĭtaphĭum -i, m. *a funeral oration*.

ĕpĭthălămĭum -i, n. *a nuptial song*.

ĕpĭthēca -ae, f. *addition*.

ĕpĭtŏma -ae and **ĕpĭtŏmē** -ēs, f. *abridgment, epitome*.

ĕpops -opis, m. *the hoopoe*.

ĕpos, n. *an epic poem*.

ēpōtus -a -um, *drunk up, drained*. Transf. (1) *spent on drink*. (2) *swallowed up*.

ĕpŭlae -arum, f. *food, dishes, a banquet, feast*.

ĕpŭlāris -e, *belonging to a banquet*.

ĕpŭlo -ōnis, m. *feaster*; Tresviri (later Septemviri) epulones, *a college of priests who had charge of sacrificial feasts*.

ĕpŭlor -ari, dep. *to feast, feast on*.

ĕpŭlum -i, n. *a banquet, feast*, esp. on public occasions.

ĕqua -ae, f. *a mare*.

ĕquĕs -ĭtis, m. *a horseman, rider, cavalryman*; polit., equites, *the knights, order between senate and plebs*; also collectively in sing.

ĕquester -stris -stre, *relating to horsemen, equestrian; relating to cavalry*; polit., *relating to the knights*.

ĕquĭdem *indeed, truly, for my part*; concessive, *of course, certainly, admittedly*.

ĕquīnus -a -um, *relating to horses*.

ĕquĭtātus -ūs, m. *cavalry*.

ĕquĭto -are, *to ride on horseback*; of winds, *to rush*.

ĕquŭlĕus = eculeus; q.v.

ĕquus -i, m. (older forms **ĕquos** and **ĕcus**) *a horse*; equus bellator, *a war-horse*; equis virisque, *with horse and foot, with all one's might*; ad equum rescribere, *to make a person a knight*.

ēra -ae, f. *mistress, lady*.

ērādīco -are, *to root out*.

ērādo -rādĕre -rāsi -rāsum, *to scratch out; to destroy, get rid of*.

Ĕrăto, f. *the Muse of lyric and love-poetry*.

ercisco, erctum = hercisco, herctum; q.v.

Ĕrĕbus -i, m. *a god of the lower world*; hence *the lower world*. Adj. **Ĕrĕbēus** -a -um.

Ĕrechtheus -ĕi, m. a mythical king of Athens; adj. **Ĕrechthēus** -a -um, m. *Athenian*; subst. **Ĕrechthīdae** -arum, m. pl. *the Athenians*.

ērectus, partic. from erigo; q.v.

ērēpo -rēpĕre -repsi -reptum, *to creep out; to creep up or over*.

ēreptĭo -ōnis, f. *taking by force, seizure*.

ēreptor -ōris, m., *one who takes by force, a robber*.

ergā, prep. with acc., *towards*, esp. of personal relations; more generally, *about*.

ergastŭlum -i, n. *a workhouse for debtors or slaves*; in plur., *the inmates of an* ergastulum.

ergō: prep., preceded by genit., *because of, on account of*; adv., *therefore, accordingly, then*.

Ērichthŏnĭus -i, m. *a mythical king of Athens*; also *a mythical king of Troy*; adj. **Ērichthŏnĭus** -a -um, *Athenian or Trojan*.

ērĭcĭus -i, m. *hedgehog*; milit. *chevaux de frise*.

ērĭgo -rĭgĕre -rexi -rectum, *to set up, place upright, erect, raise*; milit., *to march a body of soldiers up a height*. Transf., *to arouse, excite; encourage, cheer*.
    Hence partic. **ērectus** -a -um, *raised, upright, erect; high, elevated, proud; alert, anxious, intent, with minds on the stretch; resolute, cheerful*.

ērīlis -e, *of a master or mistress*.

Ērīnys -ўos, f., *one of the Furies*; plur. Erinyes, *the Furies*. Transf., *scourge, curse*.

ērĭpĭo -rĭpĕre -rĭpŭi -reptum, *to snatch away, tear out*; in good sense, *to free, rescue*.
    Hence partic. **ēreptus** -a -um, *snatched away or rescued*.

ērŏgātĭo -ōnis, f., *payment, expenditure*.

ērŏgo -are, *to ask for and obtain*; used in the sense *to pay out* money, esp. from public funds.

errābundus -a -um, *wandering*.

errātĭcus -a -um, *wandering, erratic*.

errātĭo -ōnis, f. and **errātus** -ūs m. *wandering, straying*.

¹erro -are, *to wander, stray, rove*; transit., *to wander over*. Transf., *to waver; to err, be mistaken*. N. of partic. as subst. **errātum** -i, *a fault, error, technically or morally*.

²erro -ōnis, m. *a wanderer, vagabond*.

error -ōris, m. *wandering about*. Transf., *wavering, uncertainty, error, mistake; source of error, deception*.

ērŭbesco -rŭbescĕre -rŭbŭi, *to grow red, blush*; with infin., *to blush to*; with acc., *to blush for, to respect*; gerundive **ērŭbescendus** -a -um, *of which one should be ashamed*.

ērūca -ae, f. *a colewort*.

ēructo -are, *to belch forth, throw up, vomit*. Transf. (1) *to talk drunkenly about*. (2) *to cast out, eject*.

ērŭdĭo -ire, *to free from roughness; to instruct, teach, educate*.
    Hence partic. **ērŭdītus** -a -um, *instructed, educated*; adv. **ērŭdītē**, *learnedly*.

ērŭdītĭo -ōnis, f. *teaching, instruction; knowledge, learning*.

ērumpo -rumpĕre -rūpi -ruptum: transit., *to break open, cause to burst forth; to vent, discharge*; intransit., *to break out, burst forth*; milit., *to rush forth*.

ērŭo -rŭĕre -rŭi -rŭtum, *to tear out, dig up*; of buildings, *to raze, demolish*.

ēruptiō -ōnis, f. *a bursting* or *breaking forth*; milit., *sally, attack.*

ĕrus -i, m. *master, owner, lord.*

ervum -i, n. *bitter vetch.*

Ēryx -rÿcis or **Ērÿcus** -i, m., *a mountain and city on the west coast of Sicily, with a famous temple of Venus.* Adj. **Ērÿcinus** -a -um; f. as subst. *Venus.*

esca -ae, f. *food, victuals,* esp. *as bait.*

escārius -a -um, *relating to food* or *bait.*

ēscendo -scendĕre -scendi -scensum: intransit., *to climb up, ascend; to go up from the sea-coast inland;* transit., *to ascend.*

ēscensiō -ōnis, f., *a movement inland,* esp. hostile.

ēscŭlentus -a -um, *edible, esculent.*

ēscŭletum, escŭlus; see aesc-.

ēsĭto -are, *to keep eating.*

Esquĭliae -arum, f. *one of the seven hills of Rome, the Esquiline.* Hence adj. **Esquĭlius** and **Esquĭlīnus** -a -um, *Esquiline;* f. as subst. **Esquĭlīna** -ae; *the Esquiline gate.*

essĕdārius -i, m. *a fighter in a British* or *Gallic war-chariot.*

essĕdum -i, n. *a war-chariot used by Gauls and Britons.*

ēsū, abl. sing. m., *in the eating.*

ēsŭrio -ire, *to be hungry, desire food:* in gen., *to long for.*

ēsŭrītio -ōnis, f. *hunger.*

et; as adv., *also, even;* as conj., *and; and indeed;* in narrative, *and then;* occasionally adversative, *and yet;* after alius, idem, par, *as* or *than;* repeated et . . . et . . ., *both . . . and . . .;* so -que . . . et . . .; nec (neque) . . . et, *not only not . . . but.*

ĕtĕnim, *for indeed.*

ĕtēsiae -arum, m. pl. *winds which blow about the dogdays, Etesian winds.*

ēthŏlŏgus i, m. *a mimic.*

ĕtiam, (1) as yet, still; etiam atque etiam, *again and again.* (2) *also, besides, even;* non solum (or modo) . . . sed (or verum) etiam, *not only . . . but also;* with comparatives, *still.* (3) in answers, *yes, certainly.* (4) in questions, expressing incredulity, *actually? really?*

ĕtiamnum and **ĕtiamnunc,** *yet, still, till now.*

ĕtiam-si, *even if, although.*

ĕtiam-tum and **ĕtiam-tunc,** *even then, till that time, till then.*

Etrūria -ae, f. *a district in north-west Italy;* hence adj. and subst. **Etruscus** -a -um, *Etruscan,* an *Etruscan.*

et-si, *even if, although;* elliptically, *and yet, notwithstanding.*

ĕtÿmŏlŏgia -ae, f., *etymology.*

eu, *good! well done!*

Euan or **Euhan,** m. *a name of Bacchus.*

euans or **euhans** -antis, *shouting Euan,* of Bacchanals.

euge and **eugĕpae,** *well done!*

Euias or **Euhias** -adis, f., *a Bacchante.*

Euĭus or **Euhĭus** -i, m., *a name of Bacchus.*

Eumĕnides -um, f., *Eumenides, the gracious ones,* euphem. for the Furies.

eunŭchus -i, m., *a eunuch.*

euoe, euhoe, interj., *shout of the Bacchantes.*

Eurĭpides -is, m., *the Athenian tragic poet* (c. 485-406 B.C.); adj. **Eurĭpīdēus** -a -um.

Eurĭpus -i, m. *a channel, strait,* esp. *the strait between Euboea and Boeotia; a canal* or *water-course.*

Eurōpa -ae, f. and **Eurōpē** -ēs, f.: myth., *daughter of Agenor, whom Jupiter, in the form of a bull, carried off to Crete;* geograph., *the continent of Europe.* Adj. **Eurōpaeus** -a -um, *belonging to Europa* or *to Europe.*

Eurus -i, m., *the south-east* or *east wind;* adj. **Eurōus** -a -um, *eastern.*

Euterpē -ēs, f. *Muse of harmony.*

Euxĭnus -a -um, *an epithet of the Black Sea.*

ēvādo -vādĕre -vāsi -vāsum. Intransit., *to go out, go forth;* esp. *to climb up* or *out; to escape, get off.* Transf., *to turn out, result.* Transit., *to go out through, pass over; to climb up; to escape.*

ēvăgor -ari, dep.: intransit., *to wander out, stray away;* milit. *to wheel right and left, manoeuvre;* transit., *to overstep.*

ēvălesco -vălēscĕre -vălŭi, *to grow strong, prevail, come into vogue;* in perf., *to have power, be able.*

ēvānesco -vānescĕre -vānŭi, *to vanish, disappear, pass away.*

ēvānidus -a -um, *vanishing, passing away.*

ēvasto -are, *to devastate, lay waste utterly.*

ēvĕho -vĕhĕre -vexi -vectum, *to carry out* or *up;* with reflex., or pass., of ships, *to sail away;* of riders, *to ride away.*

ēvello -vellĕre -velli -vulsum, *to tear out, pluck out.*

ēvĕnio -vĕnire -vēni -ventum, *to come out.* Transf., *to turn out, result; to befall, happen, occur.* Hence n. of partic. as subst. **ēventum** -i, *issue, consequence, result; event, occurrence, experience.*

ēventus -ūs, m. *consequence, issue, result; event, occurrence, experience.*

ēverbĕro -are, *to strike violently.*

ēverrĭcŭlum -i, n., *a fishing-net, drag-net;* fig., *a clean sweep.*

ēverro -verrĕre -verri -versum, *to sweep out; to plunder.*

ēversio -ōnis, f. *overturning, destruction, ruin.*

ēversor -ōris, m. *overturner, destroyer.*

ēverto -vertĕre -verti -versum, *to turn out, dislodge, eject; to turn up stir; to overturn, throw down, demolish destroy, ruin.*

ēvestīgātus -a -um, *tracked out, discovered.*

ēvīdens -entis, *visible, clear, plain, evident*; adv. ēvīdentĕr.

ēvīdentĭa -ae, f., *distinctness of language.*

ēvĭgĭlo -are: intransit. *to wake up; to be awake, be vigilant*; transit., *to watch through, pass in watching; to work hard at, to elaborate.*

ēvīlesco -vilescĕre -vīlŭi, *to become, contemptible.*

ēvincĭo -vincire -vinxi -vinctum, *to bind, bind round.*

ēvinco -vincĕre -vīci -victum, *to conquer entirely, utterly subdue*; in gen., *to prevail over, get through, get over; of results to bring about; of conclusions, to prove irresistibly.*

ēviscĕro -are, *to disembowel, tear in pieces.*

ēvĭtābĭlis -e, *that can be avoided.*

ēvĭto -are, *to avoid, shun.*

ēvŏcātor -ōris, m., *one who calls to arms.*

ēvŏco -are, *to call out*; esp. *to summon the spirits of the dead, or a deity*; milit. and polit. *to call out, call up, summon.* Transf., *to draw out, draw on; to call forth, produce.* M. pl. of partic. as subst. ēvŏcāti -orum, *veteran soldiers recalled to the colours.*

ēvoe; see euoe.

ēvŏlo -are, *to fly out, fly away; to come out quickly, rush forth, escape.*

ēvŏlūtĭo -ōnis, f., *the unrolling and reading of a book.*

ēvolvo -volvĕre -volvi -vŏlūtum. (1) *to roll out, roll forth*; of news, evolvi, *to spread.* (2) *to unroll, roll open*; esp. *to unroll a book to read it.* Transf., *to extricate, disentangle, detach; to unravel, disclose, explain.*

ēvŏmo -ĕre -ŭi -ĭtum, *to vomit forth, disgorge.*

ēvulgo -are, *to publish, make known.*

ēvulsĭo -ōnis, f. *pulling out.*

ex or ē, prep. with abl. (1) in space: *from or out of*; ex equo pugnare, *to fight on horseback (operating from it)*; ex adverso *opposite.* (2) in time, *since*, esp. ex quo, *from which time, since; also immediately after*; aliud ex alio, *one thing after another.* (3) in other relations: to denote origin, *from, away from, out of, of*; ex animo, *heartily*; ex industria, *on purpose*; unus ex, *one of*; pocula ex auro, *gold cups*; to denote cause or occasion, *from, on account of, by reason of*; e vulnere mori, *to die of a wound*; to denote correspondence, *in accordance with*; ex re et ex tempore, *according to time and circumstance*; to denote advantage, e.g. e republica, *for the benefit of the state*; in gen., *in regard to, with respect to*; ex parte, *in part.*

exăcerbo -are, *to provoke, exasperate, embitter.*

exactĭo -ōnis, f. *driving out, expulsion; demanding, exacting, esp. collecting of debts, tribute, etc.*; in gen., *management, direction.*

exactor -ōris, m. *one who drives out; one who demands or exacts, esp. a* collector of taxes; in gen., *superintendent, overseer.*

exactus -a -um, partic. from exigo; q.v.

exăcŭo -ŭĕre -ŭi -ūtum, *to sharpen to a point, make sharp, intensify, stimulate.*

exadversum or exadversus, *opposite.*

exaedĭfĭcātĭo -ōnis, f. *building up.*

exaedĭfĭco -are *to build up, erect, finish.*

exaequātĭo -ōnis, f. *making equal, equality.*

exaequo -are. (1) *to make level or equal, level up, relate.* (2) *to equal, be like.*

exaestŭo -are, *to be hot, boil up, foam up.*

exaggĕrātĭo -ōnis, f., *heaping up*; hence *elevation, exaltation.*

exaggĕro -are, *to heap up; to enlarge, increase; to heighten, exalt, magnify.*

exăgĭtātor -ōris, m. *a censurer.*

exăgĭto -are, *to chase about; to harass, disquiet, disturb; to scold, blame, censure, criticize; to excite, irritate.*

exalbesco -bescĕre -bŭi, *to grow white, turn pale.*

exāmen -ĭnis, n. (1) *a swarm; a throng, crowd, shoal.* (2) *the tongue of a balance; testing, consideration.*

exāmĭno -are, *to weigh; to consider.*

exāmussim, *according to rule, exactly.*

exanclo -are, *to drain, exhaust; to bear to the end, endure.*

exănĭmālis -e, *dead; deadly.*

exănĭmātĭo -ōnis, f. *want of breath, esp. from fright.*

exănĭmis -e and exănĭmus -a -um, *lifeless, dead*; also (exanimis only), *breathless, esp. from fright.*

exănĭmo -are. (1) *to take away the breath of, to wind, stun, weaken.* (2) *to deprive of life, to kill.*

exantlo = exanclo; q.v.

exardesco -ardescĕre -arsi -arsum, *to blaze up, to become hot, or inflamed*; of disturbances, *to break out.*

exāresco -ārescĕre -ārŭi, *to dry, become dry or exhausted.*

exarmo -are, *to disarm, deprive of arms.*

exăro -are, *to plough up, dig up; to produce by ploughing*; hence *to write on waxen tablets.*

exaspĕro -are, *to make rough, to irritate.*

exauctōro -are, *to dismiss from military service, discharge, cashier.*

exaudĭo -ire, *to hear plainly; to hear favourably, listen to.*

exaugĕo -ēre, *to increase much.*

exaugŭrātĭo -ōnis, f. *profanation, desecration.*

exaugŭro -are, *to desecrate, profane.*

exauspĭco -are, *to take an augury from.*

excaeco -are, *to make quite blind; to stop up a channel.*

excalcĕo -are, *to take the shoes from*; in drama, *to take the tragic cothurnus from an actor.*

excandescentĭa -ae, f., *heat, irascibility.*

excandesco -descĕre -dŭi. *to become hot, to glow.*

excanto -are, *to charm out, bring forth by incantations.*

excarnifico -are, *to tear to pieces.*

excăvo -are, *to hollow out.*

excēdo -cēdĕre -cessi -cessum: intransit., *to go out, go away, pass out;* e vita, *to die; to go beyond a point or limit; to attain to, result in;* transit., *to leave, pass beyond, exceed.*

excellentia -ae, f. *eminence, distinction.*

excello -ĕre, *to stand out, excel, be distinguished;* partic. **excellens**, *high, lofty, eminent, remarkable;* adv. **excellentĕr**, *eminently.*

excelsĭtās -ātis, f., *height, elevation.*

excelsus -a -um, adj., *lofty, high, elevated, eminent.* N. as subst. **excelsum** -i, *a height, eminence.* Adv. **excelsē**, *loftily.*

exceptĭo -ōnis, f. *exception, restriction, limitation;* esp. *an exception by the defendant to the plaintiff's statement of a case.*

excepto -are. (1) *to take up, catch;* auras, *to snuff up.* (2) *to take in succession.*

excerno -cernĕre -crēvi -crētum, *to separate, sift, sort.*

excerpo -cerpĕre -cerpsi -cerptum, *to pick out; to gather out, choose; to put on one side, separate.* N. of partic. as subst. **excerptum** -i, *an extract.*

excessus -ūs, m. *departure; from life,* i.e. *death; from subject,* i.e. *digression.*

excetra -ae, f. *a snake, viper.*

excidĭum -i, n. *overthrow, destruction.*

¹**excido** -cidĕre -cidi, *to fall out, fall away, be lost; of words, to slip out unawares, escape;* of ideas, *to pass from memory or thought, be forgotten.*

²**excido** -cidĕre -cidi -cisum, *to cut out;* lapides e terra, *to quarry.* Transf. (1) *to destroy, demolish;* portas, *to force open.* (2) *to root out, banish.*

excĭēo and **excĭo** -cire -civi and -cii -citum and citum, *to call out, arouse;* esp. *to awaken from sleep or to summon to help;* in gen., of persons, *to excite, arouse;* of feelings, *to call forth, excite, produce;* of material things, *to stir, shake.*

excipĭo -cipĕre -cēpi -ceptum. (1) *to take out; to rescue; to except.* (2) *to take up, catch; to greet, welcome* a person; *to pick up* news or ideas *by listening;* of events, *to take people, come upon them.* (3) passively, *to receive; to take over from, follow, succeed, come later.*

excisĭo -ōnis, *destruction.*

excĭto -are, *to arouse, rouse up;* of things, *to provoke, call forth, cause;* of persons, *to console, cheer, inspire;* of buildings, *to raise, erect;* of fire, *to kindle, inflame.*
  Hence partic. **excĭtātus** -a -um, *lively, vigorous, loud.*

exclāmātĭo -ōnis, f. *exclamation.*

exclāmo -are, *to shout, cry aloud; to exclaim; to call somebody by name.*

exclūdo -clūdĕre -clūsi -clūsum, *to shut out, exclude, keep away;* of things, *to knock out;* of birds, *to hatch.*

exclūsĭo -ōnis, f. *shutting out, exclusion.*

excōgĭtātĭo -ōnis, f. *contriving, devising.*

excōgĭto -are, *to think out, devise, contrive, invent.*

excŏlo -cŏlĕre -cŏlŭi -cultum, *to tend or cultivate carefully; to adorn, polish, refine; to serve, honour a deity or person.*

excŏquo -cŏquĕre -coxi -coctum, *to boil down, boil away; to cook, bake, make hard;* fig., *to cook up.*

excors -cordis, *foolish, silly, without intelligence.*

excrēmentum -i, n. *excrement;* oris, *spittle.*

excresco -crescĕre -crēvi -crētum, *to grow up, spring up.*

excrētus -a -um, partic. of excerno, or of excresco.

excrŭcio -are, *to torture, torment.*

excŭbĭae -arum, f. pl. *lying out;* milit., *keeping watch, keeping guard.* Transf., *watchfires; watchmen, guard.*

excŭbĭtor -ōris, m. *sentinel, watchman, guard.*

excŭbo -bare -bŭi -bĭtum, *to lie or sleep out of doors;* milit., *to keep watch; to be watchful, vigilant.*

excūdo -cūdĕre -cūdi -cūsum, *to strike out, beat out;* esp. *to hammer, forge;* of birds, *to hatch.* Transf., of bees, *to mould;* of writers, *to compose.*

exculco -are, *to trample firm, tread hard.*

excūrātus -a -um, *carefully seen to.*

excurro -currĕre -cŭcurri and -curri -cursum *to run out, hasten forth;* milit., *to attack, make a sortie;* with acc., *to run over;* fig., *to run out, move freely;* of places, *to run out, to project.*

excursĭo -ōnis, f. *running out; movement forwards;* fig., *outset of a speech;* milit., *attack, assault, sally.*

excursor -ōris, m. *scout, skirmisher.*

excursus -ūs, m. *running out;* rhet., *digression;* milit., *attack, sally, assault.*

excūsābĭlis -e, *excusable.*

excūsātĭo -ōnis, *an excuse, plea, defence.*

excūso -are, *to exempt from blame or accusation; to excuse a person, to make excuses for a thing; to allege in excuse, to plead.*
  Hence partic. **excūsātus** -a -um, *free from blame;* adv. **excūsātē**, *excusably.*

excŭtio -cŭtĕre -cussi -cussum. (1) *to shake out;* esp. *to shake out clothes to find anything hidden;* hence *to search, examine a person;* fig., *to investigate.* (2) *to strike off, throw out, knock away, shake off.*

exec-; see exsec-.

exēdo -esse -ēdi -ēsum, *to eat up, devour, consume; to wear down, exhaust, destroy.*

exedra -ae, f. *a hall for conversation or debate.*

exemplāris -e, *serving as a copy*; n. as subst. **exemplar** -āris, *a copy, transcript; a likeness; a pattern, ideal.*

exemplum -i, n. (1) *a sample, example*; exempli causa (or gratia), *for instance; general character, manner, fashion* (as shown by examples); *an example to be followed, model; a precedent; an example of what may happen, warning, object-lesson*; hence *a punishment intended to deter.* (2) *a copy, transcript.*

exemptus -a -um, partic. of eximo; q.v.

exentēro -are, *to torture, exhaust.*

exĕo -ire -ii (-ivi) -itum: intransit., *to go out, go away, go forth; to pass from state to state; to get out, to become known*; of time, *to come to an end, pass away*; transit., *to pass over*; also *to ward off.*

exeq-; see **exseq-**.

exercĕo -ēre -ŭi -itum, *to keep at work, exercise, train, cultivate*; of abstr. things, *to employ, exploit*; of feelings, arts, and processes, *to practise, exercise*; of the mind, *to train*; hence *to overwork, harass, trouble.*

Hence partic. **exercĭtātus** -a -um, *trained, schooled; harassed; severe, vexatious.*

exercĭtātĭo -ōnis, f. *practice, exercise; experience.*

exercĭtĭum -i, n. *practice, exercise.*

exercĭto -are, *to train hard, keep at work.*

Hence partic. **exercĭtatus** -a -um, *trained, practised, exercised; troubled, harassed.*

¹exercĭtus -a -um, partic. of exerceo; q.v.

²exercĭtus -ūs, m. *training; a trained body of soldiers, army*; esp. *the infantry*; poet. in gen., *crowd, swarm.*

exēsor -ōris, m. *one who gnaws or eats away.*

exhālātĭo -ōnis, f. *exhalation, vapour.*

exhālo -are: transit., *to exhale, breathe out*; intransit., of things, *to steam*; of persons, *to expire.*

exhaurĭo -haurire -hausi -haustum. (1) *to draw out*; in gen., *to remove, take out, take away.* (2) *to drain dry, empty out, impoverish; to finish, bring to an end; to endure, suffer.*

exhērēdo -are, *to disinherit.*

exhērēs -ēdis, *disinherited.*

exhĭbĕo -hibēre -hibŭi -hibitum, *to produce, show, display, exhibit, present; to offer, allow; to produce by making, to cause.*

exhĭlăro -are, *to make cheerful.*

exhorresco -horrescĕre -horrŭi, *to shudder exceedingly, be terrified*; transit., *to tremble at, to dread.*

exhortātĭo -ōnis, f. *exhortation, encouragement.*

exhortātīvus -a -um, *of exhortation.*

exhortor -ari, dep. *to exhort, encourage.*

exigo -igĕre -ēgi -actum. (1) *to drive out or away; to force out, exact, demand; to sell.* (2) *to drive through*; hence *to complete, finish; to determine, settle, adjust, regulate; to ascertain, decide.*

Hence partic. **exactus** -a -um. *accurate, precise, exact.*

exĭgŭĭtās -ātis, f. *littleness, smallness.*

exĭgŭus -a -um, *small, little, scanty*: of quantity, in size, *small*; in number, *scanty*; in time, *short*; of quality, *meagre.* N. as subst. **exĭgŭum** -i, *small extent.* Adv. **exĭgŭē**, *sparingly, scantily, scarcely.*

exilis -e, *thin, slender, meagre*; in possessions, *poor*; with genit., *without*; of style, *dry, dreary.* Adv. **exilitĕr**, *thinly, poorly, meagrely.*

exilitās -ātis, f. *thinness, meagreness, weakness.*

exĭmĭus -a -um, *excepted*; hence *selected; exceptional, distinguished.* Adv. **exĭmĭē**, *uncommonly, exceptionally.*

exĭmo -ĭmĕre -ēmi -emptum, *to take out, take away*, esp. off a list or out of a group; *to free, release; to take away, remove* an abstr. thing: of time, *to waste.*

exin = exinde; q.v.

exĭnānĭo -ire, *to empty; gentes, to plunder.*

exinde (**exin, exim**): in space, *thence, next*; in time, *thereupon, after that, then*; in logic, *consequently, accordingly.*

existĭmātĭo -ōnis, f. *the opinion that a man has, judgement; the opinion that others have of a man,* esp. morally, *reputation, good name, honour, character*; in finance, *credit.*

existĭmātor -ōris, m., *one who forms or gives an opinion, a critic.*

existĭmo (-ŭmo) -are, *to judge a thing according to its value*; in gen., *to judge, consider, regard.*

exĭtĭābĭlis -e, *deadly, destructive.*

exĭtĭālis -e, *destructive, fatal, deadly.*

exĭtĭo -ōnis, f. *going out.*

exĭtĭōsus -a -um, *destructive, fatal, deadly.*

exĭtĭum -i, n. *going out or away*; hence *destruction, ruin*; also *a cause of destruction.*

exĭtus -ūs, m. *going out, going forth; a means of going out, exit; end, finish; issue, result.*

exlex -lēgis, *bound by no law, lawless, reckless.*

exmŏvĕo = emoveo; q.v.

exobsĕcro -are, *to entreat earnestly.*

exŏcŭlo -are, *to deprive of eyes.*

exŏdĭum -i, n., *a comic afterpiece.*

exŏlesco -ŏlescĕre -ŏlēvi -ŏlētum, *to grow old and weak, decay, fade out*; partic. **exŏlētus** -a -um, *worn out*; m. as subst. *a dissolute person.*

exŏnĕro -are, *to unload, disburden*; in gen., *to free, release, relieve.*

exopto -are, *to desire eagerly, long for*;

partic. **exoptātus** -a -um,, *desired, longed for.*

exōrābilis -e, *able to be entreated, placable.*

exōrātor -ōris, m., *one who entreats successfully.*

exordior -ordiri -orsus, dep. *to begin to weave;* in gen., *to begin.* Partic. in pass. sense **exorsus** -a -um, *begun.*

exordium -i, n., *the warp of a web;* in gen., *a beginning;* esp. *the beginning of a speech.*

exōrior -ōriri -ortus, dep. *to rise, spring up, issue, appear, come forward.*

exornātio -ōnis, f., *adorning, ornament.*

exornātor -ōris, m., *one who adorns, an embellisher.*

exorno -are, *to furnish, provide plentifully;* also *to ornament, adorn.*

exōro -are, *to entreat successfully, obtain* a thing *by entreaty, prevail upon* a person.

¹**exorsus** -a -um, partic. of exordior; q.v.

²**exorsus** -ūs, m., *a beginning.*

exortus -ūs, m., *a rising; the East.*

exōs -ossis, *without bones.*

exoscŭlor -ari, dep. *to kiss.*

exosso -are, *to bone, take out the bones.*

exostra -ae, f. *a theatrical machine, revealing the inside of a house to the spectators.*

exōsus -a -um, *hating exceedingly.*

exōticus -a -um, *foreign, outlandish, exotic.*

expallesco -pallescěre -pallŭi, *to become very pale;* with acc., *to dread.*

expalpo -are, *to coax out.*

expando -ěre, *to stretch out, expand, spread out.* Transf., *to explain.*

expāvesco -pāvescěre -pavi, *to grow very frightened;* with acc. *to dread exceedingly.*

expědīo -ire -ivi and -ii -itum, *to free from a snare, disengage, disentangle, set free; to get things ready for action;* fig., *to release, clear, set free, set straight;* in speech, *to clear up* a point, *explain;* res expedit, or impers. expedit, *it is expedient, useful, advantageous.*

Hence partic. **expědītus** -a -um, *unshackled, unimpeded;* milit., *lightly equipped;* in gen., *free, ready;* n. as subst. *clear ground;* of abstr. things, *clear, settled, ready.* Adv. **expědītě**, *freely, easily.*

expědītio -ōnis, f., *a military operation, expedition.*

expello -pellěre -pŭli, -pulsum, *to drive out, expel, thrust away.*

expendo -penděre -pendi -pensum, *to weigh out;* esp. *to weigh out in payment, pay out, put down;* sometimes *to pay* a penalty. Transf., *to value, rate;* in gen., *to weigh up, consider.*

Hence partic. **expensus** -a -um, *weighed out,* hence *paid out;* ferre homini expensum, *to note* a thing *as paid* to a person, *charge* to. N. as subst. **expensum** -i, *payment.*

expergēfăcio -făcěre -fēci -factum, *to awaken, rouse, excite.*

expergiscor -pergisci -perrectus, dep. *to wake up, arouse oneself.*

expergo -pergěre -pergi -pergitum, *to awaken.*

expěrientia -ae, f., *trial, testing, attempt; knowledge gained by experience.*

expěrimentum -i, n. *experience; proof from experience.*

expěrior -pēriri -pertus, dep. *to try, test, prove, put to the test;* experiri ius, *to go to law;* in perf., *to know by having tried, know by experience; to try to do* a thing. Pres. partic. **expěriens** -entis, *enterprising, venturesome.* Perf. partic. **expertus** -a -um: pass., *tested, tried, approved;* act., with *experience, experienced.*

experrectus -a -um, partic. of expergiscor; q.v.

expers -pertis, *having no part in, not sharing in; wanting in, destitute of.*

expertus -a -um, partic. from experior q.v.

expětesso -ere, *to desire, wish for.*

expěto -ěre -ii and -ivi -itum: transit., *to desire, strive after, make for;* of things due, *to demand, require;* with infin., *to seek to do;* intransit. *to fall upon.*

expiātio -ōnis, f. *atonement, expiation.*

expilātio -ōnis, f. *plundering, robbing.*

expilator -ōris, m., *plunderer, robber.*

expīlo -are, *to plunder, rob.*

expingo -pingěre -pinxi -pictum, *to paint over;* fig., *to describe, depict in writing.*

expio -are, *to propitiate, appease* an offended or threatening power; *to purify* what is defiled; *to atone for* an offence.

expiscor -ari, dep. *to fish out; to search out, find out.*

explānātio -ōnis, f. *making clear, explanation;* rhet., *illustration,* also *clear articulation.*

explānātor -ōris, m., *one who explains; an interpreter.*

explāno -are, *to make level, smooth out;* hence *to explain, make clear: to set out clearly, or articulate clearly.*

explaudo = explodo; q.v.

explēmentum -i, n., *filling, stuffing.*

explěo -plēre -plēvi -plētum, *to fill, fill up; to complete* a required amount; *to make good* losses, etc.; in quality, *to complete, perfect;* of time, *to complete, finish;* of duties, *to fulfil, discharge;* of wants, *to satisfy, quench, appease.*

Hence partic. **explētus** -a -um, *perfect, complete.*

explētio -ōnis, f., *satisfying.*

explicātio -ōnis, f. *unfolding, uncoiling.* Transf., *explanation, interpretation.*

explicātor -ōris, m. and **explicātrix** -icis, f. *interpreter, explainer.*

¹**explicātus** -a -um, partic. from explico; q.v.

²**explicātus** -ūs, m. *explanation, exposition.*

explico -are -avi -atum and -ŭi -itum, *to unfold, unroll, disentangle;* in gen.

to spread out, extend, expand; milit., *to extend ranks, deploy.* Transf., *to disentangle, put in order*; of a debt, *to pay off; to explain, expound, interpret; to set free.*

Hence partic. **explĭcātus** -a -um, *ordered, arranged; made plain, clear*; also **explĭcĭtus** -a -um, *straightforward, easy*; adv. **explĭcātē, plainly.**

explōdo (-plaudo) -plōdĕre -plōsi -plōsum, *to hiss an actor off the stage*; in gen., *to scare off, reject.*

explōrātĭo -ōnis, f. *investigation.*

explōrātŏr -ōris, m. *explorer, scout, spy.*

explōro -are, *to search out, investigate, explore*; milit., *to spy out, reconnoitre; to test, try, put to proof.*

Hence partic. **explōrātus** -a -um, *established, confirmed, certain*; exploratum habeo, *I am sure*; adv. **explōrātē,** *certainly, surely, definitely.*

expōlĭo -ire -ii and -ivi -itum, *to smooth, polish, refine*; partic. **expōlĭtus** -a -um, *smooth, polished.*

expōlītĭo -ōnis, f. *smoothing, polishing.*

expōno -pōnĕre -pŏsŭi, pŏsĭtum, (1) *to put outside, cast out; to expose a child*; naut. *to land, disembark.* (2) *to put on view, display, show*; in words, *to set forth, exhibit, explain.*

Hence partic. **expŏsĭtus (expostus)** -a -um, *exposed, open, accessible*; of persons, *affable*; in bad sense, *vulgar.*

exporrĭgo -rĭgĕre -rexi -rectum, *to stretch out, expand, smooth out.*

exportātĭo -ōnis, f., *exportation.*

exporto -are, *to carry out*; esp. *to export.*

exposco -poscĕre -pŏposci, *to implore, entreat earnestly*; esp. *to demand the surrender of a person.*

expŏsĭtĭo -ōnis, f. *putting out*; hence *statement, exposition, narration.*

expostŭlātĭo -ōnis, f. *complaint, expostulation.*

expostŭlo -are. (1) *to demand earnestly*, esp. *to demand the surrender of a person.* (2) *to make a claim or complaint, to expostulate.*

expōtus = epotus; q.v.

exprĭmo -prĭmĕre -pressi -pressum. (1) *to press out, force out; to extort.* (2) *to mould or form one thing in imitation of another; hence to copy, express, portray, represent;* esp. *to express in words, describe; to translate; to articulate.* (3) *to raise up.*

Hence partic. **expressus** -a -um, *made clear, prominent, distinct.*

exprŏbrātĭo -ōnis, f. *reproach, upbraiding.*

exprŏbro -are, *to reproach; to bring up a thing against a person.*

exprōmo -prōmĕre -prompsi -promptum, *to bring forth, produce, exhibit, display; to disclose, set forth, state, utter.*

expugnābĭlis -e, *that may be taken by storm.*

expugnātĭo -ōnis, f., *the taking of a place by storm.*

expugnātŏr -ōris, m. *taker, capturer*; pudicitiae, *violator.*

expugno -are, *to take by storm, capture*; hence *to overcome, subdue; to gain forcibly, extort*: with ut and the subj., *bring it about that.*

expulsĭo -ōnis, f., *driving out, expulsion.*

expulsŏr -ōris, m. and **expultrix** -trīcis, f. *one who drives out.*

expungo -pungĕre -punxi -punctum, *to prick out*; hence *to cancel, expunge.*

expurgātĭo -ōnis, f. *vindication, justification.*

expurgo -are, *to cleanse, purify.* Hence *to cure; to purify; to justify, defend.*

expūtesco -ĕre, *to rot away.*

expūto -are, *to lop away*; hence *to consider; to comprehend.*

exquiro (-quaero) -quirĕre -quisivi -quisitum. (1) *to search for, look for, ask for.* (2) *to search through, examine.*

Hence partic. **exquīsītus** -a -um, *carefully sought or worked out, choice, exquisite, artificial.* Adv. **exquīsītē,** *accurately, carefully.*

exsaevio -ire, *to rage to an end, cease to rage.*

exsanguis -e, *bloodless, without blood; deathly pale*; act., *making pale.*

exsarcĭo -sarcire -sartum, *to patch up, make good, repair.*

exsātĭo -are, *to satisfy thoroughly, satiate.*

exsātūrābĭlis -e, *that can be satiated.*

exsātūro -are, *to satisfy, satiate.*

exscen-; see escen-.

exscindo -scindĕre -scidi -scissum, *to tear out; to destroy utterly.*

exscrĕo -are, *to cough out.*

exscrībo -scrībĕre -scripsi -scriptum, *to write out; to copy; to note down, register.*

exsculpo -sculpĕre -sculpsi -sculptum, *to scratch out, erase; to carve or scoop out.*

exsĕco -sĕcare -sĕcŭi -sectum, *to cut out, cut away.*

exsĕcrābĭlis -e, *cursing, execrating.*

exsĕcrātĭo -ōnis, f. *curse, execration; an oath containing an imprecation.*

exsĕcror -ari, dep. *to curse, execrate; to swear with an imprecation*; partic. in pass. sense, **exsĕcrātus** -a -um, *cursed, execrated.*

exsectĭo -ōnis, f. *cutting out.*

exsĕcūtĭo -ōnis, f. *performance, accomplishment*; executio Syriae, *administration*; of speech, *a discussion.*

exsĕquĭae -arum, f. pl. *a funeral procession.*

exsĕquĭālis -e, *belonging to a funeral procession.*

exsĕquor -sĕqui -sĕcūtus, dep. *to follow to the grave*; in gen., *to follow to the end; to maintain, keep up, to carry out, accomplish, execute; to avenge, punish; to relate, describe, explain a matter; to suffer, endure.*

exsĕro -sĕrĕre -sĕrŭi -sertum, *to stretch out, thrust out*; hence *to put* *forth, assert.* Perf. partic. **exsertus** -a -um, *bared, protruding.*

exserto -are, *to stretch out.*

exsibilo -are, *to hiss out;* esp. *to hiss an actor off the stage.*

exsicco -are, *to dry thoroughly; to drain dry, to empty by drinking.* Hence partic. **exsiccātus** -a -um, of style, *dry, jejune.*

exsigno -are, *to mark out.*

exsilio -silīre -silŭi, *to leap out or up.*

exsilium -i, · n. *banishment, exile.* Transf., *place of exile;* plur. = **exsules,** *exiles.*

exsisto (**existo**) -sistĕre -stiti -stitum, *to stand forth, appear; to spring forth, arise, come into existence.*

exsolvo -solvĕre -solvi -sŏlūtum. (1) *to loosen, untie, unbind, open;* glaciem, *to dissolve;* of persons, *to disentangle, free;* of things, *to explain.* (2) *to pay off; to discharge* any obligation, *perform* anything due.

exsomnis -e, *sleepless, wakeful.*

exsorbĕo -ēre, *to suck up, suck dry.*

exsors -sortis, *without lot; for which no lot has been cast, specially chosen; having no share in, deprived of,* with genit.

exspătior -ari, dep. *to deviate from the course;* fig., *to digress.*

exspectābilis -e, *that is to be expected, probable.*

exspectātio -ōnis, f. *waiting, looking for, expectation* (with objective genit.).

exspecto -are, *to look out for, wait for, await, wait to see;* esp. *with longing, fear, desire,* etc., *to hope for, dread.* Hence partic. (with compar. and superl.) **exspectātus** -a -um, *awaited, wished for, welcome.*

exspergo -spergĕre -spersum, *to sprinkle, scatter.*

exspēs, *without hope, hopeless.*

exspīrātio -ōnis, f. *exhalation.*

exspiro -are: transit., *to breathe out, exhale, emit;* intransit., *to blow forth, rush forth; to give up the ghost, to die.*

exspŏlio -are, *to plunder, rob, despoil.*

exspŭo -spŭĕre -spŭi -spūtum, *to spit out; to get rid of, cast away.*

externo -ēre, *to frighten, terrify.*

exstillo -are, *to drop moisture, drip, trickle.*

exstĭmŭlātor -ōris, m. *inciter, instigator.*

exstĭmŭlo -are, *to goad, excite, instigate.*

exstinctio -ōnis, f. *annihilation, extinction.*

exstinctor -ōris, m. *one who extinguishes, destroys, annihilates.*

exstinguo -stinguĕre -stinxi -stinctum, *to put out, extinguish;* of persons, *to kill;* in gen., *to abolish, destroy, annihilate.*

exstirpo -are, *to root out, extirpate.*

exsto (**exto**) -are, *to stand out, project; to be visible, show itself, appear; to be still in existence, be extant.*

exstructio -ōnis, f. *building up, erection.*

exstrŭo -strŭĕre -struxi -structum, *to heap up, pile up, build up.*

exsuctus -a -um, partic. of exsugo; q.v.

exsūdo -are; intransit., *to come out in sweat, exude;* transit., *to sweat out, sweat through, perform with great labour.*

exsūgo -sūgĕre -suxi -suctum, *to suck out, suck dry.*

exsul -sūlis, c., *a banished person, an exile.*

exsūlo (**exūlo**) -are, *to be banished, live in exile.*

exsultātio -ōnis, f. *leaping up; exultation, excessive rejoicing.*

exsultim, adv. *friskingly.*

exsulto (**exulto**) -are, *to leap up frequently* or *violently.* Transf., *to rejoice exceedingly, exult, triumph;* of orators, etc., *to run riot, range freely.*

exsŭpĕrābilis -e, *that can be overcome.*

exsŭpĕrantia -ae, f., *superiority, pre-eminence.*

exsŭpĕro -are: intransit., *to mount up, appear above; to be prominent, excel;* transit., *to surmount; to surpass, exceed, overcome.*

exsurdo -are, *to deafen;* of taste, *to make dull* or *blunt.*

exsurgo -surgĕre -surrexi, *to rise up, lift oneself up, stand-up; to regain strength.*

exsuscito -are, *to awaken from sleep;* of fire, *to kindle* or *fan;* mentally, *to excite, arouse;* se exsuscitare, *to make an effort.*

exta -orum, n. pl. *entrails of animals,* esp. *the heart, lungs, liver,* used by Romans for divination.

extābesco -tābescĕre -tābŭi, *to waste away entirely; to vanish, disappear.*

extāris -e, *used for cooking.*

extemplo (-**tempŭlo**), *immediately, forthwith.*

extempŏrālis -e, *extemporary, unrehearsed.*

extendo -tendĕre -tendi -tensum and -tentum, *to stretch out, expand, extend;* milit., *to extend in order of battle;* in gen., *to increase, extend;* in time, *to extend, prolong; to strain, exert.* Hence partic. **extentus** -a -um, *wide, extensive.*

extento -are, *to stretch out, strain.*

extĕnŭātio -ōnis, f. *thinning;* as a figure of speech, *diminution, lessening.*

extĕnŭo -are, *to make thin* or *small, to reduce, diminish;* milit., *to extend;* in gen., *to lessen, weaken, diminish;* in speech, *to disparage, depreciate.* Hence partic. **extĕnŭātus** -a -um, *weak, poor, slight.*

exter and **extĕrus** -a -um, *outward, foreign, strange;* compar. **extĕrior** -ius, genit. -ōris, *outer;* superl. **extrēmus** -a -um, *outermost;* n. as subst. *outer edge, extreme;* in time, *last;* n. as subst. *an end;* extremum, acc., *for the last time;* ad extremum, *to the end* or *at the end;* in degree or quality, *extreme;* esp. *lowest, worst;* extremum bonorum, malorum, *the* *highest good, evil;* superl. **extĭmus** -a -um, *outermost.*

extĕrebro -are; *to bore out, extract by boring.*

extergĕo -tergēre -tersi -tersum, *to wipe off, wipe clean; to strip clean, plunder.*

extĕrĭor, exterius; see exter.

extermĭno -are, *to drive out, expel, banish; to put aside, remove.*

externus -a -um, *outside, external, foreign, strange;* m. as subst. *a foreigner, stranger;* n. pl. as subst. *outward or foreign things.*

extĕro -tĕrĕre -trivi -tritum, *to rub out; to wear away.*

exterrĕo -terrēre -terrŭi -territum, *to frighten badly, scare, terrify.*

extĕrus; see exter.

extexo -ĕre, *to unweave; to cheat.*

extĭmesco -tĭmescĕre -tĭmŭi: intransit. *to be terrified;* transit., *to be greatly afraid of, to dread.*

extĭmus; see exter.

extispex -spĭcis, m., *a soothsayer predicting from the entrails of victims.*

extollo -ĕre, *to lift up, raise up;* of buildings, *to raise, erect;* of spirits, etc., *to elevate, exalt;* in words, *to praise or exaggerate;* sometimes *to adorn; to defer, postpone.*

extorquĕo -torquēre -torsi -tortum, *to twist out, wrest away, wrench out, dislocate.* Transf., *to obtain by force, extort.*

extorris -e, *driven from the country, exiled, banished.*

extrā: adv. *outside;* extra quam, extra quam ut, *except, unless;* prep., with acc., *beyond, outside of, without; except for;* extra iocum, *joking apart.*

extrăho -trăhĕre -traxi -tractum, *to draw out, drag out, extract, remove, extricate;* sometimes *to bring forward;* in time, *to draw out, prolong, protract.*

extrānĕus -a -um, *outside, extraneous; foreign, strange;* m. as subst. *a foreigner, stranger.*

extrāordĭnārĭus -a -um, *extraordinary, anomalous, irregular, unnatural;* milit. equites, cohortes, *picked troops of the auxiliary forces.*

extrārĭus -a -um, *outward, external, extrinsic; strange, unrelated, foreign.*

extrēmĭtās -ātis, f. *end, farthest portion, extremity.*

extrēmus -a -um; see exter.

extrĭco -are, *to disentangle, extricate; to clear up, unravel.*

extrinsĕcus, *from without, from the outside; on the outside, outwardly.*

extrūdo -trūdĕre -trūsi -trūsum, *to push out, thrust forth;* merces, *to get sold.*

extundo -tundĕre -tŭdi -tūsum. (1) *to form by beating with a hammer; to invent, devise.* (2) *to beat out violently, drive away; to extort.*

exturbo -are, *to drive away, thrust out;* mentem, *to agitate.*

exŭbĕro -are, *to grow thickly, abound.*

exul; see exsul.

exulcĕro -are, *to make worse, aggravate; to irritate, embitter.*

exŭlŭlo -are, *to howl out, howl loudly;* partic. **exŭlŭlātus** -a -um, *invoked with howlings.*

exundo -are, *to overflow, to flow out or over, to abound.*

exŭo -ŭĕre -ŭi -ūtum. (1) *to lay aside, put off, put away.* (2) *to strip, deprive* of a thing.

exūro -ūrĕre -ussi -ustum, *to burn out, burn up, consume;* also *to dry up, warm, heat.*

exustĭo -ōnis, f. *burning up, conflagration.*

exŭvĭae -arum, f. pl. *that which is taken off;* of men *dress; spoils taken from the enemy, arms, etc.; the skin, slough,* or *hide* of animals.

F

F, f, the sixth letter of the Latin Alphabet.

făba -ae, f. *the broad bean.*

făbālis -e, *of beans.*

făbella -ae, f. *a little story, fable or drama.*

făber -bra -brum, *ingenious, skilful.* M. as subst. **făber** -bri, *a worker, craftsman;* faber tignarius, *a carpenter;* ferrarius, *a blacksmith;* milit. fabri, *the engineers;* also *a fish,* perhaps dory. Adv. **făbrē,** *skilfully.*

Făbius -a -um, *name of a Roman gens.*

făbrēfăcĭo -făcĕre -fēci -factum, *to make or fashion skilfully.*

făbrĭca -ae, f. *the art of a faber; a device, trick, a workshop.*

făbrĭcātĭo -ōnis, f., *making, framing, construction.*

făbrĭcātor -ōris, m. *maker, artificer.*

Făbrĭcĭus -a, -um, *name of a Roman gens.*

făbrĭco -are, and **făbrĭcor** -ari, dep., *to form, make, forge.*

făbrīlis -e, *relating to an artificer;* n.pl. as subst., *tools.*

fābŭla -ae, f. (1) *talk, conversation:* fabulam fieri, *to get talked about.* (2) *a tale, story, fable, drama, myth;* fabulae! *nonsense!*

fābŭlor -ari, dep. (1) *to talk, converse, chatter.* (2) *to tell an untruth.*

fābŭlōsus -a -um, *renowned in story, fabled.*

făcesso făcessĕre făcessi făcessitum: transit., *to do eagerly, perform, fulfil, accomplish;* homini negotium, *to give trouble to;* intransit., *to make off, go away, depart.*

făcētĭa -ae, f.; sing., *wit;* plur., *wit, drollery, humour.*

făcētus -a -um, *fine, elegant; witty, facetious.* Adv. **făcētē,** *elegantly; wittily, humorously.*

făcĭēs -ēi, *shape, form, figure, outward appearance;* esp. *face, countenance.* Transf., *character, nature; seeming, pretence.*

făcĭlis -e, *easy to do; easy to manage,*

convenient, favourable; of movements, easy, mobile; of persons, facile, dexterous, clever; of character, affable, easy, good-natured. N. acc. as adv. **făcĭlē**, easily, without difficulty; indisputably, certainly; haud facile, not easily, hardly; facile pati, to bear willingly.

făcĭlĭtās -ātis, f. easiness, ease; of character, willingness, friendliness, affability, good-nature.

făcĭnŏrōsus -a -um, wicked, criminal.

făcĭnus -ŏris, n. a deed, action; esp. a bad deed, crime, villainy; hence instrument of crime; in plur., criminals.

făcĭo făcĕre fēci factum (the pass. is fio; q.v.). Transit., to make, form, do, perform; of feelings and circumstances, to cause, bring about; esp. copiam or potestatem, to give a chance, grant permission; with clause as object, esp. with subj., e.g. fac sciam, let me know; facere non possum quin, I cannot but; of troubles, to experience, suffer; with double acc., to make, appoint, change into; with genit., to make something the property of a person or thing, to bring into the power of, or mentally to put into a category, to regard, to esteem, value; with acc. and infin., to take it, assume or to make out, represent that a thing is so. Intransit., to act; with adverbs, to behave; facere cum, or ab, homine, to act on the side of, support; to sacrifice; to be serviceable, to suit, help, be of service; used instead of repeating another verb, to do so.

Hence partic. **factus** -a -um, done, wrought; n. of compar., factius, nearer to achievement; n. of positive as subst. **factum** -i, a deed, act, exploit.

factĭo -ōnis, f. (1) a making, doing; also the right of making or doing. (2) a party, group; esp. a political party, faction, side.

factĭōsus -a -um, busy; factious, associated with a faction.

factĭto -are. (1) to practise, be accustomed to make or do. (2) to appoint openly.

factus -a -um, partic. from facio; q.v.

făcŭla -ae, f., a little torch.

făcultās -ātis, f. feasibility, opportunity, power, means; capacity, ability; resources, stock, abundance.

făcundĭa -ae, f., eloquence, readiness of speech.

făcundus -a -um, eloquent, fluent, ready of speech; adv. **făcundē**.

faecŭla -ae, f. lees of wine.

faenebris -e, relating to interest.

faenērātĭo -ōnis, f. lending at interest, usury.

faenērātor -ōris, m. money-lender, usurer.

faenĕror -ari, dep. and **faenĕro** (**fēnĕro**) -are, to lend at interest; provincias, to despoil by usury; beneficium, to trade in benefits.

faenĕus -a -um, of hay; homines, men of straw.

faenilia -ium, n. pl. hay-loft.

faenĭsĕca -ae, m., a mower; a countryman.

faenum (**fēnum**) -i, n. hay.

faenus (**fēnus**) -ŏris, n. interest on money; pecuniam dare faenore, to lend at interest; accipere faenore, to borrow. Transf., debt, indebtedness; capital, usury.

Faesŭlae -arum, f. town in Etruria, (now Fiesole); adj. **Faesŭlanus** -a -um.

faex faecis, f. the dregs or lees of liquid, esp. of wine; fig. socially, the dregs, the lower orders.

fāgĭnĕus and **fāgĭnus** -a -um, of beech.

fāgus -i, f. beech-tree.

fāla (**phăla**) -ae, f. a wooden tower or pillar.

fălārĭca (**phălārĭca**) -ae, f. a missile covered with tow and pitch.

falcārĭus -i, m., a sickle-maker.

falcātus -a -um, furnished with sickles; sickle-shaped.

falcĭfer -fĕra -fĕrum, carrying a scythe or sickle.

Fălernus ăger, the Falernian country, in Campania; n. of adj. as subst. **Fălernum** -i, Falernian wine.

fallācĭa -ae, f. deceit, trick, fraud.

fallax -ācis, deceitful, treacherous, false; adv. **fallācĭter**.

fallo fallĕre fĕfelli falsum, to deceive, lead astray, cause to be mistaken; nisi fallor, unless I am mistaken; of abstr. things, to disappoint, fail in; poet., to beguile, wile away;—to escape the notice of, be concealed from; impers. non fallit me, I am not unaware.

Hence partic. **falsus** -a -um. (1) wrong, mistaken, misled; n. as subst., a mistake; abl. as adv., falso, falsely, mistakenly. (2) false, untrue, spurious. (3) deceitful, lying; n. as subst. a lie; abl. as adv., falso, falsely, fraudulently. Adv. **falsē**.

falsĭdĭcus -a -um, and **falsĭlŏquus** -a -um, lying.

falsus -a -um, partic. from fallo; q.v.

falx falcis, f. a sickle, bill-hook, pruning-hook; a sickle-shaped implement of war.

fāma -ae, f. talk, report, rumour, tradition; fama est, there is a rumour; public opinion; standing in public opinion, repute, good or bad.

fāmēlĭcus -a -um, hungry, famished.

fāmes -is, f. hunger, famine; insatiable desire; poverty of expression.

fāmĭgĕrātor -ōris, m. rumour-monger.

fămĭlĭa -ae, a household (of slaves), establishment; pater familias or paterfamilias, the head of the household; materfamilias, a married woman or an unmarried woman whose father was dead; filiusfamilias, a son still under his father's power. Transf., a family estate; a family, as a subdivision of a gens; any fraternity, group, sect.

fămĭlĭāris -e. (1) belonging to the

slaves of a house; as subst. **fămĭlĭāris** -is, m. *a servant, slave*. (2) *belonging to a family* or *household; known in the house* or *family, intimate, friendly*; m. and f. as subst. *a familiar friend.* (3) in augury, fissum familiare, or pars familiaris, *the part of the entrails relating to the persons sacrificing.* Adv. **fămĭlĭārĭter,** *familiarly, intimately.*

fămĭlĭārĭtās -ātis, f. *confidential friendship, intimacy*; meton., *familiar friends.*

fāmōsus -a -um: pass., *much spoken of, renowned*; in bad sense, *infamous, notorious*; act., *libellous, defamatory.*

fămŭl, fămŭla; see famulus.

fămŭlāris -e, *relating to servants* or *slaves.*

fămŭlātus -ūs, m. *servitude, slavery, service*; meton., *an establishment of slaves.*

fămŭlor -ari, dep. *to be a servant, to serve.*

fămŭlus -a -um, *serving, servile*; as subst. m. **fămŭlus (fămul)** -i, *a servant, slave, attendant*; f. **fămŭla** -ae, *a female slave, handmaid.*

fānātĭcus -a -um, *inspired; enthusiastic; frenzied.*

fānum -i, n. *a temple with the land round it, a holy place.*

fār farris, n. *spelt, grain, meal.*

farcĭo farcire farsi fartum, *to fill full, stuff full.*

fārīna -ae, f., *meal, flour.*

farrāgo -ĭnis, f. *mixed fodder for cattle, mash; a medley, mixture.*

farrātus -a -um, *provided with grain; made of corn.*

farrĕus -a -um, *made of spelt* or *corn.*

fartim (fartem), acc. sing., *stuffing, minced meat.*

fartor -ōris, m. *a fattener of fowls.*

fās, n. indecl. *divine command* or *law*; sometimes *fate, destiny*; in gen. *right, that which is allowed, lawful*; fas est, *it is allowed, is lawful.*

fascĭa -ae, f. *a bandage, band, girdle, girth.*

fascĭcŭlus -i, m., *a little bundle* or *packet*; florum, *a nosegay.*

fascĭno -are, *to bewitch; to envy.*

fascĭŏla -ae, f., *a little bandage.*

fascis -is, m. *a bundle, packet*; plur., fasces, *bundles of sticks with an axe projecting, carried by lictors before the chief Roman magistrates*; hence high office, esp. *the consulate.*

fasti -orum, m.; see fastus -a -um.

fastīdĭo -ire, *to loathe, feel distaste for, dislike.*

fastīdĭōsus -a -um, *squeamish, nice, dainty, fastidious*; with genit., *sick of, disgusted with, impatient of*; in act. sense, *disgusting, loathsome.* Adv. **fastīdĭōsē,** *fastidiously, with disgust.*

fastīdĭum -i, n. *loathing, squeamishness, disgust, dislike*; hence *scorn, haughtiness, disdain.*

fastīgātus -a -um, *pointed* or *sloping down*; adv. **fastīgātē,** *slantingly.*

fastīgĭum -i, n. *the gable end, pediment of a roof*; hence *a slope*, either up or down; of measurements looking up, *height*; looking down, *depth*; abstract, *high rank, dignity; principal point in a subject.*

¹fastus -ūs, m. *pride, haughtiness, arrogance.*

²fastus -a -um: dies fastus, plur. dies fasti, or simply fasti, *days on which the praetor could administer justice, court-days.* Transf. *a list of these days, with festivals, etc., the Roman calendar; a register, record; a list of magistrates.*

fātālis -c, *relating to destiny* or *fate; fated, destined by fate*; in bad sense, *deadly, fatal.* Adv. **fātālĭter,** *according to fate.*

fătĕor fātēri fassus, dep., *to confess, admit, allow; to reveal, make known.*

fātĭcănus and **-cĭnus** -a -um, *prophetic.*

fātĭdĭcus -a -um, *announcing fate, prophetic*; m. as subst. *a prophet.*

fātĭfer -fēra -fērum, *deadly, fatal.*

fătīgātĭo -ōnis, f. *weariness, fatigue.*

fătīgo -are, *to weary, fatigue; to vex, harass; to tease, importune, worry.*

fātĭlŏqua -ae, f. *a prophetess.*

fātisco -ere and **fātiscor** -i, dep., *to gape, crack, open; to become weak, droop.*

fătŭĭtās -ātis, f. *foolishness, silliness.*

fātum -i, n., *an utterance, esp. a divine utterance*; hence *destiny, fate; the will of a god*; personif. Fata, the Parcae or Fates; *doom, fate, natural death, misfortune, ruin, calamity.*

fătŭus -a -um, *foolish, idiotic, silly.*

Faunus -i, m. *a mythic deity of the forests.*

faustĭtās -ātis, f., *prosperity.*

faustus -a -um, *favourable, lucky, auspicious*; adv. **faustē.**

fautor -ōris, m. *patron, promoter, partisan.*

fautrix -trīcis, f., *a patroness.*

faux, f.: usually plur. **fauces** -ium, *gullet, throat, jaws.* Transf., *a chasm, gorge, defile; an isthmus, neck of land; straits.*

făvĕo făvēre făvi fautum, *to favour, be favourable to, help, support*, with dat.; with infin., *to be inclined to do.* Esp. as religious t. t., *to speak no words of bad omen*; hence *to be silent.*

făvilla -ae, f. *glowing ashes*, esp. *of the dead; a spark.*

făvĭtor -ōris, m. = fautor; q.v.

Făvōnĭus -i, m. = Zephyrus, *the west wind.*

făvor -ōris, m., *favour, good-will, support, inclinaton*; esp. *applause at the theatre, acclamation.*

făvŏrābĭlis -e, *in favour, popular.*

făvus -i, m. *honeycomb.*

fax făcis, f. (1) *a torch*, esp. as carried at weddings and funerals. (2) *a fire-brand*; of persons, *instigator*; of things, *stimulus.* (3) *light, flame*, esp. *of heavenly bodies*; fig., *brilliance* or *passion.*

febrĭcŭla -ae, f., *a slight fever, feverishness.*

febris -is, f. *fever.*

Febrŭārius -i, m. or **Febrŭārius Mensis,** *the cleansing month, February;* Kalendae Februariae, *the 1st of February.*

febrŭum -i, n. *religious purification;* Febrŭa -orum, pl. *the Roman feast of purification on the 15th of February.*

fēciālis = fetialis; q.v.

fēcundĭtās -ātis, f. *fruitfulness, fecundity.*

fēcundo -are, to *fructify, fertilize.*

fēcundus -a -um, *fruitful, prolific; abundant, full, plentiful;* with genit., *rich in, abounding in;* act., *making fruitful.*

fel fellis, n. *the gall-bladder, gall. bile; poison, venom; bitterness.*

fēles -is, f. *a cat;* hence *a thief.*

fēlīcĭtās -ātis, f. *happiness, good fortune, success;* personif., *Good Fortune as a goddess.*

felix -icis, *fruitful, fertile.* Transf., of good omen, *favourable, bringing good luck; fortunate, lucky, successful;* Felix, *the Lucky One, surname of Sulla.* Adv. **fēlīciter,** *fruitfully; auspiciously, favourably; luckily, successfully.*

fēmella -ae, f. *young woman, girl.*

fēmen = femur; q.v.

fēmina -ae, f. *a female, woman;* of animals, *the female.*

fēmĭnĕus -a -um, *female, feminine; womanish, effeminate.*

fēmur -ŏris or -ĭnis, n. *the thigh.*

fēnestra -ae, f. *a window; a breach, loophole.*

fēra -ae, f.; see ferus.

fērālis -e, *relating to the dead, funereal; deadly, fatal; mournful;* n. pl. as subst. *the festival of the dead, in February.*

fērax -ācis, *fruitful, fertile, prolific;* compar. adv. **fērācius,** *more fruitfully.*

fercŭlum -i, n. *a frame, litter, bier, tray;* of food, *a course* or *dish.*

fērē (1) *almost, nearly;* with negatives, *scarcely, hardly.* (2) *just, exactly.* (3) *as a rule, generally, usually.*

fērentārius -i, m. *a light-armed soldier.*

fēretrum -i, n., *a bier for carrying a corpse.*

fēriae -arum, f. pl. *festivals, holidays.*

fēriātus -a -um, *keeping holiday, idle, at leisure.*

fērinus -a -um, *relating to a wild beast, wild;* f. as subst. *flesh of wild animals, game.*

fērio -ire, *to strike, knock, smite, hit;* esp. *to strike dead, slay, kill;* colloq., *to cheat.*

fērĭtās -ātis, f. *wildness, savageness.*

fermē (1) *almost, nearly;* with negatives, *hardly, scarcely.* (2) *usually.*

fermentum -i, n. *leaven, yeast; a kind of beer.* Transf., *anger, passion.*

fēro ferre, with perf. tŭli, supine latum.
(1) *to bear, bring, carry;* prae se ferre,

to display, make public; often *to endure, submit to;* esp. with adv.; ferre aegre, *to take ill, be vexed at.*
(2) *to bring orth, produce.* (3) *to bring to a place or person, fetch, offer;* suffragium, sententiam, *to vote;* legem, *to propose a law;* ferre ut, *to propose that;* commercial, expensum ferre, *to set down in an account-book as paid; to cause, bring about; to report to others, spread abroad, speak of;* fama fert, *the story goes;* esp. *to publish a* person's *praises.*
(4) *to bear away, carry off;* ferre et agere, *to plunder.* Transf., *to win, get;* centuriam, tribus, *to gain the votes of.*
(5) *to bear along, move forward, put in motion;* milit., signa ferre, *to march.* Transf., *to move, impel, carry away;* without object, *to lead, tend.*

fērōcia -ae, f. *high spirit, courage;* in bad sense, *arrogance, ferocity.*

fērōcĭtās -ātis, f. *courage, untamed spirit;* in bad sense, *arrogance.*

fērox -ōcis, *courageous, high-spirited, warlike;* in bad sense, *wild, unbridled, arrogant;* adv. **fērōciter.**

ferrāmenta -orum, n. pl. *tools made of, or shod with, iron.*

ferrārius -a -um, *of iron;* m. as subst. *a blacksmith;* f. pl. as subst., *iron-mines.*

ferrātilis -e, *in irons;* of slaves.

ferrātus -a -um, *furnished* or *covered with iron;* servi, *in irons;* m. pl. as subst. *soldiers in armour.*

ferrĕus -a -um, *of iron; made of iron or like iron; hard, unfeeling, cruel; immovable, firm.*

ferritērium -i, n. = ergastulum; q.v.

ferrūgĭnĕus and **ferrūgĭnus** -a -um, *rust-coloured, dusky.*

ferrūgo -ĭnis, f. *iron rust; the colour of rust.*

ferrum -i, n. *iron;* hence *any iron instrument; plough, axe, scissors,* and esp. *sword.*

fertilis -e, *fruitful, fertile, productive; fertilizing, making fruitful.*

fertĭlĭtās -ātis, f. *fruitfulness, fertility.*

fertum (**ferctum**) -i, n. *a sacrificial cake.*

fērŭla -ae, f. (1) *the herb fennel.* (2) *a stick, cane,* esp. *to punish slaves and children.*

fērus -a -um, *wild, uncultivated, uncivilized, rough, cruel;* m. and f. as subst., *a wild animal.*

fervēfăcĭo -făcĕre -fēci -factum *to make hot, boil, melt.*

fervĕo fervēre ferbŭi (and **fervo** fervĕre fervi) *to be boiling hot, to boil, seethe, glow.* Transf., *to be in quick movement, to seethe; to be excited by passion, rage.*

Hence partic. **fervens** -entis, *glowing, hot, heated;* of character or feeling, *heated, fiery.* Adv. **fervente,** *hotly, warmly.*

fervesco -ĕre, *to become hot, begin to glow* or *boil.*

fervĭdus -a -um, *boiling, seething*

foaming; of character or feelings, *fiery, passionate, excited.*

fervo = ferveo; q.v.

fervor -ōris, m. *boiling heat, seething, foaming; ardour, passion.*

Fescennia -ae, f. *a town in Etruria famous for verse dialogues.* Adj. **Fescenninus** -a -um.

fessus -a -um, *weary, tired, exhausted*; fessa aetas, *old age*; res fessae, *distress.*

festinātio -ōnis, f. *haste, speed, hurry.*

festīno -are: intransit., *to hasten, hurry*; transit., *to hasten, accelerate.* Hence adv. **festīnanter** and **festīnātō**, *hastily.*

festinus -a -um, *hastening, hasty.*

festivitās -ātis, f. *gaiety, jollity*; of speech or writing, *cheerfulness, humour.*

festīvus -a -um, *of a holiday, festive; merry, good-humoured, cheerful*; adv. **festīvē.**

festūca -ae, f. *a stalk, 'straw, stem.* Transf., *a rod used in the manumission of slaves.*

festus -a -um, *of a holiday, festive*; of people, *keeping holiday*; n. as subst. *a feast.*

fetiālis -s, m. *one of a college of priests responsible for formally making peace or declaring war*; as adj. = *belonging to the fetiales.*

fētūra -ae, f. *the bringing forth of young, breeding*; meton. *brood, offspring.*

¹fētus -a -um. (1) *pregnant; fruitful, fertile; teeming with, full of.* (2) *that has brought forth, newly delivered.*

²fētus -ūs, m. *the bringing forth or hatching of young*; of the soil, *bearing, producing.* Transf., *that which is brought forth*: *offspring, brood*; of plants *fruit, produce, shoot.*

fibra -ae, f. *a fibre, filament; the entrails of an animal.*

fībula -ae, f. *a buckle, brooch, clasp; an iron clamp.*

ficēdūla -ae, f. *a small bird, the becafico.*

fictilis -e, *shaped*; hence *earthen, made of clay*; n. as subst., esp. pl., *earthenware, earthen vessels.*

fictio -ōnis, f. *forming, feigning; assumption.*

fictor -ōris, m. *an image-maker, a moulder*; in gen., *maker, contriver.*

fictrix -icis, f. *she that forms or fashions.*

fictūra -ae, f. *forming, fashioning.*

fictus, partic. from fingo; q.v.

ficulnus and **ficulnĕus** -a -um, *of the fig-tree.*

ficus -i, and -ūs, f. *a fig-tree; a fig.*

fideicommissum -i, n. legal, *a trust.*

fidēlia -ae, f. *an eathenware pot or vase.*

fidēlis -e, *trusty, steadfast, faithful*; m. as subst., esp. pl., *confidants, faithful friends.* Adv. **fidēliter**, *faithfully; securely, without danger.*

fidēlitās -ātis, f., *faithfulness, trust, fidelity.*

Fidēnae -arum, and **Fidēna** -ae, f. *a town in Latium*; adj. **Fidēnas** -ātis.

fidens -entis, partic. from fido; q.v.

fidentia -ae, f. *confidence, boldness.*

¹fides -ei, f., *trust, confidence, reliance, belief, faith*; fidem facere, *to create confidence, cause belief*; as mercantile t. t., *credit.* Transf., *that which produces confidence; faithfulness, conscientiousness*; fidem praestare, *to be loyal*; (ex) bona fide, *in good faith, sincerely*; of things, *credibility, actuality, fulfilment; a promise, assurance, word of honour, engagement*; fidem fallere, *to break a promise*; servare, *to keep a promise*; fide mea, *on my word of honour*; fides (or fides publica) *a promise of protection, safe-conduct*; hence, in gen., *faithful protection, constant help.*

²fides -is, f., usually plur. *a gut-string for a musical instrument*; hence *a lyre, lute, harp.*

fidicen -cinis, m., *a player on the harp, lyre, lute*; poet., *a lyric poet.*

fidicina -ae, f. *a female player on the lute or harp.*

fidicinus -a -um, *of lute-playing.*

fidicūla -ae, f., usually plur. *a little lyre or lute; an instrument for torturing slaves.*

Fidius -i, m., *a surname of Jupiter*; esp. in phrase, medius fidius! *So help me God!*

fido fidēre fisus sum, *to trust, believe, confide in*; with dat. or abl.
    Hence partic. **fidens** -entis, *without fear, confident, courageous*; adv. **fidenter.**

fidūcia -ae, f. (1) *confidence, trust, assurance*; with sui, or absol., *self-confidence, self-reliance, courage.* (2) *fidelity.*

fidūciārius -a -um, *entrusted, committed.*

fidus -a -um, *trusty, true, faithful, sure*; superl. adv. **fidissime.**

figo figĕre fixi fixum. (1) *to fix, fasten, make fast, attach, affix*; esp. with oculos, *to fix the gaze.* (2) *to thrust home a weapon, etc. so as to stick fast.* (3) *to transfix.*
    Hence partic. **fixus** -a -um, *fixed, firm, immovable.*

figūlāris -e, *of a potter.*

figūlus -i, m., *a worker in clay, potter.*

figūra -ae, f. *form, shape, figure, size; an atom; shade of a dead person*; the abstr., *kind, nature, species*; rhet., *a figure of speech.*

figūro -are, *to form, mould, shape*; rhet., *to adorn with figures.*

filātim, *thread by thread.*

filia -ae, f. *daughter.*

filicātus -a -um, *adorned with ferns; embossed with fern leaves.*

filiōla -ae, f. *little daughter.*

filiōlus -i, m. *little son.*

filius -i, m. *son.*

filix -icis, f. *fern.*

filum -i, n. *a thread*, pendere filo (tenui), *to hang by a thread; a woollen fillet.* Transf., *form, shape*; of speech or writing, *texture, thread.*

fimbriae -arum, f. pl., *fringe, border edge.*

fimbriātus -a -um, *fringed*.

fīmus -i, m. and **fimum** -i, n. *dung, dirt*.

findo findĕre fidi fissum, *to split, cleave, divide, halve*. Hence partic. **fissus** -a -um, *split, cloven*; n. as subst., *a split, cleft*; in augury, *a divided liver*.

fingo fingĕre finxi fictum, *to shape, fashion, form, mould*; also *to arrange, put in order*; *to represent, imagine, conceive*; *to feign, fabricate, devise*; fingere vultum, *to put on an artificial expression*. Hence partic. **fictus** -a -um, *feigned, false*; n. as subst. *a falsehood*.

finio -ire, *to bound, limit, enclose, restrain*; *to define, determine, appoint*; *to put an end to, conclude, finish*; esp. *to finish speaking, or to die*; pass., *to end, cease*. Perf. partic. **fīnītus** -a -um; of a phrase, *well-rounded*; adv. **fīnītē**, *moderately, within bounds*.

fĭnis -is, m. (sometimes f.) *boundary, limit, border; summit, end; object, aim*; in pl. *enclosed area, territory*.

fīnĭtĭmus and **fīnĭtŭmus** -a -um, *neighbouring, adjacent; related to, resembling, similar*. M. pl. as subst. *neighbours*.

fīnĭtor -ōris, m., *one who determines boundaries, a land surveyor*. Transf., *the horizon*.

fĭo fĭĕri factus sum, used as pass. of facio. (1) of persons and things, *to be made, come into existence*; with predicate, *to become, be appointed*; with genit., *to be valued at*. (2) of actions, *to be done*; of events, *to happen*; with abl., quid illo fiet? *what will happen to him*? fieri ut, *to come about that*; fieri non potest quin, *it must be that*.

firmāmen -inis, n. *support, prop*.

firmāmentum -i, n., *a means of support, prop; the main point in an argument*.

firmātor -ōris, m. *one who makes firm or establishes*.

firmĭtās -ātis and **firmĭtūdo** -dĭnis, f., *firmness, stability; strength of mind, constancy*.

firmo -are, *to make firm, strengthen; to make durable, make secure*; of spirits, *to encourage, cheer, animate*; of ideas, *to prove establish*, also *to assert, maintain*.

firmus -a -um, *firm, strong, stout; lasting, valid; morally strong*. Adv. **firmē** and **firmĭter**, *firmly strongly, steadfastly*.

fiscella and **fiscīna** -ae, f., *a small basket*.

fiscus -i, m. *a basket; hence a money-bag, purse; the state treasury*; under the empire, *the emperor's privy purse* (opp. aerarium, *the state treasury*).

fissĭlis -e, *that can be split*; also *split*.

fissĭo -ōnis, f. *splitting, cleaving, dividing*.

fistūca -ae, f. *a rammer, mallet*.

fistŭla -ae, f. *a water-pipe; a reed-pipe, shepherd's pipe*; eburneola, *a pitch-pipe of ivory*.

fistŭlātor -ōris, m., *one who plays the reed-pipe*.

fixus -a -um, partic. from figo; q.v.

flābellum -i, n. *a small fan*.

flābĭlis -e, *airy*.

flābra -orum, n. pl. *blasts of wind, breezes*.

flaccĕo -ēre, *to be flabby; to fail or flag*.

flaccesco flaccescĕre flaccŭi, *to begin to flag, become flabby*.

flaccĭdus -a -um, *flabby; weak, languid*.

flaccus -a -um, *flabby; of men, flap-eared*.

Flaccus; see Horatius, and Valerius.

flăgello -are, *to whip, scourge, beat*.

flăgellum -i, n. *a whip, scourge; the thong of a javelin; a young sprout vine-shoot*; plur. *the arms of a polypus*; fig., *the sting of conscience*.

flăgĭtātĭo -ōnis, f., *an earnest demand or entreaty*.

flăgĭtātor -ōris, m., *one who earnestly demands or entreats*.

flăgĭtĭōsus -a -um, *shameful, disgraceful, infamous*; adv. **flăgĭtĭōsē**.

flăgĭtium -i, n. *a disgraceful action, shameful crime; shame, disgrace*; meton., *scoundrel, rascal*.

flăgĭto -are, *to entreat, ask, demand earnestly; to demand to know; to summon before a court of justice*.

flagrantĭa -ae, f. *burning, blazing, glittering*.

flagritriba -ae, m., *one that wears out whips, whipping boy*.

flagro -are, *to blaze, burn, glow, flame*, also *to glitter*. Transf., *to glow or burn with passion; to suffer from*, with abl. Hence partic. **flagrans** -antis, *blazing, burning, glittering*. Transf., *passionate, ardent*. Adv. **flagranter**.

flagrum -i, n. *scourge, whip*.

¹**flāmen** -inis, m. *the priest of some particular god*.

²**flāmen** -inis, n. *a blowing, blast*.

flāmĭnĭca -ae, f. *the wife of a flamen*.

Flāmĭnīnus, *a surname in the patrician Gens Quinctia*; see Quinctius.

flāmĭnium -i, n., *the office of a flamen*.

Flāmĭnĭus -a -um, *name of a Roman gens*.

flamma -ae, f., *a flame, blazing fire*. Transf., *a source of light, torch, star, lightning; lustre, glitter; the fire or glow of passion; devouring flame, destruction*.

flammĕŏlum -i, n., *a small bridal veil*.

flammesco -ĕre, *to become inflamed*.

flammĕus -a -um, *fiery, flaming; flashing, fiery-red*; n. as subst. **flammĕum** -i, *a (flame-coloured) bridal veil*.

flammĭfer -fĕra -fĕrum, *flaming, fiery*.

flammo -are: intransit., *to flame, blaze, burn*; transit., *to set on fire, inflame*.

flammŭla -ae, f. *little flame*.

flātus -ūs, m. *blowing, blast, breathing*.

Transf., *haughtiness, arrogance*, gen. plur.

flāvens -entis, *yellow or gold-coloured.*

flāvesco -ĕre, *to become yellow or gold-coloured.*

Flāvius -a -um, *name of a Roman gens to which the emperors Vespasian, Titus, and Domitian belonged.*

flāvus -a -um, *gold-coloured, yellow.*

flēbilis -e: pass., *lamentable, wretched, deserving tears;* act., *tearful, doleful.* Adv. **flēbiliter.**

flecto flectĕre flexi flexum, *to bend.* (1) *to alter the shape of, to bow, twist, curve.* Transf., *to change, alter, influence.* (2) *to alter the direction of, to turn, wheel;* vocem, *to modulate.*

flĕo flēre flēvi flētum: intransit., *to weep;* *to drip, trickle;* transit., *to weep for, lament, bewail;* flendus, *to be lamented.*

¹flētus -a -um, partic. of fleo; q.v.

²flētus -ūs, m. *weeping, bewailing.*

flexibilis -e, *that can be bent, flexible;* of speech or the voice, *adaptable;* in bad sense, *fickle, changeable.*

flexilis -e, *flexible, pliant, supple.*

flexilŏquus -a -um, *equivocal, ambiguous.*

flexio -ōnis, f. *bending;* vocis, or modorum, *modulation of the voice;* deverticula flexionesque, *twists and turns.*

flexipēs -pĕdis, *crooked-footed, twining.*

flexŭōsus -a -um, *full of windings and turnings, crooked.*

flexūra -ae, f. *bending.*

¹flexus -a -um, partic. of flecto; q.v.

²flexus -ūs, m. *bending, turning;* of the voice, *modulation.* Transf., *change, alteration.*

flictus -ūs, m. *striking together, dashing against.*

flīgo -ere, *to beat or dash down.*

flo flare flavi flatum, *to blow;* intransit., of winds, persons and instruments; transit., *to blow, blow forth; to blow on* an instrument; *to cast metals, to coin.*

floccus -i, m. *a flock of wool;* flocci non facere, *to think nothing of.*

Flōra -ae, f., *the goddess of flowers, and Spring;* adj. **Flōrālis** -e, *belonging to Flora;* n. pl. as subst. *the festival of Flora.*

Flōrentia -ae, f. *a town in Etruria (now Florence);* adj. **Flōrentīnus** -a -um.

florĕo -ēre -ŭi, *to bloom, flower.* Transf., *to be in one's prime, to prosper, flourish, be in repute;* with abl., *to abound in, swarm with.* Hence partic. **flōrens** -entis, *blooming, flourishing.*

flōresco -ĕre, *to begin to blossom or flourish.*

flōrĕus -a -um, *made of flowers; rich in flowers, flowery.*

flōridus -a -um, *flowery, blossoming; made of or rich in flowers;* of age, *fresh, blooming;* of speech, *flowery, florid.*

flōrifer -fĕra fĕrum, *flower-bearing.*

flōrilĕgus -a -um, *culling flowers.*

flōs flōris, m. *a flower, blossom.* Transf., *the prime, flower of anything, the best,*

the pride; on the face, *first beard, down;* vini *bouquet;* of speech, *ornament.*

floscŭlus -i, m., *a little flower.* Transf., *best part, pride;* of speech, *ornament.*

fluctifrăgus -a -um. *wave-breaking.*

fluctŭātio -ōnis, f. *moving backwards and forwards, fluctuation; indecision.*

fluctŭo -are, *to be wave-like, move up and down;* sometimes of a *glittering effect;* of persons and passions, *to be tossed about, to waver.*

fluctŭor -ari -atus, dep. *to toss about, waver.*

fluctŭōsus -a -um, *full of waves, stormy.*

fluctus -ūs, m. *a streaming, flowing.* Transf., *commotion, disturbance.*

flŭentum -i, n., *running water, a stream.*

flŭidus -a -um, *flowing, fluid.* Transf., *lax, languid; relaxing.*

flŭito -are, *to flow hither and thither, to float, swim, sail, move up and down, be tossed about.* Transf. *to flutter; to waver, vacillate.*

flūmen -ĭnis, n. *flowing;* hence *a river, stream;* flumine secundo, *downstream;* flumine adverso, *upstream;* fig., *a stream of blood, tears, words, etc.*

flūmĭnĕus -a -um, *of a river.*

flŭo flŭĕre fluxi fluxum: of fluids, *to flow;* of a solid object, *to flow, drip with any liquid.* Transf., in gen., *to flow, stream, pour;* of abstr. things, *to proceed, issue, spread;* of circumstances, *to tend;* of language, *to flow; to sink, droop.* Hence pres. partic. **flŭens** -entis, *flowing;* hence *lax;* of speech, *fluent or diffuse;* adv. **flŭenter,** *in a flowing manner.* Past partic. **fluxus** -a -um, *flowing;* hence *leaky;* of solid objects, *waving, fluttering, loose;* of character, *lax, loose, weak;* of abstr. things, *fleeting, unstable.*

flŭto -are, *to flow, float, swim.*

flŭviālis and **flŭviātilis** -e, *of a river.*

flŭvidus -a -um, *flowing, fluid.*

flŭvius -ĭi, m., *flowing water; a stream, river.*

fluxus -a -um, partic. from flŭo; q.v.

focāle -is, n. *a wrapper for the neck.*

focillo -are, *to warm up, refresh by warmth.*

focŭla -orum, n pl. *stoves.*

focŭlus -i, m. *a brazier.*

focus -i, m. *a fireplace, hearth;* meton., *house, family, home;* sometimes *altarfire or funeral pyre.*

fŏdico -are, *to dig, jog;* latus, *to dig in the ribs.*

fŏdio fŏdĕre fōdi fossum, *to dig;* also *to dig out; to excavate.* Transf., *to prick, prod, jog.*

foecundus, **foecundo** = fecundus, fecundo; q.v.

foedĕrātus -a -um, *confederate, allied.*

foedifrăgus -a -um, *treaty-breaking.*

foedĭtās -ātis, f. *foulness, filthiness.*

foedo -are, *to make foul, make filthy, defile, disfigure;* morally, *to dishonour, disgrace.*

¹foedus -a -um, *foul, filthy, horrible, disgusting;* adv. **foedē.**

²**foedus** -ĕris, n. *a league* between states; *a compact, covenant, agreement.* Transf., *a law.*

foen-; see faen-.

foetĕo -ēre, *to have a bad smell.*

foetĭdus -a -um, *having a bad smell, stinking.*

foetor -ōris, m. *a bad smell, stink.*

foetus; see fetus.

fōlĭātus -a -um, *leafy*: n. as subst. *a salve* or *oil of spikenard leaves.*

fōlĭum -i, n. *a leaf.*

follĭcŭlus -i, m. *a little sack or bag.*

follis -is, m. *a leather bag; a pair of bellows; a purse; a puffed-out cheek.*

fōmentum -i, n. *poultice, fomentation.* Transf., *alleviation.*

fōmes -itis, m. *touchwood, tinder.*

fons fontis, m. *a spring, fountain; fresh* or *spring water.* Transf., *spring, origin, source.*

fontānus -a -um, *of a spring or fountain.*

Fontēius -a -um, *name of a Roman gens.*

fontĭcŭlus -i, m. *a little fountain or spring.*

for fāri fātus, dep. *to speak, say*; also *to speak of.*

fŏrābĭlis -e, *that can be bored through, penetrable.*

fŏrāmen -ĭnis, n. *hole, opening, aperture.*

fŏras, *out of doors, forth, out*; (scripta) foras dare, *to publish.*

forceps -cĭpis, m. and f. *a pair of tongs, pincers.*

forda -ae, *a cow in calf.*

fŏre, fŏrem, used as fut. infin. and imperf. subj. of sum; q.v.

fŏrensis -e, *relating to the market or forum*; hence *of the business of the Roman forum*, esp. *legal.*

forfex -fĭcis, f. *a pair of shears or scissors.*

¹**fŏris** -is, f. *a door*; plur. fores, *folding-doors.* Transf., *any opening, entrance.*

²**fŏris**, adv. (1) (situated) *out of doors, outside, without*; sometimes, *abroad, outside Rome.* (2) *from without, from abroad.*

forma -ae, f. *form, figure, shape; beautiful shape, beauty; image, likeness; a shape serving as model, e.g. a shoemaker's last; a mould, stamp*; abstr., *form, manner, type*; in logic, *species; outline, general notion.*

formālis -e, *formal, having a set form.*

formāmentum -i, n. *conformation.*

formātor -ōris, m. *a fashioner.*

formātūra -ae, f. *forming, shaping.*

Formiae -arum, f. *town on the coast of Latium*; adj. **Formiānus** -a -um.

formīca -ae, f. *an ant.*

formīdābĭlis -e, *fearful, formidable.*

¹**formīdo** -are, *to be terrified, to dread.*

²**formīdo** -ĭnis, f. *dread, terror*; meton., *source of fear, dreadfulness, awfulness; a scarecrow.*

formīdōlōsus -a -um: act., *causing dread, terrible, fearful*; pass. *fearful, timid.* Adv., **formīdōlōsē**, *dreadfully, terribly.*

formo -are, *to form, shape, fashion; to arrange, order, regulate, dispose.*

formōsĭtās -ātis, f. *beauty.*

formōsus -a -um, *beautifully formed, beautiful*; adv. **formōsē**.

formŭla -ae, f. *physical beauty*; legal, *set form, formula*; esp. *the form of an alliance*; in gen., *rule, principle.*

fornācālis -e, *of an oven.*

fornācŭla -ae, f., *a little oven.*

fornax -ācis, f. *oven, furnace, kiln*; Aetnae, *the crater.*

fornĭcātus -a -um, *arched, vaulted.*

fornix -ĭcis, m. *arch, vault; arcade*; milit. *an arched sallyport.*

fornus = furnus; q.v.

fŏro -are, *to bore, pierce.*

fors, *chance, luck*; in nom. **fors**, also **forsit** (fors sit), **forsăn** (fors an), and **forsĭtăn** (fors sit an), *perhaps, perchance*; abl. **fortĕ**, *by chance, accidentally, as it happened.*

fortassĕ (**fortassis**), *perhaps.*

fortĕ; see fors.

fortĭcŭlus -a -um, *fairly bold.*

fortis -e, physically, *strong, powerful, robust*; morally, *brave, courageous, steadfast*; fortes fortuna adiuvat, *fortune favours the brave*; in bad sense, *bold, audacious.* Adv. **fortiter**, *strongly, bravely.*

fortĭtūdo -ĭnis, f. *physical strength, moral bravery, courage*; plur., *deeds of bravery.*

fortŭitus -a -um, *accidental, casual, fortuitous, unpremeditated*; n. pl. as subst. *chance occurrences.* Abl. sing. as adv. **fortŭīto**, *by chance, fortuitously.*

fortūna -ae, f. *chance, fate, lot, luck, fortune*; fortuna prospera, secunda, *good fortune*; adversa, *misfortune.* Transf., *lot, condition, state, mode of life; property, possessions.*

fortūno -are, *to make happy, bless, prosper.*

Hence partic. **fortūnātus** -a -um, *blessed, lucky, fortunate; well off, wealthy, rich.* Adv. **fortūnātē**, *happily, fortunately.*

fōrŭli -orum, m., *a bookcase.*

fŏrum -i, n. *an open square, market-place*; forum bovarium, or boarium, *the cattle-market*; forum holitorium, *vegetable-market*; forum piscarium, or piscatorium, *fish-market*; in gen., *a place of public business*, commercial, political and judicial esp. in Rome. Transf., *of the business transacted in a forum*; forum agere, *to hold an assize*; forum attingere, *to apply oneself to public business.*

fŏrus -i, m. *the gangway of a ship; a block of seats in the theatre*; plur., *tiers of cells in a beehive.*

fossa -ae, f. *ditch, trench, channel.*

fossĭo -ōnis, f. *digging, excavation.*

fossor -ōris, m. *a digger, delver; a boor, clown.*

fossūra -ae, f. *digging.*

fōtus, partic. of foveo; q.v.

fŏvĕa -ae, f. *a pit, esp. as a trap for game, a pitfall.*

fŏvĕo fŏvēre fōvi fōtum, *to warm,*

keep warm, caress: fig., *to stay constantly in* a place; in gen., *to foster, cherish, support, encourage.*

fractus -a -um, partic. from frango; q.v.

frāga -orum, n. pl. *strawberries.*

frăgilis -e, *crackling; easily broken, fragile.* Transf., *fleeting, transitory; weak, feeble.*

frăgilĭtās -ātis, f., *frailty, weakness.*

fragmen -mĭnis, n. *a breaking;* hence, usually plur., *fragments, remains, ruins.*

fragmentum -i, n. *a piece broken off, fragment.*

frăgor -ōris, m., *a breaking; a noise of breaking, crack, crash.*

frăgōsus -a -um, *crashing, roaring; fragile; broken, rough.*

fragro -are, *to emit a smell*, esp. *a sweet smell;* pres. partic. **fragrans** -antis *sweet-smelling, fragrant.*

frăgum; see fraga.

frango frangĕre frēgi fractum, *to break, break in pieces, shatter;* gulam laqueo, *to strangle;* fruges saxo, *to grind;* diem morantem mero, *to shorten;* of persons, passions, etc., *to master, subdue, humble;* frangi animo, *to be discouraged.*
    Hence partic. **fractus** -a -um, *broken, humbled, enfeebled.*

frāter -tris, m. *a brother;* frater germanus, *own brother;* fratres, *brothers and sisters;* also *a cousin* or *a brother-in-law.* Transf., *a comrade, compatriot, ally.*

frātercŭlus -i, m. *little brother.*

frāternĭtās -ātis, f. *brotherhood, fraternity.*

frāternus -a -um, *of a brother, brotherly, fraternal;* sometimes *of a cousin.* Transf., *of a related person; of some thing related to another.* Adv. **frāternē**, *in a brotherly manner, like a brother.*

frātrĭcīda -ae, m. *one who kills a brother, a fratricide.*

fraudātĭo -ōnis, f. *deceit, fraud, swindling.*

fraudātor -ōris, m. *deceiver, swindler.*

fraudo -are, *to cheat, defraud, swindle; to steal, embezzle.*

fraudŭlentĭa -ae, f. *deceitfulness.*

fraudŭlentus -a -um, *deceitful, fraudulent.*

fraus, fraudis, f.: act., *deceit, fraud;* sine fraude, *honourably;* in gen., *a crime, offence; delusion, error; damage, harm;* sine fraude, *without harm.*

fraxĭnĕus and **fraxĭnus** -a -um, *of ashwood, ashen.*

fraxĭnus -i, f. *an ash-tree;* meton., *a spear* or *javelin, with a shaft of ashwood.*

Frĕgellae -arum, f. *town of Volsci, in Latium.*

frĕmĕbundus -a -um, *roaring, murmuring.*

frĕmĭtus -ūs, m. *roaring, murmuring, growling.*

frĕmo -ĕre -ŭi -ĭtum, *to roar, murmur, growl;* with acc. *to murmur out something, grumble, complain.*

frĕmor -ōris, m. *roaring, murmuring.*

frendo -ĕre: intransit., *to gnash the teeth;* transit., *to crush, bruise, grind.*

frēni -orum, m.; see frenum.

frēno -are. *to bridle, curb, restrain, check.*

frēnum -i, n., usually plur. **frēna** -orum, n.; also **frēni** -orum, m. *bridle, reins, bit, curb.* Transf., *restraint.*

frĕquens -entis, *crowded, numerous, full;* of places, *full, frequented, populous;* of time, *repeated, frequent, constant;* of persons, *often doing a thing;* of things, *often done or used.* Adv. **frĕquenter**, *in large numbers; frequently, often.*

frĕquentātĭo -ōnis, f., *frequency, crowding.*

frĕquentĭa -ae, f.: of persons, *a large concourse, numerous assembly, population;* of things, *a large number, abundance.*

frĕquento -are, *to crowd;* of number *to collect in large numbers; to fill a place with people or things; to do a thing in crowds* or *with a crowd;* of time, *to do* or *use a thing frequently:* domum, *to visit often;* Hymenaee! frequentant, *they repeat.*

frĕtum -i; n. *a strait, sound, estuary, firth, channel;* fretum Siciliae, fretum Siciliense, or fretum, *the Straits of Messina;* the *sea* in gen., usually plur.: fig., *disturbance, turmoil.*

¹**frētus** -a -um, *relying on, confiding in,* with abl.

²**frētus** -ūs, m. *a strait; an interval, difference.*

frĭco frĭcare frĭcŭi frictum and frĭcātum, *to rub, rub down.*

frīgĕo -ēre, *to be cold; to be inactive, lifeless, dull;* colloq., *to be coldly received, fall flat.*

frīgesco -ĕre, *to become cold or dull.*

frīgĭdŭlus -a -um, *somewhat cold* or *faint.*

frīgĭdus -a -um, *cold, cool, chilly;* f. sing. as subst. *cold water.* Transf., in act. sense, *chilling, causing cold;* fig., *cold, dull, lifeless;* of speech, *flat.* Adv. **frīgĭdē**, *coldly; languidly, feebly.*

frīgo frīgĕre frixi frictum, *to roast, parch.*

frĭgus -ōris n. *cold, coolness; the cold of winter; a cold place; the cold of death* or *fright.* Transf., *coldness in action, dullness, indolence; a cold reception, coolness, disfavour.*

frĭguttio -ire, *to stammer.*

frĭo -are, *to rub, crumble.*

frĭtillus -i, m. *a dice-box.*

frīvŏlus -a -um, *trifling, worthless;* n. pl. as subst. *sticks of furniture.*

frondātor -ōris, m. *a pruner of trees.*

frondĕo -ēre, *to be in leaf, be leafy.*

frondesco ĕre, *to come into leaf, put forth leaves.*

frondĕus -a -um, *leafy.*

frondĭfer -fĕra -fĕrum, *leaf-bearing, leafy.*

frondōsus -a -um, *full of leaves, leafy.*

¹**frons** frondis, f. *a leaf, foliage*; meton., *a chaplet* or *crown of leaves.*

²**frons** frontis, f. *the forehead, brow;* frontem contrahere, *to frown.* Transf., in gen., *the front, forepart;* milit., *the van; the outside end of a book roll; frontage* (in measuring land).

frontālia -ium, n. pl. *the frontlet of a horse.*

fronto -ōnis, m., *a man with a broad forehead.*

fructuārius -a -um, *fruit-bearing, fruitful.*

fructuōsus -a -um, *fruitful, fertile.*

fructus -ūs, m.: abstr., *enjoyment, enjoying;* concr., *proceeds, profit, produce, income;* esp. *the fruits of the earth.*

frūgālis -e, *frugal, economical, honest;* adv. **frūgāliter.**

frūgālitās -ātis, f., *frugality, economy, honesty;* of style, *restraint.*

frūgi; see frux.

frūgifer -fĕra -fĕrum, *fruitful, fertile, profitable, advantageous.*

frūgifĕrens -entis, *fruitful, fertile.*

frūgilĕgus -a -um, *collecting grain.*

frūgipărus -a -um, *fruitful, prolific.*

frūmentārius -a -um, *of grain or corn;* res, *the supply of corn;* m. as subst. *a corn-merchant.*

frūmentātio -ōnis, f. *a foraging; a distribution of corn.*

frūmentātor -ōris, m. *a forager* or *a provider of corn.*

frūmentor -ari, dep., *to forage, fetch corn.*

frūmentum -i, n., *corn, grain.*

fruor frŭi fructus and frūitus, dep., *to have the benefit of, to enjoy,* usually with abl.: votis, *to obtain one's wishes;* as legal t. t., *to have the use and enjoyment of.*

frustillātim, *bit by bit.*

frustrā, *in error:* frustra esse, *to be deceived, mistaken.* Transf., *in vain, without effect; wantonly, without reason.*

frustrāmen -inis, n. *deception.*

frustrātio -ōnis, f. *deception, disappointment, frustration.*

frustro -are, and frustror -ari, dep. *to disappoint, deceive, trick.*

frustum -i, n. *a bit, piece, morsel.*

frŭtex -tĭcis, m. *a shrub, bush;* as a term of reproach, *blockhead.*

frŭtĭcētum -i, n., *a thicket.*

frŭtĭco -are and **frŭtĭcor** -ari, dep. *to shoot out, become bushy.*

frŭtĭcōsus -a -um, *bushy* or *full of bushes.*

frux frūgis, f., usually plur. **frūges** -um, *fruits of the earth;* in gen., *fruits, success;* ad bonam frugem se recipere, *to improve oneself.* Dat. sing. **frŭgi,** used as adj., *useful, honest, discreet, moderate.*

fūco -are, *to colour, paint, dye;* fig., *to colour, embellish.*

Hence partic. **fūcātus** -a -um, *painted; counterfeited, simulated.*

fūcōsus -a -um, *painted; simulated, counterfeited.*

¹**fūcus** -i, m., *red* or *purple dye; red* or *purple colour; rouge;* in gen., *paint, dye* of any colour; *bee-glue.* Transf., *deceit, pretence.*

²**fūcus** -i, m. *a drone bee.*

Fūfius -a -um, *name of a Roman* gens.

fŭga -ae, f. *flight, running away;* esp. *flight from one's country, exile, banishment.* Transf., *swift course, speed; avoiding,* with genit.

fŭgax -ācis, *ready to flee, flying; speeding, fleeting, transitory;* with genit., *avoiding.* Hence compar. adv. **fŭgācius.**

fŭgio fŭgĕre fūgi fŭgĭtum, *to flee.* Intransit., *to take to flight, run away; to pass away, disappear.* Transit., *to flee from, run away from, avoid;* with infin., fuge quaerere, *do not seek;* of things, *to escape the notice of a person.*

Hence partic., **fŭgiens** -entis, *fleeing; avoiding,* with genit.; *fleeting, deteriorating.*

fŭgĭtīvus -a -um, *flying, fugitive;* m. as subst., *a fugitive,* esp. *a runaway slave.*

fŭgĭto -are, *to flee;* transit., *to fly from, avoid, shun.*

Hence partic., **fŭgĭtans** -antis, *fleeing;* with genit., *avoiding.*

fŭgo -are, *to put to flight, chase away; to drive into exile, to dismiss, avert.*

fulcīmen -inis, n., *a prop, support, pillar.*

fulcio fulcire fulsi fultum, *to prop up, support; to strengthen, secure;* morally *to support, stay, uphold.*

fulcrum -i, n., *the post* or *foot of a couch.*

fulgĕo fulgēre fulsi, *to flash, to lighten;* in gen., *to shine, gleam, glitter;* fig., *to be distinguished, to shine.*

fulgĭdus -a -um, *shining, gleaming, glittering.*

fulgo -ĕre = fulgeo; q.v.

fulgor -ōris, m., *lightning;* in gen., *glitter, brightness;* fig., *brightness, glory.*

fulgur -ŭris, n. *a flash* or *stroke of lightning;* sometimes *an object struck by lightning;* in gen., *brightness.*

fulgŭrālis -e, *relating to lightning.*

fulgŭrātor -ōris, m., *a priest who interpreted omens from lightning.*

fulgŭrītus -a -um, *struck by lightning.*

fulgŭro -are, *to lighten; to shine, be brilliant.*

fūlica -ae, f. *a coot.*

fūlīgo -inis, f. *soot; powder for darkening the eyebrows.*

fullo -ōnis, m. *a cloth-fuller.*

fullōnica -ae, f. *the art of fulling.*

fulmen -inis, n. *a stroke of lightning, a thunderbolt.* Transf. *a crushing calamity; mighty* or *irresistible power.*

fulmĭnĕus -a -um, *of lightning; like lightning, rapid* or *destructive.*

fulmĭno -are, *to lighten.*

fultūra -ae, f., *support, prop, stay.*

Fulvius -a -um, *name of a Roman* gens.

fulvus -a -um, *tawny, yellowish brown,*

fūmĕus and **fumīdus** -a -um. *smoky, full of smoke.*

fūmifer -fēra -fērum, *smoky.*

fūmifĭcus -a -um, *causing smoke.*

fūmo -are, *to smoke, steam, reek.*

fūmōsus -a -um, *smoked.*

fūmus -i, m. *smoke, steam, vapour.*

fūnālis -e, *attached to a rope.* N. as subst. **fūnāle** -is, *the thong of a sling; a wax-torch.*

fūnambŭlus -i, m. *a rope-dancer.*

functĭo -ōnis, f. *performance, execution.*

funda -ae, *a sling; a sling-stone; a casting-net.*

fundāmen -ĭnis, n. and **fundāmentum** -i, n. usually plur., *a foundation, basis.*

fundātor -ōris, m. *founder.*

fundĭto -are, *to sling.*

fundĭtor -ōris, m. *a soldier with a sling, a slinger.*

fundĭtus, *from the bottom; completely, entirely; at the bottom, below.*

¹fundo -are, *to lay the foundation of, to found; also to make firm, to strengthen.* Hence partic. **fundātus** -a -um, *founded, firm.*

²fundo **fundĕre fūdi fūsum**: of liquids, *to pour, pour out;* of metals, *to melt, cast.* Transf., *to pour out, shower, give abundantly; to squander;* se fundere, *to rush, stream;* of sounds, *to utter;* with emphasis on distribution, *to spread, extend, scatter;* milit. *to rout, defeat, scatter, put to flight.* Hence partic. **fūsus** -a -um, *spread out, extended;* crines, *flowing free;* of speech, *diffuse;* adv. **fūsē**, *widely, copiously.*

fundus -i, m. *ground; the bottom or base of anything; a farm, estate.*

fūnebris -e, *of a funeral funereal; deadly, destructive.*

fūnĕrĕus -a -um, *of a funeral, funereal; fatal, ill-omened.*

fūnĕro -are, *to bury solemnly,* inter with funeral rites; partic. **fūnĕrātus** -a -um, *done to death.*

fūnesto -are, *to defile or pollute with death.*

fūnestus -a -um: pass., *filled with mourning, defiled by death;* act., *fatal, disastrous, deadly.*

fungĭnus -a -um, *of a mushroom.*

fungor fungi functus, dep. *to occupy oneself with anything, to perform, execute, undergo,* usually with abl.; absol. in special sense, *to be affected, suffer.*

fungus -i, m. *a mushroom, fungus; a dull, stupid fellow; a 'thief' in the wick of a candle, a candlesnuff.*

fūnĭcŭlus -i, m. *thin rope, cord, string.*

fūnis -is, m. *rope, cord, line.*

fūnus -ēris, n. *a funeral, burial.* Transf., *the corpse; death; destruction, ruin; a cause of ruin.*

fŭo fŭi fŭtūrus, etc.; see sum.

fūr fūris, c. *a thief.*

fūrax -ācis, *inclined to steal, thievish.* Hence superl. adv. **fūrācissĭmē**, *most thievishly.*

furca -ae, f., *a (two-pronged) fork, a pitch-fork; a fork-shaped prop or pole; an instrument of punishment, with two prongs to which the arms were tied;* geograph., *a narrow pass.*

furcĭfer -fēra -fērum, *carrying the furca as a punishment;* applied to slaves, *gallows-bird.*

furcilla -ae, f., *a little fork.*

furcillo -are, *to support.*

furcŭla -ae, f. *a little fork; a fork-shaped prop;* geograph., *a narrow pass,* esp. of the Caudine forks.

furfur -ŭris, m. *bran; scales, scurf on the skin.*

fūrĭa -ae, f., usually plur. *rage, frenzy, madness, passion;* personif., *of the mythological Furies, avenging deities;* fig., *of persons.*

fūrĭālis -e, *furious, raging, frenzied; belonging to the Furies;* **fūrĭālĭter**, *furiously, madly.*

fūrĭbundus -a -um, *raging, furious; inspired.*

fūrĭo -are, *to make furious, madden;* partic., **fūrĭātus** -a -um, *raging.*

fūrĭōsus -a -um, *raging, raving, mad, furious;* adv. **fūrĭōsē.**

Fūrius -a -um, *name of a Roman gens.*

furnus -i, m. *an oven, bakehouse.*

fūro -ēre, *to rage, rave, be mad;* often of impassioned persons, *to rave, be frantic;* furere aliquā, *to be madly in love with.* Adv. from partic., **fūrenter**, *furiously.*

¹fūror -ari, dep. *to steal, pilfer;* fig., *to steal away, withdraw; to counterfeit, personate.*

²fūror -ōris, m. *madness, raving, insanity; furious anger, martial rage; passionate love; inspiration, poetic or prophetic frenzy;* meton., *an object of passion.*

furtĭfĭcus -a -um, *thievish.*

furtim, adv. *by stealth, stealthily.*

furtīvus -a -um, *stolen; secret, concealed, furtive.* Adv. **furtīvē.**

furtum -i, n. *theft, robbery;* in plur., *stolen property;* fig., *underhand methods; trick, deceit,* esp. *secret or stolen love.*

fūruncŭlus -i, m. *a sneak thief, pilferer.*

furvus -a -um, *dark-coloured, black.*

fuscĭna -ae, f. *a three-pronged fork, trident.*

fusco -are, *to darken, blacken.*

fuscus -a -um, *dark-coloured;* of the voice, *indistinct.*

fūsĭlis -e, *molten, liquid, soft.*

fūsĭo -ōnis, f. *pouring-out, out-pouring.*

fustis -is, m. *a stick, cudgel, club.*

fustŭārĭum -i, n. *cudgelling to death.*

¹fūsus -a -um, partic. from fundo; q.v.

²fūsus -i, m. *a spindle.*

fūtātim, *abundantly.*

futtĭlis and **fūtĭlis** -e, *brittle; vain, worthless, good for nothing.*

futtĭlĭtās and **fūtĭlĭtās** -ātis, f. *worthlessness, folly, silliness.*

fūtūrus -a -um used as future partic. of sum; q.v.

g 99 gen

G

G, g, the seventh letter of the Latin alphabet, originally represented by C.

Gābii -orum, m. *an ancient city of Latium*; adj. **Gābīnus** -a -um.

Gābīnius -a -um, *name of a Roman gens.*

Gādēs -ium, f. *a town in Hispania Baetica* (now *Cadiz*); adj. **Gādītānus** -a -um.

gaesum -i, n. *a long heavy javelin.*

Gaetūli -orum, m. pl. *a people in north-west Africa.*

Gāius, abbrev. C., *a Roman praenomen*; fem. **Gāia.**

Gălătae -arum, m. *a Celtic people settled in Asia Minor, the Galatians.*

Galba -ae, m. *a cognomen of the Sulpician gens*; esp. of Ser. Sulpicius, *Roman emperor* A.D. 68-69.

galbănĕus -a -um, *of galbanum*; q.v.

galbănum -i, n., *the resinous sap of a Syrian plant.*

galbīnus -a -um, *greenish-yellow.*

gălĕa -ae, f. *helmet.*

gălĕo -are, *to cover with a helmet*; partic., **gălĕātus** -a -um, *helmeted.*

gălēricŭlum -i, n. *skull-cap; wig.*

gălēritus -a -um, *wearing a hood or skull-cap.*

gălērum -i, n. and **gălērus** -i, m. *skull-cap; wig.*

galla -ae, f. *oakapple.*

Galli -orum, m. pl. *the Gauls, a Celtic people, to the west of the Rhine and in the north of Italy*; **Gallia** -ae, f. *Gaul, the land of the Gauls*; Cisalpina = *Northern Italy*; Transalpina = *France*; adj. **Gallicānus** and **Gallicus** -a -um, *Gaulish*; f. as subst., gallica, *a slipper.*

galliambus -i, m. *a song of the priests of Cybele.*

gallica; see Galli.

gallīna -ae, f. *hen.*

gallīnācĕus -a -um, *of poultry*; gallus, *a poultry-cock.*

gallīnārius -a -um, *of poultry*; m. as subst., *poultry-farmer.*

¹gallus -i, m. *cock.*

²Gallus, *a Gaul*; see Galli.

³Gallus -i, m. usually plur. **Galli** -orum, m. *a priest of Cybele.*

gānĕa -ae, f. and **gānĕum** -i, n. *a brothel or a low eating-house.*

gānĕo -ōnis, m. *a debauchee.*

Gangēs -is, m., *the river Ganges in India.* Adj. **Gangēticus** -a -um; f. adj. **Gangētis** -idis = *Indian.*

gannio -ire, *to yelp, snarl, growl.*

gannītus -ūs, m. *yelping, snarling.*

Gănўmēdēs -is, m. *the cup-bearer of Jove.*

garrio -ire, *to chatter, prate, babble.*

garrŭlĭtās -ātis, f. *chattering.*

garrŭlus -a -um, *talkative, chattering, babbling, noisy.*

gărum -i, n. *fish-sauce.*

Gărumna -ae, f. *a river in Gaul* (now *Garonne*); **Gărumni** -orum, m.pl. *a people living on the Garonne.*

gaudĕo gaudēre gāvīsus sum, *to rejoice, be glad*; with abl. of cause, *to delight in*; in sinu gaudere, *to rejoice in secret.*

gaudium -i, n. *joy, gladness, delight; a source of delight.*

gausāpē -is, and **gausăpum** -i, n. *woollen cloth with a long nap, frieze.*

gāza -ae, f. *the royal treasure of Persia*; in gen., *treasure, riches, wealth.*

gĕlāsīnus -i, m. *dimple.*

gĕlĭdus -a -um, *cold, frosty, icy*; in act. sense, *chilling*; f. as subst. **gĕlida** -ae, *cold water.* Adv. **gĕlĭdē,** *coldly, feebly.*

gĕlo -are, transit., *to cause to freeze*; intransit., *to freeze.*

gĕlu -ūs, n. (earlier **gĕlus** -ūs, m. and **gĕlum** -i, n.), *frost, chill.*

gĕmĕbundus -a -um, *groaning, sighing.*

gĕmellĭpăra -ae, f. adj. *twin-bearing.*

gĕmellus -a -um, *twin, paired, double*; m. as subst., *a twin.*

gĕminātĭo -ōnis, f. *doubling.*

gĕmino -are: transit., *to double; to join together, strike together, repeat*; partic. **gĕminātus** -a -um, *doubled*; intransit., *to be double.*

gĕmĭnus -a -um, *twin, double; paired or half-and-half; similar, like*; m. pl. as subst. **gemini** -orum, *twins*, esp. *Castor and Pollux.*

gĕmitus -ūs, m., *a sigh, groan*; of things, *groaning, roaring.*

gemma -ae, f. *a bud or eye of a plant.* Transf., *a jewel, gem, precious stone; a jewelled goblet; a seal-ring, seal; a literary gem.*

gemmātus -a -um, *set or adorned with jewels.*

gemmĕus -a -um, *made of or set with jewels; bright.*

gemmĭfer -fĕra -fĕrum, *bearing or producing jewels.*

gemmo -are, *to bud*; pres. partic. **gemmans** -antis, *set with jewels, glittering like jewels.*

gĕmo gĕmĕre gĕmŭi gĕmĭtum: intransit., *to sigh, groan*; of lions, *to roar*; of doves, *to coo*; of things, *to creak*; transit., *to sigh over, lament, bemoan.*

gĕna -ae, f. usually plur., *cheek, cheeks and chin.* Transf., *eye-socket, eye.*

Gĕnāva -ae, f. *a town of the Allobroges* (now *Geneva*).

gĕnĕălŏgus -i, m. *a genealogist.*

gĕner -eri, m. *a son-in-law; a grand-daughter's husband; a brother-in-law.*

gĕnĕrālis -e. (1) *belonging to a kind, generic.* (2) *universal, general.* Adv. **gĕnĕrāliter,** *in general, generally.*

gĕnĕrasco -ĕre, *to be produced, come to birth.*

gĕnĕrātim. (1) *according to kinds or classes.* (2) *in general, generally.*

gĕnĕrātor -ōris, m. *begetter, producer.*

gĕnĕro -are, *to beget, produce, bring to life.*

gĕnĕrōsus -a -um, *of noble birth noble, well-bred; of a place, producing well.* Transf., *of character, noble, mag-nanimous.* Adv. **gĕnĕrōsē,** *nobly.*

gĕnĕsis -is, f. *the constellation which presides over one's birth.*

gĕnētīvus -a -um, *inborn, innate; nomina, family names; casus, the genitive case.*

gĕnetrix -trīcis f. *one who brings forth, a mother.*

gĕniālis -e. (1) *relating to marriage.* (2) *relating to enjoyment; joyful, gay.* Adv. **gĕniālĭter,** *jovially, gaily.*

gĕnĭcŭlātus -a -um, *knotty, full of knots.*

gĕnista (gĕnesta) -ae, f. *the plant broom.*

gĕnĭtābĭlis -e, *fruitful, productive.*

gĕnĭtālis -e, *creative, fruitful; dies, birthday; of Diana, presiding over births.* Adv. **gĕnĭtālĭter,** *in a fruitful manner.*

gĕnĭtīvus; see genetivus.

gĕnĭtor -ōris, m. *a begetter, father, producer.*

gĕnĭtūra -ae, f. *begetting, engendering; in astrology, nativity.*

gĕnĭus -i, m. *the guardian spirit of a man or place, a genius; esp. as a spirit of enjoyment, one's taste, inclination; genium curare, to enjoy oneself.* Transf., *talent, genius.*

gĕno = gigno; q.v.

gens gentis, f. *a clan, stock, people, tribe, nation.* Transf., *an offspring, descendant; a district, country; esp. in partitive genit.:* ubi gentium? *where in the world?;* plur., gentes, *foreigners.*

gentīcus -a -um, *a nation, national.*

gentīlĭcius -a -um, *of a particular gens.*

gentīlis -e, *of a gens; of a country, national.*

gentīlĭtās -ātis, f. *the relationship between the members of a gens.*

gĕnu -ūs, n. *the knee.*

Gĕnŭa -ae, f. *coast-town in Liguria* (now Genoa).

gĕnŭālia -ium, n. pl. *garters.*

¹gĕnŭīnus -a -um, *natural, innate.*

²gĕnŭīnus -a -um, *belonging to the cheek or jaw:* dentes, *the jaw-teeth;* m. as subst. *a jaw-tooth.*

¹gĕnus -ĕris, n. *birth, descent, origin; race, stock, family, house; hence offspring, descendant(s); sex; in gen., class, kind, variety, sort; in logic, genus; of action, etc., fashion, manner, way.*

²genus -ūs = genu; q.v.

gĕōgrăphia -ae, f. *geography.*

gĕōmetres -ae, m. *a geometer.*

gĕōmetria -ae, f. *geometry.*

gĕōmetrĭcus -a -um, *geometrical;* m. as subst., **gĕōmetrĭcus** -i, *a geometer;* n. pl. **gĕōmetrĭca,** *geometry.*

gĕōrgĭcus -a -um, *agricultural;* n. pl. as subst. **Gĕōrgĭca** -orum, *the Georgics of Vergil.*

Germāni -orum, m. pl., *the Germans;* adj. **Germānus** -a -um, *German;* f. subst. **Germānia** -ae, *Germany;* adj. **Germānĭcus** -a -um, *German;* m. as subst. **Germānĭcus** -i. a surname assumed after victories in Germany.

germānĭtās -ātis, f. *the relationship between brothers or sisters; brotherhood, sisterhood.*

¹germānus -a -um, *having the same parents;* m. or f. as subst. *own brother, own sister.* Transf., *brotherly, sisterly; genuine, real, true.* Adv. **germāne,** *faithfully, honestly.*

²Germānus -a -um; see Germani.

germen -ĭnis, n. *an embryo; a bud, shoot or graft; fig., germ.*

germĭno -are, *to sprout forth.*

¹gĕro gĕrĕre gessi gestum. Lit. (1) *to carry, bear; esp. to wear.* (2) *to bear, give birth to.* Transf., *to carry about, display an appearance; personam gerere, to act a part; se gerere, to conduct oneself* (with adv.); *to carry about, entertain a feeling; to carry on conduct, manage business;* res gestae, *exploits, esp., warlike exploits.*

²gĕro -ōnis, m., *a carrier.*

gerrae -arum, f. pl. *wattled twigs.* Transf., *trifles, nonsense.*

gerro -ōnis, m. *a trifler, idler.*

gĕrŭlus -i, m. *porter, carrier.*

Gĕryōn -ŏnis, and Gĕryŏnēs -ae, m. *myth., a king in Spain with three bodies, killed by Hercules.*

gestāmen -ĭnis, n. *that which is carried; that by which anything is carried; a carriage or litter.*

gestĭcŭlātĭo -ōnis, f. *pantomime, gesticulation.*

gestĭcŭlor -ari, dep. *gesticulate.*

gestĭo -ōnis, f., *management, performance.*

gestĭto -are, *to carry often, wear often.*

gesto -are, *to carry, bear about;* pass. *to ride about.*

gestor -ōris, m. *a tale-bearer, gossip.*

gestus -ūs, m. *carriage of the body, posture; esp. the gestures of an actor or orator.*

Gĕtae -arum, m. pl. *a people of Thrace living near the Danube.* Adj. **Gĕtĭcus** -a -um, *Thracian;* adv. **Gĕtĭcē,** *after the Getic fashion.*

Gĕtūlus, etc. = Gaetulus, etc.; q.v.

gibba -ae, f. *hump, lunch.*

gibber -ĕra, -ĕrum, *hump-backed.*

gibbus -i, m. *hump, lunch.*

Gĭgas -gantis, m. *a giant;* adj. **Gĭgantēus** -a -um.

gigno gignĕre gĕnŭi gĕnĭtum, *to beget, bear, bring forth; to cause.*

gilvus -a -um, *pale yellow.*

gingīva -ae, f. *gum (of the mouth).*

glăber -bra -brum, *bald;* m. as subst., *a page.*

glăciālis -e, *icy.*

glăcĭes -ēi, f. *ice.* Transf., *hardness.*

glăcĭo -are, *to freeze.*

glădĭātor -ōris, m. *one hired to fight at public shows, a gladiator;* hence *bandit, brigand;* gladiatoribus, *at a show of gladiators.*

glădĭātōrĭus -a -um, *of gladiators, gladiatorial;* n. as subst. *gladiators' pay.*

glădĭātūra -ae, f. *the profession of gladiator.*

glădĭus -i, *sword.*

glaeba = gleba; q.v.

glaesum (glesum) -i, n. *amber.*

glandĭfer -fĕra -fĕrum, *acorn-bearing.*

glandĭum -i, n. *a delicate glandule in meat.*

glans glandis, f. *mast; an acorn, chestnut, etc.* Transf., *a bullet.*

glārĕa -ae, f. *gravel.*

glārĕōsus -a -um, *gravelly full of gravel.*

glaucōma -atis, n. (also -ae, f.) *a disease of the eye, cataract.*

glaucus -a -um *bluish- or greenish-grey.*

glēba (glaeba) -ae, f. *a lump or clod of earth; hence land, soil; a piece, lump of anything.*

glēbŭla -ae, f., *a little clod or lump; a little farm or estate.*

glēsum = glaesum; q.v.

glīs glīris, m. *dormouse.*

glisco -ĕre, *to grow up, swell up, blaze up.*

glŏbo -are, *to form into a ball or mass.*

glŏbōsus -a -um, *spherical.*

glŏbus -i, m. *a ball, globe, sphere; a troop, crowd, mass of people.*

glŏmĕrāmen -ĭnis, n. *a round mass, globe.*

glŏmĕro -are, *to form into a sphere, or rounded heap; in gen., to gather together collect, amass.*

glŏmus -ĕris, n. *clue, skein, ball of thread.*

glōrĭa -ae, f. *fame, renown, glory.* Transf., *of a member of a group, the pride, the glory; desire of glory, ambition, boastfulness; plur., glorious deeds.*

glōrĭātĭo -ōnis, f. *glorying, boasting.*

glōrĭŏla -ae, f. *a little glory.*

glōrĭor -ari, dep. *to glory, boast, pride oneself.*

glōrĭōsus -a -um, *famous, glorious; ambitious, pretentious, boastful.* Adv. glōrĭōsē, *gloriously; vauntingly, boastingly.*

glūbo -ĕre, *to peel.* Transf., *to rob.*

glūtĕn -tĭnis, n. *glue.*

glūtĭnātor -ōris, m., *one who glues books, a bookbinder.*

glūtĭo (gluttĭo) -ire, *to swallow, gulp down.*

glūto (glutto) -ōnis, m. *glutton.*

Gnaeus -i, m. *a Roman praenomen,* shortened Cn.

gnārĭtās -ātis, f. *knowledge.*

gnārus -a -um; act., *knowing, aquainted with, expert;* pass., *known.*

Gnătho -ōnis, m. *a parasite in the Eunuchus of Terence;* in gen. *parasite.*

Gnātĭa = Egnatia; q.v.

gnātus, gnāvus = natus, navus; q.v.

Gnīdus = Cnidus; q.v.

Gnossus (Gnōsus) -i, f., *an ancient city of Crete, the residence of Minos;* adj. Gnōsĭus and Gnōsĭăcus -a -um, *Gnosian; Cretan;* f. adj. Gnōsĭas -ădis and Gnōsĭs -ĭdis, *Cretan* and, as subst., *Ariadne.*

gōbĭus (cōbĭus) -i, and gōbĭo -ōnis, m. *a gudgeon.*

gonger; see conger.

Gorgō -gŏnis, f. *also called Medusa, slain by Perseus;* adj. Gorgŏnĕus -a -um.

Gortỹna -ae, f. *an ancient city in Crete.*

grăbātus -i, m. *a low couch, camp-bed.*

Gracchus -i, m. *a cognomen in the Gens Sempronia,* esp. of Tiberius and Gaius, *the 'Gracchi'.* Adj. Gracchānus -a -um.

grăcĭlis -e, *slender, thin, slim;* of style, etc., *simple, without ornament.*

grăcĭlĭtās -ātis, f. *thinness, slenderness.*

grăcŭlus -i, m. *jackdaw.*

grădārĭus -a -um, *going step by step.*

grădātim, adv. *step by step, by degrees.*

grădātĭo -ōnis, f., in rhetoric, *climax.*

grădĭor grădi gressus, dep. *to step, walk.*

Grădīvus -i, m. *a surname of Mars.*

grădus -ūs, m. *a step; (1) a step as made, a pace; suspenso gradu, on tiptoe; gradum facere, to step; gradum inferre, to advance;* hence in gen., *an approach.* (2) *a step as climbed, a stair;* hence any *tier, gradation; a braid of hair;* abstr., *degree; stage; rank, position;* milit. *station, post.*

Graeci -orum, m. *the Greeks;* sing. Graecus -i, m. *a Greek;* as adj. Graecus -a -um, *Greek;* adv. Graecē, *in the Greek language;* f. subst. Graecĭa -ae, f. *Greece;* Magna Graecia, *the Greek colonies in the south of Italy;* dim. Graecŭlus -i, m. *a little Greek.*

graecisso -are, and graecor -ari, dep. *to imitate the Greeks.*

Grāĭi -orum, m. = Graeci, *the Greeks;* adj. Grāĭus -a -um, *Greek.*

Grāĭŭgĕna -ae, m. *a Greek by birth.*

grallātor -ōris, m. *one that walks on stilts.*

grāmen -ĭnis, n. *grass, turf;* any *plant* or *herb.*

grāmĭnĕus -a -um, *grassy, of grass;* also *of cane or bamboo.*

grammătĭcus -a -um, *literary, grammatical;* as subst., m. *a philologist, grammarian;* f. sing. and n. pl. *grammar, philology.*

grammătista -ae, f. *a teacher of grammar or languages.*

grānārĭum -i, n. *granary.*

grandaevus -a -um, *very old.*

grandesco -ĕre, *to become great, grow.*

grandĭcŭlus -a -um, *rather large.*

grandĭfer -fĕra -fĕrum, *producing great profits.*

grandĭlŏquus -a -um, *speaking grandly; boastful.*

grandĭnat -are, impers. *it hails.*

grandĭo -ire, *to increase.*

grandis -e, *full-grown, great, large;* in stature, *tall;* in years, *old.* Transf., *great, important;* of style, *lofty, grand, sublime.*

grandĭtās -ātis, f. *of style, loftiness, sublimity.*

grandŏ -ĭnis, f. *hail, hail-storm.*

grānĭfer -fĕra -fĕrum, *grain-carrying.*

grānum -i, n. *grain, seed.*

grāphicus -a -um, *concerned with painting;* hence *masterly, skilful;* adv. **grāphĭcē.**

grāphĭum -i, n. *a stilus, a pointed instrument for writing on wax.*

grassātor -ōris, m. *an idler; a footpad.*

grassor -ari, dep. *to walk about, to loiter; to go about an undertaking; to proceed against somebody.*

grātes, f. pl. *thanks;* grates agere, *to express thanks;* habere, *to feel gratitude.*

grātĭa -ae, f.   (1) *charm, attraction, pleasantness;* personif., of *the three Graces* (Euphrosyne, Aglaia, Thalia). (2) *favour* with others; *esteem, regard, popularity.* (3) *a favour done, service, kindness;* abl. gratiā, *on account of;* meā gratiā, *for my sake.* (4) *thankfulness, thanks;* in sing. and plur.: gratias agere, with dat., *to express thanks;* gratias habere, *to feel grateful;* abl. plur. **grātĭis** or **grātis,***without recompense, for nothing, gratis.*

grātĭfĭcātĭo -ōnis, f. *complaisance, obligingness.*

grātĭfĭcor -ari, dep. *to oblige, gratify, do a favour to.*

grātĭōsus -a -um, *favoured, beloved; showing favour, complaisant.*

grātis; see gratia.

grātor -ari, dep. *to wish joy, to congratulate; to give thanks.*

grātŭĭtus -a -um, *not paid for or not provoked, gratuitous, spontaneous;* abl. sing. n. as adv. **grātŭĭto,** *gratuitously.*

grātŭlābundus -a -um, *congratulating.*

grātŭlātĭo -ōnis, f. *wishing joy, congratulation; a thanksgiving festival.*

grātŭlor -ari, dep. *to wish a person joy, congratulate* (with dat.); *to give solemn thanks,* esp. to the gods.

grātus -a -um, adj. (1) *pleasing, welcome, agreeable;* gratum facere, *to do a favour.* (2) *thankful, grateful.* Adv. **grātē,** *willingly, with pleasure; thankfully.*

grāvanter and **grāvātē;** from gravo.

grāvātim, *reluctantly.*

grāvēdĭnōsus -a -um, *subject to colds.*

grāvēdo -ĭnis, f. *cold in the head, catarrh.*

grāvēŏlens -lentis, *strong-smelling, rank.*

grāvesco -ĕre, *to become heavy; to grow worse.*

grăvĭdĭtās -ātis, f. *pregnancy.*

grăvĭdo -are, *to load, burden; to impregnate.*

grăvĭdus -a -um, *heavy; laden, filled, full; pregnant.*

grăvis -e. (1) *heavy;* of sound, *low, deep;* fig., *weighty, important;* of character, *dignified, serious;* of style, *elevated, dignified.*   (2) *burdened laden, weighed down;* esp. *pregnant.* (3) *burdensome, oppressive; grievous, painful, unpleasant.* Adv. **grăvĭter,** *heavily, weightily, reluctantly; grievously, painfully.*

grăvĭtās -ātis, f. (1) *weight;* fig., *consequence, importance;* of character,

dignity, authority, seriousness.   (2) *heaviness; pregnancy; dullness faintness.* (3) *pressure;* fig., *unpleasantness.*

grăvo -are, *to load, burden; to heighten, exaggerate, increase; to oppress, burden, trouble;* pass., *to feel burdened* or *troubled* by a thing, or *to make heavy weather of doing it.* Adv. **grăvanter,** and **grăvātē,** *reluctantly.*

grĕgālis -e, of *a herd* or *flock; common, ordinary;* m. pl. as subst. *companions, associates, accomplices.*

grĕgārĭus -a -um, of *a herd* or *flock;* miles, *a private soldier.*

grĕgātim, *in troops or crowds.*

grĕmĭum -i, n. *lap, bosom; womb.*

gressus -ūs, m. *a step;* of a ship, *course.*

grex grĕgis, m. *a herd, flock, drove;* of people, *a troop, band,* esp. *a philosophical sect or troop of soldiers;* grege facto, *in close order.*

grunnĭo (grundĭo) -ire, *to grunt like a pig.*

grunnītus -ūs, m., *the grunting of a pig.*

grus grŭis, m. and f. *a crane.*

grў, n. indecl. *scrap, crumb.*

gryllus -i, m. *cricket, grasshopper.*

gryps, grўpis, m. *griffin.*

gŭbernācŭlum (-āclum) -i, n. *rudder, helm;* hence *direction, management, government.*

gŭbernātĭo -ōnis, f. *steering; direction, government.*

gŭbernātor -ōris, m. *helmsman, steersman, pilot; director, governor.*

gŭbernātrix -īcis, f. *she that directs.*

gŭberno -are, *to steer a ship, be at the helm;* in gen., *to steer, direct, govern.*

gŭbernum -i, n. = gubernaculum; q.v.

gŭla -ae, f. *gullet, throat;* hence *greediness, gluttony.*

gŭlōsus -a -um, *gluttonous.*

gurges -itis, m. *whirlpool, eddy;* in gen., *troubled water, a stream, flood, sea;* fig., *abyss, depth.*

[1]gurgŭlĭo -ōnis, f. *windpipe.*

[2]gurgŭlĭo -ōnis, m.; see curculio.

gurgustĭum -i, n. *hut, hovel.*

gustātus -ūs, m. *taste; appetite, flavour.*

gusto -are, *to taste, take a little of; to partake of, enjoy.*

gustus -ūs, m. *tasting; taste, flavour, a whet* or *relish.*

gutta -ae, f. *a drop; a spot* or *mark.*

guttātim, *drop by drop.*

guttŭla -ae, f. *a little drop.*

guttur -ŭris, n. *the windpipe, throat; gluttony.*

guttus -i, m. *a jug.*

Gўăros -i, f. and **Gўăra** -orum, n. *a barren island in the Aegean, used as a place of exile under the empire.*

Gўgēs -is and -ae, m. *a king of Lydia, famous for his ring;* adj. **Gўgaeus** -a -um.

gymnāsĭarchus -i, m. *the master of a gymnasium.*

gymnāsĭum -i, n. *school of gymnastics, gymnasium;* also *a place for philosophical discussion.*

gymnastĭcus and **gymnĭcus** -a -um, *gymnastic.*

gўnaecēum (and **-ĭum**) -i, n. *the women's apartments in a Greek house.*

gypso -are, *to cover with gypsum*; partic. **gypsātus** -a -um, *covered with gypsum, whitened.*

gypsum -i, n. *gypsum*; meton. *a plaster figure.*

gўrus -i, m *a circle, ring*; esp. *a course for training horses*; in gen., *orbit, circuit.*

H

H, h, the eighth letter of the Latin Alphabet.

ha! hahae! hahahae! exclamations of joy or amusement.

hăbēna -ae, f. *a strap; a bridle, reins* (esp. in plur.); **habenas dare,** *to loosen the rein*; **adducere,** *to tighten it.*

hăbĕo -ēre -ŭi -ĭtum, *to have, hold; to have about one, carry, wear; to contain*; more generally, *to possess, have power over*; absol., *to possess property, be wealthy*; of places, *to own, inhabit, or rule over*; of persons, *to keep,* esp. in a certain state, or relation. Transf., **habere in animo,** *to have in mind, intend*; **habes consilia nostra,** *you know of*; **habeo dicere,** *I have it in my power to say*; **bonum animum habere,** *to be of good courage*; **odium,** *to cherish hatred*; **invidiam,** *to experience ill-will*; **misericordiam,** *to involve or cause pity*; **concilium,** *to hold a council*; **orationem,** *to make a speech*; with **reflex.,** *to keep oneself, be,* in a condition; **graviter se habere,** *to be ill*; **ut nunc res se habet,** *as things now are*; intransit., **bene habet,** *all right*; with adv., rarely, *to use, manage, treat*; with double acc., or dat., or pro and abl., *to hold, consider, regard* in a certain light. Perf. partic. **hăbĭtus** -a -um, *disposed; in a certain condition* (physical or mental).

hăbĭlis -e, *easily managed, handy; suitable, fit, convenient.*

hăbĭlĭtās -ātis, f. *aptitude, suitability.*

hăbĭtābĭlis -e, *habitable.*

hăbĭtātĭo -ōnis, f. *dwelling, habitation.*

hăbĭtātor -ōris, m. *inhabitant.*

hăbĭto -are: transit., *to inhabit*; intransit., *to dwell.*

hăbĭtūdo -ĭnis, f. *condition.*

¹hăbĭtus -a -um, partic. from habeo; q.v.

²hăbĭtus -ūs, m. *condition, habit, bearing*; of dress, *style*; of places, *lie of the land*; abstr., *nature, character, disposition, attitude.*

hāc, adv. from hic; q.v.

hactēnus, *as far as this, so far (and no farther); hitherto; up to this point.*

Hadrĭa -ae; f. *a town in the north of Italy*; m. *the Adriatic Sea.* Adj. **Hadrĭăcus** and **Hadrĭātĭcus** -a -um, *Adriatic.*

Hadrĭānus -i, m., P. Aelius, Roman emperor from A.D. 117 to 138.

haedīlĭa -ae, f. and **haedillus** -i, m., *a little kid.*

haedīnus -a -um, *of a kid.*

haedŭlus -i, m. *a little kid.*

haedus -i, m. *a kid, young goat.*

Haemŏnĭa -ae, f. *an old name of Thessaly*; adj. **Haemŏnĭus** -a -um, *Thessalian*; f. subst. **Haemŏnis** -nĭdis, *a Thessalian woman.*

haerĕo haerēre haesi haesum. (1) *to stick, cleave, adhere, hang on to a person or thing.* (2) *to come to a standstill, get stuck; be embarrassed.*

haeresco -ĕre, *to adhere, stick.*

haesĭtantĭa -ae, f. *faltering*; **linguae,** *stammering.*

haesĭtātĭo -ōnis, f.: in speech, *hesitation, stammering*; mentally, *hesitation, indecision.*

haesĭto -are, *to stick fast, to hesitate*; in speech, *to stammer*; mentally, *to be undecided, be at a loss.*

hālec; see alec.

hălĭaeëtos -i, m. *sea-eagle, osprey.*

hālĭtus -ūs, m., *breath, vapour.*

hallex -ĭcis, m. *thumb or big toe.*

hālo -are, *to breathe out, exhale.*

hālūc-; see aluc-.

hāma (**āma**) -ae, f. *bucket,* esp. *fireman's bucket.*

Hămādrўas -ādis, f., *a wood-nymph, hamadryad.*

hāmātus -a -um, *provided with hooks, hooked; curved like a hook, crooked.*

Hămilcăr -căris, m. *father of Hannibal.*

hāmĭōta -ae, m., *an angler.*

Hammon; see Ammon.

hāmus -i, m. *a hook,* esp. *a fish-hook; a talon; a thorn.*

Hannĭbăl -bălis, m. *leader of the Carthaginians in the second Punic war.*

hăra -ae, f. *a pen or coop; a pig-sty.*

hărĭŏlor -ari, dep. *to utter prophecies.* Transf., *to talk nonsense.*

hărĭŏlus -i, m. and **hărĭŏla** -ae f. *a soothsayer, prophet.*

harmŏnĭa -ae, f. *melody, concord, harmony.*

harpăgo -ōnis, m.. *a large hook, drag, grappling-iron.*

harpē -es, f. *a curved sword, scimitar.*

Harpўiae (trisyll.) -arum, f. pl., *the Harpies, mythical monsters.*

hăruspex -spĭcis, m. *soothsayer; a seer, prophet.*

hăruspĭcīnus -a -um, *concerned with divination*; f. as subst. *divination.*

hăruspĭcĭum -i, n. *inspection of entrails, divination.*

Hasdrŭbăl (Asdrŭbăl) -bălis, m. *the brother of Hannibal.*

hasta -ae, f. *a spear, pike, javelin*; milit., and in ceremonial use, at public auctions and weddings.

hastātus -a -um, *armed with a spear* m pl. as subst. **hastāti** -orum, *the front rank of a Roman army when drawn up for battle.*

hastīle -is, n., *the shaft of a spear; a spear; a prop for vines,* etc.

hau, *oh!*

haud (haut), *not, not at all, by no means*.

hauddum, *not yet*.

haudquāquam, *by no means, not at all*.

haurio haurire hausi haustum, *to draw up, draw out or in; to drink up, absorb, swallow; to shed* blood; *to drain, empty a receptacle*; in gen., *to derive, take in*; also *to exhaust, weaken, waste*.

haustrum -i, n. *a pump*.

haustus -ūs, m. *drawing of water*; legal, *the right to draw water*; of air, *inhaling*; of drink, *drinking, a draught*; of solids, *a handful*.

haut = haud; q.v.

hăvĕo; see aveo.

hebdŏmas -ădis, f. *seventh day of a disease* (supposed critical).

Hēbē -ēs, f. *the cup-bearer of the gods*.

hēbĕnus -i, f. *the ebon-tree; ebony*.

hēbĕo -ēre, *to be blunt, dull, heavy, inactive*.

hēbĕs -ētis, *blunt, dull; faint, sluggish, weak*; mentally, *dull, heavy, stupid*.

hēbesco -ēre, *to become dull, blunt, dim*.

hēbĕto -are, *to make blunt or dull, to deaden, dim*.

Hebraeus -a -um, *Hebrew, Jewish*.

Hebrus -i, m., *the chief river of Thrace*.

Hěcătē -ēs, f. *goddess of magic and enchantment*, adj. **Hěcătēius** -a -um and f. **Hěcătēis** -īdis, *Hecatean, magical*.

hěcătombē -ēs, f. *a hecatomb*.

Hector -tŏris, m. *son of Priam, husband of Andromache*; adj. **Hectŏrěus** -a -um.

Hěcŭba -ae, and **Hěcŭbē** -ēs, f. *wife of Priam*.

hědĕra -ae, f. *ivy*.

hēdychrum -i, n. *a fragrant ointment*.

hei, interj. = ei; q.v.

Hělěna -ae, and **Hělěnē** -ēs, f. *wife of Menelaus, carried off by Paris to Troy*.

Hělice -ēs, f. *a constellation, the Great Bear*.

Hělicon -ōnis, m., *a hill in Boeotia, sacred to Apollo and the Muses*; adj. **Hělicōnius** -a -um; subst. **Hělicōniădes** and **Hělicōnides** -um, f. *the Muses*.

Hellē -ēs, f. *a girl drowned in the Hellespont, so named after her*.

hellěborus; see elleborus.

Hellespontus -i, m., *the Hellespont, Dardanelles*.

hellŭo (hēlŭo) -ōnis, *glutton, squanderer*.

hellŭor (hēlŭor) -ari, dep. *to guzzle, gormandize*.

hělops (ělops, ellops) -ōpis, m. *a fish, perhaps sturgeon*.

helvella -ae, f. *a small pot-herb*.

Helvētii -orum, m. *the Helvetii, a people in what is now Switzerland*.

hem, interj. *well! just look!*

hēmĕrodrŏmus -i, m. *a special courier, express*.

hēmicillus -i, m. *mule*.

hēmicyclium -i, n. *a semi-circle* (of seats).

hēmina -ae, f. *a measure of capacity, about half a pint*.

hendĕcăsyllăbi -orum, m. pl. *verses of eleven syllables, hendecasyllables*.

Henna (Enna) -ae, f. *city of Sicily, with a temple of Ceres*; adj. **Hennensis** -e and **Hennaeus** -a -um.

heptēris -is, f. *a galley with seven banks of oars*.

hēra = ěra; q.v.

Hēra -ae, f., *the Greek goddess identified with the Roman Juno*; **Hēraea** -orum, n. pl., *her festival*.

herba -ae, f. *vegetation; a green plant; a blade or stalk, esp. of corn or grass*.

herbesco ěre, *to grow into blades or stalks*.

herbĭdus -a -um, and **herbifer** -fěra -fěrum, *grassy*.

herbōsus -a -um, *grassy*.

herbŭla -ae, f. *a little herb*.

hercisco (ercisco) -ěre, *to divide an inheritance*.

Hercle; see Hercules.

herctum -i, n. *an inheritance*; herctum ciere, *to divide an inheritance*.

Hercŭlănĕum -i, n. *town in Campania destroyed by an eruption of Vesuvius*.

Hercŭles -is and -i, m. *the son of Jupiter and Alcmena*; voc. **Hercŭles** or **Hercŭle** or **Hercle**, used as an oath, *by Hercules*; so also **Mēhercŭles**, **Mēhercŭle**, **Mēhercle**; adj. **Hercŭlěus** and **Hercŭlānĕus** -a -um.

Hercўnia silva -ae, f. *the Hercynian forest, in central Germany*.

hěrē = heri; q.v.

hērēdĭtārius -a -um, *of an inheritance; inherited, hereditary*.

hērēdĭtās -ātis, f. *inheritance*.

hērēdĭum -i, n. *patrimony*.

hērēs (haerēs) -ēdis, c. *an heir, heiress, successor; an owner*.

hěrī (hěrē), *yesterday*.

hērifūga = erifuga; q.v.

hěrilis -e = erilis; q.v.

hermaphrŏdītus -i, m. *hermaphrodite*.

Hermes or **Herma** -ae, m. *the god Hermes, identified with the Roman Mercury*.

Hērō -ūs, f., *a priestess at Sestos, loved by Leander*.

Hērōdes -is, m. *Herod*; esp. *Herod the Great*.

Hērŏdŏtus -i, m. *the Greek historian, born 484 B.C.*

hērōicus -a -um, *relating to the heroes, heroic*.

hērōina -ae and **hērōīs** -īdis, f. *a demigoddess, heroine*.

hērōs -ōis, m. *a demigod, hero*.

hērōus -a -um, *a hero, heroic*; m. as subst. *a hexameter*.

hěrus = ěrus; q.v.

Hēsiŏdus -i, m. *an early Greek poet of Boeotia*.

Hespěrus or **-os** -i, m. *the Evening Star*; adj. **Hespěrius** -a -um, *western*; f. as subst. **Hespěria** -ae, *the western land; Italy or Spain*; f. adj. **Hespěris** -idis, *western*; f. subst. **Hespěrides** -um, *daughters of Hesperus, living in the extreme west*.

hesternus -a -um, *of yesterday*.

hĕtairīa -ae, f. *a secret society.*

heu! *oh! alas!*

heus! *hallo! ho, there! hark!*

hexămĕter -tri, m.: adj., *with six feet* (of metre); as subst., *a hexameter.*

hexēris -is, f. *a galley with six banks of oars.*

hiātus -ūs, m. *a cleft, opening; the opening of the mouth, open jaws;* hence *gaping after, desire for;* gram. *hiatus.*

Hĭbēr -ēris, m. *an Iberian, Spaniard;* plur. **Hĭbēres** -ērum, and **Hĭbēri** -orum, m. *Spaniards;* **Hĭbērus** -i, m. *the river Ebro;* **Hĭbērĭa** -ae, *Spain;* adj. **Hĭbērĭcus** -a -um and **Hĭbērus** -a -um, *Spanish.*

hĭberna -orum, n.; see hibernus.

hĭbernācŭlum -i, n.: in pl., *tents or huts for winter quarters.*

Hĭbernĭa -ae, f. *Ireland.*

hĭberno -are, *to winter, spend the winter.*

hĭbernus -a -um, *wintry, of winter; like winter, cold* or *stormy, wintering, for the winter;* n. pl. as subst. *winter quarters.*

hĭbiscum -i, n. *marsh-mallow.*

hĭbrĭda (hybrĭda) -ae, *a hybrid.*

¹hīc, haec, hōc, *this, this one; this present;* in court, *my client;* strengthened form **hīce, haece, hōce;** interrog. **hīcĭne, haecĭne, hōcĭne.**

²hīc (and heic) *here; in this place, in this matter; hereupon;* strengthened **hīce** and interrog. **hīcĭne.**

hĭĕmālis -e, *of winter; wintry, stormy.*

hĭĕmo -are. (1) *to winter, spend the winter.* (2) *to be stormy.*

hĭems (hiemps) -ĕmis, f. *winter; the cold of winter; stormy weather, storm.*

Hĭĕrŏsŏlyma -orum, n. pl. *Jerusalem.*

hĭlăris -e and **hĭlărus** -a -um, *cheerful, merry, gay;* n. acc. sing. as adv. **hĭlăre,** *cheerfully.*

hĭlărĭtās -ātis, f. *cheerfulness, gaiety.*

hĭlăro -are, *to make joyful, to cheer up.*

hĭlărŭlus -a -um, *gay, cheerful.*

hillae -arum, f. pl. *intestines of animals; a kind of sausage.*

Hĭlōtae and **Ĭlōtae** -arum, m. pl., *the Helots, slaves of the Spartans.*

hīlum -i, n. *a trifle;* with neg. *not a whit, not in the least.*

hinc, adv., *from here, hence;* hinc atque illinc, *on this side and on that;* of causation, *hence, from this cause;* of time, *henceforth,* or *thereupon.*

hinnĭo -ire, *to neigh, whinny.*

hinnītus -ūs, m. *neighing.*

hinnŭlĕus -i, m. *a young roebuck, fawn.*

hinnus -i, m. *a mule.*

hĭo -are, *to open, stand open; to gape,* esp. in astonishment or longing; of speech, *to hang together badly;* with acc. object, *to pour forth.*

hippăgōgi -orum, f. pl. *transports for cavalry.*

Hippĭas -ae, m. *son of Pisistratus, tyrant of Athens.*

hippŏcentaurus -i, m. *a centaur.*

Hippŏcrătēs -is, m. *a physician of Cos* (flourishing about 430 B.C.).

Hippŏcrēnē -ēs, f. *a fountain on Mount Helicon.*

hippŏdrŏmos -i, m., *a hippodrome racecourse.*

Hippŏlўtus -i, m. *son of Theseus.*

hippŏtoxŏta -ae, m. *a mounted archer.*

hippūrus -i, m. *a fish, perhaps goldfish.*

hircīnus and **hircōsus** -a -um, *of a goat; goatlike.*

hircus -i, m. *a he-goat.*

hirnĕa -ae, f. *a can* or *jug.*

hirsūtus -a -um, *hairy, shaggy, rough; unadorned.*

Hirtĭus -a -um, *name of a Roman gens.*

hirtus -a -um, *hairy, shaggy, rough, uncultivated.*

hĭrūdo -ĭnis, f. *leech.*

hĭrundo -ĭnis, f. *swallow.*

hisco -ĕre, *to open, split open, gape; to open the mouth.*

Hispāni -orum, m. pl. *the Spaniards;* **Hispānĭa** -ae, f. *the whole of the Spanish peninsula;* adj. **Hispānĭensis** -e and **Hispānus** -a -um.

hispĭdus -a -um, *rough, hairy, bristly.*

¹hister = histrio; q.v.

²Hister (Ister) -tri, m. *name of the lower part of the Danube.*

histŏrĭa -ae, f. *inquiry; the results of inquiry; learning; historical narrative, history;* in gen., *narrative, a story.*

histŏrĭcus -a -um, *of history, historical;* m. as subst., *a historian.*

histrĭcus -a -um, *of actors.*

histrĭo -ōnis, m. *an actor.*

histrĭōnālis -e, *of actors.*

hĭulco -are, *to cause to gape, to split.*

hĭulcus -a -um, *gaping, cleft, open; gaping with desire, longing;* of speech, *badly put together;* adv. **hĭulcē,** *with hiatus.*

hŏdĭē, *today; at present, still, even now; at once.*

hŏdĭernus -a -um, *of today.*

hŏlĭtor -ōris, m. *a kitchen-gardener.*

hŏlĭtōrĭus -a -um, *of herbs;* forum, *vegetable-market.*

hŏlus (ŏlus) -ĕris, n. *vegetable, pot-herb.*

Hŏmērus -i, m. *Homer, the Greek epic poet;* adj. **Hŏmērĭcus** -a -um.

hŏmĭcīda -ae, c. *a murderer, murderess, homicide.*

hŏmĭcīdĭum -i, n. *murder, homicide.*

hŏmo -ĭnis, *a human being, man, mortal;* in pl., *men, people, the world;* used like a pronoun, *he, him;* milit. in pl., *infantry.*

hŏmullus -i, and **hŏmuncĭo** -ōnis and **hŏmuncŭlus** -i, m. *a little man, manikin.*

hŏnestās -ātis, f. (1) *honour, repute, respectability;* in pl., *notabilities.* (2) *worth, virtue, probity.* (3) *beauty.*

hŏnesto -are, *to honour, adorn, dignify.*

hŏnestus -a -um. (1) *honoured, in good repute, respectable.* (2) *honourable, proper, virtuous;* n. as subst., *morality, virtue.* (3) *fine, beautiful.* Adv. **hŏnestē,** *respectably; honourably; properly.*

hŏnor = honos; q.v.

hŏnōrābĭlis -e, *respectful.*

hŏnŏrārĭus -a -um, *done or given as an honour.*

hŏnŏrĭfĭcus -a -um, *causing honour, honouring*; adv. hŏnŏrĭfĭcē.

hŏnōro -are, *to honour, show honour to, adorn, dignify*; partic. hŏnōrātus -a -um, *honoured, distinguished, respected, or in act. sense, conferring honour*; adv. hŏnōrātē.

hŏnōrus -a -um, *honourable.*

hŏnōs and hŏnŏr -ōris, m. *honour, a mark of honour or respect, distinction;* honoris causa, *with due respect, or to honour, or for the sake of*; personif., Honour; frequently, *an office of dignity, a public office*; also *an offering to the gods, sacrifice*; poet., *beauty, grace.*

hŏplŏmăchus -i, *a gladiator.*

hōra -ae, f. *an hour, the twelfth part of a day or night*; hora quota est? *what's o'clock?* in horam vivere, *to live for the moment*; in gen., *time, season;* in plur. *a clock, dial*; personif. *the Hours, goddesses who presided over the seasons.*

Hŏrātĭus -a -um, *name of a Roman gens.*

hordĕum -i, n. *barley.*

hōrĭa -ae, f. *a small fishing-boat.*

hornōtĭnus and hornus -a -um, *of this year, this year's*; adv. hornō, *this year.*

hōrŏlŏgĭum -i, n. *a clock; a sundial or water-clock.*

horrĕo -ēre, *to bristle, be rough*; of the hair, *to stand on end*; of persons, *to shudder, dread.* Gerundive as adj. horrendus -a -um, *horrible, dreadful; awful, worthy of reverence.*

horresco horrescĕre horrŭi, *to stand on end, bristle, be rough*; of persons, *to tremble, shudder, begin to dread.*

horrĕum -i, n. *a barn, granary, store-house.*

horrĭbĭlis -e, *horrible, frightful, dreadful*; colloq., *astonishing, wonderful.*

horrĭdŭlus -a -um, *somewhat rough, unadorned.*

horrĭdus -a -um *rough, shaggy, bristly; shivering with cold.* Transf. *wild, savage; unpolished, uncouth; frightful, horrible.* Adv. horridē, *roughly.*

horrĭfer -fĕra -fĕrum, *causing shudders of cold or fear.*

horrĭfĭco -are, *to make rough; to terrify.*

horrĭfĭcus -a -um, *causing terror, dreadful*; adv. horrĭfĭcē.

horrĭsŏnus -a -um, *sounding dreadfully.*

horror -ōris, m. *bristling, shuddering; roughness of speech; dread, fright, esp. religious dread, awe*; meton., *object of dread, a terror.*

horsum, *in this direction.*

hortāmen -ĭnis, n. and hortāmentum -i, n. and hortātĭo -ōnis, f. *exhortation, encouragement, incitement.*

hortātīvus -a -um, *of encouragement.*

hortātor -ōris, m. *an inciter, encourager.*

hortātus -ūs, m. *incitement, encouragement.*

Hortensĭus -a -um *name of a Roman gens.*

hortor -ari, dep. *to exhort, incite, encourage; esp to harangue troops.*

hortŭlus -i, m. *a little garden*; plur. *grounds, a small park.*

hortus -i, m. *a garden*; in plur. *grounds, park.*

hospēs -pĭtis, m. and hospĭta -ae, f. (1) *a host, hostess.* (2) *a guest.* (3) *a guest-friend, friend.* (4) *a stranger*; used also like adj. *foreign.*

hospĭtālis -e, *of a guest or host; friendly, hospitable*; adv. hospĭtālĭter.

hospĭtālĭtās -ātis, f. *hospitality.*

hospĭtĭum -i, n. *hospitality;* meton., *a guest-chamber, inn, quarters.*

hostĭa -ae, f. *an animal slain in sacrifice, a victim.*

hostĭcus -a -um, *foreign; but usually of the enemy, hostile*; n, as subst. *enemy territory.*

hostīlis -e, *of, by or for the enemy; like an enemy, unfriendly, hostile*; adv. hostīlĭter.

Hostīlĭus -a -um, *name of a Roman gens.*

hostīmentum -i, n. *compensation, requital.*

hostĭo -ire, *to requite, recompense.*

hostis -is, c. *a stranger; but esp. an enemy, foe, opponent.*

hūc, *hither, to this place;* huc (atque) illuc, *hither and thither.* Transf., *in addition to this; to this pitch, or degree;* interrog. hūcĭnĕ?

hŭi, *exclamation of surprise, eh! hallo!*

hŭiusmŏdi or hŭiuscĕmŏdi, *of this kind.*

hum-; see also um-.

hūmānĭtās -ātis, f. *humanity, human nature, human feeling; kindness; refinement, education, culture.*

hūmānĭtŭs, *after the manner of men; also kindly.*

hūmānus -a -um, *human, of human beings*; m. as subst. *a human being;* of good qualities, *humane, kind, educated, civilized, refined.* Adv. hūmānē and hūmānĭter, *humanly, politely, courteously, kindly.*

hūmātĭo -ōnis, f. *burying, interment.*

hŭmĭlis -e, *on or near the ground, low, shallow.* Transf., of rank, etc., *humble, poor, insignificant;* of character, *abject or submissive;* of language, *mean, without elevation.* Adv. hŭmĭlĭter, *humbly, meanly, abjectly.*

hŭmĭlĭtās -ātis, f. *nearness to the ground; lowness; shallowness.* Transf., *insignificance, obscurity; submissiveness, abjectness.*

hŭmo -are, *to cover with earth, bury; to perform any funeral rites over a corpse.*

hŭmus -i, f. *ground, earth, soil;* humi, *on the ground;* meton., *land, country.*

¹Hўăcinthus (-os) -i, m., *a beautiful youth, accidentally killed by Apollo.*

hўăcinthus -i, m. *a flower*, perhaps *the martagon lily.*

Hўădes -um, f. *the Hyades, seven stars in the constellation Taurus.*

hўaena -ae, f. *hyena.*

hўălus -i, m. *glass*; colour *glassgreen.*

Hydra -ae, f. *many-headed water-snake, slain by Hercules*; also *a constellation.*

hydraulus -i, m. *a water organ.*

hydrīa -ae, f. *an urn, jug.*

hydrŏpicus -a -um, *dropsical.*

hydrops -ōpis, m. *the dropsy.*

hydrus -i, m. *a water-snake.*

Hўlas -ae, m. *companion of Hercules.*

Hўmēn -ēnis and **Hўmēnaeos** or -us -i, m. *Hymen, the god of marriage; the marriage song; a wedding* (esp. in plūr).

hўperbătŏn -i, n. *transposition of words.*

hўperbŏlē -ēs, f. *exaggeration.*

Hўperbŏrĕi -ōrum, m. pl. *a people in the extreme north*; adj. **Hўperbŏrēus** -a -um = *northern.*

hўpŏdĭdascălus -i, m. *an under-teacher.*

hўpomnēma -mătis, n. *a memorandum, note.*

I

i, the ninth letter of the Latin alphabet, used both as a vowel and as a consonant, formerly written j.

Iacchus -i, m. *name of Bacchus*; meton., *wine.*

iacĕo iacēre iacŭi, *to lie, be situated; to lie low, be flat; to lie sick or overthrown or killed*; of hair or clothes, *to hang loosely*; fig., *to be neglected, or despised; to be overthrown; to be cast down, dejected.*

iăcĭo iăcĕre iēci iactum. (1) *to lay.* (2) *to throw, cast, hurl; to fling away, shed; to scatter, diffuse; to let fall in speaking, utter.*

iactantĭa -ae, f. *boasting, bragging.*

iactātĭo -ōnis, f. *a tossing, shaking.* Transf., *violent emotion; boasting, ostentation.*

iactātor -ōris, m. *boaster, braggart.*

iactātus -ūs, m. *shaking, quick movement.*

iactĭto -are, *to toss about; to bandy.*

iacto -are, *to throw, cast, toss, fling away or about; to diffuse, spread, scatter; to harass, disturb a person; to broadcast words; to bring up, discuss a subject; to keep bringing up, to "boast of."* With reflex, or in pass., *to gesticulate*; also *to "throw one's weight about", make oneself conspicuous.* Pres. partic. **iactans** -antis, *boastful*; adv. **iactanter.**

iactūra -ae, f. *throwing away; loss, sacrifice.*

iactus -ūs, m. *cast, throw;* intra iactum, *within range.*

iăcŭlābĭlis -e, *able to be thrown.*

iăcŭlātor -ōris, m. *a thrower*; esp. *a javelin-man, light-armed soldier.*

iăcŭlātrix -icis, f. *the huntress (Diana).*

iăcŭlor -ari, dep. *to throw a javelin,*

to shoot at a target; to throw, cast, hurl a missile. Transf., *to make a verbal attack; to aim at, strive after; to utter.*

iăcŭlum -i, n. (1) *a dart, javelin.* (2) *a casting-net.*

iăcŭlus -a -um, *thrown, darting.*

iam, adv. *now, by now, already;* of future time, *immediately, presently, soon; henceforth; further, moreover; just, indeed;* iam diu, iam dudum, iam pridem, *now for a long time.*

ĭambĕus -a -um, *iambic.*

ĭambus -i, m. *an iambus, a metrical foot (˘ ¯); an iambic poem.*

iamdūdum, iamprīdem; see iam.

Iānĭcŭlum -i, n. *a hill west of Rome.*

iānitor -ōris, m. *door-keeper, porter.*

iānitrix -icis, f. *portress.*

ĭanthĭnus -a um, *violet-coloured.*

iānŭa ae, f. *door; entrance, approach.*

iānus -i, m. *a covered passage, arcade*; personif., **Iānus, Janus**, *an old Italian deity with two faces*; adj. **Iānālis** and **Iānŭālis** -e; hence also adj. **Iānŭārius** -a -um, *of Janus or of January*; Ianuarius (mensis), *January.*

Iăpyx -pўgis, m. *a west-north-west wind.*

Iāsōn -ŏnis, m. *leader of the Argonauts*; adj. **Iāsŏnĭus** -a -um.

iaspis -idis, f. *jasper.*

ĭbĕr-; see hiber-.

ĭbĭ, adv. *there, at that place; then, thereupon; therein, in that matter or person.*

ĭbĭdem, adv. *in the same place; at that moment; in that matter.*

ĭbis, genit. ibis and ibīdis, f. *the ibis.*

ibiscum=hibiscum; q.v.

Īcărus -i, m. *son of Daedalus, drowned whilst flying with wings made by his father*; adj. **Īcărĭus** -a -um, *of Icarus.*

iccirco=idcirco; q.v.

Īcēni -orum, m. *a British people in East Anglia.*

ichneumon -ŏnis, m. *the ichneumon.*

īcĭo or **īco** īci ictum, *to strike, hit, smite*; esp., *to strike a bargain.*

ictĕrĭcus -a -um, *jaundiced.*

ictus -ūs, m. *a blow, stroke;* in music, *beat.*

Īda -ae and **Īdē** -ēs, f. *name of two mountains, one in Crete, one in Phrygia, near Troy*; adj. **Īdaeus** -a -um.

idcirco (iccirco), *on that account; for that reason or purpose.*

īdem, ĕădem, idem, *the same*; with dat., or ac, et, etc., *the same as*; by way of addition, *also*; of contrast, *yet*; alter idem, *a second self.*

īdentĭdem, *repeatedly, again and again.*

īdĕo, adv. *on that account, therefore; for that reason or purpose.*

īdĭōta -ae, m. *an ignorant, uneducated man.*

īdōlon -i, n. *a spectre.*

īdōnĕus -a -um, *fit, appropriate, suitable*; adv. **īdōnēĕ.**

Īdŭmaea -ae, f. *a district in Palestine.*

Īdūs -uum, f. pl. *the Ides, a day in the Roman month; the fifteenth day in March, May, July, October; the thirteenth in other months.*

iĕcur, iĕcŏris and **iŏcĭnĕris,** n. *the liver; supposed seat of the passions.*

iĕcuscŭlum -i, n. *a little liver.*

iēiūnĭtās -ātis, f. *hungriness, emptiness; of style, etc., poverty, meagreness.*

iēiūnĭum -i, n. *fast, abstinence, hunger; hence, leanness.*

iēiūnus -a -um, *fasting, hungry, thirsty; of objects, poor, scanty; of spirit, poor, mean: of style, meagre, weak.* Adv. **iēiūnē,** *of style, meagrely.*

ientācŭlum -i, n. *breakfast.*

iento -are, *to breakfast.*

ĭgĭtur, *therefore, then; so, as I was saying;* to emphasize, *I say.*

ignārus -a -um: act., *ignorant, inexperienced in* (with genit.); pass., *unknown.*

ignāvĭa -ae, f. *idleness, listlessness; cowardice.*

ignāvus -a -um, (1) *idle, listless, inactive, inert, sluggish.* (2) *cowardly;* m. as subst. *a coward.* Adv. **ignāvē** and **ignāvĭter,** *lazily, without spirit.*

ignesco -ĕre, *to kindle, catch fire; to glow with passion.*

ignĕus -a -um, *fiery, burning, glowing, ardent.*

ignĭcŭlus -i, m. *a little fire, flame, spark.*

ignĭfĕr -fĕra -fĕrum, *fire-bearing, fiery.*

ignĭgĕna -ae, m. *born of fire.*

ignĭpēs -pĕdis, *fiery-footed.*

ignĭpŏtens -entis, *ruler of fire.*

ignis is, m. *fire, conflagration; a watch-fire, beacon; a firebrand; lightning;* in gen., *glow, glitter.* Transf., *a fire-brand* (of war); *glow of passion; the beloved.*

ignōbĭlis -e, *unknown, obscure; of humble birth.*

ignōbĭlĭtās -ātis, f. *obscurity; humble birth.*

ignōmĭnĭa -ae, f. *degradation, disgrace, dishonour.*

ignōmĭnĭōsus -a -um: *of persons, disgraced;* of things, *ignominious, disgraceful.*

ignōrābĭlis -e, *unknown.*

ignōrantĭa -ae, and **ignōrātĭo** -ōnis, f. *ignorance.*

ignōro -are, *to be ignorant of, not to know;* rarely, *to neglect, ignore.*

ignosco -noscĕre -nōvi -nōtum, *to overlook, forgive, pardon.*

ignōtus -a -um: pass., *unknown; ignoble, obscure;* act., *ignorant.*

īlĕ -is, n., plur. **īlĭa** -ium, *intestines, guts; loin, flank; ilia ducere, to become broken-winded.*

Īlerda -ae, f. *a town in Spain* (now Lerida).

īlex -ĭcis, f. *holm-oak.*

Īlĭa -ae, f. *mother of Romulus and Remus.*

Īlĭăcus; see **Ilion.**

īlĭcet. (1) a formula, *it is all over.* (2) *immediately, forthwith.*

īlĭcētum -i, n. *ilex-grove.*

īlĭco (illĭco), *on the spot; immediately.*

īlignus -a -um, *of ilex or holm-oak.*

Īlĭŏn or **Īlĭum** -i, n. and **Īlĭŏs** -i, f. *Troy;* adj. **Īlĭus** and **Īlĭăcus** -a -um, *Trojan;* **Īliensēs** -ium, m. pl., *Trojans;* **Īlĭădēs** -ae, *a son of Troy;* **Īliăs** -adis, f. *a Trojan woman, or the Iliad of Homer.*

ill-, for words compounded from in/l . . ., see in-.

illā, *by that way.*

illāc, *by that way, there;* illac facere, *to belong to that party.*

illĕ, illa, illŭd (older forms olle and ollus), pron., *that, that yonder, that one;* emphatically, *that well-known;* in contrast with hic, *the former* (sometimes *the latter*); ille qui, *he who, the one who.*

¹illĭc, illaec, illŭc, *that one;* interrog. illicine?

²illĭc or **illī,** *there, at that place; therein, in that matter.*

illim, *from that place or person.*

illinc, *from that place; on that side.*

illō, *thither, to that place; to that matter or point.*

illūc, *thither, to that place; to that matter or person.*

Īllўrĭi -ōrum, m. pl. *a people on the Adriatic.*

īmāgĭnārĭus -a -um *imaginary.*

īmāgĭnātĭo -ōnis, f. *imagination, fancy.*

īmāgĭnor -ari, *to imagine, conceive, picture to oneself.*

īmāgo -ĭnis, f. *an image, copy, likeness; any representation, portrait, statue;* in plur. *waxen figures, portraits of ancestors; the shade or ghost of the dead; an echo; a mental picture, idea, conception;* rhet., *metaphor, simile, image;* abstr., *mere form, appearance, pretence.*

imbēcillĭtās -ātis, f. *weakness, feebleness.*

imbēcillus -a -um, *weak, feeble.* Compar. adv. **imbēcillĭus,** *somewhat weakly.*

imbellis -e, *unwarlike, not fighting, indisposed or unable to fight;* hence *feeble, peaceful, quiet.*

imber -bris, m. *a shower or storm of rain, pelting rain; a rain-cloud; water or any fluid; a shower of missiles.*

imberbis -e and **imberbus** -a -um *beardless.*

imbĭbo -bĭbĕre -bĭbi, *to drink in;* mentally, *to conceive; to resolve, determine.*

imbrex -ĭcis, c. *a hollow tile used in roofing.*

imbrĭfĕr -fĕra -fĕrum, *rain-bringing.*

imbŭo -ŭĕre -ŭi -ūtum, *to wet, steep, saturate;* fig., *to stain, taint;* mentally, *to accustom, initiate, instruct.*

imĭtābĭlis -e, *that can be imitated.*

imĭtāmĕn -ĭnis, n. *an imitation;* plur., *an image.*

imĭtāmentum -i, n. *imitating, imitation.*

imĭtātĭo -ōnis, f. *imitation; pretence.*

imĭtātŏr -ōris, m. and **imĭtātrix** -ĭcis, f. *an imitator.*

imĭtor -ari, dep. *to imitate, copy; to depict; to be like, act like.*

immădŭi, infin. -isse, *to have become moist.*

immānis -e, *enormous, immense, monstrous; of character, savage, horrible, inhuman.*

immānĭtās -ātis, f. *savagery, frightfulness.*

immansuētus -a -um, *untamed, wild.*

immātūrĭtās -ātis, f. *immaturity; untimely haste.*

immātūrus -a -um, *unripe, immature; untimely.*

immĕdĭcābĭlis -e, *incurable.*

immĕmŏr -mŏris, *unmindful, forgetful, heedless.*

immĕmōrābĭlis -e, *indescribable; unworthy of mention; silent, uncommunicative.*

immĕmŏrāta -orum, n. pl. *things not related.*

immensĭtās -ātis, f. *immensity.*

immensus -a -um, *immense, vast boundless;* n. as subst., *immense size, immensity.*

immĕrens -entis, *not deserving, innocent.*

immergo -mergĕre -mersi -mersum, *to dip in, plunge in, immerse.*

immĕrĭtus -a -um: act., *not deserving (punishment), innocent;* pass., *undeserved;* adv. immĕrĭtō, *undeservedly.*

immersābĭlis -e, *that cannot be sunk.*

immētātus -a -um, *unmeasured.*

immĭgro -are, *to move away into*

immĭnĕo -ēre, *to project, overhang;* in time, *to be imminent, hang over; to threaten; to be on the watch or look out.*

immĭnŭo -ŭĕre -ŭi -ūtum, *to lessen, diminish; to weaken, infringe.*

immĭnūtĭo -ōnis, f. *diminishing, weakening;* rhet. *meiosis.*

immiscĕo -miscēre -miscŭi mixtum, *to mix in, intermingle; to join with, unite.*

immĭsērābĭlis -e, *unpitied.*

immĭsērĭcors -cordis, *unmerciful;* adv. immĭsērĭcordĭtĕr.

immissĭo -ōnis, n. *letting grow.*

immītis -e, *unripe, sour; harsh, cruel, stern.*

immitto -mittĕre -mīsi -missum. (1) *to send in, put in, work in; to engraft.* (2) *to let loose;* esp. *to let grow.* (3) *to let go against, launch against;* se in hostes, *to attack;* of feelings, *to instil.*

immixus, partic. from immisceo; q.v.

immo, *on the contrary; yes indeed, no indeed; say rather.*

immōbĭlis -e, *immovable or hard to move; inexorable.*

immŏdĕrātĭo -ōnis, f. *excess.*

immŏdĕrātus -a -um, *immeasurable, endless; immoderate, unrestrained;* adv. immŏdĕrātē.

immŏdestĭa -ae, f. *want of restraint.*

immŏdestus -a -um, *unrestrained, extravagant;* adv. immŏdestē.

immŏdĭcus -a -um, *immoderate,*

excessive; unrestrained, unbridled; adv. immŏdĭcē.

immŏdŭlātus -a -um, *inharmonious.*

immoenis; see immunis.

immŏlātĭo -ōnis, f. *sacrificer,*

immŏlātor -ōris, m. *a sacrifice.*

immŏlĭtus -a -um, *built up, erected.*

immŏlo -are, *to sacrifice; to devote to death, to slay.*

immŏrĭor -mŏri -mortuus, *to die in or over.*

immŏror -ari, *to remain in; to dwell on a subject.*

immorsus -a -um, *bitten; stimulated.*

immortālis -e, *deathless, immortal, imperishable.* Adv. immortālĭter, *infinitely.*

immortālĭtās -ātis, f. *immortality; everlasting renown; extreme happiness.*

immōtus -a -um, *unmoved, motionless; undisturbed, calm; firm, steadfast.*

immūgĭo -ire, *to bellow in or on.*

immulgĕo -ēre, *to milk into.*

immundus -a -um, *impure, foul.*

immūnĭo -ire, *to fortify.*

immūnis -e, *without duty free, exempt;* in gen., *not working or not contributing; not sharing in, devoid of; stainless.*

immūnĭtās -ātis, f. *exemption from offices or burdens; immunity.*

immūnītus -a -um, *unfortified; unpaved.*

immurmŭro -are, *to murmur at.*

immūtābĭlis, -e *unchangeable.*

immūtābĭlĭtās -ātis, f., *immutability.*

immūtātĭo -ōnis, f. *change, alteration.* rhet., *metonymy.*

[1]immūtātus -a -um, *unchanged.*

[2]immutatus -a -um, partic. from immuto; q.v.

immūto -are, *to change, alter;* immutata oratio, *allegory.*

impācātus -a um, *restless.*

impallesco -pallescĕre -pallŭi *to turn pale.*

impār -păris, *unequal, uneven; unlike, discordant; ill-matched;* of numbers, *odd;* modi impares, *hexameter and pentameter.* Adv. impărĭtĕr, *unevenly, unequally.*

impărātus -a -um *unprepared, unprovided.*

impart-; see impert-.

impastus -a -um, *unfed, hungry.*

impătĭbĭlis = impetibilis; q.v.

impătĭens -entis *unable to endure, impatient;* adv. impătĭentĕr.

impătĭentĭa -ae, f. *impatience, inability to endure.*

impăvĭdus -a -um, *fearless, undaunted;* adv. impăvĭdē.

impĕdīmentum -i, n. *hindrance, impediment;* in plur., *the baggage of an army or traveller.*

impĕdĭo -ire, *to entangle, ensnare, obstruct, surround; to embarrass, hinder, prevent.*

Hence partic. impĕdītus -a -um, *entangled, hindered;* milit., *hindered by baggage;* of places, *impassable, blocked;* in gen., *embarrassed, obstructed; awkward, complicated.*

impědĭtĭo -ōnis, f. *hindrance.*

impello -pellĕre -pŭli -pulsum. (1) *to drive against, strike upon.* (2) *to set in motion; to incite, urge on, impel;* esp. *to push over one already slipping.*

impendĕo -ēre, *to hang over, overhang; to threaten, be close at hand.*

impendĭum -i, n. *expenditure, outlay, cost; interest on money.* Abl. as adv. **impendĭō,** colloq., *by much, very much.*

impendo -pendĕre -pendi -pensum, *to weigh out;* hence *to expand, lay out;* partic. **impensus** -a -um, of price, *considerable, great;* in gen., *strong, vehement.* Adv. **impensē,** *at great cost; urgently, eagerly.*

impĕnĕtrābĭlis -e, *impenetrable.*

impensa -ac, f. *expense, outlay.*

impĕrātor -ōris, m. *commander, leader;* milit., *the commander-in-chief;* also *of the Roman emperors.*

impĕrātōrĭus -a -um, *of a general; imperial.*

impĕrātrix -īcis, f. *a female commander.*

imperceptus -a -um *unperceived, unknown.*

impercussus -a -um, *not struck.*

imperdĭtus -a -um, *not lain, undestroyed.*

imperfectus -a -um, *incomplete, unfinished.*

imperfossus -a -um *unstabbed, un-pierced.*

impĕrĭōsus -a -um, *commanding;* sibi, *master of oneself;* in bad sense, *imperious, tyrannical.*

impĕrītĭa -ae, f. *inexperience, ignorance.*

impĕrĭto -are, *to command, be in command, give an order.*

impĕrītus -a -um, *unskilled, inex-perienced, ignorant;* adv. **impĕrītē.**

impĕrĭum -i, n. *an order, a command; the right to order, power, mastery, command;* esp. *political power, autho-rity, sovereignty;* in imperio esse, *to hold office;* meton. *empire,* and in plur., *persons in authority.*

imperĭūrātus -a -um, *by which no one swears falsely.*

impermissus -a -un, *forbidden.*

impĕro -are, *to impose;* hence *to requisition, order a thing; to order an action to be done, give orders to a person; to rule over, govern, com-mand.*

imperterrĭtus -um, *undaunted, fearless.*

impertĭo -ire, *to give a person a share in; to share a thing with a person, to impart, bestow.*

imperturbātus -a -um, *undisturbed, calm.*

impervĭus -a -um, *impassable.*

impĕtĭbĭlis -e, *insufferable.*

impĕto -ĕre, *to make for, attack.*

impĕtrābĭlis -e: pass., *obtainable;* act., *successful.*

impĕtrātĭo -ōnis f *obtaining by request.*

impĕtrĭo -ire, *to seek by favourable omens.*

impĕtro -are, *to get, accomplish, effect;* esp. *to obtain by asking.*

impĕtus -ūs, m. *an attack, onset;* any *rapid motion;* mental *impulse, passion, force.*

impexus -a -um *uncombed; rude, uncouth.*

impĭĕtās -ātis, f. *undutifulness; impiety unfilial conduct, disloyalty.*

impĭgĕr -gra -grum, *diligent, active,* adv. **impĭgrē.**

impĭgrĭtās -ātis, f. *activity.*

impingo -pingĕre -pēgi -pactum, *to thrust, dash, drive against;* fig., *to press upon, bring upon a person.*

impĭus -a -um, *undutiful, disloyal; godless, unfilial, unpatriotic;* adv. **impĭē.**

implācābĭlis -e, *implacable;* compar. adv. **implācābĭlĭus.**

implācātus -a -um, *unappeased, un-satisfied.*

implĕo -plēre -plēvi -plētum, *to fill in, fill up, complete; to satisfy, content a person; to fulfil, perform; to contaminate.*

implexus -a -um *involved, entwined.*

implĭcātĭo -ōnis, f. *entwining, inter-weaving; embarrassment.*

implĭco -are, -āvi -ātum and -ūi -ītum, *to enfold, entwine, entangle, involve; to associate, unite;* partic. **implĭcātus** -a -um, *confused, entangled;* adv. **implĭcĭtē,** *confusedly.*

implōrātĭo -ōnis, f. *an imploring for help.*

implōro -are, *to call upon with tears, to beseech, implore; to call for, beg for.*

implūmis -e, *unfledged.*

implŭo -plŭere -plŭi, *to rain upon.*

implŭvĭum -i, n. *an opening in the roof of a Roman house, or the basin for rain-water below it.*

impōlītus -a -um, *rough, unpolished;* adv. **impōlītē.**

impollūtus -a -um, *undefiled.*

impōno -pōnĕre -pōsŭi -pŏsĭtum, *to put, lay, place in or upon;* naut. *to put on board ship, to embark;* fig., *to lay or put upon, impose; to put over as master; to impose upon, cheat, deceive* (with dat.).

importo -are, *to bring in, import, introduce; to bring upon, cause.*

importūnĭtās -ātis, f. *self-assertion, inconsiderateness, insolence.*

importūnus -a -um, *unsuitable, ill-adapted, unfavourable; troublesome, tiresome;* of character, *assertive, incon-siderate.*

importŭōsus -a -um, *without harbours.*

impōs -pŏtis, *having no power over.*

impōsĭtus -a -um, partic. from impono; q.v.

impŏtens -entis, *feeble, powerless;* with genit., *not master of;* esp. *unable to command oneself, violent, unrestrained.* Adv. **impŏtentēr,** *weakly; intemperately, passionately.*

impŏtentĭa -ae, f. *poverty; lack of self-restraint, violent passion.*

impraesentĭārum, *in present circum-stances, for the present.*

impransus -a -um, *without breakfast, fasting.*

imprĕcor -ari, dep. *to invoke harm upon, to call down upon.*

impressĭo -ōnis, f. *physical pressure an attack, assault*; rhet., *distinct expression, emphasis*; philos., *sense-data, the impressions of the senses.*

imprīmĭs, especially, *first of all.*

imprīmo -prīmĕre -pressi -pressum, *to press upon or into; to seal, chase, emboss; to make by pressing, imprint.*

imprŏbātĭo -ōnis, f. *disapproval, blame.*

imprŏbĭtās -ātis, f. *badness, depravity.*

imprŏbo -are, *to disapprove, blame, reject.*

imprŏbŭlus -a -um, *somewhat wicked.*

imprŏbus -a -um, *inferior, bad; morally bad, perverse, wilful; bold, persistent, mischievous*; m.pl. as subst., *the unpatriotic.* Adv. **imprŏbē**, *badly, wickedly; impudently, boldly.*

imprŏcērus -a -um, *small, low of stature.*

imprŏdictus -a -um, *not postponed.*

impromptus -a -um, *not ready.*

imprŏpĕrātus -a -um, *unhurried, slow.*

improspĕr -ĕra -ĕrum, *unfortunate*; adv. **improspĕrē.**

imprŏvĭdus -a -um, *without forethought, improvident*; adv. **imprŏvĭdē.**

imprŏvīsus -a -um, *unforeseen, unexpected*; (ex)improviso, *unexpectedly.*

imprūdens -entis, *not foreseeing, not expecting; not knowing, unaware; unwise, rash, imprudent.* Adv. **imprūdentĕr**, *without forethought; unawares; unwisely.*

imprūdentĭa -ae, f., *lack of foresight or knowledge; ignorance; lack of wisdom, imprudence.*

impūbēs -bēris and -bis. (1) *youthful; genae, beardless*; plur. as subst. *boys.* (2) *unmarried.*

impŭdens -entis, *shameless, impudent*; adv. **impŭdentĕr.**

impŭdentĭa -ae, f. *shamelessness, impudence.*

impŭdīcĭtĭa -ae, f. *incontinence, unchastity.*

impŭdīcus -a -um *shameless*; esp. *unchaste.*

impugnātĭo -ōnis, f. *assault, attack.*

impugno -are, *to attack, assail.*

impulsĭo -ōnis, f. *pressure*; fig., *impulse, instigation.*

impulsor -ōris, m. *instigator.*

impulsus -ūs, m. *pressure, impulse; incitement, instigation.*

impūnĕ, *with impunity, unpunished, safely.*

impūnĭtās -ātis, f. *impunity, exemption from punishment.*

impūnītus -a -um, *unpunished, exempt from punishment; unrestrained*; adv. **impūnītē.**

impūrātus -a -um, *vile, infamous.*

impūrĭtās -ātis, f. *moral impurity.*

impūrus -a -um, *unclean, foul; morally, impure, vile, infamous.* Adv. **impūrē.**

¹impŭtātus -a -um, *unpruned, untrimmed.*

²impŭtātus -a -um, partic. from imputo; q.v.

impŭto -are, *to lay to a charge, enter in an account; to reckon as a merit or fault in someone, to impute to; to reckon as a service done or gift given to someone.*

imus -a -um, superl. from inferus; q.v.

¹in, prep. (1) with acc., *into, on to, towards, against*; of time, *until*; in omne tempus, *for ever*; in diem vivere, *to live for the moment*; of tendency or purpose, *for*; in adverbial phrases, indicating manner or extent: in universum, *in general*; in vicem, in vices, *in turn.* (2) with abl., *in, on, among*; of time, *in, at, within; in relation to a person, in the case of.*

²in-, inseparable particle, *without, not.*

inaccessus -a -um, *inaccessible.*

ĭnăcesco -ăcescĕre -ăcŭi, *to become sour.*

Ĭnăchus (Ĭnăchŏs) -i, m. *mythical king of Argos, father of Io, after whom the river Inachus in Argolis was named.*

inadfectātus -a -um, *natural, unaffected.*

inadsuētus -a -um, *unaccustomed.*

inădustus -a -um, *unsinged.*

inaedĭfĭco -are *to build in or upon; to build up, block up, barricade.*

inaequābĭlis -e, *uneven, unequal*; adv. **inaequābĭlĭter.**

inaequālis -e. *uneven, unequal, various; making unequal, disturbing.* Adv. **inaequālĭtĕr**, *unevenly.*

inaequālĭtās -ātis, f. *unevenness.*

inaequo -are, *to make even, level up.*

inaestĭmābĭlis -e, *that cannot be estimated; hence priceless, inestimable; also having no value.*

inaestŭo -are, *to boil, rage (in).*

inaffectātus, see inadf-.

inămābĭlis -e, *unlovely, hateful.*

inămaresco -ĕre, *to become bitter.*

inambĭtĭōsus -a -um, *unpretentious.*

inambŭlātĭo -ōnis, f. *walking up and down.*

inambŭlo -are, *to walk up and down.*

inămoenus -a -um, *unlovely, dismal.*

inănĭmus -a -um, *lifeless, inanimate.*

inănĭo -ire, *to empty, make void.*

inānis -e, *empty, void*; equus, *riderless*; navis, *unloaded*; corpus, *soulless*; with genit, or abl., *empty of*; of persons, *empty-handed, poor*; fig., *vain, hollow, idle.* N. as subst., *empty space, emptiness, vanity.* Adv. **inānĭtĕr**, *vainly, uselessly.*

ĭnānĭtās -ātis, f. *emptiness, empty space; uselessness.*

ĭnărātus -a -um, *unploughed, fallow.*

inardesco -ardescĕre -arsi, *to catch fire, burn, glow.*

ināresco -ārescĕre -ārŭi, *to become dry.*

inassuētus; see inadsuetus.

inattĕnŭātus, *undiminished, unimpaired.*

inaudax -ācis, *timid, fearful.*

inaudĭo -ire, *to hear*; esp. *to hear as a secret.*

inaudītus -a -um, *unheard (esp. of accused persons); unheard of, unusual.*

inaugŭro -are: intransit., *to take the auguries*; transit., *to consecrate,* install, inaugurate; **ĭnaugŭrātō**, after taking the auguries.

inaures -ĭum, f. pl. earrings.

inauro -are, to cover with gold, gild, enrich.

ĭnauspĭcātus -a -um, without auspices; **ĭnauspĭcātō**, without consulting the auspices.

inausus -a -um, not dared, not attempted.

incaedŭus -a -um, not cut, unfelled.

incălesco -călescĕre -cālŭi, to glow, become warm or passionate.

incalfăcĭo -făcĕre, to heat, warm.

incallĭdus -a -um, ingenuous, unskilful; adv. **incallĭdē**.

incandesco -candescĕre -candŭi, to begin to whiten, esp. with heat.

incānesco -cānescĕre -cānŭi, to become grey.

incanto -are, to enchant.

incānus -a -um, quite grey.

incassum, in vain.

incastĭgātus -a -um, unchastised.

incautus -a -um, adj. incautious, careless, unwary; unguarded; not guarded against, unforeseen. Adv. **incautē**.

incēdo -cēdĕre -cessi -cessum, to walk, step, march; to proceed, come on; of feelings, with dat., to come over.

incĕlebrātus -a -um, not spread abroad.

incēnātus -a -um, without dinner.

incendiārĭus -a -um, fire-raising; incendiary.

incendĭum -i, n. a conflagration, fire; a torch, firebrand; of passion, fire, glow, heat: in gen., destruction ruin.

incendo -cendĕre -cendi -censum, to kindle, set fire to, burn; to make bright, illumine; to fire with passion, excite, incense.

incensĭo -ōnis, f. burning.

incensus -a -um, not enrolled by the censor, unassessed.

incensus, partic. from incendo; q.v.

inceptĭo -ōnis, f. a beginning; an enterprise.

incepto -are, to begin; to attempt, undertake.

inceptor -ōris, m. a beginner.

inceptum -i, n. of partic. of incipio; q.v.

incerno -cernĕre -crēvi -crētum, to sift.

incēro -are, to cover with wax.

incertus -a -um, uncertain, doubtful, not sure. (1) as to fact: act., of persons, not knowing, doubting; pass., of things, not known, obscure; n. as subst. uncertainty. (2) as to action, hesitating, irresolute, undecided; incertam securim, not surely aimed.

incesso -cessĕre -cessīvi, to attack, -assail.

incessus -ūs, m. march, walk; manner of walking, gait; attack, assault; entrance, approach.

incesto -are, to defile, pollute, dishonour.

¹**incestus** -a -um, impure, defiled; sinful, unchaste; n. as subst. unchastity, incest. Adv. **incestē**.

²**incestus** -ūs, m. unchastity, incest.

inchŏo; see incoho.

¹**incĭdo** -cĭdĕre -cĭdi -casum, to fall in or upon; to fall in with; in hostem, to attack; in aes alienum, to run into debt; in mentionem, to happen to mention; of abstr. things, to occur, happen, "crop up."

²**incīdo** -cīdĕre -cīdi cisum, to cut into, cut open; to inscribe, engrave an inscription; to make by cutting; to cut through; fig., to cut short, bring to an end, break off.

Hence, from partic., n. subst. **incīsum** -i, = incisio, q.v.; adv. **incīsē**, = incisim, q.v.

incīlĕ -is, n. a ditch, trench.

incīlo -are, to blame, scold.

incingo -cingĕre -cinxi -cinctum, to surround.

incĭno -ĕre, to sing.

incĭpĭo -cĭpĕre -cēpi -ceptum (cf. coepi), to take in hand, begin, commence; sometimes, to begin to speak. N. of partic. as subst. **inceptum** -i, a beginning; an attempt, enterprise.

incīsim, in short clauses.

incīsĭo -ōnis, f. a clause of a sentence.

incĭtāmentum -i, n. inducement, incentive.

incĭtātĭo -ōnis, f.: act., inciting, instigating; pass., violent motion excitement, vehemence.

incĭto -are, to put into rapid motion, urge on, hasten; in pass., or with reflex., to quicken one's pace, hasten. Transf., to excite, spur, inspire; to incite against, stir up; to increase.

Hence partic. **incĭtātus** -a -um, rapid, vehement; equo incitato, at full gallop; compar. adv. **incĭtātĭus**, more violently.

¹**incĭtus** -a -um, in rapid motion.

²**incĭtus** -a -um, unmoved.

inclāmo -are, to call upon loudly; esp. to scold.

inclāresco -clārescĕre -clārŭi, to become famous.

inclēmens -entis, unmerciful, harsh, rough; adv. **inclēmentĕr**.

inclēmentĭa -ae, f. unmercifulness, harshness.

inclīnātĭo -ōnis, f. leaning, bending, inclination; in gen., movement, tendency, change; good-will, liking.

inclīno -are: transit., to bend, incline, turn, change, sometimes for the worse; in pass., to fall back, waver; intransit., to take a turn, verge, incline, change; milit., to waver, yield.

Hence partic. **inclīnātus** -a -um, inclined, prone; sinking; of the voice, low, deep.

inclūdo -clūdĕre -clūsi -clūsum, to shut in, enclose; esp. to block, obstruct, confine.

inclūsĭo -ōnis, f. shutting up, confinement.

inclŭtus, inclĭtus -a -um, celebrated famous, renowned.

¹**incoctus** -a -um, uncooked, raw.

²**incoctus** -a -um, partic. from incoquo; q.v.

incōgĭtābĭlis -e, and **incōgĭtans** -antis, inconsiderate, thoughtless.

incōgĭtantĭa -ae, f. *thoughtlessness.*
incōgĭtātus -a -um: pass., *unstudied;* act., *inconsiderate.*
incōgĭto -are, *to contrive, plan.*
incognĭtus -a -um, *unexamined, unknown; unrecognized, so unclaimed.*
incŏho -are, *to take in hand, begin.* Hence partic. **incŏhātus** -a -um, *only begun, not finished.*
incŏla -ae, c. *an inhabitant, native;* sometimes *a foreign resident.*
incŏlo -cŏlĕre -cŏlŭi, *to inhabit, dwell* (in).
incŏlŭmis -e, *uninjured, safe · and sound.*
incŏlŭmĭtās -ātis, f., *safety, preservation.*
incŏmĭtātus -a -um, *unaccompanied, without retinue.*
incommendātus -a -um, *not entrusted;* hence *without protector.*
incommŏdĭtās -atis, f. *inconvenience, disadvantage, unseasonableness.*
incommŏdo -are, *to be unpleasant or troublesome.*
incommŏdus -a -um, *inconvenient, troublesome, disagreeable, · annoying;* n., as subst., *inconvenience, disadvantage;* incommodo tuo, *to your disadvantage;* adv. **incommŏdē,** *inconveniently.*
incommūtābĭlis -e, *unchangeable.*
incompărābĭlis -e, *incomparable.*
incompertus -a -um, *unknown.*
incompŏsĭtus -a -um, *not in order, irregular;* adv. **incompŏsĭtē.**
incomprěhensĭbĭlis -e, *impossible to catch; incomprehensible.*
incomptus -a -um, *unkempt, untrimmed; rude, rough.*
inconcessus -a -um, *not allowed, forbidden.*
inconcinnus -a -um, *awkward, inelegant, absurd.*
inconcussus -a -um, *unshaken, firm.*
inconditus -a -um, *not arranged, disorderly, confused;* adv. **inconditē.**
incongrŭens -entis, *not agreeing, inconsistent.*
inconsĭdĕrātus -a -um, *thoughtless, inconsiderate;* pass. *unadvised, reckless.* Adv. **inconsĭdĕrātē,** *without consideration.*
inconsōlābĭlis -e, *inconsolable; incurable.*
inconstans -stantis, *changeable, inconsistent;* adv. **inconstantēr.**
inconstantĭa -ae, f. *changeableness, inconsistency.*
inconsultus -a -um: pass., *not consulted;* act., *without asking advice, unadvised;* hence *inconsiderate, imprudent.* Adv. **inconsultē,** *indiscreetly.*
inconsumptus -a -um, *unconsumed, undiminished.*
incontāmĭnātus -a -um, *unpolluted.*
incontentus -a -um, *not stretched;* fides, *untuned.*
incontĭnens -entis, *incontinent;* adv. **incontĭnentēr.**
incontĭnentĭa -ae, f. *incontinence.*

inconvĕnĭens -entis, *not suiting, dissimilar.*
incŏquo -cŏquĕre -coxi -coctum, *to boil in or with; to dye.*
incorrectus -a -um, *unamended, unimproved.*
incorruptus -a -um, *not corrupted, untainted, unspoilt, unimpaired;* adv. **incorruptē.**
incrēbresco -ĕre -crebrŭi and **incrēbesco** -ĕre -crebŭi, *to become strong or frequent; to increase, prevail.*
incrēdĭbĭlis -e, *not to be believed, incredible;* adv. **incrēdĭbĭlĭtēr.**
incrēdŭlus -a -um, *incredulous.*
incrēmentum -i, n. *growth, increase;* meton, *the makings of anything,* also *offspring.*
increpĭto -are, *to call loudly to; to reproach, chide.*
increpo -are -ŭi (-āvi) -ĭtum (ātum), *to rustle, make a noise; to be noised abroad;* transit.. *to cause to sound.* Of persons, *to chide, rebuke.*
incresco -crescĕre -crēvi, *to grow* (in or on).
incrētus -a -um, partic. from incerno; q.v.
incrŭentātus and **incrŭentus** -a -um, *bloodless.*
incrusto -are, *to cover with rind, encrust.*
incŭbo -are -ŭi -ĭtum, *to lie in or on or over; to watch over; to hang over, lie heavily upon; to dwell in.*
inculco -are, *to trample in, press in, force upon, impress upon.*
inculpātus -a -um, *unblamed, blameless.*
¹incultus -a -um, *uncultivated, untilled;* n. pl. as subst. *wastes, deserts;* of dress, etc., *neglected, untidy;* in gen., *unpolished, rude.* Adv. **incultē.**
²incultus -ūs, m. *neglect, want of cultivation.*
incumbo -cumbĕre -cŭbŭi -cŭbĭtum, *to lie upon, put weight on, lean over, overhang; to apply oneself to, concentrate upon a thing; to incline to favour, further a cause or movement.*
incūnābŭla -orum, n. pl. *swaddling-clothes;* hence *infancy; birthplace;* in gen., *source, origin.*
incūrātus -a -um, *uncared-for, unhealed.*
incūrĭa -ae, f. *carelessness, neglect.*
incūrĭōsus -a -um: act., *careless, negligent;* pass., *neglected.* Adv. **incūrĭōsē,** *carelessly.*
incurro -currĕre -curri (cŭcurri) -cursum, *to run into;* milit., *to assail, attack, make a raid into.* Transf., *to attack with words, inveigh against; to come upon, fall in with;* in space, *to extend into;* in time, *to coincide with.*
incursĭo -ōnis, f. *a clash, onset; collision;* milit., *attack, raid, invasion.*
incurso -are, *to run against, strike against, attack.*
incursus -ūs, m. *an attack, assault;* of the mind, *efforts, impulses.*
incurvo -are, *to bend, curve, make crooked.*

incurvus -a -um, *bent, curved, crooked.*

incūs -cūdis, f. *anvil.*

incūsātĭo -ōnis, f. *blame, reproach, accusations.*

incūso -are, *to accuse, blame, find fault with.*

incussū, abl. sing. m., *by a clash.*

incustōdītus -a -um: pass., *unwatched, unguarded;* act., *incautious, imprudent.*

incūsus -a -um, *forged, fabricated.*

incūtĭo -cūtěre -cussi -cussum, *to dash, beat against; to strike into the mind, inspire with.*

indāgātĭo -ōnis, f. *investigation.*

indāgātor -ōris, m. and indāgātrix -trĭcis, f. *investigator, explorer.*

¹indāgo -are, *to track down,* as hounds hunting; *to explore, investigate.*

²indāgo -ĭnis, f. *surrounding and driving of game.*

inde, *thence, from there;* hinc . . . inde, *on this side . . . on that; from that cause, for that reason; from that time, thereafter; thereupon, then.*

indēbĭtus -a -um, *not owed, not due.*

indēcens -centis, *unbecoming, unseemly, unsightly;* adv. indēcenter.

indēclīnātus -a -um, *unchanged, firm.*

indĕcor -ris or indĕcŏris -e, *unbecoming, shameful.*

indĕcŏro -are, *to disgrace, dishonour.*

indĕcŏrus -a -um, *unbecoming; unseemly, unsightly; disgraceful.* Adv. indĕcŏrē.

indēfensus -a -um, *undefended, unprotected.*

indēfessus -a -um, *unwearied, indefatigable.*

indēflētus -a -um, *unwept.*

indēiectus -a -um, *not thrown down.*

indēlēbĭlis -e, *imperishable.*

indēlībātus -a -um, *uninjured, undiminished.*

indemnātus -a -um, *uncondemned.*

indēplōrātus -a -um, *unwept, unlamented.*

indēprensus -a -um, *undiscovered.*

indēsertus -a -um, *not forsaken.*

indēstrictus -a -um, *untouched, unhurt.*

indētonsus -a -um, *unshorn.*

indēvītātus -a -um, *unavoided.*

index -dĭcis, m. *an informer; a sign, token; the forefinger; a title; a touchstone.*

Indi -orum, m. pl. *the Indians;* sing. Indus -i, m. *an Indian,* or *Ethiopian; an elephant-driver, mahout.* Adj. Indus and Indĭcus -a -um, *Indian;* subst. Indĭa -ae, f. *India.*

indĭcente, abl. sing., *not saying:* me indicente, *without my saying a word.*

indĭcĭum -i, n. (1) *information, evidence; leave to give evidence; a reward for giving evidence.* (2) *any mark, sign, token.*

¹indĭco -are, *to make known, show, indicate;* esp. *to inform against, give evidence about; to put a price on, value.*

²indīco -dīcěre -dixi -dictum, *to make publicly known, proclaim;* bellum, *to declare war.*

¹indictus -a -um, *not said, unsaid:* indictā causā, *without a hearing.*

²indictus -a -um, partic. from ²indico; q.v.

indĭdem, *from the same place or matter.*

indifferens -entis, *indifferent; neither good nor bad; unconcerned.* Adv. indifferenter.

indĭgěna -ae, *native.*

indĭgentĭa -ae, f. *want, need; desire.*

indĭgěo -ēre -ŭi, *to want, need, require;* also *to long for.* Hence partic. indĭgens -entis, *in need.*

indĭges -gětis, m. *native, indigenous.*

indĭgestus -a -um, *disordered, confused, unarranged.*

indignābundus -a -um, *filled with indignation.*

indignātĭo -ōnis, f. *indignation; matter for indignation;* rhet., *the exciting of indignation.*

indignĭtās -ātis, f. *unworthiness, vileness; unworthy behaviour or treatment of others, indignity; indignation at unworthy treatment.*

indignor -ari, dep. *to consider unworthy, take as an indignity, be offended.* Hence partic. indignans -antis, *offended.*

indignus -a -um: of persons, *unworthy, not deserving* (with abl. or genit.); of things, *unworthy;* hence *disgraceful, shameful.* Adj. indignē, *unworthily, dishonourably; impatiently, indignantly.*

indĭgus -a -um, *needing, in want of.*

indīlĭgens -entis, *negligent;* adv. indīlĭgenter.

indīlĭgentĭa -ae, f. *carelessness, negligence.*

indĭpiscor -dīpisci -deptus, dep., and indĭpisco -ěre, *to reach, obtain; to attain, get.*

indireptus -a -um, *unpillaged.*

indiscrētus -a -um, *unsevered, undivided; undistinguished; indistinguishable.*

indisertus -a -um, *not eloquent;* adv. indisertē.

indispŏsĭtus -a -um, *disorderly, confused.*

indissŏlūbĭlis -e, *indissoluble.*

indissŏlūtus -a -um, *undissolved.*

indistinctus -a -um, *not separated; indistinct, obscure; unpretentious.*

indĭvĭdŭus -a -um, *indivisible, inseparable;* n. as subst. *an atom.*

indo -děre -dĭdi -dĭtum, *to put in* or *on;* of names, *to give, confer;* of abstr. things, *to introduce, cause, occasion.*

indŏcĭlis -e, *unteachable, untaught; ignorant, rude, artless;* of subjects, *unable to be learned.*

indoctus -a -um, *untaught, untrained, unskilled;* adv. indoctē.

indŏlentĭa -ae, f. *freedom from pain.*

indŏlēs -is, f. *native constitution* or *quality; nature, disposition, character, talents.*

indŏlesco -dŏlescěre -dŏlŭi, *to be pained* or *grieved* (at).

indŏmĭt us -a -um, *untamed, wild.*

indormīo -ire -ivi -itum, *to sleep on or over; to be negligent about,* with dat. or in.

indōtātus -a -um, *without dowry;* corpora, *without funeral honours;* ars, *unadorned, poor.*

indŭ, archaic form of in; q.v.

indŭbĭtātus -a -um, *undoubted, certain.*

indŭbĭto -are, *to feel doubt of,* with dat.

indŭbĭus -a -um, *not doubtful, certain.*

indūcĭae = indutiae; q.v.

indūco -dūcĕre -duxi -ductum. (1) *to draw over, spread over so as to cover;* also *to cover one thing with another; to put on clothing or arms; to erase writing, and hence to revoke, make invalid.* (2) *to lead or bring in, to introduce; to enter in an account-book; to lead on, induce, persuade;* with animum, *or in animum, to decide to do,* or *decide that a thing is so.*

inductĭo -ōnis, f. *leading or bringing in, introduction;* animi, *resolve, intention;* erroris, *misleading;* in logic, *induction.*

inductŭ, abl. sing. m., *by instigation.*

indulgentĭa -ae, f. *tenderness, indulgence.*

indulgĕo -dulgēre -dulsi: intransit., *to be forbearing, patient, indulgent;* fig., *to give oneself up to, indulge in;* transit. *to grant, allow, concede.*

Hence partic. **indulgens** -entis, *kind, tender, indulgent;* adv. **indulgentēr.**

indŭo -dŭĕre -dŭi -dūtum, *to put on,* esp. of dress. Transf., *to clothe, surround, cover; to put on, assume, take up, engage in;* se, with dat. or in, *to fall into, fall on; to entangle.*

indūresco -dūrescĕre -dūrŭi, *to become hard or firm.*

indūro -are, *to make hard or firm.*

industrĭa -ae, f. *industry, diligence;* de (or ex) industria, *on purpose, intentionally.*

industrĭus -a -um, *diligent, painstaking, industrious;* adv. **industrĭē.**

indūtĭae -arum, f. pl. *truce, armistice, suspension of hostilities.*

indūtus -ūs, m. *a putting on, clothing.*

inēbrĭo -are, *to intoxicate; to saturate.*

inēdĭa -ae, f. *fasting, abstinence from food.*

inēdĭtus -a -um, *not published, unknown.*

inēlĕgans -antis, *not choice, tasteless;* adv. **inēlĕgantēr.**

inēluctābĭlis -e, *from which one cannot struggle free.*

inēmŏrĭor -emori, dep. *to die in or at.*

inemptus -a -um, *unbought.*

inēnarrābĭlis -e, *indescribable, inexpressible;* adv. **inēnarrābĭlĭtēr.**

inēnōdābĭlis -e, *inextricable; inexplicable.*

inĕo -ire -ii -ĭtum: intransit., *to go* or *come in, to enter;* of time, *to begin, commence;* transit., *to go or come into; to enter upon, start, begin;* consilium, *to form a plan;* numerum, or rationem, *to go into figures, make a calculation.*

ineptĭa -ae, f. *foolish behaviour, silliness, absurdity.*

ineptĭo -ire, *to talk foolishly.*

ineptus -a -um, *unsuitable, tasteless, silly;* adv. **ineptē.**

inermis -e and **inermus** -a -um, *unarmed, defenceless, helpless.*

inerrans -antis, *not wandering, fixed.*

inerro -are, *to rove about in.*

iners -ertis, *untrained, unskilful; inactive, lazy, idle, calm; cowardly; ineffective, dull, insipid.*

inertĭa -ae, f. *unskilfulness; idleness.*

inērŭdĭtus -a -um, *illiterate, ignorant.*

inesco -are, *to allure, entice, deceive.*

inēvītābĭlis -e, *unavoidable.*

inexcĭtus -a -um, *unmoved, quiet.*

inexcūsābĭlis -e, *without excuse; inexcusable.*

inexercĭtātus -a -um, *untrained, unpractised.*

inexhaustus -a -um, *unexhausted.*

inexōrābĭlis -e, *not to be moved by entreaty, stern, severe.*

inexperrectus -a -um, *not awakened.*

inexpertus -a -um: act., *inexperienced in, unacquainted with;* pass., *untried, untested, unattempted.*

inexpĭābĭlis -e, *inexpiable; implacable irreconcilable.*

inexplēbĭlis -e, *insatiable.*

inexplētus -a -um, *unfilled, insatiate.*

inexplĭcābĭlis -e, *that cannot be untied; intricate, difficult; inexplicable, beyond explanation; inconclusive, without result.*

inexplōrātus -a -um, *unexplored, uninvestigated;* abl. **inexplōrātō,** *without reconnoitring.*

inexpugnābĭlis -e, *unconquerable, impregnable.*

inexspectātus -a -um, *unlooked-for, unexpected.*

inexstinctus -a -um, *unextinguished, inextinguishable.*

inexsŭpĕrābĭlis -e, *insurmountable.*

inextrĭcābĭlis -e, *that cannot be disentangled or unravelled.*

infabrē, *unskilfully.*

infabrĭcātus -a -um, *unwrought, unfashioned.*

infăcētĭae (infĭc-) -arum, f. pl. *crudity.*

infăcētus and **infĭcētus** -a -um, *dull, crude, without humour* or *wit;* adv. **infăcētē** (infĭc-).

infācundus -a -um, *not eloquent.*

infāmĭa -ae, f. *dishonour, disgrace;* also *a cause of disgrace.*

infāmis -e, *disgraced, disreputable.*

infāmo -are, *to put to shame, disgrace.*

infandus -a -um, *unutterable, abominable.*

infans -fantis, *speechless, unable to speak;* esp. of children; as subst., *a little child.* Transf., *tongue-tied, embarrassed; youthful, fresh; childish, silly.*

infantĭa -ae, f. *inability to speak; slowness of speech; infancy.*

infarcĭo (infercĭo) -ire, *to stuff in, cram in.*

infătŭo -are *to make a fool of.*

infaustus -a -um, *unlucky, unfortunate,*

infector -ōris, m. *a dyer.*

iinfectus -a -um, *unworked, unwrought; not done, unfinished, incomplete;* reddere infectum, *to make void, revoke; impracticable, impossible.*

²infectus, partic. from inficio; q.v.

infēcunditās -ātis, f. *barrenness, sterility.*

infēcundus -a -um, *barren, sterile.*

infēlicitās -ātis, f. *ill-luck, misfortune.*

infēlix -icis, *unfruitful, barren;* arbor, *the gallows.* Transf., *unhappy, unlucky;* act. sense, *causing unhappiness.* Adv. **infēliciter,** *unluckily.*

infenso -are, *to attack, ravage.*

infensus -a -um, *hostile, aggressive;* of weapons, *aimed, ready;* in spirit, *embittered, dangerous.* Adv. **infensē.**

infĕr -a -um, **infĕri** -orum; see inferus.

inferiae -arum, f. *offerings in honour of the dead.*

infercio; see infarcio.

infĕrior, infĕrius; see infra and inferus.

infernē, *on the lower side, beneath.*

infernus -a -um, *below, coming from below;* of the lower world, *infernal.* As subst., m. pl. **inferni,** *the shades;* n. pl. **infernā,** *the lower world.*

infĕro inferre intŭli inlātum, *to carry in, to put or place on;* templis ignes inferre, *to set fire to;* milit., signa in hostem, *to attack, charge;* bellum, with dat., *to make war on;* se inferre, and pass. inferri, *to betake oneself, to go;* of abstract things, *to bring on, introduce, occasion;* in accounts, *to enter;* in logic, *to infer, conclude.*

infĕrus -a -um, *below, lower, southern; o the lower world.* M. pl. as subst., **infĕri** -orum, *the dead, the lower world.* Compar. **infĕrior** -ius, *lower,* ex inferiore loco dicere, *to speak from the body of the court;* of time, *later, junior;* of number, rank, etc. *lower, inferior.* Superl. (1) **infĭmus (infŭmus)** -a -um, *lowest;* ab infima ara, *from the bottom of the altar;* of rank, etc., *lowest, meanest.* Superl. (2) **imus** -a -um, *lowest;* n. as subst., *the bottom;* of tone, *deepest, lowest;* of time, *last;* n. as subst., *the end.*

infervesco -fervescĕre -ferbŭi, *to begin to boil, grow hot.*

infesto -are, *to attack, disquiet.*

infestus -a -um; act., *aggressive, hostile, dangerous;* pass., *infested, beset, unsaʽe.* Adv. **infestē,** *in a hostile manner.*

inficētus, inficētē = infacetus, infacete; q.v.

inficĭo -ficĕre -fēci -fectum. (1) *to tinge, dye, stain; to steep, imbue.* (2) *to poison, taint, corrupt.*

infidēlis -e, *untrue, disloyal, faithless;* adv. **infidēliter.**

infidēlitās -ātis, f. *disloyalty.*

infidus -a -um, *untrue, disloyal.*

infigo -figĕre -fixi -fixum, *to fix, fasten or thrust in; to imprint, impress.*

infĭmus -a -um, superl. of inferus; q.v.

infindo -findĕre -fīdi -fissum, *to cut into.*

infinitās -ātis, f. *infinity, endlessness.*

infinitio, -ōnis, f. *infinity.*

infinitus -a -um, *infinite, unbounded, immense;* n. as subst., *infinite space;* of time, *endless, unceasing;* of number, *countless;* also *indefinite, general.* Adv. **infinitē,** *infinitely, endlessly.*

infirmātio -ōnis, f. *weakening; refuting, invalidating.*

infirmitās -ātis, f. *weakness, feebleness; instability, fickleness.*

infirmo -are, *to weaken, impair, shake; to refute; to annul.*

infirmus -a -um, *weak, feeble; timorous.* Adv. **infirmē,** *weakly, faintly.*

infit, defective, *he* (or *she*) *begins;* esp *begins to speak.*

infitiālis -e, *negative, containing a denial.*

infitiās ire, *to deny.*

infitiātio -ōnis, f. *denying.*

infitiātor -ōris, m. *a denier;* esp. *one who denies a debt or deposit.*

infitior -ari, *to deny;* esp. *to deny a debt, refuse to restore a deposit.*

inflammātio -ōnis, f. *setting fire:* animorum, *inspiration.*

inflammo -are, *to kindle, set fire to; to inflame, excite.*

inflātio -ōnis, f. *inflation, flatulence.*

inflātus -ūs, m. *a blowing into, blast; inspiration.*

inflecto -flectĕre -flexi -flexum, *to bend, bow, curve.* Transf., *to warp, change; to sway, affect; to modulate the voice.*

inflētus -a -um, *unwept, unlamented.*

inflexio -ōnis, f. *bending, swaying.*

inflexus -ūs, m. *bending, curving.*

infligo -fl, fligĕre -flixi -flictum, *to strike, knock, dash against; to inflict a blow, cause damage.*

inflo -are, *to blow into; to play on wind instruments; to give a blast; to blow out, puff out.* Transf., *to inspire; to puff up, elate.*

Hence partic., **inflātus** -a -um, *inflated, swollen; puffed up, pompous;* of style, *turgid.* Compar. adv. **inflātius,** *too pompously; on a grander scale.*

influo -flŭĕre -fluxi -fluxum, *to flow in.* Transf., *to steal in, to stream in, to rush in.*

infodio -fodĕre -fōdi -fossum, *to dig in, bury.*

informātio -ōnis, f. *conception, idea.*

informis -e, *formless, shapeless; deformed, hideous.*

informo -are, *to give form to, to shape, fashion; mentally, to form, dispose; to form an idea or conception of.*

infortūnātus -a -um, *unfortunate, miserable.*

infortūnium -i, n. *misfortune, ill luck: punishment.*

infrā. Prep., with acc., *below, under,* in position, size, rank; in time, *later than.* Adv., *below, underneath; in the lower world; to the south;* in rank, *lower.* Compar., **infĕrius,** *lower down.*

infractĭo -ōnis, f. *breaking*; animi, *dejection.*

infrăgilis -e, *unbreakable, strong.*

infrĕmo -frĕmĕre -frĕmŭi, *to growl.*

infrēnātus -a -um, *without bridle*, see also infreno.

infrendĕo -ēre, *to gnash with the teeth.*

infrēnis -e and **infrēnus** -a -um, *without bridle, unbridled.*

infrēno -are, *to bridle, rein* in, *to restrain, check.*

infrĕquens -entis, *scanty, thin, not crowded*; of places, *not full, scantily populated*; of time, *infrequent*; of persons, *not doing a thing often.*

infrĕquentĭa -ae, f. *fewness, scantiness thinness*; of places, *emptiness, loneliness.*

infringo -fringĕre -frēgi -fractum, *to break; to weaken, impair, discourage.* Hence partic. **infractus** -a -um, *broken, weakened, impaired.*

infrons -frondis, *leafless.*

infructŭōsus -a -um, *unfruitful, unproductive.*

infŭcātus -a -um, *coloured.*

infŭla -ae, f. *a band bandage*; esp. *a fillet, a headband worn by priests, suppliants,* etc.

infundo -fundĕre -fūdi -fūsum, *to pour in or on*; with dat., *to pour out for, hence to administer*; se infundere, or pass. infundi, *to pour over.*

infusco -are, *to make dark, blacken; to disfigure, stain.*

ingĕmĭno -are: transit., *to redouble, repeat*; intransit., *to be redoubled, to increase.*

ingĕmisco -gĕmiscĕre (-escĕre) -gĕmŭi, *to sigh or groan over.*

ingĕmo -ĕre, *to sigh, groan over* (with dat.).

ingĕnĕro -are, *to implant, generate.*

ingĕnĭōsus -a -um, *talented, able*, of things, *requiring talent or naturally fit, adapted.* Adv. **ingĕnĭōsē**, *cleverly.*

ingĕnĭum -i, n. *nature, natural quality, constitution, character*, esp. *mental power, ability, genius*; meton., *a man of genius, or a clever invention.*

ingens -entis, *monstrous, vast, enormous.*

ingĕnŭĭtās -ātis, f. *free birth; noble-mindedness, uprightness, frankness.*

ingĕnŭus -a -um, *native, natural, innate; free-born, of free birth, worthy of a free man, noble, honourable, frank.* Adv. **ingĕnŭē**.

ingĕro -gĕrĕre -gessi gestum, *to carry or put in or upon; to press upon, force upon*; of abuse, *to heap on a person.*

ingigno only in perf. indic. **ingĕnŭi,** *I implanted,* and perf. partic. **ingĕnĭtus** -a -um, *implanted.*

inglōrĭus -a -um, *without fame, inglorious, undistinguished.*

inglŭvĭēs -ēi, f. *crop, maw*; meton., *gluttony.*

ingrātiīs or **ingrātīs,** *unwillingly.*

ingrātus -a -um. (1) *unpleasant,*

unpleasing. (2) *unthankful, unrewarding.* Adv. **ingrātē**, *unwillingly; ungratefully.*

ingrăvesco -ĕre, *to become heavy; to become a burden, or become weary*; poet., *to become pregnant.*

ingrăvo -are, *to weigh down; to aggravate.*

ingrĕdĭor -grĕdi -gressus, dep. *to step in, enter, go in; to walk.* Transf., *to enter upon, begin on*; with infin., *to begin to.*

ingressĭo -ōnis, f. *an entering, going in; walking, gait, pace.* Transf., *beginning.*

ingressus -ūs, m. *going in, entering, entry*; milit., *an inroad; walking, stepping, movement.* Transf., *beginning.*

ingrŭo -ŭĕre -ŭi, *to fall upon, assail, attack.*

inguĕn -gŭinis, n. *the groin.*

ingurgĭto -are, with reflex., *to plunge oneself, or to glut, gorge oneself, gormandize.*

ingustātus -a -um, *untasted.*

inhăbĭlis -e, *unmanageable; unfit, ill-adapted.*

inhăbĭtābĭlis -e, *uninhabitable.*

inhăbĭto -are, *to inhabit.*

inhaerĕo -haerēre -haesi -haesum, *to stick in, cling to, cleave to.*

inhaeresco -haerescĕre -haesi -haesum, *to adhere to, begin to cling to.*

inhālo -are, *to breathe upon.*

inhĭbĕo -ēre -ŭi -ĭtum. (1) *to hold in, check, restrain*; naut., inhibere remis, navem retro inhibere, *to back water.* (2) *to practise, use, employ.*

inhĭbĭtĭo -ōnis, f. *restraining*; remigum, *backing water.*

inhĭo -are, *to gape*; hence *to covet, desire, long for.*

inhŏnesto -are, *to disgrace.*

inhŏnestus -a -um: morally, *degraded, dishonoured*; of things, *dishonourable, shameful*; physically, *ugly, unsightly.* Adv. **inhŏnestē**, *dishonourably.*

inhŏnōrātus -a -um, *not honoured; unrewarded.*

inhŏnōrus -a -um, *dishonoured.*

inhorrĕo -ēre, *to bristle.*

inhorresco -horrescĕre -horrŭi, *to begin to bristle, to bristle up; to shudder, quiver*, esp. from fright.

inhospĭtālis -e, *inhospitable.*

inhospĭtālĭtās -ātis, f. *want of hospitality.*

inhospĭtus -a -um, *inhospitable.*

inhūmānĭtās -ātis, f. *cruelty, inhumanity; incivility, discourtesy; stinginess, niggardliness.*

inhūmānus -a -um, *cruel, barbarous, inhuman; rude, uncivil; uncivilized.* Adv. **inhūmānē**, *inhumanly*; **inhūmānĭter,** *uncivilly.*

inhŭmātus -a -um, *unburied.*

inĭbi, adv., *therein, in that place*; of time, *near at hand.*

inĭcĭo -ĭcĕre -iēci -iectum. (1) *to throw in, put in or into.* Transf., *to cause, inspire, occasion*; in conversation, *to throw in.* (2) *to throw on or over;*

manum inicere, *to lay hands on, appropriate, take possession of.* Transf., *to impose, lay on.*

iniectio -ōnis, f. *laying on.*

iniectus -ūs, m. *throwing on* or *over.*

inimīcitia -ae, f. *enmity.*

inimīco -are, *to make hostile, set at variance.*

inimīcus -a -um, *unfriendly, adverse, hostile;* of things, *hurtful, prejudicial;* m. or f. as subst., *enemy, foe.* Adv. inimīcē, *in an unfriendly manner.*

iniquitās -ātis, f. *unevenness; unfavourableness, difficulty; unfairness, injustice, unreasonableness.*

iniquus -a -um, *uneven, unequal.* Transf., of things, *excessive, unbalanced, adverse, disadvantageous;* of contests, *ill-matched;* of terms, *unfair;* of persons, etc. *unfair, unfavourable; perverse, disgruntled;* animo iniquo ferre, *to take badly;* m. pl. as subst. *enemies.* Adv. inīque, *unequally; unfairly, adversely.*

initio -are, *to initiate.*

initium -i, n. *a beginning;* ab initio, *from the start;* initio, *at the start.* Transf., in plur. *elements, first principles; auspices; the beginning of a reign; a secret worship, mysteries.*

initus -ūs, m. *an entrance; a beginning.*

iniūcunditās -ātis, f. *unpleasantness.*

iniūcundus -a -um, *unpleasant.* Compar. adv. iniūcundius.

iniūdīcātus -a -um, *undecided.*

iniungo -iungĕre -iunxi -iunctum, *to join, attach, fasten to; to inflict upon, bring upon.*

iniūrātus -a -um, *unsworn.*

iniūria -ae, f. *injury, injustice, wrong;* iniuriā, *wrongly.* Transf., *a possession wrongfully obtained; revenge for an affront.*

iniūriōsus -a -um, *doing wrong, unjust; harmful.* Adv. iniūriōsē, *wrongfully.*

iniūrius -a -um, *wrongful, unjust.*

iniussū, abl. sing. m. *without orders.*

iniussus -a -um, *unbidden, spontaneous.*

iniustitia -ae, f. *injustice; severity.*

iniustus -a -um, *unfair, unjust; harsh, oppressive;* n. as subst. *injustice.* Adv. iniustē.

inlābĕfactus -a -um, *unshaken, firm.*

inlābor -lābi -lapsus, dep. *to glide into, fall into* or *upon.*

inlābōro -are, *to labour at.*

inlăcessītus -a -um, *unattacked, unprovoked.*

inlăcrimābilis -e, *unwept; not to be moved by tears, pitiless.*

inlăcrimo -are, and inlăcrimor -ari, dep. *to weep over, bewail.*

inlaesus -a -um, *unhurt, uninjured.*

inlaetābilis -e, *gloomy, cheerless.*

inlăquĕo -are, *to entrap, ensnare.*

inlaudātus -a -um, *unpraised, obscure; not to be praised, bad.*

inlautus = inlotus; q.v.

inlĕcebra -ae, f. *allurement, attraction, charm; a decoy bird.*

inlĕcebrōsus -a -um, *attractive, enticing;* adv. inlĕcebrōsē.

¹inlectus -a -um, *unread.*

²inlectus -ūs, m. *enticement.*

³inlectus -a -um, partic. of inlicio; q.v.

inlĕpidus -a -um, *inelegant, rude, unmannerly;* adv. inlĕpidē.

¹inlex -līcis, c. *a decoy, lure.*

²inlex -lēgis, *lawless.*

inlibātus -a -um, *undiminished, unimpaired.*

inlibĕrālis -e, *unworthy of a free man, ungenerous, sordid, mean;* adv. inlibĕrālitĕr.

inlibĕrālitās -ātis, f. *stinginess, meanness.*

inlicio -līcĕre -lexi -lectum, *to entice, allure, decoy.*

inlicitātor -ōris, m. *a sham bidder at an auction, puffer.*

inlicitus -a -um, *not allowed, illegal.*

inlido -līdĕre -lisi -lisum, *to strike, beat, dash against.*

inligo -are, *to bind, tie, fasten, attach, connect; to entangle, impede.*

inlimis -e, *free from mud, clean.*

inlino -linĕre -lēvi -litum, *to smear, daub; to spread something on a surface* or *to spread a surface with something.*

inliquĕfactus -a -um, *molten, liquefied.*

inlitterātus -a -um, *ignorant, illiterate.*

inlōtus (-lautus, -lūtus) -a -um, *unwashed, unclean.*

inlūcesco (-isco) -lūcescĕre -luxi, *to become light, begin to shine;* inlucescit, *it grows light, is daylight.*

inlūdo -lūdĕre -lūsi -lūsum, *to play with, sport with; to mock, laugh at, ridicule; to maltreat.*

inlūmino -are, *to light up, illuminate; to make clear, set off, adorn.* Adv. from perf. partic. inlūmīnātē, *luminously, clearly.*

inlūsio -ōnis, f. *irony.*

inlustris -e, *light, bright, brilliant; clear, plain, evident; distinguished, famous.* Compar. adv. inlustrius, *more clearly, more distinctly.*

inlustro -are, *to light up, make bright; to bring to light, make clear; to make illustrious, do honour to.*

inlŭviēs -ēi, f. *inundation, flood; mud, dirt.*

inm-; see imm-.

innābilis -e, *that cannot be swum in.*

innascor -nasci -nātus, dep. *to be born in, arise in* or *upon.* Hence partic. innātus -a -um, *innate, inborn.*

innăto -are, *to swim into; to swim* or *float in* or *upon.*

innecto -nectĕre -nexŭi -nexum, *to tie in, fasten, weave together;* fig., *to put together, connect, entangle, implicate.*

innitor -niti -nixus dep. *to lean upon, support oneself by.*

inno -nare, *to swim in* or *on; to flow over; to sail over, navigate.*

innŏcens -entis, *harmless, inoffensive, blameless;* adv. innŏcentĕr.

innŏcentia -ae, f. *harmlessness, innocence, integrity.*

innŏcŭus -a -um: act., *innocuous, harmless, blameless*; pass., *unhurt, unharmed*. Adv. **innŏcŭē**, *harmlessly*.

innōtesco -nōtescĕre -nōtŭi *to become known or noted*.

innŏvo -are, *to renew*.

innoxius -a -um: act., *harmless, innocent*; pass., *unhurt, unharmed*.

innūba -ae, *unmarried, without a husband*.

innūbilus -a -um, *unclouded, clear*.

innūbo -nūbĕre -nupsi -nuptum, *to marry into*.

innŭmĕrābilis -e, *countless, innumerable*; adv. **innŭmĕrābilĭtĕr**.

innŭmĕrābilĭtās -ātis, f. *an infinite number*.

innŭmĕrālis -e, and **innŭmĕrus** -a -um, *countless, innumerable*.

innŭo -nŭĕre -nŭi -nŭtum, *to give a nod to, make a sign to*.

innupta -ae, *unmarried*; as subst., *a maiden*.

innūtrio -ire, *to bring up in or among*.

inoblitus -a -um, *mindful*.

inobrŭtus -a, -um, *not overwhelmed*.

inobservābilis -e, *imperceptible*.

inobservantia -ae, f. *negligence, carelessness*.

inobservātus -a -um, *unperceived*.

inoccĭdŭus -a -um, *never setting*.

inoffensus -a -im, *not struck, not stumbling*; *unhindered, unobstructed*.

inofficiōsus -a -um, *undutiful, disobliging*.

inŏlens -entis, *without smell*.

inŏlesco -ŏlescĕre -ŏlēvi, *to grow in or on*.

inōmĭnātus -a -um, *inauspicious, unlucky*.

inŏpĭa -ae, f. *want of means, need, poverty; helplessness*.

inŏpīnans -antis, *not expecting, unawares*; adv. **inŏpīnantĕr**.

inŏpīnātus -a -um; pass., *unexpected, unlooked for*; (ex) inopinato, *unexpectedly*; act., *not expecting*.

inŏpīnus -a -um, *unexpected, unlooked for*.

inops -ŏpis, *poor, helpless, in need*; of language, *weak, poor*.

inōrātus -a -um, *not brought forward and heard*.

inordĭnātus -a -um, *disorderly, in confusion*: n. as subst. *disorder*.

inornātus -a -um, *unadorned, plain; unpraised, uncelebrated*.

inp-; see **imp-**.

inquam, inquis, inquit, etc.; perf., inquii; *say*.

inquĭēs -ētis, *unquiet, restless*.

inquĭēto -are, *to disturb*.

inquĭētus -a -um, *unquiet, restless*.

inquilīnus -i, m. *tenant, lodger*.

inquĭno -are, *to befoul, pollute, stain, corrupt*. Hence partic. **inquĭnātus** -a -um, *dirty, foul, polluted*; adv. **inquĭnātē**.

inquīro -quīrĕre -quīsīvi -quīsītum, *to search for; to investigate, inquire into*; legal, *to search for evidence against anyone*.

inquīsītĭo -ōnis, f. *looking for, search*; esp. *search for evidence against; a looking into, investigation, inquiry*.

inquīsītor -ōris, m. *an inquirer; investigator*; legal, *one who searches for evidence to support an accusation*.

inrāsus -a -um, *unshaved*.

inraucesco -raucescĕre -rausi, *to become hoarse*.

inrĕlĭgātus -a -um, *unbound*.

inrĕlĭgiōsus -a -um, *irreligious, impious*; adv. **inrĕlĭgiōsē**.

inrĕmĕābilis -e, *from which there is no return*.

inrĕpărābilis -e, *that cannot be restored, irrecoverable*.

inrĕpertus -a -um, *not discovered*.

inrēpo -rēpĕre -repsi -reptum, *to creep, crawl in; to insinuate oneself*.

inreprĕhensus -a -um, *unblamed, blameless*.

inrĕquiētus -a -um, *restless, troubled*.

inrēsectus -a -um, *uncut*.

inrĕsŏlūtus -a -um, *not loosed, not slackened*.

inrētĭo -ire, *to catch in a net, entangle*.

inrĕtortus -a -um, *not turned or twisted back*.

inrĕvĕrens -entis, *disrespectful*; adv. **inrĕvĕrentĕr**.

inrĕvĕrentia -ae, f. *want of respect, irreverence*.

inrĕvŏcābilis -e, *that cannot be called back, irrevocable; unalterable, implacable*.

inrĕvŏcātus -a -um, *not called back*.

inrīdĕo -rīdēre -risi -risum, *to laugh at, mock, ridicule*.

inrīdĭcŭlē, *without wit or humour*.

inrīdĭcŭlo, predicative dat., *for a laughing-stock*.

inrĭgātĭo -ōnis, f. *watering, irrigation*.

inrĭgo -are, *to conduct any liquid, to diffuse; to water, irrigate, inundate, flood over*.

inrĭgŭus -a -um: act., *watering, irrigating; refreshing*; pass., *watered, soaked*.

inrīsĭo -ōnis, f. *laughing at, mocking, derision*.

inrīsor -ōris, m. *a laugher, mocker, derider*.

inrīsus -ūs, m. *laughter, mockery, derision*; dat. inrisui, *for a laughing-stock*.

inrītābilis -e, *irritable, easily roused*.

inrītāmen -inis, n. *incitement, inducement*.

inrītāmentum -i, m. *incitement, incentive*.

inrītātĭo -ōnis, f. *stirring up, provoking, incitement*.

inrīto -are, *to stir up, stimulate, incite, excite*.

inrītus -a -um, *void, invalid; vain, ineffectual, useless*.

inrŏgātĭo -ōnis, f. *the imposing of fine or penalty*.

inrŏgo -are, *to propose a measure against anyone; to inflict, impose*.

inrōro -ae, *to moisten (with dew); to trickle down upon*.

inrumpo -rumpĕre -rūpi -ruptum, *to break in, burst in, rush in*.

inrŭo -rŭĕre -rŭi: transit., *to fling in*; intransit., *to rush in*.

inruptĭo -ōnis, f. *bursting in irruption*.

inruptus -a -um, *unbroken, unsevered*.

insălūbris -e, *unhealthy*.

insălūtātus -a -um, *ungreeted*

insānābĭlis -e, *incurable*.

insānĭa -ae, f. *madness, frenzy, senseless excess, extravagance; poetical rapture or inspiration*.

insānĭo -ire, *to be made, rage, rave; to be inspired*.

insānĭtās -ātis, f. *disease, unsoundness*.

insānus -a -um, *of unsound mind, mad, raving, senseless; of poets, inspired; of things, raging stormy*. Adv. insānē, *madly*.

insătĭābĭlis -e: pass., *insatiable*: act., *that does not satiate, uncloying*. Adv. insătĭābĭlĭtĕr, *insatiably*.

insătŭrābĭlis -e, *insatiable*; adv. insătŭrābĭlĭtĕr.

inscendo -scendĕre -scendi -scensum, *to climb on, ascend, mount*.

inscĭens -entis, *not knowing fact, unaware*; in gen., *ignorant*. Adv. inscĭentĕr.

inscĭentĭa -ae f. *ignorance, inexperience*.

inscĭtĭa -ae, f. *inexperience, want of skill, ignorance*.

inscītus -a -um, *ignorant unskilful, stupid*; adv. inscītē.

inscĭus -a -um, *ignorant, not knowing*.

inscrībo -scrībĕre -scripsi -scriptum, *to write in or on, inscribe; to mark, impress; to entitle, mark as something; to ascribe, mark as belonging to*.

inscriptĭo -ōnis, f. *writing in or upon*.

¹inscriptus -a -um, *unwritten*.

²inscriptus -a -um, partic. from inscribo; q.v.

insculpo -sculpĕre -sculpsi -sculptum, *to cut or carve in engrave*. Transf., *to impress*.

insĕco -sĕcare -sĕcŭi -sectum, *to cut into, notch*.

insectātĭo -ōnis, f. *close following, hot pursuit*. Transf., *abuse*.

insectātor -oris, m. *pursuer, persecutor*.

insecto -are and insector -ari, dep. *to follow closely, pursue, harry; to harry with abuse, rail at, reproach*.

insĕdăbĭlĭtĕr, *incessantly*.

insĕnesco -sĕnescĕre -sĕnŭi, *to grow old at or among*.

insensĭlis -e, *without sensation*.

insĕpultus -a -um, *unburied*.

insĕquor -sĕqui -sĕcūtus, dep., *to follow after, follow on; in time, to succeed; to pursue a subject; to pursue a person, to censure, reproach; in gen., to attack, assail*.

¹insĕro -sĕrĕre -sĕvi -situm, *to graft in, implant*. Hence partic. insĭtus -a -um, *implanted, innate; incorporated*.

²insĕro -sĕrĕre -sĕrŭi -sertum, *to let in, introduce, insert*; in gen., *to connect, put in or among*.

inserto -are, *to insert, put into*.

inservĭo -ire, *to be a slave, to serve; to be devoted to*.

insībĭlo -are, *to hiss, whistle in*.

insĭdĕo -ēre, *to sit in or on; to dwell, remain*.

insĭdĭae -arum, f. pl. *an ambush; a trap, plot*.

insĭdĭātor -oris, m. *a man in ambush; a spy, waylayer*.

insĭdĭor -ari, dep., *to lie in ambush, lie in wait; to plot against, watch for*.

insĭdĭōsus -a -um, *deceitful treacherous*; adv. insĭdĭōsē.

insĭdo -sĭdĕre -sēdi -sessum, *to sit, settle, perch upon*; milit., *to occupy, beset*; of ideas, etc., *to sink in*.

insignĕ -is, n. *a distinguishing mark, token; badge, decoration, medal*; pl. as abstr., *distinctions, beauties*.

insignĭo -ire, *to mark, distinguish*. Hence partic. insignītus -a -um, *marked; conspicuous, clear*; adv. insignītē, *remarkably*.

insignis -e, *distinguished, remarkable, extraordinary*; adv. insignĭtĕr.

insĭlĭa n. pl. *the treadles of a loom, or perhaps leash-rods*.

insĭlĭo -sĭlire -sĭlŭi, *to leap, spring, jump in or on*.

insĭmŭlātĭo -ōnis, f. *accusation, charge*.

insĭmŭlo -are, *to charge, accuse, esp. falsely*.

insincērus -a -um, *tainted*.

insinŭātĭo -ōnis, f., rhet. t. t., *gaining the favour of the audience*.

insĭnŭo -are, *to introduce by turning, to insinuate; with (and occasionally without) reflex., to penetrate, work one's way in*.

insĭpĭens -entis, *foolish*; adv. insĭpĭentĕr.

insĭpĭentĭa -ae, f. *foolishness*.

insisto -sistĕre -stĭti. (1) *to set foot on, tread on; to enter on a journey, road, etc., to set about a task*; with dat., *to follow hard upon, pursue*. (2) *to stand still in or on; to halt, stop, pause; to hesitate, doubt; to dwell upon a subject; to persist in a course*.

insĭtĭo -ōnis, f. *grafting*.

insĭtīvus -a -um, *grafted; spurious*.

insĭtor -oris, m. *a grafter*.

insĭtus -a -um, partic. from insero; q.v.

insŏcĭābĭlis -e, *unable to combine*.

insŏlābĭlĭtĕr, *inconsolably*.

insŏlens -entis, *contrary to custom*. Hence (1) *unaccustomed, unused*. (2) *unusual, excessive, extravagant; arrogant, insolent*. Adv. insŏlentĕr, *unusually, contrary to custom; excessively, extravagantly; haughtily, arrogantly*.

insŏlentĭa -ae, f. (1) *inexperience*. (2) *unusual character, novelty, extravagance, excess; pride, arrogance*.

insŏlesco -escĕre, *to become haughty or insolent*.

insŏlĭdus -a -um, *soft, tender*.

insŏlĭtus -a -um. (1) *unaccustomed*. (2) *unusual, strange, uncommon*.

insomnĭa -ae, f. *sleeplessness, loss of sleep*.

insomnis -e, *sleepless*.

insomnĭum -i, n. *a bad dream*.

insŏno -sŏnare -sŏnŭi, *to make a noise in* or *with; to sound, resound.*

insons -sontis, *innocent, guiltless, harmless.*

insōpītus -a -um, *unsleeping, watchful.*

inspectio -ōnis, f. *scrutiny, consideration.*

inspecto -are, *to look at, observe.*

inspĕrans -antis, *not hoping, not expecting.*

inspĕrātus -a -um, *unhoped-for, unexpected.*

inspergo spergĕre -spersi -spersum, *to sprinkle in* or *on.*

inspĭcĭo -spĭcĕre -spexi -spectum. (1) *to look into, see into.* (2) *to view, examine, inspect; to cónsider.*

inspīco -are, *to sharpen to a point.*

inspīro -are, *to breathe upon, blow upon, inspire.*

inspŏlĭātus -a -um, *not plundered.*

instābĭlis -e. (1) *unstable, unsteady, inconstant.* (2) *not supporting, insecure.*

instans -antis, and **instantĕr**; from insto; q.v.

instantĭa -ae, f. *presence; perseverance.*

instăr, n. (only nom. and acc. sing.), *an image, likeness;* usually with genit., in the sense *corresponding to, like.*

instaurātĭo -ōnis, f. *repetition, renewal.*

instaurātīvus -a -um, *renewed, repeated.*

instauro -are. (1) *to set up, establish.* (2) *to renew, restore;* hence *to repay, requite.*

insterno -sternĕre -strāvi -strātum, *to spread over, cover over;* equus instratus, *saddled.*

instīgātor -oris, m. and **instīgātrix** -trīcis, f. *an instigator.*

instīgo -are, *to goad, incite, stimulate.*

instillo -are, *to drop in, pour in by drops, instil.*

instīmŭlātor -ōris m. *an instigator*

instīmŭlo -are, *to incite.*

instinctor -ōris, m. *an instigator.*

instinctū, abl. sing. m. *by instigation.*

instinctus -a -um, *instigated, incited, impelled.*

instīta -ae, f. *border* or *flounce on a robe.*

instĭtĭo -ōnis, f. *standing still.*

instĭtor -ōris, m. *a hawker, pedlar.*

instĭtŭo -ŭĕre -ŭi -ūtum, *to put in place, set in order; to set up, make ready, build, construct;* abstr. *to establish, introduce, arrange; to settle on a course, to undertake, resolve, determine; to appoint a person; to instruct educate, train.*

instĭtūtĭo -ōnis, f. *arrangement; regular method; education, instruction.*

instĭtūtum -i, n. *an undertaking, purpose; an arrangement, institution, plan; an instruction, precept.*

insto -stare -stĭti. (1) *to stand in* or *on.* (2) *to be close to, follow closely, pursue eagerly; to devote oneself, persist, persevere; to insist, ask pressingly;* of time or events, *to approach, impend.*

Hence partic. **instans** -antis,

present; pressing, urgent; adv. **instanter,** *urgently.*

instrēnŭus -a -um, *inactive, lazy.*

instrĕpo -ere -ŭi -ĭtum, *to rattle, clatter, creak.*

instructĭo -ōnis, f. *drawing up in order.*

instructor -ōris, m. *a preparer.*

instructus -ūs, m. *provision; matter* (in a speech).

instrūmentum -i, n. *equipment, tool, implement; dress; store, stock: any means to an end.*

instrŭo -strŭĕre -struxi -structum, *to build in* or *into; to set up, construct; furnish,* hence *to train a person; to prepare, provide;* milit., *to draw up in order of battle.*

Hence partic. **instructus** -a -um, *equipped, supplied;* of persons, *trained, instructed.*

insuāvis -e, *unpleasant, disagreeable.*

Insubres -ium, *the Insubrians, a people in Cisalpine Gaul;* as adj. **Insūbĕr** -bris -bre, *Insubrian.*

insūdo -are, *to sweat in* or *at.*

insuēfactus -a -um, *accustomed to.*

insuesco -suescĕre -suēvi -suētum; intransit., *to become used to;* transit., *to accustom, habituate anyone to.*

¹**insuētus** -a -um: of persons, *unaccustomed, unused to;* of things, *unaccustomed, unusual.*

²**insuētus** -a -um, partic. from insuesco; q.v.

insŭla -ae, f. *an island.* Transf., *a detached house* or *block of flats.*

insŭlānus -i, m. *an islander.*

insulsĭtās -ātis, f. *tastelessness, absurdity.*

insulsus -a -um, *unsalted, insipid; tasteless, foolish;* adv. **insulsē.**

insulto -are, *to leap, prance in* or *on; to triumph over, insult.*

insum -esse -fŭi, *to be in* or *on; to be contained in, belong to.*

insūmo -sūmĕre -sumpsi -sumptum, *to take for a purpose, to expend.*

insŭo -sŭĕre -sutum, *to sew in, sew up.*

insŭpĕr: adv. *above, overhead; over and above, in addition, besides;* prep., with abl., *besides.*

insŭpĕrābĭlis -e, *insurmountable, impassable; unconquerable.*

insurgo -surgĕre -surrexi -surrectum, *to rise up, raise oneself up; to increase in power* or *force;* with dat., *to rise up against.*

insŭsurro -are, *to whisper, whisper in the ear.*

intābesco -tābescĕre -tābŭi, *to melt or wither away gradually.*

intactĭlis -e, *that cannot be touched.*

¹**intactus** -a -um, *untouched; untried unspoilt, unhurt, virgin.*

²**intactus** -ūs, m. *intangibility.*

intāmĭnātus -a -um, *unstained.*

¹**intectus** -a -um, *uncovered, unclothed; open, frank.*

²**intectus** -a -um, partic. from intego; q.v.

intĕgellus -a -um, *mor.· or less pure, undamaged.*

intĕger -gra -grum. (1) *complete,*

whole, entire, intact; fresh, sound, unexhausted; in integrum restituere, *to restore to its former condition.* (2) in quality, *unspoilt, pure, fresh*; morally, *innocent, uncorrupted*: in thought or feeling, *balanced, unbiased, impartial*; of matters for discussion or action, *unprejudiced, undecided*; integrum est mihi, *I am at liberty.* (3) *renewed, begun afresh.* Hence adv. **integrē** *wholly; honestly, uprightly, impartially*; of style, *purely, correctly.*

intĕgo -tĕgĕre -texi -tectum, *to cover, protect.*

integrasco -ĕre, *to break out afresh.*

integrātio -ōnis, f. *renewing.*

integrĭtās -ātis, f. *unimpaired condition, soundness, health; uprightness, integrity*; of style, *purity, correctness.*

integro -are, *to make whole, heal, refresh; to renew, begin afresh.*

intĕgŭmentum -i, n. *a covering, cloak, disguise.*

intellectus -ūs, m. *understanding, comprehension.*

intellĕgentia -ae, f. *perception; understanding, knowledge, taste; capacity for understanding, intelligence.*

intellĕgo -lĕgĕre -lexi -lectum, *to discern, perceive; to understand, grasp; to understand* character, *judge, appreciate; to understand by a term, take as its meaning.*
Hence partic. **intellĕgens** -entis, *intelligent, understanding; having good sense* or *taste.* Adv. **intellĕgentĕr.**

intĕmĕrātus -a -um, *unspotted, undefiled.*

intempĕrans -antis, *extravagant, unrestrained, intemperate*; adv. **intempĕrantĕr.**

intempĕrantĭa -ae, f. *want of restraint, extravagance, excess.*

intempĕrātus -a -um, *intemperate, immoderate*; adv. **intempĕrātē.**

intempĕrĭēs -ēi, f. *wildness, lack of restraint, excess.*

intempestīvus -a -um, *unseasonable, untimely; immoderate.* Adv. **intempestīvē, *unseasonably.***

intempestus -a -um, *unwholesome, unhealthy*: intempesta nox, *the dead of night.*

intemptātus -a -um, *untried.*

intendo -tendĕre -tendi -tentum. (1) *to stretch, strain*; abstr.; *to maintain, try to prove.* (2) *to extend, aim, direct*; esp. *to direct one's course; to apply the mind, direct the thoughts; to intend, aim at.*
Hence partic. **intentus** -a -um, *stretched, tense, taut*; of thought or feeling, *anxious, intent*; of speech, *earnest*; in gen, *thorough, strict, rigorous.* Adv. **intentē, *earnestly, attentively.***

¹**intentātus** -a -um; = intemptatus; q.v.

²**intentatus** -a -um, partic., from intento; q.v.

intentĭo -ōnis, f. *stretching, straining*; of the mind, *effort, exertion, attention; an attack, accusation.*

intento -are, *to stretch towards* or *against*, esp. *threateningly.*

¹**intentus** -ūs, m, *stretching out.*

²**intentus** -a -um, partic. from intendo; q.v.

intĕpesco -tĕpescĕre -tĕpui, *to become lukewarm.*

inter, prep. with acc. *between, among, amid; during, in the course of* a period; with pronouns, inter se, inter nos, etc., *between one another, mutually.*

intĕrāmenta -orum, n. pl. *woodwork of a ship.*

intĕrāresco -ĕre, *to become dry, decay.*

intercălāris -e and **intercălārĭus** -a -um, *inserted, intercalary.*

intercălo -are, *to insert*; esp. *to intercalate a day* or *month in the calendar.*

intercăpēdo -inis, f. *interval, pause, respite.*

intercēdo -cēdĕre -cessi -cessum, *to go between, come between, intervene; legal, to interpose, stand surety; to step between, withstand, protest against.*

interceptĭo -ōnis, f. *taking away.*

interceptor -ōris, m. *one who takes away, an embezzler.*

intercessĭo -ōnis, f. legal, *becoming surety, going bail*; polit., *an exercise by the tribunes of their veto.*

intercessor -ōris, m. legal, *surety, bail*; polit., *one who opposes, an obstructor.*

¹**intercīdo** -cīdĕre -cīdi -cīsum, *to cut asunder, to demolish.* Hence adv. **intercīsē, *piecemeal.***

²**intercĭdo** -cĭdĕre -cĭdi. (1) *to fall between, intervene.* (2) *to drop out, be lost, be forgotten, perish.*

intercĭno -ere, *to sing between.*

intercĭpĭo -cĭpĕre -cēpi -ceptum, *to take by the way, intercept; to embezzle, appropriate; through death, to cut off, carry off prematurely*; of roads, *to block.*

interclūdo -clūdĕre -clūsi -clūsum, *to shut off, block, hinder; to enclose, shut in.*

interclūsĭo -ōnis, f. *stopping* or *blocking up; parenthesis.*

intercŏlumnĭum -i, n. *the space between two columns.*

intercurro -currĕre -cŭcurri -cursum, *to run between, to run through; to intercede; to be among, mingle with; to hasten in the meanwhile.*

intercurso -are, *to run between, run among.*

intercursū, abl. sing. m. *by running between, by the interposition.*

intercŭs -cŭtis, *under the skin*: aqua, *the dropsy.*

interdīco -dīcĕre -dixi -dictum. (1) *to stop by interposition, forbid, prohibit*; interdicĕre aqua et igni, with dat., *to outlaw.* (2) *to make an injunction to order.*

interdictĭo -ōnis, f. *forbidding, prohibition*: aquae et ignis, *outlawing.*

interdictum -i, n. *a prohibition; a praetor's interdict* or *provisional order.*

int

interdiū (interdīus), *in the daytime, by day.*

interdo -dăre -dătum, *to put between or among, distribute.*

interductus -ū, m. *interpunctuation.*

interdum, *sometimes, now and then.*

interdŭo = interdo; q.v.

interĕā, *meanwhile*; sometimes *nevertheless, notwithstanding.*

interemptor -ōris, m. *a murderer.*

interĕo -ire -ii -ĭtum, *to be lost, to perish.*

interĕquito -are, *to ride between.*

interfātio -onis f. *speaking between, interruption.*

interfātur -fāri -fātus, dep. forms, *to speak between, interrupt.*

interfectio -ōnis, f. *slaying.*

interfector -ōris, m. *murderer.*

interfectrix -trīcis, f. *murderess.*

interfĭcĭo -fĭcĕre -fēci -fectum, *to do away with, destroy, put an end to, kill.*

interfĭo -fĭĕri, *to perish.*

interflŭo -flŭĕre -fluxi -fluxum, *to flow between.*

interfŏdĭo -fŏdĕre -fōdi -fossum, *to dig into, pierce.*

interfor; see interfatur.

interfŭgĭo -fŭgĕre, *to flee between.*

interfulgens -entis, *shining or gleaming among.*

interfūsus -a -um, *poured between, flowing between*; maculis interfusa, *stained here and there.*

interiăcĕo -ēre, *to lie between or among.*

interiăcĭo = intericio; q.v.

interĭbi, *meanwhile.*

interĭcĭo -icere -ieci -iectum, *to throw, cast, put, among or between*; anno interiecto, *after an interval of a year.*

interiectio -ōnis, f. *interjection or parenthesis.*

interiectus -ūs, m. *throwing between*; of time, *an interval.*

interim, *meanwhile*; sometimes *however.*

interĭmo -imĕre -ēmi -emptum, *to take away, destroy, make an end of; to put out of the way, kill.*

interĭor -ius, genit. -ōris, *inner, interior; remote from the sea, inland, nearer*; in racing, *on the inside.* Transf., *more secret, more intimate.* Superl. **intĭmus** -a -um; q.v. Adv. **interĭus**, *more inwardly; short, not far enough.*

interĭtio -ōnis, f. *destruction, ruin.*

interĭtus -ūs, m. *destruction, ruin.*

interiungo -iungĕre -iunxi -iunctum, *to join together, connect; also to unyoke.*

interĭus; see interior.

interlābor -lābi -lapsus, dep. *to glide, flow between.*

interlĕgo -ĕre, *to pluck here and there.*

interlĭno -lĭnĕre -lēvi -litum, *to daub between; to erase, falsify by erasure.*

interlŏquor -lŏqui -lŏcūtus, dep. *to interrupt a person speaking.*

interlūcĕo -lūcĕre -luxi, *to shine or gleam between; to be transparent, let light through gaps.*

interlūnĭum -i, n. *change of moon, time of new moon.*

interlŭo -lŭĕre, *to wash between.*

intermenstrŭus -a -um, *between two months*; n. as subst. *the time of the new moon.*

¹intermĭnātus -a -um, *unbounded, boundless.*

²intermĭnātus -a -um, partic. from interminor; q.v.

intermĭnor -ari, dep. *to threaten, forbid with threats*; perf. partic. in pass. sense, *forbidden with threats.*

intermiscĕo -miscĕre -miscŭi -mixtum, *to mix with, intermix.*

intermissĭo -ōnis, f. *leaving off, interruption.*

intermitto -mittĕre -mīsi -missum: transit., *to leave a space between, leave free*; in space, *to separate, break off*; in time, *to let pass*; in gen., *to discontinue, interrupt*; vento intermisso, *the wind having dropped*; intransit., *to cease, leave off.*

intermŏrior -mŏri -mortuus, dep. *to die off, perish suddenly*; partic. **intermortuus** -a -um, *swooning, half-dead*; fig., *lifeless.*

intermundĭa -ōrum, n. pl. *spaces between the worlds.*

intermūrālis -e, *between walls.*

internascor -nasci -natus, dep. *to grow between or among.*

internĕcĭo -ōnis, f. *extermination, massacre.*

internĕcīvus (-nĕcĭnus) -a -um, *murderous, deadly.*

internĕco -are, *to exterminate.*

internecto -ĕre, *to bind together, bind up.*

internōdĭum -i, n. *the space between two knots or joints.*

internosco -noscĕre -nōvi -nōtum, *to distinguish between.*

internuntĭa -ae, f. *a female messenger or go-between.*

internuntĭo -are, *to send messengers between parties.*

internuntĭus -i, m. *a messenger, mediator, go-between.*

internus -a, -im., *inward, internal; domestic, civil.*

interpellātĭo -ōnis, f. *interruption.*

interpellātor -ōris, m. *interrupter, disturber.*

interpello -are, *to interrupt, disturb, impede, obstruct.*

interpŏlo -are, *to furbish, vamp up; to falsify.*

interpōno -pōnĕre -pŏsŭi -pŏsĭtum, *to place between or among, interpose*; spatio interposito, *after an interval*; fidem, *to pledge one's word*; rarely, *to falsify*; with reflex., *to engage in, interfere with.*

interpŏsĭtĭo -ōnis, f. *putting in, insertion, introduction*; rhet. *parenthesis.*

interpŏsĭtū, abl. sing. m. *by putting between, by interposition.*

interprĕs -prĕtis, c. (1) *a negotiator, mediator, messenger.* (2) *an expounder, explainer; prophet, prophetess; interpreter; translator.*

interprĕtātĭo -ōnis, f., *explanation, interpretation; translation.* Transf., *meaning, signification.*

interprĕtor -ari, dep. (1) *to put an interpretation upon, understand in a certain sense.* (2) *to translate.*

interpunctio -ōnis, f. *punctuation.*

interpungo -pungĕre -punxi -punctum, *to punctuate;* partic. **interpunctus** -a -um, *well-divided.*

interquiesco -quiescĕre -quiēvi -quiētum, *to pause between.*

interregnum -i, n. *a period between two reigns, interregnum.*

interrex -rēgis m. *a regent, temporary king or chief magistrate.*

interrĭtus -a -um, *undaunted.*

interrŏgātio -ōnis, f. *questioning, interrogation:* esp. legal, *examination of witnesses;* in logic, *an argument, syllogism;* gram., *interrogation.*

interrŏgo -are, *to ask, question, interrogate;* esp. *to examine* a witness, or *to accuse, bring an action against.*

interrumpo -rumpĕre -rūpi -ruptum, *to break in the middle, sever, interrupt, disturb.* Adv. from partic. **interruptē**, *interruptedly, disconnectedly.*

intersaepio -saepire -saepsi -s.eptum, *to enclose, hem in, block up.*

interscindo -scindĕre -scidi -scissum, *to cut open, cut off, tear apart.*

interscrībo -ĕre, *to write between.*

¹**intersĕro** -sĕrĕre -sēvi -sĭtum, *to sow or plant between.*

²**intersĕro** -sĕrĕre -sĕrŭi, *to put or place between.*

interspīrātio -ōnis, f. *breathing between, taking breath.*

interstinctus -a -um, *spotted, speckled.*

interstinguo -ĕre, *to extinguish.*

interstringo -ĕre, *to squeeze tight.*

intersum -esse -fŭi, *to be between; to be among, be present at, take part in* (with dat.); in time, *to intervene;* abstr., *to be between as a difference; rarely to differ, be different.* Hence impers. **intĕrest**, *it makes a difference, it concerns;* magni (or multum) meā interest, *it makes a great difference to me.*

intertextus -a -um, *interwoven.*

intertrīmentum -i, n. *loss, damage.*

interturbātio -ōnis, f. *disturbance, disquiet.*

intervallum -i, n. *distance between, interval* (of time or space); *difference, unlikeness.*

intervĕnio -vĕnire -vēni -ventum, *to come between, intervene; to interrupt* (with dat.) *to delay* (with acc.).

interventor -ōris, m. *an interrupting visitor.*

interventus -ūs, m. *intervention, interference.*

interverto (**-vorto**) -vertĕre -verti -versum, *to intercept; to embezzle, purloin; to cheat, rob.*

intervīso -vīsĕre -vīsi -vīsum, *to look in at, visit from time to time.*

intestābĭlis -e, *disqualified, dishonoured, infamous.*

intestātus -a -um, *having made no will, intestate;* n. abl. as adv. intestato, *intestate.*

intestīnus -a -um, *inward, internal;*

n. as subst., sing. and plur. *the intestines.*

intexo -texĕre -texŭi -textum. *to weave in, plait in, interweave; to weave around, wind around.*

intĭbum -i, n. *endive, succory.*

intĭmus (**intŭmus**) -a -um, superl. (compar. interior; q.v.), *innermost, inmost; most profound, most secret, intimate;* m. as subst., *an intimate friend.* Adv. **intĭmē**. *intimately; cordially, strongly.*

intingo (**-tinguo**) -tingĕre -tinxi -tinctum, *to dip in.*

intŏlĕrābĭlis -e, *unbearable, intolerable.*

intŏlĕrandus -a -um, *unbearable, un-endurable.*

intŏlĕrans -antis: act. *impatient, unable to bear;* pass., *unbearable, intolerable.* Adv. **intŏlĕrantĕr**, *immoderately, impatiently.*

intŏlĕrantia -ae, f. *insufferable conduct, insolence.*

intŏno -tŏnare -tŏnŭi, *to thunder, thunder forth* (esp. of speakers).

intonsus -a -um, *unshorn, with long hair or beard;* hence *of persons rude, rough;* of country, *wooded, not cleared.*

intorquĕo -torquēre -torsi -tortum, *to twist or turn round;* of weapons, *to hurl;* partic. **intortus** -a -um *twisted, tangled.*

intrā: adv. *inside;* prep., with acc. *inside, within, less than, short of.*

intrābĭlis -e, *that can be entered, accessible.*

intractābĭlis -e, *unmanageable, intractable.*

intractātus -a -um, *not handled; unattempted.*

intrĕmisco -trĕmiscĕre -trĕmŭi, *to begin to tremble.*

intrĕmo -ere, *to tremble, quake.*

intrĕpĭdus -a -um, *unconfused, calm;* adv. **intrĕpĭdē**, *calmly.*

intrico -are, *to confuse, entangle.*

intrinsĕcus, *inside, inwardly, inwards.*

¹**intrĭtus** -a -um, *not worn away, unexhausted.*

²**intrĭtus** -a -um, partic. from intero, q.v.

¹**intrō**, *inwards, within.*

²**intro** -are, *to go into, enter.*

intrōdūco -dūcĕre -duxi -ductum, *to introduce, bring in, bring forward, present, suggest.*

intrōductio -ōnis, f. *bringing in, introduction.*

intrŏĕo -ire -ii -ĭtum, *to go into, enter.*

intrōfĕro -ferre -tŭli -lātum, *to carry in.*

intrōgrĕdior -grĕdi -gressus, dep. *to enter.*

intrŏĭtus -ūs, m. *an entrance; means of entrance; passage;* in gen., *beginning, introduction.*

intrōmitto -mittĕre -mīsi -missum, *to send in, allow to enter.*

introrsŭs (**-orsum**), *inwards, inwardly internally.*

intrōrumpo -rumpĕre -rūpi -ruptum, *to break into, enter by force.*

introspĭcio -spĭcĕre -spexi -spectum,

to look into, look inside, observe, examine.

intŭbum -i, n., see intibum.

intŭĕor -tŭēri -tŭitus, dep. *to look at attentively, gaze at; to consider, contemplate, look to.*

intŭmesco -tŭmescĕre -tŭmŭi, *to swell, swell up; to increase; to swell with anger.*

intŭmŭlātus -a -um, *unburied.*

intŭor -i, dep. = intueor; q.v.

inturbĭdus -a -um, *undisturbed, quiet.*

intŭs, adv. *within, inside; to or from the inside; inwardly.*

intŭtus -a -um. (1) *unprotected.* (2) *unsafe, dangerous.*

inŭla -ae, f. *the plant elecampane.*

inultus -a -um. (1) *unavenged.* (2) *unpunished.*

inumbro -are, *to shade, overshadow.*

inundātĭo -ōnis, f. *inundation, flood.*

inundo -are: transit., *to overflow, inundate, stream over;* intransit., *to overflow with.*

inungo -ungĕre -unxi -unctum, *to anoint.*

inurbānus -a -um, *rude, unpolished;* adv. **inurbānē.**

inurgĕo -urgēre -ursi, *to push, thrust against.*

inūro -ūrēre -ussi -ustum, *to burn in or on, brand, imprint; to inflict; to crimp, curl, adorn.*

inūsĭtātus -a -um, *unusual, strange, uncommon;* adv. **inūsĭtātē.**

inūtĭlis -e, *useless, unserviceable, unprofitable; injurious, harmful.* Adv. **inūtĭlĭtēr.**

inūtĭlĭtās -ātis, f. *uselessness, unprofitableness; harmfulness.*

invādo -vādēre -vāsi -vāsum. (1) *to go in, enter, get in; to undertake.* (2) *to attack, fall upon, assail, usurp, seize.*

invālesco -vālescĕre -vālŭi, *to gather strength, become strong.*

invālĭdus -a -um, *weak, powerless.*

invectĭo -ōnis, f. (1) *importation.* (2) *invective.*

invĕho -vĕhĕre -vexi -vectum, *to carry in, introduce;* pass., *or with reflex., to drive, ride or travel,* esp. *to advance against, attack;* of verbal attack, *to inveigh.*

invĕnĭo -vĕnire -vēni -ventum, *to come upon, find, meet with, discover; to invent, devise; to procure, get, earn;* pass., *or with reflex., to show oneself.* Hence partic., **inventus** -a -um, *discovered;* n. as subst. *an invention, discovery.*

inventĭo -ōnis, f. *inventing, invention; the inventive faculty.*

inventor -ōris, m. and **inventrix** -tricis, f. *inventor.*

invĕnustus -a -um, *not charming, unattractive; unhappy in love.*

invĕrēcundus -a -um, *shameless, impudent.*

invergo -ĕre, *to tip or pour upon.*

inversĭo -ōnis, f. *irony; transposition; allegory.*

inverto -vertĕre -verti -versum *to*

turn over, turn about; to transpose, alter, pervert. Hence partic. **inversus** -a -um, *overturned, upside down.*

invespĕrascit -ĕre, impers. *it grows dark.*

investĭgātĭo -ōnis, f. *inquiry, investigation.*

investĭgātor -ōris, m. *inquirer, investigator.*

investĭgo -are, *to search out, track out.*

invĕtĕrasco -ascĕre -avi, *to become old; to become obsolete; to become established, fixed, rooted.*

invĕtĕrātĭo -ōnis, f. *inveterateness, permanence.*

invĕtĕrātus -a -um, *of long standing, established.*

invĭcem, *in turn, alternately; mutually, reciprocally.*

invictus -a -um, *unconquered, unsubdued; unconquerable, invincible.*

invĭdentĭa -ae, f. *envying, envy.*

invĭdĕo -vĭdēre -vĭdi -vĭsum, *to envy, grudge, be envious of.* Hence partic. **invĭsus** -a -um: pass., *hated;* act., *hostile.*

invĭdĭa -ae, f.: act., *envy, jealously, ill-will;* pass., *odium, unpopularity.* Transf., *a source of ill-will.*

invĭdĭōsus -a -um, *envious; causing envy, envied; hateful.* Adv. **invĭdĭōsē,** *jealously, bitterly.*

invĭdus -a -um, *envious, grudging.*

invĭgĭlo -are, *to watch over* (with dat.).

invĭŏlābĭlis -e, *unassailable.*

invĭŏlātus -a -um, *uninjured, unhurt; inviolable.* Adv. **invĭŏlātē,** *inviolately.*

invĭsĭtātus -a -um, *not seen; unusual, strange.*

inviso -vīsĕre -vīsi -vīsum, *to go to see, visit; to inspect, look at.*

¹**invĭsus** -a -um, *unseen, secret.*

²**invĭsus** -a -um, partic. from invideo; q.v.

invītāmentum -i, n. *invitation, attraction.*

invītātĭo -ōnis, f. *invitation, inducement.*

invītātū, abl. sing. m. *by invitation.*

invīto -are, *to invite, summon; to receive, entertain; to induce, allure;* with reflex., *to treat oneself.*

invītus -a -um, *unwilling, against one's will;* abl. absol., me invito, *against my will.* Adv. **invītē,** *unwillingly, against one's will.*

invĭus -a -um, *impassable, impenetrable;* n. pl. as subst., *trackless places.*

invŏcātĭo -ōnis, f. *calling upon, invocation.*

¹**invŏcātus** -a -um, *uncalled, uninvited.*

²**invŏcātus** -a -um, partic. from invoco; q.v.

invŏco -are, *to call in, call upon for help, invoke.*

invŏlātū, abl. sing. m., *by the flight.*

invŏlĭto -are, *to float or wave over.*

invŏlo -are, *to fly at, seize or pounce upon.*

invŏlūcrum -i, n. *a wrap, cover.*

involvo -volvĕre -volvi -vŏlūtum, *to roll in or on; to envelop, wrap up, cover.* Hence partic. **invŏlūtus** -a -um, *rolled up; involved.*

invulgo -are, *to give information.*

invulnĕrātus -a -um, *unwounded.*

ʾĬō, interj., *hurrah! hi!*

²Ĭō (Ĭŏn) -ūs (-ōnis), f. *an Argive girl, loved by Jupiter and changed into a cow;* adj. **Ĭōnĭus** -a -um, *Ionian, of the sea between Italy and Greece, across which Io swam.*

iŏcātĭo -ōnis, f. *joke, jest.*

iŏco -are and **iŏcor** -ari, dep. *to joke, jest.*

iŏcōsus -a -um, *humorous, merry, facetious;* adv. **iŏcōsē.**

iŏcŭlārĭs -e, *jocular, laughable;* adv. **iŏcŭlārĭtĕr.**

iŏcŭlārĭus -a -um, *laughable, droll.*

iŏcŭlātor -ōris, m. *joker.*

iŏcŭlor -ari, dep. *to joke, jest.*

iŏcus -i, m. (plur. iŏci and iŏca), *a joke, jest.*

Ĭōnes -um, m. *the Ionians;* **Ĭōnĭa** -ae, f. *their country in Asia Minor;* adj. **Ĭōnĭācus** and **Ĭōnĭcus** -a -um, *Ionian.*

Ĭphĭgĕnĭa -ae, f. *daughter of Agamemnon.*

ipse -a -um, *self;* ego ipse, *I myself; the very, actual;* with numbers, etc., *just, exactly;* of action, *by oneself, of one's own accord.*

īra -ae, f. *wrath, anger, rage;* meton., *cause of anger.*

īrācundĭa -ae, f. (1) *angry disposition, irascibility.* (2) *state of anger, fury, wrath.*

īrācundus -a -um, *inclined to anger, irascible;* adv. **īrācundē,** *wrathfully.*

īrascor -i, dep. *to grow angry* (with dat.); partic. **īrātus** -a -um, *angry.*

Īris -rĭdis, f. *messenger of the gods, and goddess of the rainbow.*

īrōnĭa -ae, f. *irony.*

irr-; see **in-.**

ĭs, ĕa, ĭd, *he, she, it; this* or *that (person* or *thing);* with qui (or ut), *one (of those) who, such . . . as;* with et, -que, etc., *and that too, and what is more;* n. sing. id, *on that account;* id temporis, *at that time;* in eo est, *the position is such,* or, *it depends on this;* id est, *that is,* in explanation.

Īsis -is and -ĭdis, f., *the Egyptian goddess Isis.*

istāc, *by that way.*

iste ista istŭd, demonstr. pron. or adj. *that of yours, that beside you;* in speeches, *referring to parties opposed to the speaker* (opp. to hic, *my client); often contemptuous.*

Ister = **Hister;** q.v.

Isthmus (-os) -i, m., *the Isthmus of Corinth.*

ʾistic istaec istōc or istūc, *that of yours.*

²istic, adv. *over there, there by you; therein, in that.*

istinc, *from over there, thence.*

istĭusmŏdī or **istīus mŏdī** or **istīmŏdī,** *of that kind, such.*

istō, adv., *thither, to that place* or *thing.*

istōc and **istūc,** *thither.*

Istri; see **Histri.**

Ĭtă, *so, thus;* interrog., itane? *really?*

in answers, *certainly;* in narration *and so;* with adj. or adv., *so, so very;* ita . . . ut, with subjunc., *in such a way that,* or *only to the extent that, only on condition that.*

Ĭtălī -orum and -um, m. *the Italians;* **Ĭtălĭa** -ae, f. *Italy;* adj. **Ĭtălĭcus** and **Ĭtălus** -a -um, *Italian;* f. adj. **Ĭtălĭs** -idis.

ĭtăquĕ, *and so; therefore, for that reason.*

ĭtem, *also, likewise.*

ĭtĕr, ĭtĭnĕris, n. *going, way, direction; journey, march; right of way, permission to march;* concr., *way, road;* fig., *way, course, method.*

ĭtĕrātĭo -ōnis, f. *repetition, iteration.*

ĭtĕro -are, *to do a second time, repeat, renew.*

ĭtĕrum, *again, a second time;* iterum atque interum, *again and again.*

Ĭthăca -ae and **Ĭthăcē** -ēs, f., *an island in the Ionian Sea, home of Ulysses.*

ĭtĭdem, *likewise.*

ĭtĭo -ōnis, f. *going, travelling.*

ĭto -are, *to go.*

ĭtus -ūs, m. *movement, going, departure.*

ʾĭŭba -ae, f. *mane, crest.*

²Ĭŭba -ae, m. *name of two Numidian kings.*

iŭbar -ăris, n. *beaming light, radiance; a heavenly body, esp. the sun.*

iŭbātus -a -um, *having a mane, crested.*

iŭbĕo iŭbēre iussi iussum, *to order, command, bid;* salvere iubere, *to greet;* polit. *to ratify an order.* Hence, from perf. partic. **iussum** -i, n., *an order, command.*

iŭcundĭtās -ātis, f., *pleasantness, delightfulness, pleasure.*

iŭcundus -a -um, *pleasant, agreeable, delightful;* adv. **iŭcundē.**

Iūdaea -ae, f. *Judea* or *Palestine;* adj. and subst. **Iūdaeus** -a -um, *Jewish* or *a Jew.*

iūdex -ĭcis, m. *a judge;* in plur., *a panel of jurors.*

iūdĭcātĭo -ōnis, f. *judicial investigation; judgment, opinion.*

iūdĭcātus -ūs, m,, *the office* or *business of a judge.*

iūdĭcĭālis -e and **iūdĭcĭārĭus** -a -um, *of a court of justice, judicial.*

iūdĭcĭum -i, n., *a trial, legal investigation; a law-court; jurisdiction; judgment, considered opinion, decision; power of judging, discernment, understanding, good judgment.*

iūdĭco -are, *to be a judge, judge, decide, declare;* perf. partic. **iūdĭcātus** -a -um, of persons, *condemned;* of things, *decided.*

iŭgālis -e, *yoked together;* m. pl. as subst. *a team of horses.* Transf., *matrimonial, nuptial.*

iŭgātĭo -ōnis, f. *the training of vines on a trellis.*

iŭgĕrum -i, n. *a measure of land, about two-thirds of an English acre.*

iŭgis -e, *perpetual, continuous, esp. of water.*

iŭglans -glandis, f., *a walnut* or *walnut-tree.*

iŭgo -are, *to bind together, connect, couple.*

iŭgōsus -a -um, *mountainous.*

iŭgŭlo -are, *to cut the throat of, to butcher; to ruin, destroy.*

iŭgŭlum -i, n. and **iŭgŭlus** -i, m. *the throat.*

iŭgum -i, n. (1) *a yoke or collar.* Transf., *a team of oxen* or *horses; a pair, couple; a chariot; any bond, union; the bond of love, marriage-tie; the yoke of slavery.* (2) *a cross-bar;* esp. *the yoke under which the vanquished were sent; the beam of a pair of scales; a ridge between mountains;* plur., poet., *mountain heights.*

Iŭgurtha -ae, m. *a king of Numidia;* adj. **Iŭgurthīnus** -a -um.

Iūlĭus -a -um, *name of a Roman gens;* including the family of the Caesars; mensis Iulius *or* Iulius, *the month of July.*

Iūlus -i, m., *son of Aeneas.*

iūmentum -i n. *a beast of burden.*

iuncĕus -a -um, *made of rushes; like a rush.*

iuncōsus -a -um, *full of rushes, rushy.*

iunctio -ōnis, f. *joining, connexion.*

iunctūra -ae, f., *a joining, joint; relationship; combination, putting together.*

iuncus -i, m. *a rush.*

iungo iungĕre iunxi iunctum, *to join, unite, connect; to yoke, harness; to mate;* amicitiam, *to form.* Hence partic. **iunctus** -a -um, *connected, united, associated.*

iūnĭor; see iuvenis.

iūnĭpĕrus -i, f. *the juniper-tree.*

Iūnĭus -a -um, *the name of a Roman gens;* mensis Iunius *or* Iunius, *the month of June.*

Iūnō -ōnis, f. *the goddess Juno, Greek Hera, sister and wife of Jupiter;* adj. **Iūnōnĭus** -a -um, *Junonian.*

Iuppĭter Iŏvis, m. *Jupiter, the Roman supreme god;* sub Iove, *in the open air.*

iūrātor -ōris, m. *a sworn assessor.*

iūrĕiūro -are, *to swear an oath.*

iūrĕpĕrītus = iurisperitus; q.v.

iurgĭum -i, n., *altercation, quarrel, brawl.*

iurgo -are: intransit., *to quarrel, brawl;* transit., *to scold.*

iūrĭdĭcĭālis -e, *relating to right or justice.*

iūrisconsultus -i, m. *one learned in law, a lawyer.*

iūrisdictio -onis, f. *the administration of justice; judicial authority.*

iūrispĕrītus *or* **iūrĕpĕrītus** -i, m. *skilled or experienced in the law.*

iūro -are, *to swear, take an oath,* in verba, *to swear after a prescribed formula;* perf. partic. in act. sense **iūrātus** -a -um, *having sworn, under oath;* also *having been sworn.*

¹**iūs** iūris, n. *broth, soup.*

²**iūs** iūris, n. *right, law; a court of justice; jurisdiction; right as conferred by law;* iure, *rightly.*

iusiūrandum iūrisiūrandi (or in two words), n. *an oath.*

iussū, abl. sing m., *by order, by command.*

iussum -i, n. subst. from iubeo; q.v.

iustĭtĭa -ae, f. *justice, airness, equity.*

iustĭtĭum -i, n. *a suspension of legal business;* in gen., *pause, cessation.*

iustus -a -um, *just, equitable, fair; lawful, justified, proper; regular, perfect, complete, suitable.* N. as subst. sing. **iustum** -i, *justice, what is right;* plur. **iusta** -orum, *due forms and observances,* esp. *funeral rites.* Adv. **iustē**, *justly, rightly.*

¹**iŭvĕnālis** -e, *youthful.*

²**Iŭvĕnālis** -is, m., D. Iunius, *a Roman writer of satires.*

iŭvencus -a -um, *young;* m. as subst., **iŭvencus** -i, *a young man,* or *young bullock;* f. **iŭvenca** -ae, *a young woman,* or *young cow, heifer.*

iŭvĕnesco iŭvĕnescĕre iŭvĕnŭi, *to come* (or *come back*) *to the prime of life.*

iŭvĕnīlis -e, *youthful;* adv. **iŭvĕnīlĭtĕr**, *youthfully.*

iŭvĕnis -is, adj., *young, youthful;* as subst. *a young man, young woman.*

iŭvĕnor -ari, dep. *to act like a youth, be impetuous.*

iŭventa -ae, f. *youth.*

iŭventās -ātis, f. *youth.*

iŭventūs -ūtis, f. *youth, the prime of life* (between the ages of 20 and 45); meton., *young men.*

iŭvo -are iūvi iūtum, (1) *to help, assist, aid.* (2) *to delight, please, gratify.*

iuxtā: adv. *close by, near; in like manner, equally;* prep., *with acc., close to, near to;* in time, *just before;* in gen., *near to, just short of.*

iuxtim, *near, close by; equally.*

Ixīon -ōnis, m. *king of the Lapithae in Thessaly, bound to a perpetually revolving wheel in Tartarus.*

J

Unknown in classical Latin; invented by Italian humanists to represent the consonantal i, but now rarely used in classical texts.

K

The letter K, k, corresponding to Greek kappa (κ) belonged to the Latin Alphabet, but in some words was replaced by C.

Kălendae (Călendae) -arum, f. *the first day of a Roman month.*

Karthāgo = Carthāgo; q.v.

L

L, l, the eleventh letter of the Latin Alphabet.

lābasco -ĕre, *to totter; to give way.*

lābēcŭla -ae, f., *a little stain, slight disgrace.*

lăbĕfăcĭo -făcĕre -fēci -factum, pass.
lăbĕfīo -fīĕri -factus sum, to shake,
loosen, impair.

lăbĕfacto -are, to shake violently,
weaken, disturb.

¹lăbellum -i, n., a little lip.

²lăbellum -i, n. a small washing-vessel.

lābēs -is, f. a stain, blemish; infamy,
disgrace.

lăbĭa -ae, f., and lăbĭum -i, n., a lip.

Lăbĭēnus -i, m., T. an officer of Julius
Caesar, who went over to Pompey.

lăbĭōsus -a -um, with large lips.

lăbĭum -i, n. = labia; q.v.

lăbo -are, to totter, waver, be about to
fall, begin to sink.

¹lābor lābi lapsus, dep. to glide, slide,
flow; to slip, fall down, fall away,
decline; to make a mistake.

²lābor (lăbōs) -ōris, m. (1) work, toil,
effort, industry, capacity for work;
feat, work, result of labour. (2) hardship, fatigue, distress; labores solis,
eclipse of the sun.

lăbōrĭfer -fĕra -fĕrum, bearing toil.

lăbōrĭōsus -a -um: of things, toilsome, laborious; of persons, industrious,
toiling. Adv. lăbōrĭōsē, laboriously,
with toil.

lăbōro -are: intransit., to work, toil,
strive: to be troubled or anxious, to
care; to suffer, be distressed or
afflicted; luna laborat, is eclipsed;
transit., to work out, elaborate, prepare,
form.

lābos -ōris, m. = labor; q.v.

¹labrum -i, n. lip; edge, rim.

²labrum -i, n. basin, tub; a bathing-
place.

lābrusca -ae, f. the wild vine.

lābruscum -i, n. the wild grape.

lăbўrinthus -i, m. a labyrinth.

lăc lactis, n. milk; milky sap; milk-white
colour.

Lăcaena -ae, f. adj. (female) Spartan.

Lăcĕdaemon -ŏnis, f. the city Lace-
daemon or Sparta; adj. Lăcĕdae-
mŏnĭus -a -um, Lacedaemonian.

lăcer -cĕra -cĕrum, torn, mangled; act.,
tearing to pieces.

lăcĕrātĭo -ōnis, f. tearing, mangling.

lăcerna -ae, f. a mantle worn over the
toga.

lăcĕro -are, to tear to pieces, maim,
mangle; to squander money; to
slander, pull to pieces a character.

lăcerta -ae, f. a lizard; also a sea-fish.

lăcertōsus -a -um, muscular, powerful.

¹lăcertus -i, m., the upper arm with its
muscles; in gen., vigour.

²lăcertus -i, m. = lacerta; q.v.

lăcesso -ĕre -ivi and -ii -itum, to
provoke, exasperate, excite, induce.

Lăchĕsis -is, f., one of the three Parcae
or Fates.

lăcĭnĭa -ae, f. the flap of a garment.

Lăco (Lăcōn) -ōnis, m., a Spartan,
Lacedaemonian; adj. Lăcōnĭcus -a
-um and f. adj. Lăcōnis -ĭdis,
Spartan.

lacrĭma (lacrŭma) -ae, f. a tear;
exudation from certain plants; Helia-
dum, amber.

lacrĭmābĭlis -e, deplorable, woeful.

lacrĭmābundus -a -um, breaking into
tears, weeping.

lacrimo (lacrŭmo) -are, to weep, shed
tears; to exude, to drip.

lacrĭmōsus -a -um: tearful, shedding
tears; causing tears, mournful, piteous.

lacrĭmŭla -ae, f., a little tear.

lacrŭma, etc.; see lacrima, etc.

lactans -antis, giving milk.

lactātĭo -ōnis, f. enticement.

lactens -entis. (1) sucking milk; plur.
as subst., sucklings, unweaned animals.
(2) milky, juicy, full of sap.

lactesco -ĕre, to be changed into milk.

lactĕus -a -um, milky, of milk; milk-
white.

lacto -are, to allure, wheedle.

lactūca -ae, f. lettuce.

lăcūna -ae, f. a cavity, hollow, dip;
esp. a pool, pond. Transf., gap,
deficiency, loss.

lăcūnăr -āris, n. a panelled ceiling.

lăcūno -are, to work in panels, to panel.

lăcūnōsus -a -um, full of hollows or
gaps.

lăcus -ūs, m. a hollow; hence a lake,
pool, trough, tank, tub.

laedo laedĕre laesi laesum, to strike,
knock; hence to hurt, injure, damage;
to offend, annoy; to violate, outrage.

laena -ae, f. cloak.

Lāertēs -ae, m. father of Ulysses.

laesĭo -ōnis, f. an oratorical attack.

laetābĭlis -e, joyful, glad.

laetātĭo -ōnis, f. rejoicing, joy.

laetĭfĭco -are, to fertilize; to cheer,
gladden, delight.

laetĭfĭcus -a -um, gladdening, joyous.

laetĭtĭa -ae, f. (1) fertility; hence
richness, grace. (2) joy, delight.

laetor -ari, dep. to rejoice, be joyful.

laetus -a -um, fat, rich, fertile; glad,
joyful, happy; of style, rich, copious,
fluent. Adv. laetē.

laevus -a -um, left; f. as subst., the
left hand, the left; n. as subst., the
left side. Transf., left-handed, foolish,
silly; unlucky, unpropitious; but in-
augury, favourable. Adv. laevē,
on the left hand; awkwardly.

lăgānum -i, n., a cake.

lăgēos -ei, f., a Greek kind of vine.

lăgoena a large earthen jar with handles.

lăgōis -idis, f. a bird, perhaps heathcock
or grouse.

lăguncŭla -ae, f. a little bottle.

Lāĭus -i, m. father of Oedipus.

lāma -ae, f. a bog, slough.

lambo lambĕre lambi, to lick; of rivers,
to wash.

lāmenta -orum, n. pl. wailing, weeping.

lāmentābĭlis -e lamentable, deplorable;
expressing sorrow, mournful.

lāmentātĭo -ōnis, f. weeping, wailing.

lāmentor -ari, dep. to weep, wail,
lament; transit., to bewail.

lāmĭa -ae, f. a witch, vampire.

lāmĭna, lammĭna, and lamna -ae,
f. a plate or thin piece of metal,
marble, etc.; knife-blade; coin; nut-
shell.

lampăs -pădis, f. *a torch*; hence *brightness, esp. of the sun*; also *a meteor.*

lāna -ae, f., *wool*; also *the down on leaves, fruit,* etc.

lānātus -a -um, *wool-bearing, woolly.*

lancĕa -ae, f. *a light spear* or *lance.*

lancīno -are, *to tear to pieces; to squander.*

lānĕus -a -um, *of wool, woollen; soft as wool.*

languĕfăcĭo -făcĕre, *to make weak or faint.*

languĕo -ēre, *to be faint, weak, weary; to droop, flag*; partic. **languens** -entis, *faint, languid.*

languesco languescĕre languŭi, *to become faint, soft* or *listless.*

languĭdŭlus -a -um, *somewhat faint, limp.*

languĭdus -a -um, *faint, weak, limp*; of wine, *mild, mellow*; adv. **languĭdē.**

languor -ōris, m. *faintness, weariness, inactivity.*

lănĭātus -ūs, m. *mangling, tearing.*

lănĭēna -ae, f. *a butcher's shop.*

lānĭfĭcus -a -um, *working in wool.*

lānĭger -gĕra -gĕrum, *wool-bearing; woollen*; m. as subst. *a ram*; f., *a sheep.*

lănĭo -are, *to tear to pieces, mangle, lacerate.*

lănista -ae, m. *a trainer of gladiators; an instigator to violence, inciter.*

lānĭtĭum -i, n. *wool.*

lănĭus -i, m. *butcher.*

lanterna -ae, f. *lantern, lamp.*

lanternārĭus -i, m. *lantern-bearer.*

lānūgo -inis, f. *down, of plants* or *on the cheeks.*

Lānŭvĭum -i, n. *a town in Latium.*

lanx lancis, f. *a plate, platter; the scale of a balance.*

Lāŏcŏōn -ontis, m. *a Trojan priest.*

Lāŏmĕdōn -ontis, m. *a king of Troy, father of Priam.*

lăpăthum -i, n. and **lăpăthus** -i, f. *sorrel.*

lăpĭcīdīnae -arum, f. *stone quarries.*

lăpĭdātĭo -ōnis, f. *throwing of stones.*

lăpĭdātor -ōris, m. *thrower of stones.*

lăpĭdĕus -a -um, *of stone.*

lăpĭdo -are, *to throw stones at*; impers. lapidat, *it rains stones.*

lăpĭdōsus -a -um, *full of stones, stony.*

lăpillus -i, m. *a little stone, pebble; a precious stone, gem.*

lăpis -ĭdis, m. *a stone.*

Lăpĭthae -arum, m. pl. *the Lapithae, a mountain race in Thessaly, famous for their fight with the Centaurs.*

lappa -ae, f. *a burr.*

lapsĭo -ōnis, f. *gliding; inclination, tendency.*

lapso -are, *to slip, stumble.*

lapsus -ūs, m. *gradual movement; gliding, sliding, fall; a fault, error.*

lăquĕārĕ -is, n., esp. plur., *a panelled ceiling.*

lăquĕātus -a -um, *with a panelled ceiling.*

lăquĕus -i, m. *a noose, halter, snare, trap.*

Lār Lăris, m., usually plur. **Lăres,** *Roman tutelary deities, esp. household*

deities; meton., *hearth, dwelling, home.*

lardum (lārĭdum) -i, n. *bacon fat, lard.*

Lārentĭa -ae, f., or **Acca Lārentĭa,** *the wife of Faustulus, who brought up Romulus and Remus.*

Lăres; see Lar.

largĭfĭcus -a -um, *bountiful, liberal.*

largĭflŭus -a -um, *flowing freely.*

largĭor -iri, dep. *to give abundantly, lavish, bestow, grant; to condone.*

largĭtās -ātis, f. *liberality.*

largītĭo -ōnis, f. *free giving* or *spending, lavishing; granting, bestowing.*

largītor -ōris, m. *a liberal giver* or *spender; a briber; a waster.*

largus -a -um, of things, *abundant, plentiful, numerous*; with genit., *rich in*; of persons, *liberal, bountiful.* Adv. **largē,** *plentifully, liberally*; **largĭtĕr,** *abundantly, much.*

lārĭdum -i, n. = lardum; q.v.

larva (lārŭa) -ae, f. *a ghost, spectre; a mask.*

lascīvĭa -ae, f. *playfulness, sportiveness; wantonness, licentiousness, insolence.*

lascīvĭo -ire, *to sport, play; to wanton, run riot.*

lascīvus -a -um, *playful, wanton, licentious, insolent.* Adv. **lascīvē.**

lāserpīcĭum -i, n. *a plant from which asafoetida was obtained.*

lassĭtūdo -ĭnis, f., *weariness, exhaustion.*

lasso -are, *to make weary, exhaust.*

lassŭlus -a -um, *rather tired.*

lassus -a -um, *weary, tired, exhausted.*

lătĕbra -ae, f. *a hiding-place, retreat; a subterfuge, loophole.*

lătĕbrōsus -a -um, *full of hiding-places, secret*; pumex, *porous.* Adv. **lătĕbrōsē,** *secretly.*

lătĕo -ēre, *to lie hid, be concealed; to live in obscurity* or *safety; to be unknown.* Hence partic. **lătens** -entis, *concealed, hidden*; adv. **lătentĕr,** *secretly.*

lăter -tĕris, m. *a brick, tile.*

lătĕrāmen -inis, n. *pottery.*

lătercŭlus -i m. *a small brick* or *tile; a biscuit.*

lătērīcĭus -a -um, *built of brick.*

lăterna; see lanterna.

lătesco -ĕre, *to hide oneself.*

lătex -tĭcis, m. *fluid, liquid.*

lătĭbŭlum -i, n., *a hiding-place.*

lātĭclāvĭus -a -um, *having a broad purple stripe* (as a distinction).

lātĭfundĭum -i, n. *a large landed estate.*

Lătīnĭtās -ātis, f. *pure Latin style; Latin rights.*

¹**Lātīnus** -a -um; see Latium.

²**Lătīnus** -i, m. *king of the Laurentians, host of Aeneas.*

lātĭo -ōnis, f. *bringing; legis, proposing, bringing forward.*

lătĭto -are, *to lie hid, be concealed.*

lātĭtūdo -ĭnis, f. *breadth, extent*; verborum, *broad pronunciation, brogue.*

Lătĭum -i, n. *a district of Italy, in which Rome was situated*; adj. **Lătĭus** and **Lătīnus** -a -um, *Latin*; adv. **Lătīnē,** *in Latin.*

Lātŏ -ūs, f. and Lātōna -ae, f. *the mother of Apollo and Diana.*

lātor -ōris, m. *the proposer of a law.*

lātrātor -ōris, m. *a barker.*

lātrātus -ūs, m. *barking.*

¹lātro -are, *to bark, bay; to rant, rumble, roar;* transit., *to bark at or for.*

²latro -ōnis, m. *a hired servant or mercenary soldier; a robber, bandit, brigand; a hunter; a piece on a draught-board.*

latrōcĭnĭum -i, n. *mercenary service; highway robbery, brigandage, villainy, roguery;* meton., *a band of robbers.*

latrōcĭnor -ari, dep. *to serve as a mercenary; to practise robbery.*

latruncŭlus -i, m. *a highwayman, bandit; a piece on a draught-board.*

¹lātus -a -um, partic. from fero; q.v.

²lātus -a -um, *broad, wide, extensive; of style, diffuse, full, rich.* Hence adv. **lātē,** *broadly, widely, extensively;* longe lateque, *far and wide.*

³lātus -ĕris, n. *the side, flank;* of persons, in pl., *the lungs;* milit., a latere, *on the flank.*

lātuscŭlum -i, n. *a little side.*

laudābĭlis -e, *praiseworthy, laudable;* adv. **laudābĭlĭtĕr.**

laudātĭo -ōnis, f. *praise, commendation; a testimonial; a funeral oration.*

laudātor -ōris, m. *a praiser;* esp. *one who delivers a testimonial or funeral oration.*

laudātrix -īcis, f. *a (female) praiser.*

laudo -are, *to praise, extol, commend; to name, mention, cite, quote;* partic. **laudātus -a -um,** *praiseworthy, esteemed.*

laurĕātus -a -um, *crowned with laurel;* litterae, *bringing news of victory.*

laurĕŏla -ae, f. *a laurel branch, laurel crown;* meton., *a triumph, victory.*

laurĕus -a -um, *of laurel;* f. as subst., **laurĕa,** *laurel tree or laurel crown.*

laurĭcŏmus -a -um, *covered with laurel-trees.*

laurĭfer -fĕra -fĕrum, and laurĭger -gĕra -gĕrum, *crowned with laurels.*

laurus -i, f. *the laurel or bay-tree;* meton., *triumph, victory.*

laus laudis, f. *praise, fame, glory, commendation.* Transf., *a praiseworthy action or quality.*

lautĭa -orum, n. pl., *entertainment given to foreign ambassadors at Rome.*

lautĭtĭa -ae, f. *splendour, elegance, sumptuous living.*

lautŭmĭae (lātŏmĭae) -arum, f. *a stone-quarry.*

lautus -a -um, partic. from lavo; q.v.

lăvabrum -i, n. *a bath.*

lăvātĭo -ōnis, f. *washing, bathing; bathing apparatus.*

Lāvīnĭa -ae, f. *daughter of Latinus, wife of Aeneas.*

lăvo lăvare or lăvĕre lăvi lautum or lōtum or lăvatum, *to wash, bathe; to moisten, wet; to wash away.*

Hence partic. **lautus -a -um,** *washed;* hence *fine, elegant, sumptuous, refined;* adv. **lautē.**

laxāmentum -i, n. *widening, extending; relaxing, mitigation, respite.*

laxĭtās -ātis, f. *wideness, roominess.*

laxo -are, *to widen, loosen, extend, enlarge; to undo, slacken, relax, relieve; to release, set free.*

laxus -a -um, *wide, loose, spacious;* of time, *later, postponed; loose, lax, relaxed.* Adv. **laxē,** *widely, loosely, without restraint.*

lĕa -ae, and lĕaena -ae, f. *a lioness.*

Lĕander -dri, m. *a youth who swam nightly across the Hellespont to visit Hero, till drowned in a storm.*

lĕbēs -ētis, m. *a bronze pan, cauldron, or basin.*

lectĭca -ae, f. *a litter; a bier.*

lectĭcārĭus -i, m. *litter-bearer.*

lectĭcŭla -ae, f. *a small litter or bier; a settee.*

lectĭo -ōnis, f. *a picking out, selection, reading, perusal;* lectio senatus, *a calling over of the names of the senators.*

lectisternĭum -i, n. *a feast offered to the gods.*

lectĭto -are, *to read often or eagerly.*

lector -ōris, m. *a reader.*

lectŭlus -i, m. *a small bed, couch.*

¹lectus -a -um, partic. from lego; q.v.

²lectus -i, m. *a bed, couch.*

Lēda -ae, and Lēdē -es, f. *mother of Castor, Pollux, Helen, and Clytemnestra.*

lēgātārĭus -i, m. *a legatee.*

lēgātĭo -ōnis, f. *delegated authority;* polit., *the office of an ambassador, an embassy, legation;* milit., *the post of subordinate commander;* esp. *the command of a legion.*

lēgātor -ōris, m. *testator.*

lēgātum -i, n. and lēgātus -i, m., from lego; q.v.

lēgĭfer -fĕra -fĕrum, *law-giving.*

lēgĭo -ōnis, f. *a choosing; a chosen body;* esp. *a legion, a division of the Roman army.*

lēgĭōnārĭus -a -um, *belonging to a legion.*

lēgĭtĭmus (lēgītŭmus) -a -um, *lawful, legitimate; right, proper, appropriate.* Adv. **lēgĭtĭmē,** *lawfully, properly.*

lēgĭuncŭla -ae, f. *a small legion.*

¹lēgo -are, *to ordain, appoint;* of persons, *to make a deputy, delegate authority to;* of property, *to bequeath, leave as a legacy.* M. of partic. as subst. **lēgātus -i,** *a deputy;* polit., *an ambassador, envoy, or the deputy of a magistrate;* milit., *a subordinate commander,* esp. *commander of a legion.* N. **lēgātum -i,** *a legacy, bequest.*

²lĕgo lĕgĕre lēgi lectum, *to collect, gather, pick, pick up;* fila, *to wind up, spin;* vela, *to furl;* of places, *to pass through, traverse, coast along; with the eyes, to survey, scan, read, peruse; out of a number, to pick out, choose, select.*

Hence partic. **lectus -a -um,** *chosen, selected; choice, excellent.*

lēgŭlēius -i, m. *a pettifogging lawyer.*

lĕgūmen -ĭnis, n. *pulse; the bean.*

Lĕmannus -i, m. *the Lake of Geneva.*

lembus -i, m. *a boat, cutter, pinnace.*

lemma -ătis, n. *theme, title; an epigram.*

lemniscātus -a -um, *ribboned.*

lemniscus -i, m. *a ribbon.*

Lemnos (-us) -i, f. *the island of Lemnos in the Aegean Sea;* adj. **Lemnĭus** -a -um, *Lemnian.*

lĕmŭrēs -um, m. pl. *ghosts, spectres;* **Lĕmūrĭa** -orum, n. pl. *a festival held in May to expel ghosts.*

lēna -ae, f. *a procuress, bawd.*

Lēnaeus -a -um, *Bacchic.*

lēnīmen -ĭnis, n. *means of alleviation.*

lēnīmentum -i, n. *mitigation, alleviation.*

lēnĭo -ire, *to make mild, mitigate, relieve.*

lēnis -e, *smooth, mild, gentle;* vīnum, *mellow;* n. acc. as adv. **lēnĕ**, *gently;* adv. **lēnĭtĕr** *smoothly, gently, mildly.*

lēnĭtās -ātis, f. and **lēnĭtūdo** -ĭnis, f. *gentleness, mildness, smoothness.*

lēno -ōnis, m. *a procurer, a go-between.*

lēnōcĭnĭum -i, n. *the trade of a procurer; enticement, allurement;* of dress, *finery;* of style, 'purple patch'.

lēnōcĭnor -ari, dep. *to work as a procurer; to make up to, to flatter; to advance, promote.*

lens lentis, f. *lentil.*

lentesco -ĕre, *to become pliant, soft, sticky; to weaken, slacken.*

lentiscus -i, f. and **lentiscum** -i, n. *the mastic-tree.*

lentĭtūdo ĭnis, f. *slowness, sluggishness, apathy.*

lento -are, *to bend.*

¹**lentŭlus** -a -um, *somewhat slow.*

²**Lentŭlus** -i, m. *the name of a family in the patrician gens Cornelia.*

lentus -a -um, *tough, resistant, inert; sticky, tenacious; supple, pliant; inactive, apathetic; slow, lingering;* in dicendo, *drawling.* Adv. **lentē**, *slowly, calmly, coolly, deliberately.*

¹**lēnuncŭlus** -i, m. *a little procurer.*

²**lēnuncŭlus** -i, m. *a small boat or skiff.*

lĕo -ōnis, m. *lion.*

lĕōnīnus -a -um, *of a lion, leonine.*

Lĕontīni -orum, m. *a town on the east coast of Sicily.*

lĕpăs -ădis, f. *a limpet.*

¹**lĕpĭdus** -a -um, *pleasant, charming, elegant, witty;* adv. **lĕpĭdē**.

²**Lĕpĭdus** -i, m. *name of a family in the patrician gens Aemilia.*

lĕpor and **lĕpos** -ōris, m. *pleasantness, charm, wit.*

lĕpus -ŏris, m. *hare.*

lĕpuscŭlus -i, m. *a young hare.*

Lesbos (-us) -i, f. *an island in the Aegean Sea, birth-place of Alcaeus and Sappho.*

lētālis -e, *deadly, mortal.*

lēthargĭcus -i, m. *a drowsy, lethargic person.*

lēthargus -i, m. *drowsiness, lethargy, coma.*

Lēthē -ēs, f. *the river of forgetfulness in the underworld.*

lētĭfer -fĕra -fĕrum, *deadly.*

lēto -are, *to kill, slay.*

lētum -i, n. *death; ruin, annihilation.*

leucaspis -ĭdis, f. *having white shields.*

lĕvāmen -ĭnis, n. and **lĕvāmentum** -i, n. *alleviation, mitigation, solace.*

lĕvātĭo -ōnis, f. *alleviation, mitigation; diminution.*

lĕvĭcŭlus -a -um, *rather vain, light-headed.*

lēvĭdensis -e, *thin, slight, poor.*

¹**lĕvis** -e, *light;* milit., *light-armed;* in movement, *rapid, swift;* in value, *light, trifling, unimportant;* in character, *fickle, capricious, unstable.* Adv. **lĕvĭtĕr**, *lightly, softly, slightly.*

²**lēvis** -e, *smooth, polished, slippery; beardless, bald.*

lĕvĭsomnus -a -um, *lightly sleeping.*

¹**lĕvĭtās** -ātis, f. *lightness; levity, fickleness, inconstancy; groundlessness.*

²**lēvĭtās** -ātis, f. *smoothness, polish.*

¹**lĕvo** -are, *to raise, lift up; to make light, relieve, ease; to diminish, weaken, impair.*

²**lēvo** -are, *to make smooth, polish.*

lēvor -ōris, m. *smoothness.*

lex lēgis, f. *a set form of words, contract, covenant, agreement;* leges pacis, *conditions of peace;* esp. *a law, proposed by a magistrate as a bill,* or *passed and statutory;* legem ferre, rogare, *to propose a bill;* legem iubere, *to accept* or *pass a bill;* in gen., *a precept, rule.*

lībāmen -ĭnis, n. *a libation, offering to the gods; a sample, specimen.*

lībāmentum -i, n. *a libation, offering to the gods.*

lībātĭo -ōnis, f. *a libation.*

lībella -ae, f. (1) *a small coin, a tenth of a* denarius; *a farthing, mite.* (2) *a carpenter's level, plummet-line.*

lībellus -i, m. *a little book, note-book, diary; a memorial, petition; programme, placard; letter.*

lībens and **lŭbens** -entis, partic. from libet; q.v.

¹**līber** -ĕra -ĕrum, *free, independent, unrestrained; free from, exempt.* Adv. **līberē**, *freely, without restraint, frankly, openly, boldly.*

²**lĭber** -bri, m. *the inner bark of a tree;* from the use of this in writing, *a book, volume, catalogue, letter.*

³**Līber** -ĕri, m. *an Italian deity, identified with Bacchus.*

lībĕrālis -e, *of freedom; worthy of a free man, gentlemanlike, courteous, generous;* adv. **lībĕrālĭtĕr**.

lībĕrālĭtās -ātis, f. *courtesy, kindness, generosity.* Transf. *a grant.*

lībĕrātĭo -ōnis, f. *setting free, release, acquittal.*

lībĕrātor -ōris, m. *a liberator.*

lībĕri -ērōrum and -ērum, m. pl. *children.*

lībĕro -are, *to set free, liberate, release, exempt;* of obstacles, *to lift, raise.*

līberta -ae, f.; see libertus.

lībertās -ātis, f. *freedom, liberty, independence; freedom of speech, frankness, candour.*

lībertīnus -a -um, *of the class of freedman*; as subst. m. **lībertīnus** *a freedman*, f. **lībertīna**, *a freedwoman*.

lībertus -i, m. *a freedman*; **līberta** -ae, f. *a freedwoman*.

lĭbet (lŭbet) -bēre -bŭit or -bĭtum est, impers., *it pleases, is agreeable* (with dat. of person).
  Hence partic. **lĭbens (lŭbens)** -entis, *willing, with pleasure, pleased*; **me libente**, *with my good-will*; adv. **lĭbenter (lŭbenter)**, *willingly, with pleasure*.

lĭbīdĭnōsus -a -um, *wilful,, arbitrary, capricious; passionate, lustful*. Adv. **lĭbīdĭnōsē**, *wilfully, arbitrarily*.

lĭbīdo (lŭbīdo) -ĭnis, f. *violent desire, longing*; esp. irrational *whim, caprice*; or immoderate *passion, lust*.

Lībītīna -ae, f. *goddess of the dead*.

lĭbo -are, *to take away from, remove, derive; to taste, touch, impair, diminish; to give a taste of, offer to the gods*.

lĭbra -ae, f. (1) *a balance, pair of scales*; **aes et libra**, *a fictitious form of sale*. (2) *the Roman pound of 12 oz*.

lĭbrāmentum -i, n. (1) *weight as a source of power* or *for balancing*. (2) *a horizontal plane*.

lĭbrāria -ae, f *a female who weighed out wool to slaves*.

lĭbrārĭus -a -um, *of books*; m. as subst., *a transcriber of books, a copyist*, or *a bookseller*; n. as subst., *a bookcase*.

lībrīlis -e, *of a pound weight*.

lībrītor -ōris, m. *an artilleryman*.

lībro -are, *to balance, hold up, poise*; of weapons, *to swing, level, brandish*; hence, *to hurl*.

lībum -i, n. *a cake, offered to the gods*.

Liburni -orum, m. *the Liburnians, a people of Illyria*; f. of adj. as subst. **Līburna** -ae, *a light vessel, galley*.

Libya -ae and **Libyē** -ēs, f. *Libya*.

līcens -centis, and **līcenter** from **licet**; q.v.

līcentĭa -ae, f. *freedom, leave, liberty; licentiousness*.

līcĕo -ēre -ŭi -ĭtum, *to be on sale, be valued at*.

līcĕor -ēri, dep. *to bid* or *bid for, offer a price*.

līcet **līcēre līcŭit** or **līcĭtum est**, impers., *it is allowed, one can* or *may*; as conjunction, *granted that, although*. Hence pres. partic. **līcens** -entis, *free, unrestrained, unbridled*; adv. **līcenter**; perf. partic. **līcĭtus** -a -um, *allowed, permitted*.

Līcĭnĭus -a -um, *name of a Roman gens*.

līcĭtātĭo -onis. f. *bidding at a sale* or *auction*.

līcĭtus -a -um, partic. from licet; q.v.

līcĭum -i, n.: in weaving, *the thrum* or perhaps *a leash*; in gen., *a thread*.

lictor -ōris, m. *a lictor, attending the chief Roman magistrates*.

lĭgāmen -ĭnis, n. *string tie, bandage*.

lĭgāmentum -i, n. *bandage*.

Lĭgēr -gĕris, m. *a river* (now the *Loire*).

lignārĭus -i, m. *a carpenter*.

lignātĭo -ōnis, f. *wood-cutting*.

lignātor -ōris, m. *wood-cutter*.

lignĕŏlus -a -um, *wooden*.

lignĕus -a -um, *made of wood, wooden*.

lignor -ari, dep. *to cut* or *get wood*.

lignum -i, n. *wood, timber*; esp. *firewood*.

¹lĭgo -are, *to bind, bandage, harness; to bind together, connect, unite*.

²lĭgo -ōnis, m. *a mattock*.

lĭgŭla (lingŭla) ae, f. *a tongue of land, promontory; a shoe-strap*.

Lĭgŭrēs -um, m. pl. *the Ligurians, a people on the north-west coast of Italy*.

lĭgŭrĭo (lĭgurrĭo) -ire, *to lick, lick up; to gloat over; long for*.

lĭgŭrītĭo (lĭgurr-) -ōnis, f. *daintiness*.

lĭgustrum -i, n. *privet*.

līlĭum -i, n. *a lily*; milit. *a fortification consisting of pits and stakes*.

Lĭlȳbaeon (-baeum) -i, n. *a promontory and town at the western end of Sicily*.

līma -ae, f. *a file; polishing, revision* of a composition.

līmātŭlus -a -um *rather polished, refined*.

limbus -i, m. *a border, hem, fringe*.

līmen -ĭnis, n. *threshold, doorway, entrance; home, house, dwelling; any entrance* or *border* or *beginning*; esp. *the starting-point in a race-course*.

līmes -ĭtis, m. *a by-way, path; a course, track*; esp. *a boundary-path, a boundary-line; a distinction, difference*.

līmo -are, *to file, polish, finish off; to investigate accurately; to file down, pare down, to diminish*. Partic. **līmātus** -a -um, *refined elegant*; compar. adv. **līmātĭus**.

līmōsus -a -um, *slimy, miry, muddy*.

limpĭdus -a -um, *clear, limpid*.

¹līmus -a -um, *of the eyes, sidelong, looking sideways*.

²līmus -i, m. *slime, mud, mire*.

³līmus -i, m. *a priest's apron*.

līnĕa -ae, f. *a linen thread, string; a fishing-line, plumb-line*; ad **lineam**, *perpendicularly*. Transf., *a geometrical line; a boundary-line, goal*.

līnĕāmentum -i, n. *a line drawn with pen* or *pencil*; plur., *drawing, sketch, outline*; in gen., *a feature, lineament*.

līnĕo -are, *to make straight*.

līnĕus -a -um, *of flax* or *linen*.

lingo **lingĕre linxi linctum**, *to lick*.

lingua -ae, f. *a tongue; speech, language: a tongue of land, promontory*.

lingŭlāca -ae, f. *a chatterbox*.

līnĭger -gĕra -gĕrum, *clothed in linen*.

līno **linĕre livi** and **lēvi lĭtum**, *to smear one thing upon another*; or *to besmear one thing with another*; *to rub out writing; to befoul, dirty*.

linquo **linquĕre liqui**, *to leave, abandon, forsake*; pass., **linqui**, *to faint*.

lintĕātus -a -um, *clothed in linen*.

lintĕo -ōnis, m. *a linen-weaver*.

linter -tris, f. *a boat, skiff; a trough, tub, vat*.

lintĕus -a -um, *of linen*; n. as subst. *linen cloth, linen*, esp. *a sail*.

līnum -i, n. *flax, linen; a thread, line;* a rope, cable.

lippĭo -ire, *to have sore eyes, be blear-eyed.*

lippĭtūdo -ĭnis, f. *inflammation of the eyes.*

lippus -a -um, *blear-eyed; half-blind.*

liquĕfăcĭo -făcĕre -fēci -factum, pass. **liquēfĭo** -fĭĕri -factus sum, *to melt, dissolve; to decompose; to make weak, enervate.*

liquesco -ĕre -lĭcŭi, *to become fluid, melt, melt away, to putrefy; to become effeminate.*

liquĭdus -a -um. (1) *fluid, flowing, liquid;* n. as subst. *a liquid.* (2) *clear, bright, serene, calm, pure, evident, certain;* n. as subst. *certainty;* abl. sing. **liquĭdō** and adv. **liquĭdē**, *clearly, plainly.*

liquo -are, *to make liquid, melt; to strain, clarify.*

¹**liquor** -i, dep. *to be fluid, flow, melt; to melt away;* partic. **liquens** -entis, *flowing.*

²**liquor** -ōris, m. *fluidity; a liquid, fluid.*

līs, lītis, f. *a legal controversy, action, suit; in gen., contention, strife, quarrel.*

lītātĭo -ōnis, f. *successful sacrifice.*

lītĭgātor -ōris, m. *a party in a law-suit, litigant.*

lītĭgĭōsus -a -um, *of persons, fond of dispute, litigious; of things, full of dispute, contested at law.*

lītĭgo -are, *to go to law; in gen., to quarrel, dispute.*

līto -are: intransit., *to bring an acceptable offering,* and so *to obtain favourable omens;* transit., *to sacrifice successfully.*

lītōrālis -e, and **lītŏrĕus** -a -um *of the shore.*

littĕra (**lītĕra**) ae, f. *a letter of the alphabet; a letter, dispatch, epistle;* plur., *written records, documents, deeds; literature, letters, scholarship.*

littĕrārĭus -a -um, *of reading and writing.*

littĕrātor -ōris, m. *a philologist, grammarian, critic.*

littĕrātūra -ae, f. *the alphabet, grammar.*

littĕrātus -a -um, *lettered, inscribed with letters; learned, liberally educated.* Adv. **littĕrātē**, *in clear letters, legibly; literally, word for word; learnedly.*

littĕrŭla -ae, f. *a letter (of the alphabet) written small;* plur., *a little letter, a note, a smattering of literature.*

littus, etc.; see litus, etc.

lĭtūra -ae, f. *an erasure, correction; a passage erased; a blot.*

lītus -ōris, n. *sea-shore, beach, strand, coast; the shore of a lake or river.*

lĭtŭus -i, m. *an augur's curved staff; a curved cavalry trumpet, clarion.*

līvĕo -ēre, *to be bluish in colour; to be envious, envy;* partic. **līvens** -entis, *bluish, livid; envious.*

līvesco -ĕre, *to become bluish.*

līvĭdŭlus -a -um, *rather envious.*

līvĭdus -a -um, *bluish, livid, black and blue; envious, spiteful.*

Līvĭus -a -um, *name of a Roman gens.*

līvor -ōris, m. *bluish colour, a livid spot; envy, spite.*

lixa -ae, m. *a sutler, camp-follower.*

lŏcātĭo -ōnis, f. *placing; hence a leasing, contract, lease.*

lŏcātōrĭus -a -um, *concerned with leases.*

lŏco -are, *to place, put, set; esp. to give in marriage; commerc., to let out on hire, farm out, lease, invest; to contract for work to be done.* N. of partic. as subst. **lŏcātum** -i, *a lease, contract.*

lŏcŭlus -i, m. *a little place;* plur., loculi, *a money-box; a school satchel.*

lŏcŭplēs -plētis, *with landed property, wealthy, rich;* also *trusty, sufficient, satisfactory.*

lŏcŭplēto -are, *to enrich.*

lŏcus -i, m. (plur., loci, *single places;* loca, *region*), *a place;* milit., *position, ground, post; in time, a period, or moment; position, situation, rank; occasion, cause; passage in a book.*

¹**lŏcusta** -ae, f. *a locust; a kind of lobster.*

²**Lŏcusta** -ae, f. *a notorious poisoner, accomplice of Nero.*

lŏcūtĭo -ōnis, f. *speech; pronunciation.*

lōdix -dĭcis, f. *blanket, rug.*

lŏgĭcus -a -um, *logical;* n. pl. as subst. *logic.*

lŏgōs (-us) -i, m. *a word; a joke, jest, bon mot.*

lōlĭum -i, n. *darnel.*

lollĭgo -īgĭnis, f. *cuttle-fish.*

lōmentum -i, n. *face-cream.*

Londĭnĭum -i, n. *London.*

longaevus -a -um, *aged, old.*

longinquĭtās -ātis, f. *length, distance, remoteness; of time, duration.*

longinquus -a -um, *long, distant, far, remote, foreign; of time, long, distant.*

longĭtūdo -ĭnis, f. *length.*

longŭlus -a -um, *rather long;* adv. **longŭlē**, *rather far, at a little distance.*

longŭrĭus -i, m. *a pole, rod, rail.*

longus -a -um, *long;* navis, *a man-of-war;* poet., *spacious; of time, long, of long duration:* esp. *too long, tedious; of persons, prolix, tedious.* Adv. **longē**, *a long way off, far, at a distance; by far; in time, long, at length;* adv. **longĭter**, *far.*

lŏquācĭtās -ātis, f. *talkativeness.*

lŏquācŭlus -a -um, *rather talkative.*

lŏquax -quācis, *talkative, garrulous; babbling, noisy;* adv. **lŏquācĭter**.

lŏquella (**lŏquēla**) -ae, f. *speech, language.*

lŏquor lŏqui lŏcūtus, dep. *to speak (in conversation); to tell, say, talk of.*

lōrātus -a -um, *bound with thongs.*

lōrīca -ae, f. *cuirass, corselet, breast-plate; breastwork, parapet.*

lōrīcātus -a -um, *wearing a cuirass.*

lōrĭpēs -pĕdis, *bandy-legged.*

lōrum -i, n. *a strap or thong of leather;* plur., *reins, bridle; scourge, whip.*

lōtŏs (-us) -i, f. *the name of several plants; esp. of an African tree and its fruit.*

¹lōtus -a -um, partic. from lavo; q.v.

²lōtus -i, f. = lotos; q.v.

lŭbet, lŭbīdo, etc. = libet, libido, etc.; q.v.

lūbrĭco -are, *to make slippery.*

lūbrĭcus -a -um, *slippery, smooth; quickly moving, uncertain, insecure, perilous, deceitful.*

Lūcāni -orum, m. pl. *a people in Southern Italy.*

Lūcānus -i, m., M. Annaeus, *author of the poem Pharsalia.*

lūcar -āris, n. *a forest-tax, used for paying actors.*

lŭcellum -i, n. *little profit, small gain.*

lūcĕo lūcēre luxi, *to be bright, shine, glitter; to be clear, evident;* impers., *lucet, it is light, it is day.*

Lŭcĕrēs -um; m. *one of the three patrician tribes.*

lūcerna -ae, f. *lamp.*

lūcesco (lūcisco) lūcescĕre luxi, *to begin to shine;* impers., lucescit, *it grows light, day is breaking.*

lūcĭdus -a -um, *shining, bright; clear, lucid;* adv. **lūcĭdē.**

lūcĭfer -fĕra -fĕrum, *light-bearing, light-bringing;* m. as subst., *the morning star.*

lūcĭfŭgus -a -um, *shunning the light.*

Lūcīlius -a -um, *name of a Roman gens.*

Lūcīna -ae, f. *the goddess of births.*

lūcisco = lucesco; q.v.

Lūcius -i, m. *Roman praenomen (abbreviated to L.).*

Lucrētīus -a -um, *name of a Roman gens.*

lucrĭfăcĭo -făcĕre *to gain, receive as profit.*

Lucrīnus -i, m. *a lake on the coast of Campania, near Baiae, famous for oysters.*

lucror -ari, dep. *to gain, profit, win.*

lucrōsus -a -um, *gainful, profitable.*

lucrum -i, n. *gain, profit, advantage; love of gain, avarice.*

luctāmen -ĭnis, n. *effort, toil.*

luctātĭo -ōnis, f. *wrestling; a struggle contest.*

luctātor -ōris, m. *wrestler.*

luctĭfĭcus -a -um, *causing grief, baleful.*

luctĭsŏnus -a -um, *sad-sounding.*

luctor -ari, dep (and lucto -are), *to wrestle, struggle, strive, contend.*

luctŭōsus -a -um, (1) *causing sorrow, doleful.* (2) *feeling or showing sorrow, mourning.* Compar. adv. **luctŭōsĭus.**

luctus -ūs, m. *sorrow expressed, lamentation, mourning; mourning clothes.*

lūcubrātĭo -ōnis, f. *work done by night or lamp-light, nocturnal study.*

lūcubro -are, *to work by night;* in perf. partic. **lūcubrātus** -a -um, *done at night or spent in work.*

lūcŭlentus -a -um, *shining, bright, brilliant, splendid;* adv. **lūcŭlentē** and **lūcŭlentēr**, *splendidly.*

Lūcullus -i, m. *name of a family in the gens Licinia.*

Lūcŭmo (Lūcŏmo, Lucmo) -ōnis, m. *title given to Etruscan princes and priests.*

lūcus -i, m. *a (sacred) grove or wood.*

lūdĭa -ae, f. *an actress or female gladiator.*

lūdĭbrĭum -i, n. *derision, mockery; an object of derision, laughing-stock, plaything.*

lūdĭbundus -a -um, *playful, sportive.*

lūdĭcer -cra -crum, *sportive, done for sport; esp. of the stage.* N. as subst. **lūdicrum** -i, *a trifle, plaything; a theatrical performance.*

lūdĭfĭcātĭo -onis, f. *deriding, deceiving.*

lūdĭfĭco -are and **lūdĭfĭcor** -ari, dep. *to make game of, deride, delude, cheat, frustrate.*

lūdĭo -ōnis, m. and **lūdĭus** -i, m. *an actor.*

lūdo lūdĕre lūsi lūsum, *to play, sport; to play at or with; to imitate, banter, deceive, delude.*

lūdus -i, m. *play, game, sport, pastime;* plur., ludi, *public games or spectacles.* Transf., *a trifle, jest, joke;* ludum dare, *to give free play to; a training establishment, school.*

lŭella -ae, f. *expiation.*

lŭēs -is, f. *plague, pestilence, calamity.*

Lugdūnum -i, n. *a city in Gaul (now Lyons).* Adj. **Lugdūnensis** -e.

lūgĕo lūgēre luxi: intransit., *to mourn, be in mourning;* transit., *to bewail, lament, wear mourning for.*

lūgubris -e, *of mourning, mournful; plaintive; grievous.* N. pl. as subst. *mourning clothes.*

lumbus -i, m. *loin.*

lūmen -ĭnis, n. *light; a light, lamp; the light of day, day; the light of life; the light of the eye, the eye; an opening, a light in a building;* fig., *clearness, insight; a shining light, glory, ornament.*

lūmĭnārĕ -āris, n. *a window-shutter window.*

lūmĭnōsus -a -um, *bright.*

lūna -ae, f. *the moon; night, a month; a crescent-shaped ornament.*

lūnāris -e, *of the moon, lunar.*

lūno -are, *to bend into a crescent;* perf. partic. **lūnātus** -a -um, *crescent-shaped.*

lŭo lŭĕre lŭi lŭĭtūrus, *to loose; to expiate, atone for, make good;* luere poenam, *to pay a penalty; of trouble, to avert.*

lŭpa -ae, f. *a she-wolf; a prostitute.*

lŭpātus -a -um, *provided with iron spikes;* m. or n. pl. as subst., *a curb with jagged spikes.*

Lŭpercus -i, m. *an Italian pastoral deity, or one of his priests;* subst. **Lŭpercal** -cālis, n. *a grotto, sacred to Lupercus;* **Lŭpercālĭa** -ĭum and -iorum, n. pl., *the festival of Lupercus, celebrated in February.*

¹lŭpīnus -a -um, *of a wolf, wolfish.*

²lŭpīnus -i, m. and **lŭpīnum** -i, n., *the lupin.*

lŭpus -i, m. *a wolf; a voracious fish,*

the pike; a horse's bit with jagged
points; a hook.
lūridus -a -um, *pale yellow, lurid,
ghastly.*
lūror -ōris, m. *ghastliness, paleness.*
luscinia -ae, f. *nightingale.*
lusciōsus and **luscitiōsus** -a -um,
purblind, dim-sighted.
luscus -a -um, *one-eyed.*
lūsio -ōnis, f. *play, game.*
Lūsitānia -ae, f. *the modern Portugal,
with part of Spain.*
lūsor -ōris, m. *a player; a playful
writer; a mocker.*
lustrālis -e, *relating to expiation or
to a period of five years.*
lustrātio -ōnis, f. *purification by sacrifice; a going round, traversing.*
¹lustro -are, *to brighten, illumine.*
²lustro -are, *to purify, cleanse by sacrifices; to go round, go over, traverse;
to review, observe, examine.*
¹lustrum -i, n., usually plur., *the den
of a wild beast, woodlands; brothels,
debauchery.*
²lustrum -i, n. *an expiatory sacrifice;
a period of five years.*
lūsus -ūs, m. *playing, game, sport;
dalliance.*
lūteŏlus -a -um, *yellow.*
Lūtētia -ae, f. *a town in Gallia (now
Paris).*
¹lūteus -a -um, *saffron-yellow.*
²lūteus -a -um, *of mud or clay; dirty.*
lŭto -are, *to smear with mud.*
lŭtŭlentus -a -um, *muddy, dirty,
filthy, impure.*
¹lŭtum -i, n. *a plant used for dyeing
yellow; yellow colour.*
²lŭtum -i, n. *mud, mire, dirt; clay.*
lux, **lūcis**, f. *light; esp. daylight, day;
a day; the light of life or of day;
the eye, eyesight; illustration, eluci-
dation; hope, encouragement; ornament.*
luxŭria -ae and **luxŭries** -ei, f. *rank-
ness, exuberant growth; excess, dissipation, extravagance.*
luxŭrio -are and **luxŭrior** -ari, dep.,
*to be luxuriant, rank, grow fast; to
frisk, sport, run riot.*
luxŭriōsus -a -um, *luxuriant, rank;
immoderate, excessive; luxurious, dissolute, extravagant.* Adv. **luxŭriōsē,**
luxuriously.
luxus -ūs, m. *luxury, excess, extravagance.*
Lȳaeus -i, m. *surname of Bacchus;
wine.*
lychnūchus -i, m. *lamp-stand, candelabrum.*
lychnus -i, m. *lamp.*
Lȳcia -ae, f. *a country of Asia Minor.*
Lȳdia -ae, f. *a country of Asia Minor;*
ad. **Lȳdius** and **Lȳdus** -a -um,
Lydian.
lympha -ae, f. *water, esp. clear spring
or river water.*
lymphāticus and **lymphātus** -a -um,
raving, mad, frantic.
lynx -cis, c. *lynx.*
lȳra -ae, f. *the lyre or lute, a stringed
instrument; lyric poetry, song.*
lȳricus -a -um, *of the lyre, lyric.*

M

M, m. the twelfth letter of the Latin
Alphabet.
Măcĕdō (-ōn) -ŏnis, m. *a Macedonian;*
subst. **Măcĕdŏnia** -ae, f.; adj.
Măcĕdŏnicus, Măcĕdŏnius -a -um.
măcellum, -i, n. *a provision-market.*
măcer -cra -crum, *lean; thin, poor.*
măcĕria -ae, f. *a wall,* esp. *garden-wall.*
măcĕro -are, *to soften; to make weak,
reduce; to torment, tease, vex.*
măchaera -ae, f. *a sword.*
măchina -ae, f. *a machine, contrivance;
a crane, windlass, catapult, ballista.*
Transf., *fabric; a device, trick,
stratagem.*
măchināmentum -i, n. *machine,
instrument.*
măchinātio -ōnis, f. *contrivance,
machinery, mechanism; device, mach-
ination.*
măchinātor -ōris, m. *a maker of
machines, engineer; a deviser, contriver.*
măchinor -ari, dep. *to contrive, invent,
devise.*
măciēs -ēi, f. *leanness, thinness,
poverty, barrenness.*
macresco -ĕre, *to grow lean, become
thin.*
macrŏcollum -i, n. *paper of the
largest size.*
mactābilis -e, *deadly.*
mactātū, abl. sing. m. *by a sacrificial
stroke.*
macte; see **¹mactus.**
¹macto -are, *to magnify, honour,
glorify.*
²macto -are, *to slay, smite; to afflict,
punish.*
¹mactus -a -um, *glorified, honoured;
used only in voc. m.* **mactĕ,** *well
done! bravo! good luck!*
²mactus -a -um, *smitten.*
măcŭla -ae, f. *a spot, mark, stain;
sometimes the mesh of a net; a moral
stain, blemish, fault.*
măcŭlo -are, *to spot, stain, defile,
pollute.*
măcŭlōsus -a -um, *spotted, speckled,
stained, polluted.*
mădēfăcio -făcĕre -fēci -factum, and
pass. **mădēfīo** -fīĕri, *to mak wet,
moisten, soak.*
mădĕo -ēre, *to be wet, to stream; to
be drunk; to be boiled.* Transf., *to
be steeped in, abound in.*
mădesco mădescĕre mădŭi, *to become
wet.*
mădidus -a -um, *moist, wet; drunk;
boiled soft; dyed, steeped.* Adv.
mădidē, *drunkenly.*
mădor -ōris, m. *moisture, wetness.*
Maeandĕr and **Maeandrŏs (-us)** -dri,
m. *a river of Asia Minor, proverbial
for its winding course; a winding.*
Maecēnās -ātis, m. *C. Cilnius, the
patron of Horace and Vergil.*
maena (mēna) -ae, f. *a small sea-fish.*
Maenăs -ādis, f. *a bacchante; a
prophetess.*
maerĕo -ēre: intransit., *to grieve,*

mourn, lament; transit., *to lament, bewail.*

maeror -ōris, m. *mourning, grief, sorrow.*

maestitia -ae, f. *sadness, dejection, gloom.*

maestus -a -um, *sad, dejected, gloomy*; adv. **maestitĕr.**

măgālia -ium, n. pl. *huts.*

măgĕ; see magis.

măgĭcus -a -um, *magical.*

măgĭs (or **măgĕ**), *more, to a greater extent; rather, for preference*; non magis . . . quam, *not more . . . than, just as much . . . as*; quo magis . . . eo magis, *the more . . . the more.* Superl. **maximē (maxŭmē)**, *in the highest degree, most of all, especially, very much so*; quam maxime, *as much as possible*; with tum, cum, *just, precisely.*

măgister -tri, m. *master, chief, head, director*; populi, *dictator*; equitum, *master of the horse, the dictator's lieutenant*; magister (ludi), *a schoolmaster, teacher*; societatis, *director of a company*; elephanti, *driver*; navis, *master* or *helmsman.* Transf., *instigator, adviser, guide.*

măgisterium -i, n. *directorship, magistracy; direction, guidance.*

măgistra -ae, f. *a mistress, directress.*

măgistrātus -ūs, m. *a magistracy, official dignity, office.* Transf., *a magistrate, state official.*

magnănĭmĭtās -ātis, f. *greatness of soul, magnanimity.*

magnănĭmus -a -um, *high-minded, magnanimous.*

magnĭficentĭa -ae, f. *loftiness of thought and action; grandeur, magnificence, splendour*; in bad sense, *boasting, pomposity.*

magnĭfĭco -are, *to prize highly, esteem.*

magnĭfĭcus -a -um; compar. **magnĭficentĭor**; superl. **magnĭficentissĭmus**; *grand, splendid, fine*; in bad sense, *boastful, pompous.* Adv. **magnĭficē.**

magnĭlŏquentĭa -ae, f. *lofty* or *elevated language; pompous, boastful language.*

magnĭlŏquus -a -um, *lofty* or *elevated in language; pompous* or *boastful.*

magnĭtūdŏ -ĭnis, f. *greatness*; animi, *magnanimity.*

magnŏpĕrĕ and separately **magnō ŏpĕrĕ**, *greatly, very much.*

magnus -a -um; compar. **māior, maius**; superl. **maxĭmus (maxŭmus)** -a -um; *great, large*; of sound, *loud*; of price or value, *high*; magno, and magni, *at a high price, dear, highly.* Transf., of time, *long, old*; of standing, *great, mighty, powerful, important*; m. pl. of compar. as subst. **māiōres**, *ancestors*; in maius, *to a higher degree*; magnō ŏpĕrĕ, see magnopere; for **maximē**, see magis.

Māgo (-ōn) -ōnis, m. *brother of Hannibal.*

¹măgus -i, m. *a learned Persian; a magician.*

²măgus -a -um, *magical.*

Māia -ae, f. *the daughter of Atlas, mother of Mercury*, adj. **Māius** -a -um, *of Maia*: (mensis) Maius, *the month of May.*

māiestās -ātis, f. *greatness, grandeur, dignity, majesty*; crimen maiestatis, *treason.*

māior, māiōres; see magnus.

Māius -a -um, adj. from Maia; q.v.

māiusculus -a -um, *somewhat greater* or *older.*

māla -ae, f. *cheek-bone, jaw-bone; jaw, cheek.*

mălăcĭa -ae, f. *a calm at sea.*

mălăcus -a -um, *soft, pliable; effeminate, delicate.*

mălĕdĭco -dicĕre -dixi -dictum (sometimes separately, male dico), *to speak ill, abuse*; pres. partic., **mălĕdĭcens** -entis, *abusive*; n. of perf. partic. as subst. **mălĕdĭctum** -i, *cursing, abusive language.*

mălĕdĭctĭo -ōnis, f. *reviling, abuse.*

mălĕdĭcus -a -um, *abusive, scurrilous*; adv. **mălĕdĭcē.**

mălĕfăcĭo -făcĕre -fēci -factum (sometimes separately, male facio), *to injure*; n. of perf. partic. as subst. **mălĕfactum** -i, *an ill deed, injury.*

mălĕfactor -ōris, m. *an evil-doer.*

mălĕfĭcĭum -i, n. *wrongdoing; mischief.*

mălĕfĭcus -a -um, *evil-doing, mischievous*; adv. **mălĕfĭcē.**

mălĕsuādus -a -um, *ill-advising, seductive.*

mălĕvŏlens -entis, *spiteful, ill-disposed.*

mălĕvŏlentĭa -ae, f. *ill-will, spite, malice.*

mălĕvŏlus -a -um, *ill-disposed, spiteful, malicious.*

mālĭfer -fĕra -fĕrum, *apple-bearing.*

mălignĭtās -ātis, f. *ill-nature, malignity, spite; stinginess.*

mălignus -a -um, *ill-disposed, wicked*; esp. *stingy, niggardly; barren, unfruitful; stinted, scanty.* Adv. **mălignē.**

mălĭtĭa -ae, f. *badness, wickedness, vice*; esp. *craft, cunning, malice.*

mălĭtĭōsus -a -um, *wicked; crafty, roguish, knavish*; adv. **mălĭtĭōsē.**

mallĕŏlus -i, m. *a little hammer; a kind of fire-dart.*

mallĕus -i, m. *a hammer, mallet, pole-axe.*

mālo malle mālŭi, *to wish rather, prefer*; with dative of person, *to be more favourable to.*

mālŏbathrum -i, n. *a plant, from which ointment was prepared.*

¹mālum -i, n.; see ¹malus.

²mālum -i, n. *an apple*, or other similar fruit.

¹mălus -a -um; comp. **pēior** -us; superl. **pessĭmus** -a -um; *bad, evil* (physically or morally); *unfavourable, unsuccessful, ugly.* N. as subst. **mălum** -i, *an evil; harm, disaster; punishment; as a term of abuse, scoundrel.* Adv. **mălĕ**, compar. **pēius**; superl. **pessĭmē**, *badly, ill; male audire, to be ill spoken of; unsuccessfully, unfortunately; with* words bad in sense, *bitterly, excessively*; with words of favourable sense, with negative force, e.g., male gratus, *unthankful.*

²**mālus** -i, f. *an apple-tree.*

³**mālus** -i, m. *the mast of a ship; an upright, pole.*

malva -ae, f. *the mallow.*

Māmers -mertis, m. *the Oscan name of Mars*; hence **Māmertīni** -orum, m. *the name assumed by certain mercenary troops.*

māmilla -ae, f. *breast, teat.*

mamma -ae, f. *breast.*

mānābilis -e, *flowing, penetrating.*

manceps -cīpis, m. *a purchaser, farmer, contractor.*

mancīpium (mancŭpium) -i, n. *a formal purchase of anything.* Transf., *a slave acquired by* mancipium.

mancīpo (mancŭpo) -are, *to sell formally; to give up.*

mancus -a -um, *maimed, crippled, imperfect, defective.*

mandātū abl. sing. m. *by order.*

mandātum -i, n. subst. from mando; q.v.

¹**mando** -are, *to commit, entrust*; of actions, *to order, command, commission.* N. of partic. as subst., **mandātum** -i, *a commission charge, order.*

²**mando** mandĕre mandi mansum, *to chew, masticate, champ; to eat, consume.*

mandra -ae, f. *a stall, cattle-pen; a herd of cattle; a draughtboard.*

mānĕ, indecl. n.: as subst., *morning*; adv., *in the morning, early.*

mānĕo mānēre mansi mansum: intransit., *to remain, stay; to stay the night; to endure, last; promissis, to abide by*; transit., in gen., *to wait for, await.*

mānēs -ium, m. pl. *the shades of the departed, spirits of the dead*; poet., *the lower world, infernal regions; corpse, ashes, remains.*

mango -ōnis, m. *a salesman* esp., *slave dealer.*

mānīca -ae, f. *a sleeve, serving as a glove; handcuffs, manacles.*

mānīcātus -a -um, *having long sleeves.*

mānīcŭla -ae, f. *a little hand.*

mānifesto -are, *to show clearly, reveal.*

mānifestus -a -um, *palpable, clear, visible, evident; caught out, detected.* Abl. sing. n. as adv. **mānifestō**, *clearly*; compar. **mānifestĭus.**

Mānilius -a -um, *name of a Roman gens.*

mānīpŭlāris (mānĭplāris) *belonging to a maniple*; m. as subst. *a private soldier; a fellow-soldier.*

mānīpŭlātim, *in bundles; in maniples.*

mānĭpŭlus (poet, mānĭplus) -i, m. *a handful, bundle*; milit. *a company of infantry, a division of the Roman army.*

Manlius -a -um, *name of a Roman gens.*

mannŭlus -i, m. *a pony.*

mannus -i, m. *a pony, cob.*

māno -are, *to flow, drip, spread*; with abl., *to drip with*; with acc., *to exude.*

mansĭo -ōnis, f. *stay, sojourn; station, stage.*

mansĭto -are, *to abide, stay.*

mansuēfācĭo -fācĕre -fēci -factum, pass. **mansuēfĭo** -fĭēri -factus sum, *to tame; to soften, pacify, civilize.*

mansuēs -is or -ētis, *tame.*

mansuesco -suescĕre -suēvi -suētum: transit., *to tame*; intransit., *to grow tame or soft.*

Hence partic. **mansuētus** -a -um, *tame, mild, soft*; adv. **mansuētē.**

mansuētūdo -inis, f. *tameness: mildness, gentleness.*

mantēlē -is, n. *towel, napkin.*

mantēlum -i, n. *covering, cloak.*

mantĭca -ae, f. *wallet, knapsack.*

manto -are, *to remain, wait, wait for.*

Mantŭa -ae, f. *a town in north Italy.*

mănŭālis -e, *fitted to the hand.*

mănŭbĭae -arum, f. *money from the sale of booty*, esp. *the general's share; spoils, profits.*

mănubrium -i, n. *haft, handle.*

mănŭf-; see manif-.

mănŭlĕus -i, m. and **mănŭlĕa** -ae, f. *a long sleeve.*

mănŭmissĭo -ōnis, f. *the emancipation of a slave.*

mănŭmitto -mittĕre -mīsi -missum (or as two - words, manu mitto), *to manumit, emancipate a slave.*

mănuprĕtium (mănĭpr-) -i, n. *wages, hire, reward.*

mănus -ūs, f. *hand*; manus dare, *to surrender*; in manibus, *on hand, in preparation*; servus ad manum, *a secretary*; abl. manu, *by hand, artificially.* Transf., *the strong arm, fist, force, effort; power, jurisdiction; the hand or touch of artist or craftsman; a band or body of men; an elephant's trunk*; manus ferrea, *grappling-iron.*

māpālĭa -ium, n. *huts, hovels.*

mappa -ae, f. *a table-napkin.*

Marcellus -i, m. *the cognomen of a family of the gens* Claudia.

marcĕo -ēre, *to wither, droop, be feeble.*

marcesco -ĕre, *to begin to droop, grow feeble.*

marcĭdus -a -um, *withering, drooping, enfeebled.*

marcor -ōris, m. *rottenness, decay.*

marcŭlus -i, m. *a small hammer.*

Marcus -i, *a Roman praenomen*, abbreviated M.

măre -is, n. *the sea*; mare nostrum, *the Mediterranean*; superum, *the Adriatic*; inferum, *the Tyrrhenian Sea.*

margărīta -ae f. and **margărītum** -i n. *a pearl.*

margĭno -are, *to border.*

margo -ĭnis, m. and f. *a border, edge, boundary.*

mărīnus -a -um, *of the sea, marine*; ros, *rosemary.*

mărītālis -e, *conjugal, matrimonial.*

mărītĭmus (mărītŭmus) -a -um, *of*

or *on the sea*, *marine*; praedo, *a pirate*; n. pl. as subst. *the sea-coast.*

mărīto -are, *to marry, give in marriage*; of vines, *to bind to a tree, to train.*

mărītus -a -um, *matrimonial, nuptial*; of plants, *tied or trained together*; As subst. **mărītus** -i, m. *husband, lover, suitor*; **mărīta** -ae, f. *wife.*

Mārlus -a -um, *the name of a Roman gens.*

marmor -ŏris, n. *marble statue; stone; the white foamy surface of the sea.*

marmŏrĕus -a -um, *of marble, like marble.*

Mǎro -ōnis, m. *the cognomen of the poet P. Vergilius.*

marra -ae, f. *a hoe.*

Mars Martis, m. (old form, Māvors), *Mars, god of agriculture and of war.* Transf., *war, battle, fight.* Adj. **Martius** and poet. **Māvortius** -a -um, *of Mars*; Martius (mensis), *the month of March; warlike.* Adj. **Martiālis** -e, *of Mars*; m. as subst. *a priest of Mars or soldier of the Legio Martia.*

Marsi -ōrum, m. *an ancient people of Latium*; adj. **Marsīcus** and **Marsus** -a -um; Marsicum bellum, *the Social War.*

marsuppĭum -i, n. *purse, pouch.*

¹**Martiālis** -e, adj. from Mars; q.v.

²**Martiālis** -is, m. M. Valerius, *Martial, the writer of epigrams.*

Martigĕna -ae, m. *offspring of Mars.*

Martius -a -um, adj. from Mars; q.v.

mas măris, m. *the male; manly, vigorous.*

mascŭlus -a -um, *male; manly, bold.*

Māsinissa -ae, m. *king of Numidia.*

massa -ae, f. *a lump, mass.*

massĭcum -i, n. *Massic wine.*

Massilia -ae, f. *a town in Gallia Narbonensis* (now *Marseilles*); adj. **Massiliensis** -e.

mastigia -ae, m. *a scoundrel.*

mastrūca -ae, f. *a sheepskin.*

matăra -ae, and **matăris** -is, f. *a pike, lance.*

mătellio -ōnis, m. *a small pot, vessel.*

māter, mātris, f. *mother; source, origin.*

mātercŭla -ae, f. *little mother.*

mātĕria -ae, and **mātĕriēs** -ēi, f. *matter, material, stuff; timber.* Transf., *subject-matter; occasion, cause; natural disposition.*

mātĕrio -are, *to construct of wood.*

mātĕrior -ari, dep. *to fell wood.*

mātĕris = matara; q.v.

māternus -a -um, *of a mother, maternal.*

mātertĕra -ae, f. *maternal aunt.*

māthēmătĭcus -a -um, *mathematical*; m. as subst. *a mathematician or astrologer*; f. **māthēmătĭca** -ae, *mathematics or astrology.*

mātrĭcīda -ae, c. *a matricide.*

mātrĭcīdĭum -i, n. *slaying of a mother, matricide.*

mātrĭmōnĭum -i, n. *marriage.*

mātrimus -a -um, *having a mother still living.*

¹**mātrōna** -ae, f. *a married woman, matron.*

²**Mātrŏna** -ae, m. *a river in Gaul* (now the *Marne*).

mātrōnālis -e, *of a married woman, matronly*; n. pl. as subst. **Mātrōnālĭa** -ium, *a festival held by Roman matrons.*

matta -ae, f. *a mat of rushes.*

mattĕa (**mattўa**) -ae, f. *a dainty dish.*

mātūresco mātūrescĕre mātūrŭi, *to ripen, become ripe.*

mātūrĭtās -ātis, f. *ripeness, maturity; the right moment, fullness of time.*

mātūro -are: transit., *to make ripe, ripen; to quicken, hasten, accelerate; to anticipate, do too soon*; intransit., *to hasten, make haste.*

mātūrus -a -um, *ripe, mature, grown up, developed, perfect; timely, quick, speedy, early.* Adv. **mātūrē** *at the right time, seasonably, opportunely: in good time, betimes; early; too soon, prematurely.*

mātūtīnus -a -um, *early in the morning, of morning.*

Mauri -orum, m. *the Moors*; adj. **Maurus** -a -um; subst. **Mauritānĭa** -ae, f. *Mauritania.*

māvŏlo = malo; q.v.

Māvors -vortis, m. archaic and poet. for Mars; adj. **Māvortius** -a -um.

maxilla -ae, f. *jaw-bone, jaw.*

maximĭtās -ātis, f. *greatness, size.*

maximus, superl. of magnus; q.v.

māzŏnŏmus -i, m. or **māzŏnŏmon** -i, n. *a charger, large dish.*

mĕātus -ūs, m. *a going, motion; a way, path.*

Mēcastor; see Castor.

meddix -īcis, m. *an Oscan magistrate.*

Mēdēa -ae, f. *an enchantress, who helped Jason to obtain the golden fleece.*

mĕdĕor -ēri, dep. *to heal, to cure, assist, alleviate*; pres. partic. as subst. **mĕdens** -entis, m. *a physician.*

Mēdi -orum, m. *the Medes*; poet. = *the Persians.*

mĕdĭastīnus -i, m. *a drudge.*

mĕdĭca -ae, f. *lucerne, clover.*

mĕdĭcābĭlis -e, *curable.*

mĕdĭcāmen -ĭnis, n. *a drug, medicine, remedy; poison: dye, rouge.*

mĕdĭcāmentum -i, n. *a drug, medicine, remedy; a magic potion; poison; embellishment.*

mĕdĭcātus -ūs, m. *means of enchantment, charm.*

mĕdĭcīnus -a -um, *of the art of healing*; f. as subst. **mĕdĭcīna** -ae, *the art of healing; medicine; cure.*

mĕdĭco -are, *to drug; to dye*; partic. **mĕdĭcātus** -a -um, *steeped, drugged.*

mĕdĭcor -ari, dep., *to heal, cure.*

mĕdĭcus -a -um, *healing, medicinal*; m. as subst. **mĕdĭcus** -i, *a doctor, physician.*

mĕdimnum -i, n. and **mĕdimnus** -i, m. *a Greek measure of capacity.*

mĕdĭocris -e, *moderate, middling, ordinary*; adv. **mĕdĭocrĭter** *moderately, tolerably; with moderation.*

mĕdĭocrĭtās -ātis, f. *moderation,*

medium, the mean; mediocrity, in-significance.

Mēdĭŏlānum and **-lānĭum** -i, n. *a town in Cisalpine Gaul (now Milan).*

mĕdĭtāmentum -i, n. *preparation, practice.*

mĕdĭtātĭo -ōnis, f. (1) *a thinking over, contemplation.* (2) *practice, exercise, preparation.*

mĕdĭterrānĕus -a -um, *inland*: n. pl. as subst., *inland country.*

mĕdĭtor -ari, dep. (1) *to think over, consider;* esp. *to think about doing, to meditate, intend.* (2) *to practise.* Perf. partic. in pass. sense **mĕdĭtātus** -a -um, *meditated, considered, prepared;* adv. **mĕdĭtātē**, *thoughtfully, thoroughly.*

mĕdĭus -a -um, *middle, midmost, mid; intervening, central, neutral, 'intermediate.'* N. as subst. **mĕdĭum** -i, *the middle; the public eye, everyday life; the community, common good.* Adv. **mĕdĭē**, *moderately.*

mĕdĭus fĭdĭus; see fidius.

mĕdulla -ae, f. *the marrow of the bones.*

Mēdus; see Medi.

Mĕdūsa -ae, f. *one of the Gorgons, slain by Perseus.*

Mĕgăra -ae, f. (and -orum, n. pl.). (1) *a town in Greece.* (2) *a town in Sicily.*

mĕgĭstānes -um, m. *grandees, magnates.*

mĕhercŭle, mĕhercle; see Hercules.

mĕl mellis, n. *honey; sweetness, pleasantness.*

mĕlanchŏlĭcus -a -um, *having black bile, melancholy.*

mĕlānūrus -i, m. *small edible sea-fish.*

mĕlĭcus -a -um, *musical; lyrical, lyric.*

mĕlĭlōtŏs -i, f. *a species of clover.*

mĕlĭmēla -orum, n. pl, *honey-apples.*

mĕlĭor -us, compar. of bonus; q.v.

mĕlisphyllum and **mĕlissŏphyllŏn** -i, n. *balm.*

Mĕlĭta -ae, f. *ıne island of Malta;* adj, **Mĕlĭtensis** -e, *of Malta.*

mĕlĭuscŭlus -a -um, *somewhat better;* adv. **mĕlĭuscŭlē**, *somewhat better, pretty well* (in health).

mellĭfer -fĕra -fĕrum, *producing honey.*

mellītus -a -um, *honeyed; sweet as honey.*

¹**mĕlŏs**, n. *a tune, song.*

²**Mĕlŏs** -i, f. *an island in the Aegean Sea.*

Melpŏmĕnē -ēs, f. *the Muse of tragic poetry.*

membrāna -ae, f. *a thin skin, film, membrane; prepared skin, parchment.*

membrātim, *limb by limb; piecemeal, singly; in short sentences.*

membrum -i, n. *a limb, member, part (of the body); a clause in a sentence.*

mĕmĭni -nisse, perf. with sense of present, *to remember, recollect.* Transf. *to make mention of, to mention.*

mĕmor -ōris, *mindful, remembering; with a good memory; grateful, thoughtful, prudent; reminiscent, reminding.*

mĕmŏrābĭlis -e, *remarkable, worthy of mention, memorable.*

mĕmŏrandus -a -um, gerundive from memoro; q.v.

mĕmŏrātor -ōris, m. *a narrator.*

mĕmŏrātus -ūs, m. *mention.*

mĕmŏrĭa -ae, *memory, the capacity for remembering, remembrance; record of the past, tradition, history.*

mĕmŏrĭŏla -ae, f. *memory.*

mĕmŏrĭter, *by heart, from memory.*

mĕmŏro -are, *to mention, call to mind, relate;* gerundive **mĕmŏrandus** -a -um, *notable, memorable.*

Memphis -is and -idos, f. *a city of Egypt.*

Mĕnander -dri, m. *a Greek comic poet.*

menda -ae, f.; see mendum.

mendācĭum -i, n. *lie, falsehood.*

mendax -ācis, *lying, mendacious, false.*

mendīcĭtās -atis, f. *beggary.*

mendĭco -are and **mendĭcor** -ari, dep. *to beg, go begging; beg for.*

mendīcus -a -um, adj. *poor as a beggar, beggarly; paltry, pitiful;* m. as subst. **mendīcus** -i, *a beggar.*

mendōsus -a -um, *full of faults, inaccurate, making mistakes;* adv. **mendōsē**, *faultily.*

mendum -i, n. and **menda** -ae, f. *a fault, defect, blemish, mistake.*

Mĕnĕlāus -i, m. *brother of Agamemnon, husband of Helen.*

mens mentis, f. *mind, understanding, intellect, judgment; feelings, disposition; courage; opinion, thoughts; intention, resolve.*

mensa -ae, f. *a table, counter, altar; a course at a meal.*

mensārĭus -i, m. *a financial commissioner.*

mensĭo -ōnis, f. *measuring.*

mensis -is, m., *a month.*

mensor -ōris, m., *a measurer, surveyor; an architect.*

menstrŭus -a -um, *monthly; lasting a month;* n. as subst. *rations for a month, a month in office.*

mensūra -ae, f. *measuring; measure, standard, capacity; amount, proportion.*

menta (mentha) -ae, f. *the herb mint.*

mentĭo -ōnis, f. *mention.*

mentĭor -iri, dep. *to lie; to deceive, mislead, disappoint; to say falsely, invent; fabricate; to counterfeit, put on, assume.* Hence pres. partic. **mentĭens** -entis, *lying;* m. as subst. *a fallacy, sophism;* perf. partic. **mentītus** -a -um, *lying, fictitious.*

mentum -i, n. *the chin.*

mĕo mēare, *to go, pass.*

mĕphītis -is, f. *a noxious exhalation, malaria; personif., the goddess who protects against malaria.*

mĕrācus -a -um, *pure, unmixed.*

mercābĭlis -e, *that can be bought.*

mercātor -ōris, m. *a merchant, wholesale trader.*

mercātōrĭus -a -um, *relating to trade.*

mercātūra -ae, f. *trade, traffic; merchandise.*

mercātus -ūs, m. *trade, traffic, business; a market, fair, place of business.*

mercēdŭla -ae, f. *low wages* or *rent.*

mercennārius (mercēnārius) -a -um,
hired, paid; m. as subst. a hired
servant.

mercēs -ēdis, hire, pay, wages; a bribe;
cost, punishment; interest, rent, income.

mercimōnium -i, n. goods, merchandise.

mercor -ari, dep. to carry on trade, to
traffic; to buy.

Mercūrius -a -m. Mercury, messenger
of the gods; adj. **Mercūriālis** -e,
of Mercury; m. pl. as subst. a corporation of traders at Rome.

merda -ae, f. excrement.

mērenda -ae, f. a luncheon.

mēreo -ēre -ŭi, itum, and **mēreor**
ēri -itus, dep. to deserve, earn, obtain;
esp., to earn pay as a soldier, serve as a
soldier. Hence perf. partic. **mēritus**
-a -um, deserving; in pass. sense,
deserved. N. as subst. **mēritum** -i,
desert, merit; a good action, benefit,
service; blame, fault, grounds, reason.
Abl. as adv. **mēritō**, deservedly,
rightly.

mēretrīcius -a -um, of a harlot; adv.
mēretrīciē.

mēretrīcŭla -ae, f. a little harlot.

mēretrix -īcis, f. a harlot.

mergae -arum, f. a two-pronged fork.

mergēs -gitis, f. a sheaf of corn.

mergo mergēre mersi mersum, to dip,
plunge into liquid, immerse, sink,
overwhelm.

mergus -i, m. a sea-bird, esp. a gull.

mēridiānus -a -um, of midday,
meridian; southern.

mēridiātio -ōnis, f. midday sleep,
siesta.

mēridiēs -ēi, m., midday, noon; the
south.

mēridio -are, to take a siesta.

¹mērito -are, to earn regularly.

²mērito, adv. from mereo; q.v.

mēritōrius -a -um, hired; n. pl. as
subst., lodgings.

mēritum -i, n., subst. from mereo;
q.v.

mērops -ōpis, f., a bird, the bee-eater.

merso -are, to dip in, immerse.

mērŭla -ae, f. a blackbird; a fish, the
sea-carp.

mērus -a -um, pure, unmixed; complete, sheer; esp. of wine, undiluted;
n. as subst. **mērum** -i, wine unmixed
with water.

merx (mers) mercis, f. merchandise,
goods, wares.

Mēsŏpŏtămia -ae, f. the country between
the Euphrates and the Tigris.

Messāna -ae, f. a town in Sicily on the
straits between Italy and Sicily.

messis -is, f. harvest, crop; time of
harvest, harvest-tide.

messor -ōris, m. a reaper, mower.

messōrius -a -um, of a reaper.

mēta -ae, f. a pyramidal column used as
a turning-post or winning-post; any
turning-point; a goal, end, boundary.

mētallum -i, n. a metal; a mine,
quarry (esp. plur.).

mētămorphōsis -is, f. transformation;

plur. **Mētămorphōsēs** -ēōn, the title
of a poem by Ovid.

mētăphŏra -ae, f. metaphor.

mētātor -ōris, m. a measurer, one who
marks out.

Mētaurus -i, m. a river in Umbria.

mētior mētiri mensus, dep., to measure; to traverse, pass over; to
estimate, judge.

mēto mētēre messŭi messum, to reap,
mow, gather harvest; to mow down,
cut off.

mētor -ari, dep. (and **mēto** -are) to
measure off, lay out.

metrēta -ae, f. a Greek liquid measure.

metrum -i, n. a measure; metre.

mētŭcŭlōsus -a -um, timid; frightful.

mētŭo -ŭēre -ŭi -ūtum, to fear, be
afraid.

mētus -ūs, m. fear, dread; reverence,
awe.

mĕus -a -um, my, mine; Nero meus,
my friend Nero.

mīca -ae, f. a crumb, morsel, grain.

mīco -are -ŭi, to move rapidly to and
fro, vibrate, flicker; to shine, glitter,
sparkle.

Mīdās (Mīda) -ae, m. a king of Phrygia,
who turned to gold everything that he
touched.

migrātio -ōnis, f. removal, change of
home.

migrātŭ, abl. sing. m., in transport.

migro -are: intransit., to migrate,
depart; to change; transit., to move,
transport; to transgress.

mīlēs -ītis, c. a soldier; a private
soldier, infantryman; coll. soldiery.

mīlitāris -e, of a soldier, military; m.
as subst. a soldier; adv. **mīlitāritĕr**,
in a soldierly manner.

mīlitia -ae, f. military service, warfare;
domi militiaeque, at home and
abroad, at peace and in war; meton.,
the military, soldiery.

mīlito -are, to serve as a soldier, be a
soldier.

mīlium -i, n. millet.

millĕ, a thousand; plur. **mīlia (millĭa)**
-ium, thousands; mille passuum, a
thousand paces, a Roman mile.

mille(n)sīmus -a -um, thousandth.

milliārium (mīliārium) -i, n. a
mile-stone.

milliārius (mīliārĭus) -a -um, containing a thousand.

millie(n)s, a thousand times.

milŭīnus (milvīnus) -a -um, of a kite;
kite-like.

milŭus (milvus) -i, m. a kite; a fish,
the gurnard.

mīma -ae, f. an actress.

mīmicus -a -um, farcical; adv.
mīmicē.

mīmŭla -ae, f., a little actress.

mīmus -i, m. a mimic actor; a mime,
farce.

¹mīna, f. smooth, hairless.

²mīna -ae, f. a Greek weight; also a
Greek coin.

minae -arum, f. battlements, parapets.
Transf., threats, menaces.

minātio -ōnis, f. threatening, menace.

mĭnax -ācis, f. *projecting, overhanging.* Transf., *threatening.* Adv. **mĭnācĭtĕr**, *threateningly.*

mĭnĕo -ēre, *to project, overhang.*

Mĭnerva -ae, f. *goddess of wisdom and patroness of arts and sciences.* Transf., *wit, skill, art;* esp. *working in wool.*

mĭnĭātus -a -um, *coloured with red lead, painted vermilion.*

mĭnĭmē; see parum.

mĭnĭmus; see parvus.

mĭnister -tri, m. and mĭnistra -ae, f. *servant, attendant, assistant.*

mĭnistĕrĭum -i, n. *service, attendance, employment;* in plur., *attendants, retinue.*

mĭnistra -ae, f.; see minister.

mĭnistrātor -ōris, m., mĭnistrātrix -icis, f. *a servant, attendant, assistant.*

mĭnistro -are, *to serve, wait,* esp. *at table; to attend to, take care of, direct; to serve, supply, provide.*

mĭnĭtābundus -a -um, *threatening.*

mĭnĭto -are and mĭnĭtor -ari dep. *to threaten.*

mĭnĭum -i, n. *native cinnabar; red-lead, vermilion.*

¹mĭnor -ari, dep. *to jut out, project.* Transf., *to threaten, menace* (with dat.). Adv. from partic. **mĭnantĕr**, *threateningly.*

²mĭnor -ōris, compar. of parvus; q.v.

Mīnōs -ōis and -ōnis, *king of Crete; after his death, a judge in Tartarus.*

Mīnōtauᵣus -i, m. *a monster, half-bull, half-man, slain by Theseus.*

mĭnŭmē and mĭnŭmus; see minim-.

mĭnŭo -ŭĕre -ŭi -ŭtum, *to make smaller, lessen, diminish; to cut to pieces.* Hence partic. **mĭnūtus** -a -um, *small, petty, insignificant;* adv. **mĭnūtē.**

mĭnus; see parvus.

mĭnuscŭlus -a -um, *rather small.*

mĭnūtal -ālis, n. *a dish of minced meat.*

mĭnūtātim, *bit by bit, gradually.*

mĭnūtĭa -ae, f. *smallness.*

mĭnūtus -a -um, partic. from minuo; q.v.

mīrābĭlis -e *wonderful, extraordinary, unusual;* adv. **mīrābĭlĭtĕr.**

mīrābundus -a -um, *wondering.*

mīrācŭlum -i, n. *a wonderful thing, prodigy, miracle; wonder, surprise.*

mīrātĭo -ōnis, f. *wonder, astonishment.*

mīrātor -ōris, m. *an admirer.*

mīrātrix -icis, f. adj. *wondering.*

mīrĭfĭcus -a -um *causing wonder, wonderful, astonishing;* adv. **mīrĭfĭcē.**

mirmillo (murm-) -ōnis, m. *a kind of gladiator.*

mīror -ari, dep. *to wonder, be astonished (at); to admire, look on with admiration;* gerundive **mīrandus** -a -um, *wonderful.*

mīrus -a -um, *wonderful, astonishing, extraordinary;* adv. **mīrē.**

miscellānĕa -ōrum, n. pl., *a hash, hotchpotch.*

miscĕo miscēre miscŭi mixtum, *to mix, mingle; to combine, unite; to prepare by mixing; to confuse, confound.*

mĭsellus -a -um, *miserable, wretched, little.*

Mĭsēnus -i, m. *the trumpeter of Aeneas;* **Mĭsēnum** -i, n. *a promontory and town in Campania.*

mĭser -ĕra -ĕrum, *wretched, unhappy, sad;* adv. **mĭsērē.**

mĭsĕrābĭlis -e, *sad, wretched, mournful, plaintive;* adv. **mĭsĕrābĭlĭtĕr.**

mĭsĕrātĭo -ōnis, f. *pity, compassion; a pathetic speech or tone.*

mĭsĕrĕo -ēre and mĭsĕrĕor -ēri, dep. *to pity* (with genit.); impers. **mĭsĕret** and dep. **mĭsĕrētur,** *it excites pity, one pities.*

mĭsĕresco -ĕre, *to pity, have compassion on* (with genit.).

mĭsĕrĭa -ae, f. *wretchedness, unhappiness, distress.*

mĭsĕrĭcordĭa -ae, f. *pity, compassion, mercy; an appeal to pity.*

mĭsĕrĭcors -cordis, *pitiful, compassionate.*

mĭsĕror -ari, dep. *to bewail, deplore; to pity, have compassion on;* gerundive **mĭsĕrandus** -a -um, *pitiable, lamentable.*

missĭcĭus -a -um, *discharged from military service.*

missĭlis -e, *that can be thrown;* n. as subst., *a missile.*

missĭo -ōnis, f. *a sending off, letting go, releasing, discharge; cessation, termination.*

missĭto -are, *to send repeatedly.*

¹missus -ūs, m. *a letting go, sending, throwing; a shot, the distance shot;* in races, *a course, heat.*

²missus -a -um, partic. from mitto; q.v.

mītesco -ĕre, *to become mild, soft, or ripe; to be allayed, to subside.*

Mĭthrĭdātes -is, m. *name of several kings of Pontus.*

mītĭgātĭo -onis, f. *assuaging, appeasing.*

mītĭgo -are, *to make mild,* or *ripe; to soothe, appease, pacify.*

mītis -e, *mild, soft, ripe; gentle;* of style, *mellow;* compar. adv. **mītĭus;** superl. **mītissĭmē.**

mitra -ae, f. *a head-dress, turban.*

mitrātus -a -um, *wearing the mitra.*

mitto mittĕre misi missum, *to send, dispatch; to send as a gift; to fling; to shed; to utter; to let go, release, give up; to dismiss, discharge; to pass over a subject.*

mītŭlus (mȳtŭlus, mŭtŭlus) -i, m. *an edible mussel.*

mixtūra -ae, f. *a mixing, mixture.*

mna = ²mina; q.v.

Mnĕmŏnĭdes -um, f. pl. *the Muses.*

Mnĕmŏsynē -ēs, f. *Mnemosyne, mother of the Muses.*

mnĕmŏsynum -i, n. *a souvenir, memorial.*

mōbĭlis -e, *movable, easy to move; pliable, flexible; active, rapid; changeable, inconstant.* Adv. **mōbĭlĭtĕr,** *quickly, easily.*

mōbĭlĭtās -ātis, f. *mobility; inconstancy, changeableness.*

mōbĭlĭto -are, *to set in motion.*

mŏdĕrābĭlis -e, *moderate, restrained.*

mŏdĕrāmen -ĭnis, n. *means of guiding*; *rerum, management, government.*

mŏdĕrātim, *moderately, gradually.*

mŏdĕrātĭo -ōnis, f. *moderating, restraining; moderation, restraint.*

mŏdĕrātor -ōris, m. *a governor, controller, manager*; *equorum, a driver.*

mŏdĕrātrix -īcis, f. *she that governs or controls.*

mŏdĕror -ari, dep. (and **mŏdĕro** -are), *to keep within bounds; to regulate, restrain; to control, govern, direct.* Hence, from pres. partic. adv. **mŏdĕrantĕr,** *with controlling force*; perf. partic. **mŏdĕrātus** -a -um, *restrained, controlled*; adv. **mŏdĕrātē,** *with restraint.*

mŏdestĭa -ae, f. *moderation; restraint, propriety, orderliness; respect, obedience to authority.*

mŏdestus -a -um, *moderate, within bounds; orderly, restrained*; adv. **mŏdestē.**

mŏdĭcus -a -um, *moderate, within bounds, limited; temperate; ordinary, undistinguished.* Adv. **mŏdĭcē,** *moderately; to a limited extent; temperately, with restraint.*

mŏdĭfĭcātus -a -um, *measured.*

mŏdĭus -i, m. *a Roman corn-measure*; *pleno modio, in full measure, abundantly.*

mŏdŏ, *by measure;* hence *only, merely, but, just;* si modo, modo si, or modo alone with subj., *provided that, if only;* modo ne, *provided that . . . not;* modo non, *all but, nearly;* non modo . . . sed etiam, *not only . . . but also.* Of time, *just, lately; soon, directly;* modo . . . modo . . ., *at one time . . . at another. . . .*

mŏdŭlātĭo -ōnis, f. *rhythmical measure.*

mŏdŭlātor -ōris, m. *a musician.*

mŏdŭlor -ari, dep. *to measure;* in music, *to modulate, to sing to the accompaniment* of an instrument; *to play* an instrument. Adv. from partic. **mŏdŭlātē,** *in time* (of music).

mŏdŭlus -i, m. *a little measure.*

mŏdus -i, m. *a measure, standard of measurement;* in music, *rhythm, measure, time;* in plur., *strains, numbers.* Transf., *limit, boundary; rule; manner, mode, way, method;* servorum modo, *after the manner of slaves;* eius modi, *in that manner, of that kind.*

moecha -ae. f. *an adulteress.*

moechor -ari, dep. *to commit adultery.*

moechus -i, m. *an adulterer.*

moenĕra=*munera; see* munus.

moenĭa -ĭum, n. pl. *the walls or fortifications of a city, ramparts, bulwarks;* poet., *castle, dwelling.*

Moesi -ōrum, m. pl. *a people between Thrace and the Danube;* **Moesĭa** -ae f., *their country.*

mŏla -ae, f. *a mill-stone;* plur., *a mill.* Transf., *grits, coarse meal* or *flour.*

mŏlāris -e, *of a mill, to do with grinding;* m. as subst. *a millstone; a molar tooth, grinder.*

mōlēs -is, f. *a shapeless mass,* e.g. of *rock; a massive construction,* e.g. *dam, mole, large building;* moles belli, *large military machines.* Transf., *a mass of men; greatness, might, power; trouble, difficulty.*

mŏlestĭa -ae, f. *annoyance, troublesomeness;* of style, *affectation, stiffness.*

mŏlestus -a -um, *burdensome, troublesome, irksome;* of style, *affected, laboured.* Adv. **mŏlestē,** *with annoyance;* moleste fero, *I take it badly, am annoyed;* of style, *affectedly.*

mōlīmen -ĭnis, n. and **mōlīmentum** -i, n. *great effort, exertion, endeavour.*

mōlĭor -īri, dep.: transit., *to stir, displace, work at; to construct laboriously, build, erect, contrive; to strive after; to destroy laboriously, undermine;* intransit., *to toil, struggle, exert oneself.*

mōlītĭo -ōnis, f. *effort, laborious undertaking; demolition.*

mōlītor -ōris, m. *a builder, contriver.*

mollesco -ĕre, *to become soft or gentle.*

mollĭcŭlus -a -um, *soft, tender; effeminate.*

mollĭo -īre, *to make soft, pliable, supple; to make gentle or effeminate; to alleviate* trouble; *to ease a gradient.*

mollĭpēs -pĕdis, *soft-footed.*

mollis -e, *soft, tender, pliant, supple;* of weather, *mild;* of gradients, *easy;* of character, *tender, gentle, sensitive,* or *effeminate;* of circumstances, *easy, mild, pleasant;* of speech, *tender, moving.* Adv. **mollĭtĕr,** *softly, easily, gently, mildly; effeminately.*

mollĭtĭa -ae, and **mollĭtĭes** -ei, f. *softness, flexibility; tenderness, mildness, sensibility; effeminacy.*

mollĭtūdo -ĭnis, f. *softness, pliability; tenderness, sensibility.*

mŏlo -ĕre -ŭi -ĭtum, *to grind in a mill.*

Mŏlossi -orum, m. *a people in Epirus.* Adj. **Mŏlossus** -a -um, pes, *a metrical foot, consisting of three long syllables;* m. as subst. *a Molossian hound.*

mōly -ўos, n. *the herb moly.*

mōmen -ĭnis, n. *movement; a moving mass; momentum, impulse.*

mōmentum -i, n. *movement, motion; change, alteration; a cause of motion, impulse;* mental *impulse, influence; weight, importance;* of time, *a turning-point, minute, moment.*

Mŏna -ae, f. *the Isle of Man;* also *the Isle of Anglesey.*

mŏnēdŭla -ae, f. *jackdaw.*

mŏnĕo -ēre, *to remind, admonish, warn, advise, instruct.* N. pl. of partic. as subst. **mŏnĭta** -ōrum, *warnings; prophecies.*

mŏnēris -is, f. *a vessel with one bank of oars.*

Mŏnēta -ae, f. (1) *the mother of the Muses.* (2) *a surname of Juno.* (3) *the mint; money.*

mŏnētālis -e, *of the mint.*

mŏnīlĕ -is, n. *necklace, collar.*

mŏnīmentum = monumentum; q.v.

mŏnĭtĭo -ōnis, f. *reminding, warning.*

mŏnĭtor -ōris, m. *one who reminds or prompts; an adviser, instructor.*

mŏnĭtus -ūs, m. *warning, admonition.*

mŏnogrammos or -us -i, m. adj. *sketched, shadowy.*

mŏnŏpŏdĭum -i, n. *a table with one foot.*

mons, montis, m. *a mountain; a mass; a great rock.*

monstrātor -ōris m. *a pointer-out; an inventor.*

monstro -are, *to show, point out; to ordain, appoint; to inform against, denounce.*

monstrum -i, n. *a wonder, portent.*

monstrŭōsus (monstrōsus) -a -um, *strange, wonderful;* adv. monstrŭōsē.

montānus -a -um, *of a mountain,* or *mountainous;* m. as subst. *a mountaineer;* n. pl. as subst. *mountainous country.*

montĭcŏla -ae, c. *a highlander.*

montĭvăgus -a -um, *wandering over mountains.*

montŭōsus (montōsus) -a -um, *mountainous.*

mŏnŭmentum (mŏnĭmentum) -i, n. *a memorial, monument; a commemorative building; written memorials, annals, memoirs.*

¹mŏra -ae, f. *delay, hindrance; any space of time.*

²mŏra -ae, f. *a division of the Spartan army.*

mŏrālis -e, *moral, ethical.*

mŏrātor -ōris, m. *a delayer, retarder; an advocate who talks against time.*

¹mŏrātus, partic. from moror; q.v.

²mŏrātus -a -um, *having certain manners* or *morals; adapted to a character, in character, characteristic.*

morbĭdus -a -um, *sickly, diseased, unwholesome.*

morbus -i, m. *disease, sickness.*

mordax -ācis, *biting, snappish; stinging, pungent; satirical.* Compar. adv. mordācius, *more bitingly.*

mordĕo mordēre mŏmordi morsum, *to bite; to cut into; to nip, sting; to vex, hurt, pain.*

mordĭcus, *with the teeth, by biting.*

mōrētum -i, n. *a salad.*

mŏrĭbundus -a -um, *dying, expiring; subject to death, mortal; causing death, deadly.*

mōrĭgĕror -ari, dep. (and mōrĭgĕro -are) *to comply with, gratify.*

mōrĭgĕrus -a -um, *compliant, accommodating.*

mŏrĭor mŏri mortŭus mŏrĭtūrus, dep. *to die; to die away, wither away, decay.* Hence partic. mortŭus -a -um, *dead; decayed, extinct; half-dead;* m. as subst. *a corpse.*

mōrŏlŏgus -a -um, *talking like a fool.*

¹mŏror -ari, dep. *to delay:* intransit., *to linger, loiter, stay;* transit., *to retard, detain, hinder;* nihil (nil) morari, *to care nothing for.*

²mŏror -ari, dep. *to be foolish.*

mōrōsĭtās -ātis, f. *peevishness, fretfulness.*

mōrōsus -a -um, *peevish, captious, fretful;* adv. mōrōsē.

Morphēus -ĕos, m. *god of dreams.*

mors mortis, f. *death; a corpse; a cause of death* or *destruction.*

morsus -ūs, m. *a bite, biting; pungency; a verbal attack;* in gen. *pain, vexation.*

mortālis -e, *subject to death, mortal; transitory, perishable; human, earthly;* m. as subst. *a mortal man.*

mortālĭtās -ātis, f. *liability to death.*

mortĭfer or mortĭfĕrus -fĕra -fĕrum, *causing death, fatal, deadly;* adv. mortĭfĕrē.

mortŭālĭa -ium, n. *funeral songs, dirges.*

mortŭus -a -um, partic. from morior; q.v.

mōrum -i, n. *a mulberry; a blackberry.*

¹mōrus -i, f. *a mulberry tree.*

²mōrus -a -um, *silly, foolish.*

mōs, mōris, *the will, inclination;* morem homini gerere, *to humour a person; custom, usage, wont, rule;* in plur., *ways, conduct, character, morals.*

Mōsa -ae, f. *a river in Gaul* (now Meuse).

Mōsella -ae, f. *a river in Gaul* (now Moselle).

mōtĭo -ōnis, f. *movement.*

mōto -are, *to move about.*

¹mōtus -a -um, partic. from moveo; q.v.

²mōtus -ūs, m. *motion, movement;* terrae, *an earthquake; mental activity, emotion; political movement, rebellion, rising, riot.*

mŏvĕo mŏvēre mōvi mōtum, *to move, set in motion, stir; to remove, dispossess, dislodge;* se movere, and in middle sense, moveri, *to move* (oneself): milit., movere signa, movere castra, *to march away; to move mentally, influence, affect, excite; to cause a result; to change, shake; politically, to arouse, disturb.*

mox, *soon, presently; then, thereupon.*

mūcĭdus -a -um, *snivelling; mouldy, musty.*

Mūcĭus -a -um, *name of a Roman gens;* adj. Mūcĭānus -a -um.

mucro -ōnis, m. *a sharp point or edge; a sword.*

mūcus -i, m. *mucous matter.*

mūgil (mūgĭlis) -is, m. *a fish,* perhaps *mullet.*

mūgĭnor -ari, dep. *to loiter, dally.*

mūgĭo -ire, *to bellow, low, roar, rumble, groan.*

mūgītus -ūs, m. *lowing, bellowing, rumbling, groaning.*

mūla -ae, f. *a female mule.*

mulcĕo mulcēre mulsi mulsum, *to stroke; to soothe, appease, charm.*

Mulcĭber -ēris and -ĕri, m. *surname of Vulcan;* meton., *fire.*

mulco -are, *to thrash; to handle roughly.*

mulctra -ae, f., mulctrārĭum -i, n., and mulctrum -i, n. *milk-pail.*

mulgĕo mulgēre mulsi, *to milk.*

mŭlĭēbris -e, *of a woman, feminine; effeminate;* adv. mŭlĭēbrĭtĕr.

mŭlĭer -ĕris, f. *a woman; a wife, matron.*

mŭlĭĕrārĭus -a -um, *womanish.*

mŭlĭercŭla -ae, f. *a little woman.*

mŭlĭĕrŏsĭtās -ātis, f. *love of women.*

mŭlĭĕrōsus -a -um, *fond of women.*

mŭlīnus -a -um, *of a mule, mulish.*

mŭlĭo -ōnis, m. *a mule-keeper, mule-driver.*

mŭlĭōnĭus -a -um, *of a muleteer.*

mullus -i, m. *the red mullet.*

mulsus -a -um, *honeyed; as sweet as honey*; n. as subst. *wine sweetened with honey, mead.*

multa -ae, f. *a fine, mulct.*

multangŭlus -a -um, *many-cornered.*

multātĭcĭus -a -um, *relating to a fine.*

multātĭo -onis, f. *fining.*

multĕsĭmus -a -um, *very small.*

multĭcāvus -a -um, *porous.*

multĭcĭa -orum, n. pl. *finely woven garments.*

multĭfārĭam, *on many sides, in many places.*

multĭfĭdus -a -um, *cloven into many parts.*

multĭformis -e, *having many shapes.*

multĭfŏrus -a -um, *pierced with many holes.*

multĭgĕnĕris -e and **multĭgĕnus** -a -um, *of many kinds.*

multĭiŭgus -a -um, and **multĭiŭgis** -e, *yoked many together; manifold, of many sorts.*

multĭlŏquax -ācis, *talkative.*

multĭmŏdis, *in many ways, variously.*

multĭplex -plicis, *having many folds, winds or turnings; having many parts, manifold, many-sided, versatile; many times as large.*

multĭplĭco -are, *to increase many times, multiply.*

multĭtūdo -ĭnis, f. *a large number, multitude, crowd; common people, mob.*

multo -are, *to punish.*

multus -a -um: sing., *much, great*; plur., *many, numerous*; multi, *the common herd*; ne multa, *briefly, in brief*; ad multum diem, *till late in the day*; in re multus, *prolix on a subject, busy in a matter*; occ., in sing., many a; n. acc. sing. as adv. **multum**, *much, greatly*; abl. **multo**, *by much, by far* Compar. **plus**: in sing. n. only, *more*; genit. of value **plūris**, at *a higher price, of more value*; in plur. **plūres, plūra**, *more numerous, several, many.* Superl. **plūrĭmus**, *most, very many*: in sing., of a large number, *like* the English *full many a*; of *energy, etc., strong*; genit. of value **plūrĭmi**, *at the highest price or value.*

mūlus -i, m. *a mule.*

Mulvĭus pons, *a bridge across the Tiber.*

Mummĭus -a -um, *name of a Roman gens.*

Munda -ae, f. *town in Hispania Baetica.*

mundānus -i, m. *a citizen of the world.*

mundĭtĭa -ae, and **mundĭtĭēs** -ēi, f. *cleanness, neatness, spruceness, elegance.*

[1]mundus -a -um, *clean, neat, elegant.*

[2]mundus -i, m. (1) *toilet-things, adornment.* (2) *the universe, world; mankind.*

mūnĕro -are and **mūnĕror** -ari, dep. *to give, present.*

mūnĭa -ĭōrum, n. pl., *duties, functions*; esp. *official.*

mūnĭceps -cĭpis, c. *the citizen of a municipium; a fellow-citizen, fellow-countryman.*

mūnĭcĭpālis -e, *belonging to a municipium, municipal.*

mūnĭcĭpĭum -i, n. *a borough, free town, municipal town.*

mūnĭfĭcentĭa -ae, f. *generosity.*

mūnĭfĭco -are, *to present generously.*

mūnĭfĭcus -a -um, *generous, liberal*; of *wealth, splendid*; adv. **mūnĭfĭcē**.

mūnĭmen -ĭnis, n. *a protection, defence.*

mūnĭmentum -i, n. *a fortification, defence, protection.*

mūnĭo (moenĭo) -ire, *to build, esp. to build a wall; also to surround with a wall; to fortify; to secure, defend, protect.*
   Hence partic. **mūnītus** -a -um, *fortified, secured.*

mūnītĭo -ōnis, f. *fortifying, building up, paving, bridging*; concr., *a fortification.*

mūnĭto -are, *to pave, make passable.*

mūnītor -ōris, m. *a builder of fortifications, sapper, engineer.*

mūnus (moenus) -ĕris, n. *an office, function, duty; a charge, tax; a service, favour, gift, present; a public show,* esp. *of gladiators: a public building.*

mūnuscŭlum -i, n. *a small gift.*

mūrālis -e, *of a wall, mural*; corona, *the crown given to the first man over the wall of a besieged city.*

[1]mūrēna (muraena) -ae, f. *a sea-fish, the murry or lamprey.*

[2]Mūrēna -ae, m. *a cognomen in the gens Licinia.*

mūrex -icis, m. *the purple-fish; purple dye; a sharp stone, projecting rock.*

mūrĭa -ae, f. *brine, pickle.*

murmillo = mirmillo; q.v.

murmur -ŭris, n. *a murmur, humming, roaring, rumbling, crashing.*

murmŭro -are, *to murmur, roar, crash.*

[1]murra (myrrha) -ae, f. *the myrrh-tree; myrrh.*

[2]murra (myrrha) -ae, f. *a mineral, perhaps fluorspar.*

[1]murrĕus (myrrhĕus) -a -um, *perfumed with myrrh; myrrh-coloured.*

[2]murrĕus (myrrhĕus) -a -um, *made of fluorspar.*

mūrus -i, m. *a wall, bank* or *dyke*; fig., *protection, defence.*

mūs, mūris, c. *a mouse or rat.*

Mūsa -ae, f. *a muse: a goddess of music literature and the arts.*

mūsaeus -a -um, *poetical, musical.*

musca -ae, f. *a fly.*

muscārĭum -i, n. *a fly-trap.*

muscĭpŭla -ae, f. and **muscĭpŭlum** -i, n. *a mouse-trap.*

muscōsus -a -um, *mossy.*

muscŭlus -i, m. *a little mouse; a sea-mussel;* milit., *a shed, mantelet.*

muscus -i, m. *moss.*

mūsĕus -a -um = musaeus; q.v.

mūsĭcus -a -um, *belonging to poetry or music, musical;* m. as subst. *a musician;* f. sing. mūsĭca -ae and mūsĭcē -ēs, *music, poetry, learned studies;* adv. mūsĭcē.

mussĭto -are: intransit., *to grumble, mutter;* transit., *to keep quiet about a thing.*

musso -are, *to murmur, mutter, whisper; to keep quiet about a thing; to be at a loss.*

mustācĕum -i, n. and mustācĕus -i, m., *a must-cake, a sort of wedding-cake.*

mustēla (mustella) -ae, f. *a weasel.*

mustus -a -um, *young, new, fresh;* n. as subst. *new wine, must.*

mūtābĭlis -e, *changeable, variable, inconstant.*

mūtābĭlĭtās -ātis, f. *changeableness.*

mūtātĭo -ōnis, *changing, change, altera-tion; mutual change, exchange.*

mŭtĭlo -are, *to maim, mutilate, cut off; to curtail, diminish.*

mŭtĭlus -a -um, *maimed, mutilated.*

Mŭtĭna -ae, f. *town in Cisalpine Gaul* (now *Modena*).

mūtĭo (muttĭo) -ire, *to mutter mumble.*

mūto -are: transit., *to move, shift; to change, alter; to exchange, barter;* with abl., *to give or to get one thing in exchange for another;* intransit., *to change, alter.*

mūtŭātĭo -ōnis, f. *borrowing.*

mūtŭor -ari dep. *to borrow.*

mūtus -a -um, *inarticulate, dumb, mute, silent, still, quiet.*

mūtŭus -a -um. (1) *interchanged, mutual, reciprocal;* n. as subst. *reciprocity, equal return;* abl. as adv. mūtŭō, *mutually, reciprocally.* (2) *borrowed, lent:* pecuniam dare mutuam, *to lend;* n. as subst., *a loan.*

mўŏpăro -ōnis, m. *a small piratical galley.*

mўrīcē -ēs, f. and mўrīca -ae, f. *the tamarisk.*

myrtētum (murtētum) -i n. *a grove of myrtle-trees.*

myrtĕus (murtĕus) -a -um, *of myrtle; adorned with myrtle.*

myrtum -i, n. *myrtle-berry.*

myrtus -i and -ūs, f. *the myrtle-tree;* also *a myrtle shaft.*

mystăgōgus -i, m. *a priest who showed sacred places to strangers.*

mystērĭa -orum, n. pl. *mysteries, secrets,* esp. *of worship.*

mystēs or mysta -ae, m. *a priest at the mysteries.*

mystĭcus -a -um, *secret, mystic.*

N

N, n, the thirteenth letter of the Latin Alphabet.

nablĭum -i, n. *a kind of harp or lyre.*

nae = ¹nē; q.v.

naenĭa = nenia; q.v.

Naevĭus -a -um, *name of a Roman gens;* esp. of Cn. Naevius, *a poet of the third century B.C.*

naevus -i, m. *a mole on the body.*

Nāïās -ădis and Nāïs -idis (-idos); f. *a water-nymph. Naiad;* adj. Nāïcus -a -um.

nam and namquĕ, conj., *for.*

nanciscor nancisci nactus *and* nanctus, dep. *to light upon, obtain, meet.*

nānus -i, m. *a dwarf.*

Narbo -ōnis, m. *town in southern Gau* (now *Narbonne*); adj. Narbōnensis -e.

Narcissus -i, m. Narcissus, *a beautiful young man changed into the flower of the same name.*

nardus -i, f. and nardum, -i, n. *nard.*

nārĭs -is, f. usually plur. nārēs -ĭum, *the nostrils, nose.*

narrābĭlis -e, *able to be told.*

narrātĭo -ōnis, f. *telling, relating; a narrative.*

narrātĭuncŭla -ae, f. *a short narrative.*

narrātor -ōris, m. *a relater, narrator.*

narrātus -ūs, m. *narration, narrative.*

narro -are, *to make known; to say speak.*

narthēcĭum -i, n. *a box for perfumes and medicines.*

nārus = gnarus; q.v.

nascor -i, natus (and gnatus), dep. *to be born; to come into existence, arise, be produced.*

Hence partic. nātus -a -um, *born, naturally fitted or constituted;* pro re nata, *under present circumstances;* annos prope xc natus, *almost ninety years old.* As subst., m. *a son;* f. *a daughter.*

Nāsĭca -ae, m. *name of a family of the Scipios.*

Nāso -ōnis m. *cognomen of the poet P. Ovidius.*

nassa -ae, f. *a basket for catching fish; a trap, snare.*

nasturcium -i, n. *a kind of cress.*

nāsus -i, m. *the nose;* naso suspendere adunco, *to turn up the nose at ridicule, mock.*

nāsūtus -a -um, *having a large nose; acute, sagacious, satirical.*

nātālĭcĭus -a -um, *relating to birth;* n. pl. as subst. *a birthday-party.*

nātālĭs -e, *relating to birth, natal;* m. as subst., *a birthday;* plur. *birth, origin.*

nātātĭo -ōnis, t. *swimming.*

nātātor -ōris, m. *swimmer.*

nātĭo -ōnis, f. *being born, birth; a tribe, race, people,* esp. *uncivilized;* 1 *species stock, class.*

nātĭs -is, f., usually plur. nātēs -ĭum, *the rump, buttocks.*

nātīvus -a -um, *born; native, natural; inborn, innate.*

nāto -are, *to swim, float; to stream, flow; to swim with, be full of* (with abl.); f. pl. of partic. as subst. natantes, *fishes.*

nātrix -ĭcis, f. *a water-snake.*

nātū, abl. sing. m. *by birth*; maior natu, *older*.

nātūra -ae, f. *birth*; *nature, natura qualities* or *disposition, character*; *an element, substance, essence*; rerum natura, *nature, the world* or *universe*.

nātūrālis -e, *natural, relating to nature*; adv. **nātūrālitĕr**, *naturally, by nature*.

nātus -a -um, partic. from nascor; q.v

nauarchus -i, m. *captain of a ship.*

nauclērus -i, m. *the master of a ship.*

naucum -i, n. *a trifle*; in genit. non nauci habere, *to think nothing of.*

naufrăgĭum -i, n. *shipwreck; wreckage; ruin, loss*; naufragium facere, *to suffer shipwreck.*

naufrăgus -a -um, pass., *shipwrecked*; act., *causing shipwreck.*

naulum -i, n. *fare, passage-money.*

naumăchia, ae, f. *a naval battle performed as a show.*

nausĕa -ae, f. *sea-sickness, nausea.*

nausĕo -are, *to be sea-sick; to cause disgust, nauseate.*

nausĕŏla -ae, f. *squeamishness.*

nauta and **nāvĭta** -ae, m. *sailor, mariner.*

nautĭcus -a -um, *of a sailor, nautical*; m. pl. as subst. *sailors.*

nāvālis -e, *of ships, naval, nautical*; n. as subst. **nāvālĕ** -is, *a station for ships*; plur. *a dockyard,* or *materials for ship-building.*

nāvĭcŭla -ae, f. *a little ship, boat.*

nāvĭcŭlārĭus -a -um, *of (small) ships*; f. as subst. *the business of a ship-owner*; m. as subst. *a ship-owner.*

nāvĭfrăgus -a -um, *causing shipwreck.*

nāvĭgābĭlis -e, *navigable.*

nāvĭgātĭo -ōnis, f. *sailing, voyage.*

nāvĭgĕr -gĕra -gĕrum, *ship-bearing, navigable.*

nāvĭgĭum -i, n. *a vessel, ship.*

nāvĭgo -are: intransit., *to sail, voyage, go by sea; to swim*; transit. *to sail over, sail through, navigate.*

nāvis -is, f. *a ship, vessel*; navis longa, *a man-of-war*; oneraria, *a transport*; praetoria, *flag-ship.*

nāvĭta = nauta; q.v.

nāvĭtās (gnāvĭtās) -atis, f. *energy, zeal.*

nāvo -are, *to do energetically.*

nāvus (gnāvus) -a -um, *zealous, energetic.* Adv. **nāvĭtĕr (gnāvĭtĕr)**, *energetically; completely.*

¹nē (nae), used before pronouns, *indeed, truly.*

²nē, *not, that not, lest*; ne . . . quidem, *not even, not . . . either.*

³-nē (sometimes n') interrog., enclitic particle.

Neăpŏlis -polis, f. (1) *part of Syracuse.* (2) *a sea-port* (now *Naples*).

nēbŭla -ae, f. *vapour, fog, mist, cloud.*

nēbŭlo -ōnis, m. *a good-for-nothing fellow.*

nēbŭlōsus -a -um, *misty, foggy.*

nĕc and **nĕquĕ**, *not; and not, nor*; rarely *not even*; neque enim, *for . . . not*; nec non, *and also*; nec tamen, *and yet . . . not*; nec . . . nec, neque . . . neque, *neither . . . nor.*

necdum (nĕquĕ dum), *and not yet.*

nĕcessārĭus -a -um, *necessary, unavoidable, inevitable; pressing, urgent; closely connected*; as subst. *an intimate friend* or *relative*; n. abl. **nĕcessārĭō**, and adv. **nĕcessārĭē**, *necessarily, unavoidably.*

nĕcessĕ, indecl. adj. n., used with esse and habere; *necessary, unavoidable inevitable, indispensable.*

nĕcessĭtās -ātis, f. *inevitability, necessity, urgency*; plur. *requirements, necessary expenses.* Transf., *intimate connexion, friendship, relationship.*

nĕcessĭtūdo -ĭnis, f. *necessity, inevitableness; need, want.* Transf., *close connexion, intimate friendship*; plur., *intimate friends, near relations.*

nĕcessum =necesse; q.v.

necnĕ, *or not.*

necnōn (nĕquĕ nōn); see nec.

nĕco -are, *to kill, slay, put to death.*

nĕcŏpīnans -antis, *not expecting unaware.*

nĕcŏpīnātus (nĕc ŏpīnātus) -a -um *unexpected*; adv. **nĕcŏpīnātō**.

nĕcŏpīnus -a -um; pass., *unexpected*; act., *not expecting.*

nectar -ăris, n. *nectar, the drink of the gods; honey, milk, wine.*

nectărĕus -a -um, *of nectar.*

necto nectĕre nexŭi *and* nexi nexum, *to tie, bind, fasten; to fetter, enslave; to affix, attach; to put together, devise.*

nēcŭbi, *lest anywhere, that nowhere.*

nēcunde, *lest from any quarter, that from no direction.*

nēdum, *not to say*; after (implied) negative, *much less, still less*; after affirmative, *much more.*

nĕfandus -a -um, *not to be spoken of; abominable.*

nĕfārĭus -a -um, *impious, abominable*; adv. **nĕfārĭē**.

nĕfās, n. indecl., *what is contrary to divine command; sin, crime, abomination*; per fas et nefas, *by fair means or foul*; as interj. *monstrous! dreadful!*

nĕfastus -a -um, *forbidden, unholy; unlucky; sinful*; dies nefasti, *days on which no public business could be transacted.*

nĕgātĭo -ōnis, f. *denying.*

nĕgĭto -are, *to persist in denying.*

neglectĭo -ōnis, f. *neglect.*

neglectus -ūs, m. *neglect, disregard.*

neglĕgentĭa -ae, f. *carelessness, negligence.*

neglĕgo -lĕgĕre -lexi -lectum, *to neglect, disregard; to make light of, overlook, omit.* Hence partic. **neglĕgens** -entis. *careless*; adv. **neglĕgentĕr**.

nĕgo -are, *to say no; to deny, say that . . . not; to deny a request, refuse to give* or *do.*

nĕgōtĭālis -e, *relating to business.*

nĕgōtĭātĭo -ōnis, f. *bankers' business.*

nĕgōtĭātor -ōris, m. *a business-man*; esp. *banker.*

nĕgōtĭŏlum -i, n. *a little business.*

nĕgōtĭor -ari, dep. *to carry on business*;

esp. as *a banker*; m. of partic. as subst. **nĕgōtĭans** -antis, *a businessman.*

nĕgōtĭōsus -a -um, *full of business, busy.*

nĕgōtĭum -i, n. *business, occupation, employment, task; pains, trouble, difficulty; a matter, piece of business.*

Nĕmĕa -ae, and **Nĕmĕē** -ēs, f. *a valley in Argolis*; adj. **Nĕmĕaeus** -a -um, subst. **Nĕmĕa** -orum, n. pl., *the Nemean games.*

nēmo -ĭnis, c., *no one, nobody:* nemo non, *everyone*; non nemo, *some or many.*

nĕmŏrālis -e and **nĕmŏrensis** -e, *of woods or groves; sylvan.*

nĕmŏrōsus -a -um, *full of groves; thickly leaved, full of foliage.*

nempĕ, *truly, certainly, to be sure.*

nĕmus -ŏris, n. *a wood, grove.*

nēnĭa -ae, f. *a funeral song, dirge; an incantation; nursery ditty, lullaby.*

nĕo nēre nēvi nētum, *to spin; to interweave.*

nēpa -ae, f. *a scorpion; a crab.*

¹nĕpōs -ōtis, m. *a grandson, a nephew; a descendant; a spendthrift.*

²Nĕpos -pōtis, m., C. Cornelius, *a Roman historian, friend of Cicero.*

neptis -is, f. *a grand-daughter.*

Neptūnus -i, m. *Neptune, god of the sea;* adj. **Neptūnius** -a -um.

nēquam, indecl.; compar. **nēquĭor**, superl. **nēquissĭmus**; *worthless, good for nothing, bad;* adv. **nēquĭtĕr.**

nēquāquam, *by no means, not at all.*

nēquĕ = nec; q.v.

nēquĕdum = necdum; q.v.

nēquĕo -ire, ĭvi and -ĭi -ĭtum, *to be unable.*

nēquiquam (**nēquicquam**), *in vain to no purpose; without good reason.*

nēquĭtĭa -ae, and **nēquĭtĭēs** -ēi, f. *worthlessness, badness; esp. extravagance.*

Nerēus -ĕos and -ĕi, m. *a sea-god.*

Nĕro -ōnis, m. *a cognomen in the gens Claudia;* esp. C. Claudius Nero, *fifth Roman emperor* (54–68).

nervōsus -a -um *sinewy, nervous, strong, vigorous;* adv. **nervōsē.**

nervŭlus -i, m., *nerve, strength.*

nervus -i, m. (usually plur.), *sinew, tendon;* fig. *strength, vigour, energy; a string,* esp. *of an instrument; a strap, thong, fetter.*

nescĭo -ire -ĭvi and -ĭi -ĭtum, *not to know, to be ignorant; to fail to recognise;* with infin. *to be unable to do;* nescio quis, quid, etc., *I know not who or what, somebody, something.*

nescĭus -a -um: act., *not knowing, ignorant, unaware; not knowing how, unable,* with infin.; pass., *unknown.*

Nestŏr -ŏris, m. *the most experienced of the Greek heroes at Troy.*

neu = neve; q.v.

neuter -tra -trum, *neither.* Transf., *of neither sex, neuter.* Adv. **neutrō**, *in neither direction, towards neither side.*

neutīquam (**ne ūtīquam**), *by no means, not at all.*

nēvĕ or **neu**, *and not, or not, nor* (esp. following ut or ne).

nēvis, nēvult = nonvis, nonvult; see nolo.

nex, nĕcis, f. *death;* usually *violent death, murder.*

nexilis -e, *tied together, plainted.*

nexum -i, n. *an arrangement by which a debtor pledged his liberty as security for debt.*

nexus -ūs, m. *a tying together, connecting, restraining;* also in the sense of nexum, q.v.

ni (**nei**) and **nivē**, *if not, unless;* also in the sense of ne, q.v.; quid ni? *why not?*

nicētērĭum -i, n. *reward of victory, prize.*

nicto -are, *to wink.*

nidor -ōris, m. *vapour, reek.*

nidŭlus -i, m. *a little nest.*

nidus -i, m. *a nest.*

niger -gra -grum, *black, dark-coloured; blackening; bad, unlucky;* n. as subst. *a black spot.*

nigresco nigrescĕre nigrŭi, *to become black, grow dark.*

nigro -are, *to be black;* partic. **nigrans** -antis, *black, dark.*

nigror -ōris, m. *blackness.*

nihil and contr. **nil**, *nothing;* nihil non, *everything;* non nihil, *something;* nihil, as internal acc., or adv., *not at all.*

nihildum, *nothing as yet.*

nihilum (**nilum**), *nothing;* as adv., *not at all;* nihilominus, *nevertheless.*

nil = nihil; q.v.

Nilus -i, m. *the river Nile;* adj. **Nilĭacus** -a -um.

nimbifer -fĕra -fĕrum, *stormy.*

nimbōsus -a -um, *rainy, stormy.*

nimbus -i, m. *cloud, mist;* esp. *a black rain-cloud; a storm, shower.*

nimirum, *undoubtedly, certainly, of course* (often ironical).

nimis, *very much; too much, excessively.*

nimius -a -um, *very great; too great, excessive; intemperate, immoderate.* N. as subst. *a great deal, much;* also *excess, too much.*

ningo (**ninguo**) ningĕre ninxi, *to snow;* impers., ningit, *it snows.*

ninguēs -ĭum, f. pl. *snow.*

Nĭŏbē -es, f. and **Nĭŏba** -ae, f. *daughter of Tantalus, wife of Amphion.*

nisi, *if not, unless;* after negatives and questions, *except;* nisi quod, *except that.*

¹nisus (**nixus**) -ūs, m. *pressing, straining, effort.*

²nisus -a -um, partic. from nitor; q.v.

nitēdŭla -ae, f. *dormouse.*

nĭtĕo -ēre, *to shine, glitter, be bright; to glow, be sleek, flourish.* Hence partic. **nitens** -entis, *shining, bright, sleek, blooming.*

nitesco -ĕre, *to begin to shine; to grow sleek.*

nĭtĭdus -a -um, *bright, shining; sleek, fat; flourishing, blooming.* Transf.,

spruce, elegant; refined, polished.
Adv. nĭtĭdē.

¹nĭtor nĭti nisus or nixus, dep. (1) to rest, lean, support oneself (on); to trust (in), depend (on). (2) to strive, exert oneself, make an effort; of movement, to press on, climb up.

²nĭtor -ōris, m. brilliance, brightness, splendour, glow, elegance.

nĭvālis -e, of snow, snowy.

nĭvĕ = ni, q.v., or neve, q.v.

nĭvĕus -a -um, of snow, snowy.

nĭvōsus -a -um, snowy.

nix, nĭvis, f. snow.

nixor -ari, dep. to lean upon; to strive, strain.

¹nixus = ¹nisus; q.v.

²nixus; see ¹nitor.

no nāre nāvi, to swim. Transf., to sail, flow, fly.

nōbĭlis -e, known; celebrated, renowned, infamous, notorious; of noble birth, highly bred; of things, fine.

nōbĭlĭtās -ātis, f. fame, celebrity; noble birth, nobility; meton., the aristocrats, the nobility; in gen., excellence, worth.

nōbĭlĭto -are, to make known, make famous or notorious.

nŏcĕo -ēre, to hurt, injure, harm (with dat.); partic. nŏcens -entis, hurtful, injurious, guilty, wicked; as subst., a guilty person.

noctĭlūca -ae, f. the moon.

noctĭvăgus -a -um, wandering by night.

noctŭ, abl. from nox; q.v.

noctŭa -ae, f. owl.

noctŭābundus -a -um, travelling by night.

nocturnus -a -um, by night, nightly, nocturnal.

nŏcŭus -a -um, hurtful, injurious.

nōdo -are, to knot, tie in a knot.

nōdōsus -a -um, full of knots, knotty.

nōdus -i, m. a knot; a girdle; any tie, bond, connexion, obligation; a knotty point, difficulty.

nōlo nolle nōlŭi, to be unwilling, wish not to, refuse.

nŏmăs -ădis, c. a nomad, esp. a Numidian.

nōmen -ĭnis, n. a name; nomen dare, to go for a soldier, enlist; nomen (hominis) deferre, to give information against, accuse; nomina solvere, to pay debts; nomen Romanum, the Roman power; nomine meo, in my name, on my behalf.

nōmenclātor -ōris, m. a slave who reminded his master of names.

nōmĭnātim, by name, expressly.

nōmĭnātĭo -ōnis, f. nomination to a public office.

nōmĭnĭto -are, to call regularly by name.

nōmĭno -are, to name, give a name to, call; to mention, speak about; to make famous; to appoint, nominate to an office; to denounce, give information against.

Hence partic. nōmĭnātus -a -um, well-known, celebrated.

nŏmisma -mătis, n. a coin.

nōn (old forms noenum, noenu), not; non nihil, something; nihil non,

everything; non quod, non quo, not that, not because; non ita, not very, not particularly; in questions = nonne? q.v.; in commands = ne; in answers, no.

nōnae -arum, f. the nones; the fifth day in all months, except March, May, July and October, when it was the seventh.

nōnāgēsĭmus (-ensĭmus) -a -um, ninetieth.

nōnāgĭēs (-ĭens), ninety times.

nōnāgintā, ninety.

nōnānus -a -um, belonging to the ninth legion.

nondum, not yet.

nongenti -ae -a, nine hundred.

nonnĕ, interrog. adv., asks a question to which an affirmative answer is expected.

nonnēmo, nonnĭhil; see nemo, nihil.

nonnullus (nōn nullus) -a -um, some; in plur., several.

nonnumquam (nōn numquam), sometimes.

nōnus -a -um, ninth; f. as subst., the ninth hour (roughly 3 p.m.).

nōnusdĕcĭmus -a -um, nineteenth.

Nōrĭcum -i, n. Noricum, a country between the Alps and the Danube; adj. Nōrĭcus -a -um.

norma -ae, f. a rule, standard.

nōs, plur. of ego; q.v.

noscĭto -are, to get to know, investigate, observe, perceive; to recognize.

nosco noscĕre nōvi nōtum, to become acquainted with, get to know; hence, in perfect tenses, to be acquainted with, know. Transf., to inquire into, investigate; to recognize; to approve, acknowledge.

Hence partic. nōtus -a -um, known; famous; notorious, familiar, customary; m. pl. as subst. friends, acquaintances.

noster -tra -trum, our, ours; of us, to us, for us; m. pl. nostri, our people.

nostrās -ātis, adj. of our country, native.

nŏta -ae, f. a mark, token, note, sign; in writing, a letter, character; a distinguishing mark, brand; hence sort, quality; also mark of disgrace, stigma (esp. as imposed by the censor).

nŏtābĭlis -e, remarkable, striking; adv. nŏtābĭlĭtĕr.

nŏtārĭus -i, m. secretary or shorthand writer.

nŏtātĭo -ōnis, f. marking, noting, choice; the stigma of the censor.

nōtesco nōtescĕre nōtŭi, to become known.

nŏthus -a -um, illegitimate, bastard; hybrid, mongrel; in gen., spurious.

nōtĭo -ōnis, f. an examination, investigation; an idea, notion, conception.

nōtĭtĭa -ae, and nōtĭtĭēs -ēi, f.: pass., being known, fame, celebrity; act., knowledge, acquaintance; hence idea, notion, conception.

nŏto -are, to mark, mark out, distinguish, denote; to observe; to write; to stigmatize (esp. of the censor).

'nōtus -a -um, partic. from nosco; q.v.

²nōtus (-ōs) -i, m. *the south wind.*

nŏvācŭla -ae, f. *a sharp knife or razor.*

nŏvālis -is, f. and nŏvāle -is, n. *fallow land; a cultivated field; crops.*

nŏvātrix -icis, f. *she that renews.*

nŏvellus -a -um, *new, young; fresh, unfamiliar.*

nŏvem, *nine.*

Nŏvember and Nŏvembris -bris, m. *of the ninth month of the Roman year, of November;* m. as subst., *November.*

nŏvendĕcim, nŏvemdĕcim, *nineteen.*

nŏvendiālis -e, *of nine days; happening on the ninth day; lasting nine days.*

nŏvēni -ae -a, *nine each, nine at a time;* poet., *nine.*

Nŏvensiles dīvi, *gods whose worship had been introduced from foreign countries.*

nŏverca -ae, f. *step-mother.*

nŏvercālis -e, *of or like a step-mother.*

nŏvīcius -a -um, *new, fresh;* esp. *of persons new to slavery.*

nŏviēs (-iens), *nine times.*

nŏvĭtās -ātis, f. *newness, novelty, strangeness; the condition of a novus homo* (see novus), *newness of nobility;* in pl. *new acquaintances.*

nŏvo -are, *to make new, renew, revive; to change, alter; to invent;* novare res, *to make a revolution.*

nŏvus -a -um, *new, fresh, young; fresh, inexperienced; revived; refreshed; novel, unusual, extraordinary;* novus homo, *the first of a family to hold curule office;* novae res, *political changes, a revolution;* novae tabulae, *new account-books* (i.e. *a cancellation of debts*). N. as subst., *a new thing, news, a novelty.* Adv. nŏvē, *in a new or unusual way.* Superl., nŏvissimus -a -um, *latest, last, extreme;* agmen, *the rear;* adv. nŏvissimē, *lately, lastly, in the last place.*

nox noctis, f. *night;* meton., *sleep, darkness, gloom, death.* Abl. form as adv. noctū, *by night.*

noxa -ae, f. *harm, injury, damage; a fault, offence; punishment.*

noxia -ae, f. *fault, offence, crime.*

noxius -a -um, *hurtful, injurious; culpable, guilty.*

nūbēcŭla -ae, f. *a little cloud; a troubled expression.*

nūbes -is, f. *a cloud;* fig., *any dense mass; gloom; veil, concealment.*

nūbĭfer -fĕra -fĕrum, *cloud-bearing.*

nūbĭgĕna -ae, c. *born of a cloud.*

nūbĭlis -e, *marriageable.*

nūbĭlus -a -um, *cloudy, overcast; dark, gloomy;* n. sing. as subst., *cloudy weather;* n. pl., *clouds.*

nūbo nūbĕre nupsi nuptum, *to cover, veil;* of a bride, *to be married to, to marry* (with dat.); f. of partic. nupta, *married,* or, as subst., *a bride.*

nuclĕus -i, m. *the kernel of a nut, the stone of fruit.*

nūdĭus, *it is now the . . . day since* (always with ordinal numerals); nudius tertius, *the day before yesterday.*

nūdo -are, *to make bare, strip, uncover;* milit. *to leave undefended; to strip, spoil, divest, deprive.*

nūdus -a -um, *naked, bare, uncovered; defenceless, deprived; unadorned, plain; bare, mere, alone, only.*

nūgae -arum, f. pl., *trifles, nonsense, stuff.*

nūgātor -ōris, m. *a trifler, humbug.*

nūgātōrĭus -a -um, *trifling, frivolous, futile.*

nūgax -ācis, *trifling, frivolous.*

nūgor -ari, dep. *to trifle, talk nonsense; to trick, cheat.*

nullus -a -um, *no, none, not any; non-existent, ruined;* nullo modo, nullo pacto, *by no means;* as a strong negative, *not at all;* as subst., esp. *no one.*

num, interrog. particle, introducing a direct question, to which a negative answer is expected, or an indirect question, in the sense *whether.*

Nŭma -ae, m., Pompilius, *the second king of Rome.*

Nŭmantia -ae, f. *a town in Spain.*

nūmen -inis, n. *nodding, a nod; as an expression of will, command, consent;* of a deity, *divine will, divine command;* hence, in gen., *divine majesty, divinity, deity.*

nŭmĕrābĭlis -e, *able to be counted.*

nŭmĕro -are, *to count;* esp. *to count out money, to pay; to count over possessions,* i.e. *to own; to reckon, consider.*

Hence partic. nŭmĕrātus -a -um, *counted out; in hard cash, in ready money;* n. as subst. *hard cash, money down.*

nŭmĕrōsus -a -um. (1) *numerous.* (2) *rhythmical, metrical, melodious.* Adv. nŭmĕrōsē.

nŭmĕrus -i, m. (1) *a number, reckoning, total; a mass; a mere number, cypher; a category, band, class; rank, position, regard, consideration.* (2) *measure, part, respect;* in music, *metre, number, time.* Abl. sing. as adv. nŭmĕrō, *exactly, at the right time; too quickly, too soon.*

Nŭmĭda -ae, m. *a Numidian.*

Nŭmĭtor -ōris, m. *king of Alba, grandfather of Romulus and Remus.*

nummārĭus -a -um, *belonging to money; bribed with money, venal.*

nummātus -a -um, *provided with money, rich.*

nummŭlārĭus -i, m. *a money-changer.*

nummŭlus -i, m. *a little piece or sum of money.*

nummus -i, m. *a piece of money, coin;* esp. *the sesterce, a coin of small value.*

numquam = nunquam; q.v.

nunc, *now, at present. as things are;* of past or future time, *then, already.*

nuncŭpātĭo -ōnis, f. *naming, pronouncement.*

nuncŭpo -are, *to name, call by name to pronounce solemnly.*

nundĭnae -arum, f. pl. *market-day; the market-place; traffic, trade, business.*

nundĭnātĭo -ōnis, f. *the holding of a market, trade, business.*

nundĭnor -ari, dep. *to transact business, trade, traffic; to buy,* esp. *corruptly; to be present in great numbers.*

nundĭnum -i, n. *market-time.*

nunquam (numquam), *never;* numquam non, *always;* non numquam, *sometimes.*

nuntĭātĭo -ōnis, f. *a declaration made by the augur.*

nuntĭo -are, *to announce, give notice.*

nuntĭus -a -um, *announcing, bringing news.* M. as subst. **nuntĭus** -i: (1) *a messenger.* (2) *a message, news;* esp. *an official notice.*

nūper, *lately, not long ago.*

nupta -ae, f. subst. from nubo; q.v.

nuptĭae -arum, f. pl. *marriage, a wedding.*

nuptĭālis -e, *of marriage.*

nŭrus -us, f. *a daughter-in-law; any young married woman.*

nusquam, *nowhere, at (or to) no place; in nothing, on no occasion; to or for nothing;* nusquam esse, *not to exist.*

nūto -are, *to nod, keep nodding; to sway, waver.*

nūtrīcĭus -i, m. *a tutor, guardian.*

nūtrīco -are and **nūtrīcor** -ari, dep. *to suckle, nourish; to support, sustain.*

nūtrīcŭla -ae, f. *nurse, nanny.*

nūtrīmen -ĭnis, n. *nourishment.*

nūtrīmentum -i, n. *nourishment; support, training.*

nūtrĭo -ire and **nūtrĭor** -iri, dep. *to suckle, nourish, bring up; to make good, support, sustain.*

nūtrix -īcis, f. *a nurse, foster-mother.*

nūtus -ūs, m. *a nod; command, will; gravitation, downward movement.*

nux nŭcis, f. *a nut; a nut-tree.*

nympha -ae, and **nymphē** -es, f. *a bride;* Nymphae, *the Nymphs.*

O

O, o, the fourteenth letter of the Latin Alphabet.

o! interj. *oh!*

ob, prep. with acc., *in front of, before; in return for; because of, on account of;* ob rem, *to the purpose, with advantage.*

ŏbaerātus -a -um, *in debt;* as subst., *a debtor.*

ŏbambŭlo -are, *to walk up and down, walk about near.*

ŏbarmo -are, *to arm.*

ŏbăro -are, *to plough up.*

obbrūtesco -ĕre, *to become stupid or dull.*

obc-; see occ-.

obdo -dĕre -dĭdi -dĭtum, *to place before, put against;* fores, *to shut the door.*

obdormisco -dormiscĕre -dormīvi, *to go to sleep.*

obdūco -dūcĕre -duxi -ductum. (1) *to draw over, draw in front;* of persons, *to bring forward.* (2) *to cover, close over;* venenum, *to swallow;* frontem, *to wrinkle;* of time, *to pass, spend.*

obductĭo -ōnis, f. *covering, veiling.*

obdūresco -ĕre, *to become hard, harden.*

obdūro -are, *to be hard (against); to stand out, hold out, persist.*

ŏbēdĭo = oboedio; q.v.

ŏbĕo -ire -ĭvi and -ĭi -ĭtum. Intransit., *to go to, go to meet, go against;* of heavenly bodies, *to set;* of the living, *to die.* Transit., *to go to, go over, traverse; to go over, encompass,* by looking or speaking; *to enter upon, engage in, perform, execute* a task; with diem or mortem, *to die.*

ŏbĕquĭto -are, *to ride up to.*

ŏberro -are, *to wander about, go astray.*

ŏbēsus -a -um, *fat, plump; swollen; coarse.*

ŏbex -ĭcis, m. and f. *bolt, bar, barrier, barricade.*

obf-; see off-.

obg-; see ogg-.

ŏbhaeresco -haerescĕre -haesi -haesum. *to stick fast, adhere to.*

obĭăcĕo -ēre, *to lie at, lie against.*

obĭcĭo -icĕre -iēci -iectum, *to throw in the way, to expose; to inspire, cause, produce; to put before, hold before, as protection or obstacle; to bring up* anything as a reproach, *to throw in a person's teeth.*
Hence partic. **obiectus** -a -um, *lying near, opposite to; exposed to; brought up against* a person; n. pl. as subst., *charges.*

obiectātĭo -ōnis, f. *a reproach.*

obiecto -are, *to throw in the way, expose; to set against; to bring up* anything as a reproach, *to throw in a person's teeth.*

¹obiectus -a -um, partic. from obicio; q.v.

²obiectus -ūs, m. *placing against, putting opposite.*

ŏbīrascor -irasci -īrātus, dep. *to grow angry at.*

ŏbĭtĕr, *on the way, by the way, in passing.*

ŏbĭtus -ūs, m. *an approach;* of heavenly bodies, *setting;* of the living, *death, downfall, destruction.*

obiurgātĭo -ōnis, f. *scolding, reproving.*

obiurgātor -ōris, m. *a scolder, reprover.*

obiurgātōrĭus -a -um, *reproachful, scolding.*

obiurgo -are, *to scold, reprove, blame, chastise.*

oblanguesco -languescĕre -langŭi, *to become weary.*

oblatro -are, *to bark at; to scold.*

oblectāmen -ĭnis, n. *delight, pleasure.*

oblectāmentum -i, n. *delight, amusement, pastime.*

oblectātĭo -ōnis, f. *delighting, amusing.*

oblecto -are, *to please, amuse; to pass* time *pleasantly, while away* time.

oblīdo -līdĕre -līsi -lisum, *to crush.*

oblĭgātĭo -ōnis, f. *a bond, tie.*

oblĭgo -are, *to tie, bind up, bandage.* Transf., *to bind, make liable, oblige; to make liable to punishment, make guilty.* Hence partic. **oblĭgātus** -a -um, *bound, under an obligation.*

oblĭmo -are, *to cover with slime or mud.*

oblĭno -linĕre -lēvi -litum, *to smear, daub, besmear; to stain, defile;* perf. partic. **oblĭtus** -a -um, *overloaded.*

oblīquo -are, *to turn sideways, turn aside.*

oblīquus -a -um, *slanting, sideways, on one side;* of speech, *indirect, covert; looking askance, envious.* Adv. oblīquē, *sideways, aslant; indirectly, by implication.*

oblītesco -lītescĕre -lītŭi, *to conceal oneself.*

oblittĕro -are, *to cancel, blot out.*

oblīvĭo -ōnis, f. *forgetfulness, oblivion.*

oblīvĭōsus -a -um, *oblivious, forgetful; causing forgetfulness.*

oblivíscor oblivisci oblītus, dep. *to forget.*

oblīvĭum -i, n., usually plur., *oblivion, forgetfulness.*

oblongus -a -um, *oblong.*

oblŏquor -lŏqui -lŏcūtus, dep. *to speak against, answer back, contradict, abuse, interrupt;* in music, *to accompany.*

obluctor -ari, dep. *to struggle against.*

obmōlĭor -iri, dep. *to build against* (as barrier or defence).

obmurmŭro -are, *to roar against.*

obmūtesco -mūtescĕre -mūtŭi, *to become dumb; to cease.*

obnātus -a -um, *growing on.*

obnītor -nīti -nixus, dep. *to press against, strive against; to take up a stand, maintain a firm position;* adv. from partic., obnixē, *firmly, vigorously.*

obnoxĭōsus -a -um, *submissive, compliant.*

obnoxĭus -a -um, with dat., *liable, addicted to, guilty of; indebted, obliged, dependent on; subject to, exposed to.*

obnūbo -nūbĕre -nupsi -nuptum, *to cover.*

obnuntĭātĭo -ōnis, f. *the announcement of an unfavourable omen.*

obnuntĭo -are, *to report an unfavourable omen.*

ŏbŏedĭentĭa -ae, f. *obedience, compliance.*

ŏbŏedĭo -ire, *to obey, comply with, listen to* (with dat.); partic. ŏbŏedĭens -entis, *obedient, compliant;* adv. ŏbŏedĭentĕr.

ŏbŏrĭor -ŏrīri -ortus, dep. *to arise, appear.*

obrēpo -rēpĕre -repsi -reptum, *to creep up to; to steal upon, come on by surprise.*

obrētĭo -ire, *to catch in a net.*

obrĭgesco -rĭgescĕre -rĭgŭi, *to become stiff, esp. to freeze.*

obrŏgo -are, *to amend* or *repeal a law by introducing another.*

obrŭo -rŭĕre -rŭi -rŭtum; fut. partic. -rŭĭtūrus. Intransit., *to fall, collapse.* Transit., *to cover, bury, swamp, drown; to overwhelm, destroy, obliterate.*

obrussa -ae, f. *assay; test.*

obsaepĭo -saepire -saepsi -saeptum, *to fence in, block up, render inaccessible.*

obsătŭro -are, *to stuff, choke.*

obscēnĭtās (obscaen-) -ātis, f. *impurity, indecency.*

obscēnus (obscaenus) -a -um, *foul, filthy;* morally, *impure, indecent; ill-omened.* Adv. obscēnē.

obscūrātĭo -ōnis, f. *darkening; disappearance.*

obscūrĭtās -ātis, f. *darkness;* of language, *obscurity;* of condition, *obscurity, low birth.*

obscūro -are, *to cover, darken, obscure; to veil, conceal, suppress.*

obscūrus -a -um, *covered, dark, obscure;* n. as subst., *darkness;* of language, *obscure, unintelligible;* of origin, etc., *unknown, obscure;* of character, *secret, reserved, close.* Hence adv. obscūrē, *darkly; unintelligibly; secretly.*

obsecrātĭo -ōnis, f. *earnest entreaty, supplication; public prayer to the gods.*

obsecro -are, *to beseech, implore, entreat.*

obsĕcundo -are, *to comply with.*

obsēpĭo = obsaepio; q.v.

obsĕquella -ae, f. *compliance.*

obsĕquens -entis, partic. from obsequor; q.v.

obsĕquentĭa -ae, f. *complaisance.*

obsĕquĭum -i, n. *compliance, submission; indulgence, pliancy.*

obsĕquor -sĕqui -sĕcūtus, dep. *to comply with, yield to, obey;* partic. obsĕquens -entis, *compliant, obedient; favourable;* adv. obsĕquentĕr.

[1]obsĕro -are, *to bolt, bar.*

[2]obsĕro -sĕrĕre -sēvi -sĭtum, *to sow thickly, cover with seeds, etc.;* partic. obsĭtus -a -um, *full of, covered with, beset by* (with abl.).

observantĭa -ae, f. *respect, attention.*

observātĭo -ōnis, f. *observing, watching; care, accuracy, circumspection.*

observātor -ōris, m. *observer, watcher.*

observĭto -are, *to watch carefully.*

observo -are, *to watch, regard, attend to;* of rules, *to keep, regard;* of persons, *to respect.* Hence partic. observans -antis, *attentive, respectful.*

obses -sĭdis, c. *a hostage; a surety, security, pledge.*

obsessĭo -ōnis, f. *blockade.*

obsessor -ōris, m. *one who besets, haunts, or besieges.*

obsĭdĕo -sĭdēre -sēdi -sessum: intransit., *to sit down near;* transit., *to beset haunt, frequent;* esp. *to blockade, besiege; to watch over, be on the look-out for.*

obsĭdĭo -ōnis, f. *blockade, siege.*

[1]obsĭdĭum -i, n. *blockade, siege.*

[2]obsĭdĭum -i, n. *the condition of a hostage.*

obsīdo -sīdĕre -sēdi -sessum, *to blockade, besiege, invest.*

obsignātor -ōris, m. *one who seals; a witness to a will.*

obsigno -are, *to seal;* of a witness, *to sign and seal; to stamp, impress.*

obsisto -sistĕre -stĭti -stĭtum, *to place oneself before* or *in the way of; to oppose, withstand, resist.*

obsĭtus -a -um, partic. from [2]obsero; q.v.

obsŏlĕfīo -fīĕri -factus, *to become worn out; to be degraded.*

obsŏlesco -escĕre -ēvi, -ētum, *to go out
of use, decay, wear out;* partic.
obsŏlētus -a -um, *worn out, decayed;
obsolete; threadbare, poor;* compar.
adv. obsŏlētius, *more shabbily.*

obsōnātor -ōris, m. *a caterer.*

obsōnĭum -i, n. *what is eaten with
bread;* e.g., *vegetables, fruit, fish.*

¹obsōno -are and obsōnor -ari, dep.,
to buy food, cater, provide a meal.

²obsōno -are, *to interrupt by noise.*

obsorbĕo -ēre -ŭi, *to swallow, gulp down.*

obstetrix -icis, f. *midwife.*

obstĭnātĭo -onis, f. *persistence, firmness,
obstinacy.*

obstĭno -are, *to persist, be resolved.*
    Hence partic. obstĭnātus -a -um,
    persistent, firm, obstinate; adv.
    obstĭnātē.

obstĭpesco = obstupesco; q.v.

obstĭpus -a -um, *leaning to one side;
bent back or down.*

obsto -stare -stĭti -stātūrus, *to stand
before or in the way; to oppose, resist,
obstruct* (with dat.); n. pl. of partic.
as subst. obstantĭa, *hindrances,
obstacles, impediments.*

obstrĕpo -strĕpĕre -strĕpŭi -strĕpĭtum,
*to make a noise, clamour at, disturb,
interrupt* (with dat.); in pass., *to be
drowned by noise or filled with noise.*

obstringo -stringĕre -strinxi -strictum,
*to bind up, tie fast; to entangle,
involve, put under an obligation.*

obstructĭo -ōnis, f. *hindrance, obstruc-
tion.*

obstrūdo = obtrudo; q.v.

obstrŭo -strŭĕre -struxi -structum, *to
build against; to block up, close, stop.*

obstŭpĕfăcĭo -făcĕre -fēci -factum,
to astound, stupefy, render senseless;
pass. obstŭpĕfīo -fĭĕri -factus.

obstŭpesco (obstĭp-) -stŭpescĕre
-stŭpŭi, *to become senseless to be
astounded.*

obsum ŏbesse obfŭi, *to be in the way,
be prejudicial to* (with dat.).

obsŭo -sŭĕre -sŭi -sūtum, *to sew on;
to sew up, close up.*

obsurdesco -descĕre -dŭi, *to become
deaf; to turn a deaf ear.*

obtĕgo -tĕgĕre, -texi -tectum, *to cover
up; to protect; to conceal;* partic.
obtĕgens -entis, *concealing.*

obtempĕrātĭo -ōnis, f. *compliance,
obedience.*

obtempĕro -are, *to comply with, submit
to* (with dat.).

obtendo -tendĕre -tendi -tentum.
(1) *to stretch before, spread before.*
Transf., *to put forward as an excuse,
plead, allege.* (2) *to cover, conceal.*

¹obtentus -ūs, m. *stretching or spreading
before.* Transf., *pretext, pretence,
excuse.*

²obtentus -a -um, partic. from obtineo;
q.v.

³obtentus -a -um, partic. from obtendo; q.v.

obtĕro -tĕrĕre -trivi -tritum, *to trample,
crush, destroy.*

obtestātĭo -ōnis, f. *a calling of gods to*

witness; *an entreaty in the name of
the gods.*

obtestor -ari, dep. *to call as witness;
to adjure, implore, entreat in the name
of the gods.*

obtexo -texĕre -texŭi, *to cover.*

obtĭcĕo -ēre, *to be silent.*

obtĭcesco -tĭcescĕre -tĭcŭi, *to become
silent.*

obtĭnĕo -tĭnēre -tĭnŭi -tentum: transit.,
to hold, possess, keep, maintain; esp.
to maintain an assertion; also *to take
hold of, grasp;* intransit., *to hold,
obtain, continue.*

obtingo -tingĕre -tĭgi, *to happen, befall.*

obtorpesco -torpescĕre -torpŭi, *to
become stiff, numb, insensible.*

obtorquĕo -torquēre -torsi -tortum,
to wrench, twist round.

obtrectātĭo -ōnis, f. *disparagement,
detraction.*

obtrectātor -ōris, m. *detractor, disparager.*

obtrecto -are, *to disparage, detract from.*

obtrūdo (obstrūdo) -trūdĕre -trūsi
-trūsum. (1) *to gulp down, swallow
down.* (2) *to force, obtrude.*

obtrunco -are, *to cut down.*

obtundo -tundĕre -tŭdi -tūsum and
tunsum, *to beat upon, thump; to
make blunt, dull, weaken, weary.*
    Partic. obtūsus and obtunsus -a
    -um, *dull, blunt, blurred, insensible.*

obturbo -are, *to disturb, confuse, distract,
harass.*

obturgesco -ĕre, *to swell up.*

obturo -are, *to stop up.*

obtūsus -a -um, partic. from obtundo;
q.v.

obtūtus -ūs, m. *gaze, contemplation.*

ŏbumbro -are, *to overshadow, obscure;
to conceal, protect, cover.*

ŏbuncus -a -um, *bent inwards, hooked.*

ŏbustus -a -um, *burnt, hardened in the
fire.*

obvallo -are, *to surround with a wall,
wall round.*

obvĕnĭo -vĕnire -vēni -ventum, *to come
in the way of, to meet; to occur,
happen, fall to a person's lot.*

obversor -ari, dep. *to move before,
appear before.*

obverto (-vorto) -vertĕre -verti
-versum, *to turn towards, direct
against.* Partic. obversus -a -um,
turned towards; m. pl. as subst.,
opponents.

obvĭam, *in the way, on the way;* hence,
with dat., towards, against, to meet;
obviam ire, with dat., *to go to meet,
to oppose;* also *to help, remedy.*

obvĭus -a -um, *in the way, meeting*
(with dat.); *exposed; ready at hand;
affable, easy of access.*

obvolvo -volvĕre -volvi -vŏlūtum, *to
wrap up, cover all round.*

occaeco -are, *to make blind, to blind,
to darken; to conceal, make invisible,
to make dull or numb.*

occallesco -callescĕre -callŭi, *to become
thick-skinned, hard* or *unfeeling.*

occăno -cănĕre -cănŭi, *to sound.*

occāsĭo -ōnis, f. *a favourable moment, opportunity.*

occāsus -ūs, m. *the setting of heavenly bodies;* hence, *the west;* in gen., *fall, destruction.*

occātĭo -onis, f. *harrowing.*

occēdo -cēdĕre -cessi -cessum, *to go towards, meet.*

occento -are, *to sing a serenade to; to sing a lampoon against.*

occepto -are, *to begin.*

occĭdens -entis, m.; subst. from ²occido; q.v.

occīdĭo -ōnis, f. *slaughter, destruction, extermination.*

¹occĭdo -cīdĕre -cīdi -cīsum, *to strike down, beat to the ground; to kill, slay; to plague to death, torment.*

²occĭdo -cīdĕre -cĭdi -cāsum, *to fall, fall down;* of heavenly bodies, *to set;* of the living, *to die, perish, be ruined.* Hence pres. partic. **occĭdens** -entis, *setting;* m. as subst. (sc. sol), *the setting sun, the west.*

occĭdŭus -a -um, *setting, sinking;* hence, *western, westerly.*

occīno -cĭnĕre -cĕcĭni and -cĭnŭi, *to sing inauspiciously.*

occĭpĭo -cĭpĕre -cĕpi -ceptum, *to begin.*

occĭpĭtĭum -i, n. and **occĭput** -ĭtis, n. *the back of the head, occiput.*

occĭsĭo -ōnis, f. *killing, slaughter.*

occīsor -ōris, m. *slayer, murderer.*

occlūdo -clūdĕre -clūsi -clūsum, *to shut up, close up.*

occo -are, *to harrow.*

occŭbo -are, *to lie down,* esp. *to rest in the grave.*

occulco -are, *to trample, tread down.*

occŭlo -cŭlĕre -cŭlŭi -cultum, *to cover, hide.*
Hence partic. **occultus** -a -um, *hidden, concealed, private;* of persons, *close, reserved.* N. as subst., *concealment, secrecy, a secret.* Adv. **occultē**, *secretly, obscurely.*

occultātĭo -ōnis, f. *hiding, concealment.*

occultātor -ōris, m. *hider, concealer.*

occulto -are, *to hide, conceal.*

occultus -a -um, partic. from occulo; q.v.

occumbo -cumbĕre -cŭbŭi -cŭbĭtum, *to fall down, sink down;* esp. *to fall down dead.*

occŭpātĭo -ōnis, f. *seizing, taking possession; anticipation; business, employment, occupation.*

occŭpo -are, *to take possession of, seize, occupy, master; to fall upon, attack; to take up, employ; to invest money; to anticipate, get a start on a person, be first to do a thing.*
Hence partic. **occŭpātus** -a -um, *busy, engaged, occupied.*

occurro -currĕre -curri -cursum, *to run to meet; to fall upon, attack; to work against, oppose, counteract;* of things, *to crop up, occur, come to mind.*

occursātĭo -ōnis, f. *attention, officiousness.*

occurso -are, *to run to meet; to oppose;* of things, *to occur, come to mind.*

occursus -ūs, m. *meeting, falling in.*

Ōcĕănus -i, m. *the ocean, the sea which encompasses the earth;* personif., *the father of the Nymphs.*

ŏcellus -i, m. *a (little) eye; a darling.*

ōcĭor, ōcĭus, compar. adj., *swifter, quicker;* adv. **ōcĭus**, *more swiftly; serius, ocius, sooner or later;* sometimes = *swiftly* only.

ŏcrĕa -ae, f. *a greave.*

ŏcrĕātus -a -um, *wearing greaves.*

Octāvĭus -a -um, *name of a Roman gens;* esp. of *C. Octavius,* the *Emperor Augustus;* adj. **Octāvĭānus** -a -um.

octāvus -a -um, *eighth; octavum, for the eighth time;* f. as subst. **octāva** -ae, *the eighth hour.*

octāvusdĕcĭmus -a -um, *eighteenth.*

octĭēs (-ĭens), *eight times.*

octingentēsĭmus -a -um, *eight hundredth.*

octingenti -ae -a, *eight hundred.*

octĭpēs -pĕdis, *having eight feet.*

octō, *eight.*

Octōber -bris, *belonging to the eighth month of the Roman year,* reckoning from March; *of October;* m. as subst., *October.*

octōdĕcim, *eighteen.*

octōgēnārĭus -a -um, *consisting of eighty.*

octōgēni -ae -a, *eighty each, eighty at a time.*

octōgēsĭmus -a -um, *eightieth.*

octōgĭēs (-ĭens), *eighty times.*

octōgintā, *eighty.*

octōiŭgis -e, *yoked eight together.*

octōnārĭus -a -um, *consisting of eight together.*

octōni -ae -a, *eight each, eight at a time, eight together.*

octōphŏros -on, *borne by eight;* n. as subst. **octōphŏron** -i, *a litter carried by eight bearers.*

octŭplĭcātus -a -um, *increased eight-fold.*

octŭplus -a -um, *eight-fold;* n. as subst. *an eight-fold penalty.*

octussis -is, m. *a sum of eight asses.*

ŏcŭlātus -a -um, *having eyes; catching the eye, conspicuous.*

ŏcŭlus -i, m. *the eye; esse in oculis, to be visible; an ornament, treasure; a bud or eye of a plant.*

ōdi odisse; fut. partic. ōsūrus, *to hate, detest, dislike.*

ōdĭōsus -a -um, *hateful, troublesome, annoying;* adv. **ōdĭōsē.**

ŏdĭum -i, n. *hatred; an object of hatred; esse odio, with dat., to be hated by.*

ŏdor (older ŏdōs) -ōris, m. *a smell, odour, scent; a scent, suspicion, inkling, presentiment;* in plur., *perfumery, spices.*

ŏdōrātĭo -ōnis, f. *smelling, smell.*

¹ŏdōrātus -ūs, m. *smelling; the sense of smell.*

²ŏdōrātus -a -um, partic. from odoro; q.v.

ŏdōrĭfer, -fĕra -fĕrum, *having a pleasant smell; producing perfumes.*

ŏdōro -are, *to make odorous;* partic. **ŏdōrātus** -a -um, *sweet-smelling.*

ŏdōror -ari, dep. *to smell; to smell out, snuff at;* hence *to aim at, aspire to; to search into, investigate; to get an inkling* or *smattering of.*

ŏdōrus -a -um. (1) *sweet-smelling.* (2) *keen-scented, tracking by smell.*

ŏdōs = odor; q.v.

Ŏdyssēa -ae, f. *the Odyssey.*

oecŏnŏmĭa -ae, f. *arrangement, division.*

oecŏnŏmĭcus -a -um, *relating to domestic economy; orderly, methodical.*

Oedĭpūs -pŏdis and -i, m. *king of Thebes, son of Laius and Jocasta, fated to kill his father and marry his mother.*

Oenōnē -ēs, f. *a Phrygian nymph, loved and deserted by Paris.*

oenŏphŏrum -i, n. *a basket for wine.*

oenus = unus; q.v.

oestrus -i, m. *the gad-fly, horse-fly; inspiration, frenzy.*

oesus = usus; q.v.

oesўpum -i, n. *a cosmetic.*

ŏfella -ae, f. *a bit, morsel.*

offa -ae, f. *a pellet, mass, lump; a swelling.*

offendo -fendĕre -fendi -fensum: transit., *to strike against, knock; to hit upon, fall in with; to shock, offend, displease;* intransit., *to knock, strike; to run aground; to stumble, make a mistake, to give offence* (with dat.); also *to take offence.*

Hence partic. offensus -a -um, *injured, hurt; offensive.*

offensa -ae, f. *a striking, knocking against; injury; displeasure, offence.*

offensĭo -ōnis, f. *a striking, knocking, hitting against;* pedis, *a stumbling.* Transf., *a misfortune, setback, indisposition; displeasure, disfavour, aversion, offence.*

offensĭuncŭla -ae, f. *a slight displeasure* or *check.*

offenso -are, *to strike, knock, stumble.*

¹offensus -a -um, partic. from offensus; q.v.

²offensus -ūs, m. *shock, collision; offence, dislike.*

offĕro offerre obtŭli oblātum, *to bring forward, place before, present, offer, expose; to inflict, occasion trouble;* se offerre, and pass., offerri, *to present oneself, appear.*

officīna -ae, f. *a workshop, factory.*

officĭo -fĭcĕre -fēci -fectum, *to act against; to get in the way of, impede, hinder, injure* (with dat.).

officĭōsus -a -um, *obliging, courteous, attentive; dutiful;* adv. officĭōsē.

officĭum -i, n. *dutiful* or *respectful action; attendance, service, duty; sense of duty, respect, courtesy; submission, allegiance.*

offīgo -ĕre, *to fix in, fasten.*

offirmo -are, *to make firm, to fasten;* with reflex. or intransit., *to be determined, persevere;* partic. offirmātus -a -um, *firm, resolute.*

offūcĭa -ae, f. *paint, rouge; deceit.*

offulgĕo -fulgēre -fulsi, *to shine upon.*

offundo -fundĕre -fūdi -fūsum, *to pour over, spread round; to overspread, cover, conceal; to overwhelm; to bring trouble, etc., upon a person.*

oggannĭo -ire, *to growl at.*

oh, interj. *oh! ah!*

ōhē, interj. *ho! hi!*

oi, interj. *oh!*

ŏlĕa -ae, f. *olive, olive-tree.*

ŏlĕăgĭnus -a -um, *of the olive-tree.*

ŏlĕārĭus -a -um, *of* or *for oil.*

ŏlĕaster -tri, m. *the wild olive-tree.*

ŏlĕo -ēre, *to emit an odour; to smell of, smack of;* partic. ŏlens -entis, *smelling; fragrant* or *stinking.*

ŏlĕum -i, n. *olive-oil, oil.*

olfacĭo -făcĕre -fēci -factum, *to smell; to scent out, detect.*

ŏlĭdus -a -um, *smelling.*

ŏlim, *at that time; of the past, formerly, once; of the future, hereafter, one day; with a present, for a long time now; at times, often.*

ŏlit-; see holit-.

ŏlīva -ae, f. *olive; olive-tree; olive-wreath; staff of olive-wood.*

ŏlīvētum -i, n. *an olive-grove.*

ŏlīvĭfer -fĕra -fĕrum, *olive-bearing.*

ŏlīvum -i, n. *olive-oil, oil.*

olla -ae, f. *jar, pot.*

ollus, olle, obsolete form of ille; q.v.

ŏlo = oleo; q.v.

ŏlor -ōris, m. *swan.*

ŏlōrīnus -a -um, *of a swan.*

ŏlus; see holus.

Ŏlympĭa -ae, f. *a city in Elis, where the Olympic games were held.*

Ŏlympus -i, m. *a mountain range between Macedonia and Thessaly, supposed to be the abode of the gods.*

ōmāsum -i, n. *bullocks' tripe.*

ōmen -ĭnis, n. *an omen, sign, prognostication.*

ōmentum -i, n. *fat; entrails, bowels.*

ōmĭnor -ari, dep. *to presage prophesy, predict.*

ōmĭnōsus -a -um, *foreboding, ominous.*

ŏmitto -mittĕre -mīsi -missum, *to let go, let fall; to give up, lay aside; to disregard;* in speaking, *to leave out, omit;* with infin., *to cease.* Hence partic. ōmissus -a -um, *negligent, remiss.*

omnĭfer -fĕra -fĕrum, *bearing everything.*

omnĭgĕnus -a -um, *of all kinds.*

omnĭmŏdīs, *in every way, entirely.*

omnīnō, *altogether, entirely, wholly; in general, in all; certainly, admittedly.*

omnĭpārens -entis, *all-producing.*

omnĭpŏtens -entis, *almighty.*

omnis -e, *all, every, whole; of all kinds;* in sing., *each,* or *the whole of one person or thing.*

omnĭtŭens -entis, *all-seeing.*

omnĭvăgus -a -um, *wandering everywhere.*

ŏnăger and ŏnagrus -i, m. *wild ass.*

ŏnĕrārĭus -a -um, *of burden, freight;* iumenta, *beasts of burden;* (navis) oneraria, *a merchant* or *transport ship.*

ŏnĕro -are, *to load, burden; to fill, weigh down; to oppress, overwhelm; to make worse, aggravate.*

ŏnĕrōsus -a -um, *heavy, burdensome; troublesome.*

ŏnus -ĕris, n. *a load, burden, weight; a trouble, charge; a public burden, tax.*

ŏnustus -a -um, *laden, loaded; full.*

ŏnyx -ўchis, m. and f. *onyx; a casket of onyx.*

ŏpācĭtās -ātis, f. *shadiness.*

ŏpāco -are, *to shade, overshadow.*

ŏpācus -a -um, *shaded, shady; dark, shadowy, obscure.*

ŏpella -ae, f. *a little labour or trouble.*

ŏpĕra -ae, f. *trouble, pains, exertion;* operam dare, *with dat., to work hard at;* est operae pretium, *it is worth while;* opera mea, *thanks to me.* Transf., *time for work; work done;* in pl., *labourers, workmen,* also *mobsmen, gangsters.*

ŏpĕrārĭus -a -um, *relating to work;* m. **ŏpĕrārĭus** -i, *a labourer, workman.*

ŏpercŭlum -i, n. *a lid, cover.*

ŏpĕrĭmentum -i, n. *a cover, covering.*

ŏpĕrĭo -pĕrīre -ĕrŭi -pertum, *to cover, bury, conceal; to close, shut up; to overwhelm;* n. of partic. as subst. **ŏpertum** -i, *a secret place, or secret.*

ŏpĕror -ari, dep. *to work, labour, be busy;* esp. in perf. partic. **ŏpĕrātus** -a -um, *engaged, busy* (esp. *engaged in worship*).

ŏpĕrōsus -a -um: act., *laborious, painstaking, industrious;* pass., *toilsome, difficult.* Adv. **ŏpĕrōsē**, *laboriously.*

ŏpertum -i, subst. from operio; q.v.

ŏpes; see ops.

Ŏpĭcus -a -um, *Oscan.* Transf., *stupid, philistine.*

ŏpĭfer -fĕra -fĕrum, *helpful.*

ŏpĭfex -fĭcis, c. *a maker, framer; a workman, artisan.*

ŏpĭfĭcīna = officina; q.v.

ŏpĭlĭo and **ūpĭlĭo** -ōnis, m. *shepherd.*

ŏpīmus -a -um, *rich, fruitful, fertile; lucrative; wealthy; sumptuous, abundant, copious;* of speech, *overloaded;* spolia opima, *spoils taken by a general from the enemy's general in single combat.*

ŏpīnābĭlis -e, *conjectural.*

ŏpīnātĭo -ōnis, f. *supposition, conjecture.*

ŏpīnātor -ōris, m. *one who supposes or conjectures.*

¹ŏpīnātus -a -um, partic. from opinor; q.v.

²ŏpīnātus -ūs, m. *conjecture, supposition.*

ŏpīnĭo -ōnis, f. *opinion, conjecture, supposition; repute, rumour, report.*

ŏpīnĭōsus -a -um, *set in opinion.*

ŏpīnor -ari, dep. and **ŏpīno** -are, *to be of opinion, suppose, conjecture.* Partic. **ŏpīnātus** -a -um, in pass. sense, *supposed, fancied.*

ŏpīpărus -a -um, *splendid, rich, sumptuous;* adv. **ŏpīpărē.**

ŏpĭtŭlor -ari, dep. *to help, aid* (with dat.).

ŏportet -tēre -tŭit, impers., *it is proper, one should, one ought.*

oppēdo -ĕre, *to mock, insult.*

oppĕrĭor -pĕriri -pertus, dep. *to wait or wait for.*

oppĕto -ĕre -īvi and -ĭi -ītum, *to go to meet, encounter;* esp. *to encounter death, to die.*

oppĭdānus -a -um, *of a town;* sometimes *provincial, 'small-town';* m. pl. as subst., *the inhabitants of a town.*

oppĭdo, *quite, very much;* in answers, *certainly.*

oppĭdŭlum -i, n. *a little town.*

oppĭdum -i, n. *a town;* in Britain, *a fortified wood.*

oppignĕro -are, *to pledge, pawn, give in pledge.*

oppĭlo -are, *to stop up, block up.*

opplĕo -plēre -plēvi -plētum, *to fill up, block.*

oppōno -pōnĕre -pŏsŭi -pŏsĭtum, *to put opposite or before; to pledge against, mortgage for; to set against, oppose, interpose; to allege as an objection; to contrast.* Hence partic. **oppŏsĭtus** -a -um, *standing against, opposite.*

opportūnĭtās -ātis, f. *convenience, fitness; a fit time, opportunity; advantage.*

opportūnus -a -um, *opportune, fit, suitable, convenient;* of time, *favourable;* with dat., sometimes, *exposed, liable to.* Adv. **opportūnē**, *seasonably, conveniently.*

oppŏsĭtĭo -ōnis, f. *opposing, opposition.*

¹oppŏsĭtus -a -um, partic. from oppono; q.v.

²oppŏsĭtus -ūs, m. *placing against, opposing, interposition.*

oppressĭo -ōnis, f. *pressing down, oppression; suppression; seizure.*

¹oppressus -ūs, m. *pressing down, pressure.*

²oppressus -a -um, partic. from opprimo; q.v.

opprĭmo -prĭmĕre -pressi -pressum. (1) *to press upon, press down; to crush, smother, stamp out.* (2) *to catch, take by surprise, occupy forcibly.*

opprŏbrĭum -i, n. *reproach, scandal, disgrace; a verbal reproach, taunt; a cause of disgrace.*

opprŏbro -are, *to taunt, reproach.*

oppugnātĭo -ōnis, f. *an assault on a town;* in gen., *an attack.*

oppugnātor -ōris, m. *an assailant, attacker.*

oppugno -are, *to attack, assault.*

Ops ŏpis, f.: in nom. sing., *the goddess of abundance;* other cases **ŏpem**, **ŏpis**, **ŏpĕ**, *might, power,* esp. *power to aid; help, support;* plur. **ŏpēs**, *resources, means, wealth.*

ops-; see obs-.

optābĭlis -e, *desirable, to be wished for.*

optātĭo -ōnis, f. *a wish.*

optĭmās -ātis, *one of the best, aristocratic;* m. pl. as subst. **optĭmātēs**, *the aristocratic party, the aristocrats.*

optĭmus (**optŭmus**) -a -um, superl. of bonus; q.v.

¹optĭo -ōnis, f. *choice, option.*

²optĭo -ōnis, m. *a helper, assistant.*

optĭvus -a -um, *chosen.*

opto -are, *to choose, select; to wish for, desire.* Hence partic. **optātus** -a

-um, *wished for, desired, welcome;* n. as
subst. **optātum,** *a wish;* abl. **optātō,**
according to one's wish.

ŏpŭlens, -entis; see opulentus.

ŏpŭlentia -ae, f. *wealth, riches, opulence;
the power, greatness of a state.*

ŏpŭlento -are, *to make wealthy, enrich.*

ŏpŭlentus -a -um, also **ŏpŭlens** -entis,
adj. *rich, wealthy; powerful, mighty;
splendid, sumptuous; lucrative.* Adv.
ŏpŭlentē and **ŏpŭlentĕr,** *richly,
splendidly.*

ŏpus -ĕris, n. *work, labour; work done,
a finished work; a building; a literary
work or a work of art;* plur. milit.
works, lines, siege-engines.

    ŏpus est (or **sunt**), *there is work, there
is need; one needs, it is necessary* (with
nom., abl., or genit. of what is needed).

ŏpuscŭlum -i, n. *a little work.*

ōra -ae, f. *edge, rim, boundary;* esp.
coast-line, coast; in gen., *region,
clime, country; the people of a district;
a hawser, cable* reaching to shore.

ōrācŭlum (**ōrāclum**) -i, n. *a solemn
utterance, oracle, divine response,
prophecy;* also *the place where an
oracle is given.*

ōrātio -ōnis, f. *speaking, speech; language, style;* esp. *a set speech;
eloquence; prose; an imperial message.*

ōrātiuncŭla -ae, f. *a little speech, short
oration.*

ōrātor -ōris, m. *speaker; spokesman,
envoy; orator.*

ōrātōrius -a -um, *of an orator, oratorical;*
f. as subst. *oratory;* adv. **ōrātōriē.**

ōrātrix -īcis, f. *a female suppliant.*

ōrātū, abl. sing. m. *by request.*

orbātor -ōris, m. *one who deprives
another of children or parents.*

orbis -is, m. *a circle, ring, disk; orbit,
coil;* orbis signifer, *the Zodiac;* orbis
lacteus, *the Milky Way;* orbis terrae,
terrarum, *the world.* Transf., *rota-
tion, round;* of style, *roundness.*

orbita -ae, f. *a wheel-rut.*

orbitās -ātis, f. *bereavement, loss of
children or parents.*

orbo -are, *to bereave, deprive of parents
or children.*

orbus -a -um, *deprived of parents or
children;* as subst. *an orphan;* in
gen., *deprived, destitute.*

orca -ae, f. *a pot or jar with a large belly.*

orchăs -ădis, f. *a species of olive.*

orchestra -ae, f. *the part of a Roman
theatre reserved for senators;* meton.,
the senate.

Orcus i-, m. *Orcus, the infernal regions.*
Transf., *the god of the lower world;
death.*

ordĕum = hordeum; q.v.

ordia prima = primordia; q.v.

ordinārius -a -um, *according to order,
regular, ordinary.*

ordinātim, *in good order, regularly,
properly.*

ordinātio -ōnis, f. *setting in order,
arrangement.*

ordino -are, *to set in order, settle,
arrange, appoint; to govern a country,*

Hence partic. **ordinātus** -a -um,
arranged, orderly.

ordior ordiri orsus, dep. *to begin;* esp.
to begin speaking. N. pl. of partic. as
subst. **orsa** -orum, *beginnings, undertaking;* esp. *words uttered, speech.*

ordo -ĭnis, m. *a series, line, row, order;*
milit., *a line, rank, file;* ordinem
ducere, *to be a centurion;* polit. and
socially, *an order, rank, class;* in gen.,
order, arrangement; ordine, *in turn,
in due order, regularly;* extra ordinem,
in an unusual, irregular manner.

Ŏrēăs -ădis, f. *a mountain-nymph.*

Ŏrestes -ae and -is, m. *son of Agamemnon and Clytemnestra, who killed
his mother to avenge his father.*

ŏrexis -is, f. *desire, appetite.*

orgānĭcus -i, m. *a musician.*

organum -i, n. *an instrument;* esp., *a
musical instrument.*

orgia -orum, n. pl. *a secret festival;
mysteries; orgies.*

ŏrĭchalcum -i, n. *yellow copper ore;
brass.*

ŏrĭcŭla = auricula; q.v.

ŏriens -entis, m. partic. from orior; q.v.

ŏrīgo -ĭnis, f. *origin, source, beginning;
an ancestor.*

Ŏrīōn -ōnis, m. *the constellation Orion.*

ŏrior ŏriri ortus, dep. *to rise; to spring
up, be born, proceed from a source or
cause.* Hence partic. **ŏriens** -entis,
rising. M. as subst. *the rising sun; the
east; the morning.*

ŏriundus -a -um, *arising from, springing
from.*

ornāmentum -i, n. *equipment, trappings, furniture; ornament, decoration;
honour, distinction.*

ornātrix -icis, f. *a female hairdresser,
tire-woman.*

¹**ornātus** -ūs, m. *dress, attire, equipment;
embellishment, ornament.*

²**ornatus** -a -um, partic. from orno; q.v.

orno -are, *to equip, furnish, fit out;* also
*to adorn, decorate, embellish; to honour,
distinguish.*

    Hence partic. **ornātus** -a -um,
*furnished, equipped, provided; adorned,
decorated, embellished.* Adv. **ornātē,**
splendidly, elegantly.

ornus -i, f. *the mountain-ash.*

ōro -are, *to speak;* esp. *to speak as an
orator;* with acc., *to treat, argue,
plead; to beg, pray, entreat, beseech.*

Ŏrontes -is and -ae, m. *chief river of
Syria.*

Orpheūs -ĕi and -ĕos, *a mythical
minstrel, husband of Eurydice.*

orsa -orum, from ordior; q.v.

orsus -ūs, m. *a beginning, undertaking.*

¹**ortus** -ūs, m.: *of heavenly bodies,
rising;* of persons, *origin, birth;* in
gen., *origin, source.*

²**ortus** -a -um, partic. from orior; q.v.

ŏryx -ȳgis, m. *a wild goat or gazelle.*

ŏrȳza -ae, f. *rice.*

¹**ōs** ōris, n. (1) *the mouth;* hence *voice,
talk;* uno ore, *unanimously;* in gen.,
mouth, opening, source. (2) *the face,
countenance; presence, sight; ex-*

pression; boldness of expression, impudence; a mask.

²ŏs ossis, n. a bone.

oscen -ĭnis, m. a bird from whose note auguries were taken (e.g., raven, owl, crow).

Osci -orum, an ancient people of Italy.

oscillum -i, n. a little mask.

oscĭtātĭo -ōnis, f. gaping, yawning.

oscĭto -are, to gape, yawn; partic. oscĭtans -antis, yawning, sleepy, listless; adv. oscĭtantĕr.

oscŭlātĭo -ōnis, f. kissing.

oscŭlor -ari, dep. to kiss; to caress, make much of.

oscŭlum -i, n. a little mouth; a kiss.

ōsor -ōris, m. a hater.

Ossa -ae, m. and f. a mountain range in Thessaly.

ossĕus -a -um, bony.

ossifrăgus -i, m. and ossifrăga -ae, f. the sea-eagle, osprey.

ostendo -tendĕre -tendi -tentum and -tensum, to hold out, show, reveal, present; in speech, to make plain, declare. N. of partic. as subst. ostentum -i, a prodigy, portent.

ostentātĭo -ōnis, f. showing, revealing; showing off, display; deceitful show, pretence.

ostentātor -ōris, m. one who shows; esp., a boaster.

ostento -are, to hold out, present, offer; to show, reveal; to show off, display; in speech, to declare, make known.

ostentŭi, dat. sing. m. for a show; merely for show; as a sign or proof.

ostentum -i, n., subst. from ostendo; q.v.

Ostĭa -ae, f. and Ostĭa -orum, n. the harbour and port of Rome, at the mouth of the Tiber; adj. Ostiensis -e.

ostĭārĭum -i, n. a door-tax.

ostĭātim, from door to door.

ostĭum -i, n. door; in gen., entrance; fluminis, mouth.

ostrĕa -ae, f. and ostrĕum -i. n. an oyster.

ostrĭfer -fĕra -fĕrum, producing oysters.

ostrĭnus -a -um, purple.

ostrum -i, n. purple dye prepared from a shell-fish; a purple dress.

Ŏtho -ōnis, m. a Roman cognomen.

ōtĭor -ari, dep. to be at leisure.

ōtĭōsus -a -um, at leisure, esp. free from public duties; calm, quiet, undisturbed, neutral. Adv. ōtĭōsē, at leisure; quietly, easily.

ōtĭum -i, n. free time, leisure, ease; peace, repose.

ŏvans -antis, partic. rejoicing, exulting; esp. celebrating the minor triumph (the ovatio).

ŏvātĭo -ōnis, f. an ovation, a kind of lesser triumph.

Ŏvĭdĭus -a, name of a Roman gens; esp. of the poet P. Ovidius Naso (43 B.C.-17 A.D.).

ŏvĭle -is, n. a sheepfold, an enclosure.

ŏvillus -a -um, of sheep.

ŏvis -is, f. a sheep.

ōvum -i, n. an egg.

P

P, p, the fifteenth letter of the Latin Alphabet.

pābŭlātĭo -ōnis, f. procuring fodder, foraging.

pābŭlātor -ōris, m. a forager.

pābŭlor -ari, dep. to forage, seek fodder.

pābŭlum -i, n. food, nourishment, fodder.

pācālis -e, peaceful.

pācĭfer -fĕrum, peace-bringing.

pācĭfĭcātĭo -ōnis, f. making of peace, pacification.

pācĭfĭcātor -ōris, m. a peacemaker.

pācĭfĭcātōrĭus -a -um, peacemaking, pacific.

pācĭfĭco -are, to make peace; to appease, pacify.

pācĭfĭcus -a -um, peacemaking, pacific.

pācĭscor pācisci pactus, dep. to make a bargain or agreement, to covenant, contract; transit., to stipulate for, bargain for; also to give in exchange. Perf. partic. in pass. sense, pactus -a -um, agreed upon, stipulated; betrothed. N. as subst. pactum -i, an agreement, treaty, pact; quo pacto? how? alio pacto, in another way.

pāco -are, to pacify, make peaceful; poet., to make fruitful.
Hence partic. pācātus -a -um, peaceful, quiet; n. as subst. a peaceful country.

pactĭo -ōnis, f. a bargain, contract, agreement, treaty.

pactor -ōris, m. one who makes a contract or treaty, negotiator.

pactum -i, n., and pactus -a -um, from paciscor; q.v.

Păcŭvĭus -a -um, a Roman tragic poet.

Pădus -i, m. the river Po.

paeān -ānis, m. (1) the Healer, a surname of Apollo. (2) a hymn, paean.

paedăgōgus -i, m. a slave who accompanied children to and from school.

paedor -ōris, m. dirt, filth.

paelex (pellex) -lĭcis, f. a mistress, concubine.

paelĭcātus -ūs, m. concubinage.

Paelĭgni -orum, m. pl. an Italian tribe.

paenĕ, nearly, almost.

paeninsŭla -ae, f. a peninsula.

paenĭtentĭa -ae, f. repentance, regret.

paenĭtĕo -ēre, to repent, regret, be sorry; impers. paenĭtet hominem, a person feels regret, is sorry; gerundive paenĭtendus -a -um, regrettable, unsatisfactory.

paenŭla -ae. f. a travelling-cloak, greatcoat.

paenŭlātus -a -um, wearing the paenula; q.v.

paeōn -ōnis, m. a metrical fŏot, consisting of three short syllables and one long.

Paestum -i, n. a town in Lucania famous for roses.

paetŭlus -a -um, with a slight cast in the eye.

paetus -a -um, with a cast in the eyes, squinting.

păgānus -a -um, belonging to a village,

rural; rustic; m. as subst. *a villager, countryman.*

pāgātim, *in villages, by villages.*

pāgella -ae, f. *a little page.*

pāgina -ae, f. *a page* of a letter, book, etc.

pāgĭnŭla -ae, f. *a little page.*

pāgus -i, m. *a village* or *country district; a canton.*

pāla -ae, f. *a spade; the bezel of a ring.*

Pălaestīna -ae, and **Pălaestīnē** -ēs, f. *Palestine.*

pălaestra -ae, f. *a gymnasium* or *wrestling school; wrestling.* Transf., *training in rhetoric.*

pălaestrĭcus -a -um, *of the palaestra, gymnastic*; adv. **pălaestrĭcē.**

pălaestrīta -ae, m. *the superintendent of a* palaestra (q.v.).

pălam: adv. *openly, publicly*; prep., with abl., *in the presence of.*

Pălātĭum -i, n. *the Palatine Hill in Rome*: in plur., *a palace*; adj. **Pălātīnus** -a -um.

pălātum -i, n. and **pălātus** -i, m. *the roof of the mouth, palate; taste; critical judgment.*

pălěa -ae, f. *chaff.*

pălěar -āris, n. *the dewlap of an ox.*

Pălēs -is, f. *tutelary goddess of herds and shepherds*; adj. **Pălīlis** -e; n. pl. as subst. **Pălīlia** -ium, *the feast of Pales on the 21st of April.*

pălimpsestus -i, m. *a palimpsest.*

Pălinūrus -i, m. *the pilot of Aeneas; a promontory on the coast of Lucania.*

păliūrus -i, m. *a plant, Christ's thorn.*

palla -ae, f. *a long outer garment, esp. as worn by women and actors.*

Pallas -ădis and -ădos, f. *Athene, the Greek goddess of wisdom, identified with Minerva*; adj. **Pallădius** -a -um; n. as subst. **Pallădĭum** -i *an image of Pallas.*

pallĕo -ēre, *to be pale* or *yellow*; partic. **pallens** -entis, *pale, wan, yellow, pale green; causing paleness; drooping, weak.*

pallesco pallescěre pallui, *to grow pale* or *yellow*; with acc., *to turn pale at.*

pallĭātus -a -um, *clad in a* pallium, i.e. *as a Greek* (opp. togatus).

pallĭdŭlus -a -um, *somewhat pale.*

pallĭdus -a -um, *pale, wan; causing paleness.*

pallĭŏlum -i, n. *a little Greek cloak; a hood.*

pallĭum -i, n. *a coverlet; a Greek mantle.*

pallor -ōris, m. *paleness; fading.*

palma -ae, f. (1) *the palm of the hand; a hand; the blade of an oar.* (2) *the palm-tree; a date; a palm broom; a palm-branch* as token of victory; hence, *victory, honour, glory.*

palmāris -e, *deserving the palm* or *prize, excellent.*

palmārĭum -i, n. *a masterpiece.*

palmātus -a -um, *embroidered with palm-branches.*

palmĕs -ĭtis, m. *a young branch esp. of a vine.*

palmētum -i, n. *a palm-grove.*

palmĭfer -fěra -fěrum, *abounding in palm-trees.*

palmōsus -a -um, *full of palms.*

palmŭla -ae, f. *the blade of an oar.*

pālor -ari, dep. *to wander, stray.*

palpebra -ae, f. *eyelid.*

palpĭto -are, *to move quickly, tremble, throb.*

palpo -are and **palpor** -ari, dep. *to stroke; to coax, flatter, wheedle.*

pălūdāmentum -i, n. *the military cloak.*

pălūdātus -a -um, *clad in the military cloak.*

pălūdōsus -a -um, *marshy, boggy.*

pălumbes -is, m. and f. *a wood-pigeon, ring-dove.*

¹pālus -i, m. *a pale, stake.*

²pălūs -ūdis, f. *a swamp, marsh, bog.*

păluster -tris -tre, *marshy, boggy.*

pampĭnĕus -a -um, *attached to* or *consisting of vine-tendrils.*

pampĭnus -i, m. and f. *a vine-tendril* or *vine-leaf.*

Pān Pānos, m. *the god of flocks, woods, and shepherds.*

pănăcēa -ae, f. and **pănăcēs** -is, n. *a plant, supposed to heal all diseases; panacea, heal-all.*

pānārĭum -i, n. *a bread-basket.*

panchrestus (panchristus) -a -um, *good for everything.*

pancrătĭum (-ŏn) -i, n. *a gymnastic contest.*

pando panděre pandi pansum and passum. (1) *to stretch out, spread out, extend;* crines passi, *dishevelled hair.* (2) *to throw open, lay open, reveal, disclose.*

    Hence partic. **passus** -a -um, *spread out, esp. spread out to dry*; n. as subst. *raisin-wine.*

pandus -a -um, *bent, curved, crooked.*

pango pangěre panxi, *to fasten, fix, drive in.* Transf., *to compose, write.* In perf. **pěpĭgi** and supine **pactum**, *to fix, settle, agree upon* (cf. paciscor).

pānĭcum -i, n. *a kind of wild millet.*

pānis -is, m. *bread*; in plur., *loaves.*

pannĭcŭlus -i, m. *a little garment.*

Pannŏnia -ae, f. *Pannonia, a district on the middle Danube.*

pannōsus -a -um, *ragged, tattered.*

pannūcěus (-ĭus) -a -um, *ragged; wrinkled, shrivelled.*

pannus -i, m. *a piece of cloth; garment; rag.*

Pănormus -i, f. and **Pănormum** -i, n. *a town in Sicily* (modern *Palermo*).

pansa -ae, *splay-footed.*

panthēra -ae, f. *a panther* or *leopard.*

pantŏmīmus -i, m. and **pantŏmīma** -ae, f. *a dancer, mime.*

păpae, interj. *wonderful! indeed!*

păpās -ae and -ātis, m. *a tutor.*

păpāver -ĕris, n. *poppy.*

păpāvĕrĕus -a -um, *of the poppy.*

pāpĭlĭo -ōnis, m. *butterfly.*

păpilla -ae, f. *nipple, teat, breast.*

Păpīrĭus -a -um, *name of a Roman gens.*

pappo -are, *to eat.*

pappus -i, m. *the woolly seed of certain plants.*

păpŭla -ae, f. *a pimple.*

păpyrĭfer -fĕra -fĕrum, *producing papyrus.*

păpyrus -i, m. and f. and **păpyrum** -i, n. *the plant papyrus; clothing or paper made from papyrus.*

păr păris, *equal, like, a match*; m. and f. as subst., *a companion*; n. as subst., *the like, the equivalent, or a pair*; par impar ludere, *to play at odd and even*; par est, *it is appropriate.* Hence adv. **părĭtĕr**, *equally, alike; together, at the same time.*

părăbĭlis -e, *easily procured.*

părăbŏla -ae and **părăbŏlē** -ēs f. *a comparison.*

părăsītus -i, m. and **părăsīta** -ae, f. *a guest*; in bad sense, *a toady, parasite.*

părātĭo -ōnis, f. *preparing, preparation.*

1parātus -a -um, partic. from paro; q.v.

2parātus -ūs. m. *preparation, fitting out, equipment.*

Parca -ae, f. *a goddess of fate*; pl. Parcae, *the three Fates.*

parco parcĕre pĕperci (and parci) parsum, *to be sparing, economize; to spare, refrain from injuring* (with dat.); *to refrain from, keep oneself from*; with infin., *to forbear to.*

parcus -a -um, *sparing, thrifty, economical; moderate, sparing*; of things, *scanty, small, meagre.* Adv. **parcē**, *sparingly, economically, moderately.*

pardus -i, m. *a panther or leopard.*

1pārens -entis, partic. from pareo; q.v.

2pārens -entis, c. *a parent*; sometimes *grandfather* or *ancestor; author, cause, origin.*

părentālis -e, *parental, of parents (or ancestors)*; n. pl. as subst. **părentālĭa** -ĭum, *a festival in honour of the dead.*

părento -are, *to celebrate the parentalia.* Transf., *to avenge the dead.*

pārĕo -ere, *to appear, become evident.* Transf., *to obey, give way to; to be subject to, serve* (with dat.); partic. **pārens** -entis, *obedient.*

pārĭēs -ĕtis, m. *a wall, properly the wall of a house.*

părĭĕtīnae -arum, f. pl. *old walls, ruins.*

Părīlĭa = Palilia; see Pales.

părĭlis -e, *similar, like, equal.*

părĭo părĕre pĕperi partum; fut. partic. **păritūrus**; *to bring forth, bear, produce.* Transf., *to occasion, create, make, get.*

Păris -ĭdis, m. *a Trojan prince who carried off Helen.*

parma -ae, f. *a small round shield, a buckler.*

parmātus -a -um, *armed with the parma.*

parmŭla -ae, f. *a small round shield, buckler.*

Parnāsus (-ŏs) -i, m. *a mountain in Phocis, sacred to Apollo and the Muses*; f. adj. **Parnāsis** -ĭdis, and adj. **Parnāsĭus** -a -um.

păro -are, *to set, put; to prepare, provide, furnish, obtain; to buy.* Hence partic. **părātus** -a -um, *prepared, ready; provided, equipped*;

of persons, *skilled.* Adv. **părātē**, *with preparation, readily.*

părŏcha -ae, f. *a supplying of necessaries.*

părŏchus -i, m. *an officer who looked after travelling ambassadors and magistrates.* Transf., *a host.*

păropsis -ĭdis, f. *a dessert-dish.*

Părus (-ŏs) -i, f. *an island in the Aegean Sea, famous for marble*; adj. **Părĭus** -a -um.

parra -ae, f. *a bird of ill omen, perhaps owl.*

parrĭcīda -ae, f. *a parricide, one who murders a parent or near relative*; polit., *an assassin, traitor.*

parrĭcīdĭum -i, n. *the murder of a parent or any near relative*; polit., *assassination, treason.*

pars partis, f. *a part, piece, share; a direction, region; a side, party; an actor's role*; in gen., usually plur., *office, function, duty*; pars . . . pars, *some . . . others*; pro (sua) parte, pro virile parte, *to the best of one's ability*; magna ex parte, *to a great extent*; multis partibus, *many times, much.* Adv. **partim**, *partly*; used like a noun, *some.*

parsĭmōnĭa -ae, f. *thrift, economy.*

Parthi -orum, m. pl. *the Parthians*; adj. **Parthĭcus** and **Parthus** -a -um; subst. **Parthia** -ae, *Parthia.*

particeps -cĭpis, *sharing, participating in* (with genit.); as subst., *partner, comrade.*

particĭpo -are, *to share with a person; to cause a person to share.*

particŭla -ae, f. *a small part, particle.*

partim, adv. from pars; q.v.

partĭo -ire and **partĭor** -iri, dep. *to share out, distribute, divide*; perf. partic. in pass. sense **partītus** -a -um, *divided*; adv. **partītē**, *with proper divisions.*

partītĭo -ōnis, f. *division, sharing, distribution.*

partŭrĭo -ire, *to desire to bring forth, have the pains of labour; to teem with anything, be full of.*

1partus -a -um, partic. from pario; q.v.

2partus -ūs, m. *bearing, bringing forth, birth.* Transf., *young, offspring.*

părum, *too little, not enough* (as adv. or subst.); parum habere, *to think too little, be dissatisfied with.* Compar. **minus**, *less*; sometimes = *not, not at all*; sin minus, *but if not.* Superl. **mĭnĭmē** (**mĭnŭmē**), *in the least degree, very little, least of all*; sometimes *not at all, by no means.*

părumper, *for a little while.*

Părus = Paros; q.v.

parvĭtās -ātis, f. *littleness, smallness.*

parvŭlus -a um, *very small*; of age, *young, little.*

parvus -a -um, *little, small; slight, weak*; of time, *short*; of age, *young*; of value, *poor, insignificant*; n. as subst. *a little.* Compar. **mĭnor**, *smaller, less*; of time, *shorter*; of age, minor (natu), *younger*; of value, *inferior.* Superl. **mĭnĭmus**, *smallest, least*;

n. as adv., minimum, *very little.*
Rare superl. **parvissǐmus** -a -um.

pasco pascĕre pāvi pastum. (1)
transit., *to feed, lead to pasture; to
keep, support; to nourish;* also *to give
as pasture.* Transf., *to feast, gratify.*
Pass. as middle, *to graze on;* also *to
feast upon, delight in.* (2) intransit.,
of animals, *to graze, browse.*

pascǔus -a -um, *for pasture or grazing;*
n. as subst. *a pasture.*

Pāsǐthěa -ae and **Pāsǐthěē** -ēs, f. *one
of the three Graces.*

passer -ĕris, m. *a sparrow or other
small bird; a sea-fish, a plaice or
flounder.*

passercǔlus -i, m. *a little sparrow.*

passim, *here and there, far and wide;
indiscriminately.*

passum -i, n., subst. from pando; q.v.

¹**passus** -a -um, partic. from pando; q.v.

²**passus** -a -um, partic. from patior; q.v.

²**passus** -ūs, m. *a step, stride, pace;*
esp. as a measure of length = five
Roman feet. Transf., *footstep, track.*

pastillus -i, m. *a lozenge.*

pastǐo -ōnis, f. *pasture, pasturing.*

pastor -ōris, m. *a herd;* esp. *a shepherd.*

pastōrālis -e, **pastōrǐcǐus** -a -um and
pastōrǐus -a -um, *of shepherds,
pastoral.*

¹**pastus** -a -um, partic. from pasco; q.v.

²**pastus** -ūs, m. *pasture, feeding; food,
sustenance.*

Pătăvǐum -i, n. *a town in North Italy,
birthplace of Livy (now Padua);*
adj. **Pătăvīnus** -a -um.

pătěfǎcǐo -făcĕre -fēci -factum; pass.
pătěfīo -fīěri -factus sum; *to open,
throw open, open up, make accessible;
to bring to light, disclose, reveal.*

pătěfactǐo -ōnis, f. *throwing open,
disclosing.*

pătella -ae, f. *a dish, platter, plate.*

pătěo -ēre, *to be open, stand open, be
accessible* or *exposed; to be revealed,
disclosed, clear; to stretch out, extend.*
Hence partic. **pătens** -entis, *open,
unobstructed, accessible, exposed;* also
evident. Compar. adv. **pătentǐus,**
more openly.

păter -tris, m. *father, sire; founder,
head;* pater familias, *or* familiae,
head of a household; plur., patres,
forefathers; *also as a title of the
senators, patres,* or patres conscripti;
pater patriae, *father of his country, a
national hero.*

pătěra -ae, f. *a shallow dish, saucer.*

păternus -a -um, *of a father, paternal;
native.*

pătesco pătescĕre pătǔi, *to be opened,
lie open; to be revealed; to spread out.*

pătǐbilis -e: pass. *endurable, bearable;*
act., *sensitive.*

pătǐbǔlum -i, n. *a yoke as an instrument
of punishment, a pillory.*

pătǐentǐa -ae, f. *endurance, resignation;*
in bad sense, *want of spirit.*

pătǐna -ae, f. *a dish.*

pătǐor păti passus, dep. *to suffer,
undergo, experience; to permit, allow.*
Hence partic. **pătǐens** -entis,

enduring, capable of enduring, with
genit.; *patient;* in bad sense, *stubborn.*
Adv. **pătǐentěr.**

pătrātor -oris, m. *accomplisher, achiever.*

pătrǐa -ae, f. *fatherland;* see patrius.

pătrǐcǐus -a -um, *of the* patres,
patrician, noble; m. as subst., *a
patrician.*

pătrǐmōnǐum -i, n. *property inherited
from a father, patrimony.*

pătrǐmus -a -um, *having a father still
living.*

pătrītus -a -um, *inherited from one's
father.*

pătrǐus -a -um, *of a father, fatherly,
paternal; hereditary; ancestral;
native.* F. as subst. **pătrǐa** -ae, f.
(sc. terra), *fatherland, native land.*

pătro -are, *to accomplish, execute,
achieve.*

pătrōcǐnǐum -i, n. *the services of a
patron;* esp. *defence in a court of
law;* in gen., *defence, protection;*
plur., **pătrōcǐnǐa,** *clients.*

pătrōcǐnor -ari, dep. *to protect, defend.*

pătrōna -ae, f. *a protectress, patroness.*

pătrōnus -i, m. *a protector, defender,
patron;* esp. *an advocate in a court of
law.*

pătrǔělis -e, *descended from a father's
brother;* as subst., *a cousin.*

¹**pătrǔus** -i, m. *a father's brother,
paternal uncle.*

²**pătrǔus** -a -um, adj. *of an uncle.*

pătǔlus -a -um, *open, standing open,
spreading, extended.*

paucǐtās -ātis, f. *fewness, scarcity.*

paucǔlus -a -um, *very small;* plur.
very few.

paucus -a -um, oftener plur. **pauci** -ae
-a, *few, little;* as subst., m. pl. **pauci,**
a few, the select few, the oligarchs; n.
pl. **pauca,** *a few words.*

paulātim (paullātim), *gradually, little
by little.*

paulispěr (paullispěr), *for a little
while.*

paulǔlus (paullǔlus) -a -um, *very
little;* n. as subst. **paulǔlum** -i, *a very
little;* acc. and abl., as adv., *a little.*

¹**paulus (paullus)** -a -um, *little, small;*
as subst., **paulum,** *a little;* acc., and
abl. **paulo,** *like adv., a little.*

²**Paulus (Paullus)** -i, m. *the name of a
family of the gens Aemilia.*

pauper -ĕris, *poor;* of things, *scanty,
meagre.*

paupercǔlus -a -um, *poor.*

paupěrǐēs -ēi, f. *poverty.*

paupěro -are, *to make poor, to deprive.*

paupertās -ātis, f. *poverty.*

pausa -ae, f. *cessation, end.*

pausǐa -ae, f. *a species of olive.*

pauxillǔlus -a -um, *very little, very
small.*

pauxillus -a -um, *small, little:* n. as
subst. *a little.*

păvěfactus -a -um, *frightened, terrified.*

păvěo păvēre pāvi: intransit., *to quake
with fear, panic;* transit., *to quake at.*

păvesco -ĕre: intransit., *to begin to
quake, take fright;* transit., *to be
alarmed by.*

păvĭdus -a -um, *trembling, quaking, fearful; causing fear.* Adv. **păvĭdē,** *fearfully.*

păvĭmento -are, *to pave.*

păvĭmentum -i, n. *a pavement* of tiles, brick, stone, etc.

păvĭo -ire, *to beat.*

păvĭto -are: intransit., *to shiver, tremble, quake with fear*; transit., *to quake at.*

păvo -ōnis, m. *peacock.*

păvor -ōris, m. *trembling, quaking; fear, panic.*

pax pācis, f. *peace; calm, quiet*; of the gods, *grace, favour*; pace tua, *with your good leave.*

pecco -are, *to make a mistake, go wrong, err or sin*; n. of partic. as subst. **peccātum** -i, *an error, fault, sin.*

pĕcŏrōsus -a -um, *rich in cattle.*

pectĕn -ĭnis, m. *a comb; a weaver's comb; a rake; clasped hands; a quill,* for striking the strings of the lyre; *a shell-fish, the scallop.*

pecto pectĕre pexi pexum, *to comb; to card; to thrash*; partic. **pexus** -a -um, *with the nap on, woolly.*

pectus -ŏris, n. *breast; heart, soul; mind.*

pĕcu, n. plur. **pĕcŭa,** *sheep, flocks*; also *pastures.*

pĕcŭārĭus -a -um *of sheep or cattle*; as subst., m. *a breeder of cattle, grazier*; n. pl. *herds of sheep or cattle.*

pĕcūlātor -ōris, m. *one who embezzles public money.*

pĕcūlātus -ūs, m. *embezzlement of public money.*

pĕcūlĭāris -e, *of one's private property; one's own, special, peculiar*; adv. **pĕcūlĭārĭtĕr,** *specially.*

pĕcūlĭum -i, n. *small property, savings*; esp. *the savings of slaves or sons.*

pĕcūnĭa -ae, f. *property, wealth*; esp. *money, cash.*

pĕcūnĭārĭus -a -um, *of money, pecuniary.*

pĕcūnĭōsus -a -um, *wealthy, rich; lucrative.*

'pĕcus -ŏris, n. *cattle, a herd, flock,* esp. *of sheep.*

²pĕcus -ŭdis, f. *a single head of cattle; a beast, animal*; esp. *a sheep.*

pĕdālis -e, *a foot long* (or *wide*).

pĕdārĭus -a -um, *of a foot*; (senatores) pedarii, *senators of inferior rank.*

pĕdes -ĭtis, m.: adj., *going on foot*; subst., *a foot soldier*; coll., *infantry.*

pĕdester -tris -tre, *on foot, pedestrian*; copiae, *infantry*; sometimes, *on land.* Transf., *simple, ordinary, prosaic*: of style, *written in prose.*

pĕdĕtemptim, *feeling one's way; gradually, cautiously.*

pĕdica -ae, f. *a fetter; a trap, snare.*

pĕdĭcŭlōsus -a -um, *lousy.*

pĕdis -is, c. *a louse.*

pĕdĭsĕquus -i, m. and **pĕdĭsĕqua** -ae, f. *a follower, attendant, lackey.*

pĕdĭtātus -ūs, m. *infantry.*

pĕdum -i, n. *a shepherd's crook.*

Pēgăsus (-os) -i, m. *the winged horse which produced the fountain Hippo-*crene; adj. **Pēgăsēĭus** and **Pēgăsēus** -a -um; **Pēgăsĭdes,** *the Muses.*

pegma -ătis, n. *a bookcase; a stage, scaffolding.*

pēiĕro and **perĭūro** -are, *to commit perjury, forswear oneself*; with acc., *to swear falsely by.*

pēior, compar. of malus; q.v.

pĕlăgus -i, n., Greek plur. pelage, *the open sea, the main.*

pēlămȳs -ȳdis, f. *the young tunnyfish.*

Pĕlasgi -orum, m. pl. *the Greeks.*

Pēlēus -ĕi and -ĕos, m. *king of Thessaly, husband of Thetis, father of Achilles*; **Pēlīdēs** -ae, m. *son* or *grandson of Peleus.*

Pēlĭon -i, n. *mountain range in Thessaly*; adj. **Pēlĭăcus** and **Pēlĭus** -a -um.

pellăcĭa -ae, f. *enticing, allurement.*

pellax -ācis, *deceitful, seductive.*

pellĕgo = perlego; q.v.

pellex = paelex; q.v.

pellĭcĭo -lĭcĕre -lexi -lectum, *to entice, decoy, seduce.*

pellĭcŭla -ae, f. *a little skin* or *hide.*

pellĭo -ōnis, m. *a furrier.*

pellis -is, f. *a hide, skin; dressed hide, leather, felt*; milit., *a hut covered with skins.*

pellītus -a -um, *clothed in skins.*

pello pellĕre pĕpŭli pulsum, *to strike, knock, beat; to impel, propel, move, affect; to drive away, dislodge, banish.*

pellūcĕo = perluceo; q.v.

Pēlŏponnēsus -i, f. *the Peloponnese.*

Pēlops -ŏpis, m. *the father of Atreus and Thyestes.*

pĕlōris -ĭdis, f. *an edible shell-fish, a clam.*

pelta -ae, f. *a small shield.*

peltastes or -a -ae, m. *a soldier armed with the pelta.*

peltātus -a -um, *armed with the pelta.*

pelvis -is, f. *a basin.*

pēnārĭus -a -um, *of* or *for provisions.*

Pēnātes -ĭum, m. pl., *the Penates, Latin deities of the household and family.* Transf., *home, dwelling.*

pĕnātĭgĕr -gĕra -gĕrum, *carrying the Penates.*

pendĕo pendēre pĕpendi, *to hang; to hang upon, depend on; to hang loose, hover; to be suspended, discontinued; to be in suspense, uncertain, undecided.*

pendo pendēre pĕpendi pensum: transit., *to cause to hang down; to weigh; to pay out money; to weigh, consider, judge, value, esteem*; poenas, supplicia, *to pay a penalty, suffer punishment*; intransit., *to weigh.* Hence partic. **pensus** -a -um, *weighed; esteemed, valued, prized*; nihil pensi habere, *to put no value upon, be indifferent about.* N. as subst. **pensum** -i, *wool weighed out to a spinner*; hence, *a day's work, task, duty.*

pendŭlus -a -um, *hanging; in suspense, undecided.*

Pēnĕlŏpa -ae, and **Pēnĕlŏpē** -ēs, f. *the wife of Ulysses.*

pĕnēs, prep. with acc. *in the possession*

of, in the power of, belonging to; **penes se esse**, *to be in one's senses.*

pĕnĕtrābĭlis -e: pass., *that can be passed through, penetrable*; act., *penetrating, piercing.*

pĕnĕtrālis -e. (1) *passing through, penetrating.* (2) *inward, internal.* N. as subst. *inner chambers, interior*, esp. of a temple.

pĕnĕtro -are: transit., *to put into; to pass through or into, to penetrate*; intransit., *to make one's way in, to penetrate.*

pēnĭcillus -i, m. *a painter's brush or pencil; style.*

pēnĭcŭlus -i, m. *a brush; a sponge.*

pēnis -is, m. *a tail.*

¹**pĕnĭtus** -a -um, adj. *inward, internal.*

²**pĕnĭtus**, adv. *internally, inwardly, inside; deeply, through and through; widely.*

penna -ae, f. *a feather; a wing.*

pennātus -a -um, *feathered, winged.*

penniger -gĕra -gĕrum, *feathered, winged.*

pennĭpēs -pĕdis, *wing-footed.*

pennĭpŏtens -entis, *able to fly, winged*; plur. as subst., *birds.*

pennŭla -ae, f. *a little wing.*

pensĭlis -e, *hanging, pendent.*

pensĭo -ōnis, f. *a weighing out*; hence *paying, payment, day of payment; rent.*

pensĭto -are, *to weigh carefully, weigh out*; hence, *to pay; to ponder, consider.*

penso -are, *to weigh carefully; to estimate, ponder, consider; to counter-balance, requite; to pay for, purchase one thing with another.*

pensum -i, n. subst., from pendo; q.v.

Penthĕus -ĕi and -ĕos, *a king of Thebes.*

pēnūrĭa -ae, f. *lack, want, penury.*

pĕnus -ūs and -i, c., **pĕnum** -i, n., **pĕnus** -ōris, n. *provisions, victuals.*

peplum -i, n. and **peplus** -i, m. *a robe of state.*

per, prep. with acc.: of space, *through, along, over*; sometimes *before*, in the *presence of*; of time, *throughout, during; in the course of, in a time of*; of means or instrument, *through, by, by means of, with, by way of*; of cause, *because of, on account of*; per me licet, *you may as far as I am concerned*; in *entreaties, oaths*, etc., *in the name of.*

pēra -ae, *bag, wallet.*

pĕrabsurdus -a -um, *excessively absurd.*

pĕraccommŏdatus -a -um, *very convenient.*

pĕrăcer -cris -cre, *very sharp.*

pĕrăcerbus -a -um, *very sour, very harsh.*

pĕractĭo -ōnis, f. *finishing, completion.*

pĕrăcūtus -a -um, *very sharp; very shrill; very sharp-witted.* Adv. **pĕrăcūtē.**

pĕrădŭlescens -entis, *very young.*

pĕraequĕ, *quite equally.*

pĕrăgĭto -are, *to drive about violently, harass.*

pĕrăgo -ăgĕre -ēgi -actum. (1) *to pass through*; in words, *to go over,*

mention. (2) *to drive about, harass, disturb.* (3) *to carry through, complete, accomplish*; legal, *to prosecute till conviction.*

pĕragrātĭo -ōnis, f. *wandering through.*

pĕragro -are, *to wander through, travel through.*

pĕrămans -antis, *very loving*; adv. **pĕrămantĕr.**

pĕrambŭlo -are, *to walk through, pass through.*

pĕrămoenus -a -um, *very pleasant.*

pĕramplus -a -um, *very large.*

pĕrangustus -a -um, *very narrow*; adv. **pĕrangustē.**

pĕrantiquus -a -um, *very old.*

pĕrappŏsĭtus -a -um, *very suitable.*

pĕrardŭus -a -um, *very difficult.*

pĕrargūtus -a -um, *very witty.*

pĕrāro -are, *to plough through; to furrow the brow; to scratch letters, to write, write on.*

pĕrattentus -a -um, *very attentive*; adv. **pĕrattentē.**

perbacchor -ari, dep. *to revel through-out.*

perbĕātus -a -um, *very happy.*

perbellē, *very prettily.*

perbĕnē, *very well.*

perbĕnĕvŏlus -a -um, *very well disposed.*

perbĕnignē, *very kindly.*

perbĭbo -bĭbĕre -bĭbi, *to drink up, absorb*; mentally, *to imbibe, take in.*

perblandus -a -um, *very charming.*

perbŏnus -a -um, *very good.*

perbrĕvis -e, *very short*; perbrevi, *in a very short time*; adv. **perbrĕvĭtĕr.**

perca -ae, f. *a fish, the perch.*

percălĕfactus -a -um, *thoroughly heated.*

percălesco -călescĕre -călŭi, *to become very warm.*

percallesco -callescĕre -callŭi: intransit., *to lose sensibility, become callous*; transit., *to get a good knowledge of.*

percārus -a -um. (1) *very dear, very costly.* (2) *very dear, much loved.*

percautus -a -um, *very cautious.*

percĕlebro -are, *to speak of commonly*; pass., *to be much mentioned.*

percĕler -is -e, *very swiftly*; adv. **percĕlĕrĭtĕr.**

percello -cellĕre -cŭli -culsum, *to strike, push; to beat down, overturn, shatter, ruin*; mentally, *to daunt, unnerve.*

percensĕo -censēre -censŭi, *to count over, reckon; to survey, review; to travel through.*

perceptĭo -ōnis, f. *a receiving, grasping, gathering together.*

perceptus -a -um, partic. from percipio; q.v.

percĭo -cire -cīvi -cītum and **percĭĕo** -cĭēre, *to stir up, set in motion*; partic. **percĭtus** -a -um, *aroused, excited*; of character, *excitable.*

percĭpĭo -cĭpĕre -cēpi -ceptum, *to lay hold of, seize; to collect, gather, harvest, gain*; with the senses, *to feel, take in*; mentally, *to learn,* *grasp, understand.* N. pl. of partic. as subst. **percepta** -orum, *principles, rules.*

percītus -a -um, partic. from percio; q.v.

¹**percōlo** -are, *to strain, as through a sieve.*

²**percŏlo** -cōlĕre -cŏlŭi -cultum, *to adorn, decorate; to honour a person, revere greatly; to complete.*

percōmis -e, *very friendly.*

percommŏdus -a -um, *very fit*; adv. **percommŏdē.**

percontātĭo (percunct-) -ōnis, f. *inquiry, interrogation.*

percontātor (percunct-) -ōris, m. *an inquirer, asker of questions.*

percontor (percunctor) -ari, dep. *to sound; hence to inquire, interrogate, investigate.*

percŏquo -cŏquĕre -coxi -coctum, *to cook or heat thoroughly; to ripen; to scorch, blacken.*

percrēbresco -brescĕre -brŭi and **percrēbesco** -bescĕre -bŭi, *to become prevalent, get well known.*

percrēpo -crĕpare -crĕpŭi -crĕpĭtum, *to resound, ring.*

percunct-; see percont-.

percŭpĭdus -a -um, *very fond.*

percŭpĭo -cúpĕre, *to desire exceedingly.*

percŭrĭōsus -a -um, *very inquisitive.*

percŭro -are, *to cure, heal thoroughly.*

percurro -currĕre -cŭcurri or -curri -cursum, *to run through, hasten through, travel through;* in words, *to run over, mention in passing; to run over in the mind or with the eye; to pass through stages.*

percursātĭo -ōnis, f. *travelling through.*

percursĭo -ōnis, f. *running through; rapid consideration.*

percurso -are, *to ramble over, rove about.*

percussĭo -ōnis, f. *striking, beating;* esp. *beating time;* hence *time, rhythm.*

percussor -ōris, m. *a striker;* esp. *a murderer, assassin.*

percussus -ūs, m. *beating, knocking, striking.*

percŭtĭo -cŭtĕre -cussi -cussum, *to strike hard; to strike through, pierce, transfix; to strike down, cut down;* mentally, *to strike, shock;* colloq., *to deceive.*

perdĕcōrus -a -um, *very comely.*

perdēlirus -a -um, *senseless.*

perdifficilis -e, *very difficult;* adv. **perdifficilĭtĕr.**

perdignus -a -um, *very worthy.*

perdiligens -entis, *very diligent;* adv. **perdiligentĕr.**

perdisco -discĕre -dĭdici, *to learn thoroughly.*

perdisertē, *very eloquently.*

perditor -ōris, m. *destroyer.*

perditus -a -um, partic. from perdo; q.v.

perdiū, *for a very long time.*

perdiŭturnus -a -um, *lasting a very long time.*

perdīvĕs -vĭtis, *very rich.*

perdix -dīcis, c. *partridge.*

perdo -dĕre -dĭdi -dĭtum (in pass., usually pereo, perire), *to destroy, do away with, ruin; to lose; to waste, squander.*

Hence partic. **perdĭtus** -a -um, *miserable, ruined; morally lost, abandoned, profligate.* Adv. **perdĭtē,** *desperately, immoderately; in an abandoned manner.*

perdŏcĕo -docĕre -dŏcŭi -doctum, *to teach or instruct thoroughly;* partic. **perdoctus** -a -um, *very learned, very skilful;* adv. **perdoctē.**

perdŏmo -dŏmare -dŏmŭi -dŏmĭtum, *to tame or subdue thoroughly.*

perdūco -dūcĕre -duxi -ductum, *to lead through, bring along; conduct; to carry* or *construct buildings, from one point to another; to bring over to an opinion, to induce;* in time, *to continue, prolong; to smear over with a substance.*

perductor -ōris, m. *a guide; a pimp, pander.*

perdūdum, *a long time ago.*

perdŭellĭo -ōnis, f. *treason.*

perdŭellis -is, m. *a public enemy.*

perdŭim -is -it, alternative pres. subj. of perdo; q.v.

perdūro -are, *to last long, endure.*

pĕrĕdo -esse -ēdi -ēsum, *to eat up, devour; to consume, destroy.*

pĕregrē, adv. *in, to* or *from a foreign country; abroad, from abroad.*

pĕregrīnābundus -a -um, *travelling about.*

pĕregrīnātĭo -ōnis, f. *travelling* or *staying in foreign countries; roaming.*

pĕregrīnātor -ōris, m. *one who travels about.*

pĕregrīnĭtās -ātis, f. *the condition of a foreigner* or *alien; foreign manners.*

pĕregrīnor -ari, dep. *to stay* or *to travel in foreign countries; to roam, wander, ramble; to be strange, foreign.*

pĕregrīnus -a -um, *foreign, of a foreigner, strange;* m. and f. as subst., *a foreigner, stranger,* esp. *a foreigner resident in Rome.* Transf., *inexperienced.*

pĕrēlĕgans -antis *very elegant;* adv. **pĕrēlĕgantĕr.**

pĕrēlŏquens -entis, *very eloquent.*

pĕremnĭa, n. pl. *the auspices taken on crossing any running water.*

pĕrendĭē, *the day after tomorrow.*

pĕrendĭnus -a -um, *relating to the day after tomorrow.*

pĕrennis -e, *lasting throughout the year; durable, perennial.*

pĕrennĭtās -ātis, f. *duration, perpetuity.*

pĕrenno -are, *to last many years.*

pĕrĕo -ire -ĭi and -ĭvi -ĭtum, (often as pass. of perdo), *to go to waste, be ruined* or *lost, pass away, perish, die.*

pĕrĕquĭto -are, *to ride through, ride round.*

pĕrerro -are, *to wander through, ramble over; to look over, scan.*

pĕrērŭdĭtus -a -um, *very learned.*

pĕrexĭgŭus -a -um, *very small, very scanty;* of time, *very short.* Adv.

pĕrexĭgŭĕ, *very scantily very sparingly.*

perfăcētus -a -um, *very witty, brilliant;* adv. perfăcētē.

perfăcĭlis -e, *very easy; very courteous.* N. acc. as adv. perfăcĭle, *very easily; very readily.*

perfămĭlĭāris -e *very familiar, intimate;* m. as subst. *a very great friend.*

perfectĭo -ōnis f. *completion; perfection.*

perfector -ōris, m. *a perfecter, finisher.*

perfectus -a -um, partic. from perficĭo; q.v.

perfĕro -ferre -tŭli -lātum, *to carry through, bear to the end;* se perferre, *to betake oneself;* of news, etc., *to deliver, convey;* of tasks, *to bring to an end;* of trouble, *to bear, suffer, endure.*
Hence partic. perfĕrens -entis, *enduring, patient.*

perfĭca -ae, f. adj *accomplishing, perfecting.*

perfĭcĭo -fĭcĕre -fēci -fectum, *to bring to an end, complete, finish, achieve;* of time, *to live through;* of a pupil, *to make perfect.*
Hence partic. perfectus -a -um, *perfect, complete, finished*: adv. perfectē.

perfĭdēlis -e, *very faithful.*

perfĭdĭa -ae, f. *faithlessness, treachery, falsehood.*

perfĭdĭōsus -a -um, *faithless treacherous;* adv. perfĭdĭōsē.

perfĭdus -a -um, *faithless treacherous, false.*

perfīgo -fīgĕre -fixi -fixum, *to pierce through, stab.*

perflābĭlis -e, *able to be blown through.*

perflāgĭtĭōsus -a -um, *very shameful.*

perflo -are, *to blow through, blow over.*

perfluctŭo -are, *to surge over.*

perflŭo -flŭĕre -fluxi -fluxum, *to stream through, run away.*

perfŏdĭo -fŏdĕre -fōdi -fossum, *to dig through, pierce through; to excavate, make by digging.*

perfŏro -are, *to pierce through; to form by boring.*

perfrĕquens -entis, *much visited.*

perfrĭco -fricare -frĭcŭi -fricatum and -frictum, *to rub over;* os, frontem, etc., *to put on a bold face.*

perfrĭgesco -frĭgescĕre -frixi, *to catch a chill.*

perfrĭgĭdus -a -um, *very cold.*

perfringo -fringĕre -frēgi -fractum, *to break through; to break in pieces, shatter.*

perfrŭor -frŭi -fructus, dep. *to enjoy to the full; to execute completely.*

perfŭga -ae, m. *a deserter.*

perfŭgĭo -fŭgĕre -fŭgi -fŭgĭtum, *to flee away, take refuge;* esp. *to desert to the enemy.*

perfŭgĭum -i, n. *a place of refuge, shelter.*

perfunctĭo -ōnis, f. *performing, discharging.*

perfundo -fundĕre -fūdi -fūsum, *to pour over; to steep in a fluid, to dye;* in gen., *to steep in, fill with.*

perfungor -fungi -functus, dep. *to perform fully, execute, discharge; to go through, endure.*

perfūro -ere, *to rage furiously.*

Pergămum -i, n. and Pergămus -i, f., also plur. Pergăma -orum, n. *the citadel of Troy; Troy.*

pergaudĕo -ēre, *to rejoice exceedingly.*

pergo pergĕre perrexi perrectum. *to continue, proceed, go on with.*

pergrandis -e, *very large, very great.*

pergrātus -a -um, *very pleasant.*

pergrăvis -e, *very weighty, very important;* adv. pergrăvĭtēr.

pergŭla -ae, f., *a balcony, outhouse; a shop, workshop; a school.*

pĕrhĭbĕo -ēre -ŭi -ĭtum, *to bring forward, cite; to maintain, assert, hold, say.*

pĕrhīlum, *a very little.*

pĕrhŏnōrĭfĭcus -a -um, *very honourable; very respectful;* adv. pĕrhŏnōrĭfĭcē, *very respectfully.*

pĕrhorresco -horrescĕre -horrŭi, *to begin to shudder or tremble,* esp. with fear; transit., *to shudder at.*

pĕrhorrĭdus -a -um, *very dreadful.*

pĕrhūmānus -a -um, *very friendly, very civil;* adv. pĕrhūmānĭtēr.

Pĕrĭclēs -is, m. *Athenian statesman.*

pĕrĭclĭtātĭo -ōnis, f. *trial, experiment.*

pĕrĭclĭtor -ari, dep.: intransit., *to try, make a trial, venture; to take a risk, be in danger;* transit., *to try, test prove; to endanger, risk.*

pĕrĭcŭlōsus -a -um, *dangerous, perilous;* adv. pĕrĭcŭlōsē.

pĕrĭcŭlum (pĕrĭclum) -i, n. *a trial, proof, test, attempt; danger, peril, hazard;* at law, *a trial, action, suit;* hence, *a legal record or register.*

pĕrĭdōnĕus -a -um, *very suitable.*

pĕrillustris -e *very evident; very distinguished.*

pĕrimbēcillus -a -um, *very weak.*

pĕrĭmo (pĕrĕmo) -ĭmĕre -ēmi -emptum, *to do away with, destroy, kill, annihilate.* Transf., *to thwart, frustrate.*

pĕrincommŏdus -a -um, *very inconvenient;* adv. pĕrincommŏdē.

pĕrindĕ, adv. *in like manner;* perinde ac, ut, or quam, *just as;* perinde ac si, *just as if.*

pĕrindulgens -entis, *very indulgent, very tender.*

pĕrinfirmus -a -um, *very weak.*

pĕringĕnĭōsus -a -um, *very clever.*

pĕrinīquus -a -um, *very unfair; very discontented or unwilling.*

pĕrinsignis -e, *very remarkable.*

pĕrinvītus -a -um, *very unwilling.*

pĕrĭŏdus -i, m. *a sentence, period.*

Pĕrĭpătētĭcus -a -um, *belonging to the Peripatetic or Aristotelian school of philosophy.*

pĕrĭpĕtasma -ătis, n. *curtain, hanging.*

pĕrīrātus -a -um, *very angry.*

pĕriscēlis -ĭdis, f. *garter or anklet.*

pĕristrōma -ătis, n. *curtain, coverlet, carpet, hanging.*

pĕristўlĭum -i, n. *a court with a colonnade round it.*

pĕristўlum -i, n. *a peristyle, a colonnade round a building.*

pĕrītĭa -ae, f. *experience, skill.*

pĕrītus -a -um, *experienced, skilful, practised, expert;* adv. **pĕrītē.**

pĕriūcundus -a -um, *very pleasant;* adv. **pĕriūcundē.**

pĕriūrĭum i-, n. *false swearing, perjury.*

pĕriūro = peiero; q.v.

pĕriūrus -a -um, *perjured; lying.*

perlābor -lābi -lapsus, dep. *to glide through, glide along.*

perlaetus -a -um, *very joyful.*

perlātē, adv. *very widely.*

perlectĭo -ōnis, f. *perusal.*

perlĕgo (pellĕgo) -lĕgĕre -lēgi -lectum, *to survey thoroughly, scan; to read through;* senatum, *to call over the roll of senators.*

perlĕvis -e, *slight;* adv. **perlĕvĭtĕr.**

perlĭbens (perlŭbens) -entis, from perlibet; q.v.

perlībĕrālis -e, *well-bred, very liberal;* adv. **perlībĕrālĭtĕr.**

perlĭbet (perlŭbet) -ere, *it is very pleasing;* partic. **perlĭbens (perlŭb-)** -entis, *very willing;* adv. **perlĭbentĕr (perlŭb-).**

perlĭcĭo = pellicio; q.v.

perlĭto -are, *to offer an auspicious sacrifice.*

perlongus -a -um, *very long, tedious;* adv. **perlongē,** *very far.*

perlŭbet, etc. = perlibet, etc.; q.v.

perlūcĕo (pellūcĕo) -lūcēre -luxi, *to shine through; to be transparent.*

perlūcĭdŭlus -a -um, *transparent.*

perlūcĭdus (pellūcĭdus) -a -um, *shining, bright; transparent.*

perluctŭōsus -a -um, *very mournful.*

perlŭo -lŭĕre -lŭi -lūtum, *to wash, bathe.*

perlustro -are, *to traverse, pass through; to survey, examine.*

permagnus -a -um, *very great very large.*

permănĕo -mănēre -mansi -mansum, *to remain, stay, last, continue.*

permāno -are, *to flow through, trickle through; to penetrate, extend.* Adv. from partic. **permănantĕr,** *by flowing through.*

permansĭo -ōnis, f. *a remaining, abiding.*

permārinus -a -um, *going over the sea.*

permātūresco -mātūrescĕre -mātūrŭi, *to become thoroughly ripe.*

permĕdĭocris -e, *very moderate.*

permĕo -are, *to go through, traverse.*

permētĭor -mētīri -mensus, dep. *to measure out; to traverse.*

permīrus -a -um, *very wonderful.*

permiscĕo -miscēre -miscŭi -mixtum, *to mix together, mingle thoroughly to confuse, throw into confusion.* Hence partic. **permixtus** -a -um, *mixed; promiscuous;* adv. **permixtē.**

permissĭo -ōnis, f. *yielding, surrender; permission, leave.*

permissū, abl. sing. m. *by permission.*

permītĭālis -e, *destructive, annihilating.*

permītĭes -ēi, f. *destruction, annihilation.*

permitto -mittĕre -mīsi -missum, *to let go;* esp. of weapons, *to hurl; to give up, yield, surrender, concede, sacrifice; to make allowance for; to allow, permit.*

permixtē, adv. from permisceo; q.v.

permixtĭo -ōnis, f. *mixture; confusion.*

permŏdestus -a -um, *very modest, very moderate.*

permŏlestus -a -um, *very troublesome;* adv. **permŏlestē,** *with much difficulty.*

permŏlo -ĕre, *to grind thoroughly.*

permŏtĭo -ōnis, f. *movement, agitation.*

permŏvĕo -mŏvēre -mōvi -mōtum, *to move or stir up thoroughly; excite, agitate; to persuade, induce, influence a person.*

permulcĕo -mulcēre -mulsi -mulsum, *to stroke; to charm, soothe, soften.*

permultus -a -um, sing., *very much;* plur., *very many;* n. sing. as subst. *very much.*

permūnĭo -īre -ivi -ītum, *to fortify completely,* or *finish fortifying.*

permūtātĭo -ōnis, f. *complete change; exchange, interchange.*

permūto -are, *to change completely; to exchange, interchange.*

perna -ae, f. *ham.*

pernĕcessārĭus -a -um, *very necessary; very intimate.*

pernĕcessē, indecl. adj. *very necessary.*

pernĕgo -are, *to deny flatly; to persist in denying* or *refusing.*

pernĭcĭābilis -e, *deadly, destructive.*

pernĭcĭes -ēi, *destruction, disaster, ruin, bane.*

pernĭcĭōsus -a -um, *destructive, ruinous;* adv. **pernĭcĭōsē.**

pernĭcĭtās -ātis, f. *swiftness, agility.*

pernix -nĭcis, *swift, nimble, agile;* adv. **pernĭcĭtĕr.**

pernōbilis -e, *very famous.*

pernocto -are, *to pass the night.*

pernosco -noscĕre -nōvi -nōtum, *to investigate* or *find out thoroughly;* in perf., *to know thoroughly.*

pernōtŭit -uisse, *it has become well known.*

pernox -noctis, adj. *all-night.*

pernŭmĕro -are, *to count out, reckon up.*

pēro -ōnis, m. *a boot of untanned hide.*

pĕrobscūrus -a -um, *very obscure.*

pĕrŏdĭōsus -a -um, *very troublesome.*

pĕroffĭcĭōsē, *very attentively.*

pĕrŏlĕo -ēre, *to emit a strong smell.*

pĕrōnatus -a -um, *wearing leather boots.*

pĕropportūnus -a -um, *very convenient;* adv. **pĕropportūnē.**

pĕroptāto, abl. sing. n. *just as one would wish.*

pĕrōrātĭo -ōnis, f. *conclusion of a speech, peroration.*

pĕrornātus -a -um, *very ornate.*

pĕrorno -are, *to adorn greatly.*

pĕrōro -are, *to speak from beginning to end, to plead a cause throughout, explain* or *state thoroughly; to conclude a speech, wind up, close.*

pĕrōsus -a -um, *hating, detesting.*

perpāco -are, *to pacify thoroughly.*

perparvŭlus and perparvus -a -um, *very little.*

perpaucŭli and perpauci -ae, -a, *very few.*

perpaulum (perpaullum) i, -n. *a very little.*

perpauper -ēris, *very poor.*

perpello -pellĕre -pŭli -pulsum, *to push hard, drive along; to urge, compel, constrain.*

perpendĭcŭlum -i, n. *plumbline, plummet;* ad perpendiculum, *in a straight line.*

perpendo -pendĕre -pendi -pensum, *to weigh carefully; to consider, examine.*

perpĕram, *wrongly, falsely.*

perpēs -pĕtis, *continuous, unbroken.*

perpessĭo -ōnis, f. *suffering, endurance.*

perpessū, alb. sing. m. *in the enduring.*

perpĕtior -pĕti -pessus, dep. *to bear to the end, endure.*

perpetro -are, *to complete, accomplish, perform.*

perpĕtŭĭtās -ātis, f. *uninterrupted succession, continuity;* ad perpetuitatem, *for ever.*

¹perpĕtŭŏ, adv. from perpetuus; q.v.

²perpĕtŭo -are, *to make continual, continue, perpetuate.*

perpĕtŭus -a -um, *continuous, un-interrupted* (in space or time). Transf., *universal, general.* Abl. as adv. perpĕtŭŏ, *uninterruptedly.*

perplăcĕo -ēre, *to please greatly.*

perplexābĭlis -e, *intricate, obscure.*

perplexor -ari, dep. *to perplex.*

perplexus -a -um, *confused, intricate; obscure, ambiguous.* Adv. perplexē and perplexim.

perplĭcātus -a -um, *entangled, involved.*

perplŭit -ĕre, *to let the rain through; to run away or pour in like rain.*

perpŏlĭo -ire, *to polish thoroughly; perfect, complete.*
     Hence partic. perpŏlītus -a -um, *polished, accomplished, refined.*

perpŏpŭlor -ari, dep. *to lay waste, devastate completely.*

perpōtātĭo -ōnis, f. *continued drinking, drinking-bout.*

perpōto -are, *to continue drinking; to drink up.*

perprĭmo -primĕre -pressi -pressum, *to press hard.*

perpugnax -ācis, *very pugnacious.*

perpurgo (perpŭrĭgo) -are, *to clean thoroughly.* Transf., *to explain thoroughly, clear up.*

perpŭsillus -a -um, *very small.*

perpŭto -are, *to explain fully.*

perquam, *very much, extremely.*

perquīro -quīrĕre -quīsivi -quīsitum, *to search for eagerly; to inquire carefully into.* Compar. adv. from perf. partic. perquīsĭtius *more accurately.*

perrārus -a -um, *very uncommon;* abl. as adv. perrārŏ.

perrĕcondĭtus -a -um, *very abstruse.*

perrēpo -rēpĕre -repsi -reptum, *to crawl through, creep over.*

perrepto -are, *to crawl through, crawl about.*

perrĭdĭcŭlus -a -um, *very laughable;* adv. perrĭdĭcŭle.

perrŏgo -are, *to ask in succession, to ask one after another.*

perrumpo -rumpĕre -rūpi -ruptum, *to break through, burst through; to shatter, burst.*

Persae -arum, m. pl. *the Persians;* sing. Persa and Persēs -ae, m. *a Persian;* Persĭa -ae, f. *Persia;* Persis -ĭdis, f., as adj., *Persian,* as subst., *Persia;* adj. Persĭcus -a -um.

persaepĕ, *very often.*

persalsus -a -um, *very witty;* adv. persalsē.

persălūtātĭo -ōnis, f. *a general greeting.*

persălūto -are, *to greet in succession, greet all round.*

persăpĭens -entis, *very wise;* adv. persăpĭentĕr.

perscĭentĕr, *very discreetly.*

perscindo -scindĕre -scĭdi -scissum, *to tear to pieces.*

perscītus -a -um, *very clever.*

perscrībo -scrībĕre -scripsi -scriptum, *to write in full; to note down officially, enter; to make over or assign in writing.*

perscriptĭo -ōnis, f. *entry, noting down; assigning by written document.*

perscriptor -ōris, m. *one who makes an entry.*

perscrūto -are and perscrūtor -ari, dep. *to search through, look through, examine, investigate.*

persĕco -sĕcare -sĕcŭi -sectum, *to cut through, cut away, dissect.*

persector -ari, dep. *to pursue eagerly; to investigate.*

persĕcūtĭo -ōnis, f. *prosecution.*

persĕdĕo (persĭdĕo) -sĕdēre -sēdi -sessum, *to remain sitting.*

persegnis -e, *very languid.*

persentĭo -sentire -sensi -sensum, *to perceive distinctly, feel deeply.*

persentisco -ĕre, *to begin to perceive distinctly or feel deeply.*

Persĕphŏnē -ēs, f. *Greek name of Proserpina;* q.v.

persĕquor -sĕqui -sĕcūtus, dep. *to follow constantly, pursue to the end, hunt out, overtake; to strive after; to imitate; to proceed against an offender, punish, avenge; to accomplish an action, perform, execute; to treat a subject, expound, describe.*

¹Persēs -ae and Persēūs -ēi, m. *the last king of Macedonia, defeated by the Roman general Aemilius Paulus in* 169 B.C.; adj. Persĭcus -a -um.

²Persēs -ae, m. *a Persian;* see Persae.

Persēūs -ēi and -ĕos, m. *Perseus, who killed Medusa, and rescued Andromeda.*

persĕvĕrantĭa -ae, f. *persistence.*

persĕvĕro -are, *to persist, persevere, continue.*
     Hence partic. persĕvĕrans -antis, *enduring, persistent;* adv. persĕvĕrantĕr.

persĕvĕrus -a -um, *very strict.*

Persĭa; see Persae.

Persĭcus; see Persae and Perses.

persĭdo -sidĕre -sēdi -sessum, *to sink in,
settle down.*

persigno -are, *to note down, record.*

persimilis -e, *very like.*

persimplex -ĭcis, *very simple.*

persisto -ĕre, *to remain constant, persist.*

Persĭus -i, m. A. Persius Flaccus, *a satirist in the reign of Nero.*

persolvo -solvĕre -solvi -sŏlūtum, *to unloose; hence to explain, expound; to pay, pay off, deal out.*

persōna -ae, f. *a mask, esp. as worn by actors; hence role, part, character, personality.*

persōnātus -a -um, *masked; disguised, counterfeit.*

persōno -sŏnare -sŏnŭi -sŏnĭtum: intransit., *to resound, sound forth; to shout; to perform upon a musical instrument;* transit., *to make, resound; to proclaim loudly.*

perspergo -ĕre, *to sprinkle, moisten.*

perspĭcax -ācis, *sharp-sighted.*

perspĭcientĭa -ae, f. *full awareness or knowledge.*

perspĭcio -spĭcĕre -spexi, -spectum, *to see through, look through; to look at attentively, survey, examine;* mentally, *to regard, investigate, ascertain.* Hence partic. perspectus -a -um, *ascertained, fully known.*

perspĭcŭĭtās -ātis, f. *clearness, perspicuity.*

perspĭcŭus -a -um, *transparent, bright; clear, evident.* Adv. perspĭcŭē.

persterno -sternĕre -strāvi -strātum, *to pave thoroughly.*

perstimŭlo -are, *to goad on violently.*

persto -stare -stĭti -stātum, *to stand firm, remain standing; to remain unchanged, last, endure; to stand firm, persist, persevere.*

perstringo -stringĕre -strinxi -strictum. (1) *to press tight, bind tight; to deaden, dull the senses.* (2) *to graze, scratch; to touch upon a subject; to scold, blame, reproach a person.*

perstŭdĭōsus -a -um, *very eager;* adv. perstŭdĭōsē.

persŭādĕo -suādēre -suāsi -suāsum, *to persuade.* (1) *to convince of a fact; sibi persuadere, to satisfy oneself, be convinced.* (2) *to persuade, prevail upon a person to do a thing.*

persŭāsĭo -ōnis, f. *persuasion; a conviction, belief.*

persŭāsū, abl. sing. m. *by persuasion.*

persubtīlis -e, *very fine; very subtle.*

persulto -are, *to leap, gambol, skip about, skip over.*

pertaedet -taedēre -taesum est, *to cause weariness or disgust;* cf. taedet.

pertempto -are, *to prove, test, try; to weigh, consider, examine; to assail.*

pertendo -tendĕre -tendi, *to push on, proceed, continue.*

pertĕnŭis -e, *very slight.*

pertĕrebro -are, *to bore through.*

pertergĕo -tergēre -tersi -tersum *to wipe over; to brush.*

perterrĕo -ēre, *to terrify.*

perterrĭcrĕpus -a -um, *rattling terribly.*

pertexo -texĕre -texŭi -textum, *to weave throughout; to complete, accomplish.*

pertĭca -ae, f. *a long pole or rod.*

pertĭmesco -tĭmescĕre -tĭmŭi, *to become very much afraid.*

pertĭnācĭa -ae, f. *firmness, obstinacy, stubbornness.*

pertĭnax -ācis, adj., *tenacious; tight-fisted, mean; firm, persistent, stubborn, obstinate.* Adv. pertĭnācĭter.

pertĭnĕo -tĭnēre -tĭnŭi, *to reach to, extend to; to tend towards, have as object or result; to relate to, belong to, apply to, attach to.*

pertingo -ĕre, *to stretch out, extend.*

pertŏlĕro -are, *to endure to the end.*

pertorquĕo -ēre, *to twist, distort.*

pertractātĭo -ōnis, f. *thorough handling, detailed treatment.*

pertracto -are, *to handle, feel; to treat, study, work upon.*

pertrăho -trăhĕre -traxi -tractum, *to drag, forcibly conduct; to entice, allure.*

pertrecto = pertracto; q.v.

pertristis -e, *very sorrowful or austere.*

pertŭmultŭōsē, *in an agitated manner.*

pertundo -tundĕre -tŭdi -tūsum, *to bore through, perforate.*

perturbātĭo -ōnis, f. *confusion, disorder, disturbance;* philosoph. *a passion, emotion.*

perturbātrix -ĭcis, f. *she that disturbs.*

perturbo -are, *to disturb thoroughly, confuse, disquiet, upset.* Hence partic. perturbātus -a -um, *confused, disturbed;* adv. perturbātē.

perturpis -e, *very disgraceful.*

pertūsus -a -um, partic. from pertundo; q.v.

pĕrungo -ungĕre -unxi -unctum, *to anoint thoroughly, besmear.*

pĕrurbānus -a -um, *very polite or witty; over-sophisticated.*

pĕruro -urĕre -ussi -ustum, *to burn up, consume, inflame; to gall, chafe; to pinch, nip with cold.*

pĕrūtĭlis -e, *very useful.*

pervādo -vādĕre -vāsi -vāsum. (1) *to go through, pass through, pervade.* (2) *to reach, arrive at.*

pervăgor -ari, dep. *to wander through, to rove about; to be widely spread, pervade.* Hence partic. pervăgātus -a -um, *widespread, well known; common, general.*

pervăgus -a -um, *wandering everywhere.*

pervărĭē, *very variously.*

pervasto -are, *to lay waste completely.*

pervĕho -vĕhĕre -vexi -vectum, *to carry, lead, conduct, bring (to or through a place);* pass. pervehi, *to travel to or through.*

pervello -vellĕre -velli, *to pluck, pull, twitch; to stimulate; to pain, to disparage.*

pervĕnĭo -vĕnire -vēni -ventum, *to come through to, arrive at, reach, attain to, be passed to.*

perversĭtās -ātis, f. *perversity.*

perverto (pervorto) -vertĕre -verti -versum, *to turn upside down, overturn,* overthrow; to undermine, subvert, pervert; in speech, to trip up.

Hence partic. **perversus** -a -um, crooked, awry, askew; distorted, perverse. Adv. **perversē**.

pervespĕri, very late in the evening.

pervestigātio -ōnis, f. examination, investigation.

pervestigo -are, to track out, investigate, search into.

pervĕtus -ĕris, very old.

pervĕtustus -a -um, very old.

pervĭcācĭa -ae, f. firmness, persistence; stubbornness, obstinacy.

pervĭcax -ācis, firm, persistent; stubborn, obstinate; compar. adv. **pervĭcācĭus**, more stubbornly.

pervĭdĕo -vĭdēre -vīdi -visum, to look over, survey; to see through, discern, distinguish.

pervĭgĕo -ēre, to flourish, bloom continually.

pervĭgil -ilis, always watchful.

pervĭgĭlātĭo -ōnis, f. and **pervĭgĭlĭum** -i, n. a vigil, religious watching.

pervĭgĭlo -are, to remain awake all night.

pervīlis -e, very cheap.

pervinco -vincĕre -vici -victum, to conquer completely; to surpass, outdo; to induce, prevail upon; to carry one's point; to achieve, effect; to prove, demonstrate.

pervĭus -a -um, passable, accessible; as subst., a passage.

pervolgo = pervulgo; q.v.

pervŏlito -are, to fly round, flit about.

¹pervŏlo -are, to fly through, fly round.

²pervŏlo -velle -vŏlŭi, to wish greatly.

pervŏlūto -are, to roll round; esp. to unroll and read a book.

pervolvo -volvĕre -volvi -volutum, to roll about; to unroll and read a book.

pervorsē, etc., = perverse, etc.; q.v.

pervulgo (pervolgo) -are, to publish, make publicly known; to make generally available; to frequent, haunt a place. Hence partic. **pervulgātus** -a -um, very usual or well known.

pēs pĕdis, m. the foot; pedem referre, to return; pedibus, on foot, also by land; servus a pedibus, an attendant, lackey; pedibus ire in sententiam, to support a proposal; milit., pedibus merere, to serve in the infantry; pedem conferre, to fight hand to hand. Transf., a foot of a table, chair, etc.; a metrical foot; a measure of length; pes (veli), a rope or sheet, attached to the lower edge of a sail.

pessĭmus, pessĭme; see malus.

pessŭlus -i, m. a bolt.

pessum, to the ground, to the bottom, downwards; pessum ire, to sink, be ruined, perish; pessum dare, to destroy, ruin, put an end to.

pestĭfer -fĕra, -fĕrum, pestilential, destructive, injurious; adv. **pestĭferē**.

pestĭlens -entis, unhealthy, fatal, noxious.

pestĭlentĭa -ae, f. an unhealthy condition; a plague, infectious disease, pest.

pestĭlitās -ātis, f. = pestilentia; q.v.

pestis -is, f. pest, pestilence, plague; destruction, ruin; curse, bane.

pĕtăsātus -a -um, wearing the petasus; hence, equipped for a journey.

pĕtăso -ōnis, m. a fore-quarter of pork.

pĕtăsus -i, m. a broad-brimmed felt hat, used by travellers.

pĕtaurum -i, n. a spring-board.

pĕtesso (pĕtisso) -ĕre, to long for, strive after.

pĕtītĭo -ōnis, f. an attack, thrust, blow; a request, application; standing for office, candidature; at law, a suit, a right of claim, right to bring an action.

pĕtītor -ōris, m. a seeker; polit., a candidate; legal, a plaintiff.

pĕtītūrĭo -ire, to desire to stand for election.

pĕtītus -ūs, m. an inclining towards.

pĕto -ĕre -ivi and -ii -itum, to make for, go to; to attack, assail; to seek, strive after; to ask for, beg, request, demand; polit., to stand for, canvas for; legal, to sue for; sometimes to fetch, derive.

pĕtorrĭtum (pĕtōrĭtum) -i, n. an open four-wheeled carriage.

Petrōnius -i, m. name of a Roman gens, esp. of a satirist under Nero.

pĕtŭlans -antis, impudent, pert, wanton; adv. **pĕtŭlantĕr**.

pĕtŭlantĭa -ae, f. impudence, pertness, wantonness.

pĕtulcus -a -um, butting with the head.

pexātus -a -um, wearing a garment with the nap on.

Phaedra -ae, f. daughter of Minos, wife of Theseus.

Phaedrus -i, m. a freedman of Augustus, author of Latin fables.

Phăĕthōn -ontis, m. the son of Helios, killed trying to drive the chariot of his father.

phălangae (pălangae) -arum, f. pl. rollers.

phălangītae -arum, m. pl. soldiers belonging to a phalanx.

phălanx -angis, f. an array of soldiers in close formation.

Phălāris -ĭdis, m. a tyrant of Agrigentum.

phălĕrae -arum, f. pl. metal bosses; military decorations; horses' trappings.

phălĕratus -a -um, wearing phalerae; q.v.

Phălērum -i, n. the oldest port of Athens.

phantasma -ătis, n. an apparition.

phărĕtra -ae, f. a quiver.

phărĕtrātus -a -um, wearing a quiver.

pharmăceutrĭa -ae, f. sorceress.

pharmăcŏpōla (-es) -ae, m. a seller of drugs; a quack.

Pharsālus (-ŏs) -i, f. a town in Thessaly, where Pompey was defeated by Caesar in 48 B.C.

Phărus (-ŏs) -i, f., rarely m., an island off Alexandria, with a lighthouse; hence in gen. a lighthouse.

phăsēlus -i, m. and f. the kidney-bean or French bean; a light bean-shaped boat.

Phāsis -ĭdis and -ĭdos, m. a river in Colchis, flowing into the Black Sea;

f. adj. **Phāsis** -Idis, and **Phāsiānus** -a -um, *Colchian*.

phasma -ātis, n. *a ghost, spectre*.

phiāla -ae, f. *a drinking-vessel; a bowl, saucer*.

Phidiās -ae, m. *an Athenian sculptor*.

Philippi -orum, m. pl. *a city in Macedonia, where Octavian and Antony defeated Brutus and Cassius*.

Philippus -i, m. *the name of several kings of Macedon*; adj. **Philippēus** and **Philippĭcus** -a -um; f. as subst. **Philippĭca** -ae, *one of the speeches of Demosthenes against Philip, or of Cicero against Antony*.

philŏlŏgĭa -ae, f. *love of learning, study of literature*.

philŏlŏgus -a -um, *learned, literary*; m. as subst. *a scholar*.

Philŏmēla -ae, f. *the daughter of Pandion, turned into a nightingale*.

philŏsŏphĭa -ae, f. *philosophy*.

philŏsŏphor -ari, dep. *to philosophize, apply oneself to philosophy*.

philŏsŏphus -a -um, *philosophical*; m. and f. as subst. *a philosopher*.

philtrum -i, n. *a love-potion, philtre*.

philўra -ae, f. *the inner bark of the linden-tree*.

phĭmus -i, m. *a dice-box*.

Phlĕgĕthōn -ontis, m. *a river in the infernal regions*.

phōca -ae, f. and **phōcē** -ēs, f. *a seal*.

Phōcis -Idis, f. *a district in the north of Greece*; adj. **Phōcēus** -a -um.

Phoebē -ēs, f. *the sister of Phoebus, the Moon-goddess, Diana*.

Phoebĭgĕna -ae, m. *the son of Phoebus, Aesculapius*.

Phoebus -i, m. *Apollo, the Sun-god*; hence subst. **Phoebās** -ādis, f. *a priestess of Phoebus, a prophetess*; adj. **Phoebēĭus** and **Phoebēus** -a -um, *of Phoebus*.

Phoenīcē -ēs, f. *Phoenicia*; m. subst. **Phoenices** -um, *the Phoenicians*; f. subst. **Phoenissa** -ae, f. *a Phoenician woman*.

phoenīcoptĕros -i, m. *the flamingo*.

phoenix -īcis, m. *the phoenix, a fabulous bird of Arabia*.

phōnascus -i, m. *a teacher of music*.

phrĕnēsis -is, f. *madness, frenzy*.

phrĕnētĭcus -a -um, *mad, frantic*.

Phrixus -i, m. *brother of Helle*.

Phrўges -um, m. pl. *the Phrygians*; sing. **Phryx** -ўgis; **Phrўgĭa** -ae, f. *the country of Phrygia in Asia Minor*; adj. **Phrўgĭus** -a -um, *Phrygian*; poet. = *Trojan*.

phthĭsis -is, f. *consumption*.

phy, interj. *pish! tush!*

phўlarchus -i, m. *the head of a tribe, an emir*.

phўsĭca -ae, and **phўsĭcē** -ēs, f. *physics, natural science*.

phўsĭcus -a -um, *relating to physics, physical*; m. as subst. *a scientist*; n. pl. **phўsĭca** -orum, *physics*; adv. **phўsĭcē**, *in the manner of the scientists*.

phўsĭognōmōn -onis, m. *a physiognomist*.

phўsĭŏlŏgĭa -ae, f. *natural science*.

pĭābĭlis -e, *able to be atoned for*.

pĭācŭlāris -e, *atoning, expiating*; n. pl. as subst. *expiatory sacrifices*.

pĭācŭlum -i, n. *a means of expiating or appeasing; sacrifice, remedy; punishment; a victim; an act needing expiation, a sin, crime*.

pĭāmen -Inis, n. *means of atonement or expiation*.

pīca -ae, f. *a jay or magpie*.

pĭcārĭa -ae, f. *a place where pitch is made*.

pĭcĕa -ae, f. *the spruce-fir*.

Pĭcēnum -i, n. *a district in central Italy*.

pĭcĕus -a -um, *of pitch; pitch-black*.

pĭco -are, *to smear with pitch*.

pictor -ōris, m. *a painter*.

pictūra -ae, f. *the art of painting; a painting, picture*; pictura textilis, *embroidery*.

pictūrātus -a -um, *painted*; vestes, *embroidered*.

pīcus -i, m. *a woodpecker*.

Pĭĕris -Idis or -Idos, f. *a Muse*; plur. **Pĭĕrĭdes**, *the Muses*; adj. **Pĭĕrĭus** -a -um, *Pierian, poetic*.

pĭĕtās -ātis, f. *dutifulness, dutiful conduct; piety; patriotism; devotion; kindness*.

pĭger -gra -grum, *sluggish, unwilling, slow*; campus, *unfruitful*. Adv. **pĭgrē**.

pĭget -gēre -gŭit -gĭtum est, impers., *it causes annoyance* (or *regret* or *shame*); *it disgusts*; piget me, with genit., *I am disgusted with*.

pigmentārĭus -i, m. *a seller of paints and unguents*.

pigmentum -i, n. *paint, pigment*; of style, *ornament, decoration*.

pignĕrātor -ōris, m. *a mortgagee*.

pignĕro -are, *to give as a pledge, pawn, mortgage*.

pignĕror -ari, dep. *to take as a pledge; to claim*.

pignus -nōris and -nĕris, n. *a pledge, pawn, security; a wager, bet, stake; a token, assurance, proof*; in plur., *persons as pledges of love*.

pigrĭtĭa -ae, and **pigrĭtĭes** -ēi, f. *sluggishness, indolence*.

pigro -are and **pigror** -ari, dep. *to be sluggish*.

¹**pīla** -ae, f. *a mortar*.

²**pīla** -ae, f. *a pillar, pier; a bookstall*.

³**pīla** -ae, f. *a ball; a game of ball*.

pĭlanus -i, m. = triarius; q.v.

pīlātus -a -um, *armed with the pilum or javelin*.

pĭlentum -i, n. *a carriage, coach*.

pillĕātus (pĭlĕ-) -a -um, *wearing the felt cap*.

pillĕŏlus (pĭlĕ-) -i, m. *a little cap, skull-cap*.

pillĕus (pīlĕus) -i, m. and **pillĕum** -i, n. *a felt cap, esp. as worn by manumitted slaves*.

pĭlo -are, *to deprive of hair*.

pĭlōsus -a -um, *covered with hair, hairy*.

pīlum -i, n. *the heavy javelin of the Roman infantry*.

¹**pĭlus** -i, m. *a single hair; a trifle*.

²**pīlus** -i, m. *a division of the triarii in the Roman army*; primus pilus, *the*

chief centurion of the triarii *and of the legion.*

Pindárus -i, m. *a lyric poet of Thebes.*

pīnētum -i, n. *a pine-wood.*

pīnĕus -a -um, *made of pine-wood or deal.*

pingo pingĕre pinxi pictum, *to paint, to draw; to embroider; to stain, dye; to decorate, adorn;* in speech or writing, *to embellish, depict.*

pinguesco -ĕre, *to become fat, grow fertile.*

pinguis -e, *fat; oily; rich, fertile;* n. as subst. *fatness, fat.* Transf., *thick, dense; heavy, stupid; easy, quiet.*

pinguitūdo -ĭnis, f. *fatness, broadness.*

pīnĭfer -fĕra -fĕrum and **pīnĭgĕr** -gĕra -gĕrum, *producing pines.*

¹**pinna** -ae, f. *a feather; a feathered arrow; a wing; a battlement along the top of a wall.*

²**pinna** (**pĭna**) -ae, f. *a species of mussel.*

pinnātus -a -um, *feathered, winged.*

pinnĭgĕr -gĕra -gĕrum, *feathered, winged;* piscis, *having fins.*

pinnĭrápus -i, m. *a crestsnatcher,* i.e. *a kind of gladiator.*

pinnŭla -ae, f. *a small feather or wing.*

pinso, pinsĕre; pinsi and pinsŭi; pinsum pinsĭtum and pistum, *to stamp, pound, crush.*

pīnus -i and -ūs, f. *a fir or pine; anything made of pine-wood, e.g. a torch, oar, ship.*

pīo -are, *to appease, propitiate; to venerate; to make good, atone for.*

pĭper pĭpĕris, n. *pepper.*

pīpĭlo -are, *to twitter, chirp.*

pīpŭlus -i, m. and **pīpŭlum** -i, n. *outcry.*

Pīraeēus and **Pīraeus** -i, m. *the Piraeus, the main port of Athens.*

pīrāta -ae, m. *pirate.*

pīrātĭcus -a -um, *piratical;* f. as subst. *piracy.*

pĭrum -i, n. *a pear.*

pĭrus -i, f. *a pear-tree.*

piscātor -ōris, m. *a fisherman; a fishmonger.*

piscātōrĭus -a -um, *of fishermen or fishing.*

piscātus -ūs, m. *fishes; fishing, a catch.*

piscĭcŭlus -i, m. *a little fish.*

piscīna -ae, f. *a fish-pond; a swimming-bath.*

piscīnārĭus -i, m. *one fond of fish-ponds.*

piscis -is, m. *a fish.*

piscor -ari, dep. *to fish.*

piscōsus -a -um, *abounding in fish.*

pistillum -i, n. *a pestle.*

pistor -ōris, m. *a grinder, miller; a baker.*

pistrīnum -i, n. *a mill; a bakery.*

pistris -is, and **pistrix** -trīcis, f. *a sea monster; a whale, shark, saw-fish.* Transf., *a small fast ship.*

pĭtuīta -ae, f. *phlegm, rheum.*

pĭtuītōsus -a -um, *full of phlegm.*

pĭus -a -um, *dutiful; godly, holy; patriotic; devoted, affectionate;* in gen., *honest, upright, kind.*

pix pĭcis, f. *pitch.*

plācābĭlis -e; pass., *easy to appease;* act., *appeasing.*

plācābĭlĭtās -ātis, f. *placability.*

plācāmen -ĭnis, and **plācāmentum** -i, n. *means of appeasing.*

plācātĭo -ōnis, f. *soothing, appeasing.*

plācĕo -ēre -ŭi and -ĭtus sum, -ĭtum, *to please, be agreeable to;* impers. **plăcet,** *it seems good, it is agreed or resolved.*

Hence partic. **plăcĭtus** -a -um, *pleasing, agreeable; agreed upon.* N. as subst. *what is agreeable;* plur., *opinions, teaching.*

plăcĭdus -a -um, *quiet, still, gentle;* adv. **plăcĭdē.**

plăcĭtus -a -um, partic. from placeo; q.v.

plāco -are, *to soothe, calm; to reconcile, appease.*

Hence partic. **plācātus** -a -um, *soothed, appeased; calm, gentle, quiet;* adv. **plācātē.**

¹**plāga** -ae, f. *a blow, stroke; a wound.*

²**plăga** -ae, f. *a district, zone, region.*

³**plăga** -ae, f. *a net for hunting; a trap, snare.*

plăgiārius -i, m. *a kidnapper; a plagiarist.*

plăgōsus -a -um, *fond of flogging.*

plăgŭla -ae, f. *a bed-curtain.*

planctus -ūs, m. *beating; esp. beating of the breast, lamentations.*

plango plangĕre planxi planctum, *to beat, strike, esp. noisily; to strike the breast, head, etc., as a sign of grief;* hence plangere and pass. plangi, *to bewail.*

plangor -ōris, m. *loud striking or beating; esp. beating of the head and breast, loud lamentations.*

plānĭpēs -pĕdis, m. *an actor who wore no shoes.*

plānĭtās -ātis, f. *plainness, distinctness.*

plānĭtia -ae, and **plānĭtĭēs** -ēi, f. *a level surface, a plain.*

planta -ae, f. (1) *a green twig, cutting, graft; a plant.* (2) *the sole of the foot.*

plantārĭa -ĭum, n. pl. *young trees, slips.*

¹**plānus** -a -um, *even, flat;* n. as subst. *a plain, level ground;* de plano, *off-hand, easily.* Transf., *plain, clear, intelligible.* Adv. **plānē,** *distinctly, intelligibly; wholly, quite, thoroughly;* in answers, *certainly.*

²**plānus** -i, m. *a vagabond, a charlatan.*

plătălĕa -ae, f. *a water-bird, the spoonbill.*

plătănus -i, f. *the plane-tree.*

plătĕa -ae, f. *a street.*

Plătō (-ōn) -ōnis, m. *the Greek philosopher, disciple of Socrates.*

plaudo (**plōdo**) plaudĕre plausi plausum, *to strike, beat, clap together; to make a clapping noise, clap, applaud.*

plausĭbĭlis -e, *worthy of applause.*

plausor -ōris, m. *an applauder at the theatre.*

plaustrum (**plostrum**) -i, n. *a waggon, cart; Charles's Wain.*

plausus -ūs, m. *a noise of clapping; approbation, applause.*

Plautus -i, m., T. Maccius, *the Roman comic poet, born about* 254 B.C. Adj. **Plautīnus** -a -um.

plēbēcŭla -ae, f. *the common people, mob, rabble.*

plēbēius -a -um, *of the plebs or people, plebeian; common, low, mean.*

plēbēs -ēi and -i, f. = plebs; q.v.

plēbĭcŏla -ae, m. *a friend of the common people.*

plēbiscītum -i, n. *a decree of the people.*

plebs plēbis, f. *the plebeians, the common people, lower orders.*

¹plecto; see plexus.

²plecto -ĕre, *to punish*; usually pass. **plector** -i, *to be punished* (with blows).

plectrum -i, n. *a stick with which the strings of a stringed instrument were struck; a quill.* Transf., *the lyre; lyric poetry.*

Plēĭăs -ādis, f. *a Pleiad*; usually plur. **Plēĭădes** -ādum, f. *the Pleiads, the Seven Stars.*

plēnus -a -um, *full, full of* (with genit. or abl.); *complete; plump, thick; pregnant; filled, satisfied; well-stocked, rich;* of age, *mature:* of the voice, *strong, loud;* of style, *full, copious.* Adv. **plēnē,** *fully, completely.*

plērusquĕ -raque -rumque and plur. **plērīquĕ** -raeque -raque, *very many, a large part, the most part;* n. sing. as subst., *the greater part;* acc. as adv. *for the most part, mostly, commonly.*

plexus -a -um, partic. as from plecto, *braided, plaited.*

Plīas = Pleias; q.v.

plico -are, -ŭi and -avi, -atum and ĭtum, *to fold.*

Plīnĭus -a -um, *name of a Roman gens;* esp. of C. Plinius Secundus (Maior, *the Elder), author of a Natural History, and* C. Plinius Caecilius Secundus (Iunior, *the Younger), author of letters, etc.*

plōdo = plaudo; q.v.

plōrābĭlis -e, *deplorable.*

plōrātor -ōris, m. *a lamenter.*

plōrātus -ūs, m. *weeping, lamenting.*

plōro -are, *to lament, wail;* transit., *to weep over, deplore.*

plostellum -i, n. *a little waggon.*

plostrum = plaustrum; q.v.

plŭit plŭĕre, plŭit or plŭvit, *it rains, a shower falls.*

plūma -ae, f. *a small, soft feather; down* (esp. in pl.); meton. *bolster, featherbed; the first down on the chin.*

plūmātus -a -um, *covered with feathers.*

plumbĕus -a -um, *leaden, of lead.* Transf., *dull, stupid; heavy, oppressive; bad.*

plumbum -i, n. *lead; a bullet; a leaden pipe;* plumbum album, *tin.*

plūmĕus -a -um, *downy, of fine feathers.*

plūmōsus -a -um, *feathered, downy.*

plŭo; see pluit.

plūrĭmus and **plūs**; see multus.

pluscŭlus -a -um, *somewhat more, rather more.*

plŭtĕus -i, m. and **plŭtĕum** -i, n. *a shelter*; milit., *penthouse, shed, mantlet; breastwork, battlement.* Transf., *a board, couch, bookshelf.*

Plūtō (-ōn) -ōnis, m. *the king of the lower world;* adj. **Plūtōnĭus** -a -um.

plŭvĭālis -e, *of or from rain; bringing rain.*

plŭvĭus -a -um, *of or from rain, bringing rain;* as subst. **plŭvĭa** -ae, *rain.*

pōcillum -i, n. *a little cup.*

pōcŭlum -i, n. *a drinking-cup, goblet; a drink, draught.*

pŏdagra -ae, f. *gout in the feet.*

pōdex -icis, m. *fundament, anus.*

pŏdĭum -i, n. *a balcony,* esp. *in the amphitheatre.*

pŏēma -ătis, n. *a poem.*

poena -ae, f. *money paid as atonement, a fine;* in gen., *punishment, penalty; loss, hardship;* poenas dare, *to be punished.*

Poenī -orum, m. pl. *the Carthaginians;* sing. **Poenus** -i, m. adj. **Poenus, Pūnĭcus, Poenĭcĕus** -a -um, *Punic, Carthaginian.*

poenĭo = punio; q.v.

poenĭtet; see paenitet.

pŏēsis -is, acc. -in, f. *poetry.*

pŏēta -ae, m. *a maker;* esp. *a poet.*

pŏētĭcus -a -um, *poetical;* f. as subst. **pŏētĭca** -ae and **pŏētĭcē** -ēs, *the art of poetry;* adv. **pŏētĭcē.**

pŏētrĭa -ae, f. *a poetess.*

pōl! interj. *by Pollux! truly! really!*

pŏlenta -ae, f. *pearl-barley, barley-groats.*

pŏlĭo -ire, *to polish, file, make smooth;* esp. *to cover with white, whiten; to adorn, to finish off.* Hence partic. **pŏlītus** -a -um, *polished, refined, accomplished;* adv. **pŏlītē.**

pŏlītīa -ae, acc. -an. f. *the Republic* (Plato's work).

pŏlītĭcus -a -um *of the state, political.*

pŏlītus -a -um, partic. from polio; q.v.

pollen -ĭnis, n. and **pollis** -ĭnis, c. *fine flour, meal.*

pollentĭa -ae, f. *power, might.*

pollĕo -ēre, *to be strong, powerful, able;* partic. **pollens** -entis, *powerful, mighty.*

pollex -icis, m. *the thumb;* also *the big toe.*

pollĭcĕor -cēri -cītus, dep. *to offer, promise;* perf. partic. in pass. sense, **pollĭcĭtus** -a -um, *promised.* N. as subst. *a promise.*

pollĭcĭtātĭo -ōnis, f. *an offer, promise.*

pollĭcĭtor -ari, dep. *to keep promising.*

pollinctor -ōris, m. *an undertaker.*

pollūcĕo -lūcēre -luxi -luctum, *to offer, serve up.*

pollŭo -ŭĕre -ŭi -ūtum, *to defile, pollute, dishonour;* partic. **pollūtus** -a -um, *defiled, polluted; unchaste.*

Pollux -ūcis, m. *the twin-brother of Castor.*

pŏlus -i, m. *the end of an axis, a pole; the sky, heaven.*

Pŏlўhymnĭa -ae, f. *one of the Muses*

pŏlўpus -i, m. *polypus.*

pōmārīus -a -um, *of fruit*; m. as subst., *a fruiterer*; n. as subst., *a fruit-garden, orchard.*

pōmĕrīdiānus = postmeridianus; q.v.

pōmērium or **pōmoerium** -i, n. *a clear space beside the walls of a town.*

pōmifer -fĕra -fĕrum, *fruit-bearing.*

pōmōsus -a -um, *abounding in fruit.*

pompa -ae, f. *a solemn procession; a suite, retinue; display, parade, ostentation.*

Pompēii -orum, m. pl. *a town in Campania, destroyed by an eruption of Vesuvius*; adj. **Pompēiānus** -a -um.

Pompēius (trisyl.) or **Pompĕius** -a -um, *name of a Roman gens*; esp. of Cn. Pompeius, *Pompey the Great* (106-48 B.C.); adj. **Pompēiānus** -a -um, *belonging to Pompey.*

Pompīlius -a -um, *name of a Roman gens*; esp. of Numa Pompilius, *second king of Rome.*

pompīlus -i, m. *the pilot-fish.*

Pomptīnus -a -um, *Pomptine* or *Pontine*: palus or paludes, *a marshy district in Latium.*

pōmum -i, n. *any kind of fruit; a fruit-tree.*

pōmus -i, f. *a fruit-tree.*

pondĕro -are, *to weigh, consider, ponder.*

pondĕrōsus -a -um, *heavy, weighty; significant.*

pondo (abl.) *in weight*; as indecl. subst. *a pound, pounds.*

pondus -ĕris, n. *weight; a weight, burden, mass; balance; authority, influence.*

pōnĕ: adv. *behind, at the back*; prep. with acc., *behind.*

pōno pōnĕre pŏsŭi (pŏsīvi) pŏsĭtum (postum) *to lay, put, place, set; to put in place, settle; to put aside, lay down, discard; to lay to rest, lay out for burial*; milit., *to post, station*; of money, etc., *to store, deposit, invest; to stake, wager*; of food, *to put on table, to serve*; of buildings, *to found, set up*; of laws, etc. *to establish, ordain*; of persons, *to appoint*; of an artist, *to represent, picture; to reckon, count, regard; to lay down, assert, cite.*

Hence partic. **pŏsĭtus** -a -um, *in place*; nix, *fallen snow*; of places, *situated.*

pons pontis, m. *a bridge, gangway; the deck of a ship.*

ponticŭlus -i, m. *a little bridge.*

pontifex -fĭcis, m. *a pontiff, member of a Roman guild of priests.*

pontificālis -e, *pontifical.*

pontificātus -ūs, m. *the office of pontiff.*

pontificus -a -um, *pontifical.*

Pontius -a -um, *name of a Roman* (originally Samnite) *gens.*

ponto -ōnis, f. *a flat-bottomed boat, punt.*

¹pontus -i, n. *the sea.*

²Pontus -i, m. *the Black Sea*; also *the country on the shores of the Black Sea*; adj. **Ponticus** -a -um.

pōpa -ae, m. *a junior priest or temple-servant.*

pōpānum -i, n. *a sacrificial cake.*

pōpellus -i, m. *common people, rabble.*

pōpīna -ae, f. *a cook-shop, eating-house; the food sold there.*

pōpīno -ōnis, m. *a glutton.*

poplēs -ĭtis, m. *the ham, hough; the knee.*

pōpŭlābĭlis -e, *that can be laid waste, destructible.*

pōpŭlābundus -a -um, *laying waste, devastating.*

pōpŭlāris -e. (1) *belonging to the same people or country, native*; as subst. *fellow-countryman, adherent, partner.* (2) *of the people or state; popular; democratic*; m. pl. as subst. *the popular party, the democrats.* Adv. **pōpŭlārĭtĕr**, *after the manner of the people, vulgarly; in a popular manner, like a demagogue.*

pōpŭlārĭtās -ātis, f. *fellow-citizenship; an attempt to please the people.*

pōpŭlātĭo -ōnis, f. *laying waste, devastating, plundering.*

pōpŭlātor -ōris, m. *a devastator, plunderer.*

pōpŭlĕus -a -um, *of the poplar.*

pōpŭlifer -fĕra -fĕrum, *producing poplars.*

pōpŭlo -are and **pōpŭlor** -ari, dep. *to lay waste, devastate, plunder; to ruin, spoil, rob.*

¹pōpŭlus -i, m. *a people, political community, nation; as a section of the community, the people; in gen., the people, the public*; hence *any crowd, host, multitude.*

²pōpŭlus -i, f. *a poplar-tree.*

porca -ae, f. *a sow.*

porcīnus -a -um, *of a swine or hog.*

Porcius -a -um, *name of a Roman gens.*

porcus -i, m. *a pig, hog.*

porgo = porrigo; q.v.

porrectĭo -ōnis, f. *stretching out, extension.*

porrĭcĭo -rīcĕre -rectum, *to offer as a sacrifice.*

¹porrĭgo -rĭgĕre -rexi -rectum, *to stretch out, extend; to offer, grant*; pass., porrigi, *to lie stretched out*; partic. **porrectus** -a -um, *stretched out, extended, long.*

²porrĭgo -gĭnis, f. *scurf, dandruff.*

porro, *forward, further; next, again, in turn; in time, far back, long ago, or in future.*

porrus -i, m. and **porrum** -i, n. *a leek.*

porta -ae, f. *a gate.*

portātĭo -ōnis, f. *carrying, conveying.*

portendo -tendĕre -tendi -tentum, *to indicate, predict, presage.*

portentĭficus -a -um, *marvellous, miraculous.*

portentōsus -a -um, *extraordinary, monstrous, unnatural.*

portentum -i, n. subst. from portendo; q.v.

porthmĕus, acc. -ĕă, m. *ferryman.*

portĭcŭla -ae, f. *a little gallery or portico.*

porticus -ūs, f. *a portico, colonnade, arcade, gallery.* Transf., *the Stoic school* of philosophers.

portio -ōnis, f. *a part, section*; pro portione, *in proportion*.

portitor -ōris, m. *a customs-officer*.

portitor -ōris, m. *a carrier*; usually *a boatman, ferryman*.

porto -are, *to bear, carry, convey, bring*.

portōrium i, n. *customs, harbour-dues*; any *toll, tax*.

portula -ae, f. *a little gate, postern*.

portuōsus -a -um, *having many harbours*.

portus -ūs, m. *harbour, port; haven, refuge*.

posco poscĕre pŏposci, *to ask earnestly, request, call upon*; poscimur, *we are asked to sing*; esp. *to demand for punishment*, or *challenge to fight*; of things, *to demand, require*.

pŏsĭtio -ōnis, f. *placing, putting posture*; caeli, *situation, climate*.

pŏsĭtor -ōris, m. *founder, builder*.

pŏsĭtūra -ae, f. *placing; situation, posture; ordering, formation*.

pŏsĭtus -ūs, m. *position, place, arrangement*.

possessio -ōnis, f. *a getting possession* or *possessing; occupation, enjoyment.* Transf., *a thing possessed, possession, property*.

possessiuncula -ae, f. *a small property*.

possessor -ōris, m. *a possessor, occupier*.

possĭdĕo -sidĕre -sēdi -sessum, *to possess, have, hold*.

possĭdo -sidĕre -sēdi sessum, *to take possession of, occupy*.

possum posse pŏtŭi, *to be able*; one may, one can; *to avail, have influence.* Hence partic. **pŏtens** -entis, *able, powerful, capable; influential, efficacious*; with genit., *master of.* Adv. **pŏtentĕr**, *strongly, efficaciously; according to one's power*.

post (older **postĕ**). Adv. *behind, in the rear*; of time, *afterwards*; multo post, *much later.* Prep., with acc. *behind*; of time, *after*; in rank, etc., *next after*.

postĕā, *thereafter, afterwards, next*.

postĕāquam, conj. *after*.

postĕrĭtas -ātis, f. *future generations, posterity*.

postĕrus (**postĕr**) -a -um, *subsequent, following, next, future*; in posterum, *for the next day* or *for the future*; m. pl. as subst. *posterity.* Compar. **postĕrior** -us, *next, later; inferior, worse*; n. acc. as adv., posterius, *later.* Superl. **postrēmus** -a -um, *hindmost, last; lowest, worst.* N. abl. as adv., postremo, *at last*; n. acc. postremum, *for the last time*; ad postremum, *at last.* Superl. **postŭmus** -a -um, *the last, last-born* (esp. of children born after the father's will or death).

postfĕro -ferre, *to consider of less account*.

postgĕnĭti -ōrum, m. pl. *posterity, descendants*.

posthăbĕo -ēre -ŭi -ĭtum, *to consider of less account, put after*.

posthāc, *hereafter, in future, afterwards*.

posthinc, *next*.

posthōc, *afterwards*.

postĭcus -a -um, *hinder, back*; n. as subst. **postĭcum** -i, *a back-door*.

postĭlēna -ae, f. *a crupper*.

postillā, *afterwards*.

postis -is, m. *a door-post*; plur., *a door, doorway*.

postlīmĭnĭum -i, n. *the right to return home*.

postmĕrīdĭānus -a -um, *of the afternoon*.

postmŏdŏ and **postmŏdum**, *presently, soon*.

postpartor -ōris, m. *heir*.

postpōno -pōnĕre -pŏsŭi -pŏsĭtum, *to consider of less account, put after*.

postquam (or **post quam**), conj. *after, when*.

postrēmo, etc.; see posterus.

postrīdĭē, *the day after, on the next day*.

postscaenium -i, n. *the theatre behind the scenes*.

postscrībo -scrībĕre -scripsi -scriptum, *to write after*.

postŭlātĭo -ōnis, f. *a claim, demand, application; a complaint*.

postŭlātum -i, n. subst. from postulo; q.v.

postŭlātus -ūs, m. *a legal complaint, accusation, suit*.

postŭlo -are, *to claim, demand, request*; legal, *to demand a writ*, or *to impeach, accuse* a person; of things, *to demand, require.* N. of partic. as subst. **postŭlātum** -i, *a demand*.

postŭmus -a -um, superl. of posterus; q.v.

pōtātĭo -ōnis, f. *a drinking-bout*.

pŏtĕ; see potis.

pŏtens -entis, partic. from possum; q.v.

pŏtentātus -ūs, m. *political power, supremacy*.

pŏtentĭa -ae, f. *power, might, ability; efficacy, potency*; esp. *(unofficial) political power*.

pŏtestās -ātis, f. *power, ability, control.* Esp. *political supremacy, dominion; the authority of a magistrate, office command*; concr., *an officer, magistrate.* Transf., *opportunity, possibility, occasion*; facere potestatem, *to give opportunity* or *permission*; potestas est, *it is possible*.

pōtĭo -ōnis, f. *drinking; a drink, a draught*; esp. *a love-draught, philtre*.

pŏtĭo -ire, *to put in the power of*.

pŏtĭor -īri, dep., *to get possession of, to obtain; to possess, be master of*.

pŏtĭor; see potis.

pŏtis, **pŏtĕ**; *able, capable*; potis (or pote) est, *can, is able* (or *possible*). Compar. **pŏtĭor** -us, *preferable, better*; n. acc. as adv **pŏtĭus**, *rather, preferably.* Superl. **pŏtissimus** -a -um, *best of all, chief, principal*; n. as adv. **pŏtissĭmum**, *chiefly, above all*.

pōto pōtāre pōtāvi pōtātum or pōtum, *to drink*; esp. *to drink heavily*; of things, *to absorb.* Hence partic. **pōtus** -a -um: pass., *drunk, drained*; act., *having drunk, drunken*.

pŏtor -ōris m. *a drinker*; esp. *a tippler, drunkard.*

pŏtŭlentus (pōcŭlentus) -a -um, *drinkable; drunk, intoxicated.*

¹pōtŭs, partic. from poto; q.v.

²pōtus -ūs, m. *a drinking, draught.*

prae. Adv. *before, in front*; prae quam, *in comparison with.* Prep. with abl., *before*; prae se ferre, *to show, exhibit; in comparison with; on account of, because of.*

praeăcūtus -a -um, *sharpened to a point, pointed.*

praealtus -a -um, *very high or deep.*

praebĕo -bēre -bŭi -bĭtum, *to offer, hold out; to provide, supply, allow*; with reflex., *to present or show oneself in a certain character, behave as.*

praebĭbo -bĭbĕre -bĭbi, *to drink before, drink to.*

praebĭtor -ōris, m. *a furnisher, supplier.*

praecălĭdus -a -um, *very hot.*

praecantrix -īcis, f. *a witch.*

praecānus -a -um, *prematurely grey.*

praecăveo -căvēre -cāvi -cautum: intransit., *to take precautions, be on one's guard*; transit., *to beware of, guard against beforehand.*

praecēdo -cēdĕre -cessi -cessum, *to go before, precede*, in space or time; in rank, etc., *to surpass, excel.*

praecello -ĕre, *to surpass, excel*; genti, *to rule over*; partic. praecellens -entis,*excellent,distinguished,surpassing.*

praecelsus -a -um, *very high.*

praecentio -ōnis, f. *a musical prelude.*

praeceps -cĭpĭtis: of motion, *headlong, fast-falling, quick*; of character, *hasty, rash, blind*; of places, *steep, precipitous*; hence *dangerous.* N. as subst., *a steep place, precipice; danger*; as adv., *headlong.*

praeceptio -ōnis, f. *a pre-conception; a precept; the right to receive in advance.*

praeceptor -ōris, m. and praeceptrix -tricis, f. *a teacher, instructor.*

praeceptum -i, n. subst. from praecipio; q.v.

praecerpo -cerpĕre -cerpsi -cerptum, *to pluck prematurely; to intercept.*

praecido -cīdĕre -cīdi -cīsum, *to cut short, lop, mutilate*; ancoras, *to cut the cables*; of speech, brevi praecidam, *I will put it briefly.*

Hence partic. praecīsus -a -um, *broken off*; of places, *steep, precipitous*; of speech, *brief.* Adv. praecīsē, *briefly, in few words; absolutely, decidedly.*

praecingo -cingĕre -cinxi -cinctum, *to gird in front, surround with a girdle.*

praecino -cĭnĕre -cĭnŭi -centum: intransit. *to sing or play before; to sing an incantation*; transit. *to prophesy, predict.*

praecĭpes -is = praeceps; q.v.

praecĭpio -cĭpĕre -cēpi -ceptum, *to take before, receive in advance*; iter, *to get the start*; mentally, *to anticipate; to instruct, advise, warn.* N. of partic. as subst. praeceptum -i, *a command, rule, injunction.*

praecĭpĭto -are: transit., *to cast head-long down; to hurry along*; intransit. *to fall headlong, rush down.* Adv. from pres. partic., praecĭpĭtantĕr, *headlong.*

praecĭpŭus -a -um, *peculiar, special; excellent, distinguished, extraordinary*, as legal term *received beforehand.* N. as subst. praecĭpŭum -i, *pre-eminence, superiority.* Adv. praecĭpŭē, *especially, chiefly, particularly.*

praecīsus -a -um, partic. from praecido; q.v.

praeclārus -a -um, *very bright, very clear; striking, beautiful; remarkable, excellent, famous*; in bad sense, *notorious.* Adv. praeclārē, *very clearly; admirably, excellently.*

praeclūdo -clūdĕre -clūsi -clūsum, *to close in front, shut up, make inaccessible.*

praeco -ōnis, m. *a public crier, herald.*

praecōgĭto -are, *to consider carefully beforehand.*

praecognosco -cognoscĕre -cognĭtum, *to learn beforehand.*

praecŏlo -cŏlĕre -cultum, *to cultivate before*; partic. praecultus -a -um, *cultivated, adorned.*

praecompŏsĭtus -a -um, *composed beforehand, studied.*

praecōnĭus -a -um, *belonging to a* praeco *or crier.* N. as subst. praecōnĭum -i, *the office of a crier*; hence, *publishing, making known; a public commendation.*

praeconsūmo -sūmĕre -sumptum, *to use up beforehand.*

praecontrecto -are, *to handle beforehand.*

praecordĭa -ōrum, n. pl. *the midriff, diaphragm; the stomach; the breast, heart* (as seat of passions).

praecorrumpo -rumpĕre -ruptum, *to bribe beforehand.*

praecox -cōcis and praecŏquis -e, *ripe before the time, premature.*

praecultus -a -um, partic. from praecolo; q.v.

praecurro -currĕre -cŭcurri and -curri -cursum, *to run before, go on ahead*; in time, *to precede*; in quality, *to surpass.* N. pl. of partic. as subst. praecurrentĭa -ium, *antecedents.*

praecursĭo -ōnis, f. *going before, running ahead*; rhet., *preparation of the hearer.*

praecursor -ōris, m. *a forerunner*; milit., *vanguard, advance-guard*; spy. *scout.*

praecursōrĭus -a -um, *sent in advance.*

praecŭtio -cŭtĕre -cussi -cussum, *to shake before, brandish before.*

praeda -ae, f. *spoils of war, plunder, booty*; of animals, *prey*; in gen., *plunder, gain.*

praedābundus -a -um, *plundering.*

praedamno -are, *to condemn before*; spem, *to give up hope.*

praedātĭo -ōnis, f. *plundering, pillaging.*

praedātor -ōris, m. *plunderer, robber*; poet, *hunter.*

praedātŏrīus -a -um, *plundering, predatory.*

praedēlasso -are, *to weary beforehand.*

praedestĭno -are, *to appoint beforehand.*

praediātŏr -ōris, m. *a buyer of landed estates.*

praediātŏrīus -a -um, *relating to the sale of land.*

praedĭcābĭlis -e, *praiseworthy.*

praedĭcātĭo -ōnis, f. *making publicly known, proclamation; praising, commending.*

praedĭcātŏr -ōris, m. *a praiser, commender, public eulogist.*

¹**praedĭco** -are, *to make publicly known, publish, proclaim, declare; to praise, commend; to boast.*

²**praedīco** -dīcĕre -dīxi -dictum, *to say or name beforehand; to predict, foretell, prophesy; to warn, admonish, instruct.* Hence n. of partic. as subst. **praedictum** -i, *a prophecy, prediction; an order, command; a previous agreement.*

praedictĭo -ōnis, f. *prophesying, predicting;* rhet. *premising.*

praedictum -i, n. subst. from praedico; q.v.

praedĭōlum -i, n. *a small estate, little farm.*

praedisco -ĕre, *to learn before.*

praedispŏsĭtus -a -um, *arranged at intervals beforehand.*

praedĭtus -a -um, *endowed, furnished, provided.*

praedĭum -i, n. *a farm, landed estate.*

praedīvĕs -ĭtis, *very rich.*

praedo -ōnis, m. *robber, plunderer.*

praedŏcĕo -dŏcĕre -doctum *to teach before.*

praedor -ari, dep. *to plunder, rob; to carry off.*

praedūco -dūcĕre -duxi -ductum *to lead forward, bring in front.*

praedulcis -e, *very sweet.*

praedūrus -a -um, *very hard, very strong.*

praeēmĭnĕo -ēre, *to project; to excel.*

praeĕo -īre -īvi and -ĭi -ĭtum, *to go before, precede; hence to go over beforehand verbally, say in advance, dictate; to order, command.*

praefātĭo -ōnis, f. *saying beforehand; a religious or legal form of words, formula; a preface, introduction.*

praefectūra -ae, f. *the office of superintendent;* esp. *a subordinate provincial command.* Transf., *a town or district governed by a praefectus.*

praefectus -a -um, partic. from praeficio; q.v.

praefĕro -ferre -tŭli -lātum. (1) *carry in front; to show, display; to prefer; to anticipate.* (2) *to carry by;* praeferri, *to ride by.*

praefĕrox -ōcis, *very bold, impetuous.*

praeferrātus -a -um, *tipped with iron.*

praefervĭdus -a -um, *burning hot, very hot.*

praefestīno -are, *to hasten prematurely; to hasten by.*

praefĭcĭo -fĭcĕre -fēci -fectum, *to set over, appoint as superintendent.* M. of

partic. as subst. **praefectus** -i, *an overseer, superintendent, civil* or *military officer;* praefectus urbis, *governor of the city (Rome).*

praefīdens -entis, *over-confident.*

praefīgo -fīgĕre -fīxi -fixum, *to fix in front, fasten before; to tip, point with; to pierce through, transfix.*

praefīnĭo -ire, *to fix, prescribe, appoint beforehand.*

praeflōro -are, *to deprive of blossom;* fig., *to diminish, lessen.*

praeflŭo -flŭĕre, *to flow past.*

praefōco -are, *to choke, suffocate.*

praefŏdĭo -fŏdĕre -fōdi -fossum, *to dig in front of; to bury previously.*

praefor -fāri -fātus, dep. *to speak before, to say beforehand,* esp. *of prayers; divos, to invoke.*

praefrīgĭdus -a -um, *very cold.*

praefringo -fringĕre -frēgi -fractum, *to break off in front;* partic. **praefractus** -a -um, *of style, abrupt, disconnected;* of character, *stern, harsh;* adv. **praefractē.**

praefulcĭo -fulcire -fulsi -fultum, *to support, prop up; to use as a prop.*

praefulgĕo -fulgēre -fulsi, *to gleam, shine forth;* with dat., *to outshine.*

praegĕlĭdus -a -um, *very cold.*

praegestĭo -ire, *to desire exceedingly.*

praegnans -antis, *pregnant; full.*

praegrăcĭlis -e, *very slim, lank.*

praegrăvis -e, *very heavy; unwieldy, wearisome; stupefied.*

praegrăvo -are, *to press heavily upon, to weigh down, oppress; to outweigh.*

praegrĕdĭor -grĕdi -gressus, dep. *to go before, precede; to outstrip; to pass by, march by.*

praegressĭo -ōnis, f. *going before, precedence.*

praegustātŏr -ōris, m. *one who tastes before, a taster.*

praegusto -are, *to taste before.*

praeĭăcĕo -ēre, *to lie before.*

praeĭūdĭcĭum -i, n. *a previous judgment, preliminary decision* or *examination; a premature decision; an example, precedent.*

praeĭūdĭco -are, *to decide beforehand, give a preliminary judgment.* Hence partic. **praeĭūdĭcātus** -a -um, *previously decided;* opinio praeiudicata, *a prejudice.*

praeĭŭvo -ĭŭvare -ĭūvi, *to assist before.*

praelābor -lābi -lapsus, dep. *to glide past before or along.*

praelambo -ĕre, *to lick before, taste before.*

praelĕgo -lĕgĕre -lēgi -lectum. (1) *to read out as a teacher, to lecture upon.* (2) *to sail past, coast along.*

praelĭgo -are, *to bind in front; to bind up.*

praelongus -a -um, *very long.*

praelŏquor -lŏqui -lŏcūtus, dep. *to speak beforehand or first.*

praelūcĕo -lūcēre -luxi, *to shine or carry a light before;* with dat., *to outshine, surpass.*

praelūsĭo -ōnis, f. *prelude.*

praelustris -e, *very fine.*

praemando -are, *to order beforehand;* n. pl. of partic. as subst. **praeman-dāta** -orum, *a warrant of arrest.*

praemātūrus -a -um, *too early, premature.*

praemĕdĭcātus -a -um, *protected by medicine or charms.*

praemĕdĭtātĭo -ōnis, f. *considering beforehand.*

praemĕdĭtor -ari, dep. *to practise or consider beforehand;* perf. partic., in pass. sense, **praemĕdĭtātus** -a -um, *considered beforehand.*

praemĕtŭo -ĕre, *to fear beforehand, be apprehensive;* adv. from partic. **praemĕtŭentĕr,** *apprehensively, anxiously.*

praemitto -mittĕre -misi -missum, *to send before, send on ahead.*

praemĭum -i, n. *that which is taken first, the pick; a gift, award, reward, recompense;* poet., *notable exploit.*

praemōlestia -ae, f. *trouble beforehand.*

praemōlior -iri, dep. *to prepare beforehand.*

praemŏnĕo -ēre, *to warn, advise beforehand; to foretell, presage.*

praemŏnĭtus -ūs, m. *prediction, warning.*

praemonstro -are, *to point out the way; to prophesy, predict.*

praemordĕo -mordēre -mordi -morsum, *to bite off; to pilfer.*

praemŏrior -mŏri -mortŭus, dep. *to die prematurely.*

praemūnĭo -ire, *to fortify in front; to secure, make safe.*

praemūnĭtĭo -ōnis, f. *fortifying beforehand;* rhet., *preparation of one's hearers.*

praenăto -are, *to swim before or past.*

praenĭtĕo -ēre, *to outshine.*

praenōmen -ĭnis, n. *the first name, usually standing before the gentile name* (e.g., Marcus, in M. T. Cicero).

praenosco -ĕre, *to get to know beforehand.*

praenōtĭo -ōnis, f. *a preconception, innate idea.*

praenūbĭlus -a -um, *very cloudy or dark.*

praenuntĭo -are, *to announce beforehand, foretell.*

praenuntĭus -a -um, *foretelling;* as subst. *a harbinger, token, omen.*

praeoccŭpo -are, *to seize beforehand, to preoccupy; to anticipate, prevent.*

praeopto -are, *to choose before, to prefer.*

praepando -ĕre, *to open wide in front, extend before.*

praepărātĭo -ōnis, f. *preparation.*

praepăro -are, *to make ready, prepare;* ex praeparato, *by arrangement.*

praepĕdĭo -ire, *to entangle, shackle, fetter; to hinder, impede, obstruct.*

praependĕo -ēre, intransit., *to hang before, hang in front.*

praepĕs -pĕtis, *rapidly flying, swift;* m. and f. as subst., *a bird, esp. a bird of good omen.*

praepĭlātus -a -um, *having a button in front* (of foils, etc.).

praepinguis -e, *very fat or rich.*

praepollĕo -ēre, *to be very or more powerful.*

praepondĕro -are, *to outweigh, to turn the scale.*

praepōno -pōnĕre -pŏsŭi -pŏsĭtum, *to put before; to put over, set over as commander,* etc.; *to prefer.* Hence m. of partic., as subst. **praepŏsĭtus** -i, *a commander.*

praeporto -are, *to carry before.*

praepŏsĭtĭo -ōnis, f. *placing before; preferring, preference;* gram., *a preposition.*

praepossum -posse -pŏtŭi, *to have the chief power.*

praepostĕrus -a -um, *having the last first, inverted, perverse;* adv. **praepostĕrē.**

praepŏtens -entis, *very powerful.*

praeprŏpĕrantĕr, *very hastily.*

praeprŏpĕrus -a -um, *over-hasty, precipitate;* adv. **praeprŏpĕrē.**

praequam; see prae.

praequĕror -quĕri -questus, dep. *to complain beforehand.*

praerădĭo -are, *to outshine.*

praerăpĭdus -a -um, *very rapid.*

praerigesco -rīgescĕre -rīgŭi, *to grow very stiff.*

praerĭpĭo -rĭpĕre -rĭpŭi -reptum, *to snatch before somebody else; to carry off before the time; to anticipate, forestall.*

praerōdo -rōdĕre -rōdi -rōsum, *to gnaw off, bite through.*

praerŏgātīvus -a -um, *asked before others* (for vote, opinion, etc.); f. as subst. **praerŏgātīva** -ae, f. *the tribe or century voting first in the comitia;* hence *the first century's vote;* in gen., *a previous choice; a sure sign, indication.*

praerumpo -rumpĕre -rūpi -ruptum, *to break off in front.*

Hence partic. **praeruptus** -a -um, *broken off;* of places, *steep, precipitous;* of character, *headstrong, hasty.*

[1]**praes** praedis, m. *a surety, security, one who stands bail.*

[2]**praes,** adv. *at hand.*

praesaepes (**praesaepis**) -is, f. **praesaepe** -is, n. and **praesaepium** -i, n. *an enclosure; a crib, manger, stall; a hive; a haunt, lodging, tavern.*

praesaepĭo, *to block up in front.*

praesāgĭo -ire, *to presage, forebode, have a presentiment of.*

praesāgĭtĭo -ōnis, f. *foreboding, presentiment.*

praesāgĭum -i, n. *presage, presentiment, foreboding; prediction.*

praesāgus -a -um, *foreboding; predicting.*

praescisco -ĕre, *to find out beforehand.*

praescĭus -a -um, *knowing beforehand, prescient.*

praescrībo -scrībĕre -scripsi -scriptum, *to write before, set out in writing; to put forward or use as a pretext; to outline; dictate; to prescribe, ordain, direct beforehand.* Hence n. partic. as subst. **praescriptum** -i, *a prescribed limit, regulation, rule.*

praescriptĭo -ōnis, f. *a title, inscription, introduction; a precept, rule; a pretext; legal, an objection, demurrer.*

praesĕco -sĕcare -sĕcŭi -sectum, *to cut in front, cut short.*

praesens -entis, partic. from praesum; q.v.

praesensĭo -ōnis, f. *a presentiment, foreboding; preconception.*

praesentĭa -ae, f. *presence; animi, presence of mind; in praesentia, for the present; sometimes power, effect.*

praesentĭo -sentire -sensi -sensum, *to feel beforehand, have a presentiment of.*

praesertim, *especially, chiefly.*

praesĕs -sĭdis, *sitting before, protecting.* As subst. *a protector; also a chief, ruler, president.*

praesĭdĕo -sĭdēre -sēdi -sessum, *to sit before; to watch over, protect, guard; to preside over, manage, direct.* M. of partic. as subst. **praesĭdens** -entis, *a president, ruler.*

praesĭdĭārĭus -a, n. *on guard.*

praesĭdĭum -i, n. *sitting before; protection, help, support.* Milit., *guard, escort; a garrison; a post.*

praesignĭfĭco -are, *to indicate beforehand.*

praesignis -e, *distinguished, remarkable.*

praesŏno -sŏnare -sŏnŭi, *to sound forth.*

praespargo -ĕre, *to scatter in front.*

praestābĭlis -e, *distinguished, pre-eminent; in compar., preferable.*

praestans -antis, partic. from praesto; q.v.

praestantĭa -ae, f. *superiority, excellence.*

praestĕs -stĭtis, *protecting.*

praestīgĭae -ārum, f. pl. *deception, illusion, juggling.*

praestĭtŭo -stĭtŭere -stĭtŭi -stĭtūtum, *to prescribe, appoint beforehand.*

¹**praesto**, adv. *present, at hand ready; with esse, to be at hand, be ready to help.*

²**praesto** -stare -stĭti -stĭtum. (1) *to stand before; to be outstanding, surpass, excel;* impers., praestat, *it is better, preferable.* (2) transit., *to become surety for, answer for, be responsible for.* Transf., *to perform, execute, fulfil; to show, manifest, exhibit; to offer, present;* with se and acc. *to show oneself, behave as.* Hence partic. **praestans** -antis, *excellent, distinguished, eminent.*

praestŏlor -ari, dep., *to wait for, expect.*

praestringo -stringĕre -strinxi -strictum, *to bind up, in front.* Transf., *to make blunt or dull.*

praestrŭo -strŭĕre -struxi -structum. (1) *to build in front; to block up, make impassable.* (2) *to build beforehand, to prepare.*

praesŭl -sŭlis, c. and **praesultātor** -ōris, m. *a dancer.*

praesulto -are, *to leap or dance before.*

praesum -esse -fŭi, *to be before; to be over, preside over; to take the lead.* Hence partic. (with compar.) **praesens** -entis, *present, at hand, in*

space or time; in praesens (tempus), *for the present time;* esp. *immediate, ready; effective, powerful, helpful, resolute, determined.*

praesūmo -sūmĕre -sumpsi -sumptum, *to take beforehand; to anticipate; to take for granted.* Hence partic. **praesumptus** -a -um, *taken for granted, presumed.*

praesūtus -a -um, *sewn over in front.*

praetempto -are, *to try, test beforehand.*

praetendo -tendĕre -tendi -tentum, *to stretch or hold out;* pass., praetendi, of places, *to lie before or in front.* Transf., *to hold out as a pretext, allege in excuse.*

praetento = praetempto; q.v.

praetĕpesco -tĕpescĕre -tĕpŭi, *to glow beforehand.*

praeter. Adv., *except.* Prep. with acc., *beyond, past; beside, contrary to, beside; more than; except; in addition to.*

praetĕrăgo -ĕre, *to drive past, drive by.*

praetĕrĕā, *besides, further; after this, hereafter.*

praetĕrĕo -ire -ivi and oftener -ĭi -ĭtum, *to go by, pass by.* Transf., *to escape the notice of a person; to pass by, pass over, omit; to surpass, outstrip; to transgress.* Hence partic. **praetĕrĭtus** -a -um, *past, gone by.*

praetĕrĕquĭto -are, *to ride past, ride by.*

praeterfĕro -ferre -tŭli -lātum, *to carry past.*

praeterflŭo -flŭĕre, *to flow past, flow by.*

praetergrĕdĭor -grĕdi -gressus, dep. *to pass by, go beyond.*

praetĕrĭtus -a -um, partic. from praetereo; q.v.

praeterlābor -lābi -lapsus, dep. *to glide by, flow by, slip away.*

praetermĕo -are, *to pass by.*

praetermissĭo -ōnis, f. *leaving out, omission; passing over, neglecting.*

praetermitto -mittĕre -misi -missum, *to let pass, let go by; to neglect, omit; to pass over, overlook.*

praeterquam or **praeter quam**, *more than, beyond;* after neg., *except;* with quod, *apart from the fact that.*

praetervectĭo -ōnis, f. *a passing place.*

praetervĕhor -vĕhi -vectus sum, *to ride by, be carried past, march past, pass by.*

praetervŏlo -are, *to fly past; to slip by, escape.*

praetexo -texĕre -texŭi -textum, *to weave in front, form a border; to adorn; to cover, conceal; to put forward as a pretext.* Hence partic. **praetextus** -a -um, *bordered,* esp. *of the toga.* F. as subst. **praetexta** -ae, f. *a toga bordered with purple,* worn by magistrates and boys; also praetexta (fabula), *a tragedy with Roman characters.* N. as subst. **praetextum** -i, *a pretence, pretext.*

praetextātus -a -um, *wearing the toga praetexta; veiled; licentious.*

praetextū, abl. sing. m. *in outward appearance; under a pretext.*

praetinctus -a -um, *moistened beforehand.*

praetor -ōris, m. *leader, chief; a magistrate,* esp. one who helped the consuls by administering justice, commanding armies, etc.

praetōriānus -a -um, *belonging to the imperial body-guard, praetorian.*

praetōrius -a -um. (1) *relating to the praetor, praetorian.* (2) *relating to any general* or *commander;* praetoria navis, *flagship;* cohors, *the general's body-guard.* As subst.: m. **praetōrius** -i, *an ex-praetor* or *man of praetorian rank;* n. **praetōrium** -i, *the official residence of the praetor* or propraetor; *a palace;* also *the headquarters in a Roman camp.*

praetrēpido -are, *to be hasty* or *impatient.*

praetūra -ae, f. *the office of praetor.*

praeumbro -are, *to overshadow; to obscure.*

praeustus -a -um, *burnt at the end* or *tip; frost-bitten.*

praevăleo -vălēre -vălŭi, *to be very strong; to prevail, get the upper hand.*

praevălidus -a -um, *very strong;* terra, *too productive.*

praevāricātio -ōnis, f. *collusion.*

praevāricātor -ōris, m. *an advocate guilty of collusion.*

praevāricor -ari, dep. of an advocate, *to have a secret understanding with the other side, to be guilty of collusion.*

praevĕhor -vĕhi -vectus sum, *to ride* (or *run*) *before* or *past.*

praevĕnio -vĕnire -vĕni -ventum, *to come before, anticipate, get the start of.*

praeverro -ĕre, *to sweep before.*

praeverto (praevorto) -vertĕre -verti -versum, and **praevertor** -verti -versus sum; *of preference, to put first, take first, turn first to; of early action, to anticipate, outstrip, forestall; to surprise, preoccupy.*

praevĭdeo -vĭdēre -vidi -visum, *to see before, foresee.*

praevĭtio -are, *to corrupt beforehand.*

praevĭus -a -um, *going before, preceding.*

praevŏlo -are, *to fly before.*

pragmăticus -a -um, *skilled in business;* m. as subst. *a person who supplied speakers with material.*

prandĕo prandēre prandi pransum, *to take lunch; to lunch upon;* perf. partic. in act. sense **pransus** -a -um, *having lunched; well-fed.*

prandium -i, n. *a late breakfast* or *lunch.*

pransus -a -um, partic. from prandeo; q.v.

prăsĭnus -a -um, *leek-green.*

prātensis -e, *of a meadow.*

prātŭlum -i, n. *a little meadow.*

prātum -i, n. *a meadow; meadow-grass.*

prāvĭtās -ātis, f. *crookedness, deformity; perversity, depravity.*

prāvus -a -um, adj. *crooked, deformed; perverse; depraved.* Adv. **prāvē**.

Praxĭtĕlēs -is and -i, m. *a sculptor of Athens.*

prĕcārĭus -a -um, *begged for,* or *got by entreaty; uncertain, precarious.* N. abl. as adv. **prĕcārĭo**, *by entreaty.*

prĕcātĭo -ōnis, f. *begging, request prayer.*

prĕces; see prex.

prĕcĭae -arum, f. *a kind of vine.*

prĕcor -ari, dep. *to beg, entreat, pray, invoke.*

prĕhendo prĕhendĕre prĕhendi prehensum and prendo prendĕre prendi prensum, *to lay hold of, seize, grasp; to catch, detain, arrest; to take in,* mentally or by the senses.

prĕhenso and **prenso** -are, *to lay hold of, clutch at.* Transf., *to canvass for votes.*

prēlum -i, n. *a wine* or *olive-press.*

prĕmo prĕmĕre pressi pressum, *to press; to step on, lie on; to hug, keep close to; to press hard, squeeze; to pursue closely, press upon; to press down, strike down; to disparage, slander; to press together, close; to check, curb.*

Hence partic. **pressus** -a -um, *subdued, measured; of style, compressed, concise.* Adv. **pressē**, *accurately, precisely, distinctly; of style, briefly, concisely.*

prendo = prehendo; q.v.

prensātĭo -ōnis, f. *canvassing for office.*

prenso = prehenso; q.v.

pressĭo -ōnis, f. *leverage* or *means of leverage.*

presso -are, *to press.*

¹pressus -a -um, partic. from premo; q.v.

²pressus -ūs, m. *pressing, pressure.*

prestēr -ēris, m. *a fiery whirlwind* or *a waterspout.*

prĕtĭōsus -a -um, *costly, precious, dear; of persons, extravagant.* Adv. **prĕtĭōsē**.

prĕtĭum -i, n. *worth, value, price;* esse in pretio, *to be prized;* operae pretium, *worth while.* Transf., *prize, reward; a ransom; a bribe; punishment.*

prex prĕcis (usually plur.) f. *request, entreaty;* esp. *prayer to a god;* sometimes *a curse, execration.*

Prĭāmus -i, m. *the last king of Troy;* adj. **Prĭămēĭus** -a -um.

Prĭāpus -i, m. *the god of gardens and vineyards.*

prĭdem, *long ago, long since.*

prĭdĭē, *on the day before.*

prīmaevus -a -um, *young, youthful.*

prīmāni -orum, m. pl. *soldiers of the first legion.*

prīmārĭus -a -um, *in the first rank, distinguished.*

prīmĭgĕnus -a -um, *original, primitive.*

prīmĭpīlāris -is, m. *the centurion of the first maniple of the triarii, the chief centurion of a legion.*

prīmĭpīlus; see pilus.

prīmĭtĭae -arum, f. *first-fruits.*

prīmĭtus, *first, for the first time.*

prīmordĭum -i, n. *first beginning, origin;* plur. often = *atoms.*

prīmōris -e, *first, foremost; at the tip;* primoribus labris, *superficially;* of rank, *first, most distinguished.*

prīmus; see prior.

princeps -cipis, adj. *first, foremost.* As subst., *leader;* polit., *often as a title of the Roman emperor;* milit., plur., principes, *the second line in a Roman army, between* hastati *and* triarii.

principālis -e. (1) *first, in time or rank.* (2) *of a prince.* (3) *of the* principia *in a Roman camp.*

principātus -ūs, m. (1) *first place, pre-eminence; rule, dominion.* (2) *beginning, origin.*

principiālis -e, *original.*

principium -i, n. *beginning, origin; groundwork, foundation;* in plur., *elements, first principles;* polit., *the tribe or* curia *which voted first;* milit., in plur., *the front ranks or the head-quarters in a camp.*

prior prius, genit. -ōris, compar. adj., *fore, former,* of place or time; *higher in importance;* m. pl. as subst., *ancestors.* N. acc. as adv. prius, *before, previously; formerly; sooner, rather;* prius quam, *or* priusquam, conj., *before.* Superl. **primus** -a -um, *first, foremost,* of place or time; of rank, etc., *first, most distinguished;* (partes) primae, *the leading part;* in primis, *especially.* N. acc. as adv. primum, *at first or for the first time.* N. abl. primō, *at first.*

priscus -a -um, *ancient, antique; of the old school, venerable; former, previous.* Adv. **prisce**, *in the old-fashioned way.*

pristīnus -a -um, *former, previous, earlier.*

prius; see prior.

prīvātim, *privately, as a private person, in private life; at home.*

prīvātio -ōnis, f. *freeing, release.*

prīvigna -ae, f. *stepdaughter.*

prīvignus -i, m. *stepson.*

prīvilēgium i, n. *a special law, private law.*

prīvo -are, *to strip, deprive; to free, release.*

Hence partic. **privātus** -a -um, as adj., *private, unofficial;* in privato, *in private;* (vir) privatus, *a private person.*

prīvus -a -um, *single, every; distributively, one each; particular, special, one's own;* with genit., *deprived of.*

¹prō, prep., with abl., *before, in front of; for, on behalf of, in favour of; in place of; like, as good as;* se pro cive gerere, *to behave as a citizen; as a reward for; in proportion to, according to, by virtue of;* pro virili parte, *to the best of one's abilities;* pro eo quantum, *in proportion as.*

²pro! (**proh!**), interj. *oh! ah!*

prōăvia -ae, f. *a great-grandmother.*

prōăvitus -a -um, *ancestral.*

prōăvus -i, m. *a great-grandfather; an ancestor, forefather.*

prōbābilis -e, (1) *probable, credible.* (2) *acceptable, good.* Adv. **probā-biliter**, *probably, credibly.*

prōbābilitās -ātis, f. *probability, credibility.*

prōbātio -ōnis, f. *proving, trial, examination; approval, proof, demonstration.*

prōbātor -ōris, m. *one who approves, an approver.*

prōbitās -ātis, f. *honesty, uprightness.*

prōbo -are, *to make or find good; to approve, pronounce good;* with dat., *to recommend to;* with abl., *to judge by a standard;* in gen., *to show, prove, demonstrate.*

Hence partic. **probātus** -a -um, *found good, approved; acceptable.*

probrōsus -a -um, *shameful, disgraceful, infamous.*

probrum -i, n. *abuse, reproach; ground for reproach, disgrace; infamous conduct,* esp. *unchastity.*

prōbus -a -um, *good, excellent, fine; morally good, upright, virtuous.* Adv. **probē**, *well, rightly, properly.*

prōcācitās -ātis, f. *shamelessness, impudence.*

prōcax -cācis, *shameless, bold, impudent;* adv. **procāciter**.

prōcēdo -cēdĕre -cessi -cessum, *to go ahead, proceed, advance, continue; to come out, go out;* of actions, etc., *to turn out, result;* sometimes *to turn out well, prosper.*

prōcella -ae, f. *a storm, tempest, gale;* in fighting, *charge, onset, wave.*

prōcellōsus -a -um, *stormy, tempestuous.*

prōcer -ēris, m. *a chief noble, prince.*

prōcēritās -ātis, f. *height, length.*

prōcērus -a -um, *tall, long;* compar. adv. **procērius**, *farther forward.*

prōcessio -ōnis, f. *a (military) advance.*

prōcessus -ūs, m. *advance, progress.*

prōcido -cidĕre -cidi, *to fall forwards.*

prōcinctū, abl. sing. m. *being girded or equipped; readiness for battle.*

proclāmātor -ōris, m. *a bawler.*

proclāmo -are, *to call out, cry out.*

prōclīno -are, *to bend over, incline forwards.*

prōclivis -e and **prōclīvus** -a -um, *inclined forwards, sloping downwards;* proclive, *or per* proclive, *downwards.* Transf., *inclined, ready, prone; easy to do.*

prōclīvitās -ātis, f. *a slope.* Transf., *inclination, tendency.*

prōclīvus = proclivis; q.v.

Procnē (**Prognē**) -ēs, f. *wife of Tereus; changed into a swallow.*

prōco -are and **prōcor** -ari, dep. *to ask, demand.*

prōconsul -sūlis, m. (also **prō consūle**), *a proconsul, one who serves as a consul, in command of any army, or as governor of a province.*

prōconsulāris -e, *proconsular.*

prōconsulātus -ūs, m. *the office of proconsul.*

prōcrastinātio -ōnis, f. *procrastination.*

prŏcrastĭno -are, *to put off till tomorrow, defer.*

prŏcrĕātĭo -ōnis, f. *begetting, procreation.*

prŏcrĕātŏr -ōris, m. *begetter, creator.*

prŏcrĕātrix -icis, f. *mother.*

prŏcrĕo -are, *to beget; to produce, cause make.*

prŏcresco -ēre, *to come forth, arise; to increase.*

Procrustēs -ae, m. *a robber killed by Theseus.*

prŏcŭbo -are, *to lie stretched out.*

prŏcūdo -cūdĕre -cūdi -cūsum, *to hammer out, forge; to form, produce.*

prŏcŭl, *far; at, to, or from a distance.*

prŏculco -are, *to tread on, trample down.*

prŏcumbo -cumbĕre -cŭbŭi -cŭbĭtum, *to lean* or *bend forward; to fall down, sink down, be laid low.*

prŏcūrātĭo -ōnis, f. *taking care, management, administration.* Esp. (1) *the office of imperial procurator.* (2) *an attempt to propitiate a deity.*

prŏcūrātŏr -ōris, m. *a manager, bailiff, agent, factor;* regni, a viceroy; under the empire, *a financial agent* or *under-governor.*

prŏcūrātrix -trīcis, f. *she that governs.*

prŏcūro -are, *to take care of, look after; to manage, administer; to be a procurator; to sacrifice in order to avert evil.*

prŏcurro -currĕre -curri and -cŭcurri -cursum, *to run forward;* of places, *to project, jut out.*

prŏcursātĭo -ōnis, f. *running forward, skirmishing.*

prŏcursātŏr -ōris, m. *a skirmisher.*

prŏcurso -are, *to run forward;* milit. *to skirmish.*

prŏcursus -ūs, m. *running forward;* milit., *advance, charge.*

prŏcurvus -a -um, *bent forward.*

¹prŏcus -i. m. = procer; q.v.

²prŏcus -i, m. *a wooer, suitor; a canvasser.*

prōdĕo -ire -ii -ĭtum, *to advance, go forward; to project; to come out, appear.*

prōdīco -dicĕre -dixi -dictum, *to put off.*

prōdictātŏr -ōris, m. *one who acts as dictator.*

prōdĭgentĭa -ae, f. *profusion, prodigality.*

prōdĭgĭālis -e, *dealing in wonders;* adv. **prōdĭgĭālĭtĕr,** *wonderfully.*

prōdĭgĭōsus -a -um, *unnatural, wonderful.*

prōdĭgĭum -i, n. *a prodigy, portent; an enormity, an unnatural thing; a monster.*

prōdĭgo -ĭgĕre -ēgi -actum, *to drive forth; to spend, waste.*

prōdĭgus -a -um, *profuse, extravagant; rich, abound in.* Adv. **prōdĭgē.**

prōdĭtĭo -ōnis, f. *betrayal, treason.*

prōdĭtŏr -ōris, m. *a betrayer, traitor.*

prōdo -dĕre -dĭdi -dĭtum. (1) *to put forth, bring forth; to show, publish; to appoint.* (2) *to forsake, betray.* (3) *to hand over, deliver, transmit.*

prōdŏcĕo -ēre, *to teach, inculcate.*

prōdrŏmus -i, m. *forerunner.*

prōdūco -dūcĕre -duxi -ductum, *to bring forward, bring out, extend; to produce, bring up, advance, promote; to divulge, bring to light;* in pronunciation, *to lengthen out, make long;* in time, *to prolong, continue;* also *to put off, postpone.*

Hence partic. **prōductus** -a -um, *extended, lengthened, prolonged;* of syllables, *pronounced long;* n. pl. as subst. *preferable things* (in the Stoic philosophy). Adv. **prōductē,** *long* (of pronunciation).

prōductĭo -ōnis, f. *extending, lengthening, prolonging.*

proeliātŏr -ōris, m. *warrior.*

proelĭor -ari, dep. *to give battle, fight, strive.*

proelĭum -i, n. *battle, fight, strife.*

prŏfāno -are, *to profane, desecrate.*

prŏfānus -a -um, *not sacred; uninitiated; ordinary, common, profane; impious.*

prŏfectĭo -ōnis, f. *departure; source, origin.*

prŏfecto, *truly, really, indeed.*

prōfĕro -ferre -tŭli -lātum. (1) *to bring forth, bring forward, offer to publish, bring to light, reveal; to produce, cite, mention.* (2) *to advance, bring forward, impel.* (3) *to enlarge, extend;* in time, *to lengthen;* also *to put off, postpone.*

prŏfessĭo -ōnis, f. *declaration, profession.* Transf., *a register of persons and property; an occupation, art, profession.*

prŏfessŏr -ōris, m. *an authority, expert.*

prŏfessōrĭus -a -um, *authoritative.*

prŏfestus -a -um, *not kept as a festival, common.*

prŏfĭcĭo -fĭcĕre -fēci -fectum: of persons, *to make progress, advance;* of things, *to be of use, assist, help.*

prŏfĭciscor -fĭcisci -fectus, dep. *to start forward, set out, depart; to arise* or *spring from an origin.*

prŏfĭtĕor -fĭtēri -fessus, dep. *to acknowledge, confess; to profess* or *declare oneself anything; to profess a science, art, etc.; to make any public statement; to offer, promise.*

prōflĭgātŏr -ōris, m. *a spendthrift.*

prōflīgo -are, *to overthrow, overcome, ruin; to lower, debase; to bring almost to an end, nearly finish.*

Hence partic. **prōflīgātus** -a -um, *ruined, degraded.*

prōflo -are, *to blow forth, breathe forth.*

prōflŭentĭa -ae, f. *fluency.*

prōflŭo -flŭĕre -fluxi fluxum, *to flow forth; to proceed.*

Hence partic. **prōflŭens** -entis, *flowing;* f. as subst. (sc. aqua), *running water;* of style, *flowing, fluent.* Adv. **prōflŭentĕr.**

prōflŭvĭum -i, n. *flowing forth.*

prōfor -fari -fatus, dep. *to say, speak, declare.*

prŏfŭgĭo -fŭgĕre -fūgi: intransit., *to flee away, escape;* transit., *to flee away from.*

prŏfŭgus -a -um, *fleeing, fugitive; banished; migratory.*

prŏfundo -fundĕre -fūdi -fūsum, *to pour forth, shed, cause to flow;* pass., profundi, *to stream forth.* Transf., *to stretch at full length; to release, discharge; to utter; to spend, sacrifice. give up; to lavish, squander.*
Hence partic. prŏfūsus -a -um, *lavish, extravagant.* Adv. prŏfūsē, *in disorder; lavishly, extravagantly.*

prŏfundus -a -um, *deep, profound; high; thick, dense; boundless.* N. as subst. prŏfundum -i, *depth, abyss;* poet., *the sea.*

prŏfūsus -a -um, partic. from profundo; q.v.

prōgĕner -i, *a grand-daughter's husband.*

prōgĕnĕro -are, *to engender, produce.*

prōgĕnĭes -ēi, f. *descent, lineage; progeny, offspring, descendants.*

prōgĕnĭtor -ōris, m. *founder of a family, ancestor.*

prōgigno -gignĕre -gĕnŭi -gĕnĭtum, *to engender, bring forth.*

prognātus -a -um, *born, sprung from;* m. as subst., *a son.*

Prognē = Procne; q.v.

prōgrĕdĭor -grĕdi -gressus, dep., *to go forth, go out; to go forwards, advance, proceed.*

prōgressĭo -ōnis, f. *advance, progress; increase;* rhet., *climax.*

prōgressus -ūs, m. *going forwards, advance, progress; increase.*

proh! = pro!; q.v.

prŏhĭbĕo -ēre, *to hold back, restrain, hinder; to forbid, prohibit; to preserve, defend, protect.*

prŏhĭbĭtĭo -ōnis, f. *hindering, prohibition.*

prōĭcio -ĭcĕre -ĭēci -ĭectum, *to throw forth; to fling forward; to put forward, cause to project* (pass., *to project*); *to fling out, throw away, abandon; to defer, put off.*
Hence partic. prōĭectus -a -um, *jutting forward, prominent; stretched out, prostrate;* hence *abject, contemptible, downcast;* with ad, *addicted to.*

prōĭectĭo -ōnis, f. *throwing forward, stretching out.*

prōĭectū, abl. sing. m. *by jutting out.*

prŏinde and prŏin (o and i sometimes scanned as one syllable), *consequently, therefore;* foll. by ut or quam, *just as;* foll. by quasi, ac, ac si, *just as if.*

prōlābor -lābi -lapsus dep. (1) *to glide forward, slip along or out.* (2) *to fall forward, fall down.*

prōlapsĭo -ōnis, f. *slipping, sliding.*

prōlātĭo -ōnis, f. *bringing forward, mentioning; an extension; putting off, deferring.*

prōlāto -are, *to extend, enlarge, lengthen; to put off, defer.*

prōlecto -are, *to entice, allure.*

prōlēs -is, f. *offspring, descendants, posterity; the young men of a race; of plants, fruit.*

prōlētārĭus -i, m. *a citizen of the lowest class, serving the state only by begetting children.*

prōlĭcĭo -lĭcĕre -lixi, *to lure forth, entice.*

prōlixus -a -um, *wide, broad, long.* Transf., *willing, obliging; favourable.* Adv. prōlixē, *freely; willingly.*

prōlŏgus -i, m. *prologue.*

prōlŏquor -lŏqui -lŏcūtus, dep. *to speak out, say openly.*

prōlūdo -lūdĕre -lūsi -lūsum, *to play beforehand, to prelude.*

prōlŭo -lŭĕre -lŭi -lūtum, *to wash away or off; to wash clean.*

prōlūsĭo -ōnis, f. *a prelude, preliminary exercise.*

prōlŭvĭes -ēi, f. *an inundation; scourings, discharge.*

prōmĕrĕo -ēre -ŭi -ĭtum and prōmĕrĕor -ēri -ĭtus, dep. *to deserve;* n. of partic. as subst. prōmĕrĭtum -i, *deserts, merit.*

Prōmēthĕus -ĕi and -ĕos, m. *Prometheus, punished for stealing fire from heaven and giving it to mankind;* adj. Prōmēthĕus -a -um.

prōmĭnĕo -ēre -ŭi, *to stand out, jut out, project, extend;* partic. prōmĭnens -entis, *jutting out, projecting;* n. as subst. *a projection.*

prōmiscus and prōmiscŭus -a -um, *mixed, indiscriminate, promiscuous; commonplace, usual.* Adv. prōmiscē and prōmiscŭē.

prōmissĭo -ōnis, f. *a promise.*

prōmissor -ōris, m. *a promiser.*

prōmitto -mittĕre -mīsi -missum, *to let go forward, send forth; to let grow; to promise, undertake.*
Hence partic. prōmissus -a -um, *let grow, long, hanging down.* N. of partic. as subst. prōmissum -i, *a promise.*

prōmo prōmĕre prompsi promptum, *to bring out, produce; to bring forward, disclose, express.*
Hence partic. promptus -a -um, *ready, at hand; visible, apparent;* of persons, *prepared, resolute, prompt.* Adv. promptē.

prōmontŏrĭum -i, n. *a mountain ridge; a promontory.*

prōmŏvĕo -mŏvēre -mōvi -mōtum, *to move forwards, push onwards, make to advance; to extend; to postpone.*

promptū, abl. sing. m.: in promptu esse, *to be ready, easy, or manifest;* in promptu ponere, *to make manifest;* in promptu habere, *to have ready or have on show.*

promptus -a -um, partic. from promo; q.v.

prōmulgātĭo -ōnis, f. *publication, promulgation* (of a proposed law).

prōmulgo -are, *to publish, promulgate* (esp. a proposed law).

prōmulsis -ĭdis, f. *hors d'oeuvres.*

prōmuntŭrĭum = promontorium; q.v.

prōmus -i, m. *a steward, butler.*

prōmūtŭus -a -um, *advanced, paid beforehand.*

prōnĕpōs -pōtis, m. *great-grandson.*

prŏneptis -is, f. *great-granddaughter.*

prŏnoea -ae, f. *providence.*

prŏnŭba -ae, f. (1) *a matron attending a bride.* (2) *epithet of Juno, as the goddess presiding over marriage.*

prŏnuntiātĭo -ōnis, f. *public declaration; the decision of a judge, a judgment;* in logic, *a proposition;* in rhetoric, *delivery.*

prŏnuntiātor -ōris, m. *a relater.*

prŏnuntĭo -are, *to make publicly known, declare;* in the senate, *to announce a resolution;* at a sale, *to make a statement as to defects;* rhet. *to declaim, recite, deliver.* N. of partic. as subst. **prŏnuntĭātum** -i, in logic, *a proposition.*

prŏnŭrus -us, f. *a grandson's wife.*

prŏnus -a -um, *inclined forward, stooping forward; rushing down or past; precipitous, steep.* Transf., *inclined, well-disposed, favourable; easy.* Adv. **prŏnē**, *on a slope.*

prŏoemĭum -i, n. *preface, introduction, prelude.*

prŏpāgātĭo -ōnis, f. *spreading, propagation; extension, enlargement.*

prŏpāgātor -ōris, m. *an extender, enlarger.*

¹**prŏpāgo** -are, *to spread propagate plants; to extend, enlarge, prolong.*

²**prŏpāgo** -ĭnis, f. *a layer, slip or shoot* (esp. of the vine); of men and animals, *offspring, race, posterity.*

prŏpālam, *publicly, in public.*

prŏpātŭlus -a -um, *open, uncovered;* n. as subst. *an open place, unroofed space;* in propatulo, *publicly.*

prŏpē, adv. and prep; compar. **prŏpĭus;** superl. **prŏxĭmē.** Adv. *near,* in space or time; *nearly;* propius, *more nearly, more closely;* proxime, of time, *just now.* Prep. with acc. *near to,* in space or time; in gen., *approximating to, not far from.*

prŏpēdĭem, *at an early date, very soon.*

prŏpello -pellĕre -pŭli -pulsum, *to drive before one, drive forth or away.*

prŏpēmŏdŏ and **prŏpēmŏdum**, *almost, nearly.*

prŏpendĕo -pendĕre -pendi -pensum *to hang down; to preponderate; to incline, be favourable.*

Hence partic. **prŏpensus** -a -um, *weighty; tending, inclined, disposed;* esp. *favourably disposed.* Adv. **prŏpensē**, *readily, willingly.*

prŏpensĭo -ōnis, f. *inclination, propensity.*

prŏpĕrantĕr, adv. from propero; q.v.

prŏpĕrantĭa -ae, f. *haste, rapidity.*

prŏpĕrātĭo -ōnis, f. *haste.*

prŏpĕro -are: intransit., *to hasten;* transit., *to hasten something, to accelerate, complete quickly.* Adv. from pres. partic. **prŏpĕrantĕr**, *hastily.* Past. partic. **prŏpĕrātus** -a -um, *hasty;* n. as subst. **prŏpĕrātum** -i, *haste;* abl. **prŏpĕrātō**, *in haste.*

Prŏpertĭus -i, m., Sex. Aurelius *a poet of the Augustan age.*

prŏpĕrus -a -um. *quick, rapid, hasty;* adv. **prŏpĕrē**

prŏpexus -a -um, *combed forwards, hanging down.*

prŏpīno -are, *to drink to anyone.*

prŏpinquĭtās -ātis, f. *nearness, proximity; friendship* or *relationship.*

prŏpinquo -are: intransit., *to come near, draw near, approach;* transit. *to bring near, hasten on.*

prŏpinquus -a -um, *near, close, neighbouring; similar; nearly related, closely connected;* as subst., *a kinsman.* Adv. **prŏpinquē.**

prŏpĭor -us, genit. -ōris, *nearer,* in space or time (cf. prope); *more like; more closely connected; more suitable.* Superl. **proxĭmus (proxŭmus)** -a -um, *very near, nearest;* in time, *next, following,* or *most recent;* in rank, etc., *next, next best; most like; most nearly connected;* m. pl. as subst. *near relations* or *close friends.*

prŏpĭtĭo -are, *to soothe, appease.*

prŏpĭtĭus -a -um, *favourable, gracious.*

prŏpĭus, compar. of prope; q.v.

prŏpōla -ae, m. *a retailer, huckster.*

prŏpollŭo -ŭĕre, *to pollute worse.*

prŏpōno -pōnĕre -pŏsŭi -pŏsĭtum, *to put on view, expose, display; to publish, relate, tell; to propose, promise, offer as a reward* or *hold over as a threat; to imagine, put before the mind; to propose to oneself, purpose, intend.* N. of partic. as subst. **prŏpŏsĭtum** -i, *a design, purpose; the subject* or *theme of a discourse; the first premiss of a syllogism.*

prŏporrō, adv. *further, moreover,* or *altogether.*

prŏportĭo -ōnis, f. *proportion, analogy, similarity.*

prŏpŏsĭtĭo -ōnis, f. *a purpose; the subject of a discourse;* in logic, *the first proposition of a syllogism.*

prŏpŏsĭtum -i, n. subst. from propono; q.v.

prŏpraetor -ōris, m. (and prō praetōre) *a praetor's deputy; an ex-praetor,* sent as governor to a province or given a military command.

prŏprĭĕtās -ātis, f. *a property, peculiarity; ownership.*

prŏprĭtim, *peculiarly, specially.*

prŏprĭus -a -um, *one's own, special, peculiar characteristic; lasting, permanent.* Hence adv. **prŏprĭē**, *exclusively, peculiarly, characteristically; in a proper sense.*

propter. Adv., *near, close by.* Prep. with acc. *near; on account of, because of.*

proptĕrĕā, adv. *on that account, therefore.*

prŏpŭdĭum -i, n. *a shameful action; a wretch, villain.*

prŏpugnācŭlum -i, n. *a fortification rampart, defence.*

prŏpugnātĭo -ōnis, f. *defence.*

prŏpugnātor -ōris, m. *a defender.*

prŏpugno -are, *to skirmish in front; fight in defence, defend.*

prōpulso -are, *to drive back, repel, ward off.*

prō-quaestŏre, *an ex-quaestor who helped to govern a province.*

prōquam (or **prō quam**), *in proportion as, according as.*

prōra -ae, f. *the prow, bow of a ship;* poet., *a ship.*

prōrēpo -rēpĕre -repsi, *to creep forward, crawl forth.*

prōrēta -ae, and **prōreūs** -i, m. *a look-out man.*

prōrĭpĭo -rĭpĕre -rĭpŭi -reptum, *to snatch, tear, drag forth;* se proripere, *to rush forward.*

prōrŏgātĭo -ōnis, f. *prolongation of a term of office; deferring.*

prōrŏgo -are, *to prolong; to defer, put off.*

prorsum and **prorsŭs,** *forwards, straight ahead.* Transf., *utterly, wholly; in a word, to sum up.*

prorsus (**prōsus**) -a -um, *straight-forward; of style, in prose.*

prōrumpo -rumpĕre -rūpi -ruptum: transit., *to cause to break out; to thrust out;* prorupta audacia, *unbridled;* intransit., *to burst forth, break out.*

prōrŭo -rŭĕre -rŭi -rŭtum: intransit., *to rush forth, to fall down;* transit., *to fling forward or down, overthrow, destroy.*

prōsāpĭa -ae, f. *family, race, stock.*

proscaenĭum -i, n. *the stage of a theatre.*

proscindo -scindĕre -scĭdi -scissum, *to tear up; to break up fallow land, plough up.* Transf., *to censure, defame, satirize.*

proscrībo -scrībĕre -scripsi -scriptum, *to make publicly known, publish; to offer publicly for sale or hire, advertise; to confiscate; to proscribe, outlaw.*

proscriptĭo -ōnis, f. *an advertisement of sale; a proscription, outlawry.*

proscriptŭrĭo -ire, *to desire a proscription.*

prōsĕco -sĕcare -sĕcŭi -sectum, *to cut off; to plough up.* N. of partic. as subst. **prōsectum** -i, *part of a victim cut out to be offered to a god; the entrails.*

prōsĕda -ae, f. *a prostitute.*

prōsēmĭno -are, *to sow or scatter as seed; to disseminate.*

prōsĕquor -sĕqui -sĕcūtus, dep. *to follow or accompany out, to 'see off';* in hostile sense, *to attack, pursue;* in gen., *to attend; to go on with, continue; to imitate.*

Prŏserpĭna -ae, f. *the daughter of Ceres, carried off by Pluto to the lower world.*

prōseucha -ae. f. *a (Jewish) house of prayer, a conventicle.*

prōsĭlĭo -ire -ŭi (-īvi or -ĭi), *to spring up, leap forth.*

prōsŏcer -ĕri, m. *a wife's grandfather.*

prospecto -are, *to look forward, look out upon, survey; to look forward to, expect.*

prospectus -ūs, m. *outlook, view, prospect; sight, gaze.*

prospĕcŭlor -ari, dep. intransit., *to explore, reconnoitre;* transit., *to look out for, wait for.*

prosper (**prospĕrus**) -a -um, *fortunate, favourable, lucky, prosperous;* n. pl. as subst. *prosperity, good fortune.* Adv. **prospĕrē.**

prospĕrĭtās -ātis, f. *prosperity, good fortune.*

prospĕro -are, *to make fortunate, cause to succeed.*

prospĕrus = prosper; q.v.

prospĭcĭentĭa -ae, f. *foresight, precaution.*

prospĭcĭo -spĭcĕre -spexi -spectum: intransit., *to look forward, look out; to take care, exercise foresight;* transit., *to see ahead, make out in the distance; to look towards; to foresee; to look out for, provide, procure.*

prosterno -sternĕre -strāvi -strātum, *to cast down; to debase; to overthrow, destroy, ruin.*

prostĭtŭo -stĭtŭĕre -stĭtŭi -stĭtūtum, *to prostitute.*

prosto -stare -stĭti, *to stand out, project; to be exposed for sale; to prostitute oneself.*

prōsŭbĭgo -ĕre, *to dig up, root up.*

prōsum prōdesse prōfŭi, *to be useful, do good, benefit* (with dat.).

prōtĕgo -tĕgĕre -texi -tectum, *to cover in front; to cover over, protect; to furnish with a roof.*

prōtēlum -i, n. *a team of oxen; a series, succession.*

prōtendo -tendĕre -tendi -tentum, *to stretch forward, stretch out.*

prōtĕnŭs = protinus; q.v.

prōtĕro -tĕrĕre -trivi -tritum, *to trample under foot, tread down; to overthrow, rout, defeat; to drive away, push aside.*

prōterrĕo -ēre, *to scare away.*

prōtervĭtās -ātis, f. *boldness, impudence, pertness.*

prōtervus -a -um, *bold, impudent;* in milder sense, *pert; of things, violent.* Adv. **prōtervē.**

Prōteūs -ĕi and -ĕos, m. *a god of the sea, with the power of changing himself into different shapes.*

prōtĭnam, *immediately, at once.*

prōtĭnŭs (**prōtĕnŭs**), adv. *forward, further on; of time, continuously or immediately.*

prōtollo -ĕre, *to put forward; to lengthen, prolong.*

prōtrăho -trăhĕre -traxi -tractum, *to draw, forward, drag out; to bring to light, reveal, make known; to compel, force; to protract, defer.*

prōtrūdo -trūdĕre -trūsi -trūsum, *to push forward, thrust out; to put off, defer.*

prōturbo -are, *to drive forward, drive away; to throw down, overcome.*

prōŭt, *just as, according as.*

prŏvĕho -vĕhĕre -vexi -vectum, *to carry forward; to carry on; to advance, promote;* pass., provehi, *to ride forward, drive, sail, and fig. to be carried away.*

Hence partic. **prŏvectus** -a -um, *advanced, esp. in age.*

prōvĕnĭo -vĕnire -vēni -ventum, *to come on, appear*; of corn, *to come up, grow*; of events, *to result, come about*; esp. *to turn out well, succeed.*

prōventus -ūs, m. *coming forth, growing; product, crop; result, issue, success.*

prōverbĭum -i, n. *a proverb.*

prōvĭdentĭa -ae, f. *foresight, fore-knowledge; forethought, providence.*

prōvĭdĕo -vĭdēre -vīdi -vīsum, *to look forward to, see at a distance*; *to see beforehand, foresee*; *to take pre-cautions for or against, provide for, make preparation for.*
Hence partic. prōvĭdens -entis, *provident, prudent*; adv. prōvĭdentĕr. N. abl. of perf. partic. prōvīsō, *with forethought.*

prōvĭdus -a -um, *foreseeing; providing, taking measures for*; in gen., *cautious, prudent.*

prōvincĭa -ae, f. *employment, sphere of duty, office*, esp. that of a magistrate. Transf., *a country governed by a Roman magistrate, a province.*

prōvincĭālis -e, *of a province*; m. as subst., esp. plur., *inhabitants of provinces, provincials.*

prōvīsĭo -ōnis, f. *foresight*; hence *provision, planning.*

prōvīso -ĕre, *to look out for, go to see.*

prōvīsor -ōris, m. *one who provides for or against.*

prōvīsū, abl. sing. m. *by foreseeing; by providing for or against.*

prōvixisse, perf. infin. *to have lived on.*

prōvŏcātĭo -ōnis, f. *a challenge*; esp. *an appeal to a higher court.*

prōvŏcātor -ōris, m. *a challenger; a kind of gladiator.*

prōvŏco -are, *to call out*; *to excite, rouse, provoke*; *to challenge to a contest*; legal, *to appeal to a higher court.*

prōvŏlo -are, *to fly forth, to rush out.*

prōvolvo -volvĕre -volvi -vŏlūtum, *to roll forward, roll over and over*; provolvere se, and provolvi, *to throw oneself down, hence to abase oneself.*

prōvŏmo -ĕre, *to vomit forth.*

prŏximĭtās -atis, f. *nearness, close connexion; similarity.*

proximus -a -um, superl.; see propior.

prūdens -entis, *foreseeing, aware; skilled, experienced, practised; prudent, discreet, judicious.* Adv. prūdentĕr.

prūdentĭa -ae, f. *foresight; knowledge; sagacity, discretion.*

prūīna -ae, f. *hoar-frost, rime.*

prūīnōsus -a -um, *frosty.*

prūna -ae, f. *a live coal.*

prūnĭtĭus -a -um, *of plum-tree wood.*

prūnum -i, n. *a plum.*

prūnus -i, f. *plum-tree.*

prūrīgo -īnis, f. *the itch.*

prūrĭo -ire, *to itch.*

prўtănēum -i, n. *the town-hall in a Greek city.*

prўtănis -is, acc. -in, m. *chief magistrate in a Greek state.*

psallo psallĕre psalli, *to play on or sing to a stringed instrument.*

psaltērĭum -i, n. *a stringed instrument.*

psaltrĭa -ae, f. *a female player on the cithara.*

psēcăs -ădis, f. *an anointer of hair.*

pseudŏthўrum -i, n. *a secret door.*

psĭthĭa (vitis) -ae, f. *a kind of Greek vine.*

psittăcus -i, m. *parrot.*

psўchŏmantīum or -ēum -i n. *a place of necromancy*

-ptĕ, suffix, *self, own.*

ptĭsănārĭum -i, n. *a decoction of crushed barley* or *rice.*

pūbens -entis, of plants, *in full growth, luxuriant.*

pūbĕr -bĕris = pubes; q.v.

pūbertās -ātis, f. *puberty, the age of maturity; signs of puberty, growth of hair*, etc.

¹pūbēs -is, f. *the signs of puberty, growth of hair*, etc.; *the youth, adult male population.*

²pūbēs and pūbĕr -ĕris, *arrived at the age of puberty, adult, ripe*; m. pl. as subst. pūbĕres -um, *the men, the adult male population.*

pūbesco -bescĕre -bŭi, *to grow up, arrive at maturity.*

pūblĭcānus -a -um, *of the farming of the public taxes*; m. as subst. *a farmer of the Roman taxes.*

pūblĭcātĭo -ōnis, f. *confiscation.*

pūblĭcĭtūs, *at the public expense, in the public service; publicly.*

pūblĭco -are, *to confiscate; to make public, throw open, publish.*

pūblĭcus -a -um, *belonging to the people, public*; res publica, or respublica, *the state.* Transf., *uni-versal, general; common, ordinary.* M. as subst. pūblĭcus -i, *a state official*; N. pūblĭcum -i, *public territory; the public revenue, the treasury; an open place, the open street.* Adv. pūblĭcē, *for the people, publicly, at the public expense; all together.*

Pūblĭus -i, m. *a Roman praenomen*, abbrev. P.

pŭdĕo -ēre, *to be ashamed*; usually 3rd person, *to cause shame, fill with shame*; often impers., pŭdet; te huius templi pudet, *you are ashamed of.* Hence gerundive pŭdendus -a -um, *shameful, disgraceful.* Partic. pŭdens -entis, *modest, shamefaced*; adv. pŭdentĕr, *modestly, bashfully.*

pŭdībundus -a -um, *modest, bashful.*

pŭdĭcĭtĭa -ae, f. *modesty, chastity, virtue.*

pŭdīcus -a -um, *modest, chaste, virtuous*; adv. pŭdīcē.

pŭdor -ōris, m. *feeling of shame, bashfulness, decency, honour; chastity, purity; that which causes shame, a disgrace.*

pŭella -ae, f. *a girl, maiden; a young woman, young wife, or sweetheart.*

pŭellāris -e, *girlish, maidenly.* Adv. pŭellārĭtĕr.

pŭellŭla -ae, f. *a little girl.*

pŭellus -i, m. *a little boy.*

pŭer -i, m. *a child*; in plur., *children*; esp. *a boy, lad*; a puero, a pueris, *from boyhood*. Transf., *a serving-lad, page, slave*.

pŭerilis -e, *youthful, boyish*; *puerile, silly, childish*. Adv. **pŭerīlĭtĕr**, *boyishly*; *childishly*.

pŭerĭtia -ae, f. *boyhood*.

pŭerpĕrĭum -i, n. *childbirth, labour*.

pŭerpĕrus -a -um, *of childbirth*; f. as subst. *a woman in labour*.

pŭertĭa = pueritia; q.v.

pŭerŭlus -i, m. *a little boy, young slave*.

pūga (pȳga) -ae, f. *the rump, buttocks*.

pŭgil -ilis, m. *a boxer, fighter with the caestus*.

pŭgilātĭo -ōnis, f. *fighting with the caestus*; *boxing*.

pŭgillāris -e, *that can be grasped with the fist*; m. pl. as subst. **pŭgillāres** -ium (sc. libelli), *writing-tablets*.

pŭgĭo -ōnis, m. *a dagger, dirk, poniard*.

pŭgiunculus -i, m. *a little dagger*.

pugna -ae, f. *a fight, battle; battle-line, array*; in gen., *contest*.

pugnācĭtās -ātis, f. *desire to fight, pugnacity*.

pugnācŭlum -i, n. *a fortress*.

pugnātor -ōris, m. *a fighter, combatant*.

pugnax -ācis, *fond of fighting, combative; obstinate, contentious*. Adv. **pugnācĭtĕr**.

pugno -are, *to fight, give battle; to struggle, contend, fight, to strive, exert oneself*.

pugnus -i m. *the fist*.

pulchellus -a -um, *pretty*.

pulcher -chra -chrum and **pulcer** -cra -crum, *beautiful, lovely*; morally *excellent, fine*. Adv. **pulchrē** (**pulcrē**), *beautifully, finely*; as exclamation, *bravo! well done!*

pulchrĭtūdo -ĭnis, f. *beauty, excellence*.

pūlēĭum (pūlēgĭum) -i, n *fleabane, penny-royal*.

pūlex -ĭcis, m. *a flea*.

pullārĭus -i, m. *feeder of sacred chickens*.

pullātus -a -um, *clad in dirty or black garments*.

pullŭlo -are, *to shoot up, sprout, burgeon, luxuriate*.

'pullus -i, m. *a young animal*; esp. *a chicken, chick*.

²pullus -a -um, *dark-coloured, blackish*; poet., *sad, gloomy*. N. as subst. *a dark garment*.

pulmentārĭum -i, n. *a relish*.

pulmentum -i. n. *a relish*; in gen., *food, victuals*.

pulmo -ōnis, m. *the lung* (usually plur.).

pulpa -ae, f. *flesh*.

pulpāmentum -i, n. *flesh, esp. tit-bits*.

pulpĭtum -i, n. *a platform or stage*.

puls pultis, f. *porridge, pulse*.

pulsātĭo -ōnis, f. *knocking, beating*.

pulso -are, *to strike, beat, knock; to stir, move, affect*.

pulsus -ūs, m. *beating, blow, push; influence, impulse*.

pulto -are, *to knock, strike*.

pulvĕrĕus -a -um, *full of dust, dusty*.

pulvĕrŭlentus -a -um, *full of dust, dusty*.

pulvillus -i, m. *a little pillow*.

pulvīnar -aris, n. *a couch*, esp. *one carrying images of the gods at the Lectisternium* (q.v.).

pulvīnārĭum -i, n. *anchorage*.

pulvīnus -i, m. *pillow, cushion; a seat of honour*.

pulvis -ĕris, m. (rarely f.) *dust, powder*. Transf., *arena, scene of action*; sine pulvere palmae, *prize without effort*.

pūmex -ĭcis, m. *pumice-stone; any soft, porous stone*.

pūmĭcĕus -a -um, *made of pumice-stone*.

pūmĭco -are, *to polish with pumice-stone*.

pūmĭlĭo -ōnis, c. and **pūmĭlus** -i, m. *a dwarf*.

punctim, *by stabbing, by thrusting* (opp. caesim).

pungo pungĕre pŭpŭgi punctum, *to prick, puncture, stab; to touch, move, penetrate; to sting, vex, annoy*. N. of partic. as subst. **punctum** -i, *a prick, a little hole, small puncture; a point, spot*. Hence *a vote; a moment of time*; in speech, etc., *a short clause, section*.

pūnĭcĕus -a -um, *purple, red*.

Pūnĭcus; see Poeni.

pūnĭo (poenĭo) -ire and **pūnĭor** -iri dep. *to punish; to avenge*.

pūnĭtor -ōris, m. *punisher, avenger*.

pūpa -ae, f. *a little girl; a doll*.

pūpilla -ae, f. (1) *an orphan girl, ward, minor*. (2) *the pupil of the eye*.

pūpillāris -e, *of an orphan or ward*.

pūpillus -i, m. *an orphan or ward*.

puppis -is, f. *the poop or stern of a vessel*; poet., *the whole ship*.

pūpŭla -ae, f. *the pupil of the eye*.

purgāmen -ĭnis, n. (1) *sweepings, filth*. (2) *a means of purgation*.

purgāmentum -i, n. *sweepings, rubbish, filth*.

purgātĭo -ōnis, f. *cleaning out, cleansing; excusing, justification*.

purgo -are. (1) *to clean, cleanse, purify*. Hence *to excuse, defend, justify; to allege in defence*. (2) *to clear away, wash off*.

purpūra -ae, f. *the purple-fish*. Transf., *purple dye*; *purple cloth*; *the purple*, = *high rank*, etc.

purpūrātus -a -um, *clad in purple*. M. as subst., *a man of high rank, a courtier*.

purpŭrĕus -a -um, *purple-coloured; dark-red, dark-brown*. Transf., *clad in purple*; in gen., *gleaming, bright, beautiful*.

pūrus -a -um, *clean, pure, cleared*. Transf., *without addition, simple, plain*; morally, *upright, pure*; of style, *pure, faultless*; legally, *without conditions, absolute*. N. as subst. *the clear sky*. Adv **pūrē** and poet. **pūrĭtĕr**, *purely, cleanly*; of style, *faultlessly*.

pūs pūris, n. *corrupt matter; bitterness*.

pūsillus -a -um, tiny; puny; petty, mean.

pūsio -onis, m. little boy.

pŭtāmen -inis, n. cutting, paring, shell

pŭtātor -ōris, m. pruner.

pŭtĕal -ālis, n. stone curb round the mouth of a well or sacred place.

pŭtĕālis -e, of a well.

pŭtĕo -ēre, to stink.

pŭter -tris -tre and putris -e, rotten, putrid; loose, crumbling, friable, flabby.

pŭtesco pūtescĕre, to decay.

pŭtĕus -i, m. a well, pit.

pūtĭdus -a -um, rotten, stinking, foul; of style, affected, in bad taste; adv. pūtĭdē, affectedly.

pŭto -are, to cleanse, clear; of trees, to lop. Transf., to clear up, settle, esp. of accounts; hence to weigh up, ponder, reckon, estimate; to consider, believe, think; parenthetically, puto or ut puto, I suppose.

putrēfăcĭo -făcĕre -fēci -factum to make rotten or soft.

putresco -ĕre, to become rotten.

putrĭdus -a -um, rotten, decayed.

pŭtus -a -um, pure, unmixed, unadulterated.

pȳga = puga; q.v.

Pygmaei -orum, m. the Pygmies, a race of dwarfs in Africa.

pȳra -ae, f. funeral pyre.

pȳrămis -ĭdis, f. pyramid; hence a cone.

pȳrōpus -i, m. bronze.

Pyrrhus -i, m. (1) son of Achilles. (2) a king of Epirus, enemy of the Romans.

Pȳthăgŏras -ae, m. Greek philosopher of Samos (about 540 B.C.).

Pȳtho -ūs, f. the old name of Delphi; adj. Pȳthĭcus, Pȳthĭus -a -um, Delphic, relating to Apollo; f. as subst., the priestess of Apollo; n. pl., the Pythian games, celebrated every fourth year in honour of Apollo.

pyxis -ĭdis, f. a little box, casket.

Q

Q, q, the sixteenth letter of the Latin Alphabet, only used before u and another vowel.

quā, abl. f. of qui, as adv.: relat., by which way, where; also whereby, or as far as; qua . . . qua, partly . . . partly; interrog., by what way? how?; indef., in any way, at all.

quācumque (-cunque), wherever; by whatever way.

quādamtĕnŭs, to a certain point.

quadra -ae, f. a square; used of any square object or square piece.

quādrāgēni -ae -a, forty at a time, forty each.

quādrāgēsĭmus (-ensĭmus) -a -um, fortieth; f. as subst. the fortieth part, esp. as a tax.

quādrāgĭēs (-iens), forty times.

quādrāgintā, forty.

quādrans -antis, m. a fourth part, quarter; as a coin, the fourth part of an as.

quādrantārĭus -a -um, of a quarter; of price, costing a quarter of an as.

quadrīdŭum (quātrīdŭum) -i, n. a space of four days.

quadriennĭum -i, n. a period of four years.

quadrifārĭam, in four parts.

quadrĭfĭdus -a -um, split into four.

quadrīgae -arum, f. a team of four horses abreast, esp. drawing a chariot.

quadrīgārĭus -a -um, of a racing charioteer.

quadrīgātus -a -um, stamped with the figure of a four-horse chariot.

quadrīgŭlae -arum, f. a little team of four horses.

quadrīiŭgis -e, in a team of four.

quadrīiŭgus -a -um, in or with a team of four.

quadrimus -a -um, four years old.

quadringēnārĭus -a -um, of four hundred each.

quadringēni -ae -a, four hundred at a time, four hundred each.

quadringentēsĭmus (-ensĭmus) -a -um, four hundredth.

quadringenti -ae -a, four hundred.

quadringentiēs (-iēs), four hundred times.

quadrĭpertītus -a -um, divided into four parts, fourfold.

quadrīrēmis -e, with four banks of oars; f. as subst., a quadrireme.

quadrivĭum -i, n. a crossroads, place where four roads meet.

quadro -are: transit., to make square; to join properly together; intransit., to be square; to fit exactly, to suit; esp. of accounts, to agree. Partic. quadrātus -a -um, squared, square; n. as subst., a square.

quadrum -i, n. a square.

quadrŭpĕdans -antis, going on four feet, galloping; plur. as subst., horses.

quadrŭpēs -pĕdis, four-footed, on four feet; as subst., a quadruped.

quadrŭplātor -ōris, m. a multiplier by four; an exaggerator; an informer.

quadrŭplex -plĭcis, fourfold, quadruple.

quadrŭplor -ari, dep. to be an informer.

quadruplus -a -um, fourfold; n. as subst., four times the amount.

quaerĭto -are, to seek or enquire about eagerly.

quaero quaerĕre quaesīi or quaesīvi quaesitum, to seek, search for; sometimes to obtain, get; to miss, want; to seek to know, ask, enquire into a matter. Partic. quaesītus -a -um, sought out; unusual, select; in bad sense, far-fetched, affected; n. as subst., a question or a gain.

quaesītĭo -ōnis, f. an interrogation.

quaesītor -ōris, m. investigator, inquirer, esp. judicial.

quaeso -ĕre, to seek for, ask for; first person, quaeso, I beg.

quaestĭo -ōnis, f. seeking, searching; inquiry, investigation; esp. judicial inquiry; quaestiones perpetuae, standing courts of justice.

quaestiuncŭla -ae, f. a little question.

quaestor -ōris, m. one of the quaestors, magistrates in Rome, occupied with matters of law and finance.

quaestŏrĭus -a -um, *belonging to a* quaestor. N. as subst., *the quaestor's tent in camp,* or *residence in a province.* M. as subst., *an ex-quaestor.*

quaestŭōsus -a -um, *profitable; fond of gain; having gained much, rich.*

quaestūra -ae, f. *the office of quaestor, quaestorship.*

quaestus -ūs, m. *gaining, getting, profit; a source of profit, occupation, business.*

quālĭbĕt (quālŭbĕt) *wherever you like; in any way you please.*

quālis -e: interrog., *of what kind?;* relat. (with or without antecedent talis), *of the kind that, such as;* indef., *having some quality or other.* Adv. **quālĭtĕr,** *as, just as.*

quālĭscumque (-cunque) qualecumque: relat., *of whatever kind;* indef., *any whatever.*

quālislĭbĕt, quālēlĭbĕt, *of what · sort you will.*

quālĭtās -ātis, f. *quality, property.*

quālus -i, m. and **quālum** -i, n. *wicker-basket.*

quam, adv. *how, in what way:* interrog., *how much? how?;* exclam., *how!;* relat., *of correspondence, as* (often with tam); *with superl. adj. or adv., as . . . as possible* (with or without possum); *quam primum, as soon as possible;* of comparison, *than, as.*

quamlĭbĕt (quamlŭbĕt), *as much as you please.*

quamobrem (quam ob rem): interrog., *wherefore? why?;* relat., *for which reason, wherefore.*

quamquam (quanquam), *although, though;* at the beginning of a sentence, *nevertheless, and yet.*

quamvis, *as much as you please, ever so much;* as conj., *however much, although.*

quānam, *by what way?*

quandō, *when:* interrog., *when?;* indef., *at any time, ever;* relat., *at the time when;* sometimes causal, *since, because.*

quandōcumque (-cunque): relat., *whenever, as often as;* indef., *at some time or other.*

quandōquĕ: relat., *whenever, as often as;* indef., *at some time or other.*

quandŏquĭdem, *since, because.*

quantŏpĕrĕ (quantŏ ŏpĕrĕ), *with what great trouble; how much.*

quantŭlus -a -um, *how little, how small.*

quantŭluscumque -ācumque -um-cumque, *however small.*

quantus -a -um; interrog., *how great?;* exclam., *how great!;* relat. (with or without tantus), *(as great) as;* quantus quantus, *however great.* N. as subst. *quantum:* interrog., *how much?;* exclam., *how much!;* relat., *as much as;* quantum in me est, *as far as in me lies.* Neuter in genit. (or locative) of price, **quanti,** *for how much, at what price;* in abl., **quantō,** *(by) how much,* with compar. adj. or adv.

quantuscumque -acumque -um-cumque, *however great.*

quantuslĭbĕt -tālĭbĕt -tumlĭbĕt, *as great as you will, however great.*

quantusvis -āvis -umvis, *as great as you please, however great.*

quāpropter, *wherefore.*

quārē (quā rē), *wherefore.*

quartādĕcŭmāni -orum, m. *soldiers of the fourteenth legion.*

quartānus -a -um, *of the fourth;* f. as subst. (sc. febris) *a quartan fever;* m. pl. as subst., *the soldiers of the fourth legion.*

quartārius -i, m. *the fourth part of a sextarius.*

quartus -a -um, *the fourth;* f. as subst., *the fourth hour;* n. acc. or abl. *quartum, quartō, for the fourth time.*

quartusdĕcĭmus -a -um, *fourteenth.*

quăsi, *as if, just as,* esp. in hypothetical comparisons; also with descriptions, *as it were, a sort of;* with numerals, *about.*

quăsillus -i, m. and **quăsillum** -i, n. *little basket.*

quassātĭo -ōnis, f. *a shaking.*

quasso -are: transit., *to shake violently; to shatter, break in pieces;* intransit., *to shake.*

quătĕfăcĭo -făcĕre -fēci, *to shake, weaken.*

quătēnŭs, *how far, to what extent; in so far as, since.*

quătĕr, *four times;* hence *again and again.*

quătĭo quătĕre quassi quassum, *to shake, brandish, agitate;* sometimes *to shatter.*

quattŭor, *four.*

quattŭordĕcim, *fourteen.*

quattŭorvĭrātus -ūs, m. *the office of the quattuorviri.*

quattŭorvĭri -ōrum, m. *a board of four magistrates.*

-quĕ, enclitic conj., *and;* repeated, -que . . . -que, *both . . . and . . .*

queis = quibus; *see* qui.

quĕmadmŏdum (quem ad mŏdum), *in what manner, how* (interrog. or relat.); esp. corresponding with sic, ita, item, etc., *as, just as.*

quĕo quire quivi and quĭi quĭtum, *to be able.*

quercētum -i, n. *an oak-wood.*

quercĕus -a -um, *oaken.*

quercus -ūs, f. *the oak;* sometimes *a crown of oak leaves.*

quĕrēla (quĕrella) -ae, f. *a complaint, complaining.*

quĕrĭbundus -a -um, *complaining, plaintive.*

quĕrĭmōnĭa -ae, f. *a complaining, complaint.*

quĕrĭtor -ari, dep., *to complain excessively.*

quernus -a -um, *of oak, oaken.*

quĕror quĕri questus, dep. *to complain, lament, bewail;* of animals, *to make a plaintive sound.*

querquĕtŭlānus -a -um, *of an oak-wood.*

quĕrŭlus -a -um, *complaining, plaintive.*

questus -ūs, m. *complaint, lament.*

¹quī quae quod: interrog. adj., *which? what? what kind of?*; exclam., *what!*; indef., (with f. quae or qua) *any, some*; relat., *who, which, what, that.* Acc. n. sing., **quod**, as adv.: quod sciam, *as far as I know.* Abl. **quō**, with comparatives: quo celerius, eo melius, *the faster the better.*

²quī (old abl. of ¹quī): interrog., *in what manner? how?*; relat., *wherewith, wherefrom*; indef., *somehow.*

quiā, *because.*

quiānam, quiānĕ, *why?*

quīcum, *with whom, with which.*

quīcumque (-cunque) quaecumque quodcumque: relat., *whoever, whichever, whatever*; indef., *any available.*

quīdam quaedam quoddam (subst. quiddam), *a certain person or thing* (known but not necessarily named). Transf., *a kind of.*

quīdem, *indeed*; ne . . . quidem *not, even . . .*

quīdnī? *why not?*

quiēs -ētis, f. *rest, quiet; peace; sleep; a dream; a resting-place.*

quiēsco -escĕre -ēvi -ētum, *to rest; to be at peace; to sleep; to cease from action.*

quiētus -a -um, *resting; sleeping; at peace, undisturbed, neutral*; of character, *quiet, calm.* Adv. **quiētē.**

quīlibet quaelibet quodlibet (subst. quidlibet), *any you will, anyone, anything.*

quīn: in questions, *why not?*; in commands, to encourage, *but come now*; in statements, *rather, but indeed*; in subordinate clauses, with subjunctive, *but that, without, that not, who not.*

quīnam quaenam quodnam, *which, what?*

quīncunx -cuncis, *five-twelfths.*

quīndecięns (-iēs), *fifteen times.*

quīndecim, *fifteen.*

quīndecimprīmī -orum, m. *the fifteen chief senators of a municipium.*

quīndecimvir -i, m. *one of a board of fifteen magistrates.*

quīndecimvirālis -e, *of the quindecimviri.*

quīndēni or **quīni dēni** -ae -a, *fifteen at a time, fifteen each.*

quīngēni -ae -a, *five hundred at a time, five hundred each.*

quīngentēsimus (-ēnsimus) -a -um, *five hundredth.*

quīngenti -ae -a, *five hundred.*

quīngentięns (-iēs), *five hundred times.*

quīni -ae -a, *five at a time, five each.*

quīnīvīcēni -ae -a, *twenty-five each.*

quīnquāgēni -ae -a, *fifty at a time, fifty each.*

quīnquāgēsimus (-ēnsimus) -a -um, *fiftieth*; f. as subst. (*a tax of*) a *fiftieth part.*

quīnquāgintā, *fifty.*

quīnquātrūs -ŭum, f. pl., and **quīnquātria** -ōrum and -ium, n. pl. *a festival of Minerva.*

quīnquĕ, *five.*

quīnquennālis -e, *happening every five years, or lasting for five years.*

quīnquennis -e, *of five years; five years old.*

quīnquennium -i, n. *a period of five years.*

quīnquĕpertītus -a -um, *in five portions, fivefold.*

quīnquĕprīmi -orum, m. *the five chief senators in a municipium.*

quīnquĕrēmis -e, *having five banks of oars*; f. as subst., *a quinquereme.*

quīnquĕvir -i, m., *one of a board of five.*

quīnquĕvirātus -ūs, m. *the office of quinquevir.*

quīnquięs (-iēns), *five times.*

quīnquiplico -are, *to multiply by five.*

quīntādĕcimāni -ōrum, m. *soldiers of the fifteenth legion.*

quīntānus -a -um, *of the fifth*; f. as subst. (sc. via), *a road in a Roman camp*; m. pl., *soldiers of the fifth legion.*

Quīntiliānus (Quinct-) -i, m. M. Fabius Quintilianus, *head of a school of rhetoric at Rome.*

Quīntilis (Quinctilis) -is, m. (with or without mensis), *the fifth month afterwards called Iulius.*

¹quīntus -a -um, *fifth*; quintum, quinto, *for the fifth time.*

²Quīntus (abbrev. Q.) and f. **Quīnta**, *a Roman praenomen.*

quīntusdĕcimus -a -um, *fifteenth.*

quippĕ, *certainly, indeed, to be sure of course.*

quippīni, *why not?*

Quirīnus -i, m. *the name of Romulus after his apotheosis*; adj. **Quirīnus** -a -um, and **Quirīnālis** -e, *of Romulus*: collis, *the Quirinal Hill* at Rome; n. pl. **Quirīnālia** -ium, *a festival in honour of Romulus.*

¹Quīrīs -itis and pl. **Quirītēs** -ium and -um, m. *the inhabitants of the Sabine town Cures*; also used of *the citizens of Rome* in their civil capacity.

²quiris or **cūris,** *a spear.*

quīrītātio -ōnis, f. *a shriek, scream.*

quirīto -are, *to shriek, scream, cry out.*

¹quis quid, pron.: interrog., *who? what? which?*; indef., *anyone, anybody, anything.* N. nom. and acc. **quid?** *what?*; with genit., *how much? how many?* sometimes *why?*; quid ita? *why so?*

²quis = quibus; see qui.

quisnam quaenam quidnam, pron. *who? what?*

quispiam quaepiam quodpiam (subst. quidpiam, quippiam), *anyone, anything; someone, something*; n. acc. as adv. *at all.*

quisquam quaequam quidquam (quicquam), *anybody, anyone, anything,* esp. in negative sentences and questions.

quisque quaeque quidque (adj. quodque), *each, every, everyone, everything.*

quisquiliae -arum, f. pl. *rubbish, sweepings, refuse.*

quisquis quaequae quidquid (quicquid), and adj. quodquod: relat., *whoever, whatever, whichever*; indef., *anyone, anything.*

quīvīs quaevis quidvis (adj. quodvis), *whoever or whatever you will, anyone, anything.*

quīvīscumque quaeviscumque quodviscumque, *whosoever, whatsoever.*

¹quō: interrog., *where? to what place? whither? how far? to what extent? to what end?*; indef., *to any place, anywhither*; relat., *to the end that, in order that.*

²quō, *because, whereby*; see also quominus.

quoad, *how far; as far as, as long as; also until.*

quōcircā, *wherefore, on which account.*

quōcumque, *whithersoever*

quod, conj.; *the fact that, the point that; as to the fact that, whereas; because, on the ground that; why, on which account;* with temporal clause, *since; as far as, to the extent that;* introducing a fresh sentence, *and, but, now,* esp. foll. by si.

quōdammŏdo, *in a certain way in a certain measure.*

quŏiās = cuias; q.v.

quŏlĭbĕt, *whithersoever you please.*

quŏmĭnŭs, *by which the less, so that not.*

quŏmŏdo, *in what manner, how.*

quŏmŏdocumquĕ, *in whatever way; somehow.*

quŏmŏdonam, *how then?*

quŏnam, *whither then?*

quondam, *in the past, formerly, once; in the future, sometime; in gen., at times, sometimes.*

quŏnĭam, *since, whereas, because.*

quŏpĭam, and quŏquam, *to any place at all.*

quŏquĕ, placed after the word which it emphasizes, *also, too.*

quŏquŏ or quŏ quŏ, *whithersoever, to whatever place.*

quŏquŏversŭs (-versum, -vorsum), *in every direction.*

quorsum (quorsŭs), *whither? to what place? to what purpose?*

quŏt, indecl., *how many* (interrog. and exclam.); relat. (often with tot) *as many*; quot annis, *every year.*

quŏtannis = quot annis; see quot.

quotcumquĕ, *as many as. however many.*

quŏtēni -ae -a, *how many each.*

quŏtīdĭānus (cottīdĭānus, cŏtīd-), *daily, of every day; everyday, common, ordinary.*

quŏtīdĭē (cottīdĭē, cŏtīd-), *daily, every day.*

quŏtĭēs (quŏtĭens), *how often* (interrog. and exclam.); relat. (often with toties), *as often as.*

quŏtĭescumquĕ (-cunquĕ), *however often.*

quotquŏt, indecl., *however many.*

quŏtus -a -um, *which in number?* quota pars, *how small a fraction?*; quotus quisque, *one in how many? how rare?*

quŏtuscumquĕ (-cunquĕ) -ācumquĕ -umcumquĕ, *whatever in number*; pars quotacumque, *however small a fraction.*

quŏtusquisquĕ; see quotus.

quŏusquĕ (quŏ usquĕ), *how long? how far?*

quŏvīs, *to whatever place you will.*

quum = ¹cum; q.v.

R

R, r, seventeenth letter of the Latin Alphabet.

răbĭdus -a -um, *raging, mad, savage;* adv. răbĭdē.

răbĭes -ēi, f. *madness, rage, fury, frenzy.*

răbĭōsŭlus -a -um, *rather furious.*

răbĭōsus -a -um, *raging, mad, savage;* adv. răbĭōsē.

Răbīrius -a -um, *name of a Roman* gens.

răbŭla -ae, m. *a bawling advocate.*

răcēmĭfer -fēra -fērum, *bearing clusters.*

răcēmus -i, m. *a cluster,* esp. *of grapes.*

rădĭātus -a -um, *provided with spokes or rays.*

rādīcĭtŭs, *with or by the root; utterly.*

rādīcŭla -ae, f. *a little root.*

rădĭo -are and rădĭor -ari, dep. *to gleam, radiate.*

rădĭus -i, m. *a staff, rod; the spoke of a wheel; the radius of a circle;* in weaving, *a shuttle;* in botany, *a kind of long olive.* Transf., *a ray, beam of light.*

rādix -īcis, f. *a root; the foot of a mountain;* in gen., *foundation, basis, origin.*

rādo rādĕre rāsi rāsum, *to scrape, shave graze; to erase; to hurt, offend.*

raeda -ae, f. *a travelling carriage.*

raedārius -i, m. *coachman.*

rāmālĕ -is, n. usually plur., *sticks, brushwood.*

rāmentum -i, n., usually plur., *shavings, splinters, chips.*

rāmĕus -a -um, *of branches.*

rāmex -īcis, m. *a rupture*; plur., *the lungs.*

Ramnes and Ramnenses -ium, m. pl. *one of the three tribes into which the early Roman citizens were divided.*

rāmōsus -a -um, *full of boughs, branching.*

rāmŭlus -i, m. *a little branch, twig.*

rāmus -i, m. *a bough, branch, twig.*

rāna -ae, f. *a frog.*

rancens -entis, *stinking, putrid.*

rancĭdŭlus -a -um, *rather putrid.*

rancĭdus -a -um, *stinking, rank, offensive.*

rānuncŭlus -i, m. *a little frog, tadpole.*

răpācĭtās -ātis, f. *greediness.*

răpax -ācis, *snatching, grasping, greedy.*

răpĭdĭtās -ātis, f. *rapid flow, rapidity.*

răpĭdus -a -um, *rushing, swift, violent;* adv. răpĭdē.

răpīna -ae, f. *robbery, pillage; booty, plunder.*

răpĭo răpĕre răpŭi raptum, *to seize, snatch, tear away; to plunder a place; to hurry along a person or thing;* se rapere, *to rush off.* Transf., *to pervert, lead astray.* N. of partic. as subst. raptum -i, *plunder.*

raptim, *violently, hastily, hurriedly.*

raptio -ōnis, f. *carrying off, abduction.*

rapto -are, *to seize and carry off, to hurry away; to rob, plunder* a place

raptor -ōris, m. *a robber, plunderer.*

raptus -ūs, m. *tearing off, rending away; carrying off, abduction, rape; plundering.*

rāpŭlum -i, n. *a little turnip.*

rārĕfăcio -făcĕre -fēci -factum *to make thin, rarefy.*

rāresco -ĕre, *to become thin, to lose density; to widen out; to grow less.*

rārĭtās -ātis, f. *thinness, looseness of texture; fewness, rarity.*

rārus -a -um, *loose, thin; scattered, scanty, far apart;* milit., *in loose order;* in gen., *rare, infrequent;* sometimes *extraordinary, distinguished.* Adv. rārō, rārē, *seldom, rarely*

rāsĭlis -e, *scraped, smooth.*

rastrum -i, n., plur. gen. rastri -orum, *a hoe, rake, mattock.*

rātĭo -onis, f. *a reckoning, account, consideration, calculation;* rationem ducere, *to compute; any transaction, affair, business; a reason, motive, ground; a plan, scheme, system; reasonableness, method, order; a theory, doctrine, science; the reasoning faculty.*

rătĭōcĭnātĭo -ōnis, f. *reasoning;* esp. *a form of argument, syllogism.*

rătĭōcĭnātīvus -a -um, *argumentative; syllogistic.*

rătĭōcĭnātor -ōris, m. *a calculator, accountant.*

rătĭōcĭnor -ari, dep. *to compute calculate; to argue, infer, conclude.*

rătĭōnālis -e, *reasonable, rational.*

rătĭōnārĭum -i, n. *a statistical account*

rătis -is, f. *a raft;* poet., *a ship, boat.*

rătiuncŭla -ae, f. *a little reckoning, account; a poor reason; a petty syllogism.*

rătus -a -um, partic. from reor; q.v.

raucĭsŏnus -a -um, *hoarsely sounding.*

raucus -a -um, *hoarse, harsh-sounding.*

raudus (rōdus, rūdus) -ĕris, n. *a rough mass, lump,* esp. *of copper money.*

rauduscŭlum -i, n. *a small sum of money.*

Răvenna -ae, f. *a town in Gallia Cispadana, near the Adriatic.*

rāvus -a -um, *tawny or greyish.*

rĕa; *see* reus.

rĕapsĕ, *in truth, really.*

rĕbellātĭo = rebellio; q.v.

rĕbellātrix -icis, f. *renewing war, rebellious.*

rĕbellĭo -ōnis, f. *a renewal of war,* esp. *by the conquered; a revolt.*

rĕbellis -e, *renewing war, insurgent.*

rĕbellĭum = rebellio; q.v.

rĕbello -are, *to renew war, revolt, fight back.*

rĕbŏo -are, *to echo, resound; to make to resound.*

rĕcalcitro -are, *to kick back;* fig., *to deny access.*

rĕcălĕo -ēre, *to be warm again.*

rĕcălesco -ĕre, *to become warm again.*

rĕcalfăcio -făcĕre -fēci -factum, *to make warm again.*

rĕcandesco -candescĕre -candŭi, *to grow white; to become hot, begin to glow.*

rĕcanto -are: intransit., *to resound echo;* transit., *to recall, recant; to charm away.*

rĕcēdo -cēdĕre -cessi -cessum, *to go back, retreat, retire; to disappear.*

rĕcellŏ -ere, *to spring back, fly back.*

rĕcens -entis, *new, fresh, young, recent; vigorous.* As adv. rĕcens, *lately. recently.*

rĕcenseo -censēre -censŭi -censum, *to review, muster, examine; to recount.*

rĕcensĭo -ōnis, f. *reviewing, mustering.*

rĕceptācŭlum -i, n. *a reservoir, receptacle; a place of refuge, shelter, retreat.*

rĕcepto -are, *to draw back, receive back take in; to receive frequently, harbour.*

rĕceptor -ōris, m. and receptrix -tricis, f. *a receiver, harbourer.*

rĕceptus -ūs, m. *drawing back; withdrawal, recantation; retiring, retreat, return;* poet., *a place of retreat.*

rĕcessim, *backwards.*

rĕcessus -ūs, m. *going back, retreat, withdrawal; a place of retreat, quiet place.*

rĕcĭdīvus -a -um, *returning, repeated.*

¹rĕcĭdo -cĭdĕre -ccĭdi -cāsūrus, *to fall back; to relapse, recoil, descend, sink, fall.*

²rĕcĭdo -cĭdĕre -cĭdi -cīsum, *to cut back, lop away.*

rĕcingo -cingĕre -cinxi -cinctum, *to ungird, loosen.*

rĕcĭno -ĕre, *to resound, echo;* transit., *to cause to resound.*

rĕcĭpĭo -cĭpĕre -cēpi -ceptum, *to hold back, retain; to take back, fetch back;* se recipere, *to withdraw, retreat; to regain, recover; to receive, accept, take to oneself; to receive hospitably.* Transf., *to accept, admit, allow; to accept an obligation; hence to guarantee, promise, be responsible for.* N. of partic. as subst., receptum -i. *an engagement, guarantee.*

rĕcĭprŏco -are, *to move backwards and forwards;* animam, *to breathe.*

rĕcĭprŏcus -a -um, *going backwards and forwards; mare, ebbing.*

rĕcĭtātĭo -ōnis, f. *a reading aloud.*

rĕcĭtātor -ōris, m. *a reader aloud.*

rĕcĭto -are, *to read aloud, read out, recite.*

reclāmātĭo -ōnis, f. *loud disapprobation.*

reclāmĭto -are, *to cry out against.*

reclāmo -are, *to cry out against, contradict loudly;* poet., *to re-echo, resound.*

reclīnis -e, *leaning backwards.*

reclīno -are, *to bend back, cause to lean back.*

reclūdo -clūdĕre -clūsi -clūsum, *to open; to reveal;* fata, *to relax.*

rĕcōgĭto -are, *to think again, reconsider.*

rĕcognĭtĭo -ōnis, f. *inspection, examination.*

rĕcognosco -noscĕre -nōvi -nītum, to recognize, know again, recall; to review, inspect, investigate.

rĕcŏlo -cŏlĕre -cŏlŭi -cultum, to cultivate or work again; to resume; to set up again, rehabilitate; to reflect upon, to recall.

rĕcompōno -pōnĕre -pŏsĭtum, to readjust.

rĕconcĭlĭātĭo -ōnis, f. winning back, restoration.

rĕconcĭlĭātor -ōris, m. a restorer.

rĕconcĭlĭo -are, to restore, repair; of persons, to reunite, reconcile.

rĕconcinno -are, to restore, renovate, repair.

rĕcondo -dĕre -dĭdi -dĭtum to put away, put back, store, hide.
　　Hence partic. rĕcondĭtus -a -um, put away, concealed; abstruse, profound; of character, reserved, mysterious.

rĕconflo -are, to rekindle.

rĕconligo -lĭgĕre -lēgi -lectum, to collect again, recover.

rĕcŏquo -cŏquĕre -coxi -coctum, to boil again, heat up again, remould.

rĕcordātĭo -ōnis, f. recollection, remembrance.

rĕcordor -ari, dep. to remember, recollect; to think of, ponder over.

rĕcrĕo -are, to restore, refresh, invigorate, revive.

rĕcrĕpo -are, to echo, resound.

rĕcresco -crescĕre -crēvi -crētum, to grow again.

rĕcrūdesco -crūdescĕre -crūdŭi, to become raw again, break out afresh.

rectĭo -ōnis, f. ruling, direction.

rector -ōris, m. ruler, governor, director, guide; navis, steersman; of animals, driver or rider.

rectus; see rego.

rĕcŭbo -are, to lie back, recline.

rĕcumbo -cumbĕre -cŭbŭi, to lie back, recline (esp. at table); in gen., to sink down, fall down.

rĕcŭpĕrātĭo -ōnis, f. recovery.

rĕcŭpĕrātor (rĕcĭpĕrātor) -ōris, m. a recoverer; pl., recuperatores, a board of arbiters appointed by the praetor.

rĕcŭpĕrātōrĭus -a -um, of the recuperatores (q.v.).

rĕcŭpĕro (rĕcĭpĕro) -are, to regain, recover.

rĕcŭro -are, to restore, refresh.

rĕcurro -currĕre -curri -cursum, to run back; to revert, return.

rĕcurso -are, to run back, return.

rĕcursus -ūs, m. return, retreat.

rĕcurvo -are, to bend or curve backwards.

rĕcurvus -a -um, bent or curved backwards; winding.

rĕcūsātĭo -ōnis, f. refusal; legal, a protest, counter-plea.

rĕcūso -are, to object to, protest against, refuse; legal, to take exception, plead in defence.

rĕcŭtĭo -cŭtĕre -cussi -cussum, to strike back, cause to rebound.

rēda -ae, f. = raeda; q.v.

rĕdămo -are, to love in return.

rĕdargŭo -gŭĕre -gŭi, to refute, disprove, contradict.

reddo -dĕre -dĭdi -dĭtum. (1) to give back, restore; reddi, or se reddere, to return; in words, to repeat, recite; to reproduce by imitation, to represent, reflect. (2) to give in return; hence to answer; to translate, render interpret; to make, render, cause to be. (3) to give as due; to pay up, deliver; fulfil; reddere ius, to administer justice.

rĕdemptĭo -ōnis, f. a buying up; bribing; farming of taxes; buying back, ransoming, redemption.

rĕdempto -are, to ransom, redeem.

rĕdemptor -ōris, m. buyer, contractor, farmer (of taxes).

rĕdemptūra -ae, f. contracting, farming (of taxes, etc.).

rĕdĕo -īre -ii -(īvi) -ĭtum. (1) to go back, come back, return; ad se, come to one's senses; redit, the matter comes up again. (2) of revenue, income, etc., to come in. (3) to fall back upon, be reduced or brought to.

rĕdhālo -are, to breathe out again.

rĕdhĭbĕo -ēre -ŭi -ĭtum, to take back.

rĕdĭgo -ĭgĕre -ēgi -actum, to drive back, bring back; of money, etc., to draw in, call in; in gen., to bring or reduce to a condition; to reduce in number, value, etc.; to lessen, bring down.

rĕdĭmĭcŭlum -i, n. a fillet, chaplet.

rĕdĭmĭo -īre -ĭi -ĭtum, to bind round, wreathe, crown.

rĕdĭmo -ĭmĕre -ēmi -emptum, to buy back, redeem; to ransom, recover; in gen., to buy up, contract for, farm, hire, procure.

rĕdintĕgro -are, to restore, renew, repair.

rĕdĭpiscor -i, dep. to get back.

rĕdĭtĭo -ōnis, f. going back, return.

rĕdĭtus -ūs, m. going back, return; in gratiam, reconciliation; of money, etc., returns, income, revenue.

rĕdĭvia = reduvia; q.v.

rĕdĭvīvus -a -um, renewed, renovated; n. as subst., old building materials used again.

rĕdŏlĕo -ēre -ŭi, to emit an odour, smell of.

rĕdŏmĭtus -a -um, tamed again.

rĕdōno -are, to give back; to give up.

rĕdūco -dūcĕre -duxi -ductum, to draw backwards, bring back, lead home; also to bring to a state or condition.
　　Hence partic. rĕductus -a -um, drawn back; withdrawn, retired, remote, sequestered.

rĕductĭo -ōnis, f. bringing back, restoration.

rĕductor -ōris, one who brings back.

rĕduncus -a -um, bent back, curved.

rĕdundantĭa -ae, f. overflowing; redundancy.

rĕdundo -are, to overflow, stream over; to be in excess, be copious, diffuse, to abound in (with abl.); to be left over, overflow, spread.

rĕdŭvĭa (rĕdīvĭa) -ae, f. *a hangnail, whitlow.*

rĕdux -dūcis, adj.: act., *bringing back restoring*; pass., *brought back re-turned.*

rĕfectĭo -ōnis, f. *repairing, restoring.*

rĕfello -fellĕre -felli, *to refute, disprove.*

rĕfercĭo -fercīre -fersi -fertum, *to stuff, to cram*; partic. **rĕfertus** -a -um, *stuffed, crammed, filled.*

rĕfērĭo -ire, *to strike back, strike again.* Transf., *to reflect.*

rĕfĕro rĕferre rettŭli rĕlātum. (1) *to carry back, bring back*; referre pedem, or se, or pass., referri, *to return, go back.* (2) *to bring again, restore, repeat; to echo; to reproduce, recall.* (3) *to say back, answer.* (4) *to bring as expected, pay up, deliver; to bring back a message, report; to refer a matter to authority; to enter in a record,* etc., register, *put down, enter; to assign to a cause.*

rĕfert rĕferre rĕtŭlit, impers., *it matters, it concerns, it makes a difference*; meā, illorum refert, *it matters to me, to them.*

rĕfertus -a -um, partic. from refercio; q.v.

rĕfervĕo -ēre, *to boil over.*

rĕfervesco -ĕre, *to boil up, bubble up.*

rĕfĭcĭo -fĭcĕre -fēci -fectum. (1) *to make again, restore, repair, re-establish, refresh, revive.* (2) *to get back, receive, get.*

rĕfīgo -fīgĕre -fixi -fixum, *to unfasten, demolish, remove; of laws, to repeal, abrogate.*

rĕfingo -ĕre, *to form anew.*

rĕflăgĭto -are, *to ask back, demand again.*

rĕflātŭ, abl. sing. m. *by a contrary wind.*

reflecto -flectĕre -flexi -flexum, *to bend back, turn back, divert*; intransit., *to yield, retreat.*

reflo -are: intransit., *to blow back, blow contrary*; transit., *to blow out.*

rĕflŭo -flŭĕre -fluxi -fluxum, *to flow back; to overflow.*

rĕflŭus -a -um, *flowing back.*

rĕformātor -ōris, m. *a reviver.*

rĕformīdātĭo -ōnis, f. *dread, terror.*

rĕformīdo -are, *to dread, fear, shun, avoid.*

rĕformo -are, *to form again, mould anew.*

rĕfŏvĕo -fŏvēre -fōvi -fōtum, *to warm again, revive, restore, refresh.*

refractārĭŏlus -a -um, *somewhat contentious, stubborn.*

refrăgor -ari, dep. *to oppose, withstand, thwart.*

refrēno -are, *to rein back, hold in, restrain, curb.*

refrĭco -frĭcare -frĭcŭi -frĭcatum, *to rub again; to excite again, renew.*

refrĭgĕrātĭo -ōnis, f. *cooling, coolness.*

refrĭgĕro -are, *to cool off*; pass., refrigerari, *to cool oneself, grow cool, grow languid.*

refrĭgesco -frĭgescĕre -frixi, *to grow cold, cool down; to flag, fail, grow stale.*

refringo -fringĕre -frēgi -fractum, *to break up, break open; to curb check.*

rĕfŭgĭo -fŭgĕre -fūgi: intransit., *to flee back, run away; to shrink;* of places, *to recede*; transit., *to fly from, avoid.*

rĕfŭgĭum -i, n. *refuge.*

rĕfŭgus -a -um, *fugitive, receding, recoiling.*

rĕfulgĕo -fulgēre -fulsi, *to gleam back, shine brightly, glitter.*

rĕfundo -fundĕre -fūdi -fūsum, *to pour back, to make overflow.*

rĕfūtātĭo -ōnis, f. *refutation.*

rĕfūtātŭ, abl. sing. m. *by refutation.*

rĕfūto -are, *to drive back, check, repress; to refute, disprove.*

rēgālis -e, *of a king, royal, regal*; adv. **rēgālĭter**, *regally, tyrannically.*

rĕgĕlo -are, *to thaw, warm.*

rēgĕro -gĕrĕre -gessi -gestum, *to carry back, throw back.*

rēgĭa; see regius.

rēgĭfĭcus -a -um, *princely, splendid.*

rĕgigno -ĕre, *to bring forth again.*

Rēgillus -i, m. *a lake in Latium, scene of a victory of the Romans over the Latins,* 496 B.C.

rēgĭmen -ĭnis, n. *control, guidance, rule, direction, government; a ruler, governor;* poet., *rudder.*

rēgīna -ae, f. *queen; princess; lady. mistress, sovereign.*

rēgĭo -ōnis, f. (1) *a direction, line;* esp. *a boundary line, boundary;* e regione, *in a straight line;* also *opposite, over against* (with genit. or dat.). (2) *a region, district, province.* Transf., *sphere, department.*

rēgĭōnātim, *according to districts.*

Rēgĭum (Rhēgĭum) -i, n. (1) *a town in Gallia Cispadana.* (2) *a town in Calabria.*

rēgĭus -a -um, *of a king, royal, regal; splendid, magnificent.* F. as subst. **rēgĭa** -ae, *palace, court, the royal family; capital city.* Adv. **rēgĭē.** *royally; tyrannically.*

regnātor -ōris, m. *ruler, king.*

regnātrix -trīcis, f. adj., *ruling.*

regno -are; intransit. *to be a king, reign; to be master, be a tyrant; to prevail;* transit., in pass., regnari, *to be ruled by a king.*

regnum -i, n. (1) *royal power, mon-archy, supremacy; tyranny.* (2) *a realm, kingdom, estate.*

rēgo rĕgĕre rexi rectum, *to guide, direct, to rule, govern, administer.* Hence partic. **rectus** -a -um, *ruled;* as adj. *straight; upright.* Transf., *right, correct, proper; honest, upright; natural, plain, straight-forward;* n. as subst., *right.* Adv. **rectē**, *in a straight line; rightly properly;* recte est, *all is well.*

regrĕdĭor -grĕdi -gressus, dep. *to step back, go back;* milit., *to retire, retreat.*

regressus -ūs, m. *a going back, return; retreat; refuge, recourse.*

rēgŭla -ae, f. *a ruler, a plank.* Transf., *a rule, pattern, model.*

¹rēgŭlus -i, m. *a petty king,* or *king's son, prince.*

²**Rēgŭlus,** *a surname in the gens Atilia.*

rĕgusto -are, *to taste again or repeatedly.*

rĕicio -icĕre -iēci -iectum, *to throw back, throw behind, throw away; to drive off;* of a storm, *to drive back, cast up.* Transf., *to throw off, reject; to refer;* in time, *to put off;* legal, *to challenge a juror.*

rĕiectio -ōnis, f. *throwing back, rejection;* legal, *the challenging of a juror.*

rĕiecto -are, *to throw back.*

rĕlābor -lābi -lapsus, dep. *to glide back, fall back.*

rĕlanguesco -languescĕre -langŭi, *to become faint; to slacken.*

rĕlātĭo -ōnis, f. *carrying back, bringing back;* polit., *a report;* gram., *repetition.*

rĕlātor -ōris, m. *one who makes a report.*

rĕlātus -ūs, m. *a narrative; a report.*

rĕlaxātĭo -ōnis, f. *relaxation, easing.*

rĕlaxo -are, *to loosen, enlarge; to ease, lighten, relax.*

rĕlēgātĭo -ōnis, f. *banishment.*

¹**rĕlēgo** -are, *to send away; to put aside, reject; to banish.*

²**rĕlĕgo** -lĕgĕre -lēgi -lectum, *to gather up again;* of places, *to pass again;* of topics, *to go over again.*

rĕlentesco -ĕre, *to become languid again.*

rĕlĕvo -are, *to lift again; to lighten; to relieve, alleviate.*

rĕlictĭo -ōnis, f. *leaving, deserting.*

rĕlicŭos and rĕlicus = reliquus; q.v.

rĕligātĭo -ōnis, f. *tying up.*

rĕligĭo (relligio) -ōnis, f. of persons, *scrupulousness, conscientious exactness;* esp. *religious scruple, awe, superstition, strict observance;* in gen., *moral scruples, conscientiousness;* of gods, etc., *sanctity; an object of worship, holy thing* or *place.*

rĕligĭōsus (relligiōsus) -a -um, of persons, *scrupulous, conscientious; holy, strict, superstitious;* of actions, either *required* or *forbidden by religion;* of gods, etc., *holy, sacred.* Adv. **rĕligĭōsē,** *conscientiously, scrupulously; religiously.*

rĕligo -are, *to tie on, fasten behind.*

rĕlĭno -lĭnĕre -lēvi -lĭtum, *to unseal.*

rĕlinquo -linquĕre -lĭqui -lictum, *to leave behind;* at death, *to bequeath; to leave unchanged;* pass., *to remain; to omit, leave out, pass over; to desert, abandon, forsake.*

rĕlĭquĭae (rellĭquĭae) -ārum, f. pl. *remains, relics, remnant.*

rĕlĭquus (rĕlĭcus) -a -um, *left behind, remaining, other;* of a debt, *outstanding;* of time, *remaining, future.* N. as subst., sing. and plur., *the rest; the remainder;* in reliquum, *for the future.*

relli-; see **reli-**.

rĕlūcĕo -lūcēre -luxi, *to glitter.*

rĕlūcesco -lūcescĕre -luxi, *to become bright again.*

rĕluctor -ari, dep. *to struggle against, resist.*

rĕmănĕo -mănēre -mansi -mansum, *to remain behind, stay, continue.*

rĕmāno -are, *to flow back.*

rĕmansĭo -ōnis, f. *remaining in a place.*

rĕmĕdĭum -i, n. *means of healing, cure, remedy, medicine.*

rĕmĕo -are, *to go back, return.*

rĕmētĭor -mētĭri -mensus, dep. *to measure again, go back over;* perf. partic. sometimes pass. in meaning.

rēmex -mĭgis, m. *a rower.*

rēmĭgātĭo -ōnis, f. *rowing.*

rēmĭgĭum -i, n. *rowing.* Transf. *oars; crew.*

rēmĭgo -are, *to row.*

rēmĭgro -are, *to wander back, come back, return.*

rĕmĭniscor -i, dep. *to call to mind, recollect, remember.*

rĕmiscĕo -miscēre -mixtum, *to mix up, mingle.*

rĕmissĭo -ōnis, f. *letting go back, letting fall, lowering; breaking off, interrupting; remitting;* animi *relaxation, quiet.*

rĕmitto -mittĕre -mīsi -missum. (1) *to send back, send again; throw back; echo.* (2) *to let go back, relax, loosen; to relieve, abate;* with infin., *to give up doing;* intransit., *to ease off.* (3) *to give up, yield; abandon, sacrifice; to forgive an offence, remit punishment.* Hence partic. **rĕmissus** -a -um, *relaxed, mild, gentle;* in bad sense *negligent, remiss.* Adv. **rĕmissē.**

rĕmōlior -iri, dep. *to push back.*

rĕmollesco -ĕre, *to become soft again.*

rĕmollio -ire, *to make soft again, to weaken.*

rĕmōra -ae, f. *delay, hindrance.*

rĕmōrāmen -ĭnis, n. *delay.*

rĕmordĕo -mordēre -morsum. *to worry, harass.*

rĕmŏror -ari, dep.: intransit., *to remain behind, linger, loiter;* transit., *to obstruct, hinder.*

rĕmōtĭo -ōnis, f. *putting away, removing.*

rĕmŏvĕo -mŏvēre -mōvi -mōtum *to move back, withdraw.* Hence partic. **rĕmōtus** -a -um, *removed, withdrawn, distant, far off, remote;* adv. **rĕmōtē,** *far off, at a distance.*

rĕmūgĭo -ire, *to bellow again, bellow back.*

rĕmulcĕo -mulcēre -mulsi *to stroke back.*

rĕmulcum -i, n. *a tow-rope.*

rĕmūnĕrātĭo -ōnis, f. *a recompense, return.*

rĕmūnĕror -ari, dep. *to repay, reward.*

rĕmurmŭro -are, *to murmur back.*

¹**rēmus** -i, m. *an oar.*

²**Rēmus** -i, m. *twin brother of Romulus.*

rēnarro -are, *to relate again.*

rēnascor -nasci -nātus, dep. *to be born again, grow again.*

rēnāvĭgo -are, *to sail back.*

rĕnĕo -nēre, *to unravel.*

rēnes -um, m. pl. *the kidneys.*

rēnīdĕo -ēre, *to shine back, glitter; to beam with joy, laugh, smile.*

rēnītor -i, dep. *to oppose, withstand, resist.*

¹**rēno** -nare, *to swim back.*

²rēno (rhēno) -ōnis, m. *a garment made of fur.*

rēnōdo -are, *to tie back.*

rĕnŏvāmen -ĭnis, n. *renewal.*

rĕnŏvātĭo -ōnis, f. *renewal, renovation;* renovatio singulorum annorum, *compound interest.*

rĕnŏvo -are, *to renew, restore, repair; to repeat.*

rĕnŭmĕro -are, *to count over again; to pay back.*

rĕnuntĭātĭo -ōnis, f. *a formal report, public announcement.*

rĕnuntĭo -are. (1) *to bring back word, report, announce.* (2) *to disclaim, refuse, renounce.*

rĕnŭo -nŭĕre -nŭi, *to deny, refuse, reject.*

rĕnūto -are, *to refuse, decline.*

rĕor rēri rătus, dep. *to think suppose, judge;* partic., in pass. sense, rătus -a -um, *determined, settled;* ratum facere, *to ratify, confirm, make valid;* pro rata, *in proportion.*

rĕpāgŭla -orum, n. pl. *bars or bolts; restraints, limits.*

rĕpandus -a -um, *bent backwards, turned up.*

rĕpārābĭlis -e, *that can be restored.*

rĕparco = reperco; q.v.

rĕpāro -are, *to restore, renew, make good; to get in exchange, purchase.*

rĕpastĭnātĭo -ōnis, f. *digging up again.*

rĕpecto -pectĕre -pexum, *to comb back.*

rĕpello rĕpellĕre reppŭli, rĕpulsum, *to drive back, drive away; to banish, repel;* a spe, *to disappoint;* criminationes, *to refute.*

rĕpendo -pendĕre -pendi -pensum, *to weigh back again; to ransom; to repay, requite.*

rĕpens -entis, *sudden, unexpected; fresh, recent.* Adv. rĕpentĕ, *suddenly, unexpectedly.*

rĕpentīnus -a -um, *sudden, unexpected;* n. abl. as adv. rĕpentīnō, *suddenly.*

rĕperco (rĕparco) -percĕre -persi or -pĕrci, *to spare, be sparing, abstain.*

rĕpercussus -ūs, m. *reverberation; echo, reflection.*

rĕpercŭtĭo -cŭtĕre -cussi -cussum, *to strike back, make rebound;* perf. partic. rĕpercussus -a -um, *rebounding, reflected.*

rĕpĕrĭo rĕpĕrire reppĕri rĕpertum, *to get again; to find, discover, ascertain, invent.*

rĕpertor -ōris, m. *discoverer, inventor.*

rĕpĕtentĭa -ae, f. *recollection, remembrance.*

rĕpĕtītĭo -ōnis, f. *repetition.*

rĕpĕtītor -ōris, m. *one who demands back.*

rĕpĕto -ĕre -īvi *and* -ii -ītum, *to seek again, go back for or to; to ask back;* res repetere, *to demand satisfaction;* (pecuniae) repetundae, *money claimed back, as having been extorted; to return to, renew, begin again; to trace back, deduce; to recollect, recall.*

rĕpĕtundae; see repeto.

rĕplĕo -plēre -plēvi -plētum, *to fill again, fill up; to make full, fill, satisfy.* Hence partic. replētus -a -um, *filled, full.*

rĕplĭcātĭo -ōnis, f. *rolling again, folding round.*

rĕplĭco -are, *to unroll; to turn over, review.*

rēpo rēpĕre repsi reptum, *to creep, crawl.*

rĕpōno -pōnĕre -pŏsŭi -pŏsĭtum, *to lay back; to put aside, lay up, deposit, store; mentally, to reckon, place; to replace, restore; to replace by a substitute; to requite.*

rĕporto -are, *to bring back, carry back;* of reports, *to deliver.*

rĕposco -ĕre, *to ask back again; to demand as a right, claim.*

rĕpostor -ōris, m. *a restorer.*

rĕpōtĭa -ōrum, n. *an after-party, second entertainment.*

repraesentātĭo -ōnis, f. (1) *vivid presentation, lively description.* (2) *payment in cash.*

repraesento -are, *to bring back, reproduce; to perform immediately, hasten on;* pecuniam, *to pay cash.*

rĕprĕhendo -prĕhendĕre -prĕhendi -prĕhensum, *and* rĕprendo -prendĕre -prendi -prensum, *to catch, hold fast, detain, check; to blame, reprove; to refute.*

rĕprĕhensĭo -ōnis, f. *stopping, check; blame, censure; refutation.*

rĕprĕhenso -are, *to hold back, hold fast.*

rĕprĕhensor -ōris, m. *a censurer, reprover; an improver, reformer.*

repressor -ōris, m. *a restrainer.*

rĕprĭmo -primĕre -pressi -pressum, *to hold back, restrain, hinder, repress.*

rĕprōmissĭo -ōnis, f. *a counterpromise.*

rĕprōmitto -mittĕre -misi -missum, *to promise in return.*

repto -are, *to creep, crawl along.*

rĕpŭdĭātĭo -ōnis, f. *refusal, rejection.*

rĕpŭdĭo -are, *to refuse, reject, disdain; to divorce.*

rĕpŭdĭum -i, n. *divorce.*

rĕpŭĕrasco -ĕre, *to become a boy again, to frolic.*

rĕpugnantĭa -ae, f. *incompatibility.*

rĕpugno -are *to fight against, oppose, resist; to be opposed, repugnant, inconsistent, incompatible.* Hence partic. rĕpugnans, *contrary opposed;* n. pl. as subst. *contradictions;* adv. rĕpugnantĕr, *unwillingly.*

rĕpulsa -ae, f. *repulse, rejection; denial refusal.*

rĕpulsans -antis, partic., *beating back;* colles verba repulsantes, *echoing.*

rĕpulsū, abl. sing. m. *by striking back, by reflection, by echoing.*

rĕpungo -ĕre, *to prick again.*

rĕpurgo -are, *to clean again; to purge away.*

rĕpŭtātĭo -ōnis, f. *re-appraisal.*

rĕpŭto -are. (1) *to reckon back, count, compute.* (2) *to think over, reconsider.*

rĕquĭēs -ētis, f. *rest, repose.*

rĕquĭesco -quĭescĕre -quĭēvi -quĭētum, *to rest, repose*; pass. partic. **rĕquĭētus** -a -um, *rested, refreshed*; ager, *fallow*.

rĕquīro -quīrĕre -quīsīi *and* -quīsīvi -quīsītum, *to ask for, look for, enquire after; to demand, desire; to miss, feel the want of*.

rēs rĕi, f. *a thing, object, matter, affair, circumstance*; natura rerum, *the world, the universe, nature*; pro re, *according to circumstance*; esp. *the real thing, fact, truth, reality*; rē verā, *in truth*; *possessions, property, wealth; interest, advantage, benefit*; in rem, *to one's advantage; cause, ground, reason*; qua re, quam ob rem, *wherefore; a matter of business; a law-suit, action*; res publica or respublica, *the republic, state, commonwealth*; e republicā, *in the public interest*.

rĕsacro = resecro; q.v.

rĕsaevĭo -ire, *to rage again*.

rĕsălūto -are, *to salute back, greet in return*.

rĕsănesco -sānescĕre -sānŭi, *to become sound again*.

rĕsarcĭo -sarcīre -sartum, *to patch up, mend, repair, restore*.

rescindo -scindĕre -scĭdi -scissum, *to tear back, cut away, break open; vulnus, to reopen; of laws, etc., to rescind, repeal*.

rescisco -sciscĕre -scīvi *and* -scĭi -scĭtum, *to find out, ascertain*.

rescrībo -scrībĕre -scripsi -scriptum, *to write again, rewrite; to enrol again, transfer; to write back, answer in writing*; in book-keeping, *to pay, repay*.

rĕsĕco -sĕcare -sĕcŭi -sectum, *to cut back, cut short*.

rĕsēmĭno -are, *to produce again*.

rĕsĕquor -sĕqui -sĕcūtus, dep. *to follow again*; dictis, *to answer*.

rĕsĕro -are, *to unbolt, open up, disclose, reveal*.

rĕservo -are, *to lay up, keep back, reserve; to save, preserve, keep*.

rĕsĕs -sĭdis, *sitting; inactive, calm, quiet*.

rĕsĭdĕo -sĭdēre -sēdi -sessum, *to remain sitting, stay, rest*.

rĕsīdo -sīdĕre -sēdi, *to sit down, settle, sink, subside, abate*.

rĕsĭdŭus -a -um, *remaining, outstanding*; pecuniae, *arrears*.

rĕsigno -are, *to unseal, open, reveal; to cancel, annul; to transfer, give back, resign*.

rĕsĭlĭo -sĭlire -sĭlŭi -sultum, *to leap back, rebound; to shrink, contract*.

rĕsīmus -a -um, *bent backwards, turned up*.

rĕsīna -ae, f. *resin*.

rĕsĭpĭo -sipere, *to have a flavour of anything*.

rĕsĭpisco -sĭpiscĕre -sīpĭi, *also* -sīpīvi, *to recover one's senses; to become rational again*.

rĕsisto -sistĕre -stĭti. (1) *to stay, still, stop, continue; to recover one's footing.* (2) *to resist, oppose, withstand*; usually with dat.

rĕsolvo -solvĕre -solvi -sŏlūtum, *to untie, loosen, open; to melt; to dissipate; to dispel; to release; to reveal; to weaken*.

rĕsŏnābĭlis -e, *resounding*.

rĕsŏno -are; intransit., *to resound, echo*; transit., *to make resound*.

rĕsŏnus -a -um, *resounding, echoing*.

rĕsorbĕo -ēre, *to swallow again, suck back*.

respecto -are, *to look eagerly back (at); to have a regard for, give thought to*.

respectus -ūs, m. *looking back*; hence *care, regard, consideration; looking around one*; meton., *refuge, retreat*.

respergo -spergĕre -spersi -spersum, *to sprinkle, splash*.

respersĭo -ōnis, f. *sprinkling*.

respĭcĭo -spĭcĕre -spexi -spectum, *to look behind, look back (at); to look back upon; to look to, provide for; to look to, depend upon; to have a regard for, care for, consider*.

respīrāmen -ĭnis, n. *windpipe*.

respīrātĭo -ōnis, f. *taking breath, respiration; exhalation*.

respīrātus -ū, m. *taking breath*.

respīro -are. (1) *to breathe back, blow in a contrary direction.* (2) *to breathe again, to take breath; to recover from fear, etc.; of things, to abate, decline*.

resplendĕo -ēre, *to glitter back, gleam again*.

respondĕo -spondĕre -spondi -sponsum: intransit., *to match, correspond to, answer to; to resemble*; legal, *to answer to one's name, appear, be present*; transit., *to give an answer to person or thing, to answer, reply*. N. of partic. as subst. **responsum** -i, *an answer, reply*; a lawyer's *opinion*.

responsĭo -ōnis, f. *a reply, answer*.

responsĭto -are, *to keep giving an answer or opinion*.

responso -are, *to keep answering; to re-echo*; with dat., *to defy, withstand*.

responsum -i, n. subst. from respondeo; q.v.

respublĭca; see res.

respŭo -spŭĕre -spŭi, *to spit out, reject, refuse, repel*.

restagno -are, *to overflow, be swamped*.

restauro -are, *to restore, rebuild*.

restĭcŭla -ae, f. *a thin rope*.

restinctĭo -ōnis, f. *slaking, quenching*.

restinguo -stinguĕre -stinxi -stinctum, *to put out again, extinguish, quench, slake, destroy*.

restĭo -ōnis, m. *a rope-maker*.

restĭpŭlātĭo -ōnis, f. *a counter-engagement*.

restĭpŭlor -ari, dep. *to obtain a promise in return*.

restis -is, f. *a rope, cord*.

restĭto -are, *to remain behind, linger*.

restĭtŭo -ŭĕre -ŭi -ūtum, *to put back, replace, restore; to reinstate, re-establish; to repair, make good*.

restĭtūtĭo -ōnis, f. *restoration, reinstatement*.

restĭtūtor -ōris, m. *restorer*.

resto -stare -stĭti. (1) *to make a stand, resist, oppose.* (2) *to stand still, stay behind; to be left over, survive; to remain available or possible;* of the future, *to await, be in store.*

restringo -stringĕre -strinxi -strictum, *to bind back, draw back; to confine, restrict, restrain.*
    Hence partic. **restrictus** -a -um, *close, tight; stingy; strict, severe.* Adv. **restrictē**, *sparingly; strictly.*

rĕsulto -are *to spring back, rebound; to echo, resound;* of style, *to go jerkily.*

rĕsūmo -sūmĕre -sumpsi -sumptum, *to take again, resume; to renew, repeat.*

rĕsŭpīno -are, *to throw down, prostrate.*

rĕsŭpīnus -a -um, *bent backwards, on one's back; also with head thrown back.*

rĕsurgo -surgĕre -surrexi -surrectum, *to rise up again, appear again.*

rĕsuscĭto -are, *to revive, resuscitate.*

rĕtardātĭo -ōnis, f. *hindering.*

rĕtardo -are, *to slow down, retard, impede.*

rētĕ -is, n. *a net.*

rĕtĕgo -tĕgĕre -texi -tectum, *to uncover, reveal, open, disclose.*

rĕtempto -are, *to attempt again.*

rĕtendo -tendĕre -tendi -tensum *and* -tentum, *to slacken, unbend.*

rĕtentĭo -ōnis, f. *keeping back; withholding.*

¹**rĕtento** -are, *to hold firmly; to preserve maintain.*

²**rĕtento** = retempto; q.v.

rĕtentus -a -um, partic. from retendo or from retineo; q.v.

rĕtexo -texĕre -texŭi -textum, *to unravel, undo, reverse; to cancel, annul; to retract; to revise.*

rētĭārĭus -i, m. *a gladiator using a net.*

rĕtĭcentĭa -ae, f. *keeping silent.*

rĕtĭcĕo -ēre: intransit., *to keep silence, say nothing:* transit., *to keep silent about.*

rĕtĭcŭlum -i, n. *a little net; a net-bag; a hair-net.*

rĕtīnācŭla -ōrum, n. pl. *a rope, cable.*

rĕtĭnentĭa -ae, f. *recollection.*

rĕtĭnĕo -tĭnēre -tĭnŭi -tentum, *to hold back, detain; to restrain; to keep, reserve, maintain.*
    Hence partic. **rĕtĭnens** -entis, *tenacious.*

rĕtinnĭo -ire, *to resound, ring again.*

rĕtŏno -are, *to thunder back, resound.*

rĕtorquĕo -torquēre -torsi -tortum, *to twist back, bend back.*

retractātĭo -ōnis, f. (1) *refusal, denial.* (2) *reconsideration.*

retracto (**retrecto**) -are. (1) *to handle again, undertake anew, reconsider.* (2) *to draw back, refuse, be reluctant;* dicta, *to withdraw.*

retrăho -trăhĕre -traxi -tractum, *to draw back; to hold back, withdraw; to draw on again, induce.*
    Hence partic. **retractus** -a -um, *withdrawn; distant, remote.*

retrĭbŭo -trĭbŭĕre -trĭbŭi -trĭbūtum, *to give again or give as due.*

retrō, *backwards, back, behind.*

retrŏăgo -ăgĕre -ēgi -actum, *to drive back, reverse.*

retrorsum, *backwards, behind, in return, in reversed order.*

retrūdo -trūdĕre -trūsum, *to push back;* perf. partic. retrūsus, *remote, obscure.*

rĕtundo -tundĕre -tŭdi (rettŭdi) -tūsum (rĕtunsum), *to hammer back, blunt, dull; to check or weaken;* partic. **rĕtūsus** (**rĕtunsus**) -a -um, *dull, blunt.*

rĕus -i, m. and **rĕa** -ae, f. *a party in a law-suit, whether plaintiff or defendant;* esp. *a defendant, accused person;* in gen., *one bound or answerable.*

rĕvălesco -vălescĕre -vălŭi, *to become well again, be restored, recover.*

rĕvĕho -vĕhĕre -vexi -vectum, *to carry back;* pass., *to drive back, ride back, sail back.*

rĕvello -vellĕre -velli -vulsum, *to tear back, pull away; to remove, banish.*

rĕvēlo -are, *to unveil, lay bare.*

rĕvĕnĭo -vĕnire -vēni -ventum, *to come back, return.*

rĕvērā, adv. from res; q.v.

rĕvĕrentĭa -ae, f. *respect, fear, awe.*

rĕvĕrĕor -vĕrēri -vĕritus, dep. *to revere, respect, fear;* partic. **rĕvĕrens** -entis, *respectful, reverent;* adv. **rĕvĕrenter**; gerundive, **rĕvĕrendus** -a -um, *awesome, venerable.*

rĕversĭo (**rĕvorsĭo**) -ōnis, f. *turning back, return, recurrence.*

rĕverto (**rĕvorto**) -vertĕre -verti, and pass. **rĕvertor** (**rĕvortor**) *to return, come back, revert.*

rĕvincĭo -vincire -vinxi -vinctum, *to tie back, bind fast.*

rĕvinco -vincĕre -vici -victum, *to beat back, subdue; to refute.*

rĕvĭresco -vĭrescĕre -vĭrŭi, *to grow green or strong again; to revive.*

rĕviso -ĕre: intransit., *to pay a fresh visit, return:* transit., *to come to see again, revisit.*

rĕvivisco -vivescĕre -vixi, *to come to life again, revive.*

rĕvŏcābĭlis -e, *able to be called back.*

rĕvŏcāmen -ĭnis, n. *calling back, recall.*

rĕvŏcātĭo -ōnis, f. *calling back; withdrawing, revocation.*

rĕvŏco -are, *to call again or back; to recall; to bring or get back, recover; to refer; to revoke.*

rĕvŏlo -are, *to fly back.*

rĕvŏlūbĭlis -e, *able to be rolled back.*

rĕvolvo -volvĕre -volvi -vŏlūtum, *to roll backwards; esp. to unroll or open a book; hence to go over again;* pass., *to roll back, come round again in due course.*

rĕvŏmo -vŏmĕre -vŏmŭi, *to vomit up, disgorge.*

rĕvor-; see rever-.

rex, rēgis, m. *ruler, king, prince, chief; monarch, tyrant.*

Rhădămanthus -i, m. *brother of Minos, a judge in the lower world.*

¹**Rhēa (Rēa) Silvĭa,** *mother of Romulus and Remus.*

²**Rhēa** -ae, f. *old name of Cybele.*

rhēda = raeda; q.v.

Rhēnus -i, m. *the Rhine.*

rhētor -ŏris, m. *a teacher of rhetoric, a rhetorician.*

rhētŏrĭcus -a -um, *rhetorical*; subst., f. **rhētŏrĭca** -ae and **rhētŏrĭcē** -ēs, *the art of oratory*; m. pl. **rhētŏrĭci** -ōrum, *teachers of rhetoric*; adv. **rhētŏrĭcē,** *rhetorically.*

rhīnŏcērōs -ōtis, m. *a rhinoceros.*

rhō, n. indecl. *the Greek name of the letter R.*

Rhŏdănus -i, m. *the Rhone.*

Rhŏdus (-ŏs) -i, f. *Rhodes*; adj. **Rhŏdĭus** -a -um, and **Rhŏdĭensis** -e.

rhombus (-ŏs) -i, m. (1) *a magician's circle.* (2) *the turbot.*

rhomphaea (rumpĭa) -ae, f. *a long javelin.*

rhythmĭcus -i, m. *one who teaches rhythm.*

rhythmus (-ŏs) -i. m. *rhythm, time, harmony.*

rhȳtĭum -i, n. *a drinking-horn.*

rīca -ae, f. *a veil.*

rīcĭnum -i, n. *a small veil.*

rictus -ūs, m. and **rictum** -i, n. *the open mouth.*

rīdĕo rīdēre rīsi rīsum: intransit., *to laugh, smile, look cheerful*; with dat., *to please*; transit., *to laugh at.*

rīdĭcŭlārĭus and **rīdĭcŭlōsus** -a -um, *laughable, droll.*

rīdĭcŭlus, *exciting laughter; droll, humorous; absurd, ridiculous*; m. as subst., *a joker, jester*; n., *a joke, jest.* Adv. **rīdĭcŭlē,** *humorously; absurdly.*

rĭgĕo -ēre, *to be stiff* (esp. with cold); of hair, *to stand on end*; partic. **rĭgens** -entis, *stiff.*

rĭgesco rĭgescĕre rĭgŭi, *to grow stiff*; of hair, *to stand on end.*

rĭgĭdus -a -um, *stiff, unbending, hard; stern, inflexible.* Adv. **rĭgĭdē.**

rĭgo -are, *to lead or conduct water; to wet, moisten, bedew.*

rĭgor -ōris, m. *stiffness, hardness*, esp. from cold. Transf., *sternness.*

rĭgŭus -a -um; act., *watering*; pass., *well-watered, irrigated.*

rīma -ae, f. *a crack, fissure, leak.*

rīmor -ari, dep. *to cleave; to probe, pry into, examine.*

rīmōsus -a -um, *full of cracks, leaky.*

ringor -i, dep. *to show the teeth; to snarl, be angry.*

rīpa -ae, f. *bank, shore.*

rīpŭla -ae, f. *a little bank.*

riscus -i; m. *a box, trunk.*

rīsĭo -ōnis, f. *laughter.*

rīsor -ōris, m. *a laugher, mocker.*

rīsus -ūs, m. *laughing, laughter; ridicule; an object of laughter.*

rītē, *in due form, with proper ceremonies, properly, fitly, rightly.*

rītus -ūs, m. *usage, ceremony, rite*; abl., ritu, with genit., *after the manner of.*

rīvālis -is, m. *a rival in love.*

rīvālĭtās -ātis, f. *rivalry* (in love).

rīvŭlus -i, m. *small brook, rivulet.*

rīvus -i, m. *stream.*

rixa -ae, f. *quarrel, brawl, contention.*

rixor -ari, dep. *to quarrel brawl contend.*

rōbĭgĭnōsus -a -um, *rusty.*

rōbīgo (rūbīgo) -ĭnis, f. *rust; blight, mildew; inaction, mental rust.* Personif. **Rōbīgo (Rūb-)** -ĭnis, f. or **Rōbīgus (Rūb-)** -i, m. *a deity invoked to preserve grain from mildew*; **Rōbīgālĭa** -ĭum, n. *the festival of Robigo.*

rōbŏrĕus -a -um, *oaken.*

rōbŏro -are, *to strengthen, make firm.*

rōbur -ŏris, n. *hard wood*; esp., *oak, oak-wood; a dungeon at Rome,* also called the Tullianum; as a quality, *hardness, strength*; in gen., *the pick flower,* of anything.

rōbustus -a -um, *of hard wood*; esp. *of oak, oaken; strong, powerful, firm.*

rōdo rōdĕre rōsi rōsum, *to gnaw, nibble at; to corrode, consume; to disparage, backbite, slander.*

rŏgālis -e *of the funeral pile.*

rŏgātĭo -ōnis, f. *asking; a question; a request; a proposed law, a bill.*

rŏgātĭuncŭla -ae, f. *a minor question or bill.*

rŏgātor -ōris, m. *one who asks; the proposer of a bill; a polling-clerk.*

rŏgātū, abl. sing. m. *at the request.*

rŏgĭto -are, *to ask eagerly.*

rŏgo -are, *to ask, inquire; to ask for, request*; polit., rogare aliquem sententiam, *to ask a person his opinion*; rogare populum or legem, *to propose a law, introduce a bill*; rogare magistratum, *to offer a person for election.*

rŏgus -i, m. *funeral pile.*

Rōma -ae, f. *Rome*; adj. **Rōmānus** -a -um.

Rōmŭlus -i, m. *son of Mars, founder and first king of Rome*; adj. **Rōmŭlĕus** and **Rōmŭlus** -a -um.

rōrārĭi -ōrum, m. pl. *light-armed troops skirmishers.*

rōrĭdus -a -um, *bedewed.*

rōrĭfer -fĕra -fĕrum, *dew-bringing.*

rōro -are: intransit., *to drop dew, drip, be moist;* transit., *to bedew, moisten, water; to drip, let fall in drops.*

rōs rōris, m. *dew, moisture*; ros marinus, rosmarinus, *rosemary.*

rōsa -ae, f. *a rose; a garland of roses; a rose-tree.*

rŏsārĭus -a -um, *of roses*; n. as subst. *a rose-garden.*

roscĭdus -a -um, *bedewed, dewy; dripping like dew; moistened.*

Roscĭus -a -um, *name of a Roman gens.*

rŏsētum -i, n. *a garden of roses.*

rŏsĕus -a -um, *of roses; rose-coloured, rosy.*

rosmărīnus; see ros.

rostrātus -a -um, *having a beak, beaked curved*; columna rostrata, *a pillar in the forum, adorned with ships' prows.*

rostrum -i, n. *beak, snout; a ship's prow*; plur. **rostra** -ōrum, *the speaker's platform in the Forum* (ornamented with prows of ships).

rŏta -ae, f. *a wheel*; poet., *a chariot.*

rŏto -are, *to whirl round, swing, brandish*; pass. rotari, *to revolve, to roll round.*

rŏtundo -are, *to round, make round.*

rŏtundus -a -um, *round circular; sometimes spherical; rounded, complete, self-contained.* Adv. **rŏtundē,** of style, *elegantly, smoothly.*

rŭběfăcio -făcĕre -fēci -factum, *to redden, make red.*

rŭbellus -a -um, *reddish.*

rŭběo -ēre, *to be red; to blush*; partic. **rŭbens** -entis, *red, blushing.*

rŭber -bra -brum, *red, ruddy.*

rŭbesco -bescĕre -bŭi, *to become red.*

¹rŭbēta -ae, f. *a species of toad.*

²rŭbēta -ōrum, n. pl. *bramble-thickets.*

rŭbēus -a -um, *of bramble.*

Rŭbico -ōnis, m. *a river, once the boundary between Italia and Gallia Cisalpina.*

rŭbīcundus -a -um, *red, ruddy.*

rŭbīgo = robigo; q.v.

rŭbor -ōris, m. *redness; a blush; modesty; shame, disgrace.*

rubrīca -ae, f. *red earth; red ochre; a law with its title written in red.*

rŭbus -i, m. *a bramble-bush; a blackberry.*

ructo -are, and **ructor** -ari, dep. *to belch.*

ructus -ūs, m. *belching.*

rŭdens -entis, m. *a rope, halyard.*

rŭdīmentum -i, n. *a trial, attempt, essay.*

¹rŭdis -e, *rough, raw, uncultivated; unrefined, unskilled, awkward.*

²rŭdis -is, f. *a small stick; a foil* (given to gladiators on their discharge).

rŭdo rŭdĕre rŭdīvi rŭdītum, *to bellow, roar.*

¹rŭdus (**rōdus**) -ĕris, n. *broken fragments of stone.*

²rŭdus = raudus; q.v.

rŭfus -a -um, *red, ruddy.*

rūga -ae, f. *a wrinkle.*

rūgōsus -a -um, *wrinkled.*

rŭīna -ae, f. *falling down, collapse, ruin, destruction; the ruins of a building, debris.*

rŭīnōsus -a -um, *going to ruin.*

rūmex -īcis, f. *sorrel.*

Rūmīna -ae, f. *a Roman goddess;* **Rūmīnālis ficus,** m. *a fig-tree under which the she-wolf had suckled Romulus and Remus.*

rūmīnātĭo -ōnis, f. *chewing the cud; ruminating.*

rūmīno -are, *to chew the cud, ruminate.*

rūmor -ōris, m. *report, rumour, common talk, hearsay; general opinion, popular judgment.*

rumpo rumpĕre rūpi ruptum, *to break, shatter, burst open; to cause to break forth; to destroy, violate, annul; to break off, interrupt.*

rūmuscŭlus -i, m. *trifling rumour, idle talk, gossip.*

rūna -ae, f. *a dart.*

runco -are, *to weed, thin out.*

rŭo rŭĕre rŭi rŭtum; fut. partic. **rŭĭtūrus;** intransit., *to rush down, fall,* *collapse, be ruined; to rush along; to be precipitate;* transit., *to hurl down; also to cast up.*

rūpēs -is, f. *rock, cliff.*

ruptor -ōris, m. *breaker, violator.*

rūrĭcŏla -ae, *inhabiting* or *cultivating the country.*

rūrĭgěna -ae, m. *one born in the country, a rustic.*

rūro -are and **rūror** -ari, dep. *to live in the country.*

rursus and **rursum,** *backward, back; on the other hand, in return; again, afresh.*

rūs rūris, n. *the country, a country-seat, farm, estate;* acc., rus, *to the country*; locative, ruri (or rure), *in the country.*

russus -a -um, *red, russet.*

rustĭcānus -a -um, *of the country, rustic.*

rustĭcātĭo -ōnis, f. *living in the country.*

rustĭcĭtās -ātis, f. *rustic manners, rusticity.*

rustĭcor -ari, dep. *to live in the country.*

rustĭcŭlus -a -um, *countrified;* m. as subst., *a rustic.*

rustĭcus -a -um, *of the country, rural, rustic; plain, simple; awkward, boorish;* m. as subst. *a countryman, a boor.* Adv. **rustĭcē.**

rūta -ae, *the herb rue; bitterness, unpleasantness.*

rūtĭlo -are: intransit., *to shine reddish;* transit., *to make red.*

rŭtĭlus -a -um, *red, golden, auburn.*

rutrum -i, n. *a spade, shovel.*

rūtŭla -ae, f. *a little bit of rue.*

Rŭtŭli -ōrum, m. pl. *an ancient people of Latium.*

S

S, s, the eighteenth letter of the Latin alphabet.

Săba -ae, f. *a town in Arabia, famous for perfumes.*

sabbăta -ōrum, n. pl. *the Sabbath, the Jewish day of rest.*

Săbelli -ōrum, m. *poetic name of the Sabines.*

Săbīni -orum, m. pl. *an ancient people of Italy, northerly neighbours of the Latins.*

săbŭlum -i, n. *gravel, sand.*

săburra -ae, f. *sand used as ballast.*

sacco -are, *to strain or filter.*

saccŭlus -i, m. *a small bag.*

saccus -i, m. *a sack, bag;* esp. *a purse.*

săcellum -i, n. *a small shrine, chapel.*

săcer -cra -crum, *sacred, holy, consecrated; in bad sense, accursed, devoted to destruction, horrible.* N. sing. as subst. **sacrum** -i, *a holy thing* or *place; a sacrifice* or *victim;* n. pl. *sacred rites, worship.*

săcerdōs -dōtis, c. *a priest, priestess.*

săcerdōtālis -e, *priestly.*

săcerdōtĭum -i, n. *priesthood.*

săcrāmentum -i, n.: *legal, money deposited by the parties in a suit; hence a civil suit, legal process;* milit., *oath of allegiance; hence an oath* or *solemn promise.*

sacrārĭum -i, n. (1) *a place where sacred things are kept, sacristy.* (2) *a place of worship, chapel, shrine.*

sacrĭcŏla -ae, c. *a sacrificing priest or priestess.*

sacrĭfer -fĕra -fĕrum, *carrying sacred things.*

sacrĭfĭcālis -e, *of sacrifices.*

sacrĭfĭcātĭo -ōnis, f. *sacrificing.*

sacrĭfĭcĭum -i, n. *sacrifice.*

sacrĭfĭco -are, *to sacrifice.*

sacrĭfĭcŭlus -i, m. *a sacrificing priest.*

sacrĭfĭcus -a -um, *sacrificial, sacrificing.*

sacrĭlĕgĭum -i, n. *stealing of sacred things, sacrilege, profanation.*

sacrĭlĕgus -a -um, *stealing sacred things, sacrilegious, impious.*

sacro -are. (1) *to dedicate to a god, consecrate; to devote, allot; to doom, curse.* (2) *to make holy, make inviolable; to immortalize.*
Hence partic. **sacrātus** -a -um, *holy, consecrated.*

sacrōsanctus -a -um, *consecrated, holy, sacred, inviolable.*

sacrum; see sacer.

saecŭlāris -e, *relating to a saeculum or age;* ludi, *secular games* (celebrated at intervals of about 100 years).

saecŭlum (poet. **saeclum**) -i, n. *a generation; the spirit of the age, the times; a hundred years, a century, an age.*

saepĕ, *often, frequently;* **saepĕnŭmĕrō**, *repeatedly, again and again.*

saepes (**sēpes**) -is, f. *hedge, fence.*

saepīmentum -i, n. *hedge, enclosure.*

saepĭo saepire saepsi saeptum, *to hedge in, enclose, surround, confine;* n. of partic. as subst. **saeptum** -i, *barrier, wall, enclosure;* in plur., *the enclosure where the Romans voted at the comitia.*

saeta -ae, f. *a bristle, stiff hair; part of an angler's line.*

saetĭger -gĕra -gĕrum, *having bristles, bristly;* m. as subst. *a boar.*

saetōsus -a -um, *bristly.*

saevīdĭcus -a -um, *angrily spoken.*

saevĭo -īre -ii -itum, *to rage, be furious, take violent action.*

saevĭtĭa -ae, f. *rage, ferocity.*

saevus -a -um, *raging, fierce, furious, violent, savage, cruel;* adv. **saevē** and **saevĭtĕr**.

sāga -ae, f., *a prophetess, fortune-teller.*

săgācĭtās -ātis, f. *keenness, acuteness, shrewdness.*

săgātus -a -um, *clothed in a* sagum; q.v.

săgax -ācis, *keen, acute;* esp. *keen-scented; mentally acute, shrewd, clever.* Adv. **săgācĭtĕr**.

săgīna -ae, f. *fattening, cramming; food, nourishment.*

săgīno -are, *to fatten, cram.*

săgitta -ae, f. *arrow.*

săgittārĭus -a -um, *of an arrow;* m. as subst. *an archer.*

săgittĭfer -fĕra -fĕrum, *carrying arrows.*

săgitto -are, *to shoot arrows.*

sagmen -ĭnis, n. *a bunch of sacred herbs.*

săgŭlum -i, n. *a small military cloak.*

săgum -i, n. *a cloak of coarse wool,* as worn by servants, and esp. by soldiers, saga sumere, *to take up arms, prepare for war.*

Săguntum -i, n. and **Săguntus** (-ŏs) -i, f. *a town on the coast of Spain.*

săl, sălis, m. *salt; brine, sea-water;* fig., sing. and plur., *wit.*

sălăco -ōnis, m. *a swaggerer, braggart.*

Sălāmis -mĭnis, f. (1) *an island in the Saronic Gulf.* (2) *a town in Cyprus.*

sălăpūtĭum -i, n. *a little man, manikin.*

sălārĭus -a -um, *of salt;* n. as subst. *salt money, an allowance, pay.*

sălax -ācis, *lustful, lecherous.*

sălebra -ae, f. *jolting; a rough patch of road;* of style, *ruggedness.*

sălebrōsus -a -um, *rugged, rough.*

Sălĭātus -ūs, m. *the office of a priest of Mars;* see Salii.

sălictum -i, n. *a plantation of willows.*

sălignus -a -um, *of willow-wood.*

Sălĭi -ōrum, m. *a college of 12 priests of Mars Gradivus;* adj. **Sălĭāris** -e, *relating to the Salii; splendid, magnificent.*

sălĭlum -i, n. *a little salt-cellar.*

sălīnae -arum, f. *salt-works, brine-pits.*

sălīnum -i, n. *a salt-cellar.*

sălĭo sălire sălŭi saltum, *to spring, leap, bound;* f. pl. of partic. as subst. **sălĭentēs** -ium, *fountains.*

sălĭunca -ae, f. *wild nard.*

sălīva -ae, f. *spittle, saliva; appetite, taste.*

sălix -ĭcis, f. *a willow.*

Sallustĭus -i, m.: C. Sallustius Crispus, *the Roman historian* Sallust, *contemporary of Cicero.*

salpa -ae, f. *a kind of stock-fish.*

salsāmentum -i, n. *fish-pickle, brine; salted or pickled fish.*

salsūra -ae, f. *salting, pickling.*

salsus -a, -um, *salted, salty;* hence *sharp, biting, witty;* adv. **salsē**.

saltātĭo -ōnis, f. *a dancing, dance.*

saltātor -ōris, m. *a dancer.*

saltātōrĭus -a -um, *of dancing.*

saltātrix -trīcis, f. *a dancing-girl.*

saltātus -ūs, m. *a dancing, dance.*

saltem, *at least, at all events.*

salto -are, *to dance,* esp. *with gesticulation;* with acc., *to represent in pantomime, to sing with gestures.*

saltŭōsus -a -um, *wooded.*

¹saltus -ūs, m. *a spring, leap, bound.*

²saltus -ūs, m. *a forest or mountain pasture; a pass, dale, ravine, glade.*

sălūbris and **sălūber** -bris -bre, *healthful, healthy, wholesome; sound, useful; healthy, vigorous.* Adv. **sălūbrĭtĕr**, *wholesomely, advantageously.*

sălūbrĭtās -ātis, f. *wholesomeness; soundness, health.*

sălum -i, n. *the open sea.*

sălūs -ūtis, f. *health, soundness; safety, welfare, well-being, salvation; a wish for a person's welfare, salutation, greeting.*

sălūtāris -e, *healthful, wholesome, advantageous;* n. pl. as subst. *remedies, medicines.* Adv. sălūtārĭtĕr.

sălūtātĭo -ōnis, f. *greeting, salutation; a call, ceremonial visit;* concr., *visitors.*

sălūtātor -ōris, m. *a visitor, caller.*

sălūtātrix -tricis, f. adj. *greeting, paying a visit.*

sălūtĭfer -fĕra -fĕrum, *health-bringing.*

sălūto -are, *to wish well, greet, call upon, pay respect to, reverence.*

salvĕo -ēre, *to be well, be in good health;* salve, salvete, as a greeting, *Good day! Good morning!,* used also in bidding farewell.

salvus -a -um, *safe, unhurt, well, all right;* salvo iure, *without infraction of law.* Adv. salvē.

sambūca -ae, f. *a species of harp.*

sambūcistria -ae, f. *a female harpist.*

Samnium -i, n. *a region of central Italy;* adj. and subst. Samnīs -itis, *Samnite, a Samnite.*

Sămōs (-ŭs) -i, f. *an island in the Aegean Sea;* adj. Sămĭus -a -um.

Sămothrācē, -ēs, Sămothrāca -ae, and Sămothrācĭa -ae, f. *Samothrace, an island in the northern Aegean.*

sānābĭlis -e, *curable.*

sānātĭo -ōnis, f. *healing, curing.*

sancĭo sancire sanxi sanctum (sancitum), *to consecrate, hallow, make inviolable, confirm, ratify, decree;* also *to forbid on pain of punishment, provide against.* Hence partic. sanctus -a -um, *consecrated, holy, sacred; pure, virtuous.* Adv. sanctē, *solemnly, conscientiously.*

sanctĭmōnĭa -ae, f. *sanctity, sacredness; purity, chastity, virtue.*

sanctĭo -ōnis, f. *a clause in a law defining a penalty.*

sanctĭtās -ātis, f. *inviolability, sanctity; purity, chastity.*

sanctĭtūdo -ĭnis, f., *sanctity.*

sanctor -ōris, m., *an enacter.*

sanctus -a -um, partic. from sancio; q.v.

sandālĭum -i, n. *a slipper, sandal.*

sandăpĭla -ae, f. *a bier used for poor people.*

sandyx -dўcis, f. *vermilion.*

sanguĭnans -antis, *bloodthirsty.*

sanguĭnārĭus -a -um, *of blood; bloodthirsty, savage.*

sanguĭnĕus -a -um, *of blood, bloody; blood-red.*

sanguĭnŏlentus -a -um, *stained with blood, bloody; wounding, injuring; blood-red.*

sanguis -ĭnis, m. (and sanguen, n.) *blood.* Transf. *blood-relationship, race, family, progeny; life-blood, strength, vigour.*

sănĭēs -ēi, f. *corrupted blood, matter; slaver, venom, poison.*

sānĭtās -ātis, f. *health, soundness; good sense, sanity;* of style, *correctness, purity.*

sanna -ae, f. *a mocking grimace.*

sannĭo -ōnis, m. *a buffoon.*

sāno -are, *to heal, cure, restore, repair.*

sānus -a, -um, *sound, healthy, uninjured; of sound mind, rational, sane;* of style, *correct.* Hence adv. sănē, *rationally, sensibly.* Transf., *really, indeed, to be sure;* with imperatives, *then, if you will;* sane quam, *exceedingly, extremely.*

săpa -ae, f. *must or new wine.*

săpĭentĭa -ae, f. *wisdom, good sense, discernment;* esp. *proficiency in philosophy, science,* etc.

săpĭo săpĕre săpĭvi or săpĭi. (1) *to taste;* with acc., *to taste of or smell of.* (2) *to have taste, be able to taste.* (3) mentally, *to discern, be sensible, be wise, think.* Hence partic. săpĭens -entis, *wise, sensible, judicious;* as subst., *a sensible, judicious person;* also *wise man, philosopher, sage.* Adv. săpĭentĕr.

săpor -ōris, m. *taste, flavour, flavouring; sense of taste; taste in style or conduct.*

Sapphō -ūs, f. *a lyric poetess of Mytilene in Lesbos.*

sarcĭna -ae, f. *a bundle, pack, burden, load.*

sarcĭnārĭus -a -um, *of burdens or baggage.*

sarcĭnātor -ōris, m. *cobbler.*

sarcĭnŭla -ae, f. *a little bundle.*

sarcĭo sarcire sarsi sartum, *to mend, patch, repair, make good.* Hence partic. sartus -a -um; sartus (et) tectus, *in good condition, well-preserved.*

sarcŏphăgus -i, m. *coffin, grave.*

sarcŭlum -i, n. *a light hoe.*

Sardēs (Sardis) -ĭum, f. pl. *Sardis, the old capital of Lydia;* adj. Sardĭānus -a -um.

Sardi -ōrum, m. *the Sardinians;* adj. Sardus, Sardŏnĭus, Sardŏus -a -um, *Sardinian;* subst. Sardĭnĭa ae, f. *Sardinia.*

sardŏnyx -nŷchis, m. and f. *a precious stone, sardonyx.*

sargus -i, m. *a salt-water fish, the sargue.*

sărisa -ae, f. *the long Macedonian pike.*

sărisŏphŏrus -i, m. *a Macedonian pikeman.*

Sarmăta -ae, m. *a Sarmatian;* subst. Sarmătĭa -ae, f. *Sarmatia;* adj. Sarmătĭcus -a -um, *Sarmatic;* adv. Sarmătĭcē; f. adj. Sarmātĭs -ĭdis.

sarmentum -i, n. *twigs, brushwood.*

sarrācum -i, n. = serracum; q.v.

sarrĭo (sărĭo) -ire -ŭi and -ivi, *to hoe, weed.*

sartāgo -ĭnis, f. *frying-pan.*

sartus -a -um, partic. from sarcio; q.v.

săt, sătăgĭto, sătăgo; see satis.

sătellĕs -ĭtis, c. *a guard, attendant; an accomplice;* plur., *escort, suite, train.*

sătĭās -ātis, f. *sufficiency, abundance; satiety.*

sătĭĕtās -ātis, f. *sufficiency, abundance; satiety.*

sătĭnĕ, sătĭn = satisne; see satis.

¹sătĭo -are, *to satisfy, fill; to cloy, satiate.*

²sătĭo -ōnis, f. *a sowing or planting;* in plur. *sown fields.*

sătĭra; see satur.

sătĭs or **săt**, *enough, sufficient;* as adv., *enough, sufficiently, fairly, quite;* compar. **sătĭus**, *better, more advantageous;* **sătĭnĕ**, **sătĭn** = satisne, *introducing questions;* **sătĭs** (or **săt**) **ăgo** or **sătăgo** -**ăgĕre**, *to satisfy or pay a creditor; to have enough to do, have one's hands full;* **sătĭs dŏ dăre**, *to give bail* or *security;* **sătĭs accĭpĭo** accĭpĕre, *to take bail* or *security;* **sătĭs făcĭo** or **sătĭsfăcĭo** -făcĕre, *to give satisfaction, satisfy, pay up, make amends;* also *to prove sufficiently.*

sătisdătĭo -ōnis, f. *a giving bail* or *security.*

sătisfactĭo -ōnis, f. *amends, reparation, apology.*

sătĭus, compar. of satis; q.v.

sător -ōris, m. *a sower, planter, begetter, father, producer.*

satrăpes -is; plur. satrapae -arum; m., *the governor of a Persian province, viceroy.*

sătur -ūra -ūrum, *full, sated, rich, copious.* F. as subst. **sătŭra** -ae, *a dish of various ingredients, a medley;* per saturam, *indiscriminately;* **sătŭra** (or **sătĭra**), ' *satire* ', *as a literary form.*

sătŭrĕia -ae, f., plur. **sătŭrĕia** -ōrum, n.; *the herb savory.*

sătŭrĭtās -ātis, f. *satiety, abundance.*

Sāturnālĭa, etc.; see Saturnus.

Sāturnus -i, m. (1) *the planet Saturn.* (2) *a mythical king of Latium.* Hence adj. **Sāturnĭus** -a -um, and **Sāturnālis** -e; n. pl. as subst. **Sāturnālĭa** -ĭum and -iorum, *a festival of Saturn beginning on the 17th of December.*

sătŭro -are, *to satisfy, fill.*

¹**sătus** -a -um, partic. from sero; q.v.

²**sătus** -ūs, m. *sowing, planting; begetting, origin.*

sătyrus -i, m. *a satyr.* Transf., *Greek Satyric drama.*

saucĭātĭo -ōnis, f. *wounding.*

saucĭo -are, *to wound, hurt.*

saucĭus -a -um, *wounded, hurt, stricken, distressed.*

sāvĭor -ari, dep. *to kiss.*

sāvĭum (suāvĭum) -i, n. *a kiss.*

saxētum -i, n. *a rocky place.*

saxĕus -a -um, *of rock, stony.*

saxĭfĭcus -a -um, *petrifying.*

saxōsus -a -um, *full of rocks, rocky.*

saxŭlum -i, n. *a little rock.*

saxum -i, n. *a rock, stone;* esp. *the Tarpeian rock.*

scăbellum (scăbillum) -i, n. *footstool; a musical instrument played with the foot.*

scăber -bra -brum, *scabby; rough.*

scăbĭēs -ĕi, f. *scab, mange, itch; roughness; itching desire.*

scăbĭōsus -a -um, *scabby; rough.*

scăbo scăbĕre scăbi, *to scratch.*

scaena (scēna) -ae, f. *stage, scene, theatre; natural background; publicity, the public eye.*

scaenālis -e, *theatrical.*

scaenĭcus -a -um, *of the stage, theatrical;* m. as subst. *a stage-hero, an actor.*

Scaevŏla -ae, m. *the left-handed, a surname of the gens Mucia.*

scaevus -a -um, *left, on the left.* Transf., *awkward.*

scālae -arum, f. pl. *a flight of stairs, ladder;* milit., *scaling-ladders.*

scalmus -i, m. *a thole-pin, rowlock.*

scalpellum -i, n. *a lancet, scalpel.*

scalpo scalpĕre scalpsi scalptum, *to carve, scrape, scratch.*

scalprum -i, n. *a chisel; a penknife.*

scammōnĕa (-mōnĭa) -ae, f. *the plant scammony.*

scamnum -i, n. *a bench, stool.*

scando scandĕre scandi scansum, *to climb, mount, rise.*

scăpha -ae, f. *a small boat, skiff.*

scăphĭum -i, n. *a pot, bowl, drinking-vessel.*

scăpŭlae -ārum, f. pl. *the shoulder-blades; the shoulders, back.*

scăpus -i, m. *a weaver's beam,* or perhaps *leash-rod.*

scărus -i, m. *a salt-water fish;* perhaps *parrot-fish.*

scătebra -ae, f. *a spouting up, bubbling up.*

scătĕo -ēre and **scăto** -ĕre, *to gush, spout up; to teem, abound.*

scătŭrrĭgo -gĭnis, f. *a bubbling spring.*

scătŭrrĭo -ire,. *to gush, bubble over.*

scaurus -a -um, *with swollen ankles.*

scazōn -ontis, m. *an iambic trimeter with a spondee or trochee in the last foot.*

scĕlĕro -are, *to pollute with guilt.* Partic. **scĕlĕrātus** -a -um, *polluted with guilt; impious, wicked; tiresome, noxious;* adv. **scĕlĕrātē**, *impiously, wickedly.*

scĕlĕrōsus -a -um, *guilty, wicked.*

scĕlestus -a -um, *guilty, wicked, accursed;* adv. **scĕlestē**.

scĕlus -ĕris, n. *a crime.* Transf., *misfortune, calamity.* As a term of abuse, *scoundrel, rascal.*

scēn-; see scaen-.

sceptrĭfer -fĕra -fĕrum, *sceptre-bearing.*

sceptrum -i, n. *a sceptre;* poet., *dominion, kingdom.*

sceptūchus -i, m. *wand-bearer, a court official.*

schēda and **scĭda** -ae, f. *a strip of papyrus bark; a leaf of paper.*

schēma -ae, f. and -ătis, n. *shape, figure, form.*

schoenŏbătēs -ae, m. *a rope-walker.*

schŏla -ae, f. *learned leisure; conversation, debate; a lecture, dissertation; a school; a sect.*

schŏlastĭcus -a -um, *of a school;* esp. *rhetorical;* m. as subst. *a student or teacher of rhetoric.*

scĭda = schida; q.v.

scientĭa -ae, f. *knowing, knowledge, acquaintance, skill.*

scīlĭcĕt, *evidently, certainly, of course;* ironically, *no doubt;* in answers, *certainly;* explanatory, *namely.*

scilla (squilla) -ae, f. *a sea-leek, squill; a crayfish* or *prawn.*

scīn = scisne; see scio.

scindo scindĕre scĭdi scissum, *to cut, rend, split; to divide, separate.* Partic. **scissus** -a -um, *torn, rent;* of the voice, *harsh.*

scintilla -ae, f. *a spark; a glimmer.*

scintillo -are, *to sparkle, glitter.*

scintillŭla -ae, f. *a little spark.*

scio scīre scivi or scii scitum, *to know, understand;* with infin., *to know how to;* with adv., scire Graece, *to understand Greek.*

Hence partic. **scĭens** -entis, *knowing, aware; understanding; versed in, acquainted with* (with genit.); adv. **scientĕr;** for **scĭtus** -a -um. see scisco.

¹**scīpio** -ōnis, m. *a staff, wand.*

²**Scīpio** -ōnis, m. *a family of the gens* Cornelia; **Scīpiădēs** -ae, *one of the family of the Scipios, a Scipio.*

scirpĕus (sirpĕus) -a -um, *of rushes:* f. as subst. *basket-work.*

scirpĭcŭlus (sirpĭcŭlus) -a -um, *of rushes;* m. and f. as subst. *a rush-basket.*

scirpus (sirpus) -i, m. *a rush, bulrush.*

sciscĭtor -ari, dep. and **sciscĭto** -are, *to inquire, examine, interrogate.*

scisco sciscĕre scīvi scitum, *to investigate, inquire;* polit. *to vote, ordain, resolve.*

Hence partic. **scĭtus** -a -um, *knowing, shrewd, judicious; pretty, fine;* adv. **scĭtē,** *skilfully;* n. of partic. as subst., *a decree, statute;* plebis scitum, *a decree of the people of* Rome.

scissus -a -um, partic. from scindo; q.v.

scītor -ari, dep., *to seek to know, inquire, ask.*

scītū, abl. sing. m. *by a decree.*

scītus -a -um, partic. from scisco; q.v.

sciūrus -i, m. *a squirrel.*

scōbis -is, f. *filings, chips, shavings, sawdust.*

scomber -bri, m. *a mackerel.*

scōpae -ārum, f. pl. *a besom, broom.*

scŏpŭlōsus -a -um, *rocky, craggy.*

scŏpŭlus -i, m. *a rock, crag, cliff, danger, ruin.*

scorpĭo -ōnis, and **scorpĭus (-ŏs)** -i, m. *a scorpion;* milit., *an engine for throwing missiles; a salt-water fish,* perhaps *the sculpin.*

scortĕus -a -um, *leathern, made of leather;* f. as subst. *a leathern garment.*

scortor -ari, dep. *to whore, go with harlots.*

scortum -i, n. *a harlot, prostitute.*

scrĕo -are, *to clear the throat, hawk, hem.*

scrība -ae, m. *a clerk, secretary, notary.*

scriblīta -ae, f. *a kind of pastry.*

scrībo scrībĕre scripsi scriptum, *to engrave, draw lines, write, write on, write about;* polit., *to draw up laws, etc.;* legal, dicam scribere, *to bring an action;* with double acc., *to appoint in writing;* milit., *to enrol.* N. of partic.

as subst. **scriptum** -i *a mark or line; a composition, piece of writing;* esp. *a decree, law.*

scrīnium -i, n. *a case for books or papers.*

scriptĭo -ōnis, f. *the act of writing; authorship, composition; wording.*

scriptĭto -are, *to write often.*

scriptor -ōris, m. *a scribe, clerk, secretary; a writer, author, composer.*

scriptŭla -ōrum, n. *the lines on a draught-board.*

scriptum -i, n. subst. from scribo; q.v.

scriptūra -ae, f. *a piece of writing, composition; a testamentary disposition; a rent paid on public pastures.*

scrīpŭlum (scrŭpŭlum, scriptŭlum) -i, m. *a small weight or measure.*

scrŏbis -is, c. *a ditch; a grave.*

scrōfa -ae, f. *a breeding sow.*

scrūpĕus and **scrūpōsus** -a -um, *of sharp stones, rugged, rough.*

scrūpŭlōsus -a -um, *full of stones, rough, rugged.* Transf., *exact, scrupulous, precise.*

scrūpŭlum = scripulum; q.v.

scrūpŭlus -i, m. *a small stone.* Transf. *an anxiety, doubt, scruple.*

scrūpus -i, m. *a sharp stone.* Transf. *a worry, anxiety.*

scrūta -ōrum, n. pl. *frippery, trash.*

scrūtor -ari, dep. *to search through, investigate, examine.*

sculpo sculpĕre sculpsi sculptum, *to carve, cut, chisel.*

sculptilis -e, *carved.*

sculptor -ōris, m. *sculptor.*

scurra -ae, m. *a dandy, man-about-town; a jester, buffoon.*

scurrīlis -e, *like a buffoon; mocking, jeering.*

scurrīlĭtās -ātis, f. *buffoonery.*

scurror -ari, dep. *to play the buffoon.*

scūtāle -is, n. *the thong of a sling.*

scūtātus -a -um, *armed with a shield.*

scūtella -ae, f. *a flat dish, saucer.*

scūtĭca -ae, f. *a whip.*

¹**scūtŭla** -ae, f. *a little square-shaped dish.*

²**scūtŭla** -ae, f. *a roller, cylinder.*

scūtŭlāta -ōrum, n. pl. *checked cloths, checks.*

scūtŭlum -i, n. *a little shield.*

scūtum -i, n. *a large quadrangular shield.*

Scylla -ae, f. *a rock at the straits between* Sicily *and* Italy, *opposite to* Charybdis; adj. **Scyllaeus** -a -um.

scymnus -i, m. *cub, whelp.*

scȳphus -i, m. *a drinking-cup, goblet.*

scȳtăla -ae and **scȳtălē** ēs, f. = scutula; q.v.

Scȳthēs (Scȳthă) -ae, m. *a Scythian;* **Scȳthia** -ae, f. *Scythia.*

sē or **sēsē,** acc. sing. and plur.; **sŭī,** genit.; **sĭbi,** dat.; **se** or **sēsē,** abl.; strengthened forms, **sēpse, sēmet;** reflexive pronoun of third person, *himself, herself, itself, themselves;* sibi velle, *to mean;* secum = cum se; inter se, *reciprocally.*

sēbum -i, n. *tallow, fat.*

sēcēdo -cēdĕre -cessi -cessum, *to go apart, withdraw.*

sēcerno -cernĕre -crēvi -crētum, *to separate, part, sunder; to distinguish; to set aside, reject.*

Hence partic. **sēcrētus** -a -um, *separate, alone, special; retired, solitary; hidden, secret;* with abl., *deprived of.* N. as subst. **sēcrētum** -i, *retirement, solitude; a secret, mystery.* Abl. as adv. **sēcrētō**, *apart, separately.*

sēcessio -ōnis, f. *a going apart, withdrawal, secession.*

sēcessus -ūs, m. *a going apart, withdrawal, retirement; a retreat, recess.*

sēcius; see secus.

sēclūdo -clūdĕre -clūsi -clūsum, *to shut off; to confine, to separate from others.*

sĕco sĕcare sĕcŭi sectum, *to cut, amputate, to wound, hurt; to divĭde, part; hence to settle disputes; to cut out, make by cutting.*

sēcretus -a -um, partic. from secerno; q.v.

secta -ae, f. *a way, mode of life, procedure; a school of thought.*

sectātor -ōris, m. *a follower, hanger-on;* plur., *train, retinue.*

sectilis -e, *cut; able to be cut.*

sectio -ōnis, f. *cutting.* Transf., *thĕ buying up of state property;* concr., *auctioned property, a lot.*

¹sector -ōris, m. *a cutter.* Transf., *a buyer of state property.*

²sector -ari, dep. *to follow eagerly; to accompany, attend;* of enemies, *to run after, chase;* in gen., *to strive after, try to get or find.*

sectūra -ae, f. *cutting;* aerariae secturae, *copper-mines.*

sēcŭbitus -ūs, m. *lying alone.*

sēcŭbo -are, -ŭi, *to sleep alone.*

sēcŭl-; see saecul-.

sēcum = cum se; see se.

sēcundāni -ōrum, m. pl. *soldiers of the second legion.*

sēcundārius -a -um, *second-rate.*

sēcundo -are, *to favour, assist.*

sēcundum: adv., *after, behind;* prep., with acc., *following, after, along beside; during; in addition to; next after, next to; according to; in favour of.*

sēcundus -a -um. (1) *going after, second, following; inferior, second-rate.* (2) *going the same way, attending, favouring;* secundo flumine, *downstream;* res secundae, *prosperity, success.* As subst.: n. abl. sing. **sēcundō**, *secondly;* f. pl. **sēcundae** -ārum, *the second role, second fiddle;* n. pl. **sēcundā** -ōrum, *prosperity, success.*

sēcūrĭfer -fĕra -fĕrum, and **sēcūrĭger** -gĕra -gĕrum, *carrying an axe.*

sēcūris -is, f. *an axe, hatchet;* esp. *the headsman's axe;* hence *supreme power, Roman supremacy.*

sēcūrĭtās -ātis, f. *freedom from care; peace of mind, composure; careless-*

ness, false confidence. Transf., *freedom from danger, security.*

sēcūrus -a -um, *free from care, unconcerned, fearless, tranquil; careless;* objectively, *safe, secure.* Adv. **sēcūrē.**

¹sēcus, n. indecl., *sex.*

²sēcŭs, adv. *otherwise, not so;* foll. by atque (ac), or quam, *otherwise than, differently from;* non secus, haud secus, *just so.* Transf., *not as one would wish,* i.e. *wrongly, badly.* Compar. **sēquĭus** or **sētĭus**, *otherwise, not so; less; rather badly.*

sēcūtor -ōris, m. *a gladiator armed with sword and shield.*

sēd (sĕt), *but, however;* sed enim, *but in fact; confirming, and indeed, and what is more.*

sēdātio -ōnis, f. *allaying, soothing.*

sēdĕcim, *sixteen.*

sēdēcŭla -ae, f. *a low seat, stool.*

sēdĕo sēdēre sēdi sessum, *to sit; to sit in council or judgment; to sit about, be inactive;* milit. *to remain encamped;* of things, *to be settled, stay fixed;* of resolves, *to be firmly determined.*

sēdēs -is, f. *a seat; a chair, throne; an abode, home;* of things, *place, seat, base, foundation.*

sēdĭle -is, n. *a seat, bench.*

sēdītio -ōnis, f. *insurrection, rising, mutiny; dissension, quarrel.*

sēdītiōsus -a -um, *quarrelsome, turbulent, restless;* adv. **sēdītiōsē.**

sēdo -are, *to settle, soothe, calm, allay;* partic. **sēdātus** -a -um, *calm, composed;* adv. **sēdātē.**

sēdūco -dūcĕre -duxi -ductum, *to lead apart, turn aside, separate;* partic. **sēductus** -a -um, *remote, distant.*

sēductio -ōnis, f. *leading aside.*

sēdŭlĭtās -ātis, f. *zeal, application.*

sēdŭlus -a -um, *busy, diligent;* in bad sense, *officious.* N. abl. as adv. **sēdŭlō**, *busily; purposely, designedly.*

sĕgĕs -ĕtis, f. *a cornfield; standing corn, a crop;* in gen., *field, ground, soil; source, origin; profit.*

segmentātus -a -um, *adorned with borders or patches.*

segmentum -i, n. *a cutting, shred;* plur., *borders or patches of purple or gold.*

segnĭpēs -pēdis, *slow-footed.*

segnis -e, *slow, tardy, sluggish, lingering.* N. acc. as adv. **segnĕ,** and adv. **segnĭtĕr,** *slowly, sluggishly.*

segnĭtia -ae, and **segnĭtĭēs** -ēi, f. *sluggishness, slowness.*

segrĕgo -are, *to segregate, separate, remove.*

sēiŭgātus -a -um, *separated.*

sēiŭgis -is, m. *a chariot drawn by six horses.*

sēiunctim, *separately.*

sēiunctio -ōnis, f. *separation.*

sēiungo -iungĕre -iunxi -iunctum, *to separate, sever, disjoin.*

sēlectio -ōnis, f. *choosing out, selection.*

Sēleucus -i, m. *name of several kings of Syria.*

sēlibra -ae, f. *half a pound.*

sēligo -lĭgĕre -lēgi -lectum, *to choose, select.*

sella -ae, f. *a seat, chair, stool*; **sella** (curulis), *a magistrate's seat*; **sella** (gestatoria), *a sedan-chair.*

sellisternia -ōrum, n. pl. *religious banquets in honour of goddesses.*

sellŭla -ae, f. *a little chair.*

sellŭlārius -i, m. *a sedentary worker.*

sēmĕl, *once, a single time; for the first time; once for all*; indef., *once, ever, at any time.*

Sĕmĕla -ae, and **Sĕmĕlē** -ēs, f. *mother of Bacchus.*

sēmen -ĭnis, n. *seed; a seedling, scion, shoot; a stock, race; an element; a cause, origin; an author, instigator.*

sēmentĭfer -fĕra -fĕrum, *seed-bearing, fruitful.*

sēmentis -is, *a sowing or planting*; plur., **sementes**, *young growing corn.*

sēmentīvus -a -um, *of seed-time.*

sēmestris (**sēmenstris**) -e, *of six months, lasting six months.*

sēmēsus -a -um, *half-eaten.*

sēmĭădăpertus -a -um, *half-open.*

sēmĭănimis -e and **sēmĭănimus** -a -um, *half-alive, half-dead.*

sēmĭăpertus -a -um, *half-open.*

sēmĭbōs -bŏvis, m. *half-ox.*

sēmĭcăper -pri, m. *half-goat.*

sēmĭcrĕmātus and **sēmĭcrĕmus** -a -um, *half-burnt.*

sēmĭcŭbĭtālis -e, *half a cubit long.*

sēmĭdĕus -a -um, *half-divine*; as subst., *a demigod.*

sēmĭdoctus -a -um, *half-taught.*

sēmĭermis (**sēmĭmermis**) -e and **sēmĭermus** (**sēmĭmermus**) -a -um, *half-armed, half-equipped.*

sēmĭēsus = semesus; q.v.

sēmĭfactus -a -um, *half-done, half-finished.*

sēmĭfer -fĕra -fĕrum, *half-animal; half-savage.*

sēmĭgermānus -a -um, *half-German.*

sēmĭgrăvis -e, *half-overcome.*

sēmĭgro -are, *to go away, depart.*

sēmĭhians -antis, *half-open.*

sēmĭhŏmo -hŏmĭnis, m. *half-man; half-wild.*

sēmĭhora -ae, f. *half an hour.*

sēmĭlăcer -cĕra -cĕrum, *half-mangled.*

sēmĭlīber -bĕra -bĕrum, *half-free.*

sēmĭlixa -ae, m. *half a sutler.*

sēmĭmărīnus -a -um, *half in the sea.*

sēmĭmas -măris, m. *half-male, hermaphrodite; castrated.*

sēmĭnārĭum -i, n. *a plantation, nursery.*

sēmĭnātor -oris, m. *begetter, author.*

sēmĭnex -nĕcis, *half-dead.*

sēmĭnĭum -i, n. *a begetting; a race or breed.*

sēmĭno -are, *to sow, plant; to beget, produce.*

sēmĭnūdus -a -um, *half-naked; ill-protected.*

sēmĭplēnus -a -um, *half-full, half-manned.*

sēmĭpŭtātus -a -um, *half-pruned.*

sēmĭrēductus -a -um, *half bent back.*

sēmĭrēfectus -a -um, *half-repaired.*

sēmĭrŭtus -a -um, *half-ruined, half pulled down.*

sēmis -issis, m. *the half of anything*, e.g. of an as or iuger; as a rate of interest = 6 *per cent per annum.*

sēmĭsĕpultus -a -um, *half-buried.*

sēmĭsomnus -a -um and **sēmĭsomni̇̈s** -e, *half-asleep, drowsy.*

sēmĭsŭpīnus -a -um, *half on the back.*

sēmĭta -ae, f. *a narrow way, footpath.*

sēmĭtālis -e, and **sēmĭtārius** -a -um *of the footpaths.*

sēmĭustŭlātus = semustulatus; q.v.

sēmĭustus (**sēmustus**) -a -um, *half-burnt.*

sēmĭvir -vĭri, m. adj., *half-man half-animal; hermaphrodite; castrated, effeminate.*

sēmĭvīvus -a -um, *half-dead, very faint.*

sēmŏdĭus -i, m. *half a modius.*

sēmŏvĕo -mŏvēre -mōvi -mōtum, *to move away, set aside, separate*; partic. **sēmōtus** -a -um, *remote distant.*

semper, *always, at all times.*

sempiternus -a -um, *continual, ever-lasting.*

Semprōnĭus -a -um, *name of a Roman gens.*

sēmuncia -ae, f. *half an uncia.*

sēmunciārius -a- um, *of the fraction* 1/24: faenus, 1/24 *per cent monthly,* i.e. ½ *per cent per annum.*

sēmustŭlātus (**sēmĭustŭlātus**) -a -um *half-burnt.*

sēnācŭlum -i, n. *an open space in the Forum, used by the Senate.*

sēnārĭŏlus -i, m. *a trifling senarius.*

sēnārĭus -a -um, *composed of six in a group*; senarius (versus), m. a senarius, *a verse of six feet.*

sēnātor -ōris, m. *a member of the senate, a senator.*

sēnātōrius -a -um, *of a senator, senatorial.*

sēnātus -ūs, (or -i), m *a council of elders, the Senate*; senatus (senati) consultum, *a formal resolution of the senate.*

Sĕnĕca -ae, m. M. Annaeus Seneca, *a rhetorician from Corduba in Spain*; L. Annaeus Seneca, *his son, a Stoic philosopher, tutor of Nero.*

¹**sĕnectus** -a -um, *old, aged*; f. as subst. **sĕnecta** -ae, *old age.*

²**sĕnectūs** -ūtis, f. *old age*; concr., *old men.*

sĕnĕo -ēre, *to be old.*

sĕnesco senescĕre sĕnŭi, *to grow old; to flag, wane.*

sĕnex sĕnis; compar. **sĕnĭor**: adj., *old, aged*; subst., *an old person.*

sēni -ae -a, *six at a time, or six each.*

sĕnīlis -e, *of an old man, senile*; adv. **sĕnīlĭter.**

sĕnĭo -ōnis, m. *the number six upon dice.*

sĕnĭor, compar. of senex; q.v.

sĕnĭum -i, n. *old age; decline, decay; gloom, grief.*

sensĭcŭlus -i, m. *a little sentence.*

sensĭfer -fĕra -fĕrum, *producing sensation.*

sensĭlis -e, *having sensation, sensitive.*

sensim, *just perceptibly, gradually, by degrees.*

sensus -ūs, m. *sense, sensation; feeling, attitude; judgment, perception, understanding; sense, meaning* of words, etc.; *a sentence.*

sententĭa -ae, f. *a way of thinking, opinion, thought, meaning, purpose; a decision, vote; meaning, sense* of words, etc.; *a sentence, period;* esp., *a maxim, aphorism.*

sententĭŏla -ae, f. *a short sentence, maxim, aphorism.*

sententĭōsus -a -um, *pithy, sententious;* adv. sententĭōsē.

sentĭcētum -i, n. *a thorn-brake.*

sentĭna -ae, f. *bilge-water; rabble, dregs of the population.*

sentĭo sentire sensi sensum, *to feel, perceive; to experience, feel the force of* a thing; *to realize* a truth; *to hold* an opinion, *judge, suppose; legal, to decide, to vote.* N. pl. of partic. as subst. sensa -ōrum, *thoughts, sentiments.*

sentis -is, c. *a thorn-bush, briar.*

sentisco -ĕre, *to begin to perceive*

sentus -a -um, *neglected, rough.*

sĕorsum, sorsum, sorsus, *apart, separately.*

sēpărātim, *apart, separately, differently.*

sēpărātĭo -ōnis, f. *separation, severance.*

sēpăro -are, *to sever, separate; to consider or treat separately.* Hence partic. sēpărātus -a -um, *separate, distinct;* compar. adv. sēpărātĭŭs, *less closely.*

sēpĕlĭo -pĕlire -pĕlivi and -pĕlli -pultum, *to bury; to ruin, destroy;* partic. sĕpultus, *buried, sunk, immersed.*

sēp-; see also saep-.

sēpĭa -ae, f. *cuttle-fish.*

sēpōno -pōnĕre -pŏsŭi -pŏsĭtum, *to put on one side, place apart, reserve; to put out of the way, banish; to distinguish, divide.* Partic. sēpŏsĭtus -a -um, *distant, remote; choice, select.*

sepse = se ipse; see ipse.

septem, *seven.*

September -bris, *of September;* (mensis) September, *the seventh month of the Roman year, September.*

septemdĕcim, *seventeen.*

septemflŭus -a -um, *with seven mouths.*

septemgĕmĭnus -a -um, *sevenfold.*

septemplex -plicis, *sevenfold.*

septemtrĭōnālis -e, *northern.*

septemtrĭōnēs (septen-) -um, m. pl. *the seven stars of either the Great Bear or the Little Bear;* in gen., *the north; the north wind.*

septemvĭr -viri, m. *one of the septemviri, a college or guild of seven persons;* adj. septemvĭrālis -e, *of septemviri;* subst. septemvĭrātus -ūs, m. *the office of a septemvir.*

septēnārĭus -a -um, *containing seven;* m. pl. as subst. septēnāriī, *verses containing seven feet, heptameters.*

septendĕcim = septemdecim; q.v.

septēni -ae, -a, *seven at a time or seven each.*

septentrĭo = septemtrio; q.v.

septĭes (-iens), *seven times.*

septĭmānus -a -um, *of the seventh;* m. pl. as subst. *soldiers of the seventh legion.*

septĭmus (septŭmus) -a -um, *seventh;* septĭmum, *for the seventh time.*

septĭmus dĕcĭmus -a -um, *seventeenth.*

septingentēsĭmus (-ensĭmus) -a -um, *seven hundredth.*

septingenti -ae -a, *seven hundred.*

septŭāgēsĭmus (-ensĭmus) -a -um, *seventieth.*

septŭāginta, *seventy.*

septŭennis -e, *of seven years.*

septum = saeptum; q.v.

septunx -uncis, m. *seven-twelfths.*

sĕpulcrālis -e, *of a tomb, sepulchral.*

sĕpulcrētum -i, n. *a burial-place, cemetery.*

sĕpulcrum -i n., *a place of burial, grave, tomb.*

sĕpultūra -ae, f. *burial, interment;* also *the burning of a dead body.*

Sēquăna -ae, m. *a river of Gaul (now the Seine).*

sĕquax -ācis, *following, attending, pursuing.*

sĕquester -tri or -tris, m. *a depositary; a go-between, agent, mediator.*

sĕquestra -ae, f. *a mediator.*

sēquĭus = secius, compar. of secus; q.v.

sĕquor sĕqui sĕcūtus, dep. *to follow, accompany, attend; to pursue, chase;* in time, *to follow, ensue; to follow logically, follow as a consequence;* of property, *to go to, fall to; to conform to; to strive after, aim at.*

sēra -ae, f. *a bar or bolt.*

sērēnĭtās -ātis, f. *clear weather.*

sērēno -are, *to make clear, make bright.*

sērēnus -a -um, *clear, bright, fair;* n. as subst. *fair weather.*

Sērēs -um, m. *the Chinese famous for their silks;* adj. Sērĭcus -a -um, *Chinese; silken.*

sēresco -ere, *to become dry.*

sērĭa -ae, f. *a large jar.*

sērĭes, acc. -em, abl. -e, f. *a row, chain, series; a line of descent, lineage.*

sērĭus -a -um, *serious, earnest;* n. as subst. *earnest, seriousness;* abl. as adv. sērĭō, *in earnest, seriously.*

sermo -ōnis, m. *talk, conversation; discussion; common talk, report, rumour; a subject of conversation; a conversational style, or prose; any manner of speaking, style, expression, diction, language, dialect.*

sermōcĭnor -ari, dep. *to converse, talk, discuss.*

sermuncŭlus -i, m. *rumour, tittle-tattle.*

¹sĕro sĕrĕre sēvi sătum, *to sow, set, plant;* n. pl. of partic. as subst., sata -ōrum, *standing corn, crops; to beget, engender, bring forth;* partic. sătus -a -um, *sprung, born;* in gen., *to produce, give rise to.*

²sĕro sĕrĕre sĕrŭi sertum, *to join together, put in a row, connect,* partic. sertus -a -um, *linked, connected;* n. as subst. sertum -i, and plur. serta -orum, *a garland, wreath;* also f. serta -ae.

serpens -entis, c. *a snake, serpent.*

serpentīgĕna -ae, m. *sprung from a serpent.*

serpentīpēs -pēdis, *snake-footed.*

serpĕrastra -orum, n. *bandages or knee-splints.*

serpo serpĕre serpsi serptum, *to creep, crawl, advance slowly.*

serpyllum (-pillum, -pullum) -i, n. *wild thyme.*

serra -ae, f. *a saw.*

serrācum (sarr-) -i, n. *a kind of waggon.*

serrātus -a -um, *toothed like a saw, serrated;* m. pl. as subst. (sc. nummi), *milled coins.*

serrŭla -ae, f. *a little saw.*

sertum; see sero.

sĕrum -i, n. *whey.*

sĕrus -a -um, *late, too late;* n. as subst. serum -i, *a late hour;* n. abl. sing. as adv. sērō, *late, too late.*

serva -ae, f. see servus.

servābilis -e, *able to be saved.*

servātor -ōris, m. and servātrix -īcis, f., *a preserver, saviour; a watcher.*

servīlis -e, *of a slave, servile;* adv. servīlĭter.

Servīlius -a -um, *name of Roman gens.*

servĭo -ire, (with dat.), *to be a slave, to serve, help, gratify;* legal, of buildings, etc., *to be subject to certain rights,* e.g. *to be mortgaged.*

servĭtĭum -i, n. *slavery, servitude, subjection;* concr., *slaves, servants, a household.*

servĭtūdo -inis, f. *slavery, servitude.*

servĭtūs -ūtis, f. *slavery, servitude;* in gen., *subjection, obedience;* legal, of houses, etc., *liability to certain burdens,* e.g. *a right of way;* concr., *slaves.*

servo -are, *to watch over, observe; to keep, protect, save; to lay up, reserve; to keep, retain a promise,* etc.; *to keep to, stay in a place.* Partic., in superl., servantissimus -i, *most careful, most observant.*

servŭlus (servŏlus) -i, m. and servŭla (servŏla) -ae, f. *a young slave.*

servus -a -um, adj., *serving, servile; subject;* legal, of lands, etc., *subject to other rights;* m. and f. as subst., *a slave, servant.*

sescēnāris -e, *a year and a half old.*

sescēnārius -a -um, *consisting of six hundred.*

sescēni -ae -a, *six hundred at a time or six hundred each.*

sescentēsimus (-ensimus) -a -um, *six hundredth.*

sescenti -ae -a, *six hundred;* in gen., *countless.*

sescentiēs (-iens), *six hundred times.*

sĕsĕlis -is, f. *a plant, hartwort.*

sesquī, *one half more, half as much again.*

sesquīalter -altĕra -altĕrum, *one and a half.*

sesquīhōra -ae, f. *an hour and a half.*

sesquīmōdius -i, m. *a modius and a half.*

sesquīoctāvus -a -um, *containing 9/8 of a thing.*

sesquīpĕdālis -e, *a foot and a half long.*

sesquīpēs -pĕdis, m. *a foot and a half long, wide,* etc.

sesquīplāga -ae, f. *a blow and a half.*

sesquīplex -plīcis, *one and a half times as much.*

sesquītertius -a -um, *containing 4/3 of anything.*

sessĭbŭlum -i, n. *a seat, stool, chair.*

sessĭlis -e, *fit for sitting;* of plants, *low, dwarf.*

sessĭo -ōnis, f. *the act of sitting; loitering, idling; a session; a place for sitting, seat.*

sessĭto -are, *to sit much, sit often.*

sessĭuncŭla -ae, f. *a little company or assembly.*

sessor -ōris, m. *a sitter; an inhabitant.*

sestertius -a -um, *consisting of two and a half;* m. as subst. sestertius -i, *a sesterce, a silver coin,* = ¼ denarius, = 2½ asses.

Sestius -a -um, *name of a Roman gens.*

sēt = sed; q.v.

sēta = saeta; q.v.

seu; see sive.

sĕvērĭtās -ātis, and sĕvērĭtūdo -inis f. *gravity, sternness.*

sĕvērus -a -um, *grave, serious, strict, stern, hard;* adv. sĕvērē.

sēvŏco -are, *to call aside, withdraw, separate.*

sēvum = sebum; q.v.

sex, *six.*

sexāgēnārius -a -um, *containing sixty; sixty years old.*

sexāgēni -ae -a, *sixty at a time,* or *sixty each.*

sexāgēsĭmus (-ensĭmus) -a -um, *sixtieth.*

sexāgiēs (-iens), *sixty times.*

sexāgintā, *sixty.*

sexangŭlus -a -um, *hexagonal.*

sexcen-; see sescen-.

sexdĕcim = sedecim; q.v.

sexennis -e, *six years old.*

sexennium -i, n. *a period of six years.*

sexiēs (-iens), *six times.*

sexprimi -ōrum, m. *a board of six magistrates in a provincial town.*

sextādĕcĭmāni -orum, m. pl. *soldiers of the 16th legion.*

sextans -antis, m. *one sixth.*

sextārius -i, m. *one sixth,* esp. of a congius (about a pint).

Sextīlis -e, *of the sixth month of the old Roman year;* sextilis (mensis), *the sixth month,* afterwards called Augustus.

sextŭla -ae, f. 1/72.

sextus -a -um, *sixth;* sextum, *for the sixth time.*

sextusdĕcĭmus -a -um, *sixteenth.*

sexus -ūs, m. *sex.*

sī, *if, supposing that*; quod si, *and if, but if*; si modo, *if only*; si quis, *if anybody*; si non, si minus, nisi, *if not, unless.*

sibila -ōrum, n. pl.: as adj., *hissing*; as subst., = plur. of sibilus (q.v.).

sibĭlo -are,: intransit., *to hiss, whistle*; transit., *to hiss at.*

sibĭlus -i, m. (poet. plur. sibila; q.v.), *a hissing, whistling.*

Sĭbylla -ae, f. *a prophetess of Apollo, a Sibyl*; adj. **Sĭbyllīnus** -a -um, *of the Sibyl, Sibylline.*

sīc, *so, thus, in this way; like this, as follows; in that case, with this limitation;* leading up to consecutive clause, *so much, to such a degree;* interrog. **sīcĭnĕ**, *is it thus that?*

sīca -ae, f. *dagger, dirk, poniard.*

Sĭcāni -ōrum, m. pl. *an ancient people of Sicily*; adj. **Sĭcānus** and **Sĭcānĭus** -a -um, *Sicanian*; subst. **Sĭcānia** -ae, f. *Sicania = Sicily.*

sĭcārĭus -i, m. *an assassin, murderer.*

siccĭtās -ātis, f. *dryness, drought; sound health;* of style *plainness, simplicity.*

sicco -are, *to make dry, to dry; to stanch; to drain.*

siccus -a -um, *dry; thirsting, thirsty;* of health, *sound; sober, temperate;* of style *plain, simple;* adv. **siccē**

Sĭcĭlia -ae, f.; see Siculi.

sĭcĭnĕ ; see sic.

sīcŭbĭ, *if anywhere.*

Sĭcŭli -ōrum, m. pl., *the Sicilians*; adj. **Sĭcŭlus** -a -um, *Sicilian*; subst. **Sĭcĭlia** -ae, f. *Sicily.*

sīcunde, *if from anywhere.*

sīcŭt and **sīcŭti**, *as, just as; as for example; as it were;* with verb in subj., *just as if.*

Sĭcyŏn -ōnis, f. *a city in the Peloponnese*; adj. **Sĭcyŏnĭus** -a -um, *Sicyonian*; n. pl. as subst. *a kind of soft shoes from Sicyon.*

sīdĕrĕus -a -um, *of the stars starry; gleaming.*

sīdo sīdĕre sīdi and sēdi sessum, *to sit or sink down, settle, alight; to remain lying or fixed;* naut. *to stick fast, be stranded;* of feelings, *to subside.*

Sĭdōn -onis, f. *a city of Phoenicia*; adj. **Sĭdōnĭus** -a -um; f. adj. **Sĭdōnĭs** -īdis.

sīdus -ĕris, n. *a constellation, or a single star; any luminary, heavenly body; time of year, season, weather;* in astrology, *star, destiny;* plur., *the heavens.* Transf., *pride, glory.*

sĭgilla -ōrum, n. pl. *small figures, images; a seal.*

sĭgillātus -a -um, *adorned with small figures.*

sigma -ătis, n. *the Greek letter sigma; a semicircular dining-couch.*

signātor -ōris, m. *one who seals; a witness.*

signĭfer -fĕra -fĕrum, *bearing signs or figures; covered with constellations.* M. as subst. **signĭfer** -fĕri *a standard-bearer; a leader.*

signĭfĭcātĭo -ōnis, f. *indication, sign, token; sign of assent, approbation; emphasis; meaning, signification.*

signĭfĭco -are, *to indicate, show; to foreshow; to mean, signify;* partic. **signĭfĭcans** -antis, *distinct, clear;* adv. **signĭfĭcantĕr.**

signo -are, *to mark, inscribe; to seal, seal up; to coin, stamp money.* Transf., *to impress, indicate; to observe, notice.*

signum -i, n. *a sign, mark, token; a warning, symptom;* milit., *a standard, banner, ensign,* or *a signal, order, command,* or *a watchword, password; a figure, image, statute; a seal, signet; a group of stars, constellation.*

sĭlānus -i, m. *a fountain.*

sĭlentium -ī, n. *silence, stillness, quiet; repose; obscurity.*

sĭlĕo -ēre -ŭi, *to be still, silent;* with acc., *to be silent about; to be still, rest, be inactive;* partic. **sĭlens** -entis, *silent, still;* pl. as subst. *the dead.*

sĭler -ĕris, n. *the brook-willow.*

sĭlesco -ere, *to become silent, grow still.*

sĭlex -icis, m. (rarely f.), *any hard stone, such as flint; crag, rock, cliff.*

sĭlicernium -i, n. *a funeral feast.*

sĭlīgo -inis, f. *wheat; wheaten flour.*

sĭlĭqua -ae, f. *a husk, pod, shell;* in plur., *pulse.*

Sĭlius -a -um, *name of Roman gens.*

Sĭlūres -um, pl. *a British people.*

sĭlus -a -um, *snub-nosed, pug-nosed.*

silva, *a wood, forest; bush; a plantation, grove; a mass, plenty, abundance.*

Silvānus -i, m. *god of woods and forests.*

silvesco -ĕre, *of a vine, to run wild, run to wood.*

silvestris -e, *of woods; wooded; wild, rural.*

silvĭcŏla -ae, m. and f. and **silvĭcultrix** -tricis, f. *inhabiting woods.*

silvĭfrăgus -a -um, *shattering the woods.*

silvōsus -a -um *well wooded.*

sīmĭa -ae, f. *ape, monkey.*

sĭmĭlis -e; compar. similior, superl. simillimus; *like, resembling, similar* (with genit. or dat.); veri similis, *probable;* n. as subst. *a resemblance* or *comparison;* adv. **sĭmĭlĭtĕr**, *similarly.*

sĭmĭlĭtūdo -ĭnis, f. *likeness, resemblance;* veri similitudo, *probability; intended likeness, imitation; a metaphor, simile; uniformity, monotony.*

sĭmĭlo = simulo; q.v.

sĭmĭŏlus -i, m. *little ape.*

sĭmĭtu, *together.*

sīmĭus -i, m. *ape, monkey.*

simplex -plicis; *simple, single; unmixed, pure, plain, absolute; morally simple, straightforward.* Adv. **simplĭcĭtĕr**, *simply, plainly; artlessly; frankly.*

simplĭcĭtās -ātis, f. *simplicity; straightforwardness, honesty, candour.*

simplum -i, m. *the simple sum or number* (opp. double, etc.).

simpŭlum -i, n. *a ladle.*

simpŭvium -i, n. *a sacrificial bowl.*

sĭmul, *at once, at the same time, together;* simul atque (ac), *as soon as.*

sĭmŭlacrum -i, n. *an image, likeness, portrait; effigy, a shade, ghost, imitation, phantom, appearance.*

sĭmŭlāmen -ĭnis, n. *an imitation.*

sĭmŭlātĭo -ōnis, f. *assumed appearance, pretence, feint.*

sĭmŭlātor -ōris, m. *an imitator; a pretender, feigner.*

sĭmŭlo -are, *to make like, cause to resemble; to make a copy of, to represent; to play the part of; to pretend a thing is so, simulate, feign;* partic. **sĭmŭlans** -antis, *imitating, imitative;* adv. from perf. partic. **sĭmŭlātē,** *feignedly.*

sĭmultās -ātis, f. *a clash, rivalry, feud.*

sĭmŭlus -a -um, *rather snub-nosed.*

sĭmus -a -um, *snub-nosed.*

sĭn, conj. *but if, if however.*

sĭnāpi -is, n. and **sĭnāpis** -is, f. *mustard.*

sincērĭtās -ātis, f. *purity, soundness, integrity.*

sincērus -a -um, *pure, whole, sound, genuine, uncorrupt;* adv. **sincērē,** *honestly, frankly.*

sincĭput -pĭtis, n. *half a head; the smoked chap of a pig.*

sindōn -ōnis, f. *fine cotton cloth, muslin.*

sĭnĕ, prep. with abl., *without.*

singillātim, *singly, one by one.*

singŭlāris -e, *alone, single individual, singular; unique, extraordinary.* Adv. **singŭlārĭtĕr,** *singly; in the singular number; particularly, extraordinarily.*

singŭli; *see* singulus.

singultim, *with sobs.*

singulto -are: intransit., *to gasp, sob;* transit., *to sob out, gasp out.*

singultus -ūs, m. *a sobbing, gasping.*

singŭlus -a -um, more freq. plur. **singŭli** -ae, -a, *single, separate, one at a time;* distributive, *one each.*

sĭnister -tra -trum, *left, on the left hand; wrong, perverse;· unfavourable, adverse;* sometimes, in augury, *favourable.* F. as subst. **sĭnistra** -ae, *the left hand;* also *the left side.* Adv. **sĭnistrē,** *wrongly, unfavourably.*

sĭnistrorsus (-orsum), *to the left.*

sĭno sĭnĕre sĭvi sĭtum, *to let alone, leave; to let, allow, permit;* partic. **sĭtus** -a -um, *placed, laid down; lying, situated.*

Sĭnōpa -ae, and **Sĭnōpē** -ēs, f. *a town on the Black Sea.*

sĭnum; *see* ¹sinus.

sĭnŭo -are, *to bend, curve.*

sĭnŭōsus -a -um, *winding, sinuous.* Transf., *roundabout, diffuse.*

¹sĭnus -i, m. and **sĭnum** -i, n. *a large bowl.*

²sĭnus -ūs, m. *a curve, fold, winding;* of dress, *a fold, pocket, lap;* in a coastline, *a bay, gulf.* Transf., *heart, secret feelings.*

sĭpārium -i, n. *a curtain; a drop-scene at a theatre.*

sĭpho (sĭfo) -ōnis, m. *a siphon; a fire-engine.*

sĭquando, *if ever.*

sĭquĭdem, *if indeed;* sometimes *since, because.*

Sīrēn -ēnis, f., usually plur. **Sīrēnes** -um, *the Sirens, nymphs who by their song lured mariners to destruction.*

Sīrĭus -i, m. *the Dog-Star Sirius.*

sīs = (1) si vis; *see* volo. (2) second sing. of pres. subj. of sum; q.v. (3) dat. or abl. plur. of suus; q.v.

sisto sistĕre stĭti stătum: transit., *to cause to stand, set, place;* legal, *to cause to appear in court;* vadimonium sistere, *to appear on the appointed day; to stop, check; to establish firmly;* intransit., *to place oneself, stand;* legal, *to present oneself in court; to stand still to halt; to stand firm.*

Hence partic. **stătus** -a -um, *fixed, determined, regular.*

sistrum -i, n. *a sort of rattle used in the worship of Isis.*

sĭsymbrĭum -i, n. *an aromatic herb, perhaps mint.*

Sĭsўphus -i, m. *a robber, condemned in the lower world to roll a stone uphill for ever.*

sĭtella -ae, f. *an urn for drawing lots.*

sĭtĭcŭlōsus -a -um, *very dry, parched.*

sĭtĭo -ire: intransit., *to thirst, to be thirsty, dry, parched;* transit., *to thirst for, thirst after;* partic. **sĭtĭens** -entis, *thirsty, dry, parched; eager, desirous;* adv. **sĭtĭentĕr.**

sĭtis -is, f. *thirst; dryness, drought; eager desire.*

sĭtĭtor -ōris, m. *a thirster.*

sittўbus -i, m. *a strip of parchment showing the title of a book.*

sĭtŭla -ae, f. *a jar.*

¹sĭtus -a -um, partic. from sino; q.v.

²sĭtus -ūs, m. (1) *layout, site, position, situation.* (2) *being left; neglect, dirt, decay; mental rusting, dullness.*

sīvĕ and **sĕū,** *or if;* sive (seu) . . . sive (seu), *whether . . . or.*

smāragdus -i, m. and f. *emerald.*

sŏbŏles, sŏbŏlesco = suboles, subolesco; q.v.

sŏbrīnus -i, m. and **sōbrīna** -ae, f. *a cousin on the mother's side.*

sōbrĭus -a -um, *sober; without wine; moderate, frugal; sober-minded, reasonable, sensible.* Adv. **sōbrĭē.**

soccŭlus -i, m. *a little soccus:* q.v.

soccus -i, m. *a light shoe or slipper,* esp. *as worn by comic actors.*

sŏcer -ĕri, m. *father-in-law;* plur., soceri, *father- and mother-in-law.*

sŏcĭa -ae, f., *see* socius.

sŏcĭābĭlis -e, *easily united, compatible.*

sŏcĭālis -e, *of partners or allies; conjugal; sociable.* Adv. **sŏcĭālĭtĕr,** *sociably.*

sŏcĭĕtās -ātis, f. *partnership, fellowship, association, alliance.*

sŏcĭo -are, *to unite, combine, associate.*

sŏcĭus -a -um, *sharing, associated, allied.* M. and f. as subst. *a partner comrade, associate, ally.*

sōcordĭa (sēcordĭa) -ae, f. *folly, stupidity; negligence, indolence.*

sŏcors -cordis, *weak-minded, stupid; negligent, slothful, careless*; compar. adv. **sŏcordĭus**, *too feebly*.

Sŏcrătēs -is, m. *the Athenian philosopher, put to death in 399 B.C.* Adj. **Sŏcrătĭcus** -a -um, *Socratic*; m. pl. as subst., *followers of Socrates*.

socrus -ūs, f. *mother-in-law*.

sŏdālĭcĭum -i, n. *an association; esp. a secret society*; in gen., *comradeship*.

sŏdālĭcĭus -a -um, *of companionship*.

sŏdālis -is, c. *member of an association, esp. of a priesthood or a secret society*; in gen., *a comrade*; of things, *companion, attendant on*.

sŏdālĭtās -ātis, f. *an association; comradeship, intimacy*.

sŏdēs, *if you please, with your leave*.

sōl sōlis, m. *the sun*; poet., *a day*; personif., *the Sun-god*.

sōlācĭŏlum -i, n. *a small consolation*.

sōlācĭum -i, n. *consolation, comfort, relief*.

sōlāmen -ĭnis, n. *consolation comfort*.

sōlāris -e, *of the sun, solar*.

sōlārĭum -i, n. *a sundial; a terrace exposed to the sun*.

sōlātŏr ōris, m. *a consoler, comforter*.

soldūrĭi -ōrum, m. pl. *retainers, vassals*.

soldus = solidus; q.v.

sŏlĕa -ae, f. *a sandal; a kind of fetter; a shoe for an animal; a fish, the sole*.

sŏlĕātus -a -um, *wearing sandals*.

sŏlennis = sollemnis; q.v.

sŏlĕo sŏlēre sŏlĭtus sum, *to be accustomed*; ut solet, *as usual*; partic. **sŏlĭtus** -a -um, *accustomed, habitual, usual*; n. as subst. *that which is usual*.

sōlers = sollers; q.v.

sŏlĭdĭtās -ātis, f. *solidity*.

sŏlĭdo -are, *to make firm or solid*.

sŏlĭdus (soldus) -a -um, *dense, solid; whole, complete, entire; firm, enduring, real*; n. as subst., *firm ground, solid substance, entirety*. Adv. **sŏlĭdē**, *firmly*; scire, *to know for certain*.

sōlĭferrĕum -i, n. *a javelin entirely of iron*.

sŏlistĭmus -a -um; *see* tripudium.

sōlĭtārĭus -a -um, *alone, lonely*.

sōlĭtūdo -ĭnis, f. *solitude, loneliness; desertion, deprivation, want*.

sōlĭtus -a -um, partic. from soleo; q.v.

sŏlĭum -i, n. (1) *a chair of state, throne*; hence *dominion, regal power*. (2) *a bath-tub*.

sōlĭvăgus -a -um, *wandering alone; solitary, lonely*.

sollemnis -e, *yearly, annual, recurring; solemn, festive, religious; usual, customary*. N. as subst. **sollemnĕ** -is. *a solemn feast, religious rite; a custom*. Adv. **sollemnĭtĕr**.

sollers -ertis, *clever, skilful*; adv. **sollertĕr**.

sollertĭa -ae, f. *cleverness, skill*.

sollĭcĭtātĭo -ōnis, f. *inciting, instigation*.

sollĭcĭto -are, *to move violently, disturb, agitate; to rouse, vex, disquiet; to incite, instigate, tamper with*.

sollĭcĭtūdo -ĭnis, f. *uneasiness, disquiet, anxiety*.

sollĭcĭtus -a -um, *disturbed, agitated, restless; anxious, uneasy, worried*; of animals, *watchful*; in act. sense, *disquieting*. Adv. **sollĭcĭtē**, *anxiously, carefully*.

sōlo -are, *to make solitary*.

sŏloecismus -i, m. *a grammatical error*.

Sŏlōn -ōnis, m. *a famous Athenian legislator, active about 600 B.C.*

sōlor -ari, dep. *to comfort, console; to assuage, relieve troubles*, etc.

solstĭtĭālis -e, *of the summer solstice; of summer; of the sun*.

solstĭtĭum -i, n. *solstice, esp. the summer solstice; summer*.

sŏlum -i, n. *bottom, floor, foundation; the sole of the foot, or shoe; soil, ground, earth, land, country*.

sōlus -a -um, *alone, only, sole*; of places, *solitary, uninhabited*. N. acc. as adv. **sōlum**, *alone, only*.

sŏlūtĭo -ōnis, f. *a loosening; a paying, payment; a solution, explanation*.

solvo solvĕre solvi sŏlūtum, *to loosen; to untie, release, free; to dissolve, break up; to exempt; to break up, weaken, bring to an end; to pay off, discharge a debt*; solvendo non esse, *to be insolvent; to meet engagements, perform duties; to break down a restraining influence; to solve a problem, explain a difficulty*.

Hence partic. **sŏlūtus** -a -um, *loosened, unbound, free, unencumbered, independent*; in bad sense, *unrestrained, unbridled; lax, lazy, negligent*: of style, *fluent or in prose*. Adv. **sŏlūtē**, *loosely, freely; carelessly*.

somnĭcŭlōsus -a -um, *sleepy, drowsy*; adv. **somnĭcŭlōsē**.

somnĭfer -fĕra -fĕrum, *sleep-bringing; narcotic, deadly*.

somnĭo -are, *to dream*; with acc., *to dream of; to imagine foolishly*.

somnĭum -i, n. *a dream; a fancy, day-dream; foolishness, nonsense*.

somnus -i, m. *sleep, slumber; drowsiness, laziness, inactivity; night*.

sŏnābĭlis -e, *resounding*.

sŏnĭpēs -pĕdis, *sounding with the feet*; m. as subst., *a horse*.

sŏnĭtus -ūs, m. *a sound, noise*.

sŏnĭvĭus -a -um, *sounding*; sonivium tripudium, *the noise of the food falling from the beaks of the sacred chickens*.

sŏno sŏnāre sŏnŭi sŏnĭtum, *to sound, resound, make a noise; to sing of, to celebrate*; of words, *to mean*.

sŏnor -ōris, m. *sound, noise, din*.

sŏnōrus -a -um, *sounding, resonant, loud*.

sons sontis, *guilty*.

sontĭcus -a -um, *important, serious*.

sŏnus -i, m. *noise, sound; tone, character, style*.

sŏphĭa -ae, f. *wisdom*.

sŏphistēs -ae, m. *a sophist*.

Sŏphoclēs -is and -i, m. *the Greek tragic poet*; adj. **Sŏphoclēus** -a -um.

¹**sŏphŏs** (-ŭs) -i, m. *wise*; as subst., *a wise man.*

²**sŏphŏs**, adv. *bravo! well done!*

sōpio -ire, *to put to sleep, lull to sleep, quieten; to stun, render senseless.*

sŏpor -ōris, m. *deep sleep; laziness; a sleeping draught.*

sŏpōrātus -a -um, *full of sleep.*

sŏpōrĭfer -fĕra -fĕrum, *causing deep sleep.*

sŏpōrus -a -um, *sleep-bringing.*

Sōractĕ -is, n. *a mountain in Etruria.*

sorbĕo -ēre, *to suck in, drink, swallow.*

sorbĭlo, *by sipping; drop by drop.*

sorbum -i, n. *a service-berry.*

sordĕo -ēre, *to be dirty; to appear vile.*

sordēs -is, f. often plur. **sordēs** -ĭum, *dirt, filth; shabby or dirty garments; low rank; sordid conduct, meanness.*

sordesco sordescĕre sorduī, *to become dirty.*

sordĭdātus -a -um, *wearing shabby or dirty clothes.*

sordĭdŭlus -a -um, *somewhat dirty or mean.*

sordĭdus -a -um, *dirty, filthy, shabby; low, base in rank; mean in conduct.* Adv. **sordĭdē**, *meanly; stingily.*

sōrex -ĭcis, m. *a shrew-mouse.*

sŏror -ōris, *a sister.*

sŏrōrĭcīda -ae, m. *one who murders a sister.*

sŏrōrĭus -a -um, *of a sister, sisterly.*

sors sortis, f. *a lot; a casting of lots; an oracular response, prophecy; official duty* as allotted; with genit., *share, part; fate, fortune, destiny; money, capital out at interest.*

sortĭlĕgus -a -um, *prophetic, oracular*; m. as subst., *a soothsayer, fortune-teller.*

sortĭor -iri, dep., and **sortĭo** -ire: instransit., *to cast lots*; transit., *to allot, cast lots for; share out*; also *to obtain by lot; to choose.* Hence partic. **sortītus** -a -um; dep., *having obtained* (by lots) *or cast lots for*; pass. *gained by lot*; n. abl. as adv., **sortītō**, *by lot, by fate.*

sortītĭo -ōnis, f. *casting lots, deciding by lot.*

¹**sortītus** -ūs, m. *casting lots, deciding by lot.*

²**sortītus** -a -um, partic. from sortior; q.v.

sospĕs -ĭtis, *safe, unhurt, uninjured; lucky, favourable.*

Sospĭta -ae, f. *the Saviour*; epithet of Juno.

sospĭto -are, *to keep safe, preserve.*

sōtĕr -ēris; acc. -ēra; m. *a saviour.*

sōtēria -ōrum, n. pl. *presents given on recovery from sickness.*

spādix -dīcis, *chestnut-coloured*

spādo -ōnis, m. *a eunuch.*

spargo spargĕre sparsi sparsum, *to scatter, sprinkle, throw about; to spread, circulate, distribute; to disperse, dissipate*; with abl. *to besprinkle with.* Hence partic. **sparsus** -a -um, *spread out, scattered; speckled, spotted.*

sparsĭo -ōnis, f. *a sprinkling.*

Sparta -ae, and **Spartē** -es, f. *Sparta, the capital of Laconia*; adj. **Spartānus** -a -um, *Spartan.*

spartum -i, n. *Spanish broom.*

spărŭlus -i, m. *a fish, sea-bream.*

spărus -i, m. *a spear with a curved blade.*

spătha -ae, f. *a broad two-edged sword.*

spătĭor -ari, dep. *to walk about, take a walk*; of things, *to spread out, expand.*

spătĭōsus -a -um, *ample, wide*; of time, *long*; adv. **spătĭōsē**.

spătĭum -i, n. *space, extent, room; distance, interval; dimensions, size; a tract, course*, esp. in a race; *an open space, a walk.* Transf., *a space of time, period; leisure, opportunity; metrical time, measure, quantity.*

spĕcĭālis -e, *individual, particular, special.*

spĕcĭēs -ēi, f.: act., *a seeing, view*; pass., *sight, look; shape, form, outward appearance; beauty; a vision, phantom; a representation, image, statue.* Transf., *pretext, pretence; notion, idea; kind, species.*

spĕcillum -i, n. *a surgeon's probe.*

spĕcīmen -ĭnis, n. *a visible mark, example, model; a pattern, ideal.*

spĕcĭo (**spĭcĭo**) spĕcĕre spexi, *to look at, see.*

spĕcĭōsus -a -um, *beautiful, handsome, imposing*; in bad sense, *plausible, specious.* Adv. **spĕcĭōsē**.

spectābĭlis -e, *visible; worth seeing, notable.*

spectācŭlum -i, n. *sight, show, spectacle; the seats in the theatre or circus.*

spectātĭo -ōnis, f. *looking, watching, viewing; inspection of money.*

spectātor -ōris, m. and **spectātrix** -trīcis, f. *a watcher, spectator, observer; an examiner, critic.*

spectĭo -ōnis, f. *the right to observe auspices.*

specto -are, *to look at, contemplate, watch; to test, examine*; of places, *to look towards, face.* Transf., *to consider, contemplate, look for; to bear in mind, have in view*; of things, *to tend, incline.* Hence partic. **spectatus** -a -um, *tried, approved*; hence *esteemed, respected.*

spectrum -i, n. *a spectre, apparition.*

¹**spĕcŭla** -ae, f. *a look out, watch-tower.*

²**spĕcŭla** -ae, f. *a little hope, ray of hope.*

spĕcŭlābundus -a -um, *watching, on the watch.*

spĕcŭlāris -e, *like a mirror; transparent*; n. pl. **spĕcŭlāria** -ōrum, *window-panes.*

spĕcŭlātor -ōris, m.: milit., *scout, spy*; in gen., *observer, investigator.*

spĕcŭlātōrĭus -a -um, *of a scout*; f. as subst. *a spy-boat.*

spĕcŭlātrix -īcis, f. *a (female) observer, watcher.*

spĕcŭlor -ari, dep. *to look out, spy, watch.*

spĕcŭlum -i, n. *a mirror*; fig., *image, copy.*

spěcus -ūs, m., f., and n. *a cave, hole, hollow.*

spēlaeum -i, n. *a cave, den.*

spēlunca -ae, f. *a cave, den.*

sperno spernĕre sprēvi sprētum, *to remove; to reject, scorn, spurn.*

spēro -are, *to look for, expect;* of good things, *to hope, hope for;* of bad, *to anticipate, forebode.*

spēs -ěi, f. *expectation;* of good things, *hope;* of bad, *anticipation, foreboding.*

sphaera -ae, f. *a globe, sphere.*

sphaeristērium -i, n. *a place for playing ball.*

Sphinx Sphingis, f. *the Sphinx, a mythical monster at Thebes.*

spīca -ae, f. *a spike; an ear of corn; a tuft.*

spīcěus -a -um, *of ears of corn.*

spīcĭfer -fěra -fěrum, *carrying ears of corn.*

spīcŭlum -i, n. *sharp point; sting; spear, dart.*

spīna -ae, f. *a thorn, prickle; a thorn-bush;* in pl., *anxieties, difficulties, perplexities.*

spīnētum -i, n. *thorn-hedge, thorn-brake.*

spīněus -a -um, *of thorns, thorny.*

spīnōsus -a -um, *of thorns, thorny, prickly;* of style, *crabbed, obscure;* of feeling, *anxious.*

spīnus -i, m. *blackthorn.*

spīra -ae, f. *a coil, twist.*

spīrābĭlis -e, *that may be breathed.*

spīrācŭlum -i, n. *an air-hole.*

spīrāmen -ĭnis, n. *an air-hole; a breath, puff.*

spīrāmentum -i, n. *an air-hole; a breathing-space, pause, interval.*

spīrĭtūs -ūs, m. *breathing, breath, exhalation; a sigh, the breath of life; life; inspiration; spirit, disposition; a high spirit, pride.*

spīro -are: intransit., *to breathe, blow, draw breath; to be alive; to have inspiration, be inspired;* transit., *to breathe out, exhale.*

spissesco -ĕre, *to become thick.*

spisso -are, *to make thick, thickness.*

spissus -a -um, *close, dense, thick, crowded; slow, tardy, difficult;* adv. **spissē.**

splendĕo -ēre, *to shine, glitter, be bright.*

splendesco -ĕre, *to become bright.*

splendĭdus -a -um, *shining, bright, brilliant; distinguished, outstanding; showy, specious;* of sound, *clear.* Hence adv. **splendĭdē,** *splendidly, finely, nobly.*

splendor -ōris, m. *brilliance, brightness, lustre, distinction;* of sound, *clarity.*

splēnĭum -i, n. *an adhesive plaster.*

spŏlĭātĭo -ōnis, f. *plundering, stripping.*

spŏlĭātor -ōris, m. and **spŏlĭātrix** -trīcis, f. *plunderer.*

spŏlĭo -are, *to strip, despoil, plunder, rob.*

spŏlĭum -i, n. usually plur., *skin or hide stripped from an animal; arms, clothing,* etc., *taken from an enemy;* in gen., *spoils, plunder, booty.*

sponda -ae, f. *a bedstead, bed, sofa, bier.*

spondālĭum -i, n. *a sacrificial hymn.*

spondĕo spondēre spŏpondi sponsum, *to pledge oneself to, promise solemnly, vow; to be a security, go bail for a person.* Partic. as subst.: **sponsus** -i, m. *a betrothed man, bridegroom;* **sponsa** -ae, f. *a betrothed woman, bride;* **sponsum** -i, n. *a covenant.*

spondēus -i, m. *a spondee (— —).*

spondȳlus -i, m. *a kind of mussel.*

spongĭa (-ĕa) -ae, f. *a sponge; an open-worked cuirass.*

sponsa -ae, f. subst. from spondeo; q.v.

sponsālis -e, *of betrothal;* n. pl. as subst. **sponsālĭa** -ĭum or -ĭōrum, *a betrothal, betrothal feast.*

sponsĭo -ōnis, f. *a solemn promise, engagement, guarantee; a wager.*

sponsor -ōris, m. *a surety, bail.*

sponsū, abl. sing. m. *by an engagement.*

sponsus -i, m. and **sponsum** -i, n. subst. from spondeo; q.v.

spontē, abl. f.: of persons, *willingly, of one's own accord; unaided;* of things, *by itself, automatically;* in itself, alone.

sporta -ae, f. *a basket, hamper.*

sportella -ae, f. *a little basket.*

sportŭla -ae, f. *a little basket; a dole, given by the great to their clients.*

sprētĭo -ōnis, f. *contempt, disdain.*

sprētor -ōris, m. *a despiser.*

spūma -ae, f. *foam, froth.*

spūmesco -ĕre, *to begin to foam.*

spūměus -a -um, *foaming, frothy.*

spūmĭfer -fěra -fěrum, and **spūmĭger** -gĕra -gĕrum, *foaming.*

spūmo -are, *to foam, froth.*

spūmōsus -a -um, *foaming, frothy.*

spŭo spŭĕre spŭi spūtum, *to spit out;* n. of partic. as subst. **spūtum** -i, *spittle.*

spurcĭtĭa -ae, f. and **spurcĭtĭēs** -ēi, f. *filthiness, dirt.*

spurco -are, *to make dirty, defile;* partic. **spurcātus** -a -um, *foul.*

spurcus -a -um, *dirty, filthy, unclean;* adv. **spurcē.**

spūto -are, *to spit, spit out.*

spūtum -i, n. subst. from spuo; q.v.

squālĕo -ēre, *to be rough, stiff; to be overgrown* or *dirty from neglect; to wear mourning.*

squālĭdus -a -um, *rough, stiff, scaly; squalid, dirty;* in *mourning;* of style, *rough;* adv. **squālĭdē.**

squālor -ōris, m. *roughness, stiffness; dirt caused by neglect; mourning;* of style, *roughness.*

squālus -i, m. *a kind of fish.*

squāma -ae, f. *a scale; scale armour; a fish.*

squāměus -a -um, *scaly.*

squāmĭger -gĕra -gĕrum, *scale-bearing, scaly;* m.pl. as subst. *fishes.*

squāmōsus -a -um, *covered with scales, scaly.*

st! *hush! hist!*

stăbĭlīmentum -i, n. *a stay, support.*

stăbĭlĭo -īre, *to make firm; to establish.*

stăbĭlis -e, *firm, steady, stable*; adv. **stăbĭlĭter.**

stăbĭlĭtās -ātis, f. *firmness, stability; durability.*

stăbŭlo -are: transit., *to stable cattle*; intransit., *to have a stall.*

stăbŭlum -i, n. *standing-room, quarters, habitation; a pothouse, brothel.*

stacta -ae, and **stactē** -ēs, f. *oil of myrrh.*

stădĭum -i, n. *a stade, a Greek measure of length; a race-course.*

stagno -are: intransit. *to be stagnant, stagnate*; of places, *to lie under water*; transit., *to overflow, inundate.*

stagnum -i, n. *standing water; a pond, marsh, swamp; a lake, strait.*

stāmen -ĭnis, n. *the warp on a loom; the thread hanging from a distaff*; stamina ducere, *to spin; any thread or woven cloth.*

stāmĭnĕus -a -um, *full of threads.*

stannum -i, n. *an alloy of silver and lead.*

stătārĭus -a -um, *steady, stable, stationary*; f. as subst. **stătārĭa** -ae, *a quiet kind of comedy*; m. pl. **stătārĭi** -ōrum, *the actors in this.*

stătēra -ae, f. *a steelyard, a balance.*

stătim, *firmly, steadfastly; on the spot, at once.*

stătĭo -ōnis, f. *a standing still; a place of abode*; milit., *post, station, or picket*; naut., *roadstead, anchorage.*

Stātĭus -m.: Caecilius Statius, *a comic poet, born* 168 B.C.: P. Papinius Statius, *a poet of Domitian's time.*

stătīvus -a -um, *standing still, fixed*; n. pl. as subst. *a permanent camp.*

¹**stător** -ōris, m. *a magistrate's attendant.*

²**Stător** -ōris, m. *stayer of flight, a surname of Jupiter.*

stătŭa -ae, f. *a statue, image.*

stătŭārĭus -a -um, *of statues*; f. as subst. *the art of sculpture*; m. *a statuary.*

stătūmen -ĭnis, n. *stay, support*; in pl., *the ribs of a ship.*

stătŭo -ŭĕre -ŭi -ūtum *to cause to stand, place, set up; to establish, settle a point; to give a ruling, make arrangements; to decide* (on a course of action or matter of fact).

stătūra -ae, f. *stature, height.*

¹**stătus**, partic. from sisto; q.v.

²**stătus** -ūs, m. *a standing posture, position, condition, state*; rhet. *the answer to an action.*

stella -ae, f. *a star*; stella comans, *a comet.*

stellans -antis, *starry, set with stars, bright.*

stellātus -a -um, *set with stars, starry, bright.*

stellĭfer -fĕra -fĕrum and **stellĭger** -gĕra -gĕrum, *star-bearing, starry.*

stellĭo (**stēlĭo**) -ōnis, m. *a spotted lizard.*

stemma -ătis, n. *a garland, chaplet; a genealogical tree.*

stercŏro -are, *to dung, manure.*

stercus -ōris, n. *dung, manure.*

stĕrĭlis -e *barren; bare, empty; fruitless, vain.*

stĕrĭlĭtās -ātis, f. *barrenness.*

sternax -ācis, *throwing to the ground.*

sterno sternĕre strāvi strātum, *to stretch out, spread; se sternere, to lie down; to strike down, lay down, overthrow; to make smooth; to calm, allay; to strew, spread a thing* (with something else); lectum, *to make, make up*; equos, *to saddle*; viam, *to pave.* N. of partic. as subst. **strātum** -i, *a coverlet, blanket; a bed; a saddle-cloth, saddle; a pavement.*

sternūmentum -i, n. *a sneeze.*

sternŭo -ŭĕre -ŭi, *to sneeze*; of a light. *to sputter.*

sterquĭlĭnĭum -i, n. *a dung-heap.*

sterto -ĕre, *to snore.*

stĭbădĭum -i, n. *a semicircular seat.*

stigma -ătis, n. *a brand put upon slaves*: in gen., *infamy, stigma.*

stigmătĭas -ae, m. *a branded slave.*

stilla -ae, f. *a drop.*

stillĭcĭdĭum -i, n. *dripping moisture; rain-water falling from the eaves of houses.*

stillo -are.: intransit., *to drip, drop*; transit., *to drop, let drop; to instil* feelings or ideas

stĭlus, *a stake, pale; the pointed instrument with which the Romans wrote on waxen tablets*; hence *writing, composition; mode of writing, style.*

stĭmŭlātĭo -ōnis. f. *spurring on, stimulating.*

stĭmŭlo -are *to goad, prick; to vex, annoy; to incite, stir up.*

stĭmŭlus -i, m. *a goad; a sting, torment; spur, incentive*; milit., *a pointed stake.*

stinguo -ĕre, *to extinguish, annihilate.*

stīpātĭo -ōnis, f. *a crowd of attendants, retinue.*

stīpātor -ōris, m. *an attendant, follower*; in plur., *train, retinue.*

stīpendĭārĭus -a -um. (1) *liable to taxes, tributary*; m. pl. as subst. *tributaries.* (2) *of soldiers, serving for pay.*

stīpendĭum -i, n. (1) *a tax, tribute, contribution.* Transf., *punishment.* (2) *the pay of a soldier; military service; a year's service, campaign.*

stīpes -itis, m. *a log, stump, tree-trunk; a branch, post, club; a blockhead.*

stīpo -are, *to press closely, compress; to crowd a place; to press round a person, accompany, attend.*

stips stĭpis, f. *a small coin, gift, ee.*

stĭpŭla -ae, f. *stalk, haulm, stubble; a reed-pipe.*

stĭpŭlātĭo -onis, f. *agreement, covenant, stipulation.*

stĭpŭlor -ari, dep. *to make demands, bargain, stipulate.*

stīrĭa -ae, f. *icicle.*

stirpĭtūs, *root and branch, thoroughly.*

stirps (**stirpes**, **stirpis**), f. rarely m., *the stock or stem of a plant; a young shoot*; of men, *stock, source, origin*; of things, *root, foundation.*

stīva -ae, f. *a plough-handle.*

stlătārĭus -a -um, *brought by sea;* hence *costly.*

stlĭs, archaic, = lis; q.v.

sto stāre stĕti stătum, *to stand, stand still, remain standing; to stand up stiffly;* milit., *to be stationed, or to stand firm;* naut., *to lie at anchor;* of abstr. things, *to remain, be fixed, stand firm, persist; to be resolved;* with ab, cum, pro, *to stand by, support, favour;* with abl. of price, *to cost;* per hominem stare, *to happen through a person's fault, be due to a person.*

Stōĭcus -a -um, *Stoic;.* m. as subst., *a Stoic;* n. pl. *the Stoic philosophy;* adv. **Stōĭcē,** *like a Stoic, stoically.*

stŏla -ae, f. *a long outer garment, worn by Roman matrons and musicians.*

stŏlĭdus -a -um, *stupid, dull, obtuse;* adv. **stŏlĭdē.**

stŏmăchor -ari, dep. *to be angry.*

stŏmăchōsus -a -um, *angry, peevish, cross;* compar. adv. **stŏmăchōsĭus.**

stŏmăchus -i, m. *the gullet, oesophagus; the stomach;* stomachus bonus, *a good digestion,* hence *good humour; taste, liking; distaste, chagrin, anger.*

stŏrĕa (stŏrĭa) -ae, f. *a rush mat.*

strābo -ōnis, m. *a squinter.*

strāgēs -is, f. *an overthrow; debris; slaughter, massacre, carnage.*

strāgŭlus -a -um, *covering, serving as a cover;* n. as subst. **strāgŭlum** -i, *a covering, carpet, mattress.*

strāmen -inis, n. *straw, litter.*

strāmentum -i, n. *straw, litter; a saddle, housing* (for mules).

strāmĭnĕus -a -um, *made of straw.*

strangŭlo -are, *to choke, strangle, throttle.*

strangŭrĭa -ae, f. *strangury.*

strătēgēma -ătis, n. *a piece of generalship, a stratagem.*

strātum -i, n., subst. from sterno; q.v.

strēna -ae, f. *a favourable omen; a new year's gift.*

strēnŭĭtās -ātis, f. *briskness.*

strēnŭus -a -um, *brisk, active, vigorous;* in bad sense, *turbulent, restless;* adv. **strēnŭē.**

strĕpĭto -are, *to rustle, rattle, clatter.*

strĕpĭtus -ūs, m. *clattering, crashing, creaking, rumbling.*

strĕpo -ĕre -ŭi -ĭtum, *to clatter, creak, clash, rumble;* of persons *to cry out;* of places, *to resound.*

strictim, *so as to graze; superficially, slightly, summarily.*

strictūra -ae, f. *a mass of iron.*

strictus -a -um, partic. from stringo; q.v.

strīdĕo strīdēre strīdi and **strīdo** strīdĕre, *to make a harsh noise; to creak, grate, hiss.*

strīdor -ōris, m. *a creaking, grating or hissing noise.*

strīdŭlus -a -um, *creaking, hissing, grating.*

strĭgĭlis -is, f. *a scraper used at the baths.*

strĭgo -are, *to halt, stop.*

strĭgōsus -a -um, *lean, thin;* of style, *dry, meagre.*

stringo stringĕre strinxi strictum. (1) *to draw tight together, to bind, tie.* (2) *to strip off, pluck, prune;* esp. *to draw a weapon from its sheath.* (3) *to graze, touch lightly; to affect, injure;* in speech, *to touch upon.*

    Hence partic. **strictus** -a -um, *close, tight; strict;* of style, *brief, concise.*

stringor -ōris, m. *a shock, a twinge.*

strix strigis, f. *a screech-owl.*

strŏpha -ae, f. *a trick, artifice.*

strŏphĭum -i, n. *a breast-band; a headband, chaplet.*

structĭlis -e, *used in building.*

structor -ōris, m. (1) *a builder, mason, carpenter.* (2) *a waiter, carver.*

structūra -ae, f. *the act of building;* concr. *a building;* of style, *arrangement, putting together.*

strŭēs -is, f. *a heap.*

strūma -ae, f. *a scrofulous tumour.*

strūmōsus -a -um, *scrofulous.*

strŭo strŭĕre struxi structum, *to put together, arrange; to pile up; to build, erect, construct; to devise, contrive.*

stŭdĕo -ēre -ŭi, *to be eager, take pains, strive after* (usually with dat.); *to side with, support, favour a person; to study a subject.*

stŭdĭōsus -a -um, *eager, zealous, keen; favouring a person or side, partial, devoted;* esp. *devoted to learning, studious.* Adv. **stŭdĭōsē,** *eagerly.*

stŭdĭum -i, n. *zeal, eagerness, application, enthusiasm; devotion to, goodwill towards a person or cause; application to learning, study.*

stultĭtĭa -ae, f. *foolishness, silliness.*

stultus -a -um, *foolish, silly;* m. as subst., *a simpleton, fool;* adv. **stultē.**

stūpa = stuppa; q.v.

stŭpĕfăcĭo -făcĕre -fēci -factum, pass. **stŭpĕfĭo** -fĭĕri, *to make senseless, benumb, stun.*

stŭpĕo -ēre -ŭi, *to be stunned, astounded, amazed;* of inanimate things, *to stand still, halt, cease.*

stŭpesco stŭpescĕre stŭpŭi, *to become amazed, astounded.*

stŭpĭdĭtās -ātis, f. *dullness, senselessness.*

stŭpĭdus -a -um, *senseless, stunned; stupid, dull..*

stŭpor -ōris, m. *senselessness, insensibility; astonishment; dullness, stupidity.*

⌐tuppa (stūpa) -ae, f. *tow, oakum.*

stuppĕus -a -um, *of tow.*

stŭpro -are, *to ravish, defile, pollute.*

stŭprum -i, n. *disgrace, defilement;* esp. *ravishing, violation.*

sturnus -i, m. *a starling.*

Stўgĭālis, Stўgĭus; see Styx.

stўlus; see stilus.

Styx, Stўgis and **Stўgos;** acc. **Stўgem** and **Stўga;** f. *a river in Arcadia;* also *a river in the infernal regions;* adj. **Stўgĭālis** -e, and **Stўgĭus** -a -um, *Stygian, infernal.*

suādēla -ae, f. *persuasion.*

suādĕo suādēre suāsi suāsum, *to recommend, advise* (a course of action to a person).

suādus -a -um, *persuasive*; f. as subst., *persuasion.*

suāsĭo -ōnis, f. *advice, recommendation; persuasive eloquence.*

suāsor -ōris, m. *an adviser, recommender; one who advocates a law.*

suāsōrĭus -a -um, *of persuasion*; as subst. *persuasive discourse.*

suāsus -ūs, m. *persuasion.*

suāvĕŏlens -entis, *sweet-smelling.*

suāvĭdĭcus -a -um, *sweetly speaking.*

suāvĭlŏquens -entis, *sweetly speaking.*

suāvĭlŏquentĭa -ae, f. *sweetness of speech.*

suāvĭŏlum, suāvĭor; see sav-.

suāvis -e, *sweet, pleasant*; adv. suāvĭtĕr.

suāvĭtās -ātis, f. *sweetness, pleasantness.*

suāvĭum = savium; q.v.

sŭb, prep. (1) with abl.: *underneath, under; close under, at the foot of;* in time, *at, near to; in the power of, under; under cover of.* (2) with acc., *to* (or *along*) *the underside of; up under, down under, along under; close up to;* in time, *towards, just before;* also *immediately after; into the power of.*

sŭbabsurdus -a -um, *somewhat absurd*; adv. sŭbabsurdē.

sŭbaccūso -are, *to accuse a little.*

sŭbactĭo -ōnis, f. *preparation, discipline.*

sŭbadrōganter, *somewhat arrogantly.*

sŭbagrestis -e, *somewhat rustic* or *boorish.*

sŭbămārus -a -um, *somewhat bitter.*

sŭbausculto -are, *to listen secretly.*

subc-; see succ-.

subdĭffĭcĭlis -e, *somewhat difficult.*

subdĭffīdo -ĕre, *to be somewhat distrustful.*

subdĭtīcĭus and subdītīvus -a -um, *supposititious, substituted, counterfeit.*

subdo -dĕre -dĭdi dĭtum, *to put, place* or *lay under; to subject, subdue; to put in the place of another substitute; to counterfeit.*

subdŏcĕo -ēre, *to teach as an assistant, help in teaching.*

subdŏlus -a -um, *with secret guile; sly, crafty*; adv. subdŏlē.

subdŭbĭto -are, *to doubt* or *hesitate a little.*

subdūco -dūcĕre -duxi -ductum, *to draw up from under, pull up, raise, remove; to take away stealthily, steal;* naut., *to draw a ship up on shore;* milit., *to withdraw;* of accounts, *to balance, cast up.*

subductĭo -ōnis, f. *the drawing up of a ship on dry land; a reckoning, computing.*

sŭbĕdo -esse -ēdi, *to eat from under, wear away.*

sŭbĕo -ire -ĭi or -ĭvi -ĭtum. (1) *to go under, pass under;* of a bearer, *to to under and support; to undergo, submit to, take upon oneself.* (2) *to come from under, approach, advance, mount, climb;* of thoughts, etc., *to*

come into, or *come over, the mind.* (3) *to come on after, to follow;* sometimes *to come and support.*

Hence partic. sŭbĭtus -a -um, as adj., *sudden; coming suddenly, taking by surprise;* pass., *suddenly done, hastily contrived, improvised.* N. as subst. *a sudden occurrence, emergency.* N. abl. as adv. sŭbĭtō, *suddenly.*

sūber -ĕris, n. *cork-tree; cork.*

subf -; see suff-.

subg -; see sugg-.

subhorrĭdus -a -um, *somewhat rough.*

subĭăcĕo -ēre -ŭi, *to lie under; to be subject to, be connected with.*

subĭcĭo -ĭcĕre -ĭēci -ĭectum. (1) *to throw* or *place under; to submit, subject;* in speech or writing, *to append, reply.* (2) *to throw up from below, raise, lift; to put into a mind, suggest.* (3) *to substitute, insert by guile, counterfeit.*

Hence partic. subĭectus -a -um, *subjected;* of places, *lying near, adjacent;* superl. adv. subĭectissimē, *most submissively.*

subĭectĭo -ōnis, f. *a laying under, placing under; a counterfeiting, forging.*

subĭecto -are, *to put under;* also *to throw up from below.*

subĭector -ōris, m. *forger, counterfeiter.*

sŭbĭgo -ĭgĕre -ēgi -actum, *to drive under; to subject, constrain, subdue, compel; to drive up from below, to propel; to work the soil;* in gen., *to work at; to train, discipline.*

subimpŭdens -entis, *somewhat impudent.*

subĭnānis -e, *somewhat vain.*

subindē, *immediately afterwards; repeatedly.*

subinsulsus -a -um, *somewhat insipid.*

subinvĭdĕo -ere, *to envy somewhat;* partic. subinvīsus -a -um, *somewhat hated.*

subinvīto -are, *to invite mildly.*

sŭbīrascor -irasci -īrātus, dep. *to get a little angry.*

sŭbĭtārĭus -a -um, *hastily contrived, improvised.*

sŭbĭto, sŭbĭtus; from subeo; q.v.

subiungo -iungĕre -iunxi -iunctum, *to yoke beneath; to join on, attach; to subdue, subjugate.*

sublābor -lābi -lapsus, dep. *to glide up; to glide from beneath, slip away.*

sublātĭo -ōnis, f. *lifting up, elevation.*

sublātus -a -um, partic. from tollo; q.v.

sublēgo -lĕgĕre -lēgi -lectum, *to gather from below, pick up; to carry off secretly; to choose in the place of another.*

sublĕvātĭo -ōnis, f. *a relieving, lightening.*

sublĕvo -are, *to raise, lift, support; to encourage* a person; *to alleviate* troubles.

sublĭca -ae, f. *a pile, stake.*

sublĭcĭus -a -um, *resting upon piles.*

sublĭgācŭlum -i, and sublĭgar -āris, n. *a loincloth, kilt.*

subligo -are, *to bind below, bind on.*

sublimis -e (archaic **sublimus** -a -um), *high, raised, lofty; elevated, sublime.* N. acc. sing. as adv. **sublime**, *on high, aloft.*

sublimitas -atis, f. *loftiness height, sublimity.*

sublimus; see sublimis.

subluceo -ere, *to gleam faintly, glimmer.*

subluo -luere -lutum, *to wash below; of rivers, to flow beneath.*

sublustris -e, *gleaming faintly, glimmering.*

subm -; see summ-.

subnascor -nasci -natus, dep. *to grow up out of or after.*

subnecto -nectere -nexui -nexum, *to tie on, bind on beneath.*

subnego -are, *to deny a little, partly refuse.*

subnixus (subnisus) -a -um, *propped up, supported.*

subnoto -are, *to mark beneath, write underneath; to notice secretly.*

subnuba -ae, f. *a rival.*

subnubilus -a -um, *somewhat cloudy.*

subo -are, *to be in heat.*

subobscenus -a -um, *somewhat obscene.*

subobscurus -a -um, *somewhat obscure.*

subodiosus -a -um, *rather unpleasant.*

suboffendo -ere, *to give some offence.*

suboleo -ere (only in 3 pers.), *to emit a smell; hence to make itself felt.*

suboles -is, f. *a sprout, shoot, offspring, progeny.*

subolesco -ere, *to grow up.*

suborior -oriri, dep. *to arise after or in succession.*

suborno -are. (1) *to furnish, equip, provide.* (2) *to instigate secretly, suborn.*

subortus -us, m. *an arising after or in succession.*

subp -; see supp-.

subrancidus -a -um, *somewhat putrid.*

subraucus -a -um, *somewhat hoarse.*

subrectus (surr-), partic. from subrigo; q.v.

subremigo (surr-) -are, *to row underneath.*

subrepo (surr-) -repere -repsi, *to creep or crawl up from below.*

subrepticius = surrepticius; q.v.

subrideo (surr-) -ridere -risi -risum, *to smile.*

subridicule, *somewhat laughably.*

subrigo (surr-) -rigere -rexi -rectum, *to raise, lift up.*

subringor -i, dep. *to make a wry face.*

subripio = surripio; q.v.

subrogo (surr-) -are, *to suggest that a person be chosen as substitute for another.*

subrostrani -orum, m. *loungers about the rostra, idlers.*

subrubeo -ere, *to blush slightly, be rather red.*

subruo -ruere -rui -rutum, *to undermine, overthrow, destroy.*

subrusticus -a -um, *somewhat clownish.*

subscribo -scribere -scripsi -scriptum, *to write under, write beneath; to sign a document; to complete an indict-*

---

ment, hence to prosecute, accuse; with dat., *to support, assent to; to note down, make a note of.*

subscriptio -onis, f. *a writing beneath, signature; the completion of an indictment; a record, register.*

subscriptor -oris, m. *the signer of an indictment; an accuser.*

subsecivus = subsicivus; q.v.

subseco -secare -secui -sectum, *to cut away below.*

subsellium -i, n. *a bench, seat,* esp. *in the courts.*

subsentio -sentire -sensi, *to notice secretly.*

subsequor -sequi -secutus, dep. *to follow after; to support a cause, etc.*

subservio -ire, *to be subject to, comply with.*

subsicivus (subsec-) -a -um, *left over; extra, superfluous, spare.*

subsidiarius -a -um, *in reserve.*

subsidium -i, n.: milit., *reserve troops, auxiliary forces;* in gen., *support, help, assistance.*

subsido -sidere -sedi -sessum, *to crouch down, settle, sink, subside; to stay, remain; to lie in wait, lurk in ambush.*

subsignanus -a -um, *serving beneath the standard;* milites, *reserve legionaries.*

subsigno -are, *to write under, endorse; to enter on a list, to register.*

subsilio -silire -silui, *to leap up, spring up.*

subsisto -sistere -stiti, *to stand; to make a stand, to withstand; to come to a stand, stop, halt, cease; to stay, remain.*

subsortior -iri, dep. *to choose by lot as a substitute.*

subsortitio -onis, f. *the choice of a substitute by lot.*

substantia -ae, f. *substance, essence; property, means of subsistence.*

substerno -sternere -stravi -stratum, *to spread beneath, lay under; to set out, provide.*

substituo -uere -ui -utum, *to put next; to put under, to put in the place of another, to substitute.*

substo -stare, *to stand firm.*

substringo -stringere -strinxi -strictum, *to draw together, bind up;* partic. **substrictus** -a -um, *narrow, contracted, small.*

substructio -onis, f. *a base, foundation.*

substruo -struere -struxi -structum, *to build beneath, lay a foundation.*

subsulto -are, *to spring up, leap up.*

subsum -esse -fui, *to be near, be close at hand; to be under; to be subject; to be there, to exist.*

subsutus -a -um, *fringed, edged below.*

subtemen -inis, n. *the weft or woof in weaving.*

subter (supter), adv. and prep., *beneath, below, underneath.*

subterfugio -fugere -fugi, *to escape.*

subterlabor -labi -lapsus, dep. *to glide under, flow under; to slip away, escape.*

subtĕro -tĕrĕre -trīvi -trītum, *to wear away underneath.*

subterrānĕus -a -um, *underground, subterranean.*

subtexo -texĕre -texŭi -textum, *to weave beneath; to connect, join on; to cover, darken.*

subtīlis -e, *finely woven, slender, fine; of senses, etc., discriminating, nice; of style, plain, simple, unadorned.* Hence adv. **subtīlĭtĕr,** *by fine links or passages; of judgment, with discrimination; of style, plainly, simply.*

subtīlĭtās -ātis, f. *fineness, minuteness; of judgment, discrimination; of style, plainness, simplicity.*

subtĭmĕo -ēre, *to be a little afraid.*

subtrăho -trăhĕre -traxi -tractum, *to draw up from beneath; to draw away secretly, remove, steal away.*

subturpĭcŭlus -a -um, *rather on the disgraceful side.*

subturpis -e, *rather disgraceful.*

subtŭs, adv. *beneath, below, underneath.*

subtūsus -a -um, *somewhat bruised.*

sŭbŭcŭla -ae, f. *a shirt.*

sŭbŭla -ae, f. *a shoemaker's awl.*

sŭbulcus -i, m. *a swineherd.*

Sŭbūra -ae, f. *a part of Rome, north-east of the Forum.*

sŭburbānĭtās -ātis, f. *nearness to the city.*

sŭburbānus -a -um, *near the city (Rome), suburban;* n. as subst. *an estate near Rome.*

sŭburbĭum -i, n. *a suburb.*

sŭburgŭĕo -ēre, *to drive close.*

subvectio -ōnis, f. *carrying up, conveyance, transport.*

subvecto -are, *to carry up, convey, transport.*

subvectus -ūs, m. *a carrying up.*

subvĕho -vĕhĕre -vexi -vectum, *carry up, convey, transport.*

subvĕnĭo -vĕnīre -vēni -ventum, *to come up to aid, to succour, relieve.*

subvĕrĕor -ēri, dep. *to be rather anxious.*

subversor -ōris, m. *overthrower.*

subverto (**-vorto**) -vertĕre -verti -versum, *to overthrow, overturn, destroy.*

subvexus -a -um, *sloping upwards.*

subvŏlo -are, *to fly up.*

subvolvo -ĕre, *to roll up.*

succāvus -a -um, *hollow underneath.*

succēdo -cēdĕre -cessi -cessum. (1) *to go under; to submit to.* (2) *to go from under, ascend, mount.* (3) *to come after; to succeed, relieve, follow; of things, to turn out well, prosper, succeed.*

succendo -cendĕre -cendi -censum, *to set on fire from below; to kindle, inflame.*

succensĕo = suscenseo; q.v.

¹succentŭrĭo -are, *to put in the place of another, to substitute.*

²succentŭrĭo -ōnis, m. *an under-centurion.*

successĭo -ōnis, f. *succeeding, succession.*

successor -ōris, m. *a successor, follower, heir.*

successus -ūs, m. (1) *an advance uphill, approach.* (2) *success.*

succĭdĭa -ae, f. *a flitch of bacon.*

¹succĭdo -cīdĕre -cīdi, *to fall under; to sink, flag, fail.*

²succĭdo -cīdĕre -cīdi -cīsum *to cut from under, cut down.*

succĭdŭus -a -um, *sinking, failing.*

succingo -cingĕre -cinxi -cinctum, *to gird below, gird up; to equip, arm, provide, surround;* partic. **succinctus** -a -um, as adj., *concise, succinct.*

succingŭlum -i, n. *a girdle.*

succĭno -ĕre, *to sing to, accompany; in speech, to chime in.*

succlāmātĭo -ōnis, f. *shouting in reply.*

succlāmo -are, *to shout back.*

succontŭmēlĭōsē, *somewhat insolently.*

succresco -crescĕre -crēvi, *to grow up, increase; to grow up to, match.*

succrispus = subcrispus; q.v.

succumbo -cumbĕre -cŭbŭi -cŭbĭtum, *to lie down under, sink down, give way, succumb, surrender.*

succurro -currĕre -curri -cursum. (1) *to run beneath, go under; to undergo; of ideas, to come into the mind.* (2) *to come to aid, succour, help, assist.*

succŭtĭo -cŭtĕre -cussi -cussum, *to shake from beneath, fling aloft.*

sūcĭdus -a -um, *juicy, full of sap.*

sūcĭnus -a -um, *of amber.*

sūco -ōnis, m. *a sucker.*

sūcus (**succus**) -i, m. *juice, sap; a draught; flavour, taste; sap, vigour, energy.*

sūdārĭum -i, n. *handkerchief, towel.*

sūdātōrĭus -a -um, *of sweating;* n. as subst. *a sweating-room.*

sūdātrix -tricis, f. *causing perspiration.*

sūdis -is, f. *a stake, pile; a spike, point.*

sūdo -are: intransit., *to sweat, perspire; to make a great effort; to drip with moisture; to drip from, distil;* transit., *to sweat out, to exude; to soak with sweat.*

sūdor -ōris, m. *sweat, perspiration; great exertion; any moisture.*

sūdus -a -um, *dry; of weather, bright cloudless;* n. as subst. *fine weather.*

Suēbi (**Suēvi**) -orum, m. *a Germanic tribe.*

suemus, 1 plur. as from sueo, *we are accustomed.*

suesco -suescĕre suēvi suētum: intransit., *to become accustomed;* transit., *to accustom.* Hence partic. **suētus** -a -um *accustomed; customary, usual.*

Suētōnĭus -i, m. C. Suetonius Tranquillus, *author of the Lives of the Caesars.*

suētus -a -um, partic. from suesco; q.v.

Suēvi = Suebi; q.v.

sŭfes (**suffes**) -fētis, m. *the chief magistrate at Carthage.*

suffarcĭno -are, *to stuff, cram.*

suffĕro sufferre, *to hold up, support; to endure, suffer.*

suffĭcĭo -fĭcĕre -fēci -fectum: transit., *to put under*; hence, *to stain, steep, suffuse; to provide, supply; to put in place of another, to substitute, choose as a substitute*; intransit., *to be adequate, suffice*; with infin., *to be able.*

suffĭgo -fĭgĕre -fixi -fixum, *to fix up, fasten.*

suffimen -ĭnis and **suffimentum** -i, n. *incense.*

suffĭo -ire, *to fumigate, perfume; to warm.*

sufflāmen -ĭnis, n. *a brake, drag, hindrance.*

sufflo -are: intransit., *to blow*; transit., *to blow up, inflate.*

suffōco -are, *to strangle, choke, suffocate.*

suffōdĭo -fōdĕre -fōdi -fossum, *to pierce underneath, excavate, undermine.*

suffrāgātĭo -ōnis, f. *voting in favour, support.*

suffrāgātor -ōris, m. *a voter in favour; a (political) supporter.*

suffrāgātōrĭus -a -um, *relating to the support of a candidate.*

suffrāgĭum -i, n. *a voting tablet, a vote; the right to vote, franchise*; in gen., *judgment; approval, support.*

suffrāgor -ari, dep. *to vote for; to favour, approve, support.*

suffringo -ĕre, *to break underneath.*

suffŭgĭo -fŭgĕre -fŭgi, *to flee, escape.*

suffŭgĭum -i, n. *a shelter, place of refuge.*

suffulcĭo -fulcire -fulsi -fultum, *to support beneath, undergo, underprop.*

suffundo -fundĕre -fūdi -fūsum, *to pour over, spread through, suffuse; to steep, stain, cover.*

suffuscus -a -um, *brownish, dark.*

Sŭgambri (**Sӯg-**, **Sĭg-**) -ōrum, m. pl. *a Germanic tribe.*

suggĕro -gĕrĕre -gessi -gestum, *to bring up, supply, provide; to add, attach; to place next.*

suggestum -i, n. and **suggestus** -ūs, m. *a raised place, height, elevation*; esp., *a platform.*

suggrandis -e, *somewhat large.*

suggrĕdĭor -grĕdi -gressus, dep. *to go up to, approach, attack.*

sūgillātĭo -ōnis, f. *a bruise; mockery, insult.*

sūgillo -are, *to beat, to insult.*

sūgo sūgĕre suxi suctum, *to suck.*

sŭillus -a -um, *of swine.*

sulcātor -ōris, m. *a plougher.*

sulco -are, *to furrow, plough; to wrinkle.*

sulcus -i, m. *a furrow; ploughing; a trench or ditch; a track, path.*

sulfur (**sulpur**) -ŭris, n. *sulphur; lightning.*

sulfŭrātus -a -um, *containing sulphur.*

sulfŭrĕus -a -um, *sulphurous.*

Sulla (**Sylla**) -ae, m. *a name of a family in the gens Cornelia*; adj. **Sullānus** -a -um; verb **sullātŭrĭo** -ire, *to wish to imitate Sulla.*

Sulmo -ōnis, m. *birth-place of Ovid*; adj. **Sulmōnensis** -e.

sulpur = sulfur; q.v.

sultis = si vultis; see volo.

sum, esse, fūi, *to be, to exist, be there, be so*; with dat., *to be in one's possession*; copulative, *to be so and so*, with complement; fut. partic. fūtūrus -a -um, *future, about to be*; n. as subst. *the future.*

sūmen -ĭnis, n. *the udder of a sow; a sow.*

summa -ae; see summus.

summātim, adv. *summarily, briefly.*

summātus -ūs, m. *supremacy, chief authority.*

summergo -mergĕre -mersi -mersum, *to plunge under, to sink.*

summĭnistro -are, *to help by supplying.*

summissĭo (subm-) -ōnis, f. *a letting down, lowering.*

summitto (subm-) -mittĕre -misi -missum, (1) *to let down, send under; subject, subordinate*; with animum, or se, *to condescend, submit.* (2) *to send up from below, to raise, rear, make to grow.* (3) *to send as help.* (4) *to send secretly.* Hence partic. **summissus** (subm-) -a -um, *let down, lowered; mild, gentle, humble*; in bad sense, *mean, abject.* Adv. **summissē**, *softly, calmly; modestly, humbly.*

summŏlestus (subm-) -a -um, *somewhat troublesome*; adv. **summŏlestē**, *with some vexation.*

summŏnĕo (subm-) -ēre, *to remind secretly.*

summŏpĕrē (**summō ŏpĕrĕ**), *very much, exceedingly.*

summŏrosus (subm-) -a -um, *somewhat peevish.*

summŏvĕo (subm-) -mŏvēre -mōvi -mōtum, *to move up from below; to move away, drive off, expel*; esp. of the lictor *to clear a way for a magistrate, to keep back the crowd; to force away from, compel, to give up*; pass. partic., **summōtus**, *lying out of the way, remote.*

summūto (subm-) -are, *to exchange.*

sūmo sūmĕre sumpsi sumptum, *to take, choose, obtain, buy; of clothes, etc., to put on; to exact a punishment; to take upon oneself, claim; to take for granted, assume.*

sumptĭo -ōnis f. *the premiss of a syllogism.*

sumptŭārĭus -a -um, *relating to expense, sumptuary.*

sumptŭōsus -a -um: of things, *costly, expensive*; of persons, *lavish, extravagant*; adv. **sumptŭōsē**, *expensively, sumptuously.*

sumptus -ūs, m. *cost, expense.*

sŭo sŭĕre sŭi sūtum, *to sew, stitch together, join together.*

sŭōmet and **sŭōpte**; see suus.

sŭōvĕtaurīlĭa -ĭum, n. pl., *a sacrifice of a pig, sheep and bull.*

sŭpellex -lectĭlis, f. *household furniture.*

¹**sŭper** -a -um; see superus.

²sŭper. Adv., *over*, *above*; *besides*, *beyond*, *moreover*; *remaining*, *over and above*. Prep.: with abl., of place *over*, *above*; of time, *at*; *concerning*, *about*; *besides*, *beyond*; with acc., of place, *over*, *above*, *upon*; *besides*, *beyond*; of time, *during*; of superiority, *above*, *more than*.

sŭpĕrā; see supra.

sŭpĕrābĭlis -e, *that can be surmounted*; *conquerable*.

sŭpĕraddo -addĕre -addĭtum, *to add as well*, *put on besides*.

sŭpĕrātor -ōris, m. *a conqueror*.

sŭperbĭa -ae, f. *pride*; *haughtiness*, *arrogance*.

sŭperbĭo -ire: of persons, *to be proud*, *pride oneself*; of things, *to be splendid*, *superb*.

sŭperbus -a -um, *haughty*, *exalted*, *proud*; *arrogant*, *overbearing*; *brilliant*, *splendid*. Adv. sŭperbē, *haughtily*, *proudly*.

sŭpercĭlĭum -i, n. *an eyebrow*; *the eyebrows*; *a nod* (as expression of will); *arrogance*, *censoriousness*; of things, *ridge*, *summit*.

sŭpĕrēmĭnĕo -ēre, *to overtop*.

sŭperfĭcĭēs -ēi, f. *top*, *surface*.

sŭperfĭo -fĭēri, *to be left over*.

sŭperfixus -a -um, *fixed on the top*.

sŭperflŭo -flŭĕre, *to flow over*, *overflow*, *be superfluous*.

sŭperfundo -fundĕre -fūdi -fūsum, *to pour over*, *pour upon*; pass., *to overflow*; in gen., *to spread about*, *spread over*.

sŭpergrĕdĭor -grĕdi -gressus, dep. *to step beyond*, *overstep*; *to exceed*, *surpass*.

sŭpĕrĭācĭo -ĭăcĕre -ĭēci -ĭectum or -ĭactum, *to throw over*, *throw upon*; *to overtop*, *exceed*, *go beyond*.

sŭpĕrimmĭnĕo -ēre, *to overhang*.

sŭpĕrimpendens -entis, *overhanging*.

sŭpĕrimpŏsĭtus -a -um, *laid over*, *placed upon*.

sŭpĕrincĭdens -entis, *falling on top*.

sŭpĕrincŭbans -antis, *lying over or upon*.

sŭpĕrincumbo -cumbĕre -cŭbŭi *to lie on*, *lie over*.

sŭpĕrinĭcĭo -inĭcĕre -inĭēci -inĭectum, *to throw upon*.

sŭpĕrinsterno -sternĕre -strāvi, *to spread over*, *lay over*.

sŭpĕrĭor -ōris, compar. of superus; q.v.

sŭperlātĭo -ōnis, f. *exaggeration*, *hyperbole*.

sŭperlātus -a -um, *exaggerated*, *hyperbolical*.

sŭpernus -a -um, *above*, *upper*, *high*; adv. sŭpernē, *above or from above*.

sŭpĕro -are: intransit., *to go above*, *overtop*, *project*; *to prevail*, *conquer*; *to abound*; *to remain*, *be over*; esp. *to remain alive*, *survive*; *to be too much*, *to exceed*; transit., *to rise above*, *surmount*, *overtop*, *pass*; *to surpass*, *excel*, *exceed*; *to overcome*, *conquer*. Compar. of pres. partic. sŭperantĭor -ōris, *more dominant*.

sŭpĕrobrŭo -ŭĕre, *to overwhelm*.

sŭperpendens -entis, *overhanging*.

sŭperpōno -pōnĕre -pŏsŭi -pŏsĭtum, *to place over*, or *upon*; *to put in authority*.

sŭperscando -ĕre, *to climb over*.

sŭpersĕdĕo -sĕdēre -sēdi -sessum, *to sit above*, *sit out*; hence *to forbear*, *refrain*.

sŭperstagno -are, *to spread out into a lake*.

sŭpersterno -sternĕre -strāvi -strātum, *to spread over or upon*.

sŭperstĕs -stĭtis, *standing over or near*; *present*, *witnessing*; *surviving*, *living on*.

sŭperstĭtĭo -ōnis, f. *superstition*, *fanaticism*.

sŭperstĭtĭōsus -a -um, *superstitious*; adv. sŭperstĭtĭōsē.

sŭpersto -are, *to stand over or upon*.

sŭperstrŭo -strŭĕre -struxi -structum, *to build upon*.

sŭpersum -esse -fŭi -fŭtūrus, *to be over and above*; *to be left*, *remain*, *survive*; *to be plentiful*, *to abound*; *to be superfluous*, *be redundant*.

sŭpĕrurgĕo -ēre, *to press from above*.

sŭpĕrus (rarely sŭper) -a -um, *situated above*; *upper*, *higher*; m. pl. as subst. *the gods above*; also *men on earth*; n. pl. *heights* or *heavenly* bodies. Compar. sŭpĕrĭor -ĭus, *higher*, *upper*; of time, *earlier*, *former*, *past*; of rank, etc., *higher*, *greater*. Superl. suprēmus -a -um, of place, *highest*, *uppermost*; in time, *last*, *final*; of degree, *highest*, *greatest*; of rank, *highest*; n. sing. as subst., *the end*; n. pl., suprēma -ōrum, *death*, *funeral rites*, *last will and testament*. Used as another superl. summus -a -um, *highest*, *uppermost*, *at the top*; summa urbs, *the highest part of the city*; of the voice, *highest*, *loudest*; of time, *last*; of rank, etc., *greatest*, *highest*, *most distinguished*. F. as subst. summa -ae *the highest place*, *the main thing*, *most important point*; *a summary*, *the gist*, *the sum total of an amount*. N. as subst. summum -i, *surface*, *top*; acc. as adv., *at most*. Adv. summē, *in the highest degree*, *extremely*.

sŭpervācānĕus and sŭpervācŭus -a -um, *superfluous*, *unnecessary*, *extra*.

sŭpervado -ĕre, *to go over*, *surmount*.

sŭpervĕhor -vĕhi -vectus sum, *to ride or sail past*.

sŭpervĕnĭo -vĕnire -vēni -ventum, *to come upon*, *rise above*; *to arrive*, *come up*, esp. *unexpectedly*.

sŭperventus -ūs, m. *coming up*, *(unexpected) arrival*.

sŭpervivo -ĕre, *to survive*.

sŭpervŏlĭto -are, and sŭpervŏlo -are, *to fly over*, *fly above*.

sŭpīno -are, *to put face upwards*, *throw on the back*.

sŭpīnus -a -um, *lying on the back*, *face-upwards*; manus, *with palm upwards*; of streams, *flowing up*, *returning*; of ground, *sloping upwards*; of character, *negligent*, *lazy*.

suppaenĭtet -ēre, *to cause slight regret.*

suppăr -păris, *almost equal.*

suppĕdĭtātĭo -ōnis, f. *abundant provision.*

suppĕdĭto -are: intransit., *to be at hand, be ready, suffice;* transit., *to provide, supply, give.*

suppernātus -a -um, *lamed in the hip.*

suppĕtĭae -ārum, f. pl. *help, aid.*

suppĕtĭor -ari, dep. *to help, assist.*

suppĕto -ĕre, -ivi and -ĭi, -ĭtum, *to be in store, be at hand; to suffice, be enough.*

supplanto -are, *to trip up.*

supplēmentum -i, n. *filling up, completion;* milit., *a body of recruits, reinforcements.*

supplĕo -plēre -plēvi -plētum, *to fill up, make complete.*

supplex -plĭcis, *kneeling; entreating, suppliant;* adv. **supplĭcĭter.**

supplĭcātĭo -ōnis, f. *solemn public prayer* or *thanksgiving; a religious festival* or *fast.*

supplĭcĭum -i, n. (1) *a humble entreaty, supplication, prayer.* (2) *punishment;* esp. *capital punishment.*

supplĭco -are, *to kneel, beseech, entreat;* esp. *to pray to the gods.*

supplōdo -plōdĕre -plōsi, *to stamp.*

supplōsĭo -ōnis, f. *a stamping.*

suppōno -pōnĕre -pŏsŭi -pŏsĭtum. (1) *to put under; to subject.* (2) *to put next to, to add.* (3) *to put in the place of; to substitute, counterfeit, forge.*

supporto -are, *to carry up.*

suppŏsĭtĭcĭus -a -um, *substituted, spurious.*

suppressĭo -ōnis, f. *embezzlement.*

supprĭmo -prĭmĕre -pressi -pressum, *to press under; to hold down, check, restrain; to keep back, suppress, conceal;* pecuniam, nummos, *to embezzle.* Partic. **suppresssus** -a -um, *checked, restrained;* of the voice, *low, subdued.*

suppŭdet -ēre, *to cause some shame.*

suppus -a -um, *head-downwards.*

suppŭto -are, *to count up, compute.*

suprā. Adv. *over, on the top;* of time, *before, previously;* in writing, *above;* of amount, etc., *over, more, beyond;* supra quam, *more than.* Prep., with acc., *above, over;* of time, *before;* of amount, *more than, above, beyond.*

suprascando -ĕre, *to climb over, surmount.*

suprēmus, etc.; see superus.

sūra -ae, f. *the calf of the leg.*

surcŭlus -i, m. *a young shoot, sprout, twig; a slip, sucker.*

surdaster -tra -trum, *somewhat deaf.*

surdĭtās -ātis, f. *deafness.*

surdus -a -um, *deaf; unwilling to hear, insensible; not heard, still, silent;* of sounds, etc., *indistinct, faint.*

surēna -ae, m. *a Parthian grand vizier.*

surgo surgĕre surrexi surrectum, *to rise, get up; to spring up, arise.*

surpŭit, etc., forms from surripio; q.v.

surr-; see also subr-.

surreptĭcĭus (subr-) -a -um, *stolen, secret, surreptitious.*

surrĭpĭo -rĭpĕre -rĭpŭi -reptum, *to take away secretly; to steal, filch.*

sursum (**sursus**), *upwards, on high;* sursum deorsum, *up and down, backwards, and forwards.*

sus sŭis, c. *a sow, swine, pig, hog; a kind of fish.*

suscensĕo -ēre -ŭi, *to be angry, bear a grudge.*

susceptĭo -ōnis, f. *undertaking.*

suscĭpĭo -cĭpĕre -cēpi -ceptum, *to take up, catch up; to support, raise; to accept, receive,* esp. *to acknowledge a child as one's own; to take upon oneself, undertake, begin; to maintain a point, be ready to prove.*

suscĭto -are, *to stir up, arouse, excite.*

suspecto -are, *to keep looking at, gaze upon; to look upon with suspicion, suspect.*

¹**suspectus** -a -um, partic. from suspicio; q.v.

²**suspectus** -ūs, m. *looking upwards; respect, esteem.*

suspendĭum -i, n. *a hanging of oneself.*

suspendo -pendĕre -pendi -pensum, *to hang up; to prop up, support; to keep in suspense, leave undecided; to check, break off.*
Hence partic. **suspensus** -a -um, *hovering, hanging, suspended; dependent; ambiguous, doubtful, in suspense.*

suspĭcax -ācis: act., *suspicious, suspecting;* pass., *suspicious, suspected.*

¹**suspĭcĭo** -spĭcĕre -spexi -spectum, *to look from below, look upwards; to look up to, esteem, respect; to look askance at, suspect.*
Hence partic. **suspectus** -a -um, *suspected.*

²**suspĭcĭo** -ōnis, f. *mistrust, suspicion; a faint idea, imperfect conception.*

suspĭcĭōsus -a -um, *feeling suspicion, suspecting; exciting suspicion, suspicious;* adv. **suspĭcĭōsē,** *in a suspicious manner, suspiciously.*

suspĭcor -ari, dep. *to suspect; to conjecture, suppose, surmise.*

suspīrātus -ūs, and **suspīrĭtus** -ūs, and **suspīrĭum** -i, n. *a deep breath, a sigh.*

suspīro -are: intransit., *to draw a deep breath, to sigh;* transit., *to sigh for, long for.*

susquĕ dequĕ, *up and down.*

sustentācŭlum -i, n. *a prop, support.*

sustentātĭo -ōnis, f. *forbearance.*

sustento -are, *to hold up, support, sustain; to maintain; to put off, hinder, delay.*

sustĭnĕo -tĭnēre -tĭnŭi -tentum, *to hold up, support, sustain;* with infin., *to endure to, have the heart to; to maintain; to put off, delay; to hold back, check, restrain.*

sustollo -ĕre, *to lift up, raise; to take away, remove, destroy.*

sŭsurrātor -ōris, m. *a mutterer.*

sŭsurro -are, *to murmur, mutter, whisper;* of bees, *to hum.*

¹**sŭsurrus** -i, m. *a murmur, muttering, whisper, hum, buzz.*

²**sŭsurrus** -a -um, *whispering, muttering.*

sŭtĭlis -e, *stitched together, fastened together.*

sŭtor -ōris, m. *a shoemaker, cobbler.*

sūtōrĭus and **sūtrīnus** -a -um, *of a shoemaker.*

sūtūra -ae, f. *a seam, suture.*

sŭus -a -um, reflexive possessive pronoun of 3rd person, *his, her, its, their (own);* often strengthened by -pte *or* -met; sometimes *proper, due, suitable, favourable; independent.* As subst., *one's own people, property,* etc.

Sỹbăris -ris, f. *a town in Lucania, famous for luxury.*

sỹcŏphanta -ae, f. *an informer, trickster.*

Sylla = Sulla; q.v.

syllăba -ae, f. *a syllable;* in plur., *verses, poems.*

syllăbătim, *syllable by syllable.*

syllŏgismus (or -ŏs) -i, m. *a syllogism.*

symbŏla -ae, f. *a contribution towards a common feast.*

symphōnĭa -ae, f. *a concert, musical performance.*

symphōnĭăcus -a -um, *of or for a concert.*

sỹnedrus -i, m. *a Macedonian councillor.*

syngrăpha -ae, f. *a bond, agreement to pay.*

sỹnŏdūs -ontis, m. *a fish, perhaps bream.*

synthĕsis -is, f. *a dinner-service; a suit of clothes; a dressing-gown.*

Sỹrācūsae -ārum, f. pl. *the chief town of Sicily.*

Sỹrĭa -ae, f. *Syria;* adj. **Sỹrĭus, Sỹrus, Sỹrĭăcus** -a -um, *Syrian;* subst. **Sỹri** -orum, *the Syrians.*

syrma -mătis, n. *a long robe, worn by tragic actors.*

syrtis -is, f. *a sandbank, quicksand;* esp. *one on the coast of Northern Africa.*

T

T, t, the nineteenth letter of the Latin Alphabet.

tăbella -ae, f. *a small flat board or tablet; a writing-tablet; a document, letter, record; a votive tablet; a voting-ticket, ballot; a picture.*

tăbellārĭus -a -um, *of letters, or of voting.* M. as subst. *a letter-carrier.*

tăbĕo -ere, *to waste away; to drip, run.*

tăberna -ae, f. *a booth, hut; a cottage, hovel; a stall, shop; an inn, tavern; a block of seats in the Circus.*

tăbernācŭlum -i, n. *a hut, tent.*

tăbernārĭus -i, m. *a shopkeeper.*

tăbēs -is, f. *wasting away, decay, melting; disease, pestilence; demoralization; decayed matter, corruption.*

tăbesco **tăbescĕre** tăbŭi, *to melt, waste away; to pine, be spoiled.*

tăbĭdŭlus -a -um, *wasting, consuming.*

tăbĭdus -a -um: pass., *melting, wasting, dissolving;* act., *consuming.*

tăbĭfĭcus -a -um, *consuming.*

tăbŭla -ae, f. *a board, plank; a draught-board; a painted panel, a painting; a votive tablet; a map; a writing-tablet; a document;* in plur., *a record, register; a catalogue; an auction.*

tăbŭlārĭum -i, n. *archives, records.*

tăbŭlātĭo -ōnis, f. *flooring, planking; a storey.*

tăbŭlātus -a -um, *floored, boarded;* n. as subst., *a floor, storey; a row or layers of vines.*

tābum -i, n. *corrupt moisture, matter; a plague, pestilence.*

tăcĕo -ēre -ŭi -ĭtum, *to be silent, say nothing; to be still, quiet;* transit., *to be silent about, pass over in silence.* Hence partic. **tăcĭtus** -a -um: pass., *passed over in silence, unmentioned; implied, tacit; secret, concealed;* act., *silent, mute, still, quiet.* Adv. **tăcĭtē.**

tăcĭturnĭtās -ātis, f., *silence, taciturnity.*

tăcĭturnus -a -um, *silent, still, quiet.*

tăcĭtus -a -um, partic. from taceo; q.v.

Tăcĭtus -i, m., Cornelius, *the historian of the early Empire.*

tactĭlis -e, *able to be touched.*

tactĭo -ōnis, f. *touching, sense of touch.*

tactus -ūs, m. *touch, touching; influence, operation; the sense of touch.*

taeda -ae, f. *pine-wood; a board, a torch,* esp. *as used at weddings.*

taedet taedēre taedŭit, and taesum est, impers., *it causes weariness or boredom.*

taedĭfer -fĕra -fĕrum, *torch-bearing.*

taedĭum -i, n. *disgust, weariness, boredom.*

taenĭa -ae, f. *a fillet, head-band.*

taeter -tra -trum, *foul, hideous, offensive; disgraceful, abominable;* adv. **taetrē.**

tăgax -ācis, *thievish, given to pilfering.*

tālāris -e, *of or stretching to the ankles;* n. pl. as subst. *wings on the ankles, winged sandals,* or *a robe reaching to the ankles.*

tālārĭus -a -um, *of dice.*

tālĕa -ae, f. *a cutting, slip; a short stake or bar.*

tălentum -i, n. *a (Greek) weight;* also *a sum of money.*

tālĭo -ōnis, f. *retaliation.*

tālis -e, *of such a kind, such.*

talpa -ae, f. or m. *a mole.*

tālus -i, m. *the ankle, ankle-bone; the heel; a die* (made originally of ankle-bones of animals).

tam, *so, so far, to such a degree.*

tămărix -ĭcis, f. *the tamarisk.*

tamdĭū, *so long.*

tămĕn, *however, yet, nevertheless.*

Tămĕsis -is, m. and **Tămĕsa** -ae, *the Thames.*

tămetsi, *even if, although.*

tamquam (tanquam), *as, just as, like as; just as if.*

tandem, *at length, at last;* in questions, *after all, may I ask?*

tango tangĕre tĕtĭgi tactum, *to touch, strike, push, hit; to border on, to reach; to steal; to defile; to taste; to affect the feelings; to touch upon a subject.*

Tantălus i-, m. *a son of Jupiter, who offended the gods and was "tantalised" in Hades.*

tantillus -a -um, *so little, so small.*

tantispĕr, *just so long.*

tantŏpĕrĕ, *so greatly, so much.*

tantŭlus -a -um, *so small, so little;* n. as subst. *such a trifle.*

tantum; see tantus.

tantummŏdo, only just.

tantus -a -um, of such a size, so great. N. as subst. **tantum** -i, so much; acc. as adv., so far, or only; tantum non, all but; genit. **tanti,** for so much, worth so much; abl. **tanto,** by so much.

tantusdem tantădem tantundem, just so much, just so great.

tăpēta -ae, m. **tăpēta** -ōrum, n. pl., and **tăpētia** -ium, n. pl., drapery, tapestry.

tardesco -ěre, to become slow.

tardīpēs -pĕdis, slow-footed, limping.

tardĭtās -ātis, f. slowness, tardiness; dullness, stupidity.

tardo -are: intransit., to loiter, be slow; transit., to slow down, hinder, delay.

tardus -a -um, adj. slow, tardy; dull, stupid; poet., making slow; of speech, measured, deliberate. Adv. **tardē,** slowly.

Tărentum -i, n. a coastal town of southern Italy (now Taranto); adj. **Tărentīnus** -a -um.

Tarpēius -a -um, name of a Roman family; mons Tarpeius, the Tarpeian rock, from which criminals were thrown.

Tarquiniī -orum, m. pl. an old town in Etruria, whence came the Tarquin family, including two kings of Rome.

Tarrāco -ōnis, f. a town in Spain.

Tartărus (-ŏs) -i, m.; plur. **Tartără** -ōrum, n. the infernal regions; adj. **Tartărĕus** -a -um.

taurĕus -a -um, of a bull; f. as subst. a whip of bull's hide.

tauriformis -e, shaped like a bull.

taurinus -a -um, of or like a bull.

taurus -i, m. a bull.

Taurus -i, m. a mountain range in Asia Minor.

taxātĭo -onis, f. rating, valuing, appraising.

taxillus -i, m. a small die.

taxus -i, f. yew-tree.

¹tĕ; see tu.

²-tĕ, suffix added to tu, etc.

techna -ae, f. a cunning trick, artifice.

tector -ōris, m. a plasterer.

tectōriŏlum -i, n. plaster or stucco work.

tectōrius -a -um, used for covering, or of for plastering; n. as subst. plaster, stucco, fresco painting, cosmetic.

tectus -a -um, partic. from tego; q.v.

tēgēs -ĕtis, f. a mat, rug, covering.

tēgimen, tēgŭmen, tegmĕn -ĭnis, n. a cover, covering.

tēgimentum, tēgŭmentum, tegmentum -i, n. a covering.

tēgo tĕgĕre texi tectum, to cover; to bury; to conceal; to shield, protect. Hence partic. as adj. **tectus** -a -um, covered, concealed; close, reserved, cautious. N. as subst. **tectum** -i, a roof or ceiling; a shelter, dwelling. Adv. **tectē,** covertly.

tegu-; see also tegi-.

tēgŭla -ae, f. a roof-tile.

tela -ae, f. a web in weaving; a warp; a spider's web; a loom; a design.

Tēlĕmăchus -i, m. son of Penelope and Ulysses.

tellūs -ūris, f. earth, soil, land; a country; the world.

tēlum -i, n. a missile; a dart, javelin, spear; any weapon; a beam of light.

tĕmĕrārius -a -um, accidental; inconsiderate, thoughtless, rash.

tĕmĕrē, adv. blindly, by chance, casually, heedlessly; non temere, not for nothing, not lightly, not easily.

tĕmĕrĭtās -ātis, f. chance, accident; rashness.

tĕmĕro -are, to darken; to defile, dishonour.

tēmētum -i, n. intoxicating drink; wine, etc.

temno temnĕre tempsi temptum, to despise.

tēmŏ -ōnis, m. a pole; the pole of a waggon; a waggon; Charles's Wain.

Tempē, n. pl., indecl. a valley in Thessaly.

tempĕrāmentum -i, n. a right proportion, middle way, mean, moderation.

temperantĭa -ae, f. temperance moderation, self-control.

temperātĭo -ōnis, f. moderation, just proportion; an organizing principle.

tempĕrātor -ōris, m. one who arranges or governs.

tempĕri; see tempus.

tempĕrĭēs -ēi, f. a proper mixture, tempering; of climate, mildness.

tempĕro -are: intransit., to be moderate, control oneself; with dat. to control, use with moderation, or to spare; with ab, or with abl., to keep from, refrain from; transit., to mix properly, temper, mitigate, regulate. Hence partic. as adj. **tempĕrans** -antis, moderate, temperate, restrained; adv. **tempĕranter;** perf. partic. **tempĕrātus** -a -um, tempered, ordered, moderate; adv. **tempĕrātē.**

tempĕstās -ātis, f. a period of time, a season; weather; esp. bad weather, storm, tempest; fig., attack, fury.

tempestīvĭtās -ātis, f. fit time, proper season.

tempestīvus -a -um, opportune, fit, appropriate; early; ripe, mature. Adv. **tempestīvē,** seasonably.

templum -i, n. a section, a part cut off; a space marked out by the augur for auspices; consecrated ground, esp. a sanctuary, asylum; a place dedicated to a deity, a shrine, temple; any open space, quarter, region; a rafter, cross-beam.

tempŏrālis -e, temporary, lasting for a time.

tempŏrārius -a -um temporary; seasonable.

tempŏri; see tempus.

temptābundus -a -um, trying, attempting.

temptāmen -ĭnis, and **temptāmentum** -i, n. a trial, attempt, essay.

temptātĭo -ōnĭs, f. a trial, test; an attack.

temptātor -ōris, m. an assailant.

tempto -are, *to prove, try, test, attempt;
  *to test by attack, to assail; to work upon,
  tamper with, excite, disturb.

tempus -ŏris, n. *a division, section;* of
  the temples of the head; of time, *a
  space, period, moment;* time, in gen.);
  a fit time, occasion, opportunity; the
  state, condition of things (esp. bad);
  *time in pronouncing a syllable, quantity;
  time in grammar, tense.* As adv.
  tempŏrĕ, tempŏrī, and **tempĕrī,**
  at the right time, or *for the occasion;*
  in tempŏrĕ, *at the right moment;*
  ex tempŏrĕ, *on the spur of the
  moment.*

tēmŭlentus -a -um, *drunken, tipsy.*

tēnācĭtās -ātis, f. *tenacity; stinginess.*

tēnax -ācis, *holding fast, clinging,
  tenacious; sparing, frugal, stingy;
  firm, steady; obstinate.* Adv. **tēnā-
  cĭtĕr,** *firmly, steadily.*

tendĭcŭla -ae, f. *a snare, trap.*

tendo tendĕre tĕtendi tentum and
  tensum: transit., *to stretch, extend,
  spread; to direct, present, give;*
  barbiton, *to string;* praetorium, *to
  pitch;* intransit., *to direct one's
  course, tend, make towards; to be
  inclined, aim at, strive after;* with
  infin., *to try, attempt;* milit., *to
  pitch one's tent, encamp.*

tĕnebrae -arum, f. pl. *darkness;
  night; blindness; obscurity.*

tĕnebrĭcōsus -a -um, *dark, gloomy,
  obscure.*

tĕnebrōsus -a -um, *dark, gloomy.*

tĕnĕo tĕnēre tĕnŭi tentum, *to hold;
  to possess, keep, preserve, maintain;
  to understand, grasp, know, remember;
  to contain, comprise;* milit. *to occupy,
  garrison;* transit., *to master, restrain, keep
  back; to charm, amuse;* intransit., *to
  keep on, persevere, persist, endure.*

tĕner -ĕra -ĕrum, *tender, delicate, soft;
  young;* adv. **tĕnĕrē.**

tĕnĕrasco -ĕre, *to grow tender.*

tĕnĕrĭtās -ātis, f. *tenderness, softness.*

tĕnor -ōris, m. *course, continued movement; duration, career.*

tensa -ae, f. *a car on which images of the
  gods were carried.*

tento etc.; see tempto, etc.

tentīgo -ĭnis, f. *lecherousness.*

tentōrium -i, n. *a tent.*

tentus -a -um, partic. from tendo and
  teneo; q.v.

tĕnŭĭcŭlus -a -um, *very mean, slight.*

tĕnŭis -e, *thin, slight, slender; refined,
  subtle; little, trivial, feeble; mean,
  low.* Adv. **tĕnŭĭtĕr,** *thinly; subtly;
  slightly, poorly.*

tĕnŭĭtās -ātis, f. *thinness; refinement,
  subtlety; slightness, poverty.*

tĕnŭo -are, *to make thin, attenuate; to
  weaken, diminish.*

tĕnŭs, prep. after noun or pronoun in
  abl. or genit., *up to, down to, as far as.*

tĕpĕfācĭo -fācĕre -fēci -factum, *to make
  warm.*

tĕpĕo -ēre, *to be warm,* or *lukewarm.*

tĕpesco tĕpescĕre tĕpŭi, *to grow warm*
  or *lukewarm.*

tĕpĭdus -a -um, *warm, lukewarm,
  tepid;* compar. adv. **tĕpĭdĭus.**

tĕpor -ōris, m. *lukewarmness, moderate
  heat.*

tĕr, *three times, thrice.*

terdĕcĭēs (-ĭens) *thirteen times.*

tĕrĕbinthus -i, f. *the terebinth-tree.*

tĕrebro -are, *to bore through, pierce,
  perforate.*

tĕrēdo -ĭnis, f. *a worm that gnaws wood.*

Tĕrentĭus -a -um, *the name of a Roman
  gens;* esp. of M. Terentius Afer, *the
  comic dramatist.*

tĕrēs -rētis, *rounded, polished, well-
  turned, smooth; refined, elegant.*

tergĕmĭnus = trigeminus; q.v.

tergĕo -ēre and **tergo** -ĕre, tersi
  tersum, *to wipe, scour, clean;* partic.
  tersus -a -um, *clean, neat, correct.*

tergīversātĭo -ōnis, f. *backwardness,
  reluctance, evasion.*

tergīversor -ari, dep. *to be backward
  and reluctant, shuffle, find excuses,
  evade.*

tergo = tergeo; q.v.

tergum -i, n. *the back;* terga dare, *to
  flee;* a tergo, *in the rear; a hide, skin;*
  meton., *a thing made out of hide.*

tergus -ōris, n. *the back; skin, hide,
  leather.*

termĕs -ĭtis, m. *a branch,* esp. of olive.

Termĭnālĭa -ĭum and -ĭōrum, n. *the
  Festival of Terminus (god of boundaries).*

termĭnātĭo -ōnis, f. *limiting, determining, termination.*

termĭno -are, *to limit, set bounds to,
  restrict, define, close.*

termĭnus -i, m. *a boundary-mark,
  limit, end;* personif., *the god of
  boundaries.*

terni -ae -a, *three at a time,* or *three
  each.*

tĕro tĕrĕre trĭvi trĭtum, *to rub; to
  whet, smooth; to grind, thresh; to
  wear out, use up, spend.*
     Hence partic. as adj. **trĭtus** -a -um,
  worn; frequented; practised; of
  words, etc., *trite, well-known.*

Terpsĭchŏrē -ēs, f. *the Muse of dancing;*
  in gen., *poetry.*

terra -ae, f. *earth, land, ground, soil;
  a country, land, region;* orbis terrarum,
  the whole world.

terrēnus -a -um, *belonging to the earth,
  terrestrial; made of earth, earthen;* n.
  as subst. *land, ground.*

terrĕo terrēre, *to frighten, terrify; scare
  away; to deter.*

terrestris -e, *of the earth, terrestrial.*

terrĕus -a -um, *of earth, earthly.*

terrĭbĭlis -e, *terrible, dreadful.*

terrĭcŭla -ōrum, n. pl. *a bogey.*

terrĭfĭco -are, *to frighten, terrify.*

terrĭfĭcus -a -um, *frightful, terrible.*

terrĭgĕna -ae, m. and f. *earth-born.*

terrĭlŏquus -a -um, *terror-speaking.*

terrĭto -are, *to frighten, intimidate,
  scare.*

terrĭtōrium -i, n. *land belonging to a
  town, district, territory.*

terror -ōris, m. *fright, fear, terror; a
  frightening object.*

tersus -a -um, partic. from tergeo; q.v.

tertiădĕcĭmāni -ōrum, m. pl. *soldiers of the thirteenth legion.*

tertiānus -a -um. (1) *of the third day;* f. as subst., *a tertian fever.* (2) *belonging to the third legion;* m. pl. as subst., *soldiers of the third legion.*

tertius -a -um, *third;* acc. n. sing. **tertĭum,** *for the third time;* abl. **tertĭō,** *for the third time,* or *thirdly.*

tertĭusdĕcĭmus -a -um, *thirteenth.*

tĕruncĭus -i, m. *one quarter;* ne teruncius quidem, *not a farthing.*

tesqua (tesca) -ōrum, n. pl. *wastes, deserts.*

tessella -ae, f. *a small cube of stone.*

tessĕra -ae, f. *a cube; a piece of mosaic paving; a die* (with numbers on all six sides); *a token; a watchword.*

tessĕrārĭus -i, m. *the officer who received the watchword.*

testa -ae, f. *an earthen vessel, pot, jug, urn,* etc.; *a potsherd; a brick* or *tile; the shell of shell-fish;* any *shell, covering.*

testāmentārĭus -a -um, *relating to a will;* m. as subst., *a forger of wills.*

testāmentum -i, n. *a last will, testament.*

testātĭo -ōnis, f. *calling to witness,* or *bearing witness.*

testĭfĭcātĭo -ōnis, f. *bearing witness, testifying; evidence, proof.*

testĭfĭcor -ari, dep. *to bear witness to, give evidence of; to show, bring to light; to call to witness.*

testĭmōnĭum -i, n. *witness, evidence; proof, indication.*

¹**testis** -is, c. *one who gives evidence, a witness; an eye-witness, spectator.*

²**testis** -is, m. *a testicle.*

testor -ari, dep. (1) *to bear witness to, give evidence of; to make known, publish, declare;* as pass., *to be attested, declared.* (2) *to make a will.* (3) *to call to witness.*

testūdĭnĕus -a -um, *of a tortoise; of tortoise-shell.*

testūdo -ĭnis, f. *a tortoise; tortoise-shell; a lyre, cithara,* etc.; *an arch* or *vault;* milit. *a shed, to protect soldiers while attacking fortifications,* also *a formation with shields held over the soldiers' heads and interlocking.*

testŭla -ae, f. *a potsherd.*

testum -i, n. with abl. testo and testu, *an earthen pot.*

teter; see taeter.

Tēthys -thўos; acc. -thyn; f. *a marine goddess.*

tetrachmum or **tetradrachmum** -i, n. *a Greek coin of four drachmae.*

tetrarchēs -ae, m. *ruler over one-fourth of a country, tetrarch.*

tetrarchĭa -ae, f. *a tetrarchy.*

tetrĭcus -a -um, *harsh, gloomy, severe.*

Teucer -cri, and **Teucrus** -i, m. (1) *son of Telamon, and brother of Ajax.* (2) *first king of Troy;* hence adj. **Teucrus** -a -um, *Trojan;* m. pl. as subst. *the Trojans;* **Teucrĭa** -ae, f. *Troy.*

Teutŏni -ōrum, and **Teutŏnes** -um, m. pl. *the Teutons, a Germanic people.*

texo texĕre texŭi textum, *to weave; to twine together, plait; to put together, construct, build;* of speech or writing, *to compose.* N. of partic. as subst.

textum -i, *woven cloth, a web, fabric;* of composition, *style.*

textĭlis -e, *woven, textile, plaited.* N. as subst. *a woven fabric, piece of cloth.*

textor -ōris, m. and **textrix** -tricis, f. *a weaver.*

textrīnum -i, n. *weaving.*

textum -i, n. subst. from texo; q.v.

textūra -ae, f. *a web, texture; putting together, construction.*

textus -ūs, m. *a web; texture, structure;* of speech or writing, *connexion.*

thălămus -i, m. *a room,* esp. *a woman's bedroom; a marriage-bed; any abode, dwelling.*

thălassĭnus -a -um, *sea-green.*

Thălīa -ae, f. *the Muse of comic poetry.*

thallus -i, m. *a green branch.*

Thapsus (-ŏs) -i, f. *a town in Africa, where Caesar conquered the Pompeians.*

thĕātrālis -e, *of a theatre, theatrical.*

thĕātrum -i, n. *a theatre.*

Thēbae -arum, f. pl. *Thebes.* (1) *a city of Upper Egypt.* (2) *the chief city of Boeotia.* Adj. **Thēbānus** -a -um, *belonging to Thebes in Boeotia.*

thēca -ae, f. *a case, envelope, covering.*

thēma -ătis, n. *a topic, subject.*

thĕŏlŏgus -i, m. *a theologian.*

thermae -arum, f. pl. *warm springs, warm baths.*

thēsaurus -i, m. *a treasure, store, hoard; a treasury, store-house.*

Thēsēus -ĕi and -ĕos, m. *a king of Athens, conqueror of the Minotaur;* adj. **Thēsēus** and **Thēsēĭus** -a -um, *of Theseus.*

thĕsis -is, f. *a proposition, thesis.*

Thessălĭa -ae, f. *Thessaly, a region in the north of Greece;* adj. **Thessălĭcus** and **Thessălus** -a -um, *Thessalian;* f. adj. **Thessălĭs** -ĭdis, *Thessalian.*

Thĕtis -ĭdis or -ĭdos, f. *a sea-nymph, mother of Achilles;* poet., *the sea.*

thĭāsus -i, m. *a Bacchic rout, band of revellers.*

Thisbē -ēs, f. *a Babylonian maiden, loved by Pyramus.*

thŏlus -i, m. *a cupola, dome.*

thōrax -ācis, m. *a breastplate, cuirass.*

Thrācĭa -ae; also **Thrāca** -ae and **Thrācē** -ēs; f. *the country of Thrace;* adj. **Thrācĭus** and **Thrēĭcĭus** -a -um, *Thracian;* **Thrax** -ācis and **Thrēx** -ēcis, m. *Thracian, a Thracian.*

Thūcȳdĭdēs -is, m. *the Athenian historian of the Peloponnesian war.*

Thūlē (Thȳlē) -ēs, f. *an island in the extreme north of Europe.*

thunnus (thynnus) -i, m. *a tunny-fish.*

thūs, thūrārĭus, etc. = tus, turarius, etc.; q.v.

Thўestēs -ae and -is, m. *son of Pelops, brother of Atreus.*

Thȳĭăs and **Thȳăs** -ādis, f. *a Bacchante.*

Thȳlē = Thule; q.v.

thymbra -ae, f. *the herb savory.*

thȳmum -i, n. *the herb thyme.*

thynnus = thunnus; q.v.

thyrsus -i, m. *the stalk of a plant; a wand, as carried by Bacchus and his attendants.*

tiăra -ae, f. and tiărus -ae, m. *a turban.*

Tibĕris -bĕris, m.; also poet. Tibris or Thibris -bridis, m. *the river Tiber;* adj. Tibĕrīnus -a -um, *of the river Tiber;* m. as subst. *the river-god of the Tiber.*

Tibĕrius -i, m. *a Roman praenomen,* abbreviated Ti.

tibia -ae, f. *the shin-bone, tibia; a pipe, flute* (originally made of a hollow bone).

tibīcĕn -inis, m. *a flute-player; piper; a pillar, prop.*

tibīcĭna -ae, f. *a female flute-player.*

tibīcĭnĭum -i, *playing on the flute.*

Tibris = Tiberis; q.v.

Tibullus -i, m.; Albius, *a Roman elegiac poet.*

Tibŭr -būris, n. *an old town in Latium;* adj. Tiburs -burtis, Tīburtīnus and Tiburnus -a -um.

tigillum -i, n. *a small beam.*

tignārius -a -um, *of beams;* faber, *a carpenter.*

tignum -i, *a beam.*

Tigrānēs -is, m. *a king of Armenia.*

tigris -idis and -is, c. *a tiger.*

tilia -ae, f. *linden or lime-tree.*

tĭmĕfactus -a -um, *frightened, alarmed.*

tĭmĕo -ēre, *to be afraid, fear, dread;* partic. timens -entis, *fearing, fearful.*

tĭmĭdĭtās -ātis, f. *fearfulness, timidity.*

tĭmĭdus -a -um, *fearful, timid;* adv. tĭmĭdē.

timor -ōris, m. *fear, dread; an object exciting fear.*

tinctĭlis -e, *in which something is dipped.*

tĭnĕa -ae, f. *a grub, larva, worm.*

tingo tingĕre tinxi tinctum, *to wet, moisten; to dye, colour, imbue.*

tinnĭo -ire, *to ring, tinkle; to talk shrilly; to make to chink;* hence *to pay money.*

tinnītus -ūs, m. *ringing, tinkle, jingle.*

tinnŭlus -a -um, *ringing, tinkling, jingling.*

tintinnābŭlum -i, n. *a bell.*

tintinno (tintino) -are, *to ring, tinkle.*

tinus -i, f. *a shrub, the laurustinus.*

Tīridātēs -dātis, m. *name of several kings of Armenia.*

tīrō -ōnis, m. *a young soldier; a recruit, beginner, learner.*

tīrōcĭnĭum -i, n. *the state of a recruit, rawness, inexperience; beginning, apprenticeship;* concr. *a body of recruits.*

tīruncŭlus -i, m. *a young beginner.*

Tiryns -nthis or -nthos, f. *an Argive town where Hercules was brought up;* adj. Tīrynthĭus -a -um.

Tīsiphŏnē -ēs, f. *one of the Furies.*

Tītān -tānis, and Tītānus -i, m.; usually plur. Tītānes -um and Tītāni -ōrum, *the Titans, who warred against Jupiter and were by him cast into Hades.*

Tīthōnus -i, m. *husband of Aurora.*

Tītĭes -ium and Tītĭenses -ium, m. pl., *one of the three original tribes at Rome.*

tītillātĭo -ōnis, f. *a tickling.*

tītillo -are, *to tickle.*

tītŭbātĭo -ōnis, f. *a staggering, reeling; uncertainty.*

tītŭbo -are, *to totter, stagger; to stammer; to falter, waver, hesitate;* adv. from partic. tītŭbantĕr, *hesitatingly, uncertainly.*

tītŭlus -i, m. *an inscription, label, notice; a title, honour; pretence, pretext.*

Titus -i, m. *a Roman praenomen,* abbreviated T.

tŏcŭlio -ōnis, m. *a usurer.*

tōfus (tōphus) -i, m. *tufa.*

tŏga -ae, f. *the white woollen upper garment worn by Roman citizens.*

tŏgātŭlus -i, m. *a little client.*

tŏgātus -a -um, *wearing the toga;* m. as subst. *a Roman citizen;* f. as subst. *the national drama of the Romans.*

tŏgŭla -ae, f. *a little toga.*

tŏlĕrābĭlis -e; pass., *bearable;* act., *tolerant, patient;* compar. adv. tŏlĕrābĭlius, *rather patiently.*

tŏlĕrantia -ae and tŏlĕrātĭo -ōnis, f. *bearing, endurance.*

tŏlĕro -are, *to carry, bear, endure, sustain; to sustain; to support, keep up, maintain.* Hence pres. partic. tŏlĕrans -antis, *enduring, patient;* adv. tŏlĕrantĕr; perf. partic. tŏlĕrātus -a -um, *endurable.*

tollēno -ōnis, m. *a machine for raising weights, a crane.*

tollo tollĕre sustŭli sublātum. (1) *to lift up, raise, elevate;* in crucem, *to crucify;* tollere ancoras, *to weigh anchor;* laudibus, *to extol;* of children, *to acknowledge as one's own, to bring up.* (2) *to take away, remove, carry off, steal; to destroy, abolish.*

tŏmācŭlum (-aclum) -i, n. *a kind of sausage.*

tōmentum -i, n. *the stuffing of a pillow, mattress,* etc.

Tŏmi -ōrum, m. pl. and Tŏmis -is, f. *a town on the Black Sea, Ovid's place of exile.*

tōmus -i, m. *a cutting, chip, shred.*

tondĕo tondēre tŏtondi tonsum, *to shave, shear, clip; to mow, reap, prune; to browse on, crop; to fleece a person.*

tŏnitrus -ūs, m. and tŏnitruum -i, n. *thunder.*

tŏno -are -ūi -itum, *to thunder.* Transf.: instransit., *to make a loud noise;* transit., *to thunder forth.*

tonsa -ae, f. *an oar.*

tonsĭlis -e, *shorn, clipped, cut.*

tonsillae -arum, f. *the tonsils.*

tonsor -ōris, m. *a hair-cutter, barber.*

tonsōrĭus -a -um, *of or for clipping.*

tonstrĭcŭla -ae, f. *a little female barber.*

tonstrīna -ae, f. *a barber's shop.*

tonstrix -icis, f. *a female barber.*

tonsūra -ae, f. *clipping, shearing, shaving.*

tophus, etc. = tofus, etc.; q.v.

tŏpiārius -a -um, *of ornamental gardening*; m. as subst. *a landscape gardener*; f. as subst. *the art of landscape gardening*.

tŏrāl -ālis, n. *the valance of a couch*.

tŏreuma -ātis, n. *carved or embossed work*.

tormentum -i, n. *an instrument for twisting or pressing; a windlass; the rack; any instrument of torture; hence suasion, pressure; torture, torment*; milit., *a piece of artillery, or a missile*.

tormĭna -um, n. pl. *the colic, gripes*.

tormĭnōsus -a -um, *suffering from colic*.

torno -are, *to turn in a lathe; to round, make round*.

tornus -i, m. *a lathe*.

tŏrōsus -a -um, *muscular, brawny*.

torpēdo -ĭnis, f. (1) *lethargy, sluggishness*. (2) *a fish, the electric ray*.

torpĕo -ēre, *to be sluggish, numb, inert, inactive*.

torpesco -pescĕre -pŭi, *to become sluggish or numb*.

torpĭdus -a -um, *numb, sluggish*.

torpor -ōris, m. *numbness, sluggishness, dullness, inactivity*.

torquātus -a -um, *wearing a twisted collar or necklace*.

torquĕo torquēre torsi tortum, *to twist, wind, curl, wrench; to distort; to hurl violently, whirl; to rack, torture, torment, plague, try, test*.
  Hence partic. **tortus** -a -um, *twisted, crooked, intricate*; adv. **tortē**.

torquis (torquēs) -is, m. and f. *a twisted collar or necklace; a ring, wreath, chaplet*.

torrĕo torrēre torrŭi tostum, *to burn, parch, dry up*.
  Hence partic. as adj. **torrens** -entis, *burning, hot, parched; rushing, seething*. M. as subst. *a torrent*.

torresco -ĕre, *to become parched*.

torrĭdus -a -um, *parched, burnt, dry*. Transf., *pinched, nipped with cold*.

torris, is, m. *a firebrand*.

tortĭlis -e, *twisted, twined*.

torto -are, *to torture, torment*.

tortor -ōris, m. *a torturer, tormentor; a wielder*.

tortŭōsus -a -um, *tortuous, intricate, involved*.

¹**tortus** -a -um, partic. from torqueo; q.v.

²**tortus** -ūs, m. *a twisting, curve*.

tŏrus -i, m. *any round protuberance; a muscle; a bed, sofa; a marriage couch; a bier; a mound*; fig., *an ornament*.

torvĭtās -ātis, f. *savageness, wildness*.

torvus -a -um, *savage, grim, fierce*.

tŏt, indecl. *so many*.

tŏtĭdem, indecl. *just as many*.

tŏtĭes (-ĭens), *so often, so many times*.

tōtus -a -um, genit. tōtĭus, dat. tōti; *whole, complete, entire; whole-hearted, absorbed*. N. as subst. **tōtum** -i, *the whole*; ex toto, in toto, *on the whole*.

toxĭcum -i, n. *poison (for arrows)*.

trăbālis -e, *of beams of wood; like a beam*.

trăbĕa -ae, f. *a white robe with scarlet stripes and a purple seam, worn by kings and knights*.

trăbĕātus -a -um, *clad in the trabea*; q.v.

trabs trăbis, f. *a beam of wood; a tree-trunk; a ship; a roof; a table*.

tractābĭlis -e, *that can be handled, manageable; yielding, compliant*.

tractātĭo -ōnis, f. *handling, management*.

tractātor -ōris, m. *a masseur*.

tractātrix -īcis, f. *a masseuse*.

tractātus -ūs, m. *handling, management, treatment*.

tractim, *gradually, by degrees*.

tracto -are, *to drag along, haul, pull about; to handle, manage, treat; to behave towards a person*.

¹**tractus** -a -um, partic. from traho; q.v.

²**tractus** -ūs, m. *a dragging process; verborum, drawling; belli, extension*; concr., *a track, trail; extent, position; a tract, district*.

trādĭtĭo -ōnis, f. *giving up, surrender; instruction, relation*.

trādĭtor -ōris, m. *traitor*.

trādo (transdo) -dĕre -dĭdi -dĭtum, *to hand over, give up, surrender, betray; to hand down to posterity; esp. to hand down an account of an event, to report, relate, teach*; with reflex., *to commit, surrender, devote oneself*.

trādūco (transdūco) -dūcĕre -duxi -ductum, *to lead over, bring over or across; to lead past in front of others; to transpose, transfer; of time, to pass, spend, lead; to show, display; to expose to ridicule, " show up "*.

trāductĭo -ōnis, f. *transferring*; rhet., metonymy; temporis, *passage or lapse of time*.

trāductor -ōris, m. *a transferrer*.

trādux -ŭcis, m. *vine-layer*.

trăgĭcus -a -um, *tragic; lofty, sublime; awful, fearful*. M. as subst. *a tragic poet*. Adv. **trăgĭcē**, *tragically*.

trăgoedĭa -ae, f. *tragedy; a dramatic scene*.

trăgoedus -i, m. *tragic actor, tragedian*.

trăgŭla -ae, f. *a species of javelin*.

trăhĕa -ae, f. *sledge, drag*.

trăho trăhĕre traxi tractum, *to trail, pull along; to drag, pull violently; to draw in, take up; of air, to breathe; to draw out, hence to lengthen; to draw together, contract*. Transf., *to draw, attract; to take in or on, assume, derive; to prolong, spin out; to ascribe, refer, interpret*.
  Hence partic. **tractus** -a -um, *of speech, fluent, flowing*. N. as subst., *a flock of wool*.

trāĭcĭo (transĭcĭo) -ĭcĕre -ĭēci -ĭectum, (1) *to throw a thing (or person) across something; to convey over, transport*. (2) *to pass through or across a thing (or person); to cross, penetrate, pierce*.

trāĭectĭo -ōnis, f. *a passing over, crossing over; transferring, transposition; hyperbole*.

trāĭectus -ūs, m. *crossing over, passage*.

tralat- = translat-; q.v.

trālūcĕo = transluceo; q.v.

trāma -ae, f. *the woof in weaving.*

trāmĕo = transmeo; q.v.

trāmĕs -itis, m. *by-way, foot-path.*

trāmigro = transmigro; q.v.

trāmitto = transmitto; q.v.

trānăto (transnăto) -are, *to swim across, pass through.*

tranquillĭtās -ātis, f. *quiet, calm.*

tranquillo -are, *to calm.*

tranquillus -a -um, *quiet, calm.* N. as subst. *a calm, quietness.* Adv. tranquillē.

trans, prep. with acc., *over, across, on* or *to the other side of.*

transăbĕo -ire -ĭi, *to go through or past.*

transactor -ōris, m. *manager, accomplisher.*

transădĭgo -Igĕre -ēgi -actum, *to drive a thing through something else; also to pierce, penetrate.*

Transalpīnus -a -um, *beyond the Alps, transalpine.*

transcendo (transscendo) -scendĕre -scendi -scensum, *to climb over, pass over; to step over, transgress.*

transcrībo (transscribo) -scrībĕre -scripsi -scriptum, *to copy, transcribe.* Transf., *to transfer, convey, assign.*

transcurro -currĕre -cŭcurri and -curri -cursum, *to run across or over, hasten past.*

transcursus -ūs, m. *a running past, hastening through.*

transdo = trado; q.v.

transdūco = traduco; q.v.

transenna -ae, f. *lattice-work, grating.*

transĕo -ire -ĭi -ĭtum, *to go over, cross, pass over, go past.* Transf., *to be changed; to pass time; to pass beyond, transgress; to pass over, ignore, or touch lightly on.*

transfĕro transferre transtŭli translātum and trālātum, *to carry over or across; to transfer, transport, convey.* Transf., *to put off, defer; to change; in writing, to copy; to translate into another language; to use a word figuratively or metaphorically.*

transfīgo -fīgĕre -fixi -fixum, *to pierce through, or thrust through.*

transfōdio -fōdĕre -fōdi -fossum, *to stab through, transfix.*

transformis -e, *changed, transformed.*

transformo -are, *to change, transform.*

transfŭga -ae, *deserter.*

transfŭgio -fŭgĕre -fŭgi -fŭgitum, *to desert to the enemy.*

transfŭgium -i, n. *desertion.*

transfundo -fundĕre -fūdi -fūsum, *to pour from one vessel into another, to transfer.*

transfūsio -ōnis, f. *a pouring out, pouring off.*

transgrĕdior -grĕdi -gressus, dep. *to go across, pass over.*

transgressio -ōnis, f. *going over, passage; transposition of words.*

transgressus -ūs, m. *going over, passage.*

transĭgo -Igĕre -ēgi -actum, *to stab, pierce through; of time, to pass, spend;*

of business, *to finish, complete, accomplish, transact;* of a difference or dispute, *to settle.*

transĭlio (transsĭlio) -sĭlire -sĭlŭi, *to spring over, leap across; to pass over a thing, or to pass beyond, transgress.*

transĭtio -ōnis, f. *going across, passing over; communication, infection, contagion;* concr., *a passage.*

transĭtus -ūs, m. *passing over or across, transit; changing over, transition.*

translātĭcĭus (trālātĭcĭus) -a -um, *customary, prescriptive; common, usual.*

translātĭo (trālātĭo) -ōnis, f. *transferring, handing over;* of plants, *grafting; a translation; a metaphor, trope.*

translātīvus -a -um, *transferable.*

translātŏr -ōris, m. *transferrer.*

translūcĕo (trālūcĕo) -ēre, *to shine through or across.*

transmărīnus -a -um, *from beyond the sea, foreign.*

transmĕo (trāmĕo) -mĕare, *to go over or through.*

transmigro -are, *to migrate.*

transmissio -ōnis, f. and **transmissus** -ūs, m. *passage.*

transmitto (trāmitto) -mittĕre -misi -missum, (1) *to send across, send over, transmit; to convey, make over, entrust;* of time, *to let pass.* (2) *to go across, pass through or over; to leave unnoticed.*

transmontāni -ōrum, m. pl. *dwellers beyond the mountains.*

transmŏvĕo -mŏvēre -mōvi -mōtum, *to remove, transfer.*

transmūto -are, *to change, transmute.*

transnăto = tranato; q.v.

transpădānus -a -um, *beyond* (i.e. *north of) the Po, transpadane.*

transpectus -ūs, m. *a looking through, seeing through.*

transpĭcĭo (transspĭcĭo) -spĭcĕre, *to look through, see through.*

transpōno -pōnĕre -pŏsŭi -pŏsĭtum, *to put over, remove, transfer.*

transporto -are, *to convey across, transport.*

transrhĕnānus -a -um, *beyond the Rhine.*

transtĭbĕrīnus -a -um, *beyond the Tiber.*

transtrum -i, n. *cross-beam; thwart.*

transulto (transsulto) -are, *to spring across.*

transŭo (transsŭo) -sŭĕre, *to sew through;* hence *to pierce through.*

transvectio (trāvectĭo) -ōnis, f. *a carrying across or past; esp. the riding of a Roman knight past the censor at the periodical muster.*

transvĕho (trāvĕho) -vĕhĕre -vexi -vectum, *to carry over or past;* pass., *to ride, soil, etc., across;* of a knight, *to ride past the censor at a muster;* of time, *to pass by.*

transverbĕro -are, *to pierce through, transfix.*

transversārĭus -a, -um, *lying across, transverse.*

transversus, trāversus and **trans-vorsus** -a -um, *transverse, oblique, athwart*; transverso itinere, *obliquely*; transversum digitum, *a finger's breadth*; de transverso, *unexpectedly*.

transvŏlĭto -are, *to fly across.*

transvŏlo (trāvŏlo) -are, *to fly over or across; to hasten through* or *past.*

trăpētus -i, m. **trăpētum** -i, n. and plur. **trăpētes** -um, m. *an oil-press.*

Trăsŭmēnus (also **Trasy-** and **Trasi-**; also with double **n**) -i, m. *the Trasimene lake, where Hannibal conquered the Romans under Flaminius* (217 B.C.).

trav- = transv-; q.v.

trĕcēni -ae, -a, *three hundred at a time* or *each.*

trĕcentēsĭmus -a -um, *three-hundredth.*

trĕcenti -ae -a, *three hundred.*

trĕcentiēs (-**iens**) *three hundred times.*

trĕchēdipnum -i, n. *a light garment worn at table.*

trĕdĕcim, *thirteen.*

trĕmĕbundus -a -um, *trembling.*

trĕmĕfăcĭo -făcĕre -fēci -factum, *to cause to tremble.*

trĕmesco (-isco) -ĕre, *to tremble, quake*; with acc., *to tremble at.*

tremi-; see treme-.

trĕmo -ĕre -ŭi, *to tremble, quake*; with acc. *to tremble at*; gerundive as adj. **trĕmendus** -a -um, *fearful, terrible.*

trĕmor -ōris, m. *a trembling, quaking.*

trĕmŭlus -a -um, *trembling, quaking*; poet., *that causes trembling.*

trĕpĭdātĭo -ōnis, f. *agitation, anxiety.*

trĕpĭdo -are, *to be agitated, be busy, bustle about*; with acc., *to be anxious about*; with infin., *to be in a hurry to do a thing*; of flame, *to flicker.* Adv. from partic. **trĕpĭdantĕr**, *anxiously, hurriedly.*

trĕpĭdus -a -um, *agitated, restless, disturbed, in an emergency*; adv. **trĕpĭdē.**

trēs trĭa, *three.*

tresvĭri = triumviri; q.v.

Trēvĕri (Trēvĭri) -ōrum, m. pl. *a Germanic people.*

trĭangŭlus -a -um, *three-cornered, triangular.* N. as subst. *a triangle.*

trĭārĭi -ōrum, m. pl. *experienced Roman soldiers, drawn up in the third rank, behind the others.*

trĭbŭārĭus -a -um, *relating to a tribe.*

trĭbŭlis -is, m. *a fellow-tribesman.*

trĭbŭlum -i, n. *threshing machine.*

trĭbŭlus -i, m. *a thorny plant, the caltrop.*

trĭbūnăl -ālis, n. *the tribunal, a raised platform used by magistrates and generals.*

trĭbūnātus -ūs, m. *tribuneship.*

trĭbūnĭcĭus -a -um, *of a tribune, tribunicial*; m. as subst. *an ex-tribune.*

trĭbūnus -i, m. *a tribune;* tribuni aerarii, *paymasters who assisted the quaestors;* tribuni militum, or militares, *military officers, of whom there were six to every legion;* tribuni plebis, *tribunes of the people, magistrates who protected the plebeians.*

trĭbŭo -ŭĕre -ŭi -ūtum, *to divide out, allot, assign; to grant, give, allow, yield, ascribe, attribute.*

trĭbus -ūs, f. *a tribe, a division of the Roman people.*

trĭbūtārĭus -a -um, *relating to tribute.*

trĭbūtim, *tribe by tribe.*

trĭbūtĭo -ōnis, f. *a distribution.*

trĭbūtum -i, n. *tax, tribute.* Transf., *a gift, present.*

trĭbūtus -a -um, *arranged according to tribes.*

trīcae -ārum, f. pl. *trifles, nonsense; vexations, troubles.*

trĭcēni -ae -a, *thirty at a time* or *each.*

trĭceps -cĭpĭtis, *three-headed.*

trĭcēsĭmus (-ensĭmus) *thirtieth.*

trĭchĭla -ae, f. *summer-house, arbour.*

trĭcĭēs (-iens), *thirty times.*

trĭclīnĭum -i, n. *dining-couch;* hence *dining-room.*

trĭcor -ari, dep. *to make difficulties shuffle, trifle.*

trĭcorpŏr -pŏris, *having three bodies.*

trĭcuspis -ĭdis, *having three points.*

trĭdens -entis, *having three teeth* or *prongs.* M. as subst. *a trident, a three-pronged spear.*

trĭdentĭfer and **trĭdentĭger** -ĕri, m. *the trident-bearer* (of Neptune).

trĭdŭum -i, n. *a space of three days.*

trĭennĭa -ĭum, n. pl. *a festival celebrated every three years.*

trĭennĭum -i, n. *a space of three years.*

trĭens -entis, m. *a third part, one-third.*

trĭentābŭlum -i, n. *the equivalent in land for the third part of a sum of money.*

trĭērarchus -i, m. *the commander of a trireme.*

trĭētērĭcus -a -um, *recurring every three years, triennial.*

trĭētēris -ĭdis, f. *a space of three years* or *a triennial festival.*

trĭfārĭam, *in three places, on three sides.*

trĭfaux -faucis, *having three throats.*

trĭfĭdus -a -um, *split in three parts, three-forked.*

trĭformis -e, *having three forms.*

trĭgĕmĭnus (tergĕmĭnus) -a -um, *threefold, triple.*

trĭgintā, *thirty.*

trĭgon -ōnis, m. *a ball for playing.*

trĭlībris -e, *of three pounds' weight.*

trĭlinguis -e, *having three tongues.*

trĭlix -īcis, *having three threads.*

trĭmetrŏs (-us) -a -um, *containing three double feet.* M. as subst., *a trimeter.*

trĭmus -a -um, *three years old.*

Trīnacrĭa -ae, f. *the triangular land,* i.e. *Sicily*; adj. **Trīnacrĭus** -a -um, and f. **Trīnacris** -ĭdis, *Sicilian.*

trīni -ae, -a; *three at a time, three together.*

Trīnobantes -um, m. *a people in east Britain.*

trĭnōdis -e, *having three knots.*

trĭōnēs -um, m. pl. *the ploughing oxen; the constellations Great Bear and Little Bear.*

trĭpart-; see tripert-.

trĭpectŏrus -a -um, *having three breasts.*

trīpĕdālis -e, *of three feet in measure.*

tripertītus (**-partītus**) -a -um, *three-fold, triple.* N. abl. sing. **tripertītō** (**-partītō**), *in three parts.*

tripēs -pĕdis, *having three feet.*

triplex -līcis, *threefold, triple.* M. pl. as subst. *a writing tablet with three leaves.*

triplus -a -um, *threefold, triple.*

tripudio -are, *to beat the ground with the feet, to dance,* esp. as a religious rite.

tripŭdium -i, n. (1) *a religious dance.* (2) *a favourable omen, when the sacred chickens ate fast.*

tripūs -pŏdis, m. *three-legged seat, tripod,* esp. that at Delphi.

triquetrus -a -um, *three-cornered, triangular.*

trirēmis -e, *having three banks of oars;* f. as subst., *a trireme.*

triscurrĭa -ōrum, n. pl. *gross buffooneries.*

tristĭcŭlus -a -um, *somewhat sorrowful.*

tristis -e, *sad, gloomy, dismal, forbidding, harsh;* of taste or smell, *harsh, bitter.* N. acc. **tristĕ** used like adv. *harshly.*

tristĭtĭa -ae and **tristĭtĭēs** -ēi, f. *sadness, gloom, harshness.*

trisulcus -a -um, *three-pointed, three-pronged.*

trītĭcĕus -a -um, *wheaten.*

trītĭcum -i, n. *wheat.*

Trītōn -ōnis or -ōnos, m. (1) *Triton, son of Neptune, a god of the sea.* (2) *a lake in Africa, supposed birth-place of Minerva;* adj. **Trītōnĭăcus, Trītōnĭus** -a -um, and f. **Trītōnis** -ĭdis or -ĭdos, esp. in connexion with Minerva.

trītūra -ae, f. *threshing.*

triumphālis -e, *triumphal.* N. pl. as subst. *the distinctions of a triumphing general.*

triumpho -are, *to triumph, to have a triumph;* hence, fig., *to exult;* pass., *to be triumphed over, to be completely conquered.*

triumphus (old form **triumpus**) -i, m., *triumphal procession, triumph.*

triumvir -vĭri, m. *a triumvir;* usually plur. **triumvĭri** (also **trēsvĭri**), *a board or commission of three.*

triumvirālis -e, *of a triumvir.*

triumvirātus -ūs, m. *the office of a triumvir.*

trivĭālis -e, *ordinary, trivial.*

trivĭum -i, n. *a place where three roads meet, crossroads, public place.*

trivĭus -a -um, *of three ways, of cross-roads;* esp. *of deities worshipped at crossroads;* f. as subst. **Trivia** -ae, *Diana* or *Hecate.*

Trōas -ādis; see Tros.

trŏchaeus -i, m. *a trochee, a metrical foot* (– ⏑).

trochlĕa -ae, f. *a set of blocks and pulleys for raising weights.*

trŏchus -i, m. *child's hoop.*

Trōes; see Tros.

Trōĭa, Trōĭădes, Trōĭcus; see Tros.

Trōĭŭgĕna -ae, *born in Troy, Trojan.*

trŏpaeum, -i, n. *a trophy, monument of victory.* Transf., *any memorial.*

Trōs Trōis, m. *a king of Phrygia, after whom Troy was named;* **Trōĭā** or **Trōĭā** -ae, f. *the town of Troy, besieged and finally captured by the Greeks;* adj. **Trōus, Trōĭus, Trōĭcus, Trōĭānus** -a -um, *Trojan;* subst. **Trōs Trōis,** m. *a Trojan;* f. adj. and subst. **Trōăs** -ădos, *Trojan, a Trojan woman.*

trŭcīdātĭo -onis, f. *slaughtering, massacre.*

trŭcīdo -are, *to slaughter, massacre; to demolish, destroy.*

trŭcŭlentĭa -ae, f. *roughness, ferocity.*

trŭcŭlentus -a -um, *rough, ferocious, cruel, wild;* compar. adv. **trŭcŭlentius.**

trūdis -is, f. *pointed staff, stake.*

trūdo **trūdĕre** **trūsi** **trūsum,** *to push, thrust; to press, urge on, force.*

trulla -ae, f. *ladle, pan* or *basin.*

trunco -are, *to shorten, maim, mutilate.*

truncus -a -um, *maimed, mutilated, cut short.* M. as subst. **truncus** -i, *a lopped tree, the trunk of a tree; the trunk of the human body.* Transf., *dolt, blockhead.*

trŭtĭna -ae, f. *a balance, pair of scales.*

trux **trŭcis,** *savage, fierce, grim.*

tū; pron. of the 2nd person; strengthened forms in -te, -met, temet; *thou, you;* plur. vos, etc. *ye, you.*

tūba -ae, f. *the straight war-trumpet of the Romans.*

¹tūber -ĕris, n. *swelling, hump.* Transf., *truffle.*

²tūber -ĕris; m. *a kind of apple-tree;* f. *the fruit of this tree.*

tūbĭcĕn -ĭnis, m. *a trumpeter.*

tūbĭlustrĭum -i, n. *a feast of trumpets.*

tūdĭto -are, *to strike often.*

tŭĕor (or **tŭor**) **tŭēri** **tŭĭtus** and **tūtus,** dep., and **tŭĕo** -ēre, *to look at, regard;* esp. *to look after, watch over, guard.* Perf. partic. as pass. adj. **tūtus** -a -um, *watched over;* hence *safe, secure, out of danger; watchful, cautious.* N. as subst. **tūtum** -i, *a safe place, safety.* N. abl. **tūtō** and adv. **tūtĕ,** *safely.*

tŭgŭrĭum -i, n. *peasant's hut, cottage.*

tŭĭtĭo -ōnis, f. *a protecting, preservation.*

Tullĭus -a -um, *the name of a Roman gens;* esp. *of Servius Tullius, sixth king of Rome,* and of *M. Tullius Cicero, the Roman orator and statesman.* Hence adj. **Tulliānus** -a -um, *Tullian;* n. as subst. **Tulliānum,** -i, *part of a Roman state prison.*

tum, *then, at that time; next, thereupon, afterwards;* cum . . . tum, *both . . . and especially,* or *not only . . . but also.*

tŭmĕfăcĭo -făcĕre -fēci -factum, *to cause to swell; to puff up with pride.*

tŭmĕo -ēre, *to swell, be swollen, be puffed up; to swell with pride, anger* or *excitement;* of style, *to be pompous, tumid.*

tŭmesco tŭmescĕre tŭmŭi, *to begin to swell; to swell with anger or excitement.*

tŭmĭdus -a -um, adj. *swollen, puffed up; swollen with pride, anger or excitement;* of style, *pompous, tumid, bombastic.*

tŭmor -ōris, m. *swelling, protuberance; excitement of the mind,* esp. *in pride or anger;* in gen., *ferment, commotion;* of style, *turgidity, bombast.*

tŭmŭlo -are, *to bury.*

tŭmŭlōsus -a -um, *full of mounds, hilly.*

tŭmultŭārĭus -a -um; *of troops, hastily brought together, suddenly levied;* in gen., *sudden, hasty, improvised.*

tŭmultŭātĭo -ōnis, f. *confusion, bustle.*

tŭmultŭor -ari, dep. and **tŭmultŭo** -are, *to be confused, be in an uproar.*

tŭmultŭōsus -a -um, adj. *alarmed, disturbed, confused; disquieting, turbulent;* adv. **tŭmultŭōsē,** *confusedly, tumultuously.*

tŭmultus -ūs, m. *confusion, uproar, bustle;* esp. *of political commotion, insurrection, rebellion.* Transf., *mental disturbance, excitement.*

tŭmŭlus -i, m. *mound of earth, hillock, hill;* esp. *a sepulchral mound.*

tunc, *then, at that time; next.*

tundo tundĕre tŭtŭdi tunsum and tūsum, *to thump, pound, strike repeatedly; to deafen, importune.*

tŭnĭca -ae, f. *a sleeved garment, tunic; a jacket, coat, covering.*

tŭnĭcātus -a -um, *clothed in a tunic.*

tŭor = tueor; q.v.

turba -ae, f. *tumult, disturbance;* hence *a mob, throng, crowd.*

turbāmentum -i, n. *means of disturbance.*

turbātĭo -ōnis, f. *disturbance, confusion.*

turbātor -ōris, m. *disturber, troubler.*

turbĕn -ĭnis, n. = ¹turbo; q.v.

turbĭdus -a -um, *confused, disordered, wild;* adv. **turbĭdē.**

turbĭnĕus -a -um, *shaped like a top.*

¹turbo -are, *to disturb, throw into disorder or confusion; to upset;* esp. *to cause political disturbance, to unsettle.*
Hence partic. as adj. **turbātus** -a -um, *disturbed, disordered, restless, troubled;* sometimes *angered, exasperated;* adv. **turbātē.**

²turbo -ĭnis, m. *an eddy, whirling round; a mental or political disturbance; a child's top; a reel; a spindle.*

turbŭlentus -a -um: pass., *confused, restless, stormy, boisterous;* act., *turbulent, causing disturbance;* adv. **turbŭlentē** and **turbŭlentĕr,** *in confusion, tumultuously.*

turdus -i, m. and **turda** -ae, f. *a thrush.*

tūrĕus -a -um, *of incense.*

turgĕo turgēre tursi, *to swell up, be swollen;* of style, *to be pompous, turgid.*

turgesco -ĕre, *to begin to swell, swell up; to swell with passion;* of style, *to be pompous.*

turgĭdus -a -um, *swollen;* of style, *turgid, bombastic.*

tūrĭbŭlum -i, n. *a censer for burning incense.*

tūricrĕmus -a -um, *burning incense.*

tūrĭfer -fĕra -fĕrum, *producing incense.*

tūrĭlĕgus -a -um, *collecting incense.*

turma -ae, f. *a troop of cavalry, a squadron; any troop, throng.*

turmālis -e, *of a troop or squadron.*

turmātim, *troop by troop, in troops.*

Turnus -i, m. *a king of the Rutuli, killed by Aeneas.*

turpĭcŭlus -a -um, *somewhat ugly or deformed.*

turpĭfĭcātus -a -um, *corrupted.*

turpis -e, *ugly, foul;* morally *foul, disgraceful;* n. as subst. **turpĕ,** *a disgrace;* adv. **turpĭtĕr,** *foully, disgracefully.*

turpĭtūdo -ĭnis, f. *ugliness;* moral *baseness, disgrace.*

turpo -are, *to make ugly, befoul; to disgrace, dishonour.*

turrĭger -gĕra -gĕrum, *tower-bearing.*

turris -is, f. *tower;* esp. *as used in military operations;* sometimes *howdah.* Transf., *dove-cote.*

turrītus -a -um, *turreted, furnished with towers; towering.*

turtur -ūris, m. *turtle-dove.*

tūs (**thūs**) tūris, n. *incense, frankincense.*

Tusci -ōrum, m. *the Tuscans, Etruscans, inhabitants of Etruria;* adj. **Tuscus** -a -um, *Etruscan.*

tussĭo -ire, *to have a cough, to cough.*

tussis -is, f. *a cough.*

tūtāmen -ĭnis, and **tūtāmentum** -i, n. *a defence, protection.*

tūtēla -ae, f. *protection, guard, charge,* esp. *of wards, etc., guardianship, tutelage;* concr., act. *protector, guardian;* pass., *the person or thing protected.*

¹tūtor -ōris, m. *a watcher, protector;* esp. *the guardian of a woman, minor, or imbecile.*

²tūtor -ari dep.: also **tūto** -are; *to protect, watch, keep:* Transf., *to guard against.*

tūtus -a -um, partic. from tueo; q.v.

tŭus -a -um, possess. pron. of the 2nd pers. sing., *thy, thine, your.*

Tȳdēus -ĕi and -ĕos, m. *the son of Oeneus;* hence **Tȳdīdes** -ae, m. *son of Tydeus,* i.e. *Diomedes.*

tympănum (**tŷpănum**) -i, n. *a tambourine, kettle-drum; a drum or wheel for raising weights.*

Tyndărēus -ĕi, and **Tyndărus** -i, m. *king of Sparta, father of Castor and Pollux, Helen and Clytemnestra;* adj. **Tyndărĭus** -a -um; subst. m. **Tyndărĭdēs** -ae, *a male descendant,* and f. **Tyndăris** -ĭdis, *a female descendant of Tyndareus.*

tŷpus -i, m. *a figure on a wall.*

tŷrannĭcīda -ae, m. *the slayer of a tyrant.*

tŷrannĭcus -a -um, *tyrannical;* adv. **tŷrannĭcē.**

tŷrannis -ĭdis, f. *despotism, tyranny.*

tўrannoctŏnus -i, m. *the slayer of a tyrant.*

tўrannus -i, m. *an absolute ruler, prince, lord; a usurper, despot, tyrant.*

Tўrius, see Tyrus.

tўrŏtărichŏs -i, m. *a dish of cheese and salt-fish.*

Tyrrhēni -ōrum, m. pl. *a Pelasgian people;* subst. **Tyrrhēnĭa** -ae, f. *their country, Etruria;* adj. **Tyrrhēnus** -a -um, *Etruscan.*

Tўrus (-ŏs) -i, f. *Tyre, a city of Phoenicia, famous for its purple;* adj. **Tўrius** -a -um.

U

U, u, originally written **V, v,** the 20th letter of the Latin Alphabet.

¹ūber -ĕris, n. *an udder, teat, breast; richness, abundance, fertility.*

²ūber -eris, adj., *rich, fertile, fruitful, copious;* adv. in compar. **ūbĕrius** and superl. **ūberrĭmē,** *more and most abundantly.*

ūbertās -ātis, f. *fruitfulness, abundance.*

ūbertim, *abundantly, copiously.*

ūbĭ, *where* (interrog. and relat.); *of time, when, as soon as;* of other relations, *wherein, whereby, with whom.*

ūbĭcumquĕ (-cunquĕ): relat., *wherever;* indef., *anywhere, everywhere.*

Ubii -ōrum, m. *a Germanic people.*

ūbĭquĕ, *everywhere.*

ūbĭvis, *wherever you will, anywhere.*

ūdus -a -um, *wet, moist.*

ulcĕro -are, *to make sore, ulcerate, wound.*

ulcĕrōsus -a -um, *full of sores, ulcerous, wounded.*

ulciscor ulcisci ultus, dep. (1) *to take vengeance for, to avenge.* (2) *to take vengeance on, to punish.*

ulcus -ĕris, n. *a sore, ulcer, wound.*

ūlīgo -ĭnis, f. *moisture, damp.*

Ūlixēs -is or ei, m. *Latin name for Ulysses or Odysseus, husband of Penelope, king of Ithaca.*

ullus -a -um; genit. ullius, dat. ulli; *any;* as subst., *anyone, anything.*

ulmĕus -a -um, *of elm-wood.*

ulmus -i, f. *elm.*

ulna -ae, f. *elbow, arm; an ell.*

ultĕrior -ĭus, compar. as from ulter, *farther, more distant, more advanced, more remote.* Superl. **ultĭmus** -a -um, *most distant, farthest, extreme;* in time or succession, either *original* or *last, final;* ad ultimum, *to the last;* ultimum, *for the last time;* in rank, etc., either *highest, greatest,* or *meanest, lowest.*

ultĭo -ōnis, f. *avenging, punishment, revenge.*

ultor -ōris, m. *avenger, punisher.*

ultrā, adv. and prep. *beyond, on the far side (of), farther (than), more (than).*

ultrix -īcis, f. *avenging.*

ultrō, adv. *to the far side, beyond;* ultro et citro, *up and d wn.* Transf.,

besides, moreover; of one's own accord, spontaneously, gratuitously.

ŭlŭla -ae, f. *an owl.*

ŭlŭlātus -ūs, m. *howling, wailing, yelling.*

ŭlŭlo -are, *to howl, yell;* transit., *to howl to;* of places, *to resound with howling.*

ulva -ae, f. *sedge.*

umbella -ae, f. *a parasol.*

umbĭlicus -i, m. *the navel; middle, centre; the end of the roller of a scroll; a kind of sea-snail.*

umbo -ōnis, m. *a boss, round projection;* esp. *the centre of a shield; a shield; the elbow.*

umbra -ae, f. *a shade, shadow; a shady place; protection; idleness, pleasant rest; a phantom, ghost, shade, semblance; an uninvited guest; a fish,* perhaps grayling.

umbrācŭlum -i, n. *a shady place, arbour; quiet, retirement; a parasol.*

umbrātĭlis -e, *retired, contemplative.*

Umbri -ōrum, m. pl. *a people of central Italy;* **Umbrĭa** -ae, f. *Umbria.*

umbrĭfer -fĕra -fĕrum, *shady.*

umbro -are, *to shade, over-shadow.*

umbrōsus -a -um, *shady.*

ūmecto (hū-) -are, *to wet, moisten.*

ūmectus (hū-) -a -um, *moist.*

ūmĕo (hū-) -ēre, *to be moist;* partic. **ūmens** -entis, *moist.*

ūmĕrus (hū-) -i, m. *the upper arm or shoulder.*

ūmesco (hū-) -ĕre, *to become moist.*

ūmĭdŭlus (hū-), -a -um, *moist.*

ūmĭdus (hū-) -a -um, *wet, moist, damp;* ligna, *unseasoned;* n. as subst. *a wet place.*

ūmor (hū-) -ōris, m. *moisture, fluid.*

umquam (unquam), *at any time, ever.*

ūnā, adv. from unus; q.v.

ūnănĭmĭtās -ātis, f. *concord, unanimity.*

ūnănĭmus -a -um, *of one mind, agreeing, unanimous.*

uncĭa -ae, f. *a twelfth; an ounce.*

uncĭārĭus -a -um, *of a twelfth part;* faenus, 8⅓%.

uncĭātim, *little by little.*

uncīnātus -a -um, *hooked.*

uncĭŏla -ae, f. *a mere twelfth.*

unctĭo -ōnis, f. *anointing.*

unctĭto -are, *to anoint, besmear.*

unctor -ōris, m. *an anointer.*

unctūra -ae, f. *anointing of the dead.*

unctus -a -um, partic. from ungo; q.v.

¹uncus -i, m. *a hook.*

²uncus -a -um, *hooked, curved.*

unda -ae, f. *water, fluid,* esp. as a *wave;* fig. *a stream of people,* etc.

undĕ, *whence, from where* (interrog. and relat.). Transf., *how, from whom.*

undĕcĭēs (-ĭens) *eleven times.*

undĕcim, *eleven.*

undĕcĭmus -a -um, *eleventh.*

undĕcumquĕ (-cunquĕ), *from whatever place.*

undēni -ae -a, *eleven at a time* or *eleven each.*

undēnōnāgintā, *eighty-nine.*

undeoctōgintā, *seventy-nine.*

undēquadrāgintā, *thirty-nine.*

undēquīnquāgēsĭmus -a -um, forty-ninth.

undēquīnquāgintā, forty-nine.

undēsexāgintā, fifty-nine.

undētrīcēsĭmus -a -um, twenty-ninth.

undēvīcēsĭmus, nineteenth.

undēvīgintī, nineteen.

undĭquĕ, from or on all sides, from everywhere, everywhere; altogether, in every respect.

undĭsŏnus -a -um, resounding with waves.

undo -are: intransit., to surge, wave, undulate; transit., to flood.

undōsus -a -um, surging, billowy.

ūnetvīcēsĭmānī -ōrum, m. pl. soldiers of the twenty-first legion.

ūnetvīcēsĭmus -a -um, twenty-first.

ungo (unguo) ungĕre unxi unctum, to anoint, besmear; partic. **unctus** -a -um, besmeared, anointed, greasy; rich, copious; n. as subst. a sumptuous repast.

unguĕn -ĭnis, n. fatty substance, ointment.

unguentārĭus -a -um, of ointment; m. as subst. a dealer in unguents.

unguentātus -a -um, anointed.

unguentum -i, n. salve, ointment, perfume.

ungŭĭcŭlus -i, m. a finger or toe-nail.

unguis -is, m. a finger- or toe-nail; of animals, claw, hoof; de tenero ungui, from childhood; ad (or in) unguem, to a hair, nicely, perfectly.

ungŭla -ae, f. a hoof, claw, talon.

unguo = ungo; q.v.

ūnĭcŏlor -oris, of one colour.

ūnĭcus -a -um, one, only, sole; singular, unique; adv. **ūnĭcē**, singly, especially.

ūnĭformis -e, having one form, simple.

ūnĭgĕna -ae, of the same race; only-begotten, unique.

ūnĭmānus -a -um, having but one hand.

ūnĭo -ōnis, m. a large pearl.

ūnĭtās -ātis, f. unity, oneness.

ūnĭtĕr, in one, together.

ūnĭversālis -e, general, universal.

ūnĭversĭtās -atis, f. the whole, total; the universe, the world.

ūnĭversus (archaic **ūnĭvorsus**) -a -um, combined in one, whole, entire; plur. **ūnĭversi** -ae -a, all together; n. as subst. **ūnĭversum** -i, the whole; the world, the universe; phrase, in universum, and adv. **ūnĭversē**, generally, in general.

ūnus -a -um, genit. **ūnĭus**, dat. **ūni**, one; only one; one and the same; any one; ad unum omnes, all to a man; in unum, into one place; uno tempore, at the same time. Adv. **ūnā**, in one, together.

ūpĭlĭo (ōpĭlĭo) -ōnis, m. a shepherd.

Ūrănĭa -ae and **Ūrănĭē** -ēs, f. the Muse of Astronomy.

urbānĭtās -ātis, f. city life, esp. life in Rome. Hence politeness, urbanity, refinement; wit, pleasantry.

urbānus -a -um, of a city (esp. Rome); urban; hence refined; elegant; witty, pleasant; m. pl. as subst. the inhabitants of a city, the townsfolk. Adv.

urbānē, politely, courteously; wittily, elegantly.

urbs -bis, f. a walled town or city; esp. the city of Rome.

urcĕŏlus -i, m. a small jug or pitcher.

urcĕus -i, m. a jug, pitcher.

ūrēdo -ĭnis, f. a blight on plants.

urgĕo urgēre ursi, to push, press, drive, urge; to beset, oppress; to stress; of work, to press on with, ply hard, follow up.

ūrīna -ae, f. urine.

ūrīnātor -ōris, m. a diver.

ūrīno -are and **ūrīnor** -ari, dep. to dive.

urna -ae, f. a jug, pitcher, jar, pot.

ūro ūrēre ussi ustum, to burn; to dry up, parch; chafe, gall; to disturb, harass.

ursa -ae, f. a she-bear.

ursus -i, m. a bear.

urtĭca -ae, f. a nettle. Transf., desire.

ūrus -i, m. a kind of wild ox.

ūsĭtātus -a -um, customary, usual; adv. **ūsĭtātē**.

uspĭam, anywhere.

usquam, anywhere; at all, in any way; in any direction.

usquĕ, through and through, all the way, continuously; always; usque Romam, as far as Rome; usque a Romulo, ever since Romulus.

usquĕquāquĕ, always.

ustor -ōris, m. a burner of corpses.

ustŭlo -are, to burn, scorch, singe.

¹ūsūcăpĭo -căpĕre -cēpi -captum, to acquire ownership by long use.

²ūsūcăpĭo -ōnis, f. ownership acquired by long possession or use.

ūsūra -ae, f. use, enjoyment; esp. use of borrowed capital; interest paid for money borrowed.

ūsurpātĭo -ōnis, f. using, use; undertaking.

ūsurpo -are, to use, bring into use; to take possession of, acquire, appropriate, usurp; to perceive, to notice; to use a word, to mention; hence to call, name.

ūsus -ūs, m. use, application, practice, exercise; social intercourse, familiarity; legal, usus et fructus, ususfructus, the use of others' property. Transf., practice, skill, experience; utility, usefulness, profit; usui esse, ex usu esse, to be useful, be of use; usus est, there is need of, occasion for; usu venit, it happens.

ūsusfructus; see usus.

ŭt or **ŭtī**. (1) with indic. verb: how (interrog. and exclam.); relat., as, esp. with corresponding sic or ita; ut ut, in whatever way; explanatory, as, as being (sometimes without verb); temporal, as when, while, since; of place, where. (2) with subjunctive: in indirect questions, how; in wishes, o that; concessive, granted that; consecutive, so that, often preceded by ita, tam, etc.; explaining or defining, namely that; final, in order that (negat. ne or ut ne); in "indirect command" that, to; after verbs of fearing (= ne non), that . . . not.

utcumquĕ (-cunquĕ), *in whatever manner, however; whenever.*

ūtensĭlĭa -ĭum, n. pl., *useful things, utensils.*

¹ūter ūtris, m. *the skin of an animal used as bag or bottle.*

²ūter utra utrum; genit. utrīus, dat. utri; interrog., *which of the two?*; plur., *which side? which set?*; relat., *that (of two) which*; indef., *either of the two.*

ŭtercumquĕ (-cunquĕ) utrăcumquĕ utrumcumquĕ, *whichever of the two.*

ŭterlĭbet utrălĭbet utrumlĭbet, *whichever of the two you please.*

ŭterquĕ utrăquĕ utrumquĕ; genit. utrīusquĕ, dat. utrīquĕ; *each of two; in plur., usually, each side, each set; sometimes of individuals, both.*

ŭtĕrus -i, m. and ŭtĕrum -i, n. *womb; belly.*

ŭtervīs utrāvīs utrumvīs; genit. utrī-usvīs, dat. utrīvīs; *whichever of the two you please.*

ūtī = ut; q.v.

Ūtĭca -ae, f. *a town in Africa where Cato the younger killed himself*; adj. Ūtĭcensis -e.

ūtĭlis -e, *useful, fit, profitable*; adv. ūtĭlĭtĕr.

ūtĭlĭtās -ātis, f. *usefulness profit, advantage.*

ŭtĭnam, *would that! oh that!*

ŭtĭquĕ, *at any rate, certainly, at least.*

ūtor ūtī ūsus, dep. *to use, employ; to possess, enjoy*; of persons, *to associate with*, or, with a predicate, *to find.*

Hence partic. ūtens -entis, *possessing.*

utpŏtĕ, *seeing that, inasmuch as.*

utrārĭus -i, m. *a water-carrier.*

utrimquĕ (-inquĕ) *from or on both sides.*

utrŏ, *to which of two places? to which side?*

utrōbĭquĕ (utrŭbĭquĕ), *on each of two sides; both ways.*

utrōquĕ, *to both sides, in both directions; at each point, both ways.*

utrum, *whether*; used mainly in alternative questions, direct or indirect.

ŭtŭt, *however*; see ut.

ūva -ae, f. *a bunch of grapes*; meton., *vine.* Transf., *a cluster.*

ūvesco -ĕre, *to become moist.*

ūvĭdŭlus -a -um, *moist.*

ūvĭdus -a -um, *moist, damp, wet.* Transf., *drunken.*

uxor -ōris, f. *a wife*; uxorem ducere, *to marry a wife.*

uxōrĭus -a -um. (1) *of a wife.* (2) *too devoted to one's wife, uxorious.*

V

V, v, the twenty-first letter of the Latin Alphabet.

văcātĭo -ōnis, f. *freedom, immunity, exemption.* Transf., *money paid for exemption from military duties.*

vacca -ae, f. *a cow.*

vaccīnĭum -i, n. *the blueberry, whortle-berry; according to some, the hyacinth.*

văcēfīo -fĭĕri, *to be made empty.*

văcillātĭo -ōnis, f. *rocking, reeling.*

văcillo (vaccillo) -are, *to totter, reel stagger.*

văcīvus (vŏcīvus) -a -um, *empty.*

văco -are, *to be empty*; of property, *to be vacant, to have no master*; in gen., *to be free from anything, be without; to be free from work, be at leisure*; with dat., *to have time for*; impers., vacat, *there is time (for).*

văcŭēfăcĭo -făcĕre -fēci -factum, *to make empty.*

văcŭĭtās -ātis, f. *freedom, exemption, immunity; a vacancy in a public office.*

văcŭo -are, *to make void, to empty.*

văcŭus -a -um, *empty, void; empty-handed; vacant; devoid, exempt, without* (with abl. or *ab*); *free, at leisure*; with dat., *free for; worthless, useless, vain.* N. as subst. văcŭum -i, *an empty place, vacuum.*

vădĭmōnĭum -i, n. *bail, security recognizance.*

vādo -ĕre, *to go, hasten, rush.*

vādor -ari, dep. *to bind over by bail.*

vădōsus -a -um, *shallow.*

vădum -i, n. *a shallow, shoal, ford in river or sea*; in gen., *water, river, sea*; fig., *shallows*, typical either of *safety* or of *danger.*

vae, interj. *alas! woe!*

văfer vafra vafrum, *artful, sly, crafty*; adv. vafrē.

văgīna -ae, f. *a scabbard, sheath, case: the husk of grain.*

văgĭo -ire, *to whimper as a child.*

văgītus -ūs, m. *whimpering, crying.*

văgor -ōris, m. = vagitus; q.v.

văgor -ari, dep. *to wander, ramble, rove.*

văgus -a -um, *wandering, roaming; fickle; diffuse, aimless.* Adv. văgē, *dispersedly.*

vah (vaha), interj. *ah! oh!*

valdē, *intensely, very much*; in replies *certainly, very much so.*

vălēdico -ĕre, *to say good-bye.*

vălĕo -ĕre, *to be strong, vigorous, in good health, well; to have force, avail, prevail, be able; to be worth*; of words, *to mean, signify*; as a farewell greeting, vale, or valeas, *farewell, good-bye*; valere iubere, *to bid farewell, say good-bye to.*

Hence partic. vălens -entis, *strong, powerful, healthy*; adv. vălentĕr.

Vălĕrĭus -a -um, *name of a Roman gens.*

vălesco -ĕre, *to grow strong.*

vălētŭdo -ĭnis, f. *state of health; sometimes either ill-health, weakness, or good health.*

vălĭdus -a -um, *strong, powerful; healthy, well; mighty, influential*; of medicines, *efficacious.* Adv. vălĭdē, *strongly, powerfully*; in replies, *certainly to be sure.*

vallāris -e, *relating to the* vallum; q.v.

vallēs (vallis) -is, f. *a vale, valley, hollow.*

vallo -are, *to fortify with a palisade; to strengthen.*

vallum -i, n. *a palisade of stakes; a fortification, defence.*

vallus -i, m. *a post, stake;* collectively, *a palisade, stockade.*

valvae -ārum, f. pl. *folding-doors.*

vānesco -ěre, *to pass away, disappear.*

vānilŏquentia -ae, f. *idle talk, vaunting.*

vānilŏquus -a -um, *lying; boastful.*

vānĭtās -ātis, f. *emptiness; worthlessness, unreality; boasting, ostentation.*

vannus -i, f. *winnowing-fan.*

vānus -a -um, *empty, void; vain, idle, worthless, meaningless;* of persons, *ostentatious, boastful, unreliable.*

vāpĭdus -a -um, *spiritless, spoiled, flat.*

vāpor (vāpōs) -ōris, m. *vapour, steam; warm exhalation, warmth.*

vāpōrārium -i, n. *a steam flue.*

vāpōro -are; intransit., *to steam, reek;* transit., *to fill with vapour, heat, warm.*

vappa -ae, f. *flat wine.* Transf., *a worthless fellow.*

vāpŭlo -are, *to be flogged, beaten, knocked about;* of things, *to be wasted.*

vărĭantĭa -ae, and vărĭātĭo -ōnis, f. *difference, variation.*

vārĭco -are, *to stand with feet apart.*

vārĭcōsus -a -um, *having varicose veins.*

vārĭcus -a -um, *straddling.*

vărĭětās -ātis, f. *variety, difference, diversity.*

vărĭo -are: transit., *to vary, diversify, change, alter, do or say differently;* pass., variari, *to waver, be divided, vary;* intransit., *to be different, vary.*

¹vărĭus -a -um, *various, manifold, changeable, diverse;* of persons, in bad sense, *fickle, changeable;* adv. vărĭē, *diversely, variously.*

²Vărĭus -a -um, *name of a Roman gens.*

vārix -īcis, c. *a varicose vein.*

Varro -ōnis, m. *a surname in the gens Terentia.*

¹vārus -a -um, *knock-kneed;* in gen., *crooked, bent; diverse, different.*

²Vārus -i, m. *a Roman surname.*

¹vās vādis, m. *a bail, surety.*

²vās vāsis, n. *a utensil;* plur. (vāsa-ōrum) milit., *war materials, equipment.*

vāsārium -i, n. *an outfit allowance.*

vascŭlārĭus -i, m. *a maker of vessels,* esp. *in metal.*

vascŭlum -i, n. *a small vessel.*

vastātĭo -ōnis, f. *devastating, laying waste.*

vastātor -ōris, m. *devastator, ravager.*

vastĭfĭcus -a -um, *devastating.*

vastĭtās -ātis, f. *a waste, emptiness, desolation;* concr. in plur., *devastators.*

vasto -are, *to empty; to lay waste, ravage, devastate, prey upon.*

vastus -a -um, *empty, waste, desolate; laid waste, devastated.* Transf., *vast,*

enormous; rough, rude. Adv. vastē, *widely, extensively; rudely, roughly.*

vātēs -is, c. *a prophet, seer; a bard, poet.*

Vātĭcānus -a -um, *Vatican:* mons, collis, *the Vatican Hill on the west side of the Tiber.*

vātĭcĭnātĭo -ōnis, f. *soothsaying, prophecy.*

vātĭcĭnātor -ōris, m. *soothsayer, prophet.*

vātĭcĭnor -ari, dep. *to prophesy; to talk wildly, to rave.*

vātĭcĭnus -a -um, *soothsaying, prophetic.*

vătillum (băt-) -i, n. *a chafing-dish or shovel.*

Vātĭnĭus -a -um, *the name of a Roman gens.*

-vē, enclitic, *or, or perhaps.*

vēcordĭa (vae-) -ae, f. *folly, madness.*

vēcors (vae-) -cordis, *senseless, mad.*

vectĭgal -gālis, n. *revenue, income;* esp. *a tax, impost, duty.*

vectĭgālis -e, *relating to income or to taxes; liable to tax, tributary.*

vectĭo -ōnis, f. *carrying, conveyance.*

vectis -is, m. *a lever, crow-bar; a bar, bolt.*

vecto -are, *to carry, convey;* pass., *to ride or be driven.*

vector -ōris, m.: act., *a carrier, bearer;* pass., *a passenger, rider.*

vectōrĭus -a -um, *for carrying;* navigia, *transports.*

vectūra -ae, f. *conveying, transportation; passage-money, fare.*

vĕgĕo -ěre, *to stir up, excite.*

vĕgĕtus -a -um, *lively, vigorous, fresh.*

vēgrandis -e, *diminutive.*

vĕhĕmens (poet. vēmens) -entis, *violent, furious, impetuous;* adv. vĕhĕmentěr, *violently; forcibly, exceedingly.*

vĕhĭcŭlum -i, n. *vehicle, conveyance.*

vĕho vēhĕre vexi vectum, *to carry, convey;* pass., *to sail, ride, drive, etc.;* so also pres. partic., vehens, *riding.*

Vēii -ōrum, m. pl. *an old town in Etruria;* adj. Vēĭens -entis.

vĕl: conj., singly, or; doubled, *either . . . or;* adv. *even, actually; for example.*

vēlāmen -ĭnis, n. *covering, garment.*

vēlāmentum -i, n. *a covering, veil;* in plur., *olive-branches wrapped in wool, carried by suppliants.*

vēlārĭum -i, n. *an awning in a theatre.*

vēlāti -ōrum, m. pl., milit. *the reserve, supernumary troops.*

vēlēs -ĭtis, m. usually plur., velites, *light-armed infantry, skirmishers.*

vēlĭfer -fěra -fěrum, *carrying sail.*

vēlĭfĭcātĭo -ōnis, f. *sailing.*

vēlĭfĭco -are and vēlĭfĭcor -āri, dep. *to sail.* Transf., *to work for an end.*

vēlĭtāris -e, *of light-armed troops.*

vēlĭvŏlans -antis, and vēlĭvŏlus -a -um, *flying with sails.*

vellĭco -are, *to pluck, twitch; to taunt, criticize.*

vello vellěre velli (vulsi, volsi) vulsum (volsum), *to pull, twitch; to pluck out;* partic. vulsus -a -um, *plucked, smooth.*

vellus -ěris, n. *a fleece; skin, hide.*

vēlo -are, *to cover, veil, hide.*

vēlōcĭtās -ātis, f. *quickness, rapidity.*

vēlox -ōcis, *quick, rapid, swift*; adv. **vēlōcĭtēr.**

vēlum -i, *a sail*; vela dare, *to sail; a covering, awning, curtain.*

vēlŭt (vēlŭtī), *as, just as; even as; as for instance*; with subjunctive, velut, or velut si, *as if, just as if.*

vēmens = vehemens; q.v.

vēna -ae, f. *a blood-vessel, vein, artery; a water-course; a vein of metal; a vein of talent, disposition, natural inclination.*

vēnābŭlum -i, n. *a hunting-spear.*

Vēnăfrum -i, n. *a Samnite town in Campania.*

vēnālīcĭus -a -um, *of the sale of slaves*; m. as subst. *a slave-dealer.*

vēnālis -e, *on sale, to be sold; venal*; m. as subst. *a slave put up for sale.*

vēnātĭcus -a -um, *of or for the chase.*

vēnātĭo -ōnis, f. *the chase, hunting; game.*

vēnātor -ōris, m. *a hunter, sportsman.*

vēnātōrĭus -a -um, *of or for the chase.*

vēnātrix -īcis, f. *huntress.*

vēnātus -ūs, m. *the chase, hunting.*

vendĭbĭlis -e, *on sale, saleable; popular, acceptable.*

vendĭtātĭo -onis, f. *a putting up for sale; hence boasting, vaunting.*

vendĭtātor -ōris, m. *vaunter, boaster.*

vendĭtĭo -ōnis, f. *selling, sale.*

vendĭto -are, *to offer for sale, try to sell; to praise, advertise.*

vendĭtor -ōris, m. *seller, vendor.*

vendo -dĕre -dĭdi -dĭtum (pass. usually veneo; q.v.), *to put up for sale, sell; to betray; to recommend, advertise.*

vēnēfĭcĭum -i, n. *poisoning; magic, sorcery.*

vēnēfĭcus -a -um, *poisonous, magical*; m. as subst., *a poisoner, sorcerer; a sorceress, witch.*

vēnēnĭfer -fēra -fērum, *poisonous.*

vēnēno -are, *to poison, drug*; partic. **vēnēnātus** -a -um, *poisoned, drugged, enchanted.*

vēnēnum -i, n. *a drug; poison (fig. ruin, destruction); a love-potion; colouring matter, dye; rouge.*

vēnĕo vēnīre vēnii vēnum, *to go for sale, to be sold* (used as pass. of vendo).

vĕnĕrābĭlis -e, *venerable, reverend.*

vĕnĕrābundus -a -um, *reverent, respectful.*

vĕnĕrātĭo -ōnis, f. *reverence, respect.*

vĕnĕrātor -ōris, m. *a venerator, reverer.*

vĕnĕrĭus; see venus.

vĕnĕror -ari, dep. *to ask reverently; to revere, respect, worship.*

vĕnĭa -ae, f. *grace, indulgence, favour, permission; pardon, forgiveness.*

vĕnĭo vēnīre vēni ventum, *to come; in course of time, to happen, come, arrive; to grow, arise.*

vēnor -ari, dep, *to hunt.*

venter -tris, m. *the belly, stomach; the womb.*

ventĭlo -are, *to wave, brandish, fan.*

ventĭto -are, *to come often, resort.*

ventōsus -a -um, *full of wind, windy; swift or light as wind; puffed up, vain; changeable, inconstant.*

ventrĭcŭlus -i, m. *the belly; a ventricle.*

ventŭlus -i, m. *a slight wind.*

ventus -i, m. *wind; rumour, favour.*

vēnŭcŭla (venn-) -ae, f. *a kind of grape.*

vēnum and **vēno,** acc. and dat. n., *for sale.*

vēnumdo (vēnundo) -dăre -dĕdi -dătum, *to offer for sale, to sell.*

vĕnus -ĕris, f. *charm, loveliness; love; a loved one; personif.,* **Vĕnus,** *goddess of love; the Venus throw, highest throw of the dice*; adj. **Vĕnĕrĕus (-ĭus)** -a -um, *of Venus or of love.*

Vĕnŭsĭa -ae, f. *a town on the borders of Lucania and Apulia, birthplace of Horace.*

vĕnustās -ātis, f. *loveliness, charm, attractiveness.*

vĕnustus -a -um, *charming, lovely, graceful*; adv. **vĕnustē.**

vēpallĭdus -a -um, *very pale.*

veprēcŭla -ae, f. *a thorn-bush.*

veprēs -is, m. *a thorn-bush, briar-bush.*

vēr vēris, n. *spring*; primo vere, *in the beginning of spring*; ver sacrum, *an offering of the firstlings.*

vērātrum -i, n. *hellebore.*

vērax -ācis, *speaking the truth, truthful.*

verbēna -ae, f., often in pl., *sacred boughs carried by the Fetiales.*

verber -ĕris, n. *a lash; a whip, scourge, thong; a blow, stroke; whipping.*

¹verbĕro -are, *to beat, whip, thrash; with words; to assail, lash.*

²verbĕro -ōnis, m. *a rascal.*

verbōsus -a -um, *copious, diffuse, wordy*; adv. **verbōsē.**

verbum -i, n. *a word*; verbum facere, *to speak*; uno verbo, *in a word, briefly*; ad verbum, *word for word*; verbi causa, *for example*; grammat., *a verb; an expression, saying; mere words, mere talk*; verba dare homini, *to cheat a person.*

Vercingĕtŏrix -rīgis, m. *a Gallic chief.*

vĕrēcundĭa -ae, f. *modesty, diffidence, bashfulness*; with genit., *respect for, scruple about.*

vĕrēcundor -ari, dep. *to be bashful, ashamed, shy.*

vĕrēcundus -a -um, *bashful, modest, shy, diffident*; adv. **vĕrēcundē.**

vērēdus -i, *a swift horse, hunter.*

vĕrĕor -ēri -ĭtus, dep. *to be afraid, fear; to have respect for, revere*; gerundive **vĕrendus** -a -um, *venerable, reverend.*

Vergĭlĭus -i, m. P. Vergilius Maro, *author of the Aeneid, Georgics, and Eclogues.*

Vergĭnĭus -a -um, *the name of a Roman gens.*

vergo vergĕre versi: intransit., *to bend, be inclined, verge; of time, to draw to an end*; transit., *to bend, turn, incline.*

vērĭdĭcus -a -um, *truthful.*

vērĭlŏquĭum -i, n. *etymology.*

vērĭsĭmĭlis -e, *probable, likely.*

vērĭsĭmĭlĭtūdo inis, f. *probability.*

vērĭtās -ātis, f. *the truth, reality; truthfulness, telling of truth;* in gen., *honesty.*

vermen -ĭnis, n. *a griping pain.*

vermĭcŭlus -i, m. *little worm, grub.*

vermis -is, m. *worm.*

verna -ae, c. *a slave born in the master's house; a native.*

vernācŭlus -a -um, *of a slave born in the house; native, domestic.*

vernīlis -e, *like a slave; mean, abject, pert, forward;* adv. **vernīlĭtĕr,** *like a slave.*

verno -are, *to flourish, grow green.*

vernŭla -ae, c. *a little slave born in the house;* as adj. *native, indigenous.*

vernus -a -um, *of spring, vernal.*

Vērōna -ae, f. *a town of northern Italy, birthplace of Catullus.*

¹verrēs -is, m. *a boar.*

²Verrēs -is, m. *C. Cornelius, praetor in Sicily, prosecuted by Cicero;* adj. **Verrĭus** and **Verrīnus** -a -um.

verrīnus -a -um, *of a boar.*

verro verrĕre verri versum, *to drag, pull, sweep; sweep up; to sweep clean, brush, scour.*

verrūca -ae, f. *a wart; blemish.*

verrunco -are, *to turn out;* bene verruncare, *to turn out well.*

versābundus -a -um, *whirling round, revolving.*

versātĭlis -e, *turning round, revolving; versatile.*

versĭcŏlor -ōris, *of various colours.*

versĭcŭlus -i, m. *a little line; a poor little verse.*

versĭfĭcātĭo -ōnis, f. *making of verses.*

versĭfĭcātŏr -ōris, m. *versifier.*

versĭfĭco -are, *to write verse.*

verso (vorso) -are, *to turn about, turn this way and that; to bend, ply, twist; to influence, agitate; to turn over in the mind, think of.* Pass., *to be about, hover, resort; to be engaged, take part, be employed.*

versum = versus; q.v.

versūra -ae, f. *turning; the borrowing of money to pay a debt;* hence *a loan.*

¹versus (vors-) and **versum** (vors-), *towards;* used esp. after an accusative or prep. and acc.; sursum versus, *upwards.*

²versus (vors-) -a -um, partic. from verro or verto; q.v.

³versus (vors-) -ūs, m. *a row, line; a line of writing,* esp. *of poetry.*

versūtĭa -ae, f. *wile, stratagem.*

versūtus -a -um, *dexterous; cunning, crafty, sly;* adv. **versūtē.**

vertex (vortex) -ĭcis, m. (1) *a whirl, eddy, whirlwind, gust.* (2) *the crown of the head;* in gen., *head, summit, elevation.* (3) *the pole of the heavens.*

vertĭcōsus (vortĭc-) -a -um, *eddying.*

vertīgo -ĭnis, f. *whirling round, revolution; giddiness, vertigo.*

verto (vorto) vertĕre verti versum, *to turn, turn round, turn up;* intransit., *to turn oneself;* milit., vertere in fugam, *to put to flight, rout;* terga vertere, *to flee; to interpret, construe, understand in a certain way, to impute; to*

alter, change; *to translate; to change for another, exchange;* vertere solum, *to go into exile; to upset, overthrow;* pass. or intransit., of time, *to roll round;* pass., *to move in a certain sphere, to depend on, centre in.*

Vertumnus (vor-) -i, m. *god of the changing year.*

vērŭ -ūs, n. *a spit; a javelin.*

vērus -a -um, *true, real, genuine; truthful, veracious; just, reasonable.* N. as subst. *truth, reality; right, duty;* veri similis, *likely, probable.* N. nom. as adv. **vērum,** *but yet, still, however;* strengthened, **vērumtāmen** (vērum-), *notwithstanding, nevertheless.* N. abl. as adv. **vērō,** *in truth, indeed, in fact;* in a climax, *even, indeed;* ironically, *to be sure;* adversative, *but indeed, but in fact.* Adv. **vērē,** *truly, really, rightly.*

vērutum -i, n. *javelin.*

vērūtus -a -um, *armed with a javelin.*

vervex -vēcis, m. *a wether; a sheep, dolt.*

vēsānĭa -ae, f. *madness, insanity.*

vēsānĭens -entis, *raging.*

vēsānus -a -um, *mad, insane;* of things, *furious, wild.*

vescor -i, dep. *to eat, feed on; to use, enjoy.*

vescus -a -um: act., *consuming;* pass., *wasted, thin.*

vēsica -ae, f. *the bladder; a purse, a lantern of style, bombast.*

vēsicŭla -ae, f. *a little bladder.*

vespa -ae, f. *wasp.*

Vespăsĭānus -i, m., T. Flavius, *Roman emperor,* A.D. 69-79.

vesper -ĕris or -ĕri, m. *evening; the west; the evening star;* vespere, vesperi, *in the evening.*

vespĕrasco -ĕre, *to become evening.*

vespertīnus -a -um, *of evening; western.*

vespillo -ōnis, m. *a corpse-bearer for the poor.*

Vesta -ae, f. *goddess of the hearth and domestic life;* adj. **Vestālis** -e, *Vestal;* f. as subst. *a Vestal virgin, priestess of Vesta.*

vester (voster) -tra -trum, *your, yours.*

vestĭbŭlum -i, n. *entrance-court, court-yard;* in gen., *entrance; beginning.*

vestĭgĭum -i, n. *a foot-step, track; a trace, mark;* in plur., *the foot;* in vestigio, e vestigio, *at that moment.*

vestĭgo -are, *to track, trace.*

vestĭmentum -i, n. *clothing, a garment.*

vestĭo -ire, *to dress, clothe; to cover, adorn.*

vestis -is, f. *a covering* or *garment, clothing; a blanket, carpet, tapestry.*

vestĭtus -ūs, m. *clothing, clothes; a covering.*

Vĕsŭvĭus -i, m. *Vesuvius, the volcano in Campania.*

vĕtĕrānus -a -um, *old;* m. pl. *old soldiers, veterans.*

vĕtĕrasco -ascĕre -āvi, *to grow old.*

vĕtĕrātŏr -ōris, m. *an old hand, old stager.*

vĕtĕrātŏrĭus -a -um, *cunning, crafty*; adv. **vĕtĕrātŏrĭē.**

vĕtĕrĭnus -a -um, *of draught*; bestia, *a beast of burden.*

vĕternōsus -a -um, *lethargic, sleepy, dull.*

vĕternus -i, m. *age; lethargy, inactivity, sloth.*

vĕto (vŏto) vĕtare vĕtŭi vĕtĭtum, *to forbid, prohibit*; n. of perf. partic. as subst. **vĕtĭtum** -i, *that which is forbidden; a prohibition.*

vĕtŭlus -a -um, *little old, poor little old*; as subst., *an old man* or *woman.*

vĕtus -ĕris; superl. **vĕterrĭmus**; *old, ancient, of long standing; experienced.* M. pl. as subst. *the ancients.*

vĕtustās -ātis, f. *age; antiquity, past time; long duration, length of time* (including future time).

vĕtustus -a -um, *old, ancient, of long standing; old-fashioned, antiquated.*

vexāmen -ĭnis, n. *shaking, upheaval.*

vexātĭo -ōnis, f. *shaking, jolting, shock; ill-treatment.*

vexātor -ōris, m. *one who shakes, harasses, disturbs.*

vexillārĭus -i, m. *a standard-bearer*; in plur. *a corps of veterans, a reserve.*

vexillum -i, n. *a standard, flag; a company, troop.*

vexo -are, *to shake, toss, jostle; to harass, annoy.*

vĭa -ae, f. *a way, passage; a highway, road, street; a course, march, journey; means, way, method*; abl. **vĭā,** *methodically.*

vĭātĭcus -a -um, *relating to a journey*; n. as subst., *journey money*; also *savings* or *prize-money.*

vĭātor -ōris, m. (1) *a traveller, wayfarer.* (2) *an apparitor, messenger.*

vibro -are: transit., *to cause to vibrate, brandish, shake; to brandish and hurl a weapon; to curl, frizzle hair*; intransit., *to shake, tremble, quiver, vibrate.*

vĭburnum -i, n. *the wayfaring-tree.*

vīcānus -a -um, *dwelling in a village*; m. pl. as subst. *villagers.*

vĭcārĭus -a -um, *substituted, vicarious*; m. as subst., *a substitute*; esp. *an under-servant.*

vĭcātim, *from street to street; in villages.*

vĭcē, vĭcem,; see vicis.

vĭcēni -ae -a, *twenty at a time* or *twenty each.*

vīcēsĭmāni -ōrum, m. pl. *soldiers of the twentieth legion.*

vīcēsĭmārĭus -a -um, *relating to the vicesima.*

vīcēsĭmus (vīcens-) -a -um, *twentieth*; f. as subst. **vīcēsĭma** (vīcens-) -ae, *the twentieth part, as a toll* or *tax.*

vĭcĭa -ae, f. *vetch.*

vĭcĭēs (-iens), *twenty times.*

vīcīnālis -e, *neighbouring, near.*

vīcīnĭa -ae, and **vīcīnĭtās** -ātis, f. *neighbourhood; vicinity; likeness*; concr., *the neighbours.*

vīcīnus -a -um, *near, neighbouring*; m. and f. as subst., *a neighbour*; n. as subst., *neighbourhood, vicinity.*

vĭcis (genit. nom. not found); *change, interchange, alternation*; per vices, in vices, *alternately, reciprocally; recompense, retaliation; the vicissitude of fate, lot, destiny; one's place, office, duty*; vicem, vice, in vicem, ad vicem, *in place of, instead of, like.*

vĭcissim, *in turn.*

vĭcissĭtūdo -ĭnis, f. *change, alteration.*

victĭma -ae, f. *an animal offered in sacrifice, victim.*

victĭmārĭus -i, m. *to live on, feed on.*

victor -ōris, m. and **victrix** -trīcis, f. *conqueror, victor*; as adj., *victorious.*

victōrĭa -ae, f. *victory, conquest.*

victōrĭātus -i, m. *a silver coin stamped with a figure of Victory.*

victōrĭŏla -ae, f. *a small statue of Victory.*

victrix -trīcis, f.; see victor.

victus -ūs, m. *living; manner of life; nourishment, food.*

vīcŭlus -i, m. *a little village, hamlet.*

vīcus -i, m. *part of a town, a street; a village, hamlet; an estate, country-seat.*

vĭdēlicet, *it is clear*; as adv. *clearly, plainly, manifestly; namely*; ironically, *of course, to be sure.*

vĭdĕo vĭdēre vidi vīsum, *to see; to perceive, notice, observe; to look into a matter, see to, provide for.* Pass., *to be seen; to seem, appear, be thought; also to seem good, seem right.* N. of perf. partic. as subst. **vīsum** -i, *a sight, appearance, vision.*

vĭdŭĭtās -ātis, f. *want; widowhood.*

vĭdŭo -are, *to deprive*; f. of perf. partic. **vĭdŭāta** -ae, *widowed.*

vĭdŭus -a -um, *deprived, bereaved, widowed*; f. as subst. **vĭdŭa** -ae, *a widow,* or *an unmarried woman.*

Vienna -ae, f. *town in Gallia Narbonensis* (now Vienne).

vĭĕo -ēre, *to weave together*; partic. **vĭētus** -a -um, *shrivelled, shrunken.*

vĭgĕo -ēre, *to be vigorous, thrive, flourish.*

vĭgesco -ĕre, *to become vigorous, begin to thrive.*

vĭgēsimus = vicesimus; q.v.

vĭgil -ĭlis, *wakeful, watchful*; m. as subst., *a watchman.*

vĭgĭlantĭa -ae, f. *watchfulness, vigilance.*

vĭgĭlax -ācis, *watchful, wakeful.*

vĭgĭlĭa -ae, f. *wakefulness, sleeplessness, watch; a watch of the night; the watch, sentinels*; fig. *watchfulness, vigilance, care.*

vĭgĭlo -are: intransit., *to keep awake, watch; to be vigilant, watchful, careful*; transit. in pass, *to be watched through, watched over.* Pres. partic. **vĭgĭlans** -antis, *watch ul, vigilant*; adv. **vĭgĭlantĕr.**

vĭgintī, *twenty.*

vīgintĭvĭrātus -ūs, *the office of the vigintiviri.*

vīgintĭvĭri -ōrum, m. pl. *a commission of twenty.*

vigor -ōris, m. *force, energy.*

vilīco -are, *to manage an estate as bailiff.*

vilīcus -i, m. *a bailiff, steward, overseer of an estate;* f. **vilīca** -ae, *a bailiff's wife.*

vilis -e, *cheap, worth little;* adv. **vilītĕr.**

vilītās -ātis, f. *cheapness, low price;* in gen., *worthlessness.*

villa -ae, f. *a country-house, estate, farm.*

villĭc-; see vilic-.

villōsus -a -um, *shaggy, hairy.*

villŭla -ae, f. *a small country-house, little farm.*

villum -i, n. *a sup of wine.*

villus -i, m. *shaggy hair.*

vīmen -ĭnis, n. *an osier, twig; a basket.*

vīmentum = vimen; q.v.

Vīmĭnālis collis, *one of the seven hills of Rome.*

vīmĭnĕus -a -um, *of osiers, wicker.*

vīn = visne; see volo.

vīnācĕus -a -um, *belonging to wine or a grape.*

vīnālia -ĭum and -ĭōrum, n. pl. *wine festivals, one in April, one in August.*

vīnārĭus -a -um, *of wine;* as subst. m. *a vintner;* n. *a wine-jar.*

vincĭbĭlis -e, *easily gained.*

vincĭo vincīre vinxi vinctum, *to bind, tie up; to surround, encompass; to restrain, confine, secure.*

vinco vincĕre vici victum, *to conquer, overcome, master, surpass; to prove successfully, win one's point.*

vincŭlum (vinclum) -i, n. *a band, cord, chain, fetter, tie;* plur., *imprisonment.*

Vindĕlĭci -ōrum, m. pl. *a Germanic people.*

vindēmĭa -ae, f. *vintage; grapes, wine.*

vindēmĭātor -ōris, m. *a harvester of grapes.*

vindēmĭŏla -ae, f. *a little vintage; a perquisite.*

vindex -ĭcis, c. *a claimant or protector; an avenger, punisher.*

vindĭcātĭo -ōnis, f. *defending, protecting; avenging.*

vindĭcĭae -ārum, f. pl. *things or persons claimed as property; the making of a claim.* Transf., *protection.*

vindĭco -are, *to claim; to arrogate, assume; appropriate; to claim as free; hence to liberate, deliver or protect; to avenge, punish.*

vindicta -ae, f. *a rod used in manumitting slaves.* Transf., *deliverance; vengeance, punishment.*

vīnĕa -ae, f. *a vineyard;* milit. *a mantlet, penthouse.*

vīnĕtum -i, n. *vineyard.*

vīnĭtor -ōris, m. *a vinedresser.*

vīnŏlentĭa -ae, f. *wine-drinking, intoxication.*

vīnŏlentus -a -um, *mixed with wine; drunk, intoxicated.*

vīnōsus -a -um, *full or fond of wine.*

vīnum -i, n. *wine, wine-drinking.*

vīŏla -ae, f. *a violet or stock; the colour violet.*

vĭŏlābĭlis -e, *able to be injured.*

vĭŏlārĭum -i, n. *a bed of violets.*

vĭŏlātĭo -ōnis, f. *injury, violation, profanation.*

vĭŏlātor -ōris, m. *injurer, violator, profaner.*

vĭŏlens -entis, *violent, furious, impetuous;* adv. **vĭŏlentĕr.**

vĭŏlentĭa -ae, f. *violence, impetuosity.*

vĭŏlentus -a -um, *violent, vehement, furious, impetuous.*

vĭŏlo -are, *to violate, outrage, injure.*

vīpĕra -ae, f. *a viper; a snake, serpent.*

vīpĕrĕus -a -um, *of a viper or snake; snaky.*

vīpĕrīnus -a -um, *of a viper or snake.*

vir, viri, m. *a man, male person;* esp. *a grown man; a husband; a man of character or courage, "he-man";* milit. *a soldier,* esp. *an infantryman; a single man, individual.*

vīrāgo -ĭnis, f. *a female warrior, heroine.*

vĭrectum (-ētum) -i, n. *greensward, turf.*

vĭrĕo -ēre, *to be green, vigorous, healthy, fresh.*

vīres -ĭum, f. pl.; see vis.

vīresco -ĕre, *to grow green.*

vĭrētum = virectum; q.v.

virga -ae, f. *a green twig, a slip; a rod; a wand; a broom; a streak, stripe;* in plur., virgae, *the lictors' rods.*

virgātus -a -um, (1) *made of twigs.* (2) *striped.*

virgētum -i, n. *an osier-bed.*

virgĕus -a -um, *of twigs or rods.*

Virgilĭus = Vergilius; q.v.

virgĭnālis -e, **virgĭnārĭus, virgĭnĕus** -a -um, *maidenly.*

virgĭnĭtās -ātis, f. *virginity.*

virgo -ĭnis, f. *a maiden, virgin, girl.*

virgŭla -ae, f. *a little bough, twig; a rod, staff.*

virgultum -i, n. (1) *a thicket, copse.* (2) *a slip for planting.*

virguncŭla -ae, f. *a little girl.*

vĭrĭdans -antis, *green;* hence verb **vĭrĭdor** -ari, *to become green.*

vĭrĭdārĭum -i, n. *a pleasure-garden.*

vĭrĭdis -e, *green.* Transf., *fresh, young, vigorous.*

vĭrĭdĭtās -ātis, f. *greenness; freshness, bloom.*

vĭrīlis -e, *manly, male, virile; of a grown man, adult; courageous, spirited;* pro virili parte, *to the best of one's ability.* Adv. **vĭrīlĭtĕr,** *manfully.*

vĭrīlĭtās -ātis, f. *manhood, virility.*

vĭrītim, *man by man, individually.*

vīrōsus -a -um, *stinking, fetid.*

virtūs -ūtis, f. *manliness; excellence, worth, goodness, virtue; bravery, courage.*

vīrus -i, n. *slimy liquid, slime; poison,* esp. *of snakes, venom; any harsh taste or smell.*

vīs, acc. vim, abl. vī; plur. **vīrēs** -ĭum, f. *force, power, strength; might, influence;* in sing. also *violence; a large number, quantity; the force,* nature, meaning of a thing; plur., milit., troops, forces.

viscātus -a -um, smeared with bird-lime.

viscĕrātĭo -ōnis, f. public distribution of meat.

viscum -i, n. and viscus -i, m. mistletoe; bird-lime.

viscus -ĕris, usually plur. viscĕra -um, n. flesh; also internal organs, entrails; inmost part or heart of anything.

visĭo -ōnis, f. seeing, view; appearance; notion, idea.

visĭto -are, to see often; to visit.

viso visĕre visi visum, to look at, look into, see after; to go to see, visit, call upon; gerundive visendus -a -um, worth seeing, notable.

visum -i, n. subst. from video; q.v.

visus -ūs, m. seeing, sight; an appearance.

vita -ae, f. life.

vitābĭlis -e, that can or should be avoided.

vitābundus -a -um, trying to avoid.

vitālis -e, of life, vital; living, surviving; adv. vitālĭter, vitally.

vitātĭo -ōnis, f. avoiding, shunning.

Vitellius -a -um, the name of a Roman gens; Aulus Vitellius, the Roman emperor who succeeded Otho (A.D. 69).

vĭtellus -i, m. the yolk of an egg.

vitĕus -a -um, of a vine.

vitĭcŭla -ae, f. a little vine.

vitĭfer -fĕra -fĕrum, vine-bearing.

vitĭgĕnus -a -um, produced from the vine.

vitĭo -are, to injure, damage, corrupt; to forge, falsify.

vitĭōsĭtās -ātis, f. viciousness, corruption.

vitĭōsus -a -um, faulty, corrupt, bad, wrong; adv. vitĭōsē.

vitis -is, f. a vine; a centurion's staff.

vitĭsător -ōris, m. one who plants vines.

vitĭum -i, n. a fault, defect, blemish; crime, vice; relig., a defect in auguries or auspices.

vito -are, to avoid, shun.

vitrĕus -a -um, of glass; glassy, transparent, glittering.

vitrĭcus -i, m. stepfather.

vitrum -i, n. (1) glass. (2) woad.

vitta -ae, f. a ribbon, band, fillet.

vittātus -a -um, bound with a fillet.

vitŭla -ae, f. calf, heifer.

vitŭlinus -a -um, of a calf; assum, roast veal; f. as subst. veal.

vitŭlus -i, m. a bull-calf; also of the young of other animals.

vitŭpĕrābĭlis -e, blamable.

vitŭpĕrātĭo -ōnis, f. blaming, scolding, censure; meton., blameworthy conduct.

vitŭpĕrātor -ōris, m. a blamer.

vitŭpĕro -are, to blame, scold, censure.

vivārĭum -i, n. a warren, preserve, fish-pond.

vivātus -a -um, quickened, vivid.

vivax -ācis, long-lived, lasting, enduring; brisk, lively, vigorous.

vivesco vivescĕre vixi, to grow lively.

vividus -a -um, full of life, animated, vigorous; life-like.

vivirādix -icis, f. a cutting with a root, a layer.

vivisco = vivesco; q.v.

vivo vivĕre vixi victum, to live, be alive; to live well, to enjoy life; to survive; to live on anything; to dwell.

vivus (vīvŏs) -a -um, alive, living; lifelike; flumen, running water; ros. fresh; sulfur, natural.

vix, with difficulty, scarcely, only just; vix dum, or vixdum, hardly yet

vŏcābŭlum -i, n. name, appellation; grammat. a noun.

vŏcālis -e, vocal; speaking, singing; f. as subst. a vowel.

vŏcāmen -inis, n. name, appellation.

vŏcātĭo -ōnis, f. summons, invitation.

vŏcātor -ōris, m. an inviter.

vŏcātus -ūs, m. summons, invocation.

vŏcĭfĕrātĭo -ōnis, f. loud calling, shouting.

vŏcĭfĕror -ari, dep. to cry aloud, shout.

vŏcĭto -are, to be accustomed to name; to shout loudly or often.

vŏco -are, to call, summon, invoke, invite; to name, designate; to bring or put into any state or condition; in dubium, to call in question.

vŏcŭla -ae, f. a low, weak voice; a low tone; a petty speech.

vŏlaema pira, n. pl. a kind of large pear.

vŏlātĭcus -a -um, winged, flying; flighty, inconstant.

vŏlātĭlis -e, winged, flying; swift, rapid; fleeting, transitory.

vŏlātus -ūs, m. flying, flight.

Volcānus (Vulc-) -i, m. Vulcan, the god of fire, husband of Venus.

volgo, volgus = vulgo, vulgus; q.v.

vŏlĭto -are, to fly about, flit, flutter, rush around.

volnĕro = vulnero; q.v.

¹vŏlo velle vŏlŭi (vīn = visne; sis = si vis; sultis = si vultis); to be willing, to wish, want; to will, ordain; to suppose, maintain that; sibi velle to mean, signify.

Hence partic. vŏlens -entis, willing, favourable.

²vŏlo -are, to fly; to move rapidly, rush; f. pl. of partic. volantes, -ium = birds.

vŏlōnes -um, m. pl. volunteers (in the Second Punic War).

Volsci -ōrum, m. pl. a people in Latium.

volsella -ae, f. a pair of tweezers.

volsus -a -um, partic. from vello; q.v.

volt-; see vult-.

vŏlūbĭlis -e, rolling, revolving, turning round; changeable, inconstant; of speech, rapid, fluent; adv. vŏlūbĭlĭter, fluently.

vŏlūbĭlĭtās -ātis, f. turning, revolution; roundness; inconstancy, flow of words, fluency.

vŏlŭcer volucris volucre, flying, winged; fleet, swift, fleeting. F. as subst. vŏlucris -is, a bird or flying insect.

vŏlūmen -inis, n. a scroll, book; a roll, wreath, fold.

vŏluntārĭus -a -um, voluntary, acting or done voluntarily; m. pl. as subst. volunteers.

vŏluntās -ātis, f. *will, wish, inclination;* esp. *goodwill; last will, testament;* of words, etc., *meaning, sense.*

vŏlup, *agreeably, pleasantly.*

vŏluptārius -a -um, *pleasant; concerned with or devoted to pleasure.*

vŏluptās -ātis, f. *pleasure, delight, enjoyment;* in plur., *public shows.*

vŏluptŭōsus -a -um, *delightful.*

vŏlūtābrum -i, n. *a place for pigs, a slough.*

vŏlūtābundus -a -um, *rolling, wallowing.*

vŏlūtātĭo -ōnis, f. *rolling about, wallowing; disquiet.*

vŏlūto -are, *to roll round, tumble about;* partic. volutans, *rolling about.* Transf., *to turn over in the mind, consider; to busy, occupy.*

volva (vulva) -ae, f. *womb;* esp. *a sow's womb*

volvo volvĕre volvi vŏlūtum, *to wind, turn, roll, twist round;* in pass. *to roll.* Esp. *to unroll a book, to read.* Transf., of time, *to make roll by;* of persons, *to turn over in the mind, consider; to experience, go through.*

vōmer (vōmis) -ēris, m. *ploughshare.*

vōmĭca -ae, f. *an ulcer, sore, boil; a plague, curse.*

vōmis -eris, m. = vomer; q.v.

vŏmĭtĭo -ōnis, f. *vomiting, throwing up.*

vŏmo -ere -ŭi -ĭtum, *to vomit; to vomit forth, throw up.*

vŏrāgo -ĭnis, f. *pit, chasm, abyss.*

vŏrax -ācis, *gluttonous, voracious.*

vŏro -are, *to eat greedily, swallow up, consume, devour.*

vors-; see vers-.

vort-; see vert-.

vōs, *you,* plur. of tu; q.v.

vōtĭvus -a -um, *of a vow, votive, vowed.*

vōtum -i, n. *a vow, promise to the gods; a votive offering;* in gen., *prayer, wish, desire.*

vŏvĕo vŏvēre vōvi vōtum, *to vow, promise to a god; to pray for, wish.*

vox vōcis, f. *voice, cry, call; accent, language; sound, tone; a saying, utterance.*

Vulcānus = Volcanus; q.v.

vulgāris (volg-) -e, *common, ordinary, usual;* adv. vulgārĭtĕr, *in the ordinary way.*

vulgātus -a -um, partic. from vulgo; q.v.

vulgĭvăgus -a -um, *wandering, vagrant.*

vulgo (volgo) -are, *to make common or accessible, spread, publish, impart;* partic. vulgātus -a -um, *common, commonly known.*

vulgus (volgus) -i, n. (occ. m.) *the people, the public; a mass, crowd, rabble, mob.* Abl. as adv. vulgō, *commonly, generally, in public.*

vulnĕrātĭo (voln-) -ōnis, f. *wounding, a wound.*

vulnĕro (voln-) -are, *to wound, injure.*

vulnĭfĭcus (voln-) -a -um, *inflicting wounds.*

vulnus (volnus) -ĕris, n. *a wound, injury.*

vulpēcŭla (volp-) -ae, f. *a little fox.*

vulpēs (volpēs) -is, f. *a fox.*

vulsus -a -um, partic. from vello; q.v.

vultĭcŭlus -a -um, *grimacing, affected.*

vultŭōsus -a -um, *grimacing, affected.*

vultur (voltur) -ŭris, m. *a vulture.*

vultŭrīnus (volt-) -a -um, *of or like a vulture.*

vultŭrius (volt-) -i, m. *a vulture.* Transf., *a rapacious man.*

Vulturnus (Volt-) -i, m. *a river in Campania.*

vultus (voltus) -ūs, m. *expression of face, countenance, look, aspect.* Transf., *face.*

X

X, x, the twenty-second letter of the Latin alphabet.

xĕnĭum -i, n. *a present to a guest.*

Xĕnŏphōn -ōntis, m. *an Athenian soldier and writer.*

xĕrampĕlinae -ārum, f. pl. *dark-red garments.*

Xerxēs -is, m. *king of the Persians, defeated at Salamis.*

xĭphias -ae, m. *sword-fish.*

xystus -i, m. and xystum -i, n. *an open colonnade, a walk planted with trees.*

Y

Y, y, a letter borrowed from the Greek in order to represent the Greek upsilon.

Z

Z, z, representing the Greek zeta.

Zāma -ae, f. *a town in Numidia, where Scipio defeated Hannibal* (201 B.C.).

zēlŏtўpus -a -um, *jealous.*

Zēno (-ōn) -ōnis, m. *name of several Greek philosophers.*

zĕphўrus -i, m. *a warm west wind, zephyr.*

zm-; see sm-.

zōdĭācus -i, m. *the zodiac.*

zōna -ae, f. *a girdle, money-belt;* in pl. zonae, *terrestrial zones.*

zōnārĭus -a -um, *of a girdle;* m. as subst. *girdle-maker.*

zōthēca -ae, f. *a private room.*

adaptation, *accommodatio.*
adapted, *aptus, idoneus.*
add, *addĕre, adicĕre*; to — up, *computare.*
adder, *vipera.*
addict, v.; to — oneself, *se dare, dedĕre, tradĕre.*
addicted, *deditus.*
addition: = adding, *accessio*; in arithmetic, *additio.*
additional, *novus, additus, adiectus.*
address, v. = to speak to, *adloqui, adfari, appellare, compellare*; to address a letter, (*homini*) *epistulam inscribere.*
address, subst.: speech, *contio, oratio*; the — of a letter, *inscriptio*; = place, *locus*; = adroitness, *dexteritas, sollertia.*
adduce, *adducĕre, proferre.*
adept, *callidus, peritus.*
adequate, *aptus, idoneus*; adv. *apte, satis.*
adhere, (*in*)*haerēre.*
adherent, *socius, fautor, cliens.*
adhesive, *tenax.*
adieu! *vale!* plur. *valete*; to bid —, (*hominem*) *valēre iubēre.*
adjacent, *contiguus, vicinus, finitimus*; to be —, *adiacēre.*
adjective, *nomen adiectivum.*
adjoin; see adjacent.
adjourn, *ampliare, rem differre.*
adjournment, *dilatio.*
adjudge, *addicĕre, adiudicare.*
adjudicate; see judge.
adjunct; see addition.
adjure, = entreat, *obsecrare, obtestari.*
adjust; see arrange, adapt.
adjustment, *accommodatio.*
administer, *administrare, procurare*; to — medicine, *medicinam dare, adhibēre*; to — justice, *ius dicĕre.*
administration, the act, *administratio, procuratio*; = the government, *ei qui reipublicae praesunt.*
admirable, (*ad*)*mirabilis, praeclarus*; adv. *admirabiliter, mirum in modum, praeclare.*
admiral, *praefectus classis*
admiration, *admiratio.*
admire, (*ad*)*mirari.*
admissible, *aequus*; or use verb.
admission: = leave to enter, *aditus* (*-ūs*), *accessus* (*-ūs*); = confession, *confessio*; in argument, *concessio.*
admit; to let in, *admittĕre, recipĕre*; in argument, *concedĕre, dare*; = to confess, *fateri, confiteri*; to — of, = allow, *recipĕre, pati.*
admonish, (*ad*)*monēre, commonēre.*
admonition, (*ad*)*monitio.*
ado: with much —, *vix, aegre*; see fuss.
adolescence, *adulescentia.*
adolescent, *adulescens.*
adopt, *adoptare*; = to choose, accept, *adsumĕre, accipĕre, recipĕre*; to — a resolution, *constituĕre.*
adoption, *adoptio.*
adoptive, *adoptivus.*
adorable, *sanctus, venerandus.*
adoration, *cultus* (*-ūs*), *veneratio.*

adore, *venerari, colĕre*; = to love, *diligĕre, amare.*
adorn, (*ex*)*ornare, decorare.*
adornment, *ornatus* (*-ūs*), *exornatio.*
adrift, to be, *fluctibus iactari.*
adroit, *callidus, sollers, dexter*; adv. *callide, dextere.*
adroitness, *dexteritas.*
adulation, *adulatio, adsentatio.*
adult, *adultus, pubes.*
adulterate, *corrumpĕre, vitiare.*
adulterer, *adulter, moechus.*
adultery, *adulterium.*
adults, subst. *puberes* (plur. only).
adumbrate, *adumbrare.*
adumbration, *adumbratio.*
advance, v.: intransit., *progredi, procedĕre*; to become advanced in years, *aetate provehi*; transit., *promovēre, provehĕre, adiuvare, augēre.*
advance-guard, *primum agmen.*
advantage, *commodum, lucrum, fructus* (*-ūs*), *utilitas, bonum*; to be of — expedire, prodesse, usui esse.*
advantageous, *utilis, fructuosus, opportunus*; adv. *utiliter.*
advent, *adventus* (*-ūs*).
adventitious, *adventicius, externus.*
adventure, subst.: = exploit, *facinus* (*-oris*), *inceptum*; = happening, *casus* (*-ūs*).
adventure, v. *audēre, tentare, experiri, periclitari.*
adventurous, *audax*; adv. *audacter*
adverb, *adverbium.*
adversary, *adversarius.*
adverse, *adversus, contrarius*; adv. *contra, secus.*
adversity, *res adversae, calamitas.*
advertise; = to make known, *praedicare, pronuntiare*; of goods, *proscribĕre, inscribĕre.*
advertisement, = notice of sale, *proscriptio.*
advice, *consilium*; by my —, *me auctore.*
advise, *suadēre, monēre*; see also inform.
advisedly, *consulte, considerate, de industria.*
adviser, *suasor, auctor.*
advocate, subst.; legal, *patronus*; in gen., *suasor, auctor.*
advocate, v. *suadēre.*
adze, *ascia.*
aerial, *aerius, aetherius.*
afar, *procul, longe.*
affability, *comitas.*
affable, *adfabilis, comis*; adv. *comiter.*
affair, *res, negotium.*
affect, v.: = to influence, *adficĕre, tangĕre*, (*com*)*movēre*; = to be fond of, *diligĕre, amare*; = to make a show of, *simulare, imitari.*
affectation, *simulatio.*
affected, *quaesitus, simulatus*; of style, *putidus, molestus*; adv. *putide, moleste.*
affection: in gen., *adfectio, adfectus* (*-ūs*); = friendly sentiment, *amor, caritas, studium*; dutiful —, *pietas.*
affectionate, adj. *amans*; dutifully — *pius*; adv. *amanter, pie.*

affiance, = betroth, *(de)spondēre.*

affidavit, *testimonium per tabulas datum.*

affinity, *propinquitas, necessitudo;* in gen., = close connexion, *cognatio, coniunctio.*

affirm, *adfirmare, confirmare*

affirmation, *adfirmatio.*

affirmative, use verb.

affix, *adfigere, adligare, adnectēre.*

afflict, *adflictare, vexare.*

affliction, *aegritudo, dolor, molestia.*

affluence, *divitiae, opes, copia.*

affluent, *dives.*

afford, = supply, *praestare praebēre, sufficēre, suppeditare.*

affray, *rixa, pugna.*

affright; see frighten.

affront, subst. *contumelia.*

affront, v. *contumeliā adficēre.*

afloat: to be —, *navigare, navi vehi.*

afoot, *pedibus.*

aforesaid, *quem (quod) supra scripsi.*

afraid, *timidus, pavidus, trepidus;* to be —, *timēre, metuēre.*

afresh; see again.

after. Prep.: of place or time, *post,* with acc.; of rank, etc., *secundum,* with acc.; of conformity, = according to, *ad,* with acc. Conj., *postquam, cum, ubi.*

afterwards, *post, postea, dein(de), inde;* = after this, *posthac;* some months —, *paucis postea mensibus, aliquot post menses.*

afternoon: in the —, *post meridiem;* adj. *postmeridianus.*

again, *rursus, rursum, denuo;* = a second time, *iterum;* again and again, *identidem;* = further, moreover, *porro, autem.*

against, *contra, adversus, in,* with acc.; — the stream, *adverso flumine;* — my will, *me invito.*

age: = time (esp. time of life), *aetas;* of the same —, *aequalis;* = old age, of persons, *senectus,* of things, *vetustas.*

aged, *aetate provectus;* an — man, *senex (-is).*

agency, = instrumentality, *opera.*

agent, *procurator.*

aggrandize, *amplificare, augēre.*

aggrandizement, *amplificatio;* or use verb.

aggravate: = to make worse, *(ad)-gravare;* = to annoy, *exasperare, lacessēre.*

aggregate, *summa.*

aggression, *impetus (-ūs), incursus (-ūs), iniuria.*

aggressive, *hostilis, infensus.*

aggressor, *qui prior oppugnat qui iniuriam facit.*

aggrieve; see grieve.

aghast, *stupefactus, perturbatus;* to stand —, *stupēre, obstupescēre.*

agile, *agilis, velox, pernix.*

agility, *agilitas, pernicitas, velocitas.*

agitate: = to shake, *agitare, quatēre, vibrare;* mentally, = to disturb, *percutēre, perturbare, sollicitare;* = to discuss, *agitare, disputare, disserēre.*

agitated, *sollicitus, trepidus.*

agitation: physical, *agitatio, iactatio;* mental, *animi motus (-ūs), commotio concitatio.*

agitator, *turbator.*

ago, *abhinc;* long —, *(iam) pridem, iam dudum.*

agony, *aegritudo, dolor.*

agrarian, *agrarius.*

agree, *concinēre, consentire;* it is agreed, *constat;* to — upon, = settle, *componēre, constituēre.*

agreeable: of things, *acceptus, gratus, dulcis;* of persons, *commodus, lepidus.*

agreement; = harmony, *consensus (-ūs), concordia;* = arrangement, compact *pactum, pactio, conventum.*

agricultural, *rusticus.*

agriculture, *agri cultura, agri cultio.*

agriculturist, *agricola.*

aground, to run, *sidēre.*

ague, *febris.*

ah! aha! interj. *a, ah, aha.*

ahead, use compound verb with *prae-* or *pro-.*

aid, subst. *auxilium, adiumentum, subsidium, opem* (nom. *ops* not used).

aid, *adiuvare, subvenire, succurrēre, opem ferre.*

ailing, *aeger;* see sick.

aim, subst. *finis, propositum, consilium.*

aim, v. to take aim, *telum dirigēre* or *intendēre;* to — aim at, *telo petēre;* fig., *adfectare, petēre, quaerēre, spectare.*

air, subst. (1), *aer, aether* (upper air), *aura* (breeze), *anima* (= breath); in the open —, *sub Iove, sub divo.* (2), = look manner, *vultus (-ūs), aspectus (-ūs), species.* (3) = tune *modus, numeri.*

air, v. *ventilare.*

airy, *aerius.*

akin: = related, *consanguineus, propinquus, agnatus, cognatus;* = similar, connected, *finitimus, vicinus.*

alacrity, *alacritas, pernicitas.*

alarm, subst.: = loud noise, *clamor, strepitus (-ūs);* = disturbance, *turba, tumultus (-ūs);* = fear, *terror, trepidatio.*

alas! *heu! eheu! vae! ei!*

alcove, *zotheca.*

alder, *alnus;* adj. *alneus.*

alert, *vigil, alacer, promptus.*

alias, *nomen alienum.*

alien, adj.: = foreign, *peregrinus, externus;* = adverse, *alienus, aversus.*

alien, subst. *peregrinus, advena, alienigena.*

alienate, *(ab)alienare, avertēre.*

alienation, *(ab)alienatio.*

alight, v. *descendēre.*

alike: adj. *par, similis;* adv. *pariter, similiter, aeque.*

alive, *vivus;* to be —, *vivēre.*

all: = every single, *omnis;* = the whole, *totus;* all together, *cunctus, universus;* in —, *omnino;* not at —, *minime;* — but, *tantum non.*

allay, *lenire, sedare, mitigare.*

allegation, *adfirmatio;* see also accusation.

allege: see assert.

allegiance, *fides*; to swear — to. *in verba hominis iurare.*

allegory, *allegoria.*

alleviate, *(ad)levare*; see also allay.

alleviation, *levatio, mitigatio, levamen.*

alley, *angiportus (-ūs).*

alliance, *societas, foedus (-eris).*

allot: by lot, *sortiri*; in gen., *distribuĕre, adsignare, adiudicare.*

allotment, *adsignatio*; of land *ager adsignatus, possessio.*

allow. (1) = permit, *sinĕre, pati; permittĕre, concedĕre*; I am —ed, *licet mihi.* (2) = admit, *concedĕre, confiteri.* (3) = grant; q.v.

allowable, *concessus, licitus.*

allowance: = indulgence, *indulgentia*; to make — for, *ignoscĕre, condonare*; an — of food, *diaria, demensum.*

alloy: without —, *sincerus, purus.*

allude to, = to refer to, *significare, designare.*

allure, *adlicĕre, inlicĕre, invitare, inescare.*

allurement, *invitamentum, blanditia, inlecebra.*

alluring, *blandus.*

allusion, *significatio, mentio*; or use verb.

ally, subst. *socius.*

ally, v.: = make an alliance, *foedus facĕre* (or *ferire*), *societatem inire*; = join together as allies, *sociare.*

almanack, *fasti (-orum), ephemeris.*

almighty, *omnipotens.*

almond, *amygdala.*

almost, *prope, paene.*

alms, *stips (-is, f.: nom. not used).*

aloft, *sublime, alte; sublimis,* adj.

alone: adj. *solus, unus*; adv. = only; q.v.

along: adv., *porro, protinus*; prep., *secundum, praeter*; — with, *una cum.*

aloof, *procul.*

aloud, *clara* or *magna voce.*

already, *iam.*

also, *etiam, praeterea, quoque, item.*

altar, *ara, altaria* (plur.).

alter: transit., *mutare, commutare, immutare, (con)vertĕre*; intransit., use passive, e.g. *mutari.*

alterable, adj. *mutabilis.*

alteration, *(com)mutatio*; a sudden —, *conversio.*

altercation, *altercatio, iurgium, rixa.*

alternate, v.; transit., *alternare, variare*; intransit., *variare.*

alternate, adj. *alternus*; adv. *invicem.*

alternation, *vicissitudo.*

alternative: there is no alternative left except . . ., *nihil restat nisi ut . . . .*

although, *quamquam; etsi* (= even if); *quamvis* (= however much); *licet* (= granted that).

altitude, *altitudo.*

altogether, = wholly, *omnino.*

always, *semper.*

amalgamate, *(com)miscĕre.*

amalgamation, *coniunctio, mixtura.*

amanuensis, *librarius, servus a manu.*

amass, *(co)acervare, aggerare, accumulare.*

amaze, *obstupefacĕre.*

amazed, *(ob)stupefactus, stupidus*; to be —, *stupĕre, (ob)stupescĕre.*

amazement, *stupor.*

amazing, *mirus, admirabilis*; adj. *admirabiliter, mirum in modum.*

ambassador, *legatus.*

amber, *sucinum, electrum.*

ambiguity, *ambiguitas; ambages* (plur.; = riddle).

ambiguous, *anceps, ambiguus, dubius*; adv. *ambigue.*

ambition, *ambitio, gloria; laudis studium contentio honorum.*

ambitious, *gloriae* (or *laudis*) *cupidus.*

ambrosia, *ambrosia.*

ambush, *insidiae* (plur.).

ameliorate, *corrigĕre, emendare.*

amen! *fiat! esto!*

amenable, *(dicto) oboediens.*

amend, *emendare, corrigĕre.*

amendment, *correctio, emendatio.*

amends, *satisfactio, expiatio*: to make — for, *expiare, satisfacĕre.*

amenity, *amoenitas.*

amiability, *suavitas.*

amiable, *suavis, amabilis*; adv. *suaviter*

amicable; see friendly.

amidst, *inter,* with acc.

amiss, *male, perperam, prave*: to take —, *aegre ferre.*

ammunition, *apparatus (-ūs) belli, arma (-orum)*; see also bullet.

amnesty, use *venia,* or *ignoscĕre.*

among, *inter,* with acc.; *in,* with abl.; *apud,* with acc.

amorous, *amans*; in bad sense, *libidinosus.*

amount, *summa.*

amount to, v. *efficere*: what does it — to? *quae summa est?* it —s to the same thing, *idem est, nihil interest.*

amphitheatre, *amphitheatrum.*

ample, *amplus*; adv. *ample, abunde.*

amplify, *amplificare.*

amplitude, *amplitudo.*

amputate, *praecidĕre, amputare.*

amuse, *delectare, oblectare.*

amusement, *delectatio, oblectatio, oblectamentum.*

amusing, *facetus, festivus.*

anachronism; use phrase, e.g. *tempora miscĕre.*

analogous, *similis.*

analogy, *similitudo.*

analyse, *explicare; quasi in membra discerpĕre.*

analysis, *explicatio, enodatio.*

anarchy, *licentia.*

anatomy; refer to the structure of the body, = *compages* or *conformatio corporis.*

ancestor; sing. *auctor generis*; plur. *maiores.*

ancestral, *avitus, proavitus.*

ancestry, *origo, genus.*

anchor, subst. *ancora*; to cast —, *ancoram iacĕre*; to weigh —, *ancoram tollĕre.*

anchor, v. transit. *(navem) ad ancoras deligare.*

anchorage, *statio.*

ancient, *antiquus, vetus, vetustus, priscus*; the ancients, *veteres, antiqui.*

and, *et*; *-que* (enclitic); *atque, ac*; — so,
 itaque; — yet, *tamen*; — not, *et non,
 neque, nec.*
anecdote, *fabula, fabella.*
anew, *denuo, ab integro.*
anger, subst. *ira, iracundia, indignatio.*
anger, v. *lacessĕre, inritare.*
angle, *angulus.*
angle, v. *piscari.*
angler, *piscator.*
angry, adj. *iratus, iracundus*; to be (or
 become) angry, *irasci*; adv. *iracunde.*
anguish, *cruciatus (-ūs), dolor, angor.*
angular, *angulatus.*
animadvert, *animadvertĕre.*
animal, subst. *animal, animans*; = a
 beast, *bestia, pecus (-udis,* domestic),
 belua (large), *fera* (wild).
animal, adj. *animalis*; or genit. of
 animal, corpus, etc.
animate, v. *animare*; fig., *excitare,
 incitare.*
animate, adj. *animalis, animatus.*
animated, *animatus, animans, animalis*;
 = lively, *vegetus, alacer.*
animation, *alacritas, vigor.*
animosity, *odium, invidia.*
ankle, ankle-bone, *talus.*
annals, *annales (-ium,* plur.).
annex, v.: = add, *(ad)iungĕre, addĕre*;
 = conquer, *sibi subicĕre.*
annihilate, *delēre, exstinguĕre.*
annihilation, *exstinctio, excidium.*
anniversary, *festus dies anniversarius.*
annotate, *adnotare.*
annotation, *adnotatio.*
announce, *(re)nuntiare, praedicare.*
annoy, *lacessĕre, inritare, vexare.*
annoyance, *molestia, vexatio.*
annual, *annuus, anniversarius*; adv.
 quotannis.
annuity, *annua pecunia.*
annul, *tollĕre, delēre, abrogare, abolēre.*
anoint, *(in)unguĕre.*
anointing, subst. *unctio.*
anon, *brevi (tempore), mox.*
anonymous, *sine nomine.*
another, pron. and adj. *alius*; *alter*
 (= a second); they fear one —,
 alius alium timet, inter se timent.
answer, subst. *responsum*; to a charge,
 defensio, excusatio.
answer, v. *respondēre*; to a charge, *se
 defendĕre, excusare*; of an oracle,
 responsum dare; to — for, *(rem)
 praestare.*
answerable: to be — to a person,
 homini rationem reddĕre.
ant, *formica.*
antagonist, *adversarius.*
antagonistic, *contrarius, adversus, infensus.*
antecedent, adj. *antecedens, prior.*
antecedents, subst. *antecedentia (-ium).*
antechamber, *vestibulum, atriolum.*
antelope; see deer.
anterior, *antecedens, prior.*
anthem, *cantus (-ūs).*
anticipate, = to act first, forestall,
 occupare, praevertĕre, antevertĕre;
 = to expect, *exspectare.*
anticipation: see anticipate; = expectation, *exspectatio, spes.*

antics, *ludi, ioca.*
antidote, *remedium.*
antipathy: of things, *(rerum) discordia,
 repugnantia*; of persons, *odium.*
antiquary, antiquarian, *rerum antiquarum studiosus.*
antiquated, *obsoletus, priscus.*
antique, *antiquus.*
antiquity, *antiquitas, vetustas.*
antithesis: rhet. *contentio*; = the
 opposite, *contrarium.*
antler, *cornu.*
anvil, *incus (-udis).*
anxiety, *anxietas, cura, sollicitudo.*
anxious, *anxius, sollicitus, trepidus*; adv.
 anxie, sollicite.
any, anyone: with negative, or in
 questions, *ullus* (adj.) *quisquam* (sub-
 stantival); after *si, nisi,* or *ne,* use *qui,
 qua, quod* (adj.), *quis* (subst.); — you
 like, — you please, *quivis, quilibet.*
anywhere, *usquam*; *ubivis* (= anywhere you please); *quoquam* (= to any
 place).
apace, *celeriter.*
apart, *seorsum*; or use compound verbs
 with *dis-* and *se-.*
apartment; see room.
apathetic, *hebes, lentus.*
apathy, *stupor, lentitudo.*
ape, *simia, simius.*
ape, v. *imitari.*
Apennines, *Apenninus.*
aperture; see opening.
apex, *cacumen, apex.*
aphorism, *sententia, dictum, elogium.*
apiece, use distrib. num.
apologise, *excusare.*
apology: = defence, *defensio*; = excuse, *excusatio.*
apophthegm, *elogium, sententia, dictum.*
apostrophize; see address.
apothecary, *medicus.*
appal, *(ex)terrēre*; see frighten.
apparatus, *apparatus (-ūs).*
apparel, *vestis, vestimentum.*
apparent: = evident, *manifestus, apertus*; to be —, *apparēre*; = not real,
 fictus, simulatus; adv. *ut videtur.*
apparition: = appearing, *adventus(-ūs)*;
 = spectre, *simulacrum, species.*
appeal, subst.: legal, *appellatio, provo-
 catio*; = entreaty, *obsecratio, preces.*
appeal, v.: legal, to a magistrate,
 (hominem) appellare; to the people,
 ad populum provocare; appeal to,
 = entreat, *obtestari, obsecrare*; appeal
 to, = please, *placēre.*
appealing, *supplex.*
appear: = become visible, be evident,
 apparēre, conspici; to appear in
 public, *in publicum prodire*; —, = be
 present, put in an appearance,
 comparēre, adesse; to —, = seem,
 videri.
appearance: = arrival, *adventus (-ūs)*;
 or use verb; = looks, *species, facies,
 habitus (-ūs)*; = semblance, *species.*
appease, *placēre*; of hunger etc., *sedare.*
appeasement, *placatio.*
appellant; see appeal.
append, *addĕre, adiungĕre.*
appendage, *appendix, accessio.*

appetite, *appetentia, appetitio*; for food, *fames*.

applaud, *(ap)plaudĕre*.

applause, *plausus (-ūs)*.

apple, *malum*; — tree, *malus*, f.

appliance, *apparatus (-ūs), instrumentum*.

application: = request, *petitio*; of the mind, *animi intentio, diligentia*.

apply, v.: transit., = bring to bear, *adhibēre, admovēre*; to — oneself, *se conferre*; intransit., = refer, *pertinēre*; = make application, *adirĕ*.

appoint, *constituĕre, dicĕre, destinare*; of officials, *creare, facĕre*; to — to command, *praeponĕre, praeficĕre*.

appointment: = office, *munus (-eris), magistratus (-ūs)*; = agreement to meet, *constitutum*.

apportion, *dividĕre, distribuĕre ad-signare*.

apposite, *aptus, accommodatus.*

appraise, *aestimare*.

appreciate, *aestimare; agnoscĕre*.

apprehend, *comprehendĕre*; = to grasp mentally, *comprehendĕre, complecti (animo or mente), intellegĕre*; = fear; q.v.

apprehension: = mental grasp, *intellegentia*; = fear, *timor*.

apprehensive; see timid.

apprentice, subst. *homo (homini) addic-tus*.

apprentice, v. *addicĕre*.

approach, subst. *adventus (-ūs), aditus (-ūs)*.

approach, v. *accedĕre, appropinquare, adventare*.

approbation; see approval.

appropriate, adj. *idoneus, aptus, accom-modatus*; adv. *apte, accommodate*.

appropriate, v. *(ad)sumĕre, sibi adro-gare, sibi vindicare*.

approval, *approbatio, comprobatio*; with your approval, *pace tua*.

approve, *(ap)probare, comprobare*.

approved, *probatus, spectatus*.

approximate, adj. *propinquus*.

approximate, v., see approach.

April, *Aprilis (mensis)*.

apron, *subligaculum*.

apt: = appropriate; q.v.; = prone, *pronus, propensus*; adv. *apte*.

aptitude, *habilitas*.

aquatic, *aquatilis*.

aqueduct, *aquae ductus (-ūs)*.

aquiline, *aduncus*.

arable; see plough.

arbiter, *arbiter, disceptator*.

arbitrarily, *libidinose*.

arbitrary: = capricious, *libidinosus*; of power, use *dominari* or *dominatio*.

arbitrate, v. *disceptare, diiudicare*.

arbitration, *arbitrium*.

arbour, *umbraculum*.

arc, *arcus (-ūs)*.

arcade, *porticus (-ūs)*.

arch, subst. *arcus (-ūs), fornix*.

arch, adj. *petulans, improbus, malus*.

arch, v. *arcuare*; see curve.

archaeology, *rerum antiquarum scientia*.

archaism, *verbum obsoletum*.

archer, *sagittarius*.

architect, *architectus*.

architecture, *architectura*.

archives, *tabulae publicae*.

arctic, *septentrionalis, arctous*.

ardent, *ardens, fervens, acer*; adv., *ardenter, acriter*.

ardour, *ardor, fervor, studium*.

arduous, *arduus, difficilis*.

area, *area, superficies*.

arena, *harena*.

argue: = to discuss, *disserĕre, dis-putare*; = conclude, seek to prove, *argumentari, conligĕre*.

argument: = dispute, *disputatio*; line of —, *argumentum*.

arid, *aridus, siccus*.

aright, *recte, bene*.

arise, *surgĕre, (ex)oriri, exsistĕre*.

aristocracy: = aristocrats, *optimates, patricii, nobiles*; as a form of govern-ment, *optimatium dominatus (-ūs)*.

aristocrat, aristocratic; see aristo-cracy.

arithmetic, *arithmetica (-orum)*.

arithmetical, *arithmeticus*.

ark, = chest, *arca*.

arm, subst. *bracchium*; upper —, *lacertus*; arms, = embrace, *complexus (-ūs), manūs* (plur.); see also arms.

arm, v. transit. *armare*; intransit. *armari, arma capĕre*.

arm-chair, *sella*.

armed, *armatus*.

armistice, *indutiae (-arum)*.

armour, *arma (-orum)*; armour-bearer, *armiger*.

armourer, *faber armorum*.

armpit, *ala*.

arms, *arma (-orum), tela (-orum)*, (offen-sive).

army, *exercitus (-ūs)*; in marching array, *agmen*; in battle array, *acies*.

aromatic, *odorus, odoratus*.

around: adv. and prep., *circa, circum*.

arouse, *excitare, suscitare*.

arraign; see accuse.

arrange, *ordinare, componĕre, disponĕre, digerĕre*; abstr., *constituĕre, com-ponĕre*.

arrangement, *ordo, ratio, dispositio*; or use verb.

arrant, render by superl., or *summus*.

array: of battle, *acies*; = dress, *vestis*.

array, v. = dress, *vestire*.

arrears, *pecuniae residuae*.

arrest: = put under arrest, *compre-hendĕre, in custodiam dare*; = stop; q.v.

arrival, *adventus (-ūs), accessus (-ūs)*.

arrive, *advenire, pervenire, adventare*.

arrogance, *adrogantia, superbia*.

arrogant, *adrogans, superbus*; adv *adroganter, superbe*.

arrogate, v. *sibi adrogare, (ad)sumĕre*.

arrow, *sagitta*.

arsenal, *armamentarium*; naval — *navalia (-ium)*.

art, *ars, artificium, peritia* (= acquired skill); the fine —s, *artes ingenuae* or *liberales*.

artful, *astutus, callidus*; adv. *astute, callide*.

artfulness *astutia, calliditas, dolus*.

article, *res;* = clause or item, *caput, condicio.*

articulate, adj. *clarus.*

articulate, v. *dicěre.*

artificer, *artifex, opifex.*

artificial, adj. *artificiosus;* adv. *arte, manu, opere.*

artillery, *tormenta (-orum).*

artisan, *opifex, faber.*

artist, *artifex;* or *poeta, pictor,* etc.

artistic, adj. *artifex;* adv. *artificiose, summa arte.*

artless, adj. *simplex;* adv. *simpliciter, sine arte.*

as, adv. and conj.: see while, because, since, though; as . . . as., *tam . . . quam . . .;* such . . . as . . ., *talis . . . qualis . . .;* as great as . . ., *tantus . . . quantus;* as soon as, *simul ac;* the same as, *idem ac, atque, qui;* as far as, *tenus* (prep.), *usque* (adv., = all the way); as if, as though, *quasi, tamquam, velut;* as regards . . ., *quod ad . . . attinet.*

ascend, *scanděre, ascenděre.*

ascendency, render by *superior* or *summus.*

ascent, *ascensus (-ūs).*

ascertain, *explorare, cognoscěre, comperire.*

ascetic, render by phrase (e.g. *cibo abstinēre).*

ascribe, *ascriběre, adiudicare, attribuěre.*

ash (tree), *fraxinus;* adj. *fraxineus;* mountain-ash, *ornus.*

ashamed, *pudore adfectus;* I am ashamed, *pudet me.*

ashes, *cinis, favilla.*

ashore: of rest, *in litore;* of motion, *in litus;* to put —, *exponěre.*

aside, *seorsum;* see apart.

ask: of questions, *rogare, interrogare, quaerěre;* of favours, etc., *rogare, petěre, poscěre.*

askance: to look — at, *limis oculis adspicěre.*

aslant, *oblique, ex transverso.*

asleep, *dormiens, in somno, per somnum.*

asp, *aspis.*

aspect, *aspectus (-ūs), forma, facies, species.*

asperity, *asperitas, acerbitas.*

asperse, *infamiā aspergěre, calumniari.*

aspersion, *calumnia, opprobrium.*

aspirate, *aspiratio.*

aspire, *(ad rem) aspirare, contenděre; (rem) adfectare.*

aspiration, *appetitio, adfectatio.*

ass, *asinus;* a little —, *asellus.*

ass-driver, *asinarius.*

assail, *oppugnare, adoriri.*

assailant, *qui oppugnat.*

assassin, *sicarius, percursor.*

assassinate, *insidiis interficěre.*

assassination, *caedes;* to accuse of —, *accusare inter sicarios.*

assault, *impetus (-ūs), incursus (-ūs), oppugnatio;* legal, *vis.*

assay, subst. *obrussa.*

assemble, v. transit., *convocare;* intransit., *convenire, coire.*

assembly, *conventus (-ūs), concilium.*

assent, subst. *adsensio, adsensus (-ūs).*

assent, v. *adsentire, adnuěre.*

assert: = to state, *dicěre, adfirmare, confirmare;* to — a right, *ius retinēre, obtinēre.*

assertion: = statement, *adfirmatio;* = maintenance, *defensio, vindicatio.*

assess, *aestimare.*

assessment, *aestimatio, census (-ūs).*

assessor, *censor;* = a judge's assistant, *adsessor.*

assets, *bona (-orum).*

assiduity, *adsiduitas, sedulitas.*

assiduous, *adsiduus, sedulus, industrius;* adv. *adsidue, sedulo, industrie.*

assign, *adsignare, (at)tribuěre.*

assignation, *constitutum.*

assimilate: = to make like, *(ad) aequare, similem facěre;* = to digest, *concoquěre.*

assist, *(ad)iuvare, auxilium ferre, auxiliari, opitulari, subvenire.*

assistance, *opem* (nom. sing. not used), *auxilium, adiumentum.*

assistant, *adiutor.*

associate, subst. *socius, sodalis.*

associate, v. transit., *(con)iungěre, (con)sociare, congregare;* intransit., use pass., or reflex.

association, *societas, sodalitas, sodalicum.*

assort, *digerěre.*

assuage, *mitigare, lenire, sedare, levare.*

assume: = take to oneself, *sibi adrogare, (ad)suměre, occupare;* = take for granted, *poněre, suměre.*

assurance: = strong assertion, *confirmatio;* = confidence, *fiducia.*

assure, *homini (pro certo) adfirmare, confirmare;* = to secure; q.v.

assured: of things, *certus, exploratus;* to feel assured, *creděre, confiděre, pro certo habēre.*

assuredly, *profecto, certe.*

astern, *in* or *a puppi.*

astonish, *obstupefacěre.*

astonished, *attonitus;* to be —, *obstupescěre, stupēre.*

astonishing, *mirabilis, mirus;* adv. *mire, mirum in modum, mirabiliter.*

astonishment, *stupor, (ad)miratio.*

astray, use adj. *vagus,* or verb *vagari.*

astrologer, *astrologus, mathematicus.*

astrology, *astrologia.*

astronomy: treat as astrology; q.v.

astute, *astutus, callidus.*

asunder, *seorsum;* see apart.

asylum; see refuge.

at: of place, *ad, apud, in,* or locative case; of time, *in, ad,* or abl. case.

atheism, *deum esse negare.*

athlete, *athleta.*

athwart; see across.

atmosphere, *aer, caelum.*

atmospheric, use genit. *aeris* or *caeli.*

atom, *atomus, corpusculum.*

atone, *(ex)piare.*

atonement, *piaculum.*

atrocious, *nefandus, nefarius, atrox;* adv. *nefarie.*

atrocity: as quality, *immanitas, atrocitas;* as deed, *res atrox, nefas.*

attach, *adfigěre, adligare;* fig., *adiungěre, applicare.*

att 249 **bab**

attached, *aptus*; = fond, *studiosus*.
attachment, *studium, amor, caritas*.
attack, *impetus (-ūs), oppugnatio, incursus (-ūs)*.
attack, v. *oppugnare, adoriri, adgredi (ap)petĕre*; to be —ed by disease, *morbo corripi*.
attacker, *oppugnator*.
attain, *adsequi, consequi*.
attainment, *adeptio, comparatio*; = acquired skill, *ars, doctrina, eruditio*.
attempt, subst. *conatus (-ūs), inceptum*.
attempt, v. *conari, temptare*.
attend: of physical presence, *(hominem) comitari, prosequi, deducĕre*; as a servant, *(homini) famulari, ministrare*; at a gathering, *adesse, interesse, frequentare*; mentally, = to pay attention, *operam dare, curare, animadvertĕre, animum attendĕre, hoc agĕre*; not to attend, *aliud agĕre*.
attendance, *apparitio, adsectatio*; of large numbers, *frequentia*.
attendant: = escort, *(ad)sector, stipator*; = servant, *servus, minister, famulus*.
attention, *animus attentus, animi intentio*; = an attentive act, *officium*.
attentive: = paying attention, *attentus, intentus, erectus*; adv. *attente, intente*; = helpful, kind, *officiosus, observans*.
attenuate, v. *attenuare, extenuare*.
attest: = vouch for, *testari, testificari*; = call to witness, *testari, testem facĕre*.
attestation, *testificatio*; = evidence, *testimonium*.
attire; see dress.
attitude: physical, *(corporis) habitus (-ūs), status (-ūs)*; mental, *animus*.
attract, *attrahĕre, allicĕre*.
attraction, *vis attrahendi*; = pleasant object, *oblectamentum*.
attractive, adj. *iucundus, suavis*.
attribute, subst.; use phrase with *natura* or *proprius*; gram., *attributio, attributum*.
attribute, v. *(at)tribuĕre, adsignare*.
attrition; render by verb *terĕre*.
attune; use phrase with *concinĕre* or *consonus*.
auburn, *fulvus*.
auction, *auctio*; to hold an —, *auctionari*.
auctioneer, *magister auctionis, praeco*.
audacious, *audax, protervus, confidens*.
audacity, *audacia, protervitas*.
audience: = hearing *admissio, aditus (-ūs)*; = hearers, *audientes, corona*; a large —, *audientium frequentia*.
audit, v. *rationes dispungĕre*.
augment, v. *(ad)augēre, amplificare*.
augmentation, *amplificatio*.
augur, subst. *augur*.
augur, v., = foretell, *praedicĕre, vaticinari, augurari*.
augury, *augurium, omen*.
August, *(mensis)* Sextilis; later *Augustus*.
august, adj. *augustus, inlustris, magnificus*.
aunt, *amita* (= father's sister); *matertera* (= mother's sister).

auspices, *auspicium*.
auspicious, *felix, prosper, faustus*; adv. *feliciter, prospere, fauste*.
austere, *austerus, severus, tristis*; adv. *austere, severe*.
austerity, *austeritas, severitas*.
authentic, *certus, verus*; adv. *certo auctore*.
authenticity, *fides, auctoritas*.
author: = originator, *auctor, inventor*; = writer, *scriptor*.
authoritative, *gravis*.
authority, *auctoritas, gravitas*; an — for speech or action, *auctor*; the —s, *magistratus, potestates*.
authorize, *auctor esse, potestatem facĕre, permittĕre*.
autocrat, *dominus*.
autumn, *autumnus*.
autumnal, *autumnalis*.
auxiliaries, *auxilia, (milites) auxiliares*.
auxiliary, adj. *auxiliaris, auxiliarus*.
avail, *valēre, prodesse*; to — oneself of, *uti*.
avarice, *avaritia*.
avaricious, *avarus*.
avaunt! *abi! apage!*
avenge, *vindicare, ulcisci*.
avenger, *ultor, vindex*.
avenue, *xystus*.
aver; see affirm, assert.
averse, *aversus, alienus*.
avert, *avertĕre, prohibēre*.
aversion, *odium, animus aversus*.
avoid, *vitare, declinare, aversari*.
avow, *profitēri, confitēri*.
avowal, *confessio*.
avowed, *apertus*; adv. *aperte*.
await, *exspectare, manēre, opperiri*.
awake, adj. *vigilans*; to be —, *vigilare*.
awake, v.: transit., *(e somno) excitare*; intransit., *expergisci, excitari*.
award, subst. *arbitrium, addictio*.
award, v. *addicĕre, adiudicare*; see give.
aware, *gnarus*; to be —, *scire, novisse*.
away, *procul*; often rendered by compound verb with *ab-*.
awe, subst. *formido, reverentia, veneratio*.
awe, v. *terrēre; formidinem inicĕre*.
awe-inspiring, **awful**, *dirus, formidolosus, terribilis*.
awhile, *aliquamdiu, paulisper, parumper*.
awkward, *agrestis, rusticus, rudis, inscitus*; adv. *inscite, rustice*.
awkwardness, *rusticitas, inscitia*.
awl, *subula*.
awning, *velum*.
awry; adj. *obliquus, perversus*; adv. *oblique, perverse*.
axe, *securis, dolabra*.
axis, axle, *axis*.
ay, aye, adv. *ita, certe, sane*; I say ay, *aio*.
azure, *caeruleus*.

B

baa, v. *balare*.
babble, v. *blaterare, garrire*.
babbler, *garrulus*.
babe, baby, *infans*.

baboon: see ape.

bachelor, *caelebs.*

back, subst. *tergum:* on one's back, *supinus* (adj.).

back, v.: transit. = move backwards, *retro movēre*; = support, *favēre*; intransit., = go back, *se recipēre*, *recedēre.*

back, backwards, *retro, retrorsum*; or use compound verb with *re-.*

backbite, *rodēre, absenti maledicēre.*

bacon, *lardum.*

bad, *malus, pravus* (= crooked), *turpis* (= ugly, foul); *improbus, perversus, nequam;* in — health, *aeger;* adv. *male, prave, turpiter, improbe.*

badge, *signum, insigne, nota.*

badger, *meles.*

badness, *pravitas, turpitas, nequitia.*

baffle, *eludēre, ad irritum redigēre.*

bag, *saccus, culeus.*

baggage, *sarcinae, impedimenta* (-orum), *vasa* (-orum).

bail, subst.: = security given, *vadimonium;* = person giving security, *vas, sponsor.*

bail, v. *spondēre.*

bailiff: on an estate, *procurator, vilicus;* at law courts, *apparitor.*

bait, subst. *esca.*

bait, v. = put bait on (a hook), *escam* (*hamo*) *imponēre;* = feed, *cibum praebēre;* = worry, *vexare, lacessēre.*

bake, *coquēre, torrēre.*

baker, *pistor.*

bakery, *pistrinum.*

balance, subst.: = scales, *trutina, libra;* = remainder, use adj. *reliquus.*

balance, v. *aequis ponderibus librare;* fig., *compensare;* the accounts —, *ratio constat.*

bald, *glaber, calvus;* of language, *incultus.*

baldness, *calvitium.*

bale, subst. *fascis.*

bale (out), v. *egerēre, exhaurire.*

baleful, *perniciosus, exitiosus.*

balk, v. *frustrari, eludēre.*

ball: = round object, *globus;* a — to play with, *pila, follis* (= football); see also bullet; —, = dance, *saltatio.*

ballad, *carmen.*

ballast, *saburra.*

ballet, *pantomimus;* — dancer, *pantomimus.*

ballot, *suffragium, tabella.*

balm, *balsamum;* fig., *solatium.*

balustrade, *cancelli* (-orum).

ban; see forbid.

band, subst.: for binding, *fascia, ligamen;* = company, *manus, turba, grex, caterva.*

band (together), v.; see combine.

bandage; see band and bind.

bandit, *latro.*

bandy: to — words, *altercari.*

bandy, bandy-legged, *loripes.*

bane, *venenum, virus;* fig., *pernicies, pestis.*

baneful, *perniciosus, exitiosus.*

bang, subst., *crepitus* (-ūs), *sonitus* (-ūs).

bang, v.; see strike.

banish, v. (*homini*) *aqua et igni interdicēre;* (*hominem*) (*ex*)*pellēre, exterminare, relegare, deportare.* Transf., *exterminare,* (*ex*)*pellēre, amovēre.*

banishment, *interdictio aquae et ignis, relegatio, deportatio, exsilium.*

bank, subst.: of earth, *agger;* of a river, *ripa;* financial, *argentaria, mensa publica.*

banker, *argentarius.*

bankrupt, *decoctor;* to become —, (*rationes*) *conturbare, decoquēre.*

banner, *vexillum.*

banquet, *epulae* (-arum), *convivium, cena.*

banter, subst. *cavillatio, ludibrium.*

banter, v. *cavillari, iocari.*

bar, subst.; = a long piece, *asser, later;* = bolt, *claustrum, obex, sera;* legal, *forum;* to practise at the —, *causas agēre, dicēre, orare.*

bar, v. = bolt, *occludēre, obserare;* = hinder, *impedire, prohibēre.*

barbarian, *barbarus.*

barbaric, barbarous, *barbarus;* = savage, cruel, *immanis, saevus, crudelis;* adv. *barbare, saeve, crudeliter.*

barbarity, *immanitas.*

barbed, *hamatus.*

barber, n. *tonsor:* a —'s shop, *tonstrina.*

bard, *vates.*

bare, adj., *nudus;* = mere, *merus.*

bare, v. *nudare, aperire.*

barefaced, *impudens.*

barefoot, *pedibus nudis.*

barely, *vix, aegre.*

bargain, subst. *pactio, pactum.*

bargain, v. *pacisci.*

bark, subst.: of trees, *cortex, liber;* of dogs, *latratus.*

bark, v. *latrare.*

barley, *hordeum.*

barn, *horreum.*

barracks, *castra* (-orum).

barrel, *cupa, seria, dolium, orca.*

barren, *sterilis, infecundus.*

barrenness, *sterilitas.*

barricade, subst. *munimentum.*

barricade, v. *praesepire, obstruēre, oppilare.*

barrier, *septum, cancelli* (-orum), *claustra* (-orum).

barrister; see advocate.

barrow, *ferculum.*

barter, subst. (*per*)*mutatio mercium.*

barter, v. *merces mutare.*

base, subst. *basis, fundamentum, radix.*

base, adj. *turpis;* — coin, *nummi adulterini;* — born, *ignobilis, humili loco natus.* Adv. *turpiter.*

baseness, *turpitudo.*

bashful, *pudens, pudicus, verecundus;* adv. *verecunde.*

bashfulness, *pudor, verecundia.*

basin, *pelvis, trulla.*

basis; see base.

bask, *apricari.*

basket, *corbis, qualus, sporta, calathus.*

bas-relief, *toreuma* (-atis, n.).

bass, (in music), *gravis.*

bastard, *nothus.*

bat: the flying creature, *vespertilio;* for games, *clava.*

batch, *numerus.*

bath, subst. *balineum, balneum, balneae (-arum,* plur.).

bath, bathe, v.: transit. *lavare, abluĕre, perfundĕre;* intransit., *lavari, perlui.*

bath-tub, *alveus.*

battalion, *cohors.*

batter, *pulsare, percutĕre, verberare.*

battering-ram, *aries.*

battery: = assault, *vis;* of artillery, *tormenta (-orum).*

battle, *proelium, pugna.*

battle-array, *acies.*

battle-axe, *bipennis, securis.*

battle-cry, *clamor.*

battle-field, *locus pugnae;* sometimes *acies.*

battlement, *pinna.*

bawl, *vociferari, clamitare.*

bay, subst.: the tree, *laurea, laurus;* of the sea, *sinus (-ūs).*

bay, adj. *spadix, badius.*

bay, v. *latrare.*

be, *esse; exsistĕre, exstare.*

beach, *litus.*

beacon: = lighthouse, *pharus;* = fire, *ignis.*

bead, *baca.*

beak, *rostrum.*

beaker, *poculum.*

beam, subst.: of wood, *tignum, trabs;* of light, *radius, iubar.*

beam, v. *(ad)fulgēre.*

bean, *faba.*

bear, subst.: the animal, *ursus, ursa;* the constellation, *arctos, septentriones:* the Great —, *ursa major;* the Little —, *ursa minor.*

bear, v.: = carry, *ferre, gestare, portare;* = endure, *(per)ferre, pati, sustinēre, tolerare;* = have, (feeling, etc.), *gerĕre;* = produce, bring forth, *parĕre, ferre.*

beard, subst. *barba.*

beard, v.; see defy.

bearer: = porter, *baiulus;* — of letters, *tabellarius.*

beast, *bestia* (wild); *belua; pecus (-udis,* tame); *fera* (wild); *iumentum* (— of burden).

beastliness, *spurcitia.*

beastly, *spurcus, immundus.*

beat, v.: = strike, *ferire, percutĕre, pulsare;* to be beaten, *vapulare;* to beat down, *(pro)sternĕre;* —, = overcome, *vincĕre, superare;* intransit., *palpitare, salire.*

beating, subst. *ictus (-ūs), verbera (-um,* plur.).

beau, *homo bellus* or *elegans.*

beautiful, *pulcher, speciosus, formosus, bellus, amoenus* (of landscapes, etc.); adv. *pulchre, belle.*

beautify, *(ex)ornare.*

beauty, *pulchritudo, species, forma, amoenitas* (of places).

beaver, *castor, fiber.*

becalmed, *ventis destitutus.*

because, *quod, quia, quoniam;* because of, *propter, ob.*

beck, = nod, *nutus (-ūs).*

beckon, *digito innuĕre.*

become, v. *fieri, evadĕre;* = to suit, *decēre, convenire.*

bed: for sleeping, *lectus:* to make a —, *lectum sternĕre;* to go to —, *cubitum ire:* of a river, *alveus.*

bedaub, *(ob)linĕre, perungĕre.*

bed-clothes, bedding, *stragulum, lodix.*

bedew, *inrorare.*

bedizen, *(ex)ornare.*

bedroom, *cubiculum.*

bee, *apis:* — hive, *alvus, alveus;* a swarm of —s, *examen apium.*

beech, *fagus;* adj. *fageus, faginus.*

beef, *(caro) bubula.*

beetle, subst. *scarabaeus.*

befall, *accidĕre, contingĕre.*

befit, *convenire, aptum esse, decēre.*

before. Adv.: in space, *prae;* in time, *prius, ante.* Prep.: in space, =in presence of, *coram;* = in front of, *ante;* in time, *ante.* Conj., *antequam, priusquam.*

beforehand, *antea.*

befoul, *inquinare, foedare.*

befriend, *adiuvare, favēre.*

beg, *mendicare;* = to ask earnestly, *precari, orare, rogare.*

beget, *gignĕre, generare, procreare.*

beggar, *mendicus.*

beggarly, *miser, vilis.*

beggary, *egestas, paupertas, mendicitas.*

begin, *incipĕre, ordiri, inchoare.*

beginning, *initium, principium, primor-dium;* — of a speech, *exordium;* the —s of a science, *elementa (-orum), rudimenta (-orum).*

beginner, = novice, *tiro.*

begone! *abi! apage te!*

begrudge, *invidēre.*

beguile, *decipĕre, fallĕre.*

behalf: on — of, *pro.*

behave, *se gerĕre.*

behaviour, *mores (-um,* plur.).

behead, *detruncare, obtruncare;* in execution, *securi ferire.*

behind: adv. *pone, post, retro, a tergo;* prep. *pone, post.*

behold, v. *adspicĕre, intueri, contemplari, spectare.*

behold! *en! ecce!*

beholden, = indebted, *obnoxius.*

behove: it behoves, *decet, convenit, oportet.*

being, *natura;* a human being, *homo.*

belated, *serus.*

beleaguer, *obsidēre.*

belie: = misrepresent, *criminari, cal-umniari;* = refute, *refellĕre, refutare.*

belief, *fides, opinio, persuasio.*

believe, *credĕre, fidem habēre;* = to think, *credĕre, putare, arbitrari, opinari;* I firmly —, *mihi persuasum est.*

bell, *tintinnabulum;* sometimes *aes.*

bellow, subst. *mugitus (-ūs).*

bellow, v. *mugire.*

bellows, *follis.*

belly, *venter, alvus, abdomen.*

belong, *esse,* with genit. or possess. adj.; *attinēre, pertinēre.*

below: adv., *subter, infra*; prep., *infra, subter, sub.*

belt, *cingulum, zona, balteus.*

bench, *scamnum, subsellium*; for rowers, *transtrum.*

bend: transit., *(in)flectĕre, inclinare*; intransit., pass. or reflex.

bending, *flexus (-ūs), flexio, inclinatio.*

beneath; see below.

beneficence, *beneficentia, liberalitas.*

beneficent, *liberalis, beneficus.*

beneficial, *utilis, salutaris.*

benefit, subst. *beneficium.*

benefit, v.: transit., *prodesse,(ad)iuvare*; intransit., *proficĕre.*

benevolence, *benevolentia.*

benevolent, *benevolus.*

benign, *benignus.*

benignity, *benignitas.*

bent, subst. *animi inclinatio, voluntas.*

bent, adj. *curvus*; bent on a thing, *rei* (genit.) *studiosus, cupidus.*

benumb; to be —ed, *obtorpescĕre, torpĕre.*

bequeath, *legare.*

bequest, *legatum.*

bereave, *orbare.*

bereaved, *orbus.*

bereavement, *orbitas.*

berry, *baca, bacula, acinus.*

beseech, *orare, implorare, obtestari.*

beset, *obsidēre, urgēre, premĕre.*

beside, prep.: = near, *prope, iuxta*; = except, *praeter*; — the point, *nihil ad rem*; — oneself, *sui impotens.*

besides, *praeter (quam)*; as adv. = in addition, *praeterea, ultro.*

besiege, *obsidēre, circumsedēre.*

besmear, *(ob)linĕre.*

bespatter, *adspergĕre, conspergĕre.*

bespeak, *imperare.*

best, *optimus*; see good.

bestir: to bestir oneself, *se (com)movēre, excitare.*

bestow; see give.

bet, subst. *pignus (-oris).*

betake: to betake oneself, *se conferre.*

betimes, *mature.*

betoken, *significare.*

betray, *prodĕre.*

betrayal, *proditio.*

betrayer, *proditor.*

betroth, *(de)spondēre.*

betrothal, *sponsalia (-ium* or *-iorum).*

better, adj. *melior, potior* (= preferable); I am getting better, *convalesco.*

better, adv. *melius.*

better, v. transit. *meliorem facĕre, corrigĕre, emendare.*

between, *inter,* with acc.

beverage, *potio, potus (-ūs).*

bevy, *grex.*

bewail, *deplorare, deflēre, (con)queri.*

beware, v. *cavēre.*

bewilder, *(con)turbare.*

bewitch, *fascinare;* see also charm.

beyond: adv., *ultra, supra*; prep., *trans, ultra, extra, praeter.*

bias, subst. *inclinatio animi.*

bias, v. *inclinare (animum).*

bibulous, *bibulus.*

bid, subst. (at a sale), *licitatio.*

bid, v. := command, *iubēre, imperare;* = invite, *invitare;* at a sale, *liceri.*

bide, *manēre.*

bier, *feretrum, sandapila.*

big, *magnus, grandis, vastus.*

bile, *bilis.*

bilge-water, *sentina.*

bill: of a bird, *rostrum;* = a proposed law, *rogatio;* to bring forward a —, *rogationem ferre;* to reject a —, *antiquare;* to carry a —, *perferre.*

billet, subst., = letter, *epistula.*

billet, v.: to billet troops, *milites per domos disponĕre.*

billow, *fluctus (-ūs).*

billowy, *fluctuosus.*

bind, v. *(ad)ligare, vincire;* fig., *obligare, adstringĕre;* to — together, *conligare, constringĕre;* to — over, *vadari.*

biographer; see historian.

biped, *bipes.*

birch, *betula.*

bird, *avis, volucris, ales;* — catcher, *auceps;* — lime, *viscum.*

birth, *ortus (-ūs);* of noble —, *nobili genere natus.*

birthday, *dies natalis.*

bishop, *episcopus.*

bit: of a horse, *frenum;* = piece, *frustum.*

bitch, *canis (femina).*

bite, subst., *morsus (-ūs).*

bite, v. *mordēre.*

biting, *mordens, mordax, acidus.*

bitter, *amarus, acerbus, acidus;* adv. *amare, acerbe.*

bitterness, *acerbitas.*

bivouac, subst. *excubiae (-arum).*

black, *ater, niger;* dressed in —, *sordidatus, pullatus, atratus;* a black man, *Aethiops.*

blackberry, *rubus.*

blackbird, *merula.*

blacken, v.: transit., *nigrum facĕre;* intransit., *nigrescĕre.*

Black Sea, *Pontus Euxinus.*

blacksmith, *faber (ferrarius).*

bladder, *vesica.*

blade: of grass, *herba;* of an oar, *palma;* of a knife, *lamina.*

blame, subst. *culpa, reprehensio, vituperatio.*

blame, v. *reprehendĕre, culpare, vituperare.*

blameless, *innocens, integer, sanctus.*

blamelessness, *innocentia, integritas, sanctitas.*

bland, *blandus, lenis, mitis;* adv. *blande.*

blandishment, *blanditia, blandimentum.*

blank, *vacuus.*

blanket, *lodix.*

blast, subst. *flamen, flatus (-ūs).*

blast, v. transit.; see blight.

blaze, subst. *flamma.*

blaze, v. *ardēre, (con)flagrare.*

bleach, *candidum facĕre.*

bleak; see cold.

blear-eyed, *lippus;* to be —, *lippire.*

bleat, subst. *balatus (-ūs).*

bleat, v. *balare.*

bleed, v. *sanguinem dare* or *effundĕre.*

blemish, subst. *vitium, mendum, macula.*

blemish, v. *(com)maculare.*

blend, (com)miscēre.

bless: in words, bonis ominibus prosequi: in gen., beare, fortunare.

blessed, beatus, fortunatus.

blessedness, felicitas.

blight, subst. robigo.

blight, v. robigine adficēre; of hopes, frustrari.

blind, adj. caecus, oculis captus; adv., = rashly, temere.

blind, v. (oc)caecare, oculis privare.

blindfold, oculis opertis.

blindness, caecitas.

blink, connivēre, nictare.

bliss, felicitas.

blister, pustula.

blithe, laetus, hilaris.

bloated, turgidus, tumidus.

block, subst. stipes, truncus, caudex.

block, v. claudēre, occludēre, opplēre, obstruēre.

blockade, subst. obsessio, obsidio.

blockade, v. obsidēre, obsidēre, circum-vallare.

blockhead; see block.

blood, sanguis, cruor; = birth, race, sanguis, genus.

bloodless, exsanguis, incruentus.

blood-red, cruentus, sanguineus.

blood-relation, consanguineus.

bloodshed, caedes.

bloodshot, sanguine suffusus.

blood-stained, cruentus.

blood-thirsty, sanguinarius.

bloody, cruentus, sanguineus.

bloom, subst. flos.

bloom, v. florēre, vigēre.

blossom; see bloom.

blot, subst.; on paper, litura; in gen. macula, labes.

blot, v. (com)maculare; to — out, delēre, exstinguēre.

blow, subst. ictus (-ūs), plaga.

blow, v. flare; to — into, inflare; to — on, adflare.

blowing, subst. flatus (-ūs).

bludgeon, fustis.

blue, caeruleus.

blunder, subst. error, erratum, mendum.

blunder, v. errare.

blunt, adj. hebes; fig., = rude, agrestis, rusticus; adv., of speech, libere.

blunt, v. transit. hebetare, obtundēre.

blurt out, effutire.

blush, subst. rubor.

blush, v. erubescēre, rubēre.

bluster, subst. declamatio.

bluster, v. declamare, declamitare.

boar, verres; a wild —, aper.

board, subst.: = plank, tabula; = food, victus (-ūs), alimentum; = body of officials, conlegium.

board, v.: to — over, contabulare; to — a ship, navem conscendēre; to — with anyone, apud hominem habitare.

boast, gloriari, (se) iactare.

boaster, iactator, homo gloriosus.

boasting, subst. gloriatio, iactatio.

boastful, gloriosus; adv. gloriose.

boat, linter, scapha, navicula.

boatman, nauta.

bodily, corporeus.

body, corpus (-oris); a — of men, manus, numerus, grex.

bodyguard, stipatores, satellites.

bog, palūs (-ūdis).

boggy, uliginosus, paluster.

bogy, terricula (-orum, plur.).

boil, subst. vomica.

boil, v. transit., coquēre; intransit., fervēre, (ef)fervescēre, (ex)aestuare.

boisterous, turbidus; of weather, tur-bulentus.

bold, audax, confidens, ferox, animosus; adv. audacter, confidenter, ferociter, animose.

boldness, audacia, confidentia.

bole, truncus, stirps.

bolster, cervical, culcita, pulvinus.

bolt, subst.: = fastening, obex, sera, pessulus; = weapon, telum.

bolt, v. claudēre, occludēre, obserare.

bombast, (verborum) tumor, inflata oratio.

bombastic, inflatus.

bond, vinculum, ligamentum, compes, catena; = legal document, chiro-graphum, syngrapha.

bondage, servitūs (-ūtis), servitium.

bone, os (ossis).

bony, osseus.

book, liber, volumen, codex.

bookseller, bibliopola.

boon, beneficium.

boorish, agrestis, inurbanus, rusticus; adv. rustice, inurbane.

boot, calceus; an army —, caliga.

bootless, inutilis, inritus; adv. frustra.

booty, praeda.

border, margo; of a stream, ripa; of a country, finis.

border, v.; to border on, adiacere, attingēre.

bore, subst. homo importunus or odiosus.

bore, v.: = perforate, perforare, tere-brare; = weary, obtundere, defatigare, vexare; I am bored, taedet me.

boredom, taedium.

born; to be —, nasci.

borrow, mutuari, mutuum sumēre.

borrowed, mutuus, alienus.

bosom, sinus (-ūs), pectus (-oris), gre-mium.

boss, umbo, bulla.

botany, (ars) herbaria.

both, ambo; uterque (= each); both ... and ..., et ... et ..., cum ... tum ...

bother, subst. molestia, incommodum.

bother, v.; see annoy; = to take trouble, curare.

bottle, lagena, ampulla.

bottom, fundus, solum; the bottom of the sea, imum mare.

bough, ramus.

bounce, resilire.

bound, subst.: = limit, finis, modus, terminus; = jump, saltus (-ūs).

bound, v.: = limit, (de)finire, terminare; = jump, salire.

boundary, finis, terminus, confinium.

boundless, infinitus, immensus.

bountiful, largus, liberalis; adv. large, liberaliter.

bounty, largitas, liberalitas, munificentia.

bout, certamen; a drinking —, comissatio.

bow, subst.: the weapon, *arcus (-ūs)*; of a ship, *prora*; = movement of the body, *corporis inclinatio*.

bow, v. *flectĕre, demittĕre, inclinare*; to bow to, *salutare*; fig., *obsequi, obtemperare*.

bowman, *sagittarius*.

bowstring, *nervus*.

bowels, *viscera (-um), alvus*.

bower, *umbraculum*.

bowl, subst. *crater, cratera, patera*.

bowl, v. *volvĕre*.

box, subst.: = receptacle, *arca, cista, pyxis*; the shrub, *buxus*; adj. *buxeus*.

box, v. intransit. *pugnis certare*.

boxer, *pugil*.

boy, *puer*.

boyhood, *aetas puerilis, pueritia*.

boyish, *puerilis*; adv. *pueriliter*.

brace, subst.: = strap, *fascia, vinculum*; = stay (rigid), *fibula*; = a pair, *par*.

brace, v. *(ad)ligare*; mentally, *(con)firmare*.

bracelet, *armilla*.

brackish, *amarus*.

brag; see boast.

braid, subst. *limbus*; of hair, *gradus*.

braid, v. *texĕre, nectĕre*.

brain, *cerebrum*.

bramble, *rubus, vepris*.

branch, subst. *ramus*.

branch, v. *dividi*.

brand, subst.: = firebrand, *torris, fax*; = a mark, *nota*.

brand, v. *notam inurĕre, notare*.

brandish, *vibrare, iactare*.

brass, *orichalcum*.

bravado, *iactatio*.

brave, *fortis, strenuus, animosus*; adv. *fortiter, strenue*.

bravery, *fortitudo*.

bravo! *euge! factum bene! macte!*

brawl, subst. *rixa, iurgium*.

brawl, v. *rixari*.

brawny, *robustus, lacertosus*.

brazen, *a(h)eneus, aereus*; fig., = shameless, *impudens*; — face, *os durum*.

breach, subst.: to make a —, *perfringĕre, discutĕre*; a — of treaty, *foedus ruptum* or *violatum*.

bread, *panis*; = subsistence, *victus (-ūs)*.

breadth, *latitudo*.

break, subst. *intervallum*; — of day, *prima lux, diluculum*.

break, v. (1) transit. *frangĕre, confringĕre, rumpĕre*; to — open, *refringĕre*; fig., = to weaken, subdue, *domare, frangĕre, infringĕre*; to — a treaty, *foedus violare*; — a promise, *fidem fallĕre*. (2) intransit. *frangi, confringi, rumpi*; to break in, *inrumpĕre*; to — out, *erumpĕre*, fig. *exoriri, exardescĕre, gliscĕre*.

breaker, *fluctus (-ūs)*.

breakfast, *ientaculum*.

breakwater, *moles*.

breast, *pectus, animus* (fig.).

breast-plate, *lorica, thorax*.

breastwork, *pluteus, lorica*.

breath, *spiritus (-ūs), anima*; to put out of —, *exanimare*.

breathe, *spirare*; to — again, *respirare*; to — upon, *adflare*; to — out, *exhalare*.

breathless, *exanimatus, exanimis*.

breeches, *bracae*; wearing —, *bracatus*.

breed, subst. *genus (-eris, n.)*.

breed, v. transit. *gignĕre, generare parĕre, procreare*; intransit., *nasci*.

breeding, *cultus (-ūs)*.

breeze, *aura*.

brevity, *brevitas*.

brew, *coquĕre*; of trouble, *imminēre, impendēre*.

briar; see brier.

bribe, subst. *pretium*.

bribe, v. *(pretio, pecuniā, etc.) corrumpĕre*.

briber, *corruptor*.

bribery, *largitio*; or use verb.

brick, *later*; adj. *latericius*.

bridal, adj. *nuptialis*.

bride, **bridegroom**, *(nova) nupta, (novus) maritus*.

bridge, *pons*.

bridle, *frenum*.

bridle, v. *(in)frenare*.

brief, *brevis*; in —, *ne longus sim*. Adv. *breviter, paucis (verbis)*.

brier, **briar**, *vepris, dumus, frutex*.

brigade, *legio*.

brigand, *latro*.

bright, *clarus, lucidus, splendidus, fulgens*; of weather, *serenus*; to be —, *clarēre*. Adv. *clare, lucide*.

brighten, v.: transit., *inlustrare, inluminare*; intransit., *clarescĕre*.

brightness, *candor, splendor, nitor fulgor*; of weather, *serenitas*.

brilliant, *splendidus, inlustris, luculentus, praeclarus*.

brim, *ora, margo, labrum*.

Brindisi, *Brundisium*.

brine, *muria, salsamentum*.

bring: by carrying, *(ad)ferre, (ap)portare*; by leading, etc., *(ad)ducĕre*: to — back, *referre, reducĕre*; to — together, *cogĕre*; to — about, *efficĕre (ut)*; to — forward, *in medium proferre*; to — in, yield, *reddĕre*; to — up, *educare*.

brink, *margo, ripa*.

brisk, *alacer, vegetus*.

briskness, *alacritas*.

bristle, subst. *saeta*.

bristle, v. *horrēre*.

bristly, *saetosus*.

brittle, *fragilis*.

broach, *aperire*.

broad, *latus, amplus*; adv. *late*.

broil, subst. *rixa*.

broil, v. *torrēre*.

bronze, subst. *aes*.

bronze, adj. *a(h)eneus, aereus*.

brooch, *fibula*.

brood, subst. *fetus (-ūs)*.

brood, v. *incubare*.

brook, subst. *rivus, rivulus*.

brook, v. *ferre, tolerare*.

broom: the plant, *genista*; for sweeping, *scopae (-arum*, plur.).

broth, *ius (iuris)*.

brother, *frater*.

brotherhood, = association, *societas, sodalitas.*
brotherly, *fraternus.*
brow: = eyebrow, *supercilium*; = forehead, *frons*; of a hill, *summus collis.*
brown, *fuscus, fulvus.*
bruise, v. *contundĕre.*
bruit, v. *(di)vulgare.*
brush, subst. *penicillus*; see broom.
brush, v. transit. *verrĕre, (de)tergĕre.*
brush-wood, *virgultum, sarmentum.*
brutal, *ferus, inhumanus, immanis*; adv. *inhumane, immaniter.*
brutality, *immanitas.*
brute, *pecus, belua*; see beast.
bubble, subst. *bulla.*
buccaneer, *pirata, praedo.*
bucket, *situla, hama.*
buckle, *fibula.*
buckler, *scutum, clipeus, parma.*
bud, subst. *gemma, germen.*
bud, v. *gemmare.*
budge, *loco cedĕre.*
buff, *luteus.*
buffalo, *bos.*
buffet, = blow, *alapa, colaphus.*
buffoon, *sannio, scurra.*
buffoonery, *scurrilitas.*
bug, *cimex (-icis).*
bugbear; see bogy.
bugle, *bucina.*
build, *aedificare, (ex)struĕre.*
builder, *aedificator, structor.*
building, subst.: the process, *aedificatio, exstructio*; the thing built, *aedificium.*
bulb, *bulbus.*
bulk, *magnitudo, amplitudo, moles.*
bulky, *amplus, ingens.*
bull, *taurus.*
bullock, *iuvencus.*
bullet, *glans.*
bullion, *aurum, argentum.*
bulrush, *iuncus, scirpus.*
bulwark, *propugnaculum.*
bump, subst.: = swelling, *tumor, tuber*; = bang, *ictus (-ūs).*
bump, v.: to bump into, *offendĕre.*
bumper; see cup.
bunch, of fruit, *racemus, uva*; see bundle.
bundle, *fascis, manipulus, sarcina.*
bung, *obturamentum.*
buoyant, *levis.* Transf., *hilaris.*
burden, subst. *onus (-eris)*: beast of —, *iumentum.*
burden, v. *onerare, opprimĕre.*
burdensome, *gravis, molestus.*
bureau, *scrinium.*
burgess, burgher, *municeps, civis.*
burglar, *fur.*
burglary, *furtum.*
burial, *sepultura, humatio.*
burial-ground, *sepulturae locus, sepulcrum.*
burn, v. transit., = set on fire, *incendĕre*; to burn up, *comburĕre, (con)cremare*; intransit., = to blaze, *ardēre, flagare.*
burnish, *polire.*
burrow, *cuniculus.*
burst, v. transit. *(di)rumpĕrc.*
bury, *humare, sepelire.*
bush, *frutex, dumus.*
bushy, *fruticosus.*

bushel, *medimnus.*
business, *res, negotium.*
buskin, *cothurnus.*
bust, *effigies.*
bustle, subst. *festinatio, trepidatio.*
bustle, v. *festinare, trepidare.*
busy, *occupatus, negotiosus*; adv. *sedulo, industrie.*
busy-body, *ardelio.*
but: = except, *praeter*; all but, *tantum non*; = only, *modo, tantum, solum*; as adversat. conj., *sed, verum, at; atqui* (= and yet); *tamen* (= however); but if, *sin, quodsi.*
butcher, *lanius.*
butcher, v. *caedĕre*; of persons, *trucidare.*
butchery, *caedes.*
butler, *cellarius, promus.*
butt: = object of ridicule, *ludibrium.*
butt, v. *arietare, cornu petĕre.*
butterfly, *papilio.*
buttocks, *clunes (-ium), nates (-ium), pyga.*
buttress, v. *fulcire.*
buxom, *hilaris.*
buy, v. *(co)emĕre, mercari.*
buyer, *emptor.*
by: of place, *ad, apud, iuxta, prope*; to go —, *praeterire*; to stand —, *adesse*; of time, — night, *noctu, nocte*; — moonlight, *ad lunam*; of means or manner, *per* with acc.; of agency, *ab (homine)*; in adjuration, *per* with acc.; of distribution, one — one, *singuli, singillatim.*
by-way, *trames (-itis), semita, deverticulum.*
by-word: to become a —, *contemptui esse.*

C

cabbage, *brassica, caulis.*
cabin, *casa, tugurium.*
cabinet: = room, *conclave*; = cupboard, desk, etc., *armarium, thesaurus, scrinium.*
cable, *ancorale, funis ancorarius.*
cackle, *strepĕre.*
cadaverous, *exsanguis.*
cadence, *numerus.*
cadet, *tiro.*
Cadiz, *Gades (-ium,* plur.).
cage, *cavea.*
cajolery, *blanditiae (-arum).*
cake, subst. *placenta.*
cake, v., = stick together, *concrescĕre.*
calamitous, *calamitosus, luctuosus.*
calamity, *calamitas, clades.*
calculate, *computare.*
calculated, *accommodatus, aptus, idoneus.*
calculation, *ratio.*
caldron, *a(h)enum, cortina.*
calendar, *fasti (-orum).*
calf, *vitulus, vitula*; — of the leg, *sura.*
call, subst.: = cry, *vox*; = visit, *salutatio.*
call, v.: = cry out, *clamare*; = name, *vocare, nominare, appellare*; = summon, *(ad)vocare*; to — together.

convocare; to — for, = to demand,
(de)*poscere*, *flagitare*; to — on,
= visit, *salutare*, *visĕre*.
caller, = visitor, *salutator*.
callous, *callosus*. Transf., *durus*.
calm, subst. *quies*, *tranquillitas*, *otium*,
pax; — at sea, *malacia*.
calm, adj. *quietus*, *tranquillus*, *placidus*;
adv. *tranquille*, *placide*; *aequo animo*.
calm, v. *sedare*, *lenire*, *tranquillare*.
calumniate, *calumniari*, *criminari*.
calumniator, *obtrectator*.
calumny, *criminatio*, *calumnia*.
camel, *camelus*.
camp, *castra* (-*orum*).
campaign, *stipendium*.
can, subst.; see jug.
can, v. *posse*; see able.
canal, *fossa*.
cancel, *delēre*, *tollĕre*.
candid, *liber*, *apertus*, *verus*, *simplex*;
adv. *libere*, *aperte*.
candidate, *candidatus*.
candour, *libertas*, *candor*.
candle, *candela*.
candlestick, *candelabrum*.
cane, subst. *harundo*, *calamus*; for
walking, *baculum*; for correction,
ferula.
cane, v. (*ferulā*) *verberare*.
canine, *caninus*.
canker, v. *corrumpĕre*.
cannon, *tormentum*.
canoe, *cymba*.
canon, = a rule, *lex*, *regula*, *norma*.
canopy, *aulaeum*.
canton, *pagus*.
canvas, in a sail, *carbasus*, *velum*.
canvass, *ambire*.
canvassing, *ambitio*, *ambitus* (-*ūs*).
cap, *pileus*, *galerus*.
capability, *facultas*.
capable, *aptus*, *idoneus*; often rendered
by *posse*.
capacious, *capax*, *amplus*.
caparison, *phalerae* (-*arum*, plur.).
capital, subst.: = chief city, *caput*;
or use *urbs* with adj.: of a pillar,
capitulum; of money, *sors*, *caput*.
capital, adj., *capitalis*; see excellent,
etc.
capitulate; see surrender.
caprice, *libido*, *levitas*.
capricious, *inconstans*, *levis*.
captain, *princeps*, *dux*; of a ship,
navarchus, *magister*.
captious, *morosus*, *difficilis*.
captivate, *capĕre*.
captive, *captus*, *captivus*.
captivity, *captivitas*.
capture, *capĕre*, *comprehendĕre*.
car, *carrus*, *cisium*, *plaustrum*, *vehiculum*.
caravan, *comitatus* (-*ūs*).
carcase, *cadaver*.
card, subst. *charta*.
card, v. *pectĕre*.
care, subst.: = attention, caution,
cura, *diligentia*; = anxiety, *cura*,
sollicitudo; = management, *cura*,
curatio.
care, v.; to — for, — about, *curare*.
career, *curriculum*, *cursus* (-*ūs*).

careful, *diligens*, *accuratus*, *attentus*;
adv. *diligenter*, *accurate*.
careless, *neglegens*.
carelessness, *imprudentia*, *neglegentia*,
incuria.
caress, subst. *complexus* (-*ūs*)
caress, v. *blandiri*, *permulcēre*.
caressing, *blandus*.
cargo, *onus* (-*eris*).
carnage, *caedus*, *strages*.
carnal, render by genit. *corporis*.
carnival, *feriae* (-*arum*).
carousal, *comissatio*, *potatio*.
carouse, v. *comissari*, *potare*.
carp, v.: to — at, *carpĕre*, *vellicare*.
carpenter, *faber* (*tignarius*).
carpet, *tapeta* (-*ae*), *tapeta* (-*orum*),
tapetia (-*ium*).
carriage: = act of carrying, *gestura*;
= bearing, *habitus*; = vehicle, *vehiculum*.
carrier, *gerulus*; letter —, *tabellarius*.
carry, *ferre*, *portare*, *vehĕre*, *gerĕre*; to
— out (= perform), *conficĕre*, *exsequi*.
cart, *plaustrum*.
carve, *caelare*, *scalpĕre*, *sculpĕre*: to
— meat, *scindere*, *secare*.
carver, *caelator*, *sculptor*.
carving, *caelatura*, *scalptura*, *sculptura*.
cascade, *aquae ex alto desilientes*.
case: = receptacle, *theca*, *involucrum*;
gram., *casus* (-*ūs*); judicial, *causa*;
= chance, *res*, *casus* (-*ūs*).
casement, *fenestra*.
cash, subst. *pecunia praesens* or
numerata.
cash, v. *praesenti pecunia solvĕre*.
cashier, v. = discharge, *exauctorare*.
cask, *dolium*, *cupa*.
casket, *arcula*, *capsula*.
casque, *galea*, *cassis*.
cast, subst., = throw, *iactus* (-*ūs*).
cast, v. *iacĕre*, *conicĕre*, *iactare*, *mittĕre*;
to — in metal, *fundĕre*; to be —
down, *adfligi*.
castaway, *perditus*, *profligatus*; by
ship-wreck, *naufragus*.
castigate; see punish.
castle, *castellum*.
casual, *fortuitus*, *forte oblatus*; adv.
forte, *casu*, *fortuito*.
cat, *feles* (or *felis*).
catalogue, *index*.
catapult, *catapulta*.
cataract, in the eye, *glaucŏma*; see also
cascade.
catarrh, *gravedo*, *pituita*.
catastrophe; see disaster.
catch, *capĕre*, *excipĕre*, *deprehendĕre*,
comprehendĕre; to — up, *adsequi*,
consequi; to — fire, *ignem concipĕre*.
categorical, *simplex*, *definitus*.
category, *genus* (-*eris*), *numerus*.
cater, *obsonare*.
caterpillar, *eruca*.
cattle, *boves*; coll., *pecus* (-*oris*); a head
of —, *pecus* (-*udis*).
cauldron; see caldron.
cause, subst. *causa*; *materia* (= occasion, ground); *res* (= case, affair).
cause, v. transit., *facĕre*, *efficĕre* (*ut*);
movēre, *excitare*.
causeway, *agger*.

caustic, *mordax, acerbus.*
cauterize, *adurĕre.*
caution, = care, *cautio, cura, prudentia.*
caution, v. *monēre.*
cautious, *providus, prudens, cautus;*
adv. *prudenter, caute.*
cavalcade, *comitatus (-ūs).*
cavalier = horseman, *eques.*
cavalierly, *adroganter, insolenter.*
cavalry, *equitatus, equites (-um, plur.).*
cave, *caverna, specus, spelunca, antrum.*
cavil; see carp.
cavity; see hole.
cease, *desinĕre, desistĕre.*
ceaseless, *perpetuus, adsiduus;* adv.
perpetuo, adsidue.
cedar, *cedrus.*
cede, *concedĕre.*
ceiling, *tectum.*
celebrate, *celebrare.*
celebrated, *celeber, clarus, inlustris.*
celebration, *celebratio.*
celebrity, *gloria, laus;* = celebrated
person, *vir insignis.*
celerity, *celeritas.*
celestial, *caelestis, divinus.*
cell, *cella, cubiculum.*
cellar, *cella;* a wine — *apotheca.*
cement, subst. *gluten.*
cemetery, *sepulchra (-orum).*
censor, *censor.*
censorious, *severus.*
censure, subst. *reprehensio, vituperatio.*
censure, v. *reprehendĕre, vituperare.*
census, *census (-ūs);* to take a census,
censēre.
centaur, *centaurus.*
centre, subst. *media pars;* or use
medius (e.g. the — of the city, *media
urbs).*
centurion, *centurio.*
century, *centum anni, saeculum.*
ceremonious, *sollemnis.*
ceremony, *ritus (-ūs), caerimonia.*
certain, *certus, stabilis, fidus* (= trust-
worthy); a — person, *quidam;* to
know for —, *certo scire.*
certainly, *certo;* in answers, *profecto,
sane;* = admittedly, *certe, quidem,
sane.*
certify, *confirmare.*
cessation, *intermissio.*
chafe, v.: transit., *calĕfacĕre;* intransit., *stomachari, aestuare.*
chaff, *palea.*
chagrin, *aegritudo, stomachus, dolor.*
chain, subst., *catena, vinculum;* =
series, *series.*
chain, v. *vincire.*
chair, *sella, sedile, cathedra.*
chalice, *calix.*
chalk, *creta.*
challenge, *(ad pugnam) provocare*
chamber, *cubiculum.*
champ, *mandĕre.*
champion, *propugnator, defensor.*
chance, *casus (-ūs), fors;* by —, *forte,
casu.*
chance, v. *accidĕre;* see also happen,
risk.
change, subst. *(com)mutatio, vicissitudo.*
change, v.: transit., *(com)mutare,
convertĕre;* intransit., *(com)mutari.*

changeable, *mutabilis, inconstans, varius.*
changeableness, *mutabilitas, varietas.*
changeling, *puer subditus.*
channel, *fossa, canalis, fretum.*
chant, v. *canĕre, cantare.*
chaos, *chaos, confusio, perturbatio.*
chaotic, *confusus, perturbatus.*
chapel, *aedicula, sacellum.*
chapter, of a book, *caput.*
character: = symbol, letter, *littera;*
= disposition, nature, *natura, ingenium, mores (-um);* = part played,
persona, partes (-ium); = reputation,
fama, existimatio.
characteristic, subst. *proprietas.*
characteristic, adj. *proprius;* adj.
proprie, more suo.
characterize, *notare, designare.*
charcoal, *carbo.*
charge, subst.: = price, *pretium;*
= command, *mandatum;* = care (of),
cura, custodia; = accusation, *accu-
satio, crimen;* = attack, *impetus (-ūs),
incursus (-ūs).*
charge, v. to — to a person, *homini
imputare;* to — with a duty, *(homini)
committĕre, mandare.;* = accuse, *accusare, insimulare;* = attack, *invadĕre,
impetum facĕre, incurrĕre.*
charger: = dish, *lanx;* = horse, *equus.*
chariot, *currus (-ūs).*
charioteer, *auriga.*
charitable, *benignus, liberalis, beneficus;*
adv. *benigne, liberaliter.*
charity, *benignitas;* as conduct, *beneficentia, liberalitas.*
Charles, *Carolus.*
charm, subst.: = magic formula,
carmen; = amulet, *fascinum;* = attraction, *blandimentum, dulcedo, lepor.*
charm, v.: by magic, *fascinare;* see
delight.
charming, *suavis, lepidus;* of country,
amoenus.
chart, *tabula.*
chary, *parcus.*
chase, subst. *venatio, venatus (-ūs).*
chase, v. *venari;* = engrave, *caelare.*
chasm, *hiatus (-ūs), specus (-ūs).*
chaste, *castus, pudicus.*
chastise, *castigare;* see punish.
chastisement, *castigatio, animadversio.*
chastity, *castitas, pudicitia.*
chat, subst. *sermo.*
chat, v. *fabulari, garrire.*
chatter, *garrulitas.*
chattering, *garrulus, loquax.*
cheap, *vilis.*
cheat, subst.: = deception, *fraus, dolus;*
= deceiver, *circumscriptor, fraudator.*
cheat, v. *fallĕre, decipĕre, fraudare.*
check, subst. *impedimentum, mora.*
check, v. *continēre, impedire, reprimĕre.*
cheek, *gena;* puffed out, *bucca.*
cheer, subst.: = shout, *clamor;* to be
of good —, *bono animo esse.*
cheer, v. = shout, *clamare;* = gladden
exhilarare, erigĕre.
cheerful, *hilaris, laetus;* adv. *hilare
laete.*
cheering, subst. *favor.*
cheerless, *tristis, maestus.*

cheese, *caseus.*
chequered, *varius.*
cherish, *fovēre, colēre, tuēri.*
cherry, *cerasus.*
chest, *pectus (-oris)*; = receptacle, *arca, cista.*
Chester, *Deva.*
chestnut, *castanea.*
chew, *mandēre.*
chicanery, *dolus, calumnia.*
chicken, *pullus (gallinaceus).*
chide, *obiurgare, increpare.*
chiding, *obiurgatio.*
chief, subst. *caput, princeps, dux.*
chief, adj. *primus, praecipuus*; adv. *praecipue.*
chieftain, *regulus.*
child: male, *filius*; female, *filia*: a small —, *infans*; children, *pueri, liberi.*
child-birth, *partus (-ūs).*
childhood, *pueritia, aetas puerilis.*
childish, *puerilis*; adv. *pueriliter.*
childless, *(liberis) orbus.*
chill, subst. *horror, frigus (-oris).*
chill, v. *refrigerare.*
chin, *mentum.*
china, use *murra*; adj. *murrinus.*
chink, *rima.*
chip, *assula.*
chirp, *pipilare.*
chisel, subst. *scalprum, caelum.*
chivalrous, *magnanimus.*
chivalry, as an institution, *ordo equester*; as a spirit, *magnanimitas.*
choice, subst. *delectus (-ūs), magnanimitas.*
choice, adj. *electus, eximius.*
choir, *chorus.*
choke, v. *suffocare, animam intercludēre.*
choler; see anger.
choose, v. *eligēre, diligēre.*
chop, *abscidēre, praecidēre.*
chord, *nervus.*
chorus, *chorus.*
Christ, *Christus.*
Christian, *Christianus.*
chronic, *longinquus, diuturnus.*
chronicle, subst. *annales (-ium).*
chronicle, v. transit., *in annales referre.*
chronicler, *annalium scriptor.*
chronology, *temporum (or rerum) ordo.*
church, *ecclesia.*
churlish, *agrestis, rusticus, inurbanus.*
cinder, *cinis.*
cipher, subst.: = a secret writing, *notae*; = a nobody, *numerus.*
cipher, v. *computare.*
circle, *orbis, circulus*; of people, *corona.*
circuit, *circuitus (-ūs), orbis, circulus.*
circular, *rotundus.*
circulate, v. transit. *circumagēre, dispergēre*; of news, etc., *divulgare.*
circumlocution, *circumitio verborum.*
circumnavigate, *circumvehi (navi).*
circumscribe, *circumscribēre, definire.*
circumspect, *cautus, providus, prudens.*
circumspection, *cautio, prudentia.*
circumstance, *res, tempus*: according to —s, *pro re (natā)*; in these —s, *quae cum ita sint.*
circumvallation, *circummunitio.*

circumvent, *circumvenire, circumscribēre.*
cistern, *cisterna, lacus, puteus.*
citadel, *arx.*
cite, v. *proferre, memorare*; before a court, *citare, in ius vocare.*
citizen, *civis.*
citizenship, *civitas.*
city, *urbs.*
civic, *civilis, civicus.*
civil: = civic, *civilis, civicus*: — war, *bellum civile, intestinum, domesticum*; = polite, *urbanus*; adv. *urbane.*
civilization, *cultus (-ūs), humanitas.*
civilize, *expolire.*
civilized, *humanus.*
clad, *vestitus.*
claim, v. *postulare, vindicare*; to — back, *repetēre.*
claimant (at law), *petitor.*
clammy, *lentus.*
clamour, subst. *vociferatio, clamor.*
clamour, v. *(con)clamare, vociferari.*
clan, *gens, tribus (-ūs).*
clandestine, *clandestinus, furtivus*; adv. *clam, furtim.*
clang, subst. *sonus (-ūs), sonitus (-ūs).*
clang, v. *strepēre, (re)sonare.*
clank, subst. *crepitus (-ūs), strepitus (-ūs).*
clank, v. *crepare, crepitare.*
clap, subst.: of hands, *plausus (-ūs)*; of thunder, *tonitrus (-ūs).*
clap, v. *(manibus) plaudēre.*
clash, subst.: = collision, *concursus (-ūs)*; = loud noise, *crepitus (-ūs), strepitus (-ūs).*
clash, v. *concrepare*; = disagree, *inter se (re)pugnare, dissidēre, discrepare.*
clasp, subst.: = fastener, *fibula*; see also embrace, grasp.
class, *genus (-eris), classis, ordo.*
classical, from the Roman point of view, *Graecus.*
classify, *in genera describēre.*
clatter, subst. *crepitus (-ūs), strepitus (-ūs).*
clatter, v. *crepare, strepēre.*
clause, *pars, membrum, caput.*
claw, *unguis.*
clay, *argilla.*
clean, adj. *purus, mundus.*
clean, v. *purgare.*
cleanliness, *munditia, mundities.*
clear, adj. *clarus*; of weather, *serenus, lucidus*; of style, *lucidus*; = evident, intelligible, *planus, manifestus*; it is —, *apparet, liquet.* Adv. *clare, plane, manifeste, lucide.*
clear, v. *expedire, purgare*; to — up a matter, *expedire, explicare.*
clearness, *claritas*; of weather, *serenitas.*
cleave: = split, *(dif)findēre, scindēre*; = stick, *(ad)haerēre.*
cleaver, *culter.*
cleft, *rima.*
clemency, *clementia, mansuetudo.*
clement, *clemens, mansuetus, indulgens, lenis.*
clench: to — the fist, *digitos comprimēre.*

clerk, *scriba.*
clever, *sollers, callidus, astutus*; adv. *sollerter, callide, astute.*
cleverness, *sollertia, calliditas.*
client, *cliens, consultor.*
cliff, *scopulus, cautes.*
climate, *caelum.*
climax, *gradatio.*
climb, subst. *ascensus (-ūs).*
climb, v. *scandēre, ascendēre, eniti.*
cling, *(ad)haerēre, amplecti.*
clip, *tondēre, praecidēre, resecare.*
cloak, subst. *amiculum, pallium*; for journeys, *lacerna*; a soldier's —, *sagum.*
cloak, v. *dissimulare, tegēre.*
clod, *glaeba.*
clog, v. *impedire.*
cloister, *porticus (-ūs).*
close, subst., = end, *finis, exitus.*
close, adj.: = reserved, *taciturnus, tectus*; = niggardly, *parcus*; = near, *propinquus, vicinus, finitimus*; = closely packed, *densus, confertus, artus*; adv. *arte, dense.*
close, adv. *prope, iuxta.*
close, v.: transit., = shut, *claudēre, occludēre*; = finish, *finire*; intransit., = be shut, *claudi*; = come to an end, *finiri.*
closeness, = nearness, *propinquitas, vicinitas.*
closet, *cubiculum.*
clot, subst., of blood, *sanguis concretus.*
clot, v. *concrescēre.*
cloth, *textum, textile.*
clothe, v. *vestire, amicire.*
clothes, clothing, *vestis, vestimenta (-orum).*
cloud, subst. *nubes, nimbus.*
cloud, v. *obscurare.*
cloudless, *serenus.*
cloudy, *nubilus.*
clownish, *rusticus, agrestis.*
cloy, *satiare, saturare.*
club, subst.: = cudgel, *clava, fustis*; = association, *circulus, sodalitas.*
clubfooted, *scaurus.*
clue, *glomus (-eris), filum*; = indication, *indicium.*
clump, *globus.*
clumsiness, *inscitia.*
clumsy, *inhabilis, ineptus, inscitus*; adv. *inepte, inscite.*
cluster, = bunch, *racemus, uva.*
clutch, *comprehendēre, adripēre.*
coach; see carriage.
coachman, *raedarius, auriga.*
coagulate, v. *coire, concrescēre.*
coal, *carbo*; a live —, *pruna.*
coalesce, *coalescēre, coire.*
coalition, *coniunctio, consociatio.*
coarse, *crassus*; of behaviour, etc., *incultus, imurbanus.* Adv. *crasse*; *inculte.*
coarseness, *crassitudo*; *mores inculti.*
coast, subst. *litus (-oris), ora*; on the —, adj., *maritimus.*
coast, v. *oram legēre, praetervehi.*
coat, *toga, tunica*; = hide, *vellus (-eris), pellis.*
coax, *blandiri, permulcēre.*
cobble, *(re)sarcire.*

cobbler, *sutor.*
cock, *gallus (gallinaceus).*
code, *leges.*
coerce, *coercēre, cohibēre, cogēre.*
coercion, *coercitio, vis.*
coffer, *cista, arca.*
coffin, *arca, capulus.*
cog, of a wheel, *dens.*
cogency, *pondus (-eris), vis.*
cogent, *firmus, validus, gravis.*
cogitate, *cogitare.*
cognizance, *cognitio.*
cognizant, *conscius.*
coheir, *coheres.*
cohere, *cohaerēre.*
coherent, *cohaerens, contextus, congruens.*
cohort, *cohors.*
coin, *nummus.*
coin, v. transit. *cudēre, signare.*
coinage, *res nummaria.*
coincide, *congruēre, eodem tempore fieri.*
coincidence, = chance; q.v.
Colchester, *Camulodunum.*
cold, subst. *frigus (-oris), algor*; in the head, *gravedo.*
cold, *frigidus, gelidus*: to be —, *frigēre, algēre*; adv. *frigide, gelide.*
collapse, v. *conlabi, concidēre, corruēre.*
collar, subst. *monile, torques.*
collate, v. transit. *conferre.*
collation: = comparison, *conlatio*; = meal, *cena.*
colleague, *conlega.*
collect, v.: transit. *conligēre, congerēre*; to — money, etc., *exigēre*; intransit., *convenire, coire.*
collection, *conlatio, congeries.*
college, *conlegium, societas, sodalitas.*
collide, *configēre.*
collision, *concursus (-ūs), concursio.*
collocation, *conlocatio.*
colloquial; — speech, *sermo humilis.*
colloquy, *conloquium.*
collusion, *conlusio, praevaricatio.*
Cologne, *Colonia Agrippina.*
colonel, *tribunus militum, praefectus.*
colonist, *colonus.*
colonnade, *porticus (-ūs).*
colony, *colonia.*
colossal, *vastus, ingens.*
colour, subst. *color*; = paint, *pigmentum.*
colour, v. *colorare, tingēre, inficēre*; intransit., see blush.
colt, *eculeus.*
column: = pillar, *columna*; milit., *agmen.*
comb, *pecten*; of a cock, *crista.*
comb, v. *(de)pectēre.*
combat, subst. *pugna, certamen.*
combat, v.: see fight.
combination *(con)iunctio, societas.*
combine, v. transit. *(con)iungēre, consociare.*
come, *venire, pervenire, advenire, accedēre*; to — about, *fieri*; to — back, *redire*; to — together, *convenire*; to — upon, *invenire.*
comedy, *comoedia.*
comeliness, *venustas, decor, pulchritudo.*
comely, *bellus, venustus, pulcher.*
comet, *cometes (-ae).*

comfort, subst.; = consolation, *solatium, consolatio*; —s, *commoda (-orum)*.

comfort, v. *(con)solari, adlevare*.

comfortable, *commodus*.

comforter, *consolator*.

comic, comical: = of comedy, *comicus*; = ridiculous, *ridiculus, facetus*; adv. *ridicule, facete*.

coming, subst. *adventus (-ūs)*.

command, subst.; = right to give orders, *imperium*; supreme —, *summa imperii*; = an order given, *imperium, iussum, mandatum*; a — of the senate, *decretum*.

command, v. *(hominem) iubēre, (homini) imperare*; of places, = dominate, *imminēre, despectare*.

commander, *dux, imperator, praefectus*.

commemorate, *celebrare*.

commemoration, *celebratio*.

commence, *incipēre*; see begin.

commend: = commit, entrust, *commendare, committēre, credēre*; = praise, *laudare, commendare, probare*.

commendable, *laudabilis*.

commendation, *commendatio, laus*.

commendatory, *commendaticius*.

comment, subst. *dictum*.

comment, v. *sententiam dicēre, censēre*.

commentator, *interpres, explanator*.

commerce, *commercium, negotia (-orum), mercatura*.

commiserate, *(com)miserari*; see pity.

commissariat, *res frumentaria, commeatus (-ūs)*.

commission, subst. = allotted task, *mandatum*; = position of trust, *munus (-eris)*.

commission, v. *mandare*.

commit: = entrust, *mandare, commendare, committēre, credēre*; = do, perpetrate, *facēre, committēre, patrare*; = oblige, engage, *obligare, obstringēre*.

committee, *consilium*.

commodious, *commodus, opportunus, aptus*; adv. *commode, opportune, apte*.

commodity, *res, merx*.

common, subst. *ager publicus*.

common, adj.: = belonging to several or all, *communis*; = belonging to people or state, *publicus*; = commonplace, ordinary, *vulgaris, quotidianus*; the — people, *plebs*. Adv., = usually, *fere, ferme, plerumque*.

commonplace, subst. *locus communis*.

commonwealth, *republica, civitas*.

commotion, *tumultus (-ūs), motus (-ūs)*.

commune, *conloqui*.

communicate, *communicare*; see also share, tell.

communication, *communicatio*.

communicative, *loquax*.

communion, *commercium, societas*.

community, = state, society, *civitas, respublica*.

commute; see exchange.

compact, subst. *pactio, pactum, conventus (-ūs)*.

compact, adj. *densus, crassus, confertus*; adv. *confertim*.

companion, *comes, socius, sodalis*.

companionable, *adfabilis, facilis*.

company, *societas*; milit., *manipulus*.

comparable, *comparabilis*.

comparative, *comparativus*.

compare, *comparare, componēre, conferre*.

comparison, *comparatio, conlatio*; in — with, *prae, ad*.

compass, subst.: = extent, *ambitus (-ūs), circuitus (-ūs)*; a pair of —es, *circinus*.

compass, v.; see encompass, accomplish.

compassion, *misericordia*.

compassionate, *misericors*.

compatible, *congruens, conveniens*.

compatriot, *civis*.

compel, *cogēre, compellēre, adigēre*.

compendious, *brevis*.

compensate; to — for, *compensare, rependēre*.

compensation, *compensatio*.

compete, *contendēre, certare*.

competent: see able: to be —, *competēre*.

competition, *contentio, certamen, certatio*.

competitor, *competitor*.

compile, *componēre*.

complacent, *qui sibi placet*.

complain, *(con)queri*.

complaint, *questus (-ūs), querimonia, querela*; = illness, *morbus*.

complaisance, *obsequium, obsequentia, indulgentia*.

complaisant, *indulgens, facilis, obsequens*.

complement, *complementum*.

complete, adj. *absolutus, perfectus, iustus*; adv. *omnino, prorsus*.

complete, v. *complēre, explēre, absolvēre, conficēre*.

completion, *confectio, absolutio, finis*.

complex, *multiplex*.

complexion, *color*.

compliance, *obsequium*.

complicate, *impedire*.

complicated, *involutus, impeditus*.

complication, *implicatio*.

compliment, *laus*; to pay —s, *laudare*.

complimentary, *honorificus*.

comply, v. *obsequi, (con)cedēre, morem gerēre*.

components, *partes (-ium)*.

compose: = make up, constitute, *componēre, efficēre*; of literature, *componēre, scribēre*.

composed, = calm, *tranquillus*.

composer, *scriptor*.

composition, the act, *compositio*; literary, *scriptio, scriptura*; the product, *scriptum*.

composure, *tranquillitas, aequus animus*.

compound, adj. *compositus, multiplex*.

compound, v. *miscēre, confundēre*.

comprehend: = contain, *continēre, complecti*; = understand, *(mente) comprehendēre, complecti, intellegēre*.

comprehension, *comprehensio, intellegentia*.

comprehensive, *late patens*.

compress, *comprimēre, condensare*.

compression, of style, *compressio*.

compromise, v.: = to settle, *componēre,*

compromittĕre; = to embarrass, impedire.

compulsion, vis, necessitas; under —, coactus -a -um.

compunction, paenitentia.

compute, computare.

comrade, socius, comes, sodalis.

comradeship, sodalitas, contubernium.

concave, (con)cavus.

conceal, celare, occulĕre, occultare, abdĕre.

concede, (con)cedĕre, permittĕre.

conceit; render by sibi placēre.

conceive: physically, concipĕre; mentally, concipĕre, intellegĕre, comprehendĕre.

concentrate: = bring together, conligĕre, contrahĕre; to — on, = attend to, (animum) attendĕre.

conception: physical, conceptio, conceptus (-ūs); mental, notio, opinio.

concern, subst.: = affair, res, negotium; = anxiety, cura, anxietas, sollicitudo.

concern, v. pertinēre, attinēre; it —s, interest, refert.

concerning, = about, de.

conciliate, conciliare.

conciliation, conciliatio.

conciliatory, pacificus, blandus.

concise, brevis, pressus, adstrictus; adv. adstricte, breviter.

conciseness, brevitas.

conclave; see assembly.

conclude: = finish, finire, conficĕre; = draw a conclusion, concludĕre, conligĕre.

conclusion, finis, conclusio.

conclusive, gravis, certus.

concoct, miscēre; fig., fingĕre, excogitare, conflare.

concoction, potus (-ūs).

concord, concordia, consensus (-ūs).

concordant, concors.

concourse, concursus (-ūs), concursio.

concrete, = solid, solidus.

concur, consentire, congruĕre.

concurrence, consensio, consensus (-ūs).

concurrently, una, simul.

condemn, damnare, condemnare.

condemnation, damnatio, condemnatio.

condense, v. transit., densare, spissare; intransit., concrescĕre.

condensed, densus, spissus, concretus; of style, pressus, densus.

condescend, se submittĕre, descendĕre.

condescending, comis, facilis.

condescension, comitas, facilitas.

condign, = due, debitus, meritus.

condiment, condimentum.

condition: = state, condicio, status (-ūs); = stipulation, condicio, pactum, lex.

conditioned, adj. adfectus.

condole, casum (hominis) dolēre.

conduce, conducĕre (ad rem).

conducive, utilis.

conduct, subst.: = behaviour, vita, mores (-um, plur.); = management, administratio.

conduct, v.: = lead, (de)ducĕre; = manage, gerĕre, administrare.

conductor, dux.

conduit, canalis.

cone, conus, meta.

confederacy, foedus (-eris, n.), societas.

confederates, socii, foederati.

confer: = give, conferre, tribuĕre; = talk, conloqui, consultare.

conference, conloquium.

confess, fateri, confiteri.

confession, confessio.

confidant, conscius (f. conscia).

confide: = entrust, committĕre, mandare, credĕre; to — in, (con)fidere.

confidence, fides, fiducia, confidentia.

confident, (con)fidens; adv. (con)fidenter.

confidential; see secret.

confiding, adj. credulus.

confine, subst. finis, terminus, confinium.

confine, v. includĕre, coercēre, cohibēre.

confined, adj. artus.

confinement, inclusio; = imprisonment, custodia.

confirm, (con)firmare; = ratify, sancire, ratum facĕre.

confiscate, publicare.

confiscation, publicatio.

conflagration, incendium, ignis.

conflict, subst. certamen, pugna.

conflict, v.: = fight, pugnare, certare, contendĕre; = differ, dissentire, discrepare, repugnare.

confluence, confluens or plur. confluentes.

conform, obsequi, obtemperare.

conformable, accommodatus, congruens.

conformation, conformatio, forma, figura.

conformity, convenientia; in — with, ex, secundum.

confound; = confuse, confundĕre; = astonish, obstupefacĕre; = frustrate, frustrari.

confront, v. obviam ire, se opponĕre.

confuse, confundĕre, (per)miscēre, (per)turbare.

confused, confusus, perplexus; adv. confuse, perplexe.

confusion, confusio, perturbatio.

confute, refellĕre, redarguĕre, confutare.

congeal: transit. congelare; intransit. concrescĕre.

congenial, gratus, concors.

congratulate, gratulari.

congratulation, gratulatio.

congregate, congregari, convenire, confluĕre.

congregation, conventus (-ūs), coetus (-ūs).

congress, conventus (-ūs), concilium.

conjecture, subst. coniectura, opinio.

conjecture, v. augurari, conicĕre, coniectare.

conjugal, adj. coniugalis.

conjugate, gram., declinare.

conjugation, gram., declinatio.

conjure, v.: transit., = entreat, obtestari, obsecrare; to — up, (mortuorum) animas elicĕre; intransit., = perform tricks, praestigiis uti.

conjurer, magus, praestigiator.

connect, adligare, (con)iungĕre, connectĕre.

connexion, coniunctio; between persons, societas, necessitudo; by marriage, adfinitas.

connive, *connivēre, (rem) dissimulare.*
connivance, *indulgentia.*
connoisseur, *iudex, existimator.*
conquer, *(de)vincĕre, superare.*
conqueror, *victor.*
conquest, *victoria.*
consanguinity, *consanguinitas.*
conscience, *conscientia.*
conscientious, *religiosus, sanctus*; adv. *religiose, sancte.*
conscientiousness, *religio, sanctitas, fides.*
conscious, = aware, *gnarus, conscius*; adv., render by adj. *prudens.*
consciousness, *animus (-ūs).*
conscript: see recruit.
conscription, *delectus (-ūs).*
consecrate, *consecrare, dedicare.*
consecrated, *sacer.*
consecration, *consecratio, dedicatio.*
consecutive, *continens, continuus*; adv. *continenter.*
consent, subst. *consensus (-ūs).*
consent, v. *velle.*
consequence: = result, *exitus (-ūs), eventus (-ūs)*; in — of, *ex, propter*; = importance, *momentum, auctoritas.*
consequently, *itaque, ergo, igitur.*
conserve, *(con)servare*; of fruit, *condire.*
conservative, polit., *qui nihil in republica immutari vult.*
consider: = think about, *considerare, expendĕre, delibare, contemplari*; = take into account, *respicĕre*; to — that, *arbitrari, ducĕre*; = to regard as, *ducĕre, habēre, existimare.*
considerable, *magnus, gravis*; adv. *aliquantum.*
considerate, *humanus, officious, benignus.*
considerateness, *humanitas, benignitas.*
consideration: = thought, *consideratio, deliberatio, contemplatio*; = proper regard, *ratio, respectus (-ūs).*
consign, *committĕre, credĕre, mandare.*
consist, *consistĕre, constare.*
consistent: — with, *consentaneus, congruens*; = unchanging, *constans*; adv. *constanter.*
consolation, *solatium, consolatio.*
console, *(con)solari.*
consoler, *consolator.*
consonant, subst., gram., *consonans.*
consonant, adj. *consentaneus, congruens.*
consort, subst. *comes, socius*; = husband or wife, *coniunx.*
consort, v.: to — with, *familiariter uti.*
conspicuous, *conspicuus, clarus, insignis*; adv. *clare.*
conspiracy, *coniuratio.*
conspirator, *coniuratus.*
conspire, *coniurare, conspirare.*
constable, *lictor.*
constancy, *constantia, fides, fidelitas.*
constant, *constans, firmus*; = incessant, *continuus, perpetuus*; = faithful, *fidelis, fidus.* Adv. *constanter; semper, perpetuo.*
constellation, *sidus (-eris, n.), signum.*
consternation, *pavor, terror.*
constitute; = to make up, *componĕre, efficĕre*; = to establish, *statuĕre, constituĕre, designare*; = to appoint, *creare, facĕre.*

constitution, *constitutio, habitus (-ūs)*; of a state, *civitatis status (ūs).*
constitutional: = natural, *innatus, insitus*; = legal, *legitimus.* Adv. *naturā; legitime, e republica.*
constrain, *cogĕre, compellĕre.*
constraint, *vis.*
construct, *facĕre, fabricari.*
construction: as an act, *fabricatio, aedificatio*; = form, plan, *structura, figura, forma*; = interpretation, *interpretatio*; to put a good — on, *rem in bonam partem accipĕre.*
construe, *interpretari, accipĕre.*
consul, *consul*; ex-consul, *vir consularis.*
consulship, *consulatus (-ūs).*
consult, *consultare, deliberare*; to — a person, *hominem consulĕre.*
consume, *consumĕre, conficĕre, absumĕre.*
consummate, adj. *summus, absolutus, perfectus*; adv. *summe, absolute, perfecte.*
consummation, *absolutio, perfectio.*
contact, *(con)tactus (-ūs).*
contagion, *contagio.*
contain, *capĕre, habēre, continēre.*
contaminate, *contaminare, inquinare, polluĕre.*
contamination, *macula, labes.*
contemplate, *contemplari, intuēri.*
contemplation, *contemplatio.*
contemporary, *aequalis.*
contempt, *contemptus (-ūs), fastidium.*
contemptible, *contemptus, turpis.*
contend: = to struggle, *contendĕre, (de)certare*; = to maintain, *contendĕre, confirmare, adfirmare.*
content, subst. *animus contentus.*
content, adj. *contentus.*
content, v. *satisfacĕre* (with dat.); to — oneself with saying, *satis habēre dicĕre.*
contentedly, *aequo animo*; or use adj. *contentus.*
contentious, *pugnax.*
conterminous, *confinis.*
contest, subst. *certatio, certamen, contentio.*
contest, v. *contendĕre.*
context, *argumentum.*
contiguity, *vicinitas, propinquitas.*
contiguous, *confinis, continens.*
continence, *continentia, temperantia.*
continent, subst. *continens.*
continent, adj. *continens, castus*; adv. *continenter, caste.*
contingency, *casus (-ūs).*
contingent, subst. *auxilia (-orum).*
contingent, adj. *fortuitus, forte oblatus.*
continual, *continuus, perpetuus, adsiduus*; adv. *continenter, adsidue, perpetuo.*
continuance, continuation, *perpetuitas, adsiduitas, diuturnitas.*
continue, v.: transit. *extendĕre, producĕre, continuare*; intransit., = to persevere, *pergĕre, perseverare*; = to last, *durare, (per)manēre.*
continuity, *continuatio, perpetuitas.*
contort, *depravare, distorquēre.*
contortion, *distortio, depravatio.*
contour, *forma, figura.*

contract, subst. *pactum, conductio, locatio, redemptio.*

contract, v.: = draw in, *contrahĕre, adducĕre;* = incur, *contrahĕre;* to — for, *locare, conducĕre,* or *redimĕre;* intransit., = become smaller, *se contrahĕre, minui.*

contracted, *contractus, angustus, brevis.*

contraction, *contractio.*

contractor, *conductor, redemptor.*

contradict, *obloqui, contradicĕre;* fig., *repugnare, discrepare.*

contradictory, *contrarius, repugnans, diversus.*

contrary, subst.: on the —, *contra;* in answers, *immo.*

contrary, adj. *adversus, contrarius.*

contrary to, *contra, praeter,* with acc.

contrast, subst. *diversitas, dissimilitudo.*

contrast, v. transit. *comparare, conferre;* intransit. *discrepare.*

contravene, *violare, frangĕre.*

contribute, v.: = give, *contribuĕre, conferre;* = help, *prodesse, adiuvare.*

contrite, adj.; see penitent.

contrivance: = contriving, *inventio, excogitatio;* = thing contrived, *machina.*

contrive, *excogitare, invenire, fingĕre, efficĕre.*

control, subst. *potestas, imperium, dicio;* self —, *moderatio, temperantia.*

control, v. *moderari, temperare, coercēre.*

controversial, = disputed, *controversus.*

controversy, *controversia, contentio.*

controvert, *refellĕre, refutare.*

contumacious, *contumax, pertinax;* adv. *contumaciter, pertinaciter.*

contumacy, *pertinacia, contumacia.*

contumelious, *contumeliosus, probrosus.*

contumely, *contumelia.*

convalescent, use verb *convalescĕre.*

convene, *convocare.*

convenience, *commoditas, opportunitas.*

convenient, *commodus, opportunus, accommodatus;* adv. *commode, opportune, accommode.*

convention: = assembly, *conventus (-ūs);* = agreement, *foedus (-eris,* n.), *pactio;* = custom, *mos.*

conventional, *translaticius, usu receptus.*

converge, *coire, in unum vergĕre.*

conversant, *versatus, exercitatus, peritus.*

conversation, *sermo, conloquium.*

converse, v. *conloqui, sermonem conferre.*

conversion, *(com)mutatio, conversio.*

convert, v. *(com)mutare, convertĕre;* — to an opinion, *ad sententiam traducĕre.*

convex, *convexus.*

convey: see carry; legal, *transcribĕre, abalienare.*

convict, v. *condemnare, convincĕre.*

conviction, *damnatio;* = belief, *opinio, sententia.*

convince, *persuadĕre.*

convivial, *hilaris.*

conviviality, *hilaritas.*

convoke, *convocare.*

convoy, subst. *praesidium.*

convoy, v. *deducĕre, comitari.*

convulse, *agitare, percutĕre.* (com)-movēre.

convulsion, *motus (-ūs), turba;* medical, *convulsio.*

cook, subst. *coquus.*

cook, v. *coquĕre.*

cool, subst. *frigus (-oris,* n.).

cool, adj. *frigidus;* of temper, etc., *lentus* (= phlegmatic), *impavidus* (= undismayed), *impudens* (= impudent). Adv. *frigide; lente.*

cool, v.: transit., *refrigerare;* intransit., *refrigerari, defervescĕre.*

co-operate, *una agĕre;* to — with, *adiuvare.*

co-operation, *opera, auxilium.*

cope, v. *resistĕre, certare;* able to —, *par.*

coping, *fastigium.*

copious, *copiosus, abundans, largus;* adv. *copiose, abundanter, large.*

copiousness, *copia, abundantia.*

copper, subst. *aes.*

copper, adj. *a(h)enus.*

coppice, copse, *silva.*

copy, subst. *exemplum, exemplar.*

copy, v. *imitari;* to — out, *transcribĕre, describĕre.*

cord, *restis, funis.*

cordial, *benignus, comis;* adv. *benigne, comiter.*

cordiality, *benignitas, comitas.*

core, *nucleus, granum.*

cork, subst. *cortex.*

corn, *frumentum;* the price of — *annona;* = field, *seges.*

corner, *angulus.*

cornet, *cornu, buccina.*

corporal, subst. *decurio.*

corporal, corporeal, adj. *corporeus,* or genit. of *corpus.*

corporation, *municipium, conlegium.*

corps, *manus (-ūs).*

corpse, *cadaver.*

corpulent, *obesus, pinguis.*

correct, adj.; of conduct, *honestus, rectus;* of style, *emendatus, purus;* = true, *verus.* Adv. *recte, honeste; pure; vere.*

correct, v. *corrigĕre, emendare;* see also punish.

correction, *correctio, emendatio;* see also punishment.

correspond, v. *respondēre, congruĕre;* letter, *litteras dare et accipĕre.*

correspondence: = agreement, *congruentia, convenientia;* = letters, *litterae, epistulae.*

corresponding, *par.*

corroborate, *confirmare, comprobare.*

corroboration, *confirmatio.*

corrode, *rodĕre.*

corrupt, adj. *corruptus, impurus, pravus;* adv. *corrupte, impure, prave.*

corrupt, v. *corrumpĕre, depravare, vitiare.*

corrupter, *corruptor.*

corruptible, = venal, *venalis.*

corruption, *corruptio, depravatio, corruptela.*

corsair, *pirata.*

corslet, *thorax, lorica.*

cortege, *comitatus (-ūs).*

cosmetic, *fucus.*

cost, subst. *pretium, sumptus* (*-ūs*); — of living, *annona.*
cost, v. (*con*)*stare, venire.*
costly, *carus, pretiosus.*
costume, *vestitus* (*-ūs*), *habitus* (*-ūs*).
cot, *lectulus.*
cottage, *casa, tugurium.*
cottager, *rusticus.*
couch, subst. *lectus, lectulus, cubile.*
couch, v. *cubare, latēre, delitescēre.*
cough, subst. *tussis.*
cough, v. *tussire.*
council, *concilium;* a — of war, *consilium, praetorium.*
councillor, *senator, decurio.*
counsel, = advice, *consilium, auctoritas.*
counsel, v.; see advise.
count: = to number, (*e*)*numerare, percensēre, computare;* = to consider, *habēre, ducēre;* to — upon, *confidĕre.*
countenance, subst.: = face, *vultus* (*-ūs*), *os;* = favour, *favor.*
countenance, v.: = approve, *approbare;* = allow, *permittĕre.*
counter, subst.: for counting, *calculus;* in a shop, *mensa.*
counter, adv.: — to, *contra;* to run — to, *adversari.*
counteract, *resistĕre.*
counter-balance, (*ex*)*aequare, compensare.*
counterfeit, adj. *falsus.*
counterfeit, v. *simulare.*
counterpane, *lodix.*
countless, *innumerabilis, innumerus.*
country: opp. to town, *rus:* in the —, *ruri;* = native land, *patria;* = region, *terra, regio.*
country-house, *villa.*
countryman, (*homo*) *rusticus.*
country-town, *municipium, oppidum.*
couple, subst. *par, bini -ae -a.*
couple, v. transit. (*con*)*iungĕre, copulare.*
courage, *fortudo, virtus, animus.*
courageous, *fortis, strenuus, animosus;* adv. *fortiter, strenue.*
courier, *nuntius, tabellarius.*
course, *cursus* (*-ūs*); — of life, *vitae curriculum;* a — of action, *ratio;* of —, *scilicet, sane;* a — at dinner, *ferculum.*
court, subst.: = enclosed space, *area;* a royal —, *aula, regia;* a — of justice, *forum, basilica.*
court, v. transit., *petĕre, colĕre, captare.*
courteous, *comis, urbanus;* adv. *comiter, urbane.*
courtesy, *urbanitas, comitas.*
courtier, *aulicus.*
cousin, (*con*)*sobrinus, patruelis.*
covenant, subst. *pactio, pactum, conventio.*
covenant, v. *pacisci.*
cover, subst.: = lid, *operimentum;* = shelter, *perfugium.*
cover, v.: to — up, (*con*)*tegĕre, operire, velare;* = to protect, *protegĕre, defendĕre.*
covering, *tegmen.*
covert, subst., = thicket, *dumetum.*
covert, adj.: see secret.
covet, *adpetĕre, concupiscĕre.*

covetous, *avarus, avidus;* adv. *avare, avide.*
covetousness, *avaritia, aviditas.*
cow, subst. *vacca.*
cow, v. *domare.*
coward, *homo ignavus* or *timidus.*
cowardice, *ignavia, timiditas.*
cowardly, *ignavus, timidus.*
cowl, *cucullus.*
coy, *verecundus.*
crab, *cancer.*
crabbed: in temper, *acerbus, morosus;* of style, *implicatus, impeditus.*
crack, subst.: = noise, *crepitus* (*-ūs*), *fragor;* = fissure, *rima.*
crack, v.: transit., *frangĕre, findĕre, rumpĕre;* intransit., = break open, *dissilire, dehiscĕre;* = make a noise, *crepare.*
cradle, *cunae* (*-arum*), *cunabula* (*-orum*).
craft: = cunning, *dolus, astutia;* = skill, trade, *ars, artificium;* = boat, *cymba, scapha.*
craftsman, *artifex, opifex.*
crafty, *astutus, callidus, dolosus;* adv. *astute, callide, dolose.*
crag, *scopulus, rupes.*
cram, *farcire, refercire, stipare.*
cramp; see confine.
crane: the bird, *grus;* the machine, *trochlea, tolleno.*
crank, of a machine, *uncus.*
cranny, *rima.*
crash, subst. *fragor, strepitus* (*-ūs*).
crash, v. *strepĕre.*
crater, *crater.*
crave; see beg, need.
craving, *desiderium.*
crawl, *repĕre, serpĕre.*
crazy: = decrepit, *decrepitus, imbecillus;* = deranged, *cerritus.*
creak, v. *stridĕre, crepare.*
creaking, subst. *stridor, crepitus* (*-ūs*).
crease, v. *rugare.*
crease, subst. *ruga.*
create, *creare, gignĕre, generare, facĕre.*
creator, *creator, fabricator, auctor.*
creature, *animal.*
credibility, *fides, auctoritas.*
credible, *credibilis.*
credit, subst. *fides.*
credit, v.: = to believe, *credĕre;* to — a thing (to a person), *rem acceptam* (*homini*) *referre.*
creditable, *honestus, honorificus;* adv. *honeste.*
creditor, *creditor.*
credulity, *credulitas.*
credulous, *credulus.*
creek, *sinus* (*-ūs*), *aestuarium.*
creep; see crawl.
crest, *crista, iuba.*
crested, *cristatus, iubatus.*
crestfallen, *demissus.*
crevice; see crack.
crew: on a ship, *nautae* (*-arum*); in gen., *grex.*
crib, *praesepe.*
crime, *scelus* (*-eris*), *delictum, facinus* (*-oris*).
criminal, *scelestus, sceleratus, nefarius:* adv. *nefarie.*

crimson, *coccineus.*
cringe, *adulari.*
cringing, *abiectus.*
cripple, *debilitare, frangĕre, infringĕre.*
crippled, *claudus, mancus, debilis.*
crisis, *discrimen.*
crisp: = curled. *crispus*; = brittle, *fragilis.*
criterion, *norma, obrussa.*
critic, *iudex, criticus, existimator.*
critical: = discriminating, *elegans, subtilis*; = of a crisis, *anceps, dubius.*
criticism, *iudicium.*
criticize: = to judge, *iudicare*; = to find fault with, *reprehendĕre, culpare.*
croak, v. *crocire, queri.*
crockery, *fictilia (-ium).*
crocodile, *crocodilus.*
crocus, *crocus.*
crone, *vetula, anus (-ūs), anicula.*
crook, a shepherd's, *pedum.*
crooked, *pravus*; adv. *prave.*
crookedness, *pravitas.*
crop, subst.: of corn, etc., *messis, fruges (-um)*; of birds, *ingluvies.*
crop, v.: = to browse on, *(at)tondĕre*; = to cut short, *praecidĕre, amputare.*
cross, subst. *crux.*
cross, adj.: = transverse, *transversus, obliquus*; = annoyed, *difficilis, morosus.*
cross, v.: = to go across, *transire, transgredi*; = to oppose, *obsistĕre, adversari*; to — out, *delēre.*
cross-examine, *interrogare.*
crossing, subst. *transitus (-ūs).*
crouch, *se demittĕre.*
crow, subst. *cornix.*
crow, v. *canĕre.*
crowd, subst. *turba, vulgus, multitudo.*
crowd, v.: transit., *stipare, cogĕre*; intransit., *concurrĕre, congregari.*
crown, subst.: = garland, *corona*; a king's *diadema (-atis)*, fig., = sovereignty, *regnum*; the — of the head, *vertex.*
crown, v. *coronare, diadema (regi) imponĕre.*
crucifixion, *crucis supplicium.*
crucify, *cruci adfigĕre.*
crude: = raw, unripe, *crudus*; = rough, *informis, incultus, rudis*; adv. *inculte.*
cruel, *crudelis, saevus, atrox*; adv. *crudeliter, atrociter.*
cruelty, *crudelitas, saevitia.*
cruise, v. *(per)vagari, circumvectari, navigare.*
crumb, *mica.*
crumble: transit., *comminuĕre, conterĕre*; intransit., render by pass.
crumple, *(con)rugare.*
crush, v. *opprimĕre, contundĕre, conterĕre*; fig., *adfligĕre.*
crust, *crusta.*
crutch, *baculum.*
cry, subst. *clamor, vociferatio*; of distress, *ploratus (-ūs).*
crystal: subst. *crystallus*; adj. *crystallinus.*
cub, *catulus.*
cube, *tessera, cubus.*
cuckoo, *cuculus.*

cucumber, *cucumis.*
cud: to chew the cud, *ruminare, remandĕre.*
cudgel, subst. *baculum, fustis.*
cue, = hint, *signum, indicium.*
cuff, subst.: = blow, *alapa, colaphus*; = sleeve, *manica extrema.*
cuirass, *thorax, lorica.*
culmination, *fastigium.*
culpable, *culpandus.*
culprit; see criminal.
cultivate, *(ex)colĕre, exercēre.*
cultivation, culture, *cultus (-ūs), cultura*; = education, etc., *humanitas, litterae (-arum).*
cultivator, *cultor.*
cumber, *impedire,(prae)gravare,onerare.*
cumbrous, *gravis, incommodus.*
cunning, subst. *calliditas, astutia, dolus.*
cunning, adj. *callidus, astutus, dolosus*; adv. *callide, astute.*
cup, *poculum, scyphus, calix.*
cup-bearer, *minister, servus.*
cupboard, *armarium.*
cupidity, *cupiditas, avaritia.*
curb, subst. *frenum.*
curb, v. *frenare, coercēre, cohibēre.*
curdle, v.: transit., *coagulare*; ntransit., *concrescĕre.*
cure, subst. *medicina, sanatio.*
cure, v. *sanare, medēri.*
curiosity, *noscendi studium.*
curious: = inquisitive, *curiosus*; = strange, *insolitus, novus, mirus.*
curl, v. transit. *crispare.*
curling-irons, *calamister.*
curly, *crispus.*
currency, *nummi (-orum).*
current, subst.: in a river, *flumen*; at sea, *aestus (-ūs).*
current, adj.: = this, *hic*; = common, *usitatus, vulgaris*; adv. *vulgo.*
curse, subst.: of speech, *exsecratio, imprecatio*; = malign influence, *pernicies, pestis.*
curse, v. *exsecrari, detestari.*
cursory; see brief.
curt, *brevis, abruptus*; adv. *breviter, praecise.*
curtail, *(co)artare, (im)minuĕre.*
curtain, *velum, aulaeum.*
curve, subst. *flexus (-ūs), sinus (-ūs).*
curve, v. transit. *(in)curvare, (in)flectĕre.*
cushion, *pulvinus, pulvinar.*
custody, *custodia, vincula (-orum).*
custom, *consuetudo, mos, usus (-ūs).*
customary, *usitatus, quotidianus, solitus.*
custom-duty, *vectigal, portorium.*
customer, *emptor.*
cut, v. *secare, caedĕre*; to — corn, etc., *(de)metĕre*; to — down, *succidĕre*; to — off, = destroy, *absumĕre, exstinguĕre*; to — short, *praecidĕre, amputare.*
cutlery, *cultri (-orum).*
cut-throat, *sicarius.*
cutting, adj., of speech, *mordax.*
cuttlefish, *sepia, lolligo.*
cycle, *orbis, circulus.*
cylinder, *cylindrus.*
cymbal, *cymbalum.*
cynic, *cynicus.*

cynical, *mordax.*
cypress, *cupressus.*

D

dabble: to — in, *attingĕre.*
daffodil, *narcissus.*
dagger, *pugio, sica.*
daily: adj., *quotidianus*; adv., *quotidie.*
daintiness: = fussiness, *cuppedia*; = elegance, *venustas.*
dainty: = particular, *fastidiosus*; = elegant, *elegans, delicatus.*
dale, *vallis.*
dalliance, *lascivia, ludus.*
dally: = to linger, *morari*; = to sport, *lascivire, ludĕre.*
dam, subst.: = mother, *mater*; = breakwater, *moles, agger.*
dam, v. *obstruĕre, coercĕre.*
damage, subst. *dammum, incommodum, noxa.*
damage, v. *laedĕre, nocĕre.*
dame, *matrona, domina.*
damn, *damnare, condemnare.*
damp, subst. *umor.*
damp, adj. *umidus, udus.*
damp, v. *umectare*; fig., *comprimĕre, restinguĕre.*
damsel, *puella, virgo.*
dance, subst. *saltatio, saltatus (-ūs).*
dance, v. *saltare.*
dancer, *saltator* (f. *saltatrix*).
dandy, *homo elegans.*
danger, *periculum, discrimen.*
dangerous, *periculosus, infestus, lubricus*; adv. *periculose.*
dangle, *(de)pendĕre.*
dank, *umidus.*
Danube, *Danubius.*
dapper, *nitidus.*
dappled, *maculosus.*
dare, *audēre*; = to challenge, *provocare.*
daring, subst. *audacia.*
daring, adj. *audax.*
dark, subst.; see darkness.
dark, adj. *obscurus*; in colour, *fuscus, pullus.* Adv. *obscure.*
darken, v. *obscurare, occaecare.*
darkness, *obscuritas, tenebrae (-arum), caligo.*
darling, subst. *deliciae (-arum).*
darling, adj. *suavissimus, mellitus.*
darn, *sarcire.*
dart, subst. *telum, iaculum*; to throw —s, *iaculari.*
dart, v. = to dash, *provolare, se conicĕre.*
dash, subst., = rush, *impetus (-ūs).*
dash, v.: transit., to — one thing against another, *adfligĕre, offendĕre*; to — down, *proruĕre*; intransit., see dart.
dastardly, *ignavus.*
date, subst.: the fruit, *palmula*; = a particular time, *dies, tempus (-oris)*; out of —, *obsoletus.*
date, v.; to — a letter, *diem in epistula ascribĕre.*
dative, *(casus) dativus.*
daub, *(ob)linĕre, (per)ungĕre.*

daughter, *filia*: — -in-law, *nurus (-ūs).*
dauntless, *impavidus.*
dawdle, *cessare.*
dawn, *diluculum, prima lux, aurora* (poet.); it is —, *lucescit.*
day, *dies*: at break of —, *prima luce*; good —, *salve(te)*; a period of two —, *biduum*; on the — before, *pridie*; on the — after, *postridie.*
day-break; see dawn.
dazzle, *perstringĕre, caecare.*
dead, *mortuus.* Transf., = dull, *languidus*; at — of night, *nocte intempesta.*
deaden, *hebetare, enervare, debilitare.*
deadly, *mortifer, exitialis, perniciosus.*
deaf, *surdus, auribus captus.*
deafen, *exsurdare, obtundĕre.*
deafness, *surditas.*
deal, v.: to — out, *dividĕre, distribuĕre*; to — with, see treat.
dealer, *mercator, negotiator*; a retail —, *institor, propola.*
dealing, *commercium, negotium, usus (-ūs).*
dear: = expensive, *carus, pretiosus*; = beloved, *carus.*
dearly, = at a high price, *care, magno pretio.*
dearness, *caritas.*
dearth, *inopia, caritas, penuria.*
death, *mors, letum, obitus (-ūs).*
debar, *excludĕre, prohibēre.*
debase, *corrumpĕre, vitiare.*
debasement, *ignominia.*
debate, subst. *disceptatio, disputatio.*
debate, v. *disceptare, disputare.*
debauch, subst. *comissatio.*
debauch, v. *corrumpĕre, depravare, vitiare.*
debauchery, *stuprum.*
debenture, *syngrapha.*
debility, *infirmitas, imbecilitas, debilitas.*
debit, v.: to — a thing to a person, *homini rem expensam ferre.*
debt, *aes alienum.*
debtor, *debitor, obaeratus.*
decade, *decem anni.*
decamp, *discedĕre.*
decant, *diffundĕre.*
decanter, *lagena.*
decapitate; see behead.
decay, *tabes, defectio virium.*
decay, v. *marcescĕre, senescĕre, tabescĕre.*
decease, *obitus (-ūs).*
deceit, *fallacia, fraus, dolus.*
deceitful, *fallax, dolosus, fraudulentus*; adv. *fallaciter, dolose.*
deceive, *decipĕre, fallĕre, circumvenire.*
deceiver, *fraudator.*
December, *(mensis) December.*
decency, *honestas, decentia, decorum.*
decent, *honestus, decens, decorus*; adv. *honeste, decenter, decore.*
deception, *fraus, dolus, fallacia.*
decide, *statuĕre, constituĕre.*
decided, *certus*; of persons, *constans, firmus.* Adv. *firme, constanter*; in answers, *vero, plane, sane.*
decimate, *decimare.*
decipher, *explanare, explicare.*
decision: = settlement, *arbitrium,*

desolate, adj. *vastus, desertus.*

desolate, v. *vastare, populari.*

despair, subst. *desperare, spem abicĕre.*

despatch, *litterae (-arum), epistula.*

despatch, v.: = send, *mittĕre*; = complete, finish, *conficĕre, perficĕre*; = hasten, haste, *maturare*; = kill, *interficĕre, interimĕre.*

desperate: = hopeless, *desperatus, exspes*; = dangerous, *periculosus.* Adv. *desperanter.*

desperation, *desperatio.*

despicable, *contemptus.*

despise, *contemnĕre, despicĕre, spernĕre.*

despite: in — of, *contra.*

despond, v. *desperare, animum demittĕre.*

despondency, *animus demissus.*

despot, *tyrannus, dominus.*

despotic, *imperiosus, superbus*; adv. *superbe, tyrannice.*

despotism, *dominatus (-ūs), tyrannis, regnum.*

dessert, *mensa secunda.*

destine, *destinare, constituĕre.*

destiny, *fatum, sors.*

destitute, *inops, egens, privatus.*

destitution, *inopia, egestas.*

destroy, *perdĕre, delēre, extinguĕre.*

destruction, *excidium, exstinctio, pernicies.*

destructive, *perniciosus, exitiosus*; adv. *perniciose.*

desuetude, *desuetudo*; to fall into —, *obsolescĕre.*

desultory, *inconstans, levis.*

detach, *separare, seiungĕre, disiungĕre.*

detachment, of troops, *manus (-ūs).*

details, *singula (-orum).*

detail, v. *(singula) explicare, exsequi.*

detain, *tenēre, retinēre.*

detect, *invenire, deprehendĕre.*

detention, *retentio; custodia.*

deter, *deterrēre, absterrēre.*

deteriorate: transit., *depravare, corrumpĕre*; intransit., *in peius mutari.*

deterioration, *deterior condicio.*

determination: = intention, *institutum, consilium*; of character, *constantia, firmitas animi.*

determine, *statuĕre, constituĕre.*

determined, *certus*; = resolute, *constans, firmus.*

detest, *odisse, detestari.*

detestable, *detestabilis.*

detestation, *odium.*

dethrone, *regno expellĕre.*

detract; see derogate, depreciate.

detriment, *damnum, detrimentum.*

detrimental, *perniciosus, iniquus.*

devastate, *(per)vastare, (de)populari.*

devastation, *vastatio; vastitas.*

develop, v. transit., *educare, excolĕre, alĕre*; intransit., *crescĕre, adulescĕre, augeri.*

development, *auctus (-ūs), progressus (-ūs).*

deviate, *declinare, decedĕre, aberrare.*

deviation, *declinatio, digressio.*

device: = emblem, *insigne*; = plan, *machina, dolus.*

devil, *diabolus* (eccl.); go to the —! *abi in malam crucem.*

devious, *devius, vagus.*

devise, *excogitare, fingĕre, machinari*; see also bequeath.

devoid, *vacuus, liber.*

devolve, v.: transit., *deferre, permittĕre, mandare*; intransit., *(per)venire, permitti.*

devote, *devovēre, consecrare, (de)dicare*; fig., *dedĕre, conferre.*

devoted, *deditus, studiosus*; adv. *studiose.*

devotion, = zeal, *studium*; plur., see prayers.

devour, *(de)vorare, consumĕre.*

devouring, *edax.*

devout, *pius (erga deos)*; adv. *pie, sancte.*

dew, *ros.*

dewy, *roscidus.*

dexterity, *dexteritas, sollertia.*

dexterous, *dexter, sollers*; adv. *dext(e)re sollerter.*

diadem, *diadema (-atis, n.).*

diagonal, *diagonalis.*

diagram, *descriptio, forma.*

dial, *solarium,*

dialect, *lingua.*

dialectics, *dialectica.*

dialogue, *dialogus*; in plays, *diverbium*; = conversation, *sermo, conloquium.*

diamond, *adamas.*

diaphragm, *praecordia (-ium, plur.).*

diary, *commentarii diurni.*

dice, **die**, *talus, tessera*; — box, *fritillus.*

dictate, *dictare*; see also order.

dictator, *dictator.*

dictatorial, *dictatorius, imperiosus.*

dictatorship, *dictatura.*

diction, *dicendi or scribendi genus (-eris).*

die, v. *mori, (mortem) obire*; of wind, *cadĕre.*

diet, *victus (-ūs), diaeta.*

differ, *discrepare, differre.*

difference, *varietas, diversitas, dissensio.*

different, *alius, diversus, varius*; adv. *aliter, diverse, varie.*

difficult, *difficilis, arduus, impeditus.*

difficulty, *difficultas*; to be in difficulties, *laborare*; with —, *vix, aegre.*

diffidence, *verecundia, diffidentia.*

diffident, *verecundus, diffidens*; adv. *verecunde, diffidenter.*

diffuse, v.: transit., *diffundĕre*; intransit., *diffundi, permeare.*

diffuse, adj. *verbosus, fusus*; adv. *verbose, fuse.*

dig, *fodĕre*; to — up, *effodĕre.*

digest, v. *concoquĕre.*

digger, *fossor.*

dignified, *gravis, augustus.*

dignify, *honestare, honorare.*

dignity, *dignitas, amplitudo, auctoritas maiestas.*

digress, *digredi, aberrare.*

digression, *digressio.*

dike: = earthwork, *moles, agger*; = ditch, *fossa.*

dilapidated, *ruinosus.*

dilapidation, *ruina.*

dilate: = to extend, *dilatare*; in speech, *latius dicĕre.*

dilatory, *tardus, lentus.*

dilemma, in logic, *complexio*.

diligence, *diligentia, industria*.

diligent, *diligens, industrius*; adv. *diligenter, industrie*.

dilute, *aquâ miscēre, diluēre*.

dim, adj. *obscurus, hebes*; to grow —, *hebescēre*.

dim, v. transit., *obscurare, hebetare*.

diminish, v.: transit., *(im)minuēre, deminuēre*; intransit., render by passive.

din, subst. *strepitus (-ūs)*.

din, v.: to — into (a person), *(hominis) aures obtundēre*.

dine, *prandēre, cenare*.

dingy, *fuscus, sordidus*.

dining-room, *triclinium*.

dinner, *prandium* (morning), *cena* (evening).

dint: by — of, *per*, or abl.

dip, v.: transit., *tingēre, mergēre*; intransit., *tingi, mergi, vergēre*; to — into a book, *librum attingēre*.

diploma, *diploma (-atis, n.)*.

diplomat, *legatus*.

diplomatic, = clever, *astutus, callidus*.

dire, *dirus, atrox*.

direct, adj. *rectus*. Adv. *recte*; = immediately, *statim, confestim*.

direct, v. *regēre, dirigēre, intendēre*; *gubernare, administrare*; = to show the way, *viam monstrare*; to — a letter, *epistolam inscribēre*.

direction: = course, *cursus (-ūs), via, regio*; = management, *cura, regimen, administratio*.

director, *magister, curator, praefectus*.

dirge, *nenia*.

dirt, *caenum, sordes*.

dirty, adj. *spurcus, sordidus, turpis*; to be —, *sordēre*. Adv. *spurce*.

dirty, v. *inquinare, polluēre*.

disable, *enervare, debilitare*.

disadvantage, *incommodum, iniquitas*.

disadvantageous, *incommodus, iniquus*; adv. *incommode, inique*.

disaffected, *(ab)alienatus, aversus*.

disaffection, *animus alienus* or *aversus*.

disagree, *dissentire, dissidēre*.

disagreeable, *ingratus, gravis, molestus*; adv. *ingrate, graviter, moleste*.

disagreement, *discrepantia, dissensio, dissidium*.

disallow, *vetare*.

disappear, *e conspectu abire, evanescēre*.

disappoint, *frustrari, spem fallēre, spe depellēre*.

disapproval, *improbatio*.

disapprove, *improbare, condemnare*.

disarm, *armis exuēre*.

disarrange, *(per)turbare, confundēre*.

disarrangement, *perturbatio*.

disaster, *clades, calamitas*.

disastrous, *calamitosus, funestus*; adv. *calamitose, funeste*.

disavow, *infitiari, abnuēre*.

disavowal, *infitiatio*.

disband, *exauctorare, dimittēre*.

disbelieve, *non credēre*.

disburden, *exonerare liberare, expedire*.

disc, *orbis*.

discern, *(dis)cernēre, dispicēre*.

discerning, *perspicax, sagax, subtilis, prudens*.

discernment, *prudentia, iudicium, subtilitas*.

discharge, subst., *(di)missio*; = shooting, *emissio, coniectio, coniectus (-ūs)*.

discharge, v.: from service, *missum facēre, dimittēre*; = to shoot, *(e)mittēre, conicēre*; = to perform, *(per)fungi*.

disciple, *discipulus, auditor*.

discipline, subst. *disciplina*; sense of —, *modestia*.

discipline, v. *instituēre, exercēre*.

disclaim, *repudiare*.

disclose, *detegēre, aperire, patefacēre*.

disclosure, *patefactio, indicium*.

discolour, *decolorare*.

discomfit, *profligare, adfligēre*.

discomfiture, *clades*.

discomfort, *incommodum*.

disconcert, *percellēre, perturbare*.

disconsolate, *maestus*.

discontent, *molestia, taedium*.

discontinue, *interrumpēre, intermittēre, omittēre*.

discord, = disagreement, *dissensio, dissidium, discordia*.

discordant: in music, *dissonus, absonus*. = disagreeing, *discors, discrepans*.

discount, subst. *deductio, decessio*.

discountenance, *improbare, condemnare*.

discourage, *animum frangēre, infringēre*; to — from, *deterrēre, dissuadēre*.

discourse, subst., = conversation, *sermo, conloquium*; = set speech, *oratio, contio*.

discourse, v.: = to converse, *confabulari, conloqui*; = to make a speech, *orationem habēre, contionari*.

discourteous, *inurbanus, inlepidus*; adv. *inurbane, inlepide*.

discourtesy, *inurbanitas*.

discover, v. *invenire, reperire, cognoscēre*; see also disclose.

discoverer, *inventor*.

discovery, *inventio, investigatio*; = thing discovered, *inventum*.

discredit, subst., = disgrace, *dedecus (-oris, n.), ignominia*.

discreditable, *inhonestus, turpis*.

discreet, *prudens, cautus*; adv. *prudenter, caute*.

discretion, *prudentia, iudicium*.

discriminate, *diiudicare, discernēre, distinguēre*.

discrimination, *distinctio, discrimen*.

discursive, *varius, vagus*.

discuss, *disceptare, disputare, disserēre*.

discussion, *disceptatio, disputatio*.

disdain, subst. *fastidium, contemptio*.

disdain, v. *spernēre, fastidire, aspernari*.

disdainful, *fastidiosus*.

disease, *morbus*.

diseased, *aeger, aegrotus*.

disembark, v.: transit., *exponēre*; intransit., *egredi*.

disembarkation, *egressus (-ūs)*.

disengage, *solvēre, liberare*.

disengaged, *otiosus, vacuus*.

disentangle, *expedire, explicare*.

disfavour, *invidia, offensa*.

disfigure, *deformare.*

disfranchise, *civitatem adimĕre, suffra-gio privare.*

disgrace, *dedecus* (-oris, n.), *infamia, ignominia.*

disgrace, v. *dedecorare, dehonestare.*

disgraceful, *turpis, inhonestus, flagit-iosus;* adv. *turpiter, inhoneste, flagitiose.*

disguise, *vestis mutata, persona* (= mask); fig., *simulatio.*

disguise, v. *aliena veste occultare;* fig., *dissimulare.*

disgust, subst. *fastidium, taedium, satietas.*

disgust, v. *fastidium* (or *taedium*) *movĕre.*

disgusting, *foedus, molestus;* adv. *foede, moleste.*

dish, subst. *patina, lanx.*

dish, v.: to — up, *adponĕre.*

dishearten, *animum frangĕre.*

dishonest, *malus, improbus;* adv. *male, improbe.*

dishonesty, *improbitas, fraus.*

dishonour: see disgrace.

dishonourable, *inhonestus.*

disinclination, *declinatio, animus aversus.*

disinclined, *aversus;* to be —, *nolle.*

disinherit, *exheredare.*

disinherited, *exheres.*

disintegrate, v. transit. *dissolvĕre.*

disinter, *effodĕre, eruĕre.*

disinterested, *suae utilitatis immemor.*

disjoin, *disiungĕre, seiungĕre.*

disjointed, *incompositus;* adv. *incom-posite.*

disk, *orbis.*

dislike, subst. *odium, fastidium.*

dislike, v. *fastidire, abhorrĕre.*

dislocate, *extorquĕre, luxare.*

dislodge, (de)*pellĕre, expellĕre, deicĕre.*

disloyal, *improbus, infidus, infidelis.*

disloyalty, *infidelitas.*

dismal, *maestus, miser;* adv. *maeste, misere.*

dismantle, *nudare, diruĕre.*

dismast, *malo privare.*

dismay, *consternatio, pavor, terror.*

dismay, v. *consternare, pavefacĕre,* (per)*terrĕre.*

dismember, *discerpĕre.*

dismiss, *dimittĕre, ablegare.*

dismissal, *dimissio.*

dismount, *ex equo desilire.*

disobedience, *contumacia.*

disobey, *non parĕre.*

disoblige, *offendĕre.*

disorder, subst. *confusio, turba.*

disorder, v. (per)*turbare, miscĕre, confundĕre.*

disordered, =sick, *aeger.*

disorderly: =confused, *confusus,* (per)-*turbatus, perplexus, incompositus;* = insubordinate, *turbidus, turbulentus.*

disown, *repudiare, infitiari.*

disparage, *extenuare, elevare, obtrectare.*

disparagement, *obtrectatio.*

disparity, *dissimilitudo, differentia.*

dispassionate, *placidus, placatus, tran-quillus.*

dispatch: see despatch.

dispel, *discutĕre, dissipare, dispellĕre.*

dispense, *distribuĕre, dividĕre;* to — with, (di)*mittĕre.*

dispersal, *dissipatio, diffugium.*

disperse, v.: transit., *dissipare, disper-gĕre, dispellĕre;* intransit.. *dilabi, diffugĕre.*

displace, *loco* (suo) *movĕre.*

display, subst. *ostentatio.*

display, v. *ostentare, ostendĕre.*

displease, *displicĕre, offendĕre.*

displeasure, *offensio, offensa.*

disposal, *arbitrium:* at the — of, *penes* (with acc.).

dispose: = to arrange, *ordinare, con-stituĕre;* = to incline, *inclinare;* see also sell, use, and rid.

disposed, *inclinatus, propensus, pronus.*

disposition: = arrangement, *conlocatio, ordinatio;* = character, *ingenium, indoles, natura.*

dispossess, *possessione depellĕre.*

disproportion, *dissimilitudo.*

disproportionate, *impar.*

disprove, *refellĕre, redarguĕre.*

dispute, subst. *controversia, altercatio, rixa.*

dispute, v. *ambigĕre, disputare;* con-*tendĕre, rixari.*

disqualify, = hinder, *impedire.*

disquieted, *inquietus, sollicitus.*

disregard, subst., *neglegentia, incuria.*

disregard, v. *neglegĕre, omittĕre.*

disreputable, *infamis.*

disrepute, *infamia.*

disrespect, *insolentia.*

disrespectful, *insolens.*

dissatisfaction, *molestia, offensa, off-ensio.*

dissatisfied: I am —, *paenitet me* (with genit.).

dissatisfy, *displicĕre.*

dissect, *persecare.*

dissemble, *dissimulare.*

dissembler, *dissimulator.*

disseminate, *spargĕre, dispergĕre*

dissension, *discordia.*

dissent, subst *dissensio.*

dissent, v. *dissentire, dissidĕre.*

dissimilar, *dissimilis, dispar.*

dissimulation, *dissimulatio.*

dissipate, *dissipare.*

dissipated, *dissolutus, luxuriosus.*

dissipation, *luxuria, licentia.*

dissolute; see dissipated.

dissolution, *dissolutio.*

dissolve, v.: transit., *liquefacĕre,* (dis)-*solvĕre;* intransit., *liquescĕre,* (dis)-*solvi.*

dissonant, *dissonus, absonus.*

dissuade, *dissuadĕre, dehortari, deter-rĕre.*

dissuasion, *dissuasio.*

distaff, *colus. f.*

distance, subst. *spatium, intervallum;* at a —, *procul, longe;* from a —, *eminus.*

distance, v. *superare.*

distant, *remotus, longinquus;* to be —, *distare, abesse.*

distaste, *fastidium.*

distasteful, *molestus, ingratus.*

distemper, *morbus.*

distend, *distendĕre.*

distil, v. *stillare.*

distinct: = separate, *separatus, disiunctus;* = clear, *distinctus, clarus, perspicuus.* Adv. *distincte, clare, perspicue.*

distinction, *discrimen, distinctio;* honourable —, *honor, dignitas;* a mark of —, *insigne.*

distinctive, *proprius;* adv. *proprie.*

distinguish, *distinguĕre, secernĕre, diiudicare;* see also honour.

distinguished, *insignis (prae)clarus.*

distort, *detorquĕre, distorquĕre.*

distorted, *pravus.*

distract; = to make inattentive, *distrahĕre, distinĕre;* = to agitate, *(per)-turbare.*

distracted, distraught, *(per)turbatus, amens, vecors.*

distraction: see agitation, frenzy.

distrain, v. *bona vendĕre.*

distress, subst. *miseria, aerumna, labor.*

distress, v. *angĕre, vexare, sollicitare, adflictare.*

distressed, *sollicitus, anxius, adflictus;* to be —, *laborare.*

distressing, *gravis, acerbus.*

distribute, *distribuĕre, dividĕre.*

distribution, *distributio.*

district, *ager, regio, terra.*

distrust, subst. *diffidentia.*

distrust, v. *diffidĕre.*

distrustful, *suspiciosus, diffidens.*

disturb, *(per)turbare, commovĕre.*

disturbance, *turba, turbatio, tumultus (-ūs).*

disturber, *turbator.*

disunion, *dissensio, dissidium, discordia.*

disunite, *seiungere, secernĕre, disiungĕre.*

disused, *desuetus.*

ditch, *fossa.*

ditcher, *fossor.*

ditty, *nenia, carmen.*

diurnal, *diurnus.*

dive, *urinari, se (de)mergĕre.*

diver, *urinator.*

diverge, *decedĕre, discedĕre;* of roads, *in diversas partes ferre.*

divergence, *declinatio.*

diverse, *alius, diversus, dissimilis;* adv. *aliter, diverse, dissimiliter.*

diversify, *variare, distinguĕre.*

diversion: = turning aside, *derivatio, deductio;* = distracting, *avocatio;* = recreation, *oblectatio, oblectamentum.*

diversity, *diversitas, discrepantia.*

divert: = turn aside, *avertĕre;* = amuse, *delectare, oblectare;* see also distract.

divest, *nudare, spoliare, privare;* to — oneself of a thing, *exuĕre.*

divide: transit., *dividĕre, partiri, distribuĕre;* intransit., *dividi, discedĕre.*

divination, *divinatio, vaticinatio, auguratio.*

divine, adj. *divinus, caelestis;* adv. *divine, divinitus.*

divine, v. *divinare, vaticinari, augurari, coniectare.*

diviner, *haruspex, hariolus.*

divinity, *divinitas, numen.*

divisible, *dividuus.*
  vision, *partitio, divisio;* = part, *pars;* milit., *legio.*

divorce, subst. *divortium, repudium.*

divorce, v. *divortium facĕre.*

divulge, *(di)vulgare, (in medium) proferre, aperire, patefacĕre.*

dizziness, *vertigo.*

dizzy, *vertiginosus.*

do, *facĕre, efficĕre, agĕre, gerĕre:* how do you —? *quid agis?* he is done for, *de eo actum est.*

docile, *docilis.*

docility, *docilitas.*

dock, subst.: for ships, *navale;* in the —, *reus.*

dock, v.; see curtail.

doctor, subst. *medicus.*

doctor, v. *curare.*

doctrine, *dogma (-atis, n.), disciplina.*

document, *litterae (-arum), instrumentum.*

dodge, v. *eludĕre.*

doe, *cerva.*

doer, *actor, auctor.*

doff, *exuĕre.*

dog, subst. *canis;* of a —, *caninus.*

dog, v. *indagare, investigare.*

dogged, *pervicax, pertinax;* adv. *pertinaciter.*

dogma, *dogma, placitum.*

doing; see action.

dole, subst. *stips, diaria (-orum), sportula.*

dole, v.; see distribute.

doleful, *tristis, flebilis, maestus;* adv. *flebiliter, maeste.*

dolphin, *delphinus.*

dolt, *stipes, caudex, baro.*

domain: = kingdom, *regnum;* = estate, *possessio.*

dome, *tholus.*

domestic, subst.; see servant.

domestic, adj.; = of the home, *domesticus, familiaris, privatus;* = not foreign, *intestinus, domesticus.*

domesticate; see tame.

domicile, *domicilium, domus.*

dominate, *dominari, regnare.*

domination, *dominatio, dominatus (-ūs).*

domineer, *dominari.*

domineering, *imperiosus, superbus.*

dominion, *potestas, imperium, dicio;* of a king, *regnum.*

Don, *Tanais.*

donation, *donum.*

doom, subst. *fatum, sors.*

doom, v. *condemnare, damnare.*

door, *ostium, ianua;* back —, *posticum;* out of —s, *foras, foris.*

doorkeeper, *ianitor (f. ianitrix).*

doorpost, *postis.*

dormant: to lie —, *iacĕre.*

dormitory, *cubiculum.*

dormouse, *glis.*

dose, subst. *potio, medicamentum.*

dose, v. *medicamentum dare.*

dot, *punctum.*

dotage, *senium.*

dotard, *senex, delirus.*

dote, v.: to — upon, *deamare, deperire.*

double, adj. *duplex* (=twofold), *duplus* (=twice as much), *geminus* (= twin).

double, v. *duplicare;* = to sail round, *flectĕre, circumvehi.*

doublet, *tunica.*

double-tongued, *bilinguis.*

doubly, *bis, dupliciter.*

doubt, subst. *dubitatio, scrupulus.*

doubt, v. *dubitare, animi pendĕre.*

doubtful, adj. *dubius, incertus*; adv. *dubie, ambigue, dubitanter* (= doubtingly).

doubtless, *sine dubio.*

dough, *farina.*

doughty, *fortis, strenuus.*

dove, *columba.*

Dover, *Portus Dubris.*

dower, dowry, *dos.*

down, subst.: of feathers, etc., *pluma, lanugo*; = hill, *collis, clivus.*

down: prep., — from, *de*; — stream, *secundo flumine*; adv. rendered by compound verb with *de* —; see downwards.

downcast, *demissus, tristis, maestus.*

downfall, *(oc)casus (-ūs), ruina.*

downpour, *imber.*

downright, adj.: = complete, *merus, summus*; = straight-forward, *simplex.*

downright, adv. *prorsus, omnino.*

downtrodden, *adflictus.*

downwards, *desuper, deorsum.*

downy, *plumeus.*

doze, v. *dormitare.*

dozen, *duodecim.*

drab, *ravus*; see brown.

drag, v. *trahĕre.*

dragon, *draco, serpens.*

drain, subst. *fossa, cloaca.*

drain, v. *siccare, (ex)haurire.*

drama, *fabula.*

dramatic, *scaenicus.*

draper, *qui pannos vendit.*

draught: of drink, *haustus (-ūs), potio*; of air, *spiritus (-ūs), aura.*

draw, v. (1) transit., *trahĕre, ducĕre*; of fluids, *haurire*: to — a sword, *gladium (de)stringĕre*; to — tight, *adducĕre, adstringĕre*; = to portray by drawing, *describĕre, (de)pingĕre*; = to induce, *movĕre*; to — up (a document), *concipĕre*; to — up (troops) *instruĕre.* (2) intransit.: to — near, *accedĕre, appropinquare*; to — back, *recedĕre, se recipĕre.*

draw-bridge, *pons, ponticulus.*

drawer: of water, *aquarius*; chest of drawers, *armarium.*

drawing, *pictura.*

dray, *carrus, plaustrum.*

dread: see fear.

dream, subst. *somnium*; in a —, *in somno.*

dream, v. *somniare*; to — of, *vidēre in somnis.*

dreamy, *somniculosus.*

dreary, *tristis, miser*; adv. *misere.*

dregs, *faex.*

drench, *madefacĕre, perfundĕre.*

dress, subst. *vestis, vestitus (-ūs), ornatus (-ūs).*

dress, v. *vestire*; of food, *coquĕre*; of wounds, *curare.*

dressed, *vestitus*; — in black, *sordidatus*; — in white, *albatus.*

dressing, medic., *fomentum.*

drift, subst. = aim, *consilium, ratio.*

drift, v. *ferri, fluitare.*

drill, subst.: the tool, *terebra*; of troops, *exercitatio.*

drill, v.; = to bore, *perforare, terebrare*; = to train, *exercēre, exercitare.*

drink, subst. *potio, potus (-ūs).*

drink, v. *bibĕre, potare, haurire* (= drink up); to — to a person, *homini propinare.*

drinker, *potor, potator* (habitual).

drinking-bout, *potatio, comissatio.*

drip, *stillare.*

drive, subst. *gestatio.*

drive, v. (1) transit., *agĕre, pellĕre*; to — out, *expellĕre, exturbare*; = to force, *cogĕre, compellĕre.* (2) intransit.: in a carriage, etc., *(in)vehi, gestari*; to — at, *petĕre.*

drivel: see nonsense.

driver, *raedarius, auriga*; of animals, *agitator.*

drizzle, v. *leniter pluĕre.*

droll, *lepidus, ridiculus, facetus*; adv. *lepide, ridicule, facete.*

drone, *fucus.*

droop, v.: transit., *demittĕre*; intransit., *(de)pendēre*; = wither, *languescĕre, flaccescĕre.*

drop, subst. *gutta, stilla.*

drop, v.: transit., *demittĕre, deicĕre*; intransit., = fall in drops, *(de)stillare*; = fall to the ground, *delabi, decidĕre.*

dropsy, *hydrops.*

dross, = refuse; q.v.

drought, *siccitas.*

drove, *grex, armentum.*

drover, *pecuarius, armentarius.*

drown, *(in aquam) summergĕre*; with noise, *obstrepĕre.*

drowsy, *somniculosus, semisomnus.*

drudge, subst. *servus, mediastinus.*

drudge, v. *servire.*

drudgery, *opera servilis.*

drug, subst. *medicamentum*; poisonous —, *venenum.*

drum, *tympanum.*

drunk, *ebrius, temulentus.*

drunkenness, *ebrietas*; as habit, *ebriositas, vinolentia.*

dry, adj. *siccus, aridus, sitiens* (= thirsty). Transf., *exilis, ieiunus, aridus.* Adv., of style, *exiliter, ieiune.*

dry, v. transit. *siccare*; to — tears, *abstergĕre lacrimas*; intransit., *siccari, arescĕre.*

dryness, *siccitas.*

dubious; see doubtful.

duck, subst. *anas.*

duck, v. *(sub)mergĕre*; to — the head, *caput demittĕre.*

dudgeon, *ira, stomachus.*

due, subst. *ius (iuris), debitum*; —s, *vectigal*; harbour —, *portorium.*

due, adj. *debitus; meritus, iustus, idoneus.*

duel, *certamen.*

dulcimer, *sambuca.*

dull, adj. *hebes, obtusus, tardus*; = uninteresting, *aridus, frigidus.* Adv. *tarde, frigide.*

dull, v. *hebetare, obscurare, obtundĕre.*

dulness, of mind, *(ingenii) tarditas, stupor.*

dumb, *mutus*; to become —, *obmutescĕre.*

dumbfounder, *obstupefacĕre.*

dun, adj. *fucus, suffuscus.*

dunce, *stipes.*

dung, *stercus (-oris), fimus.*

dungeon, *carcer, robur.*

dunghill, *sterquilinium.*

dupe, subst. *homo credulus.*

duplicate; see copy.

duplicity, *allacia, fraus.*

durable, *firmus, stabilis, perpetuus;* adv. *firme, stabiliter.*

duration, *temporis spatium.*

during, *per* with acc.; *in* with abl.; *inter* with acc.

dusk, *crepusculum.*

dusky, *fuscus;* see dark.

dust, subst. *pulvis.*

dust, v. *detergĕre.*

dusty, *pulverulentus.*

dutiful, *pius, officiosus;* adv. *pie, officiose.*

dutifulness, *pietas.*

duty, *officium, munus;* sense of —, *pietas, religio;* —tax, *vectigal.*

dwarf, *nanus, pumilio.*

dwarfish, *pusillus.*

dwell, *habitare, (in)colĕre.*

dweller, *incola.*

dwelling, *domicilium, sedes, domus.*

dwindle, *(de)minui, decrescĕre.*

dye, v. *tingĕre, inficĕre.*

dyer, *infector.*

dynasty; use phrase with *domus.*

dyspepsia, *cruditas.*

dyspeptic, *crudus.*

E

each: of two, *uterque;* of three or more, *unusquisque, quisque, omnis;* — other, *inter se, alius alium.*

eager, *cupidus, studiosus, acer;* adv. *cupide, studiose, acriter.*

eagerness, *cupiditas, studium, ardor.*

eagle, *aquila.*

ear, *auris;* of corn, *spica, arista.*

early, adj. *matutinus* (= in the morning), *novus* (= fresh), *maturus, tempestivus* (= in good time).

early, adv. *mane* (in the morning); *mature, tempestive.*

earn, *merĕre* adj. *merĕri.*

earnest, adj. *intentus, gravis, serius;* in —, *serio.* Adv. *intente, impense.*

earnestness, *studium, contentio.*

earnings, *quaestus (-ūs), lucrum.*

earth: = soil, *terra, solum;* = the globe, *terra, orbis (terrarum).*

earthen, *terrenus.*

earthenware; adj., *fictilis;* subst. *fictilia (-ium).*

earthly, *terrestris; humanus.*

earthquake, *terrae motus (-ūs).*

earthwork, *agger.*

ease, subst. = rest, *tranquillitas, quies, otium, pax;* to be at ease, *quiescĕre;* = readiness, *facilitas.*

ease, v. *exonerare, expedire.*

easiness, *facilitas.*

east, subst. *oriens, orientis (solis) partes.*

eastern, easterly, *orientis; ad orientem versus.*

easy, *facilis;* = tranquil *tranquillus, quietus, otiosus.*

eat, *edĕre, (re)vesci;* to — away, *rodĕre.*

eatable, *esculentus.*

eating-house, *popina.*

eaves-dropper, *auceps.*

ebb, subst. *aestūs decessus (-ūs).*

ebb, v. *recedĕre.*

ebony, *hebenus.*

Ebro, *Hiberus.*

ebullition: use *effervescĕre;* of passions, *impetus (-ūs), aestus (-ūs).*

eccentric, *inusitatus.*

echo, subst. *imago vocis.*

echo, v. *vocem reddĕre, resonare;* see also imitate.

eclipse, subst. *defectio, defectus (-ūs).*

eclipse, v. transit. *obscurare.*

economical, *frugi, parcus;* adv. *parce.*

economy: = management, in gen., *rei familiaris administratio;* = frugality, *parsimonia.*

ecstasy: = frenzy, *insania, furor;* = bliss, *elatio voluptaria.*

ecstatic, *fanaticus, furens, insanus.*

eddy, *vertex.*

edge, a cutting —, *acies;* = margin, *margo, ora.*

edible, *esculentus.*

edict, *edictum, decretum, iussum*

edify, *docĕre.*

edit, *(librum) edĕre.*

educate, *instituĕre, erudire, educare.*

education, *educatio, disciplina, eruditio.*

eel, *anguilla.*

efface, *delĕre, abolēre.*

effect, subst. (1), = consequence, *effectus (-ūs), eventus (-ūs), consecutio.* (2), = influence, *vis, effectus (-ūs);* without —, *frustra;* in —, *revera, reapse.* (3), —s, = property, *res, bona (-orum).*

effect, v. *facĕre, efficĕre, conficĕre.*

effective, effectual, *efficiens, efficax;* adv. *efficienter, efficaciter.*

effeminacy, *mollitia, mollities.*

effeminate, *mollis, effeminatus;* adv. *molliter, effeminate.*

effervesce, *effervescĕre.*

effete, *effetus, obsoletus.*

efficacy, *efficientia, vis.*

effigy, *effigies, imago, simulacrum.*

effort, *opera, labor, conatus (-ūs);* to make an —, *operam dare, contendĕre.*

effrontery, *impudentia, os (impudens).*

effulgence, *splendor, fulgor.*

egg, *ovum.*

egoism, egotism, *sui ostentatio, sui amor.*

egoist, egotist, *qui sibi soli studet.*

egregious, *singularis, praeclarus.*

egress, *egressus (-ūs), exitus (-ūs).*

eight, adj. *octo;* — each, *octoni;* — times, *octies.*

eighteen, *duodeviginti.*

eighteenth, *duodevicesimus.*

eighth, *octavus;* an —, *octava pars.*

eightieth, *octogesimus.*

eighty, *octoginta;* — each, *octogeni;* — times, *octogies.*

either, *alteruter, utervis, uterlibet;* either . . . or, *aut . . . aut, vel. . . . vel.*

ejaculate, *vocem emittĕre.*
ejaculation, *vox.*
eject, *expellĕre, eicĕre, deicĕre.*
ejection, *expulsio, eiectio, deiectio.*
eke, v.: to — out, *rei* (dat.) *parcĕre.*
elaborate, adj. *elaboratus, exquisitus;* adv. *exquisite.*
elaborate, v. *elaborare, expolire.*
elapse, *intercedĕre, praeterire.*
elated, v. *elatus.*
elation, *animus elatus; gaudium.*
Elbe, *Albis.*
elbow, *cubitum.*
elder, *maior* (natu).
elderly, *aetate provectus.*
elect, adj. *designatus.*
elect, v. *creare, legĕre, eligĕre.*
election, *electio;* as an occasion, *comitia* (-orum).
electioneering, subst. *ambitio.*
elective, *suffragiis creatus.*
elector, *qui ius suffragii habet.*
elegance, *elegantia, venustas.*
elegant, *elegans, venustus, nitidus;* adv. *eleganter, venuste, nitide.*
elegy, *elegia* (-orum).
element: scientific, *elementum;* =part, *membrum; pars;* the —s of a subject, *elementa* (-orum), *principia* (-orum).
elementary, *primus.*
elephant, *elephantus, elephas.*
elevate, *(at)tollĕre, extollĕre.*
elevated, of places, *editus, altus;* of spirits, *elatus.*
elevation: = raising, *elatio;* of spirits, *elatio, altitudo;* = rising ground, *locus editus* or *superior.*
eleven, *undecim;* — each *undeni;* — times, *undecies.*
eleventh, *undecimus.*
elicit, *elicĕre, evocare.*
eligible, *opportunus, idoneus, dignus.*
elk, *alces.*
ell, *ulna, cubitum.*
elm, *ulnus.*
elocution, *pronuntiatio.*
elongate; see lengthen.
elope, *clam fugĕre.*
eloquence, *eloquentia, facundia.*
eloquent, *eloquens, facundus;* adv. *facunde, diserte.*
else, adj. *alius.*
else, adv.: = besides, *praeterea;* = otherwise, *aliter, alioqui(n).*
elsewhere, *alibi.*
elucidate; see explain.
elude, *(e)vitare, declinare.*
elusive, *fallax.*
Elysian, *Elysius.*
Elysium, *Elysium.*
emaciate, *attenuare, macerare.*
emaciated, *macer.*
emaciation, *macies.*
emanate, *emanare, effundi.*
emancipate, *liberare;* of slaves, *manumittĕre.*
emancipation, *liberatio;* of slaves, *manumissio.*
emancipator, *liberator.*
embalm, *condire.*
embankment, *agger, moles.*
embark, v.: transit., *imponĕre in navem;* intransit. *conscendĕre (navem).*

embarrass, *(con)turbare, impedire.*
embarrassing, *difficilis.*
embarrassment, *implicatio, conturbatio;* financial —, *angustiae* (-arum).
embassy, *legatio, legati* (-orum).
embellish, *(ex)ornare, decorare.*
embellishment, *decus* (-oris, n.), *ornamentum.*
embers, *cinis, favilla.*
embezzle, *avertĕre, supprimĕre.*
embezzlement, *peculatus* (-ūs), *suppressio.*
embezzler, *pecuniae aversor.*
embitter, *exacerbare.*
emblem, *insigne, signum.*
embody: to — troops, *milites conscribĕre;* = to include, *includĕre.*
emboss, *caelare.*
embrace, subst. *amplexus* (-ūs), *complexus* (-ūs).
embrace, v. *amplecti, amplexari, complecti;* = to contain, *comprehendĕre;* to — an opportunity, *occasionem capĕre;* to — an opinion, *in sententiam transire.*
embrocation, *fomentum.*
embroider, *(acu) pingĕre.*
embroil, *conturbare;* to — in a matter, *re implicare.*
emend, *emendare, corrigĕre.*
emendation, *emendatio.*
emerald, *smaragdus.*
emerge, *emergĕre, exsistĕre.*
emergency, *casus* (-ūs), *discrimen.*
emigrate, *(e)migrare, demigrare.*
emigration, *(e)migratio.*
eminence: = high ground, *locus editus, tumulus;* =distinction, *praestantia, fastigium.*
eminent, *insignis, (prae)clarus, egregius.* Adv. *egregie, praecipue, imprimis.*
emissary, *legatus, emissarius.*
emit, *(e)mittĕre, iacĕre.*
emolument, *emolumentum, lucrum.*
emotion, *animi motus* (-ūs) or *adfectus* (-ūs).
emperor, *imperator, princeps.*
emphasis, *vis.*
emphatic, *gravis, vehemens;* adv. *graviter, vehementer.*
empire, *imperium, principatus* (-ūs).
employ, *(re) uti; (rem) usurpare, exercēre, adhibēre;* of persons, to be —ed, *detineri, versari.*
employment: as an act, *usus* (-ūs), *usurpatio;* = business, *res, negotium.*
emptiness, *inanitas.*
empty, adj. *inanis, vacuus, vanus, cassus.*
empty, v. *vacuefacĕre, exinanire.*
emulate, *aemulari.*
emulation, *aemulatio.*
emulous, *aemulus;* adv. *certatim.*
enable, *homini rei* (genit.) *facultatem facĕre.*
enact, *(legem) sancire, iubĕre, statuĕre, constituĕre.*
enactment; see law.
enamoured; see love.
encamp, v. *castra ponĕre, ponĕre.*
enchant, *(ef)fascinare.* Transf., *capĕre, delectare.*
enchantment; see charm.
enchantress, *venefica.*

encircle, *cingĕre, circumdare.*

enclose, *includĕre, saepire, continēre.*

enclosure, *saeptum, saepimentum.*

encomium, *laus, laudatio.*

encompass; see encircle.

encounter, subst. *congressus (-ūs), concursio.*

encounter, v. *concurrĕre, congredi, obviam fieri;* = to face unwelcome things, *obire, oppetĕre.*

encourage, *(ad)hortari, confirmare, erigĕre.*

encouragement, *confirmatio, (ad)hortatio.*

encroach, v.: to — on, *occupare, invadĕre.*

encroachment, *iniuria.*

encumber, *onerare, praegravare, impedire.*

encumbrance, *onus (-eris, n.), impedimentum.*

end, subst.: = termination, *finis, exitus (-ūs);* in the —, *tandem, denique;* = aim, object, *finis, consilium, propositum.*

end, v.: transit., *finire, conficĕre, terminare;* intransit., *finem habēre, desinĕre;* to — well, *bene evenire.*

endanger, *in periculum adducĕre, periclitari.*

endear, *devincire.*

endearments, *blanditiae (-arum, plur.).*

endeavour, subst. *conatus (-ūs), nisus (-ūs).*

endeavour, v. *conari, (e)niti.*

endless, *infinitus, aeternus, perpetuus;* adv. *sine fine, perpetuo.*

endorse; see allow, sanction.

endow: to — a daughter, *dotem filiae dare;* see also give.

endowed, *ornatus, praeditus, instructus.*

endurable, *tolerabilis, patibilis.*

endurance, *patientia, perpessio.*

endure: = to bear, *(per)ferre, sustinēre, pati, perpeti;* = to last, *(per)manēre, durare.*

enemy, *hostis* (public), *inimicus* (personal or private); *adversarius.*

energetic, *acer, strenuus, impiger;* adv. *acriter, strenue, impigre.*

energy, *vis, impetus (-ūs), contentio.*

enervate, *enervare, debilitare, (e)mollire.*

enervation, *debilitatio, languor.*

enforce, *exsequi.*

enfranchise, *in civitatem adscribĕre; civitate donare.*

enfranchisement, *civitas, civitatis donatio.*

engage: = to bind, make liable, *obligare, obstringĕre;* = to promise, undertake, *spondēre, promittĕre, recipĕre;* = to join battle, *confligĕre, congredi.*

engaged: = busy, *occupatus;* — to be married, *sponsus, pactus.*

engagement: = promise, *sponsio, pactum, pactio, promissum;* an — to marry, *pactio nuptialis;* = piece of business, *negotium;* = battle *pugna, proelium.*

engaging, *blandus, suavis.*

engender, *gignĕre, generare.*

engine, *machina, machinatio, machinamentum.*

engineer, *machinator, faber.*

England, *Anglia; Britannia* (= Britain).

English, *Anglus, Anglicus; Britannus, Britannicus.*

engrave, *incidĕre, insculpĕre, scalpĕre.*

engraver, *scalptor.*

engross: = occupy exclusively, *occupare, tenēre.*

engulf, *absorbēre, (de)vorare, (ex)haurire.*

enhance, *augēre, amplificare.*

enhancement, *amplificatio.*

enigma, *aenigma (-atis, n.), ambages (-um).*

enigmatic, *obscurus, ambiguus;* adv. *ambigue, per ambages.*

enjoin; see command.

enjoy, *(re) frui, gaudēre;* = to have, *uti, habēre.*

enjoyment, *gaudium, voluptas.*

enlarge, *amplificare, dilatare, augēre;* to — upon, *pluribus (verbis) disputare.*

enlighten, *inlustrare, inluminare.* Transf., *docēre, erudire.*

enlightenment, *humanitas.*

enlist, v.: transit., of troops, *(con)scribĕre;* in gen., = win over, *conciliare;* intransit., *nomen dare.*

enliven, *excitare, exhilarare.*

enmity, *inimicitia, odium, simultas.*

ennoble, *nobilium ordini adscribĕre; ornare, honestare.*

ennui, *taedium.*

enormity, *immanitas;* = monstrous action, *scelus (-eris, n.), flagitium.*

enormous, *ingens, immanis;* adv. *praeter modum.*

enough, *sat, satis, adfatim;* more than —, *nimis;* not —, *parum.*

enquire; see ask; to — into, *quaerĕre, inquirĕre, cognoscĕre.*

enquiry, *quaestio, inquisitio, cognitio.*

enrage, *inritare, exasperare.*

enrich, *locupletare, ditare.*

enroll, *(ad)scribĕre;* see enlist.

enshrine, *dedicare, consecrare.*

ensign: = banner, *signum, vexillum;* = banner-bearer, *signifer, aquilifer.*

enslave, *(hominem) in servitutem redigĕre.*

enslaved, *servus.* Transf., *addictus, emancipatus.*

ensnare, *capĕre, inretire, inlicĕre.*

entail, *adferre, inferre;* see cause.

entangle, *impedire, implicare.*

entanglement, *implicatio.*

enter, *intrare, introire, inire, ingredi;* to — upon an undertaking, *ingredi, inire, suscipĕre, incipĕre;* to — public life, *ad rempublicam accedĕre;* to — an alliance, *societatem facĕre.*

enterprise, *inceptum, opus (-eris, n.).*

enterprising, *promptus, acer, audax.*

entertain: = to have, *habēre;* = to amuse, *delectare, oblectare;* = to receive hospitably, *hospitio accipĕre, excipĕre.*

entertaining; see amusing.

entertainment: = hospitality, *hospitium;* = banquet, *epulae (-arum) convivium.*

enthusiasm, *studium, fervor, ardor.*

enthusiastic, *fanaticus, ardens, fervidus*; adv. *ardenter, acriter.*

entice, *adlicĕre, adlectare, inlicĕre.*

enticement, *inlecebrae, esca.*

enticing, *blandus.*

entire, *totus, integer, solidus.* Adv. *omnino, plane, prorsus, penitus.*

entitle: = to name, *appellare, nominare*; = to give a title to, *ius or potestatem dare.*

entrails, *intestina* (-orum), *viscera* (-um).

entrance, subst.: as act, *ingressio, introitus* (-ūs); = place of —, *aditus* (-ūs), *introitus* (-ūs), *ostium.*

entrap; see ensnare.

entreat, *precari, rogare, orare, obsecrare.*

entrench, *fossā* (com)*munire, vallare.*

entrenchment, *vallum, munitio, munimentum.*

entrust, (con)*credĕre, committĕre, mandare, commendare.*

entry; see entrance; in accounts, *nomen.*

entwine, (in)*nectĕre, implicare, redimire.*

enumerate, (di)*numerare, enumerare.*

enunciate, *edicĕre, pronuntiare, enuntiare.*

enunciation, *enuntiatio.*

envelope, subst. *involucrum.*

envelope, v. *involvĕre, obducĕre.*

envenom, *venenare, veneno imbuĕre.*

enviable, *fortunatus, beatus.*

envious, *invidus, lividus.*

environs, render by phrase with *loca* and *circum.*

envoy, *legatus.*

envy, subst. *invidia, livor.*

envy, v. *invidĕre.*

ephemeral, *unius diei, caducus, brevis.*

epic, *epicus, heroïcus*; an — poem, *epos.*

Epicurean, *Epicureus;* = hedonist, *voluptarius.*

epidemic, *morbus, pestilentia.*

epigram, *epigramma* (-atis, n.).

epigrammatic, *salsus.*

epilepsy, *morbus comitialis.*

epilogue, *epilogus.*

episode, *embolium, excursus* (-ūs).

epistle, *epistula, litterae* (-arum).

epitaph, *titulus, elogium.*

epitome, *epitome, summarium.*

epoch, *tempus* (-oris, n.), *aetas, saeculum.*

equability, *aequus animus, aequabilitas.*

equable, *aequus, aequabilis*; adv. *aequo animo, aequabiliter.*

equal, subst. *par, compar.*

equal, adj. *aequus, aequalis, par, compar*; adv. *aeque, aequaliter, pariter.*

equal, v. (ad)*aequare, aequiparare.*

equality, *aequalitas, aequabilitas.*

equalize, (ex)*aequare, adaequare.*

equanimity, *aequus animus, aequitas animi.*

equestrian, subst. *eques* (-itis).

equestrian, adj. *equester or equestris.*

equidistant, to be, *pari intervallo inter se distare.*

equilateral, *aequis lateribus.*

equilibrium, *aequilibrium*; to hold in —, *librare.*

equinox, *aequinoctium.*

equip, *armare, instruĕre, ornare.*

equipment, *arma* (-orum), *armamenta* (-orum), *armatura.*

equitable, adj. *aequus, iustus, meritus.*

equity, *aequitas, aequum, iustitia.*

equivalent; see equal.

equivocal, *ambiguus, anceps, dubius.*

equivocate, *tergiversari.*

equivocation, *ambiguitas.*

era, *tempus.*

eradicate, *extirpare, evellĕre, eruĕre.*

erase, *delēre, inducĕre.*

erasure, *litura.*

ere; see before.

erect, adj. (e)*rectus.*

erect, v. *erigĕre, tollĕre*; = build, *aedificare, exstruĕre.*

erection: as act, *aedificatio, exstructio*; = a building, *aedificium.*

erotic, *amatorius.*

err, *errare, vagari; falli* (= be mistaken); *peccare or delinquĕre* (= do wrong).

errand, *mandatum.*

erratic, *vagus, inconstans.*

erroneous, *falsus*; adv. *falso, perperam.*

error, *error, erratum; peccatum* (= sin).

erst, *quondam, olim.*

erudite, *litteratus, doctus, eruditus.*

erudition, *doctrina, eruditio.*

eruption, *eruptio.*

escape, subst. *fuga, effugium.*

escape, v. (ef)*fugĕre, elabi, evadĕre.*

escarpment, *vallum.*

eschew, *vitare;* see avoid.

escort, *comitatus* (-ūs); under a person's —, *homine comitante.*

escort, v. *comitari, deducĕre, prosequi.*

esoteric, *arcanus, occultus.*

especial, *praecipuus*; adv. *praesertim, praecipue, maxime.*

espouse; see betroth and marry.

essay, subst.: = attempt, *conatus* (-ūs); = treatise, *libellus.*

essay, v. *conari.*

essence, *natura, vis.*

essential, *verus, proprius*; adv. *reapse, vere, necessario.*

establish: = set up, *statuĕre, instituĕre*; = make strong, *confirmare, stabilire*; = prove, *probare, vincĕre.*

establishment, *constitutio, confirmatio*; = household, *familia.*

estate: = condition, *status* (-ūs), *habitus* (-ūs), *condicio, sors*; = property, *res, fundus, praedium.*

esteem, subst. *opinio, existimatio.*

esteem, v.: = think, *existimare, putare*; = respect, *diligĕre, vereri.*

estimable, *bonus, gravis, probus.*

estimate, subst. *aestimatio*; in gen., = judgment, *iudicium.*

estimate, v., = value, *aestimare, censēre.*

estimation; see esteem.

estrange, (ab)*alienare.*

estrangement, *alienatio, discidium.*

estuary, *aestuarium.*

eternal, *aeternus, sempiternus, perpetuus*; adv. *in aeternum, perpetuo.*

eternity, *aeternitas.*

ether, *aether.*

ethereal, *aetherius.*

ethical, *moralis;* or use phrase with *mores.*

ethics, *philosophia moralis*; see ethical.

etiquette, *mos, usus (-ūs).*

eulogy, *laudatio, laus.*

euphemism; render by phrase, such as *mitiorem in partem vertĕre dicendo.*

euphony, *sonus dulcis.*

evacuate, *vacuefacĕre, (de)relinquĕre; loco discedĕre.*

evade, *(ef)fugĕre, subterfugĕre.*

evaporate, *in vaporem vertĕre.*

evasion, *ambages (-um), tergiversatio.*

evasive, *ambiguus;* adv. *ambigue.*

even, adj. *aequus, planus;* of numbers, *par.* Adv. *aequaliter, pariter.*

even, adv. *etiam, vel, adeo:* not —, *ne . . . quidem;* — if, *etsi, etiamsi.*

evening, subst. *vesper (-eris* or *-eri);* in the —, *vesperi.*

evening, adj. *vespertinus;* the — star, *Hesperus, Vesper.*

evenness, *aequalitas;* of temper, *aequus animus.*

event: = result, *eventus (-ūs), exitus (-ūs);* = occurrence, *factum, casus (-ūs):* at all —s, *certe, saltem.*

eventful, *memorabilis.*

ever, adv.: = always, *semper;* = at any time, *umquam (unquam), quando* (after *num* and *si);* for —, *in aeternum, in perpetuum.*

everlasting; see eternal.

every, *quisque, omnis:* — one, *unusquisque;* one in — ten, *decimus quisque;* — body, *omnes (-ium), nemo non;* — day, *quotidie;* — thing, *omnia (-ium);* — where, *ubique, passim.*

evict, *(ex)pellĕre, detrudĕre.*

evidence: legal, *testimonium, indicium;* in gen., *argumentum.*

evident, *manifestus, apertus;* it is —, *apparet, liquet.* Adv. *aperte, manifesto.*

evil, subst. *malum, incommodum.*

evil, adj. *malus, pravus, improbus.*

evil-doer, *maleficus.*

evil-speaking, *maledicus.*

evince, *ostendĕre, probare, praestare.*

evoke, *evocare, elicĕre, excitare.*

evolution: — of soldiers, *decursus (-ūs);* in nature, *rerum progressio.*

ewe, *ovis femina;* — lamb, *agna.*

ewer, *urceus, hydria, urna.*

exact, *exactus, subtilis, diligens;* adv. *diligenter, accurate, subtiliter.*

exacting, *rapax.*

exaction, *exactio.*

exactitude, *subtilitas, diligentia.*

exaggerate, *augēre, in maius extollĕre.*

exaggeration, *superlatio, traiectio.*

exalt, *augēre, amplificare, (ex)tollĕre.*

exaltation: of feeling, *elatio;* in rank, *dignitatis accessio.*

exalted, *altus, (ex)celsus, elatus.*

examination, *investigatio, inquisitio.*

examine, *investigare, inquirĕre.*

example, *exemplum, exemplar, documentum;* for —, *verbi causa, exempli gratia, vel.*

exasperate. *inritare, exasperare.*

exasperation, *ira.*

excavate, *(ex)cavare, effodĕre.*

excavation, *cavum.*

exceed, *excedĕre, egredi.*

excel, *excellĕre, praestare* (with dat).

excellence, *excellentia, praestantia.*

excellent, *excellens, praestans, egregius, optimus;* adv. *excellenter, egregie, optime.*

except, prep. *praeter, extra;* except you, *te excepto.*

except, v. *excipĕre, eximĕre.*

exception, *exceptio;* all without —, *omnes ad unum.*

exceptional, *rarus;* adv. *praeter modum.*

excess: — in quantity, *nimium;* in conduct, *intemperantia, licentia.*

excessive, *nimius, immodicus;* adv. *nimis, immodice, praeter modum.*

exchange, subst. *permutatio;* of money, *collybus.*

exchange, v. *(per)mutare.*

exchequer, *aerarium, fiscus.*

excitable, *inritabilis, fervidus.*

excite, *excitare, concitare, (com)movēre, incendĕre.*

excited, *trepidus.*

excitement, *concitatio, commotio.*

exclaim, *(ex)clamare, vociferari.*

exclamation, *exclamatio, vox.*

exclude, *excludĕre, prohibēre, arcēre.*

exclusive: of persons, *rari aditūs;* of properties, = belonging to one only, *proprius.*

excrescence, *tuber.*

excruciating, *acerbissimus.*

exculpate, *excusare, (ex)purgare*

exculpation, *purgatio.*

excursion, *iter (-ineris).*

excuse, subst. *excusatio.*

excuse, v.: = make excuses for, *excusare, (ex)purgare;* = pardon, *ignoscĕre, veniam dare.*

execrable; see abominable.

execrate, *exsecrari, detestari, abominari.*

execute: = carry out, *exsequi, persequi, efficĕre;* = punish by death, *necare, securi ferire.*

execution: = carrying out, *effectio;* = capital punishment, *supplicium;* = slaughter, in gen., *strages, caedes.*

executioner, *carnifex.*

executive: use phrase with *administrare.*

exegesis, *explanatio, interpretatio.*

exemplary, adj.; see excellent.

exempt, adj. *immunis, liber, solutus.*

exempt, v. *excipĕre, eximĕre, liberare.*

exemption, *immunitas.*

exercise, subst. *exercitatio;* = literary task, *thema (-atis).*

exercise, v.: = carry on, *exercēre, facĕre, efficĕre;* = work, train, *exercēre.*

exert, v. *contendĕre, intendĕre;* to — oneself, *niti, eniti, conari.*

exertion, *contentio, conatus (-ūs).*

Exeter, *Isca (Dumnoniorum).*

exhale, *(ex)halare.*

exhalation, *exhalatio.*

exhaust, *exhaurire;* = wear out, *consumĕre, conficĕre.*

exhausted, *confectus, defessus, fatigatus.*

exhaustion; see fatigue.

exhibit, v. *proponĕre, exhibēre;* see show.

exhibition, *spectaculum, ludi* (-*orum*).

exhilarate, (*ex*)*hilarare, hilarem facĕre.*

exhilaration, *hilaritas.*

exhort, (*ad*)*hortari.*

exigence, *necessitas, angustiae* (-*arum*).

exile, subst.: = banishment, *exsilium, relegatio;* to be in —, *exsulare;* = person banished, *exsul.*

exile, v. *eicĕre, relegare,* (*ex*)*pellĕre.*

exist, *esse, existĕre, exstare.*

existence; use *esse.*

exit: = going out, *exitus* (-*ūs*); = way out, *exitus* (-*ūs*), *ostium.*

exonerate, (*culpa*) *liberare.*

exorbitant, *immodicus;* adv. *immodice.*

exordium, *exordium, prooemium.*

exotic, *peregrinus, externus.*

expand, v. transit. (*ex*)*pandĕre, extendĕre, laxare.*

expanse, *spatium.*

expatiate, *pluribus* (*verbis*) *disputare.*

expatriate; see banish.

expect, *exspectare, sperare.*

expectant, *adrectus, suspensus.*

expectation, *exspectatio, spes.*

expectorate, *exscreare, exspuĕre.*

expediency, *utilitas.*

expedient, subst. *ratio, consilium.*

expedient, adj. *commodus, utilis:* it is —, *expedit.*

expedite, *expedire, maturare.*

expedition: = speed, *celeritas;* milit., *expeditio.*

expeditious, *celer, promptus;* adv. *celeriter, prompte.*

expel, (*ex*)*pellĕre, eicĕre.*

expend, *expendĕre, impendĕre.*

expense, *impensa, impendium.*

expensive, *sumptuosus, carus, pretiosus;* adv. *sumptuose, pretiose.*

expenditure, of public money, *erogatio;* see also expense.

experience, subst. *rerum usus* (-*ūs*), *experientia;* I speak from —, *expertus dico.*

experience, v. *experiri, pati.*

experienced, (*rerum*) *peritus.*

experiment, *experimentum, periculum.*

expert, *sciens, callidus, peritus.*

expertness, expertise, *calliditas, peritia.*

expiate, *luere, expiare.*

expiation, *expiatio, poena, piaculum.*

expiatory, *piacularis.*

expire, *exspirare;* of time, *exire.*

explain, *exponĕre, explicare, interpretari.*

explanation, *explicatio, interpretatio.*

explicit, *apertus, definitus;* adv. *plane, definite.*

explode: = to discredit (a theory), *explodĕre, refellĕre, confutare;* intransit., = to burst, *dirumpi.*

export, *exportare.*

exportation, *exportatio.*

exports, *merces* (*quae exportantur*).

expose, *exponĕre;* to danger, etc., *obicĕre, offerre;* = to unmask, *detegĕre.*

exposition, *expositio.*

expound; see explain.

express, (in words), *significare, declarare;* to — oneself, *loqui, dicĕre.*

expression: = thing said, *verbum, sententia, dictum, vox;* of the features, *vultus* (-*ūs*).

expressive, *significans;* adv. *significanter.*

expressiveness, *vis.*

expulsion, *exactio, expulsio.*

expunge, *delere, oblitterare.*

expurgate, (*ex*)*purgare.*

exquisite, *exquisitus, venustus;* adv. *exquisite, venuste.*

extant: to be —, *exstare.*

extempore, *subitus;* to speak —, *ex tempore dicĕre.*

extend, v.; transit., *extendĕre, augēre, amplificare;* intransit., *patēre, extendi.*

extensive, *magnus, amplus, latus;* adv. *late.*

extent, *ambitus* (-*ūs*), *spatium;* to this —, *hactenus;* to a certain —, *aliqua ex parte.*

extenuate, *levare, mitigare, minuĕre.*

extenuation, *imminutio.*

exterior, subst. *forma, species.*

exterior, adj.; see external.

exterminate, *ad unum interficĕre; eradicare, exstirpare.*

extermination, *internecio, occidio.*

external, *externus exter*(*us*), *exterior;* adv. *extrinsecus.*

extinct, *exstinctus, obsoletus.*

extinction, *exstinctio.*

extinguish, *exstinguĕre, restinguĕre.*

extirpate, *exstirpare, eradicare, excidĕre.*

extol, *laudibus,* (*ef*)*ferre,* (*con*)*laudare.*

extort, *exprimĕre, extorquĕre.*

extortion, *res repetundae.*

extortionate, *rapax, avarus.*

extra, adv. *praeterea.*

extract, v. *extrahĕre, evellĕre, exprimĕre;* from a book, *excerpĕre.*

extraction: as act, *evulsio;* = origin, *origo, genus* (-*eris,* n.).

extraneous; see external.

extraordinary, *inusitatus, insolitus, novus, mirus.* Adv. *extra ordinem, praeter morem, mire.*

extravagance: in expenditure, *sumptus* (-*ūs*); in gen., = excess, *intemperantia, immoderatio.*

extravagant: = lavish, *prodigus, sumptuosus;* in gen., = excessive, *nimius, immoderatus, intemperans.* Adv. *prodige, sumptuose; immoderate, intemperanter.*

extreme, subst.; see extremity.

extreme, adj. *extremus, ultimus, summus.* Adv. *summe;* often rendered by superl.

extremity: = top, *cacumen, fastigium;* = farthest part, *extremus;* or extreme degree, render by adj. *extremus.*

extricate, *expedire,* (*ex*)*solvĕre.*

extrude, *extrudĕre, eicĕre.*

exuberance, *ubertas, luxuria.*

exuberant, *luxuriosus, laetus;* adv. *uberrime.*

exude, (*ex*)*sudare, manare.*

exult, *exsultare, gestire, laetari.*

exultant, *laetus.*

exultation, *laetatio, exsultatio.*

eye, subst. *oculus, ocellus.*

eye, v. *adspicĕre, contemplari, intuēri.*

eye-ball, *pupula.*
eye-brow, *supercilium.*
eye-lid, *palpebra* (usually plur.)
eyesight, *acies.*
eye-witness, *arbiter, spectator et testis.*

F

fable, *fabula (commenticia).*
fabled, fabulous, *fabulosus, fictus, commenticius.*
fabric: built, *aedificium;* woven, *textum, textile;* fig., *compages.*
fabricate, *fabricari, texĕre.*
fabrication: = making, *fabricatio;* = falsehood, *commentum, mendacium.*
fabricator, *auctor.*
face, subst. *facies, vultus (-ūs), os (oris);* — to —, *coram.*
face, v.: = to be opposite, (*a*)*spectare;* = to encounter, *obire, obviam ire.*
facetious, *iocosus, facetus;* adv. *iocose, facete.*
facetiousness, *facetiae (-arum).*
facilitate, *faciliorem reddĕre.*
facility, *facilitas.*
facing, *contra, adversus.*
facsimile, *descriptio imagoque.*
fact, *res, factum;* in —, *reapse, sane.*
faction, *factio, pars.*
factious, *factiosus, seditiosus;* adv. *per factionem, seditiose.*
factiousness, *factio, studium partium.*
factitious; see false.
factory, *fabrica, officina.*
faculty, *vis, facultas.*
fade, *pallescĕre.*
faded; see pale.
fading, = transient, *caducus, fluxus.*
fagot, *fascis, sarmenta (-orum,* plur.).
fail, subst.: without —, *certo, omnino.*
fail, v.: = to give out, *deficĕre, deesse;* = not to succeed, *concidĕre, cadĕre;* transit., *deficĕre, deserĕre, destituĕre.*
failing, *peccatum, vitum.*
failure, *defectio.*
fain: I would — do, *velim facĕre, libens faciam.*
faint, adj. *languidus, defessus.*
faint, v. *conlabi,* (*animo*) *linqui.*
faint-hearted, *timidus.*
faintness, *languor.*
fair, subst. *nundinae (-arum).*
fair, adj.: = beautiful, *pulcher, venustus, formosus;* of weather, *serenus;* = favourable, *secundus, idoneus;* morally, *aequus, iustus;* = moderately good, *mediocris.* Adv., *aeque, iuste; mediocriter.*
fairness: = beauty, *pulchritudo, forma, venustas;* = justice, *iustitia, aequitas.*
fairy, *nympha.*
faith: = fidelity, *fides, fidilitas, pietas;* = belief, *opinio, persuasio, fides;* to have — in, *credĕre, confidĕre.*
faithful, *fidelis, fidus;* adv. *fideliter.*
faithfulness, *fidelitas, fides, constantia.*
faithless, *perfidus;* adv. *perfide.*
faithlessness, *perfidia, infidelitas.*
fall, subst. *casus (-ūs), lapsūs (-us);* = ruin, *ruina, excidium;* = lessening, *deminutio.*

fall, v. *cadĕre, decidĕre, ruĕre;* to — dead, *cadĕre, concidĕre, occidĕre;* of a city, *expugnari, capi;* to — back, = retreat, *pedem referre;* to — back on, *recurrĕre* or *confugĕre ad;* to — upon, = attack, *invadĕre, incurrĕre;* to — out, = happen, *evenire;* = disagree, *dissentire, dissidĕre.*
fallacious, *fallax, falsus;* adv. *fallaciter, falso.*
fallacy, *vitium, captio.*
fallible, *errori obnoxius.*
fallow: the field lies —, *ager cessat;* — ground, *novalis.*
false, *falsus; fictus, commenticius* (= made up), *subditus* (= forged), *perfidus* (= treacherous); to play —, *deesse.* Adv. *falso, perperam.*
falsehood, *mendacium, commentum.*
falsify, *vitiare, corrumpĕre.*
falter, *haesitare, haerĕre, titubare.*
falteringly, *titubanter.*
fame, *laus, gloria, fama.*
familiar: = well known, *familiaris, notus;* = acquainted, *sciens, gnarus, peritus.* Adv. *familiariter.*
familiarity, *familiaritas, consuetudo.*
family, subst. *familia* (= household); *domus; gens* (= clan); *genus (-eris,* = race, stock); of good —, *nobilis.*
family, adj. *familiaris, domesticus; gentilis; privatus* (opp. to *publicus*).
famine, *fames, cibi inopia.*
famish, *fame enecare, conficĕre.*
famous, (*prae*)*clarus, inlustris, celeber.*
fan, subst.: for winnowing, *vannus;* for fanning oneself, *flabellum.*
fan, v. *ventilare.*
fanatical, *fanaticus.*
fancied, *opinabilis, opinatus.*
fancy, subst.: as a faculty, *inventio, cogitatio;* = idea, notion, *opinio;* = liking, preference, *libido.*
fancy, v.: = to imagine, *fingĕre;* = to think, *opinari, putare.*
fang, *dens.*
fanged, *dentatus.*
far: in space, *procul, longe:* from — off, *eminus;* farther, *longius, ultra;* as — as, *tenus* (prep.), *usque* (adv. = all the way); — and wide, *longe lateque;* in degree, — better, *longe* or *multo melior;* — from it, *minime;* so —, *hactenus.*
farce, *mimus.*
farcical, *mimicus, ridiculus;* adv. *mimice, ridicule.*
fare, subst.: = food, *cibus, victus (-ūs);* = money for journey, *vectura, naulum.*
fare, v. *se habēre,* with adv.
farewell! *vale! valēte!;* to bid — *valēre iubēre.*
far-fetched, *longe repetitus, arcessitus.*
farm, subst. *fundus, praedium, ager.*
farm, v.: = till, *arare, colĕre;* = hire, *redimĕre, conducĕre;* — out, = let out on contract, (*e*)*locare.*
farmer, *agricola, colonus;* a — of revenues, *publicanus.*
farming, *agricultura, res rusticae;* = hiring, *redemptio, conductio.*
farthing, *quadrans, teruncius;* I do not care a — for, *haud flocci facio.*

fascinate, *fascinare;* see charm.

fascination, *fascinum.* Transf., *blanditia, dulcedo.*

fashion, subst.: = custom, way, *mos, consuetudo, ritus (-ūs);* = style of dress, *habitus (-ūs), ornatus (-ūs);* = what is fashionable, *saeculum;* out of —, *obsoletus.*

fashion, v. *fabricari, (ef)fingĕre.*

fashionable, *elegans;* adv. *eleganter.*

fast, subst. *ieiunium.*

fast, adj.;= quick, *celer, citus, rapidus;* = fixed, firm, *firmus, stabilis;* to make —, *firmare, stabilire.*

fast, adv.: = quickly, *celeriter, rapide;* = firmly, *firme, firmiter.*

fast, v. *ieiunium servare.*

fasten, *(ad)figĕre, (ad)ligare, adnectĕre;* to — together, *connectĕre.*

fastening, *vinculum, claustra (-orum).*

fastidious, *fastidiosus, delicatus;* adv. *fastidiose, delicate.*

fat, subst. *adeps, sebum.*

fat, adj. *pinguis, obesus.*

fatal, *perniciosus, funestus.*

fatality: = power of fate, *fatum;* = accident, *casus (-ūs).*

fate, *fatum, necessitas, sors;* the Fates, *Parcae.*

fated, *fatalis.*

father, subst. *pater, parens;* fathers= ancestors, *maiores (-um).*

father, v. *ascribĕre, tribuĕre.*

father-in-law, *socer.*

fatherless, *orbus.*

fatherly, *paternus.*

fathom, subst. *ulna.*

fathom, v. *explorare.*

fatigue, subst. *(de)fatigatio, lassitudo.*

fatigue, v. *(de)fatigare.*

fatigued, *(de)fatigatus, (de)fessus.*

fatten: transit., *saginare;* intransit., *pinguescĕre.*

fatuity, *fatuitas, ineptia.*

fatuous, *fatuus, ineptus;* adv. *inepte.*

fault, *culpa, vitium, delictum;* to find — with, *culpare, accusare.*

faultless, *integer, innocens;* adv. *integre, innocenter.*

faulty, *mendosus, vitiosus;* adv. *mendose, vitiose.*

favour, subst.; as position, *gratia;* as disposition, goodwill, *favor, benevolentia;* an act of —, *beneficium;* to do a —, *gratificari.*

favour, v. *favēre, studēre, suffragari.*

favourable, *propitius* (of gods), *commodus, secundus;* adv. *benigne, commode.*

favourer, *fautor* (f. *fautrix).*

favourite, subst. *deliciae (-arum).*

favourite, adj. *carus, gratiosus.*

fawn, subst. *hinnuleus.*

fawn, v.: to — upon, *adulari.*

fawning, subst. *adulatio.*

fealty, *fides, fidelitas.*

fear, subst. *metus (-ūs), timor, pavor.*

fear, v. *metuĕre, timēre, verēri.*

fearful: = afraid, *timidus, pavidus;* = dreadful, *dirus, terribilis.* Adv. *timide, pavide; dire.*

fearless, *impavidus, intrepidus;* adv. *sine timore, impavide.*

feasible, *quod fieri potest.*

feast, subst.: = feast-day, *dies festus;* = banquet, *convivium, epulae (-arum).*

feast, v.: transit., *pascĕre;* intransit., *epulari, convivari.*

feat, *facinus (-oris, n.), factum.*

feather, subst. *penna (pinna).*

feature, of the face, *lineamentum;* the —s, *vultus (-ūs).*

February, *(mensis) Februarius.*

fecund, *fecundus.*

fecundity, *fecunditas, fertilitas.*

federal, *foederatus, foedere sociatus.*

fee, subst. *merces.*

fee, v. *mercedem dare.*

feeble, *infirmus, invalidus, debilis;* adv. *infirme.*

feebleness, *debilitas, infirmitas.*

feed, v.: transit., *pascĕre, alĕre;* intransit., *vesci, (de)pasci.*

feel: = to touch, handle, *temptare, tangĕre;* to — an emotion, *laetitiam,* etc., *capĕre, percipĕre, sentire.*

feeler, *crinis, corniculum.*

feeling, subst. *sensus (-ūs), tactus (-ūs);* = emotion, *animus, animi motus (-ūs)* or *adfectus (-ūs).*

feeling, adj. *humanus, misericors.*

feign, *fingĕre, simulare.*

feigned, *fictus, simulatus;* adv. *ficte, simulate.*

feint, *simulatio.*

felicitate, *gratulari.*

felicitation, *gratulatio.*

felicitous, of style, *venustus.*

felicity: = happiness, *vita beata;* of style, *venustas.*

fell, adj. *dirus, saevus.*

fell, v. *caedere, excidĕre;* in gen., = knock down, *(con)sternĕre.*

fellow: = associate, *socius, comes;* = equal, *par;* = person, *homo.*

fellow-citizen, fellow-countryman, *civis.*

fellow-heir, *coheres.*

fellow-servant, *conservus.*

fellowship, *societas;* = corporation, *conlegium.*

fellow-soldier, *commilito.*

felon: see criminal.

felt, *coactum.*

female, subst. *femina, mulier.*

female, feminine, *muliebris, femineus;* gram., *femininus.*

fen, *palūs (-ūdis,* f.), *uligo.*

fence, subst. *saepes, saepimentum.*

fence, v.: = enclose, *saepire;* = fight with swords, *batuĕre.*

fencer, *gladiator.*

fenny, *uliginosus, paluster.*

ferment, *fermentum.* Transf., *frevor, aestus (-ūs).*

ferment, v. *fervēre.*

fern, *filix.*

ferocious, *ferus, saevus, atrox.*

ferocity, *saevitia, atrocitas.*

ferret, subst. *viverra.*

ferry, subst. *traiectus (-ūs);* — -boat, *scapha, cymba;* — -man, *portitor.*

ferry, v. *traicĕre, transmittĕre.*

fertile, *fecundus, fertilis, uber.*

fertility, *fertilitas, ubertas, fecunditas.*

fervent, fervid, fervidus, fervens, ardens; adv. ardenter, ferventer.
fervour, ardor, fervor.
festival, dies festus, feriae (-arum).
festive, hilaris, festus.
festivity: see festival; = mirth, festivitas, hilaritas.
festoon, subst. serta (-orum).
fetch, adferre, adducĕre.
fetid, teter, foetidus, gravis.
fetter, subst. compes, catena, vinculum.
fetter, v. vincula inicĕre. Transf., impedire.
feud, simultas; inimicitia.
fever, febris; to be in a — (fig.), trepidare, aestuare.
feverish, febriculosus. Transf., trepidus; — excitement, summa trepidatio.
few, pauci, rari.
fib, mendaciunculum.
fibre, fibra.
fickle, inconstans, levis.
fickleness, inconstantia, levitas.
fiction, res ficta, fabula, commentum.
fictitious, commenticius, fictus.
fiddle, fides (-ium).
fiddler, fidicen.
fidelity, fidelitas, fides.
fidget, v. trepidare.
fidgety, inquietus.
field: = piece of land, ager, arvum, campus (= plain); — of battle, acies; fig., = sphere, campus, locus, area.
fiendish, nefandus, immanis, atrox.
fierce, ferox, ferus, saevus; adv. ferociter, saeve.
fierceness, ferocitas, saevitia.
fiery, igneus, flammeus. Transf., ardens, fervidus, ferox.
fife, tibia.
fifteen, quindecim; — each, quini deni; — times, quindecie(n)s.
fifteenth, quintus decimus.
fifth, quintus.
fiftieth, quinquagesimus.
fifty, quinquaginta; — each, quinquageni.
fig, ficus.
fight, subst. pugna, certamen.
fight, v. (de)pugnare, dimicare, proeliari.
fighter, pugnator, proeliator.
figment: see fiction.
figurative, translatus; adv. per translationem.
figure, subst.: = form, shape, figura, forma, species; = image, representation, signum, figura, imago; a — of speech, conformatio, figura.
figure, v. fingĕre; see imagine.
figured, sigillatus, caelatus.
filament, fibra, filum.
file, subst.: the tool, lima, scobina; milit., ordo; rank and —, milites.
file, v. limare, polire.
filial, pius (erga parentes); adv. pie.
filings, scobis.
fill, v. implēre, complēre.
fillet, vitta, infula (religious).
film, membrana.
filter, subst. colum.
filter, v. (per)colare, liquare.
filth, impuritas; see dirt.
filthy, impurus, obscenus; adv. impure.
fin, pinna.

final, ultimus, extremus; adv. ad extremum, postremo.
finance, finances: domestic, res familiaris; of a state, vectigalia (-ium), aerarium.
find, v. invenire, reperire; to — out, cognoscere, invenire.
finder, inventor, repertor.
fine, subst. multa.
fine, adj. praeclarus, pulcher; the — arts, artes liberales; = thin, tenuis, subtilis; of weather, serenus, sudus. Adv. praeclare; tenuiter, subtiliter.
fine, v. multare.
fineness, elegantia; = thinness, tenuitas, subtilitas; of weather, serenitas.
finery, munditia, apparatus (-ūs).
finesse, artificium.
finger, subst. digitus.
finger, v. tangĕre, attrectare.
finish, subst. absolutio, perfectio.
finish, v.: = complete, conficĕre, absolvĕre, peragĕre; = put an end to, finire, terminare.
finished, absolutus, perfectus.
finite, finitus, circumscriptus.
fir, abies, pinus.
fire, subst. ignis, flamma, incendium; to be on —, ardēre, flagrare; to set on —, incendĕre. Transf., = ardour, (animi) vis, ardor, fervor; of missiles, telorum coniectus (-ūs).
fire, v.: transit., incendĕre; intransit., to — up, exardescĕre.
fire-brand, fax, torris.
fire-brigade, vigiles.
fire-engine, sipho(n).
fire-place, fire-side, caminus, focus.
fire-wood, lignum (usually plur.).
firm, firmus, stabilis, solidus; adv. firmiter, firme, solide.
firmness, firmitas, stabilitas; of mind, constantia.
first, adj. primus, prior (of two).
first, adv. primum, primo.
first-born, natu maximus (of two, maior).
first-fruits, primitiae (-arum).
fish, subst. piscis.
fish, v. piscari; fig., to — for, captare.
fisherman, piscator.
fishhook, hamus.
fishing, piscatus (-ūs); of —, adj., piscatorius.
fishing-line, linum.
fishing-net, rete, iaculum.
fishing-rod, harundo.
fishmonger, cetarius.
fissure, rima.
fist, pugnus.
fisticuffs, pugilatio.
fit, subst. impetus (-ūs).
fit, fitted, adj. aptus, idoneus, commodus; adv. apte, commode.
fit, v.: transit. aptare, accommodare; to — out, (ex)ornare, instruĕre; intransit. convenire.
fitness, habilitas, opportunitas.
five, quinque; — each, quini; a period of — years, lustrum, quinquennium; — times, quinquie(n)s.
fix, v. (ad)figĕre.
fixed, certus.

flabby, flaccid, *marcidus, fluidus.*
flag, subst. *signum, vexillum;* — ship, *navis praetoria.*
flagon, *lagena.*
flagrant, *impudens;* adv. *impudenter.*
flail, *pertica.*
flame, subst. *flamma.*
flame, v. *ardēre, flagrare.*
flaming, *flammeus.*
flank, *latus (-eris, n.).*
flap, subst. *lacinia.*
flap, v.: to — the wings, *alis plaudēre;* in gen., *fluitare.*
flare, v. *flagrare.*
flash, subst. *fulgor.*
flash, v. *fulgēre, splendēre.*
flask, *ampulla.*
flat: = level, *planus, aequus, pronus* (= lying —); of wine, *vapidus;* of jokes, etc., *frigidus.* Adv. *plane.*
flatter, *adulari, blandiri.*
flatterer, *adsentator.*
flattering, *blandus.*
flattery, *adulatio, blandimentum.*
flaunt, *iactare, ostentare.*
flavour, subst. *sapor, sucus.*
flavour, v. *condire.*
flaw, *vitium, mendum.*
flawless, *emendatus.*
flax, *linum, carbasus.*
flaxen, *lineus;* of colour, *flavus.*
flay, *pellem detrahēre (corpori).*
flea, *pulex.*
fledged, *plumatus.*
flee, *(ef)fugēre.*
fleece, subst. *vellus (-eris, n.).*
fleece, v. *tondēre;* = rob, *expilare, spoliare.*
fleecy, *laniger.*
fleet, subst. *classis.*
fleet, adj. *velox, celer, pernix.*
fleeting, *fugax, caducus, fluxus.*
fleetness, *velocitas, pernicitas.*
flesh, *caro* (= meat), *viscera (-um), corpus (-oris, n.).*
flexible, *flexibilis, lentus, facilis.*
flicker, *tremēre, micare.*
flight: = fleeing, *effugium, fuga;* to put to —, *fugare;* = flying, *lapsus (-ūs), volatus (-ūs);* of stairs, *scalae (-arum).*
flightiness, *mobilitas, levitas.*
flighty, *mobilis, levis, inconstans.*
flimsiness, *tenuitas.*
flimsy, *tenuis.* Transf., *inanis.*
flinch, *refugēre.*
fling, *iacēre, conicēre.*
flint, *silex.*
flippancy, *petulantia.*
flippant, *petulans.*
flirt, v., perhaps *subblandiri.*
flit, *volitare.*
flitch, *succidia.*
float, *innare, fluitare;* in the air, *pendēre, volitare.*
flock, subst. *grex.*
flock, v. *adfluēre, confluēre;* to — together, *concurrēre.*
flog, *verberare;* to be flogged, *vapulare.*
flogging, *verbera (-um).*
flood, subst. *eluvio;* — tide, *aestūs accessus (-ūs).* Transf., *vis magna, flumen.*
flood, v. transit. *inundare.*

floor, *solum, pavimentum* (of stone).
floral, *floreus* (poet).
Florence, *Florentia.*
florid, *rubicundus.* Transf., *floridus.*
flounder, *fluitare.* Transf., *titubare.*
flour, *farina.*
flourish, subst., in style, *calamister.*
flourish, v.: intransit., *florēre, vigēre;* transit., *vibrare.*
flout, *ludificari, deridēre.*
flow, subst. *fluxio, lapsus (-ūs);* of words, *volubilitas, copia (verborum).*
flow, v. *fluēre, labi* (= glide), *manare* (= ooze).
flower, subst. *flos, flosculus;* = best part, *flos, robur.*
flower, v. *florēre, (ef)florescēre.*
flowery, *floreus, floridus.*
flowing, of speech, *fluens, volubilis, fusus.*
fluctuate, *fluctuare, pendēre.*
fluency, *facundia, volubilitas.*
fluent, *volubilis, disertus;* adv. *volubiliter.*
fluid, subst. *liquor, humor.*
fluid, adj. *liquidus.*
flush, subst. *rubor.*
flush, v. *rubescēre.*
fluster, *agitare, sollicitare.*
flute, *tibia, harundo.*
flute-player, *tibicen.*
fluted, *striatus.*
flutter, subst. *trepidatio.*
flutter, v. *trepidare, volitare.*
fly, subst. *musca.*
fly, v. *volare, volitare,* see also flee.
flying, *volatilis, volucer.*
foal, *eculeus, pullus equinus.*
foam, subst. *spuma.*
foam, v. *spumare, (ex)aestuare.*
foamy, *spumeus, spumosus.*
fodder, *pabulum.*
foe, *hostis* (public), *inimicus* (private).
fog, *nebula, caligo.*
foggy, *nebulosus, caliginosus.*
foible, *vitium.*
foil, subst.: a fencer's —, *rudis;* of metal, *lamina.*
foil, v. *ad inritum redigēre, eludēre.*
foist, *supponēre, subdēre.*
fold, subst.: in fabric, etc., *sinus (-ūs);* for animals, *ovile, stabulum.*
fold, v. *(com)plicare;* with -ed hands, *compressis manibus.*
folding-doors, *valvae (-arum).*
foliage, *frons,* plur. *frondes.*
folk; see people.
follow, *(con)sequi, insequi, persequi* (to the end); to — after, succeed, *succedēre.*
follower, *(ad)sectator.*
following, subst. *secta.*
following, *(in)sequens, proximus, posterus.*
folly, *stultitia, ineptia.*
foment, *fovēre.* Transf., *excitare.*
fond: = loving, *amans, studiosus;* = foolish, *stultus.* Adv. *amanter; stulte.*
fondle, *(per)mulcēre, amplexari.*
fondness: = love, *studium, amor, caritas;* = folly, *stultitia.*
food, *cibus, victus (-ūs), alimentum;* of animals, *pabulum.*
fool, subst. *homo stultus;* to play the —, *ineptire, desipēre.*

fool, v. (e)ludĕre, ludificare.

foolery, ineptiae (-arum), nugae (-arum).

foolhardy, temerarius.

foolish, stultus, ineptus, insulsus; adv. stulte, inepte, insulse.

foot, pes; on — (adj.), pedes, pedester; the — of the mountain, infimus mons; as a measure, pes; a — in size, pedalis; a metrical —, pes.

footing, ratio, status (-ūs).

footman, pedisequus, servus a pedibus.

footpad, latro.

foot-path, semita, callis.

foot-print, vestigium.

foot-soldier, pedes.

footstool, scamnum, scabillum.

for, prep.: = on behalf of, instead of, in return for, pro, with abl.; — this reason, propter hoc; — a sum of money, render by genit. or abl. of price; of time, to last for, for the purposes of, in with acc.: = during, render by acc., or per with acc.

for, conj. nam(que), etenim enim (second word in clause).

forage, subst. pabulum.

forage, v. pabulari, frumentari.

forager, pabulator, frumentator.

foraging, subst. pabulatio, frumentatio.

forbear, parcĕre, temperare, (se) abstin-ēre.

forbearance, abstinentia, patientia.

forbid, vetare, interdicĕre; it is for-bidden, non licet.

force, subst. vis; to be in —, valēre; milit., forces, copiae (-arum).

force, v.; see compel.

forced, of language, accessitus; a — march, magnum iter.

forcible: = done by force, per vim factus; = strong, validus, gravis, vehe-mens. Adv. vi, per vim; valide, vehementer.

ford, subst. vadum.

ford, v. vado transire.

forearm, subst. bracchium.

forebode: = to prophesy, portendĕre; = to expect, praesagire, praesentire.

foreboding, subst. praesensio.

forecast, v. praevidēre, prospicĕre.

forefather, avus, proavus; —s, maiores (-um).

forefinger, digitus index.

forego, dimittĕre, (con)cedĕre.

forehead, frons (-ntis).

foreign, peregrinus, externus, adventi-cius; = incompatible, abhorrens, alienus.

foreigner, peregrinus, advena.

foremost, primus, princeps.

forenoon, dies antemeridianus.

forensic, forensis.

forerunner, praenuntius.

foresee, praevidēre, prospicĕre.

foresight, providentia.

forest, silva.

forestall, praevenire.

foretell, praedicĕre.

forethought, providentia.

forewarn, praemonēre.

forfeit, subst. poena, multa.

forfeit, v. amittĕre; multari.

forge, subst. fornax, officina.

forge, v. procudĕre, fabricari. Transf.: = make, in gen., fabricari, fingĕre; =counterfeit, subicĕre, supponĕre.

forged, of money, adulterinus.

forger, (of documents) subiector.

forgery, (of documents) subiectio.

forget, oblivisci, dediscĕre: to be forgot-ten, e memoria excidĕre.

forgetful, obliviosus, immemor.

forgetfulness, oblivio.

forgive, ignoscĕre; veniam dare.

forgiveness, venia.

forgiving, clemens, exorabilis.

fork, (for hay-making), furca, furcilla.

forked, bifurcus.

forlorn, relictus, destitutus.

form, subst.: = shape, figura, forma, facies; in proper —, rite; = bench, scamnum.

form, v.: = shape, make, (ef)fingĕre (con)formare, fabricari; milit., to — (up) troops, instruĕre, ordinare.

formality, ritus (-ūs).

formation, conformatio, forma.

former, prior, pristinus, superior; the — . . . the latter, ille . . . hic. Adv. antea, olim, quondam.

formidable, metuendus, terribilis, form-idolosus; adv. formidolose.

formless, informis, rudis.

formula, formula, carmen, verba (-orum).

forsake, deserĕre, destituĕre.

forsooth! scilicet, sane.

forswear, = swear falsely, periurare. See also abjure.

fort, arx, castellum, castrum.

forth, of place, foras; often rendered by compound verb with e- or ex-or pro; and so —, et cetera.

forthcoming, express by future tense.

forthwith, extemplo, statim.

fortification, munitio, munimentum.

fortify, (com)munire.

fortitude, fortitudo, virtūs (-ūtis, f.).

fortuitous, fortuitus, forte oblatus; adv. forte, fortuito, casu.

fortunate, felix, fortunatus, beatus; adv. feliciter, fortunate.

fortune, fortuna, fors, casus (-ūs); = wealth, divitiae (-arum), res (famili-aris), bona (-orum).

fortune-teller, sortilegus; female, saga.

forty, quadraginta; — each, quadrageni; — times, quadragie(n)s.

forward, adj., = pert, protervus.

forward, adv. porro, ante; to go —, pergĕre.

forward, v.; of letters, perferendum curare; = help, promote, adiuvare.

foster, nutrire, alĕre.

foster-child, alumnus, f. alumna.

foster-father, nutricius.

foster-mother, nutrix.

foul, foedus, turpis, immundus; adv. foede, turpiter.

foulness, foeditas.

found: of cities, etc., condĕre, fundare; = cast in metal, fundĕre.

foundation, fundamenta (-orum); from the —s, funditus.

founder, subst. conditor, auctor.

founder, v. submergi, deperire

fount, fountain, *fons, caput.* Transf., *fons, principium, origo.*

four, *quattuor:* — each, *quaterni;* — times, *quater;* a period of — years, *quadriennium;* — fold, *quadruplex.*

fourteen, *quattuordecim:* — each, *quaterni deni;* — times, *quater decie(n)s.*

fourteenth, *quartus decimus.*

fourth, *quartus:* for the — time, *quartum.*

fowl, subst. *avis, volucris, ales;* = hen, *gallina.*

fowl, v. *aucupari.*

fowler, *auceps.*

fowling, *aucupium.*

fox, *vulpes;* of a —, adj. *vulpinus.*

fraction, *pars.*

fractious, *morosus, difficilis*

fracture, v. *frangĕre.*

fragile, *fragilis.*

fragility, *fragilitas.*

fragment, *fragmentum.*

fragrance, *odor suavis.*

fragrant, *suavis; suaveolens* (poet).

frail, adj. *infirmus, debilis.*

frailty, *infirmitas.*

frame, subst. *compages:* — of mind, *animus.*

frame, v. *fingĕre, fabricari;* — draw up in words, *concipĕre, componĕre.*

framework, *compages, contignatio.*

France, *Gallia.*

franchise, *civitas, iūs (iūris, n.).*

frank, *candidus, apertus;* adv. *candide, aperte.*

frankincense, *tūs (tūris, n.).*

frankness, *simplicitas, libertas.*

frantic, *insanus, amens;* adv. *insane.*

fraternal, *fraternus;* adv. *fraterne.*

fraternity, *germanitas, fraternitas;* = society, *sodalitas, sodalicium.*

fratricide: as act, *parricidium fraternum;* as person, *fratricida.*

fraud, *fraus, dolus (malus), fallacia.*

fraudulent, *fraudulentus, dolosus;* adv. *fraudulenter, dolo malo, dolose.*

fraught, *refertus, repletus.*

fray, *pugna.*

free, adj.: = unrestricted, *liber, solutus, vacuus;* to be — from, *(re) carēre;* of space, = unoccupied, *patens, apertus;* = without cost, *gratuitus;* = generous, *largus, liberalis.* Adv. *libere, solute;* = generously, *large.*

free, v. *liberare, eximĕre, solvĕre;* of slaves, *manumittĕre.*

freebooter, *latro, praedo.*

free-born, *ingenuus.*

freedman, *libertus, libertinus.*

freedom, *libertas, licentia;* — of choice, *arbitrium;* — from punishment, *impunitas.*

freehold, *praedium liberum.*

freeholder, *possessor.*

freewill, *voluntas.*

freeze, transit., *glaciare, (con)gelare.*

freight, *onus (oneris, n.).*

French, *Gallicus;* a — man, *Gallus.*

frenzied, *furens, insanus, amens.*

frenzy, *furor, insania, amentia.*

frequency, *frequentia, crebritas.*

frequent, adj. *frequens, creber;* adv. *frequenter, crebro, saepe.*

frequent, v. *celebrare, frequentare.*

frequented, *frequens, celeber.*

fresh: = new, *recens, novus;* = refreshed, *untired, recens, integer, vegetus;* = cold, *frigidus.*

freshen, *recreare, reficere;* intransit., of wind, *increbrescere.*

freshness, *viriditas.*

fret: transit., = chafe, *atterĕre,* = distress, *sollicitare, vexare;* intransit., *dolere, macerari.*

fretful, *morosus, stomachosus;* adv. *morose, stomachose.*

fretfulness, *morositas, stomachus.*

friable, *puter* or *putris.*

friction, *tritus (-ūs).*

friend, *amicus* (f. *amica*), *sodalis.*

friendliness, *comitas, adfabilitas.*

friendly, *amicus, comis.*

friendship, *amicitia, familiaritas.*

frieze, (the cloth), *gausape* or *gausapum*

fright, *terror, pavor.*

frighten, *(ex)terrēre.*

frightful, *terribilis, formidolosus;* adv. *terribilem in modum, formidolose.*

frigid, *frigidus.*

frill, *segmenta (-orum).*

fringe, *fimbriae (-arum), limbus.*

frisk, *salire, lascivire.*

frisky, *lascivus.*

fritter, subst., *laganum.*

fritter, v. *(con)terĕre, dissipare.*

frivolity, *nugae (-arum), levitas.*

frivolous, *levis, inanis.*

fro: to and —, *huc (et) illuc, ultro citro(que).*

frog, *rana.*

frolic, subst. *ludus, lascivia.*

frolic, v. *ludĕre, lascivire.*

frolicsome, *lascivus, ludibundus, iocosus.*

from, *a, ab; ex* (= out of); *de* (=down from).

front, subst. *frons, pars prior;* in — of, *pro,* with abl.

front, v., = look towards, *aspectare.*

frontier, *finis, terminus, confinium.*

fronting, *adversus, oppositus.*

frost, *gelu, pruina; frigus (-oris, n.* = frosty weather).

frosty, *frigidus.*

froth, subst. *spuma.*

froth, v. *spumare.*

frothy, *spumosus, spumeus.*

froward, *contumax, pertinax;* adv. *contumaciter, pertinaciter.*

frowardness, *contumacia, pertinacia.*

frown, subst. *frontis contractio.*

frown, v. *frontem contrahĕre.*

frozen, *rigidus.*

frugal, *parcus, frugi* (indecl.); adv. *parce, frugaliter.*

frugality, *parsimonia, frugalitas.*

fruit, *fructus (-ūs), frux* and plur. *fruges* (esp. of grain), *pomum* (esp. = fruit of trees), *baca* (= berry).

fruitful, *fecundus, fertilis, uber;* adv. *fecunde.*

fruitfulness, *fecunditas, fertilitas.*

fruition, *fructus (-ūs).*

fruitless, *inutilis, cassus, inritus;* adv.
incassum, frustra, re infecta.
fruit-tree, *pomum.*
frustrate, *ad inritum redigĕre.*
fry, v. *frigĕre.*
frying-pan, *sartago.*
fuel, *ligna (-orum).*
fugitive, subst. *fugitivus, profugus.*
fugitive, adj. *fugax, fugitivus.*
fulfil, *explēre, exsequi, conficĕre.*
fulfilment, *confectio.*
full: = filled, *plenus, repletus;* — of
food, *satur* = complete, *plenus,*
integer; of ı writer or speaker,
copiosus. Adv. *plene; copiose, abund-*
anter.
fuller, *fullo.*
full-grown, *adultus.*
fulminate, *fulminare, intonare.*
fulsome, *putidus;* adv. *putide.*
fumble; see feel.
fume, subst. *vapor, halitus (-ūs)*
fume, v. *(ex)aestuare.*
fumigate, *suffire.*
fun, *iocus, ludus.*
function, *munus (-eris, n.), officium.*
fund, *pecunia.*
fundamental, *primus, principalis;* adv.
penitus.
fundamentals, *elementa (-orum),*
principia (-orum).
funeral, subst. *funus (-eris, n.), exse-*
quiae (-arum).
funeral, adj. *funebris;* — pile, *rogus,*
pyra.
funereal, *funebris, lugubris.*
funnel, *infundibulum.*
funny, *ridiculus, iocularis;* adv. *ridicule.*
fur, *pellis.*
furbish, *interpolare, expolire.*
furious, *rabidus, furens;* adv. *rabide.*
furl, *(vela) contrahĕre.*
furlong, *stadium.*
furlough, *commeatus (-ūs).*
furnace, *fornax.*
furnish: = equip, *(ad)ornare, instru-*
ere; = supply, give, *suppeditare, prae-*
bere.
furnished, *instructus, praeditus.*
furniture, *supellex; apparatus (-ūs).*
furrow, subst. *sulcus.*
furrow, v. *sulcare.*
further: adj. *ulterior;* adv. *ulterius,*
amplius; praeterea.
furthest, *ultimus.*
furtive, *furtivus;* adv. *furtim, furtive.*
fury, *furor, rabies.*
fuse, *liquefacĕre, fundĕre.*
fuss, subst. *trepidatio, tumultus (-ūs).*
fuss, v. *trepidare.*
fusty; see mouldy.
futile, *futilis, inanis, vanus.*
futility, *futilitas.*
future, subst. *futura (-orum);* for the
—, *in futurum.*
future, adj. *futurus, posterus.*

G

gabble, *garrire, blaterare.*
gable, *fastigium.*
gadfly, *asilus, tabanus.*

gage, *pignus (-oris, n.).*
gaiety, *hilaritas, laetitia.*
gain, subst. *lucrum, quaestus (-ūs;* =
profit), *commodum* (= advantage).
gain, v. *lucrari, lucri facĕre, consequi,*
capĕre; to — over, *conciliare.*
gainful, *quaestuosus, lucrosus.*
gait, *incessus (-ūs).*
gala; see festival.
galaxy, *orbis lacteus.*
gale, *ventus, aura* (= breeze).
gall, subst. *fel, bilis.*
gall, v. *terĕre;* = annoy, *mordĕre, urĕrc.*
gallant, *amator.*
gallant, adj.: = brave, *fortis, animosus;*
adv. *fortiter, animose;* = attentive to
females, *officiosus.*
gallantry, *virtus (-utis, f.), fortitudo;* in
love, *amores (-um).*
gallery, *porticus (-ūs).*
galley, *navis longa, triremis.*
gallon, *congius.*
gallop, subst. *gradus (-ūs) citatus:* at a
—, *equo admisso.*
gallop, v. *equo admisso vehi or currĕre.*
gallows, *crux.*
gamble, v. *aleā ludĕre.*
gambler, *aleator.*
gambling, *alea.*
gambol, subst. *lusus (-ūs).*
gambol, v. *ludĕre, lascivire.*
game, susbt.: as played, *ludus;* a — of
chance, *alea;* as hunted, *ferae*
(-arum); on table, *(caro) ferina.*
gammon, *perna.*
gammon, interj. *gerrae!*
gander, *anser (mas or masculus).*
gang, *grex, caterva.*
gangway, *forus.*
gaol, *carcer; vincula (-orum).*
gaoler, *custos.*
gap, *lacuna, hiatus (-ūs).*
gape, *(in)hiare, (de)hiscĕre.*
garbage, *purgamentum, quisquiliae*
(-arum).
garble, *corrumpĕre, vitiare.*
garden, subst. *hortus.*
garden, v. *in horto fodĕre, hortum*
colĕre.
garish, *clarus, splendidus.*
garland, *corona, sertum* (usually plur.).
garlic, *alium.*
garment, *vestimentum.*
garner, subst. *horreum.*
garner, v. *condĕre.*
garnish, *(ex)ornare, instruĕre, decorare.*
garret, *cenaculum.*
garrison, subst. *praesidium.*
garrison, v. *(urbi) praesidium imponĕre.*
garrulity, *garrulitas, loquacitas.*
garrulous, *garrulus, loquax, verbosus;*
adv. *loquaciter.*
gas, *spiritus (-ūs), vapor.*
gash, subst. *vulnus (-eris, n.).*
gash, v. *vulnerare.*
gasp, subst. *anhelitus (-ūs).*
gasp, v. *anhelare.*
gasping, adj. *anhelus.*
gate, *ianua, ostium;* of a city, *porta.*
gate-keeper, *ianitor.*
gate-post, *postis.*
gather, v.: transit., *legĕre, conligĕre.*